THE

ANTE-NICENE FATHERS

TRANSLATIONS OF

The Writings of the Fathers down to A.D. 325

THE REV. ALEXANDER ROBERTS, D.D.,

AND

JAMES DONALDSON, LL.D.,

EDITORS

AMERICAN REPRINT OF THE EDINBURGH EDITION

REVISED AND CHRONOLOGICALLY ARRANGED, WITH BRIEF PREFACES AND OCCASIONAL NOTES,

BY

A. CLEVELAND COXE, D.D.

VOLUME VII

LACTANTIUS, VENANTIUS, ASTERIUS, VICTORINUS, DIONYSIUS, APOSTOLIC TEACHING AND CONSTITUTIONS, HOMILY, AND LITURGIES.

AUTHORIZED EDITION

T&T CLARK
EDINBURGH

WM. B. EERDMANS PUBLISHING COMPANY
GRAND RAPIDS, MICHIGAN

British Library Cataloguing in Publication Data
Ante-Nicene Fathers.
1. Fathers of the church
I. Robertson, Alexander II. Donaldson, James
230′.13 BR60.A62

T&T Clark ISBN 0 567 09380 8

Eerdmans ISBN 0-8028-8093-2
Reprinted, March 1994

PHOTOLITHOPRINTED BY EERDMANS PRINTING COMPANY
GRAND RAPIDS, MICHIGAN, UNITED STATES OF AMERICA

FATHERS OF THE THIRD AND FOURTH CENTURIES:

LACTANTIUS, VENANTIUS, ASTERIUS, VICTORINUS, DIONYSIUS, APOSTOLIC TEACHING AND CONSTITUTIONS, HOMILY, AND LITURGIES.

AMERICAN EDITION

CHRONOLOGICALLY ARRANGED, WITH NOTES, PREFACES, AND ELUCIDATIONS,

BY

A. CLEVELAND COXE, D.D.

Τὰ ἀρχαῖα ἔθη κρατείτω.

THE NICENE COUNCIL.

INTRODUCTORY NOTICE

THE genius of Lactantius suffers a sad transformation when unclothed of his vernacular and stripped of the idiomatic graces of his style. But the intelligent reader will be sure to compare this translation with the Latinity of the original, and to recur to it often for the enjoyment of its charming rhetoric, and of the high sentiment it so nobly enforces and adorns. This volume will be the favourite of the series with many. The writings of the Christian Tully alone make up more than half of its contents; and it is supremely refreshing to reach, at last, an author who chronicles the triumph of the Gospel[1] over "Herod and Pontius Pilate;" over the heathen in their "rage," and the people in their "vain imaginings;" over "the kings of the earth who stood up, and the rulers who were gathered together against the Lord and against His Christ."

I love the writings of Lactantius, and two of his sayings are always uppermost when I recall his name. They touch me like plaintive but inspiring music. Let me quote them entire:[2] —

1. "Si vita est optanda sapienti profecto nullam aliam ob causam vivere optaverim, quam ut aliquid efficiam quod vita dignum sit."

2. "Satis me vixisse arbitrabor, et officium hominis implesse, si labor meus aliquos homines ab erroribus liberatos, ad iter cœleste direxerit."

The *Minor Writers* to be found in this volume are not unworthy of their place. They are chiefly valuable as an appendix to preceding volumes,[3] and illustrative of their contents.

But this series is enriched beyond its original by the *Bryennios Manuscript* and the completed form of the *pseudo-Clementine Epistle*, edited by Professor Riddle. The same hand has annotated the *Apostolic Constitutions*, so called; and the student has in his brief but learned notes all the light which has been shed by modern scholarship on these invaluable relics of antiquity, since the days of the truly illustrious Bishop Beveridge. These, and the liturgical *pseudepigraphic* treasures of early Christianity I have gathered here, to distinguish them from the mere *Apocrypha*, which will largely make up the one remaining volume of the series.

Of the *Liturgies*, I have said what seemed necessary as an introduction, in the proper place.[4] They are debased by mediæval alloy. In their English dress, and in the nudity of their appearance, without adequate notes and elucidations, they are therefore far from attractive specimens of liturgical literature. But it would have been beyond my province to say much where the original editors have said nothing, and I have contented myself with such comments only as seemed requisite to remind the student how to "take forth the precious from the vile."

JUNE, 1886. A. C. C.

---

[1] Compare Merivale, *Conversion of the Roman Empire*, p. 8, ed. New York, 1866.

[2] *De Opificio Dei*, cap. xxi. p. 395, ed. Basil, 1521.

[3] Thus the Apocalyptic comments of Victorinus must be compared with those of Commodian and Hippolytus, Dionysius with his namesake of Alexandria, Asterius with Caius, etc.

[4] Compare Canon Wescott, *The Historic Faith, Short Lectures*, etc., pp. 185–202, 237 (and same author's *Risen Lord*, etc., p. 28), London, 1883.

CONTENTS OF VOLUME VII

LACTANTIUS

[TRANSLATED BY THE REV. WILLIAM FLETCHER, D.D.]

INTRODUCTORY NOTICE

TO

LACTANTIUS

[A.D. 260–330.] Reaching, at last, the epoch of Constantine, perhaps the reader will share my own feelings, as those of—

> "One who long, in thickets and in brakes
> Entangled, winds now this way, and now that,
> His devious course uncertain, seeking home,
> But finds at last a greensward smooth and large,
> Courageous, and refreshed for future toil."

How strange it seems, after three centuries since John the Baptist suffered, to gain a moment when kings are not actually persecuting Christ in His servants!

How marvellous the change must have been in the experience of the primitive faithful; the Roman Emperor not ashamed of Jesus, and setting up the cross on the standards of his legions! Tertullian, *De Fuga*, and the troubles of Cyprian about *The Lapsed*, are matters of the past. As in a moment, God has changed the world for His people, and their perils become as suddenly reversed. The world's favour begins to be the trial of faith, as its hatred before. The mild contemplative attitude of the Church at this period is something surprising. It accepts with little exultation this miracle of the Master; but so long has it been habituated to persecution, that it finds much of its discipline, and not less of its prevailing spirit, neutralized by its very triumph. No more the martyr's heroic testimony and his crown beyond this life; no such call for the celibate as had been enforced before in tomes of the Christian literature; and what need now of Antony's invitation to the desert and the cell? But, on the other hand, these ascetic forms of heroic faith were all that were now left to minister to the martyr-spirit, and to perpetuate the habits enforced upon the early believers. The hermitage and the monastery assumed a new attractiveness, and became dear to sentiment, as to principle before. We must not be surprised, then, at the tendencies of the age now rapidly developed; but let us rejoice for a moment in the times of refreshing from the Lord now at last vouchsafed to that "little flock" to which He had promised the kingdom.

The "conversion of Constantine," as it is called, introduced the most marvellous revolution in human empire, in practical thought, and in the laws and manners of mankind, ever known in the history of the world. It is amazing how little the men of the epoch itself glorified their own introduction to "marvellous light," and how very little the Church has left us, to tell the story of its emotions when first it found itself at rest from fiery persecutions, or when came forth from the Emperor the Edict of Milan for the legal observance of "the Day of the Sun."[1] What a day that Easter was, when, emerging from the catacombs and other dens and caves of the earth, the Church herself seemed as one risen from the dead!

---

[1] He borrows from Justin, vol. i. note 1, p. 186.

We may be sure there were tears of joy and warm embraces among kindred long torn asunder by their common exposures to fire and sword. We cannot imagine, indeed, all that was in the hearts of those Christian families that now kept holyday together in the face of the world, and sang fearlessly in holy places their anthem, "Christ is risen from the dead." But a moment's thought we ought to give, as we pass into a stage of history entirely fresh and new, to the power of God thus manifested. The miracle thus wrought by the ascended Christ needs no aid from the supposed "vision of Constantine" to make it a supernatural exhibition of His glory who is "King of kings and Lord of lords."

Arnobius wrote to the minds of perplexed Pilates asking "What is truth" in a new spirit, and not indisposed to wash their own hands of the blood of Jesus, though not prepared to believe and be baptized. His pupil finds a better sort of Pilate in the Emperor and in his period. Constantine is a pagan still at heart, but he is convinced of the truth that Christ has a kingdom "not of this world;" and he must have this credit, above the Antonines, that he recognised in the Christians not only his best and most loyal subjects, but men of a character altogether superior[1] to that of the heathen, who had so long been the councillors of the empire. He was one, also, who accepted "the logic of events," and who came to terms with the inevitable in time to turn it to his own advantage.

I think Constantine had read the *Apologies* addressed to the Antonines[2] by Justin Martyr, and was at first disposed only to accept the plea for Christians so far forth as Justin had urged it. Going so far, he was led beyond his positive convictions to measures of policy which identified him with the Church. That the Church was distrustful of him, and doubted how long the imperial favour might be relied upon, is also apparent. This doubt accounts, in some degree, for the great moderation of the Church in accepting benefits from him, and in withholding notes of triumph. She instinctively foresaw Julians in the way, and expected reactionary periods. She forbore to baptize the Emperor, and encouraged his disposition to postpone. It was as when "the wolf of Benjamin" was introduced to the disciples: "they were afraid of him, and believed not that he was a disciple."

Lactantius, moved, perhaps, by Hosius or Eusebius, undertakes the instruction of the Emperor, while seeming only to copy the example of Justin writing to Antoninus Pius. The *Institutes*, it is true, had been begun at an earlier date; but he economizes, for a new purpose, the material, in which, perhaps, he had only purposed to follow up the work of his teacher, in language better fitted to the polite, for refuting heathenism. I cannot doubt that he aimed, in pure Latinity, to win the Emperor and his court to a deeper and purer conviction of divine truth: to more than a feeble and possibly superstitious idea that it was useless to contend with it, and that the gods of the empire were impotent to protect themselves against Christian progress and its masterly exposures of their shame and nothingness.

In language which has given him the title of the Christian Cicero, Lactantius employs Cicero himself as a defender of the truth; correcting him, indeed, and overruling his mistakes, rebuking his pusillanimity, and justly censuring him, (1) in philosophy, for declaring it no rule of action, however ennobling its precepts; and (2) in religion, for not venturing to profess conclusions to which his reasonings necessarily tend. All this is admirably adapted to carry on the work of Christian Fathers and Apologists under the change of times. He and Arnobius furnish but a supplement to the real teachers of the Church, and are not to be always depended on in statements of doctrine. They write like earnest converts, but not like theologians; yet, although their loose expressions are often inconsistent one with another, it is manifest that their design is to support orthodoxy as it had been defined by abler expounders. I think the large respect which Lactantius pays to the testimony of the Sibyls was addressed to the class with which he had to deal. Constantine was greatly influenced by such testimonies, if we may judge from his own

[1] e.g., Theonas, vol. vi. p. 158.

[2] While Lactantius was tutor to his son.

liberal quotations[1] and his comments on the *Pollio* of Virgil, to which, as a Christian oracle, our author may have introduced him. In short, the day had come in which it could no longer be said with strict propriety of phrase, "Not many mighty, not many noble, are called;" and Lactantius accepted, as his mission, the enforcement, before such a class, of despised truths which the great had persecuted in vain for centuries. He drew them thus to the conclusion that God had indeed "chosen the foolish things of the world to confound the wise, and the weak things of the world to confound the things which are mighty; and base things of the world, and things which are despised, hath God chosen, yea, and things which are not, to bring to nought things that are." Such was the prophecy of St. Paul, and the *Labarum* uplifted by Cæsar's legions proclaimed the fulfilment.

I have little doubt that Lactantius was of heathen parentage, and was converted late in life. To his eternal honour he was not a "fair-weather Christian," but boldly confessed the faith amid the fires of the last and most terrible of the great persecutions. Its probable date suggests that his treatise on the persecutors may have been a far-reaching effort to dissuade the Cæsars of a later age from trying to restore "the gods to Latium." I confess my own partiality to our author, and the interest with which his writings continue to impress me, even now. In youth (*Consule Planco*) I brought to his pages an enthusiastic appreciation of the genius which had adorned the very dawn of Christian civilization by works of literary merit not inferior to those of the Augustan age. The crabbed Latinity of Tertullian has charms, indeed, of its own sort: it was the shaggy raiment of the ascetic and the confessor, "always bearing about in his own body the dying of the Lord Jesus." It befitted the age and the man, and those awful realities with which Christians had then to deal. Not words, but things, were their one concern. It is pleasant to find, however, that Christianity is not incapable of meeting all sorts and conditions of men; and Lactantius was doubtless the instrument of Providence in bearing the testimony of Jesus, "even before kings," in language which promised to Roman letters the new and commanding development imparted to its language by Christianity, which has made it imperishable, and more truly "eternal" than Rome itself.

The following is the Introductory Notice of the reverend translator:[2] —

Lactantius has always held a very high place among the Christian Fathers, not only on account of the subject-matter of his writings, but also on account of the varied erudition, the sweetness of expression, and the grace and elegance of style, by which they are characterized. It appears, therefore, more remarkable that so little is known with certainty respecting his personal history. We are unable to fix with precision either the place or time of his birth, and even his name has been the subject of much discussion. It is known that he was a pupil of Arnobius, who gave lectures in rhetoric at Sicca in Africa. Hence it has been supposed that Lactantius was a native of Africa, while others have maintained that he was born in Italy, and that his birthplace probably was Firmium, on the Adriatic. He was probably born about the middle of the third century, since he is spoken of as far advanced in life about A.D. 315. He is usually denominated "Lucius Cælius Firmianus Lactantius;" but the name Cæcilius is sometimes substituted for Cælius, and it is uncertain whether Firmianus is a family name or a local[3] designation. Some have even supposed that he received the name of *Lactantius* from the milky softness of his style.

He attained to great eminence as a teacher of rhetoric, and his fame far outstripped the reputation of his master Arnobius. Such, indeed, was his celebrity, that he was invited by the Emperor Diocletian to settle at Nicomedia, and there practise his art. He appears, however, to have met with so little success in that city, as to have been reduced to extreme indigence. Abandoning his profession as a pleader, he devoted himself to literary composition. It was

[1] See his *Address to the Assembly of the Saints*, preserved by Eusebius.
[2] William Fletcher, D.D., head master of Queen Elizabeth's School, Wimborne, Dorset.
[3] i.e., of Firmium.

probably at this period that he embraced the Christian faith, and we may perhaps be justified in supposing some connection between his poverty and his change of religion.[1] He was afterwards called to settle in Gaul, probably about A.D. 315, and the Emperor Constantine entrusted to him the education of his son Crispus. He is believed to have died at Trèves about A.D. 325.

His principal work is *The Christian Institutions*, or an *Introduction to True Religion*, in seven books, designed to supersede[2] the less complete treatises of Minucius Felix, Tertullian, and Cyprian. In these books, each of which has a distinct title, and constitutes a separate essay, he demonstrates the falsehood of the pagan religion, shows the vanity of the heathen philosophy, and undertakes the defence of the Christian religion against its adversaries. He also sets forth the nature of righteousness, gives instructions concerning the true worship of God, and treats of the punishment of the wicked, and the reward of the righteous in everlasting happiness.

To the *Institutions* is appended an epitome dedicated to Pentadius. The authorship of this abridgment has been questioned in modern times; but it is expressly assigned to Lactantius by Hieronymus. The greater part of the work was wanting in the earlier editions, and it was not until the beginning of the eighteenth century that it was discovered nearly entire.[3]

The treatise on *The Anger of God* is directed mainly against the tenets of the Epicureans and Stoics, who maintained that the deeds of men could produce no emotions of pleasure or anger in the Deity. Lactantius holds that the love of the good necessarily implies the hatred of evil; and that the tenets of these philosophers, as tending to overthrow the doctrine of future rewards and punishments, are subversive of the principles of true religion.

In the treatise on *The Workmanship of God*, or *The Formation of Man*, the author dwells upon the wonderful construction of the human frame, and the adaptation of means to ends therein displayed, as proofs of the wisdom and goodness of God. The latter part of the book contains speculations concerning the nature and origin of the soul.

In the treatise[4] on the *Deaths of Persecutors*, an argument for the truth of the Christian religion is derived from the fact, that those emperors who had been most distinguished as persecutors of the Christians, were special objects of divine vengeance.

To these treatises are usually appended some poetical works which have been attributed to Lactantius, but it is very questionable whether any of them were really written by him.

The poem on the *Phœnix* appears to be of a comparatively modern date.

That on *Easter*[5] is believed to have been composed by Venantius Honorianus Clementianus Fortunatus in the sixth century.

The poem on the *Passion of the Lord*, though much admired both in its language and style of thought, bears the impress of a later age.[6]

There is also a collection of *A Hundred Enigmas*,[7] which has been attributed to Lactantius; but there is good reason to suppose that they are not the production of his pen. Heumann endeavoured to prove that *Symposium* is the title of the work, and that no such person as Symposius[8] ever existed. But this opinion is untenable. It is true that Hieronymus speaks of Lactantius as the author of a Symposium, but there are no grounds for supposing that the work was of a light and trifling character: it was probably a serious dialogue.

The style of Lactantius has been deservedly praised for the dignity, elegance, and clearness

---

1 [I see no force in this suggestion. Quite the reverse. He could not then anticipate anything but worse sufferings.]

2 [To supplement, rather.]

3 In an ancient MS. at Turin.

4 Lord Hailes' translation has been adopted in the present edition.

5 *De Paschâ*.

6 It has an allusion to the adoration of the cross. [Hence must be referred to a period subsequent to the pseudo-council called Deutero-Nicene. Comp. vol. iv. note 6, p. 191; and see Smith's *History of the Christian Church in the First Ten Centuries*, vol. i. p. 451, ed. Harpers, New York.]

7 The Enigmas have not been included in the present translation, for the reason mentioned.

8 The title prefixed to them in the MSS. is Firmianus Symposius (written also Symphosius) Cælius. See Dr. Smith's *Dictionary of Biography*, under the names Firmianus and Lactantius.

of expression by which it is characterized, and which have gained for him the appellation of the Christian Cicero. His writings everywhere give evidence of his varied and extensive erudition, and contain much valuable information respecting the systems of the ancient philosophers. But his claims as a theologian are open to question; for he holds peculiar opinions on many points, and he appears more successful as an opponent of error than as a maintainer of the truth. Lactantius has been charged with a leaning to Manicheism,[1] but the charge appears to be unfounded.

The translation has been made from Migne's edition, from which most of the notes have been taken. The quotations from Virgil have been given in the words of Conington's translation,[2] and those from Lucretius in the words of Munro.

---

[1] This question is fully discussed by Dr. Lardner in his *Credibility of the Gospel History, Works*, vol. iii. [p. 516. The whole chapter (lxv.) on Lactantius deserves study].

[2] [Which reduces many of Virgil's finest and most Homeric passages to mere song and ballad, and sacrifices all their epic dignity.]

THE DIVINE INSTITUTES

BOOK I.

OF THE FALSE WORSHIP OF THE GODS.

PREFACE. — OF WHAT GREAT VALUE THE KNOWLEDGE OF THE TRUTH IS AND ALWAYS HAS BEEN.

MEN of great and distinguished talent, when they had entirely devoted themselves to learning, holding in contempt all actions both private and public, applied to the pursuit of investigating the truth whatever labour could be bestowed upon it; thinking it much more excellent to investigate and know the method of human and divine things, than to be entirely occupied with the heaping up of riches or the accumulation of honours. For no one can be made better or more just by these things, since they are frail and earthly, and pertain to the adorning of the body only. Those men were indeed most deserving of the knowledge of the truth, which they so greatly desired to know, that they even preferred it to all things. For it is plain that some gave up their property, and altogether abandoned the pursuit of pleasures, that, being disengaged and without impediment, they might follow the simple truth, and it alone. And so greatly did the name and authority of the truth prevail with them, that they proclaimed that the reward of the greatest good was contained in it. But they did not obtain the object of their wish, and at the same time lost their labour and industry; because the truth, that is the secret of the Most High God, who created all things, cannot be attained by our own ability and perceptions. Otherwise there would be no difference between God and man, if human thought could reach to the counsels and arrangements of that eternal majesty. And because it was impossible that the divine method of procedure should become known to man by his own efforts, God did not suffer man any longer to err in search of the light of wisdom, and to wander through inextricable darkness without any result of his labour, but at length opened his eyes, and made the investigation of the truth His own gift, so that He might show the nothingness of human wisdom, and point out to man wandering in error the way of obtaining immortality.

But since few make use of this heavenly benefit and gift, because the truth lies hidden veiled in obscurity; and it is either an object of contempt to the learned because it has not suitable defenders, or is hated by the unlearned on account of its natural severity, which the nature of men inclined to vices cannot endure: for because there is a bitterness mingled with virtues, while vices are seasoned with pleasure, offended by the former and soothed by the latter, they are borne headlong, and deceived by the appearance of good things, they embrace evils for goods, — I have believed that these errors should be encountered, that both the learned may be directed to true wisdom, and the unlearned to true religion. And this profession is to be thought much better, more useful and glorious, than that of oratory, in which being long engaged, we trained young men not to virtue, but altogether to cunning wickedness.[1] Certainly we shall now much more rightly discuss respecting the heavenly precepts, by which we may be able to instruct the minds of men to the worship of the true majesty. Nor does he deserve so well respecting the affairs of men, who imparts the knowledge of speaking well, as he who teaches men to live in piety and innocence; on which account the philosophers were in greater glory among the Greeks than the orators. For they, *the philosophers*, were considered teachers of right living, which is far more excellent, since to speak well belongs only to a few, but to live well belongs to all. Yet that practice in fictitious suits has been of great advantage to us, so that we are now able to plead the cause of truth with greater copiousness and ability of speaking; for although the truth may be defended without eloquence, as it often has

---

[1] [This, St. Augustine powerfully illustrates. See *Confessions*, lib. iii. cap 3. Note also *Ib.*, lib. ix. cap 5.]

been defended by many, yet it needs to be explained, and in a measure discussed, with distinctness and elegance of speech, in order that it may flow with greater power into the minds of men, being both provided with its own force, and adorned with the brilliancy of speech.

CHAP. I. — OF RELIGION AND WISDOM.

We undertake, therefore, to discuss religion and divine things. For if some of the greatest orators, veterans as it were of their profession, having completed the works of their pleadings, at last gave themselves up to philosophy, and regarded that as a most just rest from their labours, if they tortured their minds in the investigation of those things which could not be found out, so that they appear to have sought for themselves not so much leisure as occupation, and that indeed with much greater trouble than in their former pursuit; how much more justly shall I betake myself as to a most safe harbour, to that pious, true, and divine wisdom, in which all things are ready for utterance, pleasant to the hearing, easy to be understood, honourable to be undertaken! And if some skilful men and arbiters of justice composed and published Institutions of civil law, by which they might lull the strifes and contentions of discordant citizens, how much better and more rightly shall we follow up in writing the divine Institutions, in which we shall not speak about rain-droppings, or the turning of waters, or the preferring of claims, but we shall speak of hope, of life, of salvation, of immortality, and of God, that we may put an end to deadly superstitions and most disgraceful errors.

And we now commence this work under the auspices of your name, O mighty Emperor Constantine, who were the first of the Roman princes to repudiate errors, and to acknowledge and honour the majesty of the one and only true God.[1] For when that most happy day had shone upon the world, in which the Most High God raised you to the prosperous height of power, you entered upon a dominion which was salutary and desirable for all, with an excellent beginning, when, restoring justice which had been overthrown and taken away, you expiated the most shameful deed of others. In return for which action God will grant to you happiness, virtue, and length of days, that even when old you may govern the state with the same justice with which you began in youth, and may hand down to your children the guardianship of the Roman name, as you yourself received it from your father. For to the wicked, who still rage against the righteous in other parts of the world, the Omnipotent will also repay the reward of their wickedness with a severity proportioned to its tardiness; for as He is a most indulgent Father towards the godly, so is He a most upright Judge against the ungodly. And in my desire to defend His religion and divine worship, to whom can I rather appeal, whom can I address, but him by whom justice and wisdom have been restored to the affairs of men?

Therefore, leaving the authors of this earthly philosophy, who bring forward nothing certain, let us approach the right path; for if I considered these to be sufficiently suitable guides to a good life, I would both follow them myself, and exhort others to follow them. But since they disagree among one another with great contention, and are for the most part at variance with themselves, it is evident that their path is by no means straightforward; since they have severally marked out distinct ways for themselves according to their own will, and have left great confusion to those who are seeking for the truth. But since the truth is revealed from heaven to us who have received the mystery of true religion, and since we follow God, the teacher of wisdom and the guide to truth, we call together all, without any distinction either of sex or of age, to heavenly pasture. For there is no more pleasant food for the soul than the knowledge of truth,[2] to the maintaining and explaining of which we have destined seven books, although the subject is one of almost boundless and immeasurable labour; so that if any one should wish to dilate upon and follow up these things to their full extent, he would have such an exuberant supply of subjects, that neither books would find any limit, nor speech any end. But on this account we will put together all things briefly, because those things which we are about to bring forward are so plain and lucid, that it seems to be more wonderful that the truth appears so obscure to men, and to those especially who are commonly esteemed wise, or because men will only need to be trained by us, — that is, to be recalled from the error in which they are entangled to a better course of life.

And if, as I hope, we shall attain to this, we will send them to the very fountain of learning, which is most rich and abundant, by copious draughts of which they may appease the thirst conceived within, and quench their ardour. And all things will be easy, ready of accomplishment, and clear to them, if only they are not annoyed at applying patience in reading or hearing to the perception of the discipline of wisdom.[3] For many, pertinaciously adhering to vain superstitions, harden themselves against the manifest

[1] [It thrills me to compare this modest tribute of Christian confidence, with Justin's unheeded appeal to the Stoical Antonine.]

[2] [Pilate is answered at last out of the Roman court itself.]

[3] ["How charming is divine philosophy!
Not harsh and crabbed, as dull fools suppose."
— Milton, *Comus*.]

truth, not so much deserving well of their religions, which they wrongly maintain, as they deserve ill of themselves; who, when they have a straight path, seek devious windings; who leave the level ground that they may glide over a precipice; who leave the light, that, blind and enfeebled, they may lie in darkness. We must provide for these, that they may not fight against themselves, and that they may be willing at length to be freed from inveterate errors. And this they will assuredly do if they shall at any time see for what purpose they were born; for this is the cause of their perverseness, — namely, ignorance of themselves: and if any one, having gained the knowledge of the truth, shall have shaken off this ignorance, he will know to what object his life is to be directed, and how it is to be spent. And I thus briefly define the sum of this knowledge, that neither is any religion to be undertaken without wisdom, nor any wisdom to be approved of without religion.

CHAP. II. — THAT THERE IS A PROVIDENCE IN THE AFFAIRS OF MEN.

Having therefore undertaken the office of explaining the truth, I did not think it so necessary to take my commencement from that inquiry which naturally seems the first, whether there is a providence which consults for all things, or all things were either made or are governed by chance; which sentiment was introduced by Democritus, and confirmed by Epicurus. But before them, what did Protagoras effect, who raised doubts respecting the gods; or Diagoras afterwards, who excluded them; and some others, who did not hold the existence of gods, except that there was supposed to be no providence? These, however, were most vigorously opposed by the other philosophers, and especially by the Stoics, who taught that the universe could neither have been made without divine intelligence, nor continue to exist unless it were governed by the highest intelligence. But even Marcus Tullius, although he was a defender of the Academic system, discussed at length and on many occasions respecting the providence which governs affairs, confirming the arguments of the Stoics, and himself adducing many new ones; and this he does both in all the books of his own philosophy, and especially in those which treat of the nature of the gods.[1]

And it was no difficult task, indeed, to refute the falsehoods of a few men who entertained perverse sentiments by the testimony of communities and tribes, who on this one point had no disagreement. For there is no one so uncivilized, and of such an uncultivated disposition, who, when he raises his eyes to heaven, although he knows not by the providence of what God all this visible universe is governed, does not understand from the very magnitude of the objects, from their motion, arrangement, constancy, usefulness, beauty, and temperament, that there is some providence, and that that which exists with wonderful method must have been prepared by some greater intelligence. And for us, assuredly, it is very easy to follow up this part as copiously as it may please us. But because the subject has been much agitated among philosophers, and they who take away providence appear to have been sufficiently answered by men of sagacity and eloquence, and because it is necessary to speak, in different places throughout this work which we have undertaken, respecting the skill of the divine providence, let us for the present omit this inquiry, which is so closely connected with the other questions, that it seems possible for us to discuss no subject, without at the same time discussing the subject of providence.

CHAP. III. — WHETHER THE UNIVERSE IS GOVERNED BY THE POWER OF ONE GOD OR OF MANY.

Let the commencement of our work therefore be that inquiry which closely follows and is connected with the first: Whether the universe is governed by the power of one God or of many. There is no one, who possesses intelligence and uses reflection, who does not understand that it is one Being who both created all things and governs them with the same energy by which He created them. For what need is there of many to sustain the government of the universe? unless we should happen to think that, if there were more than one, each would possess less might and strength. And they who hold that there are many gods, do indeed effect this; for those gods must of necessity be weak, since individually, without the aid of the others, they would be unable to sustain the government of so vast a mass. But God, who is the Eternal Mind, is undoubtedly of excellence, complete and perfect in every part. And if this is true, He must of necessity be one. For power or excellence, which is complete, retains its own peculiar stability. But that is to be regarded as solid from which nothing can be taken away, that as perfect to which nothing can be added.

Who can doubt that he would be a most powerful king who should have the government of the whole world? And not without reason, since all things which everywhere exist would belong to him, since all resources from all quarters would be centred in him alone. But if more than one divide the government of the world, undoubtedly each will have less power and strength, since every one must confine him-

[1] [Ingeniously introduced, and afterward very forcibly expanded.]

self within his prescribed portion.[1] In the same manner also, if there are more gods than one, they will be of less weight, others having in themselves the same power. But the nature of excellence admits of greater perfection in him in whom the whole is, than in him in whom there is only a small part of the whole. But God, if He is perfect, as He ought to be, cannot but be one, because He is perfect, so that all things may be in Him. Therefore the excellences and powers of the gods must necessarily be weaker, because so much will be wanting to each as shall be in the others; and so the more there are, so much the less powerful will they be. Why should I mention that this highest power and divine energy is altogether incapable of division? For whatever is capable of division must of necessity be liable to destruction also. But if destruction is far removed from God, because He is incorruptible and eternal, it follows that the divine power is incapable of division. Therefore God is one, if that which admits of so great power can be nothing else: and yet those who deem that there are many gods, say that they have divided their functions among themselves; but we will discuss all these matters at their proper places. In the meantime, I affirm this, which belongs to the present subject. If they have divided their functions among themselves, the matter comes back to the same point, that any one of them is unable to supply the place of all. He cannot, then, be perfect who is unable to govern all things while the others are unemployed. And so is comes to pass, that for the government of the universe there is more need of the perfect excellence of one than of the imperfect powers of many. But he who imagines that so great a magnitude as this cannot be governed by one Being, is deceived. For he does not comprehend how great are the might and power of the divine majesty, if he thinks that the one God, who had power to create the universe, is also unable to govern that which He has created. But if he conceives in his mind how great is the immensity of that divine work, when before it was nothing, yet that by the power and wisdom of God it was made out of nothing — a work which could only be commenced and accomplished by one — he will now understand that that which has been established by one is much more easily governed by one.

Some one may perhaps say that so immense a work as that of the universe could not even have been fabricated except by many. But however many and however great he may consider them, — whatever magnitude, power, excellence, and majesty he may attribute to the many, — the whole of that I assign to one, and say that it exists in one: so that there is in Him such an amount of these properties as can neither be conceived nor expressed. And since we fail in this subject, both in perception and in words — for neither does the human breast admit the light of so great understanding, nor is the mortal tongue capable of explaining such great subjects — it is right that we should understand and say this very same thing. I see, again, what can be alleged on the other hand, that those many gods are such as we hold the one God to be. But this cannot possibly be so, because the power of these gods individually will not be able to proceed further, the power of the others meeting and hindering them. For either each must be unable to pass beyond his own limits, or, if he shall have passed beyond them, he must drive another from his boundaries. They who believe that there are many gods, do not see that it may happen that some may be opposed to others in their wishes, from which circumstance disputing and contention would arise among them; as Homer represented the gods at war among themselves, since some desired that Troy should be taken, others opposed it. The universe, therefore, must be ruled by the will of one. For unless the power over the separate parts be referred to one and the same providence, the whole itself will not be able to exist; since each takes care of nothing beyond that which belongs peculiarly to him, just as warfare could not be carried on without one general and commander. But if there were in one army as many generals as there are legions, cohorts, divisions,[2] and squadrons, first of all it would not be possible for the army to be drawn out in battle array, since each would refuse the peril; nor could it easily be governed or controlled, because all would use their own peculiar counsels, by the diversity of which they would inflict more injury than they would confer advantage. So, in this government of the affairs of nature, unless there shall be one to whom the care of the whole is referred, all things will be dissolved and fall to decay.

But to say that the universe is governed by the will of many, is equivalent to a declaration that there are many minds in one body, since there are many and various offices of the members, so that separate minds may be supposed to govern separate senses; and also the many affections, by which we are accustomed to be moved either to anger, or to desire, or to joy, or to fear, or to pity, so that in all these affections as many minds may be supposed to operate; and if any one should say this, he would appear to be destitute even of that very mind, which is one. But

[1] [A hint to Cæsar himself, the force of which began soon after very sorely to be felt in the empire.]

[2] Cunei; properly, soldiers arranged in the shape of a wedge.

if in one body one mind possesses the government of so many things, and is at the same time occupied with the whole, why should any one suppose that the universe cannot be governed by one, but that it can be governed by more than one? And because those maintainers of many gods are aware of this, they say that they so preside over separate offices and parts, that there is still one chief ruler. The others, therefore, on this principle, will not be gods, but attendants and ministers, whom that one most mighty and omnipotent appointed to these offices, and they themselves will be subservient to his authority and command. If, therefore, all are not equal to one another, all are not gods; for that which serves and that which rules cannot be the same. For if God is a title of the highest power, He must be incorruptible, perfect, incapable of suffering, and subject to no *other* being; therefore they are not gods whom necessity compels to obey the one greatest God. But because they who hold this opinion are not deceived without cause, we will presently lay open the cause of this error. Now, let us prove by testimonies the unity of the divine power.

CHAP. IV. — THAT THE ONE GOD WAS FORETOLD EVEN BY THE PROPHETS.

The prophets, who were very many, proclaim and declare the one God; for, being filled with the inspiration of the one God, they predicted things to come, with agreeing and harmonious voice. But those who are ignorant of the truth do not think that these prophets are to be believed; for they say that those voices are not divine, but human. Forsooth, because they proclaim one God, they were either madmen or deceivers. But truly we see that their predictions have been fulfilled, and are in course of fulfilment daily; and their foresight, agreeing as it does to one opinion, teaches that they were not under the impulse of madness. For who possessed of a frenzied mind would be able, I do not say to predict the future, but even to speak coherently? Were they, therefore, who spoke such things deceitful? What was so utterly foreign to their nature as a system of deceit, when they themselves restrained others from all fraud? For to this end were they sent by God, that they should both be heralds of His majesty, and correctors of the wickedness of man.

Moreover, the inclination to feign and speak falsely belongs to those who covet riches, and eagerly desire gains, — a disposition which was far removed from those holy men. For they so discharged the office entrusted to them, that, disregarding all things necessary for the maintenance of life, they were so far from laying up store for the future, that they did not even labour for the day, content with the unstored food which God had supplied; and these not only had no gains, but even endured torments and death. For the precepts of righteousness are distasteful to the wicked, and to those who lead an unholy life. Wherefore they, whose sins were brought to light and forbidden, most cruelly tortured and slew them. They, therefore, who had no desire for gain, had neither the inclination nor the motive for deceit. Why should I say that some of them were princes, or even kings,[1] upon whom the suspicion of covetousness and fraud could not possibly fall, and yet they proclaimed the one God with the same prophetic foresight as the others?

CHAP. V. — OF THE TESTIMONIES OF POETS AND PHILOSOPHERS.

But let us leave the testimony of prophets, lest a proof derived from those who are universally disbelieved should appear insufficient. Let us come to authors, and for the demonstration of the truth let us cite as witnesses those very persons whom they are accustomed to make use of against us, — I mean poets and philosophers. From these we cannot fail in proving the unity of God; not that they had ascertained the truth, but that the force of the truth itself is so great, that no one can be so blind as not to see the divine brightness presenting itself to his eyes. The poets, therefore, however much they adorned the gods in their poems, and amplified their exploits with the highest praises, yet very frequently confess that all things are held together and governed by one spirit or mind. Orpheus, who is the most ancient of the poets, and coeval with the gods themselves, — since it is reported that he sailed among the Argonauts together with the sons of Tyndarus and Hercules, — speaks of the true and great God as the first-born,[2] because nothing was produced before Him, but all things sprung from Him. He also calls Him Phanes[3] because when as yet there was nothing He first appeared and came forth from the infinite. And since he was unable to conceive in his mind the origin and nature of this Being, he said that He was born from the boundless air: "The first-born, Phaethon, son of the extended air;" for he had nothing more to say. He affirms that this Being is the Parent of all the gods, on whose account He framed the heaven, and provided for His children that they might have a habitation and place of abode in common: "He built for immortals an imperishable home." Thus, under the guidance of nature and reason, he understood that there was a power of surpassing

1 [Not David merely, nor only other kings of the Hebrews. Elucidation I.]

2 πρωτόγονον.

3 φάνητα, the appearer.

greatness which framed heaven and earth. For he could not say that Jupiter was the author of all things, since he was born from Saturn; nor could he say that Saturn himself was their author, since it was reported that he was produced from the heaven; but he did not venture to set up the heaven as the primeval god, because he saw that it was an element of the universe, and must itself have had an author. This consideration led him to that first-born god, to whom he assigns and gives the first place.

Homer was able to give us no information relating to the truth, for he wrote of human rather than divine things. Hesiod was able, for he comprised in the work of one book the generation of the gods; but yet he gave us no information, for he took his commencement not from God the Creator, but from chaos, which is a confused mass of rude and unarranged matter; whereas he ought first to have explained from what source, at what time, and in what manner, chaos itself had begun to exist or to have consistency. Without doubt, as all things were placed in order, arranged, and made by some artificer, so matter itself must of necessity have been formed by some being. Who, then, made it except God, to whose power all things are subject? But he shrinks from admitting this, while he dreads the unknown truth. For, as he wished it to appear, it was by the inspiration of the Muses that he poured forth that song on Helicon; but he had come after previous meditation and preparation.

Maro was the first of our poets to approach the truth, who thus speaks respecting the highest God, whom he calls Mind and Spirit:[1] —

> "Know first, the heaven, the earth, the main,
> The moon's pale orb, the starry train,
> Are nourished by a Soul,
> A Spirit, whose celestial flame
> Glows in each member of the frame,
> And stirs the mighty whole."

And lest any one should happen to be ignorant what that Spirit was which had so much power, he has declared it in another place, saying:[2] "For the Deity pervades all lands, the tracts of sea and depth of heaven; the flocks, the herds, and men, and all the race of beasts, each at its birth, derive their slender lives from Him."

Ovid also, in the beginning of his remarkable work, without any disguising of the name, admits that the universe was arranged by God, whom he calls the Framer of the world, the Artificer of all things.[3] But if either Orpheus or these poets of our country had always maintained what they perceived under the guidance of nature, they would have comprehended the truth, and gained the same learning which we follow.[4]

But thus far of the poets. Let us come to the philosophers, whose authority is of greater weight, and their judgment more to be relied on, because they are believed to have paid attention, not to matters of fiction, but to the investigation of the truth. Thales of Miletus, who was one of the number of the seven wise men, and who is said to have been the first of all to inquire respecting natural causes, said that water was the element from which all things were produced, and that God was the mind which formed all things from water. Thus he placed the material of all things in moisture; he fixed the beginning and cause of their production in God. Pythagoras thus defined the being of God, "as a soul passing to and fro, and diffused through all parts of the universe, and through all nature, from which all living creatures which are produced derive their life." Anaxagoras said that God was an infinite mind, which moves by its own power. Antisthenes maintained that the gods of the people were many, but that the God of nature was one only; that is, the Fabricator of the whole universe. Cleanthes and Anaximenes assert that the air is the chief deity; and to this opinion our poet has assented:[5] "Then almighty father Æther descends in fertile showers into the bosom of his joyous spouse; and great himself, mingling with her great body, nourishes all her offspring." Chrysippus speaks of God as a natural power endowed with divine reason, and sometimes as a divine necessity. Zeno also speaks of Him as a divine and natural law. The opinion of all these, however uncertain it is, has reference to one point, — to their agreement in the existence of one providence. For whether it be nature, or æther, or reason, or mind, or a fatal necessity, or a divine law, or if you term it anything else, it is the same which is called by us God. Nor does the diversity of titles prove an obstacle, since by their very signification they all refer to one object. Aristotle, although he is at variance with himself, and both utters and holds sentiments opposed to one another, yet upon the whole bears witness that one Mind presides over the universe. Plato, who is judged the wisest of all, plainly and openly maintains the rule of one God; nor does he name Him Æther, or Reason, or Nature, but, as He truly is, God, and that this universe, so perfect and wonderful, was fabricated by Him. And Cicero, following and imitating him in many instances, frequently acknowledges God, and calls Him supreme, in those books which he wrote on the

1 *Æn.*, vi. 724.

2 *Georg.*, iv. 221. [These passages seem borrowed from the *Octavius* of Minucius, cap. 19, vol. iv. p. 183.]

3 [Fabricatorem mundi, rerum opificem.]

4 [Concerning the *Orphica*, see vol. i. p. 178, note 1, and pp. 279, 290. For *Sibyllina*, *Ibid.*, p. 169, note 9, and pp. 280–289. Note also vol. ii. p. 194, note 2, and T. Lewis, *Plato cont. Ath.*, p. 99.]

5 Virg., *Georg.*, ii. 325–327.

subject of laws; and he adduces proof that the universe is governed by Him, when he argues respecting the nature of the gods in this way: "Nothing is superior to God: the world must therefore be governed by Him. Therefore God is obedient or subject to no nature; consequently He Himself governs all nature." But what God Himself is he defines in his *Consolation:*[1] "Nor can God Himself, as He is comprehended by us, be comprehended in any other way than as a mind free and unrestrained, far removed from all mortal materiality, perceiving and moving all things."

How often, also, does Annæus Seneca, who was the keenest Stoic of the Romans, follow up with deserved praise the supreme Deity! For when he was discussing the subject of premature death, he said: "You do not understand the authority and majesty of your Judge, the Ruler of the world, and the God of heaven and of all gods, on whom those deities which we separately worship and honour are dependent." Also in his *Exhortations:* "This Being, when He was laying the first foundations of the most beautiful fabric, and was commencing this work, than which nature has known nothing greater or better, that all things might serve their own rulers, although He had spread Himself out through the whole body, yet He produced gods as ministers of His kingdom." And how many other things like to our own writers did he speak on the subject of God! But these things I put off for the present, because they are more suited to other parts of the subject. At present it is enough to demonstrate that men of the highest genius touched upon the truth, and almost grasped it, had not custom, infatuated by false opinions, carried them back; by which custom they both deemed that there were other gods, and believed that those things which God made for the use of man, as though they were endowed with perception, were to be held and worshipped as gods.

CHAP. VI. — OF DIVINE TESTIMONIES, AND OF THE SIBYLS AND THEIR PREDICTIONS.

Now let us pass to divine testimonies; but I will previously bring forward one which resembles a divine testimony, both on account of its very great antiquity, and because he whom I shall name was taken from men and placed among the gods. According to Cicero, Caius Cotta the pontiff, while disputing against the Stoics concerning superstitions, and the variety of opinions which prevail respecting the gods, in order that he might, after the custom of the Academics, make everything uncertain, says that there were five Mercuries; and having enumerated four in order, says that the fifth was he by whom Argus was slain, and that on this account he fled into Egypt, and gave laws and letters to the Egyptians. The Egyptians call him Thoth; and from him the first month of their year, that is, September, received its name among them. He also built a town, which is even now called in Greek Hermopolis (the town of Mercury), and the inhabitants of Phenæ honour him with religious worship. And although he was a man, yet he was of great antiquity, and most fully imbued with every kind of learning, so that the knowledge of many subjects and arts acquired for him the name of Trismegistus.[2] He wrote books, and those in great numbers, relating to the knowledge of divine things, in which he asserts the majesty of the supreme and only God, and makes mention of Him by the same names which we use — God and Father. And that no one might inquire His name, he said that He was without name, and that on account of His very unity He does not require the peculiarity of a name. These are his own words: "God is one, but He who is one only does not need a name; for He who is self-existent is without a name." God, therefore, has no name, because He is alone; nor is there any need of a proper name, except in cases where a multitude of persons requires a distinguishing mark, so that you may designate each person by his own mark and appellation. But God, because He is always one, has no peculiar name.

It remains for me to bring forward testimonies respecting the sacred responses and predictions, which are much more to be relied upon. For perhaps they against whom we are arguing may think that no credence is to be given to poets, as though they invented fictions, nor to philosophers, inasmuch as they were liable to err, being themselves but men. Marcus Varro, than whom no man of greater learning ever lived, even among the Greeks, much less among the Latins, in those books respecting divine subjects which he addressed to Caius Cæsar the chief pontiff, when he was speaking of the Quindecemviri,[3] says that the Sibylline books were not the production of one Sibyl only, but that they were called by one name Sibylline, because all prophetesses were called by the ancients Sibyls, either from the name of one, the Delphian priestess, or from their proclaiming the counsels of the gods. For in the Æolic dialect they used to call the gods by the word *Sioi*, not *Theoi;* and for counsel they used the word *bule*, not *boule;* — and so the Sibyl received her name as though *Siobule*.[4] But he says that the Sibyls

[1] [See (Sigonius) p. 144, ed. Paris, 1818.]

[2] [See vol. i. p. 289, note 2, this series.]

[3] The Quindecemviri were the fifteen men to whom the care of the Sibylline books was entrusted. At first two (Duumviri) were appointed. The number was afterwards increased to ten, and subsequently to fifteen. It appears probable that this last change was made by Sulla.

[4] [i.e., Counsel of God. See p. 14 *supra*, and 16 *infra*.]

were ten in number, and he enumerated them all under the writers, who wrote an account of each: that the *first* was from the Persians, and of her Nicanor made mention, who wrote the exploits of Alexander of Macedon; — the *second* of Libya, and of her Euripides makes mention in the prologue of the Lamia; — the *third* of Delphi, concerning whom Chrysippus speaks in that book which he composed concerning divination; — the *fourth* a Cimmerian in Italy, whom Nævius mentions in his books of the Punic war, and Piso in his annals; — the *fifth* of Erythræa, whom Apollodorus of Erythræa affirms to have been his own countrywoman, and that she foretold to the Greeks when they were setting but for Ilium, both that Troy was doomed to destruction, and that Homer would write falsehoods; — the *sixth* of Samos, respecting whom Eratosthenes writes that he had found a written notice in the ancient annals of the Samians. The *seventh was* of Cumæ, by name Amalthæa, who is termed by some Herophile, or Demophile and *they say* that she brought nine books to the king Tarquinius Priscus, and asked for them three hundred philippics, and that the king refused so great a price, and derided the madness of the woman; that she, in the sight of the king, burnt three of the books, and demanded the same price for those which were left; that Tarquinius much more considered the woman to be mad; and that when she again, having burnt three other books, persisted in asking the same price, the king was moved, and bought the remaining books for the three hundred pieces of gold: and the number of these books was afterwards increased, after the rebuilding of the Capitol; because they were collected from all cities of Italy and Greece, and especially from those of Erythræa, and were brought to Rome, under the name of whatever Sibyl they were. *Further*, that the *eighth* was from the Hellespont, born in the Trojan territory, in the village of Marpessus, about the town of Gergithus; and Heraclides of Pontus writes that she lived in the times of Solon and Cyrus; — the *ninth* of Phrygia, who gave oracles at Ancyra; — the *tenth* of Tibur, by name Albunea, who is worshipped at Tibur as a goddess, near the banks of the river Anio, in the depths of which her statue is said to have been found, holding in her hand a book. The senate transferred her oracles into the Capitol.

The predictions of all these Sibyls[1] are both brought forward and esteemed as such, except those of the Cumæan Sibyl, whose books are concealed by the Romans; nor do they consider it lawful for them to be inspected by any one but the *Quindecemviri*. And there are separate books the production of each, but because these are inscribed with the name of the Sibyl they are believed to be the work of one; and they are confused, nor can the productions of each be distinguished and assigned to their own authors, except in the case of the Erythræan Sibyl, for she both inserted her own true name in her verse, and predicted that she would be called Erythræan, though she was born at Babylon. But we also shall speak of the Sibyl without any distinction, wherever we shall have occasion to use their testimonies. All these Sibyls, then, proclaim one God, and especially the Erythræan, who is regarded among the others as more celebrated and noble; since Fenestella, a most diligent writer, speaking of the *Quindecemviri*, says that, after the rebuilding of the Capitol, Caius Curio the consul proposed to the senate that ambassadors should be sent to Erythræ to search out and bring to Rome the writings of the Sibyl; and that, accordingly, Publius Gabinius, Marcus Otacilius, and Lucius Valerius were sent, who conveyed to Rome about a thousand verses written out by private persons. We have shown before that Varro made the same statement. Now in these verses which the ambassadors brought to Rome, are these testimonies respecting the one God: —

1. "One God, who is alone, most mighty, uncreated."

This is the only supreme God, who made the heaven, and decked it with lights.

2. "But there is one only God of pre-eminent power, who made the heaven, and sun, and stars, and moon, and fruitful earth, and waves of the water of the sea."

And since He alone is the framer of the universe, and the artificer of all things of which it consists or which are contained in it, it testifies that He alone ought to be worshipped: —

3. "Worship Him who is alone the ruler of the world, who alone was and is from age to age."

Also another Sibyl, whoever she is, when she said that she conveyed the voice of God to men, thus spoke: —

4. "I am the one only God, and there is no other God."

I would now follow up the testimonies of the others, were it not that these are sufficient, and that I reserve others for more befitting opportunities. But since we are defending the cause of truth before those who err from the truth and serve false religions, what kind of proof ought we to bring forward[2] against them, rather than to refute them by the testimonies of their own gods?

[1] [Concerning the Sibyls, see also, fully, Lardner, *Credib.*, ii. 258, 334, etc. On the use here and elsewhere made of them by our author, *Ibid.*, p. 343, and iii. 544; also pp. 14 and 15, *supra*.]

[2] [Vol. ii. cap. 28, p. 143.]

CHAP. VII. — CONCERNING THE TESTIMONIES OF APOLLO AND THE GODS.

Apollo, indeed, whom they think divine above all others, and especially prophetic, giving responses at Colophon, — I suppose because, induced by the pleasantness of Asia, he had removed from Delphi, — to some one who asked who He was, or what God was at all, replied in twenty-one verses, of which this is the beginning: —

> "Self-produced, untaught, without a mother, unshaken,
> A name not even to be comprised in word, dwelling in fire,
> This is God; and we His messengers are a slight portion of God."

Can any one suspect that this is spoken of Jupiter, who had both a mother and a name? Why should I say that Mercury, that thrice greatest, of whom I have made mention above, not only speaks of God as "without a mother," as Apollo does, but also as "without a father," because He has no origin from any other source but Himself? For He cannot be produced from any one, who Himself produced all things. I have, as I think, sufficiently taught by arguments, and confirmed by witnesses, that which is sufficiently plain by itself, that there is one only King of the universe, one Father, one God.

But perchance some one may ask of us the same question which Hortensius asks in Cicero: If God is one only,[1] what solitude can be happy? As though we, in asserting that He is one, say that He is desolate and solitary. Undoubtedly He has ministers, whom we call messengers. And that is true, which I have before related, that Seneca said in his *Exhortations* that God produced ministers of His kingdom. But these are neither gods, nor do they wish to be called gods or to be worshipped, inasmuch as they do nothing but execute the command and will of God. Nor, however, are they gods who are worshipped in common, whose number is small and fixed. But if the worshippers of the gods think that they worship those beings whom we call the ministers of the Supreme God, there is no reason why they should envy us who say that there is one God, and deny that there are many. If a multitude *of gods* delights them, we do not speak of twelve, or three hundred and sixty-five, as Orpheus did; but we convict them of innumerable errors on the other side, in thinking that they are so few, Let them know, however, by what name they ought to be called, lest they do injury to the true God, whose name they set forth, while they assign it to more than one. Let them believe their own Apollo, who in that same response took away from the other gods their name, as he took away the dominion from Jupiter. For the third verse shows that the ministers of God ought not to be called gods, but angels. He spoke falsely respecting himself, indeed; for though he was of the number of demons, he reckoned himself among the angels of God, and then in other responses he confessed himself a demon. For when he was asked how he wished to be supplicated, he thus answered: —

> "O all-wise, all-learned, versed in many pursuits, hear, O demon."

And so, again, when at the entreaty of some one he uttered an imprecation against the Sminthian Apollo, he began with this verse: —

> "O harmony of the world, bearing light, all-wise demon."

What therefore remains, except that by his own confession he is subject to the scourge of the true God and to everlasting punishment? For in another respouse he also said: —

> "The demons who go about the earth and about the sea
> Without weariness, are subdued beneath the scourge of God."

We speak on the subject of both in the second book. In the meantime it is enough for us, that while he wishes to honour and place himself in heaven, he has confessed, as the nature of the matter is, in what manner they are to be named who always stand beside God.

Therefore let men withdraw themselves from errors; and laying aside corrupt superstitions, let them acknowledge their Father and Lord, whose excellence cannot be estimated, nor His greatness perceived, nor His beginning comprehended. When the earnest attention of the human mind and its acute sagacity and memory has reached Him, all ways being, as it were, summed up and exhausted,[2] it stops, it is at a loss, it fails; nor is there anything beyond to which it can proceed. But because that which exists must of necessity have had a beginning, it follows that since there was nothing before Him, He was produced from Himself before all things. Therefore He is called by Apollo "self-produced," by the Sibyl "self-created," "uncreated," and "unmade." And Seneca, an acute man, saw and expressed this in his *Exhortations*. "We," he said, "are dependent upon another." Therefore we look to some one to whom we owe that which is most excellent in us. Another brought us into being, another formed us; but God of His own power made Himself.

CHAP. VIII. — THAT GOD IS WITHOUT A BODY, NOR DOES HE NEED DIFFERENCE OF SEX FOR PROCREATION.

It is proved, therefore, by these witnesses, so numerous and of such authority, that the universe

---

1 [1 John iv. 8. The Divine Triad "is Love."]

2 Subductis et consummatis.

is governed by the power and providence of one God, whose energy and majesty Plato in the *Timæus* asserts to be so great, that no one can either conceive it in his mind, or give utterance to it in words, on account of His surpassing and incalculable power. And then can any one doubt whether any thing can be difficult or impossible for God, who by His providence designed, by His energy established, and by His judgment completed those works so great and wonderful, and even now sustains them by His spirit, and governs them by His power, being incomprehensible and unspeakable, and fully known to no other than Himself? Wherefore, as I often reflect on the subject of such great majesty, they who worship the gods sometimes appear so blind, so incapable of reflection, so senseless, so little removed from the mute animals, as to believe that those who are born from the natural intercourse of the sexes could have had anything of majesty and divine influence; since the Erythræan Sibyl says: "It is impossible for a God to be fashioned from the loins of a man and the womb *of a woman*." And if this is true, as it really is, it is evident that Hercules, Apollo, Bacchus, Mercury, and Jupiter, with the rest, were but men, since they were born from the two sexes. But what is so far removed from the nature of God as that operation which He Himself assigned to mortals for the propagation of their race, and which cannot be affected without corporeal substance?

Therefore, if the gods are immortal and eternal, what need is there of the other sex, when they themselves do not require succession, since they are always about to exist? For assuredly in the case of mankind and the other animals, there is no other reason for difference of sex and procreation and bringing forth, except that all classes of living creatures, inasmuch as they are doomed to death by the condition of their mortality, may be preserved by mutual succession. But God, who is immortal, has no need of difference of sex, nor of succession. Some one will say *that this arrangement is necessary*, in order that He may have some to minister to Him, or over whom He may bear rule. What need is there of the female sex, since God, who is almighty, is able to produce sons without the agency of the female? For if He has granted to certain minute creatures [1] that they

> "Should gather offspring for themselves with their mouth from leaves and sweet herbs,"

why should any one think it impossible for God Himself to have offspring except by union with the other sex? No one, therefore, is so thoughtless as not to understand that those were mere mortals, whom the ignorant and foolish regard and worship as gods. Why, then, some one will say, were they believed to be gods? Doubtless because they were very great and powerful kings; and since, on account of the merits of their virtues, or offices, or the arts which they discovered, they were beloved by those over whom they had ruled, they were consecrated to *lasting* memory. And if any one doubts this, let him consider their exploits and deeds, the whole of which both ancient poets and historians have handed down.

CHAP. IX. — OF HERCULES AND HIS LIFE AND DEATH.[2]

Did not Hercules, who is most renowned for his valour, and who is regarded as an Africanus among the gods, by his debaucheries, lusts, and adulteries, pollute the world, which he is related to have traversed and purified? And no wonder, since he was born from an adulterous intercourse with Alcmena.

What divinity could there have been in him, who, enslaved to his own vices, against all laws, treated with infamy, disgrace, and outrage, both males and females? Nor, indeed, are those great and wonderful actions which he performed to be judged such as to be thought worthy of being attributed to divine excellence. For what! is it so magnificent if he overcame a lion and a boar; if he shot down birds with arrows; if he cleansed a royal stable; if he conquered a virago, and deprived her of her belt; if he slew savage horses together with their master? These are the deeds of a brave and heroic man, but still a man; for those things which he overcame were frail and mortal. For there is no power so great, as the orator says, which cannot be weakened and broken by iron and strength. But to conquer the mind, and to restrain anger, is the part of the bravest man; and these things he never did or could do: for one who does these things I do not compare with excellent men, but I judge him to be most like to a god.

I could wish that he had added *something* on the subject of lust, luxury, desire, and arrogance, so as to complete the excellence of him whom he judged to be like to a god. For he is not to be thought braver who overcomes a lion, than he who overcomes the violent wild beast shut up within himself, viz. anger; or he who has brought down most rapacious birds, than he who restrains most covetous desires; or he who subdues a warlike Amazon, than he who subdues lust, the vanquisher [3] of modesty and fame; or he who cleanses a stable from dung, than he who cleanses his heart from vices, which are more destructive

[1] [The bees, according to Virgil, *Georg.*, iv. 199.]

[2] [Vol. ii. p. 179. It is interesting to observe the influence of Justin and Clement on the reasoning of the later Fathers, not excepting St. Augustine.]

[3] Debellatricem.

evils because they are peculiarly his own, than those which might have been avoided and guarded against. From this it comes to pass, that he alone ought to be judged a brave man who is temperate, moderate, and just. But if any one considers what the works of God are, he will at once judge all these things, which most trifling men admire, to be ridiculous. For they measure them not by the divine power of which they are ignorant, but by the weakness of their own strength. For no one will deny this, that Hercules was not only a servant to Eurystheus, a king, which to a certain extent may appear honourable, but also to an unchaste woman, Omphale, who used to order him to sit at her feet, clothed with her garments, and executing an appointed task. Detestable baseness! But such was the price at which pleasure was valued. What! some one will say, do you think that the poets are to be believed? Why should I not think so? For it is not Lucilius who relates these things, or Lucian, who spared not men nor gods, but these especially who sung the praises of the gods.

Whom, then, shall we believe, if we do not credit those who praise them? Let him who thinks that these speak falsely produce other authors on whom we may rely, who may teach us who these gods are, in what manner and from what source they had their origin, what is their strength, what their number, what their power, what there is in them which is admirable and worthy of adoration — what mystery, in short, more to be relied on, and more true. He will produce no such authorities. Let us, then, give credence to those who did not speak for the purpose of censure, but to proclaim their praise. He sailed, then, with the Argonauts, and sacked Troy, being enraged with Laomedon on account of the reward refused to him, by Laomedon, for the preservation of his daughter, from which circumstance it is evident at what time he lived. He also, excited by rage and madness, slew his wife, together with his children. Is this he whom men consider a god? But his heir Philoctetes did not so regard him, who applied a torch to him when about to be burnt, who witnessed the burning and wasting of his limbs and sinews, who buried his bones and ashes on Mount Œta, in return for which office he received his arrows.

CHAP. X. — OF THE LIFE AND ACTIONS OF ÆSCULAPIUS, APOLLO, NEPTUNE, MARS, CASTOR AND POLLUX, MERCURY AND BACCHUS.

What other action worthy of divine honours, except the healing of Hippolytus, did Æsculapius perform, whose birth also was not without disgrace to Apollo? His death was certainly more renowned, because he earned the distinction of being struck with lightning by a god. Tarquitius, in a dissertation concerning illustrious men, says that he was born of uncertain parents, exposed, and found by some hunters; that he was nourished by a dog, and that, being delivered to Chiron, he learned the art of medicine. He says, moreover, that he was a Messenian, but that he spent some time at Epidaurus. Tully also says that he was buried at Cynosuræ. What was the conduct of Apollo, his father? Did he not, on account of his impassioned love, most disgracefully tend the flock of another, and build walls for Laomedon, having been hired together with Neptune for a reward, which could with impunity be withheld from him? And from him first the perfidious king learned to refuse *to carry out* whatever contract he had made with gods. And he also, while in love with a beautiful boy, offered violence to him, and while engaged in play, slew him.

Mars, when guilty of homicide, and set free from the charge of murder by the Athenians through favour, lest he should appear to be too fierce and savage, committed adultery with Venus. Castor and Pollux, while they are engaged in carrying off the wives of others, ceased to be twin-brothers. For Idas, being excited with jealousy on account of the injury, transfixed one *of the brothers* with his sword. And the poets relate that they live and die alternately: so that they are now the most wretched not only of the gods, but also of all mortals, inasmuch as they are not permitted to die once only. And yet Homer, differing from the other poets, simply records that they both died. For when he represented Helen as sitting by the side of Priam on the walls of Troy, and recognising all the chieftains of Greece, but as looking in vain for her brothers only, he added to his speech a verse of this kind: —

> "Thus she; unconscious that in Sparta they,
> Their native land, beneath the sod were laid."

What did Mercury, a thief and spendthrift, leave to contribute to his fame, except the memory of his frauds? Doubtless he was deserving of heaven, because he taught the exercises of the palæstra, and was the first who invented the lyre.[1] It is necessary that Father Liber should be of chief authority, and of the first rank in the senate of the gods, because he was the only one of them all, except Jupiter, who triumphed, led an army, and subdued the Indians. But that very great and unconquered Indian commander was most shamefully overpowered by love and lust. For, being conveyed to Crete with his effeminate retinue, he met with an unchaste woman on the shore; and in the confidence inspired by his

1 [See vol. v. p. 43, and note, p. 46, this series.]

Indian victory, he wished to give proof of his manliness, lest he should appear too effeminate. And so he took to himself in marriage that woman, the betrayer of her father, and the murderer of her brother, after that she had been deserted and repudiated by another husband; and he made her Libera, and with her ascended into heaven.

What was the conduct of Jupiter, the father of all these, who in the customary prayer is styled[1] Most Excellent and Great? Is he not, from his earliest childhood, proved to be impious, and almost a parricide, since he expelled his father from his kingdom, and banished him, and did not await his death though he was aged and worn out, such was his eagerness for rule? And when he had taken his father's throne by violence and arms, he was attacked with war by the Titans, which was the beginning of evils to the human race; and when these had been overcome and lasting peace procured, he spent the rest of his life in debaucheries and adulteries. I forbear to mention the virgins whom he dishonoured. For that is wont to be judged endurable. I cannot pass by the cases of Amphitryon and Tyndarus, whose houses he filled to overflowing with disgrace and infamy. But he reached the height of impiety and guilt in carrying off the royal boy. For it did not appear enough to cover himself with infamy in offering violence to women, unless he also outraged his own sex. This is true adultery, which is done against nature. Whether he who committed these crimes can be called Greatest is a matter of question, undoubtedly he is not the Best; to which name corrupters, adulterers, and incestuous persons have no claim; unless it happens that we men are mistaken in terming those who do such things wicked and abandoned, and in judging them most deserving of every kind of punishment. But Marcus Tullius was foolish in upbraiding Caius Verres with adulteries, for Jupiter, whom he worshipped, committed the same; and in upbraiding Publius Clodius with incest with his sister, for he who was Best and Greatest had the same person both as sister and wife.

CHAP. XI. — OF THE ORIGIN, LIFE, REIGN, NAME, AND DEATH OF JUPITER, AND OF SATURN AND URANUS.[2]

Who, then, is so senseless as to imagine that he reigns in heaven who ought not even to have reigned on earth? It was not without humour that a certain poet wrote of the triumph of Cupid: in which book he not only represented Cupid as the most powerful of the gods, but also as their conqueror. For having enumerated the loves of each, by which they had come into the power and dominion of Cupid, he sets in array a procession, in which Jupiter, with the other gods, is led in chains before the chariot of him, celebrating a triumph. This is elegantly pictured by the poet, but it is not far removed from the truth. For he who is without virtue, who is overpowered by desire and wicked lusts, is not, *as the poet feigned*, in subjection to Cupid, but to everlasting death. But let us cease to speak concerning morals; let us examine the matter, in order that men may understand in what errors they are miserably engaged. The common people imagine that Jupiter reigns in heaven; both learned and unlearned are alike persuaded of this. For both religion itself, and prayers, and hymns, and shrines, and images demonstrate this. And yet they admit that he was also descended from Saturn and Rhea. How can he appear a god, or be believed, as the poet says, to be the author of men and all things, when innumerable thousands of men existed before his birth — those, for instance, who lived during the reign of Saturn, and enjoyed the light sooner than Jupiter? I see that one god was king in the earliest times, and another in the times that followed. It is therefore possible that there may be another hereafter. For if the former kingdom was changed, why should we not expect that the latter may possibly be changed, unless by chance it was possible for Saturn to produce one more powerful than himself, but impossible for Jupiter so to do? And yet the divine government is always unchangeable; or if it is changeable, which is an impossibility, it is undoubtedly changeable at all times.

Is it possible, then, for Jupiter to lose his kingdom as his father lost it? It is so undoubtedly. For when that deity had spared neither virgins nor married women, he abstained from Thetis only in consequence of an oracle which foretold that whatever son should be born from her would be greater than his father. And first of all there was in him a want of foreknowledge not befitting a god; for had not Themis related to him future events, he would not have known them of his own accord. But if he is not divine, he is not indeed a god; for the name of divinity is derived from god, as humanity is from man. Then there was a consciousness of weakness; but he who has feared, must plainly have feared one greater than himself. But he who does this assuredly knows that he is not the greatest, since something greater can exist. He also swears most solemnly by the Stygian marsh: "Which is set forth the sole object of religious dread to the gods above." What is this object of religious dread? Or by whom is it set forth?

[1] [*Nat. Deor.*, iii. 36. De Maistre, *Soirées*, i. p. 30, and note, p 63.]

[2] [Compare the remorseless satire of Arnobius, vol. vi. p. 498.]

Is there, then, some mighty power which may punish the gods who commit perjury? What is this great dread of the infernal marsh, if they are immortal? Why should they fear that which none are about to see, except those who are bound by the necessity of death? Why, then, do men raise their eyes to the heaven? Why do they swear by the gods above, when the gods above themselves have recourse to the infernal gods, and find among them an object of veneration and worship? But what is the meaning of that saying, that there are fates whom all the gods and Jupiter himself obey? If the power of the Parcæ is so great, that they are of more avail than all the heavenly gods, and their ruler and lord himself, why should not they be rather said to reign, since necessity compels all the gods to obey their laws and ordinances? Now, who can entertain a doubt that he who is subservient to anything cannot be greatest? For if he were so, he would not receive fates, but would appoint them. Now I return to another subject which I had omitted. In the case of one goddess only he exercised self-restraint, though he was deeply enamoured of her; but this was not from any virtue, but through fear of a successor. But this fear plainly denotes one who is both mortal and feeble, and of no weight: for at the very hour of his birth he might have been put to death, as his elder brother had been put to death; and if it had been possible for him to have lived, he would never have given up the supreme power to a younger brother. But *Jupiter* himself having been preserved by stealth, and stealthily nourished, was called Zeus, or Zen,[1] not, as they imagine, from the fervor of heavenly fire, or because he is the giver of life, or because he breathes life into living creatures, which power belongs to God alone; for how can he impart the breath of life who has himself received it from another source? But he was so called because he was the first who lived of the male children of Saturn. Men, therefore, might have had another god as their ruler, if Saturn had not been deceived by his wife. But it will be said the poets feigned these things. Whoever entertains this opinion is in error. For they spoke respecting men; but in order that they might embellish those whose memory they used to celebrate with praises, they said that they were gods. Those things, therefore, which they spoke concerning them as gods were feigned, and not those which they spoke concerning them as men; and this will be manifest from an instance which we will bring forward. When about to offer violence to Danae, he poured into her lap a great quantity of golden coins. This was the price which he paid for her dishonour. But the poets who spoke about him as a god, that they might not weaken the authority of his supposed majesty, feigned that he himself descended in a shower of gold, making use of the same figure with which they speak of showers of iron when they describe a multitude of darts and arrows. He is said to have carried away Ganymede by an eagle; it is a picture of the poets. But he either carried him off by a legion, which has an eagle for its standard; or the ship on board of which he was placed had its tutelary deity in the shape of an eagle, just as it had the effigy of a bull when he seized Europa and conveyed her across the sea. In the same manner, it is related that he changed Io, the daughter of Inachus, into a heifer. And in order that she might escape the anger of Juno, just as she was, now covered with bristly hair, and in the shape of a heifer, she is said to have swam over the sea, and to have come into Egypt; and there, having recovered her former appearance, she became the goddess who is now called Isis. By what argument, then, can it be proved that Europa did not sit on the bull, and that Io was not changed into a heifer? Because there is a fixed day in the annals on which the voyage of Isis is celebrated; from which fact we learn that she did not swim across the sea, but sailed over. Therefore they who appear to themselves to be wise because they understand that there cannot be a living and earthly body in heaven, reject the whole story of Ganymede as false, and perceive that the occurrence took place on earth, inasmuch as the matter and the lust itself is earthly. The poets did not therefore invent these transactions, for if they were to do so they would be most worthless; but they added a certain colour to the transactions.[2] For it was not for the purpose of detraction that they said these things, but from a desire to embellish them. Hence men are deceived; especially because, while they think that all these things are feigned by the poets, they worship that of which they are ignorant. For they do not know what is the limit of poetic licence, how far it is allowable to proceed in fiction, since it is the business of the poet with some gracefulness to change and transfer actual occurrences into other representations by oblique transformations. But to feign the whole of that which you relate, that is to be foolish and deceitful rather than to be a poet.

But grant that they feigned those things which are believed to be fabulous, did they also feign those things which are related about the female deities and the marriages of the gods? Why, then, are they so represented, and so worshipped? unless by chance not the poets only, but painters also, and statuaries, speak falsehoods. For if

[1] Ζεύς or Ζῆν. [Quod sit auctor vitæ. *Delphin note.*]

[2] [On the Poets, vol. i. cap. 2, p. 273.]

this is the Jupiter who is called by you a god, if it is not he who was born from Saturn and Ops, no other image but his alone ought to have been placed in all the temples. What meaning have the effigies of women? What the doubtful sex? in which, if this Jupiter is represented, the very stones will confess that he is a man. They say that the poets have spoken falsely, and yet they believe them: yes, truly they prove by the fact itself that the poets did not speak falsely; for they so frame the images of the gods, that, from the very diversity of sex, it appears that these things which the poets say are true. For what other conclusion does the image of Ganymede and the effigy of the eagle admit of, when they are placed before the feet of Jupiter in the temples, and are worshipped equally with himself, except that the memory of impious guilt and debauchery remains for ever? Nothing, therefore, is wholly invented by the poets: something perhaps is transferred and obscured by oblique fashioning, under which the truth was enwrapped and concealed; as that which was related about the dividing of the kingdoms by lot. For they say that the heaven fell to the share of Jupiter, the sea to Neptune, and the infernal regions to Pluto. Why was not the earth rather taken as the third portion, except that the transaction took place on the earth? Therefore it is true that they so divided and portioned out the government of the world, that the empire of the east fell to Jupiter, a part of the west was allotted to Pluto, who had the surname of Agesilaus; because the region of the east, from which light is given to mortals, seems to be higher, but the region of the west lower. Thus they so veiled the truth under a fiction, that the truth itself detracted nothing from the public persuasion. It is manifest concerning the share of Neptune; for we say that his kingdom resembled that unlimited authority possessed by Mark Antony, to whom the senate had decreed the power of the maritime coast, that he might punish the pirates, and tranquillize the whole sea. Thus all the maritime coasts, together with the islands, fell to the lot of Neptune. How can this be proved? Undoubtedly ancient stories attest it. Euhemerus, an ancient author, who was of the city of Messene, collected the actions of Jupiter and of the others, who are esteemed gods, and composed a history from the titles and sacred inscriptions which were in the most ancient temples, and especially in the sanctuary of the Triphylian Jupiter, where an inscription indicated that a golden column had been placed by Jupiter himself, on which column he wrote an account of his exploits, that posterity might have a memorial of his actions. This history was translated and followed by Ennius, whose words are these: "Where Jupiter gives to Neptune the government of the sea, that he might reign in all the islands and places bordering on the sea."

The accounts of the poets, therefore, are true, but veiled with an outward covering and show. It is possible that Mount Olympus may have supplied the poets with the hint for saying that Jupiter obtained the kingdom of heaven, because Olympus is the common name both of the mountain and of heaven. But the same history informs us that Jupiter dwelt on Mount Olympus, when it says: "At that time Jupiter spent the greatest part of his life on Mount Olympus; and they used to resort to him thither for *the administration of* justice, if any matters were disputed. Moreover, if any one had found out any new invention which might be useful for human life, he used to come thither and display it to Jupiter." The poets transfer many things after this manner, not for the sake of speaking falsely against the objects of their worship, but that they may by variously coloured figures add beauty and grace to their poems. But they who do not understand the manner, or the cause, or the nature of that which is represented by figure, attack the poets as false and sacrilegious. Even the philosophers were deceived by this error; for because these things which are related about Jupiter appeared unsuited to the character of a god, they introduced two Jupiters, one natural, the other fabulous. They saw, on the one hand, that which was true, that he, forsooth, concerning whom the poets speak, was man; but in the case of that natural Jupiter, led by the common practice of superstition, they committed an error, inasmuch as they transferred the name of a man to God, who, as we have already said, because He is one only, has no need of a name. But it is undeniable that he is Jupiter who was born from Ops and Saturn. It is therefore an empty persuasion on the part of those who give the name of Jupiter to the Supreme God. For some are in the habit of defending their errors by this excuse; for, when convinced of the unity of God, since they cannot deny this, they affirm that they worship Him, but that it is their pleasure that He should be called Jupiter. But what can be more absurd than this? For Jupiter is not accustomed to be worshipped without the accompanying worship of his wife and daughter. From which his real nature is evident; nor is it lawful for that name to be transferred thither,[1] where there is neither any Minerva nor Juno. Why should I say that the peculiar meaning of this name does not express a divine, but human power? For Cicero explains the names Jupiter and Juno as being derived from giving help;[2] and Jupiter is so called as if he were a helping father,—a name which is ill adapted to God:

[1] Eo, i.e., to those.
[2] Juvando. [*Nat. Deor.*, iii. 25, 26.]

for to help is the part of a man conferring some aid upon one who is a stranger, and in a case where the benefit is small. No one implores God to help him, but to preserve him, to give him life and safety, which is a much greater and more important matter than to help.

And since we are speaking of a father, no father is said to help his sons when he begets or brings them up. For that expression is too insignificant to denote the magnitude of the benefit derived from a father. How much more unsuitable is it to God, who is our true Father, by whom we exist, and whose we are altogether, by whom we are formed, endued with life, and enlightened, who bestows upon us life, gives us safety, and supplies us with various kinds of food! He has no apprehension of the divine benefits who thinks that he is only aided by God. Therefore he is not only ignorant, but impious, who disparages the excellency of the supreme power under the name of Jupiter. Wherefore, if both from his actions and character we have proved that Jupiter was a man, and reigned on earth, it only remains that we should also investigate his death. Ennius, in his sacred history, having described all the actions which he performed in his life, at the close thus speaks: Then Jupiter, when he had five times made a circuit of the earth, and bestowed governments upon all his friends and relatives, and left laws to men, provided them with a settled mode of life and corn, and given them many other benefits, and having been honoured with immortal glory and remembrance, left lasting memorials to his friends, and when his age [1] was almost spent, he changed [2] his life in Crete, and departed to the gods. And the Curetes, his sons, took charge of him, and honoured him; and his tomb is in Crete, in the town of Cnossus, and Vesta is said to have founded this city; and on his tomb is an inscription in ancient Greek characters, "Zan Kronou," which is in Latin, "Jupiter the son of Saturn." This undoubtedly is not handed down by poets, but by writers of ancient events; and these things are so true, that they are confirmed by some verses of the Sibyls, to this effect: —

"Inanimate demons, images of the dead,
Whose tombs the ill-fated Crete possesses as a boast."

Cicero, in his treatise concerning the Nature of the Gods, having said that three Jupiters were enumerated by theologians, adds that the third was of Crete, the son of Saturn, and that his tomb is shown in that island. How, therefore, can a god be alive in one place, and dead in another; in one place have a temple, and in another a tomb? Let the Romans then know that their Capitol, that is the chief head of their objects of public veneration, is nothing but an empty monument.

Let us now come to his father who reigned before him, and who perhaps had more power in himself, because he is said to be born from the meeting of such great elements. Let us see what there was in him worthy of a god, especially that he is related to have had the golden age, because in his reign there was justice in the earth. I find something in him which was not in his son. For what is so befitting the character of a god, as a just government and an age of piety? But when, on the same principle, I reflect that he is a son, I cannot consider him as the Supreme God; for I see that there is something more ancient than himself, — namely, the heaven and the earth. But I am in search of a God beyond whom nothing has any existence, who is the source and origin of all things. He must of necessity exist who framed the heaven itself, and laid the foundations of the earth. But if Saturn was born from these, as it is supposed, how can he be the chief God, since he owes his origin to another? Or who presided over the universe before the birth of Saturn? But this, as I recently said, is a fiction of the poets. For it was impossible that the senseless elements, which are separated by so long an interval, should meet together and give birth to a son, or that he who was born should not at all resemble his parents, but should have a form which his parents did not possess.

Let us therefore inquire what degree of truth lies hid under this figure. Minucius Felix, in his treatise which has the title of *Octavius*,[3] alleged these proofs: "That Saturn, when he had been banished by his son, and had come into Italy, was called the son of Cœlus (heaven), because we are accustomed to say that those whose virtue we admire, or those who have unexpectedly arrived, have fallen from heaven; and that he was called the son of earth, because we name those who are born from unknown parents sons of earth." These things, indeed, have some resemblance to the truth, but are not true, because it is evident that even during his reign he was so esteemed. He might have argued thus: That Saturn, being a very powerful king, in order that the memory of his parents might be preserved, gave their names to the heaven and earth, whereas these were before called by other names, for which reason we know that names were applied both to mountains and rivers. For when the poets speak of the offspring of Atlas, or of the river Inachus, they do not absolutely say that men could possibly be born from inanimate objects; but they undoubtedly indicate those who were born from those men, who either during their lives or after their death gave their

[1] Ætate pessum acta. [See plural Joves, *Nat. Deor.*, iii. 16.]
[2] Commutavit; others read consummavit, "he completed."

[3] [Condensed from cap. xxii. See vol. iv. p. 186, this series.]

names to mountains or rivers. For that was a common practice among the ancients, and especially among the Greeks. Thus we have heard that seas received the names of those who had fallen into them, as the Ægean, the Icarian, and the Hellespont. In Latium, also, Aventinus gave his name to the mountain on which he was buried; and Tiberinus, or Tiber, gave his name to the river in which he was drowned. No wonder, then, if the names of those who had given birth to most powerful kings were attributed to the heaven and earth. Therefore it appears that Saturn was not born from heaven, which is impossible, but from that man who bore the name of Uranus. And Trismegistus attests the truth of this; for when he said that very few had existed in whom there was perfect learning, he mentioned by name among these his relatives, Uranus, Saturn, and Mercury. And because he was ignorant of these things, he gave another account of the matter; how he might have argued, I have shown. Now I will say in what manner, at what time, and by whom this was done; for it was not Saturn who did this, but Jupiter. Ennius thus relates in his sacred history: "Then Pan leads him to the mountain, which is called the pillar of heaven. Having ascended thither, he surveyed the lands far and wide, and there on that mountain he builds an altar to Cœlus; and Jupiter was the first who offered sacrifice on that altar. In that place he looked up to heaven, by which name we now call it, and that which was above the world which was called the firmament,[1] and he gave to the heaven its name from the name of his grandfather; and Jupiter in prayer first gave the name of heaven to that which was called firmament,[1] and he burnt entire the victim which he there offered in sacrifice." Nor is it here only that Jupiter is found to have offered sacrifice. Cæsar also, in Aratus, relates that Aglaosthenes says that when he was setting out from the island of Naxos against the Titans, and was offering sacrifice on the shore, an eagle flew to Jupiter as an omen, and that the victor received it as a good token, and placed it under his own protection. But the sacred history testifies that even beforehand an eagle had sat upon his head, and portended to him the kingdom. To whom, then, could Jupiter have offered sacrifice, except to his grandfather Cœlus, who, according to the saying of Euhemerus,[2] died in Oceania, and was buried in the town of Aulatia?

[1] Æther. [Tayler Lewis, *Plato cont. Ath.*, pp. 126-129.]

[2] Euhemerus was a Sicilian author of the age of Alexander the Great. He wrote a sacred history containing an account of the several gods who were worshipped in Greece, whom he represents as having originally been men who had distinguished themselves by their exploits, or benefits conferred upon men, and who were therefore, after their death, worshipped as gods. The Christian writers frequently refer to Euhemerus as helping them to prove that the pagan mythology consisted only of fables invented by men. See *Dictionary of Greek and Roman Biography.*

Chap. XII. — That the Stoics Transfer the Figments of the Poets to a Philosophical System.

Since we have brought to light the mysteries of the poets, and have found out the parents of Saturn, let us return to his virtues and actions. He was, *they say*, just in his rule. First, from this very circumstance he is not now a god, inasmuch as he has ceased to be. In the next place, he was not even just, but impious not only towards his sons, whom he devoured, but also towards his father, whom he is said to have mutilated. And this may perhaps have happened in truth. But men, having regard to the element which is called the heaven, reject the whole fable as most foolishly invented; though the Stoics, (according to their custom) endeavour to transfer it to a physical system, whose opinion Cicero has laid down in his treatise concerning the Nature of the Gods. They held, he says, that the highest and ethereal nature of heaven, that is, of fire, which by itself produced all things, was without that part of the body which contained the productive organs. Now this theory might have been suitable to Vesta, if she were called a male. For it is on this account that they esteem Vesta to be a virgin, inasmuch as fire is an incorruptible element; and nothing can be born from it, since it consumes all things, whatever it has seized upon. Ovid in the *Fasti* says:[3] "Nor do you esteem Vesta to be anything else than a living flame; and you see no bodies produced from flame. Therefore she is truly a virgin, for she sends forth no seed, nor receives it, and loves the attendants of virginity."

This also might have been ascribed to Vulcan, who indeed is supposed to be fire, and yet the poets did not mutilate him. It might also have been ascribed to the sun, in whom is the nature and cause of the productive powers. For without the fiery heat of the sun nothing could be born, or have increase; so that no other element has greater need of productive organs than heat, by the nourishment of which all things are conceived, produced, and supported. Lastly, even if the case were as they would have it, why should we suppose that Cœlus was mutilated, rather than that he was born without productive organs? For if he produces by himself, it is plain that he had no need of productive organs, since he gave birth to Saturn himself; but if he had them, and suffered mutilation from his son, the origin of all things and all nature would have perished. Why should I say that they deprive Saturn himself not only of divine, but also of human intelligence, when they affirm that Saturn is he who comprises the course and change of the spaces and seasons, and that he has that very

[3] vi. 291. [Tayler Lewis (*ut supra*), note xii. p. 119.]

name in Greek? For he is called Cronos, which is the same as Chronos, that is, a space of time. But he is called Saturn, because he is satiated with years. These are the words of Cicero, setting forth the opinion of the Stoics: "The worthlessness of these things any one may readily understand. For if Saturn is the son of Cœlus, how could Time have been born from Cœlus, or Cœlus have been mutilated by Time, or afterwards could Time have been despoiled of his sovereignty by his son Jupiter? Or how was Jupiter born from Time? Or with what years could eternity be satiated, since it has no limit?" [1]

CHAP. XIII. — HOW VAIN AND TRIFLING ARE THE INTERPRETATIONS OF THE STOICS RESPECTING THE GODS, AND IN THEM CONCERNING THE ORIGIN OF JUPITER, CONCERNING SATURN AND OPS.

If therefore these speculations of the philosophers are trifling, what remains, except that we believe it to be a matter of fact that, being a man, he suffered mutilation from a man? Unless by chance any one esteems him as a god who feared a co-heir; whereas, if he had possessed any divine knowledge, he ought not to have mutilated his father, but himself, to prevent the birth of Jupiter, who deprived him of the possession of his kingdom. And he also, when he had married his sister Rhea, whom in Latin we call Ops, is said to have been warned by an oracle not to bring up his male children, because it would come to pass that he should be driven into banishment by a son. And being in fear of this, it is plain that he did not devour his sons, as the fables report, but put them to death; although it is written in sacred history that Saturn and Ops, and other men, were at that time accustomed to eat human flesh, but that Jupiter, who gave to men laws and civilization, was the first who by an edict prohibited the use of that food. Now if this is true, what justice can there possibly have been in him? But let us suppose it to be a fictitious story that Saturn devoured his sons, only true after a certain fashion; must we then suppose, with the vulgar, that he has eaten his sons, who has carried them out to burial? But when Ops had brought forth Jupiter, she stole away the infant, and secretly sent him into Crete to be nourished. Again, I cannot but blame his want of foresight. For why did he receive an oracle from another, *and not from himself?* Being placed in heaven, why did he not see the things which were taking place on earth? Why did the Corybantes with their cymbals escape his notice? Lastly, why did there exist any greater force which might overcome his power? Doubtless, being aged, he was easily overcome by one who was young, and despoiled of his sovereignty. He was therefore banished and went into exile; and after long wanderings came into Italy in a ship, as Ovid relates in his *Fasti:* —

"The cause of the ship remains to be explained. The scythe-bearing god came to the Tuscan river in a ship, having first traversed the world."

Janus received him wandering and destitute; and the ancient coins are a proof of this, on which there is a representation of Janus with a double face, and on the other side a ship; as the same poet adds: —

"But pious posterity represented a ship on the coin, bearing testimony to the arrival of the stranger god."

Not only therefore all the poets, but the writers also of ancient histories and events, agree that he was a man, inasmuch as they handed down to memory his actions in Italy: of Greek writers, Diodorus and Thallus; of Latin writers, Nepos, Cassius, and Varro. For since men lived in Italy after a rustic fashion,[2] —

"He brought the race to union first,
Erewhile on mountain tops dispersed,
And gave them statutes to obey,
And willed the land wherein he lay
Should Latium's title bear."

Does any one imagine him to be a god, who was driven into banishment, who fled, who lay hid? No one is so senseless. For he who flees, or lies hid, must fear both violence and death. Orpheus, who lived in more recent times than his, openly relates that Saturn reigned on earth and among men: —

"First Cronus ruled o'er men on earth,
And then from Cronus sprung the mighty king,
The widely sounding Zeus."

And also our own Maro says: [3] —

"This life the golden Saturn led on earth;"

and in another place: [4] —

"That was the storied age of gold,
So peacefully, serenely rolled
The years beneath his reign."

The poet did not say in the former passage that he led this life in heaven, nor in the latter passage that he reigned over the gods above. From which it appears that he was a king on earth; and this he declares more plainly in another place: [5] —

"Restorer of the age of gold,
In lands where Saturn ruled of old."

[1] *De Nat. deor.*, ii. 64.

[2] Virg., *Æneid*, viii. 321.
[3] *Georg.*, ii. 538.
[4] *Æneid*, viii. 324.
[5] *Ibid.*, vi. 793.

Ennius, indeed, in his *translation of* Euhemerus, says that Saturn was not the first who reigned, but his father Uranus. In the beginning, he says, Cœlus first had the supreme power on the earth. He instituted and prepared that kingdom in conjunction with his brothers. There is no great dispute, if there is doubt, on the part of the greatest authorities respecting the son and the father. But it is possible that each may have happened: that Uranus first began to be pre-eminent in power among the rest, and to have the chief place, but not the kingdom; and that afterwards Saturn acquired greater resources, and took the title of king.

Chap. XIV. — What the Sacred History of Euhemerus and Ennius Teaches Concerning the Gods.

Now, since the sacred history differs in some degree from those things which we have related, let us open those things which are contained in the true writings, that we may not, in accusing superstitions, appear to follow and approve of the follies of the poets. These are the words of Ennius: "Afterwards Saturn married Ops. Titan, who was older *than Saturn*, demands the kingdom for himself. Upon this their mother Vesta, and their sisters Ceres and Ops, advise Saturn not to give up the kingdom to his brother. Then Titan, who was inferior in person to Saturn, on that account, and because he saw that his mother and sisters were using their endeavours that Saturn might reign, yielded the kingdom to him. He therefore made an agreement with Saturn, that if any male children should be born to him, he would not bring them up. He did so for this purpose, that the kingdom might return to his own sons. Then, when a son was first born to Saturn, they slew him. Afterwards twins were born, Jupiter and Juno. Upon this they present Juno to the sight of Saturn, and secretly hide Jupiter, and give him to Vesta to be brought up, concealing him from Saturn. Ops also brings forth Neptune without the knowledge of Saturn, and secretly hides him. In the same manner Ops brings forth twins by a third birth, Pluto and Glauca. Pluto in Latin is Dispater; others call him Orcus. Upon this they show to Saturn the daughter Glauca, and conceal and hide the son Pluto. Then Glauca dies while yet young." This is the lineage of Jupiter and his brothers, *as these things are written*, and the relationship is handed down to us after this manner from the sacred narrative. Also shortly afterwards he introduces these things: "Then Titan, when he learned that sons were born to Saturn, and secretly brought up, secretly takes with him his sons, who are called Titans, and seizes his brother Saturn and Ops, and encloses them within a wall, and places over them a guard."

The truth of this history is taught by the Erythræan Sibyl, who speaks almost the same things, with a few discrepancies, which do not affect the subject-matter itself. Therefore Jupiter is freed from the charge of the greatest wickedness, according to which he is reported to have bound his father with fetters; for this was the deed of his uncle Titan, because he, contrary to his promise and oath, had brought up male children. The rest of the history is thus put together. *It is said* that Jupiter, when grown up, having heard that his father and mother had been surrounded with a guard and imprisoned, came with a great multitude of Cretans, and conquered Titan and his sons in an engagement, and rescued his parents from imprisonment, restored the kingdom to his father, and thus returned into Crete. Then, after these things, *they say* that an oracle was given to Saturn, bidding him to take heed lest his son should expel him from the kingdom; that he, for the sake of weakening the oracle and avoiding the danger, laid an ambush for Jupiter to kill him; that Jupiter, having learned the plot, claimed the kingdom for himself afresh, and banished Saturn; and that he, when he had been tossed over all lands, followed by armed men whom Jupiter had sent to seize or put him to death, scarcely found a place of concealment in Italy.

Chap. XV. — How They Who Were Men Obtained the Name of Gods.

Now, since it is evident from these things that they were men, it is not difficult to see in what manner they began to be called gods.[1] For if there were no kings before Saturn or Uranus, on account of the small number of men who lived a rustic life without any ruler, there is no doubt but in those times men began to exalt the king himself, and his whole family, with the highest praises and with new honours, so that they even called them gods; whether on account of their wonderful excellence, men as yet rude and simple really entertained this opinion, or, as is commonly the case, in flattery of present power, or on account of the benefits by which they were set in order and reduced to a civilized state. Afterwards the kings themselves, since they were beloved by those whose life they had civilized, after their death left regret of themselves. Therefore men formed images of them, that they might derive some consolation from the contemplation of their likenesses; and proceeding further through love of their worth,[2] they began to reverence the memory of the deceased, that

1 [Vol. ii. cap. 28, p. 143, this series.]
2 Per amorem meriti. Some editions omit "meriti."

they might appear to be grateful for their services, and might attract their successors to a desire of ruling well. And this Cicero teaches in his treatise on the Nature of the Gods, saying: "But the life of men and common intercourse led to the exalting to heaven by fame and goodwill men who were distinguished by their benefits. On this account Hercules, on this Castor and Pollux, Æsculapius and Liber" were ranked with the gods. And in another passage: "And in most states it may be understood, that for the sake of exciting valour, or that the men most distinguished for bravery might more readily encounter danger on account of the state, their memory was consecrated with the honour paid to the immortal gods." It was doubtless on this account that the Romans consecrated their Cæsars, and the Moors their kings. Thus by degrees religious honours began to be paid to them; while those who had known them, first instructed their own children and grandchildren, and afterwards all their posterity, in the practice of this rite. And yet these great kings, on account of the celebrity of their name, were honoured in all provinces.

But separate people privately honoured the founders of their nation or city with the highest veneration, whether they were men distinguished for bravery, or women admirable for chastity; as the Egyptians honoured Isis, the Moors Juba, the Macedonians Cabirus, the Carthaginians Uranus, the Latins Faunus, the Sabines Sancus, the Romans Quirinus. In the same manner truly Athens worshipped Minerva, Samos Juno, Paphos Venus, Lemnos Vulcan, Naxos Liber, and Delos Apollo. And thus various sacred rites have been undertaken among different peoples and countries, inasmuch as men desire to show gratitude to their princes, and cannot find out other honours which they may confer upon the dead. Moreover, the piety of their successors contributed in a great degree to the error; for, in order that they might appear to be born from a divine origin, they paid divine honours to their parents, and ordered that they should be paid by others. Can any one doubt in what way the honours paid to the gods were instituted, when he reads in Virgil the words of Æneas giving commands to his friends:[1] —

> "Now with full cups libation pour
> To mighty Jove, whom all adore,
> Invoke Anchises' blessed soul."

And he attributes to him not only immortality, but also power over the winds:[2] —

> "Invoke the winds to speed our flight,
> And pray that he we hold so dear
> May take our offerings year by year,
> Soon as our promised town we raise,
> In temples sacred to his praise."

In truth, Liber and Pan, and Mercury and Apollo, acted in the same way respecting Jupiter, and afterwards their successors did the same respecting them. The poets also added their influence, and by means of poems composed to give pleasure, raised them to the heaven; as is the case with those who flatter kings, even though wicked, with false panegyrics. And this evil originated with the Greeks, whose levity being furnished[3] with the ability and copiousness of speech, excited in an incredible degree mists of falsehoods. And thus from admiration of them they first undertook their sacred rites, and handed them down to all nations. On account of this vanity the Sibyl thus rebukes them: —

> "Why trustest thou, O Greece, to princely men?
> Why to the dead dost offer empty gifts?
> Thou offerest to idols; this error who suggested,
> That thou shouldst leave the presence of the mighty God,
> And make these offerings?"

Marcus Tullius, who was not only an accomplished orator, but also a philosopher, since he alone was an imitator of Plato, in that treatise in which he consoled himself concerning the death of his daughter, did not hesitate to say that those gods who were publicly worshipped were men. And this testimony of his ought to be esteemed the more weighty, because he held the priesthood of the augurs, and testifies that he worships and venerates the same gods. And thus within the compass of a few verses he has presented us with two facts. For while he declared his intention of consecrating the image of his daughter in the same manner in which they were consecrated by the ancients, he both taught that they were dead, and showed the origin of a vain superstition. "Since, in truth," he says, "we see many men and women among the number of the gods, and venerate their shrines, held in the greatest honour in cities and in the country, let us assent to the wisdom of those to whose talents and inventions we owe it that life is altogether adorned with laws and institutions, and established on a firm basis. And if any living being was worthy of being consecrated, assuredly it was this. If the offspring of Cadmus, or Amphitryon, or Tyndarus, was worthy of being extolled by fame to the heaven, the same honour ought undoubtedly to be appropriated to her. And this indeed I will do; and with the approbation of the gods, I will place you the best and most learned of all women in their assembly. and will consecrate you to the estimation of all men." Some one may perhaps say that Cicero raved through excessive grief. But, in truth, the whole of that speech, which was perfect both in learning and in its examples, and in the very style of expression, gave no indications of a dis-

1 *Æneid*, vii. 133.
2 *Ibid.*, v. 59.

3 Instructa. [Vol. ii. cap. 18, p. 137, this series.]

tempered mind, but of constancy and judgment; and this very sentence exhibits no sign of grief. For I do not think that he could have written with such variety, and copiousness, and ornament, had not his grief been mitigated by reason itself, and the consolation of his friends and length of time. Why should I mention what he says in his books concerning the Republic, and also concerning glory? For in his treatise on the Laws, in which work, following the example of Plato, he wished to set forth those laws which he thought that a just and wise state would employ, he thus decreed concerning religion:[1] "Let them reverence the gods, both those who have always been regarded as gods of heaven, and those whose services *to men* have placed them in heaven: Hercules, Liber, Æsculapius, Castor, Pollux, and Quirinus." Also in his Tusculan Disputations,[2] when he said that heaven was almost entirely filled with the human race, he said: "If, indeed, I should attempt to investigate ancient accounts, and to extract from them those things which the writers of Greece have handed down, even those who are held in the highest rank as gods will be found to have gone from us into heaven. Inquire whose sepulchres are pointed out in Greece: remember, since you are initiated, what things are handed down in the mysteries; and then at length you will understand how widely this *persuasion* is spread." He appealed, as it is plain, to the conscience of Atticus, that it might be understood from the very mysteries that all those who are worshipped were men; and when he acknowledged this without hesitation in the case of Hercules, Liber, Æsculapius, Castor and Pollux, he was afraid openly to make the same admission respecting Apollo and Jupiter their fathers, and likewise respecting Neptune, Vulcan, Mars, and Mercury, whom he termed the greater gods; and therefore he says that this opinion is widely spread, that we may understand the same concerning Jupiter and the other more ancient gods: for if the ancients consecrated their memory in the same manner in which he says that he will consecrate the image and the name of his daughter, those who mourn may be pardoned, but those who believe it cannot be pardoned. For who is so infatuated as to believe that heaven is opened to the dead at the consent and pleasure of a senseless multitude? Or that any one is able to give to another that which he himself does not possess? Among the Romans, Julius was made a god, because it pleased a guilty man, Antony; Quirinus was made a god, because it seemed good to the shepherds, though one of them was the murderer of his twin brother, the other the destroyer of his country. But if Antony had not been consul, in return for his services towards the state Caius Cæsar would have been without the honour even of a dead man, and that, too, by the advice of his father-in-law Piso, and of his relative Lucius Cæsar, who opposed the celebration of the funeral, and by the advice of Dolabella the consul, who overthrew the column in the forum, that is, his monuments, and purified the forum. For Ennius declares that Romulus was regretted by his people, since he represents the people as thus speaking, through grief for their lost king: "O Romulus, Romulus, say what a guardian of your country the gods produced you? You brought us forth within the regions of light. O father, O sire, O race, descended from the gods." On account of this regret they more readily believed Julius Proculus uttering falsehoods, who was suborned by the fathers to announce to the populace that he had seen the king in a form more majestic than that of a man; and that he had given command to the people that a temple should be built to his honour, that he was a god, and was called by the name of Quirinus. By which deed he at once persuaded the people that Romulus had gone to the gods, and freed the senate from the suspicion of having slain the king.

Chap. XVI. — By What Argument It Is Proved That Those Who Are Distinguished by a Difference of Sex Cannot Be Gods.[3]

I might be content with those things which I have related, but there still remain many things which are necessary for the work which I have undertaken. For although, by destroying the principal part of superstitions, I have taken away the whole, yet it pleases me to follow up the remaining parts, and more fully to refute so inveterate a persuasion, that men may at length be ashamed and repent of their errors. This is a great undertaking, and worthy of a man. "I proceed to release the minds of men from the ties of superstitions," as Lucretius[4] says; and he indeed was unable to effect this, because he brought forward nothing true. This is our duty, who both assert the existence of the true God and refute false deities. They, therefore, who entertain the opinion that the poets have invented fables about the gods, and yet believe in the existence of female deities, and worship them, are unconsciously brought back to that which they had denied — that they have sexual intercourse, and bring forth. For it is impossible that the two sexes can have been instituted except for the sake of generation. But a difference of sex being admitted, they do not perceive that conception follows as a consequence. And this cannot

1 [*De Legibus*, ii. cap. 8.]
2 [Liber i. capp. 12, 13.]

3 And that the office of propagating (his race) does not fall within the nature of God.
4 i. 931. [i.e., *De Rerum Natura*, lib. i. verse 931.]

be the case with a God. But let the matter be as they imagine; for they say that there are sons of Jupiter and of the other gods. Therefore new gods are born, and that indeed daily, for gods are not surpassed in fruitfulness by men. It follows that all things are full of gods without number, since forsooth none of them dies. For since the multitude of men is incredible, and their number not to be estimated — though, as they are born, they must of necessity die — what must we suppose to be the case with the gods who have been born through so many ages, and have remained immortal? How is it, then, that so few are worshipped? Unless we think by any means that there are two sexes of the gods, not for the sake of generation, but for mere gratification, and that the gods practise those things which men are ashamed to do, and to submit to. But when any are said to be born from any, it follows that they always continue to be born, if they are born at any time; or if they ceased at any time to be born, it is befitting that we should know why or at what time they so ceased. Seneca, in his books of moral philosophy, not without some pleasantry, asks, "What is the reason why Jupiter, who is represented by the poets as most addicted to lust, ceased to beget children? Was it that he was become a sexagenarian, and was restrained by the Papian law?[1] Or did he obtain the privileges conferred by having three children? Or did the sentiment at length occur to him, 'What you have done to another, you may expect from another;' and does he fear lest any one should act towards him as he himself did to Saturn?" But let those who maintain that they are gods, see in what manner they can answer this argument which I shall bring forward. If there are two sexes of the gods, conjugal intercourse follows; and if this takes place, they must have houses, for they are not without virtue and a sense of shame, so as to do this openly and promiscuously, as we see that the brute animals do. If they have houses, it follows that they also have cities; and for this we have the authority of Ovid, who says, "The multitude of gods occupy separate places; in this front the powerful and illustrious inhabitants of heaven have placed their dwellings." If they have cities, they will also have fields. Now who cannot see the consequence, — namely, that they plough and cultivate their lands? And this is done for the sake of food. Therefore they are mortal. And this argument is of the same weight when reversed. For if they have no lands, they have no cities; and if they have no cities, they are also without houses. And if they have no houses, they have no conjugal intercourse; and if they are without this, they have no female sex. But we see that there are females among the gods also. Therefore there are not gods. If any one is able, let him do away with this argument. For one thing so follows the other, that it is impossible not to admit these last things. But no one will refute even the former argument. Of the two sexes the one is stronger, the other weaker. For the males are more robust, the females more feeble. But a god is not liable to feebleness; therefore there is no female sex. To this is added that last conclusion of the former argument, that there are no gods, since there are females also among the gods.

CHAP. XVII. — CONCERNING THE SAME OPINION OF THE STOICS, AND CONCERNING THE HARDSHIPS AND DISGRACEFUL CONDUCT OF THE GODS.

On these accounts the Stoics form a different conception of the gods; and because they do not perceive what the truth is, they attempt to join them with the system of natural things. And Cicero, following them, brought forward this opinion respecting the gods and their religions. Do you see then, he says, how an argument has been drawn from physical subjects which have been well and usefully found out, to the existence of false and fictitious gods? And this circumstance gave rise to false opinions and turbulent errors, and almost old-womanly superstitions. For both the forms of the gods, and their ages, and clothing and ornaments, are known to us; and moreover their races, and marriages, and all their relationships, and all things reduced to the similitude of human infirmity. What can be said more plain, more true? The chief of the Roman philosophy, and invested with the most honourable priesthood, refutes the false and fictitious gods, and testifies that their worship consists of almost old-womanly superstitions: he complains that men are entangled in false opinions and turbulent errors. For the whole of his third book respecting the Nature of the Gods altogether overthrows and destroys all religion. What more, therefore, is expected from us? Can we surpass Cicero in eloquence? By no means; but confidence was wanting to him, being ignorant of the truth, as he himself simply acknowledges in the same work. For he says that he can more easily say what is not, than what is; that is, that he is aware that *the received system* is false, but is ignorant of the truth.[2] It is plain, therefore, that those who are supposed to be gods were but men, and that their memory was consecrated after their death. And on this account also different ages and established representations of form are assigned to each, be-

[1] [Cicero, *De Officiis*, lib. iii. 11.]

[2] [*Nat. Deor.*, liber i. 32.]

cause their images were fashioned in that dress and *of that* age at which death arrested each.

Let us consider, if you please, the hardships of the unfortunate gods. Isis lost her son; Ceres her daughter; Latona, expelled and driven about over the earth, with difficulty found a small island [1] where she might bring forth. The mother of the gods both loved a beautiful youth, and also mutilated him when found in company with a harlot; and on this account her sacred rites are now celebrated by the Galli [2] as priests. Juno violently persecuted harlots, because she was not able to conceive by her brother.[3] Varro writes, that the island Samos was before called Parthenia, because Juno there grew up, and there also was married to Jupiter. Accordingly there is a most noble and ancient temple of hers at Samos, and an image fashioned in the dress of a bride; and her annual sacred rites are celebrated after the manner of a marriage. If, therefore, she grew up, if she was at first a virgin and afterwards a woman, he who does not understand that she was a human being confesses himself a brute. Why should I speak of the lewdness of Venus, who ministered to the lusts of all, not only gods, but also men? For from her infamous debauchery with Mars she brought forth Harmonia; from Mercury she brought forth Hermaphroditus, who was born of both sexes; from Jupiter Cupid; from Anchises Æneas; from Butes Eryx; from Adonis she could bring forth no offspring, because he was struck by a boar, and slain, while yet a boy. And she first instituted the art of courtesanship, as is contained in the sacred history; and taught women in Cyprus to seek gain by prostitution, which she commanded for this purpose, that she alone might not appear unchaste and a courter of men beyond other females. Has she, too, any claim to religious worship, on whose part more adulteries are recorded than births? But not even were those virgins who are celebrated able to preserve their chastity inviolate. For from what source can we suppose that Erichthonius was born? Was it from the earth, as the poets would have it appear? But the circumstance itself cries out. For when Vulcan had made arms for the gods, and Jupiter had given him the option of asking for whatever reward he might wish, and had sworn, according to his custom, by the infernal lake, that he would refuse him nothing which he might ask, then the lame artificer demanded Minerva in marriage. Upon this the excellent and mighty Jupiter, being bound by so great an oath, was not able to refuse; he, however, advised Minerva to oppose and defend her chastity. Then in that struggle they say that Vulcan shed his seed upon the earth, from which source Erichthonius was born: and that this name was given to him from ἔριδος and χθονός, that is, from the contest and the ground. Why, then, did she, a virgin, entrust that boy shut up with a dragon and sealed to three virgins born from Cecrops? An evident case of incest, as I think, which can by no means be glossed over. Another, when she had almost lost her lover, who was torn to pieces by his madened horses, called in the most excellent physician Æsculapius for the treatment of the youth; and when he was healed,

> "Trivia kind her favourite hides,
> And to Egeria's care confides,
> To live in woods obscure and lone,
> And lose in Virbius' name his own." [4]

What is the meaning of this so diligent and anxious care? Why this secret abode? Why this banishment, either to so great a distance, or to a woman, or into solitude? Why, in the next place, the change of name? Lastly, why such a determined hatred of horses? What do all these things imply, but the consciousness of dishonour, and a love by no means consistent with a virgin? There was evidently a reason why she undertook so great a labour for a youth so faithful, who had refused compliance with the love of his stepmother.

CHAP. XVIII. — ON THE CONSECRATION OF GODS, ON ACCOUNT OF THE BENEFITS WHICH THEY CONFERRED UPON MEN.

In this place also they are to be refuted, who not only admit that gods have been made from men, but even boast of it as a subject of praise, either on account of their valour, as Hercules, or of their gifts, as Ceres and Liber, or of the arts which they discovered, as Æsculapius or Minerva. But how foolish these things are, and how unworthy of being the causes why men should contaminate themselves with inexpiable guilt, and become enemies to God, in contempt of whom they undertake offerings to the dead, I will show from particular instances. They say that it is virtue [5] which exalts man to heaven, — not, however, that concerning which philosophers discuss, which consists in goods of the soul, but this connected with the body, which is called fortitude; and since this was pre-eminent in Hercules, it is believed to have deserved immortality. Who is so foolishly senseless as to judge strength of body to be a divine or even a human good, when it has been assigned in greater measure to cattle, and it is often impaired by one disease, or is lessened by old age

[1] Delos.
[2] The priests of Cybele were called Galli.
[3] Jupiter.
[4] Virg., *Æneid*, vii 774.
[5] Virtus in its first meaning denotes valour, the property of a man (*vir*); then it is used to signify moral excellence.

itself, and altogether fails? And so Hercules, when he perceived that his muscles were disfigured by ulcers, neither wished to be healed nor to grow old, that he might not at any time appear to have less strength or comeliness than he once had.[1] They supposed that he ascended into heaven from the funeral pile on which he had burnt himself alive; and those very qualities which they most foolishly admired, they expressed by statues and images, and consecrated, so that they might for ever remain as memorials of the folly of those who had believed that gods owed their origin to the slaughter of beasts. But this, perchance, may be the fault of the Greeks, who always esteemed most trifling things as of the greatest consequence. What is the case of our own countrymen? Are they more wise? For they despise valour in an athlete, because it produces no injury; but in the case of a king, because it occasions widely-spread disasters, they so admire it as to imagine that brave and warlike generals are admitted to the assembly of the gods, and that there is no other way to immortality than to lead armies, to lay waste the territory of others, to destroy cities, to overthrow towns, to put to death or enslave free peoples. Truly the greater number of men they have cast down, plundered, and slain, so much the more noble and distinguished do they think themselves; and ensnared by the show of empty glory, they give to their crimes the name of virtue. I would rather that they should make to themselves gods from the slaughter of wild beasts, than approve of an immortality so stained with blood. If any one has slain a single man, he is regarded as contaminated and wicked, nor do they think it lawful for him to be admitted to this earthly abode of the gods. But he who has slaughtered countless thousands of men, has inundated plains with blood, and infected rivers, is not only admitted into the temple, but even into heaven. In Ennius Africanus thus speaks: "If it is permitted any one to ascend to the regions of the gods above, the greatest gate of heaven is open to me alone." Because, in truth, he extinguished and destroyed a great part of the human race. Oh how great the darkness in which you were involved, O Africanus, or rather O poet, in that you imagined the ascent to heaven to be open to men through slaughters and bloodshed! And Cicero also assented to this delusion. It is so in truth, he said, O Africanus, for the same gate was open to Hercules; as though he himself had been doorkeeper in heaven at the time when this took place. I indeed cannot determine whether I should think it a subject of grief or of ridicule, when I see grave and learned, and, as they appear to themselves, wise men, involved in such miserable waves of errors. If this is the virtue which renders us immortal, I for my part should prefer to die, rather than to be the cause of destruction to as many as possible. If immortality can be obtained in no other way than by bloodshed, what will be the result if all shall agree to *live in* harmony? And this may undoubtedly be realized, if men would cast aside their pernicious and impious madness, and live in innocence and justice. Shall no one, then, be worthy of heaven? Shall virtue perish, because it will not be permitted men to rage against their fellow-men? But they who reckon the overthrow of cities and people as the greatest glory will not endure public tranquillity: they will plunder and rage; and by the infliction of outrageous injuries will disturb the compact of human society, that they may have an enemy whom they may destroy with greater wickedness than that with which they attacked.

Now let us proceed to the remaining subjects. The conferring of benefits gave the name of gods to Ceres and Liber. I am able to prove from the sacred writings that wine and corn were used by men before the offspring of Cœlus and Saturnus. But let us suppose that they were introduced by these. Can it appear to be a greater thing to have collected corn, and having bruised it, to have taught men to make bread; or to have pressed grapes gathered from the vine, and to have made wine, than to have produced and brought forth from the earth corn itself, or the vine? God, indeed, may have left these things to be drawn out by the ingenuity of man; yet all things must belong to Him, who gave to man both wisdom to discover, and those very things which might be discovered. The arts also are said to have gained immortality for their inventors, as medicine for Æsculapius, the craft of the smith for Vulcan. Therefore let us worship those also who taught the art of the fuller and of the shoemaker. But why is not honour paid to the discoverer of the potter's art? Is it that those rich men despise Samian vessels? There are also other arts, the inventors of which greatly profited the life of man. Why have not temples been assigned to them also? But doubtless it is Minerva who discovered all, and therefore workmen offer prayers to her. Such, then, was the low condition[2] from which Minerva ascended to heaven. Is there truly any reason why any one should leave the worship of Him who created[3] the earth with its living creatures, and the heaven with its stars, for the adoration of her who taught men to set up the woof? What place does he hold who taught the healing of wounds in the

[1] Lit., than himself.

[2] Ab his sordibus.

[3] Exorsus est. The word properly denotes to begin a web, to lay the warp; hence the use of "ordiri" in the following clause.

body? Can he be more excellent than Him who formed the body itself, and the power of sensibility and of life? Finally, did he contrive and bring to light the herbs themselves, and the other things in which the healing art consists?

Chap. XIX. — That it is impossible for any one to worship the true God together with false deities.

But some one will say that this supreme Being, who made all things, and those also who conferred on men particular benefits, are entitled to their respective worship. First of all, it has never happened that the worshipper of these has also been a worshipper of God. Nor can this possibly happen. For if the honour paid to Him is shared by others, He altogether ceases to be worshipped, since His religion requires us to believe that He is the one and only God. The excellent poet exclaims, that all those who refined life by the invention of arts are in the lower regions, and that even the discoverer himself of such a medicine and art was thrust down by lightning to the Stygian waves, that we may understand how great is the power of the Almighty Father, who can extinguish even gods by His lightnings. But ingenious men perchance thus reasoned with themselves: Because God cannot be struck with lightning, it is manifest that the occurrence never took place; nay, rather, because it did take place, it is manifest that the person in question was a man, and not a god. For the falsehood of the poets does not consist in the deed, but in the name. For they feared evil, if, in opposition to the general persuasion, they should acknowledge that which was true. But if this is agreed upon among themselves, that gods were made from men, why then do they not believe the poets, if at any time they describe their banishments and wounds, their deaths, and wars, and adulteries? From which things it may be understood that they could not possibly become gods, since they were not even good men, and during their life they performed those actions which bring forth everlasting death.

Chap. XX. — Of the gods peculiar to the Romans, and their sacred rites.

I now come to the superstitions peculiar to the Romans, since I have spoken of those which are common. The wolf, the nurse of Romulus, was invested with divine honours. And I could endure this, if it had been the animal itself whose figure she bears. Livy relates that there was an image of Larentina, and indeed not of her body, but of her mind and character. For she was the wife of Faustulus, and on account of her prostitution she was called among the shepherds wolf,[1] that is, harlot, from which also the brothel[2] derives its name. The Romans doubtless followed the example of the Athenians in representing her figure. For when a harlot, by name Leæna, had put to death a tyrant among them, because it was unlawful for the image of a harlot to be placed in the temple, they erected the effigy of the animal whose name she bore. Therefore, as the Athenians erected a monument from the name, so did the Romans from the profession *of the person thus honoured*. A festival was also dedicated to her name, and the Larentinalia were instituted. Nor is she the only harlot whom the Romans worship, but also Faula, who was, as Verrius writes, the paramour of Hercules. Now how great must that immortality be thought which is attained even by harlots! Flora, having obtained great wealth by this practice, made the people her heir, and left a fixed sum of money, from the annual proceeds of which her birthday might be celebrated by public games, which they called Floralia. And because this appeared disgraceful to the senate, in order that a kind of dignity might be given to a shameful matter, they resolved that an argument should be taken from the name itself. They pretended that she was the goddess who presides over flowers, and that she must be appeased, that the crops, together with the trees or vines, might produce a good and abundant blossom. The poet followed up this idea in his *Fasti*, and related that there was a nymph, by no means obscure, who was called Chloris, and that, on her marriage with Zephyrus, she received from her husband as a wedding gift the control over all flowers. These things are spoken with propriety, but to believe them is unbecoming and shameful. And *when the truth is in question*, ought disguises of this kind to deceive us? Those games, therefore, are celebrated with all wantonness, as is suitable to the memory of a harlot. For besides licentiousness of words, in which all lewdness is poured forth, women are also stripped of their garments at the demand of the people, and then perform the office of mimeplayers, and are detained in the sight of the people with indecent gestures, even to the satiating of unchaste eyes.

Tatius consecrated an image of Cloacina, which had been found in the great sewer; and because he did not know whose likeness it was, he gave it a name from the place. Tullus Hostilius fashioned and worshipped Fear and Pallor. What shall I say respecting him, but that he was worthy of having his gods always at hand, as men commonly wish? The conduct of Marcus Marcellus concerning the consecration of Honour and Valour differs from this in goodness of the names, but agrees with it in reality. The senate

[1] Lupa. [See vol. iii. cap. 10, p. 138, this series.]
[2] Lupanar.

acted with the same vanity in placing Mind[1] among the gods; for if they had possessed any intelligence, they would never have undertaken sacred rites of this kind. Cicero says that Greece undertook a great and bold design in consecrating the images of Cupids and Loves in the gymnasia: it is plain that he flattered Atticus, and jested with his friend. For that ought not to have been called a great design, or a design at all, but the abandoned and deplorable wickedness of unchaste men, who exposed their children, whom it was their duty to train to an honourable course, to the lust of youth, and wished them to worship gods of profligacy, in those places especially where their naked bodies were exposed to the gaze of their corruptors, and at that age which, through its simplicity and incautiousness, can be enticed and ensnared before it can be on its guard. What wonder, if all kinds of profligacy flowed from this nation, among whom vices themselves have the sanction of religion, and are so far from being avoided, that they are even worshipped? And therefore, as though he surpassed the Greeks in prudence, he subjoined to this sentence as follows: "Vices ought not to be consecrated, but virtues." But if you admit this, O Marcus Tullius, you do not see that it will come to pass that vices will break in together with virtues, because evil things adhere to those which are good, and have greater influence on the minds of men; and if you forbid these to be consecrated, the same Greece will answer you that it worships some gods that it may receive benefits, and others that it may escape injuries.

For this is always the excuse of those who regard their evils as gods, as the Romans esteem Blight and Fever. If, therefore, vices are not to be consecrated, in which I agree with you, neither indeed are virtues. For they have no intelligence or perception of themselves; nor are they to be placed within walls or shrines made of clay, but within the breast; and they are to be enclosed within, lest they should be false if placed without man. Therefore I laugh at that illustrious law of yours which you set forth in these words: "But those things on account of which it is given to man to ascend into heaven — *I speak of* mind, virtue, piety, faith — let there be temples for their praises." But these things cannot be separated from man. For if they are to be honoured, they must necessarily be in man himself. But if they are without man, what need is there to honour those things which you do not possess? For it is virtue which is to be honoured, and not the image of virtue; and it is to be honoured not by any sacrifice, or incense, or solemn prayer, but only by the will and purpose. For what else is it to honour virtue, but to comprehend it with the mind, and to hold it fast? And as soon as any one begins to wish for this, he attains it. This is the only honour of virtue; for no other religion and worship is to be held but that of the one God. To what purport is it, then, O wisest man, to occupy with superfluous buildings places which may turn out to the service of men? To what purport is it to establish priests for the worship of vain and senseless objects? To what purport to immolate victims? To what purport to bestow such great expenditure on the forming or worshipping of images? The human breast is a stronger and more uncorrupted temple: let this rather be adorned, let this be filled with the true deities. For they who thus worship the virtues — that is, who pursue the shadows and images of virtues — cannot hold the very things which are true. Therefore there is no virtue in any one when vices bear rule; there is no faith when each individual carries off all things for himself; there is no piety when avarice spares neither relatives nor parents, and passion rushes to poison and the sword: no peace, no concord, when wars rage in public, and in private enmities prevail even to bloodshed; no chastity when unbridled lusts contaminate each sex, and the whole body in every part. Nor, however, do they cease to worship those things which they flee from and hate. For they worship with incense and the tips of their fingers those things which they ought to have shrunk from with their inmost feelings; and this error is altogether derived from their ignorance of the principal and chief good.

When their city was occupied by the Gauls, and the Romans, who were besieged in the Capitol, had made military engines from the hair of the women, they dedicated a temple to the Bald Venus. They do not therefore understand how vain are their religions, even from this very fact, that they jeer at them by these follies. They had perhaps learned from the Lacedæmonians to invent for themselves gods from events. For when they were besieging the Messenians, and they (the Messenians) had gone out secretly, escaping the notice of the besiegers, and had hastened to plunder Lacedæmon, they were routed and put to flight by the Spartan women. But the Lacedæmonians, having learned the stratagem of the enemy, followed. The women in arms went out to a distance to meet them; and when they saw that their husbands were preparing themselves for battle, supposing them to be Messenians, they laid bare their persons. But the men, recognising their wives, and excited to passion by the sight, rushed to promiscuous intercourse, for there was not time for discrimination. In like manner, the youths who had on a

[1] Mens. [Tayler Lewis, *Plato*, etc., p. 219.]

former occasion been sent by the same people, having intercourse with the virgins, from whom the Partheniæ were born, in memory of this deed erected a temple and statue to armed Venus. And although this originated in a shameful cause, yet it seems better to have consecrated Venus as armed than bald. At the same time an altar was erected also to Jupiter Pistor (the baker), because he had admonished them in a dream to make all the corn which they had into bread, and throw it into the camp of the enemy; and when this was done, the siege was ended, since the Gauls despaired of being able to reduce the Romans by want.

What a derision of religious rites is this! If I were a defender of these, what could I complain of so greatly as that the name of gods had come into such contempt as to be mocked by the most disgraceful names? Who would not laugh at the goddess Fornax, or rather that learned men should be occupied with celebrating the Fornacalia? Who can refrain from laughter on hearing of the goddess Muta? They say that she is the goddess from whom the Lares were born, and they call her Lara, or Larunda. What advantage can she, who is unable to speak, afford to a worshipper? Caca also is worshipped, who informed Hercules of the theft of his oxen, having obtained immortality through the betrayal of her brother; and Cunina, who protects infants in the cradle, and keeps off witchcraft; and Stercutus, who first introduced the method of manuring the land; and Tutinus, before whom brides sit, as an introduction to the marriage rites; and a thousand other fictions, so that they who regarded these as objects of worship may be said to be more foolish than the Egyptians, who worship certain monstrous and ridiculous images. These, however, have some delineation of form. What shall I say of those who worship a rude and shapeless stone under the name of Terminus? This is he whom Saturnus is said to have swallowed in the place of Jupiter; nor is the honour paid to him undeservedly. For when Tarquinius wished to build the Capitol, and there were the chapels of many gods on that spot, he consulted them by augury whether they would give way to Jupiter; and when the rest gave way, Terminus alone remained. From which circumstance the poet speaks of the immoveable stone of the Capitol. Now from this very fact how great is Jupiter found to be, to whom a stone did not give way, with this confidence, perhaps, because it had rescued him from the jaws of his father! Therefore, when the Capitol was built, an aperture was left in the roof above Terminus himself, that, since he had not given way, he might enjoy the free heaven; but they did not themselves enjoy this, who imagined that a stone enjoyed it. And therefore they make public supplications to him, as to the god who is the guardian of boundaries; and he is not only a stone, but sometimes also a stock. What shall I say of those who worship such objects, unless—that they above all others are stones and stocks?

CHAP. XXI.—OF CERTAIN DEITIES PECULIAR TO BARBARIANS, AND THEIR SACRED RITES; AND IN LIKE MANNER CONCERNING THE ROMANS.

We have spoken of the gods themselves who are worshipped; we must now speak a few words respecting their sacrifices and mysteries. Among the people of Cyprus, Teucer sacrificed a human victim to Jupiter, and handed down to posterity that sacrifice which was lately abolished by Hadrian when he was emperor. There was a law among the people of Tauris, a fierce and inhuman nation, *by which it was ordered* that strangers should be sacrificed to Diana; and this sacrifice was practised through many ages. The Gauls used to appease Hesus and Teutas with human blood. Nor, indeed, were the Latins free from this cruelty, since Jupiter Latialis is even now worshipped with the offering of human blood. What benefit do they who offer such sacrifices implore from the gods? Or what are such deities able to bestow on the men by whose punishments they are propitiated? But this is not so much a matter of surprise with respect to barbarians, whose religion agrees with their character. But are not our countrymen, who have always claimed for themselves the glory of gentleness and civilization, found to be more inhuman by these sacrilegious rites? For these ought rather to be esteemed impious, who, though they are embellished with the pursuits of liberal training, turn aside from such refinement, than those who, being ignorant and inexperienced, glide into evil practices from their ignorance of those which are good. And yet it is plain that this rite of immolating human victims is ancient, since Saturn was honoured in Latium with the same kind of sacrifice; not indeed that a man was slain at the altar, but that he was thrown from the Milvian bridge into the Tiber. And Varro relates that this was done in accordance with an oracle; of which oracle the last verse is to this effect: "And offer heads to Ades, and to the father a man."[1] And because this appears ambiguous, both a torch and a man are accustomed to be thrown to him. But it is said that sacrifices of this kind were put an end to by Hercules when he returned from Spain; the custom still continuing, that instead of real men, images made from rushes were cast forth, as Ovid informs us in his *Fasti*:[2] "Until the Tirynthian

[1] Or, lights. The oracle is ambiguous, since the word φως signifies a man, and also light. [i.e., φὼς = man, and φῶς = light.]

[2] v. 629.

came into these lands, gloomy sacrifices were annually offered in the Leucadian manner: he threw into the water Romans made of straw; do you, after the example of Hercules, cast[1] in the images of human bodies."

The Vestal virgins make these sacred offerings, as the same poet says:[2] "Then also a virgin is accustomed to cast from the wooden bridge the images of ancient men made from rushes."

For I cannot find language to speak of the infants who were immolated to the same Saturn, on account of his hatred of Jupiter. To think that men were so barbarous, so savage, that they gave the name of sacrifice to the slaughter of their own children, that is, to a deed foul, and to be held in detestation by the human race; since, without any regard to parental affection, they destroyed tender and innocent lives, at an age which is especially pleasing to parents, and surpassed in brutality the savageness of all beasts, which — savage as they are — still love their offspring! O incurable madness! What more could those gods do to them, if they were most angry, than they now do when propitious, when they defile their worshippers with parricide, visit them with bereavements, and deprive them of the sensibilities of men? What can be sacred to these men? Or what will they do in profane places, who commit the greatest crimes amidst the altars of the gods? Pescennius Festus relates in the books of his History by a Satire, that the Carthaginians were accustomed to immolate human victims to Saturn; and when they were conquered by Agathocles, the king of the Sicilians, they imagined that the god was angry with them; and therefore, that they might more diligently offer an expiation, they immolated two hundred sons of their nobles: "So great the ills to which religion could prompt, which has ofttimes produced wicked and impious deeds." What advantage, then, did the men propose by that sacrifice, when they put to death so large a part of the state, as not even Agathocles had slain when victorious?

From this kind of sacrifices those public rites are to be judged *signs* of no less madness; some of which are in honour of the mother of the gods, in which men mutilate themselves; others are in honour of Virtus, whom they also call Bellona, in which the priests make offsprings not with the blood of another victim, but with their own.[3] For, cutting their shoulders, and thrusting forth drawn swords in each hand, they run, they are beside themselves, they are frantic. Quintilian therefore says excellently in his *Fanatic:* "If a god compels this, he does it in anger." Are even these things sacred? Is it not better to live like cattle, than to worship deities so impious. profane, and sanguinary? But we will discuss at the proper time the source from which these errors and deeds of such great disgrace originated. In the meantime, let us look also to other matters which are without guilt, that we may not seem to select the worse parts through the desire of finding fault. In Egypt there are sacred rites in honour of Isis, since she either lost or found her little son. For at first her priests, having made their bodies smooth, beat their breasts, and lament, as the goddess herself had done when her child was lost. Afterwards the boy is brought forward, as if found, and that mourning is changed into joy. Therefore Lucan says, "And Osiris never sufficiently sought for." For they always lose, and they always find him. Therefore in the sacred rites there is a representation of a circumstance which really occurred; and which assuredly declares, if we have any intelligence, that she was a mortal woman, and almost desolate, had she not found one person. And this did not escape the notice of the poet himself; for he represents Pompey when a youth as thus speaking, on hearing the death of his father: "I will now draw forth the deity Isis from the tomb, *and send her* through the nations; and I will scatter through the people Osiris covered with wood." This Osiris is the same whom the people call Serapis. For it is customary for the names of the dead who are deified to be changed, that no one, as I believe, may imagine them to be men. For Romulus after his death became Quirinus, and Leda became Nemesis, and Circe Marica; and Ino, when she had leapt into the sea, was called Leucothea; and the mother Matuta; and her son Melicerta was called Palæmon and Portumnus. And the sacred rites of the Eleusinian Ceres are not unlike these. For as in those *which have been mentioned* the boy Osiris is sought with the wailing of his mother, so in these Proserpine is carried away to contract an incestuous marriage with her uncle; and because Ceres is said to have sought for her in Sicily with torches lighted from the top of Etna, on this account her sacred rites are celebrated with the throwing of torches.

At Lampsacus the victim to be offered to Priapus is an ass, and the cause of the sacrifice of this animal is thus set forth in the *Fasti:* — When all the deities had assembled at the festival of the Great Mother, and when, satiated with feasting, they were spending the night in sport, they say that Vesta had laid herself on the ground for rest, and had fallen asleep, and that Priapus upon this formed a design against her honour as she slept; but that she was aroused by the unseasonable braying of the ass on which Silenus used to ride, and that the design of the insidi-

[1] Jace. Others read "jaci."
[2] v. 621.
[3] So the priests of Baal cut themselves, 1 Kings xviii. 28.

ous plotter was frustrated. On this account they say that the people of Lampsacus were accustomed to sacrifice an ass to Priapus, as though it were in revenge; but among the Romans the same animal was crowned at the Vestalia (festival of Vesta) with loaves,[1] in honour of the preservation of her chastity. What is baser, what more disgraceful, than if Vesta is indebted to an ass for the preservation of her purity? But the poet invented a fable. But was that more true which is related by those[2] who wrote "Phenomena," when they speak concerning the two stars of Cancer, which the Greeks call asses? That they were asses which carried across father Liber when he was unable to cross a river, and that he rewarded one of them with the power of speaking with human voice; and that a contest arose between him and Priapus; and Priapus, being worsted *in the contest*, was enraged, and slew the victor. This truly is much more absurd. But poets have the licence of saying what they will. I do not meddle with a mystery so odious; nor do I strip Priapus of his disguise, lest something deserving of ridicule should be brought to light. It is true the poets invented these fictions, but they must have been invented for the purpose of concealing some greater depravity. Let us inquire what this is. But in fact it is evident. For as the bull is sacrificed to Luna,[3] because he also has horns as she has; and as "Persia propitiates with a horse Hyperion surrounded with rays, that a slow victim may not be offered to the swift god;" so in this case no more suitable victim could be found than that which resembled him to whom it is offered.

At Lindus, which is a town of Rhodes, there are sacred rites in honour of Hercules, the observance of which differs widely from all other rites; for they are not celebrated with words of good omen[4] (as the Greeks term it), but with revilings and cursing. And they consider it a violation of the sacred rites, if at any time during the celebration of the solemnities a good word shall have escaped from any one even inadvertently. And this is the reason assigned for this practice, if indeed there can be any reason in things utterly senseless. When Hercules had arrived at the place, and was suffering hunger, he saw a ploughman at work, and began to ask him to sell one of his oxen. But the ploughman replied that this was impossible, because his hope of cultivating the land depended altogether upon those two bullocks. Hercules, with his usual violence, because he was not able to receive one of them, killed both. But the unhappy man, when he saw that his oxen were slain, avenged the injury with revilings,—a circumstance which afforded gratification to the man of elegance and refinement. For while he prepares a feast for his companions, and while he devours the oxen of another man, he receives with ridicule and loud laughter the bitter reproaches with which the other assails him. But when it had been determined that divine honours should be paid to Hercules in admiration of his excellence, an altar was erected in his honour by the citizens, which he named, from the circumstance, the yoke of oxen;[5] and at this altar two yoked oxen were sacrificed, like those which he had taken from the ploughman. And he appointed the same man to be his priest, and directed him always to use the same revilings in offering sacrifice, because he said that he had never feasted more pleasantly. Now these things are not sacred, but sacrilegious, in which that is said to be enjoined, which, if it is done in other things, is punished with the greatest severity. What, moreover, do the rites of the Cretan Jupiter himself show, except the manner in which he was withdrawn from his father, or brought up? There is a goat belonging to the nymph Amalthea, which gave suck to the infant; and of this goat Germanicus Cæsar thus speaks, in his poem translated from Aratus:[6]—

> "She is supposed to be the nurse of Jupiter; if in truth the infant Jupiter pressed the faithful teats of the Cretan goat, which attests the gratitude of her lord by a bright constellation."

Musæus relates that Jupiter, when fighting against the Titans, used the hide of this goat as a shield, from which circumstance he is called by the poets shield-bearer.[7] Thus, whatever was done in concealing the boy, that also is done by way of representation in the sacred rites. Moreover, the mystery of his mother also contains the same *story* which Ovid sets forth in the *Fasti*:—

> "Now the lofty Ida resounds with tinklings, that the boy may cry in safety with infant mouth. Some strike their shields with stakes, some beat their empty helmets. This is the employment of the Curetes, this of the Corybantes. The matter was concealed, and imitations of the ancient deed remain; the attendant goddesses shake instruments of brass, and hoarse hides. Instead of helmets they strike cymbals, and drums instead of shields; the flute gives Phrygian strains, as it gave before."

Sallust rejected this opinion altogether, as though invented by the poets, and wished to give an ingenious explanation of the reasons for

1 Panibus, loaves made in the shape of crowns.

2 [See this page, note 6, *infra*.]

3 The moon.

4 εὐφημια. It was supposed that words of ill omen, if uttered during the offering of a sacrifice, would render the gods unpropitious: the priest therefore, at the commencement of a sacrifice, called upon the people to abstain from ill-omened words: εὐφημεῖτε, "favete linguis."

5 Βούζυγον.

6 Aratus was the author of two Greek astronomical poems, the Φαινόμενα and the Διοσημεῖα. Virgil, in his *Georgics*, has borrowed largely from the latter. Germanicus Cæsar, the grandson of Augustus, as stated in the text, translated the Φαινόμενα.

7 αιγιοχος; "scutum habens."

which the Curetes are said to have nourished Jupiter; and he speaks to this purport: Because they were the first to understand the worship of the deity, that therefore antiquity, which exaggerates all things, made them known as the nourishers of Jupiter. How much this learned man was mistaken, the matter itself at once declares. For if Jupiter holds the first place, both among the gods and in religious rites, if no gods were worshipped by the people before him, because they who are worshipped were not yet born; it appears that the Curetes, on the contrary, were the first who did not understand the worship of the deity, since all error was introduced by them, and the memory of the true God was taken away. They ought therefore to have understood from the mysteries and ceremonies themselves, that they were offering prayers to dead men. I do not then require that any one should believe the fictions of the poets. If any one imagines that these speak falsely, let him consider the writings of the pontiffs themselves, and weigh whatever there is of literature pertaining to sacred rites: he will perhaps find more things than we bring forward, from which he may understand that all things which are esteemed sacred are empty, vain, and fictitious. But if any one, having discovered wisdom, shall lay aside his error, he will assuredly laugh at the follies of men who are almost without understanding: I mean those who either dance with unbecoming gestures, or run naked, anointed, and crowned with chaplets, either wearing a mask or besmeared with mud. What shall I say about shields now putrid with age? When they carry these, they think that they are carrying gods themselves on their shoulders. For Furius Bibaculus is regarded among the chief examples of piety, who, though he was prætor, nevertheless carried the sacred shield,[1] preceded by the lictors, though his office *as prætor* gave him an exemption from this duty. He was therefore not Furius, but altogether mad,[2] who thought that he graced his prætorship by this service. Deservedly then, since these things are done by men not unskilful and ignorant, does Lucretius exclaim: —

> "O foolish minds of men! O blinded breasts! In what darkness of life and in how great dangers is passed this term of life, whatever be its duration!"

Who that is possessed of any sense would not laugh at these mockeries, when he sees that men, as though bereft of intelligence, do those things seriously, which if any one should do in sport, he would appear too full of sport and folly?

[1] *Ancile*, the sacred shield, carried by the *Salii*, or priests of Mars, in the processions at the festival of that deity.

[2] Non Furius, sed plane furiosus.

CHAP. XXII. — WHO WAS THE AUTHOR OF THE VANITIES BEFORE DESCRIBED IN ITALY AMONG THE ROMANS, AND WHO AMONG OTHER NATIONS.

The author and establisher of these vanities among the Romans was that Sabine king who especially engaged[3] the rude and ignorant minds of men with new superstitions: and that he might do this with some authority, he pretended that he had meetings by night with the goddess Egeria. There was a very dark cavern in the grove of Aricia, from which flowed a stream with a never failing spring. Hither he was accustomed to withdraw himself without any witnesses, that he might be able to pretend that, by the admonition of the goddess his wife, he delivered to the people those sacred rites which were most acceptable to the gods. It is evident that he wished to imitate the craftiness of Minos, who concealed himself in the cave of Jupiter, and, after a long delay there, brought forward laws, as though delivered to him by Jupiter, that he might bind men to obedience not only by the authority of his government, but also by the sanction of religion. Nor was it difficult to persuade shepherds. Therefore he instituted pontiffs, priests, *Salii*, and augurs; he arranged the gods in families; and by these means he softened the fierce spirits of the new people, and called them away from warlike affairs to the pursuit of peace. But though he deceived others, he did not deceive himself. For after many years, in the consulship of Cornelius and Bebius, in a field belonging to the scribe Petilius, under the Janiculum, two stone chests were found by men who were digging, in one of which was the body of Numa, in the other seven books in Latin respecting the law of the pontiffs, and the same number written in Greek respecting systems of philosophy, in which he not only annulled the religious rites which he himself had instituted, but all others also. When this was referred to the senate, it was decreed that these books should be destroyed. Therefore Quintus Petilius, the prætor who had jurisdiction in the city, burnt them in an assembly of the people. This was a senseless proceeding; for of what advantage was it that the books were burnt, when the cause on account of which they were burnt — that they took away the authority due to religion — was itself handed down to memory? Every one then in the senate was most foolish; for the books might have been burnt, and yet the matter itself have been unknown. Thus, while they wish to prove even to posterity with what piety they defended religious institutions, they lessened the authority of the institutions themselves by their testimony.

But as Pompilius was the institutor of foolish

[3] Implicavit.

superstitions among the Romans, so also, before Pompilius, Faunus was in Latium, who both established impious rites to his grandfather Saturnus, and honoured his father Picus with a place among the gods, and consecrated his sister Fatua Fauna, who was also his wife; who, as Gabius Bassus relates, was called Fatua because she had been in the habit of foretelling their fates to women, as Faunus did to men. And Varro writes that she was a woman of such great modesty, that, as long as she lived, no male except her husband saw her or heard her name. On this account women sacrifice to her in secret, and call her the Good Goddess. And Sextus Claudius, in that book which he wrote in Greek, relates that it was the wife of Faunus who, because, contrary to the practice and honour of kings, she had drunk a jar of wine, and had become intoxicated, was beaten to death by her husband with myrtle rods. But afterwards, when he was sorry for what he had done, and was unable to endure his regret for her, he paid her divine honours. For this reason they say that a covered jar of wine is placed at her sacred rites. Therefore Faunus also left to posterity no slight error, which all that are intelligent see through. For Lucilius in these verses derides the folly of those who imagine that images are gods: "The terrestrial[1] Lamiæ, which Faunus and Numa Pompilius and others instituted; at these he trembles, he places everything in this. As infant boys believe that every statue of bronze is a living man, so these imagine that all things feigned are true: they believe that statues of bronze contain a heart. It is a painter's gallery;[2] there is nothing true; all things are fictitious." The poet, indeed, compares foolish men to infants. But I say that they are much more senseless than infants. For they (infants) suppose that images are men, whereas these take them for gods: the one through their age, the others through folly, imagine that which is not true: at any rate, the one soon ceased to be deceived; the foolishness of the others is permanent, and always increases. Orpheus was the first who introduced the rites of father Liber into Greece; and he first celebrated them on a mountain of Bœotia, very near to Thebes, where Liber was born; and because this mountain continually resounded with the strains of the lyre, it was called Cithæron.[3] Those sacred rites are even now called Orphic, in which he himself was lacerated and torn in pieces; and he lived about the same time with Faunus. But which of them was prior in age admits of doubt, since Latinus and Priam reigned during the same years, as did also their fathers Faunus and Laomedon, in whose reign Orpheus came with the Argonauts to the coast of the Trojans.

Let us therefore advance further, and inquire who was really the first author of the worship of the gods. Didymus,[4] in the books of his commentary on Pindar, says that Melisseus, king of the Cretans, was the first who sacrificed to the gods, and introduced new rites and parades of sacrifices. He had two daughters, Amalthæa and Melissa, who nourished the youthful Jupiter with goats' milk and honey. Hence that poetic fable derived its origin, that bees flew to the child, and filled his mouth with honey. Moreover, he says that Melissa was appointed by her father the first priestess of the Great Mother; from which circumstance the priests of the same Mother are still called Melissæ. But the sacred history testifies that Jupiter himself, when he had gained possession of power, arrived at such insolence that he built temples in honour of himself in many places. For when he went about to different lands, on his arrival in each region, he united to himself the kings or princes of the people in hospitality and friendship; and when he was departing from each, he ordered that a shrine should be dedicated to himself in the name of his host, as though the remembrance of their friendship and league could thus be preserved. Thus temples were founded in honour of Jupiter Atabyrius and Jupiter Labrandius; for Atabyrius and Labrandius were his entertainers and assistants in war. Temples were also built to Jupiter Laprius, to Jupiter Molion, to Jupiter Casius, and others, after the same manner. This was a very crafty device on his part, that he might both acquire divine honour for himself, and a perpetual name for his entertainers in conjunction with religious observances. Accordingly they were glad, and cheerfully submitted to his command, and observed annual rites and festivals for the sake of *handing down* their own name. Æneas did something like this in Sicily, when he gave the name of his host[5] Acestes to a city which he had built, that Acestes might afterwards joyfully and willingly love, increase, and adorn it. In this manner Jupiter spread abroad through the world the observance of his worship, and gave an example for the imitation of others. Whether, then, the practice of worshipping the gods proceeded from Melisseus, as Didymus related, or from Jupiter also himself, as Euhemerus says, the

[1] Terricolas. Another reading is *terriculas*, bugbears.

[2] Pergula. The word properly means a projection attached to a house. Apelles is said to have placed his pictures in such an adjunct, and to have concealed himself behind them, that he might hear the comments of persons passing by.

[3] Cithæron, from "cithara," a lyre.

[4] *Didymus.* A celebrated Alexandrian grammarian, a follower of the school of Aristarchus. He is distinguished from other grammarians who bore the name of Didymus, by the surname *Chalcenteros*, which he is said to have received from his unwearied diligence in study. Among his productions, which are all lost, was one on the Homeric poems. He also wrote a commentary on Pindar, to which allusion is made in the text. See Smith's *Dictionary of Greek and Roman Biography*.

[5] Cf. Virg., *Æneid*, v. [verse 718].

time is still agreed upon when the gods began to be worshipped. Melisseus, indeed, was much prior in time, inasmuch as he brought up Jupiter his grandson. It is therefore possible that either before, or while Jupiter was yet a boy, he taught the worship of the gods, namely, the mother of his foster-child, and his grandmother Tellus, who was the wife of Uranus, and his father Saturnus; and he himself, by this example and institution, may have exalted Jupiter to such pride, that he afterwards ventured to assume divine honours to himself.

CHAP. XXIII. — OF THE AGES OF VAIN SUPERSTITIONS, AND THE TIMES AT WHICH THEY COMMENCED.

Now, since we have ascertained the origin of vain superstitions, it remains that we should also collect the times during which they whose memory is honoured lived. Theophilus,[1] in his book written to Autolycus respecting the times,[2] says that Thallus relates in his history, that Belus, who is worshipped by the Babylonians and Assyrians, is found to have lived 322 years before the Trojan war; that Belus, moreover, was contemporary with Saturnus, and that they both grew up at one time; — which is so true, that it may be inferred by reason itself. For Agamemnon, who carried on the Trojan war, was the fourth[3] in descent from Jupiter; and Achilles and Ajax were of the third[4] descent from him; and Ulysses was related in the same degree. Priam, indeed, was distant by a long series of descents. But according to some authorities, Dardanus and Iasius were sons of Coritus, not of Jupiter. For if it had been so, Jupiter could not have formed that unchaste connection with Ganymede, his own descendant. Therefore, if you divide the years which are in agreement, the number will be found in harmony with the parents of those whom I have named above. Now, from the destruction of the Trojan city fourteen hundred and seventy years are made up. From this calculation of times, it is manifest that Saturnus has not been born more than eighteen hundred years, and he also was the father of all the gods. Let them not glory, then, in the antiquity of their sacred rites, since both their origin and system and times have been ascertained. There still remain some things which may be of great weight for the disproving of false religions; but I have determined now to bring this book to an end, that it may not exceed moderate limits. For those things must be followed up more fully, that, having refuted all things which seem to oppose the truth, we may be able to instruct in true religion men who, through ignorance of good things, wander in uncertainty. But the first step towards wisdom is to understand what is false; the second, to ascertain what is true. Therefore he who shall have profited by this first discussion of mine, in which we have exposed false things, will be excited to the knowledge of the truth, than which no pleasure is more gratifying to man; and he will now be worthy of the wisdom of heavenly training, who shall approach with willingness and preparation to the knowledge of the other subjects.

1 Theophilus was bishop of Antioch in the latter part of the second century. He was originally a heathen, and was converted to Christianity, as he tells us, by the reading of the Scriptures. [See vol. ii. pp. 87 and 120, this series.]

2 *De Temporibus*. Among the extant works of Theophilus there is not any with this title, but his work to Autolycus contains an apology for Christianity in three books. It is to this that Lactantius here refers.

3 Abnepos, son of a great-grandchild.

4 Pronepotes, great-grandsons.

THE DIVINE INSTITUTES.

BOOK II.

OF THE ORIGIN OF ERROR.

CHAP. I.—THAT FORGETFULNESS OF REASON MAKES MEN IGNORANT OF THE TRUE GOD, WHOM THEY WORSHIP IN ADVERSITY AND DESPISE IN PROSPERITY.

ALTHOUGH I have shown in the first book that the religious ceremonies of the gods are false, because those in whose honour the general consent of men throughout the world by a foolish persuasion undertook various and dissimilar rites were mortals, and when they had completed their *term of* life, yielded to a divinely appointed necessity and died, yet, lest any doubt should be left, this second book shall lay open the very fountain of errors, and shall explain all the causes by which men were deceived, so that at first they believed that they were gods, and afterwards with an inveterate persuasion persevered in the religious observances which they had most perversely undertaken. For I desire, O Emperor Constantine, now that I have proved the emptiness of these things, and brought to light the impious vanity of men, to assert the majesty of the one God, undertaking the more useful and greater duty of recalling men from crooked paths, and of bringing them back into favour with themselves, that they may not, as some philosophers do, so greatly despise themselves, nor think that they are weak and useless, and of no account, and altogether born in vain. For this notion drives many to vicious pursuits. For while they imagine that we are a care to no God, or that we are about to have no existence after death, they altogether give themselves to the indulgence of their passions; and while they think that it is allowed them, they eagerly apply themselves to the enjoyment of pleasures, by which they unconsciously run into the snares of death; for they are ignorant as to what is reasonable conduct on the part of man: for if they wished to understand this, in the first place they would acknowledge their Lord, and would follow after virtue and justice; they would not subject their souls to the influence of earth-born fictions, nor would they seek the deadly fascinations of their lusts; in short, they would value themselves highly, and would understand that there is more in man than appears; and that they cannot retain their power and standing unless men lay aside depravity, and undertake the worship of their true Parent. I indeed, as I ought, often reflecting on the sum of affairs, am accustomed to wonder that the majesty of the one God, which keeps together and rules all things, has come to be so forgotten, that the only befitting object of worship is, above all others, the one which is especially neglected; and that men have sunk to such blindness, that they prefer the dead to the true and living God, and those who are of the earth, and buried in the earth, to Him who was the Creator of the earth itself.

And yet this impiety of men might meet with some indulgence if the error entirely arose from ignorance of the divine name. But since we often see that the worshippers of other gods themselves confess and acknowledge the Supreme God, what pardon can they hope for their impiety, who do not acknowledge the worship of Him whom man cannot altogether be ignorant of? For both in swearing, and in expressing a wish, and in giving thanks, they do not name Jupiter, or a number of gods, but God;[1] so entirely does the truth of its own accord break forth by the force of nature even from unwilling breasts. And this, indeed, is not the case with men in their prosperity. For then most of all does God escape the memory of men, when in the enjoyment of His benefits they ought to honour His divine beneficence. But if any weighty necessity shall press them, then they remember God. If the terror of war shall have resounded, if the pestilential force of diseases shall have overhung them, if long-continued drought shall have denied nourishment to the

1 [See Tertullian, vol. iii. p. 176, this series.]

crops, if a violent tempest or hail shall have assailed them, they betake themselves to God, aid is implored from God, God is entreated to succour them. If any one is tossed about on the sea, the wind being furious, it is this *God* whom he invokes. If any one is harassed by any violence, he implores His aid. If any one, reduced to the last extremity of poverty, begs for food, he appeals to God alone, and by His divine and matchless name [1] alone he seeks to gain the compassion of men. Thus they never remember God, unless it be while they are in trouble. When fear has left them, and the dangers have withdrawn, then in truth they quickly hasten to the temples of the gods: they pour libations to them, they sacrifice to them, they crown [2] them with garlands. But to God, whom they called upon in their necessity itself, they do not give thanks even in word. Thus from prosperity arises luxury; and from luxury, together with all other vices, there arises impiety towards God.

From what cause can we suppose this to arise? Unless we imagine that there is some perverse power which is always hostile to the truth, which rejoices in the errors of men, whose one and only task it is perpetually to scatter darkness, and to blind the minds of men, lest they should see the light, — lest, in short, they should look to heaven, and observe the nature [3] of their own body, the origin [4] of which we shall relate at the proper place; but now let us refute fallacies. For since other animals look down to the ground, with bodies bending forward, because they have not received reason and wisdom, whereas an upright position and an elevated countenance have been given to us by the Creator God, it is evident that these ceremonies paid to the gods are not in accordance with the reason of man, because they bend down the heaven-sprung being to the worship of earthly objects. For that one and only Parent of ours, when He created man, — that is, an animal intelligent and capable of exercising reason, — raised him from the ground, and elevated him to the contemplation of his Creator. As an ingenious poet [5] has well represented it: —

> "And when other animals bend forward and look to the earth, He gave to man an elevated countenance, and commanded him to look up to the heaven, and to raise his countenance erect to stars."

From this circumstance the Greeks plainly derived the name ἄνθρωπος,[6] because he looks upward. They therefore deny themselves, and renounce the name of man, who do not look up, but downward: unless they think that the fact of our being upright is assigned to man without any cause. God willed that we should look up to heaven, and undoubtedly not without reason. For both the birds and almost all of the dumb creation see the heaven, but it is given to us in a peculiar manner to behold the heaven as we stand erect, that we may seek religion there; that since we cannot see God with our eyes, we may with our mind contemplate Him, whose throne is there: and this cannot assuredly be done by him who worships brass and stone, which are earthly things. But it is most incorrect that the nature of the body, which is temporary, should be upright, but that the soul itself, which is eternal, should be abject; whereas the figure and position have no other signification, except that the mind of man ought to look in the same direction as his countenance, and that his soul ought to be as upright as his body, so that it may imitate that which it ought to rule. But men, forgetful both of their name and nature, cast down their eyes from the heaven, and fix them upon the ground, and fear the works of their own hands, as though anything could be greater than its own artificer.

CHAP. II. — WHAT WAS THE FIRST CAUSE OF MAKING IMAGES; OF THE TRUE LIKENESS OF GOD, AND THE TRUE WORSHIP OF HIM.

What madness is it, then, either to form those objects which they themselves may afterwards fear, or to fear the things which they have formed? But, they say, we do not fear the images themselves, but those beings after whose likeness they were formed, and to whose names they are dedicated. You fear them doubtless on this account, because you think that they are in heaven; for if they are gods, the case cannot be otherwise. Why, then, do you not raise your eyes to heaven, and, invoking their names, offer sacrifices in the open air? Why do you look to walls, and wood, and stone, rather than to the place where you believe them to be? What is the meaning of temples [7] and altars? what, in short, of the images themselves, which are memorials either of the dead or absent? For the plan of making likenesses was invented by men for this reason, that it might be possible to retain the memory of those who had either been removed by death or separated by absence.

---

1 Nomen. Another reading is *numen*, deity.

2 It was a custom among the heathen nations to crown the images of the gods with garlands of flowers.

3 The allusion is to the upright attitude of man, as compared with other created beings. The argument is often used by Lactantius.

4 This sentence is omitted in some editions.

5 Ovid, *Metamorphosis* [book i. 85.

> Os homini sublime dedit: cœlumque tueri
> Jussit, et erectos ad sidera tollere vultus].

6 The allusion is to the supposed derivation of the word ἄνθρωπος, from ἀνὰ, τρέπω, ὢψ, to turn the face upwards.

7 The word *temples* is not here applied to the buildings which the faithful set apart for the worship of God, but to the places used by the heathens for their rites and sacrifices. [For three centuries *templa* was the word among Christians for the idolatrous places.] That buildings were set apart by Christians from the earliest ages for their religious assemblies, is gathered from the express testimony of Tertullian, Cyprian, and other early writers. They were called *ecclesiæ;* churches, not temples. [For *κυριακὸν*, *dominicum*, *basilica*, etc., see Bingham, book viii. cap i. sec. 2.]

In which of these classes, then, shall we reckon the gods? If among the dead, who is so foolish as to worship them? If among the absent, then they are not to be worshipped, if they neither see our actions nor hear our prayers. But if the gods cannot be absent, — for, since they are divine, they see and hear all things, in whatever part of the universe they are, — it follows that images are superfluous, since the gods are present everywhere, and it is sufficient to invoke with prayer the names of those who hear us. But if they are present, they cannot fail to be at hand at their own images. It is entirely so, as the people imagine, that the spirits of the dead wander [1] about the tombs and relics of their bodies. But after that the deity has begun to be near, there is no longer need of his statue.

For I ask, if any one should often contemplate the likeness of a man who has settled in a foreign land, that he may thus solace himself for him who is absent, would he also appear to be of sound mind, if, when the other had returned and was present, he should persevere in contemplating the likeness, and should prefer the enjoyment of it, rather than the sight of the man himself? Assuredly not. For the likeness of a man appears to be necessary at that time when he is far away; and it will become superfluous when he is at hand. But in the case of God, whose spirit and influence are diffused everywhere, and can never be absent, it is plain that an image is always superfluous. But they fear lest their religion should be altogether vain and empty if they should see nothing present which they may adore, and therefore they set up images; and since these are representations of the dead, they resemble the dead, for they are entirely destitute of perception. But the image of the ever-living God ought to be living and endued with perception. But if it received this name [2] from resemblance, how can it be supposed that these images resemble God, which have neither perception nor motion? Therefore the image of God is not that which is fashioned by the fingers of men out of stone, or bronze, or other material, but man himself, since he has both perception aud motion, and performs many and great actions. Nor do the foolish men understand, that if images could exercise perception and motion, they would of their own accord adore men, by whom they have been adorned and embellished, since they would be either rough and unpolished stone, or rude and unshapen wood,[3] had they not been fashioned by man.

Man, therefore, is to be regarded as the parent of these images; for they were produced by his instrumentality, and through him they first had shape, figure, and beauty. Therefore he who made them is superior to the objects which were made. And yet no one looks up to the Maker Himself, or reverences Him: he fears the things which he has made, as though there could be more power in the work than in the workman. Seneca, therefore, rightly says in his moral treatises: They worship the images of the gods, they supplicate them with bended knee, they adore them, they sit or stand beside them through the whole day, they offer to them contributions,[4] they slay victims; and while they value these *images* so highly, they despise the artificers who made them. What is so inconsistent, as to despise the statuary and to adore the statue; and not even to admit to your society him who makes your gods? What force, what power can they have, when he who made them has none? But he was unable to give to these even those powers which he had, the power of sight, of hearing, of speech, and of motion. Is any one so foolish as to suppose that there is anything in the image of a god, in which there is nothing even of a man except the mere resemblance? But no one considers these things; for men are imbued with this persuasion, and their minds have thoroughly imbibed the deception [5] of folly. And thus beings endowed with sense adore objects which are senseless, rational beings adore irrational objects, those who are alive adore inanimate objects, those sprung from heaven adore earthly objects. It delights me, therefore, as though standing on a lofty watch-tower, from which all may hear, to proclaim aloud that saying of Persius: [6] —

> "O souls bent down to the earth, and destitute of heavenly things?"

Rather look to the heaven, to the sight of which God your Creator raised you. He gave to you an elevated countenance; you bend it down to the earth; you depress to things below those lofty minds, which are raised together with their bodies to their parent, as though it repented you that you were not born quadrupeds. It is not befitting that the heavenly being should make himself equal to things which are earthly, and incline to the earth. Why do you deprive yourselves of heavenly benefits, and of your own accord fall prostrate upon the ground? For you do wretchedly roll yourselves [7] on the ground,

---

[1] The heathens thought that the souls of the unburied dead wandered about on the earth, until their remains were committed to the tomb.

[2] The words *simulacrum*, "an image," and *similitudo*, "a likeness" or "resemblance," are connected together through the common root *similis*, "like."

[3] Materia is especially used in the sense of wood or timber.

[4] Stipem jaciunt, "they throw a coin." The word properly means a "coin," money bearing a stamped impression; hence *stipendium*, "soldiers' pay."

[5] Fucus, "colouring juice;" hence anything not genuine, but artificial. Others read succum, "juice."

[6] Persius, Satire 2d, 6. Lactantius uses the testimony of heathen writers against the heathen.

[7] Or wallow — "voluto."

when you seek here below that which you ought to have sought above. For as to those vain[1] and fragile productions, the work of man's hands, from whatever kind of material they are formed, what are they but earth, out of which they were produced? Why, then, do you subject yourselves to lower objects? why do you place the earth above your heads? For when you lower yourselves to the earth, and humiliate yourselves, you sink of your own accord to hell, and condemn yourselves to death; for nothing is lower and more humble than the earth, except death and hell. And if you wished to escape these, you would despise the earth lying beneath your feet, preserving the position of your body, which you received upright, in order that you might be able to direct your eyes and your mind to Him who made it. But to despise and trample upon the earth is nothing else than to refrain from adoring images, because they are made of earth; also not to desire riches, and to despise the pleasures of the body, because wealth, and the body itself, which we make use of as a lodging, is but earth. Worship a living being, that you may live; for he must necessarily die who has subjected[2] himself and his soul to the dead.

CHAP. III. — THAT CICERO AND OTHER MEN OF LEARNING ERRED IN NOT TURNING AWAY THE PEOPLE FROM ERROR.

But what does it avail thus to address the vulgar and ignorant, when we see that learned and prudent men, though they understand the vanity of these ceremonies, nevertheless through some perverseness persist in the worship of those very objects which they condemn? Cicero was well aware that the deities which men worshipped were false. For when he had spoken many things which tended to the overthrow of religious ceremonies, he said nevertheless that these matters ought not to be discussed by the vulgar, lest such discussion should extinguish the system of religion which was publicly received. What can you do respecting him, who, when he perceives himself to be in error, of his own accord dashes himself against the stones, that all the people may stumble? or tears out his own eyes, that all may be blind? who neither deserves well of others, whom he suffers to be in error, nor of himself, since he inclines to the errors of others, and makes no use of the benefit of his own wisdom, so as to carry out[3] in action the conception of his own mind, but knowingly and consciously thrusts his foot into the snare, that he also may be taken with the rest, whom he ought, as the more prudent, to have extricated? Nay rather, if you have any virtue, Cicero, endeavour to make the people wise: that is a befitting subject, on which you may expend all the powers of your eloquence. For there is no fear lest speech should fail you in so good a cause, when you have often defended even bad ones with copiousness and spirit. But truly you fear the prison of Socrates,[4] and on that account you do not venture to undertake the advocacy of truth. But, as a wise man, you ought to have despised death. And, indeed, it would have been much more glorious to die on account of good words than on account of revilings. Nor would the renown of your Philippics have been more advantageous to you than the dispersion of the errors of mankind, and the recalling of the minds of men to a healthy state by your disputation.

But let us make allowance for timidity, which ought not to exist in a wise man. Why, then, are you yourself engaged in the same error? I see that you worship things of earth made by the hand: you understand that they are vain, and yet you do the same things which they do, whom you confess to be most foolish. What, therefore, did it profit you, that you saw the truth, which you were neither about to defend nor to follow? If even they who perceive themselves to be in error err willingly, how much more so do the unlearned vulgar, who delight in empty processions, and gaze at all things with boyish minds! They are delighted with trifling things, and are captivated with the form of images; and they are unable to weigh every object in their own minds, so as to understand that nothing which is beheld by the eyes of mortals ought to be worshipped, because it must necessarily be mortal. Nor is it matter of surprise if they do not see God, when they themselves do not even see man, whom they believe that they see. For this, which falls under the notice of the eyes,[5] is not man, but the receptacle of man, the quality and figure of which are not seen from the lineaments of the vessel which contains them, but from the actions and character. They, therefore, who worship images are *mere* bodies without men, because they have given themselves to corporeal things, and do not see anything with the mind more than with the body; whereas it is the office of the soul to perceive those things more clearly which the eye of the body cannot behold. And that philosopher and poet severely accuses those men as humble and abject, who, in opposition to the design of their nature, prostrate them-

1 Ludicra, "diversions." The word is applied to stage-plays.

2 Adjudicavit, adjudged, made over. Cf. Hor., *Ep.*, i. 18: "Et, si quid abest, Italis adjudicat armis."

3 Fill up and complete the outline which he has conceived.

4 Lactantius charges Cicero with want of courage, in being unwilling to declare the truth to the Romans, lest he should incur the peril of death. The fortitude with which Socrates underwent death, when condemned by the Athenians, is related by Xenophon and Plato.

5 Lactantius here follows Plato, who placed the essence of man in the intellectual soul. The body, however, as well as the soul, is of the essence of man; but Lactantius seems to limit the name of man to the higher and more worthy part. [Rhetorically, not dogmatically.]

selves to the worship of earthly things; for he says: [1] —

> "And they abase their souls with fear of the gods, and weigh and press them down to earth."

When he said these things, indeed, his meaning was different — that nothing was to be worshipped, because the gods do not regard the affairs of men.

In another place, at length, he acknowledges that the ceremonies and worship of the gods is an unavailing office: [2] —

> "Nor is it any piety to be often seen with veiled head to turn to a stone, and approach every altar, and fall prostrate on the ground, and spread the hands before the shrines of the gods, and sprinkle the altars with much blood of beasts, and to offer vow after vow."

And assuredly if these things are useless, it is not right that sublime and lofty souls should be called away and depressed to the earth, but that they should think only of heavenly things.

False religious systems, therefore, have been attacked by more sagacious men, because they perceived their falsehood; but the true *religion* was not introduced, because they knew not what and where it was. They therefore so regarded it as though it had no existence, because they were unable to find it in its truth. And in this manner they fell into a much greater error than they who held a religion which was false. For those worshippers of fragile images, however foolish they may be, inasmuch as they place heavenly things in things which are earthly and corruptible, yet retain something of wisdom, and may be pardoned, because they hold the chief duty of man, if not in reality, yet still in their purpose; since, if not the only, yet certainly the greatest difference between men and the beasts consists in religion. But this latter class, in proportion to their superior wisdom, in that they understood the error of false religion, rendered themselves so much the more foolish, because they did not imagine that some religion was true. And thus, because it is easier to judge of the affairs of others than of their own, while they see the downfall of others, they have not observed what was before their own feet. On either side is found the greatest folly, and a certain trace [3] of wisdom; so that you may doubt which are rather to be called more foolish — those who embrace a false religion, or those who embrace none. But (as I have said) pardon may be granted to those who are ignorant and do not own themselves to be wise; but it cannot be extended to those who, while they profess [4] wisdom, rather exhibit folly. I am not, indeed, so unjust as to imagine that they could divine, so that they might find out the truth by themselves; for I acknowledge that this is impossible. But I require from them that which they were able to perform by reason [5] itself. For they would act more prudently, if they both understood that some *form of* religion is true, and if, while they attacked false *religions*, they openly proclaimed that men were not in possession of that which is true.

But this consideration may perhaps have influenced them, that if there were any true religion, it would exert itself and assert its authority, and not permit the existence of anything opposed to it. For they were unable to see at all, on what account, or by whom, and in what manner true religion was depressed, which partakes of a divine mystery [6] and a heavenly secret. And no man can know [7] this by any means, unless he is taught. The sum of the matter is this: The unlearned and the foolish esteem false religions as true, because they neither know the true nor understand the false.[8] But the more sagacious, because they are ignorant of the true, either persist in those religions which they know to be false, that they may appear to possess something; or worship nothing at all, that they may not fall into error, whereas this very thing partakes largely of error, under the figure of a man to imitate the life of cattle. To understand that which is false is truly the part of wisdom, but of human wisdom. Beyond this step man cannot proceed, and thus many of the philosophers have taken away religious institutions, as I have pointed out; but to know the truth is the part of divine wisdom. But man by himself cannot attain to this knowledge, unless he is taught by God. Thus philosophers have reached the height of human wisdom, so as to understand that which is not; but they have failed in attaining the power of saying that which really is. It is a well-known saying of Cicero: [9] "I wish that I could as easily find out the truth as I can refute false things." And because this is beyond the power of man's condition, the capability of this office is assigned to us, to whom God has delivered the knowledge of the truth; to the explaining of which the four last books shall be devoted. Now, in the meantime, let us bring to light false things, as we have begun to do.

CHAP. IV. — OF IMAGES, AND THE ORNAMENTS OF TEMPLES, AND THE CONTEMPT IN WHICH THEY ARE HELD EVEN BY THE HEATHENS THEMSELVES.

What majesty, then, can images have, which were altogether in the power of puny man, either

[1] Lucretius, *De Rerum Natura*, vi. 5. ["Premunt ad terram."]
[2] Lucretius, v. 1197.
[3] Odor quidam sapientiæ.
[4] Rom. i. 22: "Professing themselves to be wise, they became fools."
[5] The apostle teaches the same, Rom. i. 19–21.
[6] Divini sacramenti. 1 Cor. ii. 7: "We speak the wisdom of God in a mystery."
[7] 1 Cor ii. 14: "The natural man receiveth not the things of the Spirit of God, for they are foolishness unto him; neither can he know them, because they are spiritually discerned."
[8] [2 Pet. iii. 16. Even among believers such perils exist.]
[9] *De Natura Deorum*, lib. i. [cap. 32. Quam falsa convincere].

that they should be formed into something else, or that they should not be made at all? On which account Priapus thus speaks in Horace:[1]

> "Formerly I was the trunk of a fig-tree,[2] a useless log, when the carpenter, at a loss whether he should make a bench or a Priapus, decided that it should be a god. Accordingly I am a god, a very great terror to thieves and birds."

Who would not be at ease with such a guardian as this? For thieves are so foolish as to fear the figure of Priapus; though the very birds, which they imagine to be driven away by fear of his scythe, settle upon the images which are skilfully made, that is, which altogether resemble men, build their nests there, and defile them. But Flaccus, as a writer of satire, ridiculed the folly of men. But they who make the images fancy that they are performing a serious business. In short, that very great poet, a man of sagacity in other things, in this alone displayed folly, not like a poet, but after the manner of an old woman, when even in those most highly-finished[3] books he orders this to be done:—

> "And let the guardianship of Priapus of the Hellespont,[4] who drives away thieves and birds with his willow scythe, preserve them."

Therefore they adore mortal things, as made by mortals. For they may be broken, or burnt, or be destroyed. For they are often apt to be broken to pieces, when houses fall through age, and when, consumed by conflagration, they waste away to ashes; and in many instances, unless aided by their own magnitude, or protected by diligent watchfulness, they become the prey of thieves. What madness is it, then, to fear those objects for which either the downfall of a building, or fires, or thefts, may be feared! What folly, to hope for protection from those things which are unable to protect themselves! What perversity, to have recourse to the guardianship of those which, when injured, are themselves unavenged, unless vengeance is exacted by their worshippers! Where, then, is truth? Where no violence can be applied to religion; where there appears to be nothing which can be injured; where no sacrilege can be committed.

But whatever is subjected to the eyes and to the hands, that, in truth, because it is perishable, is inconsistent with the whole subject of immortality. It is in vain, therefore, that men set off and adorn their gods with gold, ivory, and jewels, as though they were capable of deriving any pleasure from these things. What is the use of precious gifts to insensible objects? Is it the same which the dead have? For as they embalm the bodies of the dead, wrap them in spices and precious garments, and bury them in the earth, so they honour the gods, who when they were made did not perceive it, and when they are worshipped have no knowledge of it; for they did not receive sensibility on their consecration. Persius was displeased that golden vessels should be carried into the temples, since he thought it superfluous that that should be reckoned among religious offerings which was not an instrument of sanctity, but of avarice. For these are the things which it is better to offer as a gift to the god whom you would rightly worship:—

> "Written law[5] and the divine law of the conscience, and the sacred recesses of the mind, and the breast imbued with nobleness."[6]

A noble and wise sentiment. But he ridiculously added this: that there is this gold in the temples, as there are dolls[7] presented to Venus by the virgin; which perhaps he may have despised on account of their smallness. For he did not see that the very images and statues of the gods, wrought in gold and ivory by the hand of Polycletus, Euphranor, and Phidias, were nothing more than large dolls, not dedicated by virgins, to whose sports some indulgence may be granted, but by bearded men. Therefore Seneca deservedly laughs at the folly even of old men. We are not (he says) boys twice,[8] as is commonly said, but are always so. But there is this difference, that *when men* we have greater subjects of sport. Therefore men offer to these dolls, which are of large size, and adorned as though for the stage, both perfumes, and incense, and odours: they sacrifice to these costly and fattened victims, which have a mouth,[9] but one that is not suitable for eating; to these they bring robes and costly garments, though they have no need of clothing; to these they dedicate gold and silver, of which they who receive them are as destitute[10] as they who have given them.

And not without reason did Dionysius, the despot of Sicily, when after a victory he had become master of Greece,[11] despise, and plunder and jeer at such gods, for he followed up his sacrilegious acts by jesting words. For when he

---

1 Horat., 1 Serm. 8. 1.

2 The wood of the fig-tree is proverbially used to denote that which is worthless and contemptible.

3 The *Georgics*, which are much more elaborately finished than the other works of Virgil.

4 Priapus was especially worshipped at Lampsacus on the Hellespont; hence he is styled Hellespontiacus.

5 Compositum jus, fasque animi. *Compositum jus* is explained as "the written and ordained laws of men;" *fas*, "divine and sacred law." Others read *animo*, "human and divine law settled in the mind."

6 Persius, *Sat.*, ii. 73.

7 Pupæ, dolls or images worn by girls, as *bullæ* were by boys. On arriving at maturity, they dedicated these images to Venus. See Jahn's note on the passage from Persius.

8 The allusion is to the proverb that "old age is second childhood."

9 An allusion to Ps. cxv. 5: "They have mouths, but they speak not."

10 Quæ tam non habent qui accipiunt, quam qui illa donarunt. The senseless images can make no use of the treasures.

11 Justin relates that Græcia Magna, a part of Italy, was subdued by Dionysius. Cicero says that he sailed to Peloponnesus, and entered the temple of the Olympian Jupiter. [*De Nat. Deor.*, iii. 34.]

had taken off a golden robe from the statue of the Olympian Jupiter, he ordered that a woollen garment should be placed upon him, saying that a golden robe was heavy in summer and cold in winter, but that a woollen one was adapted to each season. He also took off the golden beard from Æsculapius, saying that it was unbecoming and unjust, that while his father Apollo was yet smooth and beardless, the son should be seen to wear a beard before his father. He also took away the bowls, and spoils, and some little images [1] which were held in the extended hands of the statues, and said that he did not take them away, but received them: for that it would be very foolish and ungrateful to refuse to receive good things, when offered voluntarily by those from whom men were accustomed to implore them. He did these things with impunity, because he was a king and victorious. Moreover, his usual good fortune also followed him; for he lived even to old age, and handed down the kingdom in succession to his son. In his case, therefore, because men could not punish his sacrilegious deeds, it was befitting that the gods should be their own avengers. But if any humble person shall have committed any such crime, there are at hand for his punishment the scourge, fire, the rack,[2] the cross, and whatever torture men can invent in their anger and rage. But when they punish those who have been detected in the act of sacrilege, they themselves distrust the power of their gods. For why should they not leave to them especially the opportunity of avenging themselves, if they think that they are able to do so? Moreover, they also imagine that it happened through the will of the deities that the sacrilegious robbers were discovered and arrested; and their cruelty is instigated not so much by anger as by fear, lest they themselves should be visited with punishment if they failed to avenge the injury done to the gods. And, in truth, they display incredible shallowness in imagining that the gods will injure them on account of the guilt of others, who by themselves were unable to injure those very persons by whom they were profaned and plundered. But, in fact, they have often themselves also inflicted punishment on the sacrilegious: that may have occurred even by chance, which has sometimes happened, but not always. But I will show presently how that occurred. Now in the meantime I will ask, Why did they not punish so many and such great acts of sacrilege in Dionysius, who insulted the gods openly, and not in secret? Why did they not repel this sacrilegious man, possessed of such power, from their temples, their ceremonies, and their images? Why, even when he had carried off their sacred things, had he a prosperous voyage—as he himself, according to his custom, testified in joke? Do you see, he said to his companions who feared shipwreck, how prosperous a voyage the immortal gods themselves give to the sacrilegious? But perhaps he had learnt from Plato that the gods have no[3] power.

What of Caius Verres? whom his accuser Tully compares to this same Dionysius, and to Phalaris, and to all tyrants. Did he not pillage the whole of Sicily, carrying away the images of the gods, and the ornaments of the temples? It is idle to follow up each particular instance: I would fain make mention of one, in which the accuser, with all the force of eloquence—in short, with every effort of voice and of body—lamented about Ceres of Catina, or of Henna: the one of whom was of such great sanctity, that it was unlawful for men to enter the secret recesses of her temple; the other was of such great antiquity, that all accounts relate that the goddess herself first discovered grain in the soil of Henna, and that her virgin daughter was carried away from the same place. Lastly, in the times of the Gracchi, when the state was disturbed both by seditions and by portents, on its being discovered in the Sibylline predictions that the most ancient Ceres ought to be appeased, ambassadors were sent to Henna. This Ceres, then, either the most holy one, whom it was unlawful for men to behold even for the sake of adoration, or the most ancient one, whom the senate and people of Rome had appeased with sacrifices and gifts, was carried away with impunity by Caius Verres from her secret and ancient recesses, his robber slaves having been sent in. The same *orator*, in truth, when he affirmed that he had been entreated by the Sicilians to undertake the cause of the province, made use of these words: "That they had now not even any gods in their cities to whom they might betake themselves, since Verres had taken away the most sacred images from their most venerable shrines." As though, in truth, if Verres had taken them away from the cities and shrines, he had also taken them from heaven. From which it appears that those gods have nothing in them more than the material of which they are made. And not without reason did the Sicilians have recourse to you, O Marcus Tullius, that is, to a man; since they had for three years experienced that those gods had no power. For they would have been most foolish if they had fled for protection against the injuries of men, to those who were unable to be angry with Caius Verres on their own behalf. But, *it will be urged*, Verres was condemned on account of these deeds. Therefore he was not punished by the gods, but by the energy of Cicero, by which he either

[1] Sigilla. The word is also used to denote seals, or signets.

[2] Equuleus: an instrument of torture resembling a horse, on which slaves were stretched and tortured.

[3] Nihil esse [= are nothing.]

crushed his defenders or withstood his influence.[1] Why should I say that, in the case of Verres himself, that was not so much a condemnation as a respite from labour? So that, as the immortal gods had given a prosperous voyage to Dionysius when he was carrying off the spoils of gods, so also they appear to have bestowed on Verres quiet repose, in which he might with tranquillity enjoy the fruits of his sacrilege. For when civil wars afterwards raged, being removed from all danger and apprehension, under the cloak of condemnation he heard of the disastrous misfortunes and miserable deaths of others; and he who appeared to have fallen while all retained their position, he alone, in truth, retained his position while all fell; until the proscription of the triumvirs,—that very proscription, indeed, which carried off Tully, the avenger of the violated majesty of the gods,—carried him off, satiated at once with the enjoyment of the wealth which he had gained by sacrilege, and with life, and worn out by old age. Moreover, he was fortunate in this very circumstance, that before his own death he heard of the most cruel end of his accuser; the gods doubtless providing that this sacrilegious man and spoiler of their worship should not die before he had received consolation from revenge.

CHAP. V.—THAT GOD ONLY, THE CREATOR OF ALL THINGS, IS TO BE WORSHIPPED, AND NOT THE ELEMENTS OR HEAVENLY BODIES; AND THE OPINION OF THE STOICS IS REFUTED, WHO THINK THAT THE STARS AND PLANETS ARE GODS.

How much better, therefore, is it, leaving vain and insensible objects, to turn our eyes in that direction where is the seat and dwelling-place of the true God; who suspended the earth[2] on a firm foundation, who bespangled the heaven with shining stars; who lighted up the sun, the most bright and matchless light for the affairs of men, in proof of His own single majesty; who girded the earth with seas, and ordered the rivers to flow with perpetual course!

> "He also commanded the plains to extend themselves, the valleys to sink down, the woods to be covered with foliage, the stony mountains to rise."[3]

All these things truly were not the work of Jupiter, who was born seventeen hundred years ago; but of the same, "that framer of all things, the origin of a better world,"[3] who is called God, whose beginning cannot be comprehended, and ought not to be made the subject of inquiry. It is sufficient for man, to his full and perfect wisdom, if he understands the existence of God: the force and sum of which understanding is this, that he look up to and honour the common Parent of the human race, and the Maker of wonderful things. Whence some persons of dull and obtuse mind adore as gods the elements, which are both created objects and are void of sensibility; who, when they admired the works of God, that is, the heaven with its various lights, the earth with its plains and mountains, the seas with their rivers and lakes and fountains, struck with admiration of these things, and forgetting the Maker Himself, whom they were unable to see, began to adore and worship His works. Nor were they able at all to understand how much greater and more wonderful He is, who made these things out of nothing. And when they see that these things, in obedience to divine laws, by a perpetual necessity are subservient to the uses and interests of men, they nevertheless regard them as gods, being ungrateful towards the divine bounty, so that they preferred their own works to their most indulgent God and Father. But what wonder is it if uncivilized or ignorant men err, since even philosophers of the Stoic sect are of the same opinion, so as to judge that all the heavenly bodies which have motion are to be reckoned in the number of gods; inasmuch as the Stoic Lucilius thus speaks in Cicero:[4] "This regularity, therefore, in the stars, this great agreement of the times in such various courses during all eternity, are unintelligible to me without the exercise of mind, reason, and design; and when we see these things in the constellations, we cannot but place these very objects in the number of the gods." And he thus speaks a little before: "It remains," he says, "that the motion of the stars is voluntary; and he who sees these things, would act not only unlearnedly, but also impiously, if he should deny it." We in truth firmly deny it; and we prove that you, O philosophers, are not only unlearned and impious, but also blind, foolish, and senseless, who have surpassed in shallowness the ignorance of the uneducated. For they regard as gods *only* the sun and moon, but you the stars also.

Make known to us, therefore, the mysteries of the stars, that we may erect altars and temples to each; that we may know with what rites and on what day to worship each, with what names and with what prayers we should call on them; unless perhaps we ought to worship gods so innumerable without any discrimination, and gods so minute in a mass. Why should I mention that the argument by which they infer that all the heavenly bodies are gods, tends to the opposite conclusion? For if they imagine that they are gods on this account, because they have their courses fixed and in accordance with reason,

---

1 The allusion is to the efforts made by the partisans of Verres to prevent Cicero from obtaining the necessary evidence for the condemnation of Verres. But all these efforts were unavailing: the evidence was overwhelming, and before the trial was over Verres went into exile.

2 Ps. cxlviii. 6: "He hath established them for ever and ever."

3 Ovid, *Metam.*, lib. i. [79. Jussit et extendi campos, etc.].

4 [*De Nat. Deor.*, ii cap. 21.]

they are in error. For it is evident from this that they are not gods, because it is not permitted them to deviate[1] from their prescribed orbits. But if they were gods, they would be borne hither and thither in all directions without any necessity, as living creatures on the earth, who wander hither and thither as they please, because their wills are unrestrained, and each is borne wherever inclination may have led it. Therefore the motion of the stars is not voluntary, but of necessity, because they obey[2] the laws appointed for them. But when he was arguing about the courses of the stars, while he understood from the very harmony of things and times that they were not by chance, he judged that they were voluntary; as though they could not be moved with such order and arrangement, unless they contained within them an understanding acquainted with its own duty. Oh, how difficult is truth to those who are ignorant of it! how easy to those who know it! If, he says, the motions of the stars are not by chance, nothing else remains but that they are voluntary; nay, in truth, as it is plain that they are not by chance, so is it clear that they are not voluntary. Why, then, in completing their courses, do they preserve their regularity? Undoubtedly God, the framer of the universe, so arranged and contrived them, that they might run through their courses[3] in the heaven with a divine and wonderful order, to accomplish the variations of the successive seasons. Was Archimedes[4] of Sicily able to contrive a likeness and representation of the universe in hollow brass, in which he so arranged the sun and moon, that they effected, as it were every day, motions unequal and resembling the revolutions of the heavens, and that sphere, while it revolved,[5] exhibited not only the approaches and withdrawings of the sun, or the increase and waning of the moon, but also the unequal courses of the stars, whether fixed or wandering? Was it then impossible for God to plan and create the originals,[6] when the skill of man was able to represent them by imitation? Would the Stoic, therefore, if he should have seen the figures of the stars painted and fashioned in that brass, say that they moved by their own design, and not by the genius of the artificer? There is therefore in the stars design, adapted to the accomplishment of their courses; but it is the design of God, who both made and governs all things, not of the stars themselves, which are thus moved. For if it had been His will that the sun should remain[7] fixed, it is plain that there would be perpetual day. Also if the stars had no motions, who doubts that there would have been eternal night? But that there might be vicissitudes of day and night, it was His will that the stars should move, and move with such variety that there might not only be mutual interchanges of light and darkness, by which alternate courses[8] of labour and rest might be established, but also *interchanges* of cold and heat, that the power and influence of the different seasons might be adapted either to the production or the ripening of the crops. And because philosophers did not see this skill of the divine power in contriving the movements of the stars, they supposed them to be living, as though they moved with feet and of their own accord, and not by the divine intelligence. But who does not understand why God contrived them? Doubtless lest, as the light of the sun was withdrawn, a night of excessive darkness should become too oppressive with its foul and dreadful gloom, and should be injurious to the living. And so He both bespangled the heaven with wondrous variety, and tempered the darkness itself with many and minute lights. How much more wisely therefore does Naso judge, than they who think that they are devoting themselves to the pursuit of wisdom, in thinking that those lights were appointed by God to remove the gloom of darkness! He concludes the book, in which he briefly comprises the phenomena *of nature*, with these three verses: —

> "These images, so many in number, and of such a figure,
> God placed in the heaven; and having scattered
> them through the gloomy darkness, He ordered
> them to give a bright light to the frosty night."

But if it is impossible that the stars should be gods, it follows that the sun and moon cannot be gods, since they differ from the light of the stars in magnitude only, and not in their design. And if these are not gods, the same is true of the heaven, which contains them all.

CHAP. VI. — THAT NEITHER THE WHOLE UNIVERSE NOR THE ELEMENTS ARE GOD, NOR ARE THEY POSSESSED OF LIFE.

In like manner, if the land on which we tread, and which we subdue and cultivate for food, is not a god, then the plains and mountains will not be gods; and if these are not so, it follows that the whole of the earth cannot appear to be God. In like manner, if the water, which is

1 Exorbitare, "to wander from their orbits."
2 Deserviunt, "they are devoted to."
3 Spatium; a word borrowed from the chariot-course, and applied with great beauty to the motions of the stars.
4 Archimedes was the greatest of ancient mathematicians, and possessed in an eminent degree inventive genius. He constructed various engines of war, and greatly assisted in the defence of Syracuse when it was besieged by the Romans. His most celebrated work, however, was the construction of a sphere, or "orrery," representing the movements of the heavenly bodies. To this Lactantius refers.
5 Dum vertitur.
6 Illa vera. [Newton showed his *orrery* to Halley the atheist, who was charmed with the contrivance, and asked the name of the maker. "Nobody," was the *ad hominem* retort.]
7 Staret.
8 Spatia.

adapted to the wants[1] of living creatures for the purpose of drinking and bathing, is not a god, neither are the fountains *gods* from which the water flows. And if the fountains are not gods, neither are the rivers, which are collected from the fountains. And if the rivers also are not gods, it follows that the sea, which is made up of rivers, cannot be considered as God. But if neither the heaven, nor the earth, nor the sea, which are the parts of the world, can be gods, it follows that the world altogether is not God; whereas the same Stoics contend that it is both living and wise, and therefore God. But in this they are so inconsistent, that nothing is said by them which they do not also overthrow. For they argue thus: It is impossible that that which produces from itself sensible objects should itself be insensible. But the world produces man, who is endowed with sensibility; therefore it must also itself be sensible. Also they argue: that cannot be without sensibility, a part of which is sensible; therefore, because man is sensible, the world, of which man is a part, also possesses sensibility. The propositions[2] themselves are true, that that which produces a being endowed with sense is itself sensible; and that that possesses sense, a part of which is endowed with sense. But the assumptions by which they draw their conclusions are false; for the world does not produce man, nor is man a part of the world. For the same God who created the world, also created man from the beginning: and man is not a part of the world, in the same manner in which a limb is a part of the body; for it is possible for the world to be without man, as it is for a city or house. Now, as a house is the dwelling-place of one man, and a city of one people, so also the world is the abode[3] of the whole human race; and that which is inhabited is one thing, that which inhabits another. But these persons, in their eagerness to prove that which they had falsely assumed, that the world is possessed of sensibility, and is God, did not perceive the consequences of their own arguments. For if man is a part of the world, and if the world is endowed with sensibility because man is sensible, therefore it follows that, because man is mortal, the world must also of necessity be mortal, and not only mortal, but also liable to all kinds of disease and suffering. And, on the contrary, if the world is God, its parts also are plainly immortal: therefore man also is God, because he is, as you say, a part of the world. And if man, then also both beasts of burden and cattle, and the other kinds of beasts and of birds, and fishes, since these also in the same manner are possessed of sensibility, and are parts of the world. But this is endurable; for the Egyptians worship even these. But the matter comes to this: that even frogs, and gnats, and ants appear to be gods, because these also have sensibility, and are parts of the world. Thus arguments drawn from a false *source* always lead to foolish and absurd conclusions. Why should I mention that the same *philosophers* assert that the world was constructed[4] for the sake of gods and men as a common dwelling? Therefore the world is neither god, nor living, if it has been made: for a living creature is not made, but born; and if it has been built, it has been built as a house or ship *is built*. Therefore there is a builder of the world, *even* God; and the world which has been made is distinct from Him who made it. Now, how inconsistent and absurd is it, that when they affirm that the heavenly fires[5] and the other elements of the world are gods, they also say that the world itself is God! How is it possible that out of a great heap of gods one God can be made up? If the stars are gods, it follows that the world is not God, but the dwelling-place of gods. But if the world is God, it follows that all the things which are in it are not gods, but members[6] of God, which clearly cannot by themselves[7] take the name of God. For no one can rightly say that the members of one man are many men; but, however, there is no similar comparison between a living being and the world. For because a living being is endowed with sensibility, its members also have sensibility; nor do they become senseless[8] unless they are separated from the body. But what resemblance does the world present to this? Truly they themselves tell us, since they do not deny that it was made, that it might be, as it were, a common abode for gods and men. If, therefore, it has been constructed as an abode, it is neither itself God, nor are the elements which are its parts; because a house cannot bear rule over itself, nor can the parts of which a house consists. Therefore they are refuted not only by the truth, but even by their own words. For as a house, made for the purpose of being inhabited, has no sensibility by itself, and is subject to the master who built or inhabits it; so the world, having no sensibility of itself, is subject to God its Maker, who made it for His own use.

---

1 Is subservient to.

2 Lactantius speaks after the manner of Cicero, and uses the word *proposition* to express that which logicians call the *major* proposition, as containing the major term: the word *assumption* expresses that which is called the *minor* proposition, as containing the minor term.

3 Thus Cicero, *De Finibus*, iii., says: "But they think that the universe is governed by the power of the gods, and that it is, as it were, a city and state common to men and gods, and that every one of us is a part of that universe."

4 If the world was created out of nothing, as Christians are taught to believe, it was not born; for birth (γένεσις) takes place when matter assumes another substantial form. — BETULEIUS.

5 The stars.

6 Membra, "limbs," "parts."

7 Sola, "alone." Another reading is solius, "of the only God."

8 Brutescunt.

Chap. VII. — Of God, and the Religious Rites of the Foolish; of Avarice, and the Authority of Ancestors.

The foolish, therefore, err in a twofold manner: first, in preferring the elements, that is, the works of God, to God *Himself;* secondly, in worshipping the figures of the elements themselves under human form. For they form the images of the sun and moon after the fashion of men; also those of fire, and earth, and sea, which they call Vulcan, Vesta, and Neptune. Nor do they openly sacrifice to the elements themselves. Men are possessed with so great a fondness for representations,[1] that those things which are true are now esteemed of less value: they are delighted, in fact, with gold, and jewels, and ivory. The beauty and brilliancy of these things dazzle their eyes, and they think that there is no religion where these do not shine. And thus, under pretence of *worshipping* the gods, avarice and desire are worshipped. For they believe that the gods love whatever they themselves desire, whatever it is, on account of which thefts and robberies and murders daily rage, on account of which wars overthrow nations and cities throughout the whole world. Therefore they consecrate their spoils and plunder to the gods, who must undoubtedly be weak, and destitute of the highest excellence, if they are subject to desires. For why should we think them celestial if they long for anything from the earth, or happy if they are in want of anything, or uncorrupted if they take pleasure in those things in the pursuit of which the desire of men is not unreservedly condemned? They approach the gods, therefore, not so much on account of religion, which can have no place in badly acquired and corruptible things, as that they may gaze upon[2] the gold, and view the brilliancy of polished marble or ivory, that they may survey with unwearied contemplation garments adorned with precious stones and colours, or cups studded with glittering jewels. And the more ornamented are the temples, and the more beautiful the images, so much the greater majesty are they believed to have: so entirely is their religion confined[3] to that which the desire of men admires.

These are the religious institutions handed down to them by their ancestors, which they persist in maintaining and defending with the greatest obstinacy. Nor do they consider of what character they are; but they feel assured of their excellence and truth on this account, because the ancients have handed them down; and so great is the authority of antiquity, that it is said to be a crime to inquire into it. And thus it is everywhere believed as ascertained truth. In short, in Cicero,[4] Cotta thus speaks to Lucilius: "You know, Balbus, what is the opinion of Cotta, what the opinion of the pontiff. Now let me understand what are your sentiments: for since you are a philosopher, I ought to receive from you a reason for your religion; but in the case of our ancestors it is reasonable to believe them, though no reason is alleged by them." If you believe, why then do you require a reason, which may have the effect of causing you not to believe? But if you require a reason, and think that the subject demands inquiry, then you do not believe; for you make inquiry with this view, that you may follow it when you have ascertained it. Behold, reason teaches you that the religious institutions of the gods arc not true: what will you do? Will you prefer to follow antiquity or reason? And this, indeed, was not imparted[5] to you by another, but was found out and chosen by yourself, since you have entirely uprooted all religious systems. If you prefer reason, you must abandon the institutions and authority of our ancestors, since nothing is right but that which reason prescribes. But if piety advises you to follow your ancestors, then admit that they were foolish, who complied with religious institutions invented contrary to reason; and that you are senseless, since you worship that which you have proved to be false. But since the name of ancestors is so greatly objected to us, let us see, I pray, who those ancestors were from whose authority it is said to be impious to depart.[6]

Romulus, when he was about to found the city, called together the shepherds among whom he had grown up; and since their number appeared inadequate to the founding of the city, he established an asylum. To this all the most abandoned men flocked together indiscriminately from the neighbouring places, without any distinction of condition. Thus he brought together the people from all these; and he chose into the senate those who were oldest, and called them Fathers, by whose advice he might direct all things. And concerning this senate, Propertius the elegiac poet thus speaks: —

> "The trumpet used to call the ancient Quirites to an assembly;[7] those hundred in the field often formed the senate. The senate-house, which now is raised aloft and shines with the well-robed senate, received the Fathers clothed in skins, rustic spirits."

These are the Fathers whose decrees learned and sagacious men obey with the greatest devotion; and all posterity must judge that to be true and unchangeable which an hundred old men clothed in skins established at their will; who, however,

---

1 Imaginum.
2 Ut oculis hauriant.
3 Nihil aliud est.

4 Cicero, *De Nat. Deor.*, iii. 2.
5 Insinuata.
6 [See Clement, vol. ii. cap. 10, p. 197, this series.]
7 Ad verba.

as has been mentioned in the first book,[1] were enticed by Pompilius to believe the truth of those sacred rites which he himself delivered. Is there any reason why their authority should be so highly esteemed by posterity, since during their life no one either high or low judged them worthy of affinity?[2]

CHAP. VIII. — OF THE USE OF REASON IN RELIGION; AND OF DREAMS, AUGURIES, ORACLES, AND SIMILAR PORTENTS.

It is therefore right, especially in a matter on which the whole plan of life turns, that every one should place confidence in himself, and use his own judgment and individual capacity for the investigation and weighing of the truth, rather than through confidence in others to be deceived by their errors, as though he himself were without understanding. God has given wisdom to all alike,[3] that they might be able both to investigate things which they have not heard, and to weigh things which they have heard. Nor, because they preceded us in time, did they also outstrip us in wisdom; for if this is given equally to all, we cannot be anticipated[4] in it by those who precede us. It is incapable of diminution, as the light and brilliancy of the sun; because, as the sun is the light of the eyes, so is wisdom the light of man's heart. Wherefore, since wisdom — that is, the inquiry after truth — is natural to all, they deprive themselves of wisdom, who without any judgment approve of the discoveries of their ancestors, and like sheep are led by others. But this escapes their notice, that the name of ancestors being introduced, they think it impossible that they themselves should have more knowledge because they are called descendants, or that the others should be unwise because they are called ancestors.[5] What, therefore, prevents us from taking a precedent[6] from them, that as they handed down to posterity their false inventions, so we who have discovered the truth may hand down better things to our posterity? There remains therefore a great subject of inquiry, the discussion of which does not come from talent, but from knowledge: and this must be explained at greater length, that nothing at all may be left in doubt. For perhaps some one may have recourse to those things which are handed down by many and undoubted authorities; that those very persons, whom we have shown to be no gods, have often displayed their majesty both by prodigies, and dreams, and auguries, and oracles. And, indeed, many wonderful things may be enumerated, and especially this, that Accius Navius, a consummate augur, when he was warning Tarquinius Priscus to undertake the commencement of nothing new without the previous sanction of auguries,[7] and the king, detracting from[8] the credit due to his art, told him to consult the birds, and then to announce to him whether it was possible for that which he himself had conceived in his mind to be accomplished, and Navius affirmed that it was possible; then take this whetstone, he said, and divide it with a razor. But the other without any hesitation took and cut it.

In the next place is the fact of Castor and Pollux having been seen in the Latin war at the lake of Juturna washing off the sweat of their horses, when their temple which adjoins the fountain had been open of its own accord. In the Macedonian war the same *deities*, mounted on white horses, are said to have presented themselves to Publius Vatienus as he went to Rome at night, announcing that King Perseus had been vanquished and taken captive on that day, the truth of which was proved by letters received from Paulus[9] a few days afterwards. That also is wonderful, that the statue of Fortune, in the form[10] of a woman, is reported to have spoken more than once; also that the statue of Juno Moneta,[11] when, on the capture of Veii, one of the soldiers, being sent to remove it, sportively and in jest asked whether she wished to remove to Rome, answered that she wished it. Claudia also is set forth as an example of a miracle. For when, in accordance with the Sibylline books, the Idæan mother was sent for, and the ship in which she was conveyed had grounded on a shoal of the river Tiber, and could not be moved by any force, they report that Claudia, who had been always regarded as unchaste on account of her excess in personal adornment, with bended knees entreated the goddess, if she judged her to be chaste, to follow her girdle; and thus the ship, which could not be moved by all the strong men,[12] was moved by a single woman. It is equally wonderful, that during the prevalence of a pestilence, Æsculapius, being called from Epidaurus, is said to have released the city of Rome from the long-continued plague.

---

1 Twenty-second chapter.

2 Relationship by marriage. The allusion is to the well-known story, that all the neighbouring towns refused to intermarry with the Romans.

3 Pro virili portione. The phrase properly denotes the share that falls to a person in the division of an inheritance, hence equality.

4 It cannot be forestalled or preoccupied.

5 Majores. There is a play upon the words for ancestors and descendants in Latin which our translation does not reproduce. The word translated ancestors may also mean "men who are greater or superior;" the word translated descendants may mean "men who are less or inferior."

6 Exemplum, "an example for imitation."

7 Until he had consulted auguries.

8 Elevans, "disparaging," or "diminishing from."

9 Paulus Æmilius, who subdued Macedonia.

10 Muliebre. Others read Fortunæ muliebris.

11 The name is said to be derived from *monendo*, "giving warning," or "admonition."

12 The youth of military age.

Sacrilegious persons can also be mentioned, by the immediate punishment of whom the gods are believed to have avenged the injury done to them. Appius Claudius the censor having, against the advice of the oracle, transferred the sacred rites of Hercules to the public slaves,[1] was deprived of his eyesight; and the Potitian *gens*, which abandoned [2] its privilege, within the space of one year became extinct. Likewise the censor Fulvius, when he had taken away the marble tiles from the temple of the Lacinian [3] Juno, to cover the temple of the equestrian Fortuna, which he had built at Rome, was deprived of his senses, and having lost his two sons who were serving in Illyricum, was consumed with the greatest grief of mind. Turullius also, the lieutenant of Mark Antony, when he had cut down a grove of Æsculapius in Cos,[4] and built a fleet, was afterwards slain at the same place by the soldiers of Cæsar. To these examples is added Pyrrhus, who, having taken away money from the treasure of the Locrian Proserpine, was shipwrecked, and dashed against the shores near to the temple of the goddess, so that nothing was found uninjured except that money. Ceres of Miletus also gained for herself great veneration among men. For when the city had been taken by Alexander, and the soldiers had rushed in to plunder her temple, a flame of fire suddenly thrown upon them blinded them all.

There are also found dreams which seem to show the power of the gods. For it is said that Jupiter presented himself to Tiberius Atinius, a plebeian, in his sleep, and enjoined him to announce to the consuls and senate, that in the last Circensian [5] games a public dancer had displeased him, because a certain Antonius Maximus had severely scourged a slave under the *furca* [6] in the middle of the circus, and had led him to punishment, and that on this account the games ought to be repeated. And when he had neglected this command, he is said on the same day to have lost his son, and to have been himself seized by a severe disease; and that when he again perceived the same image asking whether he had suffered sufficient punishment for the neglect of his command, he was carried on a litter to the consuls; and having explained the whole matter in the senate, he regained strength of body, and returned to his house on foot. And that dream also was not less wonderful, to which it is said that Augustus Cæsar owed his preservation. For when in the civil war with Brutus he was afflicted with a severe disease, and had determined to abstain from battle, the image of Minerva presented itself to his physician Artorius, advising him that Cæsar should not confine himself to the camp on account of his bodily infirmity. He was therefore carried on a litter to the army, and on the same day the camp was taken by Brutus. Many other examples of a similar nature may be brought forward; but I fear that, if I shall delay too long in the setting forth of contrary subjects, I may either appear to have forgotten my purpose, or may incur the charge of loquacity.

[1] The circumstance is related by Livy, book ix. c. 29.
[2] Prodidit, "betrayed."
[3] Lacinian, so called from the promontory Lacinia, near Croton.
[4] The island of Cos lies off the coast of Caria; it had a celebrated temple of Æsculapius.
[5] The Circensian games were instituted by Romulus, according to the legend, when he wished to attract the Sabine population to Rome for the purpose of obtaining wives for his people. They were afterwards celebrated with great enthusiasm.
[6] Furca, an instrument of punishment to which the slave was bound and scourged.

CHAP. IX. — OF THE DEVIL, THE WORLD, GOD, PROVIDENCE, MAN, AND HIS WISDOM.

I will therefore set forth the method of all these things, that difficult and obscure subjects may be more easily understood; and I will bring to light all these deceptions [7] of the pretended deity, led by which men have departed very far from the way of truth. But I will retrace the matter far back from its source; that if any, unacquainted with the truth and ignorant, shall apply himself to the reading *of this book*, he may be instructed, and may understand what can in truth be "the source and origin of these evils;" and having received light, may perceive his own errors and those of the whole human race.

Since God was possessed [8] of the greatest foresight for planning, and of the greatest skill for carrying out in action, before He commenced this business of the world, — inasmuch as there was in Him, and always is, the fountain of full and most complete goodness, — in order that goodness might spring as a stream from Him, and might flow forth afar, He produced a Spirit like to Himself, who might be endowed with the perfections of God the Father. But how He willed that, I will endeavour to show in the fourth book.[9] Then He made another being, in whom the disposition of the divine origin did not remain. Therefore he was infected with his own envy as with poison, and passed from good to evil; and at his own will, which had been given to him by God unfettered,[10] he acquired for himself a contrary name. From which it appears that the source of all evils is envy. For he envied his predecessor,[11] who through his stedfastness [12] is acceptable and dear to God the Father. This being, who from good became

[7] The tricks of a juggler.
[8] Most prudent.
[9] Chap. vi., *infra*.
[10] Free.
[11] The Son of God, afterwards spoken of.
[12] By perseverance. There seems to be a contrast between the Son, who remained stedfast, and the evil spirits who fell.

evil by his own act, is called by the Greeks *diabolus:*[1] we call him accuser, because he reports to God the faults to which he himself entices us. God, therefore, when He began the fabric of the world, set over the whole work that first and greatest Son, and used Him at the same time as a counsellor and artificer, in planning, arranging, and accomplishing, since He is complete both in knowledge,[2] and judgment, and power; concerning whom I now speak more sparingly, because in another place[3] both His excellence, and His name, and His nature must be related by us. Let no one inquire of what materials God made these works so great and wonderful: for He made all things out of nothing.

Nor are the poets to be listened to, who say that in the beginning was a chaos, that is, a confusion of matter and the elements; but that God afterwards divided all that mass, and having separated each object from the confused heap, and arranged them in order, He constructed and adorned the world. Now it is easy to reply to these persons, who do not understand the power of God: for they believe that He can produce nothing, except out of materials already existing[4] and prepared; in which error philosophers also were involved. For Cicero, while discussing the nature of the gods,[5] thus speaks: "First of all, therefore, it is not probable[6] that the matter[7] from which all things arose was made by divine providence, but that it has, and has had, a force and nature of its own. As therefore the builder, when he is about to erect any building, does not himself make the materials, but uses those which are already prepared, and the statuary[8] also *uses* the wax; so that divine providence ought to have had materials at hand, not of its own production, but already prepared for use. But if matter was not made by God, then neither was the earth, and water, and air, and fire, made by God." Oh, how many faults there are in these ten lines! First, that he who in almost all his other disputations and books was a maintainer of the divine providence, and who used very acute arguments in assailing those who denied the existence of a providence, now himself, as a traitor or deserter, endeavoured to take away providence; in whose case, if you wish to oppose[9] him, neither consideration nor labour is required: it is only necessary to remind him of his own words. For it will be impossible for Cicero to be more strongly refuted by any one than by Cicero himself. But let us make this concession to the custom and practice of the Academics,[10] that men are permitted to speak with great freedom, and to entertain what sentiments they may wish. Let us examine the sentiments themselves. It is not probable, he says, that matter was made by God. By what arguments do you prove this? For you gave no reason for its being improbable. Therefore, on the contrary, it appears to me exceedingly probable; nor does it appear so without reason, when I reflect that there is something more in God, whom you verily reduce to the weakness of man, to whom you allow nothing else but the mere workmanship. In what respect, then, will that divine power differ from man, if God also, as man does, stands in need of the assistance of another? But He does stand in need of it, if He can construct nothing unless He is furnished with materials by another. But if this is the case, it is plain that His power is imperfect, and he who prepared the material[11] must be judged more powerful. By what name, therefore, shall he be called who excels God in power? — since it is greater to make that which is one's own, than to arrange those things which are another's. But if it is impossible that anything should be more powerful than God, who must necessarily be of perfect strength, power, and intelligence, it follows that He who made the things which are composed of matter, made matter also. For it was neither possible nor befitting that anything should exist without the exercise of God's power, or against His will. But it is probable, he says, that matter has, and always has had, a force and nature of its own.[12] What force could it have, without any one to give it? what nature, without any one to produce it? If it had force, it took that force from some one. But from whom could it take it, unless it were from God? Moreover, if it had a nature, which plainly is so called from being produced, it must have been produced. But from whom could it have derived its existence, except God? For nature, from which you say that all things had their origin, if it has no understanding, can make nothing. But if it has the power of producing and making, then it has understanding, and must be God. For that force can be called by no other name, in which there is both the foresight[13] to plan, and the skill and power to carry into effect. Therefore Seneca, the most intelligent of all the Stoics, says better, who saw "that nature was nothing else but God." Therefore he

1 διάβολος, "slanderer or accuser." The Greek and Latin words employed by Lactantius have the same meaning.
2 Providence.
3 Book iv. ch. vi., etc. [Deus, igitur, machinator constitutorque rerum, etc.]
4 Lying under; answering to the Greek expression ὑποκειμένη ὕλη, subject matter.
5 Not now found in the treatise which bears this title.
6 Capable of proof.
7 Materia; perhaps from "mater," mother stuff — matter out of which anything is composed.
8 The moulder. The ancients made statues of wax or clay, as well as of wood, ivory, and marble.
9 Contradict.

10 Alluding to the well-known practice of the Academics, viz., of arguing on both sides of a question.
11 The founder or preparer of the material.
12 [Quam *vim* potuit habere nullo dante?]
13 Providentia.

says, "Shall we not praise God, who possesses natural excellence?" For He did not learn it from any one. Yes, truly, we will praise Him; for although it is natural to Him, He gave it to Himself,[1] since God Himself is nature. When, therefore, you assign the origin of all things to nature, and take it from God, you are in the same difficulty: —

"You pay your debt by borrowing,[2] Geta."

For while simply changing the name, you clearly admit that it was made by the same person by whom you deny that it was made.

There follows a most senseless comparison. "As the builder," he says, "when he is about to erect any building, does not himself make the materials, but uses those which are already prepared, and the statuary also the wax; so that divine providence ought to have had materials at hand, not of its own production, but already prepared for use." Nay rather it ought not; for God will have less power if He makes from materials already provided, which is the part of man. The builder will erect nothing without wood, for he cannot make the wood itself; and not to be able to do this is the part of human weakness. But God Himself makes the materials for Himself, because He has the power. For to have the power is the property of God; for if He is not able, He is not God. Man produces *his works* out of that which already exists, because through his mortality he is weak, and through his weakness his power is limited and moderate; but God produces His works out of that which has no existence, because through His eternity He is strong, and through His strength His power is immense, which has no end or limit, like the life of the Maker Himself. What wonder, then, if God, when He was about to make the world, first prepared the material from which to make it, and prepared it out of that which had no existence? Because it is impossible for God to borrow anything from another source, inasmuch as all things are in Himself and from Himself. For if there is anything before Him, and if anything has been made, *but* not by Him, He will therefore lose both the power and the name of God. But it may be said matter was never made, like God, who out of matter made this world. In that case, it follows that two eternal *principles* are established, and those indeed opposed to one another, which cannot happen without discord and destruction. For those things which have a contrary force and method must of necessity come into collision. In this manner it will be impossible that both should be eternal, if they are opposed to one another, because one must overpower the other. Therefore the nature of that which is eternal cannot be otherwise than simple, so that all things descended from that source as from a fountain. Therefore either God proceeded from matter, or matter from God. Which of these is more true, is easily understood. For of these two, one is endued with sensibility, the other is insensible. The power of making anything cannot exist, except in that which has sensibility, intelligence, reflection, and the power of motion. Nor can anything be begun, or made, or completed, unless it shall have been foreseen by reason how it shall be made before it exists, and how it shall endure[3] after it has been made. In short, he *only* makes anything who has the will to make it, and hands to complete that which he has willed. But that which is insensible always lies inactive and torpid; nothing can originate in that source where there is no voluntary motion. For if every animal is possessed of reason, it is certain that it cannot be produced from that which is destitute of reason, nor can that which is not present in the original source[4] be received from any other quarter. Nor, however, let it disturb any one, that certain animals appear to be born from the earth. For the earth does not give birth to these of itself, but the Spirit of God, without which nothing is produced. Therefore God did not arise from matter, because a being endued with sensibility can never spring from one that is insensible, a wise one from one that is irrational, one that is incapable of suffering from one that can suffer, an incorporeal being from a corporeal one; but matter is rather from God. For whatever consists of a body solid, and capable of being handled, admits of an external force. That which admits of force is capable of dissolution; that which is dissolved perishes; that which perishes must necessarily have had an origin; that which had an origin had a source[5] from which it originated, that is, some maker, who is intelligent, foreseeing, and skilled in making. There is one assuredly, and that no other than God. And since He is possessed of sensibility, intelligence, providence, power, and vigour, He is able to create and make both animated and inanimate objects, because He has the means of making everything. But matter cannot always have existed, for if it had existed it would be incapable of change. For that which always was, does not cease always to be; and that which had no beginning must of necessity be without an end. Moreover, it is easier for that which had a beginning to be without an end, than for that which had no beginning

[1] Sibi illam dedit. There is another reading, illa sibi illam dedit, but it does not give so good a sense.

[2] A proverbial expression, signifying "to get out of one difficulty by getting into another." The passage in the text is a quotation from Terence, *Phorm.*, v. 2. 15. [Not in some editions of our author; e.g., Basil, 1521.]

[3] Stand firm and stedfast.

[4] Which does not exist there, from whence it is sought.

[5] Fountain.

to have an end. Therefore if matter was not made, nothing can be made from it. But if nothing can be made from it, then matter itself can have no existence. For matter is that out of which something is made. But everything out of which anything is made, inasmuch as it has received the hand of the artificer, is destroyed,[1] and begins to be some other thing. Therefore, since matter had an end, at the time when the world was made out of it, it also had a beginning. For that which is destroyed[1] was *previously* built up; that which is loosened was *previously* bound up; that which is brought to an end was begun. If, then, it is inferred from its change and end, that matter had a beginning, from whom could that beginning have been, except from God? God, therefore, is the only being who was not made; and therefore He can destroy other things, but He Himself cannot be destroyed. That which was in Him will always be permanent, because He has not been produced or sprung from any other source; nor does His birth depend on any other object, which being changed may cause His dissolution. He is of Himself, as we said in the first book;[2] and therefore He is such as He willed that He should be, incapable of suffering, unchangeable, incorruptible, blessed, and eternal.

But now the conclusion, with which Tully finished the sentiment, is much more absurd.[3] "But if matter," he says, "was not made by God, the earth indeed, and water, and air, and fire, were not made by God." How skilfully he avoided the danger! For he stated the former point as though it required no proof, whereas it was much more uncertain than that on account of which the statement was made. If matter, he says, was not made by God, the world was not made by God. He preferred to draw a false inference from that which is false, than a true one from that which is true. And though uncertain things ought to be proved from those which are certain, he drew a proof from an uncertainty, to overthrow that which was certain. For, that the world was made by divine providence (not to mention Trismegistus, who proclaims this; not to mention the verses of the Sibyls, who make the same announcement; not to mention the prophets,[4] who with one impulse and with harmonious[5] voice bear witness that the world was made,[6] and that it was the workmanship of God), even the philosophers almost universally agree; for this is the opinion of the Pythagoreans, the Stoics, and the Peripatetics, who are the chief of every sect.[7] In short, from those first seven wise men,[8] even to Socrates and Plato, it was held as an acknowledged and undoubted fact; until many ages afterwards[9] the crazy Epicurus lived, who alone ventured to deny that which is most evident, doubtless through the desire of discovering novelties, that he might found a sect in his own name. And because he could find out nothing new, that he might still appear to disagree with the others, he wished to overthrow old opinions. But in this all the philosophers who snarled[10] around him, refuted him. It is more certain, therefore, that the world was arranged by providence, than that matter was collected[11] by providence. Wherefore he ought not to have supposed that the world was not made by divine providence, because its matter was not made by divine providence; but because the world was made by divine providence, *he ought to have concluded* that matter also was made by the Deity. For it is more credible that matter was made by God, because He is all-powerful, than that the world was not made by God, because nothing can be made without mind, intelligence, and design. But this is not the fault of Cicero, but of the sect. For when he had undertaken a disputation, by which he might take away the nature of the gods, respecting which philosophers prated, in his ignorance of the truth he imagined that the Deity must altogether be taken away. He was able therefore to take away the gods, for they had no existence. But when he attempted to overthrow the divine providence, which is in the one God, because he had begun to strive against the truth, his arguments failed, and he necessarily fell into this pitfall, from which he was unable to withdraw himself. Here, then, I hold him firmly fixed; I hold him fastened to the spot, since Lucilius, who disputed on the other side, was silent. Here, then, is the turning-point;[12] on this everything depends. Let Cotta disentangle himself, if he can, from this difficulty;[13] let him bring forward arguments by which he may prove that matter has always existed, which no providence made. Let him show how anything ponderous and heavy either could exist without an author or could be changed, and how that which

[1] Distruitur, "pulled to pieces." The word is thus used by Cicero.
[2] Ch. 3 and 7. [See pp. 11, 17, *supra*.]
[3] [Multo absurdior.]
[4] Lactantius seems to refer not to the true prophets, but to those of other nations, such as Orpheus and Zoroaster, or the magi of the Persians, the gymnosophists of the Indians, or the Druids of the Gauls. St. Augustine often makes mention of these. It would seem inconsistent to mention Moses and the prophets of God with the prophets of the heathens. [Compare, however, "Christian analogies," etc., in Justin. See vol. i. 169; also *Ibid.*, pp. 182, 283–286.]
[5] Pari voce.
[6] The work of the world, and the workmanship of God.
[7] Qui sunt principes omnis disciplinæ. There is another reading: quæ sunt principes omnium disciplinæ, "which are the leading sects of all."
[8] Thales said that the world was the work of God.
[9] This statement is incorrect, as Plato was born B.C. 430, and Epicurus B.C. 337.
[10] There is probably an allusion to the Cynics.
[11] Conglobatam. Another reading is, quàm materiâ providentiam conglobatam.
[12] Hinge.
[13] Abyss.

always was ceased to be, so that that which never was might begin to be. And if he shall prove these things, then, and not till then, will I admit that the world itself was not established by divine providence, and yet in making this admission I shall hold him fast by another snare. For he will turn round again to the same point, to which he will be unwilling *to return*, so as to say that both the matter of which the world consists, and the world which consists of matter, existed by nature; though I contend that nature itself is God. For no one can make wonderful things, that is, things existing with the greatest order, except one who has intelligence, foresight, and power. And thus it will come to be seen that God made all things, and that nothing at all can exist which did not derive its origin from God.

But the same, as often as he follows the Epicureans,[1] and does not admit that the world was made by God, is wont to inquire by what hands, by what machines, by what levers, by what contrivance, He made this work of such magnitude. He might see, if he could have lived at that time in which *God* made it. But, that man might not look into the works of God, He was unwilling to bring him into this world until all things were completed. But he could not be brought in: for how could he exist while the heaven above was being built, and the foundations of the earth beneath were being laid; when humid things, perchance, either benumbed with excessive stiffness were becoming congealed, or seethed with fiery heat and rendered solid were growing hard? Or how could he live when the sun was not yet established, and neither corn nor animals were produced? Therefore it was necessary that man should be last made, when the finishing[2] hand had now been applied to the world and to all other things. Finally, the sacred writings teach that man was the last work of God, and that he was brought into this world as into a house prepared and made ready; for all things were made on his account. The poets also acknowledge the same. Ovid, having described the completion of the world, and the formation of the other animals, added:[3] —

> "An animal more sacred than these, and more capacious of a lofty mind, was yet wanting, and which might exercise dominion over the rest. Man was produced."

So impious must we think it to search into those things which God wished to be kept secret! But his inquiries were not made through a desire of hearing or learning, but of refuting; for he was confident that no one could assert that. As though, in truth, it were to be supposed that these things were not made by God, because it cannot be plainly seen in what manner they were created! If you had been brought up in a well-built and ornamented house, and had never seen a workshop,[4] would you have supposed that that house was not built by man, because you did not know how it was built? You would assuredly ask the same question about the house which you now ask about the world — by what hands, with what implements, man had contrived such great works; and especially if you should see large stones, immense blocks,[5] vast columns, the whole work lofty and elevated, would not these things appear to you to exceed the measure of human strength, because you would not know that these things were made not so much by strength as by skill and ingenuity?

But if man, in whom nothing is perfect, nevertheless effects more by skill than his feeble strength would permit, what reason is there why it should appear to you incredible, when it is alleged that the world was made by God, in whom, since He is perfect, wisdom can have no limit, and strength no measure? His works are seen by the eyes; but how He made them is not seen even by the mind, because, as Hermes says, the mortal cannot draw nigh to (that is, approach nearer, and follow up with the understanding) the immortal, the temporal[6] to the eternal, the corruptible to the incorruptible. And on this account the earthly animal is as yet incapable of perceiving[7] heavenly things, because it is shut in and held as it were in custody by the body, so that it cannot discern all things with free and unrestrained perception. Let him know, therefore, how foolishly he acts, who inquires into things which are indescribable. For this is to pass the limits of one's own condition, and not to understand how far it is permitted man to approach. In short, when God revealed the truth to man, He wished us only to know those things which it concerned man to know for the attainment of life; but as to the things which related to a profane and eager curiosity[8] He was silent, that they might be secret. Why, then, do you inquire into things which you cannot know, and if you knew them you would not be happier. It is perfect wisdom in man, if he knows that there is but one God, and that all things were made by Him.

Chap. X. — Of the World, and Its Parts, the Elements and Seasons.

Now, having refuted those who entertain false sentiments respecting the world and God its

1 As often as he is an Epicurean.
2 The last hand.
3 *Metamorph.*, book i.

4 Fabrica. The word is also used to denote the *exercise* of skill in workmanship.
5 Cæmenta, rough stones from the quarry.
6 Pertaining to time, as opposed to eternal.
7 Looking into.
8 A curious and profane eagerness.

Maker, let us return to the divine workmanship of the world, concerning which we are informed in the sacred[1] writings of our holy religion. Therefore, first of all, God made the heaven, and suspended it on high, that it might be the seat of God Himself, the Creator. Then He founded the earth, and placed it under the heaven, as a dwelling-place for man, with the other races of animals. He willed that it should be surrounded and held together by water. But He adorned and filled His own dwelling-place with bright lights; He decked it with the sun, and the shining orb of the moon, and with the glittering signs of the twinkling stars; but He placed on the earth the darkness, which is contrary to these. For of itself the earth contains no light, unless it receives it from the heaven, in which He placed perpetual light, and the gods above, and eternal life; and, on the contrary, He placed on the earth darkness, and the inhabitants of the lower regions, and death. For these things are as far removed from the former ones, as evil things are from good, and vices from virtues. He also established two parts of the earth itself opposite to one another, and of a different character, — namely, the east and the west; and of these the east is assigned to God, because He Himself is the fountain of light, and the enlightener[2] of all things, and because He makes us rise to eternal life. But the west is ascribed to that disturbed and depraved mind, because it conceals the light, because it always brings on darkness, and because it makes men die and perish in their sins. For as light belongs to the east, and the whole course of life depends upon the light, so darkness belongs to the west: but death and destruction are contained in darkness.[3] Then He measured out in the same way the other parts, — namely, the south and the north, which parts are closely united with the two former. For that which is more glowing with the warmth of the sun, is nearest to and closely united with the east; but that which is torpid with colds and perpetual ice belongs to the same division as the extreme west. For as darkness is opposed to light, so is cold to heat. As, therefore, heat is nearest to light, so is the south to the east; and as cold is nearest to darkness, so is the northern region to the west. And He assigned to each of these parts its own time, — namely, the spring to the east, the summer to the southern region, the autumn belongs to the west, and the winter to the north. In these two parts also, the southern and the northern, is contained a figure of life and death, because life consists in heat, death in cold. And as heat arises from fire, so does cold from water. And according to the division of these parts He also made day and night, to complete by alternate succession with each other the courses[4] and perpetual revolutions of time, which we call years. The day, which the first east supplies, must belong to God, as all things do, which are of a better character. But the night, which the extreme west brings on, belongs, indeed, to him whom we have said to be the rival of God.

And even in the making of these God had regard to the future; for He made them so, that a representation of true religion and of false superstitions might be shown from these. For as the sun, which rises daily, although it is but one, — from which Cicero would have it appear that it was called Sol,[5] because the stars are obscured, and it alone is seen, — yet, since it is a true light, and of perfect fulness, and of most powerful heat, and enlightens all things with the brightest splendour; so God, although He is one only, is possessed of perfect majesty, and might, and splendour. But night, which we say is assigned to that depraved adversary of God,[6] shows by a resemblance the many and various superstitions which belong to him. For although innumerable stars appear to glitter and shine,[7] yet, because they are not full and solid lights, and send forth no heat, nor overpower the darkness by their multitude, therefore these two things are found to be of chief importance, which have power differing from and opposed to one another — heat and moisture, which God wonderfully designed for the support and production of all things. For since the power of God consists in heat and fire, if He had not tempered its ardour and force by mingling matter of moisture and cold, nothing could have been born or have existed, but whatever had begun to exist must immediately have been destroyed by conflagration. From which also some philosophers and poets said that the world was made up of a discordant concord; but they did not thoroughly understand the matter. Heraclitus said that all things were produced from fire; Thales of Miletus from water. Each saw something *of the truth*, and yet each was in error: for if one *element* only had existed, water could not have been produced from fire, nor, on the other hand, could fire from water; but it is more true that all things were produced from a mingling of the two. Fire, indeed, cannot be mixed with water, because they are opposed to each other; and if they came into collision, the one which proved superior must destroy the other. But their sub-

[1] Secret writings.

[2] *Apos. Const.* (so-called), book ii. cap. 57. See Bingham, book viii. cap. 3, sec. 3; also vol. ii. note 1, p. 535, this series, and vol. iii. note 1, p. 31. So Cyril of Jerusalem, Augustine, and later Fathers. Bingham, book xiii. cap. 8, sec. 15.]

[3] [In baptism, the renunciations were made with face turned to the west. Bingham, book xi. cap. 7, sec. 4.]

[4] Spatia; an expression derived from the chariot-race.

[5] A play upon the words *Sol*, the sun, and *solus*, alone.

[6] Antitheus, one who takes the place of God; as Antichrist, ἀντίχριστος, one who sets himself in the place of Christ.

[7] Emit rays.

stances may be mingled. The substance of fire is heat; of water, moisture. Rightly therefore does Ovid say:[1] —

> "For when moisture and heat have become mingled, they conceive, and all things arise from these two. And though fire is at variance with water, moist vapour produces all things, and discordant concord[2] is adapted to production."

For the one element is, as it were, masculine; the other, as it were, feminine: the one active, the other passive. And on this account it was appointed by the ancients that marriage contracts should be ratified by the solemnity[3] of fire and water, because the young of animals are furnished with a body by heat and moisture, and are thus animated to life.

For, since every animal consists of soul[4] and body, the material of the body is contained in moisture, that of the soul in heat: which we may know from the offspring of birds; for though these are full of thick moisture, unless they are cherished by creative[5] heat, the moisture cannot become a body, nor can the body be animated with life. Exiles also were accustomed to be forbidden the use of fire and water: for as yet it seemed unlawful to inflict capital punishment on any, however guilty, inasmuch as they were men. When, therefore, the use of those things in which the life of men consists was forbidden, it was deemed to be equivalent to the actual infliction of death on him who had been thus sentenced. Of such importance were these two elements considered, that they believed them to be essential for the production of man, and for the sustaining of his life. One of these is common to us with the other animals, the other has been assigned to man alone. For we, being a heavenly and immortal race,[6] make use of fire, which is given to us as a proof of immortality, since fire is from heaven; and its nature, inasmuch as it is moveable and rises upward, contains the principle of life. But the other animals, inasmuch as they are altogether mortal, make use of water only, which is a corporeal and earthly element. And the nature of this, because it is moveable, and has a downward inclination, shows a figure of death. Therefore the cattle do not look up to heaven, nor do they entertain religious sentiments, since the use of fire is removed from them. But from what source or in what manner God lighted up or caused[7] to flow these two principal elements, fire and water, He who made them alone can know.[8]

[1] *Metamorph.*, i. 430.
[2] [Discors concordia.]
[3] Sacramento. Torches were lighted at marriage ceremonies, and the bride was sprinkled with water.
[4] The living principle.
[5] The artificer.
[6] Animal.
[7] Eliquaverit, "strained off," "made liquid."
[8] [So Izaak Walton: "Known only to Him whose name is Wonderful."]

CHAP. XI. — OF LIVING CREATURES, OF MAN; PROMETHEUS, DEUCALION, THE PARCÆ.

Therefore, having finished the world, He commanded that animals of various kinds and of dissimilar forms should be created, both great and smaller. And they were made in pairs, that is, one of each sex; from the offspring of which both the air and the earth and the seas were filled. And God gave nourishment to all these by their kinds[9] from the earth, that they might be of service to men: some, for instance, were for food, others for clothing; but those which are of great strength He gave, that they might assist in cultivating the earth, whence they were called beasts of burthen.[10] And thus, when all things had been settled with a wonderful arrangement, He determined to prepare for Himself an eternal kingdom, and to create innumerable souls, on whom He might bestow immortality. Then He made for Himself a figure endowed with perception and intelligence, that is, after the likeness of His own image, than which nothing can be more perfect: He formed man out of the dust of the ground, from which he was called man,[11] because He was made from the earth. Finally, Plato says that the human form[12] was godlike; as does the Sibyl, who says, —

> "Thou art my image, O man, possessed of right reason."[13]

The poets also have not given a different account respecting this formation of man, however they may have corrupted it; for they said that man was made by Prometheus from clay. They were not mistaken in the matter itself, but in the name of the artificer. For they had never come into contact with a line of the truth; but the things which were handed down by the oracles of the prophets, and contained in the sacred book[14] of God; those things collected from fables and obscure opinion, and distorted, as the truth is wont to be corrupted by the multitude when spread abroad by various conversations, every one adding something to that which he had heard, — those things they comprised in their poems; and in this, indeed, *they acted* foolishly, in that they attributed so wonderful and divine a work to man. For what need was there that man should be formed of clay, when he might be generated in the same way in which Prometheus himself was born from Iapetus? For if he was a man, he was able to beget a man, but not to make one. But his punishment on Mount

[9] By species.
[10] Jumenta, "beasts of burthen," as though derived from juvo, "to aid."
[11] Homo, "man," from humus, "the ground." [P. 56, *supra*.]
[12] This image, or likeness of God, in which man was originally created, is truly described not by Plato, but by St. Paul: 2 Cor. iv. 6; Col. iii 10; Eph. iv. 24.
[13] Another reading is, "Man is my image."
[14] Sacrario, "the shrine."

Caucasus declares that he was not of the gods. But no one reckoned his father Iapetus or his uncle [1] Titan as gods, because the high dignity of the kingdom was in possession of Saturn only, by which he obtained divine honours, together with all his descendants. This invention of the poets admits of refutation by many arguments. It is agreed by all that the deluge took place for the destruction of wickedness, and for its removal from the earth. Now, both philosophers and poets, and writers of ancient history, assert the same, and in this they especially agree with the language of the prophets. If, therefore, the flood took place for the purpose of destroying wickedness, which had increased through the excessive multitude of men, how was Prometheus the maker of man, when his son Deucalion is said by the same writers to have been the only one who was preserved on account of his righteousness? How could a single descent [2] and a single generation have so quickly filled the world with men? But it is plain that they have corrupted this also, as they did the former account; since they were ignorant both at what time the flood happened on the earth, and who it was that deserved on account of his righteousness to be saved when the human race perished, and how and with whom he was saved: all of which are taught by the inspired [3] writings. It is plain, therefore, that the account which they give respecting the work of Prometheus is false.

But because I had said [4] that the poets are not accustomed to speak that which is altogether untrue, but to wrap up in figures and thus to obscure their accounts, I do not say that they spoke falsely in this, but that first of all Prometheus made the image of a man of rich and soft clay, and that he first originated the art of making statues and images; inasmuch as he lived in the times of Jupiter, during which temples began to be built, and new modes of worshipping the gods introduced. And thus the truth was corrupted by falsehood; and that which was said to have been made by God began also to be ascribed to man, who imitated the divine work. But the making of the true and living man from clay is the work of God. And this also is related by Hermes,[5] who not only says that man was made by God, after the image of God, but he even tried to explain in how skilful a manner He formed each limb in the human body, since there is none of them which is not as available for the necessity of use as for beauty. But even the Stoics, when they discuss the subject of providence, attempt to do this; and Tully followed them in many places. But, however, he briefly treats of a subject so copious and fruitful, which I now pass over on this account, because I have lately written a particular book on this subject to my disciple Demetrianus. But I cannot here omit that which some erring philosophers say, that men and the other animals arose from the earth without any author; whence that expression of Virgil:[6] —

> "And the earth-born [7] race of men raised its head from the hard fields."

And this opinion is especially entertained by those who deny the existence of a *divine* providence. For the Stoics attribute the formation of animals to divine skill. But Aristotle freed himself from labour and trouble, by saying that the world always existed, and therefore that the human race, and the other things which are in it, had no beginning, but always had been, and always would be. But when we see that each animal separately, which had no previous existence, begins to exist, and ceases to exist, it is necessary that the whole race must at some time have begun to exist, and must cease at some time because it had a beginning.

For all things must necessarily be comprised in three periods of time — the past, the present, and the future. The commencement [8] belongs to the past, existence to the present, dissolution to the future. And all these things are seen in the case of men individually: for we begin when we are born; and we exist while we live; and we cease when we die. On which account they would have it that there are three Parcæ: [9] one who warps the web of life for men; the second, who weaves it; the third, who cuts and finishes it. But in the whole race of men, because the present time only is seen, yet from it the past also, that is, the commencement, and the future, that is, the dissolution, are inferred. For since it exists, it is evident that at some time it began to exist, for nothing can exist without a beginning; and because it had a beginning, it is evident that it will at some time have an end. For that cannot, as a whole, be immortal, which consists of mortals. For as we all die individually, it is possible that, by some calamity, all may perish simultaneously: either through the unproductiveness of the earth, which sometimes happens in particular cases; or through the general spread of pestilence, which often desolates separate cities and countries; or by the conflagration of the world, as is said to have happened in the case of Phaethon; or by a deluge, as is reported in the time of Deucalion, when

1 Father's brother.
2 Gradus.
3 Prophetical writings.
4 Book i. [ch. 11, p. 22, *supra*].
5 The title ὁ δημιουργὸς, the Architect, or Creator, is used by Plato and Hermes.

6 *Georg.*, ii. 341. [Terrea progenies duris caput extulit arvis.]
7 Terrea. Another reading is ferrea, "the race of iron."
8 The origin.
9 The fable of the three Parcæ — Clotho, Lachesis, and Atropos — is derived from Hesiod.

the whole race was destroyed with the exception of one man. And if this deluge happened by chance, it might assuredly have happened that he who was the only survivor should perish. But if he was reserved by the will of divine providence, as it cannot be denied, to recruit mankind, it is evident that the life and the destruction of the human race are in the power of God. And if it is possible for it to die altogether, because it dies in parts, it is evident that it had an origin at some time; and as the liability to decay[1] bespeaks a beginning, so also it gives proof of an end. And if these things are true, Aristotle will be unable to maintain that the world also itself had no beginning. But if Plato and Epicurus extort this from Aristotle, yet Plato and Aristotle, who thought that the world would be everlasting, will, notwithstanding their eloquence, be deprived of this also by Epicurus, because it follows, that, *as it had a beginning*, it must also have an end. But we will speak of these things at greater length in the last book. Now let us revert to the origin of man.

CHAP. XII. — THAT ANIMALS WERE NOT PRODUCED SPONTANEOUSLY, BUT BY A DIVINE ARRANGEMENT, OF WHICH GOD WOULD HAVE GIVEN US THE KNOWLEDGE, IF IT WERE ADVANTAGEOUS FOR US TO KNOW IT.

They say that at certain changes of the heaven, and motions of the stars, there existed a kind of maturity[2] for the production of animals; and thus that the new earth, retaining the productive seed, brought forth of itself certain vessels[3] after the likeness of wombs, respecting which Lucretius[4] says, —

> "Wombs grew attached to the earth by roots;"

and that these, when they had become mature, being rent by the compulsion of nature, produced tender animals; afterwards, that the earth itself abounded with a kind of moisture which resembled milk, and that animals were supported by this nourishment. How, then, were they able to endure or avoid the force of the cold or of heat, or to be born at all, since the sun would scorch them or the cold contract them? But, they say, at the beginning of the world there was no winter nor summer, but a perpetual spring of an equable temperature.[5] Why, then, do we see that none of these things now happens? Because, they say, it was necessary that it should once happen, that animals might be born; but after they began to exist, and the power of generation was given to them, the earth ceased to bring forth, and the condition of time[6] was changed. Oh, how easy it is to refute falsehoods! In the first place, nothing can exist in this world which does not continue permanent, as it began. For neither were the sun and moon and stars then uncreated; nor, having been created, were they without their motions; nor did that divine government, which manages and rules their courses, fail to begin *its exercise* together with them. In the next place, if it is as they say, there must of necessity be a providence, and they fall into that very condition which they especially avoid. For while the animals were yet unborn, it is plain that some one provided that they should be born, that the world might not appear gloomy[7] with waste and desolation. But, that they might be produced from the earth without the office of parents, provision must have been made with great judgment; and in the next place, that the moisture condensed from the earth might be formed into the various figures of bodies; and also that, having received from the vessels with which they were covered the power of life and sensation, they might be poured forth, as it were, from the womb of mothers, is a wonderful and indescribable[8] provision. But let us suppose that this also happened by chance; the circumstances which follow assuredly cannot be by chance, — that the earth should at once flow with milk, and that the temperature of the atmosphere should be equable. And if these things plainly happened, that the newly born animals might have nourishment, or be free from danger, it must be that some one provided these things by some divine counsel.

But who is able to make this provision except God? Let us, however, see whether the circumstance itself which they assert could have taken place, that men should be born from the earth. If any one considers during how long a time and in what manner an infant is reared, he will assuredly understand that those earth-born children could not possibly have been reared without some one to bring them up. For they must have lain for many months cast forth, until their sinews were strengthened, so that they had power to move themselves and to change their place, which can scarcely happen within the space of one year. Now see whether an infant could have lain through many months in the same manner and in the same place where it was cast forth, without dying, overwhelmed and corrupted by that moisture of the earth which it supplied for the sake of nourishment, and by the excrements of its own body mixed together. Therefore it is impossible but that it was reared by some one; unless, indeed, all animals are born not in a tender con-

1 Frailty.
2 Ripeness, or suitableness.
3 Little bags, or follicles.
4 Book v. 806. [Uteri terram radicibus apti.]
5 A perpetual temperature and an equable spring.
6 The seasons were varied.
7 Be rough.
8 Inextricabilis that cannot be disentangled.

dition, but grown up: and it never came into their mind to say this. Therefore the whole of that method is impossible and vain; if that can be called method by which it is attempted that there shall be no method. For he who says that all things are produced of their own accord, and attributes nothing to divine providence, he assuredly does not assert, but overthrows method. But if nothing can be done or produced without design, it is plain that there is a divine providence, to which that which is called design peculiarly belongs. Therefore God, the Contriver of all things, made man. And even Cicero, though ignorant of the sacred writings, saw this, who in his treatise on the Laws, in the first book,[1] handed down the same thing as the prophets; and I add his words: "This animal, foreseeing, sagacious, various, acute, gifted with memory, full of method and design, which we call man, was produced by the supreme Deity under remarkable circumstances; for this alone of so many kinds and natures of animals, partakes of judgment and reflection, when all other animals are destitute of them." Do you see that the man, although far removed from the knowledge of the truth, yet, inasmuch as he held the image of wisdom, understood that man could not be produced except by God? But, however, there is need of divine[2] testimony, lest that of man should be insufficient. The Sibyl testifies that man is the work of God:—

> "He who is the only God being the invincible Creator,
> He Himself fixed[3] the figure of the form of men,
> He Himself mixed the nature of all belonging to the generation of life."

The sacred writings contain statements to the same effect. Therefore God discharged the office of a true father. He Himself formed the body; He Himself infused the soul with which we breathe. Whatever we are, it is altogether His work. In what manner He effected this He would have taught us, if it were right for us to know; as He taught us other things, which have conveyed to us the knowledge both of ancient error and of true light.

CHAP. XIII. — WHY MAN IS OF TWO SEXES; WHAT IS HIS FIRST DEATH, AND WHAT THE SECOND; AND OF THE FAULT AND PUNISHMENT OF OUR FIRST PARENTS.

When, therefore, He had first formed the male after His own likeness, then He also fashioned woman after the image of the man himself, that the two by their union might be able to perpetuate their race, and to fill the whole earth with a multitude. But in the making of man himself He concluded and completed the nature of those two materials which we have spoken of as contrary to each other, fire and water. For having made the body, He breathed into it a soul from the vital source of His own Spirit, which is everlasting, that it might bear the similitude of the world itself, which is composed of opposing elements. For he[4] consists of soul and body, that is, as it were, of heaven and earth: since the soul by which we live, has its origin, as it were, out of heaven from God, the body out of the earth, of the dust of which we have said that it was formed. Empedocles — whom you cannot tell whether to reckon among poets or philosophers, for he wrote in verse respecting the nature of things, as did Lucretius and Varro among the Romans — determined that there were four elements, that is, fire, air, water, and earth; perhaps following Trismegistus, who said that our bodies were composed of these four elements by God, for *he said* that they contained in themselves something of fire, something of air, something of water, and something of earth, and *yet* that they were neither fire, nor air, nor water, nor earth. And these things indeed are not false; for the nature of earth is contained in the flesh, that of moisture in the blood, that of air in the breath, that of fire in the vital heat. But neither can the blood be separated from the body, as moisture is from the earth; nor the vital heat from the breath, as fire from the air: so that of all things only two elements are found, the whole nature of which is included in the formation of our body. Man, therefore, was made from different and opposite substances, as the world itself was made from light and darkness, from life and death; and he has admonished us that these two things contend against each other in man: so that if the soul, which has its origin from God, gains the mastery, it is immortal, and lives in perpetual light; if, on the other hand, the body shall overpower the soul, and subject it to its dominion, it is in everlasting darkness and death.[5] And the force of this is not that it altogether annihilates[6] the souls of the unrighteous, but subjects them to everlasting punishment.[7]

We term that punishment the second death, which is itself also perpetual, as also is immortality. We thus define the first death: Death is the dissolution of the nature of living beings; or thus: Death is the separation of body and

[1] [*De Legibus*, book i. cap. 7.]
[2] That is, according to the notions of the heathen.
[3] Made fast, established.

[4] i.e., man.
[5] It was necessary to remove ambiguity from the heathen, to whom the word death conveys no such meaning. In the sacred writings the departure of the soul from the body is often spoken of as sleep, or rest. Thus Lazarus is said to sleep. 1 Thess. iv. 14, "Them that sleep in Jesus will God bring with Him," — an expression of great beauty and propriety as applied to Christians. On the other hand, the prophets speak of "the shadow of death."
[6] Extinguishes. Compare the words of Christ Himself, John v. 29; Acts xxiv. 15.
[7] [Must not be overlooked. See vol. iv. p. 495, and elucidation (after book. iv.) on p. 542.]

soul. But we thus define the second death: Death is the suffering of eternal pain; or thus: Death is the condemnation of souls for their deserts to eternal punishments. This does not extend to the dumb cattle, whose spirits, not being composed of God,[1] but of the common air, are dissolved by death. Therefore in this union of heaven and earth, the image of which is developed[2] in man, those things which belong to God occupy the higher part, namely the soul, which has dominion over the body; but those which belong to the devil occupy the lower[3] part, manifestly the body: for this, being earthly, ought to be subject to the soul, as the earth is to heaven. For it is, as it were, a vessel which this heavenly spirit may employ as a temporary dwelling. The duties of both are — for the latter, which is from heaven and from God, to command; but for the former, which is from the earth and the devil, to obey. And this, indeed, did not escape the notice of a dissolute man, Sallust,[4] who says: "But all our power consists in the soul and body; we use the soul to command, the body rather to obey." It had been well if he had lived in accordance with his words; for he was a slave to the most degrading pleasures, and he destroyed the efficacy of his sentiment by the depravity of his life. But if the soul is fire, as we have shown, it ought to mount up to heaven as fire, that it may not be extinguished; that is, *it ought to rise* to the immortality which is in heaven. And as fire cannot burn and be kept alive unless it be nourished[5] by some rich fuel[6] in which it may have sustenance, so the fuel and food of the soul is righteousness alone, by which it is nourished unto life. After these things, God, having made man in the manner in which I have pointed out, placed him in paradise,[7] that is, in a most fruitful and pleasant garden, which He planted in the regions of the East with every kind of wood and tree, that he might be nourished by their various fruits; and being free from all labours,[8] might devote himself entirely to the service of God his Father.

Then He gave to him fixed commands, by the observance of which he might continue immortal; or if he transgressed them, be punished with death. It was enjoined that he should not taste of one tree only which was in the midst of the garden,[9] in which He had placed the knowledge of good and evil. Then the accuser, envying the works of God, applied all his deceits and artifices to beguile[10] the man, that he might deprive him of immortality. And first he enticed the woman by fraud to take the forbidden fruit, and through her instrumentality he also persuaded the man himself to transgress the law of God. Therefore, having obtained the knowledge of good and evil, he began to be ashamed of his nakedness, and hid himself from the face of God, which he was not before accustomed to do. Then God drove out the man from the garden, having passed sentence upon the sinner, that he might seek support for himself by labour. And He surrounded[11] the garden itself with fire, to prevent the approach of the man until He execute the last judgment on earth; and having removed death, recall righteous men, His worshippers, to the same place; as the sacred writers teach, and the Erythræan Sibyl, when she says: "But they who honour the true God inherit everlasting life, themselves inhabiting together paradise, the beautiful garden, for ever." But since these are the last things,[12] we will treat of them in the last part of this work. Now let us explain those which are first. Death therefore followed man, according to the sentence of God, which even the Sibyl teaches in her verse, saying: "Man made by the very hands of God, whom the serpent treacherously beguiled that he might come to the fate of death, and receive the knowledge of good and evil." Thus the life of man became limited in duration;[13] but still, however, long, inasmuch as it was extended to a thousand[14] years. And when Varro was not ignorant of this, handed down as it is in the sacred writings, and spread abroad by the knowledge of all, he endeavoured to give reasons why the ancients were supposed to have lived a thousand years. For he says that among the Egyptians months are accounted[15] as years: so that the circuit of the sun through the twelve signs *of the zodiac* does not make a year, but the moon, which traverses that sign-bearing circle in the space of thirty days; which argument is manifestly false. For no one then exceeded the thousandth year. But now they who attain to the hundredth year, which frequently happens,

1 [Eccles. iii. 18–21. Answered, Eccles. xii. 7.]
2 Portrayed or expressed.
3 It is not to be supposed that Lactantius, following the error of Marcion, believed that the body of man had been formed by the devil, for he has already described its creation by God. He rather speaks of the devil as exercising a power permitted to him over the earth and the bodies of men. Compare 2 Cor. iv. 4.
4 Preface to *Catiline*.
5 The word *teneo* is used in this sense by Cicero (*De Nat. Deor.*, ii. 54): "Tribus rebus animantium vita tenetur, cibo, potione, spiritu."
6 Material.
7 Gen. ii.
8 We are not to understand this as asserting that the man lived in idleness, and without any employment in paradise; for this would be inconsistent with the Scripture narrative, which tells us that Adam was placed there to keep the garden and dress it. It is intended to exclude painful and anxious labour, which is the punishment of sin. See Gen. iii. 17.

9 Paradise.
10 Another reading is, ad *dejiciendum* hominem, "to overthrow the man."
11 Circumvallavit, "placed a barrier round." See Gen. iii. 24: "He placed at the east of the garden of Eden cherubims, and a flaming sword, which turned every way, to keep the way of the tree of life."
12 [Not *novissima*, but *extrema* here. He refers to book vii. cap. 11, etc.]
13 Temporary. The word is opposed to everlasting.
14 No one actually lived a thousand years. They who approached nearest to it were Methuselah, who lived 969 years, Jared 962, and Noah 950.
15 It appears that the practice of the Egyptians varied as to the computation of the year.

undoubtedly live a thousand and two hundred months. And competent[1] authorities report that men are accustomed to reach one hundred and twenty years.[2] But because Varro did not know why or when the life of man was shortened, he himself shortened it, since he knew that it was possible for man to live a thousand and four hundred months.

CHAP. XIV. — OF NOAH THE INVENTOR OF WINE, WHO FIRST HAD KNOWLEDGE OF THE STARS, AND OF THE ORIGIN OF FALSE RELIGIONS.

But afterwards God, when He saw the earth filled with wickedness and crimes, determined to destroy mankind with a deluge; but, however, for renewing the multitude, He chose one man, who,[3] when all were corrupted, stood forth preeminent, as a remarkable example of righteousness. He, when six hundred years old, built an ark, as God had commanded him, in which he himself was saved, together with his wife and three sons, and as many daughters-in-law, when the water had covered all the loftiest mountains. Then when the earth was dry, God, execrating the wickedness of the former age, that the length of life might not again be a cause of meditating evils, gradually diminished the age of man by each successive generation, and placed a limit at a hundred and twenty years,[4] which it might not be permitted to exceed. But he, when he went forth from the ark, as the sacred writings inform us, diligently cultivated the earth, and planted a vineyard with his own hand. From which circumstance they are refuted who regard Bacchus as the author of wine. For he not only preceded Bacchus, but also Saturn and Uranus, by many generations. And when he had first taken the fruit from the vineyard, having become merry, he drank even to intoxication, and lay naked. And when one of his sons, whose name was Cham,[5] had seen this, he did not cover his father's nakedness, but went out and told the circumstance to his brothers also. But they, having taken a garment, entered with their faces turned backwards, and covered their father.[6] And when their father became aware of what had been done, he disowned and sent away his son. But he went into exile, and settled in a part of that land which is now called Arabia; and that land was called from him Chanaan, and his posterity Chanaanites. This was the first nation which was ignorant of God, since its prince and founder did not receive from his father the worship of God, being cursed by him;[7] and thus he left to his descendants ignorance of the divine nature.[8]

From this nation all the nearest people flowed as the multitude increased. But the descendants of his father were called Hebrews, among whom the religion of the true God was established.[9] But from these also in after times, when their number was multiplied exceedingly, since the small extent of their settlements could not contain them, then young men, either sent by their parents or of their own accord, by the compulsion of poverty, leaving their own lands to seek for themselves new settlements, were scattered in all directions, and filled all the islands and the whole earth; and thus being torn away from the stem of their sacred root, they established for themselves at their own discretion new customs and institutions. But they who occupied Egypt were the first of all who began to look up to and adore the heavenly bodies. And because they did not shelter themselves in houses on account of the quality of the atmosphere, and the heaven is not overspread with any clouds in that country, they observed the courses of the stars, and their obscurations,[10] while in their frequent adorations they more carefully and freely beheld them. Then afterwards, induced by certain prodigies, they invented monstrous figures of animals, that they might worship them; the authors of which we will presently disclose. But the others, who were scattered over the earth, admiring the elements of the world, began to worship the heaven, the sun, the earth, the sea, without any images and temples, and offered sacrifices to them in the open air, until in process of time they erected temples and statues to the most powerful kings, and originated the practice of honouring them with victims and odours; and thus wandering from the knowledge of God, they began to be heathens. They err, therefore, who contend that the worship of the gods was from the beginning of the world, and that heathenism was prior to the religion of God: for they think that this was discovered afterwards, because they are ignorant of the source and origin of the truth. Now let us return to the beginning of the world.

1 Philo and Josephus.

2 [" Old Parr," born in Shropshire, A.D. 1483, died in 1635: i.e., born before the discovery of America, he lived to the beginning of Hampden's career in England.]

3 The reading is *quod*, which in construction refers not to the preceding, but to the following substantive. *Qui* has been suggested as a preferable reading.

4 Lactantius understands the hundred and twenty years (mentioned Gen. vi. 3) as the limit of human life, and regards it as a mark of severity on God's part. But Chrysostom, Jerome, Augustine, and most commentators, regard it rather as a sign of God's patience and long-suffering, in giving them that space for repentance. And this appears to be confirmed by the Apostle Peter, 1 Ep. iii. 20, " When once the long-suffering of God waited in the days of Noah, while the ark was a preparing."

5 Ham.

6 Gen. ix. 23.

7 This refers to that prophetic denunciation of divine judgment on the impiety of Ham, which Noah, by the suggestion of the Holy Spirit, uttered against the posterity of the profane man. Gen. ix. 25: "Cursed be Canaan." The curse was not uttered in a spirit of vengeance or impatience on account of the injury received, but by the prophetic impulse of the Divine Spirit. [The prophet fixes on the descendant of Ham, whose *impiety* was foreseen, and to whom *it* brought a curse so signal.]

8 [Our author falls into a *hysteron-proteron:* the curse did not work the ignorance, but wilful ignorance and idolatry wrought the curse, which was merely foretold, not fore-ordained.]

9 Resedit.

10 Eclipses.

CHAP. XV. — OF THE CORRUPTION OF ANGELS, AND THE TWO KINDS OF DEMONS.

When, therefore, the number of men had begun to increase, God in His forethought, lest the devil, to whom from the beginning He had given power over the earth, should by his subtilty either corrupt or destroy men, as he had done at first, sent angels for the protection and improvement[1] of the human race; and inasmuch as He had given these a free will, He enjoined them above all things not to defile themselves with contamination from the earth, and thus lose the dignity of their heavenly nature.[2] He plainly prohibited them from doing that which He knew that they would do, that they might entertain no hope of pardon. Therefore, while they abode among men, that most deceitful ruler[3] of the earth, by his very association, gradually enticed them to vices, and polluted them by intercourse with women. Then, not being admitted into heaven on account of the sins into which they had plunged themselves, they fell to the earth. Thus from angels the devil makes them to become his satellites and attendants. But they who were born from these, because they were neither angels nor men, but bearing a kind of mixed[4] nature, were not admitted into hell, as their fathers were not into heaven. Thus there came to be two kinds of demons; one of heaven, the other of the earth. The latter are the wicked[5] spirits, the authors of all the evils which are done, and the same devil is their prince. Whence Trismegistus calls him the ruler of the demons. But grammarians say that they are called demons, as though *dæmones*,[6] that is, skilled and acquainted with matters: for they think that these are gods. They are acquainted, indeed, with many future events, but not all, since it is not permitted them entirely to know the counsel of God; and therefore they are accustomed to accommodate[7] their answers to ambiguous results. The poets both know them to be demons, and so describe them. Hesiod thus speaks: —

"These are the demons according to the will of Zeus,
Good, living on the earth, the guardians of mortal men."

And this is said for this purpose, because God had sent them as guardians to the human race; but they themselves also, though they are the destroyers of men, yet wish themselves to appear as their guardians, that they themselves may be worshipped, and God may not be worshipped. The philosophers also discuss the subject of these beings. For Plato attempted even to explain their natures in his "Banquet;" and Socrates said that there was a demon continually about him, who had become attached to him when a boy, by whose will and direction his life was guided. The art also and power of the Magi altogether consists in the influences[8] of these; invoked by whom they deceive the sight of men with deceptive illusions,[9] so that they do not see those things which exist, and think that they see those things which do not exist. These contaminated and abandoned spirits, as I say, wander over the whole earth, and contrive a solace for their own perdition by the destruction of men. Therefore they fill every place with snares, deceits, frauds, and errors; for they cling to individuals, and occupy whole houses from door to door, and assume to themselves the name of *genii;* for by this word they translate demons in the Latin language. They consecrate these in their houses, to these they daily pour out[10] libations of wine, and worship the wise demons as gods of the earth, and as averters of those evils which they themselves cause and impose. And these, since spirits are without substance[11] and not to be grasped, insinuate themselves into the bodies of men; and secretly working in their inward parts, they corrupt the health, hasten diseases, terrify their souls with dreams, harass their minds with phrenzies, that by these evils they may compel men to have recourse to their aid.

CHAP. XVI. — THAT DEMONS HAVE NO POWER OVER THOSE WHO ARE ESTABLISHED IN THE FAITH.

And the nature of all these deceits[12] is obscure to those who are without the truth. For they think that those demons profit them when they cease to injure, whereas they have no power except to injure.[13] Some one may perchance say that they are therefore to be worshipped, that they may not injure, since they have the power to injure. They do indeed injure, but those only by whom they are feared, whom the powerful and lofty hand of God does not protect, who are un-

1 Cultum.
2 Substantiæ, "essence."
3 See 2 Cor. iv. 4, "the god of this world."
4 Middle.
5 Unclean.
6 δαήμονες. Other derivations have been proposed; but the word probably comes from δαιω, "to distribute destinies." Plato approves of the etymology given by Lactantius; for he says that good men, distinguished by great honours, after their death became demons, in accordance with this title of prudence and wisdom. [See the whole subject in Lewis' *Plato*, etc., p. 347]
7 To combine, qualify, or temperate.

8 Aspirations.
9 Blinding tricks, juggleries.
10 They lavish. The word implies a profuse and excessive liberality.
11 Thin, unsubstantial, as opposed to corporeal. The ancients inclined to the opinion that angels had a body, not like that of man, but of a slight and more subtle nature. Probably Lactantius refers to this idea in using the word *tenuis*. How opposed this view is to Scripture is manifest. [Not so *manifest* as our translator supposes. I do not assert what Lactantius says to be scripturally correct: but it certainly is not *opposed* to many facts as Scripture states them; whether figuratively or otherwise, I do not venture a suggestion.]
12 Augustine gives an account of these deceits, *De Civit. Dei*, ix. 18.
13 Thus the ancient Romans worshipped Fever, Fear, etc., to avoid injury from them.

initiated in the mystery[1] of truth. But they fear the righteous,[2] that is, the worshippers of God, adjured by whose name they depart[3] from the bodies *of the possessed:* for, being lashed by their words as though by scourges, they not only confess themselves to be demons, but even utter their own names — those which are adored in the temples — which they generally do in the presence of their own worshippers; not, it is plain, to the disgrace of religion, but[4] *to the disgrace* of their own honour, because they cannot speak falsely to God, by whom they are adjured, nor to the righteous, by whose voice they are tortured. Therefore ofttimes having uttered the greatest howlings, they cry out that they are beaten, and are on fire, and that they are just on the point of coming forth: so much power has the knowledge of God, and righteousness! Whom, therefore, can they injure, except those whom they have in their own power? In short, Hermes affirms that those who have known God are not only safe from the attacks of demons, but that they are not even bound by fate. "The only protection," he says, "is piety, for over a pious man neither evil demon nor fate has any power: for God rescues the pious man from all evil; for the one and only good thing among men is piety." And what piety is, he testifies in another place, in these words: "For piety is the knowledge of God." Asclepius also, his disciple, more fully expressed the same sentiment in that finished discourse which he wrote to the king. Each of them, in truth, affirms that the demons are the enemies and harassers of men, and on this account Trismegistus calls them wicked angels; so far was he from being ignorant that from heavenly beings they were corrupted, and began to be earthly.

CHAP. XVII. — THAT ASTROLOGY, SOOTHSAYING, AND SIMILAR ARTS ARE THE INVENTION OF DEMONS.

These were the inventors of astrology, and soothsaying, and divination, and those productions which are called oracles, and necromancy, and the art of magic, and whatever evil practices besides these men exercise, either openly or in secret. Now all these things are false of themselves, as the Erythræan Sibyl testifies: —

"Since all these things are erroneous,
Which foolish men search after day by day."

But these same authorities by their countenance[5] cause it to be believed that they are true. Thus they delude the credulity of men by lying divination, because it is not expedient for them to lay open the truth. These are they who taught men to make images and statues; who, in order that they might turn away the minds of men from the worship of the true God, cause the countenances of dead kings, fashioned and adorned with exquisite beauty, to be erected and consecrated, and assumed to themselves their names, as though *they were assuming* some characters. But the magicians, and those whom the people truly call enchanters,[6] when they practise their detestable arts, call upon them by their true names, those heavenly names which are read in the sacred writings. Moreover, these impure and wandering spirits, that they may throw all things into confusion, and overspread the minds of men with errors, interweave and mingle false things with true. For they themselves feigned that there are many heavenly beings, and one king of all, Jupiter; because there are many spirits of angels in heaven, and one Parent and Lord of all, God. But they have concealed the truth under false names, and withdrawn it from sight.

For God, as I have shown in the beginning,[7] does not need a name, since He is alone; nor do the angels, inasmuch as they are immortal, either suffer or wish themselves to be called gods: for their one and only duty is to submit to the will of God, and not to do anything at all except at His command. For we say that the world is so governed by God, as a province is by its ruler; and no one would say that his attendants[8] are his sharers in the administration of the province, although business is carried on by their service. And yet these can effect something contrary to the commands of the ruler, through his ignorance; which is the result of man's condition. But that guardian of the world and ruler of the universe, who knows all things, from whose divine eyes nothing is concealed,[9] has alone with His Son the power over all things; nor is there anything in the angels except the necessity of obedience. Therefore they wish no honour to be paid to them, since all their honour is in God. But they who have revolted from the service of God, because they are enemies of the truth, and betrayers[10] of God attempt to claim for themselves the name and worship of gods; not that they desire any hon-

1 Sacramento.
2 See Acts of Apostles xvi. 18, and xix. 15, 16. In the Gospels the demons say to Jesus, "Art Thou come to torment us before the time?" [Suggestive of 2 Pet. ii. 4.]
3 The practice of exorcism was used in the early ages of the Church, and the faithful were supposed to possess power over demons. See book iv. ch. 27. Justin, Tertullian, and other writers attest the same. There were also exorcists in the Jewish synagogues. See Acts xix. 13.
4 Sed. Other editions read *et;* but the one adopted in the text brings out the meaning more distinctly by contrast = they did not disgrace religion, but their own honour.
5 By their presence.
6 Malefici — evil-doers. The word is specially used of enchanters.
7 Book i. ch. vi.
8 Apparitors. The word is especially applied to public servants, as lictors, etc.
9 Surrounded, shut in.
10 Prævaricatores. The word is properly applied to an advocate who is guilty of collusion with his antagonist, and thus betrays his client.

our (for what honour is there to the lost?), nor that they may injure God, who cannot be injured, but that they may injure men, whom they strive to turn away from the worship and knowledge of the true Majesty, that they may not be able to obtain immortality, which they themselves have lost through their wickedness. Therefore they draw on darkness, and overspread the truth with obscurity, that men may not know their Lord and Father. And that they may easily entice them, they conceal themselves in the temples, and are close at hand at all sacrifices; and they often give prodigies, that men, astonished by them, may attach to images a belief in their divine power and influence. Hence it is that the stone was cut by the augur with a razor; that Juno of Veii answered that she wished to remove to Rome; that Fortuna Muliebris[1] announced the threatening danger; that the ship followed the hand of Claudia; that Juno when plundered, and the Locrian Proserpine, and the Milesian Ceres, punished the sacrilegious; that Hercules exacted vengeance from Appius, and Jupiter from Atinius, and Minerva from Cæsar. Hence it was that the serpent sent for from Epidaurus freed the city of Rome from pestilence. For the chief of the demons was himself carried thither in his own form, without any dissembling; if indeed the ambassadors who were sent for that purpose brought with them a serpent of immense size.

But they especially deceive in the case of oracles, the juggleries of which the profane[2] cannot distinguish from the truth; and therefore they imagine that commands,[3] and victories, and wealth, and prosperous issues of affairs, are bestowed by them, — in short, that the state has often been freed from imminent dangers by their interposition;[4] which dangers they have both announced, and when appeased with sacrifices, have averted. But all these things are deceits. For since they have a presentiment[5] of the arrangements of God, inasmuch as they have been His ministers, they interpose themselves in these matters, that whatever things have been accomplished or are in the course of accomplishment by God, they themselves may especially appear to be doing or to have done; and as often as any advantage is hanging over any people or city, according to the purpose of God, either by prodigies, or dreams, or oracles, they promise that they will bring it to pass, if temples, honours, and sacrifices are given to them. And on the offering of these, when the necessary[6] result comes to pass, they acquire for themselves the greatest veneration. Hence temples are vowed, and new images consecrated; herds of victims are slain; and when all these things are done, yet the life and safety of those who have performed them are not the less sacrificed. But as often as dangers threaten, they profess that they are angry on account of some light and trifling cause; as Juno was with Varro, because he had placed a beautiful boy on the carriage[7] of Jupiter to guard the dress, and on this account the Roman name was almost destroyed at Cannæ. But if Juno feared a second Ganymede, why did the Roman youth suffer punishment? Or if the gods regard the leaders only, and neglect the rest of the multitude, why did Varro alone escape who acted thus, and why was Paulus, who was innocent,[8] slain? Assuredly nothing then happened to the Romans by "the fates of the hostile Juno,"[9] when Hannibal by craft and valour despatched two armies of the Roman people. For Juno did not venture either to defend Carthage, where were her arms and chariot, or to injure the Romans; for

> "She had heard that sons of Troy
> Were born her Carthage to destroy."[10]

But these are the delusions of those who, concealing themselves under the names of the dead, lay snares for the living. Therefore, whether the impending danger can be avoided, they wish it to appear that they averted it, having been appeased; or if it cannot be avoided, they contrive that it may appear to have happened through disregard[11] of them. Thus they acquire to themselves authority and fear from men, who are ignorant of them. By this subtilty and by these arts they have caused the knowledge of the true and only God to fail[12] among all nations. For, being destroyed by their own vices, they rage and use violence that they may destroy others. Therefore these enemies of the human race even devised human victims, to devour as many lives as possible.

Chap. XVIII. — Of the Patience and Vengeance of God, the Worship of Demons, and False Religions.

Some one will say, Why then does God permit these things to be done, and not apply a remedy to such disastrous errors? That evils may be at variance with good; that vices may be opposed to virtues; that He may have some whom He may punish, and others whom He

1 Womanly Fortune.
2 Unbelievers.
3 Governments.
4 At their nod, or suggestion.
5 They presage.
6 That which was necessary according to the purpose and arrangement of God.

7 Tensa; a carriage on which the images of the gods were carried to the circus at the Circensian games.
8 Deserved nothing, had nothing worthy of punishment. Varro and Paulus Æmilius were the two consuls who commanded at Cannæ. Varro escaped, Paulus was slain.
9 Virg., *Æn.*, viii. 292.
10 *Ibid.*, i. 19.
11 Contempt.
12 They have made old.

may honour. For He has determined at the last times to pass judgment on the living and the dead, concerning which judgment I shall speak in the last book. He delays,[1] therefore, until the end of the times shall come, when He may pour out His wrath with heavenly power and might, as

> "Prophecies of pious seers
> Ring terror in the 'wildered ears."[2]

But now He suffers men to err, and to be impious even towards Himself, just, and mild, and patient as He is. For it is impossible that He in whom is perfect excellence should not also be of perfect patience. Whence some imagine, that God is altogether free from anger, because He is not subject to affections, which are perturbations of the mind; for every animal which is liable to affections and emotions is frail. But this persuasion altogether takes away truth and religion. But let this subject of discussing the anger of God be laid aside for the present; because the matter is very copious, and to be more widely treated in a work devoted to the subject. Whoever shall have worshipped and followed these most wicked spirits, will neither enjoy heaven nor the light, which are God's; but will fall into those things which we have spoken of as being assigned in the distribution of things to the prince of the evil ones himself, — namely, into darkness, and hell, and everlasting punishment.

I have shown that the religious rites of the gods are vain in a threefold manner: In the first place, because those images which are worshipped are representations of men who are dead; and that is a wrong and inconsistent thing, that the image of a man should be worshipped by the image of God, for that which worships is lower and weaker *than that which is worshipped:* then that it is an inexpiable crime to desert the living in order that you may serve memorials of the dead, who can neither give life nor light to any one, for they are themselves without it: and that there is no other God but one, to whose judgment and power every soul is subject. In the second place, that the sacred images themselves, to which most senseless men do service, are destitute of all perception, since they are earth. But who cannot understand that it is unlawful for an upright animal to bend itself that it may adore the earth? which is placed beneath our feet for this purpose, that it may be trodden upon, and not adored by us, who have been raised from it, and have received an elevated position beyond the other living creatures, that we may not turn ourselves again downward, nor cast this heavenly countenance to the earth, but may direct our eyes to that quarter to which the condition of their nature has directed, and that we may adore and worship nothing except the single deity of our only Creator and Father, who made man of an erect figure, that we may know that we are called forth to high and heavenly things. In the third place, because the spirits which preside over the religious rites themselves, being condemned and cast off by God, wallow[3] over the earth, who not only are unable to afford any advantage to their worshippers, since the power of all things is in the hands of one alone, but even destroy them with deadly attractions and errors; since this is their daily business, to involve men in darkness, that the true God may not be sought by them. Therefore they are not to be worshipped, because they lie under the sentence of God. For it is a very great crime to devote[4] one's self to the power of those whom, if you follow righteousness, you are able to excel in power, and to drive out and put to flight by adjuration of the divine name. But if it appears that these religious rites are vain in so many ways as I have shown, it is manifest that those who either make prayers to the dead,[5] or venerate the earth, or make over[6] their souls to unclean spirits, do not act as becomes men, and that they will suffer punishment for their impiety and guilt, who, rebelling against God, the Father of the human race, have undertaken inexpiable rites, and violated every sacred law.

CHAP. XIX. — OF THE WORSHIP OF IMAGES AND EARTHLY OBJECTS.

Whoever, therefore, is anxious to observe the obligations to which man is liable, and to maintain a regard for his nature, let him raise himself from the ground, and, with mind lifted up, let him direct his eyes to heaven: let him not seek God under his feet, nor dig up from his footprints an object of veneration, for whatever lies beneath man must necessarily be inferior to man; but let him seek it aloft, let him seek it in the highest place: for nothing can be greater than man, except that which is above man. But God is greater than man: therefore He is above, and

---

[1] Jerome says: "Great is the anger of God when He does not correct sins, but punishes blindness with blindness. On this very account God sends strong delusion, as St. Paul writes to the Thessalonians, that they should believe a lie, that they all may be damned who have not believed the truth. They are unworthy of the living fountain who dig for themselves cisterns."

[2] Virg., *Æn.*, iv. 464. Some read *priorum* instead of *piorum*.

[3] Roll themselves.

[4] Addico, "to adjudge," is the legal term, expressing the sentence by which the prætor gave effect to the right which he had declared to exist.

[5] [Let this be noted.]

[6] Mancipo. The word implies the making over or transferring by a formal act of sale. Debtors, who were unable to satisfy the demands of their creditors, were made over to them, and regarded as their slaves. They were termed addicti. Our Lord said (John viii. 34), "Whosoever committeth sin, is the servant of sin." Thus also St. Paul, Rom. vi. 16, 17.

not below; nor is He to be sought in the lowest, but rather in the highest region. Wherefore it is undoubted that there is no religion wherever there is an image.[1] For if religion consists of divine things, and there is nothing divine except in heavenly things; it follows that images are without religion, because there can be nothing heavenly in that which is made from the earth. And this, indeed, may be plain to a wise man from the very name.[2] For whatever is an imitation, that must of necessity be false; nor can anything receive the name of a true object which counterfeits the truth by deception and imitation. But if all imitation is not particularly a serious matter, but as it were a sport and jest, then there is no religion in images, but a mimicry of religion. That which is true is therefore to be preferred to all things which are false; earthly things are to be trampled upon, that we may obtain heavenly things. For this is the state of the case, that whosoever shall prostrate his soul, which has its origin from heaven, to the shades[3] beneath, and the lowest things, must fall to that place to which he has cast himself. Therefore he ought to be mindful of his nature and condition, and always to strive and aim at things above. And whoever shall do this, he will be judged altogether wise, he just, he a man: he, in short, will be judged worthy of heaven whom his Parent will recognise not as abject, nor cast down to the earth after the manner of the beasts,[4] but rather standing and upright as He made him.

CHAP. XX. — OF PHILOSOPHY AND THE TRUTH.

A great and difficult portion of the work which I have undertaken, unless I am deceived, has been completed; and the majesty of heaven supplying the power of speaking, we have driven away inveterate errors. But now a greater and more difficult contest with philosophers is proposed to us, the height of whose learning and eloquence, as some massive structure, is opposed to me. For as in the former[5] case we were oppressed by a multitude, and almost by the universal agreement of all nations, so in this subject we are oppressed by the authority of men excelling in every kind of praise. But who can be ignorant that there is more weight in a smaller number of learned men than in a greater number of ignorant persons?[6] But we must not despair that, under the guidance of God and the truth, these also may be turned aside from their opinion; nor do I think that they will be so obstinate as to deny that they behold with sound and open eyes the sun as he shines in his brilliancy. Only let that be true which they themselves are accustomed to profess, that they are possessed with the desire of investigation, and I shall assuredly succeed in causing them to believe that the truth which they have long sought for has been at length found, and to confess that it could not have been found by the abilities of man.

1 [Quare non est dubium quin religio nulla sit ubicunque simulacrum est. Such is the uniform Ante-Nicene testimony.]

2 Simulacrum, "an image," from simulo, "to imitate."

3 The infernal regions.

4 Quadrupeds.

5 In this second book.

6 [Quis autem nesciat plus esse momenti in paucioribus doctis, quam in pluribus imperitis?]

THE DIVINE INSTITUTES

BOOK III.

OF THE FALSE WISDOM OF PHILOSOPHERS.

CHAP. I. — A COMPARISON OF THE TRUTH WITH ELOQUENCE: WHY THE PHILOSOPHERS DID NOT ATTAIN TO IT. OF THE SIMPLE STYLE OF THE SCRIPTURES.

SINCE it is supposed that the truth still lies hidden in obscurity — either through the error and ignorance of the common people, who are the slaves of various and foolish superstitions, or through the philosophers, who by the perverseness of their minds confuse rather than throw light upon it — I could wish that the power of eloquence had fallen to my lot, though not such as it was in Marcus Tullius, for that was extraordinary and admirable, but in some degree approaching it;[1] that, being supported as much by the strength of talent as it has weight by its own force, the truth might at length come forth, and having dispelled and refuted public errors, and the errors of those who are considered wise, might introduce among the human race a brilliant light. And I could wish that this were so, for two reasons: either that men might more readily believe the truth when adorned with embellishments, since they even believe falsehood, being captivated by the adornment of speech and the enticement of words; or, at all events, that the philosophers themselves might be overpowered by us, most of all by their own arms, in which they are accustomed to pride themselves and to place confidence.

But since God has willed this to be the nature of the case, that simple and undisguised truth should be more clear, because it has sufficient ornament of itself, and on this account it is corrupted when embellished[2] with adornings from without, but that falsehood should please by means of a splendour not its own, because being corrupt of itself it vanishes and melts away, unless it is set off[3] and polished with decoration sought from another source; I bear it with equanimity that a moderate degree of talent has been granted to me. But it is not in reliance upon eloquence, but upon the truth, that I have undertaken this work, — a work, perhaps, too great to be sustained by my strength; which, however, even if I should fail, the truth itself will complete, with the assistance of God, whose office this is. For when I know that the greatest orators have often been overcome by pleaders of moderate ability, because the power of truth is so great that it defends itself even in small things by its own clearness: why should I imagine that it will be overwhelmed in a cause of the greatest importance by men who are ingenious and eloquent, as I admit, but who speak false things; and not that it should appear bright and illustrious, if not by our speech, which is very feeble, and flows from a slight fountain, but by its own light? Nor, if there have been philosophers worthy of admiration on account of their literary erudition, should I also yield to them the knowledge and learning of the truth, which no one can attain to by reflection or disputation. Nor do I now disparage the pursuit of those who wished to know the truth, because God has made the nature of man most desirous of arriving at the truth; but I assert and maintain this against them, that the effect did not follow their honest and well-directed will, because they neither knew what was true in itself, nor how, nor where, nor with what mind it is to be sought. And thus, while they desire to remedy the errors of men, they have become entangled in snares and the greatest errors. I have therefore been led to this task of refuting philosophy by the very order of the subject which I have undertaken.

For since all error arises either from false religion or from wisdom,[4] in refuting error it is necessary to overthrow both. For inasmuch as

[1] [A modest confession of his desire to "find out acceptable words." Eccles. xii. 10. His success is proverbial.]
[2] Stained, counterfeit.
[3] Embellished.

[4] [i.e., false *sophia* = "philosophy falsely so called." Vol. v. p. 81.]

it has been handed down to us in the sacred writings that the thoughts of philosophers are foolish, this very thing is to be proved by fact and by arguments, that no one, induced by the honourable name of wisdom, or deceived by the splendour of empty eloquence, may prefer to give credence to human rather than to divine things. Which things, indeed, are related in a concise and simple manner. For it was not befitting that, when God was speaking to man, He should confirm His words by arguments, as though He would not otherwise[1] be regarded with confidence: but, as it was right, He spoke as the mighty Judge of all things, to whom it belongs not to argue, but to pronounce sentence. He Himself, as God, is truth. But we, since we have divine testimony for everything, will assuredly show by how much surer arguments truth may be defended, when even false things are so defended that they are accustomed to appear true. Wherefore there is no reason why we should give so much honour to philosophers as to fear their eloquence. For they might speak well as men of learning; but they could not speak truly, because they had not learned the truth from Him in whose power it was. Nor, indeed, shall we effect anything great in convicting them of ignorance, which they themselves very often confess. Since they are not believed in that one point alone in which alone they ought to have been believed, I will endeavour to show that they never spoke so truly as when they uttered their opinion respecting their own ignorance.

CHAP. II. — OF PHILOSOPHY, AND HOW VAIN WAS ITS OCCUPATION IN SETTING FORTH THE TRUTH.

Now, since the falsehood of superstitions[2] has been shown in the two former books, and the origin itself of the whole error has been set forth, it is the business of this book to show the emptiness and falsehood of philosophy also, that, all error being removed, the truth may be brought to light and become manifest. Let us begin, therefore, from the common name of philosophy, that when the head itself is destroyed, an easier approach may be open to us for demolishing the whole body; if indeed that can be called a body, the parts and members of which are at variance with one another, and are not united together by any connecting link,[3] but, as it were, dispersed and scattered, appear to palpitate rather than to live. Philosophy is (as the name indicates, and they themselves define it) the love of wisdom. By what argument, then, can I prove that philosophy is not wisdom, rather than by that derived from the meaning of the name itself? For he who devotes himself to wisdom is manifestly not yet wise, but devotes himself to the subject that he may be wise. In the other arts it appears what this devotedness effects, and to what it tends: for when any one by learning has attained to these, he is now called, not a devoted follower of the profession, but an artificer. But it is said it was on account of modesty that they called themselves devoted to wisdom, and not wise. Nay, in truth, Pythagoras, who first invented this name, since he had a little more wisdom than those of early times, who regarded themselves as wise, understood that it was impossible by any human study to attain to wisdom, and therefore that a perfect name ought not to be applied to an incomprehensible and imperfect subject. And, therefore, when he was asked what was his profession,[4] he answered that he was a philosopher, that is, a searcher after wisdom. If, therefore, philosophy searches after wisdom, it is not wisdom itself, because it must of necessity be one thing which searches, and another which is searched for; nor is the searching itself correct, because it can find nothing.

But I am not prepared to concede even that philosophers are devoted to the pursuit of wisdom, because by that pursuit there is no attaining to wisdom. For if the power of finding the truth were connected[5] with this pursuit, and if this pursuit were a kind of road to wisdom, it would at length be found. But since so much time and talent have been wasted in the search for it, and it has not yet been gained, it is plain that there is no wisdom there. Therefore they who apply themselves to philosophy do not devote themselves to the pursuit of wisdom; but they themselves imagine that they do so, because they know not where that is which they are searching for, or of what character it is. Whether, therefore, they devote themselves to the pursuit of wisdom or not, they are not wise, because that can never be discovered which is either sought in an improper manner, or not sought at all. Let us look to this very thing, whether it is possible for anything to be discovered by this kind of pursuit, or nothing.

CHAP. III. — OF WHAT SUBJECTS PHILOSOPHY CONSISTS, AND WHO WAS THE CHIEF FOUNDER OF THE ACADEMIC SECT.

Philosophy appears to consist of two subjects, knowledge and conjecture, and of nothing more. Knowledge cannot come from the understanding, nor be apprehended by thought; because

1 Aliter. This word is usually read in the former clause, but it gives a better meaning in this position.

2 [*Religionum* falsitas. He does not here employ *superstitio*. By the way, Lactantius derives this word from those "qui *superstitem* memoriam hominum, tanquam deorum, colerent." Cicero, however, derives it from those who bother the gods with petitions,—"pro *superstite* prole." See note of the annotator of the Delphin Cicero, on the *Natura Deor.*, i. 17.]

3 A joint or fastening.

4 What he professed—gave himself out to be.

5 Subjaceret.

to have knowledge in oneself as a peculiar property does not belong to man, but to God. But the nature of mortals does not receive knowledge, except that which comes from without. For on this account the divine intelligence has opened the eyes and ears and other senses in the body, that by these entrances knowledge might flow through to the mind. For to investigate or wish to know the causes of natural things, — whether the sun is as great as it appears to be, or is many times greater than the whole of this earth; also whether the moon be spherical or concave; and whether the stars are fixed to the heaven, or are borne with free course through the air; of what magnitude the heaven itself is, of what material it is composed; whether it is at rest and immoveable, or is turned round with incredible swiftness; how great is the thickness of the earth, or on what foundations it is poised and suspended, — to wish to comprehend these things, I say, by disputation and conjectures, is as though we should wish to discuss what we may suppose to be the character of a city in some very remote country, which we have never seen, and of which we have heard nothing more than the name. If we should claim to ourselves knowledge in a matter of this kind, which cannot be known, should we not appear to be mad, in venturing to affirm that in which we may be refuted? How much more are they to be judged mad and senseless, who imagine that they know natural things, which cannot be known by man! Rightly therefore did Socrates, and the Academics[1] who followed him, take away knowledge, which is not the part of a disputant, but of a diviner. It remains that there is in philosophy conjecture only; for that from which knowledge is absent, is entirely occupied by conjecture. For every one conjectures that of which he is ignorant. But they who discuss natural subjects, conjecture that they are as they discuss them. Therefore they do not know the truth, because knowledge is concerned with that which is certain, conjecture with the uncertain.

Let us return to the example before mentioned. Come, let us conjecture about the state and character of that city which is unknown to us in all respects except in name. It is probable that it is situated on a plain, with walls of stone, lofty buildings, many streets, magnificent and highly adorned temples. Let us describe, if you please, the customs and deportment of the citizens. But when we shall have described these, another will make opposite statements; and when he also shall have concluded, a third will arise, and others after him; and they will make very different conjectures to those of ours. Which therefore of all is more true? Perhaps none of them. But all things have been mentioned which the nature of the circumstances admits, so that some one of them must necessarily be true. But it will not be known who has spoken the truth. It may possibly be that all have in some degree erred *in their description*, and that all have in some degree attained to the truth. Therefore we are foolish if we seek this by disputation; for some one may present himself who may deride our conjectures, and esteem us as mad, since we wish to conjecture the character of that which we do not know. But it is unnecessary to go in quest of remote cases, from which perhaps no one may come to refute us. Come, let us conjecture what is now going on in the forum, what in the senate-house. That also is too distant. Let us say what is taking place with the interposition of a single wall;[2] no one can know this but he who has heard or seen it. No one therefore ventures to say this, because he will immediately be refuted not by words, but by the presence of the fact itself. But this is the very thing which philosophers do, who discuss what is taking place in heaven, but think that they do that with impunity, because there is no one to refute their errors. But if they were to think that some one was about to descend who would prove them to be mad and false, they would never discuss those subjects at all which they cannot possibly know. Nor, however, is their shamelessness and audacity to be regarded as more successful because they are not refuted; for God refutes them to whom alone the truth is known, although He may seem to connive at their conduct, and He reckons such wisdom of men as the greatest folly.

CHAP. IV. — THAT KNOWLEDGE IS TAKEN AWAY BY SOCRATES, AND CONJECTURE BY ZENO.

Zeno and the Stoics, then, were right in repudiating conjecture. For to conjecture that you know that which you do not know, is not the part of a wise, but rather of a rash and foolish man. Therefore if nothing can be known, as Socrates taught, or ought to be conjectured, as Zeno taught, philosophy is entirely removed. Why should I say that it is not only overthrown by these two, who were the chiefs of philosophy, but by all, so that it now appears to have been long ago destroyed by its own arms? Philosophy has been divided into many sects; and they all entertain various sentiments. In which do we place the truth? It certainly cannot be in

[1] It is evident that the Academy took its rise from the doctrine of Socrates. Plato, the disciple of Socrates, founded the Academy. However excellent their system may appear to many, the opinion of Carneades the Stoic seems just, who said that "the wise man who is about to conjecture is about to err, for he who conjectures knows nothing." Thus knowledge is taken from them by themselves. — BETUL.

[2] With nothing but an inner wall between.

all. Let us point out some one; it follows that all the others will be without wisdom. Let us pass through them separately; in the same manner, whatever we shall give to one we shall take away from the others. For each particular sect overturns all others, to confirm itself and its own *doctrines:* nor does it allow wisdom to any other, lest it should confess that it is itself foolish; but as it takes away others, so is it taken away itself by all others. For they are nevertheless philosophers who accuse it of folly. Whatever sect you shall praise and pronounce true, that is censured by philosophers as false. Shall we therefore believe one which praises itself and its doctrine, or the many which blame the ignorance of each other? That must of necessity be better which is held by great numbers, than that which is held by one only. For no one can rightly judge concerning himself, as the renowned poet testifies;[1] for the nature of men is so arranged, that they see and distinguish the affairs of others better than their own. Since, therefore, all things are uncertain, we must either believe all or none: if we are to believe no one, then the wise have no existence, because while they separately affirm different things they think themselves wise; if all, it is equally true that there are no wise men, because all deny the wisdom of each individually. Therefore all are in this manner destroyed; and as those fabled *sparti*[2] of the poets, so these men mutually slay one another, so that no one remains of all; which happens on this account, because they have a sword, but have no shield. If, therefore, the sects individually are convicted of folly by the judgment of many sects, it follows that all are found to be vain and empty; and thus philosophy consumes and destroys itself. And since Arcesilas the founder of the Academy understood this, he collected together the mutual censures of all, and the confession of ignorance made by distinguished philosophers, and armed himself against all. Thus he established a new philosophy of not philosophizing. From this founder, therefore, there began to be two kinds of philosophy: one the old one, which claims to itself knowledge; the other a new one, opposed to the former, and which detracts from it. Between these two kinds of philosophy I see that there is disagreement, and as it were civil war. On which side shall we place wisdom, which cannot be torn asunder?[3] If the nature of things can be known, this troop of recruits will perish; if it cannot, the veterans will be destroyed: if they shall be equal, nevertheless philosophy, the guide of all, will still perish, because it is divided; for nothing can be opposed to itself without its own destruction. But if, as I have shown, there can be no inner and peculiar knowledge in man on account of the frailty of the human condition, the party of Arcesilas prevails. But not even will this stand firm, because it cannot be the case that nothing at all is known.

CHAP. V.—THAT THE KNOWLEDGE OF MANY THINGS IS NECESSARY.

For there are many things which nature itself, and frequent use, and the necessity of life, compel us to know. Accordingly you must perish, unless you know what things are useful for life, in order that you may seek them; and what are dangerous, that you may shun and avoid them. Moreover, there are many things which experience finds out. For the various courses of the sun and moon, and the motions of the stars, and the computation of times, have been discovered, and the nature of bodies, and the strength of herbs by students of medicine, and by the cultivators of the land the nature of soils, and signs of future rains and tempests have been collected. In short, there is no art which is not dependent on knowledge. Therefore Arcesilas ought, if he had any wisdom, to have distinguished the things which were capable of being known, and those which were incapable. But if he had done this, he would have reduced himself to the common herd. For the common people have sometimes more wisdom, because they are only so far wise as is necessary. And if you inquire of them whether they know anything or nothing, they will say that they know the things which they know, and will confess that they are ignorant of what they are ignorant. He was right, therefore, in taking away the systems of others, but he was not right in laying the foundations of his own. For ignorance of all things cannot be wisdom, the peculiar property of which is knowledge. And thus, when he overcame the philosophers, and taught that they knew nothing, he himself also lost the name of philosopher, because his system is to know nothing. For he who blames others because they are ignorant, ought himself to have knowledge; but when he knows nothing, what perverseness or what insolence it is, to constitute himself a philosopher on account of that very thing for which he takes away the others! For it is in their power to answer thus: If you convict us of knowing nothing, and therefore of being unwise because we know nothing, does it follow that you are not wise, because you confess that you know nothing? What progress, therefore, did Arcesilas make, except that, having despatched all the philosophers, he pierced himself also with the same sword?

[1] Terent., *Heautont.*, iii. sec. 97.
[2] σπαρτοί, those who sprung from the dragon's teeth.
[3] Distrahi, which is the reading of some editions, is here followed in preference to the common reading, detrahi.

CHAP. VI.—OF WISDOM, AND THE ACADEMICS, AND NATURAL PHILOSOPHY.

Does wisdom therefore nowhere exist? Yes, indeed, it was amongst them, but no one saw it. Some thought that all things could be known: these were manifestly not wise. Others thought that nothing could be known; nor indeed were these wise: the former, because they attributed too much to man; the latter, because they attributed too little. A limit was wanting to each on either side. Where, then, is wisdom? It consists in thinking neither that you know all things, which is the property of God; nor that you are ignorant of all things, which is the part of a beast. For it is something of a middle character which belongs to man, that is, knowledge united and combined with ignorance. Knowledge in us is from the soul, which has its origin from heaven; ignorance from the body, which is from the earth: whence we have something in common with God, and with the animal creation. Thus, since we are composed of these two elements, the one of which is endowed with light, the other with darkness, a part of knowledge is given to us, and a part of ignorance. Over this bridge, so to speak, we may pass without any danger of falling; for all those who have inclined to either side, either towards the left hand or the right, have fallen. But I will say how each part has erred. The Academics argued from obscure subjects, against the natural philosophers, that there was no knowledge; and satisfied with the examples of a few incomprehensible subjects, they embraced ignorance as though they had taken away the whole of knowledge, because they had taken it away in part. But natural philosophers, on the other hand, derived their argument from those things which are open, *and inferred* that all things could be known, and, satisfied with things which were manifest, retained knowledge; as if they had defended it altogether, because they had defended it in part. And thus neither the one saw what was clear, nor the others what was obscure; but each party, while they contended with the greatest ardour either to retain or to take away knowledge only, did not see that there would be placed in the middle that which might guide them to wisdom.

But Arcesilas, who teaches that there is no knowledge,[1] when he was detracting from Zeno, the chief of the Stoics, that he might altogether overthrow philosophy on the authority of Socrates, undertook this opinion to affirm that nothing could be known. And thus he disproved the judgment of the philosophers, who had thought that the truth was drawn forth,[2] and found out by their talents,—namely, because that wisdom was mortal, and, having been instituted a few ages before, had now attained to its greatest increase, so that it was now necessarily growing old and perishing, the Academy[3] suddenly arose, the old age, as it were, of philosophy, which might despatch it now withering. And Arcesilas rightly saw that they are arrogant, or rather foolish, who imagine that the knowledge of the truth can be arrived at by conjecture. But no one can refute one speaking falsely, unless he who shall have previously known what is true; but Arcesilas, endeavouring to do this without a knowledge of the truth, introduced a kind of philosophy which we may call unstable or inconstant.[4] For, that nothing may be known, it is necessary that something be known. For if you know nothing at all, the very knowledge that nothing can be known will be taken away. Therefore he who pronounces as a sentiment that nothing is known, professes, as it were, some conclusion already arrived at and known: therefore it is possible for something to be known.

Of a similar character to this is that which is accustomed to be proposed in the schools as an example of the kind of fallacy called *asystaton;* that some one had dreamt that he should not believe dreams. For if he did believe them, then it follows that he ought not to believe them. But if he did not believe them, then it follows that he ought to believe them. Thus, if nothing can be known, it is necessary that this fact must be known, that nothing is known. But if it is known that nothing can be known, the statement that nothing can be known must as a consequence be false. Thus there is introduced a tenet opposed to itself, and destructive of itself. But the evasive[5] man wished to take away learning from the other philosophers, that he might conceal it at his home. For truly he is not for taking it from himself who affirms anything that he may take it from others: but he does not succeed; for it shows itself, and betrays its plunderer. How much more wisely and truly he would act, if he should make an exception, and say that the causes and systems of heavenly things only, or natural things, because they are hidden, cannot be known, for there is no one to teach them; and ought not to be inquired into, for they cannot be found out by inquiry! For if he had brought forward this exception, he would both have admonished the natural philosophers not to search into those things which exceeded the limit of human reflection; and would have freed himself from the ill-will arising from calumny, and would certainly

1 The master of ignorance.
2 Erutam.
3 The New Academy.
4 In Greek, ἀσύστατον, "without consistency, not holding together;" in Latin, "instabile" or "inconstans."
5 Versutus, one who turns and shifts.

have left us something to follow. But now, since he has drawn us back from following others, that we may not wish to know more than we are capable of knowing, he has no less drawn us back from himself also. For who would wish to labour lest he should know anything? or to undertake learning of this kind that he may even lose ordinary knowledge? For if this learning exists, it must necessarily consist of knowledge; if it does not exist, who is so foolish as to think that that is worthy of being learned, in which either nothing is learned, or something is even unlearned? Wherefore, if all things cannot be known, as the natural philosophers thought, nor nothing, as the Academics taught, philosophy is altogether extinguished.

CHAP. VII. — OF MORAL PHILOSOPHY, AND THE CHIEF GOOD.

Let us now pass to the other part of philosophy, which they themselves call moral, in which is contained the method of the whole of philosophy, since in natural philosophy there is only delight, in this there is utility also. And since it is more dangerous to commit a fault in arranging the condition of life and in forming the character, greater diligence must be used, that we may know how we ought to live. For in the former subject [1] some indulgence may be granted: for whether they say anything, they bestow no advantage; or if they foolishly rave, they do no injury. But in this subject there is no room for difference of opinion, none for error. All must entertain the same sentiments, and philosophy itself must give instructions as it were with one mouth; because if any error shall be committed, life is altogether overthrown. In that former part, as there is less danger, so there is more difficulty; because the obscurity of the subject compels us to entertain different and various opinions. But in this, as there is more danger, so there is less difficulty; because the very use of the subjects and daily experiments are able to teach what is truer and better. Let us see, therefore, whether they agree, or what *assistance* they give us for the better guidance of life. It is not necessary to enlarge on every point; let us select one, and especially that which is the chief and principal thing, in which the whole of wisdom centres and depends.[2] Epicurus deems that the chief good consists in pleasure of mind, Aristippus in pleasure of the body. Callipho and Dinomachus united virtue with pleasure, Diodorus with the privation of pain. Hieronymus placed the chief good in the absence of pain; the Peripatetics, again, in the goods of the mind, the body, and fortune. The chief good of Herillus is knowledge; that of Zeno, to live agreeably to nature; that of certain Stoics, to follow virtue. Aristotle placed the chief good in integrity and virtue. These are the sentiments of nearly all. In such a difference of opinions, whom do we follow? whom do we believe? All are of equal authority. If we are able to select that which is better, it follows that philosophy is not necessary for us; because we are already wise, inasmuch as we judge respecting the opinions of the wise. But since we come for the sake of learning wisdom, how can we judge, who have not yet begun to be wise? especially when the Academic is close at hand, to draw us back by the cloak, and forbid us to believe any one, without bringing forward that which we may follow.

CHAP. VIII. — OF THE CHIEF GOOD, AND THE PLEASURES OF THE SOUL AND BODY, AND OF VIRTUE.

What then remains, but that we leave raving and obstinate wranglers, and come to the judge, who is in truth the giver of simple and calm wisdom? which is able not only to mould us, and lead us into the way, but also to pass an opinion on the controversies of those men. This teaches us what is the true and highest good of man; but before I begin to speak on this subject, all those opinions must be refuted, that it may appear that no one of those *philosophers* was wise. Since the inquiry is respecting the duty of man, the chief good of the chief animal ought to be placed in that which it cannot have in common with the other animals. But as teeth are the peculiar property of wild beasts, horns of cattle, and wings of birds, so something peculiar to himself ought to be attributed to man, without which he would lose the fixed [3] order of his condition. For that which is given to all for the purpose of life or generation, is indeed a natural good; but still it is not the greatest, unless it be peculiar to each class. Therefore he was not a wise man who believed that pleasure of the mind is the chief good, since that, whether it be freedom from anxiety or joy, is common to all. I do not consider Aristippus even worthy of an answer; for since he is always rushing into pleasures of the body, and is only the slave of sensual indulgences, no one can regard him as a man: for he lived in such a manner that there was no difference between him and a brute, except this only, that he had the faculty of speech. But if the power of speaking were given to the ass, or the dog, or swine, and you were to inquire from these why they so furiously pursue the females, that they can scarcely be separated from them, and even neglect their food and drink; why they either drive away other males,

[1] Natural philosophy.
[2] The hinge of wisdom altogether turns.
[3] Rationem, "the plan or method of his condition."

or do not abstain from the pursuit even when vanquished, but often, when bruised by stronger animals, they are more determined in their pursuit; why they dread neither rain nor cold; why they undertake labour, and do not shrink from danger; — what other answer will they give, but that the chief good is bodily pleasure? — that they eagerly seek it, in order that they may be affected with the most agreeable sensations; and that these are of so much importance, that, for the sake of attaining them, they imagine that no labour, nor wounds, nor death itself, ought to be refused by them? Shall we then seek precepts of living from these men, who have no other feelings than those of the irrational creatures?

The Cyrenaics say that virtue itself is to be praised on this account, because it is productive of pleasure. True, says the filthy dog, or the swine wallowing in the mire.[1] For it is on this account that I contend with my adversary with the utmost exertion of strength, that my valour may procure for me pleasure; of which I must necessarily be deprived if I shall come off vanquished. Shall we therefore learn wisdom from these men, who differ from cattle and the brutes, not in feeling, but in language? To regard the absence of pain as the chief good, is not indeed the part of Peripatetic and Stoic, but of clinical philosophers. For who would not imagine that the discussion was carried on by those who were ill, and under the influence of some pain? What is so ridiculous, as to esteem that the chief good which the physician is able to give? We must therefore feel pain in order that we may enjoy good; and that, too, severely and frequently, that afterwards the absence of pain may be attended with greater pleasure. He is therefore most wretched who has never felt pain, because he is without that which is good; whereas we used to regard him as most happy, because he was without evil. He was not far distant from this folly, who said that the entire absence of pain was the chief good. For, besides the fact that every animal avoids pain, who can bestow upon himself that good, towards the obtaining of which we can do no more than wish? But the chief good cannot make any one happy, unless it shall be always in his power; and it is not virtue, nor learning, nor labour, which affords this to man, but nature herself bestows it upon all living creatures. They who joined pleasure with virtuous principle, wished to avoid this common blending together of all, but they made a contradictory kind of good; since he who is abandoned to pleasure must of necessity be destitute of virtuous principle, and he who aims at principle must be destitute of pleasure.

The *chief* good of the Peripatetics may possibly appear excessive, various, and — excepting those goods which belong to the mind, and what they are is a great subject of dispute — common to man with the beasts. For goods belonging to the body — that is, safety, freedom from pain, health — are no less necessary for dumb creatures than for man; and I know not if they are not more necessary for them, because man can be relieved by remedies and services, the dumb animals cannot. The same is true of those which they call the goods of fortune; for as man has need of resources for the support of life, so have they[2] need of prey and pasture. Thus, by introducing a good which is not within the power of man, they made man altogether subject to the power of another. Let us also hear Zeno, for he at times dreams of virtue. The chief good, he says, is to live in accordance with nature. Therefore we must live after the manner of the brutes. For in these are found all the things which ought to be absent from man: they are eager for pleasures, they fear, they deceive, they lie in wait, they kill; and that which is especially to the point, they have no knowledge of God. Why, therefore, does he teach me to live according to nature, which is of itself prone to a worse course, and under the influence of some more soothing blandishments plunges headlong into vices? Or if he says that the nature of brutes is different from the nature of man, because man is born to virtue, he says something to the purpose; but, however, it will not be a definition of the chief good, because there is no animal which does not live in accordance with its nature.

He who made knowledge the chief good, gave something peculiar to man; but men desire knowledge for the sake of something else, and not for its own sake. For who is contented with knowing, without seeking some advantage from his knowledge? The arts are learned for the purpose of being put into exercise; but they are exercised either for the support of life, or pleasure, or for glory. That, therefore, is not the chief good which is not sought for on its own account. What difference, therefore, does it make, whether we consider knowledge to be the chief good, or those very things which knowledge produces from itself, that is, means of subsistence, glory, pleasure? And these things are not peculiar to man, and therefore they are not the chief goods; for the desire of pleasure and of food does not exist in man alone, but also in the brutes. How is it with regard to the desire of glory? Is it not discovered in horses, since they exult in victory, and are grieved when vanquished? "So great is their love of praises, so great is their eagerness for victory."[3] Nor with-

[1] [Sus ille lutulentus. 2 Pet. ii. 22.]

[2] They, i.e., the beasts of prey and the tame animals.

[3] Virg., *Georg.*, iii. 112, 102.

out reason does that most excellent poet say that we must try "what grief they feel when overcome, and how they rejoice in victory." But if those things which knowledge produces are common to man with other animals, it follows that knowledge is not the chief good. Moreover, it is no slight fault of this definition that bare knowledge is set forth. For all will begin to appear happy who shall have the knowledge of any art, even those who shall know mischievous subjects; so that he who shall have learned to mix poisons, is as happy as he who has learned to apply remedies. I ask, therefore, to what subject knowledge is to be referred. If to the causes of natural things, what happiness will be proposed to me, if I shall know the sources of the Nile, or the vain dreams of the natural philosophers respecting the heaven? Why should I mention that on these subjects there is no knowledge, but mere conjecture, which varies according to the abilities of men? It only remains that the knowledge of good and evil things is the chief good. Why, then, did he call knowledge the chief good more than wisdom, when both words have the same signification and meaning? But no one has yet said that the chief good is wisdom, though this might more properly have been said. For knowledge is insufficient for the undertaking of that which is good and avoiding that which is evil, unless virtue also is added. For many of the philosophers, though they discussed the nature of good and evil things, yet from the compulsion of nature lived in a manner different from their discourse, because they were without virtue. But virtue united with knowledge is wisdom.

It remains that we refute those also who judged virtue itself to be the chief good, and Marcus Tullius was also of this opinion; and in this they were very inconsiderate.[1] For virtue itself is not the chief good, but it is the contriver and mother of the chief good; for this cannot be attained without virtue. Each point is easily understood. For I ask whether they imagine that it is easy to arrive at that distinguished good, or that it is reached only with difficulty and labour? Let them apply their ingenuity, and defend error. If it is easily attained to, and without labour, it cannot be the chief good. For why should we torment ourselves, why wear ourselves out with striving day and night, seeing that the object of our pursuit is so close at hand, that any one who wishes may grasp it without any effort of the mind? But if we do not attain even to a common and moderate good except by labour, since good things are by their nature arduous and difficult,[2] whereas evil things have a downward tendency, it follows that the greatest labour is necessary for the attainment of the greatest good. And if this is most true, then there is need of another virtue, that we may arrive at that virtue which is called the chief good; but this is incongruous and absurd, that virtue should arrive at itself by means of itself. If no good can be reached unless by labour, it is evident that it is virtue by which it is reached, since the force and office of virtue consist in the undertaking and carrying through of labours. Therefore the chief good cannot be that by which it is necessary to arrive at another. But they, since they were ignorant of the effects and tendency of virtue, and could discover nothing more honourable, stopped at the very name of virtue, and said that it ought to be sought, though no advantage was proposed from it; and thus they fixed for themselves a good which itself stood in need of a good. From these Aristotle was not far removed, who thought that virtue together with honour was the chief good; as though it were possible for any virtue to exist unless it were honourable, and as though it would not cease to be virtue if it had any measure of disgrace. But he saw that it might happen that a bad opinion is entertained respecting virtue by a depraved judgment, and therefore he thought that deference should be paid to what in the estimation of men constitutes a departure from what is right and good, because it is not in our power that virtue should be honoured simply for its own deserts. For what is honourable[3] character, except perpetual honour, conferred on any one by the favourable report of the people? What, then, will happen, if through the error and perverseness of men a bad reputation should ensue? Shall we cast aside virtue because it is judged to be base and disgraceful by the foolish? And since it is capable of being oppressed and harassed, in order that it may be of itself a peculiar and lasting good, it ought to stand in need of no outward assistance, so as not to depend by itself upon its own strength, and to remain stedfast. And thus no good is to be hoped by it from man, nor is any evil to be refused.

CHAP. IX. — OF THE CHIEF GOOD, AND THE WORSHIP OF THE TRUE GOD, AND A REFUTATION OF ANAXAGORAS.

I now come to the chief good of true wisdom, the nature of which is to be determined in this manner: first, it must be the property of man alone, and not belong to any other animal; secondly, it must belong to the soul only, and

[1] [*De Finibus*, book v. cap. 28.]

[2] Literally, "since the nature of good things is placed on a steep ascent, that of evil things on a precipitous descent."

[3] *Honestas* is used with some latitude of meaning, to express respectability of character, or honourable feeling, or the principle of honour, or virtue itself. [See Philipp. iv. 8.]

not be shared with the body; lastly, it cannot fall to the lot of any one without knowledge and virtue. Now this limitation excludes and does away with all the opinions of those *whom I have mentioned;* for their sayings contain nothing of this kind. I will now say what this is, that I may show, as I designed, that all philosophers were blind and foolish, who could neither see, nor understand, nor surmise at any time what was fixed as the chief good for man. Anaxagoras, when asked for what purpose he was born, replied that he might look upon the heaven and the sun. This expression is admired by all, and judged worthy of a philosopher. But I think that he, being unprepared with an answer, uttered this at random, that he might[1] not be silent. But if he had been wise, he ought to have considered and reflected with himself; for if any one is ignorant of his own condition, he cannot even be a man. But let us imagine that the saying was not uttered on the spur of the moment. Let us see how many and what great errors he committed in three words. First, he erred in placing the whole duty of man in the eyes alone, referring nothing to the mind, but everything to the body. But if he had been blind, would he lose the duty of a man, which cannot happen without the ruin[2] of the soul? What of the other parts of the body? Will they be destitute, each of its own duty? Why should I say that more depends upon the ears than upon the eye, since learning and wisdom can be gained by the ears only, but not by the eyes only? Were you born for the sake of seeing the heaven and the sun? Who introduced you to this[3] sight? or what does your vision contribute to the heaven and the nature of things? Doubtless that you may praise this immense and wonderful work. Therefore confess that God is the Creator of all things, who introduced you into this world, as a witness and praiser of His great work. You believe that it is a great thing to behold the heaven and the sun: why, therefore, do you not give thanks to Him who is the author of this benefit? why do you not measure with your mind the excellence, the providence, and the power of Him whose works you admire? For it must be, that He who created objects worthy of admiration, is Himself much more to be admired. If any one had invited you to dinner, and you had been well entertained, should you appear in your senses, if you esteemed the mere pleasure more highly than the author of the pleasure? So entirely do philosophers refer all things to the body, and nothing at all to the mind, nor do they see beyond that which falls under their eyes. But all the offices of the body being put aside, the business of man is to be placed in the mind alone. Therefore we are not born for this purpose, that we may see those things which are created, but that we may contemplate, that is, behold with our mind, the Creator of all things Himself. Wherefore, if any one should ask a man who is truly wise for what purpose he was born, he will answer without fear or hesitation, that he was born for the purpose of worshipping God, who brought us into being for his cause, that we may serve Him. But to serve God is nothing else than to maintain and preserve justice by good works. But he, as a man ignorant of divine things, reduced a matter of the greatest magnitude to the least, by selecting two things only, which he said were to be beheld by him. But if he had said that he was born to behold the world, although he would comprise all things in this, and would use an expression of greater[4] sound, yet he would not have completed the duty of man; for as much as the soul excels the body, so much does God excel the world, for God made and governs the world. Therefore it is not the world which is to be contemplated by the eye, for each is a body;[5] but it is God who is to be contemplated by the soul: for God, being Himself immortal, willed that the soul also should be everlasting. But the contemplation of God is the reverence and worship of the common Parent of mankind. And if the philosophers were destitute of this, and in their ignorance of divine things prostrated themselves to the earth, we must suppose that Anaxagoras neither beheld the heaven nor the sun, though he said that he was born that he might behold them. The object proposed to man is therefore plain[6] and easy, if he is wise; and to it especially belongs humanity.[7] For what is humanity itself, but justice? what is justice, but piety? And piety[8] is nothing else than the recognition of God as a parent.

CHAP. X. — IT IS THE PECULIAR PROPERTY OF MAN TO KNOW AND WORSHIP GOD.

Therefore the chief good of man is in religion only; for the other things, even those which are supposed to be peculiar to man, are found in the other animals also. For when they discern and distinguish their own voices[9] by peculiar marks among themselves, they seem to converse: they also appear to have a kind of smile, when with soothed ears, and contracted mouth, and with

1 That he might be able to make some answer.
2 The fall or overthrow.
3 This sight or spectacle, that is, into this world. This expression is used for the place from which the sight is beheld.

4 Would use a greater sound.
5 Each, viz., the world and the eye.
6 Expedita, "free from obstacles," "unembarrassed."
7 Humanity, properly that which is characteristic of man, then kindness and humaneness.
8 Pietas. The word denotes not only piety towards God, but also the affection due to a parent.
9 The sounds uttered by the beasts, by which they are able to distinguish one another. [Rousseau's theory goes further.]

eyes relaxed to sportiveness, they fawn upon man, or upon their own mates and young. Do they not give a greeting which bears some resemblance to mutual love and indulgence? Again, those creatures which look forward to the future and lay up for themselves food, plainly have foresight. Indications of reason are also found in many of them. For since they desire things useful to themselves, guard against evils, avoid dangers, prepare for themselves lurking-places standing open in different places with various outlets, assuredly they have some understanding. Can any one deny that they are possessed of reason, since they often deceive man himself? For those which have the office of producing honey, when they inhabit the place assigned to them, fortify a camp, construct dwellings with unspeakable skill, and obey their king; I know not if there is not in them perfect prudence. It is therefore uncertain whether those things which are given to man are common to him with other living creatures: they are certainly without religion. I indeed thus judge, that reason is given to all animals, but to the dumb creatures only for the protection of life, to man also for its prolongation. And because reason itself is perfect in man, it is named wisdom, which renders man distinguished in this respect, that to him alone it is given to comprehend divine things. And concerning this the opinion of Cicero is true: "Of so many kinds of animals," he says, "there is none except man which has any knowledge of God; and among men themselves, there is no nation either so uncivilized or so savage, which, even if it is ignorant of due conceptions of the Deity, does not know that some conception of Him ought to be entertained." From which it is effected, that he acknowledges God, who, as it were, calls to mind the source from which he is sprung. Those philosophers, therefore, who wish to free the mind from all fear, take away even religion, and thus deprive man of his peculiar and surpassing good, which is distinct from living uprightly, and from everything connected with man, because God, who made all living creatures subject to man, also made man subject to Himself. What reason is there why they should also maintain that the mind is to be turned in the same direction to which the countenance is raised? For if we must look to the heaven, it is undoubtedly for no other reason than on account of religion; if religion is taken away, we have nothing to do with the heaven. Therefore we must either look in that direction or bend down to the earth. We are not able to bend down to the earth, even if we should wish, since our posture is upright. We must therefore look up to the heaven, to which the nature of the body calls us. And if it is admitted that this must be done, it must either be done with this view, that we may devote ourselves to religion, or that we may know the nature of the heavenly objects. But we cannot by any means know the nature of the heavenly objects, because nothing of that kind can be found out by reflection, as I have before shown. We must therefore devote ourselves to religion, and he who does not undertake this prostrates himself to the ground, and, imitating the life of the brutes, abdicates the office of man. Therefore the ignorant are more wise; for although they err in choosing religion, yet they remember their own nature and condition.

CHAP. XI. — OF RELIGION, WISDOM, AND THE CHIEF GOOD.

It is agreed upon, therefore, by the general consent of all mankind, that religion ought to be undertaken; but we have to explain what errors are committed on this subject. God willed this to be the nature of man, that he should be desirous and eager for two things, religion and wisdom. But men are mistaken in this, that they either undertake religion and pay no attention to wisdom, or they devote themselves to wisdom alone, and pay no attention to religion, though the one cannot be true without the other. The consequence is, that they fall into a multiplicity of religions, but false ones, because they have left wisdom, which could have taught them that there cannot be many gods; or they devote themselves to wisdom, but a false wisdom, because they have paid no attention to the religion of the Supreme God, who might have instructed them to the knowledge of the truth. Thus men who undertake either of these courses follow a devious path, and one full of the greatest errors, inasmuch as the duty of man, and all truth, are included in these two things which are inseparably connected. I wonder, therefore, that there was none at all of the philosophers who discovered the abode and dwelling-place of the chief good. For they might have sought it in this manner. Whatever the greatest good is, it must be an object proposed to all men. There is pleasure, which is desired by all; but this is common also to man with the beasts, and has not the force of the honourable, and brings a feeling of satiety, and when it is in excess is injurious, and it is lessened by advance of age, and does not fall to the lot of many: for they who are without resources, who constitute the greater part of men, must also be without pleasure. Therefore pleasure is not the chief good; but it is not even a good. What shall we say of riches? This is much more [1] true of them. For they fall to the lot of fewer men, and that generally by chance; and they often fall to the indolent, and

[1] Multo magis is the reading of the MSS.; but multo minus — "much less" — seems preferable.

sometimes by guilt, and they are desired by those who already possess them. What shall we say of sovereignty itself? That does not constitute the chief good: for all cannot reign, but it is necessary that all should be capable of attaining the chief good.

Let us therefore seek something which is held forth to all. Is it virtue? It cannot be denied that virtue is a good, and undoubtedly a good for all men. But if it cannot be happy because its power and nature consist in the endurance of evil, it assuredly is not the chief good. Let us seek something else. But nothing can be found more beautiful than virtue, nothing more worthy of a wise man. For if vices are to be avoided on account of their deformity, virtue is therefore to be desired on account of its beauty. What then? Can it be that that which is admitted to be good and honourable should be requited with no reward, and be so unproductive as to procure no advantage from itself? That great labour and difficulty and struggling against evils with which this life is filled, must of necessity produce some great good. But what shall we say that it is? Pleasure? But nothing that is base can arise from that which is honourable. Shall we say that it is riches? or commands? But these things are frail and uncertain.[1] Is it glory? or honour? or a lasting name? But all these things are not contained in virtue itself, but depend upon the opinion and judgment of others. For virtue is often hated and visited with evil. But the good which arises from it ought to be so closely united with it as to be incapable of being separated or disunited from it; and it cannot appear to be the chief good in any other way than if it belongs peculiarly to virtue, and is such that nothing can be added to it or taken from it. Why should I say that the duties of virtue consist in the despising of all these things? For not to long for, or desire, or love pleasures, riches, dominions, and honours, and all those things which are esteemed as goods, as others do overpowered by desire, that assuredly is virtue. Therefore it effects something else more sublime and excellent; nor does anything struggle against these present goods but that which longs for greater and truer things. Let us not despair of being able to find it, if we turn our thoughts in all directions; for no slight or trifling rewards are sought.

CHAP. XII. — OF THE TWOFOLD CONFLICT OF BODY AND SOUL; AND OF DESIRING VIRTUE ON ACCOUNT OF ETERNAL LIFE.

But our inquiry is as to the object for which we are born: and thus we are able to trace out what is the effect of virtue. There are two[2] parts of which man is made up, soul and body. There are many things peculiar to the soul, many peculiar to the body, many common to both, as is virtue itself; and as often as this is referred to the body, it is called fortitude for the sake of distinction. Since, therefore, fortitude is connected with each, a contest is proposed to each, and victory held forth to each from the contest: the body, because it is solid, and capable of being grasped, must contend with objects which are solid and can be grasped; but the soul, on the other hand, because it is slight[3] and subtle, and invisible, contends with those enemies who cannot be seen and touched. But what are the enemies of the soul, but lusts, vices, and sins? And if virtue shall have overcome and put to flight these, the soul will be pure and free from stain. Whence, then, are we able to collect what are the effects of fortitude of soul? Doubtless from that which is closely connected with it, and resembles it, that is, from fortitude of the body; for when this has come to any encounter and contest, what else does it seek from victory but life? For whether you contend with a man or beast, the contest is for safety. Therefore, as the body obtains by victory its preservation from destruction, so the soul obtains a continuation of its existence; and as the body, when overcome by its enemies, suffers death, so the soul, when overpowered by vices, must die. What difference, therefore, will there be between the contest carried on by the soul and that carried on by the body, except that the body seeks for temporal, but the soul eternal life? If, therefore, virtue is not happy by itself, since its whole force consists, as I have said, in the enduring of evils; if it neglects all things which are desired as goods; if in its highest condition it is exposed to death, inasmuch as it often refuses life, which is desired by others, and bravely undergoes death, which others fear; if it must necessarily produce some great good from itself, because labours, endured and overcome even until death, cannot fail of obtaining a reward; if no reward, such as it deserves, is found on earth, inasmuch as it despises all things which are frail and transitory, what else remains but that it may effect some heavenly reward, since it treats with contempt all earthly things, and may aim at higher things, since it despises things that are humble? And this *reward* can be nothing else but immortality.

With good reason, therefore, did Euclid, no obscure philosopher, who was the founder of the system of the Megareans, differing from the others, say that that was the chief good which

[1] Liable to fall, perishable.

[2] According to St. Paul, man consists of three parts — body, soul, and spirit. Lactantius appears to use the word *soul* in the same sense in which the Scriptures speak of spirit. [Vol. i. p. 532.]

[3] Tenuis, as applied to the soul, opposed to *solidus*, applied to the body.

was unvarying and always the same. He certainly understood what is the nature of the chief good, although he did not explain in what it consisted; but it consists of immortality, nor anything else at all, inasmuch as it alone is incapable of diminution, or increase, or change. Seneca also unconsciously happened to confess that there is no other reward of virtue than immortality. For in praising virtue in the treatise which he wrote on the subject of premature death, he says: "Virtue is the only thing which can confer upon us immortality, and make us equal to the gods." But the Stoics also, whom he followed, say that no one can be made happy without virtue. Therefore, the reward of virtue is a happy life, if virtue, as it is rightly said, makes a happy life. Virtue, therefore, is not, as they say, to be sought on its own account, but on account of a happy life, which necessarily follows virtue. And this argument might have taught them in what the chief good consisted. But this present and corporeal life cannot be happy, because it is subjected to evils through the body. Epicurus calls God happy and incorruptible, because He is everlasting. For a state of happiness ought to be perfect, so that there may be nothing which can harass, or lessen, or change it. Nor can anything be judged happy in other respects, unless it be incorruptible. But nothing is incorruptible but that which is immortal. Immortality therefore is alone happy, because it can neither be corrupted nor destroyed. But if virtue falls within the power of man, which no one can deny, happiness also belongs to him. For it is impossible for a man to be wretched who is endued with virtue. If happiness falls within his power, then immortality, which is possessed of the attribute of happiness, also belongs to him.

The chief good, therefore, is found to be immortality alone, which pertains to no other animal or body; nor can it happen to any one without the virtue of knowledge, that is, without the knowledge of God and justice. And how true and right is the seeking for this, the very desire of this life shows: for although it be but temporary, and most full of labour, yet it is sought and desired by all; for both old men and boys, kings and those of the lowest station, in fine, wise as well as foolish, desire this. Of such value, as it seemed to Anaxagoras, is the contemplation of the heaven and the light itself, that men willingly undergo any miseries on this account. Since, therefore, this short and laborious life, by the general consent not only of men, but also of other animals, is considered a great good, it is manifest that it becomes also a very great and perfect good if it is without an end and free from all evil. In short, there never would have been any one who would despise this life, however short it is, or undergo death, unless through the hope of a longer life. For those who voluntarily offered themselves to death for the safety of their countrymen, as Menœceus did at Thebes, Codrus at Athens, Curtius and the two Mures at Rome, would never have preferred death to the advantages of life, unless they had thought that they should attain to immortality through the estimation of their countrymen; and although they were ignorant of the life of immortality, yet the reality itself did not escape their notice. For if virtue despises opulence and riches because they are frail, and pleasures because they are of brief continuance, it therefore despises a life which is frail and brief, that it may obtain one which is substantial and lasting. Therefore reflection itself, advancing by regular order, and weighing everything, leads us to that excellent and surpassing good, on account of which we are born. And if philosophers had thus acted, if they had not preferred obstinately to maintain that which they had once apprehended, they would undoubtedly have arrived at this truth, as I have lately shown. And if this was not the part of those who extinguish the heavenly souls together with the body, yet those who discuss the immortality of the soul ought to have understood that virtue is set before us on this account, that, lusts having been subdued, and the desire of earthly things overcome, our souls, pure and victorious, may return to God, that is, to their original source. For it is on this account that we alone of living creatures are raised to the sight of the heaven, that we may believe that our chief good is in the highest place. Therefore we alone receive religion, that we may know from this source that the spirit of man is not mortal, since it longs for and acknowledges God, who is immortal.

Therefore, of all the philosophers, those who have embraced either knowledge or virtue as the chief good, have kept the way of truth, but have not arrived at perfection. For these are the two things which together make up that which is sought for. Knowledge causes us to know by what means and to what end we must attain; virtue causes us to attain to it. The one without the other is of no avail; for from knowledge arises virtue, and from virtue the chief good is produced. Therefore a happy life, which philosophers have always sought, and still do seek, has no existence either in the worship of the gods or in philosophy; and on this account they were unable to find it, because they did not seek the highest good in the highest place, but in the lowest. For what is the highest but heaven, and God, from whom the soul has its origin? And what is the lowest but the earth, from which the body is made? Therefore, although some philosophers have assigned the chief good, not to the body, but to the soul, yet, inasmuch as they have referred it to this life, which has its ending with the body, they have gone back to the body, to which the whole of this time which is passed on earth has reference. Therefore it was not without reason that they did not attain to the highest good; for whatever looks to the body only, and is without immortality, must necessarily be the lowest. Therefore happiness does not fall to the condition of man in that manner in which philosophers thought; but it so falls to him, not that he should then be happy, when he lives in the body, which must undoubtedly be corrupted in order to its dissolution; but then, when, the soul being freed from intercourse with the body, he lives in the spirit only. In this one thing alone can we be happy in this life, if we appear to be unhappy; if, avoiding the enticements of pleasures, and giving ourselves to the service of virtue only, we live in all labours and miseries, which are the means of exercising and strengthening virtue; if, in short, we keep to that rugged and difficult path which has been opened for us to happiness. The chief good therefore which makes men happy cannot exist, unless it be in that religion and doctrine to which is annexed the hope of immortality.

CHAP. XIII. — OF THE IMMORTALITY OF THE SOUL, AND OF WISDOM, PHILOSOPHY, AND ELOQUENCE.

The subject seems to require in this place, that since we have taught that immortality is the chief good, we should prove this also, that the soul is immortal. On which subject there is great disputation among philosophers; nor have they who held true opinions respecting the soul been able to explain or prove anything: for, being destitute of divine knowledge, they neither brought forward true arguments by which they might overcome, nor evidence by which they might convince. But we shall treat of this question more conveniently in the last book, when we shall have to discuss the subject of a happy life. There remains that third part of philosophy, which they call Logic, in which the whole subject of dialectics and the whole method of speaking are contained. Divine learning does not stand in need of this, because the seat of wisdom is not the tongue, but the heart; and it makes no difference what kind of language you employ, for the question is not about words,[1] but facts. And we are not disputing about the grammarian or the orator, whose knowledge is concerned with the proper manner of speaking, but about the wise man, whose learning is concerned with the right manner of living. But if that system of natural philosophy before mentioned is not necessary, nor this of logic, because they are not able to render a man happy, it remains that the whole force of philosophy is contained in the ethical part alone, to which Socrates is said to have applied himself, laying aside the others. And since I have shown that philosophers erred in this part also, who did not grasp the chief good, for the sake of gaining which we are born; it appears that philosophy is altogether false and empty, since it does not prepare us for the duties of justice, nor strengthen the obligations and settled course of man's life. Let them know, therefore, that they are in error who imagine that philosophy is wisdom; let them not be drawn away by the authority of any one; but rather let them incline to the truth, and approach it. There is no room for rashness here; we must endure the punishment of our folly to all eternity, if we shall be deceived either by an empty character or a false opinion. But man,[2] such as he is, if he trusts in himself, that is, if he trusts in man, is (not to say foolish, in that he does not see his own error) undoubtedly arrogant, in venturing to claim for himself that which the condition of man does not admit of.

And how much that greatest author of the Roman language is deceived, we may see from that sentiment of his; for when, in his "Books on Offices,"[3] he had said that philosophy is nothing else than the desire of wisdom, and that wisdom itself is the knowledge of things divine and human, added: "And if any one censures the desire of this, I do not indeed understand what there is which he imagines praiseworthy. For if enjoyment of the mind and rest from cares is sought, what enjoyment can be compared with the pursuits of those who are always inquiring into something which has reference to and tends to promote a good and happy life? Or if any account is taken of consistency and virtue, either this is the study[4] by which we may attain them, or there is none at all. To say that there is no system in connection with the greatest subjects, when none of the least is without a system, is the part of men speaking inconsiderately, and erring in the greatest subjects. But if there is any discipline of virtue, where shall it be sought when you have departed from that kind of learning?" For my own part, although I endeavoured to attain in some degree to the means of acquiring learning, on account of my desire to teach others, yet I have never been eloquent, inasmuch as I never even engaged in

[1] There is a memorable story related by ecclesiastical historians, about a very clever disputant, whose sophistries could not be answered by his fellow-disputants, but who was completely silenced by the simple answers of a Christian otherwise unknown. When questioned about his sudden silence, the sophist replied that others exchanged words for words, but that this simple Christian fought with virtue.

[2] There seems to be a reference to a passage of Terence, in which the poet represents it as the property of man to err. [Or to Cicero, rather: Cujusvis hominis est errare, etc. Philipp. xii. 2.]

[3] Cicero, *De Officiis*, ii. 2.

[4] Ars denotes study, method, or system. The word is applied both to theoretical knowledge and practical skill.

public speaking; but the goodness of the cause cannot fail of itself to make me eloquent, and for its clear and copious defence the knowledge of divinity and the truth itself are sufficient. I could wish, therefore, that Cicero might for a short time rise from the dead, that a man of such consummate eloquence might be taught by an insignificant person who is devoid of eloquence, first, what that is which is deemed worthy of praise by him who blames that study which is called philosophy; and in the next place, that it is not that study by which virtue and justice are learned, nor any other, as he thought; and lastly, that since there is a discipline of virtue, he might be taught where it is to be sought, when you have laid aside that kind of learning, which he did not seek for the sake of hearing and learning. For from whom could he hear when no one knew it? But, as his usual practice was in pleading causes, he wished to press *his opponent* by questioning, and thus to lead him to confession, as though he were confident that no answer could be given to show that philosophy was not the instructress of virtue. And in the Tusculan disputations he openly professed this, turning his speech to philosophy, as though he was showing himself off by a declamatory style of speaking. "O philosophy, thou guide of life," he says; "O thou investigator of virtue, and expeller of vices; what could not only we, but the life of men, have effected at all without thee? Thou hast been the inventor of laws, thou the teacher of morals and discipline;" — as though, indeed, she could perceive anything by herself, and he were not rather to be praised who gave her. In the same manner he might have given thanks to food and drink, because without these life could not exist; yet these, while they minister to sense, confer no benefit. But as these things are the nourishment of the body, so wisdom is of the soul.

CHAP. XIV. — THAT LUCRETIUS AND OTHERS HAVE ERRED, AND CICERO HIMSELF, IN FIXING THE ORIGIN OF WISDOM.

Lucretius, accordingly, acts more correctly in praising him who was the first discoverer of wisdom; but he acts foolishly in this, that he supposed it to be discovered by a man, — as though that man whom he praises had found it lying somewhere as flutes at the fountain,[1] according to the legends of the poets. But if he praised the inventor of wisdom as a god, — for thus he speaks:[2] —

> "No one, I think, who is formed of mortal body. For if we must speak, as the acknowledged majesty of the subject itself demands, he was a god, he was a god, most noble Memmius," —

yet God ought not to have been praised on this account, because He discovered wisdom, but because He created man, who might be capable of receiving wisdom. For he diminishes the praise who praises a part only of the whole. But he praised Him as a man; whereas He ought to have been esteemed as a God on this very account, because He found out wisdom. For thus he speaks:[3] —

> "Will it not be right that this man should be enrolled among the gods?"

From this it appears, either that he wished to praise Pythagoras, who was the first, as I have said,[4] to call himself a philosopher; or Thales of Miletus, who is reported to have been the first who discussed the nature of things. Thus, while he seeks to exalt, he has depressed the thing itself. For it is not great if it could have been discovered by man. But he may be pardoned as a poet. But that same accomplished orator, that same consummate philosopher, also censures the Greeks, whose levity he always accuses, and yet imitates. Wisdom itself, which at one time he calls the gift, at another time the invention, of the gods, he fashions after the manner of the poets, and praises on account of its beauty. He also grievously complains that there have been some who disparaged it. "Can any one," he says, "dare to censure the parent of life, and to defile himself with this guilt of parricide, and to be so impiously ungrateful?"

Are we then parricides, Marcus Tullius, and in your judgment worthy to be sewed[5] up in a bag, who deny that philosophy is the parent of life? Or you, who are so impiously ungrateful towards God (not this god whose image you worship as he sits in the Capitol, but Him who made the world and created man, who bestowed wisdom also among His heavenly benefits), do you call her the teacher of virtue or the parent of life, having learned[6] from whom, one must be in much greater uncertainty than he was before? For of what virtue is she the teacher? For philosophers to the present time do not explain where she is situated. Of what life is she the parent? since the teachers themselves have been worn out by old age and death before they have determined upon the befitting course of life. Of what truth can you hold her forth as an explorer? since you often testify that, in so great a multitude of philosophers, not a single wise man has yet existed. What, then, did that mistress of life teach you? Was it to assail with reproaches the most powerful consul,[7] and by

[1] A proverbial expression, denoting an accidental occurrence.
[2] Book v. 6.

[3] Book v. 51.
[4] Ch. ii.
[5] The allusion is to the punishment of parricides, who were sewed into a bag with an ape, a serpent, and a cock, and thus thrown into the sea.
[6] If any one has approached her as a learner.
[7] Marcus Antonius, who was consul with C. Cæsar in the year when Cæsar was assassinated. It was against Antonius that Cicero

your envenomed speeches to render him the enemy of his country? But let us pass by those things, which may be excused under the name of fortune. You applied yourself, in truth, to the study of philosophy, and so, indeed, that no one ever applied himself more diligently; since you were acquainted with all the systems of philosophy, as you yourself are accustomed to boast, and elucidated the subject itself in Latin writings, and displayed yourself as an imitator of Plato. Tell us, therefore, what you have learned, or in what sect you have discovered the truth. Doubtless it was in the Academy which you followed and approved. But this teaches nothing, excepting that you know your own ignorance.[1] Therefore your own books refute you, and show the nothingness of the learning which may be gained from philosophy for life. These are your words: "But to me we appear not only blind to wisdom, but dull and obtuse to those very things which may appear in some degree to be discerned." If, therefore, philosophy is the teacher of life, why did you appear to yourself blind, and dull, and obtuse? whereas you ought, under her teaching, both to perceive and to be wise, and to be engaged in the clearest light. But how you confessed the truth of philosophy we learn from the letters addressed to your son, in which you advise him that the precepts of philosophy ought to be known, but that we must live as members of a community.[2]

What can be spoken so contradictory? If the precepts of philosophy ought to be known, it is on this account that they ought to be known, in order to our living well and wisely. Or if we must live as members of a community, then philosophy is not wisdom, if it is better to live in accordance with society than with philosophy. For if that which is called philosophy be wisdom, he assuredly lives foolishly who does not live according to philosophy. But if he does not live foolishly who lives in accordance with society, it follows that he who lives according to philosophy lives foolishly. By your own judgment, therefore, philosophy is condemned of folly and emptiness. And you also, in your *Consolation*, that is, not in a work of levity and mirth, introduced this sentiment respecting philosophy: "But I know not what error possesses us, or deplorable ignorance of the truth." Where, then, is the guidance of philosophy? or what has that parent of life taught you, if you are deplorably ignorant of the truth? But if this confession of error and ignorance has been extorted almost against your will from your innermost breast, why do you not at length acknowledge to yourself the truth, that philosophy which, though it teaches nothing, you extolled with praises to the heavens, cannot be the teacher of virtue?

wrote those speeches full of invectives, which, in imitation of Demosthenes, he named Philippics.

1 This point is discussed by Cicero in his Academic questions.

2 [Advice which he took to heart as a swinish debauchee.]

CHAP. XV. — THE ERROR OF SENECA IN PHILOSOPHY, AND HOW THE SPEECH OF PHILOSOPHERS IS AT VARIANCE WITH THEIR LIFE.

Under the influence of the same error (for who could keep the right course when Cicero is in error?), Seneca said: "Philosophy is nothing else than the right method of living, or the science of living honourably, or the art of passing a good life. We shall not err in saying that philosophy is the law of living well and honourably. And he who spoke of it as a rule of life, gave to it that which was its due." He evidently did not refer to the common name of philosophy; for, since this is diffused into many sects and systems, and has nothing certain — nothing, in short, respecting which all agree with one mind and one voice, — what can be so false as that philosophy should be called the rule of life, since the diversity of its precepts hinders the right way and causes confusion? or the law of living well, when its subjects are widely discordant? or the science of passing life, in which nothing else is effected by its repeated contradictions than general[3] uncertainty? For I ask whether he thinks that the Academy is philosophy or not? I do not think that he will deny it. And if this is so, none of these things, therefore, is in agreement with philosophy; which renders all things uncertain, abrogates law, esteems art as nothing, subverts method, distorts rule, entirely takes away knowledge. Therefore all those things are false, because they are inconsistent with a system which is always uncertain, and up to this time explaining nothing. Therefore no system, or science, or law of living well, has been established, except in this the only true and heavenly wisdom, which had been unknown to philosophers. For that earthly wisdom, since it is false, becomes varied and manifold, and altogether opposed to itself. And as there is but one founder and ruler of the world, God, and as truth is one; so wisdom must be one and simple, because, if anything is true and good, it cannot be perfect unless it is the only one of its kind. But if philosophy were able to form the life, no others but philosophers would be good, and all those who had not learned it would be always bad. But since there are, and always have been, innumerable persons who are or have been good without any learning, but of philosophers there has seldom been one who has done anything praiseworthy in his life; who is there, I pray, who does not see that those men are not teachers

3 Than — that no one knows anything.

of virtue, of which they themselves are destitute? For if any one should diligently inquire into their character, he will find that they are passionate, covetous, lustful, arrogant, wanton, and, concealing their vices under a show of wisdom, doing those things at home which they had censured in the schools.[1]

Perhaps I speak falsely for the sake of bringing an accusation. Does not Tullius both acknowledge and complain of the same thing? "How few," he says, "of philosophers are found of such a character, so constituted in soul and life, as reason demands! how few who think true instruction not a display of knowledge, but a law of life! how few who are obedient to themselves, and submit to their own decrees! We may see some of such levity and ostentation, that it would be better for them not to have learned at all; others eagerly desirous of money, others of glory; many the slaves of lusts, so that their speech wonderfully disagrees with their life." Cornelius Nepos also writes to the same Cicero: "So far am I from thinking that philosophy is the teacher of life and the completer of happiness, that I consider that none have greater need of teachers of living than many who are engaged in the discussion of this subject. For I see that a great part of those who give most elaborate precepts in their school respect-modesty and self-restraint, live at the same time in the unrestrained desires of all lusts." Seneca also, in his *Exhortations*, says: "Many of the philosophers are of this description, eloquent to their own condemnation: for if you should hear them arguing against avarice, against lust and ambition, you would think that they were making a public disclosure[2] of their own character, so entirely do the censures which they utter in public flow back upon themselves; so that it is right to regard them in no other light than as physicians, whose advertisements[3] contain medicines, but their medicine chests poison. Some are not ashamed of their vices; but they invent defences for their baseness, so that they may appear even to sin with honour." Seneca also says: "The wise man will even do things which he will not approve of, that he may find means of passing to the accomplishment of greater things; nor will he abandon good morals, but will adapt them to the occasion; and those things which others employ for glory or pleasure, he will employ for the sake of action." Then he says shortly afterwards: "All things which the luxurious and the ignorant do, the wise man also will do, but not in the same manner, and with the same purpose. But it makes no difference with what intention you act, when the action itself is vicious; because acts are seen, the intention is not seen."

Aristippus, the master of the Cyrenaics, had a criminal intimacy with Lais, the celebrated courtesan; and that grave teacher of philosophy defended this fault by saying, that there was a great difference between him and the other lovers of Lais, because he himself possessed Lais, whereas others were possessed by Lais. O illustrious wisdom, to be imitated by good men! Would you, in truth, entrust your children to this man for education, that they might learn to possess a harlot? He said that there was some difference between himself and the dissolute, that they wasted their property, whereas he lived in indulgence without any cost. And in this the harlot was plainly the wiser, who had the philosopher as her creature, that all the youth, corrupted by the example and authority of the teacher, might flock together to her without any shame. What difference therefore did it make, with what intention the philosopher betook himself to that most notorious harlot, when the people and his rivals saw him more depraved than all the abandoned? Nor was it enough to live in this manner, but he began also to teach lusts; and he transferred his habits from the brothel to the school, contending that bodily pleasure was the chief good. Which pernicious and shameful doctrine has its origin not in the heart of the philosopher, but in the bosom of the harlot.

For why should I speak of the Cynics, who practised licentiousness in public? What wonder if they derived their name and title from dogs,[4] since they also imitated their life? Therefore there is no instruction of virtue in this sect, since even those who enjoin more honourable things either themselves do not practise what they advise; or if they do (which rarely happens), it is not the system which leads them to that which is right, but nature which often impels even the unlearned to praise.

Chap. XVI. — That the Philosophers Who Give Good Instructions Live Badly, by the Testimony of Cicero; Therefore We Should Not So Much Devote Ourselves to the Study of Philosophy as to Wisdom.

But when they give themselves up to perpetual sloth, and undertake no exercise of virtue, and pass their whole life in the practice of speaking, in what light ought they to be regarded rather than as triflers? For wisdom, unless it is engaged on some action on which it may exert its force, is empty and false; and Tullius rightly

[1] [Sallust as a writer abounds in denunciations of vice. But see book ii. cap. 13, note 4, p. 62, *supra*.]

[2] Indicium sui professos putes; others read *judicium*, "you would think that they were passing sentence on themselves."

[3] Tituli, "titles."

[4] Augustine in many places expresses his opinion that the Cynics were so called from their immodesty. Others suppose that the name was given to them on account of their snarling propensity.

gives the preference, above teachers of philosophy, to those men employed in civil affairs, who govern the state, who found new cities or maintain with equity those already founded, who preserve the safety and liberty of the citizens either by good laws or wholesome counsels, or by weighty judgments. For it is right to make men good rather than to give precepts about duty to those shut up in corners, which precepts are not observed even by those who speak them; and inasmuch as they have withdrawn themselves from true actions, it is manifest that they invented the system of philosophy itself, for the purpose of exercising the tongue, or for the sake of pleading. But they who merely teach without acting, of themselves detract from the weight of their own precepts; for who would obey, when they who give the precepts themselves teach disobedience? Moreover, it is a good thing to give right and honourable precepts; but unless you also practise them it is a deceit, and it is inconsistent and trifling to have goodness not in the heart, but on the lips.

It is not therefore utility, but enjoyment, which they seek from philosophy. And this Cicero indeed testified. "Truly," he says, "all their disputation, although it contains most abundant fountains of virtue and knowledge, yet, when compared with their actions and accomplishments, I fear lest it should seem not to have brought so much advantage to the business of men as enjoyment to their times of relaxation." He ought not to have feared, since he spoke the truth; but as if he were afraid lest he should be arraigned by the philosophers on a charge of betraying a mystery, he did not venture confidently to pronounce that which was true, that they do not dispute for the purpose of teaching, but for their own enjoyment in their leisure; and since they are the advisers of actions, and do not themselves act at all, they are to be regarded as mere talkers.[1] But assuredly, because they contributed no advantage to life, they neither obeyed their own decrees, nor has any one been found, through so many ages, who lived in accordance with their laws. Therefore philosophy[2] must altogether be laid aside, because we are not to devote ourselves to the pursuit of wisdom, for this has no limit or moderation; but we must be wise, and that indeed quickly. For a second life is not granted to us, so that when we seek wisdom in this life we may be wise in that; each result must be brought about in this life. It ought to be quickly found, in order that it may be quickly taken up, lest any part of life should pass away, the end of which is uncertain. Hortensius in Cicero, contending against philosophy, is pressed by a clever argument; inasmuch as, when he said that men ought not to philosophize, he seemed nevertheless to philosophize, since it is the part of the philosophers to discuss what ought and what ought not to be done in life. We are free and exempt from this calumny, who take away philosophy, because it is the invention of human thought; we defend wisdom, because it is a divine tradition, and we testify that it ought to be taken up by all. He, when he took away philosophy without introducing anything better, was supposed to take away wisdom; and on that account was more easily driven from his opinion, because it is agreed upon that man is not born to folly, but to wisdom.

Moreover, the argument which the same Hortensius employed has great weight also against philosophy, — namely, that it may be understood from this, that philosophy is not wisdom, since its beginning and origin are apparent. When, he says, did philosophers begin to exist? Thales, *as I imagine*, was the first, and his age was recent. Where, then, among the more ancient men did that love of investigating the truth lie hid? Lucretius also says:[3] —

> "Then, too, this nature and system of things has been discovered lately, and I the very first of all have only now been found able to transfer it into native words."

And Seneca says: "There are not yet a thousand years since the beginnings of wisdom were undertaken." Therefore mankind for many generations lived without system. In ridicule of which, Persius says:[4] —

> "When wisdom came to the city,
> Together with pepper and palms;"

as though wisdom had been introduced into the city together with savoury merchandise.[5] For if it is in agreement with the nature of man, it must have had its commencement together with man; but if it is not in agreement with it, human nature would be incapable of receiving it. But, inasmuch as it has received it, it follows that wisdom has existed from the beginning: therefore philosophy, inasmuch as it has not existed from the beginning, is not the same true wisdom. But, in truth, the Greeks, because they had not attained to the sacred letters of truth, did not know how wisdom was corrupted. And, therefore, since they thought that human life was destitute of wisdom, they invented philosophy; that is, they wished by discussion to tear up the truth which was lying hid and unknown to them: and this employment, through ignorance of the truth, they thought to be wisdom.

[1] [See p. 83, note 2, and p. 84, note 1.]

[2] Lactantius must be understood as speaking of that kind of philosophy which teaches errors and deceits, as St. Paul speaks, Col. ii. 8: "Beware lest any man spoil you through philosophy and vain deceit."

[3] Lucretius, v. 336.

[4] Persius, *Sat.*, vi. 38.

[5] [The force of the poet's satire is in this *petty* merchandise.]

CHAP. XVII. — HE PASSES FROM PHILOSOPHY TO THE PHILOSOPHERS, BEGINNING WITH EPICURUS; AND HOW HE REGARDED LEUCIPPUS AND DEMOCRITUS AS AUTHORS OF ERROR.

I have spoken on the subject of philosophy itself as briefly as I could; now let us come to the philosophers, not that we may contend with these, who cannot maintain their ground, but that we may pursue those who are in flight and driven from our battle-field. The system of Epicurus was much more generally followed than those of the others; not because it brings forward any truth, but because the attractive name of pleasure invites many.[1] For every one is naturally inclined to vices. Moreover, for the purpose of drawing the multitude to himself, he speaks that which is specially adapted to each character separately. He forbids the idle to apply himself to learning; he releases the covetous man from giving largesses to the people; he prohibits the inactive man from undertaking the business of the state, the sluggish from bodily exercise, the timid from military service. The irreligious is told that the gods pay no attention to the conduct of men; the man who is unfeeling and selfish is ordered to give nothing to any one, for that the wise man does everything on his own account. To a man who avoids the crowd, solitude is praised. One who is too sparing, learns that life can be sustained on water and meal. If a man hates his wife, the blessings of celibacy are enumerated to him; to one who has bad children, the happiness of those who are without children is proclaimed; against unnatural[2] parents it is said that there is no bond of nature. To the man who is delicate and incapable of endurance, it is said that pain is the greatest of all evils; to the man of fortitude, it is said that the wise man is happy even under tortures. The man who devotes himself to the pursuit of influence and distinction is enjoined to pay court to kings; he who cannot endure annoyance is enjoined to shun the abode of kings. Thus the crafty man collects an assembly from various and differing characters; and while he lays himself out to please all, he is more at variance with himself than they all are with one another. But we must explain from what source the whole of this system is derived, and what origin it has.

Epicurus saw that the good are always subject to adversities, poverty, labours, exile, loss of dear friends. On the contrary, he saw that the wicked were happy; that they were exalted with influence, and loaded with honours; he saw that innocence was unprotected, that crimes were committed with impunity: he saw that death raged without any regard to character, without any arrangement or discrimination of age; but that some arrived at old age, while others were carried off in their infancy; that some died when they were now robust and vigorous, that others were cut off by an untimely death in the first flower of youth; that in wars the better men were especially overcome and slain. But that which especially moved him, was the fact that religious men were especially visited with weightier evils, whereas he saw that less evils or none at all fell upon those who altogether neglected the gods, or worshipped them in an impious manner; and that even the very temples themselves were often set on fire by lightning. And of this Lucretius complains,[3] when he says respecting the god: —

> "Then he may hurl lightnings, and often throw down his temples, and withdrawing into the deserts, there spend his rage in practising his bolt, which often passes the guilty by, and strikes dead the innocent and unoffending."

But if he had been able to collect even a small particle of truth, he would never say that the god throws down his own temples, when he throws them down on this account, because they are not his. The Capitol, which is the chief seat of the Roman city and religion, was struck with lightning and set on fire not once only, but frequently. But what was the opinion of clever men respecting this is evident from the saying of Cicero, who says that the flame came from heaven, not to destroy that earthly dwelling-place of Jupiter, but to demand a loftier and more magnificent abode. Concerning which transaction, in the books respecting his consulship, he speaks to the same purport as Lucretius: —

> "For the father thundering on high, throned in the lofty Olympus, himself assailed his own citadels and famed temples, and cast fires upon his abode in the Capitol.

In the obstinacy of their folly, therefore, they not only did not understand the power and majesty of the true God, but they even increased the impiety of their error, in endeavouring against all divine law to restore a temple so often condemned by the judgment of Heaven.

Therefore, when Epicurus reflected on these things, induced as it were by the injustice of these matters (for thus it appeared to him in his ignorance of the cause and subject), he thought that there was no providence.[4] And having persuaded himself of this, he undertook also to defend it, and thus he entangled himself in inextricable errors. For if there is no providence,

[1] [See Plato's remark upon what he calls *this disease*, *De Leg.*, x., finely expounded in *Plato cont. Atheos* (note ix. p. 114) by Tayler Lewis.]

[2] There is another reading, "adversus parentes impio," "to the son whose conduct to his parents is unnatural."

[3] Lucretius, *De Rerum Natura*, ii. 1101, Munro.

[4] [This age is favoured with a reproduction of these absurdities; and what has happened in consequence before, will be repeated now.]

how is it that the world was made with such order and arrangement? He says: There is no arrangement, for many things are made in a different manner from that in which they ought to have been made. And the divine man found subjects of censure. Now, if I had leisure to refute these things separately, I could easily show that this man was neither wise nor of sound mind. Also, if there is no providence, how is it that the bodies of animals are arranged with such foresight, that the various members, being disposed in a wonderful manner, discharge their own offices individually? The system of providence, he says, contrived nothing in the production of animals; for neither were the eyes made for seeing, nor the ears for hearing, nor the tongue for speaking, nor the feet for walking; inasmuch as these were produced before it was possible to speak, to hear, to see, and to walk. Therefore these were not produced for use; but use was produced from them. If there is no providence, why do rains fall, fruits spring up, and trees put forth leaves? These things, he says, are not always done for the sake of living creatures, inasmuch as they are of no benefit to providence; but all things must be produced of their own accord. From what source, therefore, do they arise,[1] or how are all things which are carried on brought about? There is no need, he says, of supposing a providence; for there are seeds floating through the empty void, and from these, collected together without order, all things are produced and take their form. Why, then, do we not perceive or distinguish them? Because, he says, they have neither any colour, nor warmth, nor smell; they are also without flavour and moisture; and they are so minute, that they cannot be cut and divided.

Thus, because he had taken up a false principle at the commencement, the necessity of the subjects which followed led him to absurdities. For where or from whence are these atoms? Why did no one dream of them besides Leucippus only? from whom Democritus,[2] having received instructions, left to Epicurus the inheritance of his folly. And if these are minute bodies, and indeed solid, as they say, they certainly are able to fall under the notice of the eyes. If the nature of all things is the same, how is it that they compose various objects? They meet together, he says, in varied order and position; as the letters which, though few in number, by variety of arrangement make up innumerable words. But it is urged the letters have a variety of forms. And so, he says, have these first principles; for they are rough, they are furnished with hooks, they are smooth. Therefore they can be cut and divided, if there is in them any part which projects. But if they are smooth and without hooks, they cannot cohere. They ought therefore to be hooked, that they may be linked together one with another. But since they are said to be so minute that they cannot be cut asunder by the edge of any weapon, how is it that they have hooks or angles? For it must be possible for these to be torn asunder, since they project. In the next place, by what mutual compact, by what discernment, do they meet together, so that anything may be constructed out of them? If they are without intelligence, they cannot come together in such order and arrangement; for nothing but reason can bring to accomplishment anything in accordance with reason. With how many arguments can this trifling be refuted! But I must proceed with my subject. This is he

> "Who surpassed in intellect the race of man, and quenched the light of all, as the ethereal sun arisen quenches the stars."[3]

Which verses I am never able to read without laughter. For this was not said respecting Socrates or Plato, who are esteemed as kings of philosophers, but concerning a man who, though of sound mind and vigorous health, raved more senselessly than any one diseased. And thus the most vain poet, I do not say adorned, but overwhelmed and crushed, the mouse with the praises of the lion. But the same man also releases us from the fear of death, respecting which these are his own exact words:—

> "When we are in existence, death does not exist; when death exists, we have no existence: therefore death is nothing to us."

How cleverly he has deceived us! As though it were death now completed which is an object of fear, by which sensation has been already taken away, and not the very act of dying, by which sensation is being taken from us. For there is a time in which we ourselves even yet[4] exist, and death does not yet exist; and that very time appears to be miserable, because death is beginning to exist, and we are ceasing to exist.

Nor is it said without reason that death is not miserable. The approach of death is miserable; that is, to waste away by disease, to endure the thrust, to receive the weapon in the body, to be burnt with fire, to be torn by the teeth of beasts. These are the things which are feared, not because they bring death, but because they bring great pain. But rather make out that pain is not an evil. He says it is the greatest of all evils.

---

[1] See Lucretius, book ii.

[2] [See vol. ii. p. 465, the whole of 14th chapter.]

[3] Lucretius, iii. 1056.

[4] The reading of the text, which appears to be the true one, is, "quo nos etiamnum sumus." There is another reading, "quo et nos jam non sumus." This latter reading would be in accordance with the sentiment of Epicurus, which is totally opposed to the view taken by Lactantius.

How therefore can I fail to fear, if that which precedes or brings about death is an evil? Why should I say that the argument is false, inasmuch as souls do not perish? But, he says, souls do perish; for that which is born with the body must perish with the body. I have already stated that I prefer to put off the discussion of this subject, and to reserve it for the last part of my work, that I may refute this persuasion of Epicurus, whether it was that of Democritus or Dicæarchus, both by arguments and divine testimonies. But perhaps he promised himself impunity in the indulgence of his vices; for he was an advocate of most disgraceful pleasure, and said that man was born for its enjoyment.[1] Who, when he hears this affirmed, would abstain from the practice of vice and wickedness? For if the soul is doomed to perish, let us eagerly pursue riches, that we may be able to enjoy all kinds of indulgence; and if these are wanting to us, let us take them away from those who have them by stealth, by stratagem, or by force, especially if there is no God who regards the actions of men: as long as the hope of impunity shall favour us, let us plunder and put to death.[2] For it is the part of the wise man to do evil, if it is advantageous to him, and safe; since, if there is a God in heaven, He is not angry with any one. It is also equally the part of the foolish man to do good; because, as he is not excited with anger, so he is not influenced by favour. Therefore let us live in the indulgence of pleasures in every possible way; for in a short time we shall not exist at all. Therefore let us suffer no day, in short, no moment of time, to pass away from us without pleasure; lest, since we ourselves are doomed to perish, the life which we have already spent should itself also perish.

Although he does not say this in word, yet he teaches it in fact. For when he maintains that the wise man does everything for his own sake, he refers all things which he does to his own advantage. And thus he who hears these disgraceful things, will neither think that any good thing ought to be done, since the conferring of benefits has reference to the advantage of another; nor that he ought to abstain from guilt, because the doing of evil is attended with gain. If any chieftain of pirates or leader of robbers were exhorting his men to acts of violence, what other language could he employ than to say the same things which Epicurus says: that the gods take no notice; that they are not affected with anger nor kind feeling; that the punishment of a future state is not to be dreaded, because souls die after death, and that there is no future state of punishment at all; that pleasure is the greatest good; that there is no society among men; that every one consults for his own interest; that there is no one who loves another, unless it be for his own sake; that death is not to be feared by a brave man, nor any pain; for that he, even if he should be tortured or burnt, should say that he does not regard it. There is evidently sufficient cause why any one should regard this as the expression of a wise man, since it can most fittingly be applied to robbers!

CHAP. XVIII. — THE PYTHAGOREANS AND STOICS, WHILE THEY HOLD THE IMMORTALITY OF THE SOUL, FOOLISHLY PERSUADE A VOLUNTARY DEATH.

Others, again, discuss things contrary to these, namely, that the soul survives after death; and these are chiefly the Pythagoreans and Stoics. And although they are to be treated with indulgence because they perceive the truth, yet I cannot but blame them, because they fell upon the truth not by their opinion, but by accident. And thus they erred in some degree even in that very matter which they rightly perceived. For, since they feared the argument by which it is inferred that the soul must necessarily die with the body, because it is born with the body, they asserted that the soul is not born with the body, but rather introduced into it, and that it migrates from one body to another. They did not consider that it was possible for the soul to survive the body, unless it should appear to have existed previously to the body. There is therefore an equal and almost similar error on each side. But the one side are deceived with respect to the past, the other with respect to the future. For no one saw that which is most true, that the soul is both created and does not die, because they were ignorant why that came to pass, or what was the nature of man. Many therefore of them, because they suspected that the soul is immortal, laid violent hands upon themselves, as though they were about to depart to heaven. Thus it was with Cleanthes[3] and Chrysippus,[4] with Zeno,[5] and Empedocles,[6] who in the dead of night cast himself into a cavity of the burning Ætna, that when he had suddenly disappeared it might be believed that he had departed to the gods; and thus also of the Romans Cato died, who through the whole of his life was an imitator of Socratic

---

[1] [For his pious talk, however, see T. Lewis, *Plato*, etc., p. 258.]

[2] [These operations of the unbelieving mind have appeared in our day in the *Communisme* of Paris. They already threaten the American Republic, the mass of the population being undisciplined in moral principle, and our lawgivers as well.]

[3] Cleanthes was a Stoic philosopher, who used to draw water by night for his support, that he might devote himself to the study of philosophy by day. He ended his life by refusing to take food.

[4] Chrysippus was a disciple of Zeno, and, after Cleanthes, the chief of the Stoic sect. According to some accounts, he died from an excessive draught of wine; according to others, from excessive laughter.

[5] Zeno, the chief of the Stoic sect. He is said to have died from suffocation.

[6] Empedocles was a philosopher and poet. There are various accounts of his death; that mentioned in the text is usually received.

ostentation. For Democritus[1] was of another persuasion. But, however,

"By his own spontaneous act he offered up his head to death;"[2]

and nothing can be more wicked than this. For if a homicide is guilty because he is a destroyer of man, he who puts himself to death is under the same guilt, because he puts to death a man. Yea, that crime may be considered to be greater, the punishment of which belongs to God alone. For as we did not come into this life of our own accord; so, on the other hand, we can only withdraw from this habitation of the body which has been appointed for us to keep, by the command of Him who placed us in this body that we may inhabit it, until He orders us to depart from it; and if any violence is offered to us, we must endure it with equanimity, since the death of an innocent person cannot be unavenged, and since we have a great Judge who alone always has the power of taking vengeance in His hands.

All these philosophers, therefore, were homicides; and Cato himself, the chief of Roman wisdom, who, before he put himself to death, is said to have read through the treatise of Plato which he wrote on the immortality of the soul, and was led by the authority of the philosopher to the commission of this great crime; yet he, however, appears to have had some cause for death in his hatred of slavery. Why should I speak of the Ambraciot,[3] who, having read the same treatise, threw himself into the sea, for no other cause than that he believed Plato?—a doctrine altogether detestable and to be avoided, if it drives men from life. But if Plato had known and taught by whom, and how, and to whom, and on account of what actions, and at what time, immortality is given, he would neither have driven Cleombrotus nor Cato to a voluntary death, but he would have trained them to live with justice. For it appears to me that Cato sought a cause for death, not so much that he might escape from Cæsar, as that he might obey the decrees of the Stoics, whom he followed, and might make his name distinguished by some great action; and I do not see what evil could have happened to him if he had lived. For Caius Cæsar, such was his clemency, had no other object, even in the very heat of civil war, than to appear to deserve well of the state, by preserving two excellent citizens, Cicero and Cato. But let us return to those who praise death as a benefit. You complain of life as though you had lived, or had ever settled with yourself why you were born at all. May not therefore the true and common Father of all justly find fault with that saying of Terence:[4]—

"First, learn in what life consists; then, if you shall be dissatisfied with life, have recourse to death."

You are indignant that you are exposed to evils; as though you deserved anything good, who are ignorant of your Father, Lord, and King; who, although you behold with your eyes the bright light, are nevertheless blind in mind, and lie in the depths of the darkness of ignorance. And this ignorance has caused that some have not been ashamed to say, that we are born for this cause, that we may suffer the punishment of our crimes; but I do not see what can be more senseless than this. For where or what crimes could we have committed when we did not even exist? Unless we shall happen to believe that foolish old man,[5] who falsely said that *he had lived before, and* that in his former life he had been Euphorbus. He, I believe, because he was born of an ignoble race, chose for himself a family from the poems of Homer. O wonderful and remarkable memory of Pythagoras! O miserable forgetfulness on the part of us all, since we know not who we were in our former life! But perhaps it was caused by some error, or favour, that he alone did not touch the abyss of Lethe, or taste the water of oblivion; doubtless the trifling old man (as is wont to be the case with old women who are free from occupation) invented fables as it were for credulous infants. But if he had thought well of those to whom he spoke these things; if he had considered them to be men, he would never have claimed to himself the liberty of uttering such perverse falsehoods. But the folly of this most trifling man is deserving of ridicule. What shall we do in the case of Cicero, who, having said in the beginning of his *Consolation* that men were born for the sake of atoning for their crimes, afterwards repeated the assertion, as though rebuking him who does not imagine that life is a punishment? He was right, therefore, in saying beforehand that he was held by error and wretched ignorance of the truth.

CHAP. XIX.—CICERO AND OTHERS OF THE WISEST MEN TEACH THE IMMORTALITY OF THE SOUL, BUT IN AN UNBELIEVING MANNER; AND THAT A GOOD OR AN EVIL DEATH MUST BE WEIGHED FROM THE PREVIOUS LIFE.

But those who assert the advantage of death, because they know nothing of the truth, thus reason: If there is nothing after death, death is

[1] There are various accounts respecting the death of Democritus.
[2] Lucretius, iii. 1041.
[3] Cleombrotus of Ambracia.
[4] *Heautontim.*, v. 2. 18. This advice is given to a young man, who, not knowing the value of life, is prepared rashly to throw it away in consequence of some check to his plans.
[5] Pythagoras taught the doctrine of the transmigration of souls, and affirmed that he had lived already as Euphorbus, one of the heroes of Troy, who was slain by Menelaus in the Trojan war. Lactantius again refers to this subject, book vii. ch. 23, *infra*.

not an evil; for it takes away the perception of evil. But if the soul survives, death is even an advantage; because immortality follows. And this sentiment is thus set forth by Cicero concerning the Laws:[1] "We may congratulate ourselves, since death is about to bring either a better state than that which exists in life, or at any rate not a worse. For if the soul is in a state of vigour without the body, it is a divine life; and if it is without perception, assuredly there is no evil." Cleverly argued, as it appeared to himself, as though there could be no other state. But each conclusion is false. For the sacred writings[2] teach that the soul is not annihilated; but that it is either rewarded according to its righteousness, or eternally punished according to its crimes. For neither is it right, that he who has lived a life of wickedness in prosperity should escape the punishment which he deserves; nor that he who has been wretched on account of his righteousness, should be deprived of his reward. And this is so true, that Tully also, in his *Consolation*, declared that the righteous and the wicked do not inhabit the same abodes. For those same wise men, he says, did not judge that the same course was open for all into the heaven; for they taught that those who were contaminated by vices and crimes were thrust down into darkness, and lay in the mire; but that, on the other hand, souls that were chaste, pure, upright, and uncontaminated, being also refined by the study and practice of virtue, by a light and easy course take their flight to the gods, that is, to a nature resembling their own. But this sentiment is opposed to the former argument. For that is based on the assumption that every man at his birth is presented with immortality. What distinction, therefore, will there be between virtue and guilt, if it makes no difference whether a man be Aristides or Phalaris, whether he be Cato or Catiline? But a man does not perceive this opposition between sentiments and actions, unless he is in possession of the truth. If any one, therefore, should ask me whether death is a good or an evil, I shall reply that its character depends upon the course of the life. For as life itself is a good if it is passed virtuously, but an evil if it is spent viciously, so also death is to be weighed in accordance with the past actions of life. And so it comes to pass, that if life has been passed in the service of God, death is not an evil, for it is a translation to immortality. But if not so, death must necessarily be an evil, since it transfers men, as I have said, to everlasting punishment.[3]

What, then, shall we say, but that they are in error who either desire death as a good, or flee from life as an evil? unless they are most unjust, who do not weigh the fewer evils against the greater number of blessings. For when they pass all their lives in a variety of the choicest gratifications, if any bitterness has chanced to succeed to these, they desire to die; and they so regard it as to appear never to have fared well, if at any time they happen to fare ill. Therefore they condemn the whole of life, and consider it as nothing else than filled with evils. Hence arose that foolish sentiment, that this state which we imagine to be life is death, and that that which we fear as death is life; and so that the first good is not to be born, that the second is an early death. And that this sentiment may be of greater weight, it is attributed to Silenus.[4] Cicero in his *Consolation* says: "Not to be born is by far the best thing, and not to fall upon these rocks of life. But the next thing is, if you have been born, to die as soon as possible, and to flee from the violence of fortune as from a conflagration." That he believed this most foolish expression appears from this, that he added something of his own for its embellishment. I ask, therefore, for whom he thinks it best not to be born, when there is no one at all who has any perception; for it is the perception which causes anything to be good or bad. In the next place, why did he regard the whole of life as nothing else than rocks, and a conflagration; as though it were either in our power not to be born, or life were given to us by fortune, and not by God, or as though the course of life appeared to bear any resemblance to a conflagration?

The saying of Plato is not dissimilar, that he gave thanks to nature, first that he was born a human being rather than a dumb animal; in the next place, that he was a man rather than a woman; that he was a Greek rather than a barbarian;[5] lastly, that he was an Athenian, and that he was born in the time of Socrates. It is impossible to say what great blindness and errors are produced by ignorance of the truth. I would altogether contend that nothing in the affairs of men was ever spoken more foolishly. As though, if he had been born a barbarian, or a woman, or, in fine, an ass, he would be the same Plato, and not that very being which had been produced. But he evidently believed Pythagoras, who, in order that he might prevent men from feeding on animals, said that souls passed from the bodies of men to the bodies of other animals; which is both foolish and impossible. It is foolish, because it was unnecessary to introduce souls that have long existed into new bod-

[1] This passage is not contained in Cicero's treatise on the Laws, but the substance of it is in the *Tusculan Questions*.

[2] See Dan. xii.; Matt. iii., xiii., xxv.; John xii.

[3] [See vol. iii. p. 231, and same treatise *sparsim*.]

[4] Silenus was the constant companion of Dionysus. He was regarded as an inspired prophet, who knew all the past and the most distant future, and as a sage who despised all the gifts of fortune.

[5] The Greeks included all nations, except themselves, under the general name of barbarians.

ies, when the same Artificer who at one time had made the first, was always able to make fresh ones; it is impossible, because the soul endued with right reason can no more change the nature of its condition, than fire can rush downwards, or, like a river, pour its flame obliquely.[1] The wise man therefore imagined, that it might come to pass that the soul which was then in Plato might be shut up in some other animal, and might be endued with the sensibility of a man, so as to understand and grieve that it was burthened with an incongruous body. How much more rationally would he have acted, if he had said that he gave thanks because he was born with a good capacity, and capable of receiving instruction, and that he was possessed of those resources which enabled him to receive a liberal education! For what benefit was it that he was born at Athens? Have not many men of distinguished talent and learning lived in other cities, who were better individually than all the Athenians? How many thousands must we believe that there were, who, though born at Athens, and in the times of Socrates, were nevertheless unlearned and foolish? For it is not the walls or the place in which any one was born that can invest a man with wisdom. Of what avail was it to congratulate himself that he was born in the times of Socrates? Was Socrates able to supply talent to learners? It did not occur to Plato that Alcibiades also, and Critias, were constant hearers of the same Socrates, the one of whom was the most active enemy of his country, the other the most cruel of all tyrants.

CHAP. XX. — SOCRATES HAD MORE KNOWLEDGE IN PHILOSOPHY THAN OTHER MEN, ALTHOUGH IN MANY THINGS HE ACTED FOOLISHLY.

Let us now see what there was so great in Socrates himself, that a wise man deservedly gave thanks that he was born in his times. I do not deny that he was a little more sagacious than the others who thought that the nature of things could be comprehended by the mind. And in this I judge that they were not only senseless, but also impious; because they wished to send their inquisitive eyes into the secrets of that heavenly providence. We know that there are at Rome, and in many cities, certain sacred things which it is considered impious for men to look upon. Therefore they who are not permitted to pollute those objects abstain from looking upon them; and if by error or some accident a man has happened to see them, his guilt is expiated first by his punishment, and afterwards by a repetition of sacrifice. What can you do in the case of those who wish to pry into unpermitted things? Truly they are much more wicked who seek to profane the secrets of the world and this heavenly temple with impious disputations, than those who entered the temple of Vesta, or the Good Goddess, or Ceres. And these shrines, though it is not lawful for men to approach them, were yet constructed by men. But these men not only escape the charge of impiety, but, that which is much more unbecoming, they gain the fame of eloquence and the glory of talent. What if they were able to investigate anything? For they are as foolish in asserting as they are wicked in searching out; since they are neither able to find out anything, nor, even if they had found out anything, to defend it. For if even by chance they have seen the truth — a thing which often happens — they so act that it is refuted by others as false. For no one descends from heaven to pass sentence on the opinions of individuals; wherefore no one can doubt that those who seek after these things are foolish, senseless, and insane.

Socrates therefore had something of human wisdom,[2] who, when he understood that these things could not possibly be ascertained, removed himself from questions of this kind; but I fear that he so acted in this alone. For many of his actions are not only undeserving of praise, but also most deserving of censure, in which things he most resembled those of his own class. Out of these I will select one which may be judged of by all. Socrates used this well-known proverb: "That which is above us is nothing to us." Let us therefore fall down upon the earth, and use as feet those hands which have been given us for the production of excellent works. The heaven is nothing to us, to the contemplation of which we have been raised;[3] in fine, the light itself can have no reference to us; undoubtedly the cause of our sustenance is from heaven. But if he perceived this, that we ought not to discuss the nature of heavenly things, he was unable even to comprehend the nature of those things which he had beneath his feet. What then? did he err in his words? It is not probable; but he undoubtedly meant that which he said, that we are not to devote ourselves to religion; but if he were openly to say this, no one would suffer it.

For who cannot perceive that this world, completed with such wonderful method, is governed by some providence, since there is nothing which can exist without some one to direct it? Thus, a house deserted by its inhabitant falls to decay; a ship without a pilot goes to the bottom; and a body abandoned by the soul wastes away. Much less can we suppose that so great a fabric could either have been constructed without an

[1] In transversum, "crosswise or transversely."

[2] Lactantius here uses cor, "the heart," for wisdom, regarding the heart as the seat of wisdom.

[3] The allusion is to the upright figure of man, as opposed to the other animals, which look down upon the earth, whereas man looks upward. [Our author is partial to this idea. See p. 41, *supra*.]

Artificer, or have existed so long without a Ruler. But if he wished to overthrow those public superstitions, I do not disapprove of this; yea, I shall rather praise it, if he shall have found anything better *to take their place*. But the same man swore[1] by a dog and a goose. Oh buffoon (as Zeno the Epicurean[2] says), senseless, abandoned, desperate man, if he wished to scoff at religion; madman, if he did this seriously, so as to esteem a most base animal as God! For who can dare to find fault with the superstitions of the Egyptians, when Socrates confirmed them at Athens by his authority? But was it not a mark of consummate vanity, that before his death he asked his friends to sacrifice for him a cock which he had vowed to Æsculapius? He evidently feared lest he should be put upon his trial before Rhadamanthus, the judge, by Æsculapius on account of the vow. I should consider him most mad if he had died under the influence of disease. But since he did this in his sound mind, he who thinks that he was wise is himself of unsound mind. Behold one in whose times the wise man congratulates himself as having been born!

CHAP. XXI. — OF THE SYSTEM OF PLATO, WHICH WOULD LEAD TO THE OVERTHROW OF STATES.

Let us, however, see what it was that he learned from Socrates, who, having entirely rejected natural philosophy, betook himself to inquiries about virtue and duty. And thus I do not doubt that he instructed his hearers in the precepts of justice. Therefore, under the teaching of Socrates, it did not escape the notice of Plato, that the force of justice consists in equality, since all are born in an equal condition. Therefore (he says) they must have nothing private or their own; but that they may be equal, as the method of justice requires, they must possess all things in common. This is capable of being endured, as long as it appears to be spoken of money. But how impossible and how unjust this is, I could show by many things. Let us, however, admit its possibility. For grant that all are wise, and despise money. To what, then, did that community lead him? Marriages also, he says, ought to be in common; so that many men may flock together like dogs to the same woman, and he who shall be superior in strength may succeed in obtaining her; or if they are patient as philosophers, they may await their turns, as in a brothel. Oh the wonderful equality of Plato! Where, then, is the virtue of chastity? where conjugal fidelity? And if you take away these, all justice is taken away. But he also says that states would be prosperous, if either philosophers were their kings, or their kings were philosophers. But if you were to give the sovereignty to this man of such justice and equity, who had deprived some of their own property, and given to some the property of others, he would prostitute the modesty of women; a thing which was never done, I do not say by a king, but not even by a tyrant.

But what motive did he advance for this most degrading advice? The state will be in harmony, and bound together with the bonds of mutual love, if all shall be the husbands, and fathers, and wives, and children of all. What a confusion of the human race is this? How is it possible for affection to be preserved where there is nothing certain to be loved? What man will love a woman, or what woman a man, unless they shall always have lived together, — unless devotedness of mind, and faith mutually preserved, shall have made their love indivisible? But this virtue has no place in that promiscuous pleasure. Moreover, if all are the children of all, who will be able to love children as his own, when he is either ignorant or in doubt whether they are his own? Who will bestow honour upon any one as a father, when he does not know from whom he was born? From which it comes to pass, that he not only esteems a stranger as a father, but also a father as a stranger. Why should I say that it is possible for a wife to be common, but impossible for a son, who cannot be conceived except from one? The community, therefore, is lost to him alone, nature herself crying out against it. It remains that it is only for the sake of concord that he would have a community of wives. But there is no more vehement cause of discords, than the desire of one woman by many men. And in this Plato might have been admonished, if not by reason, yet certainly by example, both of the dumb animals, which fight most vehemently on this account, and of men, who have always carried on most severe wars with one another on account of this matter.

CHAP. XXII. — OF THE PRECEPTS OF PLATO, AND CENSURES OF THE SAME.

It remains that the community of which we have spoken admits of nothing else but adulteries and lusts, for the utter extinction of which virtue is especially necessary. Therefore he did not find the concord which he sought, because he did not see whence it arises. For justice has no weight in outward circumstances, not even in the body,[3] but it is altogether employed on the mind of man. He, therefore, who wishes to

[1] This oath is mentioned by Athenæus. Tertullian makes an excuse for it, as though it were done in mockery of the gods. Socrates was called the Athenian buffoon, because he taught many things in a jesting manner.

[2] To be distinguished from Zeno of Citium, the Stoic, and also from Zeno of Elea.

[3] The Stoics not only regarded accidental things, but also our bodies themselves, as being without us.

place men on an equality, ought not to take away marriage and wealth, but arrogance, pride, and haughtiness, that those who are powerful and lifted up on high may know that they are on a level even with the most needy. For insolence and injustice being taken from the rich, it will make no difference whether some are rich and others poor, since they will be equal in spirit, and nothing but reverence towards God can produce this result. He thought, therefore, that he had found justice, whereas he had altogether removed it, because it ought not to be a community of perishable things, but of minds. For if justice is the mother[1] of all virtues, when they are severally taken away, it is also itself overthrown. But Plato took away above all things frugality, which has no existence when there is no property of one's own which can be possessed; he took away abstinence, since there will be nothing belonging to another from which one can abstain; he took away temperance and chastity, which are the greatest virtues in each sex; he took away self-respect, shame, and modesty, if those things which are accustomed to be judged base and disgraceful begin to be accounted honourable and lawful. Thus, while he wishes to confer virtue upon all, he takes it away from all. For the ownership of property contains the material both of vices and of virtues, but a community of goods contains nothing else than the licentiousness of vices. For men who have many mistresses can be called nothing else than luxurious and prodigal. And likewise women who are in the possession of many men, must of necessity be not adulteresses, because they have no fixed marriage, but prostitutes and harlots. Therefore he reduced human life, I do not say to the likeness of dumb animals, but of the herds and brutes. For almost all the birds contract marriages, and are united in pairs, and defend their nests, as though their marriage-beds, with harmonious mind, and cherish their own young, because they are well known to them; and if you put others in their way, they repel them. But this wise man, contrary to the custom of men, and contrary to nature, chose more foolish objects of imitation; and since he saw that the duties of males and females were not separated in the case of other animals, he thought that women also ought to engage in warfare, and take a share in the public counsels, and undertake magistracies, and assume commands. And therefore he assigned to them horses and arms: it follows that he should have assigned to men wool and the loom, and the carrying of infants. Nor did he see the impossibility of what he said, from the fact that no nation has existed in the world so foolish or so vain as to live in this manner.[2]

[1] Justice comprises within herself all the virtues. And thus Aristotle calls her the mother of the other virtues, because she cherishes as it were in her bosom all the rest.

CHAP. XXIII. — OF THE ERRORS OF CERTAIN PHILOSOPHERS, AND OF THE SUN AND MOON.

Since, therefore, the leading men among the philosophers are themselves discovered to be of such emptiness, what shall we think of those lesser[3] ones, who are accustomed never to appear to themselves so wise, as when they boast of their contempt of money? Brave spirit! But I wait to see their conduct, and what are the results of that contempt. They avoid as an evil, and abandon the property handed down to them from their parents. And lest they should suffer shipwreck in a storm, they plunge headlong of their own accord in a calm, being resolute not by virtue, but by perverse fear; as those who, through fear of being slain by the enemy, slay themselves, that by death they may avoid death. So these men, without honour and without influence, throw away the means by which they might have acquired the glory of liberality. Democritus is praised because he abandoned his fields, and suffered them to become public pastures. I should approve of it, if he had given them. But nothing is done wisely which is useless and evil if it is done by all. But this negligence is tolerable. What shall I say of him who changed his possessions into money, which he threw into the sea? I doubt whether he was in his senses, or deranged. Away, he says, ye evil desires, into the deep. I will cast you away, lest I myself should be cast away by you. If you have so great a contempt for money, employ it in acts of kindness and humanity, bestow it upon the poor; this, which you are about to throw away, may be a succour to many, so that they may not die through famine, or thirst, or nakedness. Imitate at least the madness and fury of Tuditanus;[4] scatter abroad your property to be seized by the people. You have it in your power both to escape the possession of money, and yet to lay it out to advantage; for whatever has been profitable to many is securely laid out.

But who approves of the equality of faults as laid down by Zeno? But let us omit that which is always received with derision by all. This is sufficient to prove the error of this madman, that he places pity among vices and diseases. He deprives us of an affection, which involves almost the whole course of human life. For since the nature of man is more feeble than that of the other animals, which divine provi-

[2] [This caustic review of Plato is painfully just. Alas! that such *opprobria* should be incapable of reply.]

[3] That is, philosophers of less repute and fame.

[4] Cicero speaks of Tuditanus as scattering money from the rostrum among the people.

dence has armed with natural means of protection,[1] either to endure the severity of the seasons or to ward off attacks from their bodies, because none of these things has been given to man, he has received in the place of all these things the affection of pity, which is truly called humanity, by which we might mutually protect each other. For if a man were rendered savage by the sight of another man, which we see happen in the case of those animals which are of a solitary[2] nature, there would be no society among men, no care or system in the building of cities; and thus life would not even be safe, since the weakness of men would both be exposed to the attacks of the other animals, and they would rage among themselves after the manner of wild beasts. Nor is his madness less in other things.

For what can be said respecting him who asserted that snow was black? How naturally it followed, that he should also assert that pitch was white! This is he who said that he was born for this purpose, that he might behold the heaven and the sun, who beheld nothing on the earth when the sun was shining. Xenophanes most foolishly believed mathematicians who said that the orb of the moon was eighteen times larger than the earth; and, as was consistent with this folly, he said that within the concave surface of the moon there was another earth, and that there another race of men live in a similar manner to that in which we live on this earth. Therefore these lunatics have another moon, to hold forth to them a light by night, as this does to us. And perhaps this globe of ours may be a moon to another earth below this.[3] Seneca says that there was one among the Stoics who used to deliberate whether he should assign to the sun also its own inhabitants; he acted foolishly in doubting. For what injury would he have inflicted if he had assigned them? But I believe the heat deterred him, so as not to imperil so great a multitude; lest, if they should perish through excessive heat, so great a calamity should be said to have happened by his fault.

CHAP. XXIV. — OF THE ANTIPODES, THE HEAVEN, AND THE STARS.

How is it with those who imagine that there are antipodes[4] opposite to our footsteps? Do they say anything to the purpose? Or is there any one so senseless as to believe that there are men whose footsteps are higher than their heads? or that the things which with us are in a recumbent position, with them hang in an inverted direction? that the crops and trees grow downwards? that the rains, and snow, and hail fall upwards to the earth? And does any one wonder that hanging gardens[5] are mentioned among the seven wonders of the world, when philosophers make hanging fields, and seas, and cities, and mountains? The origin of this error must also be set forth by us. For they are always deceived in the same manner. For when they have assumed anything false in the commencement of their investigations, led by the resemblance of the truth, they necessarily fall into those things which are its consequences. Thus they fall into many ridiculous things; because those things which are in agreement with false things, must themselves be false. But since they placed confidence in the first, they do not consider the character of those things which follow, but defend them in every way; whereas they ought to judge from those which follow, whether the first are true or false.

What course of argument, therefore, led them to the idea of the antipodes? They saw the courses of the stars travelling towards the west; they saw that the sun and the moon always set towards the same quarter, and rise from the same. But since they did not perceive what contrivance regulated their courses, nor how they returned from the west to the east, but supposed that the heaven itself sloped downwards in every direction, which appearance it must present on account of its immense breadth, they thought that the world is round like a ball, and they fancied that the heaven revolves in accordance with the motion of the heavenly bodies; and thus that the stars and sun, when they have set, by the very rapidity of the motion of the world[6] are borne back to the east. Therefore they both constructed brazen orbs, as though after the figure of the world, and engraved upon them certain monstrous images, which they said were constellations. It followed, therefore, from this rotundity of the heaven, that the earth was enclosed in the midst of its curved surface. But if this were so, the earth also itself must be like a globe; for that could not possibly be anything but round, which was held enclosed by that which was round. But if the earth also were round, it must necessarily happen that it should present the same appearance to all parts of the heaven; that is, that it should raise aloft mountains, extend plains, and have level seas. And if this were so, that last consequence also followed, that there would be no part of the earth uninhabited by men and the other animals. Thus the rotundity of the earth leads, in addition, to the invention of those suspended antipodes.

---

1 [Anacreon, *Ode* 2. τοῖς ἀνδράσιν φρόνημα.]

2 Animals of a solitary nature, as opposed to those of gregarious habits.

3 [He was nearer truth than he imagined, if the planet Mars may be called below us.]

4 [Vol. v. p. 14.]

5 He alludes to the hanging gardens of Semiramis at Babylon.

6 [*World* here means universe. See vol. ii. p. 136, note 2.]

But if you inquire from those who defend these marvellous fictions, why all things do not fall into that lower part of the heaven, they reply that such is the nature of things, that heavy bodies are borne to the middle, and that they are all joined together towards the middle, as we see spokes in a wheel; but that the bodies which are light, as mist, smoke, and fire, are borne away from the middle, so as to seek the heaven. I am at a loss what to say respecting those who, when they have once erred, consistently persevere in their folly, and defend one vain thing by another; but that I sometimes imagine that they either discuss philosophy for the sake of a jest, or purposely and knowingly undertake to defend falsehoods, as if to exercise or display their talents on false subjects. But I should be able to prove by many arguments that it is impossible for the heaven to be lower than the earth, were it not that this book must now be concluded, and that some things still remain, which are more necessary for the present work. And since it is not the work of a single book to run over the errors of each individually, let it be sufficient to have enumerated a few, from which the nature of the others may be understood.

CHAP. XXV. — OF LEARNING PHILOSOPHY, AND WHAT GREAT QUALIFICATIONS ARE NECESSARY FOR ITS PURSUIT.

We must now speak a few things concerning philosophy in general, that having strengthened our cause we may conclude. That greatest imitator of Plato among our writers thought that philosophy was not for the multitude, because none but learned men could attain to it. "Philosophy," says Cicero,[1] "is contented with a few judges, of its own accord designedly avoiding the multitude." It is not therefore wisdom, if it avoids the concourse of men; since, if wisdom is given to man, it is given to all without any distinction, so that there is no one at all who cannot acquire it. But they so embrace virtue, which is given to the human race, that they alone of all appear to wish to enjoy that which is a public good; being as envious as if they should wish to bind or tear out the eyes of others that they may not see the sun. For what else is it to deny wisdom to men, than to take away from their minds the true and divine light? But if the nature of man is capable of wisdom, it was befitting that both workmen, and country people, and women, and all, in short, who bear the human form, should be taught to be wise; and that the people should be brought together from every language, and condition, and sex, and age. Therefore it is a very strong argument that philosophy neither tends to wisdom, nor is of itself wisdom, that its mystery is only made known by the beard and cloak of the philosophers.[2] The Stoics, moreover, perceived this, who said that philosophy was to be studied both by slaves and women; Epicurus also, who invites those who are altogether unacquainted with letters to philosophy; and Plato also, who wished to compose a state of wise men.

They attempted, indeed, to do that which truth required; but they were unable to proceed beyond words. First, because instruction in many arts is necessary for an application to philosophy. Common learning must be acquired on account of practice in reading, because in so great a variety of subjects it is impossible that all things should be learned by hearing, or retained in the memory. No little attention also must be given to the grammarians, in order that you may know the right method of speaking. That must occupy many years. Nor must there be ignorance of rhetoric, that you may be able to utter and express the things which you have learned. Geometry also, and music, and astronomy, are necessary, because these arts have some connection with philosophy; and the whole of these subjects cannot be learned by women, who must learn within the years of their maturity the duties which are hereafter about to be of service to them for domestic uses; nor by servants, who must live in service during those years especially in which they are able to learn; nor by the poor, or labourers, or rustics, who have to gain their daily support by labour. And on this account Tully says that philosophy is averse from the multitude. But yet Epicurus will receive the ignorant.[3] How, then, will they understand those things which are said respecting the first principles of things, the perplexities and intricacies of which are scarcely attained to by men of cultivated minds?

Therefore, in subjects which are involved in obscurity, and confused by a variety of intellects, and set off by the studied language of eloquent men, what place is there for the unskilful and ignorant? Lastly, they never taught any women to study philosophy, except Themiste[4] only, within the whole memory of man; nor slaves, except Phædo[5] only, who is said, when living in oppressive slavery, to have been ransomed and taught by Cebes. They also enumerate Plato and Diogenes: these, however, were not slaves, though they had fallen into servitude, for they

[1] *Tusc.*, ii. 1.

[2] A long beard and cloak were the badges of the philosophers. [See vol. ii. p. 321, note 9.]

[3] [Platonic philosophy being addressed to the mind, and the Epicurean to lusts and passions.]

[4] Themiste is said to have been the wife of Leontius; Epicurus is reported to have written to her. Themistoclea, the sister of Pythagoras, is mentioned as a student of philosophy; besides many other women in different ages.

[5] Plato dedicated to Phædo his treatise on the immortality of the soul: according to other accounts, Phædo was ransomed by Crito or Alcibiades at the suggestion of Socrates.

had been taken captive. A certain Aniceris is said to have ransomed Plato for eight sesterces. And on this account Seneca severely rebuked the ransomer himself, because he set so small value upon Plato. He was a madman, as it seems to me, who was angry with a man because he did not throw away much money; doubtless he ought to have weighed gold as though to ransom the corpse of Hector, or to have insisted upon the payment of more money than the seller demanded. Moreover, they taught none of the barbarians, with the single exception of Anacharsis the Scythian, who never would have dreamed of philosophy had he not previously learned both language and literature.

CHAP. XXVI. — IT IS DIVINE INSTRUCTION ONLY WHICH BESTOWS WISDOM; AND OF WHAT EFFICACY THE LAW OF GOD IS.

That, therefore, which they perceived to be justly required by the demands of nature, but which they were themselves unable to perform, and saw that the philosophers could not effect, is accomplished only by divine instruction; for that only is wisdom. Doubtless they were able to persuade any one who do not even persuade themselves of anything; or they will crush the desires, moderate the anger, and restrain the lusts of any one, when they themselves both yield to vices, and acknowledge that they are overpowered by nature. But what influence is exerted on the souls of men by the precepts of God, because of their simplicity and truth, is shown by daily proofs. Give me a man who is passionate, scurrilous, and unrestrained; with a very few words of God,

"I will render him as gentle as a sheep."[1]

Give me one who is grasping, covetous, and tenacious; I will presently restore him to you liberal, and freely bestowing his money with full hands. Give me a man who is afraid of pain and death; he shall presently despise crosses, and fires, and the bull of Phalaris.[2] Give me one who is lustful, an adulterer, a glutton; you shall presently see him sober, chaste, and temperate. Give me one who is cruel and bloodthirsty: that fury shall presently be changed into true clemency. Give me a man who is unjust, foolish, an evil-doer; forthwith he shall be just, and wise, and innocent: for by one laver[3] all his wickedness shall be taken away. So great is the power of divine wisdom, that, when infused into the breast of man, by one impulse it once for all expels folly, which is the mother of faults, for the effecting of which there is no need of payment, or books, or nightly studies. These results are accomplished gratuitously, easily, and quickly, if only the ears are open and the breast thirsts for wisdom. Let no one fear: we do not sell water, nor offer the sun for a reward. The fountain of God, most abundant and most full, is open to all; and this heavenly light rises for all,[4] as many as have eyes. Did any of the philosophers effect these things, or is he able to effect them if he wishes? For though they spend their lives in the study of philosophy, they are neither able to improve any other person nor themselves (if nature has presented any obstacle). Therefore their wisdom, doing its utmost, does not eradicate, but hide vices. But a few precepts of God so entirely change the whole man, and having put off the old man, render him new, that you would not recognise him as the same.

CHAP. XXVII. — HOW LITTLE THE PRECEPTS OF PHILOSOPHERS CONTRIBUTE TO TRUE WISDOM, WHICH YOU WILL FIND IN RELIGION ONLY.

What, then? Do they enjoin nothing similar? Yes, indeed, many things; and they frequently approach the truth. But those precepts have no weight, because they are human, and are without a greater, that is, that divine authority. No one therefore believes them, because the hearer imagines himself to be a man, just as he is, who enjoins them. Moreover, there is no certainty with them, nothing which proceeds from knowledge. But since all things are done by conjecture, and many differing and various things are brought forward, it is the part of a most foolish man to be willing to obey their precepts, since it is doubted whether they are true or false; and therefore no one obeys them, because no one wishes to labour for an uncertainty. The Stoics say that it is virtue which can alone produce a happy life. Nothing can be said with greater truth. But what if he shall be tormented, or afflicted with pain? Will it be possible for any one to be happy in the hands of the executioners? But truly pain inflicted upon the body is the material of virtue; therefore he is not wretched even in tortures. Epicurus speaks much more strongly. The wise man, he says, is always happy; and even when shut up in the bull of Phalaris he will utter this speech: "It is pleasant, and I do not care for it." Who would not laugh at him? Especially, because a man who is devoted to pleasure took upon himself the character of a man of fortitude, and that to an immoderate degree; for it is impossible that any one should esteem tortures of the body as pleasures, since it is sufficient for discharging the office of virtue that one sustains and endures them. What do you, Stoics, say? What do

[1] Terence, *Adelphi*, iv. 1.
[2] Perillus invented the brazen bull, which the tyrant Phalaris used as an instrument of torture. It was so constructed that the groans of the victims appeared to resemble the bellowing of the bull.
[3] The baptismal font. [i.e., as signifying Zech. xiii. 1.]
[4] See John i. 9.

you, Epicurus? The wise man is happy even when he is tortured. If it is on account of the glory of his endurance, he will not enjoy it, for perchance he will die under the tortures. If it is on account of the recollection of the deed, either he will not perceive it if souls shall perish, or, if he shall perceive it, he will gain nothing from it.

What other advantage is there then in virtue? what happiness of life? Is it that a man may die with equanimity? You present to me the advantage of a single hour, or perhaps moment, for the sake of which it may not be expedient to be worn out by miseries and labours throughout the whole of life. But how much time does death occupy? on the arrival of which it now makes no difference whether you shall have undergone it with equanimity or not. Thus it happens that nothing is sought from virtue but glory. But this is either superfluous and short-lived, or it will not follow from the depraved judgments of men. Therefore there is no fruit from virtue where virtue is subject to death and decay. Therefore they who said these things saw a certain shadow[1] of virtue; they did not see virtue itself. For they had their eyes fixed on the earth, nor did they raise their countenances on high that they might behold her

"Who showed herself from the quarters of heaven."[2]

This is the reason why no one obeys their precepts; inasmuch as they either train men to vices, if they defend pleasure; or if they uphold virtue, they neither threaten sin with any punishment, except that of disgrace only, nor do they promise any reward to virtue, except that of honour and praise only, since they say that virtue is to be sought for its own sake, and not on account of any other object. The wise man therefore is happy under tortures; but when he suffers torture on account of his faith, on account of justice, or on account of God, that endurance of pain will render him most happy. For it is God alone who can honour virtue, the reward of which is immortality alone. And they who do not seek this, nor possess religion, with which eternal life is connected, assuredly do not know the power of virtue, the reward of which they are ignorant; nor look towards heaven, as they themselves imagine that they do, when they inquire into subjects which do not admit of investigation, since there is no other cause for looking towards heaven, unless it be either to undertake religion, or to believe that one's soul is immortal. For if any one understands that God is to be worshipped, or has the hope of immortality set before him, his mind[3] is in heaven; and although he may not behold it with his eyes, yet he does behold it with the eye of his soul. But they who do not take up religion are of the earth, for religion is from heaven; and they who think that the soul perishes together with the body, equally look down towards the earth: for beyond the body, which is earth, they see nothing further, which is immortal. It is therefore of no profit that man is so made, that with upright body he looks towards heaven, unless with mind raised aloft he discerns God, and his thoughts are altogether engaged upon the hope of everlasting life.

[1] A shadow; outline, or resemblance.
[2] Lucretius, i. 65.

CHAP. XXVIII. — OF TRUE RELIGION AND OF NATURE, WHETHER FORTUNE IS A GODDESS, AND OF PHILOSOPHY.

Wherefore there is nothing else in life on which our plan and condition can depend but the knowledge of God who created us, and the religious and pious worship of Him; and since the philosophers have wandered from this, it is plain that they were not wise. They sought wisdom, indeed; but because they did not seek it in a right manner, they sunk down to a greater distance, and fell into such great errors, that they did not even possess common wisdom. For they were not only unwilling to maintain religion, but they even took it away; while, led on by the appearance of false virtue, they endeavour to free the mind from all fear: and this overturning of religion gains the name of nature. For they, either being ignorant by whom the world was made, or wishing to persuade men that nothing was completed by divine intelligence, said that nature was the mother of all things, as though they should say that all things were produced of their own accord: by which word they altogether confess their own ignorance. For nature, apart from divine providence and power, is absolutely nothing. But if they call God nature, what perverseness is it, to use the name of nature rather than of God![4] But if nature is the plan, or necessity, or condition of birth, it is not by itself capable of sensation; but there must necessarily be a divine mind, which by its foresight furnishes the beginning of their existence to all things. Or if nature is heaven and earth, and everything which is created, nature is not God, but the work of God.

By a similar error they believe in the existence of fortune, as a goddess mocking the affairs of men with various casualties, because they know not from what source things good and evil hap-

[3] Thus St. Paul, Col. iii. 2, exhorts us to set our affections on things above, not on things of the earth.
[4] [Quod si Deum *naturam* vocant quæ perversitas est naturam potius quam Deum nominare. Observe this terse maxim of our author. It rebukes the teachers and scientists of our day, who seem afraid to "look through nature up to nature's God," in their barren instruction. They go back to Lucretius, and call it *progress!*]

pen to them. They think that they are brought together to do battle with her; nor do they assign any reason by whom and on what account they are thus matched; but they only boast that they are every moment carrying on a contest for life and death with fortune. Now, as many as have consoled any persons on account of the death and removal of friends, have censured the name of fortune with the most severe accusations; nor is there any disputation of theirs on the subject of virtue, in which fortune is not harassed. M. Tullius, in his *Consolation*, says that he has always fought against fortune, and that she was always overpowered by him when he had valiantly beaten back the attacks of his enemies; that he was not subdued by her even then, when he was driven from his home and deprived of his country; but then, when he lost his dearest daughter, he shamefully confesses that he is overcome by fortune. I yield, he says, and raise my hand.[1] What is more wretched than this man, who thus lies prostrate? He acts foolishly, he says; but it is one who professes that he is wise. What, then, does the assumption of the name imply? What that contempt of things which is laid claim to with magnificent words? What that dress, so different from others? Or why do you give precepts of wisdom at all, if no one has yet been found who is wise? And does any one bear ill-will to us because we deny that philosophers are wise, when they themselves confess that they neither have knowledge nor wisdom? For if at any time they have so failed that they are not even able to feign anything, as their practice is in other cases, then in truth they are reminded of their ignorance; and, as though in madness, they spring up and exclaim that they are blind and foolish. Anaxagoras pronounces that all things are overspread with darkness. Empedocles complains that the paths of the senses are narrow, as though for his reflections he had need of a chariot and four horses. Democritus says that the truth lies sunk in a well so deep that it has no bottom; foolishly, indeed, as he says other things. For the truth is not, as it were, sunk in a well to which it was permitted him to descend, or even to fall, but, as it were, placed on the highest top of a lofty mountain, or in heaven, which is most true. For what reason is there why he should say that it is sunk below rather than that it is raised aloft? unless by chance he preferred to place the mind also in the feet, or in the bottom of the heels, rather than in the breast or in the head.

So widely removed were they from the truth itself, that even the posture of their own body did not admonish them, that the truth must be sought for by them in the highest place.[2] From this despair arose that confession of Socrates, in which he said that he knew nothing but this one thing alone, that he knew nothing. From this flowed the system of the Academy, if that is to be called a system in which ignorance is both learnt and taught. But not even those who claimed for themselves knowledge were able consistently to defend that very thing which they thought that they knew. For since they were not in agreement[3] with one another, through their ignorance of divine things they were so inconsistent and uncertain, and often asserting things contrary to one another, that you are unable to determine and decide what their meaning was. Why therefore should you fight against those men who perish by their own sword? Why should you labour to refute those whom their own speech refutes and presses?[4] Aristotle, says Cicero, accusing the ancient philosophers, declares that they are either most foolish or most vainglorious, since they thought that philosophy was perfected by their talents; but that he saw, because a great addition had been made in a few years, that philosophy would be complete in a short time. What, then, was that time? In what manner, when, or by whom, was philosophy completed? For that which he said, that they were most foolish in supposing that philosophy was made perfect by their talents, is true; but he did not even himself speak with sufficient discretion, who thought that it had either been begun by the ancients, or increased by those who were more recent, or that it would shortly be brought to perfection by those of later times. For that can never be investigated which is not sought by its own way.

CHAP. XXIX. — OF FORTUNE AGAIN, AND VIRTUE.

But let us return to the subject which we laid aside. Fortune, therefore, by itself, is nothing; nor must we so regard it as though it had any perception, since fortune is the sudden and unexpected occurrence of accidents. But philosophers, that they may not sometimes fail to err, wish to be wise in a foolish matter; and say that she is not a goddess, as is generally believed, but a god. Sometimes, however, they call this god nature, sometimes fortune, "because he brings about," says the same Cicero, "many things unexpected by us, on account of our want of intelligence and our ignorance of causes." Since, therefore, they are ignorant of the causes on account of which anything is done, they must also be ignorant of him who does them. The

---

[1] To raise or stretch out the hand was an acknowledgment of defeat.

[2] [See p. 91, note 3, *supra*, and *sparsim* in this work.]

[3] Literally, "their accounts did not square."

[4] Afficit, "presses and harasses." Another reading is affligit, "casts to the ground."

same writer, in a work of great seriousness, in which he was giving to his son precepts of life drawn from philosophy, says, "Who can be ignorant that the power of fortune is great on either side? For both when we meet with a prosperous breeze from her we gain the issues which we desire, and when she has breathed contrary to us we are dashed on the rocks."[1] First of all, he who says that nothing can be known, spoke this as though he himself and all men had knowledge. Then he who endeavours to render doubtful even the things which are plain, thought that this was plain, which ought to have been to him especially doubtful; for to a wise man it is altogether false. Who, he says, knows not? I indeed know not. Let him teach me, if he can, what that power is, what that breeze, and what the contrary breath.

It is disgraceful, therefore, for a man of talent to say that, which if you were to deny it, he would be unable to prove. Lastly, he who says that the assent must be withheld because it is the part of a foolish man rashly to assent to things which are unknown to him, he, I say, altogether believed the opinions of the vulgar and uninstructed, who think that it is fortune which gives to men good and evil things. For they represent her image with the horn of plenty and with a rudder, as though she both gave wealth and had the government of human affairs. And to this opinion Virgil[2] assented, who calls fortune omnipotent; and the historian[3] who says, But assuredly fortune bears sway in everything. What place, then, remains for the other gods? Why is she not said to reign by herself, if she has more power than others; or why is she not alone worshipped, if she has power in all things? Or if she inflicts evils only, let them bring forward some cause why, if she is a goddess, she envies men, and desires their destruction, though she is religiously worshipped by them; why she is more favourable to the wicked and more unfavourable to the good; why she plots, afflicts, deceives, exterminates; who appointed her as the perpetual harasser of the race of men; why, in short, she has obtained so mischievous a power, that she renders all things illustrious or obscure according to her caprice rather than in accordance with the truth. Philosophers, I say, ought rather to have inquired into these things, than rashly to have accused fortune, who is innocent: for although she has some existence, yet no reason can be brought forward by them why she should be as hostile to men as she is supposed to be. Therefore all those speeches in which they rail at the injustice of fortune, and in opposition to fortune arrogantly boast of their own virtues, are nothing else but the ravings of thoughtless levity.

Wherefore let them not envy us, to whom God has revealed the truth: who, as we know that fortune is nothing, so also know that there is a wicked and crafty spirit who is unfriendly to the good, and the enemy of righteousness, who acts in opposition to God; the cause of whose enmity we have explained in the second book.[4] He therefore lays plots against all; but those who are ignorant of God he hinders by error, he overwhelms with folly, he overspreads with darkness, that no one may be able to attain to the knowledge of the divine name, in which alone are contained both wisdom and everlasting life. Those, on the other hand, who know God, he assails with wiles and craft, that he may ensnare them with desire and lust, and when they are corrupted by the blandishments of sin, may impel them to death; or, if he shall have not succeeded by stratagem, he attempts to cast them down by force and violence. For on this account he was not at once thrust down by God to punishment at the original transgression, that by his malice he may exercise man to virtue: for unless this is in constant agitation, unless it is strengthened by continual harassing, it cannot be perfect, inasmuch as virtue is dauntless and unconquered patience in enduring evils. From which it comes to pass that there is no virtue if an adversary is wanting. When, therefore, they perceived the force of this perverse power opposed to virtue, and were ignorant of its name, they invented for themselves the senseless name of fortune; and how far this is removed from wisdom, Juvenal declares in these verses:[5] —

> "No divine power is absent if there is prudence; but we make you a goddess, O Fortune, and place you in heaven."

It was folly, therefore, and error, and blindness, and, as Cicero says,[6] ignorance of facts and causes, which introduced the names of Nature and Fortune. But as they are ignorant of their adversary, so also they do not indeed know virtue, the knowledge of which is derived from the idea of an adversary. And if this is joined with wisdom, or, as they say, is itself also wisdom, they must be ignorant in what subjects it is contained. For no one can possibly be furnished with true arms if he is ignorant of the enemy against whom he must be armed; nor can he overcome his adversary, who in fighting does not attack his real enemy, but a shadow. For he will be overthrown, who, having his at-

[1] Cicero, *De Offic.*, ii. 6. The expressions are borrowed from the figure of a ship at sea.
[2] *Æn.*, viii. 33.
[3] Sallust, *Cat.*, viii.
[4] Chapter xvi.
[5] *Satire* x. 365: Nullum numen abest. Others read, Nullum numen habes. You have no divine power, O Fortune, if there is prudence, etc.
[6] *Acad.*, i. 7. [Let our sophists feel this rebuke of Tully.]

tention fixed on another object, shall not previously have foreseen or guarded against the blow aimed at his vitals.

CHAP. XXX. — THE CONCLUSION OF THE THINGS BEFORE SPOKEN ; AND BY WHAT MEANS WE MUST PASS FROM THE VANITY OF THE PHILOSOPHERS TO TRUE WISDOM, AND THE KNOWLEDGE OF THE TRUE GOD, IN WHICH ALONE ARE VIRTUE AND HAPPINESS.

I have taught, as far as my humble talents permitted, that the philosophers held a course widely deviating from the truth. I perceive, however, how many things I have omitted, because it was not my province to enter into a disputation against philosophers. But it was necessary for me to make a digression to this subject, that I might show that so many and great intellects have expended themselves in vain on false subjects, lest any one by chance being shut out by corrupt superstitions, should wish to betake himself to them as though about to find some certainty. Therefore the only hope, the only safety for man, is placed in this doctrine, which we defend. All the wisdom of man consists in this alone, the knowledge and worship of God: this is our tenet, this our opinion. Therefore with all the power of my voice I testify, I proclaim, I declare: Here, here is that which all philosophers have sought throughout their whole life; and yet, they have not been able to investigate, to grasp, and to attain to it, because they either retained a religion which was corrupt, or took it away altogether. Let them therefore all depart, who do not instruct human life, but throw it into confusion. For what do they teach? or whom do they instruct, who have not yet instructed themselves? whom are the sick able to heal, whom can the blind guide? Let us all, therefore, who have any regard for wisdom, betake ourselves to this subject. Or shall we wait until Socrates knows something? or Anaxagoras finds light in the darkness? or until Democritus draws forth truth from the well? or Empedocles extends the paths of his soul? or until Arcesilas and Carneades see, and feel, and perceive?

Lo, a voice from heaven teaching the truth, and displaying to us a light brighter than the sun itself.[1] Why are we unjust to ourselves, and delay to take up wisdom, which learned men, though they wasted their lives in its pursuit, were never able to discover. Let him who wishes to be wise and happy hear the voice of God, learn righteousness, understand the mystery of his birth, despise human affairs, embrace divine things, that he may gain that chief good to which he was born. Having overthrown all false religions, and having refuted all the arguments, as many as it was customary or possible to bring forward in their defence; then, having proved the systems of philosophy to be false, we must now come to true religion and wisdom, since, as I shall teach, they are both connected together; that we may maintain it either by arguments, or by examples, or by competent witnesses, and may show that the folly with which those worshippers of gods do not cease to upbraid us, has no existence with us, but lies altogether with them. And although, in the former books, when I was contending against false religions, and in this, when I was overthrowing false wisdom, I showed where the truth is, yet the next book will more plainly indicate what is true religion and what true wisdom.

1 [A noble utterance from Christian philosophy, now first gaining the ear and heart of humanity.]

THE DIVINE INSTITUTES

BOOK IV.

OF TRUE WISDOM AND RELIGION.

CHAP. I.—OF THE FORMER RELIGION OF MEN, AND HOW ERROR WAS SPREAD OVER EVERY AGE, AND OF THE SEVEN WISE MEN OF GREECE.

WHEN I reflect, O Emperor Constantine, and often revolve in my mind the original condition of men, it is accustomed to appear alike wonderful and unworthy that, by the folly of one age embracing various superstitions, and believing in the existence of many gods, they suddenly arrived at such ignorance of themselves, that the truth being taken away from their eyes, the religion of the true God was not observed, nor the condition of human nature, since men did not seek the chief good in heaven, but on earth. And on this account assuredly the happiness of the ancient ages was changed. For, having left God, the parent and founder of all things, men began to worship the senseless works[1] of their own hands. And what were the effects of this corruption, or what evils it introduced, the subject itself sufficiently declares. For, turning away from the chief good, which is blessed and everlasting on this account, because it cannot be seen,[2] or touched, or comprehended, and from the virtues which are in agreement with that good, and which are equally immortal, gliding down to these corrupt and frail gods, and devoting themselves to those things by which the body only is adorned, and nourished, and delighted, they sought eternal death for themselves, together with their gods and goods relating to the body, because all bodies are subject to death. Superstitions of this kind, therefore, were followed by injustice and impiety, as must necessarily be the case. For men ceased to raise their countenances to the heaven; but, their minds being depressed downwards, clung to goods of the earth, as they did to earth-born superstitions. There followed the disagreement of mankind, and fraud, and all wickedness; because, despising eternal and incorruptible goods, which alone ought to be desired by man, they rather chose temporal and short-lived things, and greater trust was placed by men in evil, inasmuch as they preferred vice to virtue, because it had presented itself as nearer at hand.[3]

Thus human life, which in former ages had been occupied with the clearest light, was overspread with gloom and darkness; and in conformity with this depravity, when wisdom was taken away, then at length men began to claim for themselves the name of wise. For at the time when all were wise, no one was called by that name. And would that this name, once common to all the class, though reduced to a few, still retained its power! For those few might perhaps be able, either by talent, or by authority, or by continual exhortations, to free the people from vices and errors. But so entirely had wisdom died out, that it is evident, from the very arrogance of the name, that no one of those who were so called was really wise. And yet, before the discovery of this philosophy, as it is termed, there are said to have been seven,[4] who, because they ventured to inquire into and discuss natural subjects, deserved to be esteemed and called wise men.

O wretched and calamitous age, in which through the whole world there were only seven who were called by the name of men, for no one can justly be called a man unless he is wise! But if all the others besides themselves were foolish, even they themselves were not wise, because no one can be truly wise in the judgment of the foolish. So far were they removed from wisdom, that not even afterwards, when learning increased, and many and great intellects were always intent upon this very subject, could the

---

1 Figmenta. [Rom. i. 21–23.]

2 Thus St. Paul, 1 Cor. ii. 9: "Eye hath not seen, nor ear heard, neither have entered into the heart of man, the things which God hath prepared for them that love Him."

3 In its rewards.

4 The seven wise men were, Thales, Pittacus, Bias, Solon, Cleobulus, Chilo, and Periander. To these some add Anacharsis the Scythian. [Vol. v. p. 11, *supra*. For Thales, vol. ii. p. 140.]

truth be perceived and ascertained. For, after the renown of those seven wise men, it is incredible with how great a desire of inquiring into the truth all Greece was inflamed. And first of all, they thought[1] the very name of wisdom arrogant, and did not call themselves wise men, but desirous of wisdom. By which deed they both condemned those who had rashly arrogated to themselves the name of wise men, of error and folly, and themselves also of ignorance, which indeed they did not deny. For wherever the nature of the subject had, as it were, laid its hands upon their minds, so that they were unable to give any account, they were accustomed to testify that they knew nothing, and discerned nothing. Wherefore they are found to be much wiser, who in some degree saw themselves, than those who had believed that they were wise.

CHAP. II. — WHERE WISDOM IS TO BE FOUND; WHY PYTHAGORAS AND PLATO DID NOT APPROACH THE JEWS.

Wherefore, if they were not wise who were so called, nor those of later times, who did not hesitate to confess their want of wisdom, what remains but that wisdom is to be sought elsewhere, since it has not been found where it was sought. But what can we suppose to have been the reason why it was not found, though sought with the greatest earnestness and labour by so many intellects, and during so many ages, unless it be that philosophers sought for it out of their own limits? And since they traversed and explored all parts, but nowhere found any wisdom, and it must of necessity be somewhere, it is evident that it ought especially to be sought there where the title of folly[2] appears; under the covering of which God hides the treasury of wisdom and truth, lest the secret of His divine work should be exposed to view.[3] Whence I am accustomed to wonder that, when Pythagoras, and after him Plato, inflamed with the love of searching out the truth, had penetrated as far as to the Egyptians, and Magi, and Persians, that they might become acquainted with their religious rites and institutions (for they suspected that wisdom was concerned with religion), they did not approach the Jews only, in whose possession alone it then was, and to whom they might have gone more easily. But I think that they were turned away from them by divine providence, that they might not know the truth, because it was not yet permitted for the religion of the true God and righteousness to become known to men of other nations.[4] For God had determined, as the last time drew near,[5] to send from heaven a great leader,[6] who should reveal to foreign nations that which was taken away from a perfidious[7] and ungrateful people. And I will endeavour to discuss the subject in this book, if I shall first have shown that wisdom is so closely united with religion, that the one cannot be separated from the other.

CHAP. III. — WISDOM AND RELIGION CANNOT BE SEPARATED: THE LORD OF NATURE MUST NECESSARILY BE THE FATHER OF EVERY ONE.

The worship of the gods, as I have taught in the former book, does not imply wisdom; not only because it gives up man, who is a divine animal, to earthly and frail things, but because nothing is fixed in it which may avail for the cultivation of the character and the framing of the life; nor does it contain any investigation of the truth, but only the rite of worship, which does not consist in the service of the mind, but in the employment of the body. And therefore that is not to be deemed true religion, because it instructs and improves men by no precepts of righteousness and virtue. Thus philosophy, inasmuch as it does not possess true religion, that is, the highest piety, is not true wisdom. For if the divinity which governs this world supports mankind with incredible beneficence, and cherishes it as with paternal indulgence, wishes truly that gratitude should be paid, and honour given to itself, man cannot preserve his piety if he shall prove ungrateful for the heavenly benefits; and this is certainly not the part of a wise man. Since, therefore, as I have said, philosophy and the religious system of the gods are separated, and far removed from each other; seeing that some are professors of wisdom, through whom it is manifest that there is no approach to the gods, and that others are priests of religion, through whom wisdom is not learned; it is manifest that the one is not true wisdom, and that the other is not true religion. Therefore philosophy was not able to conceive the truth, nor was the religious system of the gods able to give an account of itself, since it is without it. But where wisdom is joined by an inseparable connection with religion, both must necessarily be true; because in our worship we ought to be wise, that is, to know the proper object and mode of worship, and in our wisdom to worship, that is, to complete our knowledge by deed and action.

Where, then, is wisdom joined with religion? There, indeed, where the one God is worshipped, where life and every action is referred to one

1 This was the opinion of Pythagoras. See Book iii. 2.
2 See 1 Cor. i. 20–22.
3 [" Thou art a God that hidest thyself," Isa. xlv. 15. Wisdom must be searched after as hidden treasure.]
4 See Eph. i. 9, 10; Col. i. 26, 27. [This is a mysterious truth: God's election of men and nations has been according to their desire to be enlightened. Christ must be the "Desire of Nations."]
5 The last time is the last dispensation, the time of the new covenant. Heb. i. 2.
6 See Isa. lv. 4: "Behold, I have given Him for a leader and commander to the people."
7 Matt. xxi.

source, and to one supreme authority: in short, the teachers of wisdom are the same, who are also the priests of God.[1] Nor, however, let it affect any one, because it often has happened, and may happen, that some philosopher may undertake a priesthood of the gods; and when this happens, philosophy is not, however, joined with religion; but philosophy will both be unemployed amidst sacred rites, and religion will be unemployed when philosophy shall be treated of. For that system of religious rites is dumb, not only because it relates to gods who are dumb, but also because its observance is by the hand and the fingers, not by the heart and tongue, as is the case with ours, which is true. Therefore religion is contained in wisdom, and wisdom in religion. The one, then, cannot be separated from the other; because wisdom is nothing else but the worship of the true God with just and pious adoration. But that the worship of many gods is not in accordance with nature, may be inferred and conceived even by this argument: that every god who is worshipped by man must, amidst the solemn rites and prayers, be invoked as father, not only for the sake of honour, but also of reason; because he is both more ancient than man, and because he affords life, safety, and sustenance, as a father does. Therefore Jupiter is called father by those who pray to him, as is Saturnus, and Janus, and Liber, and the rest in order; which Lucilius[2] laughs at in the council of the gods: "So that there is none of us who is not called excellent father of the gods; so that father Neptunus, Liber, father Saturnus, Mars, Janus, father Quirinus, are called after one name." But if nature does not permit that one man should have many fathers (for he is produced from one only), therefore the worship of many gods is contrary to nature, and contrary to piety.

One only, therefore, is to be worshipped, who can truly be called Father. He also must of necessity be Lord, because as He has power to indulge, so also has He power to restrain. He is to be called Father on this account, because He bestows upon us many and great things; and Lord on this account, because He has the greatest power of chastising and punishing. But that He who is Father is also Lord, is shown even by reference to civil law.[3] For who will be able to bring up sons, unless he has the power of a lord over them? Nor without reason is he called father of a household,[4] although he only has sons: for it is plain that the name of father embraces also slaves, because "household" follows; and the name of "household" comprises also sons, because the name of "father" precedes: from which it is evident, that the same person is both father of his slaves[5] and lord of his sons. Lastly, the son is set at liberty as if he were a slave; and the liberated slave receives the name[6] of his patron, as if he were a son. But if a man is named father of a household, that it may appear that he is possessed of a double power, because as a father he ought to indulge, and as a lord to restrain, it follows that he who is a son is also a slave, and that he who is a father is also a lord. As, therefore, by the necessity of nature, there cannot be more than one father, so there can only be one lord. For what will the slave do if many lords[7] shall give commands at variance with each other? Therefore the worship of many gods is contrary to reason and to nature, since there cannot be many fathers or lords; but it is necessary to consider the gods both as fathers and lords.

Therefore the truth cannot be held where the same man is subject to many fathers and lords, where the mind, drawn in different directions to many objects, wanders to and fro, hither and thither. Nor can religion have any firmness, when it is without a fixed and settled dwelling-place. Therefore there can be no true worship of many gods; just as that cannot be called matrimony, in which one woman has many husbands, but she will either be called a harlot or an adulteress. For when a woman is destitute of modesty, chastity, and fidelity, she must of necessity be without virtue. Thus also the religious system of the gods is unchaste and unholy, because it is destitute of faith, for that unsettled and uncertain honour has no source or origin.

CHAP. IV. — OF WISDOM LIKEWISE, AND RELIGION, AND OF THE RIGHT OF FATHER AND LORD.

By these things it is evident how closely connected are wisdom and religion. Wisdom relates to sons, and this relation requires love; religion to servants, and this relation requires fear. For as the former are bound to love and honour their father, so are the latter bound to respect and venerate their lord. But with respect to God, who is one only, inasmuch as He sustains the twofold character both of Father and Lord, we are bound both to love Him, inasmuch as we are sons, and to fear Him, inasmuch

1 [Iidem sunt doctores sapientiæ qui et De. sacerdotes.]

2 [The satirist, not Cicero's friend; *Nat. Deor.*, iii.]

3 Fathers in ancient times had the greatest power over their children, so that they had the right of life and death, as masters had over their slaves.

4 Pater familias — a title given to the master of a household, whether he had sons or not; the slaves of a house were called *familia*.

5 It has been judged better to keep the words "slave" and "lord" throughout the passage, for the sake of uniformity of expression, though in some places "servant" and "master" might seem more appropriate.

6 Among the Romans slaves had no *prænomen* or distinguishing name; when a slave was set at liberty, he was allowed to assume the name of his master as a *prænomen*. Thus, in Persius (*Sat.*, v.), "Dama," the liberated slave, becomes "Marcus Dama."

7 Thus the slave in Terence wished to know how many masters he had.

as we are servants.[1] Religion, therefore, cannot be divided from wisdom, nor can wisdom be separated from religion; because it is the same God, who ought to be understood, which is the part of wisdom, and to be honoured, which is the part of religion. But wisdom precedes, religion follows; for the knowledge of God comes first, His worship is the result of knowledge. Thus in the two names there is but one meaning, though it seems to be different in each case. For the one is concerned with the understanding, the other with action. But, however, they resemble two streams flowing from one fountain. But the fountain of wisdom and religion is God; and if these two streams shall turn aside from Him, they must be dried up: for they who are ignorant of Him cannot be wise or religious.

Thus it comes to pass that philosophers, and those who worship *many* gods, either resemble disinherited sons or runaway slaves, because the one do not seek their father, nor the other their master. And as they who are disinherited do not attain to the inheritance of their father, nor runaway slaves impunity, so neither will philosophers receive immortality, which is the inheritance of the heavenly kingdom, that is, the chief good, which they especially seek; nor will the worshippers of gods escape the penalty of everlasting death, which is the punishment of the true Master against those who are deserters[2] of His majesty and name. But that God is Father and also Lord was unknown to both, to the worshippers of the gods as well as to the professors of wisdom themselves: inasmuch as they either thought that nothing at all was to be worshipped; or they approved of false religions; or, although they understood the strength and power of the Supreme God (as Plato, who says that there is one God, Creator of the world, and Marcus Tullius, who acknowledges that man has been produced by the Supreme God in an excellent condition), nevertheless they did not render the worship due to Him as to the supreme Father, which was their befitting and necessary duty. But that the gods cannot be fathers or lords, is declared not only by their multitude, as I have shown above,[3] but also by reason: because it is not reported that man was made by gods, nor is it found that the gods themselves preceded the origin of man, since it appears that there were men on the earth before the birth of Vulcan, and Liber, and Apollo, and Jupiter himself. But the creation of man is not accustomed to be assigned to Saturnus, nor to his father Cœlus.

But if none of those who are worshipped is said to have originally formed and created man, it follows that none of these can be called the father of man, and so none of them can be God. Therefore it is not lawful to worship those by whom man was not produced, for he could not be produced by many. Therefore the one and only God ought to be worshipped, who was before Jupiter, and Saturnus, and Cœlus himself, and the earth. For He must have fashioned man, who, before the creation of man, finished the heaven and the earth. He alone is to be called Father who created us; He alone is to be considered Lord who rules, who has the true and perpetual power of life and death. And he who does not adore Him is a foolish servant, who flees from or does not know his Master; and an undutiful son, who either hates or is ignorant of his true Father.

CHAP. V. — THE ORACLES OF THE PROPHETS MUST BE LOOKED INTO; AND OF THEIR TIMES, AND THE TIMES OF THE JUDGES AND KINGS.

Now, since I have shown that wisdom and religion cannot be separated, it remains that we speak of religion itself, and wisdom. I am aware, indeed, how difficult it is to discuss heavenly subjects; but still the attempt must be ventured, that the truth may be made clear and brought to light, and that many may be freed from error and death, who despise and refuse the truth, while it is concealed under a covering of folly. But before I begin to speak of God and His works, I must first speak a few things concerning the prophets, whose testimony I must now use, which I have refrained from doing in the former books. Above all things, he who desires to comprehend the truth ought not only to apply his mind to understand the utterances of the prophets, but also most diligently to inquire into the times during which each one of them existed, that he may know what future events they predicted, and after how many years their predictions were fulfilled.[4] Nor is there any difficulty in making these computations; for they testified under what king each of them received the inspiration of the Divine Spirit. And many have written and published books respecting the times, making their commencement from the prophet Moses, who lived about seven hundred years before the Trojan war. But he, when he had governed the people for forty years, was succeeded by Joshua, who held the chief place twenty-seven years.

After this they were under the government of judges during *three hundred and seventy* years.

[1] Fear, in the language of the prophets often implies reverence of the divine majesty. Lactantius seems to refer to Mal. i. 6: "A son honoureth his father, and a servant his master: if then I be a father, where is mine honour? and if I be a master, where is my fear?"

[2] Literally, runaways. The reference is, as before, to runaway slaves.

[3] Chap. iii. [p. 103].

[4] [See Pusey's *Daniel*; also *Minor Prophets*.]

Then their condition was changed, and they began to have kings; and when they had ruled during *four hundred and fifty* years, until the reign of Zedekiah, the Jews having been besieged by the king of Babylon, and carried into captivity,[1] endured a long servitude, until, in the seventieth year afterwards, the captive Jews were restored to their own lands and settlements by Cyrus the elder, who attained the supreme power over the Persians, at the time when Tarquinius Superbus reigned at Rome. Wherefore, since the whole series of times may be collected both from the Jewish histories and from those of the Greeks and Romans, the times of the prophets individually may also be collected; the last of whom was Zechariah, and it is agreed on that he prophesied in the time of King Darius, in the second year of his reign, and in the eighth month. Of so much greater antiquity[2] are the prophets found to be than the Greek writers. And I bring forward all these things, that they may perceive their error who endeavour to refute Holy Scripture, as though it were new and recently composed, being ignorant from what fountain the origin of our holy religion flowed. But if any one, having put together and examined the times, shall duly lay the foundation of learning, and fully ascertain the truth, he will also lay aside his error when he has gained the knowledge of the truth.

CHAP. VI. — ALMIGHTY GOD BEGAT HIS SON; AND THE TESTIMONIES OF THE SIBYLS AND OF TRISMEGISTUS CONCERNING HIM.

God, therefore, the contriver and founder of all things, as we have said in the second book, before He commenced this excellent work of the world, begat a pure and incorruptible Spirit, whom He called His Son. And although He had afterwards created by Himself innumerable other beings, whom we call angels, this first-begotten, however, was the only one whom He considered worthy of being called by the divine name, as being powerful in His Father's excellence and majesty. But that there is a Son of the Most High God, who is possessed of the greatest power, is shown not only by the unanimous utterances of the prophets, but also by the declaration of Trismegistus and the predictions of the Sibyls. Hermes, in the book which is entitled *The Perfect Word*, made use of these words: "The Lord and Creator of all things, whom we have thought right to call God, since He made the second God visible and sensible. But I use the term sensible, not because He Himself perceives (for the question is not whether He Himself perceives), but because He leads[3] to perception and to intelligence. Since, therefore, He made Him first, and alone, and one only, He appeared to Him beautiful, and most full of all good things; and He hallowed Him, and altogether loved Him as His own Son." The Erythræan Sibyl, in the beginning of her poem, which she commenced with the Supreme God, proclaims the Son of God as the leader and commander of all, in these verses: —

> "The nourisher and creator of all things, who placed the sweet breath in all, and made God the leader of all."

And again, at the end of the same poem: —

> "But whom God gave for faithful men to honour."

And another Sibyl enjoins that He ought to be known: —

> "Know Him as your God, who is the Son of God."

Assuredly He is the very Son of God, who by that most wise King Solomon, full of divine inspiration, spake these things which we have added:[4] "God founded[5] me in the beginning of His ways, in His work before the ages. He set me up in the beginning, before He made the earth, and before He established the depths, before the fountains of waters came forth: the Lord begat me before all the hills; He made the regions, and the uninhabitable[6] boundaries under the heaven. When He prepared the heaven, I was by Him: and when He separated His own seat, when He made the strong clouds above the winds, and when He strengthened the mountains, and placed them under heaven; when He laid the strong foundations of the earth, I was with Him arranging all things. I was He in whom He delighted: I was daily delighted, when He rejoiced, the world being completed." But on this account Trismegistus spoke of Him as "the artificer of God," and the Sibyl calls Him "Counsellor," because He is endowed by God the Father with such wisdom and strength, that God employed both His wisdom and hands in the creation of the world.

CHAP. VII. — OF THE NAME OF SON, AND WHENCE HE IS CALLED JESUS AND CHRIST.

Some one may perhaps ask who this is who is so powerful, so beloved by God, and what name He has, who was not only begotten at first before the world,[7] but who also arranged it by His

[1] See 2 Kings xxv.: Jer. xxxix. and lii.

[2] The same is asserted by Justin Martyr [vol. i. p. 277], Eusebius, Augustine, and other writers. See Augustine, *De Civitate Dei*, book xviii. 37. Pythagoras, one of the most ancient of the Greek philosophers, was contemporary with the latest prophets.

[3] Literally, "sends." The passage appears to be corrupt; ὑποπίπτει has been suggested instead of ὑποπέμπει, "falls under perception," "is an object of perception."

[4] Prov. viii. 22–31. Lactantius quotes from the Septuagint.

[5] According to the Hebrew, "possessed me in the beginning," and so the authorized version.

[6] Fines inhabitabiles. Other editions read *terras inhabitabiles*, "uninhabitable lands."

[7] Literally, "whose first nativity not only preceded the world." He speaks of the eternal generation of the Son, as distinguished from His incarnation, which he afterwards speaks of as His second nativity. [See vol. vi. p. 7.]

wisdom and constructed it by His might. First of all, it is befitting that we should know that His name is not known even to the angels who dwell in heaven, but to Himself only, and to God the Father; nor will that name be published, as the sacred writings relate, before that the purpose of God shall be fulfilled. In the next place, we must know that this name cannot be uttered by the mouth of man, as Hermes teaches, saying these things: "Now the cause of this cause is the will of the divine good which produced God, whose name cannot be uttered by the mouth of man." And shortly afterwards to His Son: "There is, O Son, a secret word of wisdom, holy respecting the only Lord of all things, and the God first perceived[1] by the mind, to speak of whom is beyond the power of man." But although His name, which the supreme Father gave Him from the beginning, is known to none but Himself, nevertheless He has one name among the angels, and another among men, since He is called Jesus[2] among men: for Christ is not a proper name, but a title of power and dominion; for by this the Jews were accustomed to call their kings. But the meaning of this name must be set forth, on account of the error of the ignorant, who by the change of a letter are accustomed to call Him Chrestus.[3] The Jews had before been directed to compose a sacred oil, with which those who were called to the priesthood[4] or to the kingdom might be anointed. And as now the robe of purple[5] is a sign of the assumption of royal dignity among the Romans, so with them the anointing with the holy oil conferred the title and power of king. But since the ancient Greeks used the word χρίεσθαι to express the art of anointing, which they now express by ἀλείφεσθαι, as the verse of Homer shows,

> "But the attendants washed, and anointed[6] them with oil;"

on this account we call Him Christ, that is, the Anointed, who in Hebrew is called the Messias. Hence in some Greek writings, which are badly translated[7] from the Hebrew, the word *eleimmenos*[8] is found written, from the word *aleiphesthai*,[9] anointing. But, however, by either name a king is signified: not that He has obtained this earthly kingdom, the time for receiving which has not yet arrived, but that He sways a heavenly and eternal kingdom, concerning which we shall speak in the last book. But now let us speak of His first nativity.

CHAP. VIII. — OF THE BIRTH OF JESUS IN THE SPIRIT AND IN THE FLESH: OF SPIRITS AND THE TESTIMONIES OF PROPHETS.

For we especially testify that He was twice born, first in the spirit, and afterwards in the flesh. Whence it is thus spoken by Jeremiah:[10] "Before I formed Thee in the womb I knew Thee." And likewise by the same: "Who was blessed before He was born;"[11] which was the case with no one else but Christ. For though He was the Son of God from the beginning,[12] He was born again[13] a second time[14] according to the flesh: and this twofold birth of His has introduced great terror into the minds of men, and overspread with darkness even those who retained the mysteries of true religion. But we will show this plainly and clearly, that they who love wisdom may be more easily and diligently instructed. He who hears the Son of God mentioned ought not to conceive in his mind so great impiety as to think that God begat Him by marriage and union with a woman, which none does but an animal possessed of a body, and subject to death. But with whom could God unite Himself, since He is alone? or since His power was so great, that He accomplished whatever He wished, assuredly He did not require the co-operation[15] of another for procreation. Unless by chance we shall [profanely] imagine, as Orpheus supposed, that God is both male and female, because otherwise He would have been unable to beget, unless He had the power of each sex, as though He could have intercourse with Himself, or without such intercourse be unable to produce.

But Hermes also was of the same opinion, when he says that He was "His own father," and "His own mother."[16] But if this were so, as He is called by the prophets father, so also He would be called mother. In what manner, then, did He beget Him? First of all, divine operations cannot be known or declared[17] by any one; but nevertheless the sacred writings teach us, in which it is laid down[18] that this Son of God is the speech, or even the reason[19] of God, and also

1 Or, perceiving.

2 Jesus, that is, [Joshua =] Saviour.

3 Suetonius speaks of Christ as Chrestus. The Christians also were called Chrestians, as Tertullian shows in his *Apology*. The word χρηστός has the signification of kind, gentle, good. [Vol. i. p. 163.]

4 Each has reference to Christ, as He is King and Priest. Of the anointing of kings, see 1 Sam., and of priests, Lev. viii. [Of prophets, 1 Kings xix. 16.] The priesthood of Christ is most fully set forth in the Epistle to the Hebrews.

5 Thus Horatius, *Carm.*, i. 35, "Purpurei metuunt tyranni;" and Gray, *Ode to Adversity*, "Purple tyrants vainly groan."

6 χρισαν.

7 Interpretatæ sunt, used here in a passive sense.

8 ἠλειμμένος.

9 ἀλείφεσθαι.

10 Jer. i. 5. It can only be in a secondary sense that this prophecy refers to Christ; in its primary sense it refers to the prophet himself, as the context plainly shows.

11 This passage is not found in Jeremiah, or in the Bible.

12 [See vol. iii. p. 612.]

13 Regeneratus est.

14 Denuo, i.e., de novo, "afresh."

15 Societate alterius. [Profanely arguing to God from man. Humanity has a procreant power of a lower sort; but the ideal is divine, and needs no process like that of man's nature.]

16 αὐτοπάτορα καὶ αὐτομήτορα.

17 Thus Isa. liii. 8: "Who shall declare His generation?"

18 Cautum est.

19 Thus λόγος includes the two senses of word and reason.

that the other angels are spirits[1] of God. For speech is breath sent forth with a voice signifying something. But, however, since breath and speech are sent forth from different parts, inasmuch as breath proceeds from the nostrils, speech from the mouth, the difference between the Son of God and the other angels is great. For they proceeded from God as silent spirits, because they were not created to teach[2] the knowledge of God, but for His service. But though He is Himself also a spirit, yet He proceeded from the mouth of God with voice and sound, as the Word, on this account indeed, because He was about to make use of His voice to the people; that is, because He was about to be a teacher of the knowledge of God, and of the heavenly mystery[3] to be revealed to man: which word also God Himself first spoke, that through Him He might speak to us, and that He might reveal to us the voice and will of God.

With good reason, therefore, is He called the Speech and the Word of God, because God, by a certain incomprehensible energy and power of His majesty, enclosed the vocal spirit proceeding from His mouth, which he had not conceived in the womb, but in His mind, within a form which has life through its own perception and wisdom, and He also fashioned other spirits of His into angels. Our spirits[4] are liable to dissolution, because we are mortal: but the spirits of God both live, and are lasting, and have perception; because He Himself is immortal, and the Giver both of perception[5] and life. Our expressions, although they are mingled with the air, and fade away, yet generally remain comprised in letters; how much more must we believe that the voice of God both remains for ever, and is accompanied with perception and power, which it has derived from God the Father, as a stream from its fountain! But if any one wonders that God could be produced from God by a putting forth of the voice and breath, if he is acquainted with the sacred utterances of the prophets he will cease to wonder. That Solomon and his father David were most powerful kings, and also prophets, may perhaps be known even to those who have not applied themselves to the sacred writings; the one of whom, who reigned subsequently to the other, preceded the destruction of the city of Troy by *one hundred and forty* years. His father, the writer of sacred hymns, thus speaks in the thirty-second Psalm:[6] "By the word of God were the heavens made firm; and all their power[7] by the breath of His mouth." And also again in the forty-fourth Psalm:[8] "My heart hath given utterance to a good word; I speak of my doings towards the king;" testifying, in truth, that the works of God are known to no other than to the Son alone, who is the Word of God, and who must reign for ever. Solomon also shows that it is the Word of God, and no other,[9] by whose hands these works of the world were made. "I," He says, "came forth out of the mouth of the Most High before all creatures: I caused the light that faileth not to arise in the heavens, and covered the whole earth with a cloud. I have dwelt in the height, and my throne is in the pillar of the cloud."[10] John also thus taught: "In the beginning was the Word, and the Word was with God, and the Word was God. The same was in the beginning with God. All things were made by Him, and without Him was not anything made."[11]

CHAP. IX. — OF THE WORD OF GOD.

But the Greeks speak of Him as the *Logos*,[12] more befittingly than we do as the word, or speech: for *Logos* signifies both speech and reason, inasmuch as He is both the voice and the wisdom of God. And of this divine speech not even the philosophers were ignorant, since Zeno represents the *Logos* as the arranger of the established order of things, and the framer of the universe: whom also He calls Fate, and the necessity of things, and God, and the soul of Jupiter, in accordance with the custom, indeed, by which they are wont to regard Jupiter as God. But the words are no obstacle, since the sentiment is in agreement with the truth. For it is the spirit of God which he named the soul of Jupiter. For Trismegistus, who by some means or other searched into almost all truth, often described the excellence and majesty of the word, as the instance before mentioned declares, in which he acknowledges that there is an ineffable and sacred speech, the relation of which exceeds the measure of man's ability. I have spoken briefly, as I have been able, concerning the first nativity. Now I must more fully discuss the second, since this is the subject most controverted, that we may hold forth the light of understanding to those who desire to know the truth.

---

1 There is great difficulty in translating this passage, on account of the double sense of spiritus (as in Greek, πνεῦμα), including "*spirit*" and "breath." It is impossible to express the sense of the whole passage by either word singly. There is the same difficulty with regard to πνεῦμα, as in Heb. i. 7: "He maketh His angels spirits," more correctly "winds." See Delitzsch on Hebrews, and comp. Ps. civ. 4.

2 Ad tradendam.

3 Cœlestis arcani. See Rom. xvi. 25.

4 Lactantius is speaking of the breath: he cannot refer to the soul, which he everywhere speaks of as immortal.

5 Sensus.

6 In our version, Ps. xxxiii. 6.

7 Quoted from the Septuagint version.

8 Ps. xlv. 1. [See vol. i. p. 213.]

9 Ipsum.

10 Ecclus. xxiv. 5-7. This book is attributed to Solomon by many of the Fathers, though it bears the title of the Wisdom of Jesus the son of Sirach.

11 John i. 1-3.

12 λόγος.

CHAP. X. — OF THE ADVENT OF JESUS; OF THE FORTUNES OF THE JEWS, AND THEIR GOVERNMENT, UNTIL THE PASSION OF THE LORD.

In the first place, then, men ought to know that the arrangements of the Most High God have so advanced from the beginning, that it was necessary, as the end of the world[1] approached, that the Son of God should descend to the earth, that He might build a temple for God, and teach righteousness; but, however, not with the might of an angel or with heavenly power, but in the form of man and in the condition of a mortal, that when He had discharged the office of His ministry,[2] He might be delivered into the hands of wicked men, and might undergo death, that, having subdued this also by His might, He might rise again, and bring to man, whose nature He had put on[3] and represented, the hope of overcoming death, and might admit him to the rewards of immortality. And that no one may be ignorant of this arrangement, we will show that all things were foretold which we see fulfilled in Christ. Let no one believe our assertion unless I shall show that the prophets before a long series of ages published that it should come to pass at length that the Son of God should be born as a man, and perform wonderful deeds, and sow[4] the worship of God throughout the whole earth, and at last be crucified, and on the third day rise again. And when I shall have proved all these things by the writings of those very men who treated with violence their God who had assumed a mortal body, what else will prevent it from being manifest that true wisdom is conversant with this religion only? Now the origin of the whole mystery is to be related.

Our ancestors,[5] who were chiefs of the Hebrews, when they were distressed by famine and want, passed over into Egypt, that they might obtain a supply of corn; and sojourning there a long time, they were oppressed with an intolerable yoke of slavery. Then God pitied them, and led them out, and freed them from the hand of the king of the Egyptians, after *four hundred and thirty*[6] years, under the leadership of Moses, through whom the law was afterwards given to them by God; and in this leading out God displayed the power of His majesty. For He made His people to pass through the midst of the Red Sea, His angel[7] going before and dividing the water, so that the people might walk over the dry land, of whom it might more truly be said (as the poet says[8]), that "the wave, closing over him after the appearance of a mountain, stood around him." And when he heard of this, the tyrant of the Egyptians followed with this great host of his men, and rashly entering the sea which still lay open, was destroyed, together with his whole army, by the waves returning[9] to their place. But the Hebrews, when they had entered into the wilderness, saw many wonderful deeds. For when they suffered thirst, a rock having been struck with a rod, a fountain of water sprung forth and refreshed the people. And again, when they were hungry, a shower[10] of heavenly nourishment descended. Moreover, also, the wind[11] brought quails into their camp, so that they were not only satisfied with heavenly bread, but also with more choice banquets. And yet, in return for these divine benefits, they did not pay honour to God; but when slavery had been now removed from them, and their thirst and hunger laid aside, they fell away into luxury, and transferred their minds to the profane rites of the Egyptians. For when Moses, their leader, had ascended into the mountain, and there tarried forty days, they made the head[12] of an ox in gold, which they call Apis,[13] that it might go before them as a standard.[14] With which sin and crime God was offended, and justly visited the impious and ungrateful people with severe punishments, and made them subject to the law[15] which He had given by Moses.

But afterwards, when they had settled in a desert part of Syria, the Hebrews[16] lost their ancient name; and since the leader of their host[17] was Judas, they were called Jews,[18] and the land which they inhabited Judæa. And at

1 The boundary of the age. Thus the Scriptures speak of the end of the world, the last days.

2 Magisterio, "teaching."

3 An expression frequently used by the Fathers to denote the assumption of our nature by Christ.

4 Seminaret, "sow" or "spread." [I have put "sow" into the text, and brought down "spread," for an obvious reason.]

5 The patriarchs. The idea appears to be that Christians from the Gentiles, having succeeded to the privileges of the Jews, are, as it were, their posterity.

6 The duration of the captivity in Egypt was two hundred and fifteen years. The period of four hundred and thirty years is reckoned from the call of Abram out of Ur of the Chaldees to the final departure from Egypt.

7 The Angel of the Covenant, who so often presented Himself to the Hebrews. See Ex. xxiii. 20. [The Jehovah-Angel. Compare Justin, vol. i. pp. 223-226, and others *passim*, this series.]

8 Virgil, *Georg.*, iv. 361. He describes Aristæus as descending to the chamber of his mother Cyrene, in the depths of the river Peneus. The waters separate on each side to make a way for him, and then close over his head.

9 Coeuntibus aquis, "meeting together."

10 See Ps. lxxviii. 24: "He rained down manna upon them to eat."

11 See Num. xi 31.

12 Some of the Fathers think, with Lactantius, that it was the head only, and not the whole figure, of a calf which they made.

13 Apis is the name given by the Egyptians to the calf which they worshipped.

14 In signo.

15 The moral law had been already given to Moses on the mount before the making of the golden calf. The law here referred to may well be taken to express the burthensome routine of the ceremonial law, which Peter (Acts xv. 10) describes as "a yoke which neither their fathers nor they were able to bear." [Our author expresses himself with accuracy: He *subjected* them by the oppresive *ceremonial* law to the *moral* law He had just given.]

16 The Hebrews are said to have derived their name from Heber, the descendant of Noah by Shem; or more probably from Abram the Hebrew, that is, the man who had crossed the river, — a name given to him by the Canaanites. See Gen. xiv. 13.

17 Examinis.

18 There seems to be no authority for this derivation of the name. They were doubtless called Jews from Judah. As those who returned from the captivity at Babylon were principally of the tribe of Judah, though some from the other tribes returned with them, they were called Jews after the captivity.

first, indeed, they were not subject to the dominion of Kings, but civil Judges presided over the people and the law: they were not, however, appointed only for a year, as the Roman consuls, but supported by a perpetual jurisdiction. Then, the name of Judges being taken away, the kingly power was introduced. But during the government of the Judges the people had often undertaken corrupt religious rites; and God, offended by them, as often brought them into bondage to strangers, until again, softened by the repentance of the people, He freed them from bondage. Likewise under the Kings, being oppressed by wars with their neighbours on account of their iniquities, and at last taken captive and led to Babylon, they suffered punishment for their impiety by oppressive slavery, until Cyrus came to the kingdom, who immediately restored the Jews by an edict. Afterwards they had tetrarchs until the time of Herod, who was in the reign of Tiberius Cæsar; in whose fifteenth year, in the consulship of the two Gemini, on the 23d of March,[1] the Jews crucified Christ. This series of events, this order, is contained in the secrets of the sacred writings. But I will first show for what reason Christ came to the earth, that the foundation and the system of divine religion may be manifest.

CHAP. XI. — OF THE CAUSE OF THE INCARNATION OF CHRIST.

When the Jews often resisted wholesome precepts, and departed from the divine law, going astray to the impious worship of false gods, then God filled just and chosen men with the Holy Spirit, appointing them as prophets in the midst of the people, by whom He might rebuke with threatening words the sins of the ungrateful people, and nevertheless exhort them to repent of their wickedness; for unless they did this, and, laying aside their vanities, return to their God, it would come to pass that He would change His covenant,[2] that is, bestow[3] the inheritance of eternal life upon foreign nations, and collect to Himself a more faithful people out of those who were aliens[4] by birth. But they, when rebuked by the prophets, not only rejected their words; but being offended because they were upbraided for their sins, they slew the prophets themselves with studied[5] tortures: all which things are sealed up and preserved in the sacred writings. For the prophet Jeremiah says:[6] "I sent to you my servants the prophets; I sent them before the morning light; but ye did not hearken, nor incline your ears to hear, when I spake unto you: let every one of you turn from his evil way, and from your most corrupt affections; and ye shall dwell in the land which I gave to you and to your fathers for ever.[7] Walk ye not after strange gods, to serve them; and provoke me not to anger with the works of your hands, that I should destroy you." The prophet Ezra[8] also, who was in the times of the same Cyrus by whom the Jews were restored, thus speaks: "They rebelled against Thee, and cast Thy law behind their backs, and slew Thy prophets which testified against them, that they might turn unto Thee."

The prophet Elias also, in the third book of Kings:[9] "I have been very jealous[10] for the Lord God of hosts, because the children of Israel have forsaken Thee, thrown down Thine altars, and slain Thy prophets with the sword; and I only am left, and they seek my life to take it away." On account of these impieties of theirs He cast them off for ever;[11] and so He ceased to send to them prophets. But He commanded His own Son, the first-begotten,[12] the maker of all things, His own counsellor, to descend from heaven, that He might transfer the sacred religion of God to the Gentiles,[13] that is, to those who were ignorant of God, and might teach them righteousness, which the perfidious people had cast aside. And He had long before threatened that He would do this, as the prophet Malachi[14] shows, saying: "I have no pleasure in you, saith the Lord, and I will not accept an offering from your hands; for from the rising of the sun even unto its setting, my name shall be great[15] among the Gentiles." David also in the seventeenth Psalm[16] says: "Thou wilt make me the head of the heathen; a people whom I have not known shall serve me" Isaiah[17] also thus speaks: "I come to gather all nations and tongues; and they shall come and see my glory; and I will send among them a sign, and I will send those that escape of them unto the nations which are afar off, which have not heard my fame; and they shall declare my glory among

1 There appears to be no reasonable doubt that the day on which our Lord suffered was the 14th of Nisan, that is, April 7. See Gresswell's *Dissertations*, vol. iii. p. 168; also Ellicott's *Lectures on the Life of Christ*. [Gresswell is not to be too readily accepted in this. See the learned inquiry of Dr. Jarvis, of whom, vol. ii. p. 477.]

2 Testamentum, properly the solemn declaration of a will.

3 Converteret, "turn to."

4 Alienigenis. Comp. Eph. ii. 12: "Aliens from the commonwealth of Israel, and strangers from the covenants of promise."

5 Exquisitis.

6 Jer. xxv. 4–6.

7 From generation to generation.

8 Neh. ix. 26. The book of Nehemiah is called by the Greek writers the second book of Ezra. The words quoted are spoken by the Levites.

9 1 Kings xix. 10. The 1st and 2d Samuel are in the Septuagint 1st and 2d Kings, and 1st and 2d Kings are 3d and 4th.

10 I have been jealous with jealousy — Æmulando æmulatus sum, — a Hebraism. So Luke xxii. 15; John iii. 29.

11 Fathers were said to disown (abdicare) and cast off degenerate sons.

12 Thus Col. i. 18, "who is the beginning, the first-born from the dead."

13 The nations.

14 Mal. i. 10, 11.

15 In the Septuagint δεδόξασται, "has been glorified."

16 Ps. xviii. 43. The quotation is from the Septuagint, καταστήσεις; our version reads, "Thou hast made me."

17 Isa. lxvi. 18, 19. The quotation is again taken from the Septuagint.

the Gentiles." Therefore, when God wished to send to the earth one who should measure[1] His temple, He was unwilling to send him with heavenly power and glory, that the people who had been ungrateful towards God might be led into the greatest error, and suffer punishment for their crimes, since they had not received their Lord and God, as the prophets had before foretold that it would thus happen. For Isaiah, whom the Jews most cruelly slew, cutting him asunder with a saw,[2] thus speaks:[3] "Hear, O heaven; and give ear, O earth: for the Lord hath spoken, I have begotten sons, and lifted[4] them up on high, and they have rejected me. The ox knoweth his owner, and the ass his master's stall; but Israel hath not known, my people has not understood." Jeremiah also says, in like manner:[5] "The turtle and the swallow hath known her time, and the sparrows of the field have observed[6] the times of their coming: but my people have not known the judgment of the Lord. How do you say, We are wise, and the law of the Lord is with us? The meting out[7] is in vain; the scribes are deceived and confounded: the wise men are dismayed and taken, for they have rejected the word of the Lord."

Therefore (as I had begun to say), when God had determined to send to men a teacher of righteousness, He commanded Him to be born again a second time in the flesh, and to be made in the likeness of man himself, to whom he was about to be a guide, and companion, and teacher. But since God is kind and merciful[8] to His people, He sent Him to those very persons whom He hated,[9] that He might not close the way of salvation against them for ever, but might give them a free opportunity of following God, that they might both gain the reward of life if they should follow Him (which many of them do, and have done), and that they might incur the penalty of death by their fault if they should reject their King. He ordered Him therefore to be born again among them, and of their seed, lest, if He should be born of another nation, they might be able to allege a just excuse from the law for their rejection of Him; and at the same time, that there might be no nation at all under heaven to which the hope of immortality should be denied.

CHAP. XII. — OF THE BIRTH OF JESUS FROM THE VIRGIN; OF HIS LIFE, DEATH, AND RESURRECTION, AND THE TESTIMONIES OF THE PROPHETS RESPECTING THESE THINGS.

Therefore the Holy Spirit of God, descending from heaven, chose the holy Virgin, that He might enter into her womb.[10] But she, being filled by the possession[11] of the Divine Spirit, conceived; and without any intercourse with a man, her virgin womb was suddenly impregned. But if it is known to all that certain animals are accustomed to conceive[12] by the wind and the breeze, why should any one think it wonderful when we say that a virgin was made fruitful by the Spirit of God, to whom whatever He may wish is easy? And this might have appeared incredible, had not the prophets many ages previously foretold its occurrence. Thus Solomon speaks:[13] "The womb of a virgin was strengthened, and conceived; and a virgin was made fruitful, and became a mother in great pity." Likewise the prophet Isaiah,[14] whose words are these: "Therefore God Himself shall give you a sign: Behold, a virgin shall conceive, and bear a son; and ye shall call His name Emmanuel." What can be more manifest than this? This was read by the Jews, who denied Him. If any one thinks that these things are invented by us, let him inquire of them, let him take especially from them: the testimony is sufficiently strong to prove the truth, when it is alleged by enemies themselves. But He was never called Emmanuel, but Jesus, who in Latin is called Saving, or Saviour,[15] because He comes bringing salvation to all nations. But by this name the prophet declared that God incarnate was about to come to men. For Emmanuel signifies God with us; because when He was born of a virgin, men ought to confess that God was with them, that is, on the earth and in mortal flesh. Whence David[16] says in the eighty-fourth Psalm, "Truth has sprung out of the earth;" because God, in whom is truth, hath taken a body of earth, that He might open a way of salvation to those of the earth. In like manner Isaiah also:[17] "But they disbelieved, and vexed His Holy

[1] See Ezek. xli., where an angel measures the temple; and Rev. xi., where an angel directs John to measure it.

[2] The Scriptures do not make mention of the death of Isaiah. It is supposed that there is an allusion to it in Heb. xi. 37.

[3] Isa. i. 2, 3.

[4] Filios genui et exaltavi. This is quoted from the Septuagint.

[5] Jer. viii. 7–9.

[6] This is quoted from the Septuagint; literally, have watched for, custodierunt.

[7] Metatura. There is considerable difference in the readings of this passage. The text, as given above, deviates considerably from the Septuagint, which is more nearly expressed by the reading of other editions: "Incassum facta est metatura falsa, scribæ confusi sunt."

[8] Pius. The word is often used to represent kindness.

[9] Men are represented as being enemies to God. The enmity is on man's side, but if persisted in, must make God his enemy. See Rom. v. 9, 10, and Isa. lxiii. 10.

[10] Se insinuaret.

[11] Divino spiritu hausto.

[12] So Virgil, *Georgic* iii. 274: —

> "Et sæpe sine ullis
> Conjugiis vento gravidæ, mirabile dictu."

This theory of the impregnation of mares by the wind was general among the ancients.

[13] This passage does not occur in the writings of Solomon, or in the Old Testament. [Possibly from some copy (North African) of the "Book of Wisdom," interpolated from a marginal comment.]

[14] Isa. vii. 14.

[15] Salutaris, sive Salvator.

[16] Ps. lxxxv. 12, quoted from the Septuagint.

[17] Isa. lxiii. 10.

Spirit; and He was turned to be their enemy. And He Himself fought against them, and He remembered the days of old,[1] who raised up from the earth a shepherd of the sheep." But who this shepherd was about to be, he declared in another place,[2] saying: "Let the heavens rejoice, and let the clouds put on righteousness; let the earth open, and put forth a Saviour. For I the Lord have begotten Him." But the Saviour is, as we have said before, Jesus. But in another place the same prophet also thus proclaimed:[3] "Behold, unto us a child is born, unto us a Son is given, whose dominion is upon His shoulders, and His name is called Messenger of great counsel." For on this account He was sent by God the Father, that He might reveal to all the nations which are under heaven the sacred mystery of the only true God, which was taken away from the perfidious people, who ofttimes sinned against God. Daniel also foretold similar things:[4] "I saw," he said, "in a vision of the night, and, behold, one like the Son of man coming with the clouds of heaven, and He came even to the Ancient of days. And they who stood by brought Him near[5] before Him. And there was given unto Him a kingdom, and glory, and dominion; and all people, tribes, and languages shall serve Him: and His dominion is everlasting, which shall never pass away, and His kingdom shall not be destroyed." How then do the Jews both confess and expect the Christ of God? who rejected Him on this account, because He was born of man. For since it is so arranged by God that the same Christ should twice come to the earth, once to announce to the nations the one God, then again to reign, why do they who did not believe in His first advent believe in the second?

But the prophet comprises both His advents in few words. Behold, he says, one like the Son of man coming with the clouds of heaven. He did not say, like the Son of God, but the Son of man, that he might show that He had[6] to be clothed with flesh on the earth, that having assumed the form of a man and the condition of mortality, He might teach men righteousness; and when, having completed the commands of God, He had revealed the truth to the nations, He might also suffer death, that He might overcome and lay open[7] the other world also, and thus at length rising again, He might proceed to His Father borne aloft on a cloud.[8] For the prophet said in addition: And came even to the Ancient of days, and was presented to Him. He called the Most High God the Ancient of days, whose age and origin cannot be comprehended; for He alone was from generations, and He will be always to generations.[9] But that Christ, after His passion and resurrection, was about to ascend to God the Father, David bore witness in these words in the cixth Psalm:[10] "The Lord said unto my Lord, Sit Thou at my right hand, until I make Thine enemies Thy footstool." Whom could this prophet, being himself a king, call his Lord, who sat at the right hand of God, but Christ the Son of God, who is King of kings and Lord of lords? And this is more plainly shown by Isaiah,[11] when he says: "Thus saith the Lord God to my Lord Christ, whose right hand I have holden; I will subdue nations before Him, and will break the strength of kings. I will open before Him gates, and the cities shall not be closed. I will go before Thee, and will make the mountains level; and I will break in pieces the gates of brass, and shatter the bars of iron; and I will give Thee the hidden and invisible treasures, that Thou mayest know that I am the Lord God, which call Thee by Thy name, the God of Israel." Lastly, on account of the goodness and faithfulness which He displayed towards God on earth, there was given to Him a kingdom, and glory, and dominion; and all people, tribes, and languages shall serve Him; and His dominion is everlasting, and that which shall never pass away, and His kingdom shall not be destroyed. And this is understood in two ways: that even now He has an everlasting dominion, when all nations and all languages adore His name, confess His majesty, follow His teaching, and imitate His goodness: He has power and glory, in that all tribes of the earth obey His precepts. And also, when He shall come again with majesty and glory to judge every soul, and to restore the righteous to life, then He shall truly have the government of the whole earth: then, every evil having been removed from the affairs of men, a golden age (as the poets call it), that is, a time of righteousness and peace, will arise. But we will speak of these things more fully in the last book, when we shall speak of His second advent; now let us treat of His first advent, as we began.

CHAP. XIII. — OF JESUS, GOD AND MAN; AND THE TESTIMONIES OF THE PROPHETS CONCERNING HIM.

Therefore the Most High God, and Parent of all, when He had purposed to transfer[12] His

1 The days of the age. In the next clause the text differs both from the Hebrew and the Septuagint — which the English authorized version follows — "who raised up out of the sea."
2 Isa. xlv. 8, quoted from the Septuagint.
3 Isa. ix. 6, from the Septuagint.
4 Dan. vii. 13, 14.
5 Obtulerunt eum, "presented Him."
6 Quod carne indui haberet in terrâ. Another reading is "deberet," but the present is in accordance with the style of Lactantius.
7 Inferos resignaret.
8 Acts i. 9: "A cloud received Him out of their sight."
9 Ps. xc. 2.
10 Ps. cx. 1.
11 Isa. xlv. 1–3. The quotation is from the Septuagint. It expressly refers to Cyrus, whom God raised up to accomplish His will; but the prophecy may have a further reference to Christ, as is here supposed.
12 From the Israelites, to whom He first revealed Himself, to the Gentile world at large.

religion, sent from heaven a teacher of righteousness, that in Him or through Him He might give a new law to new worshippers; not as He had before done, by the instrumentality of man. Nevertheless it was His pleasure that He should be born as a man, that in all things He might be like His supreme Father. For God the Father Himself, who is the origin and source of all things, inasmuch as He is without parents, is most truly named by Trismegistus "fatherless" and "motherless,"[1] because He was born from no one. For which reason it was befitting that the Son also should be twice born, that He also might become "fatherless" and "motherless." For in His first nativity, which was spiritual, He was "motherless," because He was begotten by God the Father alone, without the office of a mother. But in His second, which was in the flesh, He was born of a virgin's womb without the office of a father, that, bearing a middle substance between God and man, He might be able, as it were, to take by the hand this frail and weak nature of ours, and raise it to immortality. He became both the Son of God through the Spirit, and the Son of man through the flesh,—that is, both God and man. The power of God was displayed in Him, from the works which He performed; the frailty of the man, from the passion which He endured: on what account He undertook it I will mention a little later. In the meantime, we learn from the predictions of the prophets that He was both God and man—composed[2] of both natures. Isaiah testifies that He was God in these words:[3] "Egypt is wearied,[4] and the merchandise of Ethiopia, and the Sabæans, men of stature, shall come over unto Thee, and shall be Thy servants: and they shall walk behind Thee; in chains they shall fall down unto Thee, and shall make supplication unto Thee, Since God is in Thee, and there is no other God besides Thee. For Thou art God, and we knew Thee not, the God of Israel, the Saviour. They shall all be confounded and ashamed who oppose Thee, and shall fall into confusion." In like manner the prophet Jeremiah[5] thus speaks: "This is our God, and there shall none other be compared unto Him. He hath found out all the way of knowledge, and hath given it unto Jacob His servant, and to Israel His beloved. Afterward He was seen upon earth, and dwelt among men."

David also, in the forty-fourth Psalm:[6] "Thy throne, O God, is for ever and ever; a sceptre of righteousness is the sceptre of Thy kingdom. Thou hast loved righteousness, and hated wickedness; therefore God, Thy God, hath anointed Thee with the oil of gladness." By which word he also shows His name, since (as I have shown above) He was called Christ from His anointing. Then, that He was also man, Jeremiah teaches, saying:[7] "And He is a man, and who hath known Him?" Also Isaiah:[8] "And God shall send to them a man, who shall save them, shall save them by judging." But Moses also, in Numbers,[9] thus speaks: "There shall arise a star out of Jacob, and a man[10] shall spring forth from Israel." On which account the Milesian Apollo,[11] being asked whether He was God or man, replied in this manner: "He was mortal as to His body, being wise with wondrous works; but being taken with arms under Chaldean judges, with nails and the cross He endured a bitter end." In the first verse he spoke the truth, but he skilfully deceived him who asked the question, who was entirely ignorant of the mystery of the truth. For he appears to have denied that He was God. But when he acknowledges that He was mortal as to the flesh, which we also declare, it follows that as to the spirit He was God, which we affirm. For why would it have been necessary to make mention of the flesh, since it was sufficient to say that He was mortal? But being pressed by the truth, he could not deny the real state of the case; as that which he says, that He was wise.

What do you reply to this, Apollo? If he is wise, then his system of instruction is wisdom, and no other; and they are wise who follow it, and no others. Why then are we commonly esteemed as foolish, and visionary, and senseless, who follow a Master who is wise even by the confession of the gods themselves? For in that he said that He wrought wonderful deeds, by which He especially claimed faith is His divinity, he now appears to assent to us, when he says the same things in which we boast. But, however, he recovers himself, and again has recourse to demoniacal frauds. For when he had been compelled to speak the truth, he now appeared to be a betrayer of the gods and of himself, unless he had, by a deceptive falsehood, concealed that which the truth had extorted from him. He says, therefore, that He did indeed perform won-

1 ἀπάτωρ and ἀμήτωρ. See Heb. vii. 3, where Melchisedec is a type of Christ.

2 Ex utroque genere permistum. Though the Godhead and the manhood are joined together in one person in our Lord Jesus Christ, there is no confounding of the two natures: each is whole and perfect. While Nestorius held that there were two persons in Christ, Eutyches fell into the opposite error, and taught that the two natures were so blended together as to form one mixed nature. The expression in the text is not very clear.

3 Isa. xlv. 14–16.

4 Fatigata est Ægyptus. This is taken from the Septuagint.

5 This quotation is from the apocryphal book of Baruch iii. 35–37, which is sometimes spoken of as the book of Jeremiah Baruch.

6 Ps. xlv. 6, 7.

7 Jer. xvii. 9. The passage is quoted from the Septuagint.

8 Isa. xix. 20, quoted from the Septuagint.

9 Num. xxiv. 17. The well-known prophecy of Balaam is here spoken of as though given by Moses, who only records it. [In an elucidation touching the Sibyls, I shall recur to the case of Balaam.]

10 Exsurget homo ex Israel. This is taken from the Septuagint, instead of the ordinary reading, "A sceptre shall rise out of Israel."

11 [The oracle of Apollo Didymæus; from the Milesian temple burnt by Xerxes. Readers will remember the humour of Arnobius about these divers names, vol. vi. p. 419, this series.]

derful works, yet not by divine power, but by magic. What wonder if Apollo thus persuaded men ignorant of the truth, when the Jews also, worshippers (as they seemed to be) of the Most High God, entertained the same opinion, though they had every day before their eyes those miracles which the prophets had foretold to them as about to happen, and yet they could not be induced by the contemplation of such powers to believe that He whom they saw was God? On this account, David, whom they especially read above the other prophets, in the twenty-seventh Psalm [1] thus condemns them: "Render to them their desert, because they regard not the works of the Lord." Both David himself and other prophets announced that of the house of this very David, Christ should be born according to the flesh. Thus it is written in Isaiah: [2] "And in that day there shall be a root of Jesse, and He who shall arise to rule over the nations, in Him shall the Gentiles trust; and His rest shall be glorious." And in another place: [3] "There shall come forth a rod out of the stem of Jesse, and a blossom [4] shall grow out of his root; and the Spirit of God shall rest upon Him, the spirit of wisdom and understanding, the spirit of counsel and of might, the spirit of knowledge and of piety; and He shall be filled [5] with the spirit of fear of the Lord." Now Jesse was the father of David, from whose root he foretold that a blossom would arise; namely him of whom the Sibyl speaks, "A pure blossom shall spring forth."

Also in the second book of Kings, the prophet Nathan was sent to David, who wished to build a temple for God; and this was the word of the Lord to Nathan, saying: [6] "Go and tell my servant David, Thus saith the Lord Almighty, Thou shalt not build me a house for me to dwell in; but when thy days be fulfilled, and thou shalt sleep with thy fathers, I will raise up thy seed after thee, and I will establish His kingdom. He shall build me a house for my name, and I will set up His throne for ever; and I will be to Him for a father, and He shall be to me for a son; and His house shall be established,[7] and His kingdom for ever." But the reason why the Jews did not understand these things was this, because Solomon the son of David built a temple for God, and the city which he called from his own name, Jerusalem.[8] Therefore they referred the predictions of the prophets to him. Now Solomon received the government of the kingdom from his father himself. But the prophets spoke of Him who was then born after that David had slept with his fathers. Besides, the reign of Solomon was not everlasting; for he reigned forty years. In the next place, Solomon was never called the son of God, but the son of David; and the house which he built was not firmly established,[9] as the Church, which is the true temple of God, which does not consist of walls, but of the heart [10] and faith of the men who believe on Him, and are called faithful. But that temple of Solomon, inasmuch as it was built by the hand, fell by the hand. Lastly, his father, in the cxxvith Psalm, prophesied in this manner respecting the works of his son: [11] "Except the Lord build the house, they have laboured in vain that built it; except the Lord keep the city, the watchman hath waked but in vain."

CHAP. XIV. — OF THE PRIESTHOOD OF JESUS FORETOLD BY THE PROPHETS.

From which things it is evident that all the prophets declared concerning Christ, that it should come to pass at some time, that being born with a body [12] of the race of David, He should build an eternal temple in honour of God, which is called the Church, and assemble all nations to the true worship of God. This is the faithful house, this is the everlasting temple; and if any one hath not sacrificed in this, he will not have the reward of immortality. And since Christ was the builder of this great and eternal temple, He must also have an everlasting priesthood in it; and there can be no approach to the shrine of the temple, and to the sight of God, except through Him who built the temple. David in the cixth Psalm teaches the same, saying: [13] "Before the morning-star I begat Thee. The Lord hath sworn, and will not repent; Thou art a priest for ever, after the order of Melchisedec." Also in the first book of Kings: [14] "And I will raise me up a faithful Priest, who shall do all things that are in mine heart; and I will build him a sure [15] house; and he shall walk in my sight [16] all his days." But who this was about to be, to whom God promised an everlasting priesthood, Zechariah most plainly teaches, even mentioning His name: [17] "And the Lord God showed

---

1 Ps. xxviii. 4, 5.
2 Isa. xi. 10.
3 Isa. xi. 1, 2.
4 Flos. Quoted from the Septuagint, ἄνθος.
5 Implebit eum spiritus timoris Dei.
6 2 Sam. vii. 4, 5, 12–14, 16.
7 Fidem consequetur, following the Septuagint πιστωθήσεται.
8 Hierosolyma. As though derived from ἱερόν and Σολομῶν. But Solomon was not the founder of the city. The name is probably derived from Salem, of which city Melchisedec was king. Some derive it from Jebus (the ancient name of the city) and Salem. [See vol. ii. p. 107, note 3, this series.]
9 Non est fidem consecuta, as above.
10 Thus Peter speaks, 1 Ep. ii. 5, "Ye are built up a spiritual house."
11 Ps. cxxvii. 1.
12 Corporaliter.
13 Ps. cx. 3, 4, quoted from the Septuagint. With reference to this priesthood, see Heb. v.
14 1 Sam. ii. 35.
15 Fidelem, i.e., firm and stedfast.
16 In conspectu meo. The Septuagint, ἐνώπιον χριστοῦ μου; and so the English authorized version, "before my anointed."
17 Zech. iii. 1–8.

me Jesus[1] the great Priest standing before the face of the angel of the Lord, and the adversary[2] was standing at His right hand to resist Him. And the Lord said unto the adversary, The Lord who hath chosen Jerusalem rebuke thee ; and lo, a brand plucked out of the fire. And Jesus was clothed with filthy garments, and He was standing before the face of the angel. And He answered and spake unto those that stood around before His face, saying, Take away the filthy garments from Him, and clothe Him with a flowing[3] garment, and place a fair mitre[4] upon His head ; and they clothed Him with a garment, and placed a fair mitre upon His head. And the angel of the Lord stood, and protested, saying to Jesus : Thus saith the Lord of hosts, If Thou wilt walk in my ways, and keep my precepts, Thou shalt judge my house, and I will give Thee those that may walk with Thee in the midst of these that stand by. Hear, therefore, O Jesus, Thou great Priest."

Who, therefore, would not believe that the Jews were then deprived of understanding, who, when they read and heard these things, laid impious hands upon their God? But from the time in which Zechariah lived, until the fifteenth year of the reign of Tiberius Cæsar, in which Christ was crucified, nearly five hundred years are reckoned ; since he flourished in the time of Darius and Alexander,[5] who lived not long after the banishment of Tarquinius Superbus. But they were again misled and deceived in the same manner, in supposing that these things were spoken concerning Jesus[6] the son of Nave, who was the successor of Moses, or concerning Jesus the high priest the son of Josedech ; to whom none of those things which the prophet related was suited. For they were never clothed in filthy garments, since one of them was a most powerful prince, and the other high priest ; or suffered any adversity, so that they should be regarded as a brand plucked from the fire : nor did they ever stand in the presence of God and the angels ; nor did the prophet speak of the past so much as of the future. He spoke, therefore, of Jesus the Son of God, to show that He would first come in humility and in the flesh. For this is the filthy garment, that He might prepare a temple for God, and might be scorched[7] as a brand with fire — that is, might endure tortures from men, and at last be extinguished. For a half-burnt brand drawn forth from the hearth and extinguished, is commonly so called.[8] But in what manner and with what commands He was sent by God to the earth, the Spirit of God declared through the prophet, teaching us that when He had faithfully and uniformly fulfilled the will of His supreme Father, He should receive judgment[9] and an everlasting dominion. If, He says, Thou wilt walk in my ways, and keep my precepts, then Thou shalt judge my house. What these ways of God were, and what His precepts, is neither doubtful nor obscure. For God, when He saw that wickedness and the worship of false gods had so prevailed throughout the world, that His name had now also been taken away from the memory of men (since even the Jews, who alone had been entrusted with the secret of God, had deserted the living God, and, ensared by the deceits of demons, had gone astray, and turned aside to the worship of images, and when rebuked by the prophets did not choose to return to God), He sent His Son[10] as an ambassador to men, that He might turn them from their impious and vain worship to the knowledge and worship of the true God ; and also that He might turn their minds from foolishness to wisdom, and from wickedness to deeds of righteousness. These are the ways of God, in which He enjoined Him to walk. These are the precepts which He ordered to be observed. But He exhibited faith towards God. For He taught that there is but one God, and that He alone ought to be worshipped. Nor did He at any time say that He Himself was God ; for He would not have maintained His faithfulness, if, when sent to abolish the false gods, and to assert the existence of the one God, He had introduced another besides that one. This would have been not to proclaim one God, nor to do the work of Him who sent Him, but to discharge a peculiar office for Himself, and to separate Himself from Him whom He came to reveal. On which account, because He was so faithful, because He arrogated nothing at all to Himself, that He might fulfil the commands of Him who sent Him, He received the dignity of everlasting Priest, and the honour of supreme King, and the authority of Judge, and the name of God.

CHAP. XV. — OF THE LIFE AND MIRACLES OF JESUS, AND TESTIMONIES CONCERNING THEM.

Having spoken of the second nativity, in which He showed Himself in the flesh to men, let us come to those wonderful works, on account of

[1] The authorized version reads Joshua, which has the same meaning with Jesus. See Heb. iv. 8. [Compare Justin, vol. i. note 4, p. 227.]

[2] Diabolus, i.e., the calumniator. To stand on the right hand is to accuse with authority. See Ps. cix. 6.

[3] Tunica talaris, a garment reaching to the ankles; in Greek, ποδήρης.

[4] Cidarim; an Eastern word denoting a head-dress worn by the Persian kings, or, as in this passage, the mitre of the Jewish high priest.

[5] Not the Great, but the tenth, a much earlier king of Macedon.

[6] i.e., Joshua the son of Nun, as he is generally called. [Justin, vol. i. pp. 174, 266.]

[7] Ambureretur. The word is applied to anything which is partly burned, burnt around, scorched. Hence Cicero jestingly speaks of Munatius Plancus, at whose instigation the people set fire to the senate-house, as tribunus ambustus. Cic., *pro Milone*.

[8] i.e., the word *titio*, "a firebrand," is thus used.

[9] i.e., authority to judge. [Ps. lxxii. 1 and John v. 22.]

[10] After these words some editions, "principem angelorum," the chief of angels.

which, though they were signs of heavenly power, the Jews esteemed Him a magician. When He first began to reach maturity [1] He was baptized by the prophet John in the river Jordan, that He might wash [2] away in the spiritual laver not His own sins, for it is evident that He had none, but those of the flesh,[3] which He bare; that as He saved the Jews by undergoing circumcision, so He might save the Gentiles also by baptism — that is, by the pouring forth [4] of the purifying dew. Then a voice from heaven was heard: "Thou art my Son, to-day have I begotten Thee."[5] Which voice is found to have been foretold by David. And the Spirit of God descended upon Him, formed after the appearance of a white dove.[6] From that time He began to perform the greatest miracles, not by magical tricks, which display nothing true and substantial, but by heavenly strength and power, which were foretold even long ago by the prophets who announced Him; which works are so many, that a single book is not sufficient to comprise them all. I will therefore enumerate them briefly and generally, without any designation of persons and places, that I may be able to come to the setting forth of His passion and cross, to which my discourse has long been hastening. His powers were those which Apollo called wonderful: [7] that wherever He journeyed, by a single word, and in a single moment, He healed the sick and infirm, and those afflicted with every kind of disease: so that those who were deprived of the use of all their limbs, having suddenly received power, were strengthened, and themselves carried their couches, on which they had a little time before been carried. But to the lame, and to those afflicted with some defect [8] of the feet, He not only gave the power of walking, but also of running. Then, also, if any had their eyes blinded in the deepest darkness, He restored them to their former sight. He also loosened the tongues of the dumb, so that [9] they discoursed and spake eloquently. He also opened the ears of the deaf, and caused them to hear;[10] He cleansed the polluted and the blemished.[11] And He performed all these things not by His hands, or the application of any remedy,[12] but by His word and command, as also the Sibyl had foretold: "Doing all things by His word, and healing every disease."

Nor, indeed, is it wonderful that He did wonderful things by His word, since He Himself was the Word of God, relying upon heavenly strength and power. Nor was it enough that He gave strength to the feeble, soundness of body to the maimed, health to the sick and languishing, unless He also raised the dead, as it were unbound from sleep, and recalled them to life.

And the Jews, then, when they saw these things, contended that they were done by demoniacal power, although it was contained in their secret writings that all things should thus come to pass as they did. They read indeed the words of other prophets, and of Isaiah,[13] saying: "Be strong, ye hands that are relaxed; and ye weak knees, be comforted. Ye who are of a fearful [14] heart, fear not, be not afraid: our Lord shall execute judgment; He Himself shall come and save us. Then shall the eyes of the blind be opened, and the ears of the deaf shall hear: then shall the lame man leap as a deer, and the tongue of the dumb speak plainly: [15] for in the wilderness water hath broken forth, and a stream in the thirsty land." But the Sibyl also foretold the same things in these verses: —

> "And there shall be a rising again of the dead; and the course of the lame shall be swift, and the deaf shall hear, and the blind shall see, the dumb shall speak."

On account of these powers and divine works wrought by Him when a great multitude followed Him of the maimed, or sick, or of those who desired to present their sick to be healed, He went up into a desert mountain to pray there. And when He had tarried there three days, and the people were suffering from hunger, He called His disciples, and asked what quantity of food [16] they had with them. But they said that they had five loaves and two fishes in a wallet. Then He commanded that these should be brought forward, and that the multitude, distributed by fifties, should recline *on the ground*. When the disciples did this, He Himself broke the bread in pieces, and divided the flesh of the fishes, and in His hands both of them were increased. And when He had ordered the disciples to set them before the people, five thousand men were satisfied, and moreover twelve baskets [17] were filled from the fragments which remained. What can be more wonderful, either in narration or in ac-

1 Cum primus cœpit adolescere.
2 Aboleret.
3 Not of His own flesh, but of human nature. Our Lord Himself gives a better explanation of His baptism, in His reply to the Baptist, who at first forbade him: "Suffer it to be so now, for thus it becometh us to fulfil all righteousness" (Matt. iii. 15).
4 Perfusione.
5 Compare Matt. iii. 17 with Ps. ii. 7.
6 ["A brilliant dove" is the idea. Ps. lxviii. 13. Comp. Justin, vol. i. note 6, p. 243.]
7 Portentificas.
8 Pedum vitio afflictos.
9 In eloquium sermonemque solvebat.
10 Insinuabat auditum.
11 Aspersos maculis, i.e., lepers.
12 Except in the case of the blind man, whose eyes He anointed with clay. John ix. 9.
13 Isa. xxxv. 3–6. The passage is quoted from the Septuagint. The authorized English version follows the Hebrew, "Strengthen ye the weak hands," etc.
14 Pusilli animi.
15 Plana erit, "shall be intelligible."
16 Quantos secum cibos gestarent. See Matt. xiv.; Mark vi.; Luke ix.; John vi.
17 Cophini. This miracle is always distinguished from the feeding of the four thousand by the use of this word. Thus Juvenal: "Judæis, quorum cophinus, fœnumque supellex."

tion? But the Sibyl had before foretold that it would take place, whose verses are related to this effect: —

"With five loaves at the same time, and with two fishes,
He shall satisfy five thousand men in the wilderness;
And afterwards taking all the fragments that remain,
He shall fill twelve baskets to the hope of many."

I ask, therefore, what the art of magic could have contrived in this case, the skill of which is of avail for nothing else than for deceiving [1] the eyes? He also, when He was about to retire to a mountain, as He was wont, for the sake of prayer, directed His disciples to take a small ship and go before Him. But they, setting out when evening was now coming on, began to be distressed [2] through a contrary wind. And when they were now in the midst of the sea,[3] then, setting His feet on the sea,[4] He came up to them, walking as though on the solid ground,[5] not as the poets fable Orion walking on the sea, who, while a part of his body was sunk in the water,

"With his shoulder rises above the waves."[6]

And again, when He had gone to sleep in the ship, and the wind had begun to rage, even to the extremity of danger, being aroused from sleep, He immediately ordered the wind to be silent; and the waves, which were borne with great violence, were still, and immediately at His word there followed a calm.

But perhaps the sacred writings [7] speak falsely, when they teach that there was such power in Him, that by His command He compelled the winds to obey, the seas to serve Him, diseases to depart, the dead to be submissive. Why should I say that the Sibyls before taught the same things in their verses? one of whom, already mentioned, thus speaks: —

"He shall still the winds by His word, and calm the sea
As it rages, treading with feet of peace and in faith."

And again another, which says: —

"He shall walk on the waves, He shall release men from disease.
He shall raise the dead, and drive away many pains;
And from the bread of one wallet there shall be a satisfying of men."

Some, refuted by these testimonies, are accustomed to have recourse to the assertion that these poems were not by the Sibyls, but made up and composed by our own writers. But he will assuredly not think this who has read Cicero,[8] and Varro, and other ancient writers, who make mention of the Erythræan and the other Sibyls, from whose books we bring forward these examples; and these authors died before the birth of Christ according to the flesh. But I do not doubt that these poems were in former times regarded as ravings, since no one then understood them. For they announced some marvellous wonders, of which neither the manner, nor the time, nor the author was signified. Lastly, the Erythræan Sibyl says that it would come to pass that she would be called mad and deceitful. But assuredly

"They will say that the Sibyl
Is mad, and deceitful: but when all things shall come to pass,
Then ye will remember me; and no one will any longer
Say that I, the prophetess of the great God, am mad."

Therefore they were [9] neglected for many ages; but they received attention after the nativity and passion of Christ had revealed secret things. Thus it was also with the utterances of the prophets, which were read by the people of the Jews for fifteen hundred years and more, but yet were not understood until after Christ had explained [10] them both by His word and by His works. For the prophets spoke of Him; nor could the things which they said have been in any way understood, unless they had been altogether fulfilled.

CHAP. XVI. — OF THE PASSION OF JESUS CHRIST; THAT IT WAS FORETOLD.

I come now to the passion itself, which is often cast in our teeth as a reproach: [11] that we worship a man, and one who was visited and tormented with remarkable punishment: that I may show that this very passion was undergone by Him in accordance with a great and divine plan, and that goodness and truth and wisdom are contained in it alone. For if He had been most happy on the earth, and had reigned through all His life in the greatest prosperity, no wise man would either have believed Him to be a God, or judged Him worthy of divine honour: which is the case with those who are destitute of true divinity, who not only look up [12] to perishable riches, and frail power, and the advantages arising from the benefit of another, but even consecrate them, and knowingly do service to the memory of the dead, worshipping fortune when it is now extinguished, which the wise never regarded as an object of worship even when alive and present with them. For nothing among earthly things can be venerable and worthy of heaven; but it is virtue alone, and justice

[1] Ad circumscribendos oculos. Cicero also uses the word "circumscriptio" to denote "fraud and deceit."
[2] Laborare.
[3] Pedibus mare ingressus.
[4] Matt. xiv. 24.
[5] In solido. So Virg., *Georg.*, ii. 231: —
"Alteque jubebis
In solido puteum demitti."
[6] Virg., *Æn.*, x. 765.
[7] Matt. viii.; Mark iv.; Luke viii.
[8] Cicero, *De Natura Deorum*, ii.
[9] Jacuerunt. [Elucidation II.]
[10] Interpretatus est.
[11] The pagans upbraided Christians, that they worshipped a man who was put to death as a slave.
[12] Suspiciunt, "view with admiration."

alone, which can be judged a true, and heavenly, and perpetual good, because it is neither given to any one, nor taken away. And since Christ came upon earth, supplied with virtue and righteousness, yea rather, since He Himself is virtue, and Himself righteousness, He descended that He might teach it and mould the character of man. And having performed this office and embassy from God, on account of this very virtue which He at once taught and practised, He deserved, and was able, to be believed a God by all nations. Therefore, when a great multitude from time to time flocked to Him, either on account of the righteousness which He taught or on account of the miracles which He worked, and heard His precepts, and believed that He was sent by God, and that He was the Son of God, then the rulers and priests of the Jews, excited with anger because they were rebuked by Him as sinners, and perverted by envy, because, while the multitude flocked to Him, they saw themselves despised and deserted, and (that which was the crowning point of their guilt) blinded by folly and error, and unmindful of the instructors sent from heaven, and of the prophets, they caballed against Him, and conceived the impious design of putting Him to death, and torturing Him: of which the prophets had long before written.

For both David, in the beginning of his Psalms, foreseeing in spirit what a crime they were about to commit, says,[1] "Blessed is the man who hath not walked in the way of the ungodly;" and Solomon in the book of Wisdom used these words:[2] "Let us defraud the righteous, for he is unpleasant to us, and upbraideth us with our offences against the law. He maketh his boast that he has the knowledge of God; and he calleth himself the Son of God. He is made to reprove[3] our thoughts: it grieveth us even to look upon him: for his life is not like the life of others; his ways are of another fashion.[4] We are counted by him as triflers,[5] he withdraweth himself from our ways as from filthiness; he commendeth greatly[6] the latter end of the just, and boasteth that he has God for his Father. Let us see, therefore, if his words be true; let us prove what end[7] he shall have; let us examine him with rebukes and torments, that we may know his meekness,[8] and prove his patience; let us condemn him to a shameful death. Such things have they imagined, and have gone astray. For their own folly hath blinded them, and they do not understand the mysteries[9] of God." Does he not describe that impious design entered into by the wicked against God, so that he clearly appears to have been present? But from Solomon, who foretold these things, to the time of their accomplishment, ten hundred and ten years intervened. We feign nothing; we add nothing. They who performed the actions had these accounts; they, against whom these things were spoken, read them. But even now the inheritors of their name and guilt have these accounts, and in their daily readings re-echo their own condemnation as foretold by the voice of the prophets; nor do they ever admit them into their heart, which is also itself a part of their condemnation. The Jews, therefore, being often reproved by Christ, who upbraided them with their sins and iniquities, and being almost deserted by the people, were stirred up to put Him to death.

Now His humility emboldened them to this deed. For when they read with what great power and glory the Son of God was about to descend from heaven, but on the other hand saw Jesus humble, peaceful, of low condition,[10] without comeliness, they did not believe that He was the Son of God, being ignorant that two advents on His part were foretold by the prophets: the first, obscure in humility of the flesh; the other, manifest in the power of His majesty. Of the first David thus speaks in the seventy-first Psalm:[11] "He shall descend as rain upon a fleece; and in His days shall righteousness spring forth, and abundance of peace, as long as the moon is lifted up." For as rain, if it descends upon a fleece, cannot be perceived, because it makes no sound; so he said that Christ would come to the earth without exciting the notice[12] of any, that He might teach righteousness and peace. Isaiah also thus spoke:[13] "Lord, who hath believed our report? and to whom is the arm of the Lord revealed? We made proclamation[14] before Him as children, and as a root in a thirsty land: He has no form nor glory; and we saw Him, and He had no form nor comeliness. But His form was without honour, and defective beyond the rest of men. He is a man acquainted[15] with grief, and knowing how to endure infirmity, because He turned[16] His face away from us; and He was not esteemed. He

1 Ps. i. 1.
2 Wisd. ii. 12–22.
3 In traductionem cogitationum nostrarum. Traductio is sometimes used, as here, to denote exposure to ignominy.
4 Immutatæ sunt.
5 Nugaces. In the Greek it is *εἰς κίβδηλον*, as a counterfeit.
6 Præfert. The Greek has *μακαρίζει*, "deems happy."
7 Quæ ventura sunt illi.
8 Reverentiam.
9 Sacramenta Dei.
10 Sordidum.
11 Ps. lxxii. 6, 7, quoted from the Septuagint.
12 Sine cujusquam suspicione.
13 Isa. liii. 1–6.
14 Annuntiavimus coram ipso sicut pueri; and so the Septuagint, *ἀνηγγείλαμεν ἐνάντιον αὐτοῦ ὡς παιδίον*. It is most difficult to account for this remarkable translation. The meaning of the passage is plain, that the Messiah would spring from an obscure source. [Elucidation III.]
15 Homo in plagâ positus. The Septuagint, *ἄνθρωπος ἐν πληγῇ ὤν*.
16 Aversus est. So also the Septuagint, *ἀπέστραπται τὸ πρόσωπον αὐτοῦ*. Some have supposed that there is a reference to lepers, who were compelled to cover their faces.

carries our sins, and He endures pain for us: and we thought that He Himself [1] was in pain, and grief, and vexation. But He was wounded for our transgressions, He was bruised [2] for our offences; the chastisement [3] of our peace was upon Him, by His bruises [4] we are healed. All we like sheep have gone astray, and God hath delivered Him up for our sins." And in the same manner the Sibyl spoke: "Though an object of pity, dishonoured, without form, He will give hope to those who are objects of pity." On account of this humility they did not recognise their God, and entered into the detestable design of depriving Him of life, who had come to give them life.

CHAP. XVII. — OF THE SUPERSTITIONS OF THE JEWS, AND THEIR HATRED AGAINST JESUS.

But they alleged other causes for their anger and envy, which they bore shut up [5] within in their hearts — namely, that He destroyed the obligation [6] of the law given by Moses; that is, that He did not rest [7] on the Sabbath, but laboured for the good [8] of men; that He abolished circumcision; that He took away the necessity of abstaining from the flesh of swine; [9] — in which things the mysteries of the Jewish religion consist. On this account, therefore, the rest of the people, who had not yet withdrawn [10] to Christ, were incited by the priests to regard Him as impious, because He destroyed the obligation of the law of God, though He did this not by His own judgment, but according to the will of God, and after the predictions of the prophets. For Micah announced that He would give a new law, in these terms: [11] "The law shall go forth of Zion, and the word of the Lord from Jerusalem. And He shall judge among many people, and rebuke strong nations." [12] For the former law, which was given by Moses, was not given on Mount Zion, but on Mount Horeb; [13] and the Sibyl shows that it would come to pass that this law would be destroyed by the Son of God: —

> "But when all these things which I told you shall be accomplished, then all the law is fulfilled with respect to Him."

But even Moses himself, by whom the law was given which they so tenaciously maintain, though they have fallen away from God, and have not acknowledged God, had foretold that it would come to pass that a very great prophet would be sent by God, who should be above the law, and be a bearer of the will of God to men. In Deuteronomy he thus left it written: [14] "And the Lord said unto me, I will raise them up a Prophet from among their brethren, like unto thee; and I will put my word in His mouth, and He shall speak unto them all that I shall command Him. And whosoever will not hearken to those things which that Prophet shall speak in my name, I will require [15] it of him." The Lord evidently announced by the law-giver himself that He was about to send His own Son — that is, a law alive, and present [16] in person, and destroy that old law given by a mortal,[17] that by Him who was eternal He might ratify afresh a law which was eternal.

In like manner, Isaiah [18] thus prophesied concerning the abolition of circumcision: "Thus saith the Lord to the men of Judah who dwell at Jerusalem, Break up your fallow ground, and sow not among thorns. Circumcise yourselves to the Lord your God, and take away the foreskins of your heart, lest my fury come forth like fire, and burn that none can quench it." Also Moses himself says: [19] "In the last days the Lord shall circumcise thine heart to love the Lord thy God." Also Jesus [20] the son of Nun, his successor, said: "And the Lord said unto Jesus, Make thee knives of flint very sharp, and sit and circumcise the children of Israel the second time." He said that this second circumcision would be not of the flesh, as the first was, which the Jews practise even now, but of the heart and spirit, which was delivered by Christ, who was the true Jesus. For the prophet does not say, "And the Lord said unto me," but "unto Jesus," that he might show that God was not speaking of him, but of Christ, to whom God was then speaking. For that Jesus represented [21] Christ: for when he was at first called Auses,[22] Moses, foreseeing the future, ordered that he should be called Jesus; that since he had been chosen as the leader of the warfare

1 i.e., for Himself, as though He were bearing the punishment of His own sins.
2 Infirmatus est.
3 Doctrina pacis nostræ, "the correction."
4 Livore ejus nos sanati sumus. The word "livor" properly denotes the blackness arising from a bruise.
5 Intus inclusam. Another reading is, "Intus inclusâ malitia," with malice shut up within.
6 Solveret, "He loosened or relaxed."
7 Non vacaret.
8 Operans in salutem hominum, "by healing diseases and doing good."
9 There is no mention of this in the Gospels.
10 Secesserat: "withdrawn themselves from the teaching of the scribes and Pharisees, and betaken themselves to Christ."
11 Mic. iv. 2, 3.
12 Some read, "evincet et deliget validas nationes;" but the reading "deliget" seems to have arisen from a corrupt reading of the Septuagint, — ἐκλέξει, "he shall choose," having been substituted for ἐξελέγξει, "he shall rebuke."
13 The scene of the giving of the law is sometimes spoken of as Horeb, as Ex. iii., and sometimes as Sinai, as Ex. xix. The difficulty of discriminating the two is very great. See Stanley's *Sinai and Palestine* [pp. 29, 32, 36-37, 40-42, etc. Robinson, vol. i. 177, 551.]

14 Deut. xviii. 17-19.
15 Ego vindicabo in eum.
16 Vivam præsentemque legem.
17 Another reading is, "per Moysen," by Moses.
18 The quotation is not from Isaiah, but from Jer. iv. 3, 4.
19 Deut. xxx. 6.
20 i.e., Joshua. See Josh. v. 2.
21 "Figuram gerebat," typified, or set forth as in a figure.
22 i.e., Osee, Oshea, or Hoshea, as Joshua was first called. See Num. xiii. 8. [But note Num. xiii. 16. The change was significant. See Pearson *On the Creed*, art. ii. 125-128. Thus, "Jehovah-Saviour" = Jesus, and the change was prophetic of "the Name which is above every name." Compare Gen. xxxii. 29 and Phil. ii. 9, 10.]

against Amalek, who was the enemy of the children of Israel, he might both subdue the adversary by the emblem[1] of the name, and lead the people into the land of promise. And for this reason he was also successor to Moses, to show that the new law given by Christ Jesus was about to succeed to the old law which was given by Moses. For that circumcision of the flesh is plainly irrational; since, if God had so willed it, He might so have formed man from the beginning, that he should be without a foreskin. But it was a figure of this second circumcision, signifying that the breast is to be laid bare; that is, that we ought to live with an open and simple heart, since that part of the body which is circumcised has a kind of resemblance to the heart, and is to be treated with reverence. On this account God ordered that it should be laid bare, that by this argument He might admonish us not to have our breast hidden[2] in obscurity; that is, not to veil any shameful deed within the secrets of conscience. This is the circumcision of the heart of which the prophets speak, which God transferred from the mortal flesh to the soul, which alone is about to endure. For, being desirous of promoting our life and salvation in accordance with His own goodness, in that circumcision He hath set before us repentance, that if we lay open our hearts, — that is, if we confess our sins and make satisfaction to God, — we shall obtain pardon, which is denied to those who are obstinate and conceal their faults, by Him who regards not the outward appearance, as man does, but the innermost secrets of the heart.[3]

The forbidding of the flesh of swine also has the same intention; for when God commanded them to abstain from this, He willed that this should be especially understood, that they should abstain from sins and impurities. For this animal is filthy and unclean,[4] and never looks up to heaven,[5] but prostrates itself to the earth with its whole body and face: it is always the slave of its appetite and food; nor during its life can it afford any other service, as the other animals do, which either afford a vehicle for riding,[6] or aid in the cultivation of the fields, or draw waggons by their neck, or carry burthens on their back, or furnish a covering with their skins,[7] or abound with a supply of milk, or keep watch for guarding our houses. Therefore He forbade them to use the flesh of the pig for food, that is, not to imitate the life of swine, which are nourished only for death; lest, by devoting themselves to their appetite and pleasures, they should be useless for working righteousness, and should be visited with death. Also that they should not immerse themselves in foul lusts, as the sow, which wallows in the mire;[8] or that they do not serve earthly images, and thus defile themselves with mud: for they do bedaub themselves with mud who worship gods, that is, who worship mud and earth. Thus all the precepts of the Jewish law have for their object the setting forth of righteousness, since they are given in a mysterious[9] manner, that under the figure of carnal things those which are spiritual might be known.

CHAP. XVIII. — OF THE LORD'S PASSION, AND THAT IT WAS FORETOLD.

When, therefore, Christ fulfilled these things which God would have done, and which He foretold many ages before by His prophets, incited by these things, and ignorant of the sacred Scriptures, they conspired together to condemn their God. And though He knew that this would come to pass, and repeatedly[10] said that He must suffer and be put to death for the salvation of many, nevertheless He withdrew Himself with His disciples, not that He might avoid that which it was necessary for Him to undergo and endure, but that He might show what ought to take place in every persecution, that no one should appear to have fallen into it through his own fault: and He announced that it would come to pass that He should be betrayed by one of them. And thus Judas, induced by a bribe, delivered up to the Jews the Son of God. But they took and brought Him before Pontius Pilate, who at that time was administering the province of Syria as governor,[11] and demanded that He should be crucified, though they laid nothing else to His charge except that He said that He was the Son of God, the King of the Jews; also His own saying,[12] "Destroy this temple, which was forty-six years in building, and in three days I will raise it up again without hands,"

[1] Per figuram nominis. The name Jesus or Joshua signifies a deliverer or saviour. [Nay, more, Jehovah-Salvator, thus: Hoshea + Jah = Jehoshua = Joshua = Jesus.]

[2] Involutum. Thus Seneca: "Non est tibi frons ficta, nec in alienam voluptatem sermo compositus, nec cor involutum."

[3] 1 Sam. xvi. 7: "The Lord seeth not as man seeth; for man looketh on the outward appearance, but the Lord looketh on the heart."

[4] Lutulentum (besmeared with mud) "et immundum." See 2 Pet. ii. 22.

[5] ["The swine gorges his acorns, and never looks up to the tree from which they fall," as a parable of nature for swinish men.]

[6] Sedendi vehiculum. "Sedeor" is sometimes used in this sense for riding.

[7] Exuviis, used in the same sense as "pellibus."

[8] Ingurgitat cœno, "plunges into the mire." ["Sus lota in volutabro luti." 2 Pet. ii. 22, *Vulgate*.]

[9] Per figuram. [This *Typology* has never yet been fully or satisfactorily treated. Yet the volumes of Dr. Fairbairn (*Typology of Scripture*, Clarks, Edin.) ought to be known to every Bible student.]

[10] Subinde, "from time to time."

[11] Legatus. This title was given, in the time of the Roman emperors, to the governors sent by them into the provinces. Pontius Pilate was procurator of Judæa, which was not a separate province, but a dependency of the province of Syria, which was at this time governed by Silanus.

[12] John ii. 19, 20. The forty-six years spoken of were not occupied with the rebuilding of the temple, which was completed in nine years, but with the additional works which Herod the Great and his successors were continually carrying on for the adorning and beautifying of the temple. See Prideaux. [I regret the loose references of the translator, and yet more that the inexorable demands of the press give me time to supply only the more important ones. See *Connections*, book ix. vol. ii. p. 394.]

— signifying that His passion would shortly take place, and that He, having been put to death by the Jews, would rise again on the third day. For He Himself was the true temple of God. They inveighed against these expressions of His, as ill-omened and impious. And when Pilate had heard these things, and He said nothing in His own defence, he gave sentence that there appeared nothing deserving of condemnation in Him. But those most unjust accusers, together with the people whom they had stirred up, began to cry out, and with loud voices to demand His crucifixion.

Then Pontius [1] was overpowered both by their outcries, and by the instigation of Herod the tetrarch,[2] who feared lest he should be deposed from his sovereignty. He did not, however, himself pass sentence, but delivered Him up to the Jews, that they themselves might judge Him according to their law.[3] Therefore they led Him away when He had been scourged with rods, and before they crucified Him they mocked Him; for they put upon Him a scarlet [4] robe, and a crown of thorns, and saluted Him as King, and gave Him gall for food, and mingled for Him vinegar to drink. After these things they spat upon His face, and struck Him with the palms of their hands; and when the executioners [5] themselves contended about His garments, they cast lots among themselves for His tunic and mantle.[6] And while all these things were doing, He uttered no voice from His mouth, as though He were dumb. Then they lifted Him up in the midst between two malefactors, who had been condemned for robbery, and fixed Him to the cross. What can I here deplore in so great a crime? or in what words can I lament such great wickedness? For we are not relating the crucifixion of Gavius,[7] which Marcus Tullius followed up with all the spirit and strength of his eloquence, pouring forth as it were the fountains of all his genius, proclaiming that it was an unworthy deed that a Roman citizen should be crucified in violation of all laws. And although He was innocent, and undeserving of that punishment, yet He was put to death, and that, too, by an impious man, who was ignorant of justice. What shall I say respecting the indignity of this cross, on which the Son of God was suspended and nailed?[8] Who will be found so eloquent, and supplied with so great an abundance of deeds and words, what speech flowing with such copious exuberance,[9] as to lament in a befitting manner that cross, which the world itself, and all the elements of the world, bewailed?

But that these things were thus about to happen, was announced both by the utterances of the prophets and by the predictions of the Sibyls. In Isaiah it is found thus written: [10] "I am not rebellious, nor do I oppose: I gave my back to the scourge, and my cheeks to the hand: [11] I turned not away my face from the foulness of spitting." In like manner David, in the thirty-fourth Psalm: [12] "The abjects [13] were gathered together against me,[14] and they knew me not: [15] they were dispersed, nor did they feel remorse; they tempted me, and greatly [16] derided me; and they gnashed upon me with their teeth." The Sibyl also showed that the same things would happen: —

> "He shall afterwards come into the hands of the unjust and the faithless; and they shall inflict on God blows with impure hands, and with polluted mouths they shall send forth poisonous spittle; and He shall then absolutely [17] give His holy back to stripes."

Likewise respecting His silence, which He perseveringly maintained even to His death, Isaiah thus spoke again: [18] "He was led as a sheep to the slaughter; and as a lamb before the shearer is dumb, so He opened not His mouth." And the above-mentioned Sibyl said: —

> "And being beaten, He shall be silent, lest any one should know what the Word is, or whence it came, that it may speak with mortals; and He shall wear the crown of thorns."

But respecting the food and the drink which they offered to Him before they fastened Him to the cross, David thus speaks in the sixty-eighth Psalm: [19] "And they gave me gall for my meat;

---

1 [It is probable, that, owing to the perpetual and universal recitation of the Creed, this unhappy name has been more frequently uttered and recalled to human memory than that of any other human being.]

2 Herod Antipas the tetrarch of Galilee. According to St. Luke (xxiii. 15), Herod agreed with Pilate in declaring the innocency of Jesus.

3 This statement requires some modification. Pilate did indeed say to the Jews, "Take ye Him, and judge Him according to your law;" but they declared that it was not lawful for them to put any man to death. The punishment was entirely Roman, the mode of death Roman, the executioners Roman soldiers. There were two distinct trials, — one before the Jewish Sanhedrim on a charge of impiety, the other before the Roman governor on a charge of treason.

4 Punicei coloris. The colour was a kind of red, not purple. [It was mixed with blue, so as to be at once purple and in some reflections scarlet.]

5 The quaternion of Roman soldiers who carried out the execution.

6 De tunicâ et pallio. The "tunica" was the inner garment, the "pallium" a mantle or cloak. Thus the proverbial phrase, "tunica proprior pallio." [Vol. iv. p. 13, Elucidation I., this series.]

7 Gavius was crucified by Verres. [*In Verrem*, act ii. cap. 62. This event providentially illustrated the extreme wickedness of what was done to our Lord, but so quickened the Roman conscience that it prevented like injustice to St. Paul, although a Roman citizen, over and over again. Acts xvi. 37, 38, and xxii. 24, 25.]

8 Suffixus.

9 Tantæ affluentiæ ubertate. [Compare Cicero (*ut supra*): Crux, *crux!* inquam infelici et ærumnoso, qui nunquam istam potestatem viderat, comparabatur.]

10 Isa. l. 5, 6, quoted from the Septuagint.

11 i.e., of the smiters; Gr. *εἰς ῥαπίσματα*, "blows with the hand."

12 Ps. xxxv. 15, 16. The quotation is from the Septuagint, and differs widely from the authorized English version.

13 Flagella, said to be used for men deserving the scourge; wicked men.

14 Super me, "over me."

15 Ignoraverunt. Others read "ignoravi," I knew it not.

16 Deriserunt me derisu. So the Greek, *ἐξεμυκτήρισάν με μυκτηρισμόν.*

17 ἁπλῶς.

18 Isa. liii. 7.

19 Ps. lxix. 21.

and in my thirst they gave me vinegar to drink." The Sibyl foretold that this also would happen: —

"They gave me gall for my food, and for my thirst vinegar; this inhospitable table they will show."

And another Sibyl rebukes the land of Judæa in these verses: —

"For you, entertaining hurtful thoughts, did not recognise your God sporting[1] with mortal thoughts; but you crowned Him with a crown of thorns, and mingled dreadful gall."

Now, that it would come to pass that the Jews would lay hands upon their God, and put Him to death, these testimonies of the prophets foretold. In Esdras it is thus written:[2] "And Ezra said to the people, This passover is our Saviour and our refuge. Consider and let it come into your heart, that we have to abase Him in a figure; and after these things we will hope in Him, lest this place be deserted for ever, saith the Lord God of hosts. If you will not believe Him, nor hear His announcement, ye shall be a derision among the nations." From which it appears that the Jews had no other hope, unless they purified themselves from blood, and put their hopes in that very person whom they denied.[3] Isaiah also points out their deed, and says:[4] "In His humiliation His judgment was taken away. Who shall declare His generation? for His life shall be taken away from the earth; from the transgressions of my people He was led away to death. And I will give Him the wicked for His burial, and the rich for His death, because He did no wickedness, nor spoke guile with His mouth. Wherefore He shall obtain[5] many, and shall divide the spoils of the strong; because He was delivered up to death, and was reckoned among the transgressors; and He bore the sins of many, and was delivered up on account of their transgressions." David also, in the ninety-third Psalm:[6] "They will hunt after the soul of the righteous, and condemn the innocent blood; and the Lord is become my refuge." Also Jeremiah:[7] "Lord, declare it unto me, and I shall know. Then I saw their devices; I was led as an innocent[8] lamb to the sacrifice;[9] they meditated a plan against me, saying, Come, let us send wood into his bread,[10] and let us sweep away his life from the earth, and his name shall no more be remembered." Now the wood[11] signifies the cross, and the bread His body; for He Himself is the food and the life of all who believe in the flesh which He bare, and on the cross upon which He was suspended.

Respecting this, however, Moses himself more plainly spoke to this effect, in Deuteronomy:[12] "And Thy life shall hang[13] before Thine eyes; and Thou shalt fear day and night, and shalt have no assurance of Thy life." And the same again in Numbers:[14] "God is not in doubt as a man, nor does He suffer threats[15] as the son of man." Zechariah also thus wrote:[16] "And they shall look on me, whom they pierced." Also David in the twenty-first Psalm:[17] "They pierced my hands and my feet; they numbered all my bones; they themselves looked and stared upon me; they divided my garments among them; and upon my vesture they did cast lots." It is evident that the prophet did not speak these things concerning himself. For he was a king, and never endured these sufferings; but the Spirit of God, who was about to suffer these things, after *ten hundred and fifty* years, spoke by him. For this is the number of years from the reign of David to the crucifixion of Christ. But Solomon also, his son, who built Jerusalem, prophesied that this very city would perish in revenge for the sacred cross:[18] "But if ye turn away from me, saith the Lord, and will not keep my truth, I will drive Israel from the land which I have given them; and this house which I have built for them in my name, I will cast it out from all:[19] and Israel shall be for perdition[20] and a reproach to the people; and this house shall be desolate, and every one that shall pass by it shall be astonished, and shall say, Why hath God done these evils to this land and to this house? And they shall say, Because they forsook the Lord their God, and persecuted their King most beloved by God, and crucified Him with great degradation,[21] therefore hath God brought upon them these evils."

---

1 παίζοντα. Another reading is πταίοντα, which would imply that they regarded Christ as a transgressor.

2 Justin Martyr quotes this passage in his *Dialogue with Trypho*, and complains that it had been expunged by the Jews. [See vol. i. p. 234, and remarks of Bishop Kaye, *Justin Martyr*, p. 44, on passages suppressed by the Jews.]

3 Negaverunt. Another reading is "necaverunt," they put to death.

4 Isa. liii. 8–10, 12. The quotation is made from the Septuagint.

5 Consequetur. In the Greek, κληρονομήσει, "shall inherit."

6 Ps. xciv. 21, 22.

7 Jer. xi. 18, 19, quoted from the Septuagint.

8 Sine malitiâ. Another reading is "sine maculâ," without spot.

9 Ad victimam.

10 For the various explanations, see Pole's *Synopsis*. Some suppose that there is a reference to the corruption of food by poisonous wood; others that the meaning is a substitution of wood for bread. Another explanation is, that the word translated bread denotes fruit, as in the English authorized version, "Let us destroy the tree, with the fruit thereof." But see Pole on the passage. [Jer. xi. 19. Here is a very insufficient note, the *typology* of Scripture not being duly observed. Compare Tertullian, vol. iii. p. 166, especially at note 10, which illustrates the uniform spirit of the Fathers in dealing with the Jews. And note Bishop Kaye's remark, vol. ii. p. 206, note 5, this series.]

11 This explanation appears altogether fanciful and unwarranted.

12 Deut. xxviii. 66.

13 So the Septuagint. The English authorized version appears accurately to express the idea intended to be conveyed: "Thy life shall hang in doubt before Thee."

14 The idea is that God is not in doubt, as a man, as to His conduct, nor is He liable to change His mind, or to be influenced by threats or in any other way.

15 Minas patitur.

16 Zech. xii. 10.

17 Ps. xxii. 16–18. [Compare vol. i. p. 176, note 4, this series.]

18 1 Kings ix. 6–9, with some additions and omissions; and 1 Chron. vii. 19–22.

19 Ex omnibus. The English authorized version has, "out of my sight."

20 In perditionem et improperium.

21 This is not taken from the passages cited, nor from the Old Testament.

CHAP. XIX. — OF THE DEATH, BURIAL, AND RESURRECTION OF JESUS; AND THE PREDICTIONS OF THESE EVENTS.

What more can now be said respecting the crime of the Jews, than that they were then blinded and seized with incurable madness, who read these things daily, and yet neither understood them, nor were able to be on their guard so as not to do them? Therefore, being lifted up and nailed to the cross, He cried to the Lord with a loud voice, and of His own accord gave up His spirit. And at the same hour there was an earthquake; and the veil of the temple, which separated the two tabernacles, was rent into two parts; and the sun suddenly withdrew its light, and there was darkness from the sixth [1] even to the ninth hour. Of which event the prophet Amos testifies: [2] "And it shall come to pass in that day, saith the Lord, that the sun shall go down at noon, and the daylight shall be darkened; and I will turn your feasts into mourning, and your songs into lamentation." Also Jeremiah: [3] "She who brings forth is affrighted, and vexed in spirit; her sun is gone down while it was yet mid-day; she hath been ashamed and confounded; [4] and the residue of them will I give to the sword in the sight of their enemies." And the Sibyl: —

> "And the veil of the temple shall be rent, and at mid-day there shall be dark vast night for three hours."

When these things were done, even by the heavenly prodigies, they were not able to understand their crime.

But since He had foretold that on the third day He should rise again from the dead, fearing lest, the body having been stolen by the disciples, and removed, all should believe that He had risen, and there should be a much greater disturbance among the people, they took Him down from the cross, and having shut Him up in a tomb, they securely surrounded it with a guard of soldiers. But on the third day, before light, there was an earthquake, and the sepulchre was suddenly opened; and the guard, who were astonished and stupefied with fear, seeing nothing, He came forth uninjured and alive from the sepulchre, and went into Galilee to seek His disciples: but nothing was found in the sepulchre except the grave-clothes in which they had enclosed and wrapt His body. Now, that He would not remain in hell,[5] but rise again on the third day, had been foretold by the prophets. David says, in the fifteenth Psalm: [6] "Thou wilt not leave my soul in hell; neither wilt Thou suffer Thine holy one to see corruption." Also in the third Psalm: [7] "I laid me down to sleep, and took my rest, and rose again, for the Lord sustained me." Hosea also, the first of the twelve prophets, testified of His resurrection: [8] "This my Son is wise, therefore He will not remain in the anguish of His sons: and I will redeem Him from the power [9] of the grave. Where is thy judgment, O death? or where is thy sting?" The same also in another place: [10] "After two days, He will revive us in the third day." And therefore the Sibyl said, that after three days' sleep he would put an end to death: —

> "And after sleeping three days, He shall put an end to the fate of death; and then, releasing Himself from the dead, He shall come to light, first showing to the called ones the beginning of the resurrection."

For He gained life for us by overcoming death. No hope, therefore, of gaining immortality is given to man, unless he shall believe on Him, and shall take up that cross to be borne and endured.

CHAP. XX. — OF THE DEPARTURE OF JESUS INTO GALILEE AFTER HIS RESURRECTION; AND OF THE TWO TESTAMENTS, THE OLD AND THE NEW.

Therefore He went into Galilee, for He was unwilling to show Himself to the Jews, lest He should lead them to repentance, and restore them from their impiety to a sound mind.[11] And *there He* opened to His disciples again assembled the writings of Holy Scripture, that is, the secrets of the prophets; which before His suffering could by no means be understood, for they told of Him and of His passion. Therefore Moses, and the prophets also themselves, call the law which was given to the Jews a testament: for unless the testator shall have died, a testament cannot be confirmed; nor can that which is written in it be known, because it is closed and sealed. And thus, unless Christ had undergone death, the testament could not have been opened; that is, the mystery of God could not have been unveiled [12] and understood.

But all Scripture is divided into two Testaments. That which preceded the advent and passion of Christ — that is, the law and the prophets — is called the Old; but those things which were written after His resurrection are named the New Testament. The Jews make use of the Old, we of the New: but yet they are not discordant, for the New is the fulfilling of the Old, and in both there is the same testator, even Christ, who, having suffered death for us,

[1] i.e., from noon. [Elucidation IV.]
[2] Amos viii. 9, 10.
[3] Jer. xv. 9.
[4] Confusa est et maledicta.
[5] i.e., Hades, the place of departed spirits.
[6] Ps. xvi. 10.
[7] Ps. iii. 5.
[8] Hos. xiii 13, 14.
[9] De manu inferorum.
[10] Hos. vi. 2.
[11] [A very feeble exposition of Luke xix. 42, 44.]
[12] Revelari, to be laid bare, uncovered, brought to light.

made us heirs of His everlasting kingdom, the people of the Jews being deprived and disinherited.[1] As the prophet Jeremiah testifies when he speaks such things:[2] "Behold, the days come, saith the Lord, that I will make a new testament[3] to the house of Israel and the house of Judah, not according to the testament which I made to their fathers, in the day that I took them by the hand to bring them out of the land of Egypt; for they continued not in my testament, and I disregarded[4] them, saith the Lord." Also in another place he says in like manner:[5] "I have forsaken my house, I have given up mine heritage into the hand of its enemies. Mine heritage is become unto me as a lion in the forest; it hath cried out against me, therefore have I hated it." Since the inheritance is His heavenly kingdom, it is evident that He does not say that He hates the inheritance itself, but the heirs, who have been ungrateful towards Him, and impious. Mine heritage, he says, is become unto me as a lion; that is, I am become a prey and a devouring to my heirs, who have slain me as the flock. It hath cried out against me; that is, they have pronounced against me the sentence of death and the cross. For that which He said above, that He would make[6] a new testament to the house of Judah, shows that the old testament which was given by Moses was not perfect;[7] but that that which was to be given by Christ would be complete. But it is plain that the house of Judah does not signify the Jews, whom He casts off, but us, who have been called by Him out of the Gentiles, and have by adoption succeeded to their place, and are called sons[8] of the Jews, which the Sibyl declares when she says:—

"The divine race of the blessed, heavenly Jews."

But what that race was about to be, Isaiah teaches, in whose book the Most High Father addresses His Son:[9] "I the Lord God have called Thee in righteousness, and will hold Thine hand, and will keep Thee:[10] and I have given Thee for a covenant of my race,[11] for a light of the Gentiles; to open the eyes of the blind, to bring out the prisoners from the prison, and them that sit in darkness out of the prison-house." When, therefore, we who were in time past as it were blind, and as it were shut up in the prison of folly, were sitting in darkness, ignorant of God and of the truth, we have been enlightened by Him, who adopted us by His testament; and having freed us from cruel chains, and brought us out to the light of wisdom, He admitted us to the inheritance of His heavenly kingdom.

CHAP. XXI.—OF THE ASCENSION OF JESUS, AND THE FORETELLING OF IT; AND OF THE PREACHING AND ACTIONS OF THE DISCIPLES.

But when He had made arrangements with His disciples for the preaching of the Gospel and His name, a cloud suddenly surrounded Him, and carried Him up into heaven, on the fortieth day after His passion, as Daniel had shown that it would be, saying:[12] "And, behold, one like the Son of man came with the clouds of heaven, and came to the Ancient of days." But the disciples, being dispersed through the provinces, everywhere laid the foundations of the Church, themselves also in the name of their divine[13] Master doing many and almost incredible miracles; for at His departure He had endowed them with power and strength, by which the system[14] of their new announcement might be founded and confirmed. But He also opened to them all things which were about to happen, which Peter and Paul preached at Rome; and this preaching being written for the sake of remembrance,[15] became permanent, in which they both declared other wonderful things, and also said that it was about to come to pass, that after a short time God would send against them a king who would subdue[16] the Jews, and level their cities to the ground, and besiege the people themselves, worn out with hunger and thirst. Then it should come to pass that they should feed on the bodies of their own children, and consume one another. Lastly, that they should be taken captive, and come into the hands of their enemies, and should see their wives most cruelly harassed before their eyes, their virgins ravished and polluted, their sons torn in pieces, their little ones dashed to the ground; and lastly, everything laid waste with fire and sword, the captives banished for ever from their own lands, because they had exulted over the well-beloved and most approved Son of God. And so, after their decease, when Nero had put them to death, Vespasian destroyed the name and nation of the Jews, and did all

[1] Abdicato et exhæredato. The two expressions are joined together, to give strength. "Abdicati" were sons deprived of a share in their father's possessions during his life; "exhæredati," disinherited, those who have forfeited the right of succession after their father's death.

[2] Jer. xxxi. 31, 32.

[3] Or rather "covenant," διαθήκη, for this signification is much more in accordance with the general meaning of the passage.

[4] Neglexi; Gr. ἠμέλησα.

[5] Jer. xii. 7, 8.

[6] Consummaturum, "would complete," "make perfect," as in the next clause.

[7] See Heb. viii. 13, "In that He saith, a new covenant, He hath made the first old."

[8] St. John's testimony is more distinct, i. 12: "But as many as received Him, to them gave He power to become the sons of God, even to them that believe on His name."

[9] Isa. xlii. 6, 7

[10] Confirmabo te, "will strengthen Thee."

[11] In testamentum generis mei. The word here rendered "covenant" is the same (testamentum) as that translated in other places "testament," which does not supply the sense here required. The attempt to give the meaning "testament" in all places causes much confusion, as in this passage.

[12] Dan. vii. 13.

[13] Magistri Dei.

[14] i.e., the new doctrine which they announced.

[15] In memoriam scripta. This is said to have been the title of a spurious book now lost.

[16] Expugnaret. The word properly signifies to take by storm.

things which they had foretold as about to come to pass.

CHAP. XXII. — ARGUMENTS OF UNBELIEVERS AGAINST THE INCARNATION OF JESUS.

I have now confirmed, as I imagine, the things which are thought false and incredible by those who are not instructed in the true knowledge of heavenly learning. But, however, that we may refute those also who are too wise, not without injury to themselves, and who detract from the credit due to divine things, let us disprove their error, that they may at length perceive that the fact ought to have been as we show that it actually was. And although with good judges either testimonies are of sufficient weight without arguments, or arguments without testimonies, we, however, are not content with the one or the other, since we are supplied with both, that we may not leave room for any one of depraved ingenuity either to misunderstand or to dispute on the opposite side. They say that it was impossible for anything to be withdrawn[1] from an immortal nature. They say, in short, that it was unworthy of God to be willing to become man, and to burthen Himself with the infirmity of flesh; to become subject of His own accord to sufferings, to pain, and death: as though it had not been easy for Him to show Himself to men without[2] the weakness incident to a body, and to teach them righteousness (if He so wished) with greater authority, as of one who acknowledged[3] Himself to be God. For in that case all would have obeyed the heavenly precepts, if the influence and power of God enjoining them had been united with them. Why, then (they say), did He not come as God to teach men? Why did He render Himself so humble and weak, that it was possible for Him both to be despised by men and to be visited with punishment? why did He suffer violence from those who are weak and mortal? why did He not repel by strength, or avoid by His divine knowledge,[4] the hands of men? why did He not at least in His very death reveal His majesty? but He was led as one without strength to trial, was condemned as one who was guilty, was put to death as one who was mortal. I will carefully refute these things, nor will I permit any one to be in error. For these things were done by a great and wonderful plan; and he who shall understand this, will not only cease to wonder that God was tortured by men, but also will easily see that it could not have been believed that he was God if those very things which he censures had not been done.

CHAP. XXIII. — OF GIVING PRECEPTS, AND ACTING.

If any one gives to men precepts for living, and moulds the characters of others, I ask whether he is bound himself to practise the things which he enjoins, or is not bound. If he shall not do so, his precepts are annulled. For if the things which are enjoined are good, if they place the life of men in the best condition, the instructor ought not to separate himself from the number and assemblage of men among whom he acts; and he ought himself to live in the same manner in which he teaches that men ought to live, lest, by living in another way, he himself should disparage[5] his own precepts, and make his instruction of less value, if in reality he should relax the obligations of that which he endeavours to establish by his words. For every one, when he hears another giving precepts, is unwilling that the necessity of obeying should be imposed upon him, as though the right of liberty were taken from him. Therefore he answers his teacher in this manner: I am not able to do the things which you command, for they are impossible. For you forbid me to be angry, you forbid me to covet, you forbid me to be excited by desire, you forbid me to fear pain or death; but this is so contrary to nature, that all animals are subject to these affections. Or if you are so entirely of opinion that it is possible to resist nature, do you yourself practise the things which you enjoin, that I may know that they are possible? But since you yourself do not practise them, what arrogance is it, to wish to impose upon a free man laws which you yourself do not obey! You who teach, first learn; and before you correct the character of others, correct your own. Who could deny the justice of this answer? Nay! a teacher of this kind will fall into contempt, and will in his turn be mocked, because he also will appear to mock others.

What, therefore, will that instructor do, if these things shall be objected to him? how will he deprive the self-willed[6] of an excuse, unless he teach them by deeds before their eyes[7] that he teaches things which are possible? Whence it comes to pass, that no one obeys the precepts of the philosophers.[8] For men prefer examples rather than words, because it is easy to speak, but difficult to accomplish.[9] Would to heaven that there were as many who acted well as there are who speak well! But they who give pre-

1 Ut naturæ immortali quidquam decederet.
2 Citra.
3 Professi Dei. The expression denotes one who shows himself in his real character, without any veiling or concealment. There is another reading — "professi Deum."
4 Divinitate.

5 Ipse præceptis suis fidem detrahat.
6 Contumacibus.
7 Præsentibus factis.
8 [See Augustine, quoted in elucidation, vol. vi. p. 541.]
9 Præstare.

cepts, without carrying them out into action, are distrusted;[1] and if they shall be men, will be despised as inconsistent:[2] if it shall be God, He will be met with the excuse of the frailty of man's nature. It remains that words should be confirmed by deeds, which the philosophers are unable to do. Therefore, since the instructors themselves are overcome by the affections which they say that it is our duty to overcome, they are able to train no one to virtue, which they falsely proclaim;[3] and for this cause they imagine that no perfect wise man has as yet existed, that is, in whom the greatest virtue and perfect justice were in harmony with the greatest learning and knowledge. And this indeed was true. For no one since the creation of the world has been such, except Christ, who both delivered wisdom by His word, and confirmed His teaching by presenting virtue to the eyes of men.[4]

CHAP. XXIV. — THE OVERTHROWING OF THE ARGUMENTS ABOVE URGED BY WAY OF OBJECTION.

Come, let us now consider whether a teacher sent from heaven can fail to be perfect. I do not as yet speak of Him whom they deny to have come from God. Let us suppose that some one were to be sent from heaven to instruct the life of men in the first principles of virtue, and to form them to righteousness. No one can doubt but that this teacher, who is sent from heaven, would be as perfect in the knowledge of all things as in virtue, lest there should be no difference between a heavenly and an earthly teacher. For in the case of a man his instruction can by no means be from within and of himself.[5] For the mind, shut in by earthly organs, and hindered by a corrupt[6] body, of itself can neither comprehend nor receive the truth, unless it is taught from another source.[7] And if it had this power in the greatest degree, yet it would be unable to attain to the highest virtue, and to resist all vices, the materials of which are contained in our bodily[8] organs. Hence it comes to pass, that an earthly teacher cannot be perfect. But a teacher from heaven, to whom His divine nature gives knowledge, and His immortality gives virtue, must of necessity in His teaching also, as in other things, be perfect and complete. But this cannot by any means happen, unless He should take to Himself a mortal body. And the reason why it cannot happen is manifest. For if He should come to men as God, not to mention that mortal eyes cannot look upon and endure the glory of His majesty in His own person, assuredly God will not be able to teach virtue; for, inasmuch as He is without a body, He will not practise the things which He will teach, and through this His teaching will not be perfect. Otherwise, if it is the greatest virtue patiently to endure pain for the sake of righteousness and duty, if it is virtue not to fear death itself when threatened, and when inflicted to undergo it with fortitude; it follows that the perfect teacher ought both to teach these things by precept, and to confirm them by practice. For he who gives precepts for the life, ought to remove every method[9] of excuse, that he may impose upon men the necessity of obedience, not by any constraint, but by a sense of shame, and yet may leave them liberty, that a reward may be appointed for those who obey, because it was in their power not to obey if they so wished; and a punishment for those who do not obey, because it was in their power to obey if they so wished. How then can excuse be removed, unless the teacher should practise what he teaches, and as it were go before[10] and hold out his hand to one who is about to follow? But how can one practise what he teaches, unless he is like him whom he teaches? For if he be subject to no passion, a man may thus answer him who is the teacher: It is my wish not to sin, but I am overpowered; for I am clothed with frail and weak flesh: it is this which covets, which is angry, which fears pain and death. And thus I am led on against my will;[11] and I sin, not because it is my wish, but because I am compelled. I myself perceive that I sin; but the necessity imposed by my frailty, which I am unable to resist, impels me. What will that teacher of righteousness say in reply to these things? How will he refute and convict a man who shall allege the frailty of the flesh as an excuse for his faults, unless he himself also shall be clothed with flesh, so that he may show that even the flesh is capable of virtue? For obstinacy cannot be refuted except by example. For the things which you teach cannot have any weight unless you shall be the first to practise them; because the nature of men is inclined to faults, and wishes to sin not only with indulgence, but also with a reasonable plea.[12] It is befitting

[1] Abest ab iis fides.
[2] Leves.
[3] [What neither Platonists nor Censors, in their judgments, could effect by their *sophia*, the crucified Jesus has done by His Gospel. The impotence of philosophers as compared with the Carpenter's Son, to change the morals of nations, cannot be gainsaid. See Young's *Christ of History*.]
[4] Præsenti virtute.
[5] Propria.
[6] Tabe corporis.
[7] Thus our Lord tells us that flesh and blood cannot reveal to us mysteries.
[8] Visceribus.

[9] Omnium excusationum vias. [Here is the defect of Cicero's philosophy. See William Wilberforce, *Practical Christianity*, p. 25, ed. London, 1815.]
[10] Prævius.
[11] Thus St. Paul complains, Rom. vii. 15: "What I would, that do I not; but what I hate, that do I;" and ver. 21, "I find then a law, that when I would do good, evil is present with me." But (viii. 3) he says, "What the law could not do, in that it was weak through the flesh, God, sending His own Son in the likeness of sinful flesh, condemned sin in the flesh."
[12] Cum ratione.

that a master and teacher of virtue should most closely resemble man, that by overpowering sin he may teach man that sin may be overpowered by him. But if he is immortal, he can by no means propose an example to man. For there will stand forth some one persevering in his opinion, and will say: You indeed do not sin, because you are free from this body; you do not covet, because nothing is needed by an immortal; but I have need of many things for the support of this life. You do not fear death, because it can have no power against you. You despise pain, because you can suffer no violence. But I, a mortal, fear both, because they bring upon me the severest tortures, which the weakness of the flesh cannot endure. A teacher of virtue therefore ought to have taken away this excuse from men, that no one may ascribe it to necessity that he sins, rather than to his own fault. Therefore, that a teacher may be perfect, no objection ought to be brought forward by him who is to be taught, so that if he should happen to say, You enjoin impossibilities; the teacher may answer, See, I myself do them. But I am clothed with flesh, and it is the property of flesh to sin.[1] I too bear the same flesh, and yet sin does not bear rule in me. It is difficult for me to despise riches, because otherwise I am unable to live in this body. See, I too have a body, and yet I contend against every desire. I am not able to bear pain or death for righteousness, because I am frail. See, pain and death have power over me also; and I overcome those very things which you fear, that I may make you victorious over pain and death. I go before you through those things which you allege that it is impossible to endure: if you are not able to follow me giving directions, follow me going before you. In this way all excuse is taken away, and you must confess that man is unjust through his own fault, since he does not follow a teacher of virtue, who is at the same time a guide. You see, therefore, how much more perfect is a teacher who is mortal, because he is able to be a guide to one who is mortal, than one who is immortal, for he is unable to teach patient endurance who is not subject to passions. Nor, however, does this extend so far that I prefer man to God; but to show that man cannot be a perfect teacher unless he is also God, that he may by his heavenly authority impose upon men the necessity of obedience; nor God, unless he is clothed with a mortal body, that by carrying out his precepts to their completion[2] in actions, he may bind others by the necessity of obedience. It plainly therefore appears, that he who is a guide of life and teacher of righteousness must have a body, and that his teaching cannot otherwise be full and perfect, unless it has a root and foundation, and remains firm and fixed among men; and that he himself must undergo weakness of flesh and body, and display in himself[3] the virtue of which he is a teacher, that he may teach it at the same time both by words and deeds. Also, he must be subject to death and all sufferings, since the duties of virtue are occupied with the enduring of suffering, and the undergoing death; all which, as I have said, a perfect teacher ought to endure, that he may teach the possibility of their being endured.

CHAP. XXV. — OF THE ADVENT OF JESUS IN THE FLESH AND SPIRIT, THAT HE MIGHT BE MEDIATOR BETWEEN GOD AND MAN.

Let men therefore learn and understand why the Most High God, when He sent His ambassador and messenger to instruct mortals with the precepts of His righteousness, willed that He should be clothed with mortal flesh, and be afflicted with torture, and be sentenced to death. For since there was no righteousness on earth, He sent a teacher, as it were a living law, to found a new name and temple,[4] that by His words and example He might spread throughout the earth a true and holy worship. But, however, that it might be certain that He was sent by God, it was befitting that He should not be born as man is born, composed of a mortal on both sides;[5] but that it might appear that He was heavenly even in the form of man, He was born without the office of a father. For He had a spiritual Father, God; and as God was the Father of His spirit without a mother, so a virgin was the mother of His body without a father. He was therefore both God and man, being placed in the middle between God and man. From which the Greeks call Him Mesites,[6] that He might be able to lead man to God — that is, to immortality: for if He had been God only (as we have before said), He would not have been able to afford to man examples of goodness; if He had been man only, He would not have been able to compel men to righteousness, unless there had been added an authority and virtue greater than that of man.

For, since man is composed of flesh and

[1] This is urged as an excuse by him to whom the precept is addressed. In this and the following sentences there is a dialogue between the teacher and the taught.

[2] Præcepta sua factis adimplendo.

[3] Virtutem in se recipere.

[4] Thus, Heb. viii. 2, Christ is spoken of as "a minister of the sanctuary, and the true tabernacle."

[5] Having a human father and mother.

[6] *μεσίτης*, a mediator, one who stands between two parties to bring them together. Thus 1 Tim. ii. 5, "There is one God, and one mediator (*μεσίτης*) between God and men, the man Christ Jesus." In the Epistle to the Hebrews Christ is spoken of as the "mediator of the new covenant." And Gal. iii. 20, "A mediator is not of one:" the very idea of a mediator implies that he stands between two parties as a reconciler.

spirit, and the spirit must earn[1] immortality by works of righteousness, the flesh, since it is earthly, and therefore mortal, draws with itself the spirit linked to it, and leads it from immortality to death. Therefore the spirit, apart from the flesh, could by no means be a guide to immortality for man, since the flesh hinders the spirit from following God. For it is frail, and liable to sin; but sin is the food and nourishment[2] of death. For this cause, therefore, a mediator came — that is, God in the flesh — that the flesh might be able to follow Him, and that He might rescue man from death, which has dominion over the flesh. Therefore He clothed Himself with flesh, that the desires of the flesh being subdued, He might teach that to sin was not the result of necessity, but of *man's* purpose and will. For we have one great and principal struggle to maintain with the flesh, the boundless desires of which press upon the soul, nor allow it to retain dominion, but make it the slave of pleasures and sweet allurements, and visit it with everlasting death. And that we might be able to overcome these, God has opened and displayed to us the way of overcoming the flesh. And this perfect and absolutely complete[3] virtue bestows on those who conquer, the crown and reward of immortality.

CHAP. XXVI. — OF THE CROSS, AND OTHER TORTURES OF JESUS, AND OF THE FIGURE OF THE LAMB UNDER THE LAW.

I have spoken of humiliation, and frailty, and suffering — why God thought fit to undergo them. Now an account must be taken of the cross itself, and its meaning must be related. What the Most High Father arranged from the beginning, and how He ordained all things which were accomplished, not only the foretelling by the prophets, which preceded and was proved true[4] in Christ, but also the manner of His suffering itself teaches. For whatever sufferings He underwent were not without meaning;[5] but they had a figurative meaning[6] and great significance, as had also those divine works which He performed, the strength and power of which had some weight indeed for the present, but also declared something for the future. Heavenly influence opened the eyes of the blind, and gave light to those who did not see; and by this deed He signified that it would come to pass that, turning to the nations which were ignorant of God, He might enlighten the breasts of the foolish with the light of wisdom, and open the eyes of their understanding to the contemplation of the truth. For they are truly blind who, not seeing heavenly things, and surrounded with the darkness of ignorance, worship earthly and frail things. He opened the ears of the deaf. It is plain that this divine power did not limit its exercise to this point;[7] but He declared that it would shortly come to pass, that they who were destitute of the truth would both hear and understand the divine words of God. For you may truly call those deaf who do not hear the things which are heavenly and true, and worthy of being performed. He loosed the tongues of the dumb, so that they spake plainly.[8] A power worthy of admiration,[9] even when it was in operation: but there was contained in this display[10] of power another meaning, which showed that it would shortly come to pass that those who were lately ignorant of heavenly things, having received the instruction of wisdom, might speak respecting God and the truth. For he who is ignorant of the divine nature, he truly is speechless and dumb, although he is the most eloquent of all men. For when the tongue has begun to speak truth — that is, to set forth the excellency and majesty of the one God — then only does it discharge the office of its nature; but as long as it speaks false things it is not rightly employed:[11] and therefore he must necessarily be speechless who cannot utter divine things. He also renewed the feet of the lame to the office of walking, — a strength of divine work worthy of praise; but the figure implied this, that the errors of a worldly and wandering life being restrained, the path of truth was opened by which men might walk to attain the favour of God. For He is truly to be considered lame, who, being enwrapped in the gloom and darkness of folly, and ignorant in what direction to go, with feet liable to stumble and fall, walks in the way of death.

Likewise He cleansed the stains and blemishes of defiled bodies, — no slight exercise of immortal power; but this strength prefigured that by the instruction of righteousness His doctrine was about to purify those defiled by the stains of sins and the blemishes of vices. For they ought truly to be accounted as leprous and unclean,[12] whom either boundless lusts compel to crimes, or insatiable pleasures to disgraceful deeds, and affect with an everlasting stain those who are branded with the marks of dis-

[1] Emereri, "to earn or obtain." The word is specially applied to soldiers who have served their time, and are entitled to their discharge.
[2] Pabulum.
[3] Omnibus numeris absoluta.
[4] i.e., was shown by the event to be true, not doubtful or deceptive.
[5] Inania, "empty."
[6] Figuram.
[7] Hactenus operata est.
[8] In eloquium solvit
[9] See Matt. ix. 33, "The dumb spake, and the multitudes marvelled:" Mark vii. 37, "They were beyond measure astonished, saying, He hath done all things well: He maketh both the deaf to hear and the dumb to speak."
[10] Inerat huic virtuti.
[11] In usu suo non est.
[12] Elephantiaci, those afflicted with "elephantiasis," a kind of leprosy, covering the skin with incrustations resembling the hide of an elephant.

honourable actions. He raised the bodies of the dead as they lay prostrate; and calling them aloud by their names, He brought them back from death. What is more suitable to God, what more worthy of the wonder of all ages, than to have recalled [1] the life which has run its course, to have added times to the completed times of men, to have revealed the secrets of death? But this unspeakable power was the image of a greater energy, which showed that His teaching was about to have such might, that the nations throughout the world, which were estranged from God and subject to death, being animated by the knowledge of the true light, might arrive at the rewards of immortality. For you may rightly deem those to be dead, who, not knowing God the giver of life, and depressing their souls from heaven to earth, run into the snares of eternal death. The actions, therefore, which He then performed for the present, were representations of future things; the things which He displayed in injured and diseased bodies were figures [2] of spiritual things, that at present He might display to us the works of an energy which was not of earth, and for the future might show the power of His heavenly majesty.[3]

Therefore, as His works had a signification also of greater power, so also His passion did not go before us as simple, or superfluous, or by chance. But as those things which He did signified the great efficacy and power of His teaching, so those things which He suffered announced that wisdom would be held in hatred. For the vinegar which they gave Him to drink, and the gall which they gave Him to eat, held forth hardships and severities [4] in this life to the followers of truth. And although His passion, which was harsh and severe in itself, gave to us a sample of the future torments which virtue itself proposes to those who linger in this world, yet drink and food of this kind, coming into the mouth of our teacher, afforded us an example of pressures, and labours, and miseries. All which things must be undergone and suffered by those who follow the truth; since the truth is bitter, and detested by all who, being destitute of virtue, give up their life to deadly pleasures. For the placing of a crown of thorns upon His head, declared that it would come to pass that He would gather to Himself a holy people from those who were guilty. For people standing around in a circle are called a *corona*.[5] But we, who before that we knew God were unjust, were thorns — that is, evil and guilty, not knowing what was good; and estranged from the conception and the works of righteousness, polluted all things with wickedness and lust. Being taken, therefore, from briars and thorns, we surround the sacred head of God; for, being called by Himself, and spread around Him, we stand beside God, who is our Master and Teacher, and crown Him King of the world, and Lord of all the living.

But with reference to the cross, it has great force and meaning, which I will now endeavour to show. For God (as I have before explained), when He had determined to set man free, sent as His ambassador to the earth a teacher of virtue, who might both by salutary precepts train men to innocence, and by works and deeds before their eyes [6] might open the way of righteousness, by walking in which, and following his teacher, man might attain to eternal life. He therefore assumed a body, and was clothed in a garment of flesh, that He might hold out to man, for whose instruction He had come, examples of virtue and incitements to its practice. But when He had afforded an example of righteousness in all the duties of life, in order that He might teach man also the patient endurance of pain and contempt of death, by which virtue is rendered perfect and complete, He came into the hands of an impious nation, when, by the knowledge of the future which He had, He might have avoided them, and by the same power by which He did wonderful works He might have repelled them. Therefore He endured tortures, and stripes, and thorns. At last He did not refuse even to undergo death, that under His guidance man might triumph over death, subdued and bound in chains with all its terrors. But the reason why the Most High Father chose that kind of death in preference to others, with which He should permit Him to be visited, is this. For some one may perchance say: Why, if He was God, and chose to die, did He not at least suffer by some honourable kind of death? why was it by the cross especially? why by an infamous kind of punishment, which may appear unworthy even of a man if he is free,[7] although guilty? First of all, because He, who had come in humility that He might bring assistance to the humble and men of low degree, and might hold out to all the hope of safety, was to suffer by that kind of punishment by which the humble and low usually suffer, that there might be no one at all who might not be able to imitate Him. In the next place, it was in order that His body might be

1 Resignasse, "to have unsealed or opened."
2 Figuram gerebant.
3 [It is undoubtedly true that all our Lord's miracles are also *parables*. Such also is the entire history of the Hebrews.]
4 Acerbitates et amaritudines.
5 The word "corona" denotes a crown," and also, as here, a "ring" of persons standing around. The play on the word cannot be kept up in English. [Thus "corona tibi et judices defuerunt." Cicero, *Nat. Deor.*, ii. 1. So Ignatius, στέφανον τοῦ πρεσβυτερίου = corona presbyterii, vol i. p. 64, this series.]

6 Præsentibus.
7 The cross was the usual punishment of slaves.

kept unmutilated,[1] since He must rise again from the dead on the third day.

Nor ought any one to be ignorant of this, that He Himself, speaking before of His passion, also made it known that He had the power, when He willed it, of laying down His life and of taking it again. Therefore, because He had laid down His life while fastened to the cross, His executioners did not think it necessary to break His bones (as was their prevailing custom), but they only pierced His side. Thus His unbroken body was taken down from the cross, and carefully enclosed in a tomb. Now all these things were done lest His body, being injured and broken, should be rendered unsuitable[2] for rising again. That also was a principal cause why God chose the cross, because it was necessary that He should be lifted up on it, and the passion of God become known to all nations. For since he who is suspended upon a cross is both conspicuous to all and higher than others, the cross was especially chosen, which might signify that He would be so conspicuous, and so raised on high, that all nations from the whole world should meet together at once to know and worship Him. Lastly, no nation is so uncivilized, no region so remote, to which either His passion or the height of His majesty would be unknown. Therefore in His suffering He stretched forth His hands and measured out the world, that even then He might show that a great multitude, collected together out of all languages and tribes, from the rising of the sun even to his setting, was about to come under His wings, and to receive on their foreheads that great and lofty sign.[3] And the Jews even now exhibit a figure of this transaction when they mark their thresholds with the blood of a lamb. For when God was about to smite the Egyptians, to secure the Hebrews from that infliction He had enjoined them to slay a white[4] lamb without spot, and to place on their thresholds a mark from its blood. And thus, when the first-born of the Egyptians had perished in one night, the Hebrews alone were saved by the sign of the blood: not that the blood of a sheep had such efficacy in itself as to be the safety of men, but it was an image of things to come. For Christ was the white lamb without spot; that is, He was innocent, and just, and holy, who, being slain by the same Jews, is the salvation of all who have written on their foreheads the sign of blood — that is, of the cross, on which He shed His blood. For the forehead is the top of the threshold in man, and the wood sprinkled with blood is the emblem[5] of the cross. Lastly, the slaying of the lamb by those very persons who perform it is called the paschal feast, from the word "paschein,"[6] because it is a figure of the passion, which God, foreknowing the future, delivered by Moses to be celebrated by His people. But at that time the figure was efficacious at the present for averting the danger, that it may appear what great efficacy the truth itself is about to have for the protection of God's people in the extreme necessity of the whole world. But in what manner or in what region all will be safe who have marked on the highest part of their body this sign of the true and divine blood,[7] I will show in the last book.

CHAP. XXVII. — OF THE WONDERS EFFECTED BY THE POWER OF THE CROSS, AND OF DEMONS.

At present it is sufficient to show what great efficacy the power of this sign has. How great a terror this sign is to the demons, he will know who shall see how, when adjured by Christ, they flee from the bodies which they have besieged. For as He Himself, when He was living among men, put to flight all the demons by His word, and restored to their former senses the minds of men which had been excited and maddened by their dreadful attacks; so now His followers, in the name of their Master, and by the sign of His passion, banish the same polluted spirits from men. And it is not difficult to prove this. For when they sacrifice to their gods, if any one bearing a marked forehead stands by, the sacrifices are by no means favourable.[8]

"Nor can the diviner, when consulted, give answers."[9]

And this has often been the cause of punishment to wicked kings. For when some of their attendants who were of our religion[10] were standing by their masters as they sacrificed, having the sign placed on their foreheads, they caused the gods of their masters to flee, that they might not be able to observe[11] future events in the entrails of the victims. And when the soothsayers understood this, at the instigation of the same

1 Integrum.

2 A weak and senseless reason. The true cause is given by St. John xix. 36: "These things were done that the scripture should be fulfilled, A bone of Him shall not be broken." [The previous question, however, remains: Why was the Paschal lamb to be of unbroken bones, and why the special providence that fulfilled the type? Doubtless He who raised up His body could have restored it, had the bones also been broken; but the *preciousness* of Christ's body was thus indicated, as in the new tomb, the fine linen and spices, and the ministry of "the rich in his death, because He had done no violence," etc. — Isa. liii. 9.]

3 The sign of the cross used in baptism.

4 The account, Ex. xii., makes no mention of colour. "Without spot" is equivalent to "without blemish." [But the whiteness is implied. "Without spot" excludes "the ring-streaked and speckled," and a black lamb *a fortiori*. — 1 Pet. i. 19. "Without spot" settles the case. Isa. i. 18 proves that the *normal* wool is white.]

5 Significatio.

6 ἀπο τοῦ πάσχειν, "from suffering." The word "pascha" is not derived from Greek, as Lactantius supposes, but from the Hebrew "pasach," to pass over.

7 [See book vii., and the *Epitome*, cap. li., *infra*.]

8 Litant, a word peculiar to the soothsayers, used when the sacrifices are auspicious.

9 Virg., *Georg.*, iii. 491.

10 Nostri, i.e., Christians.

11 Depingere; to make observations on the entrails of the victims, so as to foretell future events.

demons to whom they had sacrificed,[1] complaining that profane men were present at the sacrifices, they drove their princes to madness, so that they attacked the temple of the god, and contaminated themselves by true sacrilege, which was expiated by the severest punishments on the part of their persecutors. Nor, however, are blind men able to understand even from this, either that this is the true religion, which contains such great power for overcoming, or that that is false, which is not able to hold its ground or to come to an engagement.

But they say that the gods do this, not through fear, but through hatred; as though it were possible for any one to hate another, unless it be him who injures, or has the power of injuring. Yea, truly, it would be consistent with their majesty to visit those whom they hated with immediate punishment,[2] rather than to flee from them. But since they can neither approach those in whom they shall see the heavenly mark, nor injure those whom the immortal sign[3] as an impregnable wall protects, they harass them by men, and persecute them by the hands of others: and if they acknowledge the existence of these demons, we have overcome; for this must necessarily be the true religion, which both understands the nature of demons, and understands their subtlety, and compels them, vanquished and subdued, to yield to itself. If they deny it, they will be refuted by the testimonies of poets and philosophers. But if they do not deny the existence and malignity of demons, what remains except that they affirm that there is a difference between gods and demons?[4] Let them therefore explain to us the difference between the two kinds, that we may know what is to be worshipped and what to be held in execration; whether they have any mutual agreement, or are really opposed to one another. If they are united by some necessity, how shall we distinguish them? or how shall we unite the honour and worship of each kind? If, on the other hand, they are enemies, how is it that the demons do not fear the gods, or that the gods cannot put to flight the demons? Behold, some one excited by the impulse of the demon is out of his senses, raves, is mad: let us lead him into the temple of the excellent and mighty Jupiter; or since Jupiter knows not how to cure men, into the fane of Æsculapius or Apollo. Let the priest of either, in the name of his god, command the wicked spirit to come out of the man: that can in no way come to pass. What, then, is the power of the gods, if the demons are not subject to their control? But, in truth, the same demons, when adjured by the name of the true God, immediately flee. What reason is there why they should fear Christ, but not fear Jupiter, unless that they whom the multitude esteem to be gods are also demons? Lastly, if there should be placed in the midst one who is evidently suffering from an attack of a demon, and the priest of the Delphian Apollo, they will in the same manner dread the name of God; and Apollo will as quickly depart from his priest as the spirit of the demon from the man; and his god being adjured and put to flight, the priest will be for ever silent.[5] Therefore the demons, whom they acknowledge to be objects of execration, are the same as the gods to whom they offer supplications.

If they imagine that we are unworthy of belief, let them believe Homer, who associated the supreme Jupiter[6] with the demons; and also other poets and philosophers, who speak of the same beings at one time as demons, and at another time as gods, — of which names one is true, and the other false. For those most wicked spirits, when they are adjured, then confess that they are demons; when they are worshipped, then falsely say that they are gods; in order that they may lead men into errors,[7] and call them away from the knowledge of the true God, by which alone eternal death can be escaped. They are the same who, for the sake of overthrowing man, have founded various systems of worship for themselves through different regions,[8] — under false and assumed names, however, that they might deceive. For because they were unable by themselves to aspire to divinity, they took to themselves the names of powerful kings, under whose titles they might claim for themselves divine honours; which error may be dispelled, and brought to the light of truth. For if any one desires to inquire further into the matter, let him assemble those who are skilled in calling forth spirits from the dead. Let them call forth[9] Jupiter, Neptune, Vulcan, Mercury, Apollo, and Saturnus the father of all. All will answer from the lower regions; and being questioned they will speak, and confess respecting themselves and

---

1 Prosecrârant. Others read "prosecârant," a sacrificial word, properly denoting the setting apart some portion of the victim for offering to the gods.

2 Præsentibus pœnis, "on the spot."

3 i.e., the sign of the cross, with which the early Christians frequently marked themselves [So long as Christians were mocked and despised as followers of a crucified one, there was a silent testimony and bold confession in this act which must be wholly separated from the mere superstition of degenerate Christians. It used to mean just what the Apostle says, Gal. vi. 14. In this sense it is retained among Anglicans.]

4 [See vol. iii. pp. 37, 176, 180, and iv. 189-190.]

5 [The cessation of oracles is attested by Plutarch. See also Tertullian, vol. iii. p. 38, this series, and Minucius, vol. iv. p. 190. Demonology needs further exposition, for Scripture is express in its confirmation of patristic views of the subject.]

6 There is probably a reference to *Iliad*, i. 221, where Athene is represented as going to Olympus: —

ἡ δ' Οὔλυμπόνδε βεβήκει
δώματ' ἐς αἰγιόχοιο Διὸς μετὰ δαίμονας ἄλλους.

7 Ut errores hominibus immittant.

8 Per diversa regionum. There is another reading, "perversâ religione" — by perverted religion.

9 The reference is to necromancy, or calling up the spirits of the dead by magic rites.

God. After these things let them call up Christ; He will not be present, He will not appear, for He was not more than two days in the lower regions. What proof can be brought forward more certain than this? I have no doubt that Trismegistus arrived at the truth by some proof of this kind, who spoke many things [1] respecting God the Son which are contained in the divine secrets.

CHAP. XXVIII. — OF HOPE AND TRUE RELIGION, AND OF SUPERSTITION.

And since these things are so, as we have shown, it is plain that no other hope of life is set before man, except that, laying aside vanities and wretched error, he should know God,[2] and serve God; except he renounce this temporary life, and train himself by the principles of righteousness for the cultivation of true religion. For we are created on this condition, that we pay just and due obedience to God who created us, that we should know and follow Him alone. We are *bound* and *tied* to God by this *chain of piety;*[3] from which religion itself received its name, not, as Cicero explained it, from carefully gathering,[4] for in his second book respecting the nature of the gods he thus speaks: "For not only philosophers, but our ancestors also, separated superstition from religion. For they who spent whole days in prayers and sacrifices, that their children might survive [5] them, were called superstitious. But they who handled again, and as it were carefully gathered all things which related to the worship of the gods, were called religious from carefully gathering,[6] as some were called elegant from choosing out, and diligent from carefully selecting and intelligent from understanding. For in all these words there is the same meaning of gathering which there is in the word religious: thus it has come to pass, that in the names superstitious and religious, the one relates to a fault, the other belongs to praise." How senseless this interpretation is, we may know from the matter itself. For if both religion and superstition are engaged in the worship of the same gods, there is little or rather no difference between them. For what cause will he allege why he should think that to pray once for the health of sons is the part of a religious man, but to do the same ten times is the part of a superstitious man? For if it is an excellent thing to pray once, how much more so to do it more frequently! If it is well to do it at the first hour, then it is well to do it throughout the day. If one victim renders the deity propitious, it is plain that many victims must render him more propitious, because multiplied services oblige [7] rather than offend. For those servants do not appear to us hateful who are assiduous and constant in their attendance, but more beloved. Why, therefore, should he be in fault, and receive a name which implies censure,[8] who either loves his children more, or sufficiently honours the gods; and he, on the contrary, be praised, who loves them less? And this argument has weight also from the contrary. For if it is wrong [9] to pray and sacrifice during whole days, therefore it is wrong to do so once. If it is faulty frequently to wish for the preservation of our children, therefore he also is superstitious who conceives that wish even rarely. Or why should the name of a fault be derived from that, than which nothing can be wished more honourable, nothing more just? For as to his saying, that they who diligently take in hand again the things relating to the worship of the gods are called religious from their carefully gathering; how is it, then, that they who do this often in a day lose the name of religious men, when it is plain from their very assiduity that they more diligently gather those things by which the gods are worshipped?

What, then, is it? Truly religion is the cultivation of the truth, but superstition of that which is false. And it makes the entire difference what you worship, not how you worship, or what prayer you offer.[10] But because the worshippers of the gods imagine themselves to be religious, though they are superstitious, they are neither able to distinguish religion from superstition, nor to express the meaning of the names. We have said that the name of religion is derived from *the bond* of piety,[11] because God has *tied* man to Himself, and *bound* him by piety; [12] for we must serve Him as a master, and be obedient to Him as a father. And therefore Lucre-

1 There is another reading: "qui de Deo patre omnia, et de filio locutus est multa;" but this is manifestly erroneous.

2 So our Lord, John xvii. 3: "This is life eternal, that they might know Thee the only true God, and Jesus Christ, whom Thou hast sent."

3 ["Hoc vinculo pietatis obstricti Deo et *religati* sumus." He returns to this in the same chapter, *infra.*]

4 A religendo. There is little doubt that the true derivation of "religio" is from *religere*, not from *religare.* According to this, the primary meaning is, "the dwelling upon a subject, and continually recurring to it."

5 Superstites, et superstitiosi.

6 [Here the famous passage should be given with accurate reference to its place, as much of its force vanishes in translation. Cicero's etymology is thus given: "Qui autem omnia quæ ad cultum deorum pertinerent, diligentes retractarent et tamquam *relegerent* sunt dicti *religiosi*, ex *relegendo*, ut *elegantes* ex *eligendo*, tamquam a *diligendo diligentes*, ex *intelligendo intelligentes*." — *De Nat. Deor.*, lib. ii. cap. 28.]

7 Demerentur, "they lay under an obligation."

8 Criminis est.

9 Vitiosum.

10 [This seems very loose language when compared with Matt. vi. 9 and 1 Cor. xi. 1, 2. The whole epistle shows the *how* and the *what* to be important in worship, and that the Apostle had prescribed certain laws about these.]

11 [See note 4, *supra.*]

12 [Lactantius has generally been sustained by Christian criticism in the censures thus passed upon Cicero, and in making the word *religio* out of *religare.* His own words are desirable here, to be compared with those which he endeavours to refute (note 4, *supra*): "Diximus nomen *religionis* a vinculo pietatis esse deductum, quod hominem sibi Deus *religarit*," etc.; i.e., it *binds again* what was loosed.]

tius[1] better explained this name, who says that He loosens the knots of superstitions.[2] But they are called superstitious, not who wish their children to survive them, for we all wish this; but either those who reverence the surviving memory of the dead, or those who, surviving their parents, reverenced their images at their houses as household gods. For those who assumed to themselves new rites, that they might honour the dead as gods, whom they supposed to be taken from men and received into heaven, they called superstitious. But those who worshipped the public and ancient gods[3] they named religious. From which Virgil says:[4] —

> "Superstition vain, and ignorant of ancient gods."

But since we find that the ancient gods also were consecrated in the same manner after their death, therefore they are superstitious who worship many and false gods. We, on the other hand, are religious, who make our supplications to the one true God.

CHAP. XXIX. — OF THE CHRISTIAN RELIGION, AND OF THE UNION OF JESUS WITH THE FATHER.

Some one may perhaps ask how, when we say that we worship one God only, we nevertheless assert that there are two, God the Father and God the Son: which assertion has driven many into the greatest error. For when the things which we say seem to them probable, they consider that we fail in this one point alone, that we confess that there is another God, and that He is mortal. We have already spoken of His mortality: now let us teach concerning His unity. When we speak of God the Father and God the Son, we do not speak of them as different, nor do we separate each: because the Father cannot exist without the Son, nor can the Son be separated from the Father, since the name of Father[5] cannot be given without the Son, nor can the Son be begotten without the Father. Since, therefore, the Father makes the Son, and the Son the Father, they both have one mind, one spirit, one substance; but the former[6] is as it were an overflowing fountain, the latter[7] as a stream flowing forth from it: the former as the sun, the latter as it were a ray[8] extended from the sun. And since He is both faithful to the Most High Father, and beloved by Him, He is not separated from Him; just as the stream is not separated from the fountain, nor the ray from the sun: for the water of the fountain is in the stream, and the light of the sun is in the ray: just as the voice cannot be separated from the mouth, nor the strength or hand from the body. When, therefore, He is also spoken of by the prophets as the hand, and strength, and word of God, there is plainly no separation; for the tongue, which is the minister of speech, and the hand, in which the strength is situated, are inseparable portions of the body.

We may use an example more closely connected with us. When any one has a son whom he especially loves, who is still in the house, and in the power[9] of his father, although he concede to him the name and power of a master, yet by the civil law the house is one, and one person is called master. So this world[10] is the one house of God; and the Son and the Father, who unanimously inhabit the world, are one God, for the one is as two, and the two are as one. Nor is that wonderful, since the Son is in the Father, for the Father loves the Son, and the Father is in the Son; for He faithfully obeys the will of the Father, nor does He ever do nor has done anything except what the Father either willed or commanded. Lastly, that the Father and the Son are but one God, Isaiah showed in that passage which we have brought forward before,[11] when he said:[12] "They shall fall down unto Thee, and make supplication unto Thee, since God is in Thee, and there is no other God besides Thee." And he also speaks to the same purport in another place:[13] "Thus saith God the King of Israel, and His Redeemer, the everlasting God; I am the first, and I am the last; and beside me there is no God." When he had set forth two persons, one of God the King, that is, Christ, and the other of God the Father, who after His passion raised Him from the dead, as we have said[14] that the prophet Hosea showed,[15] who said, "I will redeem Him from the power of the grave:" nevertheless, with reference to each person, he introduced the words, "and beside me there is no God," when he might have said "beside us;" but it was not right that a separation of so close a relationship should be made by the use of the plural number. For there is one God alone, free, most high, without any origin; for He Himself is the origin of all things, and in Him at once both the Son and all things are contained. Wherefore, since the mind and will of the one is in the other, or rather, since there is one in both,

1 Lucret., i. 931.
2 Religionum.
3 i.e., those worshipped in public temples, and with public sacrifices, as opposed to the household gods of a family, and ancient as opposed to those newly received as gods.
4 Virg., *Æneid*, viii. 187.
5 [i.e, the Everlasting Father implies the Everlasting Son.]
6 Ille, i.e., the Father.
7 Hic, i e., the Son.
8 Thus, Heb. i. 3, the Son is described as the effulgence of the Father's glory: ἀπαύγασμα τῆς δόξης αὐτοῦ.
9 In manu patris. Among the Romans the father had the power of life and death over his children.
10 [Mundus una Dei domus. World here = universe. See vol. ii. p. 136, note 2, this series.]
11 Ch. xiii.
12 Isa. xlv. 14.
13 Isa. xliv. 6.
14 Ch. xix.
15 Hos. xiii. 14.

both are justly called one God; for whatever is in the Father[1] flows on to the Son, and whatever is in the Son descends from the Father. Therefore that highest and matchless God cannot be worshipped except through the Son. He who thinks that he worships the Father only, as he does not worship the Son, so he does not worship even the Father. But he who receives the Son, and bears His name, he truly together with the Son worships the Father also, since the Son is the ambassador, and messenger, and priest of the Most High Father. He is the door of the greatest temple, He the way of light, He the guide to salvation, He the gate of life.

CHAP. XXX. — OF AVOIDING HERESIES AND SUPERSTITIONS, AND WHAT IS THE ONLY TRUE CATHOLIC CHURCH.

But since many heresies have existed, and the people of God have been rent into divisions at the instigation of demons, the truth must be briefly marked out by us, and placed in its own peculiar dwelling-place, that if any one shall desire to draw the water of life, he may not be borne to broken cisterns[2] which hold no water, but may know the abundant fountain of God, watered by which he may enjoy perpetual light. Before all things, it is befitting that we should know both that He Himself and His ambassadors foretold that there must be numerous sects and heresies,[3] which would break the unity[4] of the sacred body; and that they admonished us to be on our guard with the greatest prudence, lest we should at any time fall into the snares and deceits of that adversary of ours, with whom God has willed that we should contend. Then that He gave us sure commands, which we ought always to treasure in our minds; for many, forgetting them, and abandoning the heavenly road, have made for themselves devious paths amidst windings and precipices, by which they might lead away the incautious and simple part of the people to the darkness of death: I will explain how this happened. There were some of our religion whose faith was less established, or who were less learned or less cautious, who rent the unity and divided the Church. But they whose faith was unsettled,[5] when they pretended that they knew and worshipped God, aiming at the increase of their wealth and honour, aspired to the highest sacerdotal power; and when overcome by others more powerful, preferred to secede with their supporters, than to endure those set over them, over whom they themselves before desired to be set.[6]

But some, not sufficiently instructed in heavenly learning, when they were unable to reply to the accusers of the truth, who objected that it was either impossible or inconsistent that God should be shut up in the womb of a woman, and that the Majesty of heaven could not be reduced to such weakness as to become an object of contempt and derision, a reproach and mockery to men; lastly, that He should even endure tortures, and be affixed to the accursed cross; and when they could defend and refute all these things neither by talent nor learning, for they did not thoroughly perceive their force and meaning, they were perverted[7] from the right path, and corrupted the sacred writings, so that they composed for themselves a new doctrine without any root and stability. But some, enticed by the prediction of false prophets, concerning whom both the true prophets and he himself had foretold, fell away from the knowledge of God, and left the true tradition. But all of these, ensnared by frauds of demons, which they ought to have foreseen and guarded against, by their carelessness lost the name and worship of God. For when they are called Phrygians,[8] or Novatians,[9] or Valentinians,[10] or Marcionites,[11] or Anthropians,[12] or Arians,[13] or by any other name, they have ceased to be Christians, who have lost the name of Christ, and assumed human and external names. Therefore it is the Catholic Church alone which retains true worship.

This is the fountain of truth, this is the abode of the faith, this is the temple of God; into which if any one shall not enter, or from which if any shall go out, he is estranged from the hope of life and eternal salvation. No one ought to flatter himself with persevering strife. For the contest is respecting life and salvation, which,

1 Thus Christ Himself speaks, John x. 30, "I and my Father are one;" and iii. 35, "The Father loveth the Son, and hath given all things into His hand."

2 So Jer. ii. 13.

3 See Matt. xviii. 7; Luke xvii. 1; 1 Cor. xi. 19; 2 Pet. ii. 1.

4 Concordiam.

5 Lubrica.

6 [N.B. — The Callistians, Novatians, etc.; vol. v. Elucidation XIV. p. 160; and *Ibid.*, p. 319, 321–333.]

7 Depravati sunt.

8 The Phrygians were the followers of Montanus, who was the founder of a sect in the second century. He is supposed to have been a native of Ardaba, on the borders of Phrygia, on which account his followers were called the Phrygian or Cataphrygian heretics. Montanus gave himself out for the Paraclete or Comforter whom our Lord promised to send. The most eminent of his followers were Priscilla and Maximilla. [But see vol. ii. pp. 4 and 5; also vol. iii. and iv. this series, and notes on Tertullian, *passim*.]

9 The Novatians were the followers of Novatus, in the third century. They assumed to themselves the title of Cathari, or the pure. They refused to re-admit to their communion those who had once fallen away, and allowed no place for repentance.

10 The Valentinians were the followers of Valentinus, an Egyptian who founded a sect in the second century. His system somewhat resembled the Gnostics. He taught that Christ had a heavenly or spiritual body, and assumed nothing from the Virgin Mary.

11 The Marcionites were the followers of Marcion, a heretic of the second century, who held the Oriental belief of two independent, eternal, co-existing principles, one of good, the other of evil. He applied this doctrine to Christianity. His chief opponent was Tertullian.

12 The Anthropians held that Jesus Christ was nothing but man (ἄνθρωπος).

13 This word is omitted by some editors, as Lactantius wrote before the Arian heresy had gained strength. [See vol. vi. p. 291.]

unless it is carefully and diligently kept in view, will be lost and extinguished. But, however, because all the separate assemblies of heretics call themselves Christians in preference to others, and think that theirs is the Catholic Church, it must be known that the true Catholic Church is that in which there is confession and repentance,[1] which treats in a wholesome manner the sins and wounds to which the weakness of the flesh is liable. I have related these things in the meanwhile for the sake of admonition, that no one who desires to avoid error may be entangled in a greater error, while he is ignorant of the secret[2] of the truth. Afterwards, in a particular and separate work, we will more fully and copiously[3] contend against all divisions of falsehoods. It follows that, since we have spoken sufficiently on the subject of true religion and wisdom, we discuss the subject of justice in the next book.

[1] This is directed against the Novatians. See preceding note on the Novatians, [and vol. v., this series, *passim*].

[2] Penetrale, "the interior of a house or temple."

[3] Uberius. Others read "verius," more truly; but the reading of the text is preferable.

GENERAL NOTES BY THE AMERICAN EDITOR.

I.

(On cap. 29.)

HERE we should look for something also concerning the Holy Spirit. But our author's principle is doubtless a reflection of the prevailing sentiment of the Church at this period, which was perhaps a violent exaggeration of our Lord's example (Mark iv. 33). And see something of this on p. 140, note 6, *infra;* also Matt. vii. 6.

II.

(On cap. 30.)

The simplicity with which our author gives a note of the Catholic Church, in accordance with African canons and the teaching of Cyprian, is very noteworthy. It never occurred to him that communion with any one particular See was the note. Hippolytus alone would have reminded him that the worst heretics had been in communion with both Zephyrinus and Callistus in his days (see vol. v. pp. 156 and 160; also *Ibid.*, 125, 130), and that orthodoxy had been persecuted by these bishops of Rome.

THE DIVINE INSTITUTES

BOOK V.

OF JUSTICE.

CHAP. I.—OF THE NON-CONDEMNATION OF ACCUSED PERSONS WITHOUT A HEARING OF THEIR CAUSE; FROM WHAT CAUSE PHILOSOPHERS DESPISED THE SACRED WRITINGS; OF THE FIRST ADVOCATES OF THE CHRISTIAN RELIGION.

I ENTERTAIN no doubt, O mighty Emperor Constantine,[1]—since they are impatient through excessive superstition,—that if any *one* of those who are foolishly religious should take in hand this work of ours, in which that matchless Creator of all things and Ruler of this boundless world is asserted, he would even assail it with abusive language, and perhaps, having scarcely read the beginning, would dash it to the ground, cast it from him, curse it, and think himself contaminated and bound by inexpiable guilt if he should patiently read or hear these things. We demand, however, from this man, if it is possible, by the right of human nature,[2] that he should not condemn before that he knows the whole matter. For if the right of defending themselves is given to sacrilegious persons, and to traitors and sorcerers, and if it is lawful for no one to be condemned beforehand, his cause being as yet untried, we do not appear to ask unjustly, that if there shall be any one who shall have fallen upon this, subject, if he shall read it, he read it throughout; if he shall hear it, that he put off the forming of an opinion until the end. But I know the obstinacy of men; we shall never succeed in obtaining this. For they fear lest they should be overcome by us, and be compelled at length to yield, truth itself crying out. They interrupt, therefore, and make hindrances, that they may not hear; and close their eyes, that they may not see the light which we present to them. Wherefore they themselves plainly show their distrust in their own abandoned system, since they neither venture to investigate, nor to engage with us, because they know that they are easily overpowered. And therefore, discussion being taken away,

> "Wisdom is driven from among them, they have recourse to violence,"

as Ennius says; and because they eagerly endeavour to condemn as guilty those whom they plainly know to be innocent, they are unwilling to be agreed respecting innocence itself; as though, in truth, it were a greater injustice to have condemned innocence, when proved to be such, than unheard. But, as I said, they are afraid lest, if they should hear, they should be unable to condemn.

And therefore they torture, put to death, and banish the worshippers of the Most High God, that is, the righteous; nor are they, who so vehemently hate, themselves able to assign the causes of their hatred. Because they are themselves in error, they are angry with those who follow the path of truth; and when they are able to correct themselves, they greatly increase[3] their errors by cruel deeds, they are stained with the blood of the innocent, and they tear away with violence souls dedicated to God from the lacerated bodies. Such are the men with whom we now endeavour to engage and to dispute: these are the men whom we would lead away from a foolish persuasion to the truth, men who would more readily drink blood than imbibe the words of the righteous. What then? Will our labour be in vain? By no means. For if we shall not be able to deliver these from death, to which they are hastening with the greatest speed; if we cannot recall them from that devious path to life and light, since they themselves oppose their own safety; yet we shall strengthen those who belong to us, whose opinion is not settled, and founded and fixed

[1] These words are omitted in some editions. The chapter is a kind of preface to the whole book, in which he complains that punishment has been inflicted on the Christians, without due inquiry into their cause. [Religious = *superstitious*. See p. 131, *supra*.]

[2] Jure humanitatis.

[3] Coacervant, "they heap up."

with solid roots. For many of them waver, and especially those who have any acquaintance with literature. For in this respect philosophers, and orators, and poets are pernicious, because they are easily able to ensnare unwary souls by the sweetness of their discourse, and of their poems flowing with delightful modulation. These are sweets [1] which conceal poison. And on this account I wished to connect wisdom with religion, that that vain system may not at all injure the studious; so that now the knowledge of literature may not only be of no injury to religion and righteousness, but may even be of the greatest profit, if he who has learned it should be more instructed in virtues and wiser in truth.

Moreover, even though it should be profitable to no other, it certainly will be so to us: the conscience will delight itself, and the mind will rejoice that it is engaged in the light of truth, which is the food of the soul, being overspread with an incredible kind of pleasantness. But we must not despair. Perchance

"We sing not to the deaf." [2]

For neither are affairs in so bad a condition that there are no sound minds to which the truth may be pleasing, and which may both see and follow the right course when it is pointed out to them. Only let the cup be anointed [3] with the heavenly honey of wisdom, that the bitter remedies may be drunk by them unawares, without any annoyance, whilst the first sweetness of taste by its allurement conceals, under the cover [4] of pleasantness, the bitterness of the harsh flavour. For this is especially the cause why, with the wise and the learned, and the princes of this world, the sacred Scriptures are without credit, because the prophets spoke in common and simple language, as though they spoke to the people. And therefore they are despised by those who are willing to hear or read nothing except that which is polished and eloquent; nor is anything able to remain fixed in their minds, except that which charms their ears by a more soothing sound. But those things which appear humble [5] are considered anile, foolish, and common. So entirely do they regard nothing as true, except that which is pleasant to the ear; nothing as credible, except that which can excite [6] pleasure: no one estimates [7] a subject by its truth, but by its embellishment. Therefore they do not believe the sacred writings, because they are without any pretence; [8] but they do not even believe those who explain them, because they also are either altogether ignorant, or at any rate possessed of little learning. For it very rarely happens that they are wholly eloquent; and the cause of this is evident. For eloquence is subservient to the world, it desires to display itself to the people, and to please in things which are evil; since it often endeavours to overpower the truth, that it may show its power; it seeks wealth, desires honours; in short, it demands the highest degree of dignity. Therefore it despises these subjects as low; it avoids secret things as contrary to itself, inasmuch as it rejoices in publicity, and longs for the multitude and celebrity. Hence it comes to pass that wisdom and truth need suitable heralds. And if by chance any of the learned have betaken themselves to it, they have not been sufficient for its defence.

Of those who are known to me, Minucius Felix was of no ignoble rank among pleaders. His book, which bears the title of *Octavius*, declares how suitable a maintainer of the truth he might have been, if he had given himself altogether to that pursuit. [9] Septimius Tertullianus also was skilled in literature of every kind; but in eloquence he had little readiness, and was not sufficiently polished, and very obscure. Not even therefore did he find sufficient renown. Cyprianus, therefore, was above all others [10] distinguished and renowned, since he had sought great glory to himself from the profession of the art of oratory, and he wrote very many things worthy of admiration in their particular class. For he was of a turn of mind which was ready, copious, agreeable, and (that which is the greatest excellence of style) plain and open; so that you cannot determine whether he was more embellished in speech, or more ready in explanation, or more powerful in persuasion. And yet he is unable to please those who are ignorant of the mystery except by his words; inasmuch as the things which he spoke are mystical, and prepared with this object, that they may be heard by the faithful only: in short, he is accustomed to be derided by the learned men of this age, to whom his writings have happened to be known. I have heard of a certain man who was skilful indeed, who by the change of a single letter called him Coprianus, [11] as though he were one who had applied to old women's fables a mind which was elegant and fitted for better things. But if this happened to him whose eloquence is

[1] Mella.

[2] Virgil, *Bucol.*, x. 8.

[3] There is a reference here to a well-known passage of Lucretius, i. 935: "As physicians, when they purpose to give nauseous wormwood to children, first smear the rim round the bowl with the sweet yellow juice of honey, that the unthinking age of children may be fooled as far as the lips, but though beguiled, not be betrayed."

[4] Sub prætextu.

[5] Sordida.

[6] Incutere. So Lucretius, i. 19, "incutiens amorem."

[7] Ponderat.

[8] Sine fuco.

[9] [Vol. iv. 173. Note our author's reference to the founders of Latin Christianity, all North-Africans, like Arnobius and himself. See vol. iv. pp. 169, 170.]

[10] Unus.

[11] The word κοπρίας is applied to sycophants and low buffoons and jesters, who, for the sake of exciting laughter, made boastful and extravagant promises.

not unpleasant, what then must we suppose happens to those whose discourse is meagre and displeasing, who could have had neither the power of persuasion, nor subtlety in arguing, nor any severity at all for refuting?

CHAP. II. — TO WHAT AN EXTENT THE CHRISTIAN TRUTH HAS BEEN ASSAILED BY RASH MEN.

Therefore, because there have been wanting among us suitable and skilful teachers, who might vigorously and sharply refute public errors, and who might defend the whole cause of truth with elegance and copiousness, this very want incited some to venture to write against the truth, which was unknown to them. I pass by those who in former times in vain assailed it. When I was teaching rhetorical learning in Bithynia, having been called thither, and it had happened that at the same time the temple of God was overthrown, there were living at the same place two men who insulted the truth as it lay prostrate and overthrown, I know not whether with greater arrogance or harshness: the one of whom professed himself the high priest of philosophy;[1] but he was so addicted to vice, that, though a teacher of abstinence, he was not less inflamed with avarice than with lusts; so extravagant in his manner of living, that though in his school he was the maintainer of virtue, the praiser of parsimony and poverty, he dined less sumptuously in a palace than at his own house. Nevertheless he sheltered[2] his vices by his hair[3] and his cloak, and (that which is the greatest screen[4]) by his riches; and that he might increase these, he used to penetrate with wonderful effort[5] to the friendships of the judges; and he suddenly attached them to himself by the authority of a fictitious name, not only that he might make a traffic of their decisions, but also that he might by this influence hinder his neighbours, whom he was driving from their homes and lands, from the recovery of their property. This man, in truth, who overthrew his own arguments by his character, or censured his own character by his arguments, a weighty censor and most keen accuser against himself, at the very same time in which a righteous people were impiously assailed, vomited forth three books against the Christian religion and name; professing, above all things, that it was the office of a philosopher to remedy the errors of men, and to recall them to the true way, that is, to the worship of the gods, by whose power and majesty, as he said, the world is governed; and not to permit that inexperienced men should be enticed by the frauds of any, lest their simplicity should be a prey and sustenance to crafty men.

Therefore he said that he had undertaken this office, worthy of philosophy, that he might hold out to those who do not see the light of wisdom, not only that they may return to a healthy state of mind, having undertaken the worship of the gods, but also that, having laid aside their pertinacious obstinacy, they may avoid tortures of the body, nor wish in vain to endure cruel lacerations of their limbs. But that it might be evident on what account he had laboriously worked out that task, he broke out profusely into praises of the princes, whose piety and foresight, as he himself indeed said, had been distinguished both in other matters, and especially in defending the religious rites of the gods; that he had, in short, consulted the interests of men, in order that, impious and foolish superstition having been restrained, all men might have leisure for lawful sacred rites, and might experience the gods propitious to them. But when he wished to weaken the grounds of that religion against which he was pleading, he appeared senseless, vain, and ridiculous; because that weighty adviser of the advantage of others was ignorant not only what to oppose, but even what to speak. For if any of our religion were present, although they were silent on account of the time, nevertheless in their mind they derided him; since they saw a man professing that he would enlighten others, when he himself was blind; that he would recall others from error, when he himself was ignorant where to plant his feet; that he would instruct others to the truth, of which he himself had never seen even a spark at any time; inasmuch as he who was a professor of wisdom, endeavoured to overthrow wisdom. All, however, censured this, that he undertook this work at that time in particular, in which odious cruelty raged. O philosopher, a flatterer, and a time-server! But this man was despised, as his vanity deserved; for he did not gain the popularity which he hoped for, and the glory which he eagerly sought for was changed into censure and blame.[6]

Another[7] wrote the same subject with more bitterness, who was then of the number of the judges, and who was especially the adviser of enacting persecution; and not contented with this crime, he also pursued with writings those whom he had persecuted. For he composed

---

1 [Let us call him *Barbatus;* for one so graphically described by our author deserves a name worthy of his sole claim to be a philosopher.]

2 Protegebat.

3 It was the custom of the philosophers to wear a beard; to which practice Horace alludes, *Serm.*, ii. 3, "Sapientem pascere barbam," to nourish a philosophic beard. [The readers of this series no longer require this information: but it may be convenient to recur to vol. ii. note 9, p. 321: also, perhaps, to Clement's *terrible* defence of beards, *Ibid.*, pp. 276–277.]

4 Velamentum.

5 Ambitu. The word denotes the unlawful striving for a post.

6 [On the reference to these two adversaries, see Lardner, *Credib.*, iii. cap. 65, p. 491; vii. cap. 39, p. 471; also vii. 207.]

7 Hierocles is referred to, who was a great persecutor of the Christians in the beginning of the fourth century. He was the chief promoter of the persecution which the Christians suffered under Diocletian. [Wrote a work (*Philalethes*) to show the contradictions of Scripture. Acts xiii. 10.]

two books, not *against* the Christians, lest he might appear to assail them in a hostile manner, but *to* the Christians, that he might be thought to consult for them with humanity and kindness. And in these writings he endeavoured so to prove the falsehood of sacred Scripture, as though it were altogether contradictory to itself; for he expounded some chapters which seemed to be at variance with themselves, enumerating so many and such secret [1] things, that he sometimes appears to have been one of the same sect. But if this was so, what Demosthenes will be able to defend from the charge of impiety him who became the betrayer of the religion to which he had given his assent,[2] and of the faith the name of which he had assumed,[3] and of the mystery [4] which he had received, unless it happened by chance that the sacred writings fell into his hands? What rashness was it, therefore, to dare to destroy that which no one explained to him! It was well that he either learned nothing or understood nothing. For contradiction is as far removed from the sacred writings as he was removed from faith and truth. He chiefly, however, assailed Paul and Peter, and the other disciples, as disseminators of deceit, whom at the same time he testified to have been unskilled and unlearned. For he says that some of them made gain by the craft of fishermen, as though he took it ill that some Aristophanes or Aristarchus did not devise that subject.

CHAP. III. — OF THE TRUTH OF THE CHRISTIAN DOCTRINE, AND THE VANITY OF ITS ADVERSARIES; AND THAT CHRIST WAS NOT A MAGICIAN.

The desire of inventing,[5] therefore, and craftiness were absent from these men, since they were unskilful. Or what unlearned man could invent things adapted to one another, and coherent, when the most learned of the philosophers, Plato and Aristotle, and Epicurus and Zeno, themselves spoke things at variance with one another, and contrary? For this is the nature of falsehoods, that they cannot be coherent. But their teaching, because it is true, everywhere agrees,[6] and is altogether consistent with itself; and on this account it effects persuasion, because it is based on a consistent plan. They did not therefore devise that religion for the sake of gain and advantage, inasmuch as both by their precepts and in reality they followed that course of life which is without pleasures, and despised all things which are reckoned among good things, and since they not only endured death for their faith, but also both knew and foretold that they were about to die, and afterwards that all who followed their system would suffer cruel and impious things. But he [7] affirmed that Christ Himself was put to flight by the Jews, and having collected a band of nine hundred men, committed robberies. Who would venture to oppose so great an authority? We must certainly believe this, for perchance some Apollo announced it to him in his slumbers. So many robbers have at all times perished, and do perish daily, and you yourself have certainly condemned many: which of them after his crucifixion was called, I will not say a God, but a man? But you perchance believed it from the circumstance of your having consecrated the homicide Mars as a god, though you would not have done this if the Areopagites had crucified him.

The same man, when he endeavoured to overthrow his wonderful deeds, and did not however deny them, wished to show that Apollonius [8] performed equal or even greater deeds. It is strange that he omitted to mention Apuleius,[9] of whom many and wonderful things are accustomed to be related. Why therefore, O senseless one, does no one worship Apollonius in the place of God? unless by chance you alone do so, who are worthy forsooth of that god, with whom the true God will punish you everlastingly. If Christ is a magician because He performed wonderful deeds, it is plain that Apollonius, who, according to your description, when Domitian wished to punish him, suddenly disappeared on his trial, was more skilful than He who was both arrested and crucified. But perhaps he wished from this very thing to prove the arrogance of Christ, in that He made Himself God, that the other may appear to have been more modest, who, though he performed greater actions, as this one thinks, nevertheless did not claim that for himself. I omit at present to compare the works themselves, because in the second and preceding book I have spoken respecting the fraud and tricks of the magic art. I say that there is no one who would not wish that that should especially befall him after death which even the greatest kings desire. For why do men prepare for themselves magnificent sepulchres? why statues and images? why by some illustrious deeds, or even by death undergone in behalf of their countrymen, do they endeavour

[1] Intima, i.e., of an esoteric character, known only to those within the school or sect.]

[2] Cui fuerat assensus. Other editions read "accensus," i.e., reckoned among.

[3] Induerat.

[4] Sacramenti.

[5] Fingendi.

[6] Undique quadrat.

[7] Hierocles, referred to in chapter 2.

[8] Apollonius, a celebrated Pythagorean philosopher of Tyana: his works and doctrines are recorded by Philostratus, from whom Lactantius appears to have derived his account. The pagans compared his life and actions with those of Christ. [See Origen, vol. iv. p. 591, this series.]

[9] Apuleius, a native of Madaura, a city on the borders of the province of Africa, he professed the Platonic philosophy. He was reputed a magician by the Christian writers. [Author of *The Golden Ass*, a most entertaining but often indecent satire, which may have inspired Cervantes, and concerning which see Warburton, *Div. Legat.*, vol. ii. p. 177 (*et alibi*), ed. London, 1811.]

to deserve the good opinions of men? Why, in short, have you yourself wished to raise a monument of your talent, built with this detestable folly, as if with mud, except that you hope for immortality from the remembrance of your name? It is foolish, therefore, to imagine that Apollonius did not desire that which he would plainly wish for if he were able to attain to it; because there is no one who refuses immortality, and especially when you say that he was both adored by some as a god, and that his image was set up under the name of Hercules, the averter of evil, and is even now honoured by the Ephesians.

He could not therefore after death be believed to be a god, because it was evident that he was both a man and a magician; and for this reason he affected[1] divinity under the title of a name belonging to another, for in his own name he was unable to attain it, nor did he venture to make the attempt. But he of whom we speak[2] could both be believed to be a god, because he was not a magician, and was believed to be such because he was so in truth. I do not say this, he says, that Apollonius was not accounted a god, because he did not wish it, but that it may be evident that we, who did not at once connect a belief in his divinity with wonderful deeds, are wiser than you, who on account of slight wonders believed that he was a god. It is not wonderful if you, who are far removed from the wisdom of God, understand nothing at all of those things which you have read, since the Jews, who from the beginning had frequently read the prophets, and to whom the mystery[3] of God had been assigned, were nevertheless ignorant of what they read. Learn, therefore, if you have any sense, that Christ was not believed by us to be God on this account, because He did wonderful things, but because we saw that all things were done in His case which were announced to us by the prediction of the prophets. He performed wonderful deeds: we might have supposed Him to be a magician, as you now suppose Him to be, and the Jews then supposed Him, if all the prophets did not with one accord[4] proclaim that Christ would do those very things. Therefore we believe Him to be God, not more from His wonderful deeds and works, than from that very cross which you as dogs lick, since that also was predicted at the same time. It was not therefore on His own testimony (for who can be believed when he speaks concerning himself?), but on the testimony of the prophets who long before foretold all things which He did and suffered, that He gained a belief in His divinity, which could have happened neither to Apollonius,[5] nor to Apuleius, nor to any of the magicians; nor can it happen at any time. When, therefore, he had poured forth such absurd ravings[6] of his ignorance, when he had eagerly endeavoured utterly to destroy the truth, he dared to give to his books which were impious and the enemies of God the title of "truth-loving." O blind breast! O mind more black than Cimmerian darkness, as they say! He may perhaps have been a disciple of Anaxagoras,[7] to whom snows were as black as ink. But it is the same blindness, to give the name of falsehood to truth, and of truth to falsehood. Doubtless the crafty man wished to conceal the wolf under the skin of a sheep,[8] that he might ensnare the reader by a deceitful title. Let it be true; grant that you did this from ignorance, not from malice: what truth, however, have you brought to us, except that, being a defender of the gods, you had at last betrayed those very gods? For, having set forth the praises of the Supreme God, whom you confessed to be king, most mighty, the maker of all things, the fountain of honours, the parent of all, the creator and preserver of all living creatures, you took away the kingdom from your own Jupiter; and when you had driven him from the supreme power, you reduced him to the rank of servants. Thus your own conclusion[9] convicts you of folly, vanity, and error. For you affirm that the gods exist, and yet you subject and enslave them to that God whose religion you attempt to overturn.

CHAP. IV. — WHY THIS WORK WAS PUBLISHED, AND AGAIN OF TERTULLIAN AND CYPRIAN.

Since, therefore, they of whom I have spoken had set forth their sacrilegious writings in my presence, and to my grief, being incited both by the arrogant impiety of these, and by the consciousness of truth itself, and (as I think) by God, I have undertaken this office, that with all the strength of my mind I might refute the accusers of righteousness; not that I should write against these, who might be crushed with a few words, but that I might once for all by one attack overthrow all who everywhere effect, or have effected, the same work. For I do not doubt that very many others, and in many places, and that not only in Greek, but also in Latin writings, have raised a monument of their own unrighteousness. And since I was not able to reply to these separately, I thought that this cause was to be so

1 Affectavit divinitatem.
2 Noster.
3 Sacramentum.
4 With one spirit, "uno spiritu."

5 [But Apollonius was set up as an Antichrist by Philostratus, as Cudworth supposes, and so other men of learning. But no student should overlook Lardner's valuable commentary on this character, and his quotations from Bishop Parker of Oxford, *Credib.*, vol. vii. p. 486, and also p. 508, cap. 29, and appendix.]
6 Deliramenta.
7 See book ii. ch. 23.
8 Cf. Matt. vii. 15.
9 Epilogus.

pleaded by me that I might overthrow former writers, together with all their writings, and cut off from future writers the whole power of writing and of replying.[1] Only let them attend, and I will assuredly effect that whosoever shall know these things, must either embrace that which he before condemned, or, which is next to it, cease at length to deride it. Although Tertullian fully pleaded the same cause in that treatise which is entitled the *Apology*,[2] yet, inasmuch as it is one thing to answer accusers, which consists in defence or denial only, and another thing to instruct, which we do, in which the substance of the whole system must be contained, I have not shrunk from this labour, that I might complete the subject, which Cyprian did not fully carry out in that discourse in which he endeavours to refute Demetrianus (as he himself says) railing at and clamouring[3] against the truth. Which subject he did not handle as he ought to have done; for he ought to have been refuted not by the testimonies of Scripture, which he plainly considered vain, fictitious, and false, but by arguments and reason. For, since he was contending against a man who was ignorant of the truth, he ought for a while to have laid aside divine readings, and to have formed from the beginning this man as one who was altogether ignorant,[4] and to have shown to him by degrees the beginnings of light, that he might not be dazzled,[5] the whole of its brightness being presented to him.[6]

For as an infant is unable, on account of the tenderness of its stomach, to receive the nourishment of solid and strong food, but is supported by liquid and soft milk, until, its strength being confirmed, it can feed on stronger nourishment; so also it was befitting that this man, because he was not yet capable of receiving divine things, should be presented with human testimonies — that is, of philosophers and historians — in order that he might especially be refuted by his own authorities. And since he did not do this, being carried away by his distinguished knowledge of the sacred writings, so that he was content with those things alone in which faith consists, I have undertaken, with the favour of God, to do this, and at the same time to prepare the way for the imitation of others. And if, through my exhortation, learned and eloquent men shall begin to betake themselves to this subject, and shall choose to display their talents and power of speaking in this field of truth, no one can doubt that false religions will quickly disappear, and philosophy altogether fall, if all shall be persuaded that this alone is religion and the only true wisdom. But I have wandered from the subject further than I wished.

CHAP. V. — THERE WAS TRUE JUSTICE UNDER SATURNUS, BUT IT WAS BANISHED BY JUPITER.

Now the promised disputation concerning justice must be given; which is either by itself the greatest virtue, or by itself the fountain of virtue, which not only philosophers sought, but poets also, who were much earlier, and were esteemed as wise before the origin of the name of philosophy. These clearly understood that this *justice* was absent from the affairs of men; and they feigned that it, being offended with the vices of men, departed from the earth, and withdrew to heaven; and that they may teach what it is to live justly (for they are accustomed to give precepts by circumlocutions), they repeat examples of justice from the times of Saturnus, which they call the golden times, and they relate in what condition human life was while it delayed on the earth.[7] And this is not to be regarded as a poetic fiction, but as the truth. For, while Saturnus reigned, the religious worship of the gods not having yet been instituted, nor any[8] race being as yet set apart in the belief of its divinity, God was manifestly worshipped. And therefore there were neither dissensions, nor enmities, nor wars.

> "Not yet had rage unsheathed maddened swords,"

as Germanicus Cæsar speaks in his poem translated from Aratus,[9]

> "Nor had discord been known among relatives."

No, nor even among strangers: but there were no swords at all to be unsheathed. For who, when justice was present and in vigour, would think respecting his own protection, since no one plotted against him; or respecting the destruction of another, since no one desired anything?

> "They preferred to live content with a simple mode of life,"

as Cicero[10] relates in his poem; and this is peculiar to our religion. "It was not even allowed to mark out or to divide the plain with a boundary: men sought all things in common;"[11] since God

[1] [*Future writers.* This laying of an anchor to windward is characteristic of Lactantius.]

[2] [See elucidations, vol. iii. pp. 56-60, this series.]

[3] Oblatrantem atque obstrepentem veritati. These words are taken from Cyprian, vol. v. p. 457, this series.

[4] Rudem.

[5] Caligaret.

[6] [This censure of Cyprian fully exculpates Minucius, Arnobius, and others, superficially blamed for their few quotations from Holy Writ. Also, it explains our author's quotations from the Sibyl, etc.]

[7] [Striking is the language of the *Pollio* ("Redit et Virgo," etc.), in which the true Virgin seems to be anticipated.]

[8] Ulla. Another reading is "illâ," as though there were a reference to the family of Saturnus.

[9] Germanicus Cæsar, the grandson of Augustus, translated in verse a part of the poems of Aratus. [See p. 36, *supra*.]

[10] Cicero translated in verse part of the poems of Aratus. [This poet is quoted by St. Paul, *τοῦ γὰρ καὶ γένος ἐσμέν*, Acts xvii. 28. Archdeacon Farrar does not consider the natural and *impedantic* spirit of the Apostle in suiting this quotation to time and place; and, if it was a common-place proverb, all the more suggestive is the *accuracy* of the reference to "one of your own poets."]

[11] Virg., *Georg.*, i. 126.

had given the earth in common to all, that they might pass their life in common, not that mad and raging avarice might claim all things for itself, and that that which was produced for all might not be wanting to any. And this saying of the poet ought so to be taken, not as suggesting the idea that individuals at that time had no private property, but it must be regarded as a poetical figure; that we may understand that men were so liberal, that they did not shut up the fruits of the earth produced for them, nor did they in solitude brood over the things stored up, but admitted the poor to share the fruits of their labour: —

> "Now streams of milk, now streams of nectar flowed."[1]

And no wonder, since the storehouses of the good liberally lay open to all. Nor did avarice intercept the divine bounty, and thus cause hunger and thirst in common; but all alike had abundance, since they who had possessions gave liberally and bountifully to those who had not. But after that Saturnus had been banished from heaven, and had arrived in Latium, —

> "Exiled from his throne
> By Jove, his mightier heir,"[2] —

since the people either through fear of the new king, or of their own accord, had become corrupted and ceased to worship God, and had begun to esteem the king in the place of God, since he himself, almost a parricide, was an example to others to the injury of piety, —

> "The most just Virgin in haste deserted the lands;"[3]

but not as Cicero says,[4]

> "And settled, in the kingdom of Jupiter, and in a part of the heaven."

For how could she settle or tarry in the kingdom of him who expelled his father from his kingdom, harassed him with war, and drove him as an exile over the whole world?

> "He gave to the black serpents their noxious poison,
> And ordered wolves to prowl;"[6]

that is, he introduced among men hatred, and envy, and stratagem; so that they were poisonous as serpents, and rapacious as wolves. And they truly do this who persecute those who are righteous and faithful towards God, and give to judges the power of using violence against the innocent. Perhaps Jupiter may have done something of this kind for the overthrow and removal of righteousness; and on this account he is related to have made serpents fierce, and to have whetted the spirit of wolves.

> "Then war's indomitable rage,
> And greedy lust of gain;"[7]

and not without reason. For the worship of God being taken away, men lost the knowledge of good and evil. Thus the common intercourse of life perished from among men, and the bond of human society was destroyed. Then they began to contend with one another, and to plot, and to acquire for themselves glory from the shedding of human blood.

CHAP. VI. — AFTER THE BANISHMENT OF JUSTICE, LUST, UNJUST LAWS, DARING, AVARICE, AMBITION, PRIDE, IMPIETY, AND OTHER VICES REIGNED.

And the source of all these evils was lust; which, indeed, burst forth from the contempt of true majesty. For not only did they who had a superfluity fail to bestow a share upon others, but they even seized the property of others, drawing everything to their private gain; and the things which formerly even individuals laboured to obtain for the common use of men,[8] were now conveyed to the houses of a few. For, that they might subdue others by slavery, they began especially to withdraw and collect together the necessaries of life, and to keep them firmly shut up, that they might make the bounties of heaven their own; not on account of kindness,[9] a feeling which had no existence in them, but that they might sweep together all the instruments of lust and avarice. They also, under the name of justice, passed most unequal and unjust laws, by which they might defend their plunder and avarice against the force of the multitude. They prevailed, therefore, as much by authority as by strength, or resources, or malice. And since there was in them no trace of justice, the offices of which are humanity, equity, pity, they now began to rejoice in a proud and swollen inequality, and made[10] themselves higher than other men, by a retinue of attendants, and by the sword, and by the brilliancy of their garments. For this reason they invented for themselves honours, and purple robes, and fasces, that, being supported by the terror produced by axes and swords, they might, as it were by the right of masters, rule them, stricken with fear, and alarmed. Such was the condition in which the life of man was placed by that king who, having defeated and put to flight a parent, did not seize his kingdom, but set up an impious tyranny by violence and armed men, and took away that

---

1 Ovid, *Metam.*, i. 111.
2 Virg., *Æn.*, viii. 320.
3 Germ. Cæs., *Arat.*, 136.
4 [That is, in his translation of the poetry of Aratus.]
5 [Et Jovis in regno, cœlique in parte resedit. For this fragmentary verse we are indebted to our author; other fragments are given in good editions of Cicero. He translated the *Phenomena* of Aratus in his youth. My (Paris) edition contains nearly the whole.]
6 Virg. *Georg.*, i. 129.
7 Virg., *Æn.*, viii. 327.
8 Hominum. Another reading is "omnium," of all, as opposed to the few.
9 Propter humanitatem.
10 Altiores se . . . faciebant. Another reading is, "altiores cæteris . . . fulgebant."

golden age of justice, and compelled men to become wicked and impious, even from this very circumstance, that he turned them away from God to the worship of himself; and the terror of his excessive power had extorted this.

For who would not fear him who was girded about with arms, whom the unwonted gleam of steel and swords surrounded? Or what stranger would he spare who had not even spared his own father? Whom, in truth, should he fear, who had conquered in war, and destroyed by massacre the race of the Titans, which was strong and excelling in might? What wonder if the whole multitude, pressed by unusual fear, had given themselves up to the adulation of a single man? Him they venerated, to him they paid the greatest honour. And since it is judged to be a kind of obsequiousness to imitate the customs and vices of a king, all men laid aside piety, lest, if they should live piously, they might seem to upbraid the wickedness of the king. Thus, being corrupted by continual imitation, they abandoned divine right, and the practice of living wickedly by degrees became a habit. And now nothing remained of the pious and excellent condition of the preceding age; but justice being banished, and drawing with her the truth, left to men error, ignorance, and blindness. The poets therefore were ignorant, who sung that she fled to heaven, to the kingdom of Jupiter. For if justice was on the earth in the age which they call "golden," it is plain that she was driven away by Jupiter, who changed the golden age. But the change of the age and the expulsion of justice is to be deemed nothing else, as I have said, than the laying aside of divine religion, which alone effects that man should esteem man dear, and should know that he is bound to him by the tie of brotherhood, since God is alike a Father to all, so as to share the bounties of the common God and Father with those who do not possess them; to injure no one, to oppress no one, not to close his door against a stranger, nor his ear against a suppliant, but to be bountiful, beneficent, and liberal, which Tullius[1] thought to be praises suitable to a king. This truly is justice, and this is the golden age, which was first corrupted when Jupiter reigned, and shortly afterwards, when he himself and all his offspring were consecrated as gods, and the worship of many deities undertaken, had been altogether taken away.

CHAP. VII. — OF THE COMING OF JESUS, AND ITS FRUIT; AND OF THE VIRTUES AND VICES OF THAT AGE.

But God, as a most indulgent parent, when the last time approached, sent a messenger to bring back that old age, and justice which had been put to flight, that the human race might not be agitated by very great and perpetual errors. Therefore the appearance of that golden time returned, and justice was restored to the earth, but was assigned to a few; and this justice is nothing else than the pious and religious worship of the one God. But perhaps some may be inclined to ask, why, if this be justice, it is not given to all mankind, and the whole multitude does not agree to it. This is a matter of great disputation, why a difference was retained by God when He gave justice to the earth; and this I have shown in another place, and whenever a favourable opportunity shall occur it shall be explained. Now it is sufficient very briefly to signify it: that virtue can neither be discerned, unless it has vices opposed to it; nor be perfect, unless it is exercised by adversity.[2] For God designed that there should be this distinction between good and evil things, that we may know from that which is evil the quality of the good, and also the quality of the evil from the good; nor can the nature of the one be understood if the other is taken away. God therefore did not exclude evil, that the nature of virtue might be evident. For how could patient endurance[3] retain its meaning and name if there were nothing which we were compelled to endure?[4] How could faith devoted to its God deserve praise, unless there were some one who wished to turn us away from God? For on this account He permitted the unjust to be more powerful, that they might be able to compel to evil; and on this account to be more numerous, that virtue might be precious, because it is rare. And this very point is admirably and briefly shown by Quintilian in "the muffled head."[5] "For what virtue," he says, "would there be in innocence, had not its rarity furnished it with praises? But because it is provided by nature that hatred, desire, and anger drive men blindly to that object to which they have applied themselves, to be free from fault appears to be beyond the power of man. Otherwise, if nature had given to all men equal affections, piety would be nothing."

How true this is, the necessity of the case itself teaches. For if it is virtue to resist with fortitude evils and vices, it is evident that, without evil and vice, there is no *perfected* virtue; and that God might render this complete and perfect, He retained that which was contrary to it, with which it might contend. For, being agitated by evils which harass it, it gains stability; and in proportion to the frequency with which

[1] [Compare Cicero, *De Officiis*, i. 14, with Luke xxii. 25.]

[2] [To establish this, would be to go far in a *theodicy* to reconcile the permission of evil with the divine goodness.]

[3] Patientia.

[4] Pati.

[5] Caput obvolutum. This appears to be the title of a lost declamation of Quintilian.

it is urged onward, is the firmness with which it is strengthened. This is evidently the cause which effects that, although justice is sent to men, yet it cannot be said that a golden age exists; because God has not taken away evil, that He might retain that diversity which alone preserves the mystery of a divine religion.

CHAP. VIII. — OF JUSTICE KNOWN TO ALL, BUT NOT EMBRACED; OF THE TRUE TEMPLE OF GOD, AND OF HIS WORSHIP, THAT ALL VICES MAY BE SUBDUED.

They, therefore, who think that no one is just, have justice before their eyes, but are unwilling to discern it. For what reason is there why they should describe it either in poems or in all their discourse, complaining of its absence, when it is very easy for them to be good if they wish? Why do you depict to yourselves justice as worthless,[1] and wish that she may fall from heaven, as it were, represented in some image? Behold, she is in your sight; receive her, if you are able, and place her in the abode of your breast; and do not imagine that this is difficult, or unsuited to the times. Be just and good, and the justice which you seek will follow you of her own accord. Lay aside every evil thought from your hearts, and that golden age will at once return to you, which you cannot attain to by any other means than by beginning to worship the true God. But you long for justice on the earth, while the worship of false gods continues, which cannot possibly come to pass. But it was not possible even at that time when you imagine, because those deities whom you impiously worship were not yet produced, and the worship of the one God must have prevailed throughout the earth; of that God, I say, who hates wickedness and requires goodness; whose temple is not stones or clay, but man himself, who bears the image of God. And this temple is adorned not with corruptible gifts of gold and jewels, but with the lasting offices of virtues. Learn, therefore, if any intelligence is left to you, that men are wicked and unjust because gods are worshipped; and that all evils daily increase to the affairs of men on this account, because God the Maker and Governor of this world has been neglected; because, contrary to that which is right, impious superstitions have been taken up; and lastly, because you do not permit God to be worshipped even by a few.

But if God only were worshipped, there would not be dissensions and wars, since men would know that they are the sons of one God; and, therefore, among those who were connected by the sacred and inviolable bond of divine relationship, there would be no plottings, inasmuch as they would know what kind of punishments God prepared for the destroyers of souls, who sees through secret crimes, and even the very thoughts themselves. There would be no frauds or plunderings if they had learned, through the instruction of God, to be content with that which was their own, though little, so that they might prefer solid and eternal things to those which are frail and perishable. There would be no adulteries, and debaucheries, and prostitution of women, if it were known to all, that whatever is sought beyond the desire of procreation is condemned by God.[2] Nor would necessity compel a woman to dishonour her modesty, to seek for herself a most disgraceful mode of sustenance; since the males also would restrain their lust, and the pious and religious contributions of the rich would succour the destitute. There would not, therefore, as I have said, be these evils on the earth, if there were by common consent a general observance[3] of the law of God, if those things were done by all which our people alone perform. How happy and how golden would be the condition of human affairs, if throughout the world gentleness, and piety, and peace, and innocence, and equity, and temperance, and faith, took up their abode! In short, there would be no need of so many and varying laws to rule men, since the law of God alone would be sufficient for perfect innocence; nor would there be any need of prisons, or the swords of rulers, or the terror of punishments, since the wholesomeness of the divine precepts infused into the breasts of men would of itself instruct them to works of justice. But now men are wicked through ignorance of what is right and good. And this, indeed, Cicero saw; for, discoursing on the subject of the laws,[4] he says: "As the world, with all its parts agreeing with one another, coheres and depends upon one and the same nature, so all men, being naturally confused among themselves, disagree through depravity; nor do they understand that they are related by blood, and that they are all subject to one and the same guardianship: for if this were kept in mind, assuredly men would live the life of gods." Therefore the unjust and impious worship of the gods has introduced all the evils by which mankind in turn destroy one another. For they could not retain their piety, who, as prodigal and rebellious children, had renounced the authority of God, the common parent of all.

CHAP. IX. — OF THE CRIMES OF THE WICKED, AND THE TORTURES INFLICTED ON THE CHRISTIANS.

At times, however, they perceive that they are wicked, and praise the condition of the former

1 Inanem.

2 [This is not consistent with the Church's allowance of matrimony to women past child-bearing, nor with the language of the Apostle, 1 Cor. vii. 2-7. See my note (2), vol. ii. p. 262.]

3 Si ab omnibus in legem Dei conjuraretur. The word "conjuro," contrary to its general use, is here employed in a good sense.

4 [See ed. Klotz, vol. ii. p. 403, Lips., 1869.]

ages, and conjecture that justice is absent because of their characters and deserts; for, though she presents herself to their eyes, they not only fail to receive or recognise her, but they even violently hate, and persecute, and endeavour to banish her. Let us suppose, in the meantime, that she whom we follow is not justice: how will they receive her whom they imagine to be the true justice, if she shall have come, when they torture and kill those whom they themselves confess to be imitators of the just, because they perform good and just actions; whereas, if they should put to death the wicked only, they would deserve to be unvisited by justice, who had no other reason for leaving the earth than the shedding of human blood? How much more so when they slay the righteous, and account the followers of justice themselves as enemies, yea, as more than enemies; who, though they eagerly seek their lives, and property, and children by sword and fire, yet are spared when conquered; and there is a place for clemency even amidst arms; or if they have determined to carry their cruelty to the utmost, nothing more is done towards them, except that they are put to death or led away to slavery! But this is unutterable which is done towards those who are ignorant of crime, and none are regarded as more guilty than those who are of all men innocent. Therefore most wicked men venture to make mention of justice, men who surpass wild beasts in ferocity, who lay waste the most gentle flock of God,—

> "Like gaunt wolves rushing from their den,
> Whom lawless hunger's sullen growl
> Drives forth into the night to prowl."[1]

But these have been maddened not by the fury of hunger, but of the heart; nor do they prowl in a black mist, but by open plundering; nor does the consciousness of their crimes ever recall them from profaning the sacred and holy name of justice with that mouth which, like the jaws of beasts, is wet with the blood of the innocent. What must we say is especially the cause of this excessive and persevering hatred?

> "Does truth produce hatred,"[2]

as the poet says, as though inspired by the Divine Spirit, or are they ashamed to be bad in the presence of the just and good? Or is it rather from both causes? For the truth is always hateful on this account, because he who sins wishes to have free scope for sinning, and thinks that he cannot in any other way more securely enjoy the pleasure of his evil doings, than if there is no one whom his faults may displease. Therefore they endeavour entirely to exterminate and take them away as witnesses of their crimes and wickedness, and think them burthensome to themselves, as though their life were reproved. For why should any be unseasonably good, who, when the public morals are corrupted, should censure them by living well? Why should not all be equally wicked, rapacious, unchaste, adulterers, perjured, covetous, and fraudulent? Why should they not rather be taken out of the way, in whose presence they are ashamed to lead an evil life, who, though not by words, for they are silent, but by their very course of life, so unlike their own, assail and strike the forehead of sinners? For whoever disagrees with them appears to reprove them.

Nor is it greatly to be wondered at if these things are done towards men, since for the same cause the people who were placed in hope,[3] and not ignorant of God, rose up against God Himself; and the same necessity follows the righteous which attacked the Author of righteousness Himself. Therefore they harass and torment them with studied kinds of punishments, and think it little to kill those whom they hate, unless cruelty also mocks their bodies. But if any through fear of pain or death, or by their own perfidy, have deserted the heavenly oath,[4] and have consented to deadly sacrifices, these they praise and load[5] with honours, that by their example they may allure others. But upon those who have highly esteemed their faith, and have not denied that they are worshippers of God, they fall with all the strength of their butchery, as though they thirsted for blood; and they call them desperate,[6] because they by no means spare their body; as though anything could be more desperate, than to torture and tear in pieces him whom you know to be innocent. Thus no sense of shame remains among those from whom all kind feeling is absent, and they retort upon just men reproaches which are befitting to themselves. For they call them impious, being themselves forsooth pious, and shrinking from the shedding of human blood; whereas, if they would consider their own acts, and the acts of those whom they condemn as impious, they would now understand how false they are, and more deserving of all those things which they either say or do against the good. For they are not of our number, but of theirs who besiege the roads in arms, practise piracy by sea; or if it has not been in their power openly to assail, secretly mix poisons; who kill their wives that they may gain their dowries, or their husbands that they may marry adulterers; who either strangle the sons born from themselves, or if

---

1 Virg., *Æn.*, ii. 355.
2 Ter., *Andr.*, i. 1, 41.

3 The Jewish people. Thus St. Paul speaks, Acts xxvi. 6: "I stand and am judged for the hope of the promise made of God unto our fathers."
4 i.e., the Christian religion.
5 Mactant.
6 Desperati, equivalent to παράβολοι, a word borrowed from combats with wild beasts, and applied to Christians as being ready to devote their lives to the cause of God.

they are too pious, expose them; who restrain their incestuous passions neither from a daughter, nor sister, nor mother, nor priestess; who conspire against their own citizens and country; who do not fear the sack;[1] who, in fine, commit sacrilege, and despoil the temples of the gods whom they worship; and, to speak of things which are light and usually practised by them, who hunt for inheritances, forge wills, either remove or exclude the just heirs; who prostitute their own persons to lust; who, in short, unmindful of what they were born, contend with women in passivity;[2] who, in violation of all propriety,[3] pollute and dishonour the most sacred part of their body; who mutilate themselves, and that which is more impious, in order that they may be priests of religion; who do not even spare their own life, but sell their lives to be taken away in public; who, if they sit as judges, corrupted by a bribe, either destroy the innocent or set free the guilty without punishment; who grasp at the heaven itself by sorceries, as though the earth would not contain their wickedness. These crimes, I say, and more than these, are plainly committed by those who are worshippers of the gods.

Amidst these crimes of such number and magnitude, what place is there for justice? And I have collected a few only out of many, not for the purpose of censure, but to show their nature. Let those who shall wish to know all take in hand the books of Seneca, who was at the same time a most true describer and a most vehement accuser of the public morals and vices. But Lucilius also briefly and concisely described that dark life in these verses: "But now from morn to night, on festival and ordinary day alike, the whole people and the fathers with one accord display themselves in[4] the forum, and never depart from it. They have all given themselves to one and the same pursuit and art, that they may be able cautiously to deceive, to fight treacherously, to contend in flattery, each to pretend that he is a good man, to lie in wait, as if all were enemies to all." But which of these things can be laid to the charge of our people,[5] with whom the whole of religion consists in living without guilt and without spot? Since, therefore, they see that both they and their people do those things which we have said, but that ours practise nothing else but that which is just and good, they might, if they had any understanding, have perceived from this, both that they who do what is good are pious, and that they themselves who commit wicked actions are impious. For it is impossible that they who do not err in all the actions of their life, should err in the main point, that is, in religion, which is the chief of all things. For impiety, if taken up in that which is the most important, would follow through all the rest. And therefore[6] it is impossible that they who err in the whole of their life should not be deceived also in religion; inasmuch as piety, if it kept its rule in the chief point, would maintain its course in others. Thus it happens, that on either side the character of the main subject may be known from the state of the actions which are carried on.

CHAP. X. — OF FALSE PIETY, AND OF FALSE AND TRUE RELIGION.

It is worth while to investigate their piety, that from their merciful and pious actions it may be understood what is the character of those things which are done by them contrary to the laws of piety. And that I may not seem to attack any one with harshness, I will take a character from the poets, and one which is the greatest example of piety. In Maro, that king

> "Than who
> The breath of being none e'er drew,
> More brave, more pious, or more true,"[7] —

what proofs of justice did he bring forward to us?

> "There walk with hands fast bound behind
> The victim prisoners, designed
> For slaughter o'er the flames."[8]

What can be more merciful than this piety? *what more merciful* than to immolate human victims to the dead, and to feed the fire with the blood of men as with oil? But perhaps this may not have been the fault of the hero himself, but of the poet, who polluted with distinguished wickedness "a man distinguished by his piety."[9] Where then, O poet, is that piety which you so frequently praise? Behold the pious Æneas: —

> "Four hapless youths of Sulmo's breed,
> And four who Ufens call their sire,
> He takes alive, condemned to bleed
> To Pallas' shade on Pallas' pyre."[10]

Why, therefore, at the very same time when he was sending the men in chains to slaughter, did he say,

> "Fain would I grant the living peace,"[11]

when he ordered that those whom he had in his power alive should be slain in the place of cattle? But this, as I have said, was not his fault — for

---

[1] There is an allusion to the punishment of parricides, who were enclosed in a bag with a dog, a serpent, an ape, and a cock, and thrown into the sea.

[2] Patientia, in a bad sense. [The text of the translator gives "endurance," for which I venture to substitute as above.]

[3] Contra fas omne.

[4] Induforo. "Indu" and "endo" are archaisms, used by Lucretius and other writers in the same sense as "in."

[5] i.e., Christians. [See vol. i. pp. 26, 27.]

[6] Eoque fieri non potest. Others read "æque fieri," etc.

[7] Virg., *Æn.*, i. 544.

[8] *Ibid.*, xi. 81.

[9] *Ibid.*, i. 10.

[10] *Ibid.*, x. 517.

[11] *Ibid.*, xi. 111.

he perhaps had not received a liberal education — but yours; for, though you were learned, yet you were ignorant of the nature of piety, and you believed that that wicked and detestable action of his was the befitting exercise of piety. He is plainly called pious on this account only, because he loved his father. Why should I say that

"The good Æneas owned their plea,"[1]

and yet slew them? For, though adjured by the same father, and

"By young Iulus' dawning day,"[2]

he did not spare them,

"Live fury kindling every vein"[3]

What! can any one imagine that there was any virtue in him who was fired with madness as stubble, and, forgetful of the shade of his father, by whom he was entreated, was unable to curb his wrath? He was therefore by no means pious who not only slew the unresisting, but even suppliants. Here some one will say: What then, or where, or of what character is piety? Truly it is among those who are ignorant of wars, who maintain concord with all, who are friendly even to their enemies, who love all men as brethren, who know how to restrain their anger, and to soothe every passion of the mind with calm government. How great a mist, therefore, how great a cloud of darkness and errors, has overspread the breasts of men who, when they think themselves especially pious, then become especially impious? For the more religiously they honour those earthy images, so much the more wicked are they towards the name of the true divinity. And therefore they are often harassed with greater evils as the reward of their impiety; and because they know not the cause of these evils, the blame is altogether ascribed to fortune, and the philosophy of Epicurus finds a place, who thinks that nothing extends to the gods, and that they are neither influenced by favour nor moved by anger, because they often see their despisers happy, and their worshippers in misery. And this happens on this account, because when they seem to be religious and naturally good, they are believed to deserve nothing of that kind which they often suffer. However, they console themselves by accusing fortune; nor do they perceive that if she had any existence, she would never injure her worshippers. Piety of this kind is therefore deservedly followed by punishment; and the deity offended with the wickedness of men who are depraved in their religious worship,[4] punishes them with heavy misfortune; who, although they live with holiness in the greatest faith and innocence, yet because they worship gods whose impious and profane rites are an abomination to the true God, are estranged from justice and the name of true piety. Nor is it difficult to show why the worshippers of the gods cannot be good and just. For how shall they abstain from the shedding of blood who worship bloodthirsty deities, Mars and Bellona? or how shall they spare their parents who worship Jupiter, who drove out his father? or how shall they spare their own infants who worship Saturnus? how shall they uphold chastity who worship a goddess who is naked, and an adulteress, and who prostitutes herself as it were among the gods? how shall they withhold themselves from plunder and frauds who are acquainted with the thefts of Mercurius, who teaches that to deceive is not the part of fraud, but of cleverness? how shall they restrain their lusts who worship Jupiter, Hercules, Liber, Apollo, and the others, whose adulteries and debaucheries with men and women are not only known to the learned, but are even set forth in the theatres, and made the subject of songs, so that they are notorious[5] to all? Among these things is it possible for men to be just, who, although they were naturally good, would be trained to injustice by the very gods themselves? For, that you may propitiate the god whom you worship, there is need of those things with which you know that he is pleased and delighted. Thus it comes to pass that the god fashions the life of his worshippers according to the character of his own will,[6] since the most religious worship is to imitate.

CHAP. XI. — OF THE CRUELTY OF THE HEATHENS AGAINST THE CHRISTIANS.

Therefore, because justice is burthensome and unpleasant to those men who agree with the character of their gods, they exercise with violence against the righteous the same impiety which they show in other things. And not without reason are they spoken of by the prophets as beasts. Therefore it is excellently said by Marcus Tullius:[7] "For if there is no one who would not prefer to die than to be changed into the figure of a beast, although he is about to have the mind of a man, how much more wretched is it to be of a brutalized mind in the figure of a man! To me, indeed, it seems as much worse as the mind is more excellent than the body." Therefore they view with disdain the bodies of beasts, though they are themselves more cruel than these; and they pride themselves on this account, that they were born men,

1 Virg., *Æn.*, xi. 106.
2 *Ibid.*, x. 524.
3 *Ibid.*, xii. 946.
4 Hominum prave religiosorum.

5 Omnibus notiora.
6 Pro qualitate numinis sui.
7 [*De Republica*, iv. i. 3.]

though they have nothing belonging to man except the features and the eminent figure. For what Caucasus, what India, what Hyrcania ever nourished beasts so savage and so bloodthirsty? For the fury of all wild beasts rages until their appetite is satisfied; and when their hunger is appeased, immediately is pacified. That is truly a beast by whose command alone

"With rivulets of slaughter reeks
The stern embattled field."
"Dire agonies, wild terrors swarm,
And Death glares grim in many a form."[1]

No one can befittingly describe the cruelty of this beast, which reclines in one place, and yet rages with iron teeth throughout the world, and not only tears in pieces the limbs of men, but also breaks their very bones, and rages over their ashes, that there may be no place for their burial, as though they who confess God aimed at this, that their tombs should be visited, and not rather that they themselves may reach the presence of God.

What brutality is it, what fury, what madness, to deny light to the living, earth to the dead? I say, therefore, that nothing is more wretched than those men whom necessity has either found or made the ministers of another's fury, the satellites of an impious command. For that was no honour, or exaltation of dignity, but the condemnation of a man to torture, and also to the everlasting punishment of God. But it is impossible to relate what things they performed individually throughout the world. For what number of volumes will contain so infinite, so varied kinds of cruelty? For, having gained power, every one raged according to his own disposition. Some, through excessive timidity, proceeded to greater lengths than they were commanded; others thus acted through their own particular hatred against the righteous; some by a natural ferocity of mind; some through a desire to please, and that by this service they might prepare the way to higher offices: some were swift to slaughter, as an individual in Phrygia, who burnt a whole assembly of people, together with their place of meeting. But the more cruel he was, so much the more merciful[2] is he found to be. But that is the worst kind *of persecutors* whom a false appearance of clemency flatters; he is the more severe, he the more cruel torturer, who determines to put no one to death. Therefore it cannot be told what great and what grievous modes of tortures judges of this kind devised, that they might arrive at the accomplishment of their purpose. But they do these things not only on this account, that they may be able to boast that they have slain none of the innocent, — for I myself have heard some boasting that their administration has been in this respect without bloodshed, — but also for the sake of envy, lest either they themselves should be overcome, or the others should obtain the glory due to their virtue. And thus, in devising modes of punishment, they think of nothing else besides victory. For they know that this is a contest and a battle. I saw in Bithynia the præfect wonderfully elated with joy, as though he had subdued some nation of barbarians, because one who had resisted for two years with great spirit appeared at length to yield. They contend, therefore, that they may conquer and inflict exquisite[3] pains on their bodies, and avoid nothing else but that the victims may not die under the torture: as though, in truth, death alone could make them happy, and as though tortures also in proportion to their severity would not produce greater glory of virtue. But they with obstinate folly give orders that diligent care shall be given to the tortured, that their limbs may be renovated for other tortures, and fresh blood be supplied for punishment. What can be so pious, so beneficent, so humane? They would not have bestowed such anxious care on any whom they loved. This is the discipline of the gods: to these deeds they train their worshippers; these are the sacred rites which they require. Moreover, most wicked murderers have invented impious laws against the pious. For both sacrilegious ordinances and unjust disputations of jurists are read. Domitius, in his seventh book, concerning the office of the proconsul, has collected wicked rescripts of princes, that he might show by what punishments they ought to be visited who confessed themselves to be worshippers of God.

CHAP. XII. — OF TRUE VIRTUE; AND OF THE ESTIMATION OF A GOOD OR BAD CITIZEN.

What would you do to those who give the name of justice to the tortures inflicted by tyrants of old, who fiercely raged against the innocent; and though they are teachers of injustice and cruelty, wish to appear just and prudent, being blind and dull, and ignorant of affairs and of truth? Is justice so hateful to you, O abandoned minds, that ye regard it as equal with the greatest crimes? Is innocence so utterly lost in your eyes, that you do not think it worthy of death only,[4] but it is esteemed as beyond all crimes to commit no crime, and to have a breast pure from all contagion of guilt? And since we are speaking generally with those who worship

[1] Virg., *Æn.*, xi. 646, ii. 368. [Dan. vii. 7.]
[2] The more severe torture, as causing immediate death, may be regarded as merciful, in comparison with a slow and lingering punishment. [This by an eye-witness of Diocletian's day.]
[3] Exquisitis, "carefully studied."
[4] Ne morte quidem simplici dignum putetis.

gods, let us have your permission to do good with you; for this is our law, this our business, this our religion. If we appear to you wise, imitate us; if foolish, despise us, or even laugh at us, if you please; for our folly is profitable to us. Why do you lacerate, why do you afflict us? We do not envy your wisdom. We prefer this folly of ours — we embrace this. We believe that this is expedient for us, — to love you, and to confer all things upon you, who hate us.

There is in the writings of Cicero[1] a passage not inconsistent with the truth, in that disputation which is held by Furius against justice: "I ask," he says, "if there should be two men, and one of them should be an excellent man, of the highest integrity, the greatest justice, and remarkable faith, and the other distinguished by crime and audacity; and if the state should be in such error as to regard that good man as wicked, vicious, and execrable, but should think the one who is most wicked to be of the highest integrity and faith; and if, in accordance with this opinion of all the citizens, that good man should be harassed, dragged away, should be deprived of his hands, have his eyes dug out, should be condemned, be bound, be branded, be banished, be in want, and lastly, should most justly appear to all to be most wretched; but, on the other hand, if that wicked man should be praised, and honoured, and loved by all, — if all honours, all commands, all wealth, and all abundance should be bestowed upon him, — in short, if he should be judged in the estimation of all an excellent man, and most worthy of all fortune, — who, I pray, will be so mad as to doubt which of the two he would prefer to be?" Assuredly he put forth this example as though he divined what evils were about to happen to us, and in what manner, on account of righteousness; for our people suffer all these things through the perverseness of those in error. Behold, the state, or rather the whole world itself, is in such error, that it persecutes, tortures, condemns, and puts to death good and righteous men, as though they were wicked and impious. For as to what he says, that no one is so infatuated as to doubt which of the two he would prefer to be, he indeed, as the one who was contending against justice, thought this, that the wise man would prefer to be bad if he had a good reputation, than to be good with a bad reputation.

But may this senselessness be absent from us, that we should prefer that which is false to the true? Or does the character of our good man depend upon the errors of the people, more than upon our own conscience and the judgment of God? Or shall any prosperity ever allure us, so that we should not rather choose true goodness, though accompanied with all evil, than false goodness together with all prosperity? Let kings retain their kingdoms, the rich their riches, as Plautus says,[2] the wise their wisdom; let them leave to us our folly, which is evidently proved to be wisdom, from the very fact that they envy us its possession: for who would envy a fool, but he who is himself most foolish? But they are not so foolish as to envy fools; but from the fact of their following us up with such care and anxiety, they allow that we are not fools. For why should they rage with such cruelty, unless it is that they fear lest, as justice grows strong from day to day, they should be deserted together with their decaying[3] gods? If, therefore, the worshippers of gods are wise, and we are foolish, why do they fear lest the wise shall be allured by the foolish?

CHAP. XIII. — OF THE INCREASE AND THE PUNISHMENT OF THE CHRISTIANS.[4]

But since our number is continually increased from the worshippers of gods, but is never lessened, not even in persecution itself, — since men may commit sin, and be defiled by sacrifice, but they cannot be turned away from God, for the truth prevails by its own power, — who is there, I pray, so foolish and so blind as not to see on which side wisdom is? But they are blinded by malice and fury, that they cannot see; and they think that those are foolish who, when they have it in their power to avoid punishments, nevertheless prefer to be tortured and to be put to death; whereas they might see from this very circumstance, that it is not folly to which so many thousands throughout the world agree with one and the same mind. For if women fall into error through the weakness of their sex (for these persons sometimes call it a womanish and anile superstition), men doubtless are wise. If boys, if youths are improvident through their age, the mature and aged doubtless have a fixed judgment. If one city is unwise, it is evident that the other innumerable cities cannot be foolish. If one province or one nation is without prudence, the rest must have understanding of that which is right. But since the divine law has been received from the rising even to the setting of the sun, and each sex, every age, and nation, and country, with one and the same mind obeys God — since there is everywhere the same patient endurance, the same contempt of death — they ought to have understood that there is some reason in that matter, that it is not without a cause that it is defended even to death, that there is some foundation and solidity, which not

[1] [From the *Republic*, iii. xvii. 27.]

[2] *Curcul.*, i. 3, 22.

[3] Cariosis. There is a great variety of readings in this place.

[4] [Vol. iv. p. 116; same vol., p. 125.]

only frees that religion from injuries and molestation, but always increases and makes it stronger. For in this respect also the malice of those is brought to light, who think that they have utterly overthrown the religion of God if they have corrupted men, when it is permitted them to make satisfaction also to God; and there is no worshipper of God so evil who does not, when the opportunity is given him, return to appease God, and that, too, with greater devotedness. For the consciousness of sin and the fear of punishment make a man more religious, and the faith is always much stronger which is replaced through repentance. If, therefore, they themselves, when they think that the gods are angry with them, nevertheless believe that they are appeased by gifts, and sacrifices, and incense, what reason is there why they should imagine our God to be so unmerciful and implacable, that it should appear impossible for him to be a Christian, who by compulsion and against his will has poured a libation to their gods? Unless by chance they think that those who are once contaminated are about to change their mind, so that they may now begin of their own accord to do that which they have done under the influence of torture. Who would willingly undertake that duty which began with injury? Who, when he sees the scars on his own sides, would not the more hate the gods, on account of whom he bears the traces of lasting punishment, and the marks imprinted upon his flesh? Thus it comes to pass, that when peace is given from heaven, those who were estranged[1] from us return, and a fresh crowd[2] of others are added, on account of the wonderful nature[3] of the virtue displayed. For when the people see that men are lacerated by various kinds of tortures, and that they retain their patience unsubdued while the executioners are wearied, they think, as is really the case, that neither the agreement of so many nor the constancy of the dying is without meaning, and that patience itself could not surmount such great tortures without the aid of God. Robbers and men of robust frame are unable to endure lacerations of this kind: they utter exclamations, and send forth groans; for they are overcome by pain, because they are destitute of patience infused[4] into them. But in our case (not to speak of men), boys and delicate women in silence overpower their torturers, and even the fire is unable to extort from them a groan. Let the Romans go and boast in their Mutius or Regulus, — the one of whom gave himself up to be slain by the enemy, because he was ashamed to live as a captive; the other being taken by the enemy, when he saw that he could not escape death, laid his hand upon the burning hearth, that he might make atonement for his crime to the enemy whom he wished to kill, and by that punishment received the pardon which he had not deserved. Behold, the weak sex and fragile age endure to be lacerated in the whole body, and to be burned: not of necessity, for it is permitted them to escape if they wished to do so; but of their own will, because they put their trust in God.[5]

CHAP. XIV. — OF THE FORTITUDE OF THE CHRISTIANS.

But this is true virtue, which the vaunting philosophers also boast of, not in deed, but with empty words, saying that nothing is so befitting the gravity and constancy of a wise man as to be able to be driven away from his sentiment and purpose by no torturers, but that it is worth his while[6] to suffer torture and death rather than betray a trust or depart from his duty, or, overcome by fear of death or severity of pain, commit any injustice. Unless by chance Flaccus appears to them to rave in his lyrics, when he says,

> "Not the rage of the million commanding things evil;
> Not the doom frowning near in the brows of the tyrant,
> Shakes the upright and resolute man
> In his solid completeness of soul."[7]

And nothing can be more true than this, if it is referred to those who refuse no tortures, no kind of death, that they may not turn aside from faith and justice; who do not tremble at the commands of tyrants nor the swords of rulers,[8] so as not to maintain true and solid liberty with constancy of mind, which wisdom is to be observed in this alone. For who is so arrogant, who so lifted up, as to forbid me to raise my eyes to heaven? Who can impose upon me the necessity either of worshipping that which I am unwilling to worship, or of abstaining from the worship of that which I wish to worship? What further will now be left to us, if even this, which must be done of one's own will,[9] shall be extorted from me by the caprice of another? No one will effect this, if we have any courage to despise death and pain. But if we possess this constancy, why are we judged foolish when we do those things which philosophers praise? Seneca, in charging men with inconsistency, rightly says the highest virtue appears to them to consist in greatness of spirit; and yet the same persons regard him who despises death as a madman, which is plainly a mark of the greatest perverseness. But those followers of vain

1 Et qui fuerint aversi, redeant. The common reading is, "et qui fugerunt, universi redeant."
2 Alius novus populus.
3 Propter miraculum virtutis.
4 Deest illis inspirata patientia.
5 [Vol. iii. p. 700, this series.]
6 Tanti est . . . ne.
7 Horat., *Carm.*, iii. 3, Lord Lytton's translation.
8 i.e., of provinces.
9 Voluntate.

religions urge this with the same folly with which they fail to understand the true God; and these the Erythræan Sibyl calls "deaf and senseless,"[1] since they neither hear nor perceive divine things, but fear and adore an earthen image moulded by their own fingers.

CHAP. XV. — OF FOLLY, WISDOM, PIETY, EQUITY, AND JUSTICE.

But the reason on account of which they imagine those who are wise to be foolish has strong grounds of support (for they are not deceived without reason). And this must be diligently explained by us, that they may at length (if it is possible) recognise their errors. Justice by its own nature has a certain appearance of folly, and I am able to confirm this both by divine and human testimonies. But perhaps we should not succeed with them, unless we should teach them from their own authorities that no one can be just, a matter which is united with true wisdom, unless he also appears to be foolish. Carneades was a philosopher of the Academic sect; and one who knows not what power he had in discussion, what eloquence, what sagacity, will nevertheless understand the character of the man himself from the praises of Cicero or of Lucilius, in whose writings Neptune, discoursing on a subject of the greatest difficulty, shows that it cannot be explained, even if Orcus should restore Carneades himself to life. This Carneades, when he had been sent by the Athenians as ambassador to Rome, disputed copiously on the subject of justice, in the hearing of Galba and Cato, who had been censor, who were at that time the greatest of orators. But on the next day the same man overthrew his own argument by a disputation to the contrary effect, and took away the justice which he had praised on the preceding day, not indeed with the gravity of a philosopher, whose prudence ought to be firm and his opinion settled, but as it were by an oratorical kind of exercise of disputing on both sides. And he was accustomed to do this, that he might be able to refute others who asserted anything. L. Furius, in Cicero, makes mention of that discussion in which justice is overthrown.[2] I believe, inasmuch as he was discussing the subject of the state, he did it that he might introduce the defence and praise of that without which he thought that a state could not be governed. But Carneades, that he might refute Aristotle and Plato, the advocates of justice, in that first disputation collected all the arguments which were alleged in behalf of justice, that he might be able to overthrow them, as he did. For it was very easy to shake justice, having no roots, inasmuch as there was then none on the earth, that its nature or qualities might be perceived by philosophers. And I could wish that men, so many and of such a character, had possessed knowledge also, in proportion to their eloquence and spirit, for completing the defence of this greatest virtue, which has its origin in religion, its principle in equity! But those who were ignorant of that first part could not possess the second. But I wish first to show, summarily and concisely, what it is, that it may be understood that the philosophers were ignorant of justice, and were unable to defend that with which they were unacquainted. Although justice embraces all the virtues together, yet there are two, the chief of all, which cannot be torn asunder and separated from it — piety and equity. For fidelity, temperance, uprightness, innocence, integrity, and the other things of this kind, either naturally or through the training of parents, may exist in those men who are ignorant of justice, as they have always existed; for the ancient Romans, who were accustomed to glory in justice, used evidently to glory in those virtues which (as I have said) may proceed from justice, and be separated from the very fountain itself. But piety and equity are, as it were, its veins: for in these two fountains the whole of justice is contained; but its source and origin is in the first, all its force and method in the second. But piety is nothing else but the conception[3] of God, as Trismegistus most truly defined it, as we have said in another place. If, therefore, it is piety to know God, and the sum of this knowledge is that you worship Him, it is plain that he is ignorant of justice who does not possess the knowledge of God. For how can he know justice itself, who is ignorant of the source from which it arises? Plato, indeed, spoke many things respecting the one God, by whom he said that the world was framed; but he spoke nothing respecting religion: for he had dreamed of God, but had not known Him. But if either he himself or any other person had wished to complete the defence of justice, he ought first of all to have overthrown the religions of the gods, because they are opposed to piety. And because Socrates indeed tried to do this, he was thrown into prison; that even then it might be seen what was about to happen to those men who had begun to defend true justice, and to serve the only God.

The other part of justice, therefore, is equity; and it is plain that I am not speaking of the equity of judging well, though this also is praiseworthy in a just man, but of making himself equal to others, which Cicero calls equability.[4] For God, who produces and gives breath to

[1] κωφοὺς καὶ ἀνοήτους.
[2] [See *Rep.*, iii. cap. 6, part iv. vol. 2, p. 300, ed. Klotz.]
[3] Notio.
[4] [*De Officiis*, i. 26; and see vol. ii. p. 421, this series.]

men, willed that all should be equal, that is, equally matched.[1] He has imposed on all the same condition of living; He has produced all to wisdom; He has promised immortality to all; no one is cut off from His heavenly benefits. For as He distributes to all alike His one light, sends forth His fountains to all, supplies food, and gives the most pleasant rest of sleep; so He bestows on all equity and virtue. In His sight no one is a slave, no one a master; for if all have the same Father, by an equal right we are all children. No one is poor in the sight of God, but he who is without justice; no one is rich, but he who is full of virtues; no one, in short, is excellent, but he who has been good and innocent; no one is most renowned, but he who has abundantly performed works of mercy; no one is most perfect, but he who has filled all the steps of virtue. Therefore neither the Romans nor the Greeks could possess justice, because they had men differing from one another by many degrees, from the poor to the rich, from the humble to the powerful; in short, from private persons to the highest authorities of kings. For where all are not equally matched, there is not equity; and inequality of itself excludes justice, the whole force of which consists in this, that it makes those equal who have by an equal lot arrived at the condition of this life.

CHAP. XVI. — OF THE DUTIES OF THE JUST MAN, AND THE EQUITY OF CHRISTIANS.

Therefore, since those two fountains of justice are changed, all virtue and all truth are taken away, and justice itself returns to heaven. And on this account the true good was not discovered by philosophers, because they were ignorant both of its origin and effects: which has been revealed to no others but to our people.[2] Some one will say, Are there not among you some poor, and others rich; some servants, and others masters? Is there not some difference between individuals? There is none; nor is there any other cause why we mutually bestow upon each other the name of brethren, except that we believe ourselves to be equal. For since we measure all human things not by the body, but by the spirit, although the condition of bodies is different, yet we have no servants, but we both regard and speak of them as brothers in spirit, in religion as fellow-servants. Riches also do not render men illustrious, except that[3] they are able to make them more conspicuous by good works. For men are rich, not because they possess riches, but because they employ them on works of justice; and they who seem to be poor, on this account are rich, because they are not[4] in want, and desire nothing.

Though, therefore, in lowliness of mind we are on an equality, the free with slaves, and the rich with the poor, nevertheless in the sight of God we are distinguished by virtue. And every one is more elevated in proportion to his greater justice. For if it is justice for a man to put himself on a level even with those of lower rank, although he excels in this very thing, that he made himself equal to his inferiors; yet if he has conducted himself not only as an equal, but even as an inferior, he will plainly obtain a much higher rank of dignity in the judgment of God[5] For assuredly, since all things in this temporal life are frail and liable to decay, men both prefer themselves to others, and contend about dignity; than which nothing is more foul, nothing more arrogant, nothing more removed from the conduct of a wise man: for these earthly things are altogether opposed to heavenly things. For as the wisdom of men is the greatest foolishness with God, and foolishness is (as I have shown) the greatest wisdom; so he is low and abject in the sight of God who shall have been conspicuous and elevated on earth. For, not to mention that these present earthly goods to which great honour is paid are contrary to virtue, and enervate the vigour of the mind, what nobility, I pray, can be so firm, what resources, what power, since God is able to make kings themselves even lower than the lowest? And therefore God has consulted our interest in placing this in particular among the divine precepts: "He that exalteth himself shall be abased; and he that humbleth himself shall be exalted."[6] And the wholesomeness of this precept teaches that he who shall *simply* place himself on a level with *other* men, and carry himself with humility, is esteemed excellent and illustrious in the sight of God. For the sentiment is not false which is brought forward in Euripides to this effect: —

> "The things which are here considered evil are esteemed good in heaven."

CHAP. XVII. — OF THE EQUITY, WISDOM, AND FOOLISHNESS OF CHRISTIANS.

I have explained the reason why philosophers were unable either to find or to defend justice. Now I return to that which I had purposed. Carneades, therefore, since the arguments of the philosophers were weak, undertook the bold task of refuting them, because he understood that they were capable of refutation. The substance of his disputation was this: "That men[7] enacted

1 [A striking parallel to Cyprian's saying, vol. v. note 2, p. 460, this series.]
2 [Cap. xv. p. 150, *supra*.]
3 Nisi quòd. Some editions read, "nisi quos," except those whom, etc.
4 Quia non egent. Some editors omit *non*; but this is not so good.
5 [Jas. i. 9, 10, and ii. 1-8.]
6 Luke xiv. ii.
7 [From the *Republic*, book iii. cap. 12, sec. 21.]

laws for themselves, with a view to their own advantage, differing indeed according to their characters, and in the case of the same persons often changed according to the times; but that there was no natural law: that all, both men and other animals, were borne by the guidance of nature to their own advantage; therefore that there was no justice, or if any did exist, it was the greatest folly, because it injured itself by promoting the interests of others." And he brought forward these arguments: "That all nations which flourished with dominion, even the Romans themselves, who were masters of the whole world, if they wish to be just, that is, to restore the possessions of others, must return to cottages, and lie down in want and miseries." Then, leaving general topics, he came to particulars. "If a good man," he says, "has a runaway slave, or an unhealthy and infected house, and he alone knows these faults, and on this account offers it for sale, will he give out that the slave is a runaway, and the house which he offers for sale is infected, or will he conceal it from the purchaser? If he shall give it out, he is good indeed, because he will not deceive; but still he will be judged foolish, because he will either sell at a low price or not sell at all. If he shall conceal it, he will be wise indeed, because he will consult his own interest; but he will be also wicked, because he will deceive. Again, if he should find any one who supposes that he is selling copper ore when it is gold, or lead when it is silver, will he be silent, that he may buy it at a small price; or will he give information of it, so that he may buy it at a great price? It evidently appears foolish to prefer to buy it at a great price." From which he wished it to be understood, both that he who is just and good is foolish, and that he who is wise is wicked; and yet that it may possibly happen without ruin, for men to be contented with poverty. Therefore he passed to greater things, in which no one could be just without danger of his life. For he said: "Certainly it is justice not to put a man to death, not to take the property of another. What, then, will the just man do, if he shall happen to have suffered shipwreck, and some one weaker than himself shall have seized a plank? Will he not thrust him from the plank, that he himself may get upon it, and supported by it may escape, especially since there is no witness in the middle of the sea? If he is wise, he will do so; for he must himself perish unless he shall thus act. But if he choose rather to die than to inflict violence upon another, in this case he is just, but foolish, in not sparing his own life while he spares the life of another. Thus also, if the army of his own people shall have been routed, and the enemy have begun to press upon them, and that just man shall have met with a wounded man on horseback, will he spare him so as to be slain himself, or will he throw him from his horse, that he himself may escape from the enemy? If he shall do this, he will be wise, but also wicked; if he shall not do it, he will be just, but also of necessity foolish." When, therefore, he had thus divided justice into two parts, saying that the one was civil, the other natural, he subverted both: because the civil part is wisdom, but not justice; but the natural part is justice, but not wisdom. These arguments are altogether subtle and acute,[1] and such as Marcus Tullius was unable to refute. For when he represents Lælius as replying to Furius, and speaking in behalf of justice, he passed them by as a pitfall without refuting them; so that the same Lælius appears not to have defended natural justice, which had fallen under the charge of folly, but that civil justice which Furius had admitted to be wisdom, but unjust.[2]

CHAP. XVIII. — OF JUSTICE, WISDOM, AND FOLLY.

With reference to our present discussion, I have shown how justice bears the resemblance of folly, that it may appear that those are not deceived without reason who think that men of our religion are foolish in appearing to do such things as he proposed. Now I perceive that a greater undertaking is required from me, to show why God wished to enclose justice under the appearance of folly, and to remove it from the eyes of men, when I shall have first replied to Furius, since Lælius has not sufficiently replied to him; who, although he was a wise man, as he was called, yet could not be the advocate of true justice, because he did not possess the source and fountain of justice. But this defence is easier for us, to whom by the bounty of Heaven this justice is familiar and well known, and who know it not in name, but in reality. For Plato and Aristotle desired with an honest will to defend justice, and would have effected something, if their good endeavours, their eloquence, and vigour of intellect had been aided also by a knowledge of divine things. Thus their work, being vain and useless, was neglected: nor were they able to persuade any of men to live according to their precept, because that system had no foundation from heaven. But our work must be more certain, since we are taught of God. For they represented justice in words, and pictured it when it was not in sight; nor were they able to confirm their assertions by present examples. For the hearers might have answered that it was impossible to live as they prescribed in their disputation; so that none have as yet existed who followed that course of life. But we show

---

1 Venenata. [See *De Finibus*, book v. cap. 23.]
2 [See p. 150, *supra*.]

the truth of our statements not only by words, but also by examples derived from the truth. Therefore Carneades understood what is the nature of justice, except that he did not sufficiently perceive that it was not folly; although I seem to myself to understand with what intention he did this. For he did not really think that he who is just is foolish; but when he knew that he was not so, but did not comprehend the cause why he appeared so, he wished to show that the truth lay hidden, that he might maintain the dogma of his own sect,[1] the chief opinion of which is, "that nothing can be fully comprehended."

Let us see, therefore, whether justice has any agreement with folly. The just man, he says, if he does not take away from the wounded man his horse, and from the shipwrecked man his plank, in order that he may preserve his own life, is foolish. First of all, I deny that it can in any way happen that a man who is truly just should be in circumstances of this kind; for the just man is neither at enmity with any human being, nor desires anything at all which is the property of another. For why should he take a voyage, or what should he seek from another land, when his own is sufficient for him? Or why should he carry on war, and mix himself with the passions of others, when his mind is engaged in perpetual peace with men? Doubtless he will be delighted with foreign merchandise or with human blood, who does not know how to seek gain, who is satisfied with his mode of living, and considers it unlawful not only himself to commit slaughter, but to be present with those who do it, and to behold it! But I omit these things, since it is possible that a man may be compelled even against his will to undergo these things. Do you then, O Furius — or rather O Carneades, for all this speech is his — think that justice is so useless, so superfluous, and so despised by God, that it has no power and no influence in itself which may avail for its own preservation? But it is evident that they who are ignorant of the mystery[2] of man, and who therefore refer all things to this present life, cannot know how great is the force of justice. For when they discuss the subject of virtue, although they understand that it is very full of labours and miseries, nevertheless they say that it is to be sought for its own sake; for they by no means see its rewards, which are eternal and immortal. Thus, by referring all things to the present life, they altogether reduce virtue to folly, since it undergoes such great labours of this life in vain and to no purpose. But more on this subject at another opportunity.

In the meanwhile let us speak of justice, as we began, the power of which is so great, that when it has raised its eyes to heaven, it deserves all things from God. Flaccus therefore rightly said, that the power of innocence is so great, that wherever it journeys, it needs neither arms nor strength for its protection: —

"He whose life hath no flaw, pure from guile, need not borrow
Or the bow or the darts of the Moor, O my Fuscus!
He relies for defence on no quiver that teems with
Poison-steept arrows.
Though his path be along sultry African Syrtes,
Or Caucasian ravines, where no guest finds a shelter,
Or the banks which Hydaspes, the stream weird[3] with fable,
Licks languid-flowing."[4]

It is impossible, therefore, that amidst the dangers of tempests and of wars the just man should be unprotected by the guardianship of Heaven; and that even if he should be at sea in company with parricides and guilty men, the wicked also should not be spared, that this one just and innocent soul may be freed from danger, or at any rate may be alone preserved while the rest perish. But let us grant that the case which the philosopher proposes is possible: what, then, will the just man do, if he shall have met with a wounded man on a horse, or a shipwrecked man on a plank? I am not unwilling to confess he will rather die than put another to death. Nor will justice, which is the chief good of man, on this account receive the name of folly. For what ought to be better and dearer to man than innocence? And this must be the more perfect, the more you bring it to extremity, and choose to die rather than to detract from the character of innocence. It is folly, he says, to spare the life of another in a case which involves the destruction of one's own life. Then do you think it foolish to perish even for friendship?

Why, then, are those Pythagorean friends praised by you, of whom the one gave himself to the tyrant as a surety for the life of the other, and the other at the appointed time, when his surety was now being led to execution, presented himself, and rescued him by his own interposition? Whose virtue would not be held in such glory, when one of them was willing to die for his friend, the other even for his word[5] which had been pledged, if they were regarded as fools. In fine, on account of this very virtue the tyrant rewarded them by preserving both, and thus the disposition of a most cruel man was changed. Moreover, it is even said that he entreated[6] them to admit him as a third party to their friendship, from which it is plain that he regarded them not

[1] i.e., The Academic School.
[2] Sacramentum, "the true theory of human life."
[3] Fabulosus.
[4] Hor., *Carm.*, i. 22. 1, Lord Lytton's translation.
[5] Pro fide.
[6] Deprecatus esse dicitur.

as fools, but as good and wise men. Therefore I do not see why, since it is reckoned the highest glory to die for friendship and for one's word, it is not glorious to a man to die even for his innocence. They are therefore most foolish who impute it as a crime to us that we are willing to die for God, when they themselves extol to the heavens with the highest praises him who was willing to die for a man. In short, to conclude this disputation, reason itself teaches that it is impossible for a man to be at once just and foolish, wise and unjust. For he who is foolish is unacquainted with that which is just and good, and therefore always errs. For he is, as it were, led captive by his vices; nor can he in any way resist them, because he is destitute of the virtue of which he is ignorant. But the just man abstains from all fault, because he cannot do otherwise, although he has the knowledge of right and wrong.

But who is able to distinguish right from wrong except the wise man? Thus it comes to pass, that he can never be just who is foolish, nor wise who is unjust. And if this is most true, it is plain that he who has not taken away a plank from a shipwrecked man, or a horse from one who is wounded, is not foolish; because it is a sin to do these things, and the wise man abstains from sin. Nevertheless I myself also confess that it has this appearance, through the error of men, who are ignorant of the peculiar character[1] of everything. And thus the whole of this inquiry is refuted not so much by arguments as by definition. Therefore folly is the erring in deeds and words, through ignorance of what is right and good. Therefore he is not a fool who does not even spare himself to prevent injury to another, which is an evil. And this, indeed, reason and the truth itself dictate.[2] For we see that in all animals, because they are destitute of wisdom, nature is the provider of supplies for itself. Therefore they injure others that they may profit themselves, for they do not understand that the[3] committing an injury is evil. But man, who has the knowledge of good and evil, abstains from committing an injury even to his own damage, which an animal without reason is unable to do; and on this account innocence is reckoned among the chief virtues of man. Now by these things it appears that he is the wisest man who prefers to perish rather than to commit an injury, that he may preserve that sense of duty[4] by which he is distinguished from the dumb creation. For he who does not point out the error of one who is offering the gold for sale, in order that he may buy it for a small sum, or he who does not avow that he is offering for sale a runaway slave or an infected house, having an eye to his own gain or advantage, is not a wise man, as Carneades wished it to appear, but crafty and cunning. Now craftiness and cunning exist in the dumb animals also: either when they lie in wait for others, and take them by deceit, that they may devour them; or when they avoid the snares of others in various ways. But wisdom falls to man alone. For wisdom is understanding either with the purpose of doing that which is good and right, or for the abstaining from improper words and deeds. Now a wise man never gives himself to the pursuit of gain, because he despises these earthly advantages: nor does he allow any one to be deceived, because it is the duty of a good man to correct the errors of men, and to bring them back to the right way; since the nature of man is social and beneficent, in which respect alone he bears a relation to God.

CHAP. XIX. — OF VIRTUE AND THE TORTURES OF CHRISTIANS, AND OF THE RIGHT OF A FATHER AND MASTER.

But undoubtedly this is the cause[5] why he appears to be foolish who prefers to be in want, or to die rather than to inflict injury or take away the property of another, — namely, because they think that man is destroyed by death. And from this persuasion all the errors both of the common people and also of the philosophers arise. For if we have no existence after death, assuredly it is the part of the most foolish man not to promote the interests of the present life, that it may be long-continued, and may abound with all advantages. But he who shall act thus must of necessity depart from the rule of justice. But if there remains to man a longer and a better life — and this we learn both from the arguments of great philosophers, and from the answers of seers, and the divine words of prophets — it is the part of the wise man to despise this present life with its advantages, since its entire loss is compensated by immortality. The same defender of justice, Lælius, says in Cicero:[6] "Virtue altogether wishes for honour; nor is there any other reward of virtue." There is indeed another, and that most worthy of virtue, which you, O Lælius, could never have supposed; for you had no knowledge of the sacred writings. And this reward it easily receives, and does not harshly demand. You are greatly mistaken, if you think that a reward can be paid to virtue by man, since you yourself most truly said in another

1 Proprietatem.
2 Conciliatricem sui.
3 Nesciunt, quia malum est nocere.
4 Officium.

5 Thus far he has refuted the arguments of Furius, the advocate of injustice. He now shows the reasons why Lælius, who was esteemed most wise, does not worthily maintain the cause of justice, i.e., because he was ignorant of heavenly wisdom. [See cap. xvii. p. 152, *supra*.]
6 *De Republ.*, i. 3.

place: "What riches will you offer to this man? what commands? what kingdoms? He who regards these things as human, judges his own advantages to be divine." Who, therefore, can think you a wise man, O Lælius, when you contradict yourself, and after a short interval take away from virtue that which you have given to her? But it is manifest that ignorance of the truth makes your opinion uncertain and wavering.

In the next place, what do you add? "But if all the ungrateful, or the many who are envious, or powerful enemies, deprive virtue of its rewards." Oh how frail, how worthless, have you represented virtue to be, if it can be deprived of its reward! For if it judges its goods to be divine, as you said, how can there be any so ungrateful, so envious, so powerful, as to be able to deprive virtue of those goods which were conferred upon it by the gods? "Assuredly it delights itself," he says, "by many comforts, and especially supports itself by its own beauty." By what comforts? by what beauty? since that beauty is often charged upon it as a fault, and turned into a punishment. For what if, as Furius said,[1] a man should be dragged away, harassed, banished, should be in want, be deprived of his hands, have his eyes put out, be condemned, put into chains, be burned, be miserably tortured also? will virtue lose its reward, or rather, will it perish itself? By no means. But it will both receive its reward from God the Judge, and it will live, and always flourish. And if you take away these things, nothing in the life of man can appear to be so useless, so foolish, as virtue, the natural goodness and honour of which may teach us that the soul is not mortal, and that a divine reward is appointed for it by God. But on this account God willed that virtue itself should be concealed under the character of folly, that the mystery of truth and of His religion might be secret; that He might show the vanity and error of these superstitions, and of that earthly wisdom which raises itself too highly, and exhibits great self-complacency, that its difficulty being at length set forth, that most narrow path might lead to the lofty reward of immortality.

I have shown, as I think, why our people are esteemed foolish by the foolish. For to choose to be tortured and slain, rather than to take incense in three fingers, and throw it upon the hearth,[2] appears as foolish as, in a case where life is endangered, to be more careful of the life of another than of one's own. For they do not know how great an act of impiety it is to adore any other object than God, who made heaven and earth, who fashioned the human race, breathed into them the breath of life, and gave them light. But if he is accounted the most worthless of slaves who runs away and deserts his master, and if he is judged most deserving of stripes and chains, and a prison, and the cross, and of all evil; and if a son, in the same manner, is thought abandoned and impious who deserts his father, that he may not pay him obedience, and on this account is considered deserving of being disinherited, and of having his name removed for ever from his family, — how much more so does he who forsakes God, in whom the two names entitled to equal reverence, of Lord and Father, alike meet? For what benefit does he who buys a slave bestow upon him, beyond the nourishment with which he supplies him for his own advantage? And he who begets a son has it not in his power to effect that he shall be conceived, or born, or live; from which it is evident that he is not the father, but only the instrument[3] of generation. Of what punishments, therefore, is he deserving, who forsakes Him who is both the true Master and Father, but those which God Himself has appointed? who has prepared everlasting fire for the wicked spirits; and this He Himself threatens by His prophets to the impious and the rebellious.[4]

CHAP. XX. — OF THE VANITY AND CRIMES OF IMPIOUS SUPERSTITIONS, AND OF THE TORTURES OF THE CHRISTIANS.

Therefore, let those who destroy their own souls and the souls of others learn what an inexpiable crime they commit; in the first place, because they cause their own death by serving most abandoned demons, whom God has condemned to everlasting punishments; in the next place, because they do not permit God to be worshipped by others, but endeavour to turn men aside to deadly rites, and strive with the greatest diligence that no life may be without injury on earth, which looks to heaven with its condition secured. What else shall I call them but miserable men, who obey the instigations of their own plunderers,[5] whom they think to be gods? of whom they neither know the condition, nor origin, nor names, nor nature; but, clinging to the persuasion of the people, they willingly err, and favour their own folly. And if you should ask them the grounds of their persuasion, they can assign none, but have recourse to the judgment of their ancestors, saying that they were wise, that they approved them, that they knew what was best; and thus they deprive themselves of all power of perception: they bid adieu to reason, while they place confidence in the errors of others. Thus, involved in ignorance

1 *Vid.* ch. xii.

2 [In focum. Here it means the *brazier* placed before an image.]

3 Generandi ministrum.

4 [Perpetually recurring are such ideas and interpretations of God's warnings. Vol. iv. p. 542.]

5 Prædonum. Some refer this to the priests; others, with greater probability, to the demons alluded to in the sentence.

of all things, they neither know themselves nor their gods. And would to heaven that they had been willing to err by themselves, and to be unwise by themselves! But they hurry away others also to be companions of their evil, as though they were about to derive comfort from the destruction of many. But this very ignorance causes them to be so cruel in persecuting the wise; and they pretend that they are promoting their welfare, that they wish to recall them to a good mind.

Do they then strive to effect this by conversation, or by giving some reason? By no means; but they endeavour to effect it by force and tortures. O wonderful and blind infatuation! It is thought that there is a bad mind in those who endeavour to preserve their faith, but a good one in executioners. Is there, then, a bad mind in those who, against every law of humanity, against every principle of justice, are tortured, or rather, in those who inflict on the bodies of the innocent such things, as neither the most cruel robbers, nor the most enraged enemies, nor the most savage barbarians have ever practised? Do they deceive themselves to such an extent, that they mutually transfer and change the names of good and evil? Why, therefore, do they not call day night — the sun darkness? Moreover, it is the same impudence to give to the good the name of evil, to the wise the name of foolish, to the just the name of impious. Besides this, if they have any confidence in philosophy or in eloquence, let them arm themselves, and refute these arguments of ours if they are able; let them meet us hand to hand, and examine every point. It is befitting that they should undertake the defence of their gods, lest, if our affairs should increase (as they do increase daily), theirs should be deserted, together with their shrines and their vain mockeries;[1] and since they can effect nothing by violence (for the religion of God is increased the more it is oppressed), let them rather act by the use of reason and exhortations.

Let their priests come forth into the midst, whether the inferior ones or the greatest; their flamens, augurs, and also sacrificing kings, and the priests and ministers of their superstitions. Let them call us together to an assembly; let them exhort us to undertake the worship of their gods; let them persuade us that there are many beings by whose deity and providence all things are governed; let them show how the origins and beginnings of their sacred rites and gods were handed down to mortals; let them explain what is their source and principle; let them set forth what reward there is in their worship, and what punishment awaits neglect; why they wish to be worshipped by men; what the piety of men contributes to them, if they are blessed: and let them confirm all these things not by their own assertion (for the authority of a mortal man is of no weight), but by some divine testimonies, as we do. There is no occasion for violence and injury, for religion cannot be imposed by force; the matter must be carried on by words rather than by blows, that the will may be affected. Let them unsheath the weapon of their intellect; if their system is true, let it be asserted. We are prepared to hear, if they teach; while they are silent, we certainly pay no credit to them, as we do not yield to them even in their rage. Let them imitate us in setting forth the system of the whole matter: for we do not entice, as they say; but we teach, we prove, we show. And thus no one is detained by us against his will, for he is unserviceable to God who is destitute of faith and devotedness; and yet no one departs from us, since the truth itself detains him. Let them teach in this manner, if they have any confidence in the truth; let them speak, let them give utterance; let them venture, I say, to discuss with us something of this nature; and then assuredly their error and folly will be ridiculed by the old women, whom they despise, and by our boys. For, since they are especially clever, they know from books the race of the gods, and their exploits, and commands, and deaths, and tombs; they may also know that the rites themselves, in which they have been initiated, had their origin either in human actions, or in casualties, or in deaths.[2] It is the part of incredible madness to imagine that they are gods, whom they cannot deny to have been mortal; or if they should be so shameless as to deny it, their own writings, and those of their own people, will refute them; in short, the very beginnings of the sacred rites will convict them.[3] They may know, therefore, even from this very thing, how great a difference there is between truth and falsehood; for they themselves with all their eloquence are unable to persuade, whereas the unskilled and the uneducated are able, because the matter itself and the truth speaks.

Why then do they rage, so that while they wish to lessen their folly, they increase it? Torture[4] and piety are widely different; nor is it possible for truth to be united with violence, or justice with cruelty. But with good reason they do not venture to teach anything concerning divine things, lest they should both be derided by our people and be deserted by their own. For the common people for the most part, if they ascertain that these mysteries were instituted in memory of the dead, will condemn them, and seek for some truer object of worship.

[1] Ludibriis.

[2] Ex mortibus. Another reading is, ex moribus.

[3] [That is, the introductions, historically recorded, of such rites; e.g., by Numa. See vol. iii. p. 36, this series.]

[4] Carnificina.

"Hence rites of mystic awe"[1]

were instituted by crafty men, that the people may not know what they worship. But since we are acquainted with their systems, why do they either not believe us who are acquainted with both, or envy us because we have preferred truth to falsehood? But, they say, the public rites of religion[2] must be defended. Oh with what an honourable inclination the wretched men go astray! For they are aware that there is nothing among men more excellent than religion, and that this ought to be defended with the whole of our power; but as they are deceived in the matter of religion itself, so also are they in the manner of its defence. For religion is to be defended, not by putting to death, but by dying; not by cruelty, but by patient endurance; not by guilt, but by good faith: for the former belong to evils, but the latter to goods; and it is necessary for that which is good to have place in religion, and not that which is evil. For if you wish to defend religion by bloodshed, and by tortures, and by guilt, it will no longer be defended, but will be polluted and profaned. For nothing is so much a matter of free-will as religion; in which, if the mind of the worshipper is disinclined to it, religion is at once taken away, and ceases to exist. The right method therefore is, that you defend religion by patient endurance or by death; in which the preservation of the faith is both pleasing to God Himself, and adds authority to religion. For if he who in this earthly warfare preserves his faith to his king in some illustrious action, if he shall continue to live, because more beloved and acceptable, and if he shall fall, obtains the highest glory, because he has undergone death for his leader; how much more is faith to be kept towards God, the Ruler of all, who is able to pay the reward of virtue, not only to the living, but also to the dead! Therefore the worship of God, since it belongs to heavenly warfare, requires the greatest devotedness and fidelity. For how will God either love the worshipper, if He Himself is not loved by him, or grant to the petitioner whatever he shall ask, when he draws nigh to offer his prayer without sincerity or reverence? But these men, when they come to offer sacrifice, present to their gods nothing from within, nothing of their own — no uprightness of mind, no reverence or fear. Therefore, when the worthless sacrifices are completed, they leave their religion altogether in the temple, and with the temple, as they had found it; and neither bring with them anything of it, nor take anything back. Hence it is that religious observances of this kind are neither able to make men good, nor to be firm and unchangeable. And thus men are easily led away from them, because nothing is learned in them relating to the life, nothing relating to wisdom, nothing to faith.[3] For what is the religion of those gods? what is its power? what its discipline? what its origin? what its principle? what its foundation? what its substance? what is its tendency? or what does it promise, so that it may be faithfully preserved and boldly defended by man? I see nothing else in it than a rite pertaining to the fingers only.[4] But our religion is on this account firm, and solid, and unchangeable, because it teaches justice, because it is always with us, because it has its existence altogether in the soul of the worshipper, because it has the mind itself for a sacrifice. In that religion nothing else is required but the blood of animals, and the smoke of incense, and the senseless pouring out of libations; but in this of ours, a good mind, a pure breast, an innocent life: those rites are frequented by unchaste adulteresses without any discrimination, by impudent procuresses, by filthy harlots; they are frequented by gladiators, robbers, thieves, and sorcerers, who pray for nothing else but that they may commit crimes with impunity. For what can the robber ask when he sacrifices, or the gladiator, but that they may slay? what the poisoner, but that he may escape notice? what the harlot, but that she may sin to the uttermost? what the adulteress, but either the death of her husband, or that her unchastity may be concealed? what the procuress, but that she may deprive many of their property? what the thief, but that he may commit more peculations? But in our religion there is no place even for a slight and ordinary offence; and if any one shall come to a sacrifice without a sound conscience, he hears what threats God denounces against him: that God, I say, who sees the secret places of the heart, who is alway hostile to sins, who requires justice, who demands fidelity. What place is there here for an evil mind or for an evil prayer? But those unhappy men neither understand from their own crimes how evil it is to worship, since, defiled by all crimes, they come to offer prayer; and they imagine that they offer a pious sacrifice if they wash their skin; as though any streams could wash away, or any seas purify, the lusts which are shut up within their breast. How much better it is rather to cleanse the mind, which is defiled by evil desires, and to drive away all vices by the one laver of virtue and faith! For he who shall do this, although he bears a body which is defiled and sordid, is pure enough.

---

[1] Virg., *Æn.*, iii. 112.

[2] Suscepta publicè sacra.

[3] ["Parcus Deorum cultor et infrequens:" so Horace describes himself in this spirit. *Odes*, book i. 34, p. 215, ed. Delphin.]

[4] [See p. 155, note 2, *supra*.]

CHAP. XXI.—OF THE WORSHIP OF OTHER GODS AND THE TRUE GOD, AND OF THE ANIMALS WHICH THE EGYPTIANS WORSHIPPED.

But they, because they know not the object or the mode of worship, blindly and unconsciously fall into the contrary practice. Thus they adore their enemies, they appease with victims their robbers and murderers, and they place their own souls to be burned with the very incense on detestable altars. The wretched men are also angry, because others do not perish in like manner, with incredible blindness of minds. For what can they see who do not see the sun? As though, if they were gods, they would need the assistance of men against their despisers. Why, therefore, are they angry with us, if they have no power to effect anything? Unless it be that they destroy their gods, whose power they distrust, they are more irreligious than those who do not worship them at all. Cicero, in his Laws,[1] enjoining men to approach with holiness to the sacrifices, says, "Let them put on piety, let them lay aside riches; if any one shall act otherwise, God Himself will be the avenger." This is well spoken; for it is not right to despair about God, whom you worship on this account, because you think Him powerful. For how can He avenge the wrongs of His worshippers, if He is unable to avenge His own? I wish therefore to ask them to whom especially they think that they are doing a service in compelling them to sacrifice against their will, Is it to those whom they compel? But that is not a kindness which is done to one who refuses it. But we must consult their interests, even against their will, since they know not what is good. Why, then, do they so cruelly harass, torture, and weaken them, if they wish for their safety? or whence is piety so impious, that they either destroy in this wretched manner, or render useless, those whose welfare they wish to promote? Or do they do service to the gods? But that is not a sacrifice which is extorted from a person against his will. For unless it is offered spontaneously, and from the soul, it is a curse; when men sacrifice, compelled by proscription, by injuries, by prison, by tortures. If they are gods who are worshipped in this manner, if for this reason only, they ought not to be worshipped, because they wish to be worshipped in this manner: they are doubtless worthy of the detestation of men, since libations are made to them with tears, with groaning, and with blood flowing from all the limbs.

But we, on the contrary, do not require that any one should be compelled, whether he is willing or unwilling, to worship our God, who is the God of all men; nor are we angry if any one does not worship Him. For we trust in the majesty of Him who has power to avenge contempt shown towards Himself, as also He has power to avenge the calamities and injuries inflicted on His servants. And therefore, when we suffer such impious things, we do not resist even in word; but we remit vengeance to God, not as they act who would have it appear that they are defenders of their gods, and rage without restraint against those who do not worship them. From which it may be understood how it is not good to worship their gods, since men ought to have been led to that which is good by good, and not by evil; but because this is evil, even its office is destitute of good. But they who destroy religious systems must be punished. Have we destroyed them in a worse manner than the nation of the Egyptians, who worship the most disgraceful figures of beasts and cattle, and adore as gods some things which it is even shameful to speak of? Have we done worse than those same who, when they say that they worship the gods, yet publicly and shamefully deride them?—for they even allow pantomimic[2] representations of them to be acted with laughter and pleasure. What kind of a religion is this, or how great must that majesty be considered, which is adored in temples and mocked in theatres? And they who have done these things do not suffer the vengeance of the injured deity, but even go away honoured and praised. Do we destroy them in a worse manner than certain philosophers, who say that there are no gods at all, but that all things are spontaneously produced, and that all things which are done happen by chance? Do we destroy them in a worse manner than the Epicureans, who admit the existence of gods, but deny that they regard anything, and say that they are neither angry nor are influenced by favour? By which words they plainly persuade men that they are not to be worshipped at all, inasmuch as they neither regard their worshippers, nor are angry with those who do not worship them. Moreover, when they argue against fears, they endeavour to effect nothing else than that no one should fear the gods. And yet these things are willingly heard by men, and discussed with impunity.

CHAP. XXII.—OF THE RAGE OF THE DÆMONS AGAINST CHRISTIANS, AND THE ERROR OF UNBELIEVERS.

They do not therefore rage against us on this account, because their gods are not worshipped by us, but because the truth is on our side, which (as it has been said most truly) produces hatred. What, then, shall we think, but that they

[1] [Lib. ii. cap. 10. A noble reference in this chapter to *equality* among men.]

[2] Mimos agi.

are ignorant of what they suffer? For they act[1] with a blind and unreasonable fury, which we see, but of which they are ignorant. For it is not the men themselves who persecute, for they have no cause of anger against the innocent; but those contaminated and abandoned spirits by whom the truth is both known and hated, insinuate themselves into their minds, and goad them in their ignorance to fury. For these, as long as there is peace among the people of God, flee from the righteous, and fear them; and when they seize upon the bodies of men, and harass their souls, they are adjured by them, and at the name of the true God are put to flight. For when they hear this name they tremble, cry out, and assert that they are branded and beaten; and being asked who they are, whence they are come, and how they have insinuated themselves into a man, confess it. Thus, being tortured and excruciated by the power of the divine name, they come out of the man.[2] On account of these blows and threats, they always hate holy and just men; and because they are unable of themselves to injure them, they pursue with public hatred those whom they perceive to be grievous to them, and they exercise cruelty, with all the violence which they can employ, that they may either weaken their faith by pain, or, if they are unable to effect that, may take them away altogether from the earth, that there may be none to restrain their wickedness. It does not escape my notice what reply can be made on the other side. Why, then, does that God of surpassing power, that mighty One, whom you confess to preside over all things, and to be Lord of all, permit these things to be done, and neither avenge nor defend His worshippers? Why, in short, are they who do not worship Him rich, and powerful, and happy? and why do they enjoy honours and kingly state, and have these very persons[3] subject to their power and sway?

We must also give a reason for this, that no error may remain. For this is especially the cause why it is thought that religion has not the power of God, because men are influenced by the appearance of earthly and present goods, which in no way have reference to the care of the mind; and because they see that the righteous are without these goods, and that the unrighteous abound in them, they both judge that the worship of God is worthless, in which they do not see these things contained, and they imagine that the rites of other gods are true, since their worshippers enjoy riches and honours and kingdoms. But they who are of this opinion do not attentively consider the power and method of man, which consists altogether in the mind, and not in the body. For they see nothing more than is seen, namely the body; and because this is to be seen and handled,[4] it is weak, frail, and mortal; and to this belong all those goods which are their desire and admiration, wealth, honours, and governments, since they bring pleasures to the body, and therefore are as liable to decay as the body itself. But the soul, in which alone man consists, since it is not exposed to the sight of the eyes, and its goods cannot be seen, for they are placed in virtue only, must therefore be as firm, and constant, and lasting as virtue itself, in which the good of the soul consists.

CHAP. XXIII. — OF THE JUSTICE AND PATIENCE OF THE CHRISTIANS.

It would be a lengthened task to draw forth all the appearances of virtue, to show respecting each how necessary it is for a wise and just man to be far removed from those goods, the enjoyment of which by the unjust causes the worship of their gods to be regarded as true and efficacious. As our present inquiry is concerned, it will be sufficient to prove our point from the case of a single virtue. For instance, patience is a great and leading virtue, which the public voices of the people and philosophers and orators alike extol with the highest praises. But if it cannot be denied that this is a virtue of the highest kind, it is necessary that the just and wise man should be in the power of the unjust, for obtaining patience; for patience is the bearing with equanimity of the evils which are either inflicted or happen to fall upon us. Therefore the just and wise man, because he exercises virtue, has patience in himself; but he will be altogether free from this if he shall suffer no adversity. On the other hand, the man who lives in prosperity is impatient, and is without the greatest virtue. I call him impatient, because he suffers nothing. He is also unable to preserve innocency, which virtue is peculiar to the just and wise man. But he often acts unjustly also, and desires the property of others, and seizes upon that which he has desired by injustice, because he is without virtue, and is subject to vice and sin; and forgetful of his frailty, he is puffed up with a mind elated with insolence.

From this cause the unjust, and those who are ignorant of God, abound with riches, and power, and honours. For all these things are the rewards of injustice, because they cannot be perpetual, and they are sought through lust and violence. But the just and wise man, because he deems all these things as human, as it has been said by Lælius, and his own goods as divine,

[1] Pergitur enim . . . furore. Another reading is, "Perciti enim perferuntur . . . furore."
[2] Exsulantur. Other readings are, "exsolantur," "expelluntur," "exultantur." [Compare p. 393, note 1, vol. v., this series.]
[3] Eos ipsos, i.e., Christians.
[4] Quia oculis manuque tractabile est.

neither desires anything which belongs to another, lest he should injure any one at all in violation of the law of humanity; nor does he long for any power or honour, that he may not do an injury to any one. For he knows that all are produced by the same God, and in the same condition, and are joined together by the right of brotherhood.[1] But being contented with his own, and *that* a little, because he is mindful of his frailty, he does not seek for anything beyond that which may support his life; and even from that which he has he bestows a share on the destitute, because he is pious; but piety is a very great virtue. To this is added, that he despises frail and vicious pleasures, for the sake of which riches are desired; since he is temperate, and master of his passions. He also, having no pride or insolence, does not raise himself too highly, nor lift up his head with arrogance; but he is calm and peaceful, lowly[2] and courteous, because he knows his own condition. Since, therefore, he does injury to none, nor desires the property of others, and does not even defend his own if it is taken from him by violence, since he knows how even to bear with moderation an injury inflicted upon him, because he is endued with virtue; it is necessary that the just man should be subject to the unjust, and that the wise should be insulted by the foolish, that the one may sin because he is unjust, and the other may have virtue in himself because he is just.

But if any one shall wish to know more fully why God permits the wicked and the unjust to become powerful, happy, and rich, and, on the other hand, suffers the pious to be humble, wretched, and poor, let him take the book of Seneca which has the title, "Why many evils happen to good men, though there is a providence;" in which book he has said many things, not assuredly with the ignorance of this world, but wisely, and almost with divine inspiration.[3] "God," he says, "regards men as His children, but He permits the corrupt and vicious to live in luxury and delicacy, because He does not think them worthy of His correction. But He often chastises the good whom He loves, and by continual labours exercises them to the practice of virtue: nor does He permit them to be corrupted and depraved by frail and perishable goods." From which it ought to appear strange to no one if we are often chastised by God for our faults. Yea, rather, when we are harassed and pressed, then we especially give thanks to our most indulgent Father, because He does not permit our corruption to proceed to greater lengths, but corrects it with stripes and blows. From which we understand that we are an object of regard to God, since He is angry when we sin. For when He might have bestowed upon His people both riches and kingdoms, as He had before given them to the Jews, whose successors and posterity we are; on this account He would have them live under the power and government of others, lest, being corrupted by the happiness of prosperity, they should glide into luxury and despise the precepts of God; as those ancestors of ours, who, ofttimes enervated by these earthly and frail goods, departed from discipline and burst the bonds of the law. Therefore He foresaw how far He would afford rest to His worshippers if they should keep His commandments, and yet correct them if they did not obey His precepts. Therefore, lest they should be as much corrupted by ease as their fathers had been by indulgence,[4] it was His will that they should be oppressed by those in whose power He placed them, that He may both confirm them when wavering, and renew them to fortitude when corrupted, and try and prove them when faithful. For how can a general prove the valour of his soldiers, unless he shall have an enemy? And yet there arises an adversary to him against his will, because he is mortal, and is able to be conquered; but because God cannot be opposed, He Himself stirs up adversaries to His name, not to fight against God Himself, but against His soldiers, that He may either prove the devotedness and fidelity of His servants, or may strengthen them, until He corrects their wasting discipline by the stripes of affliction.[5]

There is also another cause why He permits persecutions to be carried on against us, that the people of God may be increased.[6] Nor is it difficult to show why or how this happens. First of all, great numbers are driven from the worship of the false gods by their hatred of cruelty. For who would not shrink from such sacrifices? In the next place, some are pleased with virtue and faith itself. Some suspect that it is not without reason that the worship of the gods is considered evil by so many men, so that they would rather die than do that which others do that they may preserve their life. Some one desires to know what that good is which is defended even to death, which is preferred to all things which are pleasant and beloved in this life, from which neither the loss of goods, nor of the light, nor bodily pain, nor tortures of the vitals deter them. These things have great effect; but these causes have always especially increased

1 [See vol. iii. (cap. 36), p. 45, note 1, this series.]
2 Planus et communis.
3 [" Deus homines pro liberis habet sed corruptos." He attributes a sort of inspiration to such a writer, as to Orpheus and the Sibyl.]
4 Licentiâ.
5 Pressuræ verberibus. The word "pressura" is used by the Fathers to express persecution or calamity.
6 [See Tertullian, vol. iii. pp. 36 (note 1), 45 (note 2), 49, 55, and 60.]

the number of our followers. The people who stand around hear them saying in the midst of these very torments that they do not sacrifice to stones wrought by the hand of man, but to the living God, who is in heaven: many understand that this is true, and admit it into their breast. In the next place, as it is accustomed to happen in matters of uncertainty while they make inquiry of one another, what is the cause of this perseverance, many things which relate to religion, being spread abroad and carefully observed by rumour among one another, are learned; and because these are good they cannot fail to please. Moreover, the revenge which follows, as always happens, greatly impels men to believe. Nor, indeed, is it a slight cause that the unclean spirits of demons, having received permission, throw themselves into the bodies of many; and when these have afterwards been driven out, they who have been healed cling to the religion, the power of which they have experienced. These numerous causes being collected together, wonderfully gain over a great multitude to God.[1]

CHAP. XXIV. — OF THE DIVINE VENGEANCE INFLICTED ON THE TORTURERS OF THE CHRISTIANS.

Whatever, therefore, wicked princes plan against us, God Himself permits to be done. And yet most unjust persecutors, to whom the name of God was a subject of reproach and mockery, must not think that they will escape with impunity, because they have been, as it were, the ministers of His indignation against us. For they will be punished with the judgment of God, who, having received power, have abused it to an inhuman degree, and have even insulted God in their arrogance, and placed His eternal name beneath their feet, to be impiously and wickedly trampled upon. On this account He promises that He will quickly take vengeance upon them, and exterminate the evil monsters[2] from the earth. But He also, although He is accustomed to avenge the persecutions[3] of His people even in the present world, commands us, however, to await patiently that day of heavenly judgment, in which He Himself will honour or punish every man according to his deserts. Therefore let not the souls of the sacrilegious expect that those whom they thus trample upon will be despised and unavenged. Those ravenous and voracious wolves who have tormented just and innocent souls, without the commission of any crimes, will surely meet with their reward. Only let us labour, that nothing else in us may be punished by men but righteousness alone: let us strive with all our power that we may at once deserve at the hands of God the avenging of our suffering and a reward.

[1] [A most important *résumè* of the effects upon the heathen of Christian fortitude and patience. See Tertullian on "the Seed of the Church," vol. iii. pp. 55 and 60; also vol. iv. p. 126.]

[2] Bestias malas. Lactantius in several passages applies this expression to the persecutors of the Christians. [A quotation from the Cretian poet cited by St. Paul. "Cretenses semper mendaces *malæ bestiæ*, ventres pigri." Tit. ii. 12.]

[3] Vexationes."

THE DIVINE INSTITUTES

BOOK VI.

OF TRUE WORSHIP.

CHAP. I.—OF THE WORSHIP OF THE TRUE GOD, AND OF INNOCENCY, AND OF THE WORSHIP OF FALSE GODS.

WE have completed that which was the object of our undertaking, through the teaching of the Divine Spirit, and the aid of the truth itself; the cause of asserting and explaining which was imposed upon me both by conscience and faith, and by our Lord Himself, without whom nothing can be known or clearly set forth. I come now to that which is the chief and greatest part of this work—to teach in what manner or by what sacrifice God must be worshipped. For that is the duty of man, and in that one object the sum of all things and the whole course of a happy life consists, since we were fashioned and received the breath of life from Him on this account, not that we might behold the heaven and the sun, as Anaxagoras supposed, but that we might with pure and uncorrupted mind worship Him who made the sun and the heaven. But although in the preceding books, as far as my moderate talent permitted, I defended the truth, yet it may especially be elucidated [1] by the mode of worship itself. For that sacred and surpassing majesty requires from man nothing more than innocence alone; and if any one has presented this to God, he has sacrificed with sufficient piety and religion. But men, neglecting justice, though they are polluted by crimes and outrages of all kinds, think themselves religious if they have stained the temples and altars with the blood of victims, if they have moistened the hearths with a profusion of fragrant and old wine. Moreover, they also prepare sacred feasts and choice banquets, as though they offered to those who would taste something from them. Whatever is rarely to be viewed, whatever is precious in workmanship or in fragrance, that they judge to be pleasing to their gods, not by any reference to their divinity, of which they are ignorant, but from their own desires; nor do they understand that God is in no want of earthly resources.

For they have no knowledge of anything except the earth, and they estimate good and evil things by the perception and pleasure of the body alone. And as they judge of religion according to its pleasure, so also they arrange the acts of their whole life. And since they have turned away once for all from the contemplation of the heaven, and have made that heavenly faculty the slave of the body, they give the reins to their lusts, as though they were about to bear away pleasure with themselves, which they hasten to enjoy at every moment; whereas the soul ought to employ the service of the body, and not the body to make use of the service of the soul. The same men judge riches to be the greatest good. And if they cannot obtain them by good practices, they endeavour to obtain them by evil practices; they deceive, they carry off by violence, they plunder, they lie in wait, they deny on oath; in short, they have no consideration or regard for anything,[2] if only they can glitter with gold, and shine conspicuous with plate, with jewels, and with garments, can spend riches upon their greedy appetite, and always walk attended with crowds of slaves through the people compelled to give way.[3] Thus devoting [4] themselves to the service of pleasures, they extinguish the force and vigour of the mind; and when they especially think that they are alive, they are hastening with the greatest precipitation to death. For, as we showed in the second book, the soul is concerned with heaven, the body with the earth.[5] They who neglect the goods of the soul, and seek those of the body,

[1] Elucere potest.

[2] Nihil moderati aut pensi habent. The expression is borrowed from Sallust, *Catiline*, xii.

[3] Per dimotum populum.

[4] Addicti et servientes voluptatibus.

[5] [See book ii. cap. 2, p. 43, *supra*.]

are engaged with darkness and death, which belong to the earth and to the body, because life and light are from heaven; and they who are without this, by serving the body, are far removed from the understanding of divine things. The same blindness everywhere oppresses the wretched men; for as they know not who is the true God, so they know not what constitutes true worship.

CHAP. II. — OF THE WORSHIP OF FALSE GODS AND THE TRUE GOD.

Therefore they sacrifice fine and fat victims to God, as though He were hungry; they pour forth wine to Him, as though He were thirsty; they kindle lights to Him, as though He were in darkness.[1] But if they were able to conjecture or to conceive in their mind what those heavenly goods are, the greatness of which we cannot imagine, while we are still encompassed with an earthly body, they would at once know that they are most foolish with their empty offices. Or if they would contemplate that heavenly light which we call the sun, they will at once perceive how God has no need of their candles, who has Himself given so clear and bright a light for the use of man.[1] And when, in so small a circle, which on account of its distance appears to have a measure no greater than that of a human head, there is still so much brilliancy that mortal eye cannot behold it, and if you should direct your eye to it for a short time mist and darkness would overspread your dimmed eyes, what light, I pray, what brightness, must we suppose that there is in God, with whom there is no night? For He has so attempered this very light, that it might neither injure living creatures by excessive brightness or vehement heat, and has given it so much of these properties as mortal bodies might endure or the ripening of the crops require. Is that man, therefore, to be thought in his senses, who presents the light of candles and torches as an offering to Him who is the Author and Giver of light? The light which He requires from us is of another kind, and that indeed not accompanied with smoke, but (as the poet says) clear and bright; I mean the light of the mind, on account of which we are called by the poets *photes*,[2] which light no one can exhibit unless he has known God. But their gods, because they are of the earth, stand in need of lights, that they may not be in darkness; and their worshippers, because they have no taste for anything heavenly, are recalled to the earth even by the religious rites to which they are devoted.[1] For on the earth there is need of a light, because its system and nature are dark. Therefore they do not attribute to the gods a heavenly perception, but rather a human one. And on this account they believe that the same things are necessary and pleasing to them as to us, who, when hungry, have need of food; or, when thirsty, of drink; or, when we are cold, require a garment; or, when the sun has withdrawn himself, require a light that we may be able to see.[3]

From nothing, therefore, can it be so plainly proved and understood that those gods, since they once lived, are dead, as from their worship itself, which is altogether of the earth. For what heavenly influence can there be in the shedding of the blood of beasts, with which they stain their altars? unless by chance they imagine that the gods feed upon that which men shrink from touching. And whoever shall have offered to them this food,[4] although he be an assassin, an adulterer, a sorcerer, or a parricide, he will be happy and prosperous. Him they love, him they defend, to him they afford all things which he shall wish for. Persius therefore deservedly ridicules superstitions of this kind in his own style:[5] "With what bribe," he says, "dost thou win the ears of gods? Is it with lungs and rich intestines?" He plainly perceived that there is no need of flesh for appeasing the majesty of heaven, but of a pure mind and a just spirit, and a breast, as he himself says, which is generous with a natural love of honour. This is the religion of heaven — not that which consists of corrupt things, but of the virtues of the soul, which has its origin from heaven; this is true worship, in which the mind of the worshipper presents itself as an undefiled offering to God. But how this is to be obtained, how it is to be afforded, the discussion of this book will show; for nothing can be so illustrious and so suited to man as to train men to righteousness.[6]

In Cicero, Catulus in the *Hortensius*, while he prefers philosophy to all things, says that he would rather have one short treatise respecting duty, than a long speech in behalf of a seditious man Cornelius. And this is plainly to be regarded not as the opinion of Catulus, who perhaps did not utter this saying, but as that of Cicero, who wrote it. I believe that he wrote it for the purpose of recommending these books which he was about to write on Offices, in which very books he testifies that nothing in the whole

1 [The ritual use of lights was unknown to primitive Christians, however harmless it may be.]

2 φῶτες. There is here a play on the double meaning of the word — φῶς, a light, and φώς, a man. Some editions read "φῶς nuncupatur."

3 [The Lutherans retain altar-lights in Europe, and their use has never been wholly obsolete in the Anglican churches; but it is evident from our author that "from the beginning it was not so." This is not said with any scruple against their use where it is authorized by competent legislation.]

4 Saginam, thick coarse food, such as that which was given to gladiators.

5 Persius, *Sat.*, ii. 29.

6 [Ad justitiam. In Christian use, it means more than "justice," which is put here by the translator.]

range of philosophy is better and more profitable than to give precepts for living. But if this is done by those who do not know the truth, how much more ought we to do it, who are able to give true precepts,[1] being taught and enlightened by God? Nor, however, shall we so teach as though we were delivering the first elements of virtue, which would be an endless task, but as though we had undertaken the instruction of him who, with them, appears to be already perfect. For while their precepts remain, which they are accustomed to give correctly, with a view to uprightness, we will add to them things which were unknown to them, for the completion and consummation of righteousness, which they do not possess. But I will omit those things which are common to us with them, that I may not appear to borrow from those whose errors I have determined to convict and bring to light.

CHAP. III. — OF THE WAYS, AND OF VICES AND VIRTUES; AND OF THE REWARDS OF HEAVEN AND THE PUNISHMENTS OF HELL.

There are two ways,[2] O Emperor Constantine, by which human life must proceed — the one which leads to heaven, the other which sinks to hell; and these *ways* poets have introduced in their poems, and philosophers in their disputations. And indeed philosophers have represented the one as belonging to virtues, the other to vices; and they have represented that which belongs to virtues as steep and rugged at the first entrance, in which if any one, having overcome the difficulty, has climbed to the summit, they say that he afterwards has a level path, a bright and pleasant plain, and that he enjoys abundant and delightful fruits of his labours; but that those whom the difficulty of the first approach has deterred, glide and turn aside into the way of vices, which at its first entrance appears to be pleasant and much more beaten, but afterwards, when they have advanced in it a little further, that the appearance of its pleasantness is withdrawn, and that there arises a steep way, now rough with stones, now overspread with thorns, now interrupted by deep waters or violent with torrents, so that they must be in difficulty, hesitate, slip about, and fall. And all these things are brought forward that it may appear that there are very great labours in undertaking virtues, but that when they are gained there are the greatest advantages, and firm and incorruptible pleasures; but that vices ensnare the minds of men with certain natural blandishments, and lead them captivated by the appearance of empty pleasures to bitter griefs and miseries, — an altogether wise discussion, if they knew the forms and limits of the virtues themselves. For they had not learned either what they are, or what reward awaits them from God: but this we will show in these two books.

But these men, because they were ignorant or in doubt that the souls of men are immortal, estimated both virtues and vices by earthly honours or punishments. Therefore all this discussion respecting the two ways[3] has reference to frugality and luxury. For they say that the course of human life resembles the letter Y, because every one of men, when he has reached the threshold of early youth, and has arrived at the place "where the way divides itself into two parts,"[4] is in doubt, and hesitates, and does not know to which side he should rather turn himself. If he shall meet with a guide who may direct him wavering to better things — that is, if he shall learn philosophy or eloquence, or some honourable arts by which he may turn to good conduct,[5] which cannot take place without great labour — they say that he will lead a life of honour and abundance; but if he shall not meet with a teacher of temperance,[6] that he falls into the way on the left hand, which assumes the appearance of the better, — that is, he gives himself up to idleness, sloth, and luxury, which seem pleasant for a time to one who is ignorant of true goods, but that afterwards, having lost all his dignity and property, he will live in all wretchedness and ignominy. Therefore they referred the end of those ways[3] to the body, and to this life which we lead on earth. The poets perhaps did better, who would have it that this twofold way was in the lower regions; but they are deceived in this, that they proposed these ways to the dead. Both therefore spoke with truth, but yet both incorrectly; for the ways themselves ought to have been referred to life, their ends to death. We therefore speak better and more truly, who say that the two ways[3] belong to heaven and hell, because immortality is promised to the righteous, and everlasting punishment is threatened to the unrighteous.

But I will explain how these ways either exalt to heaven or thrust down to hell, and I will set forth what these virtues are of which the philosophers were ignorant; then I will show what are their rewards, and also what are vices, and what their punishments. For perhaps some one may expect that I shall speak separately of vices and virtues; whereas, when we discuss the subject of good or evil, that which is contrary may also

[1] [1 John iii. 1–8. The *ethical truth* of the Gospel was understood and exemplified by the primitive faithful.]

[2] [One wonders whether the *Duæ Viæ* here be not a reference to the "Apost. Constitutions" (book vii.), which, with the Bryennios discovery, will receive attention hereafter.]

[3] [Again the *Duæ Viæ*. See capp. 1 and 5, in (eds. Hitchcock and Brown) the Bryennios MS., pp. 3 and 13.]

[4] Virg., *Æneid*, vi. 540.

[5] Evadat ad bonam frugem.

[6] Frugalitatis.

be understood. For, whether you introduce virtues, vices will spontaneously depart; or if you take away vices, virtues will of their own accord succeed. The nature of good and evil things is so fixed, that they always oppose and drive out one another: and thus it comes to pass that vices cannot be removed without virtues, nor can virtues be introduced without the removal of vices. Therefore we bring forward these ways in a very different manner from that in which the philosophers are accustomed to present them: first of all, because we say that a guide is proposed to each, and in each case an immortal: but that the one is honoured who presides over virtues and good qualities, the other condemned who presides over vices and evils. But they place a guide only on the right side, and that not one only, nor a lasting one; inasmuch as they introduce any teacher of a good art, who may recall men from sloth, and teach them to be temperate. But they do not represent any as entering upon that way except boys and young men; for this reason, that the arts are learned at these ages. We, on the other hand, lead those of each sex, every age and race, into this heavenly path, because God, who is the guide of that way, denies immortality to no human being.[1] The shape also of the ways themselves is not as they supposed. For what need is there of the letter Y in matters which are different and opposed to one another? But the one which is better is turned towards the rising of the sun, the other which is worse towards its setting: since he who follows truth and righteousness, having received the reward of immortality, will enjoy perpetual light; but he who, enticed by that evil guide, shall prefer vices to virtues, falsehood to truth, must be borne to the setting of the sun, and to darkness.[2] I will therefore describe each, and will point out their properties and habits.

CHAP. IV. — OF THE WAYS OF LIFE, OF PLEASURES, ALSO OF THE HARDSHIPS OF CHRISTIANS.

There is one way, therefore, of virtue and the good, which leads, not, as the poets say, to the Elysian plains, but to the very citadel of the world: —

> "The left gives sinners up to pain,
> And leads to Tartarus' guilty reign." [3]

For it belongs to that accuser who, having invented false religions, turns men away from the heavenly path, and leads them into the way of perdition. And the appearance and shape of this way is so composed to the sight, that it appears to be level and open, and delightful with all kinds of flowers and fruits. For there are placed[4] in it all things which are esteemed on earth as good things — I mean wealth, honour, repose, pleasure, all kinds of enticements; but together with these also injustice, cruelty, pride, perfidy, lust, avarice, discord, ignorance, falsehood, folly, and other vices. But the end of this way is as follows: When they have reached the point from which there is now no return, it is so suddenly removed, together with all its beauty, that no one is able to foresee the fraud before that he falls headlong into a deep abyss. For whoever is captivated by the appearance of present goods, and occupied with the pursuit and enjoyment of these, shall not have foreseen the things which are about to follow after death, and shall have turned aside from God; he truly will be cast down to hell, and be condemned to eternal punishment.

But that heavenly way is set forth as difficult and hilly, or rough with dreadful thorns, or entangled with stones jutting out; so that every one must walk with the greatest labour and wearing of the feet, and with great precautions against falling. In this he has placed justice, temperance, patience, faith, chastity, self-restraint, concord, knowledge, truth, wisdom, and the other virtues; but together with these, poverty, ignominy, labour, pain, and all kinds of hardship. For whoever has extended his hope beyond the present, and chosen better things, will be without these earthly goods, that, being lightly equipped and without impediment, he may overcome the difficulty of the way. For it is impossible for him who has surrounded himself with royal pomp, or loaded himself with riches, either to enter upon or to persevere in these difficulties. And from this it is understood that it is easier for the wicked and the unrighteous to succeed in their desires, because their road is downward and on the decline; but that it is difficult for the good to attain to their wishes, because they walk along a difficult and steep path. Therefore the righteous man, since he has entered upon a hard and rugged way, must be an object of contempt, derision, and hatred. For all whom desire or pleasure drags headlong, envy him who has been able to attain to virtue, and take it ill that any one possesses that which they themselves do not possess. Therefore he will be poor, humble, ignoble, subject to injury, and yet enduring all things which are grievous; and if he shall continue his patience unceasingly to that last step and end, the crown of virtue will be given to him, and he will be rewarded by God with immortality for the labours which he has endured in life for the sake of righteousness. These are the ways which

---

[1] [Universal redemption is lovingly set forth by our author.]

[2] [A reference to the baptismal rite; the catechumen renouncing the works of darkness with his face to the west, and turning eastward to confess the Sun of Righteousness.]

[3] Virg., *Æneid*, vi. 542.

[4] Posita sunt omnia. There is another reading, "posuit Deus omnia."

God has assigned to human life, in each of which he has shown both good and evil things, but in a changed and inverted order. In the one he has pointed out in the first place temporal evils followed by eternal goods, which is the better order; in the other, first temporal goods followed by eternal evils, which is the worse order: so that, whosoever has chosen present evils together with righteousness, he will obtain greater and more certain goods than those were which he despised; but whoever has preferred present goods to righteousness, will fall into greater and more lasting evils than those were which he avoided. For as this bodily life is short, therefore its goods and evils must also be short; but since that spiritual life, which is contrary to this earthly life, is everlasting, therefore its goods and evils are also everlasting. Thus it comes to pass, that goods of short duration are succeeded by eternal evils, and evils of short duration by eternal goods.

Since, therefore, good and evil things are set before man at the same time, it is befitting that every one should consider with himself how much better it is to compensate evils of short duration by perpetual goods, than to endure perpetual evils for short and perishable goods. For as, in this life, when a contest with an enemy is set before you, you must first labour that you may afterwards enjoy repose, you must suffer hunger and thirst, you must endure heat and cold, you must rest on the ground, must watch and undergo dangers, that your children,[1] and house, and property being preserved, you may be able to enjoy all the blessings of peace and victory; but if you should choose present ease in preference to labour, you must do yourself the greatest injury: for the enemy will surprise you offering no resistance, your lands will be laid waste, your house plundered, your wife and children become a prey, you yourself will be slain or taken prisoner; to prevent the occurrence of these things, present advantage must be put aside, that a greater and more lasting advantage may be gained; — so in the whole of this life, because God has provided an adversary foi us, that we might be able to acquire virtue, present gratification must be laid aside, lest the enemy should overpower us. We must be on the watch, must post guards, must undertake military expeditions, must shed our blood to the uttermost; in short, we must patiently submit to all things which are unpleasant and grievous, and the more readily because God our commander has appointed for us eternal rewards for our labours. And since in this earthly warfare men expend so much labour to acquire for themselves those things which may perish in the same manner as that in which they were acquired, assuredly no labour ought to be refused by us, by whom that is gained which can in no way be lost.

For God, who created men to this warfare, desired that they should stand prepared in battle array, and with minds keenly intent should watch against the stratagems or open attacks of our single enemy, who, as is the practice of skilful and experienced generals, endeavours to ensnare us by various arts, directing his rage according to the nature and disposition of each. For he infuses into some insatiable avarice, that, being chained by their riches as by fetters, he may drive them from the way of truth. He inflames others with the excitement of anger, that while they are rather intent upon inflicting injury, he may turn them aside from the contemplation of God. He plunges others into immoderate lusts, that, giving themselves to pleasure of the body, they may be unable to look towards virtue. He inspires others with envy, that, being occupied with their own torments, they may think of nothing but the happiness of those whom they hate. He causes others to swell with ambitious desires. These are they who direct the whole occupation and care of their life to the holding of magistracies, that they may set a mark upon the annals,[2] and give a name to the years. The desire of others mounts higher, not that they may rule provinces with the temporal sword, but with boundless and perpetual power may wish to be called lords of the whole human race.[3] Moreover, those whom he has seen to be pious he involves in various[4] superstitions, that he may make them impious. But to those who seek for wisdom, he dashes philosophy before their eyes,[5] that he may blind them with the appearance of light, lest any one should grasp and hold fast the truth. Thus he has blocked up all the approaches against men, and has occupied the way, rejoicing in public errors; but that we might be able to dispel these errors, and to overcome the author of evils himself, God has enlightened us, and has armed us with true and heavenly virtue, respecting which I must now speak.

CHAP. V. — OF FALSE AND TRUE VIRTUE; AND OF KNOWLEDGE.

But before I begin to set forth the separate virtues, I must mark out the character of virtue itself, which the philosophers have not rightly

[1] Pignoribus.

[2] It was customary in many of the ancient states to connect the year with the name of the chief magistrate who was then in office. Thus at Athens the title of the chief magistrate was Archon Eponymus, giving name to the year; and at Rome, the year was reckoned by the names of the consuls then in office.

[3] [Ut infinita et perpetua potestate dominos se dici velint universi generis humani. A bold hint to Constantine.]

[4] Variis. Another reading is "vanis."

[5] Philosophiam in oculos impingit. [A warning to the emperor, a reflection on such as the Antonines, and a *prolepsis* of Julian.]

defined, as to its nature, or in what things it consisted; and I must describe its operation and office. For they only retained the name, but lost its power, and nature, and effect. But whatever they are accustomed to say in their definition of virtue, Lucilius puts together and expresses in a few verses, which I prefer to introduce, lest, while I refute the opinions of many, I should be longer than is necessary:—

"It is virtue, O Albinus, to pay the proper price,
To attend to the matters in which we are engaged, and in which we live.
It is virtue for a man to know the nature of everything.
It is virtue for a man to know what is right and useful and honourable,
What things are good, and what are evil.
What is useless,[1] base, and dishonourable.
It is virtue to know the end of an object to be sought, and the means *of procuring it.*
It is virtue to be able to assign their value to riches.
It is virtue to give that which is really due to honour;
To be the enemy and the foe[2] of bad men and manners, but, on the other hand, the defender of good men and manners;
To esteem these highly, to wish them well, to live in friendship with them,
Moreover, to consider the interest of one's country first;
Then those of parents, to put our own interests in the third and last place."

From these definitions, which the poet briefly puts together, Marcus Tullius derived the offices of living, following Panætius the Stoic,[3] and included them in three books.

But we shall presently see how false these things are, that it may appear how much the divine condescension has bestowed on us in opening to us the truth. He says that it is virtue to know what is good and evil, what is base, what is honourable, what is useful, what is useless. He might have shortened his treatise if he had only spoken of that which is good and evil; for nothing can be useful or honourable which is not also good, and nothing useless and base which is not also evil. And this also appears to be thus to philosophers, and Cicero shows it likewise in the third book of the above-mentioned treatise.[4] But knowledge cannot be virtue, because it is not within us, but it comes to us from without. But that which is able to pass from one to the other is not virtue, because virtue is the property of each individual. Knowledge therefore consists in a benefit derived from another; for it depends upon hearing. Virtue is altogether our own; for it depends upon the will of doing that which is good. As, therefore, in undertaking a journey, it is of no profit to know the way, unless we also have the effort and strength for walking, so truly knowledge is of no avail if our virtue fails. For, in general, even they who sin perceive what is good and evil, though not perfectly; and as often as they act improperly, they know that they sin, and therefore endeavour to conceal their actions. But though the nature of good and evil does not escape their notice, they are overpowered by an evil desire to sin, because they are wanting in virtue, that is, the desire of doing right and honourable things. Therefore that the knowledge of good and evil is one thing, and virtue another, appears from this, because knowledge can exist without virtue, as it has been in the case of many of the philosophers; in which, since not to have done what you knew to be right is justly censurable, a depraved will and a vicious mind, which ignorance cannot excuse, will be justly punished. Therefore, as the knowledge of good and evil is not virtue, so the doing that which is good and the abstaining from evil is virtue. And yet knowledge is so united with virtue, that knowledge precedes virtue, and virtue follows knowledge; because knowledge is of no avail unless it is followed up by action. Horace therefore speaks somewhat better: "Virtue is the fleeing from vice, and the first wisdom is to be free from folly."[5] But he speaks improperly, because he defined virtue by its contrary, as though he should say, That is good which is not evil. For when I know not what virtue is, I do not know what vice is. Each therefore requires definition, because the nature of the case is such that each must be understood or not understood.[6]

But let us do that which he ought to have done. It is a virtue to restrain anger, to control desire, to curb lust; for this is to flee from vice. For almost all things which are done unjustly and dishonestly arise from these affections. For if the force of this emotion which is called anger be blunted, all the evil contentions of men will be lulled to rest; no one will plot, no one will rush forth to injure another. Also, if desire be restrained, no one will use violence by land or by sea, no one will lead an army to carry off and lay waste the property of others. Also, if the ardour of lusts be repressed, every age and sex will retain its sanctity; no one will suffer, or do anything disgraceful. Therefore all crimes and disgraceful actions will be taken away from the life and character of men, if these emotions are appeased and calmed by virtue. And this calming of the emotions and affections has this meaning, that we do all things which are right. The whole duty of virtue then is, not to sin. And assuredly he cannot discharge this who is ignorant of God, since igno-

1 [Inutilia.]
2 Hostem atque inimicum: the former word signifies a "public," the latter a "private enemy."
3 [*De Officiis, passim.* Notably, to begin with, book i. cap. 3: "Triplex igitur," etc.]
4 [*De Nat. Deor.*, iii. See also *De Off.*, cap. 5, sec. 18.]
5 *Epist.*, i. 1. 41.
6 [To be taken with a grain of salt, but apparently comprehended in our author's personal theodicy.]

rance of Him from whom good things proceed must thrust a man unawares into vices. Therefore, that I may more briefly and significantly fix the offices of each subject, knowledge is to know God, virtue is to worship Him: the former implies wisdom, the latter righteousness.

CHAP. VI. — OF THE CHIEF GOOD AND VIRTUE, AND OF KNOWLEDGE AND RIGHTEOUSNESS.

I have said that which was the first thing, that the knowledge of good is not virtue; and secondly, I have shown what virtue is, and in what it consists. It follows that I should show this also, that the philosophers were ignorant of what is good and evil; and this briefly, because it has been almost[1] made plain in the third book, when I was discussing the subject of the chief good. And because they did not know what the chief good was, they necessarily erred in the case of the other goods and evils which are not the chief; for no one can weigh these with a true judgment who does not possess the fountain itself from which they are derived. Now the source of good things is God; but of evils, he who is always the enemy of the divine name, of whom we have often spoken. From these two sources good and evil things have their origin. Those which proceed from God have this object, to procure immortality, which is the greatest good; but those which arise from the other have this office, to call man away from heavenly things and sink him in earthly things, and thus to consign him to the punishment of everlasting death, which is the greatest evil. Is it therefore doubtful but that all those were ignorant of what was good and evil, who neither knew God nor the adversary of God? Therefore they referred the end of good things to the body, and to this short life, which must be dissolved and perish: they did not advance further. But all their precepts, and all the things which they introduce as goods, adhere to the earth, and lie on the ground, since they die with the body, which is earth; for they do not tend to procure life for man, but either to the acquisition or increase of riches, honour, glory, and power, which are altogether mortal things, as much so indeed as he who has laboured to obtain them. Hence is that saying,[2] "It is virtue to know the end of an object[3] to be sought, and the means of procuring it;" for they enjoin by what means and by what practices property is to be sought, for they see that it is often sought unjustly. But virtue of this kind is not proposed to the wise man; for it is not virtue to seek riches, of which neither the finding nor the possession is in our power: therefore they are more easy to be gained and to be retained by the bad than by the good. Virtue, then, cannot consist in the seeking of those things in the despising of which the force and purport of virtue appears; nor will it have recourse to those very things which, with its great and lofty mind, it desires to trample upon and bruise under foot; nor is it lawful for a soul which is earnestly fixed on heavenly goods to be called away from its immortal pursuits, that it may acquire for itself these frail things. But the course[4] of virtue especially consists in the acquisition of those things which neither any man, nor death itself, can take away from us. Since these things are so, that which follows is true: "It is virtue to be able to assign their value to riches:" which verse is nearly of the same meaning as the first two. But neither he nor any of the philosophers was able to know the price itself, either of what nature or what it is; for the poet, and all those whom he followed, thought that it meant to make a right use of riches, — that is, to be moderate in living, not to make costly entertainments, not to squander carelessly, not to expend property on superfluous or disgraceful objects.[5]

Some one will perhaps say, What do you say? Do you deny that this is virtue? I do not deny it indeed; for if I should deny it, I should appear to prove the opposite. But I deny that it is true virtue; because it is not that heavenly principle, but is altogether of the earth, since it produces no effect but that which remains on the earth.[6] But what it is to make a right use of wealth, and what advantage is to be sought from riches, I will declare more openly when I shall begin to speak of the duty of piety. Now the other things which follow are by no means true; for to proclaim enmity against the wicked, or to undertake the defence of the good, may be common to it with the evil. For some, by a pretence of goodness, prepare the way for themselves to power, and do many things which the good are accustomed to do, and that the more readily because they do them for the sake of deceiving; and I wish that it were as easy to carry out goodness in action as it is to pretend to it. But when they have begun to attain to their purpose and their wish in reaching the highest step of power, then, truly laying aside pretence, these men discover their character; they seize upon everything, and offer violence, and lay waste; and they press upon the good themselves, whose cause they had undertaken; and they cut away the steps by which they mounted, that no one

[1] Pœne: others read "plenè," and "planè." [c. 30, p. 100, *supra.*]

[2] [The first of the three *inutilia* of Lucilius, *ut supra*, thus: (1) "Virtus quærendæ rei finem scire, modumque;" (2) "Virtus divitiis pretium persolvere posse;" (3) "Virtus id dare quod re ipsa debetur honori." See p. 167, *supra.*]

[3] See chap. v. [p. 167, *supra*].

[4] Ratio virtutis.

[5] [How I love our author for his winning reproof of mere philosophical virtue in contrast with evangelical righteousness!]

[6] [See the *Quis Dives Salvetur* of Clement, vol. ii. p. 591, this series.]

may be able to imitate them against themselves. But, however, let us suppose that this duty of defending the good belongs only to the good man. Yet to undertake it is easy, to fulfil it is difficult; because when you have committed yourself to a contest and an encounter, the victory is placed at the disposal of God, not in your own power. And for the most part the wicked are more powerful both in number and in combination than the good, so that it is not so much virtue which is necessary to overcome them as good fortune. Is any one ignorant how often the better and the juster side has been overcome? From this cause harsh tyrannies have always broken out against the citizens. All history is full of examples, but we will be content with one. Cnœus Pompeius wished to be the defender of the good, since he took up arms in defence of the commonwealth, in defence of the senate, and in defence of liberty; and yet the same man, being conquered, perished together with liberty itself,[1] and being mutilated by Egyptian eunuchs, was cast forth unburied.[2]

It is not virtue, therefore, either to be the enemy of the bad or the defender of the good, because virtue cannot be subject to uncertain chances.

"Moreover, to reckon the interests of our country as in the first place."

When the agreement of men is taken away, virtue has no existence at all; for what are the interests of our country, but the inconveniences of another state or nation? — that is, to extend the boundaries which are violently taken from others, to increase the power of the state, to improve the revenues, — all which things are not virtues, but the overthrowing of virtues: for, in the first place, the union of human society is taken away, innocence is taken away, the abstaining from the property of another is taken away; lastly, justice itself is taken away, which is unable to bear the tearing asunder of the human race, and wherever arms have glittered, must be banished and exterminated from thence. This saying of Cicero[3] is true: "But they who say that regard is to be had to citizens, but that it is not to be had to foreigners, these destroy the common society of the human race; and when this is removed, beneficence, liberality, kindness, and justice are entirely[4] taken away." For how can a man be just who injures, who hates, who despoils, who puts to death? And they who strive to be serviceable to their country do all these things: for they are ignorant of what this being serviceable is, who think nothing useful, nothing advantageous, but that which can be held by the hand; and this alone cannot be held, because it may be snatched away.

Whoever, then, has gained for his country these goods — as they themselves call them — that is, who by the overthrow of cities and the destruction of nations has filled the treasury with money, has taken lands and enriched his countrymen — he is extolled with praises to the heaven: in him there is said to be the greatest and perfect virtue. And this is the error not only of the people and the ignorant, but also of philosophers, who even give precepts for injustice, lest folly and wickedness should be wanting in discipline and authority. Therefore, when they are speaking of the duties relating to warfare, all that discourse is accommodated neither to justice nor to true virtue, but to this life and to civil institutions;[5] and that this is not justice the matter itself declares, and Cicero has testified.[6] "But we," he says, "are not in possession of the real and life-like figure of true law and genuine justice, we have nothing but delineations and sketches;[7] and I wish that we followed even these, for they are taken from the excellent copies made by nature and truth." It is then a delineation and a sketch which they thought to be justice. But what of wisdom? does not the same man confess that it has no existence in philosophers? "Nor," he says,[8] "when Fabricius or Aristides is called just, is an example of justice sought from these as from a wise man; for none of these is wise in the sense in which we wish the truly wise to be understood. Nor were they who are esteemed and called wise, Marcus Cato and Caius Lælius, actually wise, nor those well-known seven;[9] but from their constant practice of the 'middle duties,'[10] they bore a certain likeness and appearance[11] of wise men." If therefore wisdom is taken away from the philosophers by their own confession, and justice is taken away from those who are regarded as just, it follows that all those descriptions of virtue must be false, because no one can know what true virtue is but he who is just and wise. But no one is just and wise but he whom God has instructed with heavenly precepts.

CHAP. VII. — OF THE WAY OF ERROR AND OF TRUTH: THAT IT IS SINGLE, NARROW, AND STEEP, AND HAS GOD FOR ITS GUIDE.

For all those who, by the confessed folly of others, are thought wise, being clothed with the

1 [Haggai ii. 7. "La journée de Pharsale fut la dernière heure de la liberté. Le sénat, les lois, le peuple, les mœurs, le mond romain étaient anéantis avec Pompée." — LAMARTINE.]

2 [See, on Pharsalia, etc., Lamartine's eloquent remarks, *Vie des Grands Hommes* (César), vol. v. pp. 276–277, ed. Paris, 1856.]

3 *De Offic.*, iii. 6

4 Funditus, "from the very foundation."

5 Moremque civilem.

6 *De Offic.*, iii. 17.

7 Umbrâ et imaginibus. The figure is borrowed partly from sculpture and partly from painting. "Effigies" is the moulded form, as opposed to the mere outline, "umbra" and "imago."

8 *De Offic.*, iii. 4. The words, "aut ab illis fortitudinis, aut," have not been translated, because they refer to the "Decii" and the "Scipiones," who are mentioned by Cicero as examples of bravery, but are omitted by Lactantius.

9 [See p 101, *supra*.]

10 [Ex *mediorum officiorum* frequentia, etc.]

11 [Rom. i. 22.]

appearance of virtue, grasp at shadows and outlines, but at nothing true. Which happens on this account, because that deceitful road which inclines to the west has many paths, on account of the variety of pursuits and systems which are dissimilar and varied in the life of men. For as that way of wisdom contains something which resembles folly, as we showed in the preceding book, so this way, which belongs altogether to folly, contains something which resembles wisdom, and they who perceive the folly of men in general seize upon this; and as it has its vices manifest, so it has something which appears to resemble virtue: as it has its wickedness open, so it has a likeness and appearance of justice. For how could the forerunner[1] of that way, whose strength and power are altogether in deceit, lead men altogether into fraud, unless he showed them some things which resembled the truth?[2] For, that His immortal secret might be hidden, God placed in his way things which men might despise as evil and disgraceful, that, turning away from wisdom and truth, which they were searching for without any guide, they might fall upon that very thing which they desired to avoid and flee from. Therefore he points out that way of destruction and death which has many windings, either because there are many kinds of life, or because there are many gods who are worshipped.

The deceitful[3] and treacherous guide of this way, that there may appear to be some distinction between truth and falsehood, good and evil, leads the luxurious in one direction, and those who are called temperate[4] in another; the ignorant in one direction, the learned in another; the sluggish in one direction, the active in another; the foolish in one direction, the philosophers in another, and even these not in one path. For those who do not shun pleasures or riches, he withdraws a little from this public and frequented road; but those who either wish to follow virtue, or profess a contempt for things, he drags over certain rugged precipices. But nevertheless all those paths which display an appearance of honours are not different roads, but turnings off[5] and bypaths, which appear indeed to be separated from that common one, and to branch off to the right, but yet return to the same, and all lead at the very end to one issue. For that guide unites them all, where it was necessary that the good should be separated from the bad, the strong from the inactive, the wise from the foolish; namely, in the worship of the gods, in which he slays them all with one sword, because they were all foolish without any distinction, and plunges them into death. But this way — which is that of truth, and wisdom, and virtue, and justice, of all which there is but one fountain, one source of strength, one abode — is both simple,[6] because with like minds, and with the utmost agreement, we follow and worship one God; and it is narrow, because virtue is given to the smaller number; and steep, because goodness, which is very high and lofty, cannot be attained to without the greatest difficulty and labour.

CHAP. VIII. — OF THE ERRORS OF PHILOSOPHERS, AND THE VARIABLENESS OF LAW.

This is the way which philosophers seek, but do not find on this account, because they prefer to seek it on the earth, where it cannot appear. Therefore they wander, as it were, on the great sea, and do not understand whither they are borne, because they neither discern the way nor follow any guide. For this way of life ought to be sought in the same manner in which their course is sought by ships over the deep: for unless they observe some light of heaven, they wander with uncertain courses. But whoever strives to hold the right course of life ought not to look to the earth, but to the heaven: and, to speak more plainly, he ought not to follow man, but God; not to serve these earthly images, but the heavenly God; not to measure all things by their reference to the body, but by their reference to the soul; not to attend to this life, but the eternal life. Therefore, if you always direct your eyes towards heaven, and observe the sun, where it rises, and take this as the guide of your life, as in the case of a voyage, your feet will spontaneously be directed into the way; and that heavenly light, which is a much brighter sun[7] to sound minds than this which we behold in mortal flesh, will so rule and govern you as to lead you without any error to the most excellent harbour of wisdom and virtue.

Therefore the law of God must be undertaken, which may direct us to this path; that sacred, that heavenly law, which Marcus Tullius, in his third book respecting the Republic,[8] has described almost with a divine voice; whose words I have subjoined, that I might not speak at greater length: "There is indeed a true law, right reason, agreeing with nature, diffused among all, unchanging, everlasting, which calls to duty by commanding, deters from wrong by forbidding; which, however, neither commands nor forbids the good in vain, nor affects the wicked by commanding or forbidding. It is not allow-

[1] Præcursor: the exact meaning of the word is a "scout."
[2] Verisimilia: the word generally means "probabilities."
[3] Prævaricator; properly an advocate who, by collusion, favours the cause of his opponent.
[4] Frugi.
[5] Diverticula.

[6] Simplex, as opposed to the various paths of the other.
[7] Multo clarior sol est, quàm hic Others read, "Multo clarius sole est, quàm hic," etc.
[8] [*Repub.*, iii. cap. 22, 16.]

able to alter[1] the provisions of this law, nor is it permitted us to modify it, nor can it be entirely abrogated.[1] Nor, truly, can we be released from this law, either by the senate or by the people; nor is another person to be sought to explain or interpret it. Nor will there be one law at Rome and another at Athens; one law at the present time, and another hereafter: but the same law, everlasting and unchangeable, will bind all nations at all times; and there will be one common Master and Ruler of all, even God, the framer, arbitrator, and proposer of this law; and he who shall not obey this will flee from himself, and, despising the nature of man, will suffer the greatest punishments through this very thing, even though he shall have escaped the other punishments which are supposed to exist." Who that is acquainted with the mystery of God could so significantly relate the law of God, as a man far removed from the knowledge of the truth has set forth that law? But I consider that they who speak true things unconsciously are to be so regarded as though they prophesied[2] under the influence of some spirit. But if he had known or explained this also, in what precepts the law itself consisted, as he clearly saw the force and purport of the divine law, he would not have discharged the office of a philosopher, but of a prophet. And because he was unable to do this, it must be done by us, to whom the law itself has been delivered by the one great Master and Ruler of all, God.

CHAP. IX. — OF THE LAW AND PRECEPT OF GOD; OF MERCY, AND THE ERROR OF THE PHILOSOPHERS.

The first head of this law is, to know God Himself, to obey Him alone, to worship Him alone. For he cannot maintain the character of a man who is ignorant of God, the parent of his soul: which is the greatest impiety. For this ignorance causes him to serve other gods, and no greater crime than this can be committed. Hence there is now so easy a step to wickedness through ignorance of the truth and of the chief good; since God, from the knowledge of whom he shrinks, is Himself the fountain of goodness. Or if he shall wish to follow the justice of God, yet, being ignorant of the divine law, he embraces the laws of his own country as true justice, though they were clearly devised not by justice, but by utility. For why is it that there are different and various laws amongst all people, but that each nation has enacted for itself that which it deemed useful for its own affairs? But how greatly utility differs from justice the Roman people themselves teach, who, by proclaiming war through the Fecials, and by inflicting injuries according to legal forms, by always desiring and carrying off the property of others, have gained for themselves the possession of the whole world.[3] But these persons think themselves just if they do nothing against their own laws; which may be even ascribed to fear, if they abstain from crimes through dread of present punishment. But let us grant that they do that naturally, or, as the philosopher says, of their own accord, which they are compelled to do by the laws. Will they therefore be just, because they obey the institutions of men, who may themselves have erred, or have been unjust? — as it was with the framers of the twelve tables, who certainly promoted the public advantage according to the condition of the times. Civil law is one thing, which varies everywhere according to customs; but justice is another thing, which God has set forth to all as uniform and simple: and he who is ignorant of God must also be ignorant of justice.

But let us suppose it possible that any one, by natural and innate goodness, should gain true virtues, such a man as we have heard that Cimon was at Athens, who both gave alms to the needy, and entertained the poor, and clothed the naked; yet, when that one thing which is of the greatest importance is wanting — the acknowledgment of God — then all those good things are superfluous and empty, so that in pursuing them he has laboured in vain.[4] For all his justice will resemble a human body which has no head, in which, although all the limbs are in their proper position, and figure, and proportion, yet, since that is wanting which is the chief thing of all, it is destitute both of life and of all sensation. Therefore those limbs have only the shape of limbs, but admit of no use, as much so as a head without a body; and he resembles this who is not without the knowledge of God, but yet lives unjustly. For he has that only which is of the greatest importance; but he has it to no purpose, since he is destitute of the virtues, as it were, of limbs.

Therefore, that the body may be alive, and capable of sensation, both the knowledge of God is necessary, as it were the head, and all the virtues, as it were the body. Thus there will exist a perfect and living man; but, however, the whole substance is in the head; and although this cannot exist in the absence of all, it may exist in the absence of some. And it will be an imperfect and faulty animal, but yet it will be alive, as he who knows God and yet sins in some respect. For God pardons sins. And

[1] Abrogo is to repeal or abrogate wholly; "derogo," to abrogate in part, or modify; "obrogo," to supersede by another law.

[2] Divinent. [Illustrative of the *Sibyllina*, and, in short, of Balaam; and not less of Rom. ii. 14, 15.]

[3] [Dan. vii. 23. An appeal for reformation.]

[4] [1 Cor. iii. 11–15. But are the heathen to be judged by the New Covenant? See vol. ii. (Clement, *sparsim*), this series.]

thus it is possible to live without some of the limbs, but it is by no means possible to live without a head. This is the reason why the philosophers, though they may be naturally good, yet have no knowledge and no intelligence. All their learning and virtue is without a head, because they are ignorant of God, who is the Head of virtue and knowledge; and he who is ignorant of Him, though he may see, is blind; though he may hear, is deaf; though he may speak, is dumb. But when he shall know the Creator and Parent of all things, then he will both see, and hear, and speak. For he begins to have a head, in which all the senses are placed, that is, the eyes, and ears, and tongue. For assuredly he sees who has beheld with the eyes of his mind the truth in which God is, or God in whom the truth is; he hears, who imprints on his heart the divine words and life-giving precepts; he speaks, who, in discussing heavenly things, relates the virtue and majesty of the surpassing God. Therefore he is undoubtedly impious who does not acknowledge God; and all his virtues, which he thinks that he has or possesses, are found in that deadly road which belongs altogether to darkness. Wherefore there is no reason why any one should congratulate himself if he has gained these empty virtues, because he is not only wretched who is destitute of present goods, but he must also be foolish, since he undertakes the greatest labours in his life without any purpose. For if the hope of immortality is taken away, which God promises to those who continue in His religion, for the sake of obtaining which virtue is to be sought, and whatever evils happen are to be endured, it will assuredly be the greatest folly to wish to comply with virtues which in vain bring calamities and labours to man. For if it is virtue to endure and undergo with fortitude, want, exile, pain, and death, which are feared by others, what goodness, I pray, has it in itself, that philosophers should say that it is to be sought for on its own account? Truly they are delighted with superfluous and useless punishments, when it is permitted them to live in tranquillity.

For if our souls are mortal, if virtue is about to have no existence after the dissolution of the body, why do we avoid the goods assigned to us, as though we were ungrateful or unworthy of enjoying the divine gifts? For, that we may enjoy these blessings, we must live in wickedness and impiety, because virtue, that is, justice, is followed by poverty. Therefore he is not of sound mind, who, without having any greater hope set before him, prefers labours, and tortures, and miseries, to those goods which others enjoy in life.[1] But if virtue is to be taken up, as is most rightly said by these, because it is evident that man is born to it, it ought to contain some greater hope, which may apply a great and illustrious solace for the ills and labours which it is the part of virtue to endure. Nor can virtue, since it is difficult in itself, be esteemed as a good in any other way than by having its hardship compensated by the greatest good. We can in no other way equally abstain from these present goods, than if there are other greater goods on account of which it is worth while to leave the pursuit of pleasures, and to endure all evils. But these are no other, as I have shown in the third book,[2] than the goods of everlasting life. Now who can bestow these except God, who has proposed to us virtue itself? Therefore the sum and substance of everything is contained in the acknowledging and worship of God; all the hope and safety of man centres in this; this is the first step of wisdom, to know who is our true Father, and to worship Him alone with the piety which is due to Him, to obey Him, to yield ourselves to His service with the utmost devotedness: let our entire acting, and care, and attention, be laid out in gaining His favour.[3]

CHAP. X. — OF RELIGION TOWARDS GOD, AND MERCY TOWARDS MEN; AND OF THE BEGINNING OF THE WORLD.

I have said what is due to God, I will now say what is to be given to man; although this very thing which you shall give to man is given to God, for man is the image of God. But, however, the first office of justice is to be united with God, the second with man. But the former is called religion; the second is named mercy or kindness;[4] which virtue is peculiar to the just, and to the worshippers of God, because this alone comprises the principle of common life. For God, who has not given wisdom to the other animals, has made them more safe from attack in danger by natural defences. But because He made him naked and defenceless,[5] that He might rather furnish him with wisdom, He gave him, besides other things, this feeling of kindness;[6] so that man should protect, love, and cherish man, and both receive and afford assistance against all dangers. Therefore kindness is the greatest bond of human society; and he who has broken this is to be deemed impious, and a parricide. For if we all derive our origin from one man, whom God

---

[1] [1 Cor. xv. 19.]

[2] [See cap. 12, p. 79, *supra*.]

[3] In eo promerendo. [John xvii. 3.]

[4] Humanitas.

[5] Fragilem.

[Φύσις κέρατα ταύροις
ὁπλὰς δ' ἔδωκεν ἵπποίς
τοῖς ἀνδράσιν φρόνημα, κ.τ.λ.
Anacreon, *Ode* 2.]

[6] Hunc pietatis affectum.

created, we are plainly of one blood; and therefore it must be considered the greatest wickedness to hate a man, even though guilty. On which account God has enjoined that enmities are never to be contracted by us, but that they are always to be removed, so that we soothe those who are our enemies, by reminding them of their relationship. Likewise, if we are all inspired and animated by one God, what else are we than brothers? And, indeed, the more closely united, because we are united in soul rather than in body.[1] Accordingly Lucretius does not err when he says:[2] "In short, we are all sprung from a heavenly seed; all have that same father." Therefore they are to be accounted as savage beasts who injure man; who, in opposition to every law and right of human nature, plunder, torture, slay, and banish.

On account of this relationship of brotherhood, God teaches us never to do evil, but always good. And He also prescribes[3] in what this doing good consists: in affording aid to those who are oppressed and in difficulty, and in bestowing food on those who are destitute. For God, since He is kind,[4] wished us to be a social animal. Therefore, in the case of other men, we ought to think of ourselves. We do not deserve to be set free in our own dangers, if we do not succour others; we do not deserve assistance, if we refuse to render it. There are no precepts of philosophers to this purport, inasmuch as they, being captivated by the appearance of false virtue, have taken away mercy from man, and while they wish to heal, have corrupted.[5] And though they generally admit that the mutual participation of human society is to be retained, they entirely separate themselves from it by the harshness of their inhuman virtue. This error, therefore, is also to be refuted, of those who think that nothing is to be bestowed on any one. They have introduced not one origin only, and cause of building a city; but some relate that those men who were first born from the earth, when they passed a wandering life among the woods and plains, and were not united by any mutual bond of speech or justice, but had leaves and grass for their beds, and caves and grottos for their dwellings, were a prey to the beasts and stronger animals. Then, that those who had either escaped, having been torn, or had seen their neighbours torn, being admonished of their own danger, had recourse to other men, implored protection, and at first made their wishes known by nods; then that they tried the beginnings of conversation, and by attaching names to each object, by degrees completed the system of speech. But when they saw that numbers themselves were not safe against the beasts, they began also to build towns, either that they might make their nightly repose safe, or that they might ward off the incursions and attacks of beasts, not by fighting, but by interposing barriers.[6]

O minds unworthy of men, which produced these foolish trifles! O wretched and pitiable men, who committed to writing and handed down to memory the record of their own folly; who, when they saw that the plan of assembling themselves together, or of mutual intercourse, or of avoiding danger, or of guarding against evil, or of preparing for themselves sleeping-places and lairs, was natural even to the dumb animals, thought, however, that men could not have been admonished and learned, except by examples, what they ought to fear, what to avoid, and what to do, or that they would never have assembled together, or have discovered the method of speech, had not the beasts devoured them! These things appeared to others senseless, as they really were; and they said that the cause of their coming together was not the tearing of wild beasts, but rather the very feeling of humanity itself; and that therefore they collected themselves together, because the nature of men avoided solitude, and was desirous of communion and society. The discrepancy between them is not great; since the causes are different, the fact is the same. Each might have been true, because there is no direct opposition. But, however, neither is by any means true, because men were not born from the ground throughout the world, as though sprung from the teeth of some dragon, as the poets relate; but one man was formed by God, and from that one man all the earth was filled with the human race, in the same way as again took place after the deluge, which they certainly cannot deny.[7] Therefore no assembling together of this kind took place at the beginning; and that there were never men on the earth who could not speak except those who were infants,[8] every one who is possessed of sense will understand. Let us suppose, however, that these things are true which idle and foolish old men vainly say, that we may refute them especially by their own feelings and arguments.

If men were collected together on this account,

1 Conjunctiores, quòd animis, quàm quòd (others read "qui") corporibus.

2 [Modern followers of Lucretius may learn from him:—

Denique cœlesti sumus omnes semine oriundi;
Omnibus ille idem pater est.]

ii. 991.

3 Isa. lviii. 6, 7; Ezek. xviii. 7; Matt. xxv. 35.

4 Pius.

5 Dum volunt sanare, vitiaverunt. There is another reading: "dum volunt sanare vitia, auxerunt," while they wish to apply a remedy to vices, have increased them.

6 Objectis aggeribus. "Agger" properly signifies a mound of earth or other material.

7 [Gen. x. 32.]

8 Præter infantiam—others read "propter infans"—properly means, one unable to speak. [See fine remarks on language, etc., in De Maistre, *Soirées*, etc., vol. i. p. 105 and notes, ed. Lyon, 1836.]

that they might protect their weakness by mutual help, therefore we must succour man, who needs help. For, since men entered into and contracted fellowship with men for the sake of protection, either to violate or not to preserve that compact which was entered into among men from the commencement of their origin, is to be considered as the greatest impiety. For he who withdraws himself from affording assistance must also of necessity withdraw himself from receiving it; for he who refuses his aid to another thinks that he stands in need of the aid of none. But he who withdraws and separates himself from the body[1] at large, must live not after the custom of men, but after the manner of wild beasts. But if this cannot be done, the bond of human society is by all means to be retained, because man can in no way live without man. But the preservation[2] of society is a mutual sharing of kind offices; that is, the affording help, that we may be able to receive it. But if, as those others assert, the assembling together of men has been caused on account of humanity itself, man ought undoubtedly to recognise man. But if those ignorant and as yet uncivilized men did this, and that, when the practice of speaking was not yet established, what must we think ought to be done by men who are polished, and connected together by interchange of conversation and all business, who, being accustomed to the society of men, cannot endure solitude?

CHAP. XI. — OF THE PERSONS UPON WHOM A BENEFIT IS TO BE CONFERRED.

Therefore humanity is to be preserved, if we wish rightly to be called men. But what else is this preservation of humanity than the loving a man because he is a man, and the same as ourselves? Therefore discord and dissension are not in accordance with the nature of man; and that expression of Cicero is true, which says[3] that man, while he is obedient to nature, cannot injure man. Therefore, if it is contrary to nature to injure a man, it must be in accordance with nature to benefit a man; and he who does not do this deprives himself of the title of a man, because it is the duty of humanity to succour the necessity and peril of a man. I ask, therefore, of those who do not think it the part of a wise man to be prevailed upon and to pity, If a man were seized by some beast, and were to implore the aid of an armed man, whether they think that he ought to be succoured or not? They are not so shameless as to deny that that ought to be done which humanity demands and requires. Also, if any one were surrounded by fire, crushed by the downfall of a building, plunged in the sea, or carried away by a river, would they think it the duty of a man not to assist him? They themselves are not men if they think so; for no one can fail to be liable to dangers of this kind. Yes, truly, they will say that it is the part of a human being, and of a brave man too, to preserve one who was on the point of perishing. If, therefore, in casualties of this nature which imperil the life of man, they allow that it is the part of humanity to give succour, what reason is there why they should think that succour is to be withheld if a man should suffer from hunger, thirst, or cold? But though these things are naturally on an equality with those accidental circumstances, and need one and the same humanity, yet they make a distinction between these things, because they measure all things not by the truth itself, but by present utility. For they hope that those whom they rescue from peril will make a return of the favour to them. But because they do not hope for this in the case of the needy, they think that whatever they bestow on men of this kind is thrown away. Hence that sentiment of Plautus is detestable:[4] —

> "He deserves ill who gives food to a beggar;
> For that which he gives is thrown away, and
> It lengthens out the life of the other to his misery."

But perhaps the poet spoke for the actor.[5]

What does Marcus Tullius say in his books respecting Offices? Does he not also advise that bounty should not be employed at all? For thus he speaks:[6] "Bounty, which proceeds from our estate, drains the very source of our liberality; and thus liberality is destroyed by liberality: for the more numerous they are towards whom you practise it, the less you will be able to practise it towards many." And he also says shortly afterwards: "But what is more foolish than so to act that you may not be able to continue to do that which you do willingly?" This professor of wisdom plainly keeps men back from acts of kindness, and advises them carefully to guard their property, and to preserve their money-chest in safety, rather than to follow justice. And when he perceived that this was inhuman and wicked, soon afterwards, in another chapter, as though moved by repentance, he thus spoke: "Sometimes, however, we must exercise bounty in giving: nor is this kind of liberality altogether to be rejected; and we must give from our property to suitable[7] persons when they are in need of assistance." What is the meaning of "suit-

[1] A corpore, that is, from society.
[2] Retentio. The word sometimes signifies a "withholding," or "drawing back;" but here, as in other passages, Lactantius uses it to express "preservation."
[3] *De Offic.*, iii. 5.
[4] *Trinumm.*, ii. 2. 58.
[5] Pro personâ.
[6] *De Offic.*, ii. 15.
[7] Idoneis. Lactantius uses this word as though its meaning were "the rich;" and though it seems to have passed into this sense in later times, it is plain from the very words of Cicero himself that he uses it of deserving persons who need assistance.

able?" Assuredly those who are able to restore and give back the favour.[1] If Cicero were now alive, I should certainly exclaim: Here, here, Marcus Tullius, you have erred from true justice; and you have taken it away by one word, since you measured the offices of piety and humanity by utility. For we must not bestow our bounty on suitable objects, but as much as possible on unsuitable objects. For that will be done with justice, piety, and humanity, which you shall do without the hope of any return!

This is that true and genuine justice, of which you say that you have no real and life-like figure.[2] You yourself exclaim in many places that virtue is not mercenary; and you confess in the books of your Laws[3] that liberality is gratuitous, in these words: "Nor is it doubtful that he who is called liberal and generous is influenced by a sense of duty, and not by advantage." Why therefore do you bestow your bounty on suitable persons, unless it be that you may afterwards receive a reward? With you, therefore, as the author and teacher of justice, whosoever shall not be a suitable person will be worn out with nakedness, thirst, and hunger; nor will men who are rich and abundantly supplied, even to luxuriousness, assist his last extremity. If virtue does not exact a reward; if, as you say, it is to be sought on its own account, then estimate justice, which is the mother and chief of the virtues, at its own price, and not according to your advantage: give especially to him from whom you hope for nothing in return. Why do you select persons? Why do you look at bodily forms? He is to be esteemed by you as a man, whoever it is that implores you, because he considers you a man. Cast away those outlines and sketches of justice, and hold fast justice itself, true and fashioned to the life. Be bountiful to the blind, the feeble, the lame, the destitute, who must die unless you bestow your bounty upon them. They are useless to men, but they are serviceable to God, who retains them in life, who endues them with breath, who vouchsafes to them the light. Cherish as far as in you lies, and support with kindness, the lives of men, that they may not be extinguished. He who is able to succour one on the point of perishing, if he fails to do so, kills him. But they, because they neither retain their nature, nor know what reward there is in this, while they fear to lose, do lose, and fall into that which they chiefly guard against; so that whatever they bestow is either lost altogether, or profits only for the briefest time. For they who refuse a small gift to the wretched, who wish to preserve humanity without any loss to themselves, squander their property, so that they either acquire for themselves frail and perishable things, or they certainly gain nothing by their own great loss.

For what must be said of those who, induced by the vanity of popular favour,[4] expend on the exhibition of shows wealth that would be sufficient even for great cities? Must we not say that they are senseless and mad who bestow upon the people that which is both lost to themselves, and which none of those on whom it is bestowed receives? Therefore, as all pleasure is short and perishable, and especially that of the eyes and ears, men either forget and are ungrateful for the expenses incurred by another, or they are even offended if the caprice of the people is not satisfied: so that most foolish men have even acquired evil for themselves by evil; or if they have thus succeeded in pleasing, they gain nothing more than empty favour and the talk[5] of a few days. Thus every day the estates of most trifling men are expended on superfluous matters. Do they then act more wisely who exhibit to their fellow-citizens more useful and lasting gifts? They, for instance, who by the building of public works seek a lasting memory for their name? Not even do they act rightly in burying their property in the earth; because the remembrance of them neither bestows anything upon the dead, nor are their works eternal, inasmuch as they are either thrown down and destroyed by a single earthquake, or are consumed by an accidental fire, or they are overthrown by some attack of an enemy, or at any rate they decay and fall to pieces by mere length of time. For there is nothing, as the orator says,[6] made by the work of man's hand which length of time does not weaken and destroy. But this justice of which we speak, and mercy, flourish more every day. They therefore act better who bestow their bounty on their tribesmen and clients, for they bestow something on men, and profit them; but that is not true and just bounty, for there is no conferring of a benefit where there is no necessity. Therefore, whatever is given to those who are not in need, for the sake of popularity, is thrown away; or it is repaid with interest, and thus it will not be the conferring of a benefit. And although it is pleasing to those to whom it is given, still it is not just, because if it is not done, no evil follows. Therefore the only sure and true office of liberality is to support the needy and unserviceable.

CHAP. XII. — OF THE KINDS OF BENEFICENCE, AND WORKS OF MERCY.

This is that perfect justice which protects human society, concerning which philosophers

[1] [Luke vi. 32-34.]
[2] *De Offic.*, iii. 17. Solidam et expressam.
[3] [*De Leg.*, iii., and *De Offic.*, i. cap. 16.]
[4] Populari levitate ducti: an expression somewhat similar to "popularis aura."
[5] Fabulam.
[6] Cic., *Pro Marcello.* [Nihil opere et manu factum.]

speak. This is the chief and truest advantage of riches; not to use wealth for the particular pleasure of an individual, but for the welfare of many; not for one's own immediate enjoyment, but for justice, which alone does not perish. We must therefore by all means keep in mind, that the hope of receiving in return must be altogether absent from the duty of showing mercy: for the reward of this work and duty must be expected from God alone; for if you should expect it from man, then that will not be kindness, but the lending of a benefit at interest;[1] nor can he seem to have deserved well who affords that which he does, not to another, but to himself. And yet the matter comes to this, that whatever a man has bestowed upon another, hoping for no advantage from him, he really bestows upon himself, for he will receive a reward from God. God has also enjoined, that if at any time we make a feast, we should invite to the entertainment those who cannot invite us in return, and thus make us a recompense, so that no action of our life should be without the exercise of mercy. Nor, however, let any one think that he is debarred from intercourse with his friends or kindness with his neighbours. But God has made known to us what is our true and just work: we ought thus to live with our neighbours, provided that we know that the one manner of living relates to man, the other to God.[2]

Therefore hospitality is a principal virtue, as the philosophers also say; but they turn it aside from true justice, and forcibly apply[3] it to advantage. Cicero says:[4] "Hospitality was rightly praised by Theophrastus. For (as it appears to me) it is highly becoming that the houses of illustrious men should be open to illustrious guests." He has here committed the same error which he then did, when he said that we must bestow our bounty on "suitable" persons. For the house of a just and wise man ought not to be open to the illustrious, but to the lowly and abject. For those illustrious and powerful men cannot be in want of anything, since they are sufficiently protected and honoured by their own opulence. But nothing is to be done by a just man except that which is a benefit. But if the benefit is returned, it is destroyed and brought to an end; for we cannot possess in its completeness that for which a price has been paid to us. Therefore the principle of justice is employed about those benefits which have remained safe and uncorrupted; but they cannot thus remain by any other means than if they are bestowed upon those men who can in no way profit us. But in receiving illustrious men, he looked to nothing else but utility; nor did the ingenious man conceal what advantage he hoped from it. For he says that he who does that will become powerful among foreigners by the favour of the leading men, whom he will have bound to himself by the right of hospitality and friendship. O by how many arguments might the inconsistency of Cicero be proved, if this were my object! Nor would he be convicted so much by my words as by his own. For he also says, that the more any one refers all his actions to his own advantage, the less he is a good man. He also says, that it is not the part of a simple and open man to ingratiate himself in the favour of others,[5] to pretend and allege anything, to appear to be doing one thing when he is doing another, to feign that he is bestowing upon another that which he is bestowing upon himself; but that this is rather the part of one who is designing[6] and crafty, deceitful and treacherous. But how could he maintain that that ambitious hospitality was not evil intention?[7] "Do you run round through all the gates, that you may invite to your house the chief men of the nations and cities as they arrive, that by their means you may acquire influence with their citizens; and wish yourself to be called just, and kind, and hospitable, though you are studying to promote your own advantage?" But did he not say this rather incautiously? For what is less suitable for Cicero? But through his ignorance of true justice he knowingly and with foresight fell into this snare. And that he might be pardoned for this, he testified that he does not give precepts with reference to true justice, which he does not hold, but with reference to a sketch and outline of justice. Therefore we must pardon this teacher who uses sketches and outlines,[8] nor must we require the truth from him who admits that he is ignorant of it.

The ransoming of captives is a great and noble exercise of justice, of which the same Tullius also approved.[9] "And this liberality," he says, "is serviceable even to the state, that captives should be ransomed from slavery, and that those of slender resources should be provided for. And I greatly prefer this practice of liberality to lavish expenditure on shows. This is the part of great and eminent men." Therefore it is the appropriate work of the just to support the poor and to ransom captives, since

[1] Beneficii fœneratio.

[2] The meaning appears to be this: To benefit our friends and relatives, relates to man, i.e., is a merely human work; but to benefit those who cannot make a recompense is a divine work, and its reward is to be expected from God.

[3] Rapiunt.

[4] *De Offic.*, ii. 18.

[5] Ambire.

[6] Malitiosi et astuti.

[7] Malitia, roguery. The word properly signifies some legal trick by which the ends of justice are frustrated, though the letter of the law is not broken.

[8] Umbratico et imaginario præceptori.

[9] *De Officiis*, ii. 18.

among the unjust if any do these things they are called great and eminent. For it is deserving of the greatest praise for those to confer benefit from whom no one expected such conduct. For he who does good to a relative, or neighbour, or friend, either deserves no praise, or certainly no great praise, because he is bound to do it, and he would be impious and detestable if he did not do that which both nature itself and relationship require; and if he does it, he does it not so much for the sake of obtaining glory as of avoiding censure. But he who does it to a stranger and an unknown person, he truly is worthy of praise, because he was led to do it by kindness only. Justice therefore exists there, where there is no obligation of necessity for conferring a benefit. He ought not therefore to have preferred this duty of generosity to expenditure on shows; for this is the part of one making a comparison, and of two goods choosing that which is the better. For that profusion of men throwing away their property into the sea is vain and trifling, and very far removed from all justice. Therefore they are not even to be called gifts,[1] in which no one receives but he who does not deserve to receive.

Nor is it less a great work of justice to protect and defend orphans and widows who are destitute and stand in need of assistance; and therefore that divine law prescribes this to all, since all good judges deem that it belongs to their office to favour them with natural kindness, and to strive to benefit them. But these works are especially ours, since we have received the law, and the words of God Himself giving us instructions. For they perceive that it is naturally just to protect those who need protection, but they do not perceive why it is so. For God, to whom everlasting mercy belongs, on this account commands that widows and orphans should be defended and cherished, that no one through regard and pity for his pledges[2] should be prevented from undergoing death in behalf of justice and faith, but should encounter it with promptitude and boldness, since he knows that he leaves his beloved ones to the care of God, and that they will never want protection. Also to undertake the care and support of the sick, who need some one to assist them, is the part of the greatest kindness, and of great beneficence;[3] and he who shall do this will both gain a living sacrifice to God, and that which he has given to another for a time he will himself receive from God for eternity. The last and greatest office of piety is the burying of strangers and the poor; which subject those teachers of virtue and justice have not touched upon at all. For they were unable to see this, who measured all their duties by utility. For in the other things which have been mentioned above, although they did not keep the true path, yet, since they discovered some advantage in these things, retained as it were by a kind of inkling[4] of the truth, they wandered to a less distance; but they abandoned this because they were unable to see any advantage in it.

Moreover, there have not been wanting those who esteemed burial as superfluous, and said that it was no evil to lie unburied and neglected; but their impious wisdom is rejected alike by the whole human race, and by the divine expressions which command the performance of the rite.[5] But they do not venture to say that it ought not to be done, but that, if it happens to be omitted, no inconvenience is the result. Therefore in that matter they discharge the office, not so much of those who give precepts, as of those who suggest consolation, that if this shall by chance have occurred to a wise man, he should not deem himself wretched on this account. But we do not speak of that which ought to be endured by a wise man, but of that which he himself ought to do. Therefore we do not now inquire whether the whole system of burial is serviceable or not; but this, even though it be useless, as they imagine, must nevertheless be practised, even on this account only, that it appears among men to be done rightly and kindly. For it is the feeling which is inquired into, and it is the purpose which is weighed. Therefore we will not suffer the image and workmanship of God to lie exposed as a prey to beasts and birds, but we will restore it to the earth, from which it had its origin; and although it be in the case of an unknown man, we will fulfil the office of relatives, into whose place, since they are wanting, let kindness succeed; and wherever there shall be need of man, there we will think that our duty is required.[6] But in what does the nature of justice more consist than in our affording to strangers through kindness, that which we render to our own relatives through affection? And this kindness is much more sure and just when it is now afforded, not to the man who is insensible, but to God alone, to whom a just work is a most acceptable sacrifice. Some one will perhaps say: If I shall do all these things, I shall have no possessions. For what if a great number of men shall be in want, shall suffer cold, shall be taken captive, shall die, since one who acts thus must deprive himself of his property even in a single day, shall I throw away the es-

---

1 Munera. The same word is used for "shows," as of gladiators, or contests of wild beasts, exhibited to the people.

2 i.e., children.

3 Operationis.

4 Quasi odore quodam veritatis. The word "odor" is sometimes used to express "a presentiment" or "suspicion."

5 [Gen. xlix. 29-31; Mark xiv. 8, 9.]

6 [Ennius; also in Cicero, *De Offic.*, i. cap. 16.]

tate acquired by my own labour or by that of my ancestors, so that after this I myself must live by the pity of others?

Why do you so pusillanimously fear poverty, which even your philosophers praise, and bear witness that nothing is safer and nothing more calm than this? That which you fear is a haven against anxieties. Do you not know to how many dangers, to how many accidents, you are exposed with these evil resources? These will treat you well if they shall pass without your bloodshed. But you walk about laden with booty, and you bear spoils which may excite the minds even of your own relatives. Why, then, do you hesitate to lay that out well which perhaps a single robbery will snatch away from you, or a proscription suddenly arising, or the plundering of an enemy? Why do you fear to make a frail and perishable good everlasting, or to entrust your treasures to God as their preserver, in which case you need not fear thief and robber, nor rust, nor tyrant? He who is rich towards God can never be poor.[1] If you esteem justice so highly, lay aside the burthens which press you, and follow it; free yourself from fetters and chains, that you may run to God without any impediment. It is the part of a great and lofty mind to despise and trample upon mortal affairs. But if you do not comprehend this virtue, that you may bestow your riches upon the altar[2] of God, in order that you may provide for yourself firmer possessions than these frail ones, I will free you from fear. All these precepts are not given to you alone, but to all the people who are united in mind, and hold together as one man. If you are not adequate to the performance of great works alone, cultivate justice with all your power, in such a manner, however, that you may excel others in work as much as you excel them in riches. And do not think that you are advised to lessen or exhaust your property; but that which you would have expended on superfluities, turn to better uses. Devote to the ransoming of captives that from which you purchase beasts; maintain the poor with that from which you feed wild beasts; bury the innocent dead with that from which you provide men for the sword.[3] What does it profit to enrich men of abandoned wickedness, who fight with beasts,[4] and to equip them for crimes? Transfer things about to be miserably thrown away to the great sacrifice, that in return for these true gifts you may have an everlasting gift from God. Mercy has a great reward; for God promises it, that He will remit all sins. If you shall hear, He says, the prayers of your suppliant, I also will hear yours; if you shall pity those in distress, I also will pity you in your distress. But if you shall not regard nor assist them, I also will bear a mind like your own against you, and I will judge you by your own laws.[5]

CHAP. XIII. — OF REPENTANCE, OF MERCY, AND THE FORGIVENESS OF SINS.

As often, therefore, as you are asked for aid, believe that you are tried by God, that it may be seen whether you are worthy of being heard. Examine your own conscience, and, as far as you are able, heal your wounds. Nor, however, because offences are removed by bounty, think that a licence is given you for sinning. For they are done away with, if you are bountiful to God because you have sinned; for if you sin through reliance on your bounty, they are not done away with. For God especially desires that men shall be cleansed from their sins, and therefore He commands them to repent. But to repent is nothing else than to profess and to affirm that one will sin no more. Therefore they are pardoned who unawares and incautiously glide into sin; he who sins wilfully has no pardon. Nor, however, if any one shall have been purified from all stain of sin, let him think that he may abstain from the work of bounty because he has no faults to blot out. Nay, in truth, he is then more bound to exercise justice when he is become just, so that that which he had before done for the healing of his wounds he may afterwards do for the praise and glory of virtue. To this is added, that no one can be without fault as long as he is burthened with a covering of flesh, the infirmity of which is subject to the dominion of sin in a threefold manner — in deeds, in words, and thoughts.

By these steps justice advances to the greatest height. The first step of virtue is to abstain from evil works; the second, to abstain also from evil words; the third, to abstain even from the thoughts of evil things. He who ascends the first step is sufficiently just; he who ascends the second is now of perfect virtue, since he offends neither in deeds nor in conversation;[6] he who ascends the third appears truly to have attained the likeness of God. For it is almost beyond the measure of man not even to admit to the thought[7] that which is either bad in action or improper in speech. Therefore even just men, who can refrain from every unjust work, are sometimes, however, overcome by frailty itself, so that they either speak evil in anger, or, at the sight of delightful things, they desire them with silent thought. But if the condition of mortality does not suffer a man to

[1] [1 Tim. vi. 8–10.]
[2] In aram Dei. Others read "arcam," the chest.
[3] i.e., "gladiators purchased from a trainer for the gratification of the people."
[4] Bestiarios: men who fought with beasts in the amphitheatre.
[5] [Matt. xviii. 21–35. Exposition of vi. 14.]
[6] [Jas. iii. 2.]
[7] In cogitationem. Others read "cogitatione."

be pure from every stain, the faults of the flesh ought therefore to be done away with by continual bounty. For it is the single work of a man who is wise, and just, and worthy of life, to lay out his riches on justice alone; for assuredly he who is without this, although he should surpass Crœsus or Crassus in riches, is to be esteemed as poor, as naked, as a beggar. Therefore we must use our efforts that we may be clothed with the garment of justice and piety, of which no one may deprive us, which may furnish us with an everlasting ornament. For if the worshippers of gods adore senseless images, and bestow upon them whatever they have which is precious, though they can neither make use of them nor give thanks because they have received them, how much more just and true is it to reverence the living images of God, that you may gain the favour of the living God! For as these make use of what they have received, and give thanks, so God, in whose sight you shall have done that which is good, will both approve of it and reward your piety.

CHAP. XIV. — OF THE AFFECTIONS, AND THE OPINION OF THE STOICS RESPECTING THEM; AND OF VIRTUE, THE VICES, AND MERCY.

If, therefore, mercy is a distinguished and excellent gift in man, and that is judged to be very good by the consent both of the good and the evil, it appears that philosophers were far distant from the good of man, who neither enjoined nor practised anything of this kind, but always esteemed as a vice that virtue which almost holds the first place in man. It pleases me here to bring forward one subject of philosophy, that we may more fully refute the errors of those who call mercy, desire, and fear, diseases of the soul. They indeed attempt to distinguish virtues from vices, which is truly a very easy matter. For who cannot distinguish a liberal man from one who is prodigal (as they do), or a frugal man from one who is mean, or a calm man from one who is slothful, or a cautious man from one who is timid? Because these things which are good have their limits, and if they shall exceed these limits, fall into vices; so that constancy, unless it is undertaken for the truth, becomes shamelessness. In like manner, bravery, if it shall undergo certain danger, without the compulsion of any necessity, or not for an honourable cause, is changed into rashness. Freedom of speech also, if it attack others rather than oppose those who attack it, is obstinacy. Severity also, unless it restrain itself within the befitting punishments of the guilty, becomes savage cruelty.

Therefore they say, that those who appear evil do not sin of their own accord, or choose evils by preference, but that, erring [1] through the appearance of good, they fall into evils, while they are ignorant of the distinction between good things and evil. These things are not indeed false, but they are all referred to the body. For to be frugal, or constant, or cautious, or calm, or grave, or severe, are virtues indeed, but virtues which relate to this short [2] life. But we who despise this life have other virtues set before us, respecting which philosophers could not by any means even conjecture. Therefore they regarded certain virtues as vices, and certain vices as virtues. For the Stoics take away from man all the affections, by the impulse of which the soul is moved — desire, joy, fear, sorrow: the two former of which arise from good things, either future or present; the latter from evil things. In the same manner, they call these four (as I said) diseases, not so much inserted in us by nature as undertaken through a perverted opinion; and therefore they think that these can be eradicated, if the false notion of good and evil things is taken away. For if the wise man thinks nothing good or evil, he will neither be inflamed with desire, nor be transported with joy, nor be alarmed with fear, nor suffer his spirits to droop [3] through sadness. We shall presently see whether they effect that which they wish, or what it is which they do effect: in the meantime their purpose is arrogant and almost mad, who think that they apply a remedy, and that they are able to strive in opposition to the force and system of nature.

CHAP. XV. — OF THE AFFECTIONS, AND THE OPINION OF THE PERIPATETICS RESPECTING THEM.

For, that these things are natural and not voluntary, the nature of all living beings shows, which is moved by all these affections. Therefore the Peripatetics act better, who say that all these cannot be taken from us, because they were born with us; and they endeavour to show how providently and how necessarily God, or nature (for so they term it), armed us with these affections; which, however, because they generally become vicious if they are in excess, can be advantageously regulated by man, — a limit being applied, so that there may be left to man as much as is sufficient for nature. Not an unwise disputation, if, as I said, all things were not referred to this life. The Stoics therefore are mad who do not regulate but cut them out, and wish by some means or other to deprive man of powers implanted in him by nature. And this is equivalent to a desire of taking away timidity from stags, or poison from serpents, or

---

1 Lapsos. [All this shows the need of an Augustine.]
2 Temporariæ. [Admirable so far as our author goes.]
3 Contrahetur.

rage from wild beasts, or gentleness from cattle. For those qualities which have been given separately to dumb animals, are altogether given to man at the same time. But if, as physicians affirm, the affection of joy has its seat in the spleen,[1] that of anger in the gall, of desire in the liver, of fear in the heart, it is easier to kill the animal itself than to tear anything from the body; for this is to wish to change the nature of the living creature. But the skilful men do not understand that when they take away vices from man, they also take away virtue, for which alone they are making a place. For if it is virtue in the midst of the impetuosity of anger to restrain and check oneself, which they cannot deny, then he who is without anger is also without virtue. If it is virtue to control the lust of the body, he must be free from virtue who has no lust which he may regulate. If it is virtue to curb the desire from coveting that which belongs to another, he certainly can have no virtue who is without that, to the restraining of which the exercise of virtue is applied. Where, therefore, there are no vices, there is no place even for virtue, as there is no place for victory where there is no adversary. And so it comes to pass that there can be no good in this life without evil. An affection therefore is a kind of natural fruitfulness[2] of the powers of the mind. For as a field which is naturally fruitful produces an abundant crop of briars,[3] so the mind which is uncultivated is overgrown with vices flourishing of their own accord, as with thorns. But when the true cultivator has applied himself, immediately vices give way, and the fruits of virtues spring up.

Therefore God, when He first made man, with wonderful foresight first implanted in him these emotions of the mind, that he might be capable of receiving virtue, as the earth is of cultivation; and He placed the subject-matter of vices in the affections, and that of virtue in vices. For assuredly virtue will have no existence, or not be in exercise, if those things are wanting by which its power is either shown or exists. Now let us see what they have effected who altogether removes vices. With regard to those four affections[4] which they imagine to arise from the opinion of things good and evil, by the eradication of which they think that the mind of the wise man is to be healed, since they understand that they are implanted by nature, and that without these nothing can be put in motion, nothing be done, they put certain other things into their place and room: for desire they substitute inclination, as though it were not much better to desire a good than to feel inclination for it; they in like manner substitute for joy gladness, and for fear caution. But in the case of the fourth they are at a loss for a method of exchanging the name. Therefore they have altogether taken away grief, that is, sadness and pain of mind, which cannot possibly be done. For who can fail to be grieved if pestilence has desolated his country, or an enemy overthrown it, or a tyrant crushed its liberty? Can any one fail to be grieved if he has beheld the overthrow of liberty,[5] and the banishment or most cruel slaughter of neighbours, friends, or good men? — unless the mind of any one should be so struck with astonishment that all sensibility should be taken from him. Wherefore they ought either to have taken away the whole, or this defective[6] and weak discussion ought to have been completed; that is, something ought to have been substituted in the place of grief, since, the former ones having been so arranged, this naturally followed.

For as we rejoice in good things that are present, so we are vexed and grieved with evil things. If, therefore, they gave another name to joy because they thought it vicious, so it was befitting that another name should be given to grief because they thought it also vicious. From which it appears that it was not the object itself which was wanting to them, but a word, through want of which they wished, contrary to what nature allowed, to take away that affection which is the greatest. For I could have refuted those changes of names at greater length, and have shown that many names are attached to the same objects, for the sake of embellishing the style and increasing its copiousness, or at any rate that they do not greatly differ from one another. For both desire takes its beginning from the inclination, and caution arises from fear, and joy is nothing else than the expression of gladness. But let us suppose that they are different, as they themselves will have it. Accordingly they will say that desire is continued and perpetual inclination, but that joy is gladness bearing itself immoderately; and that fear is caution in excess, and passing the limits of moderation. Thus it comes to pass, that they do not take away those things which they think ought to be taken away, but regulate them, since the names only are changed, the things themselves remain. They therefore return unawares to that point at which the Peripatetics arrive by argument, that vices, since they cannot be taken away, are to be regulated with moderation. Therefore they err, because they do not succeed in effecting that which they aim at, and by a circuitous route, which is long and rough, they return to the same path.

[1] [After fifteen centuries, physicians know as little about the spleen as ever. See Dunglison, *Med. Dict.*, *sub voce* "spleen."]
[2] Ubertas animorum.
[3] Exuberat in sentes, "luxuriates into briars."
[4] [Cap. xiv. p. 179, *supra*.]
[5] [After Pharsalia. Note this love of freedom.]
[6] Curta, i.e., "maimed."

CHAP. XVI. — OF THE AFFECTIONS, AND THE REFUTATION OF THE OPINION OF THE PERIPATETICS CONCERNING THEM; WHAT IS THE PROPER USE OF THE AFFECTIONS, AND WHAT IS A BAD USE OF THEM.

But I think that the Peripatetics did not even approach the truth, who allow that they are vices, but regulate them with moderation. For we must be free even from moderate vices; yea, rather, it ought to have been at first effected that there should be no vices. For nothing can be born vicious;[1] but if we make a bad use of the affections they become vices, if we use them well they become virtues. Then it must be shown that the causes of the affections, and not the affections themselves, must be moderated. We must not, they say, rejoice with excessive joy, but moderately and temperately. This is as though they should say that we must not run swiftly, but walk quietly. But it is possible that he who walks may err, and that he who runs may keep the right path. What if I show that there is a case in which it is vicious not only to rejoice moderately, but even in the smallest degree; and that there is another case, on the contrary, in which even to exult with transports of joy is by no means faulty? What then, I pray, will this mediocrity profit us? I ask whether they think that a wise man ought to rejoice if he sees any evil happening to his enemy; or whether he ought to curb his joy, if by the conquest of enemies, or the overthrow of a tyrant, liberty and safety have been acquired by his countrymen.[2]

No one doubts but that in the former case to rejoice a little, and in the latter to rejoice too little, is a very great crime. We may say the same respecting the other affections. But, as I have said, the object of wisdom does not consist in the regulation of these, but of their causes, since they are acted upon from without; nor was it befitting that these themselves should be restrained; since they may exist in a small degree with the greatest criminality, and in the greatest degree without any criminality. But they ought to have been assigned to fixed times, and circumstances, and places, that they may not be vices, when it is permitted us to make a right use of them. For as to walk in the right course is good, but to wander from it is evil, so to be moved by the affections to that which is right is good, but to that which is corrupt is evil. For sensual desire, if it does not wander from its lawful object, although it be ardent, yet is without fault. But if it desires an unlawful object, although it be moderate, yet it is a great vice. Therefore it is not a disease to be angry, nor to desire, nor to be excited by lust; but to be passionate, to be covetous or licentious, is a disease. For he who is passionate is angry even with him with whom he ought not to be angry, or at times when he ought not. He who is covetous desires even that which is unnecessary. He who is licentious pursues even that which is forbidden by the laws. The whole matter ought to have turned on this, that since the impetuosity of these things cannot be restrained, nor is it right that it should be, because it is necessarily implanted for maintaining the duties of life, it might rather be directed into the right way, where it may be possible even to run without stumbling and danger.

CHAP. XVII. — OF THE AFFECTIONS AND THEIR USE; OF PATIENCE, AND THE CHIEF GOOD OF CHRISTIANS.

But I have been carried too far in my desire of refuting them; since it is my purpose to show that those things which the philosophers thought to be vices, are so far from being vices, that they are even great virtues. Of others, I will take, for the sake of instruction, those which I think to be most closely related to the subject. They regard dread or fear as a very great vice, and think that it is a very great weakness of mind; the opposite to which is bravery: and if this exists in a man, they say that there is no place for fear. Does any one then believe that it can possibly happen that this same fear is the highest fortitude? By no means. For nature does not appear to admit that anything should fall back to its contrary. But yet I, not by any skilful conclusion, as Socrates does in the writings of Plato, who compels those against whom he disputes to admit those things which they had denied, but in a simple manner, will show that the greatest fear is the greatest virtue. No one doubts but that it is the part of a timid and feeble mind either to fear pain, or want, or exile, or imprisonment, or death; and if any one does not dread all these, he is judged a man of the greatest fortitude. But he who fears God is free from the fear of all these things. In proof of which, there is no need of arguments: for the punishments inflicted on the worshippers of God have been witnessed at all times, and are still witnessed through the world, in the tormenting of whom new and unusual tortures have been devised. For the mind shrinks from the recollection of various kinds of death, when the butchery of savage monsters has raged even beyond death itself. But a happy and unconquered patience endured these execrable lacerations of their bodies without a groan. This virtue afforded the greatest astonishment to all people and provinces, and to the torturers themselves, when

[1] [See Augustine against Pelagius; another view.]
[2] [Again this love of liberty, but loosely said.]

cruelty was overcome by patience. But this virtue was caused by nothing else than the fear of God. Therefore (as I said) fear is not to be uprooted, as the Stoics maintain, nor to be restrained, as the Peripatetics wish, but to be directed into the right way; and apprehensions are to be taken away, but so that this one only may be left: for since this is the only lawful and true one, it alone effects that all other things may not be feared. Desire also is reckoned among vices; but if it desires those things which are of the earth, it is a vice; on the other hand, if it desires heavenly things, it is a virtue. For he who desires to obtain justice, God, perpetual life, everlasting light, and all those things which God promises to man, will despise these riches, and honours, and commands, and kingdoms themselves.

The Stoic will perhaps say that inclination is necessary for the attainment of these things, and not desire; but, in truth, the inclination is not sufficient. For many have the inclination; but when pain has approached the vitals, inclination gives way, but desire perseveres: and if it effects that all things which are sought by others are objects of contempt to him, it is the greatest virtue, since it is the mother of self-restraint. And therefore we ought rather to effect this, that we may rightly direct the affections, a corrupt use of which is vice. For these excitements of the mind resemble a harnessed chariot, in the right management of which the chief duty of the driver is to know the way; and if he shall keep to this, with whatever swiftness he may go, he will not strike against an obstacle. But if he shall wander from the course, although he may go calmly and gently, he will either be shaken over rough places, or will glide over precipices, or at any rate will be carried where he does not need to go. So that chariot of life which is led by the affections as though by swift horses, if it keeps the right way, will discharge its duty. Dread, therefore, and desire, if they are cast down to the earth, will become vices, but they will be virtues if they are referred to divine things. On the other hand, they esteem parsimony as a virtue; which, if it is eagerness for possessing, cannot be a virtue, because it is altogether employed in the increase or preservation of earthly goods. But we do not refer the chief good to the body, but we measure every duty by the preservation of the soul only. But if, as I have before taught, we must by no means spare our property that we may preserve kindness and justice, it is not a virtue to be frugal; which name beguiles and deceives under the appearance of virtue. For frugality is, it is true, the abstaining from pleasures; but in this respect it is a vice, because it arises from the love of possessing, whereas we ought both to abstain from pleasures, and by no means to withhold money. For to use money sparingly, that is, moderately, is a kind of weakness of mind, either of one fearing lest he should be in want, or of one despairing of being able to recover it, or of one incapable of the contempt of earthly things. But, on the other hand, they call him who is not sparing of his property prodigal. For thus they distinguish between the liberal man and the prodigal: that he is liberal who bestows on deserving objects, and on proper occasions, and in sufficient quantities; but that he is prodigal who lavishes on undeserving objects, and when there is no need, and without any regard to his property.

What then? shall we call him prodigal who through pity gives food to the needy? But it makes a great difference, whether on account of lust you bestow your money on harlots, or on account of benevolence on the wretched; whether profligates, gamesters, and pimps squander your money, or you bestow it on piety and God; whether you expend it upon your own appetite,[1] or lay it up in the treasury of justice. As, therefore, it is a vice to lay it out badly, so it is a virtue to lay it out well. If it is a virtue not to be sparing of riches, which can be replaced, that you may support the life of man, which cannot be replaced; then parsimony is a vice. Therefore I can call them by no other name than mad, who deprive man, a mild and sociable animal, of his name; who, having uprooted the affections, in which humanity altogether consists, wish to bring him to an immoveable insensibility of mind, while they desire to free the soul from perturbations, and, as they themselves say, to render it calm and tranquil; which is not only impossible, because its force and nature consist in motion, but it ought not even to be so. For as water which is always still and motionless is unwholesome and more muddy, so the soul which is unmoved and torpid is useless even to itself: nor will it be able to maintain life itself; for it will neither do nor think anything, since thought itself is nothing less than agitation of the mind. In fine, they who assert this immoveableness of the soul wish to deprive the soul of life; for life is full of activity, but death is quiet. They also rightly esteem some things as virtues, but they do not maintain their due proportion.[2]

Constancy is a virtue; not that we resist those who injure us, for we must yield to these; and why this ought to be done I will show presently: but that when men command us to act in opposition to the law of God, and in opposition to justice, we should be deterred by no threats or punishments from preferring the command of God to the command of man. Likewise

[1] Ventri ac gulæ ingeras.

[2] Sed earum modum non tenent. [Augustine's anthropology better.]

it is a virtue to despise death; not that we seek it, and of our own accord inflict it upon ourselves, as many and distinguished philosophers have often done, which is a wicked and impious thing; but that when compelled to desert God, and to betray our faith, we should prefer to undergo death, and should defend our liberty against the foolish and senseless violence of those who cannot govern themselves, and with fortitude of spirit we should challenge all the threats and terrors of the world. Thus with lofty and invincible mind we trample upon those things which others fear — pain and death. This is virtue; this is true constancy — to be maintained and preserved in this one thing alone, that no terror and no violence may be able to turn us away from God. Therefore that is a true sentiment of Cicero:[1] "No one," he says, "can be just who fears death, or pain, or exile, or want." Also of Seneca, who says, in his books of moral philosophy: "This is that virtuous man, not distinguished by a diadem or purple, or the attendance of lictors, but in no respect inferior, who, when he sees death at hand, is not so disturbed as though he saw a fresh object; who, whether torments are to be suffered by his whole body, or a flame is to be seized by his mouth, or his hands are to be stretched out on the cross,[2] does not inquire what he suffers, but how well." But he who worships God suffers these things without fear. Therefore he is just. By these things it is effected, that he cannot know or maintain at all either the virtues or the exact limits of the virtues, whoever is estranged from the religion of the one God.

CHAP. XVIII. — OF SOME COMMANDS OF GOD, AND OF PATIENCE.

But let us leave the philosophers, who either know nothing at all, and hold forth this very ignorance as the greatest knowledge; or who, inasmuch as they think they know that of which they are ignorant, are absurdly and arrogantly foolish. Let us therefore (that we may return to our purpose), to whom alone the truth has been revealed by God, and wisdom has been sent from heaven, practise those things which God who enlightens us commands: let us sustain and endure the labours of life, by mutual assistance towards each other; nor, however, if we shall have done any good work, let us aim at glory from it. For God admonishes us that the doer of justice ought not to be boastful, lest he should appear to have discharged the duties of benevolence, not so much from a desire of obeying the divine commands, as of pleasing men, and should already have the reward of glory which he has aimed at, and should not receive the recompense of that heavenly and divine reward. The other things which the worshipper of God ought to observe are easy, when these virtues are comprehended, that no one should ever speak falsely for the sake of deceiving or injuring. For it is unlawful for him who cultivates truth to be deceitful in anything, and to depart from the truth itself which he follows. In this path of justice and all the virtues there is no place for falsehood. Therefore the true and just traveller will not use the saying of Lucilius:[3] —

> "It is not for me to speak falsely to a man who is a friend and acquaintance;"

but he will think that it is not his part to speak falsely even to an enemy and a stranger; nor will he at any time so act, that his tongue, which is the interpreter of his mind, should be at variance with his feeling and thought. If he shall have lent any money, he will not receive interest, that the benefit may be unimpaired which succours necessity, and that he may entirely abstain from the property of another. For in this kind of duty he ought to be content with that which is his own; since it is his duty in other respects not to be sparing of his property, in order that he may do good; but to receive more than he has given is unjust. And he who does this lies in wait in some manner, that he may gain booty from the necessity of another.

But the just man will omit no opportunity of doing anything mercifully: nor will he pollute himself with gain of this kind; but he will so act that without any loss to himself, that which he lends may be reckoned among his good works. He must not receive a gift from a poor man; so that if he himself has afforded anything, it may be good, inasmuch as it is gratuitous. If any one reviles, he must answer him with a blessing;[4] he himself must never revile, that no evil word may proceed out of the mouth of a man who reverences the good Word.[5] Moreover, he must also diligently take care, lest by any fault of his he should at any time make an enemy; and if any one should be so shameless as to inflict injury on a good and just man, he must bear it with calmness and moderation, and not take upon himself his revenge, but reserve it for the judgment of God.[6] He must at all times and in all places guard innocence. And this precept is not limited to this, that he should not himself inflict injury, but that he should not avenge it when inflicted on himself. For there sits on the judgment-seat a very great and impartial Judge, the observer and witness of all. Let him prefer Him to man; let him rather

---

1 *De Offic.*, ii. 11.
2 Per patibulum.
3 [Homini amico ac familiari non est mentiri meum.]
4 Matt. v. 44; Luke vi. 28; Rom. xii. 14.
5 i.e., Jesus Christ the Son of God = the Word of God.
6 Rom. xii. 19; Heb. x. 30.

choose that He should pronounce judgment respecting his cause, whose sentence no one can escape, either by the advocacy of any one or by favour. Thus it comes to pass, that a just man is an object of contempt to all; and because it will be thought that he is unable to defend himself, he will be regarded as slothful and inactive; but if any one shall have avenged himself upon his enemy, he is judged a man of spirit and activity — all honour and reverence him. And although the good man has it in his power to profit many, yet they look up to him who is able to injure, rather than to him who is able to profit. But the depravity of men will not be able to corrupt the just man, so that he will not endeavour to obey God; and he would prefer to be despised, provided that he may always discharge the duty of a good man, and never of a bad man. Cicero says in those same books respecting Offices: "But if any one should wish to unravel this indistinct conception of his soul,[1] let him at once teach himself that he is a good man who profits those whom he can, and injures no one[2] unless provoked by injury."

Oh how he marred a simple and true sentiment by the addition of two words! For what need was there of adding these words, "unless provoked by injury?" that he might append vice as a most disgraceful tail to a good man, and might represent him as without patience, which is the greatest of all the virtues. He said that a good man would inflict injuries if he were provoked: now he must necessarily lose the name of a good man from this very circumstance, if he shall inflict injury. For it is not less the part of a bad man to return an injury than to inflict it. For from what source do contests, from what source do fightings and contentions, arise among men, except that impatience opposed to injustice often excites great tempests? But if you meet injustice with patience, than which virtue nothing can be found more true, nothing more worthy of a man, it will immediately be extinguished, as though you should pour water upon a fire. But if that injustice which provokes opposition has met with impatience equal[3] to itself, as though overspread with oil, it will excite so great a conflagration, that no stream can extinguish it, but only the shedding of blood. Great, therefore, is the advantage of patience, of which the wise man has deprived the good man. For this alone causes that no evil happens; and if it should be given to all, there will be no wickedness and no fraud in the affairs of men. What, therefore, can be so calamitous to a good man, so opposed to his character, as to let loose the reins to anger, which deprives him not only of the title of a good man, but even of a man; since to injure another, as he himself most truly says, is not in accordance with the nature of man? For if you provoke cattle or horses,[4] they turn against you either with their hoof or their horn; and serpents and wild beasts, unless you pursue them that you may kill them, give no trouble. And to return to examples of men, even the inexperienced and the foolish, if at any time they receive an injury, are led by a blind and irrational fury, and endeavour to retaliate upon those who injure them. In what respect, then, does the wise and good man differ from the evil and foolish, except that he has invincible patience, of which the foolish are destitute; except that he knows how to govern himself, and to mitigate his anger, which those, because they are without virtue, are unable to curb? But this circumstance manifestly deceived him, because, when inquiry is made respecting virtue, he thought that it is the part of virtue to conquer in every kind of contention. Nor was he able in any way to see, that a man who gives way to grief and anger, and who indulges these affections, against which he ought rather to struggle, and who rushes wherever injustice shall have called him, does not fulfil the duty of virtue. For he who endeavours to return an injury, desires to imitate that very person by whom he has been injured. Thus he who imitates a bad man can by no means be good.

Therefore by two words he has taken away from the good and wise man two of the greatest virtues, innocence and patience. But, as Sallustius relates was said by Appius, because he himself practised that canine[5] eloquence, he wished man also to live after the manner of a dog, so as, when attacked, to bite in return. And to show how pernicious this repayment of insult is, and what carnage it is accustomed to produce, from what can a more befitting example be sought, than from the most melancholy disaster of the teacher himself, who, while he desired to obey these precepts of the philosophers, destroyed himself? For if, when attacked with injury, he had preserved patience — if he had learned that it is the part of a good man to dissemble and to endure insult, and his impatience, vanity, and madness had not poured forth those noble orations, inscribed with a name derived from another source,[6] he would never, by his head affixed to them, have polluted the *rostra* on which he had formerly distinguished himself, nor would that proscription have utterly destroyed

---

1 Animi sui complicitam notionem evolvere.
2 [Nisi lacessitus injuria.]
3 Comparem. Injustice and impatience are here represented as a pair of gladiators well matched against each other.
4 Pecudes, including horses and cattle.
5 Caninam, i.e., resembling a dog, cutting.
6 The allusion is to the *Philippics* of Cicero, a title borrowed from Demosthenes.

the state. Therefore it is not the part of a wise and good man to wish to contend, and to commit himself to danger, since to conquer is not in our power, and every contest is doubtful; but it is the part of a wise and excellent man not to wish to remove his adversary, which cannot be done without guilt and danger, but to put an end to the contest itself, which may be done with advantage and with justice. Therefore patience is to be regarded as a very great virtue; and that the just man might obtain this, God willed, as has been before said, that he should be despised as sluggish. For unless he shall have been insulted, it will not be known what fortitude he has in restraining himself. Now if, when provoked by injury, he has begun to follow up his assailant with violence, he is overcome. But if he shall have repressed that emotion by reasoning, he altogether has command over himself: he is able to rule himself. And this restraining[1] of oneself is rightly named patience, which single virtue is opposed to all vices and affections. This recalls the disturbed and wavering mind to its tranquillity; this mitigates, this restores a man to himself. Therefore, since it is impossible and useless to resist nature, so that we are not excited at all; before, however, the emotion bursts forth to the infliction of injury, as far[2] as is possible let it be calmed[3] in time. God has enjoined us not to let the sun go down upon our wrath,[4] lest he should depart as a witness of our madness. Finally, Marcus Tullius, in opposition to his own precept, concerning which I have lately spoken, gave the greatest praises to the forgetting of injuries. "I entertain hopes," he says, "O Cæsar, who art accustomed to forget nothing except injuries."[5] But if he thus acted — a man most widely removed not only from heavenly, but also from public and civil justice — how much more ought we to do this, who are, as it were, candidates for immortality?

CHAP. XIX. — OF THE AFFECTIONS AND THEIR USE; AND OF THE THREE FURIES.

When the Stoics attempt to uproot the affections from man as diseases, they are opposed by the Peripatetics, who not only retain, but also defend them, and say that there is nothing in man which is not produced in him with great reason and foresight. They say this indeed rightly, if they know the true limits of each subject. Accordingly they say that this very affection of anger is the whetstone of virtue, as though no one could fight bravely against enemies unless he were excited by anger; by which they plainly show that they neither know what virtue is, nor why God gave anger to man. And if this was given to us for this purpose, that we may employ it for the slaying of men, what is to be thought more savage than man, what more resembling the wild beasts, than that animal which God formed for communion and innocence? There are, then, three affections which drive men headlong to all crimes: (1) anger, (2) desire, and (3) lust.[6] On which account the poets have said that there are three furies which harass the minds of men: anger longs for revenge, desire for riches, lust for pleasures. But God has appointed fixed limits to all of these; and if they pass these limits and begin to be too great, they must necessarily pervert their nature, and be changed into diseases and vices. And it is a matter of no great labour to show what these limits are.[7] Cupidity[8] is given us for providing those things which are necessary for life; concupiscence,[9] for the procreation of offspring; the affection of indignation,[10] for restraining the faults of those who are in our power, that is, in order that tender age may be formed by a severer discipline to integrity and justice: for if this *time of life* is not restrained by fear,[11] licence will produce boldness, and this will break out into every disgraceful and daring action. Therefore, as it is both just and necessary to employ anger towards the young, so it is both pernicious and impious to use it towards those of our own age. It is impious, because humanity is injured; pernicious, because if they oppose, it is necessary either to destroy them or to perish. But that this which I have spoken of is the reason why the affection of anger has been given to man, may be understood from the precepts of God Himself, who commands that we should not be angry with those who revile and injure us, but that we should always have our hands over the young; that is, that when they err, we should correct them with continual stripes,[12] lest by useless love and excessive indulgence they should be trained to evil and nourished to vices. But those who are inexperienced in affairs and ignorant of reason, have expelled those affections which have been given to man for good uses, and they wander more widely than reason de-

---

1 Sustentatio sui.
2 Quoad fieri potest. Others read, "quod fieri potest."
3 Maturius sopiatur.
4 Eph. iv. 26.
5 Cicero, *Pro Ligar.*, 12.

6 [Rather, indignation, cupidity, and concupiscence, answering to our author's "ira, cupiditas, libido." The difference involved in this choice of words, I shall have occasion to point out.]
7 [Here he treats the "three furies" as not in themselves vices, but implanted for good purposes, and becoming "diseases" only when they pass the limits he now defines. Hence, while indignation is *virtuous* anger, it is not a disease; *cupidity*, while amounting to honest *thrift*, is not evil; and *concupiscence*, until it becomes "*evil* concupiscence" (επιθυμιαν κακὴν, Col. iii. 5), is but natural *appetite*, working to good ends.]
8 Desire. [See note 6, *supra*.]
9 Lust.
10 Anger.
11 [Quæ, nisi in metu cohibetur.]
12 [*Assiduis* verberibus. This might be rendered "careful punishments."]

mands. From this cause they live unjustly and impiously. They employ anger against their equals in age: hence disagreements, hence banishments, hence wars have arisen contrary to justice. They use desire for the amassing of riches: hence frauds, hence robberies, hence all kinds of crimes have originated. They use lust only for the enjoyment of pleasures: hence debaucheries, hence adulteries, hence all corruptions have proceeded. Whoever, therefore, has reduced those affections within their proper limits, which they who are ignorant of God cannot do, he is patient, he is brave, he is just.[1]

Chap. XX. — Of the Senses, and Their Pleasures in the Brutes and in Man; and of Pleasures of the Eyes, and Spectacles.

It remains that I should speak against the pleasures of the five senses, and this briefly, for the measure of the book itself now demands moderation; all of which, since they are vicious and deadly, ought to be overcome and subdued by virtue, or, as I said a little before respecting the affections, be recalled to their proper office. The other animals have no pleasure, except the one only which relates to generation. Therefore they use their senses for the necessity of their nature: they see, in order that they may seek those things which are necessary for the preservation of life; they hear one another, and distinguish one another, that they may be able to assemble together; they either discover from the smell, or perceive from the taste, the things which are useful for food; they refuse and reject the things which are useless, they measure the business of eating and drinking by the fulness of their stomach. But the foresight of the most skilful Creator gave to man pleasure without limit, and liable to fall into vice, because He set before him virtue, which might always be at variance with pleasure, as with a domestic enemy. Cicero says, in the *Cato Major:*[2] "In truth, debaucheries, and adulteries, and disgraceful actions are excited by no other enticements than those of pleasure. And since nature or some God has given to man nothing more excellent than the mind, nothing is so hostile to this divine benefit and gift as pleasure. For when lust bears sway there is no place for temperance, nor can virtue have any existence when pleasure reigns supreme." But, on the other hand, God gave virtue on this account, that it might subdue and conquer pleasure, and that, when it passed the boundaries assigned to it, it might restrain it within the prescribed limits, lest it should soothe and captivate man with enjoyments, render him subject to its control, and punish him with everlasting death.

The pleasure arising from the eyes is various and manifold, which is derived from the sight of objects which are pleasant in intercourse with men, or in nature or workmanship. The philosophers rightly took this away. For they say that it is much more excellent and worthy of man to look upon the heaven[3] rather than carved works, and to admire this most beautiful work adorned with the lights of the stars shining through,[4] as with flowers, than to admire things painted and moulded, and varied with jewels. But when they have eloquently exhorted us to despise earthly things, and have urged us to look up to the heaven, nevertheless they do not despise these public spectacles. Therefore they are both delighted with these, and are gladly present at them; though, since they are the greatest incitement to vices, and have a most powerful tendency to corrupt our minds, they ought to be taken away from us; for they not only contribute in no respect to a happy life, but even inflict the greatest injury. For he who reckons it a pleasure, that a man, though justly condemned, should be slain in his sight, pollutes his conscience as much as if he should become a spectator and a sharer of a homicide which is secretly committed.[5] And yet they call these sports in which human blood is shed. So far has the feeling of humanity departed from the men, that when they destroy the lives of men, they think that they are amusing themselves with sport, being more guilty than all those whose blood-shedding they esteem a pleasure.

I ask now whether they can be just and pious men, who, when they see men placed under the stroke of death, and entreating mercy, not only suffer them to be put to death, but also demand it, and give cruel and inhuman votes for their death, not being satiated with wounds nor contented with bloodshed. Moreover, they order them, even though wounded and prostrate, to be attacked again, and their carcases to be wasted[6] with blows, that no one may delude them by a pretended death. They are even angry with the combatants, unless one of the two is quickly slain; and as though they thirsted for human blood, they hate delays. They demand that other and fresh combatants should be given to them, that they may satisfy their eyes

[1] [Quod ignorantes Deum facere non possunt. In a later age Lactantius might have been charged with *Semi-Pelagianism*, many of his expressions about human nature being unstudied. But I note this passage, as, like many others, proving that he recognises the need of divine grace.]

[2] C. 12.

[3] Cœlum potius quàm cœlata. There appears to be an allusion to the supposed derivation of "cœlum" from "cœlando."

[4] [Intermicantibus astrorum luminibus. It does not seem to me that the learned translator does full justice here to our author's idea. "Adorned with the twinkling lights of the stars" would be an admissible rendering.]

[5] [It is unbecoming for a Christian, unless as an officer of the law or a minister of mercy, to be a spectator of any execution of criminals. Blessed growth of Christian morals.]

[6] Dissipari. [A very graphic description of the brutal shows of the arena, which were abolished by the first Christian emperor, perhaps influenced by these very pages.]

as soon as possible. Being imbued with this practice, they have lost their humanity. Therefore they do not spare even the innocent, but practise upon all that which they have learned in the slaughter of the wicked. It is not therefore befitting that those who strive to keep to the path of justice should be companions and sharers in this public homicide. For when God forbids us to kill, He not only prohibits us from open violence,[1] which is not even allowed by the public laws, but He warns us against the commission of those things which are esteemed lawful among men. Thus it will be neither lawful for a just man to engage in warfare, since his warfare is justice itself, nor to accuse any one of a capital charge, because it makes no difference whether you put a man to death by word, or rather by the sword, since it is the act of putting to death itself[2] which is prohibited. Therefore, with regard to this precept of God, there ought to be no exception at all; but that it is always unlawful to put to death a man, whom God willed to be a sacred animal.[3]

Therefore let no one imagine that even this is allowed, to strangle[4] newly-born children, which is the greatest impiety; for God breathes into their souls for life, and not for death. But men, that there may be no crime with which they may not pollute their hands, deprive souls as yet innocent and simple of the light which they themselves have not given. Can any one, indeed, expect that they would abstain from the blood of others who do not abstain even from their own? But these are without any controversy wicked and unjust. What are they whom a false piety[5] compels to expose their children? Can they be considered innocent who expose their own offspring[6] as a prey to dogs, and as far as it depends upon themselves, kill them in a more cruel manner than if they had strangled them? Who can doubt that he is impious who gives occasion[7] for the pity of others? For, although that which he has wished should befall the child — namely, that it should be brought up — he has certainly consigned his own offspring either to servitude or to the brothel? But who does not understand, who is ignorant what things may happen, or are accustomed to happen, in the case of each sex, even through error? For this is shown by the example of Œdipus alone, confused with twofold guilt. It is therefore as wicked to expose as it is to kill. But truly parricides complain of the scantiness of their means, and allege that they have not enough for bringing up more children; as though, in truth, their means were in the power of those who possess them, or God did not daily make the rich poor, and the poor rich. Wherefore, if any one on account of poverty shall be unable to bring up children, it is better to abstain from marriage[8] than with wicked hands to mar the work of God.

If, then, it is in no way permitted to commit homicide, it is not allowed us to be present at all,[9] lest any bloodshed should overspread the conscience, since that blood is offered for the gratification of the people. And I am inclined to think that the corrupting influence of the stage is still more contaminating.[10] For the subject of comedies are the dishonouring of virgins, or the loves of harlots; and the more eloquent they are who have composed the accounts of these disgraceful actions, the more do they persuade by the elegance of their sentiments; and harmonious and polished verses more readily remain fixed in the memory of the hearers. In like manner, the stories of the tragedians place before the eyes the parricides and incests of wicked kings, and represent tragic[11] crimes. And what other effect do the immodest gestures of the players produce, but both teach and excite lusts? whose enervated bodies, rendered effeminate after the gait and dress of women, imitate[12] unchaste women by their disgraceful gestures. Why should I speak of the actors of *mimes*,[13] who hold forth instruction in corrupting influences, who teach adulteries while they feign them, and by pretended actions train to those which are true? What can young men or virgins do, when they see that these things are practised without shame, and willingly beheld by all? They are plainly admonished of what they can do, and are inflamed with lust, which is especially excited by seeing; and every one according to his sex forms[14] himself in these representations. And they approve of these things, while they laugh at them, and with vices clinging to them, they return more corrupted to their apartments; and not boys only, who ought not to be inured to vices prematurely, but also old men, whom it does not become at their age to sin.

---

1 Lactrocinari.

2 i.e., without reference to the manner in which death is inflicted. [Lactantius goes further here than the Scriptures seem to warrant, if more than *private* warfare be in his mind. The influence of Tertullian is visible here. See Elucidation II. p. 76, and cap. xi. p. 99, vol. iii., this series.]

3 [Sanctum animal. See p. 56, *supra*. But the primal law on this very subject contains a sanction which our author seems to forget. Because he is an animal of such sacred dignity, therefore "whoso sheddeth man's blood," etc. (Gen. ix. 6). The impunity of Cain had led to bloodshed (Gen. vi. 11), to which as a necessary remedy this sanction was prescribed.]

4 Oblidere.

5 They thought it less criminal to expose children than to strangle them.

6 Sanguinem suum.

7 i.e., by exposing them, that others may through compassion bring them up.

8 Ab uxoris congressione.

9 i.e., at the shows of gladiators.

10 [How seriously this warning should be considered in our days, when American theatricals have become so generally licentious beyond all bounds, I beg permission to suggest. See Elucidation I. p. 595, vol. v.; also *Ibid.*, pp. 277, 575, this series.]

11 Cothurnata scelera.

12 Mentiuntur.

13 The *mimus* was a species of dramatic representation, containing scenes from common life, which were expressed by gesture and mimicry more than by dialogue.

14 Præfigurat, not a word of classical usage.

What else does the practice of the Circensian games contain but levity, vanity, and madness? For their souls are hurried away to mad excitement with as great impetuosity as that with which the chariot races are there carried on; so that they who come for the sake of beholding the spectacle now themselves exhibit more of a spectacle, when they begin to utter exclamations, to be thrown into transports, and to leap from their seats. Therefore all spectacles ought to be avoided, not only that no vice may settle in our breasts, which ought to be tranquil and peaceful; but that the habitual indulgence of any pleasure may not soothe and captivate us, and turn us aside from God and from good works.[1] For the celebrations of the games are festivals in honour of the gods, inasmuch as they were instituted on account of their birthdays, or the dedication of new temples. And at first the huntings, which are called shows, were in honour of Saturnus, and the scenic games in honour of Liber, but the Circensian in honour of Neptune. By degrees, however, the same honour began to be paid also to the other gods, and separate games were dedicated to their names, as Sisinnius Capito teaches in his book on the games. Therefore, if any one is present at the spectacles to which men assemble for the sake of religion, he has departed from the worship of God, and has betaken himself to those deities whose birthdays and festivals he has celebrated.[2]

CHAP. XXI. — OF THE PLEASURES OF THE EARS, AND OF SACRED LITERATURE.

Pleasure of the ears is received from the sweetness of voices and strains, which indeed is as productive of vice as that delight of the eyes of which we have spoken. For who would not deem him luxurious and worthless who should have scenic arts at his house? But it makes no difference whether you practise luxury alone at home, or with the people in the theatre. But we have already spoken of spectacles:[3] there remains one thing which is to be overcome by us, that we be not captivated by those things which penetrate to the innermost perception. For all those things which are unconnected with words, that is, pleasant sounds of the air and of strings, may be easily disregarded, because they do not adhere to us, and cannot be written. But a well-composed poem, and a speech beguiling with its sweetness, captivate the minds of men, and impel them in what direction they please. Hence, when learned men have applied themselves to the religion of God, unless they have been instructed[4] by some skilful teacher, they do not believe. For, being accustomed to sweet and polished speeches or poems, they despise the simple and common language of the sacred writings as mean. For they seek that which may soothe the senses. But whatever is pleasant to the ear effects persuasion, and while it delights fixes itself deeply within the breast. Is God, therefore, the contriver both of the mind, and of the voice, and of the tongue, unable to speak eloquently? Yea, rather, with the greatest foresight, He wished those things which are divine to be without adornment, that all might understand the things which He Himself spoke to all.

Therefore he who is anxious for the truth, who does not wish to deceive himself, must lay aside hurtful and injurious pleasures, which would bind the mind to themselves, as pleasant food does the body: true things must be preferred to false, eternal things to those which are of short duration, useful things to those which are pleasant. Let nothing be pleasing to the sight but that which you see to be done with piety and justice; let nothing be agreeable to the hearing but that which nourishes the soul and makes you a better man. And especially this sense ought not to be distorted to vice, since it is given to us for this purpose, that we might gain the knowledge of God. Therefore, if it be a pleasure to hear melodies and songs, let it be pleasant to sing and hear the praises of God. This is true pleasure, which is the attendant and companion of virtue. This is not frail and brief, as those which they desire, who, like cattle, are slaves to the body; but lasting, and affording delight without any intermission. And if any one shall pass its limits, and shall seek nothing else from pleasure but pleasure itself, he designs *for himself* death; for as there is perpetual life in virtue, so there is death in pleasure. For he who shall choose temporal things will be without things eternal; he who shall prefer earthly things will not have heavenly things.

CHAP. XXII. — OF THE PLEASURES OF TASTE AND SMELL.

But with regard to the pleasures of taste and smell, which two senses relate only to the body, there is nothing to be discussed by us; unless by chance any one requires us to say that it is disgraceful to a wise and good man if he is the slave of his appetite, if he walks along besmeared with unguents and crowned with flowers: and he who does these things is plainly foolish and senseless, and is worthless, and one whom not even a notion of virtue has reached. Perhaps some one will say, Why, then, have these things been made, except that we may enjoy them? However, it has often been said that there would have been no virtue unless it had things which it

---

1 [See Tertullian, vol. iii cap. 25, p.89, this series.]

2 [See p. 27, *supra;* also vol. vi. pp. 487, 488.]

3 [See p. 187, *supra.*]

4 Fundati, having the foundation well laid, trained. Some read, "Ab aliquo imperito doctore fundati."

might overpower. Therefore God made all things to supply a contest between two things. Those enticements of pleasures, then, are the instruments of that whose only business it is to subdue virtue, and to shut out justice from men. With these soothing influences and enjoyments it captivates their souls; for it knows that pleasure is the contriver of death. For as God calls man to life only through virtue and labour, so the other calls us to death by delights and pleasures; and as men arrive at real good through deceitful evils, so they arrive at real evil through deceitful goods. Therefore those enjoyments are to be guarded against, as snares or nets, lest, captivated by the softness of enjoyments, we should be brought under the dominion of death with the body itself, to which we have enslaved ourselves.

CHAP. XXIII.[1] — DE TACTUS VOLUPTATE ET LIBIDINE, ATQUE DE MATRIMONIO ET CONTINENTIÂ.

Venio nunc ad eam, quæ percipitur ex tactu, voluptatem: qui sensus est quidem totius corporis. Sed ego non de ornamentis, aut vestibus, sed de solâ libidine dicendum mihi puto; quæ maximè coercenda est, quia maximè nocet. Cum excogitasset Deus duorum sexuum rationem, attribuit iis, ut se invicem appeterent, et conjunctione gauderent. Itaque ardentissimam cupiditatem cunctorum animantium corporibus admiscuit, ut in hos affectus avidissimè ruerent, eâque ratione propagari et multiplicari genera possent. Quæ cupiditas et appetentia in homine vehementior et acrior invenitur; vel quia hominum multitudinem voluit esse majorem, vel quoniam virtutem soli homini dedit, ut esset laus et gloria in coercendis voluptatibus, et abstinentiâ sui. Scit ergò adversarius ille noster, quanta sit vis hujus cupiditatis, quam quidam necessitatem dicere maluerunt; eamque a recto et bono, ad malum et pravum transfert. Illicita enim desideria immittit, ut aliena contaminent, quibus habere propria sine delicto licet. Objicit quippe oculis irritabiles formas, suggeritque fomenta, et vitiis pabulum subministrat: tum intimis visceribus stimulos omnes conturbat et commovet, et naturalem illum incitat atque inflammat ardorem, donec irretitum hominem implicatumque decipiat. Ac ne quis esset, qui pœnarum metu abstineret alieno, lupanaria quoque constituit; et pudorem infelicium mulierum publicavit, ut ludibrio haberet tam eos qui faciunt, quàm quas pati necesse est.

His obscœnitatibus animas, ad sanctitatem genitas, velut in cœni gurgite demersit, pudorem extinxit, pudicitiam profligavit. Idem etiam mares maribus admiscuit; et nefandos coitus contra naturam contraque institutum Dei machinatus est: sic imbuit homines, et armavit ad nefas omne. Quid enim potest esse sanctum iis, qui ætatem imbecillam et præsidio indigentem, libidini suæ depopulandam fœdandamque substraverint? Non potest hæc res pro magnitudine sceleris enarrari. Nihil amplius istos appellare possum, quàm impios et parricidas, quibus non sufficit sexus a Deo datus, nisi etiam suum profanè ac petulanter illudant. Hæc tamen apud illos levia, et quasi honesta sunt. Quid dicam de iis, qui abominandam non libidinem, sed insaniam potius exercent! Piget dicere: sed quid his fore credamus, quos non piget facere? et tamen dicendum est, quia fit. De istis loquor, quorum teterrima libido et execrabilis furor ne capiti quidem parcit. Quibus hoc verbis, aut quâ indignatione tantum nefas prosequar? Vincit officium linguæ sceleris magnitudo. Cùm igitur libido hæc edat opera, et hæc facinora designet, armandi adversus eam virtute maximâ sumus. Quisquis affectus illos frænare non potest, cohibeat eos intra præscriptum legitimi tori, ut et illud, quod avidè expetat, consequatur, et tamen in peccatum non incidat. Nam quid sibi homines perditi volunt? Nempe honesta opera voluptas sequitur: si ipsam per se appetunt, justâ et legitimâ frui licet.

Quod si aliqua necessitas prohibebit tum verò maxima adhibenda virtus erit, ut cupiditati continentia reluctetur. Nec tantum alienis, quæ attingere non licet, verùm etiam publicis vulgatisque corporibus abstinendum, Deus præcepit; docetque nos, cùm duo inter se corpora fuerint copulata, unum corpus efficere. Ita qui se cœno immerserit, cœno sit oblitus necesse est; et corpus quidem citò ablui potest: mens autem contagione impudici corporis inquinata non potest, nisi et longo tempore, et multis bonis operibus, ab eâ quæ inhæserit colluvione purgari. Oportet ergo sibi quemque proponere, duorum sexuum conjunctionem generandi causâ datam esse viventibus, eamque legem his affectibus positam, ut successionem parent. Sicut autem dedit nobis oculos Deus, non ut spectemus, voluptatemque capiamus, sed ut videamus propter eos actus, qui pertinent ad vitæ necessitatem, ita genitalem corporis partem, quod nomen ipsum docet, nullâ aliâ causâ nisi efficiendæ sobolis accepimus. Huic divinæ legi summâ devotione parendum est. Sint omnes, qui se discipulos Dei profitebuntur, ita morati et instituti, ut imperare sibi possint. Nam qui voluptatibus indulgent, qui libidini obsequuntur, ii animam suam corpori mancipant, ad mortemque condemnant: quia se corpori addixerunt, in quod habet mors potestatem. Unusquisque igitur, quantum potest, formet se ad verecundiam, pudorem colat, castitatem conscientiâ et mente tueatur; nec tantum legibus publicis pareat: sed sit supra omnes leges, qui legem Dei sequitur. Quibus

[1] It has been judged advisable to give this chapter in the original Latin. [Compare Clement, vol. ii. p. 259, notes 3, 7, this series.]

bonis si assueverit, jam pudebit eum ad deteriora desciscere: modò placeant recta et honesta, quæ melioribus jucundiora sunt quàm prava et inhonesta pejoribus.

Nondum omnia castitatis officia exsecutus sum: quam Deus non modo intra privatos parietes, sed etiam præscripto lectuli terminat; ut cùm quis habeat uxorem, neque servam, neque liberam habere insuper velit, sed matrimonio fidem servet. Non enim, sicut juris publici ratio est, sola mulier adultera est, quæ habet alium, maritus autem, etiam si plures habeat, a crimine adulterii solutus est. Sed divina lex ita duos in matrimonium, quod est in corpus unum, pari jure conjungit, ut adulter habeatur, quisquis compagem corporis in diversa distraxerit. Nec ob aliam causam Deus, cùm cæteras animantes suscepto fœtu maribus repugnare voluisset, solam omnium mulierem patientem viri fecit; scilicet ne fœminis repugnantibus, libido cogeret viros aliud appetere, eoque facto, castitatis gloriam non tenerent.[1] Sed neque mulier virtutem pudicitiæ caperet, si peccare non posset. Nam quis mutum animal pudicum esse dixerit, quòd suscepto fœtu mari repugnat? Quod ideo facit, quia necesse est in dolorem atque in periculum veniat, si admiserit. Nulla igitur laus est, non facere quod facere non possis. Ideo autem pudicitia in homine laudatur, quia non naturalis est, sed voluntaria. Servanda igitur fides ab utroque alteri est: immo exemplo continentiæ docenda uxor, ut se caste gerat. Iniquum est enim, ut id exigas, quod præstare ipse non possis. Quæ iniquitas effecit profectò, ut essent adulteria, fœminis ægre ferentibus præstare se fidem non exhibentibus mutuam charitatem. Denique nulla est tam perditi pudoris adultera, quæ non hanc causam vitiis suis prætendat; injuriam se peccando non facere, sed referre. Quod optimè Quintilianus expressit: Homo, inquit, neque alieni matrimonii abstinens, neque sui custos, quæ inter se naturâ connexa sunt. Nam neque maritus circa corrumpendas aliorum conjuges occupatus potest vacare domesticæ sanctitati; et uxor, cùm in tale incidit matrimonium, exemplo ipso concitata, aut imitari se putat, aut vindicari.

Cavendum igitur, ne occasionem vitiis nostrâ intemperantiâ demus: sed assuescant invicem mores duorum, et jugum paribus animis ferant. Nos ipsos in altero cogitemus. Nam fere in hoc justitiæ summa consistit, ut non facias alteri, quidquid ipse ab altero pati nolis. Hæc sunt quæ ad continentiam præcipiuntur a Deo. Sed tamen ne quis divina præcepta circumscribere se putet posse, adduntur illa, ut omnis calumnia, et occasio fraudis removeatur, adulterum esse, qui a marito dimissam duxerit, et eum qui præter crimen adulterii uxorem dimiserit, ut alteram ducat; dissociari enim corpus et distrahi Deus noluit. Præterea non tantum adulterium esse vitandum, sed etiam cogitationem; ne quis aspiciat alienam, et animo concupiscat: adulteram enim fieri mentem, si vel imaginem voluptatis sibi ipsa depinxerit. Mens est enim profecto quæ peccat; quæ immoderatæ libidinis fructum cogitatione complectitur; in hâc crimen est, in hâc omne delictum. Nam etsi corpus nullâ sit labe maculatum, non constat tamen pudicitiæ ratio, si animus incestus est; nec illibata castitas videri potest, ubi conscientiam cupiditas inquinavit. Nec verò aliquis existimet, difficile esse frænos imponere voluptati, eamque vagam et errantem castitatis pudicitiæque limitibus includere, cùm propositum sit hominibus etiam vincere, ac plurimi beatam atque incorruptam corporis integritatem retinuerint, multique sint, qui hoc cœlesti genere vitæ felicissimè perfruantur. Quod quidem Deus non ita fieri præcepit, tanquam astringat, quia generari homines oportet; sed tanquam sinat. Scit enim, quantam his affectibus imposuerit necessitatem. Si quis hoc, inquit, facere potuerit, habebit eximiam incomparabilemque mercedem. Quod continentiæ genus quasi fastigium est, omniumque consummatio virtutum. Ad quam si quis eniti atque eluctari potuerit, hunc servum dominus, hunc discipulum magister agnoscet; hic terram triumphabit, hic erit consimilis Deo, qui virtutem Dei cepit. Hæc quidem difficilia videntur; sed de eo loquimur, cui calcatis omnibus terrenis, iter in cœlum paratur. Nam quia virtus in Dei agnitione consistit, omnia gravia sunt, dum ignores; ubi cognoveris, facilia: per ipsas difficultates nobis exeundum est, qui ad summum bonum tendimus.

CHAP. XXIV. — OF REPENTANCE, OF PARDON, AND THE COMMANDS OF GOD.

Nor, however, let any one be disheartened, or despair concerning himself, if, overcome by passion, or impelled by desire, or deceived by error, or compelled by force, he has turned aside to the way of unrighteousness. For it is possible for him to be brought back, and to be set free, if he repents of his actions, and, turning to better things, makes satisfaction to God. Cicero, indeed, thought that this was impossible, whose words in the third book of the Academics[2] are: "But if, as in the case of those who have gone astray on a journey, it were permitted those who have followed a devious course to correct their error by repentance, it would be more easy to amend rashness." It is altogether permitted them. For if we think that our children are

[1] [Non bene conveniunt igitur legibus divinis quæ supradicta sunt auctore nostro (vide p 143, apud n. 2) sed hæc verba de naturâ muliebri minime imperita, esse videntur.]

[2] [From a lost book.]

corrected when we perceive that they repent of their faults, and though we have disinherited and cast them off, we again receive, cherish, and embrace them, why should we despair that the mercy of God our Father may again be appeased by repentance? Therefore He who is at once the Lord and most indulgent Parent promises that He will remit the sins of the penitent, and that He will blot out all the iniquities of him who shall begin afresh to practise righteousness. For as the uprightness of his past life is of no avail to him who lives badly, because the subsequent wickedness has destroyed his works of righteousness, so former sins do not stand in the way of him who has amended his life, because the subsequent righteousness has effaced the stain of his former life. For he who repents of that which he has done, understands his former error; and on this account the Greeks better and more significantly speak of *metanoia*,[1] which we may speak of in Latin as a return to a right understanding.[2] For he returns to a right understanding, and recovers his mind as it were from madness, who is grieved for his error; and he reproves himself of madness, and confirms his mind to a better course of life: then he especially guards against this very thing, that he may not again be led into the same snares. In short, even the dumb animals, when they are ensnared by fraud, if by any means they have extricated themselves so as to escape, become more cautious for the future, and always avoid all those things in which they have perceived wiles and snares. Thus repentance makes a man cautious and diligent to avoid the faults into which he has once fallen through deceit.

For no one can be so prudent and so circumspect as not at some time to slip; and therefore God, knowing our weakness, of His compassion[3] has opened a harbour of refuge for man, that the medicine of repentance might aid this necessity to which our frailty is liable.[4] Therefore, if any one has erred, let him retrace his step, and as soon as possible recover and reform himself.

"But upward to retrace the way,
And pass into the light of day,
Then comes the stress of labour."[5]

For when men have tasted sweet pleasures to their destruction,[6] they can scarcely be separated from them: they would more easily follow right things if they had not tasted their attractions. But if they tear themselves away from this pernicious slavery, all their error will be forgiven them, if they shall have corrected their error by a better life. And let not any one imagine that he is a gainer if he shall have no witness of his fault: for all things are known to Him in whose sight we live; and if we are able to conceal anything from all men, we cannot conceal it from God, to whom nothing can be hidden, nothing secret. Seneca closed his exhortations with an admirable sentiment: "There is," he says, "some great deity, and greater than can be imagined; and for him we endeavour to live. Let us approve ourselves to him. For it is of no avail that conscience is confirmed; we lie open to the sight of God." What can be spoken with greater truth by him who knew God, than has been said by a man who is ignorant of true religion? For he both expressed the majesty of God, by saying that it is too great for the reflecting powers of the human mind to receive; and he touched upon the very fountain of truth, by perceiving that the life of men is not superfluous,[7] as the Epicureans will have it, but that they make it their endeavour to live to God, if indeed they live with justice and piety. He might have been a true worshipper of God, if any one had pointed out to him God;[8] and he might assuredly have despised Zeno, and his teacher Sotion, if he had obtained a true guide of wisdom. Let us approve ourselves to him, he says. A speech truly heavenly, had it not been preceded by a confession of ignorance. It is of no avail that conscience is confined; we lie open to the sight of God. There is then no room for falsehood, none for dissimulation; for the eyes of men are removed by walls, but the divine power of God cannot be removed by the inward parts from looking through and knowing the entire man. The same writer says, in the first book of the same work: "What are you doing? what are you contriving? what are you hiding? Your guardian follows you; one is withdrawn from you by foreign travel, another by death, another by infirm health; this one adheres to you, and you can never be without him. Why do you choose a secret place, and remove the witness? Suppose that you have succeeded in escaping the notice of all, foolish man! What does it profit you not to have a witness,[9] if you have the witness of your own conscience?

And Tully speaks in a manner no less remarkable concerning conscience and God: "Let him

---

1 μετάνοια. The word properly denotes a change of mind, resulting in a change of conduct.

2 Resipiscentiam. [Note the admitted superiority of the Greek.]

3 Pro pietate suâ. Augustine (*De Civitate Dei*, x. 1) explains the use of this expression as applied to God.

4 [Concerning the "planks after shipwreck," see Tertullian, pp. 659 and 666, vol. iii., this series.]

5 Virg., *Æneid*, vi. 128.

6 Male.

7 Supervacuum, i.e., useless, without an object. [P. 171, n. 2.]

8 [May I be pardoned for asking my reader to refer to *The Task* of the poet Cowper (book ii.): "All truth is from the sempiternal source," etc. The concluding lines illustrate the kindly judgment of our author: —

"How oft, when Paul has served us with a text,
Has Epictetus, Plato, Tully, preached!
Men that, if now alive, would sit content
And humble learners of a Saviour's worth,
Preach it who might. Such was their love of truth,
Their thirst of knowledge, and their candour too."

But turn to our author's last sentence in cap. 17, p. 183, *supra*.]

9 Conscium.

remember," he says, "that he has God as a witness, that is, as I judge, his own mind, than which God has given nothing more divine to man."[1] Likewise, in speaking of the just and good man, he says: "Therefore such a man will not dare, not merely to do, but even to think, anything which he would not dare to proclaim." Therefore let us cleanse our conscience, which is open to the eyes of God; and, as the same writer says, "let us always so live as to remember that we shall have to give an account;"[2] and let us reckon that we are looked upon at every moment, not, as he said, in some theatre of the world by men, but from above by Him who is about to be both the judge and also the witness, to whom, when He demands an account of our life, it will not be permitted any one to deny his actions. Therefore it is better either to flee from conscience, or ourselves to open our mind of our own accord, and tearing open our wounds to pour forth destruction; which wounds no one else can heal but He alone who made the lame to walk, restored sight to the blind, cleansed the polluted limbs, and raised the dead. He will quench the ardour of desires, He will root out lusts, He will remove envy, He will mitigate anger. He will give true and lasting health. This remedy should be sought by all, inasmuch as the soul is harassed by greater danger than the body, and a cure should be applied as soon as possible to secret diseases. For if any one has his eyesight clear, all his limbs perfect, and his entire body in the most vigorous health, nevertheless I should not call him sound if he is carried away by anger, swollen and puffed up with pride, the slave of lust, and burning with desires; but I should rather call him sound who does not raise his eyes to the prosperity of another, who does not admire riches, who looks upon another's wife with chaste eye, who covets nothing at all, does not desire that which is another's, envies no one, disdains no one; who is lowly, merciful, bountiful, mild, courteous: peace perpetually dwells in his mind.

That man is sound, he is just, he is perfect. Whoever, therefore, has obeyed all these heavenly precepts, he is a worshipper of the true God, whose sacrifices are gentleness of spirit, and an innocent life, and good actions. And he who exhibits all these qualities offers a sacrifice as often as he performs any good and pious action. For God does not desire the sacrifice of a dumb animal, nor of death and blood, but of man and life. And to this sacrifice there is neither need of sacred boughs, nor of purifications,[3] nor of sods of turf, which things are plainly most vain, but of those things which are put forth from the innermost breast. Therefore, upon the altar of God, which is truly very great,[4] and which is placed in the heart of man, and cannot be defiled with blood, there is placed righteousness, patience, faith, innocence, chastity, and abstinence. This is the truest ceremony, this is that law of God, as it is called by Cicero, illustrious and divine, which always commands things which are right and honourable, and forbids things which are wrong and disgraceful; and he who obeys this most holy and certain law cannot fail to live justly and lawfully. And I have laid down a few chief points of this law, since I promised that I would speak only of those things which completed the character[5] of virtue and righteousness. If any one shall wish to comprise all the other parts, let him seek them from the fountain itself, from which that stream flowed to us.

CHAP. XXV. — OF SACRIFICE, AND OF AN OFFERING WORTHY OF GOD, AND OF THE FORM OF PRAISING GOD.

Now let us speak briefly concerning sacrifice itself. "Ivory," says Plato, "is not a pure offering to God." What then? Are embroidered and costly textures? Nay, rather nothing is a pure offering to God which can be corrupted or taken away secretly. But as he saw this, that nothing which was taken from a dead body ought to be offered to a living being, why did he not see that a corporeal offering ought not to be presented to an incorporeal being? How much better and more truly does Seneca speak: "Will you think of God as great and placid, and a friend to be reverenced with gentle majesty, and always at hand? not to be worshipped with the immolation of victims and with much blood — for what pleasure arises from the slaughter of innocent animals? — but with a pure mind and with a good and honourable purpose. Temples are not to be built to Him with stones piled up on high; He is to be consecrated by each man in his own breast." Therefore, if any one thinks that garments, and jewels, and other things which are esteemed precious, are valued by God, he is altogether ignorant of what God is, since he thinks that those things are pleasing to Him which even a man would be justly praised for despising. What, then, is pure, what is worthy of God, but that which He Himself has demanded in that divine law of His?

There are two things which ought to be offered, the gift[6] and the sacrifice; the gift as a per-

1 *De Offic.*, iii. 10.
2 *Ibid.*, iii. 19.
3 Februis, a word used in the Sabine language for purgations. Others read "fibris," entrails, offered in sacrifice.

4 There is an allusion to the altar of Hercules, called "ara maxima." [Christian philosophy is heard at last among Latins.]
5 Quæ summum fastigium imponerent. The phrase properly means to complete a building by raising the pediment or gable. Hence its figurative use. [See cap 2, p. 164.]
6 Donum, a free-will offering or gift. See Ex. xxv. 2.

petual offering, the sacrifice for a time. But with those who by no means understand the nature of the Divine Being, a gift is anything which is wrought of gold or silver; likewise anything which is woven of purple and silk: a sacrifice is a victim, and as many things as are burnt upon the altar. But God does not make use either of the one or the other, because He is free from corruption, and that is altogether corruptible. Therefore, in each case, that which is incorporeal must be offered to God, for He accepts this. His offering is innocency of soul; His sacrifice praise and a hymn.[1] For if God is not seen, He ought therefore to be worshipped with things which are not seen. Therefore no other religion is true but that which consists of virtue and justice. But in what manner God deals with the justice of man is easily understood. For if man shall be just, having received immortality, he will serve God for ever. But that men are not born except for justice, both the ancient philosophers and even Cicero suspects. For, discussing the Laws,[2] he says: "But of all things which are discussed by learned men, nothing assuredly is of greater importance than that it should be entirely understood that we are born to justice." We ought therefore to hold forth and offer to God that alone for the receiving of which He Himself produced us. But how true this twofold kind of sacrifice is, Trismegistus Hermes is a befitting witness, who agrees with us, that is, with the prophets, whom we follow, as much in fact as in words. He thus spoke concerning justice: "Adore and worship this word, O son." But the worship of God consists of one thing, not to be wicked. Also in that perfect discourse, when he heard Asclepius inquiring from his son whether it pleased him that incense and other odours for divine sacrifice were offered to his father, exclaimed: "Speak words of good omen, O Asclepius. For it is the greatest impiety to entertain any such thought concerning that being of pre-eminent goodness. For these things, and things resembling these, are not adapted to Him. For He is full of all things, as many as exist, and He has need of nothing at all. But let us give Him thanks, and adore Him. For His sacrifice consists only of blessing." And he spoke rightly.[3]

For we ought to sacrifice to God in word; inasmuch as God is the Word, as He Himself confessed. Therefore the chief ceremonial in the worship of God is praise from the mouth of a just man directed towards God.[3] That this, however, may be accepted by God, there is need of humility, and fear, and devotion in the greatest degree, lest any one should chance to place confidence in his integrity and innocence, and thus incur the charge of pride and arrogance, and by this deed lose the recompense of his virtue. But that he may obtain the favour of God, and be free from every stain, let him always implore the mercy of God, and pray for nothing else but pardon for his sins, even though he has none.[4] If he desires anything else, there is no need of expressing it in word to one who knows what we wish; if anything good shall happen to him, let him give thanks; if any evil, let him make amends,[5] and let him confess that the evil has happened to him on account of his faults; and even in evils let him nothing less give thanks, and make amends in good things, that he may be the same at all times, and be firm, and unchangeable, and unshaken. And let him not suppose that this is to be done by him only in the temple, but at home, and even in his very bed. In short, let him always have God with himself, consecrated in his heart, inasmuch as he himself is a temple of God. But if he has served God, his Father and Lord, with this assiduity, obedience, and devotion, justice is complete and perfect; and he who shall keep this, as we before testified, has obeyed God, and has satisfied the obligations of religion and his own duty.

---

[1] [i.e., "the Eucharist," as a sacrifice of praise and thanksgiving. And mark what follows, note 3, *infra*.]

[2] [Nos ad justitiam esse natos.]

[3] [Ps. l. 23.]

[4] i.e., no known sins. Thus the Psalmist prays: "Cleanse thou me from my secret faults." [So St. Paul, 1 Cor. iv. 4, where the archaic "by" = adversus.]

[5] Satisfaciat, "let him make satisfaction by fruits worthy of repentance."

THE DIVINE INSTITUTES

BOOK VII.

OF A HAPPY LIFE.

CHAP. I.—OF THE WORLD, AND THOSE WHO ARE ABOUT TO BELIEVE, AND THOSE WHO ARE NOT; AND IN THIS THE CENSURE OF THE FAITHLESS.

It is well: the foundations are laid, as the illustrious orator says. But we have not only laid the foundations, which might be firm and suitable for the support of the work; but we have raised the entire edifice, with great and strong buildings, almost to the summit. There remains, a matter which is much easier, either to cover or adorn it; without which, however, the former works are both useless and displeasing. For of what avail is it, either to be freed from false religions [1] or to understand the true [2] one? Of what avail, either to see the vanity of false wisdom,[3] or to know what is true?[4] Of what avail is it, I say, to defend that heavenly justice?[5] Of what avail to hold the worship of God [2] with great difficulties, which is the greatest virtue, unless the divine reward of everlasting blessedness attends it? Of which subject we must speak in this book, lest all that is gone before should appear vain and unprofitable: if we should leave this, on account of which they were undertaken, in uncertainty, lest any one should by chance think that such great labours are undertaken in vain; while he distrusts their heavenly reward, which God has appointed for him who shall have despised the present sweet enjoyments of earth in comparison of solitary and unrewarded [6] virtue. Let us satisfy this part of our subject also, both by the testimonies of the sacred writings and also by probable arguments, that it may be equally manifest that future things are to be preferred to those which are present; heavenly things to earthly; and eternal things to those which are temporal: since the rewards of vices are temporal, those of virtues are eternal.

I will therefore set forth the system of the world, that it may easily be understood both when and how it was made by God; which Plato, who discoursed about the making of the world, could neither know nor explain, inasmuch as he was ignorant of the heavenly mystery, which is not learned except by the teaching of prophets and God; and therefore he said that it was created for eternity. Whereas the case is far different, since whatever is of a solid and heavy body, as it received a beginning at some time, so it must needs have an end. For Aristotle, when he did not see how so great a magnitude of things could perish, and wished to escape this objection,[7] said that the world always had existed, and always would exist. He did not at all see, that whatever *material thing* exists must at some time have had a beginning, and that nothing can exist at all unless it had a beginning. For when we see that earth, and water, and fire perish, are consumed, and extinguished, which are clearly parts of the world, it is understood that *that* is altogether mortal the members of which are mortal. Thus it comes to pass, that whatever is liable to destruction must have been produced. But everything which comes within the sight of the eyes must of necessity be material, and capable of dissolution. Therefore Epicurus alone, following the authority of Democritus, spoke truly in this matter, who said that it had a beginning at some time, and that it would at some time perish. Nor, however, was he able to assign any reason, either through what causes or at what time this work of such magnitude should be destroyed. But since God has revealed this to us, and we do not arrive at it by conjectures, but by instruction from heaven, we will carefully teach it, that it may at length be evident to those who are desirous of the truth, that the

---

1 The subject of the first and second books.
2 The subject of the sixth book.
3 The subject of the third book.
4 The subject of the fourth book.
5 The subject of the fifth book.
6 Nuda.

7 Præscriptionem.

philosophers did not see nor comprehend the truth; but that they had so slight a knowledge[1] of it, that they by no means perceived from what source that fragrance[2] of wisdom, which was so pleasant and agreeable, breathed upon them.

In the meantime, I think it necessary to admonish those who are about to read this, that depraved and vicious minds, since the acuteness of their mind is blunted by earthly passions, which weigh down all the perceptions and render them weak, will either altogether fail to understand these things which we relate, or, even if they shall understand them, they will dissemble and be unwilling for them to be true: because they are drawn away by vices, and they knowingly favour their own evils, by the pleasantness of which they are captivated, and they desert the way of virtue, by the bitterness of which they are offended. For they who are inflamed with avarice and a certain insatiable thirst for riches — because, when they have sold or squandered the things in which they delight, they are unable to live in a simple style — undoubtedly prefer that by which they are compelled to renounce their eager desires. Also, they who, urged on by the incitements of lusts, as the poet says,[3]

> "Rush into madness and fire,"

say that we bring forward things plainly incredible; because the precepts about self-restraint wound their ears, which restrain them from their pleasures, to which they have given[4] up their soul, together with their body. But those who, swollen with ambition or inflamed with the love of power, have bestowed all their efforts on the acquisition of honours, will not, even if we should bear the sun himself in our hands, believe that teaching which commands them to despise all power and honour, and to live in humility, and in such humility that they may be able to receive an injury, and if they have received one, be unwilling to return it. These are the men who cry out[5] in any way against the truth with closed eyes. But they who are or shall be of sound mind, that is, not so immersed in vices as to be incurable, will both believe these things, and will readily approach them; and whatever things we say, they will appear to them open, and plain, and simple, and that which is chiefly necessary, true and unassailable.

No one favours virtue but he who is able to follow it; but it is not easy for all to follow it: they can do so whom poverty and want have exercised, and made capable of virtue. For if the endurance of evils is virtue, it follows that they are not capable of virtue who have always lived in the enjoyment of good things; because they have never experienced evils, nor can they endure them, through their long-continued use and desire of good things, which alone they know. Thus it comes to pass that the poor and humble, who are unencumbered, more readily believe God than the rich, who are entangled with many hindrances;[6] yea, rather, in chains and fetters they are enslaved to the nod of desire, their mistress, which has ensnared them with inextricable bonds; nor are they able to look up to heaven, since their mind is bent down to the earth, and fixed on the ground. But the way of virtue does not admit those carrying great burthens. The path is very narrow by which justice leads man to heaven; no one can keep this unless he is unencumbered and lightly equipped. For those wealthy men, who are loaded with many and great burthens, proceed along the way of death, which is very broad, since destruction rules with extended sway. The precepts which God gives for justice, and the things which we bring forward under the teaching of God respecting virtue and the truth, are bitter and as poisons to these. And if they shall dare to oppose these things, they must own themselves to be enemies of virtue and justice. I will now come to the remaining part of the subject, that an end may be put to the work. But this remains, that we should treat of the judgment of God, which will then be established when our Lord shall return to the earth to render to every one either a reward or punishment, according to his desert. Therefore, as we spoke in the fourth book concerning His first advent,[7] so in this book we will relate His second advent, which the Jews also both confess and hope for; but in vain, since He must return to the confusion[8] of those for whose call He had before come. For they who impiously treated Him with violence in His humiliation, will experience Him in His power as a conqueror; and, God requiting them, they will suffer all those things which they read and do not understand; inasmuch as, being polluted with all sins, and moreover sprinkled with the blood of the Holy One, they were devoted to eternal punishment by that very One on whom they laid wicked hands. But we shall have a separate subject against the Jews, in which we shall convict them of error and guilt.

CHAP. II. — OF THE ERROR OF THE PHILOSOPHERS, AND OF THE DIVINE WISDOM, AND OF THE GOLDEN AGE.

Now let us instruct those who are ignorant of the truth. It has been so determined by the

1 Ita leviter odoratos.
2 Odor.
3 Virg., *Georg.*, iii. 244.
4 Adjudicaverunt.
5 Latrant.
6 Impedimentis.
7 [See p. 108, *supra*.]
8 Ad confundendos. Others read "consolandos."

arrangement of the Most High God, that this unrighteous age, having run the course[1] of its appointed times, should come to an end; and all wickedness being immediately extinguished, and the souls of the righteous being recalled to a happy life, a quiet, tranquil, peaceful, in short, golden age, as the poets call it, should flourish, under the rule of God Himself. This was especially the cause of all the errors of the philosophers, that they did not comprehend the system of the world, which comprises the whole of wisdom. But it cannot be comprehended by our own perception and innate intelligence, which they wished to do by themselves without a teacher. Therefore they fell into various and ofttimes contradictory opinions, out of which they had no way of escape,

And they remained fixed in the same mire,

as the comic writer[2] says, since their conclusion does not correspond with their assumptions;[3] inasmuch as they had assumed things to be true which could not be affirmed, and proved without the knowledge of the truth and of heavenly things. And this knowledge, as I have often said already, cannot exist in a man unless it is derived from the teaching of God. For if a man is able to understand divine things, he will be able also to perform them; for to understand is, as it were, to follow in their track. But he is not able to do the things which God does, because he is clothed with a mortal body; therefore he cannot even understand those things which God does. And whether this is possible is easy for every one to measure, from the immensity of the divine actions and works. For if you will contemplate the world, with all the things which it contains, you will assuredly understand how much the work of God surpasses the works of men. Thus, as great as is the difference between divine and human works, so great must be the distance between the wisdom of God and man. For because God is incorruptible and immortal, and therefore perfect because He is everlasting, His wisdom also is perfect, as He Himself is; nor can anything oppose it, because God Himself is subject to nothing.

But because man is subject to passion, his wisdom also is subject to error; and as many things hinder the life of man, so that it cannot be perpetual, so also his wisdom must be hindered by many things: so that it is not perfect in entirely perceiving the truth. Therefore there is no human wisdom, if it strives by itself to attain to the conception and knowledge of the truth; inasmuch as the mind of man, being bound up with a frail body, and enclosed in a dark abode, is neither able to wander at large, nor clearly to perceive the truth, the knowledge of which belongs to the divine nature. For His works are known to God alone. But man cannot attain this knowledge by reflection or disputation, but by learning and hearing from Him who alone is able to know and to teach. Therefore Marcus Tullius,[4] borrowing from Plato the sentiment of Socrates, who said that the time had come for himself to depart from life, but that they before whom he was pleading his cause were still alive, says: Which is better is known to the immortal gods; but I think that no man knows. Wherefore all the sects of philosophers must be far removed from the truth, because they who established them were men; nor can those things have any foundation or firmness which are unsupported by any utterances of divine voices.

CHAP. III. — OF NATURE, AND OF THE WORLD; AND A CENSURE OF THE STOICS AND EPICUREANS.

And since we are speaking of the errors of philosophers, the Stoics divide nature into two parts — the one which effects, the other which affords itself tractable for action. They say that in the former is contained all the power of perception, in the latter the material, and that the one cannot act without the other. How can that which handles and that which is handled be one and the same thing? If any one should say that the potter is the same as the clay, or that the clay is the same as the potter, would he not plainly appear to be mad? But these men comprehend under the one name of nature two things which are most widely different, God and the world, the Maker and the work; and say that the one can do nothing without the other, as though God were mixed up in nature with the world. For sometimes they so mix them together, that God Himself is the mind of the world, and that the world is the body of God; as though the world and God began to exist at the same time, and God did not Himself make the world. And they themselves also confess this at other times, when they say that it was made for the sake of men, and that God could, if He willed it, exist without the world, inasmuch as God is the divine and eternal mind, separate and free from a body. And since they were unable to understand His power and majesty, they mixed Him[5] with the world, that is, with His own work. Whence is that saying of Virgil:[6] —

"A spirit whose celestial flame
Glows in each member of the frame,
And stirs the mighty whole."

1 Decurso temporum spatio. A metaphor taken from the chariot course; *spatium* being used for the length of the course, between the *metæ*, or goals.
2 Ter., *Phorm.*, v. 2.
3 Assumptio: often used for the minor proposition in a syllogism.
4 *Tusc. Disp.*, i. 41.
5 Eum. Others read "eam," referring it to "majestatem."
6 *Æneid*, vi. 726.

What, then, becomes of their own saying, that the world was both made and is governed by the divine providence? For if He made the world, it follows that He existed without the world; if He governs it, it is plain that it is not as the mind governs the body, but as a master rules the house, as a pilot the ship, as a charioteer the chariot. Nor, however, are they mixed with those things which they govern. For if all these things which we see are members of God, then God is rendered insensible by them, since the members are without sensibility, and mortal, since we see that the members are mortal.

I can enumerate how often lands shaken by sudden motions[1] have either opened or sunk down precipitously; how often cities and islands have been overwhelmed by waves, and gone into the deep; marshes have inundated fruitful plains, rivers and pools have been dried up;[2] mountains also have either fallen precipitously, or have been levelled with plains. Many districts, and the foundations of many mountains, are laid waste by latent and internal fire. And this is not enough, if God does not spare His own members, unless it is permitted man also to have some power over the body of God. Seas are built up, mountains are cut down, and the innermost bowels of the earth are dug out to draw forth riches. Why, should I say that we cannot even plough without lacerating the divine body? So that we are at once wicked and impious in doing violence to the members of God. Does God, then, suffer His body to be harassed, and endure to weaken Himself, or permit this to be done by man? Unless by chance that divine intelligence which is mixed with the world, and with all parts of the world, abandoned the first outer aspect[3] of the earth, and plunged itself into the lowest depths, that it might be sensible of no pain from continual laceration. But if this is trifling and absurd, then they themselves were as devoid of intelligence as those are who have not perceived that the divine spirit is everywhere diffused, and that all things are held together by it, not however in such a manner that God, who is incorruptible, should Himself be mixed with heavy and corruptible elements. Therefore that is more correct which they derived from Plato, that the world was made by God, and is also governed by His providence. It was therefore befitting that Plato, and those who held the same opinion, should teach and explain what was the cause, what the reason, for the contriving of so great a work; why or for the sake of whom He made it.

But the Stoics also say the world was made for the sake of men. I hear. But Epicurus is ignorant on what account or who made men themselves. For Lucretius, when he said that the world was not made by the gods, thus spoke:[4]

> "To say, again, that for the sake of men they have willed to set in order the glorious nature of the world"—

then he introduced:—

> "Is sheer folly. For what advantage can our gratitude bestow on immortal and blessed beings, that for our sake they should take in hand to administer aught?"

And with good reason. For they brought forward no reason why the human race was created or established by God. It is our business to set forth the mystery of the world and man, of which they, being destitute, were able neither to reach nor see the shrine of truth. Therefore, as I said a little before, when they had assumed that which was true, that is, that the world was made by God, and was made for the sake of men, yet, since their argument failed them in the consequences, they were unable to defend that which they had assumed. In fine, Plato, that he might not make the work of God weak and subject to ruin, said that it would remain for ever. If it was made for the sake of men, and so made as to be eternal, why then are not they on whose account it was made eternal? If they are mortal on account of whom it was made, it must also itself be mortal and subject to dissolution, for it is not of more value than those for whose sake it was made. But if his argument[5] were consistent, he would understand that it must perish because it was made, and that nothing can remain for ever except that which cannot be touched.

But he who says that it was not made for the sake of men has no argument. For if he says that the Creator contrived these works of such magnitude on His own account, why then were we produced? Why do we enjoy the world itself? what means the creation of the human race, and of the other living creatures? why do we intercept the advantages of others? why, in short, do we grow, decrease, and perish? What reason is implied in our production itself? what in our perpetual succession? Doubtless God wished us to be seen, and to frame, as it were, impressions[6] with various representations of Himself, with which He might delight Himself. Nevertheless, if it were so, He would esteem living creatures as His care, and especially man, to whose command He made all things subject. But with regard to those who say that the world always existed: I omit that point, that itself cannot exist without some beginning, from which they are unable to extricate themselves; but I

1 i.e., earthquakes.
2 Siccaverunt: rarely used in a neuter sense.
3 Primam terræ faciem: as opposed to the inner depths.
4 *De Rer. Nat.*, v. 157-166.
5 Quòd si ratio ei quadraret.
6 Little images, sigilla.

say this, if the world always existed, it can have no systematic arrangement.[1] For what could arrangement have effected in that which never had a beginning? For before anything is done or arranged, there is need of counsel that it may be determined how it should be done; nor can anything be done without the foresight of a settled plan. Therefore the plan precedes every work. Therefore that which has not been made has no plan. But the world has a plan by which it both exists and is governed; therefore also it was made: if it was made, it will also be destroyed. Let them therefore assign a reason, if they can, why it was either made in the beginning or will hereafter be destroyed.

And because Epicurus or Democritus was unable to teach this, he said that it was produced of its own accord, the seeds[2] coming together in all directions; and that when these are again resolved, discord and destruction will follow. Therefore he perverted[3] that which he had correctly seen, and by his ignorance of system entirely overthrew the whole system, and reduced the world, and all things which are done in it, to the likeness of a most trifling dream, if no plan exists in human affairs. But since the world and all its parts, as we see, are governed by a wonderful plan; since the framing of the heaven, and the course of the stars and of the heavenly bodies, which is harmonious[4] even in variety itself, the constant and wonderful arrangement of the seasons, the varied fruitfulness of the lands, the level plains, the defences and heapings up of mountains, the verdure and productiveness of the woods, the most salubrious bursting forth of fountains, the seasonable overflowings of rivers, the rich and abundant flowing[5] in of the sea, the opposite and useful breathing[6] of the winds, and all things, are fixed with the greatest regularity: who is so blind as to think that they were made without a cause, in which a wonderful disposition of most provident arrangement shines forth? If, therefore, nothing at all exists nor is done without a cause; if the providence of the Supreme God is manifest from the disposition of things, His excellency from their greatness, and His power from their government: therefore they are dull and mad who have said that there is no providence. I should not disapprove if they denied the existence of gods with this object, that they might affirm the existence of one; but when they did it with this intent, that they might say that there is none, he who does not think that they were senseless is himself senseless.

1 Rationem.
2 i.e., atoms.
3 Corrupit.
4 Æqualis.
5 Interfusio.
6 Aspiratio.

CHAP. IV. — THAT ALL THINGS WERE CREATED FOR SOME USE, EVEN THOSE THINGS WHICH APPEAR EVIL; ON WHAT ACCOUNT MAN ENJOYS REASON IN SO FRAIL A BODY.

But we have spoken sufficiently on the subject of providence in the first book. For if it has any existence, as appears from the wonderful nature of its works, it must be that the same providence created man and the other animals. Let us therefore see what reason there was for the creation of the human race, since it is evident, as the Stoics say, that the world was made for the sake of men, although they make no slight error in this very matter, in saying it was not made for the sake of man, but of men. For the naming of one individual comprehends the whole human race. But this arises from the fact that they are ignorant that one man only was made by God, and they think that men were produced in all lands and fields like mushrooms. But Hermes was not ignorant that man was both made by God and after the likeness of God. But I return to my subject. There is nothing, as I imagine, which was made on its own account; but whatever is made at all must necessarily be made for some purpose. For who is there either so senseless or so unconcerned as to attempt to do anything at random, from which he expects no utility, no advantage? He who builds a house does not build it merely for this purpose, that it may be a house, but that it may be inhabited. He who builds a ship does not bestow his labour on this account, only that the ship may be visible, but that men may sail in it. Likewise he who designs and forms any vessel does not do it on this account, that he may only appear to have done it, but that the vessel when made may contain something necessary for use. In like manner, other things, whatever are made, are plainly not made superfluously, but for some useful purposes.

It is plain, therefore, that the world was made by God, not on account of the world itself; for since it is without sensibility, it neither needs the warmth of the sun, or light, or the breath of the winds, or the moisture of showers, or the nourishment of fruits. But it cannot even be said that God made the world for His own sake, since He can exist without the world, as He did before it was made; and God Himself does not make use of all those things which are contained in it, and which are produced. It is evident, therefore, that the world was constructed for the sake of living beings, since living beings enjoy those things of which it consists; and that these may live and exist, all things necessary for them are supplied at fixed times. Again, that the other living beings were made for the sake of man, is plain from this, that they are subservient to man, and were given for his protection and service; since, whether they are of the earth or of the water, they do not perceive the system of the world as man does. We must here reply to the philosophers, and especially to Cicero, who says: "Why should God, when He made all things on our account, make so large a quantity of snakes and vipers? why should He scatter so many pernicious things by land and by sea?" A very wide subject for discussion, but it must be briefly touched upon, as in passing. Since man is formed of different and opposing elements, soul and body, that is, heaven and earth, that which is slight and that which is perceptible to the senses, that which is eternal and that which is temporal, that which has sensibility and that which is senseless, that which is endued with light and that which is dark, reason itself and necessity require that both good and evil things should be set before man — good things which he may use, and evil things which he may guard against and avoid.

For wisdom has been given to him on this account, that, knowing the nature of good and evil things, he may exercise the force of his reason in seeking the good and avoiding the evil. For because wisdom was not given to the other animals, they were both defended with natural clothing and were armed; but in the place of all these He gave to man that which was most excellent, reason only. Therefore He formed him naked and unarmed, that wisdom might be both his defence and covering. He placed his defence and ornament not without, but within; not in the body, but in the heart. Unless, therefore, there were evils which he might guard against, and which he might distinguish from good and useful things, wisdom was not necessary for him. Therefore let Marcus Tullius know that reason was either given to man that he might take fishes on account of his own use, and avoid snakes and vipers for the sake of his own safety; or that good and evil things were set before him on this account, because he had received wisdom, the whole force of which is occupied in distinguishing things good and evil.[1] Great, therefore, and right, and admirable is the force, and reason, and power of man, for whose sake God made the world itself and all things, as many as exist, and gave him so much honour that He set him over all things, since he alone could admire the works of God. Most excellently, therefore, does our Asclepiades,[2] in discussing the providence of the Supreme God in that book which he wrote to me, say: "And on this account any one may with good reason think that the divine providence gave the place nearest to itself to him who was able to understand its arrangement. For that is the sun: who so beholds it as to understand why it is the sun, and what amount of influence it has upon the other parts of the system? this is the heaven, who looks up to it? this is the earth, who inhabits it? this is the sea, who sails upon it? this is fire, who makes use of it?" Therefore the Supreme God did not arrange these things on account of Himself, because He stands in need of nothing, but on account of man, who might fitly make use of them.

CHAP. V. — OF THE CREATION OF MAN, AND OF THE ARRANGEMENT OF THE WORLD, AND OF THE CHIEF GOOD.

Let us now assign the reason why He made man himself. For if the philosophers had known this, they would either have maintained those things which they had found to be true, or would not have fallen into the greatest errors. For this is the chief thing; this is the point on which everything turns. And if any one does not possess this, the truth altogether glides away from him. It is this, in short, which causes them to be inconsistent with reason;[3] for if this had shone upon them, if they had known all the mystery[4] of man, the Academy would never have been in entire opposition[5] to their disputations, and to all philosophy. As, therefore, God did not make the world for His own sake, because He does not stand in need of its advantages, but for the sake of man, who has the use of it, so also He made man himself for His own sake. What advantage is there to God in man, says Epicurus, that He should make him for His own sake? Truly, that there might be one who might understand His works; who might be able both to admire with his understanding, and to express with his voice, the foresight displayed in their arrangement, the order of their creation, the power exerted in their completion. And the sum of all these things is, that he should worship God.[6] For he who understands these things worships Him; he follows Him with due veneration as the Maker of all things, He as his true Father, who measures the excellence of His majesty according to the invention, the commencement, and completion of His works.

1 [The parables of nature are admirably expounded by Jones of Nayland. See his *Zoologica Ethica*, his *Book of Nature*, and his *Moral Character of the Monkey*, vols. iii., xi., and xii., *Works*, London, 1801.]

2 Asclepiades was a Christian writer, and contemporary of Lactantius, to whom he wrote a book on the providence of God. [According to Eusebius, a bishop of this name presided at Antioch from A.D. 214 to 220; but this is evidently another.]

3 Illis non quadrare rationem.

4 Sacramentum.

5 De transverso jugulasset. The Academics, affirming that nothing was certain, opposed the tenets of the other philosophers, who maintained their own opinions respectively.

6 [The law of his being is stated in Bacon's words: "Homo naturæ *minister et interpres*," *Nov. Org.*, i. 1. It is his duty to comprehend what he expounds, and to lend his voice to nature in the worship of God. See the *Benedicite*, or "Song of the Three Children," in the apocryphal Bible.]

What more evident argument can be brought forward that God both made the world for the sake of man, and man for His own sake, than that he alone of all living creatures has been so formed that his eyes are directed towards heaven, his face looking towards God, his countenance is in fellowship with his Parent, so that God appears, as it were, with outstretched hand to have raised man from the ground, and to have elevated him to the contemplation of Himself. "What, then," he says, "does the worship paid by man confer on God, who is blessed, and in want of nothing? Or if He gave such honour to man as to create the world for his sake, to furnish him with wisdom, to make him lord of all things living, and to love him as a son, why did He make him subject to death and decay? why did He expose the object of His love to all evils? when it was befitting that man should be happy, as though closely connected with God, and everlasting as He is, to the worship and contemplation of whom he was formed."

Although we have taught these things for the most part in a scattered manner in the former books, nevertheless, since the subject now specially requires it, because we have undertaken to discuss the subject of a happy life, these things are to be explained by us more carefully and fully, that the arrangement made by God, and His work and will, may be known. Though He was always able by His own immortal Spirit to produce innumerable souls, as He produced the angels, to whom there exists immortality without any danger and fear of evils, yet He devised an unspeakable work, in what manner He might create an infinite multitude of souls, which being at first united with frail and feeble bodies, He might place in the midst between good and evil, that He might set virtue before them composed as they were of both natures; that they might not attain to immortality by a delicate and easy course of life, but might arrive at that unspeakable reward of eternal life with the utmost difficulty and great labours. Therefore, that He might clothe them with limbs which were heavy and liable to injury,[1] since they were unable to exist in the middle void, the weight and gravity of the body sinking downwards, He determined that an abode and dwelling-place should first be built for them. And thus with unspeakable energy and power He contrived the surpassing works of the world; and having suspended the light elements on high, and depressed the heavy ones to the depths below, He strengthened the heavenly things, and established the earthly. It is not necessary at present to follow out each point separately, since we discussed them all together in the second book.

Therefore He placed in the heaven lights, whose regularity, and brightness, and motion, were most suitably proportioned to the advantage of living beings. Moreover, He gave to the earth, which He designed as their dwelling-place, fruitfulness for bringing forth and producing various[2] things, that by the abundance of fruits and green herbs it might supply nourishment according to the nature and requirements of each kind. Then, when He had completed all things which belonged to the condition of the world, He formed man from the earth itself, which He prepared for him from the beginning as a habitation; that is, He clothed and covered his spirit with an earthly body, that, being compacted of different and opposing materials, he might be susceptible of good and evil; and as the earth itself is fruitful for the bringing forth of grain, so the body of man, which was taken from the earth, received the power of producing offspring, that, inasmuch as he was formed of a fragile substance, and could not exist for ever, when the space of his temporal life was past, he might depart, and by a perpetual succession renew that which he bore, which was frail and feeble. Why, then, did He make him frail and mortal, when He had built the world for his sake? First of all, that an infinite number of living beings might be produced, and that He might fill all the earth with a multitude; in the next place, that He might set before man virtue, that is, endurance of evils and labours, by which he might be able to gain the reward of immortality. For since man consists of two parts, body and soul, of which the one is earthly, the other heavenly, two lives have been assigned to man: the one temporal, which is appointed for the body; the other everlasting, which belongs to the soul. We received the former at our birth; we attain to the latter by striving, that immortality might not exist to man without any difficulty. That earthly one is as the body, and therefore has an end; but this heavenly one is as the soul, and therefore has no limit. We received the first when we were ignorant of it, this second knowingly; for it is given to virtue, not to nature, because God wished that we should procure life for ourselves in life.

For this reason He has given us this present life, that we may either lose that true and eternal life by our vices, or win it[3] by virtue. The chief good is not contained in this bodily life, since, as it was given to us by divine necessity, so it will again be destroyed by divine necessity. Thus that which has an end does not contain the chief good. But the chief good is contained in that spiritual life which we acquire by ourselves, because it cannot contain evil, or have

[1] Vexabilibus.

[2] Varia. Others read, "fæcunditatem variam generandi."

[3] Mereamur.

an end; to which subject nature and the system of the body afford an argument. For other animals incline towards the ground, because they are earthly, and are incapable of immortality, which is from heaven; but man is upright and looks towards heaven,[1] because immortality is proposed to him; which, however, does not come, unless it is given to man by God. For *otherwise* there would be no difference between the just and the unjust, since every man who is born would become immortal. Immortality, then, is not the consequence[2] of nature, but the reward and recompense of virtue. Lastly, man does not immediately upon his birth walk upright, but at first on all fours,[3] because the nature of his body and of this present life is common to us with the dumb animals; afterwards, when his strength is confirmed, he raises himself, and his tongue is loosened so that he speaks plainly, and he ceases to be a dumb animal. And this argument teaches that man is born mortal; but that he afterwards becomes immortal, when he begins to live in conformity with the will[4] of God, that is, to follow righteousness,[5] which is comprised in the worship of God, since God raised man to a view of the heaven and of Himself. And this takes place when man, purified in the heavenly laver, lays aside[6] his infancy together with all the pollution of his past life, and having received an increase of divine vigour, becomes a perfect and complete man.

Therefore, because God has set forth virtue before man, although the soul and the body are connected together, yet they are contrary, and oppose one another. The things which are good for the soul are evil to the body, that is, the avoiding of riches, the prohibiting of pleasures, the contempt of pain and death. In like manner, the things which are good for the body are evil to the soul, that is, desire and lust, by which riches are desired, and the enjoyments of various pleasures, by which the soul is weakened and destroyed.[7] Therefore it is necessary that the just and wise man should be engaged in all evils, since fortitude is victorious over evils; but the unjust in riches, in honours, in power. For these goods relate to the body, and are earthly; and these men also lead an earthly life, nor are they able to attain to immortality, because they have given themselves up to pleasures which are the enemies of virtue. Therefore this temporal life ought to be subject to that eternal life, as the body is to the soul. Whoever, then, prefers the life of the soul must despise the life of the body; nor will he in any other way be able to strive after that which is highest, unless he shall have despised the things which are lowest. But he who shall have embraced the life of the body, and shall have turned his desires downwards[8] to the earth, is unable to attain to that higher life. But he who prefers to live well for eternity, will live badly[9] for a time, and will be subjected to all troubles and labours as long as he shall be on earth, that he may have divine and heavenly consolation. And he who shall prefer to live well[10] for a time, will live ill to eternity; for he will be condemned by the sentence of God to eternal punishment, because he has preferred earthly to heavenly goods. On this account, therefore, God seeks to be worshipped, and to be honoured by man as a Father, that he may have virtue and wisdom, which alone produce immortality. For because no other but Himself is able to confer that immortality, since He alone possesses it, He will grant[11] to the piety of the man, with which he has honoured God, this reward, to be blessed to all eternity, and to be for ever in the presence of God and in the society of God.

N.B.—The following paragraphs to the end of the chapter are wanting in many MSS., and it is very doubtful whether they were written by Lactantius.

Nor can any one shelter himself under the pretext that the fault belongs to Him who made both good and evil. For why did He will that evil should exist if He hated it? Why did He not make good only, that no one might sin, no one commit evil? Although I have explained this in almost all the former books, and have touched upon it, though slightly, above, yet it must be mentioned repeatedly, because the whole matter turns on this point. For there could be no virtue unless He had made contrary things; nor can the power of good be at all manifest, except from a comparison with evil. Thus evil is nothing else but the explanation of good. Therefore if evil is taken away, good must also be taken away. If you shall cut off

1 [Our author never wearies of this reference to Ovid's beautiful verses. Compare Cowper (*Task*, book v.) as follows:—

"Brutes graze the mountain-top with faces prone
And eyes intent upon the scanty herb
It yields them; or, recumbent on its brow,
Ruminate heedless of the scene outspread
Beneath, beyond, and stretching far away
From inland regions to the distant main.
Not so the mind that has been touched from heaven.
. . . She often holds,
With those fair ministers of light to man
That nightly fill the skies with silent pomp,
Sweet conference," etc.]

2 Sequela.

3 Quadrupes.

4 Ex Deo.

5 [Justitiam sequi. I have substituted *righteousness* for the translator's *justice* here (see c. 25, p. 126, *supra*). Coleridge remarks on the weakness of the latter word. It may be, our author is quoting St. Paul (1 Tim. vi. 11 and 2 Tim. ii.), sectare justitiam, "follow after righteousness."]

6 Exponit.

7 Enervatus exstinguitur.

8 In terram dejecerit.

9 i.e., "in discomfort," liable to the evils of this life.

10 i.e., in comfort and luxury. On the whole passage see John xii. 25: "He that loveth his life shall lose it; and he that hateth his life in this world, shall keep it unto life eternal."

11 Afficiet. Others read "afficit."

your left hand or foot, your body will not be entire, nor will life itself remain the same. Thus, for the due adjustment of the framework of the body, the left members are most suitably joined with the right. In like manner, if you make chessmen [1] all alike, no one will play. If you shall give one colour [2] only to the circus, no one will think it worth while to be a spectator, all the pleasure of the Circensian games being taken away. For he who first instituted the games was a favourer of one colour; but he introduced another as a rival, that there might be a contest, and some partisanship [3] in the spectacle. Thus God, when He was fixing that which was good, and giving virtue, appointed also their contraries, with which they might contend. If an enemy and a fight be wanting, there is no victory. Take away a contest, and even virtue is nothing. How many are the mutual contests of men, and with what various arts are they carried on! No one, however, would be regarded as surpassing in bravery, swiftness, or excellence, if he had no adversary with whom he might contend. And where victory is wanting, there also glory and the reward of victory must be absent together with it. Therefore, that he might strengthen virtue itself by continual exercise, and might make it perfect from its conflict with evils, He gave both together, because each of the two without the other is unable to retain its force. Therefore there is diversity, on which the whole system of truth depends.

It does not escape my notice what may here be urged in opposition by more skilful persons. If good cannot exist without evil, how do you say that, before he had offended God, the first man lived in the exercise of good only, or that he will hereafter live in the exercise of good only? This question is to be examined by us, for in the former books I omitted it, that I might here fill up the subject. We have said above that the nature of man is made up of opposing elements; for the body, because it is earth, is capable of being grasped, of temporary duration, senseless, and dark. But the soul, because it is from heaven, is unsubstantial,[4] everlasting, endued with sensibility, and full of lustre;[5] and because these qualities are opposed to one another, it follows of necessity that man is subject to good and evil. Good is ascribed to the soul, because it is incapable of dissolution; evil to the body, because it is frail. Since, therefore, the body and the soul are connected and united together, the good and the evil must necessarily hold together; nor can they be separated from one another, unless when they (the body and soul) are separated. Finally, the knowledge of good and of evil was given at the same time to the first man; and when he understood this, he was immediately driven from the holy place in which there is no evil; for when he was conversant with that which was good only, he was ignorant that this itself was good. But after that he had received the knowledge of good and evil, it was now unlawful for him to remain in that place of happiness, and he was banished to this common world, that he might at once experience both of those things with the nature of which he had at once become acquainted. It is plain, therefore, that wisdom has been given to man that he may distinguish good from evil — that he may discriminate between things advantageous and things disadvantageous, between things useful and things useless — that he may have judgment and consideration as to what he ought to guard against, what to desire, what to avoid, and what to follow. Wisdom therefore cannot exist without evil; and that first author [6] of the human race, as long as he was conversant with good only, lived as an infant, ignorant of good and evil. But, indeed, hereafter man must be both wise and happy without any evil; but this cannot take place as long as the soul is clothed with the abode of the body.

But when a separation shall have been made between the body and the soul, then evil will be disunited from good; and as the body perishes and the soul remains, so evil will perish and good be permanent. Then man, having received the garment of immortality, will be wise and free from evil, as God is. He, therefore, who wishes that we should be conversant with good only, especially desires this, that we should live without the body, in which evil is. But if evil is taken away, either wisdom, as I have said, or the body, will be taken from man; wisdom, that he may be ignorant of evil; the body, that he may not be sensible of it. But now, since man is furnished with wisdom to know, and a body to perceive, God willed that both should exist alike in this life, that virtue and wisdom may be in agreement. Therefore He placed man in the midst, between both, that he might have liberty to follow either good or evil. But He mingled with evil some things which appear good, that is, various and delightful enjoyments, that by the

[1] Calculi, called also "latrunculi." There were two sets, the one white, the other red or black.

[2] The chariot-drivers in the contests of the circus were distinguished by different colours. Originally there were but two factions or parties, the white and the red; afterwards they were increased to four, the green and the azure being added. Domitian increased the number to six, but this was not in accordance with the usual practice.

[3] Gratia. Thus Pliny, "Tanta gratia, tanta auctoritas in unâ vilissimâ tunicâ." Cf. Juv., *Sat.*, xi. 195. Gibbon thus describes the scene: "The spectators remained in eager attention, their eyes fixed on the charioteers, their minds agitated with hope and fear for the success of the colour which they favoured."

[4] Tenuis.

[5] Illustris.

[6] Princeps.

enticements of these He might lead men to the concealed evil. And He likewise mingled with good some things which appear evil — that is, hardships, and miseries, and labours — by the harshness and unpleasantness of which the soul, being offended, might shrink back from the concealed good. But here the office of wisdom is needed, that we may see more with the mind than with the body, which very few are able to do; because while virtue is difficult and rarely to be found, pleasure is common and public. Thus it necessarily happens that the wise man is accounted as a fool, who, while he seeks good things which are not seen, permits those which are seen to slip from his hands; and while he avoids evils which are not seen, runs into evils which are before the eyes; which happens to us when we refuse neither torture nor death in behalf of the faith, since we are driven to the greatest wickedness, so as to betray the faith and deny the true God, and to sacrifice to dead and death-bearing gods. This is the cause why God made man mortal, and made him subject to evils, although he had framed the world for his sake, namely, that he might be capable of virtue, and that his virtue might reward him with immortality. Now virtue, as we have shown, is the worship of the true God.

CHAP. VI. — WHY THE WORLD AND MAN WERE CREATED. HOW UNPROFITABLE IS THE WORSHIP OF FALSE GODS.

Now let us mark the whole argument by a brief definition.[1] The world has been created for this purpose, that we may be born; we are born for this end, that we may acknowledge the Maker of the world and of ourselves — God; we acknowledge Him for this end, that we may worship Him; we worship Him for this end, that we may receive immortality as the reward of our labours, since the worship of God consists of the greatest labours; for this end we are rewarded with immortality, that being made like to the angels, we may serve the Supreme Father and Lord for ever, and may be to all eternity a kingdom to God. This is the sum of all things, this the secret of God, this the mystery of the world, from which they are estranged, who, following present gratification, have devoted themselves to the pursuit of earthly and frail goods, and by means of deadly enjoyments have sunk as it were in mire and mud their souls, which were born for heavenly pursuits.

Let us now, in the next place, inquire whether there is anything reasonable in the worship of these gods; for if they are many, if they are worshipped only on this account by men, that they may afford them riches, victories, honours, and all things, which are of no avail except for the present; if we are produced without cause — if no providence is employed in the production of men — if we are brought forth by chance for ourselves, and for the sake of our own pleasure — if we are nothing after death, — what can be so superfluous, so empty, so vain, as the affairs of man, and the world itself? which, though it is of incredible magnitude, and constructed with such wonderful arrangement, is nevertheless occupied with trifling subjects. For why should the breathings of the winds put the clouds in motion? Why should lightnings shine forth, thunders roar, or showers fall, that the earth may bring forth its increase, and nourish its various productions? Why, in short, should all nature labour that nothing may be wanting of those things by which the life of man is sustained, if it is vain, if we utterly perish, if there is in us nothing of greater advantage to God? But if it is unlawful to be spoken, and is not to be thought possible, that that which you see to be most in accordance with reason was not established on account of some reason of importance, what reason can there be in these errors of depraved religions, and in this persuasion of philosophers, by which they imagine that souls perish? Assuredly there is none; for what have they to say why the gods so regularly supply to men everything in its season? Is it that we may present to them corn and wine, and the odour of incense, and the blood of cattle? Which things cannot be acceptable to the immortals, because they are perishable; nor can they be of use to beings destitute of bodies, because these things have been given for the use of those possessed of bodies; and yet if they required these things, they could bestow them upon themselves when they wished. Whether, therefore, souls perish or exist for ever, what principle is involved in the worship of the gods, or by whom was the world established? Why, or when, or how long, or how far were men produced, or on what account? Why do they arise, die, succeed one another, are renewed? What do the gods obtain from the worship of those who after death are about to have no existence? What do they perform, what do they promise, what do they threaten, which is worthy of men or of gods? Or if souls remain after death, what do they do or are they about to do respecting them? What need is there to them of a treasure-house of souls? From what source do they themselves arise? How, or why, or whence are they so many? Thus it comes to pass, that if you depart from that sum of things which we comprised above, all system is destroyed, and all things return[2] to nothing.

[1] Circumscriptione.

[2] Revolvantur. Others read "resolvantur."

CHAP. VII. — OF THE VARIETY OF PHILOSOPHERS, AND THEIR TRUTH.

And because the philosophers did not comprehend this main point, they were neither able to comprehend truth, although they for the most part both saw and explained those things of which the main point itself consists. But different persons brought forward all these things, and in different ways, not connecting the causes of things, nor the consequences, nor the reasons, so that they might join together and complete that main point which comprises the whole. But it is easy to show that almost the whole truth has been divided by philosophers and sects. For we do not overthrow philosophy, as the Academics are accustomed to do, whose plan was to reply to everything, which is rather to calumniate and mock; but we show that no sect was so much out of the way, and no philosopher so vain, as not to see something of the truth.[1] But while they are mad with the desire of contradicting, while they defend their own arguments even though false, and overthrow those of others even though true, not only has the truth escaped from them, which they pretended that they were seeking, but they themselves lost it chiefly through their own fault. But if there had been any one to collect together the truth which was dispersed amongst individuals and scattered amongst sects, and to reduce it to a body, he assuredly would not disagree with us. But no one is able to do this, unless he has experience[2] and knowledge of the truth. But to know the truth belongs to him only who has been taught by God. For he cannot in any other way reject the things which are false, or choose and approve of those which are true; but if even by chance he should effect this, he would most surely act the part of the philosopher; and though he could not defend those things by divine testimonies, yet the truth would explain itself by its own light. Wherefore the error of those is incredible, who, when they have approved of any sect, and have devoted themselves to it, condemn all others as false and vain, and arm themselves for battle, neither knowing what they ought to defend nor what to refute; and make attacks everywhere, without distinction,[3] upon all things which are brought forward by those who disagree with them.

On account of these most obstinate contentions of theirs, no philosophy existed which made a nearer approach to the truth, for the whole truth has been comprised by these in separate portions.[4] Plato said[5] that the world was made by God: the prophets[6] speak the same; and the same is apparent from the verses of the Sibyl. They therefore are in error, who have said either that all things were produced of their own accord or from an assemblage of atoms;[7] since so great a world, so adorned and of such magnitude, could neither have been made nor arranged and set in order without some most skilful author, and that very arrangement by which all things are perceived to be kept together and to be governed bespeaks[8] an artificer with a most skilful mind. The Stoics say that the world, and all things which are in it, were made for the sake of men: the sacred writings[9] teach us the same thing. Therefore Democritus was in error, who thought that they were poured forth from the earth like worms, without any author or plan. For the reason of man's creation belongs to a divine mystery; and because he was unable to know this, he drew[10] down man's life to nothing. Aristo asserted that men were born to the exercise of virtue; we are also reminded of and learn the same from the prophets. Therefore Aristippus is deceived, who made man subject to pleasure, that is, to evil, as though he were a beast. Pherecydes and Plato contended that souls were immortal; but this is a peculiar doctrine in our religion. Therefore Dicæarchus was mistaken, together with Democritus, who argued that souls perished with the body and were dissolved. Zeno the Stoic taught that there were infernal regions, and that the abodes of the good were separated from the wicked; and that the former enjoyed peaceful and delightful regions, but that the latter suffered punishment in dark places, and in dreadful abysses of mire: the prophets show the same thing. Therefore Epicurus was mistaken, who thought that that was an invention[11] of the poets, and explained those punishments of the infernal regions, which are spoken of, as happening in this life. Therefore the philosophers touched upon the whole truth, and every secret of our holy religion; but when others denied it, they were unable to defend that which they had found, because the system did not agree[12] with the particulars; nor were they able to reduce to a summary those things which they had perceived to be true, as we have done above.

CHAP. VIII. — OF THE IMMORTALITY OF THE SOUL.

The one chief good, therefore, is immortality, for the reception of which we were originally formed and born. To this we direct our course; human nature regards this; to this virtue exalts us. And because we have discovered this good, it remains that we should also speak of immor-

1 [See Clement, *sparsim*, and notably (cap. 5 of *Stromata*) vol. ii. p. 305, this series.]
2 Veri peritus ac sciens.
3 Sine delectu.
4 Particulatim.
5 In the *Timæus*.
6 Gen. i.; Ps. xxxiii.
7 Minutis seminibus conglobatis.
8 Confitetur.
9 Gen. i.; Ps. viii.; Heb. ii.
10 Deduxit ad nihilum.
11 Figmentum.
12 Singulis ratio non quadravit.

tality itself. The arguments of Plato, although they contribute much to the subject, have little strength to prove and fill up the truth, since he had neither summed up and collected into one the plan of the whole of this great mystery, nor had he comprehended the chief good. For although he perceived the truth respecting the immortality of the soul, yet he did not speak respecting it as though it were the chief good. We, therefore, are able to elicit the truth by more certain signs; for we have not collected it by doubtful surmise,[1] but have known it by divine instruction. Now Plato thus reasoned, that whatever has perception by itself, and always moves, is immortal; for that that which has no beginning of motion is not about to have an end, because it cannot be deserted by itself. But this argument would give eternal existence even to dumb animals, unless he had made a distinction by the addition of wisdom. He added, therefore, that he might escape this common[2] linking together, that the soul of man could not be otherwise than immortal, since its wonderful skill in invention, its quickness in reflection, and its readiness in perceiving and learning, its memory of the past, and its foresight of the future, and its knowledge of innumerable arts and subjects, which other living creatures do not possess, appear divine and heavenly; because of the soul, which conceives such great things, and contains such great things, no origin can be found on earth, since it has nothing of earthly admixture united with it. But that which is ponderous in man, and liable to dissolution, must be resolved into earth; whereas that which is slight and subtle is incapable of division, and when freed from the abode of the body, as from prison, it flies to the heaven, and to its own nature. This is a brief summary of the tenets of Plato, which are widely and copiously explained in his own writings.

Pythagoras also was previously of the same sentiments, and his teacher Pherecydes, whom Cicero reported to have been the first who discoursed respecting the immortality of the soul. And although all these excelled in eloquence, nevertheless in this contest at least, those who argued against this opinion had no less authority; Dicæarchus first, then Democritus, and lastly Epicurus: so that the matter itself, respecting which they were contending, was called into doubt. Finally, Tullius also having set forth the opinions of all these respecting immortality and death, declared that he did not know what was the truth. "Which of these opinions is true," he said, "some God may see."[3] And again he says in another place: "Since each of these opinions had most learned defenders, it cannot be divined what is certainty." But we have no need of divination, since the divinity itself has laid open to us the truth.

CHAP. IX. — OF THE IMMORTALITY OF THE SOUL, AND OF VIRTUE.

By these arguments, therefore, which neither Plato nor any other invented, the immortality of souls can be proved and perceived: which arguments we will briefly collect, since my discourse hastens on to relate the great judgment of God, which will be celebrated on the earth at the approaching end of the world.[4] Before all things, since God cannot be seen by man, lest any one should imagine from this circumstance that God does not exist, because He was not seen by mortal eyes, among other wonderful arrangements[5] He also made many things the power of which is manifest, but the substance is not seen, as the voice, smell, the wind, that by the token and example of these things we might perceive God from His power and operation and works, although He did not fall under the notice of our eyes. What is clearer than the voice, or stronger than the wind, or more forcible than smell? Yet these, when they are borne through the air and come to our senses, and impel them by their efficacy, are not distinguished by the eyesight, but are perceived by other parts of the body. In like manner, God is not to be perceived by us through the sight or other frail sense; but He is to be beheld by the eyes of the mind, since we see His illustrious and wonderful works. For as to those who have altogether denied the existence of God, I should not only refuse to call them philosophers, but even deny them the name of men, who, with a close resemblance to dumb animals, consisted of body only, discerning nothing with their mind, and referring all things to the bodily senses, who thought that nothing existed but that which they beheld with their eyes. And because they saw that adversity befell the wicked, or prosperity happened to the good, they believed that all things were carried on by fortune, and that the world was established by nature, and not by providence.

Hence they at once fell into the absurdities[6] which necessarily followed such a sentiment. But if there is a God who is incorporeal, invisible, and eternal, therefore it is credible that the soul, since it is not seen, does not perish after its departure from the body; for it is manifest that something exists which perceives and is vigorous, and yet does not come into sight.

1 Suspicione.
2 Communitatem.
3 [" We must wait patiently," said Socrates, " until some one, either a god or man, teach us our moral and religious duties, and remove the darkness from our eyes." — *Alcibiad.*, ii., *Opera*, vol. v. p. 101, Bipont.]

4 Appropinquante sæculorum fine.
5 Institutorum miracula.
6 Deliramenta.

But, it is said, it is difficult to comprehend with the mind how the soul can retain its perception without those parts of the body in which the office of perception is contained. What about God? Is it easy to comprehend how He is vigorous without a body? But if they believe in the existence of gods who, if they exist, are plainly destitute of bodies, it must be that human souls exist in the same way, since it is perceived from reason itself, and discernment, that there is a certain resemblance in man and God. Finally, that proof which even Marcus Tullius[1] saw is of sufficient strength: that the immortality of the soul may be discerned from the fact that there is no other animal which has any knowledge of God; and religion is almost the only thing which distinguishes man from the dumb creation. And since this falls to man alone, it assuredly testifies that we may aim at, desire, and cultivate that which is about to be familiar and very near.

Can any one, when he has considered the nature of other animals, which the providence of the Supreme God has made abject, with bodies bending down and prostrated to the earth, so that it may be understood from this that they have no intercourse with heaven, fail to understand that man alone of all animals is heavenly and divine, whose body raised from the ground,[2] elevated countenance, and upright position, goes in quest of its origin, and despising, as it were, the lowliness of the earth, reaches forth to that which is on high, because he perceives that the highest good is to be sought by him in the highest place, and mindful of his condition in which God made him illustrious, looks towards his Maker? And Trismegistus most rightly called this looking a contemplation of God,[3] which has no existence in the dumb animals. Since therefore wisdom, which is given to man alone, is nothing else but the knowledge of God, it is evident that the soul does not perish, nor undergo dissolution, but that it remains for ever, because it seeks after and loves God, who is everlasting, by the impulse of its very nature perceiving either from what source it has sprung, or to what it is about to return. Moreover, it is no slight proof of immortality that man alone makes use of the heavenly element. For, since the nature of the world consists of two elements[4] which are opposed to one another — fire and water — of which the one is assigned to the heaven, the other to the earth, the other living creatures, because they are of the earth and mortal, make use of the element which is earthly and heavy: man alone makes use of fire, which is an element light, rising upward,[5] and heavenly. But those things which are weighty depress to death, and those which are light elevate to life; because life is on high, and death below. And as there cannot be light without fire, so there cannot be life without light. Therefore fire is the element of light and life; from which it is evident that man who uses it is a partaker of an immortal condition, because that which causes life is familiar to him.

The gift of virtue also to man alone is a great proof that souls are immortal. For this will not be in accordance with nature if the soul is extinguished; for it is injurious to this present life. For that earthly life, which we lead in common with dumb animals, both seeks pleasure, by the varied and agreeable fruits of which it is delighted, and avoids pain, the harshness of which, by its unpleasant sensations, injures the nature of living beings, and endeavours to lead them to death, which dissolves the living being. If, therefore, virtue both prohibits man from those goods which are naturally desired, and impels him to endure evils which are naturally avoided, it follows that virtue is an evil, and opposed to nature; and he must necessarily be judged foolish who pursues it, since he injures himself both by avoiding present goods, and by seeking equally evils, without hope of greater advantage. For when it is permitted us to enjoy the sweetest pleasures, should we not appear to be without sense if we should not prefer to live in lowliness, in want, in contempt and ignominy, or not to live at all, but to be tormented with pain, and to die, when from these evils we should gain nothing to compensate us for the pleasure which we have given up? But if virtue is not an evil, and acts honourably, inasmuch as it despises vicious and shameful pleasures, and bravely, inasmuch as it neither fears pain nor death, that it may discharge its duty, therefore it must obtain some greater good than those things are which it despises. But when death has been undergone, what further good can be hoped for except immortality?

CHAP. X. — OF VICES AND VIRTUES, AND OF LIFE AND DEATH.

Let us now in turn pass on to those things which are opposed to virtue, that from these also the immortality of the soul may be inferred. All vices are for a time; for they are excited for the present. The impetuosity of anger is appeased when vengeance has been taken; the pleasure of the body puts an end[6] to lust; desire is destroyed either by the full enjoyment of the ob-

[1] *De Leg.*, i. 8.

[2] [Here again the reference to Ovid's maxim. See pp. 41, 56, and 58, *supra*.]

[3] θεώπιδα. Others read θεωρίαν, i.e., "a contemplation."

[4] [See the most instructive pages of Tayler Lewis again: *Plato against the Atheists*, p. 121.]

[5] Sublime.

[6] Libidinis finis est.

jects which it seeks, or by the excitement of other affections; ambition, when it has gained the honours which it wished for, loses[1] its strength; likewise the other vices are unable to stand their ground and remain, but they are ended by the very enjoyment which they desire. Therefore they withdraw and return. But virtue is perpetual, without any intermission; nor can he who has once taken it up depart from it. For if it should have any interruption,[2] if we can at any time do without it, vices, which always oppose virtue, will return. Therefore it has not been grasped, if it deserts its post, if at any time it withdraws itself. But when it has established for itself a firm abode, it must necessarily be engaged in every act; nor can it faithfully drive away and put to flight vices, unless it shall fortify with a perpetual guard the breast which it inhabits. Therefore the uninterrupted duration[3] of virtue itself shows that the soul of man, if it has received virtue, remains permanent, because virtue is perpetual, and it is the human mind alone which receives virtue. Since, therefore, vices are contrary to virtue, the whole systems must of necessity differ from and be contrary to each other. Because vices are commotions and perturbations of the soul; virtue, on the contrary, is mildness and tranquillity of mind. Because vices are temporary, and of short duration; virtue is perpetual and constant, and always consistent with itself. Because the fruits of vices, that is, pleasures, equally with themselves, are short and temporary, therefore the fruit and reward of virtue are everlasting. Because the advantage of vices is immediate, therefore that of virtue is future.

Thus it happens that in this life there is no reward of virtue, because virtue itself still exists. For as, when vices are completed in their performance, pleasure and their rewards follow; so, when virtue has been ended, its reward follows. But virtue is never ended except by death, since its highest office is in the undergoing of death; therefore the reward of virtue is after death. In fine, Cicero, in his *Tusculan Disputations*,[4] perceived, though with doubt, that the chief good does not happen to man except after death. "A man will go," he says, "with confident spirit, if circumstances shall so happen, to death, in which we have ascertained that there is either the chief good or no evil." Death, therefore, does not extinguish man, but admits him to the reward of virtue. But he who has contaminated himself,[5] as the same writer says, with vices and crimes, and has been the slave of pleasure, he truly, being condemned, shall suffer eternal punishment, which the sacred writings call the second death, which is both eternal and full of the severest torments.[6] For as two lives are proposed to man, of which the one belongs to the soul, the other to the body; so also two deaths are proposed, — one relating to the body, which all must undergo according to nature, the other relating to the soul, which is acquired by wickedness and avoided by virtue. As this life is temporary and has fixed limits, because it belongs to the body; so also death is in like manner temporary and has a fixed end, because it affects the body.

CHAP. XI. — OF THE LAST TIMES, AND OF THE SOUL AND BODY.

Therefore, when the times which God has appointed for death shall be completed, death itself shall be ended. And because temporal death follows temporal life, it follows that souls rise again to everlasting life, because temporal death has received an end. Again, as the life of the soul is everlasting, in which it receives the divine and unspeakable fruits of its immortality; so also its death must be eternal, in which it suffers perpetual punishments and infinite torments for its faults. Therefore things are in this position, that they who are happy in this life, pertaining to the body and the earth, are about to be miserable for ever, because they have already enjoyed the good things which they preferred, which happens to those who adore false gods and neglect the true God. In the next place, they who, following righteousness, have been miserable, and despised, and poor in this life, and have often been harassed with insults and injuries on account of righteousness itself, because virtue cannot otherwise be attained, are about to be always happy, that since they have already endured evils, they may also enjoy goods. Which plainly happens to those who, having despised gods of the earth and frail goods, follow the heavenly religion of God, whose goods are everlasting, as He Himself who gave them. What shall I say of the works of the body and soul? Do not they show that the soul is not subject to death? For, as to the body, since it is itself frail and mortal, whatever works it contrives are equally perishable. For Tullius says that there is nothing which is wrought by the hands of man which is not at some time reduced to destruction, either through injury caused by men, or through length of time, which is the destroyer of all things.

But truly we see that the productions of the mind are immortal. For as many as, devoting themselves to the contempt of present things,

1 Senescit.
2 Intervallum.
3 Perpetuitas.
4 *Tusc. Disp.*, i. 46.
5 *Ibid.*, i. 30.

6 [Tayler Lewis, *Plato*, etc., pp. 294-300; more especially, pp. 318-322.]

have handed down to memory the monuments of their genius and great deeds, have plainly gained by these an imperishable name for their mind and virtue. Therefore, if the deeds of the body are mortal for this reason, because the body itself is mortal, it follows that the soul is shown to be immortal from this, because we see that its productions are not mortal. In the same manner also, the desires of the body and of the soul declare that the one is mortal, the other everlasting. For the body desires nothing except what is temporal, that is, food, drink, clothing, rest, and pleasure; and it cannot desire or attain to these very things without the assent and assistance [1] of the soul. But the soul of itself desires many things which do not extend [2] to the duty or enjoyment of the body; and those are not frail, but eternal, as the fame of virtue, as the remembrance of the name. For the soul even in opposition to the body desires the worship of God, which consists in abstinence from desires and lusts, in the enduring of pain, in the contempt of death. From which it is credible that the soul does not perish, but is separated from the body, because the body can do nothing without the soul, but the soul can do many and great things without the body. Why should I mention that those things which are visible to the eyes, and capable of being touched by the hand, cannot be eternal, because they admit of external violence; but those things which neither come under the touch nor under the sight, but are apparent *only* in their force and method and effect, are eternal because they suffer no violence from without? But if the body is mortal on this account, because it is equally open to the sight and to the touch, therefore the soul is immortal for this reason, because it can be neither touched nor seen.

CHAP. XII. — OF THE SOUL AND THE BODY, AND OF THEIR UNION AND SEPARATION AND RETURN.

Now let us refute the arguments of those who maintain the opposite opinions, which Lucretius has related in his third book. Since, he says, the soul is born together with the body, it must necessarily die with the body. But the two cases are not similar. For the body is solid, and capable of being grasped [3] both by the eyes and the hand; but the soul is slight,[4] and eluding the touch and sight. The body is formed from the earth, and made firm; the soul has in it nothing concrete, nothing of earthly weight, as Plato maintained. For it could not have such great force, such great skill, such great rapidity, unless it derived its origin from heaven. The body, therefore, since it is made up of a ponderous and corruptible element, and is tangible and visible, is corrupted and dies; nor is it able to repel violence, because it comes under the sight and under the touch; but the soul, which by its slightness avoids all touch, can be dissolved by no attack. Therefore, although they are joined and connected together from birth, and the one which is formed of earthly material [5] is, as it were, the vessel of the other, which is drawn out from heavenly fineness, when any violence has separated the two, which separation is called death, then each returns into its own nature; that which was of earth is resolved into earth; that which is of heavenly breath remains fixed, and flourishes always, since the divine spirit is everlasting. In fine, the same Lucretius, forgetting what he asserted, and what dogma he defended, wrote these verses: [6] —

> "That also which before was from the earth passes back into the earth, and that which was sent from the borders of ether is carried again by the quarters of heaven." [7]

But this language was not for him to employ, who contended that souls perished with the bodies; but he was overcome by the truth, and the true system stole upon him unawares. Moreover, that very inference which he draws, that the soul suffers dissolution, that is, that it perishes together with the body, since they are produced together, is both false, and is capable of being turned to the opposite direction. For the body does not perish together with the soul; but when the soul departs it remains entire for many days, and frequently by medical preparations it remains entire for a very long time. For if they both perished together, as they are produced together, the soul would not hastily depart and desert the body, but both would be dispersed alike at one point of time; and the body also, while the breath still remained in it, would dissolve and perish as quickly as the soul departs: yes, truly, the body being dissolved, the soul would vanish, as moisture poured forth from a broken vessel. For if the earthly and frail body after the departure of the soul does not immediately flow away and waste into earth, from which it has its origin, therefore the soul, which is not frail, endures to eternity, since its origin is eternal. He says, since the understanding increases in boys, and is vigorous in young men, and is lessened in the aged, it is evident that it is mortal. First, the soul is not the same thing as the mind; for it is one thing that we live, another that we reflect. For it is the mind of those who are asleep which is at rest,[8] not

[1] Sine nutu et adminiculo animi.
[2] Redundent.
[3] Comprehensibile.
[4] Tenuis.
[5] De terrenâ concretione.
[6] *De Rer. Nat.*, ii. 999.
[7] [Ex ætheris oris. Concerning αἰθήρ consult Lewis, *Plato*, etc., pp. 127–129.]
[8] Sopitur.

the soul; and in those who are mad, the mind is extinguished, the soul remains; and therefore they are not said to be without a soul, but to be deprived of their mind.[1] Therefore the mind, that is, the understanding, is either increased or lessened according to age. The soul is always in its own condition; and from the time when it receives the power of breathing, it remains the same even to the end, until, being sent forth from the confinement of the body, it flies back to its own abode. In the next place, the soul, although inspired by God, yet, because it is shut up in a dark abode of earthly flesh, does not possess knowledge, which belongs to divinity. Therefore it hears and learns all things, and receives wisdom by learning and hearing; and old age does not lessen wisdom, but increases it, if the age of youth has been passed in virtue; and if excessive old age shall have enfeebled the limbs, it is not the fault of the mind if the sight has vanished, if the tongue has become benumbed, if the hearing has grown deaf, but it is the fault of the body. But, it is said, the memory fails. What wonder, if the mind is oppressed by the ruin of the falling house, and forgets the past, not about to be divine on any other condition than if it shall have escaped the prison in which it is confined?

But the soul, he says, is also subject to pain and grief, and loses its senses through drunkenness, whence it is evidently frail and mortal. On this account, therefore, virtue and wisdom are necessary, that both grief, which is contracted by the suffering and the sight of unworthy objects, may be repelled by fortitude, and that pleasure may be overcome, not only by abstaining from drinking, but also from other things. For if it be destitute of virtue, if it be given up to pleasure, and thus rendered effeminate, it will become subject to death, since virtue, as we have shown, is the contriver of immortality, as pleasure is of death. But death, as I have set forth, does not entirely extinguish and destroy, but visits with eternal torments. For the soul cannot entirely perish, since it received its origin from the Spirit of God, which is eternal. The soul, he says, is sensible even of disease of the body, and suffers forgetfulness of itself; and as it grows ill, so also it is often healed. This is therefore the reason why virtue is especially to be used, that the mind — not the soul[2] — may not be harassed by any pain of the body, or undergo oblivion of itself. And since this has its seat in a certain part of the body, when any violence of disease has vitiated that part, it is moved from its place; and as though shaken, it departs from its station, about to return when a cure and health shall have remodelled its abode. For, since the soul is united with the body, if it is destitute of virtue, it grows sick by the contagion of the body, and from sharing its frailty the weakness extends to the mind. But when it shall be disunited from the body it will flourish by itself; nor will it now be assailed by any condition of frailty, because it has laid aside its frail covering. As the eye, he says, when torn out and separated from the body, can see nothing, so also the soul, when separated, can perceive nothing, because it is itself also a part of the body. This is false, and dissimilar to the case supposed; for the soul is not a part of the body, but in the body. As that which is contained in a vessel is not a part of the vessel, and these things which are in a house are not said to be a part of the house; so the mind is not a part of the body, because the body is either the vessel or the receptacle of the soul.

Now, that is a much more empty argument which says that the soul appears to be mortal because it is not quickly sent forth from the body, but gradually unfolds itself from all the members, beginning from the extremity of the feet; as though, if it were eternal, it would burst forth in a single moment of time, which takes place in those who die by the sword. But they who are slain by disease are longer in breathing forth their spirit, so that as the limbs grow cold the soul is breathed forth. For, since it is contained in the material of the blood, as light is in the oil, that material being consumed by the heat of fevers, the extremities of the limbs must grow cold; since the more slender veins are extended into the extremities of the body, and the extreme and smaller streams are dried up when the fountain-spring fails. It must not, however, be supposed that, because the perception of the body fails, the sensibility of the soul is extinguished and perishes. For it is not the soul that becomes senseless when the body fails, but it is the body which becomes senseless when the soul takes its departure, because it draws all sensibility with it. But since the soul by its presence gives sensibility to the body, and causes it to live, it is impossible that it should not live and perceive by itself, since it is in itself both consciousness and life. For as to that which says,

> "But if our mind were immortal, it would not when dying complain so much of its dissolution as it would rejoice in passing abroad and quitting its vesture like a snake,"[3]

I never saw any one who complained of his dissolution in death; but he perhaps had seen some Epicurean philosophizing even in death,

---

[1] Non exanimes, sed dementes vocantur.

[2] [The original must be compared: Ne ullo corporis dolore frangatur et oblivionem sui non anima, sed mens patiatur. For *νοῦς* and *ψυχή*, see Lewis, *ut supra*, pp. 219, etc.]

[3] Lucret., iii. 611.

and with his latest breath discoursing about his dissolution.

How can it be known whether he feels that he is in a state of dissolution, or that he is being set free from the body, when his tongue grows dumb at his departure? For as long as he perceives and has the power of speech, he is not yet dissolved; when he has suffered dissolution, he is now unable either to perceive or to speak, so that either he is not yet able to complain of his dissolution, or he is no longer able. But, it is said, he understands before he undergoes dissolution, that he must undergo it. Why should I mention that we see many of the dying, not complaining that they are undergoing dissolution, but testifying that they are passing out, and setting forth on their journey and walking? and they signify this by gesture, or if they still are able, they express it also by their voice. From which it is evident that it is not a dissolution which takes place, but a separation; and this shows that the soul continues to exist. Other arguments of the Epicurean system are opposed to Pythagoras, who contends that souls migrate from bodies worn out with old age and death, and gain admission [1] into those which are new and recently born; and that the same souls are always reproduced at one time in a man, at another time in a sheep, at another in a wild beast, at another in a bird; and that they are immortal on this account, because they often change their abodes, consisting of various and dissimilar bodies. And this opinion of a senseless man, since it is ridiculous and more worthy of a stage-player than of a school of philosophy, ought not even to have been refuted seriously; for he who does this appears to be afraid lest any one should believe it. Therefore we must pass by those things which have been discussed in behalf of falsehood against falsehood; it is sufficient to have refuted those things which are against the truth.

CHAP. XIII. — OF THE SOUL, AND THE TESTIMONIES CONCERNING ITS ETERNITY.

I have made it evident, as I think, that the soul is not subject to dissolution. It remains that I bring forward witnesses by whose authority my arguments may be confirmed. And I will not now allege the testimony of the prophets, whose system and divination consist in this alone, the teaching that man was created for the worship of God, and for receiving immortality from Him; but I will rather bring forward those whom they who reject the truth cannot but believe. Hermes, describing the nature of man, that he might show how he was made by God, introduced this statement: "And the same out of two natures — the immortal and the mortal — made one nature, that of man, making the same partly immortal, and partly mortal; and bringing this, he placed it in the midst, between that nature which was divine and immortal, and that which was mortal and changeable, that seeing all things, he may admire all things." But some one may perhaps reckon him in the number of the philosophers, although he has been placed among the gods, and honoured by the Egyptians under the name of Mercury, and may give no more authority to him than to Plato or Pythagoras. Let us therefore seek for greater testimony. A certain Polites asked Apollo of Miletus whether the soul remains after death or goes to dissolution; and he replied in these verses: —

> "As long as the soul is bound by fetters to the body, perceiving corruptible sufferings, it yields to mortal pains; but when, after the wasting of the body, it has found a very swift dissolution of mortality, it is altogether borne into the air, never growing old, and it remains always uninjured; for the first-born providence of God made this disposition."

What do the Sibylline poems say? Do they not declare that this is so, when they say that the time will come when God will judge the living and the dead? — whose authority we will hereafter bring forward.[2] Therefore the opinion entertained by Democritus, and Epicurus, and Dicæarchus concerning the dissolution of the soul is false; and they would not venture to speak concerning the destruction of souls, in the presence of any magician, who knew that souls are called forth from the lower regions by certain incantations, and that they are at hand, and afford themselves to be seen by human eyes, and speak, and foretell future events; and if they should thus venture, they would be overpowered by the fact itself, and by proofs presented to them. But because they did not comprehend the nature of the soul, which is so subtle that it escapes the eyes of the human mind, they said that it perishes. What of Aristoxenus, who denied that there is any soul at all, even while it lives in the body? But as on the lyre harmonious sound, and the strain which musicians call harmony, is produced by the tightening of the strings, so he thought that the power of perception existed in bodies from the joining together of the vitals, and from the vigour of the limbs; than which nothing can be said more senseless. Truly he had his eyes uninjured, but his heart was blind, with which he did not see that he lived, and had the mind by which he had conceived that very thought. But this has happened to many philosophers,

[1] Se insinuare.

[2] [" Dies iræ, dies illa, . . .
Teste David *et Sibylla*."
i.e., divine and ethnic oracles alike are full of it. See note 9, p. 116, *supra*. Elucidation V.]

that they did not believe in the existence of any object which is not apparent to the eyes; whereas the sight of the mind ought to be much clearer than that of the body, for perceiving those things the force and nature of which are rather felt than seen.

CHAP. XIV. — OF THE FIRST AND LAST TIMES OF THE WORLD.

Since we have spoken of the immortality of the soul, it follows that we teach how and when it is given to man; that in this also they may see the errors of their perverseness and folly, who imagine that some mortals have become gods by the decrees and dogmas of mortals; either because they had invented arts, or because they had taught the use of certain productions of the earth, or because they had discovered things useful for the life of men, or because they had slain savage beasts. How far these things were from deserving immortality we have both shown in the former books, and we will now show, that it may be evident that it is righteousness alone which procures for man eternal life, and that it is God alone who bestows the reward of eternal life. For they who are said to have been immortalized by their merits, inasmuch as they possessed neither righteousness nor any true virtue, did not obtain for themselves immortality, but death by their sins and lusts; nor did they deserve the reward of heaven, but the punishment of hell, which impends over them, together with all their worshippers. And I show that the time of this judgment draws near, that the due reward may be given to the righteous, and the deserved punishment may be inflicted on the wicked.

Plato and many others of the philosophers, since they were ignorant of the origin of all things, and of that primal period at which the world was made, said that many thousands of ages had passed since this beautiful arrangement of the world was completed; and in this they perhaps followed the Chaldeans, who, as Cicero has related in his first book respecting divination,[1] foolishly say[2] that they possess comprised in their memorials four hundred and seventy thousand years; in which matter, because they thought that they could not be convicted, they believed that they were at liberty[3] to speak falsely. But we, whom the Holy Scriptures instuct to the knowledge of the truth, know the beginning and the end of the world, respecting which we will now speak in the end of our work, since we have explained respecting the beginning in the second book. Therefore let the philosophers, who enumerate thousands of ages from the beginning of the world, know that the six thousandth year is not yet completed, and that when this number is completed the consummation must take place, and the condition of human affairs be remodelled for the better, the proof of which must first be related, that the matter itself may be plain. God completed the world and this admirable work of nature in the space of six days, as is contained in the secrets of Holy Scripture, and consecrated the seventh day, on which He had rested from His works. But this is the Sabbath-day, which in the language of the Hebrews received its name from the number,[4] whence the seventh is the legitimate and complete number. For there are seven days, by the revolutions of which in order the circles of years are made up; and there are seven stars which do not set, and seven luminaries which are called planets,[5] whose differing and unequal movements are believed to cause the varieties of circumstances and times.[6]

Therefore, since all the works of God were completed in six days, the world must continue in its present state through six ages, that is, six thousand years. For the great day of God is limited by a circle of a thousand years, as the prophet shows, who says,[7] "In Thy sight, O Lord, a thousand years are as one day." And as God laboured during those six days in creating such great works, so His religion and truth must labour during these six thousand years, while wickedness prevails and bears rule. And again, since God, having finished His works, rested the seventh day and blessed it, at the end of the six thousandth year all wickedness must be abolished from the earth, and righteousness reign for a thousand years; and there must be tranquillity and rest from the labours which the world now has long endured. But how that will come to pass I will explain in its order. We have often said that lesser things and things of small importance are figures and previous shadowings forth of great things; as this day of ours, which is bounded by the rising and the setting of the sun, is a representation[8] of that great day to which the circuit of a thousand years affixes its limits.[9]

In the same manner also the fashioning of the earthly man held forth to the future the formation of the heavenly people. For as, when all things were completed which were contrived for the use of man, last of all, on the sixth day, He

---

[1] i. 19.
[2] Delirant.
[3] Liberum esse.

[4] The word Sabbath means rest. [He derives it from שֶׁבַע: but one wonders how these divers etymologies came into the use of Gentile believers. Compare vol. ii. Elucidation VIII. p. 443.]
[5] Errantia.
[6] [Efficere *creduntur*. Our author seems to guard himself against affirming the verity of the science of his times.]
[7] Ps. xc. 4; see also 2 Pet. iii. 8.
[8] Speciem gerere.
[9] Determinat. [Compare p. 220, *infra*.]

made man also, and introduced him into this world as into a home now carefully prepared; so now on the great sixth day the true man is being formed by the word of God, that is, a holy people is fashioned for righteousness by the doctrine and precepts of God. And as then a mortal and imperfect man was formed from the earth, that he might live a thousand years in this world; so now from this earthly age is formed a perfect man, that being quickened by God, he may bear rule in this same world through a thousand years. But in what manner the consummation will take place, and what end awaits the affairs of men, if any one shall examine the divine writings he will ascertain. But the voices also of prophets of the world, agreeing with the heavenly, announce the end and overthrow of all things after a short time, describing as it were the last old age of the wearied and wasting world. But the things which are said by prophets and seers to be about to happen before that last ending comes upon the world, I will subjoin, being collected and accumulated from all quarters.

Chap. XV. — Of the Devastation of the World and Change of the Empires.

It is contained in the mysteries of the sacred writings, that a prince of the Hebrews, compelled by want of corn, passed into Egypt with all his family and relatives. And when his posterity, remaining long in Egypt, had increased into a great nation, and were oppressed by the heavy and intolerable yoke of slavery, God smote Egypt with an incurable stroke, and freed His people, leading them through the midst of the sea, when, the waves being cut asunder and parted on either side, the people went over on dry ground. And the king of the Egyptians endeavouring to follow them as they fled, the sea returning to its place, he was cut off, with all his people. And this deed so illustrious and so wonderful, although for the present it displayed to men the power of God, was also a foreshadowing and figure of a greater deed, which the same God was about to perform at the last consummation of the times, for He will free His people from the oppressive bondage of the world. But since at that time the people of God were one, and in one nation only, Egypt only was smitten. But now, because the people of God are collected out of all languages, and dwell among all nations, and are oppressed by those bearing rule over them, it must come to pass that all nations, that is, the whole world, be beaten with heavenly stripes, that the righteous people, who are worshippers of God, may be set free. And as then signs were given by which the coming destruction was shown to the Egyptians, so at the last time wonderful prodigies will take place throughout all the elements of the world, by which the impending destruction may be understood by all nations.

Therefore, as the end of this world approaches, the condition of human affairs must undergo a change, and through the prevalence of wickedness become worse; so that now these times of ours, in which iniquity and impiety have increased even to the highest degree, may be judged happy and almost golden in comparison of that incurable evil. For righteousness will so decrease, and impiety, avarice, desire, and lust will so greatly increase, that if there shall then happen to be any good men, they will be a prey to the wicked, and will be harassed on all sides by the unrighteous; while the wicked alone will be in opulence, but the good will be afflicted in all calumnies and in want. All justice will be confounded, and the laws will be destroyed. No one will then have anything except that which has been gained or defended by the hand: boldness and violence will possess all things. There will be no faith among men, nor peace, nor kindness, nor shame, nor truth; and thus also there will be neither security, nor government, nor any rest from evils. For all the earth will be in a state of tumult; wars will everywhere rage; all nations will be in arms, and will oppose one another; neighbouring states will carry on conflicts with each other; and first of all, Egypt will pay the penalties of her foolish superstitions, and will be covered with blood as if with a river. Then the sword will traverse the world, mowing down everything, and laying low all things as a crop. And — my mind dreads to relate it, but I will relate it, because it is about to happen — the cause of this desolation and confusion will be this; because the Roman name, by which the world is now ruled, will be taken away from the earth, and the government return to Asia; and the East will again bear rule, and the West be reduced to servitude.[1] Nor ought it to appear wonderful to any one, if a kingdom founded with such vastness, and so long increased by so many and such men, and in short strengthened by such great resources, shall nevertheless at some time fall. There is nothing prepared by human strength which cannot equally be destroyed by human strength, since the works of mortals are mortal. Thus also other kingdoms in former times, though they had long flourished, were nevertheless destroyed. For it is related that the Egyptians, and Persians, and Greeks, and Assyrians had the government of the world; and after the destruction of them all, the chief power came to the Romans also. And inasmuch as they excel all other kingdoms in magnitude, with so much

[1] [This could not have been ventured before Constantine's time, and must have been bold even then. 2 Thess. ii. 7. P. 213, *infra*.]

greater an overthrow will they fall, because those buildings which are higher than others have more weight for a downfall.[1]

Seneca therefore not unskilfully divided the times of the Roman city by ages. For he said that at first was its infancy under King Romulus, by whom Rome was brought into being, and as it were educated; then its boyhood under the other kings, by whom it was increased and fashioned with more numerous systems of instruction and institutions; but at length, in the reign of Tarquinius, when now it had begun as it were to be grown up, it did not endure slavery; and having thrown off the yoke of a haughty tyranny, it preferred to obey laws rather than kings; and when its youth was terminated by the end of the Punic war, then at length with confirmed strength it began to be manly.[2] For when Carthage was taken away, which was long its rival in power, it stretched out its hands by land and sea over the whole world, until, having subdued all kings and nations, when the materials[3] for war now failed, it abused its strength, by which it destroyed itself. This was its first old age, when, lacerated by civil wars and oppressed by intestine evil, it again fell back to the government of a single ruler, as it were revolving to a second infancy.[4] For, having lost the liberty which it had defended under the guidance and authority of Brutus, it so grew old, as though it had no strength to support itself, unless it depended on the aid of its rulers. But if these things are so, what remains, except that death follow old age? And that it will so come to pass, the predictions of the prophets briefly announce under the cover[5] of other names, so that no one can easily understand them. Nevertheless the Sibyls openly say that Rome is doomed to perish, and that indeed by the judgment of God, because it held His name in hatred; and being the enemy of righteousness, it destroyed the people who kept[6] the truth. Hystaspes also, who was a very ancient king of the Medes, from whom also the river which is now called Hydaspes received its name, handed down to the memory of posterity a wonderful dream upon the interpretation of a boy who uttered divinations, announcing long before the founding of the Trojan nation, that the Roman empire and name would be taken away from the world.

CHAP. XVI. — OF THE DEVASTATION OF THE WORLD, AND ITS PROPHETIC OMENS.[7]

But, lest any one should think this incredible, I will show how it will come to pass. First, the kingdom will be enlarged, and the chief power, dispersed among many and divided,[8] will be diminished. Then civil discords will perpetually be sown; nor will there be any rest from deadly wars, until ten kings arise at the same time, who will divide the world, not to govern, but to consume it. These, having increased their armies to an immense extent, and having deserted the cultivation of the fields, which is the beginning of overthrow and disaster, will lay waste and break in pieces and consume all things. Then a most powerful enemy will suddenly arise against him from the extreme boundaries of the northern region, who, having destroyed three of that number who shall then be in possession of Asia, shall be admitted into alliance by the others, and shall be constituted prince of all. He shall harass the world with an intolerable rule; shall mingle things divine and human; shall contrive things impious to relate, and detestable; shall meditate new designs in his breast, that he may establish the government for himself: he will change the laws, and appoint his own; he will contaminate, plunder, spoil, and put to death. And at length, the name being changed and the seat of government being transferred, confusion and the disturbance of mankind will follow. Then, in truth, a detestable and abominable time shall come, in which life shall be pleasant to none of men.

Cities shall be utterly overthrown, and shall perish; not only by fire and the sword, but also by continual earthquakes and overflowings of waters, and by frequent diseases and repeated famines. For the atmosphere will be tainted, and become corrupt and pestilential — at one time by unseasonable rains, at another by barren drought, now by colds, and now by excessive heats. Nor will the earth give its fruit to man: no field, or tree, or vine will produce anything; but after they have given the greatest hope in the blossom, they will fail in the fruit. Fountains also shall be dried up, together with the rivers; so that there shall not be a sufficient supply for drinking; and waters shall be changed into blood or bitterness. On account of these things, beasts shall fail on the land, and birds in the air, and fishes in the sea. Wonderful prodigies also in heaven shall confound the minds of men with the greatest terrors, and the trains of comets, and the darkness of the sun, and the colour of the moon, and the gliding of the falling stars. Nor, however, will these things take place in the accustomed manner; but there will suddenly appear stars unknown and unseen by the eyes; the sun will be perpetually darkened, so that there will be scarcely any distinction between the night and the day; the moon will now fail, not for three hours only, but overspread with perpetual blood, will go through extraordinary movements, so that

1 [The Colosseum and its traditions may have influenced our author in this passage. See vol. iii. p. 108, *supra*.]
2 Juvenescere.
3 Materia
4 [See p 169, notes 1, 2, *supra*.]
5 Sub ambage; properly a "circumlocution."
6 Alumnum veritatis. [P. 212, note 1, *supra*.]
7 Prodigiis. [These primitive interpretations of Daniel and St. John may be compared with the expositions of Victorinus, *infra*.]

8 Concisa.

it will not be easy for man to ascertain the courses of the heavenly bodies or the system of the times; for there will either be summer in the winter, or winter in the summer. Then the year will be shortened, and the month diminished, and the day contracted into a short space; and stars shall fall in great numbers, so that all the heaven will appear dark without any lights. The loftiest mountains also will fall, and be levelled with the plains; the sea will be rendered unnavigable.

And that nothing may be wanting to the evils of men and the earth, the trumpet shall be heard from heaven, which the Sibyl foretells in this manner: —

"The trumpet from heaven shall utter its wailing voice."

And then all shall tremble and quake at that mournful sound.[1] But then, through the anger of God against the men who have not known righteousness, the sword and fire, famine and disease, shall reign; and, above all things, fear always overhanging. Then they shall call upon God, but He will not hear them; death shall be desired, but it will not come; not even shall night give rest to their fear, nor shall sleep approach to their eyes, but anxiety and watchfulness shall consume the souls of men; they shall deplore and lament, and gnash their teeth; they shall congratulate the dead, and bewail the living. Through these and many other evils there shall be desolation on the earth, and the world shall be disfigured and deserted, which is thus expressed in the verses of the Sibyl: —

"The world shall be despoiled of beauty, through the destruction of men."

For the human race will be so consumed, that scarcely the tenth part of men will be left; and from whence a thousand had gone forth, scarcely a hundred will go forth. Of the worshippers of God also, two parts will perish; and the third part, which shall have been proved, will remain.

CHAP. XVII. — OF THE FALSE PROPHET, AND THE HARDSHIPS OF THE RIGHTEOUS, AND HIS DESTRUCTION.

But I will more plainly set forth the manner in which this happens. When the close of the times draws nigh, a great prophet shall be sent from God to turn men to the knowledge of God, and he shall receive the power of doing wonderful things.[2] Wherever men shall not hear him, he will shut up the heaven, and cause it to withhold its rains; he will turn their water into blood, and torment them with thirst and hunger; and if any one shall endeavour to injure him, fire shall come forth out of his mouth, and shall burn that man. By these prodigies and powers he shall turn many to the worship of God; and when his works shall be accomplished, another king shall arise out of Syria, born from an evil spirit, the overthrower and destroyer of the human race, who shall destroy that which is left by the former evil, together with himself. He shall fight against the prophet of God, and shall overcome, and slay him, and shall suffer him to lie unburied; but after the third day he shall come to life again; and while all look on and wonder, he shall be caught up into heaven. But that king will not only be most disgraceful in himself, but he will also be a prophet of lies; and he will constitute and call himself God, and will order himself to be worshipped as the Son of God; and power will be given him to do signs and wonders, by the sight of which he may entice men to adore him. He will command fire to come down from heaven, and the sun to stand and leave his course, and an image to speak; and these things shall be done at his word, — by which miracles[3] many even of the wise shall be enticed by him. Then he will attempt to destroy the temple of God, and persecute the righteous people; and there will be distress and tribulation,[4] such as there never has been from the beginning of the world.

As many as shall believe him and unite themselves to him, shall be marked by him as sheep; but they who shall refuse his mark will either flee to the mountains, or, being seized, will be slain with studied[5] tortures. He will also enwrap righteous men with the books of the prophets, and thus burn them; and power will be given him to desolate[6] the whole earth for forty-two months. That will be the time in which righteousness shall be cast out, and innocence be hated; in which the wicked shall prey upon the good as enemies; neither law, nor order, nor military discipline shall be preserved; no one shall reverence hoary locks, nor recognise the duty of piety, nor pity sex or infancy; all things shall be confounded and mixed together against right, and against the laws of nature. Thus the earth shall be laid waste, as though by one common robbery. When these things shall so happen, then the righteous and the followers of truth shall separate themselves from the wicked, and flee into solitudes. And when he hears of this, the impious king, inflamed with anger, will come with a great army, and bringing up all his forces, will surround all the mountain in which the righteous shall be situated, that he may seize them. But they, when they shall see themselves

[1] [P. 210, note 2, *supra*. Tuba spargens mirum sonum.]

[2] [A final apparition of Elijah was anticipated by primitive believers, who regarded Mal. i. 5 as only partially fulfilled in the Baptist and the typical judgment of Jerusalem and the Jews under Vespasian. See Enoch and Elias, vol. v. p. 213; also iii. 591.]

[3] Rev. xiii.; 2 Thess. ii.

[4] Pressura et contritio.

[5] Exquisitis cruciatibus.

[6] Dan. vii.; Rev. ii.

to be shut in on all sides and besieged, will call upon God with a loud voice, and implore the aid of heaven; and God shall hear them, and send from heaven a great king to rescue and free them, and destroy all the wicked with fire and sword.

CHAP. XVIII. — OF THE FORTUNES OF THE WORLD AT THE LAST TIME, AND OF THE THINGS FORETOLD BY THE SOOTHSAYERS.

That these things will thus take place, all the prophets have announced from the inspiration of God, and also the soothsayers at the instigation of the demons. For Hystaspes, whom I have named above, having described the iniquity of this last time, says that the pious and faithful, being separated from the wicked, will stretch forth their hands to heaven with weeping and mourning, and will implore the protection of Jupiter: that Jupiter will look to the earth, and hear the voices of men, and will destroy the wicked. All which things are true except one, that he attributed to Jupiter those things which God will do. But that also was withdrawn from the account, not without fraud on the part of the demons, viz., that the Son of God would then be sent, who, having destroyed all the wicked, would set at liberty the pious. Which, however, Hermes did not conceal. For in that book which is entitled the *Complete Treatise*, after an enumeration of the evils concerning which we have spoken, he added these things: "But when these things thus come to pass, then He who is Lord, and Father, and God, and the Creator of the first and one God, looking upon what is done, and opposing to the disorder His own will, that is, goodness, and recalling the wandering and cleansing wickedness, partly inundating it with much water, and partly burning it with most rapid fire, and sometimes pressing it with wars and pestilences, He brought His world to its ancient state and restored it." The Sibyls also show that it would not be otherwise than that the Son of God should be sent by His supreme Father, to set free the righteous from the hands of the wicked, and to destroy the unrighteous, together with their cruel tyrants. One of whom thus wrote: —

"He shall come also, wishing to destroy the city of the blest; and a king sent against him from the gods shall slay all the great kings and chief men: then judgment shall thus come from the Immortal to men."

Also another Sibyl: —

"And then God shall send a king from the sun, who shall cause all the earth to cease from disastrous war."

And again another: —

"He will take away the intolerable yoke of slavery which is placed on our neck, and he will do away with impious laws and violent chains."

CHAP. XIX. — OF THE ADVENT OF CHRIST TO JUDGMENT, AND OF THE OVERCOMING OF THE FALSE PROPHET.

The world therefore being oppressed, since the resources of men shall be insufficient for the overthrow of a tyranny of immense strength, inasmuch as it will press upon the captive world with great armies of robbers, that calamity so great will stand in need of divine assistance. Therefore God, being aroused both by the doubtful danger and by the wretched lamentation of the righteous, will immediately send a deliverer. Then the middle of the heaven shall be laid open in the dead and darkness of the night, that the light of the descending God may be manifest in all the world as lightning: of which the Sibyl spoke in these words: —

"When He shall come, there will be fire and darkness in the midst of the black night."

This is the night which is celebrated by us in watchfulness on account of the coming of our King and God:[1] of which night there is a twofold meaning; because in it He then received life when He suffered, and hereafter He is about to receive the kingdom of the world. For He is the Deliverer, and Judge, and Avenger, and King, and God, whom we call Christ, who before He descends will give this sign: There shall suddenly fall from heaven a sword, that the righteous may know that the leader of the sacred warfare is about to descend; and He shall descend with a company of angels to the middle of the earth, and there shall go before Him an unquenchable fire, and the power of the angels shall deliver into the hands of the just that multitude which has surrounded the mountain, and they shall be slain from the third hour until the evening, and blood shall flow like a torrent; and all his forces being destroyed, the wicked one shall alone escape, and his power shall perish from him.

Now this is he who is called Antichrist; but he shall falsely call himself Christ, and shall fight against the truth, and being overcome shall flee; and shall often renew the war, and often be conquered, until in the fourth battle, all the wicked being slain, subdued, and captured, he shall at length pay the penalty of his crimes. But other princes also and tyrants who have harassed the world, together with him, shall be led in chains to the king; and he shall rebuke them, and reprove them, and upbraid them with their crimes, and condemn them, and consign them to deserved tortures. Thus, wickedness being extinguished and impiety suppressed, the world will be at rest, which having been subject

[1] [Not the eve of Easter, but that of the Nativity. This corroborates St. Chrysostom's testimony concerning the observance of that feast in the West. See *Opp.*, Serm. 287, tom. v. 804.]

to error and wickedness for so many ages, endured dreadful slavery. No longer shall gods made by the hands be worshipped; but the images being thrust out from their temples and couches, shall be given to the fire, and shall be burnt, together with their wonderful gifts: which also the Sibyl, in accordance with the prophets, announced as about to take place: —

> "But mortals shall break in pieces the images and all the wealth."

The Erythræan Sibyl also made the same promise: —

> "And the works made by the hand of the gods shall be burnt up."

CHAP. XX. — OF THE JUDGMENT OF CHRIST, OF CHRISTIANS, AND OF THE SOUL.

After these things the lower regions shall be opened, and the dead shall rise again, on whom the same King and God shall pass judgment, to whom the supreme Father shall give the great power both of judging and of reigning. And respecting this judgment and reign, it is thus found in the Erythræan Sibyl: —

> "When this shall receive its fated accomplishment, and the judgment of the immortal God shall now come to mortals, the great judgment shall come upon men, and the beginning."

Then in another: —

> "And then the gaping earth shall show a Tartarean chaos; and all kings shall come to the judgment-seat of God."

And in another place in the same: —

> "Rolling along the heavens, I will open the caverns of the earth; and then I will raise the dead, loosing fate and the sting of death; and afterwards I will call them into judgment, judging the life of pious and impious men."

Not all men, however, shall then be judged by God, but those only who have been exercised in the religion of God. For they who have not known God, since sentence cannot be passed upon them for their acquittal, are already judged and condemned, since the Holy Scriptures testify that the wicked shall not arise to judgment.[1] Therefore they who have known God shall be judged, and their deeds, that is, their evil works, shall be compared and weighed against their good ones: so that if those which are good and just are more [2] and weighty, they may be given to a life of blessedness; but if the evil exceed, they may be condemned to punishment. Here, perhaps, some one will say, If the soul is immortal, how is it represented as capable of suffering, and sensible of punishment? For if it shall be punished on account of its deserts, it is plain that it will be sensible of pain, and even of death. If it is not liable to death, not even to pain, it follows that it is not capable of suffering.

This question or argument is thus met by the Stoics: that the souls of men continue to exist, and are not annihilated [3] by the intervention of death: that the souls, moreover, of those who have been just, being pure, and incapable of suffering, and happy, return to the heavenly abodes from which they had their origin, or are borne to some happy plains, where they may enjoy wonderful pleasures; but that the wicked, since they have defiled themselves with evil passions, have a kind of middle nature, between that of an immortal and a mortal, and have something of weakness, from the contagion of the flesh; and being enslaved to its desires and lusts, they contract an indelible stain and earthly blot; and when this has become entirely inherent through length of time, souls are given over to its nature, so that, though they cannot altogether be extinguished, inasmuch as they are from God, nevertheless they become liable to torment through the taint of the body, which being burnt in by means of sins, produces a feeling of pain. Which sentiment is thus expressed by the poet: [4] —

> Nay, when at last the life has fled,
> And left the body cold and dead,
> E'en then there passes not away
> The painful heritage of clay:
> Full many a long contracted stain
> Perforce must linger deep in grain.
> So penal sufferings they endure
> For ancient crime, to make them pure."

These things are near to the truth.[5] For the soul, when separated from the body, is, as the same poet says,[6] such as

> "No vision of the drowsy night,
> No airy current half so light,"

because it is a spirit, and by its very slightness incapable of being perceived, but only by us who are corporeal; but capable of being perceived by God, since it belongs to Him to be able to do all things.

CHAP. XXI. — OF THE TORMENTS AND PUNISHMENTS OF SOULS.

First of all, therefore, we say that the power of God is so great, that He perceives even incorporeal things, and manages them as He will.

---

1 The reference is to Ps. i. 5: "The ungodly shall not stand in the judgment." They shall indeed arise, but it will be to "the resurrection of damnation." See Dan. xii. 2; John v. 28, 29; Acts xxiv. 15.

2 Good and bad actions will not be compared by reference to number: "For whosoever shall keep the whole law, and yet offend in one point, he is guilty of all." — Jas. ii. 10. [The figure, however, is not dissimilar in Job xxxi. 6. We must be judged by our works, though saved by faith in Christ.]

3 In nihilum resolvi.

4 Virg., *Æneid*, vi. 735.

5 [1 Cor. iii. 13–15. An *approximation* to this truth is recognised by our author in a heathen poet. See p. 217, n. 2.]

6 Virg., *Æneid*, vi. 702.

For even angels fear God, because they can be chastised by Him in some unspeakable manner; and devils dread Him, because they are tormented and punished by Him. What wonder is it, therefore, if souls, though they are immortal, are nevertheless capable of suffering at the hand of God? For since they have nothing solid and tangible in themselves, they can suffer no violence from solid and corporeal beings; but because they live in their spirits only, they are capable of being handled by God alone, whose energy and substance is spiritual. But, however, the sacred writings inform us in what manner the wicked are to undergo punishment. For because they have committed sins in their bodies, they will again be clothed with flesh, that they may make atonement in their bodies; and yet it will not be that flesh with which God clothed man, like this our earthly body, but indestructible, and abiding for ever, that it may be able to hold out against tortures and everlasting fire, the nature of which is different from this fire of ours, which we use for the necessary purposes of life, and which is extinguished unless it be sustained by the fuel of some material. But that divine fire always lives by itself, and flourishes without any nourishment; nor has it any smoke mixed with it, but it is pure and liquid, and fluid, after the manner of water. For it is not urged upwards by any force, as our fire, which the taint of the earthly body, by which it is held, and smoke intermingled, compels to leap forth, and to fly upwards to the nature of heaven, with a tremulous movement.[1]

The same divine fire, therefore, with one and the same force and power, will both burn the wicked and will form them again, and will replace as much as it shall consume of their bodies, and will supply itself with eternal nourishment: which the poets transferred to the vulture of Tityus. Thus, without any wasting of bodies, which regain their substance, it will only burn and affect them with a sense of pain. But when He shall have judged the righteous, He will also try them with fire. Then they whose sins shall exceed either in weight or in number, shall be scorched by the fire and burnt:[2] but they whom full justice and maturity of virtue has imbued will not perceive that fire; for they have something of God in themselves which repels and rejects the violence of the flame. So great is the force of innocence, that the flame shrinks from it without doing harm; which has received from God this power, that it burns the wicked, and is under the command of the righteous. Nor, however, let any one imagine that souls are immediately judged after death. For all are detained in one and a common place of confinement, until the arrival of the time in which the great Judge shall make an investigation of their deserts.[3] Then they whose piety shall have been approved of will receive the reward of immortality; but they whose sins and crimes shall have been brought to light will not rise again, but will be hidden in the same darkness with the wicked, being destined to certain punishment.

CHAP. XXII. — OF THE ERROR OF THE POETS, AND THE RETURN OF THE SOUL FROM THE LOWER REGIONS.

Some imagine that these things are figments of the poets, not knowing whence the poets received them, and they say that these things are impossible; and it is no wonder that it so appears to them. For the matter is related by the poets in a manner which is different from the truth; for although they are much more ancient than the historians and orators, and other kinds of writers, yet because they were ignorant of the secret of the divine mystery, and mention of a future resurrection had reached them by an obscure rumour, yet they handed it down, when carelessly and lightly heard, after the manner of a feigned story. And yet they also testified that they did not follow a sure authority, but mere opinion, as Maro, who says,[4]

> "What ear has heard let tongue make known."

Although, therefore, they have partly corrupted the secrets of the truth, yet the matter itself is found to be more true, because it partly agrees with the prophets: which is sufficient for us as a proof of the matter. Yet some reason is contained in their error. For when the prophets proclaimed with continual announcements that the Son of God was about to judge the dead, and this announcement did not escape their notice; inasmuch as they supposed that there was no other ruler of heaven but Jupiter, they reported that the son of Jupiter was king in the lower regions, but not Apollo, or Liber, or Mercurius, who are supposed to be gods of heaven, but one who was both mortal and just, either Minos, or Æacus, or Rhadamanthus. Therefore with poetic licence they corrupted that which they had received; or, the opinion being scattered through different mouths and various discourses, changed the truth. For inasmuch as they foretold that, when a thousand years had been passed in the lower regions, they should again be restored to life, as Maro said:[5] —

> "All these, when centuries ten times told
> The wheel of destiny have rolled,

[1] Cum trepidatione mobili. [See vol. vi. p. 375, note 1.]

[2] Perstringentur igni atque amburentur. [See p. 216, n. 5, *supra*.] This idea of passing through flames of the final judgment has in it nothing in common with "purgatory" as a *place* and as a punishment from which admission into heaven may be gained *before* judgment.]

[3] [See vol. iii. p. 59, *supra*, Elucidation X.]

[4] Virg., *Æn.*, vi. 266.

[5] *Ibid.*, 748.

The voice divine from far and wide
Calls up to Lethe's river side,
That earthward they may pass once more,
Remembering not the things before,
And with a blind propension yearn
To fleshly bodies to return:"

this matter escaped their notice, that the dead will rise again, not after a thousand years from their death, but that, when again restored to life, they may reign with God a thousand years. For God will come, that, having cleansed the world from all defilement, He may restore the souls of the righteous to their renewed bodies, and raise them to everlasting blessedness. Therefore the other things are true, except the water of oblivion, which they feigned on this account, that no one might make this objection: why, therefore, did they not remember that they were at one time alive, or who they were, or what things they accomplished? But nevertheless it is not thought probable, and the whole matter is rejected, as though licentiously and fabulously invented. But when we affirm the doctrine of the resurrection, and teach that souls will return to another life, not forgetful of themselves, but possessed of the same perception and figure, we are met with this objection: So many ages have now passed; what individual ever arose from the dead, that through his example we may believe it to be possible? But the resurrection cannot take place while unrighteousness still prevails. For in this world men are slain by violence, by the sword, by ambush, by poisons, and are visited with injuries, with want, with imprisonment, with tortures, and with proscriptions. Add to this that righteousness is hated, that all who wish to follow God are not only held in hatred, but are harassed with all reproaches, and are tormented by manifold kinds of punishments, and are driven to the impious worship of gods made with hands, not by reason or truth, but by dreadful laceration of their bodies.

Ought men therefore to rise again to these same things, or to return to a life in which it is impossible for them to be safe? Since the righteous, then, are so lightly esteemed, and so easily taken away, what can we suppose would have happened if any one returning from the dead had recovered life by a recovery[1] of his former condition? He would assuredly be taken away from the eyes of men, lest, if he were seen or heard, all men with one accord should leave the gods and betake themselves to the worship and religion of the one God. Therefore it is necessary that the resurrection should take place once only when evil shall have been taken away, since it is befitting that those who have risen again should neither die any more, nor be injured in any way, that they may be able to pass a happy life whose death has been annulled.[2] But the poets, knowing that this life abounds with all evils, introduced the river of oblivion, lest the souls, remembering their labours and evils, should refuse to return to the upper regions; whence Virgil says:[3] —

"O Father! and can thought conceive
That happy souls this realm would leave,
And seek the upper sky,
With sluggish clay to reunite?
This dreadful longing for the light,
Whence comes it, say, and why?"

For they did not know how or when it must take place; and therefore they supposed that souls were born again, and that they returned afresh to the womb, and went back to infancy. Whence also Plato, while discussing the nature of the soul, says that it may be known from this that souls are immortal and divine, because in boys minds are pliant, and easy of perception, and because they so quickly comprehend the subjects which they learn, that they appear not then to be learning for the first time, but to be recalling them to mind and recollecting them: in which matter the wise man most foolishly believed the poets.

CHAP. XXIII. — OF THE RESURRECTION OF THE SOUL, AND THE PROOFS OF THIS FACT.

Therefore they will not be born again, which is impossible, but they will rise again, and be clothed by God with bodies, and will remember their former life, and all its actions; and being placed in the possession of heavenly goods, and enjoying the pleasure of innumerable resources, they will give thanks to God in His immediate presence, because He has destroyed all evil, and because He has raised them to His kingdom and to perpetual life. Respecting which resurrection the philosophers also attempted to speak as corruptly as the poets. For Pythagoras asserted that souls passed into new bodies; but foolishly, that they passed from men into cattle, and from cattle into men; and that he himself was restored from Euphorbus. Chrysippus says better, whom Cicero speaks of as supporting the portico of the Stoics, who, in the books which he wrote concerning providence, when he was speaking of the renewing of the world, introduced these words: "But since this is so, it is evident that nothing is impossible, and that we, after our death, when certain periods of time have again come round, are restored to this state in which we now are." But let us return from human to divine things. The Sibyl thus speaks: —

"For the whole race of mortals is hard to be believed; but when the judgment of the world and of mortals shall now come, which God Himself shall

[1] Postliminio. For the uses of this word, see Smith's *Dictionary of Greek and Roman Antiquities*.

[2] Resignata est, properly "unsealed."

[3] Virg., *Æn.*, vi. 719.

institute, judging the impious and the holy at the same time, then at length He shall send the wicked to darkness in fire. But as many as are holy shall live again on the earth, God giving them at the same time a spirit, and honour, and life."

But if not only prophets, but even bards, and poets, and philosophers, agree that there will be a resurrection of the dead, let no one ask of us how this is possible: for no reason can be assigned for divine works; but if from the beginning God formed man in some unspeakable manner, we may believe that the old man can be restored by Him who made the new man.

CHAP. XXIV. — OF THE RENEWED WORLD.

Now I will subjoin the rest. Therefore the Son of the most high and mighty God shall come to judge the quick and the dead, as the Sibyl testifies and says: —

"For then there shall be confusion of mortals throughout the whole earth, when the Almighty Himself shall come on His judgment-seat to judge the souls of the quick and dead, and all the world."

But He, when He shall have destroyed unrighteousness, and executed His great judgment, and shall have recalled to life the righteous, who have lived from the beginning, will be engaged among men a thousand years, and will rule them with most just command. Which the Sibyl proclaims in another place, as she utters her inspired predictions: —

"Hear me, ye mortals; an everlasting King reigns."

Then they who shall be alive in their bodies shall not die, but during those thousand years shall produce an infinite multitude, and their offspring shall be holy, and beloved by God; but they who shall be raised from the dead shall preside over the living as judges.[1] But the nations shall not be entirely extinguished, but some shall be left as a victory for God, that they may be the occasion of triumph to the righteous, and may be subjected to perpetual slavery. About the same time also the prince of the devils, who is the contriver of all evils, shall be bound with chains, and shall be imprisoned during the thousand years of the heavenly rule in which righteousness shall reign in the world, so that he may contrive no evil against the people of God. After His coming the righteous shall be collected from all the earth, and the judgment being completed, the sacred city shall be planted in the middle of the earth, in which God Himself the builder may dwell together with the righteous, bearing rule in it. And the Sibyl marks out this city when she says: —

"And the city which God made, this He made more brilliant than the stars, and sun, and moon."

Then that darkness will be taken away from the world with which the heaven will be overspread and darkened, and the moon will receive the brightness of the sun, nor will it be further diminished: but the sun will become seven times brighter than it now is; and the earth will open its fruitfulness, and bring forth most abundant fruits of its own accord; the rocky mountains shall drop with honey; streams of wine shall run down, and rivers flow with milk: in short, the world itself shall rejoice, and all nature exult, being rescued and set free from the dominion of evil and impiety, and guilt and error. Throughout this time beasts shall not be nourished by blood, nor birds by prey; but all things shall be peaceful and tranquil. Lions and calves shall stand together at the manger, the wolf shall not carry off the sheep, the hound shall not hunt for prey; hawks and eagles shall not injure; the infant shall play with serpents. In short, those things shall then come to pass which the poets spoke of as being done in the reign of Saturnus. Whose error arose from this source, — that the prophets bring forward and speak of many future events as already accomplished. For visions were brought before their eyes by the divine Spirit, and they saw these things, as it were, done and completed in their own sight. And when fame had gradually spread abroad their predictions, since those who were uninstructed in the mysteries[2] of religion did not know why they were spoken, they thought that all those things were already fulfilled in the ancient ages, which evidently could not be accomplished and fulfilled under the reign of a man.[3] But when, after the destruction of impious religions and the suppression of guilt, the earth shall be subject to God, —

"The sailor[4] himself also shall renounce the sea, nor shall the naval pine
Barter merchandise; all lands shall produce all things.
The ground shall not endure the harrow, nor the vineyard the pruning hook;
The sturdy ploughman also shall loose the bulls from the yoke.
The plain shall by degrees grow yellow with soft ears of corn,
The blushing grape shall hang on the uncultivated brambles,
And hard oaks shall distil the dewy honey.
Nor shall the wool learn to counterfeit various colours;
But the ram himself in the meadows shall change his fleece,
Now for a sweetly blushing purple, now for saffron dye;
Scarlet of its own accord shall cover the lambs as they feed.
The goats of themselves shall bring back home their udders distended with milk;
Nor shall the herds dread huge lions."[5]

---

1 [This is "the first resurrection" as conceived of by the ancients, and the (Phil. iii. 11) ἐξανάστασις of St. Paul.]

2 Profani a sacramentis.

3 [This *rationale* of the *Orphica* and *Sibyllina* deserves thought.]

4 Vector, i.e., the passenger, as opposed to one who sails in a ship of war.

5 Virg., *Bucol.*, iv. 21–45. The order of the lines is changed. [This, the famous *Pollio*, greatly influenced Constantine. See p. 140, note 7, *supra*.]

Which things the poet foretold according to the verses of the Cumæan Sibyl. But the Erythræan thus speaks: —

> "But wolves shall not contend with lambs on the mountains, and lynxes shall eat grass with kids; boars shall feed with calves, and with all flocks; and the carnivorous lion shall eat chaff at the manger, and serpents shall sleep with infants deprived of their mothers."

And in another place, speaking of the fruitfulness of all things: —

> "And then shall God give great joy to men; for the earth, and the trees, and the numberless flocks of the earth shall give to men the true fruit of the vine, and sweet honey, and white milk, and corn, which is the best of all things to mortals."

And another in the same manner: —

> "The sacred land of the pious only will produce all these things, the stream of honey from the rock and from the fountain, and the milk of ambrosia will flow for all the just."

Therefore men will live a most tranquil life, abounding with resources, and will reign together with God; and the kings of the nations shall come from the ends of the earth with gifts and offerings, to adore and honour the great King, whose name shall be renowned and venerated by all the nations which shall be under heaven, and by the kings who shall rule on earth.

CHAP. XXV. — OF THE LAST TIMES, AND OF THE CITY OF ROME.

These are the things which are spoken of by the prophets as about to happen hereafter: but I have not considered it necessary to bring forward their testimonies and words, since it would be an endless task; nor would the limits of my book receive so great a multitude of subjects, since so many with one breath speak similar things; and at the same time, lest weariness should be occasioned to the readers if I should heap together things collected and transferred from all; moreover, that I might confirm those very things which I said, not by my own writings, but in an especial manner by the writings of others, and might show that not only among us, but even with those very persons who revile us, the truth is preserved,[1] which they refuse to acknowledge.[2] But he who wishes to know these things more accurately may draw from the fountain itself, and he will know more things worthy of admiration than we have comprised in these books. Perhaps some one may now ask when these things of which we have spoken are about to come to pass? I have already shown above, that when six thousand years shall be completed this change must take place, and that the last day of the extreme conclusion is now drawing near. It is permitted us to know respecting the signs, which are spoken by the prophets, for they foretold signs by which the consummation of the times is to be expected by us from day to day, and to be feared. When, however, this amount will be completed, those teach, who have written respecting the times, collecting them from the sacred writings and from various histories, how great is the number of years from the beginning of the world. And although they vary, and the amount of the number as reckoned by them differs considerably, yet all expectation does not exceed the limit of two hundred years. The subject itself declares that the fall and ruin of the world will shortly take place; except that while the city of Rome remains it appears that nothing of this kind is to be feared.[3] But when that capital of the world shall have fallen, and shall have begun to be a street,[4] which the Sibyls say shall come to pass, who can doubt that the end has now arrived to the affairs of men and the whole world? It is that city, that only, which still sustains all things; and the God of heaven is to be entreated by us and implored — if, indeed, His arrangements and decrees can be delayed — lest, sooner than we think for, that detestable tyrant should come who will undertake so great a deed, and dig out that eye, by the destruction of which the world itself is about to fall. Now let us return, to set forth the other things which are then about to follow.

CHAP. XXVI. — OF THE LOOSING OF THE DEVIL, AND OF THE SECOND AND GREATEST JUDGMENT.

We have said, a little before, that it will come to pass at the commencement of the sacred reign, that the prince of the devils will be bound by God. But he also, when the thousand years of the kingdom, that is, seven thousand *of the world*, shall begin to be ended, will be loosed afresh, and being sent forth from prison, will go forth and assemble all the nations, which shall then be under the dominion of the righteous, that they may make war against the holy city; and there shall be collected together from all the world an innumerable company of the nations, and shall besiege and surround the city. Then the last anger of God shall come upon the nations, and shall utterly[5] destroy them; and first He shall shake the earth most violently, and by its motion the mountains of Syria shall be rent, and the hills shall sink down precipitously, and the walls of all cities shall fall, and God shall cause the sun to stand, so that he set not for three days, and shall set it on fire; and excessive heat and great burning shall descend upon the hostile and impious people, and showers of brim-

1 Consignatam teneri.
2 [See p. 218, *supra*, and Victorinus, *sparsim*, *infra*.]
3 [Again a reference, as on p. 213, note 1, *supra*.]
4 ῥύμη. There are other readings, as πῦρ and "pyra."
5 Usque ad unum.

stone, and hailstones, and drops of fire; and their spirits shall melt through the heat, and their bodies shall be bruised by the hail, and they shall smite one another with the sword. The mountains shall be filled with carcases, and the plains shall be covered with bones; but the people of God during those three days shall be concealed under caves of the earth, until the anger of God against the nations and the last judgment shall be ended.

Then the righteous shall go forth from their hiding-places, and shall find all things covered with carcases and bones. But the whole race of the wicked shall utterly perish; and there shall no longer be any nation in this world, but the nation of God alone. Then for seven continuous years the woods shall be untouched, nor shall timber be cut from the mountains, but the arms of the nations shall be burnt; and now there shall be no war, but peace and everlasting rest. But when the thousand years shall be completed, the world shall be renewed by God, and the heavens shall be folded together, and the earth shall be changed, and God shall transform men into the similitude of angels, and they shall be white as snow; and they shall always be employed in the sight of the Almighty, and shall make offerings to their Lord, and serve Him for ever. At the same time shall take place that second and public resurrection [1] of all, in which the unrighteous shall be raised to everlasting punishments. These are they who have worshipped the works of their own hands, who have either been ignorant of, or have denied the Lord and Parent of the world. But their lord with his servants shall be seized and condemned to punishment, together with whom all the band of the wicked, in accordance with their deeds, shall be burnt for ever with perpetual fire in the sight of angels and the righteous.

This is the doctrine of the holy prophets which we Christians follow; this is our wisdom, which they who worship frail objects, or maintain an empty philosophy, deride as folly and vanity, because we are not accustomed to defend and assert it in public, since God orders us in quietness and silence to hide His secret, and to keep it within our own conscience; and not to strive with obstinate contention against those who are ignorant of the truth, and who rigorously assail God and His religion not for the sake of learning, but of censuring and jeering. For a mystery ought to be most faithfully concealed and covered, especially by us, who bear the name of faith.[2] But they accuse this silence of ours, as though it were the result of an evil conscience; whence also they invent some detestable things respecting those who are holy and blameless, and willingly believe their own inventions.

The address to Constantine is wanting in some MSS. and editions, but is inserted in the text by Migne, as found in some important MSS., and as in accordance with the style and spirit of Lactantius.

But all fictions have now been hushed, most holy Emperor, since the time when the great God raised thee up for the restoration of the house of justice, and for the protection of the human race; for while thou rulest the Roman state, we worshippers of God are no more regarded as accursed and impious. Since the truth now comes forth [3] from obscurity, and is brought into light, we are not censured as unrighteous who endeavour to perform the works of righteousness. No one any longer reproaches us with the name of God. None of us, who are alone of all men religious, is any more called irreligious; since despising the images of the dead, we worship the living and true God. The providence of the supreme Deity has raised thee to the imperial dignity, that thou mightest be able with true piety to rescind the injurious decrees of others, to correct faults, to provide with a father's clemency for the safety of men, — in short, to remove the wicked from the state, whom being cast down by pre-eminent piety, God has delivered into your hands, that it might be evident to all in what true majesty consists.

For they who wished to take away the worship of the heavenly and matchless [4] God, that they might defend impious superstitions, lie in ruin.[5] But thou, who defendest and lovest His name, excelling in virtue and prosperity, enjoyest thy immortal glories with the greatest happiness. They suffer and have suffered the punishment of their guilt. The powerful right hand of God protects thee from all dangers; He bestows on thee a quiet and tranquil reign, with the highest congratulations of all men. And not undeservedly has the Lord and Ruler of the world chosen thee in preference to all others, by whom He might renew His holy religion, since thou alone didst exist of all, who mightest afford a surpassing example of virtue and holiness: in which thou mightest not only equal, but also, which is a very great matter, excel the glory of ancient princes, whom nevertheless fame reckons among the good. They indeed perhaps by nature only resembled the righteous. For he who is ignorant of God, the Ruler of the universe, may attain to a resemblance of righteousness, but he cannot attain to righteousness itself. But thou, both by the innate sanctity of thy character, and by thy acknowledgment of the truth and of God in every action, dost fully perform [6] the works of right-

1 [This clearly proves that the better sort of Chiliasm was not extinct in the Church.]

2 [i.e., "the faithful," a title often used to designate Christians. This discipline was based on Heb. v. 14 and Matt. vii. 6.]

3 Jam emergente atque illustratâ veritate.

4 Singularis.

5 Profligati jacent.

6 Consummas. [Art fulfilling; i.e., as a catechumen.]

eousness.[1] It was therefore befitting that, in arranging the condition of the human race, the Deity should make use of thy authority and service. Whom we supplicate with daily prayers, that He may especially guard thee whom He has wished to be the guardian of the world: then that He may inspire thee with a disposition by which thou mayest always continue in the love of the divine name. For this is serviceable to all, both to thee for happiness, and to others for repose.

CHAP. XXVII. — AN ENCOURAGEMENT AND CONFIRMATION OF THE PIOUS.

Since we have completed the seven courses[2] of the work which we undertook, and have advanced to the goal, it remains that we exhort all to undertake wisdom together with true religion, the strength and office of which depends on this, that, despising earthly things, and laying aside the errors by which we were formerly held while we served frail things, and desired frail things, we may be directed to the eternal rewards of the heavenly treasure. And that we may obtain these, the alluring pleasures of the present life must as soon as possible be laid aside, which soothe the souls of men with pernicious sweetness. How great a happiness must it be thought, to be withdrawn from these stains of the earth, and to go to that most just Judge and indulgent Father, who in the place of labours gives rest, in the place of death life, in the place of darkness brightness, and in the place of short and earthly goods, gives those which are eternal and heavenly: with which reward the hardships and miseries which we endure in this world, in accomplishing the works of righteousness, can in no way be compared and equalled. Therefore, if we wish to be wise and happy, not only must those sayings of Terence be reflected upon and proposed to us,

> "That we must ever grind at the mill, we must be beaten, and put in fetters;"[3]

but things much more dreadful than these must be endured, namely, the prison, chains, and tortures: pains must be undergone, in short, death itself must be undertaken and borne, when it is clear to our conscience that that frail pleasure will not be without punishment, nor virtue without a divine reward. All, therefore, ought to endeavour either to direct themselves to the right way as soon as possible, or, having undertaken and exercised virtues, and having patiently performed the labours of this life, to deserve to have God as their comforter. For our Father and Lord, who built and strengthened the heaven, who placed in it the sun, with the other heavenly bodies, who by His power weighed the earth and fenced it with mountains, surrounded it with the sea, and divided it with rivers, and who made and completed out of nothing whatever there is in this workmanship of the world; having observed the errors of men, sent a Guide, who might open to us the way of righteousness: let us all follow Him, let us hear Him, let us obey Him with the greatest devotedness, since He alone, as Lucretius says,[4]

> "Cleansed men's breasts with truth-telling precepts, and fixed a limit to lust and fear, and explained what was the chief good which we all strive to reach, and pointed out the road by which, along a narrow track, we might arrive at it in a straightforward course."

And not only pointed it out, but also went before us in it, that no one might dread the path of virtue on account of its difficulty. Let the way of destruction and deceit, if it is possible, be deserted, in which death is concealed, being covered by the attractions of pleasure.

And the more nearly each one, as his years incline to old age, sees to be the approach of that day in which he must depart from this life, let him reflect how he may leave it in purity, how he may come to the Judge in innocency; not as they do, to whose dark minds the light is denied,[5] who, when the strength of their body now fails, are admonished in this of the last pressing necessity, that they should with greater eagerness and ardour apply themselves to the satisfying of their lusts. From which abyss let everyone free himself while it is permitted him, while the opportunity is present, and let him turn himself to God with his whole mind, that he may without anxiety await that day, in which God, the Ruler and Lord of the world, shall judge the deeds and thoughts of each. Whatever things are here desired, let him not only neglect, but also avoid them, and let him judge that his soul is of greater value than those deceitful goods, the possession of which is uncertain and transitory; for they take their departure every day, and they go forth much more quickly than they had entered, and if it is permitted us to enjoy them even to the last, they must still, without doubt, be left to others. We can take nothing with us, except a well and innocently spent life. That man will appear before God with abundant resources, that man will appear in opulence, to whom there shall belong self-restraint, mercy, patience, love, and faith. This is our inheritance, which can neither be taken away from any one, nor transferred to another.

---

1 [In admonishing the great, the form was to ascribe to them the characters they should cultivate. Lactantius here speaks as a courtier, but guardedly.]

2 Decursis septem spatiis, — an expression borrowed from the chariot race: here applied to the seven books of this treatise.

3 Terent., *Phorm.*, ii. 1. 19.

4 *De Nat. Rer.*, vi. 24.

5 Quorum cæcis mentibus lux negatur. Others read, "Quidam cæcis mentibus viri."

And who is there who would wish to provide and acquire for himself these goods?

Let those who are hungry come, that being fed with heavenly food, they may lay aside their lasting hunger; let those who are athirst come, that they may with full mouth draw forth the water of salvation from an ever-flowing fountain.[1] By this divine food and drink the blind shall both see, and the deaf hear, and the dumb speak, and the lame walk, and the foolish shall be wise, and the sick shall be strong, and the dead shall come to life again. For whoever by his virtue has trampled upon the corruptions of the earth, the supreme and truthful arbiter will raise him to life and to perpetual light. Let no one trust in riches, no one in badges of authority, no one even in royal power: these things do not make a man immortal. For whosoever shall cast away the conduct becoming a man,[2] and, following present things, shall prostrate himself upon the ground, will be punished as a deserter from his Lord, his commander, and his Father. Let us therefore apply ourselves to righteousness, which will alone, as an inseparable companion, lead us to God; and "while a spirit rules these limbs,"[3] let us serve God with unwearied service, let us keep our posts and watches, let us boldly engage with the enemy whom we know, that victorious and triumphant over our conquered adversary, we may obtain from the Lord that reward of valour which He Himself has promised.

[1] [This evident quotation from Rev. xxi. 7 and xxii. 17 is noteworthy as proof of the currency of the Apocalypse in North Africa.]

[2] Rationem hominis.

[3] Virg., *Æneid*, iv. 336.

GENERAL NOTE.

FOR remarks on the dubious passages which bear upon that of p. 221, *supra*, see the *General Note* suffixed to the tractate on the *Workmanship of God*, p. 300, *infra*.

THE EPITOME OF THE DIVINE INSTITUTES

ADDRESSED TO HIS BROTHER PENTADIUS.

THE PREFACE. — THE PLAN AND PURPORT OF THE WHOLE EPITOME,[1] AND OF THE INSTITUTIONS.

ALTHOUGH the books of the *Divine Institutions* which we wrote a long time since to illustrate the truth and religion, may so prepare and mould the minds of the readers, that their length may not produce disgust, nor their copiousness be burthensome; nevertheless you desire, O brother Pentadius, that an epitome of them should be made for you, I suppose for this reason, that I may write something to you, and that your name may be rendered famous by my work, such as it is. I will comply with your desire, although it seems a difficult matter to comprise within the compass of one book those things which have been treated of in seven large volumes.[2] For the whole matter becomes less full when so great a multitude of subjects is to be compressed within a narrow space; and it becomes less clear by its very brevity, especially since many arguments and examples, on which the elucidation of the proofs depends, must of necessity be omitted, since their copiousness is so great, that even by themselves they are enough to make up a book. And when these are removed, what can appear useful, what plain? But I will strive as much as the subject permits, both to contract that which is diffuse and to shorten that which is long; in such a manner, however, that in this work, in which truth is to be brought to light, matter may not seem to be wanting for copiousness, nor clearness for understanding it.[3]

CHAP. I. — OF THE DIVINE PROVIDENCE.

First a question arises: Whether there is any providence which made or governs the world? That there is, no one doubts, since of almost all the philosophers, except the school of Epicurus, there is but one voice and one opinion, that the world could not have been made without a contriver, and that it cannot exist without a ruler. Therefore Epicurus is refuted not only by the most learned men, but also by the testimonies and perceptions of all mortals. For who can doubt respecting a providence, when he sees that the heavens and the earth have been so arranged, and that all things have been so regulated, that they might be most befittingly adapted, not only to wonderful beauty and adornment, but also to the use of men, and the convenience of the other living creatures? That, therefore, which exists in accordance with a plan, cannot have had its beginning without a plan: thus[4] it is certain that there is a providence.

CHAP. II. — THAT THERE IS BUT ONE GOD, AND THAT THERE CANNOT BE MORE.

Another question follows: Whether there be one God or more? And this indeed contains much ambiguity. For not only do individuals differ among themselves, but also peoples and nations. But he who shall follow the guidance of reason will understand that there cannot be a Lord except one, nor a Father except one. For if God, who made all things, is also Lord and Father, He must be one only, so that the same may be the head and source of all things. Nor is it possible for the world[5] to exist unless all things be referred to one person, unless one hold the rudder, unless one guide the reins, and, as it were, one mind direct all the members of the body. If there are many kings in a swarm of bees, they will perish or be scattered abroad, while

"Discord attacks the kings with great commotion."[6]

If there are several leaders in a herd, they will contend until one gains the mastery.[7] If there

[1] [A specimen of the abridgments made by authors and editors, owing to the great expense of books in manuscript. They have been sources of great injury to literature.]

[2] [We have here only a fragment of the *Epitome*. The rest is lost.]

[3] [Christian morals were now to be taught openly in schools: hence the need of such manuals.]

[4] Quoniam. This word appears to be out of place, as its proper meaning is "since." Either it must be taken as above, or, with some editors, the last clause of this chapter may be taken as the beginning of the next chapter — "Since there is a providence," etc.

[5] Rerum summa.

[6] Virg., *Georg.*, iv. 68.

[7] Obtineat.

are many commanders in an army, the soldiers cannot obey, since different commands are given; nor can unity be maintained by themselves, since each consults his own interests according to his humours.[1] Thus, in this commonwealth of the world, unless there were one ruler, who was also its founder, either this mass would be dissolved, or it could not have been put together at all.

Moreover, the whole *authority* could not exist in many *deities*, since they separately maintain their own duties and their own prerogatives. No one, therefore, of them can be called omnipotent, which is the true title of God, since he will be able to accomplish that only which depends upon himself, and will not venture to attempt that which depends upon others. Vulcan will not claim for himself water, nor Neptune fire; nor will Ceres claim acquaintance with the arts, nor Minerva with fruits; nor will Mercury lay claim to arms, nor Mars to the lyre; Jupiter will not claim medicine, nor Æsculapius the thunderbolt: he will more easily endure it when thrown by another, than he will brandish it himself. If, therefore, individuals cannot do all things, they have less strength and less power; but he is to be regarded as God who can accomplish the whole, and not he who can only accomplish the smallest part of the whole.

CHAP. III. — THE TESTIMONIES OF THE POETS CONCERNING THE ONE GOD.

There is, then, one God, perfect, eternal, incorruptible, incapable of suffering, subject to no circumstance or power, Himself possessing all things, ruling all things, whom the human mind can neither estimate in thought nor mortal tongue describe in speech. For He is too elevated and great to be conceived by the thought, or expressed by the language of man. In short, not to speak of the prophets, the preachers of the one God, poets also, and philosophers, and inspired women,[2] utter their testimony to the unity of God. Orpheus speaks of the surpassing God who made the heaven and the sun, with the other heavenly bodies; who made the earth and the seas. Also our own Maro calls the Supreme God at one time a spirit, at another time a mind, and says that it, as though infused into limbs, puts in motion the body of the whole world; also, that God permeates the heights of heaven, the tracts of the sea and lands, and that all living creatures derive their life from Him. Even Ovid was not ignorant that the world was prepared by God, whom he sometimes calls the framer of all things, sometimes the fabricator of the world.[3]

CHAP. IV. — THE TESTIMONIES OF THE PHILOSOPHERS TO THE UNITY OF GOD.

But let us come to the philosophers, whose authority is regarded as more certain than that of the poets. Plato asserts His monarchy, saying that there is but one God, by whom the world was prepared and completed with wonderful order. Aristotle, his disciple, admits that there is one mind which presides over the world. Antisthenes says that there is one who is God by nature,[4] the governor of the whole system. It would be a long task to recount the statements which have been made respecting the Supreme God, either by Thales, or by Pythagoras and Anaximenes before him, or afterwards by the Stoics Cleanthes and Chrysippus and Zeno, or of our countrymen, by Seneca following the Stoics, and by Tullius himself, since all these attempted to define the being of God,[5] and affirmed that the world is ruled by Him alone, and that He is not subject to any nature, since all nature derives its origin from Him.

Hermes, who, on account of his virtue and his knowledge of many arts, deserved the name of Trismegistus, who preceded the philosophers in the antiquity of his doctrine, and who is reverenced by the Egyptians as a god, in asserting the majesty of the one God with infinite praises, calls Him Lord and Father, and says that He is without a name because He does not stand in need of a proper name, inasmuch as He is alone, and that He has no parents, since He exists of Himself and by Himself. In writing to his son he thus begins: To understand God is difficult, to describe Him in speech is impossible, even for one to whom it is possible to understand Him; for the perfect cannot be comprehended by the imperfect, nor the invisible by the visible.

CHAP. V. — THAT THE PROPHETIC WOMEN — THAT IS, THE SIBYLS — DECLARE THAT THERE IS BUT ONE GOD.

It remains to speak of the prophetic women. Varro relates that there were ten Sibyls, — the first of the Persians, the second the Libyan, the third the Delphian, the fourth the Cimmerian, the fifth the Erythræan, the sixth the Samian, the seventh the Cumæan, the eighth the Hellespontian, the ninth the Phrygian, the tenth the Tiburtine, who has the name of Albunea. Of all these, he says that there are three books of the Cumæan alone which contain the fates of the Romans, and are accounted sacred, but that there exist, and are commonly regarded as separate, books of almost all the others, but that they are entitled, as though by one name, Sibylline books,

[1] Pro moribus. Another reading is "pro viribus," with all their power.
[2] Vates, i e., the Sibyls.
[3] [I shall not multiply references to the seven books, which are so readily compared by turning back to the pages here epitomized.]
[4] Naturalem.
[5] Quid sit Deus.

excepting that the Erythræan, who is said to have lived in the times of the Trojan war, placed her name in her book: the writings of the others are mixed together.[1]

All these Sibyls of whom I have spoken, except the Cumæan, whom none but the Quindecemviri[2] are allowed to read, bear witness that there is but one God, the ruler, the maker, the parent, not begotten of any, but sprung from Himself, who was from all ages, and will be to all ages; and therefore is alone worthy of being worshipped, alone of being feared, alone of being reverenced, by all living beings; — whose testimonies I have omitted because I was unable to abridge them; but if you wish to see them, you must have recourse to the books themselves. Now let us follow up the remaining subjects.

CHAP. VI. — SINCE GOD IS ETERNAL AND IMMORTAL, HE DOES NOT STAND IN NEED OF SEX AND SUCCESSION.

These testimonies, therefore, so many and so great, clearly teach that there is but one government in the world, and one power, the origin of which cannot be imagined, or its force described. They are foolish, therefore, who imagine that the gods were born of marriage, since the sexes themselves, and the intercourse between them, were given to mortals by God for this reason, that every race might be preserved by a succession of offspring. But what need have the immortals either of sex or succession, since neither pleasure nor death affects them? Those, therefore, who are reckoned as gods, since it is evident that they were born as men, and that they begat others, were plainly mortals: but they were believed to be gods, because, when they were great and powerful kings, on account of the benefits which they had conferred upon men, they deserved to obtain divine honours after death; and temples and statues being erected to them, their memory was retained and celebrated as that of immortals.

CHAP. VII. — OF THE WICKED LIFE AND DEATH OF HERCULES.

But though almost all nations are persuaded that they are gods, yet their actions, as related both by poets and historians, declare that they were men. Who is ignorant of the times in which Hercules lived, since he both sailed with the Argonauts on their expedition, and having stormed Troy, slew Laomedon, the father of Priam, on account of his perjury? From that time rather more than fifteen hundred years are reckoned. He is said not even to have been born honourably, but to have been sprung from Alcmena by adultery, and to have been himself addicted to the vices of his father. He never abstained from women, or males, and traversed the whole world, not so much for the sake of glory as of lust, nor so much for the slaughter of beasts as for the begetting of children. And though he was unvanquished, yet he was triumphed over by Omphale alone, to whom he gave up his club and lion's skin; and being clothed in a woman's garment, and crouching at a woman's feet, he received his task[3] to execute. He afterwards, in a transport of frenzy, killed his little children and his wife Megara. At last, having put on a garment sent by his wife Deianyra, when he was perishing through ulcers, being unable to endure the pain, he constructed for himself a funeral pile on Mount Œta, and burnt himself alive. Thus it is effected, that although on account of his excellence[4] he might have been believed to be a god, nevertheless on account of these things he is believed to have been a man.

CHAP. VIII. — OF ÆSCULAPIUS, APOLLO, MARS, CASTOR AND POLLUX, AND OF MERCURIUS AND BACCHUS.

Tarquitius relates that Æsculapius was born of doubtful parents, and that on this account he was exposed; and being taken up by hunters, and fed by the teats of a hound, was given to Chiron for instruction. He lived at Epidaurus, and was buried at Cynosuræ, as Cicero says,[5] when he had been killed by lightning. But Apollo, his father, did not disdain to take charge of another's flock that he might receive a wife;[6] and when he had unintentionally killed a boy whom he loved, he inscribed his own lamentations on a flower. Mars, a man of the greatest bravery, was not free from the charge of adultery, since he was made a spectacle, being bound with a chain together with the adulteress.

Castor and Pollux carried off the brides of others, but not with impunity, to whose death and burial Homer bears witness, not with poetical, but simple faith. Mercurius, who was the father of Androgynus by his intrigue with Venus, deserved to be a god, because he invented the lyre and the *palæstra*. Father Bacchus, after subduing India as a conqueror, having by chance come to Crete, saw Ariadne on the shore, whom Theseus had forced and deserted. Then, being inflamed by love, he united her in marriage to

---

[1] [See Cyprian on Balaam, vol. v. p. 502, note 7. A hint as to the qualified inspiration of these women.]

[2] The appointed guardians of the Sibylline books. At first there were two; the number was afterwards increased to ten, and subsequently to fifteen, termed Quindecemviri.

[3] Pensa quæ faceret. "Pensum" properly signifies the wool daily weighed out and given to each servant.

[4] Ob virtutem.

[5] Cicero, *De Nat. Deor.*, iii. 22.

[6] When Pelias had promised his daughter Alcestis to Admetus, on condition of his coming to her in a chariot drawn by lions and boars, Apollo enabled Admetus to fulfil this condition.

himself, and placed her crown, as the poets say, conspicuously among the stars. The mother of the gods[1] herself, while she lived in Phrygia after the banishment and death of her husband, though a widow, and aged, was enamoured of a beautiful youth; and because he was not faithful, she mutilated, and rendered him effeminate: on which account even now she delights in the Galli[2] as her priests.

CHAP. IX. — OF THE DISGRACEFUL DEEDS OF THE GODS.

Whence did Ceres bring forth Proserpine, except from debauchery? Whence did Latona bring forth her twins, except from crime? Venus having been subject to the lusts of gods and men, when she reigned in Cyprus, invented the practice of courtesanship, and commanded women to make traffic of themselves, that she might not alone be infamous. Were the virgins themselves, Minerva and Diana, chaste? Whence, then, did Erichthonius arise? Did Vulcan shed his seed upon the ground, and was man born from that as a fungus? Or why did Diana banish Hippolytus either to a retired place, or give him up to a woman, where he might pass his life in solitude among unknown groves, and having now changed his name, might be called Virbius? What do these things signify but impurity, which the poets do not venture to confess?

CHAP. X. — OF JUPITER, AND HIS LICENTIOUS LIFE.

But respecting the king and father of all these, Jupiter, whom they believe to possess the chief power in heaven, — what power[3] had he, who banished his father Saturnus from his kingdom, and pursued him with arms when he fled? What self-restraint had he, who indulged every kind of lust? For he made Alcmena and Leda, the wives of great men, infamous through his adultery: he also, captivated with the beauty of a boy, carried him off with violence as he was hunting and meditating manly things, that he might treat him as a woman. Why should I mention his debaucheries of virgins? and how great a multitude of these there was, is shown by the number of his sons. In the case of Thetis alone he was more temperate. For it had been predicted that the son whom she should bring forth would be more powerful than his father. Therefore he struggled with his love, that one might not be born greater than himself. He knew, therefore, that he was not of perfect virtue, greatness, and power, since he feared that which he himself had done to his father. Why, therefore, is he called best and greatest, since he both contaminated himself with faults, which is the part of one who is unjust and bad, and feared a greater than himself, which is the part of one who is weak and inferior?

CHAP. XI. — THE VARIOUS EMBLEMS UNDER WHICH THE POETS VEILED THE TURPITUDE OF JUPITER.

But some one will say that these things are feigned by the poets. This is not the usage of the poets, to feign in such a manner that you fabricate the whole, but so that you cover the actions themselves with a figure, and, as it were, with a variegated veil. Poetic licence has this limit, not that it may invent the whole, which is the part of one who is false and senseless, but that it may change something consistently with reason. They said that Jupiter changed himself into a shower of gold, that he might deceive Danae. What is a shower of gold? Plainly golden coins, by offering a great quantity of which, and pouring them into her bosom, he corrupted the frailty of her virgin soul by this bribe. Thus also they speak of a shower of iron, when they wish to signify a multitude of javelins. He carried off his catamite upon an eagle. What is the eagle? Truly a legion, since the figure of this animal is the standard of the legion. He carried Europa across the sea on a bull. What is the bull? Clearly a ship, which had its tutelary image[4] fashioned in the shape of a bull. So assuredly the daughter of Inachus was not turned into a cow, nor as such did she swim across, but she escaped the anger of Juno in a ship which had the form of a cow. Lastly, when she had been conveyed to Egypt, she became Isis, whose voyage is celebrated on a fixed day, in memory of her flight.

CHAP. XII. — THE POETS DO NOT INVENT ALL THOSE THINGS WHICH RELATE TO THE GODS.

You see, then, that the poets did not invent all things, and that they prefigured some things, that, when they spoke the truth, they might add something like this of divinity to those whom they called gods; as they did also respecting their kingdoms. For when they say that Jupiter had by lot the kingdom of Cœlus, they either mean Mount Olympus, on which ancient stories relate that Saturnus, and afterwards Jupiter, dwelt, or a part of the East, which is, as it were, higher, because the light arises thence; but the region of the West is lower, and therefore they say that Pluto obtained the lower regions; but that the sea was given to Neptune, because he

[1] Rhea, or Cybele.

[2] Galli, the priests of Cybele, were so called: they mutilated themselves, and performed many raving ceremonies.

[3] Quid potestatis. Others read "pietatis," which appears more suitable to the sense of the passage.

[4] Tutela. The image of some deity, supposed to be the tutelary guardian of the ship, was usually painted on the stern.

had the maritime coast, with all the islands. Many things are thus coloured by the poets; and they who are ignorant of this, censure them as false, but only in word: for in fact they believe them, since they so fashion the images of the gods, that when they make them male and female, and confess that some are married, some parents, and some children, they plainly assent to the poets; for these relations cannot exist without intercourse and the generation of children.

CHAP. XIII. — THE ACTIONS OF JUPITER ARE RELATED FROM THE HISTORIAN EUHEMERUS.

But let us leave the poets; let us come to history, which is supported both by the credibility of the facts and by the antiquity of the times. Euhemerus was a Messenian, a very ancient writer, who gave an account of the origin of Jupiter, and his exploits, and all his posterity, gathered from the sacred inscriptions of ancient temples; he also traced out the parents of the other gods, their countries, actions, commands, and deaths, and even their sepulchres. And this history Ennius translated into Latin, whose words are these: —

> "As these things are written, so is the origin and kindred of Jupiter and his brothers; after this manner it is handed down to us in the sacred writing."

The same Euhemerus therefore relates that Jupiter, when he had five times gone round the world, and had distributed governments to his friends and relatives, and had given laws to men, and had wrought many other benefits, being endued with immortal glory and everlasting remembrance, ended his life in Crete, and departed to the gods, and that his sepulchre is in Crete, in the town of Gnossus, and that upon it is engraved in ancient Greek letters Zankronou, which is Jupiter the son of Saturnus. It is plain, therefore, from the things which I have related, that he was a man, and reigned on the earth.

CHAP. XIV. — THE ACTIONS OF SATURNUS AND URANUS TAKEN FROM THE HISTORIANS.

Let us pass on to former things, that we may discover the origin of the whole error. Saturnus is said to have been born of Cœlus and Terra. This is plainly incredible; but there is a certain reason why it is thus related, and he who is ignorant of this rejects it as a fable. That Uranus was the father of Saturnus, both Hermes affirms, and sacred history teaches. When Trismegistus said that there were very few men of perfect learning, he enumerated among them his relatives, Uranus, Saturnus, and Mercurius. Euhemerus relates that the same Uranus was the first who reigned on earth, using these words: "In the beginning Cœlus first had the chief power on earth: he instituted and prepared that kingdom for himself together with his brothers." [1]

CHAP. XX. — OF THE GODS PECULIAR TO THE ROMANS.

I have spoken of the religious rites which are common to all nations. I will now speak of the gods which the Romans have peculiar to themselves. Who does not know that the wife of Faustulus, the nurse of Romulus and Remus, in honour of whom the Larentinalia were instituted, was a harlot? And for this reason she was called Lupa, and represented in the form of a wild beast. Faula also and Flora were harlots, of whom the one was the mistress of Hercules, as Verrius relates; the other, having acquired great wealth by her person, made the people her heir, and on this account the games called Floralia are celebrated in her honour.

Tatius consecrated the statue of a woman which had been found in the principal sewer, and called it by the name of the goddess Cloacina. The Romans, being besieged by the Gauls, made engines for throwing weapons of the hair of women; and on this account they erected an altar and temple to Venus Calva: [2] also to Jupiter Pistor,[3] because he had advised them in a dream to make all their corn into bread, and to throw it upon the enemy; and when this had been done, the Gauls, despairing of being able to reduce the Romans by famine, had abandoned the siege. Tullus Hostilius made Fear and Pallor gods. Mind is also worshipped; but if they had possessed it, they would never, I believe, have thought that it ought to be worshipped. Marcellus originated Honour and Virtue.

CHAP. XXI. — OF THE SACRED RITES OF THE ROMAN GODS.

But the senate also instituted other false gods of this kind, — Hope, Faith, Concord, Peace, Chastity, Piety; all of which, since they ought truly to be in the minds of men, they have falsely placed within walls. But although these have no substantial existence outside of man, nevertheless I should prefer that they should be worshipped, rather than Blight or Fever, which ought not to be consecrated, but rather to be execrated; than Fornax, together with her sacred ovens; than Stercutus, who first showed men to enrich the ground with manure; than the goddess Muta, who brought forth the Lares; than Cumina, who presides over the cradles of infants; than Caca, who gave information to Hercules respecting the stealing of his cattle, that he might slay her brother. How many other monstrous and

---

1 From this point the manuscripts are defective to ch. xx.
2 i.e., Venus the bald.
3 i.e., Jupiter the baker.

ludicrous fictions there are, respecting which it is grievous to speak! I do not, however, wish to omit notice of Terminus, since it is related that he did not give way even to Jupiter, though he was an unwrought stone. They suppose that he has the custody of the boundaries, and public prayers are offered to him, that he may keep the stone of the Capitol immoveable, and preserve and extend the boundaries of the Roman empire.

CHAP. XXII. — OF THE SACRED RITES INTRODUCED BY FAUNUS AND NUMA.

Faunus was the first in Latium who introduced these follies, who both instituted bloody sacrifices to his grandfather Saturnus, and wished that his father Picus should be worshipped as a god, and placed Fatua Fauna his wife and sister among the gods, and named her the good goddess. Then at Rome, Numa, who burthened those rude and rustic men with new superstitions, instituted priesthoods, and distributed the gods into families and nations, that he might call off the fierce spirits of the people from the pursuits of arms. Therefore Lucilius, in deriding the folly of those who are slaves to vain superstitions, introduced these verses: —

> "Those bugbears [1] the Lamiæ, which Faunus and Numa Pompilius and others instituted, at these he trembles; he places everything in this. As infant boys believe that every statue of bronze is a living man, so these imagine that all things feigned are true: they believe that statues of bronze contain a heart. It is a painter's [2] gallery; nothing is real, everything fictitious."

Tullius also, writing of the nature of the gods, complains that false and fictitious gods have been introduced, and that from this source have arisen false opinions, and turbulent errors, and almost old womanly superstitions, which opinion ought in comparison [3] with others to be esteemed more weighty, because these things were spoken by one who was both a philosopher and a priest.

CHAP. XXIII. — OF THE GODS AND SACRED RITES OF THE BARBARIANS.

We have spoken respecting the gods: now we will speak of the rites and practices of their sacred institutions. A human victim used to be immolated to the Cyprian Jupiter, as Teucer had appointed. Thus also the Tauri used to offer strangers to Diana; the Latian Jupiter also was propitiated with human blood. Also before Saturnus, men of sixty years of age, according to the oracle [4] of Apollo, were thrown from a bridge into the Tiber. And the Carthaginians not only offered infants to the same Saturnus; but being conquered by the Sicilians, to make an expiation, they immolated two hundred sons of nobles. And not more mild than these are those offerings which are even now made to the Great Mother and to Bellona, in which the priests make an offering, not with the blood of others, but with their own blood; when, mutilating themselves, they cease to be men, and yet do not pass over to the women; or, cutting their shoulders, they sprinkle the loathsome altars with their own blood. But these things are cruel.

Let us come to those which are mild. The sacred rites of Isis show nothing else than the manner in which she lost and found her little son, who is called Osiris. For first her priests and attendants, having shaved all their limbs, and beating their breasts, howl, lament, and search, imitating the manner in which his mother was affected; afterwards the boy is found by Cynocephalus. Thus the mournful rites are ended with gladness. The mystery of Ceres also resembles these, in which torches are lighted, and Proserpine is sought for through the night; and when she has been found, the whole rite is finished with congratulations and the throwing about of torches. The people of Lampsacus, offer an ass to Priapus as an appropriate victim.[5] Lindus is a town of Rhodes, where sacred rites in honour of Hercules are celebrated with revilings. For when Hercules had taken away his oxen from a ploughman, and had slain them, he avenged his injury by taunts; and afterwards having been himself appointed priest, it was ordained that he himself, and other priests after him, should celebrate sacrifices with the same revilings. But the mystery of the Cretan Jupiter represents the manner in which he was withdrawn from his father, or brought up. The goat is beside him, by the teats of which Amalthea nourished the boy. The sacred rites of the mother of the gods also show the same thing. For because the Corybantes then drowned the cry of the boy by the tinkling of their helmets and the striking of their shields, a representation of this circumstance is now repeated in the sacred rites; but cymbals are beaten instead of helmets, and drums instead of shields, that Saturnus may not hear the cries of the boy.

CHAP. XXIV. — OF THE ORIGIN OF SACRED RITES AND SUPERSTITIONS.

These are the mysteries of the gods. Now let us inquire also into the origin of superstitions, that we may search out by whom and at what times they were instituted. Didymus, in those books which are inscribed *Of the Explanation*

---

1 Terriculas. There is another reading, "terricolas." See note at *Institutes*, book i. ch. 22, p 38, *supra*.
2 See preceding note and reference.
3 Comparari. Others read "compatari."
4 Ex responso. The common reading is "ex persona."

5 Ea enim visa est aptior victima, quæ ipsi, cui mactatur, magnitudine virilis obsceni posset æquari.

of Pindar, relates that Melisseus was king of the Cretans, whose daughters were Amalthea and Melissa, who nourished Jupiter with goats' milk and honey; that he introduced new rites and ceremonies of sacred things, and was the first who sacrificed to gods, that is, to Vesta, who is called Tellus, — whence the poet says: —

> "And the first of the gods,
> Tellus," —

and afterwards to the mother of the gods. But Euhemerus, in his sacred history, says that Jupiter himself, after that he received the government, erected temples in honour of himself in many places. For in going about the world, as he came to each place he united the chiefs of the people to himself in friendship and the right of hospitality; and that the remembrance of this might be preserved, he ordered that temples should be built to him, and annual festivals be celebrated by those connected with him in a league of hospitality. Thus he spread the worship of himself through all lands. But at what time they lived can easily be inferred. For Thallus writes in his history, that Belus, the king of the Assyrians, whom the Babylonians worship, and who was the contemporary and friend of Saturnus, was three hundred and twenty-two years before the Trojan war, and it is fourteen hundred and seventy years since the taking of Troy. From which it is evident, that it is not more than eighteen hundred years from the time when mankind fell into error by the institution of new forms of divine worship.

CHAP. XXV. — OF THE GOLDEN AGE, OF IMAGES, AND PROMETHEUS, WHO FIRST FASHIONED MAN.

The poets, therefore, with good reason say that the golden age, which existed in the reign of Saturnus, was changed. For at that time no gods were worshipped, but they knew of one God only. After that they subjected themselves to frail and earthly things, worshipping idols of wood, and brass, and stone, a change took place from the golden age to that of iron. For having lost the knowledge of God, and broken off that one bond of human society, they began to harass one another, to plunder and subdue. But if they would raise their eyes aloft and behold God, who raised them up to the sight of heaven and Himself, they never would bend and prostrate themselves by worshipping earthly things, whose folly Lucretius severely rebukes, saying:[1]

> "And they abase their souls with fear of the gods, and weigh and press them down to the earth."

Wherefore they tremble, and do not understand how foolish it is to fear those things which you have made, or to hope for any protection from those things which are dumb and insensible, and neither see nor hear the suppliant. What majesty, therefore, or deity can they have, which were in the power of a man, that they should not be made, or that they should be made into some other thing, and are so even now? For they are liable to injury and might be carried off by theft, were it not that they are protected by the law and the guardianship of man. Does he therefore appear to be in possession of his senses, who sacrifices to such deities the choicest victims, consecrates gifts, offers costly garments, as if they who are without motion could use them? With reason, then, did Dionysius the tyrant of Sicily plunder and deride the gods of Greece when he had taken possession of it as conqueror; and after the sacrilegious acts which he had committed, he returned to Sicily with a prosperous voyage, and held the kingdom even to his old age: nor were the injured gods able to punish him.

How much better is it to despise vanities, and to turn to God, to maintain the condition which you have received from God, to maintain your name! For on this account he is called *anthropos*,[3] because he looks upward. But he looks upward who looks up to the true and living God, who is in heaven; who seeks after the Maker and Parent of his soul, not only with his perception and mind, but also with his countenance and eyes raised aloft. But he who enslaves himself to earthly and humble things, plainly prefers to himself that which is below him. For since he himself is the workmanship of God, whereas an image is the workmanship of man, the human workmanship cannot be preferred to the divine; and as God is the parent of man, so is the man of the statue. Therefore he is foolish and senseless who adores that which he himself has made, of which detestable and foolish handicraft Prometheus was the author, who was born from Iapetus the uncle of Jupiter. For when first of all Jupiter, having obtained supreme dominion, wished to establish himself as a god, and to found temples, and was seeking for some one who was able to imitate the human figure, at that time Prometheus lived, who fashioned the image of a man from thick clay with such close resemblance, that the novelty and cleverness of the art was a wonder. At length the men of his own time, and afterwards the poets, handed him down as the maker of a true and living man; and we, as often as we praise wrought statues, say that they live and breathe. And he indeed was the inventor of earthenware images. But posterity, following him, both carved them out of marble, and moulded them

[1] *De Nat. Deor.*, vi. 52.
[2] Quare tremunt. Another reading is, "qua reddunt," which is unintelligible.

[3] ἄνθρωπος, man; said to be compounded of ἄνω, τρέπω, and ὤψ, to turn the face upwards. [Needlessly repeated from p. 41, *supra*.]

out of bronze; then in process of time ornament was added of gold and ivory, so that not only the likenesses, but also the gleam itself, might dazzle the eyes. Thus ensnared by beauty, and forgetful of true majesty, sensible beings considered that insensible objects, rational beings that irrational objects, living beings that lifeless objects, were to be worshipped and reverenced by them.

CHAP. XXVI. — OF THE WORSHIP OF THE ELEMENTS AND STARS.

Now let us refute those also who regard the elements of the world as gods, that is, the heaven, the sun, and the moon; for being ignorant of the Maker of these things, they admire and adore the works themselves. And this error belongs not to the ignorant only, but also to philosophers; since the Stoics are of opinion that all the heavenly bodies are to be considered as among the number of the gods, since they all have fixed and regular motions, by which they most constantly preserve the vicissitudes of the times which succeed them. They do not then possess voluntary motion, since they obey prescribed laws, and plainly not by their own sense, but by the workmanship of the supreme Creator, who so ordered them that they should complete unerring [1] courses and fixed circuits, by which they might vary the alternations of days and nights, of summer and winter. But if men admire the effects of these, if they admire their courses, their brightness, their regularity, their beauty, they ought to have understood how much more beautiful, more illustrious, and more powerful than these is the maker and contriver Himself, even God. But they estimated the Divinity by objects which fall under the sight of men; [2] not knowing that objects which come within the sight cannot be eternal, and that those which are eternal cannot be discerned by mortal eyes.

CHAP. XXVII. — OF THE CREATION, SIN, AND PUNISHMENT OF MAN; AND OF ANGELS, BOTH GOOD AND BAD.

One subject remains, and that the last: that, since it usually happens, as we read in histories, that the gods appear to have displayed their majesty by auguries, by dreams, by oracles, and also by the punishments of those who had committed sacrilege, I may show what cause produced this effect, so that no one even now may fall into the same snares into which those of old fell. When God, according to His excellent majesty, had framed the world out of nothing, and had decked the heaven with lights, and had filled the earth and the sea with living creatures, then He formed man out of clay, and fashioned him after the resemblance of His own likeness, and breathed into him that he might live,[3] and placed him in a garden [4] which He had planted with every kind of fruit-bearing tree, and commanded him not to eat of one tree in which He had placed the knowledge of good and evil, warning him that it would come to pass, that if he did so he would lose his life, but that if he observed the command of God he would remain immortal. Then the serpent, who was one of the servants of God, envying man because he was made immortal, enticed him by stratagem to transgress the command and law of God. And in this manner he did indeed receive the knowledge of good and evil, but he lost the life which God had given him to be for ever.

Therefore He drove out the sinner from the sacred place, and banished him into this world, that he might seek sustenance by labour, that he might according to his deserts undergo difficulties and troubles; and He surrounded the garden itself with a fence of fire, that none of men even till the day of judgment might attempt secretly [5] to enter into that place of perpetual blessedness. Then death came upon man according to the sentence of God; and yet his life, though it had begun to be temporary, had as its boundary a thousand years, and that was the extent of human life even to the deluge. For after the flood the life of men was gradually shortened, and was reduced to a hundred and twenty years. But that serpent, who from his deeds received the name of devil, that is, accuser or informer, did not cease to persecute the seed of man, whom he had deceived from the beginning. At length he urged him who was first born in this world, under the impulse of envy, to the murder of his brother, that of the two men who were first born he might destroy the one, and make the other a parricide.[6] Nor did he cease upon this from infusing the venom of malice into the breasts of men through each generation, from corrupting and depraving them; in short, from overwhelming them with such crimes, that an instance of justice was now rare, but men lived after the manner of the beasts.

But when God saw this, He sent His angels to instruct the race of men, and to protect them from all evil. He gave these a command to abstain from earthly things, lest, being polluted by any taint, they should be deprived of the honour of angels. But that wily accuser, while they tarried among men, allured these also to

[1] Inerrabiles. There is another reading, "inenarrabiles," indescribable.
[2] Humanis visibus.

[3] Inspiravit ad vitam.
[4] Paradiso.
[5] Irrepere.
[6] Parricidam. The word first means the murderer of a parent or near relative; then simply a murderer.

pleasures, so that they might defile themselves with women. Then, being condemned by the sentence of God, and cast forth on account of their sins, they lost both the name and substance of angels. Thus, having become ministers of the devil, that they might have a solace of their ruin, they betook themselves to the ruining of men, for whose protection they had come.[1]

CHAP. XXVIII. — OF THE DEMONS, AND THEIR EVIL PRACTICES.

These are the demons, of whom the poets often speak in their poems, whom Hesiod calls the guardians of men. For they so persuaded men by their enticements and deceits, that they believed that the same were gods. In fine, Socrates used to give out that he had a demon as the guardian and director of his life from his first childhood, and that he could do nothing without his assent and command. They attach themselves, therefore, to individuals, and occupy houses under the name of Genii or Penates. To these temples are built, to these libations are daily offered as to the Lares, to these honour is paid as to the averters of evils. These from the beginning, that they might turn away men from the knowledge of the true God, introduced new superstitions and worship of gods. These taught that the memory of dead kings should be consecrated, temples be built, and images made, not that they might lessen the honour of God, or increase their own, which they lost by sinning, but that they might take away life from men, deprive them of the hope of true light, lest men should arrive at that heavenly reward of immortality from which they fell. They also brought to light astrology, and augury, and divination; and though these things are in themselves false, yet they themselves, the authors of evils, so govern and regulate them that they are believed to be true. They also invented the tricks of the magic art, to deceive the eyes. By their aid it comes to pass, that that which is appears not to be, and that which is not appears to be. They themselves invented necromancies, responses, and oracles, to delude the minds of men with lying divination by means of ambiguous issues. They are present in the temples and at all sacrifices; and by the exhibition of some deceitful prodigies, to the surprise of those who are present, they so deceive men, that they believe that a divine power is present in images and statues. They even enter secretly into bodies, as being slight spirits; and they excite diseases in the vitiated limbs, which when appeased with sacrifices and vows they may again remove. They send dreams either full of terror,[2] that they themselves may be invoked, or the issues of which may correspond with the truth, that they may increase the veneration paid to themselves. Sometimes also they put forth something of vengeance against the sacrilegious, that whoever sees it may become more timid and superstitious. Thus by their frauds they have drawn darkness over the human race, that truth might be oppressed, and the name of the supreme and matchless God might be forgotten.

CHAP. XXIX. — OF THE PATIENCE AND PROVIDENCE OF GOD.

But some one says: Why, then, does the true God permit these things to be done? Why does He not rather remove or destroy the wicked? Why, in truth, did He from the beginning give power[3] to the demon, so that there should be one who might corrupt and destroy all things? I will briefly say why He willed that this should be so. I ask whether virtue is a good or an evil. It cannot be denied that it is a good. If virtue is a good, vice, on the contrary, is an evil. If vice is an evil on this account, because it opposes virtue, and virtue is on this account a good, because it overthrows vice, it follows that virtue cannot exist without vice; and if you take away vice, the merits of virtue will be taken away. For there can be no victory without an enemy. Thus it comes to pass, that good cannot exist without an evil.

Chrysippus, a man of active mind, saw this when discussing the subject of providence, and charges those with folly who think that good is caused by God, but say that evil is not thus caused. Aulus Gellius[4] has interpreted his sentiment in his books of *Attic Nights;* thus saying: "They to whom it does not appear that the world was made for the sake of God and men, and that human affairs are governed by providence, think that they use a weighty argument when they thus speak: If there were a providence, there would be no evils. For they say that nothing is less in agreement with providence, than that in this world, on account of which it is said that God made men,[5] the power of troubles and evils should be so great. In reply to these things, Chrysippus, when he was arguing, in his fourth book respecting providence, said: Nothing can be more foolish than those who think that good things could have existed, if there were not evils in the same place. For since good things are contrary to evil, they must of necessity be opposed to each other, and must stand resting, as it were, on mutual and opposite support.[6] Thus there is no contrary without another contrary.

[1] [This is a curious enlargement of the idea as taught elsewhere. See vol. ii. p. 142, this series.]

[2] Plena terroris. Another reading is, "aut plane terrores."

[3] ἀρχήν. Others read δαιμοναρχίαν, "the power of demons."

[4] Lib. vi. 1.

[5] Propter quem homines fecisse dicatur Deus. Others read, "Quem propter homines," etc.

[6] Quasi mutuo adversoque fulta nisu consistere.

For how could there be any perception of justice, unless there were injuries? or what else is justice, but the removal of injustice? In like manner, the nature of fortitude cannot be understood except by placing[1] beside it cowardice, or the nature of self-control except by intemperance. Likewise, in what manner would there be prudence, unless there were the contrary, imprudence? On the same principle, he says, why do the foolish men not require this also, that there should be truth and not falsehood? For there exist together good and evil things, prosperity and trouble, pleasure and pain. For the one being bound to the other at opposite poles, as Plato says, if you take away one, you take away both." You see, therefore, that which I have often said, that good and evil are so connected with one another, that the one cannot exist without the other. Therefore God acted with the greatest foresight in placing the subject-matter of virtue in evils which He made for this purpose, that He might establish for us a contest, in which He would crown the victorious with the reward of immortality.[2]

CHAP. XXX. — OF FALSE WISDOM.

I have taught, as I imagine, that the honours paid to gods are not only impious, but also vain, either because they were men whose memory was consecrated after death; or because the images themselves are insensible and deaf, inasmuch as they are formed of earth, and that it is not right for man, who ought to look up to heavenly things, to subject himself to earthly things; or because the spirits who claim to themselves those acts of religious service are unholy and impure, and on this account, being condemned by the sentence of God, fell to the earth, and that it is not lawful to submit to the power of those to whom you are superior, if you wish to be a follower of the true God. It remains that, as we have spoken of false religion, we should also discuss the subject of false wisdom, which the philosophers profess, — men endued with the greatest learning and eloquence, but far removed from the truth, because they neither know God nor the wisdom of God. And although they are clever and learned, yet, because their wisdom is human, I shall not fear to contend with them, that it may be evident that falsehood can be easily overcome by truth, and earthly things by heavenly.

They thus define the nature of philosophy. Philosophy is the love or pursuit of wisdom. Therefore it is not wisdom itself; for that which loves must be different from that which is loved. If it is the pursuit of wisdom, not even thus is philosophy *identical with* wisdom. For wisdom is the object itself which is sought, but the pursuit is that which seeks it. Therefore the very definition or meaning of the word plainly shows that philosophy is not wisdom itself. I will say that it[3] is not even the pursuit of wisdom, in which wisdom is not comprised. For who can be said to devote himself to the pursuit of that to which he can by no means attain? He who gives himself to the pursuit of medicine, or grammar, or oratory, may be said to be studious of that art which he is learning; but when he has learned, he is now said to be a physician, a grammarian, or an orator. Thus also those who are studious of wisdom, after they had learned it, ought to have been called wise. But since they are called students of wisdom as long as they live, it is manifest that that is not the pursuit, because it is impossible to arrive at the object itself which is sought for in the pursuit, unless by chance they who pursue wisdom even to the end of life are about to be wise in another world. Now every pursuit is connected with some end. That, therefore, is not a right pursuit which has no end.

CHAP. XXXI. — OF KNOWLEDGE AND SUPPOSITION.

Moreover, there are two things which appear to fall under the subject of philosophy — knowledge and supposition; and if these are taken away, philosophy altogether falls to the ground. But the chief of the philosophers themselves have taken away both from philosophy. Socrates took away knowledge, Zeno supposition. Let us see whether they were right in doing so. Wisdom is, as Cicero defined it,[4] the knowledge of divine and human things. Now if this definition is true, wisdom does not come within the power of man. For who of mortals can assume this to himself, to profess that he knows divine and human things? I say nothing of human affairs; for although they are connected with divine, yet, since they belong to man, let us grant that it is possible for man to know them. Certainly he cannot know divine things by himself, since he is a man; whereas he who knows them must be divine, and therefore God. But man is neither divine nor God. Man, therefore, cannot thoroughly know divine things by himself. No one, therefore, is wise but God, or certainly that man whom God has taught. But they, because they are neither gods, nor taught by God, cannot be wise, that is, acquainted with divine and human things. Knowledge, therefore, is rightly taken away by Socrates and the Academics. Supposition also does not agree with the wise man. For every

[1] Appositione. Others read "oppositione."

[2] [Philosophically, not dogmatically, asserted. God's wisdom in permitting evil (which originated in the fall of free intellects) to last for a season, will vindicate itself in judgment.]

[3] Philosophy.

[4] *De Offic.*, ii. 2.

one supposes that of which he is ignorant. Now, to suppose that you know that of which you are ignorant, is rashness and folly. Supposition, therefore, was rightly taken away by Zeno. If, therefore, there is no knowledge in man, and there ought to be no supposition, philosophy is cut up by the roots.

CHAP. XXXII. — OF THE SECTS OF PHILOSOPHERS, AND THEIR DISAGREEMENT.

To this is added, that it[1] is not uniform; but being divided into sects, and scattered into many and discordant opinions, it has no fixed state. For since they all separately attack and harass one another, and there is none of them which is not condemned of folly in the judgment of the rest, while the members are plainly at variance with one another, the whole body of philosophy is brought to destruction. Hence the Academy afterwards originated. For when the leading men of that sect saw that philosophy was altogether overthrown by philosophers mutually opposing each other, they undertook war against all, that they might destroy all the arguments of all; while they themselves assert nothing except one thing — that nothing can be known. Thus, having taken away knowledge, they overthrew the ancient philosophy. But they did not even themselves retain the name of philosophers, since they admitted their ignorance, because to be ignorant of all things is not only not the part of a philosopher, but not even of a man. Thus the philosophers, because they have no defence, must destroy one another with mutual wounds, and philosophy itself must altogether consume and put an end to itself by its own arms. But they say it is only natural philosophy which thus gives way. How is it with moral? Does that rest on any firm foundation? Let us see whether philosophers are agreed in this part at any rate, which relates to the condition of life.

CHAP. XXXIII. — WHAT IS THE CHIEF GOOD TO BE SOUGHT IN LIFE.

What is the chief good must be an object of inquiry, that our whole life and actions may be directed to it. When inquiry is made respecting the chief good of man, it ought to be settled to be of such a kind, first, that it have reference to man alone; in the next place, that it belong peculiarly to the mind; lastly, that it be sought by virtue. Let us see, therefore, whether the chief good which the philosophers mark out be such that it has reference neither to a dumb animal nor to the body, and cannot be attained without virtue.

Aristippus, the founder of the Cyrenaic sect, who thought that bodily pleasure was the chief good, ought to be removed from the number of philosophers, and from the society of men, because he compared himself to a beast. The chief good of Hieronymus is to be without pain, that of Diodorus to cease to be in pain. But the other animals avoid pain; and when they are without pain, or cease to be in pain, are glad. What distinction, then, will be given to man, if his chief good is judged to be common with the beasts? Zeno thought that the chief good was to live agreeably to nature. But this definition is a general one. For all animals live agreeably to nature, and each has its own nature.

Epicurus maintained that it was pleasure of the soul. What is pleasure of the soul but joy, in which the soul for the most part luxuriates, and unbends itself either to sport or to laughter? But this good befalls even dumb animals, which, when they are satisfied with pasture, relax themselves to joy and wantonness. Dinomachus and Callipho approved of honourable pleasure; but they either said the same that Epicurus did, that bodily pleasure is dishonourable; or if they considered bodily pleasures to be partly base and partly honourable, then that is not the chief good which is ascribed to the body. The Peripatetics make up the chief good of goods of the soul, and body, and fortune. The goods of the soul may be approved of; but if they require assistance for the completion of happiness, they are plainly weak. But the goods of the body and of fortune are not in the power of man; nor is that now the chief good which is assigned to the body, or to things placed without us, because this double good extends even to the cattle, which have need of being well, and of a due supply of food. The Stoics are believed to have entertained much better views, who said that virtue was the chief good. But virtue cannot be the chief good, since, if it is the endurance of evils and of labours, it is not happy of itself; but it ought to effect and produce the chief good, because it cannot be attained without the greatest difficulty and labour. But, in truth, Aristotle wandered far from reason, who connected honour with virtue, as though it were possible for virtue at any time to be separated from honour, or to be united with baseness.

Herillus the Pyrrhonist made knowledge the chief good. This indeed belongs to man, and to the soul only, but it may happen to him without virtue. For he is not to be considered happy who has either learnt anything by hearing, or has gained the knowledge of it by a little reading; nor is it a definition of the chief good, because there may be a knowledge either of bad things, or at any rate of things that are useless. And if it is the knowledge of good and useful things which you have acquired by labour, nevertheless it is not the chief good, because knowledge is

[1] i.e., philosophy.

not sought on its own account, but on account of something else. For the arts are learnt on this account, that they may be to us the means of gaining support, or a source of glory, or even of pleasure; and it is plain that these things cannot be the chief goods. Therefore the philosophers do not observe the rule even in moral philosophy, inasmuch as they are at variance with one another on the main point[1] itself, that is, in that discussion by which the life is moulded. For the precepts cannot be equal, or resembling one another, when some train men to pleasure, others to honour, others indeed to nature, others to knowledge; some to the pursuit, others to the avoiding of riches; some to entire insensibility to pain, others to the endurance of evils: in all which, as I have shown before, they turn aside from reason, because they are ignorant of God.

CHAP. XXXIV. — THAT MEN ARE BORN TO JUSTICE.

Let us now see what is proposed to the wise man as the chief good.[2] That men are born to justice is not only taught by the sacred writings, but is sometimes acknowledged even by these same philosophers. Thus Cicero says: "But of all things which fall under the discussion of learned men, nothing assuredly is more excellent than that it should be clearly understood that we are born to justice." This is most true.[3] For we are not born to wickedness, since we are a social and sociable animal. The wild beasts are produced to exercise their fierceness; for they are unable to live in any other way than by prey and bloodshed. These, however, although pressed by extreme hunger, nevertheless refrain from animals of their own kind. Birds also do the same, which must feed upon the carcases of others. How much more is it befitting, that man, who is united with man both in the interchange of language and in communion of feeling, should spare man, and love him! For this is justice.

But since wisdom has been given to man alone, that he may understand God, and this alone makes the difference between man and the dumb animals, justice itself is bound up in two duties. He owes the one to God as to a father, the other to man as to a brother; for we are produced by the same God. Therefore it has been deservedly and rightly said, that wisdom is the knowledge of divine and human affairs. For it is right that we should know what we owe to God, and what to man; namely, to God religion, to man affection. But the former belongs to wisdom, the latter to virtue; and justice comprises both. If, therefore, it is evident that man is born to justice, it is necessary that the just man should be subject to evils, that he may exercise the virtue with which he is endued. For virtue is the enduring of evils. He will avoid pleasures as an evil: he will despise riches, because they are frail; and if he has them, he will liberally bestow them, to preserve the wretched: he will not be desirous of honours, because they are short and transitory; he will do injury to no one; if he shall suffer, he will not retaliate; and he will not take vengeance upon one who plunders his property. For he will deem it unlawful to injure a man; and if there shall be any one who would compel him to depart from God, he will not refuse tortures nor death. Thus it will come to pass, that he must necessarily live in poverty and lowliness, and in insults, or even tortures.

CHAP. XXXV. — THAT IMMORTALITY IS THE CHIEF GOOD.

What, then, will be the advantage of justice and virtue, if they shall have nothing but evil in life? But if virtue, which despises all earthly goods, most wisely endures all evils, and endures death itself in the discharge of duty, cannot be without a reward, what remains but that immortality alone is its reward? For if a happy life falls to the lot of man, as the philosophers will have it, and in this point alone they do not disagree, therefore also immortality falls to him. For that only is happy which is incorruptible; that only is incorruptible which is eternal. Therefore immortality is the chief good, because it belongs both to man, and to the soul, and to virtue. We are only directed to this; we are born to the attainment of this. Therefore God proposes to us virtue and justice, that we may obtain that eternal reward for our labours. But concerning that immortality[4] itself we will speak in the proper place. There remains the philosophy of Logic,[5] which contributes nothing to a happy life. For wisdom does not consist in the arrangement of speech, but in the heart and the feeling. But if natural philosophy is superfluous, and this of logic, and the philosophers have erred in moral philosophy, which alone is necessary, because they have been unable in any way to find out the chief good; therefore all philosophy is found to be empty and useless, which was unable to comprehend the nature of man, or to fulfil its duty and office.

CHAP. XXXVI. — OF THE PHILOSOPHERS, — NAMELY, EPICURUS AND PYTHAGORAS.

Since I have spoken briefly of philosophy, now also I will speak a few things about the

1 In ipso cardine. [Horace, *Sat.*, book ii. 6, 71–76.]

2 Some editions repeat the words "summum bonum," but these words appear to obstruct the sense.

3 [i.e., *philosophically;* our moral constitution dictating what is just.]

4 Non mortalitate.

5 λογικὴ philosophia. Under this is included everything connected with the system of speaking.

philosophers. This is especially the doctrine of Epicurus, that there is no providence. And at the same time he does not deny the existence of gods. In both respects he acts contrary to reason. For if there are gods, it follows that there is a providence. For otherwise we can form no intelligible idea of God, for it is His peculiar province to foresee.[1] But Epicurus says He takes no care about anything. Therefore He disregards not only the affairs of men, but also heavenly things. How, therefore, or from what, do you affirm that He exists? For when you have taken away the divine providence and care, it would naturally follow that you should altogether deny the existence of God; whereas now you have left Him in name, but in reality you have taken Him away. Whence, then, did the world derive its origin, if God takes no care of anything? There are, he says, minute atoms, which can neither be seen nor touched, and from the fortuitous meeting of these all things arose, and are continually arising. If they are neither seen nor perceived by any part of the body, how could you know of their existence? In the next place, if they exist, with what mind do they meet together to effect anything? If they are smooth, they cannot cohere: if they are hooked and angular, then they are divisible; for hooks and angles project, and can be cut off. But these things are senseless and unprofitable. Why should I mention that he also makes souls capable of extinction? who is refuted not only by all philosophers and general persuasion, but also by the answers of bards, by the predictions of the Sibyls, and lastly, by the divine voices of the prophets themselves; so that it is wonderful that Epicurus alone existed, who should place the condition of man on a level with the flocks and beasts.

What of Pythagoras, who was first called a philosopher, who judged that souls were indeed immortal, but that they passed into other bodies, either of cattle, or of birds, or of beasts? Would it not have been better that they should be destroyed, together with their bodies, than thus to be condemned to pass into the bodies of other animals? Would it not be better not to exist at all, than, after having had the form of a man, to live as a swine or a dog? And the foolish man, to gain credit for his saying, said that he himself had been Euphorbus in the Trojan war, and that, when he had been slain, he passed into other figures of animals, and at last became Pythagoras. O happy man! to whom alone so great a memory was given; or rather unhappy, who, when changed into a sheep, was not permitted to be ignorant of what he was! And would to Heaven that he alone had been thus senseless! He found also some to believe him, and some indeed among the learned,[2] to whom the inheritance of folly passed.

CHAP. XXXVII. — OF SOCRATES AND HIS CONTRADICTION.

After him Socrates held the first place in philosophy, who was pronounced most wise even by the oracle, because he confessed that he knew one thing only, — namely, that he knew nothing. And on the authority of this oracle it was right that the natural philosophers should restrain themselves, lest they should either inquire into those things which they could not know, or should think that they knew things which they did not know. Let us, however, see whether Socrates was most wise, as the Pythian god proclaimed. He often made use of this proverb, that that which is above us has also no reference to us. He has now passed beyond the limits of his opinion. For he who said that he knew one thing only, found another thing to speak of, as though he knew it; but that in vain. For God, who is plainly above us, is to be sought for; and religion is to be undertaken, which alone separates us from the brutes, which indeed Socrates not only rejected, but even derided, in swearing by a goose and a dog, as if in truth he could not have sworn by Æsculapius, to whom he had vowed a cock. Behold the sacrifice of a wise man! And because he was unable to offer this in his own person, since he was at the point of death, he entreated his friends to perform the vow after his death, lest forsooth he should be detained as a debtor in the lower regions. He assuredly both pronounced that he knew nothing, and made good his statement.[3]

CHAP. XXXVIII. — OF PLATO, WHOSE DOCTRINE APPROACHES MORE NEARLY TO THE TRUTH.

His disciple Plato, whom Tully speaks of as the god of philosophers, alone of all so studied philosophy that he approached nearer to the truth; and yet, because he was ignorant of God, he so failed in many things, that no one fell into worse errors, especially because in his books respecting the state he wished all things to be common to all. This is endurable concerning property, though it is unjust. For it ought not to be an injury to any one, if he possesses more than another through his own industry; or to be a profit to any one, if through his own fault he possesses less. But, as I have said, this is capable of being endured in some way. Shall there be a com-

[1] Providere.

[2] Inter doctos homines. Others read "indoctos homines," but this does not convey so good a meaning.

[3] [Other and more creditable explanations are given. Socrates recognised the rites of his countrymen. See Tayler Lewis in a noble chapter, *Plato*, etc., p. 250.]

munity of wives also, and of children? Shall there be no distinction of blood, or certainty of race? Shall there be neither families, nor relationships, nor affinities, but all things confused and indiscriminate, as in herds of cattle? Shall there be no self-restraint in men, no chastity in women? What conjugal affection can there be in these, between whom on either side there is no sure or peculiar [1] love? Who will be dutiful towards a father, when he knows not from whom he was born? Who will love a son, whom he will reckon as not his own? [2] Moreover, he opened [3] the senate house to women, and entrusted to them warfare, magistracies, and commands.[4] But how great will be the calamity of that city, in which women shall discharge the duties of men! But of this more fully at another opportunity.

Zeno, the master of the Stoics, who praises virtue, judged that pity, which is a very great virtue, should be cut away, as though it were a disease of the mind, whereas it is at the same time dear to God and necessary for men. For who is there who, when placed in any evil, would be unwilling to be pitied, and would not desire the assistance of those who might succour them, which is not called forth so as to render aid, except by the feeling of pity? Although he calls this humanity and piety, he does not change the matter itself, only the name. This is the affection which has been given to man alone, that by mutual assistance we might alleviate our weakness; and he who removes this affection reduces us to the life of the beasts. For his assertion that all faults are equal, proceeds from that inhumanity with which also he assails pity as a disease. For he who makes no difference in faults, either thinks that light offences ought to be visited with severe punishments, which is the part of a cruel judge, or that great offences should be visited with slight punishments, which is the part of a worthless judge. In either case there is injury to the state. For if the greatest crimes are lightly punished, the boldness of the wicked will increase, and go on to deeds of greater daring; and if a punishment of too great severity is inflicted for slight offences, inasmuch as no one can be exempt from fault, many citizens will incur peril, who by correction might become better.

CHAP. XXXIX. — OF VARIOUS PHILOSOPHERS, AND OF THE ANTIPODES.

These things, truly, are of small importance, but they arise from the same falsehood. Xenophanes said that the orb of the moon is eighteen times larger than this earth of ours; and that within its compass is contained another earth, which is inhabited by men and animals of every kind. About the antipodes also one can neither hear nor speak without laughter. It is asserted as something serious, that we should believe that there are men who have their feet opposite to ours. The ravings of Anaxagoras are more tolerable, who said that snow was black. And not only the sayings, but the deeds, of some are ridiculous. Democritus neglected his land which was left to him by his father, and suffered it to become a public pasture. Diogenes with his company of dogs,[5] who professes that great and perfect virtue in the contempt of all things, preferred to beg for his support, rather than to seek it by honest labour, or to have any property. Undoubtedly the life of a wise man ought to be to others an example of living. If all should imitate the wisdom of these, how will states exist? But perhaps the same Cynics were able to afford an example of modesty, who lived with their wives in public. I know not how they could defend virtue, who took away modesty.

Nor was Aristippus better than these, who, I believe, that he might please his mistress Lais, instituted the Cyrenaic system, by which he placed the end of the chief good in bodily pleasure, that authority might not be wanting to his faults, or learning to his vices. Are those men of greater fortitude to be more approved, who, that they might be said to have despised death, died by their own hands? Zeno, Empedocles, Chrysippus, Cleanthes, Democritus, and Cato, imitating these, did not know that he who put himself to death is guilty of murder, according to the divine right and law. For it was God who placed us in this abode of flesh: it was He who gave us the temporary habitation of the body, that we should inhabit it as long as He pleased. Therefore it is to be considered impious, to wish to depart from it without the command of God. Therefore violence must not be applied to nature. He knows how to destroy[6] His own work. And if any one shall apply impious hands to that work, and shall tear asunder the bonds of the divine workmanship, he endeavours to flee from God, whose sentence no one will be able to escape, whether alive or dead. Therefore they are accursed and impious, whom I have mentioned above, who even taught what are the befitting reasons for voluntary death; so that it was not enough of guilt that they were self-murderers, unless they instructed others also to this wickedness.[7]

---

1 Proprius.
2 Alienum.
3 Reseravit. Others read "reservavit."
4 [A republic of "philosophers" (*credula gens*) was set up in France (A.D. 1793), to prove their idiotic incompetency for practical affairs.]
5 i.e., the Cynics.
6 Resolvat.
7 [A succinct statement of the sixth command in its bearing on suicide.]

CHAP. XL. — OF THE FOOLISHNESS OF THE PHILOSOPHERS.

There are innumerable sayings and doings of the philosophers, by which their foolishness may be shown. Therefore, since we are unable to enumerate them all, a few will be sufficient. It is enough that it is understood that the philosophers were neither teachers of justice, of which they were ignorant, nor of virtue, of which they falsely boast. For what can they teach, who often confess their own ignorance? I omit to mention Socrates, whose opinion is well known. Anaxagoras proclaims that all things are overspread with darkness. Empedocles says that the paths for finding out the truth of the senses are narrow. Democritus asserts that truth lies sunk in a deep well; and because they nowhere find it, they therefore affirm that no wise man has as yet existed. Since, therefore, human wisdom has no existence (Socrates says in the writings of Plato), let us follow that which is divine, and let us give thanks to God, who has revealed and delivered it to us; and let us congratulate ourselves, that through the divine bounty we possess the truth and wisdom, which, though sought by so many intellects through so many ages, philosophy [1] was not able to discover.

CHAP. XLI. — OF TRUE RELIGION AND WISDOM.

Now, since we have refuted false religion, which is in the worship of the gods, and false wisdom, which is in the philosophers, let us come to true religion and wisdom. And, indeed, we must speak of them both conjointly, because they are closely connected. For to worship the true God, that and nothing else is wisdom. For that God who is supreme and the Maker of all things, who made man as the image of Himself, on this account conferred on him alone of all animals the gift of reason, that he might pay back honour to Him as his Father and his Lord, and by the exercise of this piety and obedience might gain the reward of immortality. This is a true and divine mystery. But among those,[2] because they are not true, there is no agreement. Neither are sacred rites performed in philosophy, nor is philosophy treated of in sacred things; and on this account their religion is false, because it does not possess wisdom; and on this account their wisdom is false, because it does not possess religion. But where both are joined together, there the truth must necessarily be; so that if it is asked what the truth itself is, it may be rightly said to be either wise religion or religious wisdom.

[1] Philosophia non potuit invenire. Other editions have, "philosophiam nemo potuit invenire." ["The world by wisdom (σοφία) knew not God," etc.; 1 Cor. i. 21.]

[2] i.e., the philosophers before mentioned.

CHAP. XLII. — OF RELIGIOUS WISDOM: THE NAME OF CHRIST KNOWN TO NONE, EXCEPT HIMSELF AND HIS FATHER.

I will now say what wise religion, or religious wisdom, is. God, in the beginning, before He made the world, from the fountain of His own eternity, and from the divine and everlasting Spirit,[3] begat for Himself a Son incorruptible, faithful, corresponding to His Father's excellence and majesty. He is virtue, He is reason, He is the word of God, He is wisdom. With this artificer, as Hermes says, and counsellor, as the Sibyl says, He contrived the excellent and wondrous fabric of this world. In fine, of all the angels, whom the same God formed from His own breath,[4] He alone was admitted into a participation of His supreme power, He alone was called God. For all things were through Him, and nothing was without Him. In fine, Plato, not altogether as a philosopher, but as a seer, spoke concerning the first and second God, perhaps following Trismegistus in this, whose words I have translated from the Greek, and subjoined: "The Lord and Maker of all things, whom we have thought to be called God, created [5] a second God, who is visible and sensible. But by sensible I mean, not that He Himself receives sensation, but that He causes sensation and sight. When, therefore, He had made this, the first, and one, and only one, He appeared to Him most excellent, and full of all good qualities." The Sibyl also says that God the guide of all was made by God; and another, that

"God the Son of God must be known,"

as those examples which I have brought forward in my books declare. Him the prophets, filled with the inspiration of the Divine Spirit, proclaimed; of whom especially Solomon in the book of Wisdom, and also his father, the writer of divine hymns — both most renowned kings, who preceded the times of the Trojan war by a hundred and eighty years [6] — testify that He was born of God. His name is known to none, except to Himself and the Father, as John teaches in the Revelation.[7] Hermes says that His name cannot be uttered by mortal mouth. Yet by men He is called by two names — Jesus, which is Saviour, and Christ, which is King. He is called Saviour on this account, because He is the health and safety of all who believe in God through Him. He is called Christ on this account, because He Himself will come from

[3] [This refers to the Spirit of the Father, as Cyprian (vol. v. p. 516), "My heart hath *breathed* out a good Word."]

[4] De suis spiritibus.

[5] [Plato does not speak dogmatically, but with a marvellous intuition of truth. The Son is "begotten, not made."]

[6] This is an error. Both David and Solomon lived after the supposed taking of Troy.

[7] Rev. xix. 12.

heaven at the end of this dispensation[1] to judge the world, and, having raised the dead, to establish for Himself an everlasting kingdom.

CHAP. XLIII. — OF THE NAME OF JESUS CHRIST, AND HIS TWOFOLD NATIVITY.

But lest by any chance there should be any doubt in your mind why we call Him Jesus Christ, who was born of God before the world, and who was born of man three hundred years ago, I will briefly explain to you the reason. The same person is the son of God and of man. For He was twice born: first of God, in the spirit, before the origin of the world; afterwards in the flesh of man, in the reign of Augustus; and in connection with this fact is an illustrious and great mystery, in which is contained both the salvation of men and the religion of the Supreme God, and all truth. For when first the accursed and impious worship of gods crept in through the treachery of the demons, then the religion of God remained with the Hebrews alone, who, not by any law, but after the manner of their fathers, observed the worship handed down to them by successive generations,[2] even until the time when they went forth out of Egypt under the leadership of Moses, the first of all the prophets, through whom the law was given to them from God; and they were afterwards called Jews. Therefore they served God, being bound by the chains of the law. But they also, by degrees going astray to profane rites, undertook the worship of strange gods, and, leaving the worship of their fathers, sacrificed to senseless images. Therefore God sent to them prophets filled with the Divine Spirit, to upbraid them with their sins and proclaim repentance, to threaten them with the vengeance which would follow, and announce that it would come to pass, if they persisted in the same faults, that He would send another as the bearer of a new law; and having removed the ungrateful people from their inheritance, He would assemble to Himself a more faithful people from foreign nations. But they not only persisted in their course, but even slew the messengers themselves. Therefore He condemned them on account of these deeds: nor did He any longer send messengers to a stubborn people; but He sent His own Son, to call all nations to the favour of God. Nor, however, did He shut them out, impious and ungrateful as they were, from the hope of salvation; but He sent Him to them before all others,[3] that if they should by chance obey, they might not lose that which they had received; but if they should refuse to receive their God, then, the heirs being removed,[4] the Gentiles would come into possession. Therefore the supreme Father ordered Him to descend to the earth, and to put on a human body, that, being subject to the sufferings of the flesh, He might teach virtue and patience not only by words, but also by deeds. Therefore He was born a second time as man, of a virgin, without a father, that, as in His first spiritual birth, being born of God alone, He was made a sacred spirit, so in His second and fleshly birth, being born of a mother only, He might become holy flesh, that through Him the flesh, which had become subject to sin, might be freed from destruction.

CHAP. XLIV. — THE TWOFOLD NATIVITY OF CHRIST IS PROVED FROM THE PROPHETS.

That these things should thus take place as I have set them forth, the prophets had before predicted. In the writings of Solomon it is thus written:[5] "The womb of a virgin was strengthened, and conceived: and a virgin was impregned, and became a mother in great pity." In Isaiah[6] it is thus written: "Behold, a virgin shall conceive, and bear a son, and ye shall call His name Immanuel;" which, being interpreted, is God with us.[7] For He was with us on the earth, when He assumed flesh; and He was no less God in man, and man in God. That He was both God and man was declared before by the prophets. That He was God, Isaiah[8] thus declares: "They shall fall down unto Thee, they shall make supplication unto Thee; since God is in Thee, and we knew it not, even the God of Israel. They shall be ashamed and confounded, all of them who oppose themselves to Thee, and shall go to confusion." Also Jeremiah:[9] "This is our God, and there shall none other be compared unto Him; He hath found out all the way of knowledge, and hath given it unto Jacob His servant, and to Israel His beloved. Afterward He was seen upon earth, and dwelt among men." Likewise that He was man, the same Jeremiah[10] says: "And He is man, and who knew Him?" Isaiah also thus speaks:[11] "And the Lord shall send them a man who shall save them, and with judgment shall He heal them." Also Moses himself in the book of Numbers:[12] "There shall come a star out of Jacob, and a man shall arise out of Israel." For this cause, therefore, being God, He took upon Him flesh, that, becoming a mediator[13] between God and man, having over-

1 In sæculi hujus consummatione.
2 Per successiones.
3 Potissimum.
4 Hæredibus abdicatis.
5 See *Instit.*, iv. 12.
6 Isa. vii. 14.
7 Matt. i. 23.
8 Isa. xlv. 14–16.
9 Baruch iii. 35–37.
10 xvii. 9. This and the following quotations are from the Septuagint.
11 Isa. xix. 20.
12 Num. xxiv. 17. The prophecy of Balaam.
13 Inter deum et hominem medius factus.

come death, He might by His guidance lead man to God.

CHAP. XLV. — THE POWER AND WORKS OF CHRIST ARE PROVED FROM THE SCRIPTURES.

We have spoken of His nativity; now let us speak of His power and works, which, when He wrought them among men, the Jews, seeing them to be great and wonderful, supposed that they were done by the influence of magic, not knowing that all those things which were done by Him had been foretold by the prophets. He gave strength to the sick, and to those languishing under various diseases, not by any healing remedy, but instantaneously, by the force and power of His word; He restored the weak, He made the lame to walk, He gave sight to the blind, He made the dumb to speak, the deaf to hear; He cleansed the polluted and unclean, He restored their right mind to those who were maddened with the attack of demons, He recalled to life and light those who were dead or now buried. He also fed and satisfied[1] five thousand men with five loaves and two fishes. He also walked upon the sea. He also in a tempest commanded the wind to be still, and immediately there was a calm; all which things we find predicted both in the books of the prophets and in the verses of the Sibyls.

When a great multitude resorted to Him on account of these miracles, and, as He truly was, believed Him to be the Son of God, and sent from God, the priests and rulers of the Jews, filled with envy, and at the same time excited with anger, because He reproved their sins and injustice, conspired to put Him to death; and that this would happen, Solomon had foretold a little more than a thousand years before, in the book of Wisdom, using these words:[2] "Let us defraud the righteous, for he is unpleasant to us, and upbraideth us with our offences against the law. He maketh his boast that he has the knowledge of God, and he calleth himself the Son of God. He is made to reprove our thoughts: it grieveth us even to look upon him; for his life is not like the life of others, his ways are of another fashion. We are counted by him as triflers; he withdraweth himself from our ways, as from filthiness; he commendeth greatly the latter end of the just, and boasteth that he has God for his father. Let us see, therefore, if his words be true; let us prove what end he shall have; let us examine him with rebukes and torments, that we may know his meekness and prove his patience; let us condemn him to a shameful death. Such things have they imagined, and have gone astray; for their own folly hath blinded them, and they do not understand the mysteries of God."

Therefore, being unmindful of these writings which they read, they incited the people as though against an impious man, so that they seized and led Him to trial, and with impious words demanded His death. But they alleged against Him as a crime this very thing, that He said that He was the Son of God, and that by healing on the Sabbath He broke the law, which He said that He did not break, but fulfilled. And when Pontius Pilate, who then as legate had authority in Syria, perceived that the cause did not belong to the office of the Roman judge, he sent Him to Herod the Tetrarch, and permitted the Jews themselves to be the judges of their own law: who, having received the power of punishing His guilt, sentenced[3] Him to the cross, but first scourged and struck him with their hands, put on Him a crown of thorns, spat upon His face, gave Him gall and vinegar to eat and drink; and amidst these things no word was heard to fall from His lips. Then the executioners, having cast lots over His tunic and mantle, suspended Him on the cross, and affixed Him to it, though on the next day they were about to celebrate the Passover, that is, their festival. Which crime was followed by prodigies, that they might understand the impiety which they had committed; for at the same moment in which He expired, there was a great earthquake, and a withdrawing[4] of the sun, so that the day was turned into night.

CHAP. XLVI. — IT IS PROVED FROM THE PROPHETS THAT THE PASSION AND DEATH OF CHRIST HAD BEEN FORETOLD.

And the prophets had predicted that all these things would thus come to pass. Isaiah thus speaks:[5] "I am not rebellious, nor do I oppose: I gave my back to the scourge, and my cheeks to the hand: I turned not away my face from the foulness of spitting." The same prophet says respecting His silence:[6] "I was brought as a sheep to the slaughter, and as a lamb before its shearers is dumb, so He opened not His mouth." David also, in the xxxivth Psalm:[7] "The abjects were gathered together against me, and they knew me not: they were scattered, yet felt no remorse: they tempted me, and gnashed upon me with their teeth." The same also says respecting food and drink in the lxviiith Psalm:[8] "They gave me also gall for my meat, and in my thirst they gave me vinegar to drink." Also

[1] Saturavit.
[2] Wisd. ii. 12-22. See *Instit.*, iv. 16, p. 117, *supra*.

[3] Addixerunt. Some read "affixerunt," affixed Him to the cross.
[4] Deliquium solis. [Elucidation IV.]
[5] Isa. l. 5.
[6] Isa. liii. 7.
[7] Ps. xxxv. 15, 16. See *Instit.*, iv. 18.
[8] Ps. lxix. 21.

respecting the cross of Christ:[1] "And they pierced my hands and my feet, they numbered all my bones: they themselves have looked and stared upon me; they parted my garments among them, and cast lots upon my vesture." Moses also says in Deuteronomy:[2] "And thy life shall hang in doubt before thine eyes, and thou shalt fear day and night, and shalt have none assurance of thy life." Also in Numbers:[3] "God is not in doubt as a man, nor does He suffer threats as the son of man." Also Zechariah says:[4] "And they shall look on me whom they pierced." Amos[5] thus speaks of the obscuring of the sun: "In that day, saith the Lord, the sun shall go down at noon, and the clear day shall be dark; and I will turn your feasts into mourning, and your songs into lamentation." Jeremiah[6] also speaks of the city of Jerusalem, in which He suffered: "Her sun is gone down while it was yet day; she hath been confounded and reviled, and the residue of them will I deliver to the sword." Nor were these things spoken in vain. For after a short time the Emperor Vespasian subdued the Jews, and laid waste their lands with the sword and fire, besieged and reduced them by famine, overthrew Jerusalem, led the captives in triumph, and prohibited the others who were left from ever returning to their native land. And these things were done by God on account of that crucifixion of Christ, as He before declared this to Solomon in their Scriptures, saying,[7] "And Israel shall be for perdition and a reproach[8] to the people, and this house shall be desolate; and every one that shall pass by shall be astonished, and shall say, Why hath God done these evils to this land, and to this house? And they shall say, Because they forsook the Lord their God, and persecuted their King, who was dearly beloved by God, and crucified Him with great degradation, therefore hath God brought upon them these evils." For what would they not deserve who put to death their Lord, who had come for their salvation?

CHAP. XLVII. — OF THE RESURRECTION OF JESUS CHRIST, THE SENDING OF THE APOSTLES, AND THE ASCENSION OF THE SAVIOUR INTO HEAVEN.

After these things they took His body down from the cross, and buried it in a tomb. But on the third day, before daybreak, there was an earthquake, and the stone with which they had closed the sepulchre was removed, and He arose. But nothing was found in the sepulchre except the clothes in which the body had been wrapped.[9] But that He would rise again on the third day, the prophets had long ago foretold. David, in the xvth Psalm:[10] "Thou wilt not leave my soul in hell, neither wilt Thou suffer Thine Holy One to see corruption." Likewise Hosea:[11] "This my Son is wise, therefore He shall not stay long in the anguish of His sons: and I will ransom Him from the hand of the grave. Where is thy judgment, O death, where is thy sting?" The same again says:[12] "After two days He will revive us on the third day."

Therefore, after His resurrection He went into Galilee, and again assembled His disciples, who had fled through fear; and having given them commands which He wished to be observed, and having arranged for the preaching of the Gospel throughout the whole world, He breathed into them the Holy Spirit,[13] and gave them the power of working miracles, that they might act for the welfare of men as well by deeds as words; and then at length, on the fortieth day, He returned to His Father, being carried up into a cloud. The prophet Daniel[14] had long before shown this, saying, "I saw in the night vision, and, behold, one like the Son of man came with the clouds of heaven, and came to the Ancient of days; and they who stood beside Him brought Him near before Him. And there was given Him a kingdom, and glory, and dominion, and all people, tribes, and languages shall serve Him; and His power is an everlasting one, which shall not pass away, and His kingdom that which shall not be destroyed." Also David in the cixth Psalm:[15] "The Lord said unto my Lord, Sit Thou at my right hand, until I make Thine enemies Thy footstool."

CHAP. XLVIII. — OF THE DISINHERITING OF THE JEWS, AND THE ADOPTION OF THE GENTILES.

Since, therefore, He sits at the right hand of God, about to tread down His enemies, who tortured Him, when He shall come to judge the world, it is evident that no hope remains to the Jews, unless, turning themselves to repentance, and being cleansed from the blood with which they polluted themselves, they shall begin to hope in Him whom they denied.[16] Therefore Esdras thus speaks:[17] "This passover is our Saviour and our refuge. Consider and let it come into your heart, that we have to abase

1 Ps. xxii. 16–18.
2 Deut. xxviii. 66.
3 Num. xxiii. 19.
4 Zech. xii. 10.
5 Amos viii. 9, 10.
6 Jer. xv. 9.
7 1 Kings ix. 7–9.
8 See *Instit.*, iv. 18, p. 121, *supra.*

9 Exuviæ corporis.
10 Ps. xvi. 10.
11 Hos. xiii. 13, Septuagint version.
12 Hos. vi. 2.
13 [Here is an incidental token of the orthodoxy of our Christian philosopher as to the Third Person. He is deficient, however, in practically enforcing the Spirit's work and our need of His grace. This may have been from a worthy motive, and according to discipline.]
14 Dan. vii. 13.
15 Ps. cx. 1.
16 Negaverunt; others read "necaverunt," killed.
17 See *Instit.*, iv. 18, p. 121, *supra.*

Him in a figure: and after these things we have hoped [1] in Him."

Now that the Jews were disinherited, because they rejected Christ, and that we, who are of the Gentiles, were adopted into their place, is proved by the Scriptures. Jeremiah [2] thus speaks: "I have forsaken mine house, I have given mine heritage into the hands of her enemies. Mine heritage is become unto me as a lion in the forest; it hath given forth its voice against me: therefore have I hated it." Also Malachi: [3] "I have no pleasure in you, saith the Lord, neither will I accept an offering at your hand. For from the rising of the sun even unto the going down thereof, my name shall be great among the Gentiles." Isaiah also thus speaks: [4] "I come to gather all nations and tongues: and they shall come and see my glory." The same says in another place,[5] speaking in the person of the Father to the Son: "I the Lord have called Thee in righteousness, and will hold Thine hand, and will keep Thee, and give Thee for a covenant of my people, for a light of the Gentiles; to open the eyes of the blind, to bring out the prisoners from the prison, and them that sit in darkness out of the prison-house."

CHAP. XLIX. — THAT GOD IS ONE ONLY.

If therefore the Jews have been rejected by God, as the faith due to the sacred writings shows, and the Gentiles, as we see, brought in, and freed from the darkness of this present life and from the chains of demons, it follows that no other hope is proposed to man, unless he shall follow true religion and true wisdom, which is in Christ, and he who is ignorant of Him is always estranged from the truth and from God. Nor let the Jews, or philosophers, flatter themselves respecting the Supreme God. He who has not acknowledged the Son has been unable to acknowledge the Father.[6] This is wisdom, and this is the mystery of the Supreme God. God willed that He should be acknowledged and worshipped through Him.[7] On this account He sent the prophets beforehand to announce His coming, that when the things which had been foretold were fulfilled in Him, then He might be believed by men to be both the Son of God and God.

Nor, however, must the opinion be entertained that there are two Gods, for the Father and the Son are one. For since the Father loves the Son, and gives all things to Him, and the Son faithfully obeys the Father, and wills nothing except that which the Father does, it is plain that so close a relationship cannot be separated, so that they should be said to be two in whom there is but one substance, and will, and faith. Therefore the Son is through the Father, and the Father through the Son. One honour is to be given to both, as to one God, and is to be so divided through the worship of the two, that the division itself may be bound by an inseparable bond of union. He will leave nothing to himself, who separates either the Father from the Son, or the Son from the Father.[8]

CHAP. L. — WHY GOD ASSUMED A MORTAL BODY, AND SUFFERED DEATH.

It remains to answer those also, who deem that it was unbecoming and unreasonable that God should be clothed with a mortal body; that He should be in subjection to men; that He should endure insults; that He should even suffer tortures and death. I will speak my sentiments, and I will sum up, as I shall be able, an immense subject in few words. He who teaches anything, ought, as I think, himself to practise what he teaches, that he may compel men to obey. For if he shall not practise them, he will detract from the faith due to his precepts. Therefore there is need of examples, that the precepts which are given may have firmness, and if any one shall prove contumacious, and shall say that they cannot be carried out in practice, the instructor may refute him by actual fact.[9] Therefore a system of teaching cannot be perfect, when it is delivered by words only; but it then becomes perfect, when it is completed by deeds.

Since therefore Christ was sent to men as a teacher of virtue, for the perfection of His teaching it was plainly befitting that He should act as well as teach. But if He had not assumed a human body, He would not have been able to practise what He taught, — that is, not to be angry, not to desire riches, not to be inflamed with lust, not to fear pain, to despise death. These things are plainly virtues, but they cannot be done without flesh. Therefore He assumed a body on this account, that, since He taught that the desires of the flesh must be overcome, He might in person first practise it, that no one might allege the frailty of the flesh as an excuse.

CHAP. LI. — OF THE DEATH OF CHRIST ON THE CROSS.

I will now speak of the mystery of the cross, lest any one should happen to say, If death must be endured by Him, it should have been not one

1 Speravimus; others "sperabimus."
2 Jer. xii. 7, 8.
3 Mal. i. 10, 11.
4 Isa. lxvi. 18.
5 Isa. xlii. 6, 7.
6 [1 John iv. 15.]
7 [John xiv. 6, 13, and v. 23.]
8 [1 John i. 22, 23.]
9 Præsenti opere convincat.

that was manifestly infamous and dishonourable, but one which had some honour. I know, indeed, that many, while they dislike the name of the cross, shrink from the truth, though there is in it great reasonableness and power. For since He was sent for this purpose, that He might open to the lowest men the way to salvation, He made Himself humble that He might free them. Therefore He underwent that kind of death which is usually inflicted on the humble, that an opportunity of imitation might be given to all. Moreover, since He was about to rise again, it was not allowable that His body should be in any way mutilated, or a bone broken, which happens to those who are beheaded. Therefore the cross was preferred, which reserved the body with the bones uninjured for the resurrection.

To these grounds it was also added, that having undertaken to suffer and to die, it was befitting that He should be lifted up. Thus the cross exalted Him both in fact and in emblem,[1] so that His majesty and power became known to all, together with His passion. For in that He extended His hands on the cross, He plainly stretched out His wings towards the east and the west, under which all nations from either side of the world might assemble and repose. But of what great weight this sign is, and what power it has, is evident, since all the host of demons is expelled and put to flight by this sign. And as He Himself before His passion put to confusion demons by His word and command, so now, by the name and sign of the same passion, unclean spirits, having insinuated themselves into the bodies of men, are driven out, when racked and tormented, and confessing themselves to be demons, they yield themselves to God, who harasses them. What therefore can the Greeks expect from their superstitions and with their wisdom, when they see that their gods, whom they do not deny to be demons also, are subdued by men through the cross?

CHAP. LII. — THE HOPE OF THE SALVATION OF MEN CONSISTS IN THE KNOWLEDGE OF THE TRUE GOD, AND OF THE HATRED OF THE HEATHENS AGAINST THE CHRISTIANS.

There is therefore but one hope of life for men, one harbour of safety, one refuge of liberty, if, laying aside the errors by which they were held, they open the eyes of their mind and recognise God, in whom alone is the abode of truth; despise earthly things, and those made from the ground; esteem as nothing philosophy, which is foolishness with God; and having undertaken true wisdom, that is, religion, become heirs of immortality. But indeed they are not so much opposed to the truth as to their own safety; and when they hear these things, they abominate them as some inexpiable wickedness. But they do not even endure[2] to hear: they think that their ears are polluted with impiety[3] if they hear; nor do they now refrain from reproaches, but assail them with the most insulting words; and also, if they have obtained the power, persecute them as public enemies, yea, even as worse than enemies; for enemies, when they have been vanquished, are punished with death or slavery; nor is there any torturing after the laying down of arms, although those deserved to suffer all things who wished so to act, that piety might have place among swords.

Cruelty, combined with innocence, is unheard of, nor is it worthy of the condition of victorious enemies. What is the so powerful cause of this fury? Doubtless, because they cannot contend on the ground of reason, they urge forward their cause by means of violence; and, with the subject not understood, they condemn those as most pernicious persons who have declined to make a stand respecting the fact of their innocence. Nor do they deem it sufficient that those whom they unreasonably hate should die by a speedy and simple death; but they lacerate them with refined tortures, that they may satisfy their hatred, which is not produced by any fault, but by the truth, which is hateful to those who live wickedly, because they take it ill that there are some whom their deeds cannot please. They desire in every way to destroy these, that they may be able to sin without restraint in the absence of any witness.

CHAP. LIII. — THE REASONS OF THE HATRED AGAINST THE CHRISTIANS ARE EXAMINED AND REFUTED.

But they say that they do these things for the defence of their gods. In the first place, if they are gods, and have any power and influence, they have no need of the defence and protection of men, but they manifestly defend themselves. Or how is man able to hope for aid from them, if they are unable to avenge even their own injuries? Therefore it is a vain and foolish thing to wish to be avengers of the gods, except that their distrust is more apparent from this. For he who undertakes the protection of the god whom he worships, admits the worthlessness of that god; but if he worships him on this account, because he thinks him powerful, he ought not to wish to defend him, by whom he himself ought to be defended. We therefore act rightly. For when those defenders of false gods, who are rebellious against the true God, persecute His name in us, we resist not

---

[1] Significatione.

[2] Ne audire quidem patiuntur; others read " patienter."

[3] Sacrilegio.

either in deed or in word, but with meekness, and silence, and patience, we endure whatever cruelty is able to contrive against us. For we have confidence in God, from whom we expect that retribution will hereafter follow. Nor is this confidence ungrounded, since we have in some cases heard, and in other cases seen, the miserable ends of all those who have dared to commit this crime. Nor has any one had it in his power to insult God with impunity; but he who has been unwilling to learn by word has learned by his own punishment who is the true God.

I should wish to know, when they compel men to sacrifice against their will, what reasoning they have with themselves, or to whom they make that offering. If it is made to the gods, that is not worship, nor an acceptable sacrifice, which is made by those who are displeasing to them, which is extorted by injury, which is enforced by pain. But if it is done to those whom they compel, it is plainly not a benefit, which any one would not receive, he even prefers rather to die. If it is a good to which you call me, why do you invite me with evil? why with blows, and not with words? why not by argument, but by bodily tortures? Whence it is manifest that that is an evil, to which you do not allure me willing, but drag me refusing. What folly is it to wish to consult the good of any one against his will! If any one, under the pressure of evils, attempts to have recourse to death, can you, if you either wrest the sword from his hand, or cut the halter, or drag him away from the precipice, or pour out the poison, boast yourself as the preserver of the man, when he, whom you think that you have preserved, does not thank you, and thinks that you have acted ill towards him, in averting from him the death which he desired, and in not permitting him to reach the end and rest from his labours? For a benefit ought not to be weighed according to the quality of the action, but according to the feelings of him who receives it. Why should you reckon as a benefit that which is an injury to me? Do you wish me to worship your gods, which I consider deadly to myself? If it is a good, I do not envy it. Enjoy your good by yourself. There is no reason why you should wish to succour my error, which I have undertaken by my judgment and inclination. If it is evil, why do you drag me to a participation in evil? Use your own fortune. I prefer to die in the practice of that which is good, than to live in evil.

CHAP. LIV. — OF THE FREEDOM OF RELIGION IN THE WORSHIP OF GOD.

These things may indeed be said with justice. But who will hear, when men of furious and unbridled spirit think that their authority is diminished if there is any freedom in the affairs of men? But it is religion alone in which freedom has placed its dwelling. For it is a matter which is voluntary above all others, nor can necessity be imposed upon any, so as to worship that which he does not wish to worship.[1] Some one may perhaps pretend, he cannot wish it. In short, some, through fear of torments, or overcome by tortures, have assented to detestable sacrifices: they never do that voluntarily which they did from necessity; but when the opportunity is again given to them, and liberty restored, they again betake themselves to God, and appease Him with prayers and tears, repenting not of the will, which they had not, but of the necessity which they endured; and pardon is not denied to those who make satisfaction. What then does he accomplish who pollutes the body, since he cannot change the will?

But, in fact, men of weak understanding, if they have induced any man of spirit[2] to sacrifice to their gods, with incredible alacrity insolently exult, and rejoice, as though they had sent an enemy under the yoke. But if any one, neither frightened by threats nor by tortures, shall have chosen to prefer his faith to his life, cruelty puts forth all its ingenuity against him, plans dreadful and intolerable things; and because they know that death for the cause of God is glorious, and that this is a victory on our side, if, having overcome the torturers, we lay down our life in behalf of the faith and religion, they also themselves strive to conquer us. They do not put us to death, but they search out new and unheard-of tortures, that the frailty of the flesh may yield to pains, and if it does not yield, they put off further punishment, and apply diligent care to the wounds, that while the scars are yet fresh, a repetition of the torture may inflict more pain; and while they practise this torture[3] upon the innocent, they evidently consider themselves pious, and just, and religious (for they are delighted with such sacrifices to their gods), but they term the others impious and desperate. What perversity is this, that he who is punished, though innocent, should be called desperate and impious, and that the torturer, on the other hand, should be called just and pious!

CHAP. LV. — THE HEATHENS CHARGE JUSTICE WITH IMPIETY IN FOLLOWING GOD.

But they say that those are rightly and deservedly punished, who dislike the public rites of religion handed down to them by their ancestors. What if those ancestors were foolish in undertaking vain religious rites, as we have shown before,

[1] [Religious liberty maintained and introduced by the Gospel. Corrupted Christianity only is responsible for the reverse.]
[2] Fortem; some read "forte," by chance.
[3] Carnificinam.

shall we be prohibited from following true and better things? Why do we deprive ourselves of liberty, and become enslaved to the errors of others, as though bound[1] to them? Let it be permitted us to be wise, let it be permitted us to inquire into the truth. But, however, if it pleases them to defend *the folly*[2] of their ancestors, why are the Egyptians suffered to escape, who worship cattle and beasts of every kind as deities? Why are the gods themselves made the subjects of comic[3] representations? and why is he honoured who derides them most wittily? Why are philosophers attended to, who either say that there are no gods, or that, if there are any, they take no interest in, and do not regard the affairs of men, or argue that there is no providence at all, which rules the world?

But they alone of all are judged impious who follow God and the truth. And since this is at once justice, and wisdom, they lay to its charge either impiety or folly, and do not perceive what it is which deceives them, when they call evil good, and good evil. Many indeed of the philosophers, and especially Plato and Aristotle, spoke many things about justice, asserting and extolling that virtue with the greatest praise, because it gives to each its due, because it maintains equity in all things; and whereas the other virtues are as it were silent, and shut up within, that it is justice alone which is neither concerned[4] for itself only, nor hidden, but altogether shows itself[5] abroad, and is ready for conferring a benefit, so as to assist as many as possible: as though in truth justice ought to be in judges only, and those placed in any post of authority, and not in all men.

And yet there is no one of men, not even of the lowest and of beggars, who is not capable of justice. But because they did not know what it was, from what source it proceeded, and what was its mode of operation, they assigned to a few only that highest virtue, that is, the common good of all, and said that it aimed at[6] no advantages peculiar to itself, but only the interests of others. And not without reason was Carneades raised up, a man of the greatest talent and penetration, to refute their speech, and overthrow the justice, which had no firm foundation; not because he thought that justice was to be blamed, but that he might show that its defenders brought forward no firm or certain argument respecting justice.

CHAP. LVI. — OF JUSTICE, WHICH IS THE WORSHIP OF THE TRUE GOD.

For if justice is the worship of the true God (for what is so just with respect to equity, so pious with respect to honour, so necessary with respect to safety, as to acknowledge God as a parent, to reverence Him as Lord, and to obey His law or precepts?), it follows that the philosophers were ignorant of justice, for they neither acknowledged God Himself, nor observed His worship and law; and on this account they might have been refuted by Carneades, whose disputation was to this effect, that there is no natural justice, and therefore that all animals defended their own interests by the guidance of nature itself, and therefore that justice, if it promotes the advantages of others and neglects its own, is to be called foolishness. But if all people who are possessed of power, and the Romans themselves, who are masters of the whole world, were willing to follow justice, and to restore to every one his property which they have seized by force and arms, they will return to cottages and a condition of want. And if they did this, they might indeed be just, but they must of necessity be considered foolish, who proceed to injure themselves for the advantage of others. Then, if any one should find a man who was through a mistake offering for sale gold as mountain-brass, or silver as lead, and necessity should compel him to buy it, will he conceal his knowledge and buy it for a small sum, or will he rather inform the seller of its value? If he shall inform him, he will manifestly be called just; but he will also be foolish, for conferring an advantage upon another, and injuring himself. But it is easy *to judge* in a case of injury. What if he shall incur danger of his life, so that it shall be necessary for him either to kill another or to die, what will he do? It may happen that, having suffered shipwreck, he may find some feeble person clinging to a plank; or, his army having been defeated, in his flight he may find a wounded man on horseback: will he thrust the one from the plank, the other from his horse, that he himself may be able to escape? If he shall wish to be just, he will not do it; but he will also be judged foolish, who in sparing the life of another shall lose his own. If he shall do it, he will indeed appear wise, because he will provide for his own interests; but he will also be wicked, because he will commit a wrong.

CHAP. LVII. — OF WISDOM AND FOOLISHNESS.

These things indeed are said with acuteness; but we are able very readily to reply to them. For the imitation of names causes it thus to appear. For justice bears a resemblance to foolishness, and yet it is not foolishness; and at the same time malice bears a resemblance to wisdom, and yet it is not wisdom. But as that malice is intelligent and shrewd in preserving its own interests, it is not wisdom, but cunning and craftiness; so likewise justice ought not to be called foolishness, but innocence, because

[1] Addicti.
[2] Stultitiam. This word is wanting in the MSS., but this or some such word is necessary to complete the sense.
[3] Mimi; wanting in some editions.
[4] Sibi tantum conciliata sit.
[5] Foras tota promineat.
[6] Aucupari.

the just man must be wise, and the foolish man unjust. For neither reason nor nature itself permits that he who is just should not be wise, since it is plain that the just man does nothing except that which is right and good, and always avoids that which is perverted [1] and evil. But who will be able to distinguish between good and evil, depravity and rectitude, but he who shall be wise? But the fool acts badly, because he is ignorant of what is good and evil. Therefore he does wrong, because he is unable to distinguish between things which are perverted and those which are right. Therefore justice cannot be befitting to the foolish man, nor wisdom to the unjust. He is not then a foolish person who has not thrust off a shipwrecked man from a plank, nor a wounded man from his horse, because he has abstained from injury, which is a sin; and it is the part of the wise man to avoid sin.

But that he should appear foolish at first sight is caused by this, that they suppose the soul to be extinguished together with the body; and for this reason they refer all advantage to this life. For if there is no existence after death, it is plain that he acts foolishly who spares the life of another to his own loss, or who consults the gain of another more than his own. If death destroys the soul, we must use our endeavours to live for a longer time, and more to our own advantage; but if there remains after death a life of immortality and blessedness, the just and wise man will certainly despise this corporeal existence, with all earthly goods, because he will know what kind of a reward he is about to receive from God. Therefore let us maintain innocency, let us maintain justice, let us undergo the appearance of foolishness, that we may be able to maintain true wisdom. And if it appears to men senseless and foolish to prefer torture and death rather than to sacrifice to gods, and to escape without harm, let us however strive to exhibit faithfulness towards God by all virtue and by all patience. Let not death terrify us, nor pain subdue us, so as to prevent the vigour of our mind and constancy from being preserved unshaken. Let them call us foolish, whilst they themselves are most foolish, and blind and dull, and like sheep; who do not understand that it is a deadly thing to leave the living God, and prostrate themselves in the adoration of earthly objects; who do not know that eternal punishment awaits those who have worshipped senseless images; and that those who have neither refused tortures nor death for the worship and honour of the true God will obtain eternal life. This is the highest faith; this is true wisdom; this is perfect justice. It matters nothing to us what fools may judge, what trifling men may think. We ought to await the judgment of God, that we may hereafter judge those who have passed judgment on us.

CHAP. LVIII. — OF THE TRUE WORSHIP OF GOD, AND SACRIFICE.

I have spoken of justice, what was its nature. It follows that I show what is true sacrifice to God, what is the most just manner of worshipping Him, lest any one should think that victims, or odours, or precious gifts, are desired by God, who, if He is not subject to hunger, and thirst, and cold, and desire of all earthly things, does not therefore make use of all these things which are presented in temples and to gods of earth; but as corporeal offerings are necessary for corporeal beings, so manifestly an incorporeal sacrifice is necessary for an incorporeal being. But God has no need of those things which He has given to man for his use, since all the earth is under His power: He needs not a temple, since the world is His dwelling; He needs not an image, since He is incomprehensible both to the eyes and to the mind; He needs not earthly lights, for He was able to kindle the light of the sun, with the other stars, for the use of man. What then does God require from man but worship of the mind, which is pure and holy? For those things which are made by the hands, or are outside of man, are senseless, frail, and displeasing. This is true sacrifice, which is brought forth not from the chest but from the heart; not that which is offered by the hand, but by the mind. This is the acceptable victim, which the mind sacrifices of itself. For what do victims bestow? What does incense? What do garments? What does silver? What gold? What precious stones, — if there is not a pure mind on the part of the worshipper? Therefore it is justice only which God requires. In this is sacrifice; in this the worship of God, respecting which I must now speak, and show in what works justice must necessarily be contained.

CHAP. LIX. — OF THE WAYS OF LIFE, AND THE FIRST TIMES OF THE WORLD.

That there are two ways [2] of human life was unknown neither to philosophers nor to poets, but both introduced them in a different manner. The philosophers wished the one to be the way of industry, the other of idleness; but in this respect they were less correct in their statements, that they referred them to the advantages of this life only. The poets spoke better who said that one of them was the way of the just, the other

[1] Pravum.

[2] [The *Duæ Viæ*. A feature in the primitive catechising. See *Epistle of Barnabas*, vol. i. p. 148; also this volume, *infra*.]

of the unjust; but they err in this, that they say that they are not in this life, but in the shades below. We manifestly speak more correctly, who say that the one is the way of life, the other that of death. And here, however, we say that there are two ways; but the one on the right hand, in which the just walk, does not lead to Elysium, but to heaven, for they become immortal; the other on the left leads to Tartarus,[1] for the unjust are sentenced to eternal tortures. Therefore the way of justice, which leads to life, is to be held by us. Now the first duty of justice is to acknowledge God as a parent, and to fear Him as a master, to love Him as a father. For the same Being who begat us, who animated us with vital breath, who nourishes and preserves us, has over us, not only as a father but also as a master, authority to correct us, and the power of life and death; wherefore twofold honour is due to Him from man, that is, love combined with fear. The second duty of justice is to acknowledge man as a brother. For if the same God made us, and produced all men on equal terms to justice and eternal life, it is manifest that we are united by the relationship of brotherhood; and he who does not acknowledge this is unjust. But the origin of this evil, by which the mutual society of men, by which the bond of relationship has been torn asunder, arises from ignorance of the true God. For he who is ignorant of that fountain of bounty can by no means be good. Hence it is that, from the time when a multitude of gods began to be consecrated and worshipped by men, justice, as the poets relate, being put to flight, every compact was destroyed, the fellowship of human justice was destroyed. Then every one, consulting his own interest, reckoned might to be right, injured another, attacked by frauds, deceived[2] by treachery, increased his own advantages by the inconvenience of others, did not spare relatives, or children, or parents, prepared poisoned cups for the destruction of men, beset the ways with the sword, infested the seas, gave the rein to his lust, wherever passion led him, — in short, esteemed nothing sacred which his dreadful desire did not violate. When these things were done, then men instituted laws for themselves to promote the public advantage, that they might meanwhile protect themselves from injuries. But the fear of laws did not suppress crimes, but it checked licentiousness. For laws were able to punish offences, they were unable to punish the conscience. Therefore the things which before were done openly began to be done secretly. Justice also was evaded by stealth, since they who themselves presided over the administration of the laws, corrupted by gifts and rewards, made a traffic of their sentences, either to the escape[3] of the evil or to the destruction of the good. To these things were added dissensions, and wars, and mutual depredations; and the laws being crushed, the power of acting with violence was assumed without restraint.

CHAP. LX. — OF THE DUTIES OF JUSTICE.

When the affairs of men were in this condition, God pitied us, revealed and displayed Himself to us, that in Himself we might learn religion, faith, purity, and mercy; that having laid aside the error of our former life, together with God Himself we might know ourselves, whom impiety had disunited from Him, and we might choose[4] the divine law, which unites human affairs with heavenly, the Lord Himself delivering it to us; by which law all the errors with which we have been ensnared, together with vain and impious superstitions, might be taken away. What we owe to man, therefore, is prescribed by that same divine law which teaches that whatever you render to man is rendered to God. But the root of justice, and the entire foundation of equity, is that you should not do that which you would be unwilling to suffer, but should measure the feelings of another by your own. If it is an unpleasant thing to bear an injury, and he who has done it appears unjust, transfer to the person of another that which you feel respecting yourself, and to your own person that which you judge respecting another, and you will understand that you act as unjustly if you injure another as another would if he should injure you. If we consider these things, we shall maintain innocence, in which the first step of justice is, as it were, contained. For the first thing is, not to injure; the next is, to be of service. And as in uncultivated lands, before you begin to sow, the fields must be cleansed by tearing up the thorns and cutting off all the roots of trunks, so vices must first be thrust out from our souls, and then at length virtues must be implanted, from which the fruits of immortality, being engendered by the word of God, may spring up.

CHAP. LXI. — OF THE PASSIONS.

There are three passions, or, so to speak, three furies, which excite such great perturbations in the souls of men, and sometimes compel them to offend in such a manner, as to permit them to have regard neither for their reputation nor for their personal safety: these are anger, which desires vengeance; love of gain, which longs for riches; lust, which seeks for pleasures. We must above all things resist these vices: these

1 [See vol. v. p. 153, note 1, and pp. 161, 174, this series.]

2 Circumscribere.

3 In remissionem.

4 Sumere, "to take by selection and choice."

trunks must be rooted up, that virtues may be implanted. The Stoics are of opinion that these passions must be cut off; the Peripatetics think that they must be restrained. Neither of them judge rightly, because they cannot entirely be taken away, since they are implanted by nature, and have a sure and great influence; nor can they be diminished, since, if they are evil, we ought to be without them, even though restrained and used with moderation; if they are good, we ought to use them in their completeness.[1] But we say that they ought not to be taken away nor lessened. For they are not evil of themselves, since God has reasonably implanted them in us; but inasmuch as they are plainly good by nature, — for they are given us for the protection of life, — they become evil by their evil use. And as bravery, if you fight in defence of your country, is a good, if against your country, is an evil, so the passions, if you employ them to good purposes, will be virtues, if to evil uses, they will be called vices. Anger therefore has been given by God for the restraining of offences, that is, for controlling the discipline of subjects, that fear may suppress licentiousness and restrain audacity. But they who are ignorant of its limits are angry with their equals, or even with their superiors. Hence they rush to deeds of cruelty, hence they rise to slaughters, hence to wars. The love of gain also has been given that we may desire and seek for the necessaries of life. But they who are unacquainted with its boundaries strive insatiably to heap up riches. Hence poisoning, hence defraudings,[2] hence false wills, hence all kinds of frauds have burst forth. Moreover, the passion of lust is implanted and innate in us for the procreation of children; but they who do not fix its limits in the mind use it for pleasure only. Thence arise unlawful loves, thence adulteries and debaucheries, thence all kinds of corruption. These passions, therefore, must be kept within their boundaries and directed into their right course, in which, even though they should be vehement, they cannot incur blame.

CHAP. LXII. — OF RESTRAINING THE PLEASURES OF THE SENSES.

Anger is to be restrained when we suffer an injury, that the evil may be suppressed which is imminent from a contest, and that we may retain two of the greatest virtues, harmlessness and patience. Let the desire of gain be broken when we have that which is enough. For what madness is it to labour in heaping up those things which must pass to others, either by robbery, or theft, or by proscription, or by death? Let lust not go beyond the marriage-bed, but be subservient to the procreation of children. For a too great eagerness for pleasure both produces danger and generates disgrace, and that which is especially to be avoided, leads to eternal death. Nothing is so hateful to God as an unchaste mind and an impure soul. Nor let any one think that he must abstain from this pleasure only, quæ capitur ex fœminei corporis copulatione, but also from the other pleasures which arise from the rest of the senses, because they also are of themselves vicious, and it is the part of the same virtue to despise them. The pleasure of the eyes is derived from the beauty of objects, that of the ears from harmonious and pleasant sounds, that of the nostrils from pleasant odour, that of taste from sweet food, — all of which virtue ought strongly to resist, lest, ensnared by these attractions, the soul should be depressed from heavenly to earthly things, from things eternal to things temporal, from life immortal to perpetual punishment. In pleasures of the taste and smell there is this danger, that they are able to draw us to luxury. For he who shall be given up to these things, either will have no property, or, if he shall have any, he will expend it, and afterwards live a life to be abominated. But he who is carried away by hearing (to say nothing respecting songs,[3] which often so charm the inmost senses that they even disturb with madness a settled state of the mind by certain elaborately composed speeches and harmonious poems, or skilful disputations) is easily led aside to impious worship. Hence it is that they who are either themselves eloquent, or prefer to read eloquent writings, do not readily believe the sacred writings, because they appear unpolished; they do not seek things that are true, but things that are pleasant; nay, to them those things appear to be most true which soothe the ears. Thus they reject the truth, while they are captivated by the sweetness of the discourse. But the pleasure which has reference to the sight is manifold. For that which is derived from the beauty of precious objects excites avarice, which ought to be far removed from a wise and just man; but that which is received from the appearance of woman hurries a man to another pleasure, of which we have already spoken above.

CHAP. LXIII. — THAT SHOWS ARE MOST POWERFUL TO CORRUPT THE MINDS.

It remains to speak of public shows, which, since they have a more powerful influence on the corruption of the mind, ought to be avoided by the wise, and to be altogether guarded against,

[1] Integris abutendum est. Lactantius sometimes uses "abuti" for "uti."
[2] Circumscriptiones.
[3] [See vol. ii. p. 79, notes 1 and 2.]

because it is said that they were instituted in celebration of the honours of the gods. For the exhibitions of shows are festivals of Saturnus. The stage belongs to Father Liber; but the Circensian games are supposed to be dedicated to Neptunus: so that now he who takes part in these shows appears to have left the worship of God, and to have passed over to profane rites. But I prefer to speak of the matter itself rather than of its origin. What is so dreadful, what so foul, as the slaughter of man? Therefore our life is protected by the most severe laws; therefore wars are detestable. Yet custom finds how a man may commit homicide without war, and without laws; and this is a pleasure to him, that he has avenged guilt. But if to be present at homicide implies a consciousness of guilt, and the spectator is involved in the same guilt as the perpetrator, then in these slaughters of gladiators, he who is a spectator is no less sprinkled with blood than he who sheds it; nor can he be free from the guilt of bloodshed who wished it to be poured out, or appear not to have slain, who both favoured the slayer and asked a reward for him. What of the stage? Is it more holy, — on which comedy converses on the subject of debaucheries and amours, tragedy of incest and parricide? The immodest gestures also of players, with which they imitate disreputable women, teach the lusts, which they express by dancing. For the pantomime is a school of corruption,[1] in which things which are shameful are acted by a figurative representation,[2] that the things which are true may be done without shame. These spectacles are viewed by youths, whose dangerous age, which ought to be curbed and governed, is trained by these representations to vices and sins. The circus, in truth, is considered more innocent, but there is greater madness in this, since the minds of the spectators are transported with such great madness, that they not only break out into revilings, but often rise to strifes, and battles, and contentions. Therefore all shows are to be avoided, that we may be able to maintain a tranquil state of mind. We must renounce hurtful pleasures, lest, charmed by pestilential sweetness, we fall into the snares of death.

CHAP. LXIV. — THE PASSIONS ARE TO BE SUBDUED, AND WE MUST ABSTAIN FROM FORBIDDEN THINGS.

Let virtue alone please us, whose reward is immortal when it has conquered pleasure. But when the passions have been overcome and pleasures subdued, labour in suppressing other things is easy to him who is a follower of God and of truth: he will never revile, who shall hope for a blessing from God; he will not commit perjury, lest he should mock God; but he will not even swear, lest at any time, either by necessity or through habit, he should fall into perjury. He will speak nothing deceitfully, nothing with dissimulation; he will not refuse that which he has promised, nor will he promise that which he is unable to perform; he will envy no one, since he is content with himself and with his own possessions; nor will he take away from, or wish ill to another, upon whom, perhaps, the benefits of God are more plenteously[3] bestowed. He will not steal, nor will he covet anything at all belonging to another. He will not give his money to usury, for that is to seek after gain from the evils of others; nor, however, will he refuse to lend, if necessity shall compel any one to borrow. He must not be harsh towards a son, nor towards a slave: he must remember that he himself has a Father and a Master. He will so act towards these as he will wish that others should act towards him. He will not receive excessive gifts from those who have less resources than himself; for it is not just that the estates of the wealthy should be increased by the losses of the wretched.

It is an old precept not to kill, which ought not to be taken in this light, as though we are commanded to abstain only from homicide, which is punished even by public laws. But by the intervention of this command, it will not be permitted us to apply peril of death by word, nor to put to death or expose an infant, nor to condemn one's self by a voluntary death. We are likewise commanded not to commit adultery; but by this precept we are not only prohibited from polluting the marriage of another, which is condemned even by the common law of nations, but even to abstain from those who prostitute their persons. For the law of God is above all laws; it forbids even those things which are esteemed lawful, that it may fulfil justice. It is a part of the same law not to utter false witness, and this also itself has a wider meaning. For if false witness by falsehood is injurious to him against whom it is spoken, and deceives him in whose presence it is spoken, we must therefore never speak falsely, because falsehood always deceives or injures. Therefore he is not a just man who, even without inflicting injury, speaks in idle discourse. Nor indeed is it lawful for him to flatter, for flattery is pernicious and deceitful; but he will everywhere guard the truth. And although this may for the present be unpleasant, nevertheless, when its advantage and usefulness shall appear, it will not produce hatred, as the poet says,[4] but gratitude.

[1] Mimus corruptelarum disciplina est.
[2] Per imaginem.
[3] Proniora sunt.
[4] Terent., *And.*, i. 1.

CHAP. LXV. — PRECEPTS ABOUT THOSE THINGS WHICH ARE COMMANDED, AND OF PITY.

I have spoken of those things which are forbidden; I will now briefly say what things are commanded. Closely connected with harmlessness is pity. For the former does not inflict injury, the latter works good; the former begins justice, the latter completes it. For since the nature of men is more feeble than that of the other animals, which God has provided with means of inflicting violence, and with defences for repelling it, He has given to us the affection of pity, that we might place the whole protection of our life in mutual aid. For if we are created by one God, and descended from one man, and are thus connected by the law of consanguinity, we ought on this account to love every man; and therefore we are bound not only to abstain from the infliction of injury, but not even to avenge it when inflicted on us, that there may be in us complete harmlessness. And on this account God commands us to pray always even for our enemies. Therefore we ought to be an animal fitted for companionship and society, that we may mutually protect ourselves by giving and receiving assistance. For our frailty is liable to many accidents and inconveniences. Expect that that which you see has happened to another may happen to you also. Thus you will at length be excited to render aid, if you shall assume the mind of him who, being placed in evils, implores your aid. If any one is in need of food, let us bestow it; if any one meets us who is naked, let us clothe him; if any one suffers injury from one who is more powerful than himself, let us rescue him. Let our house be open to strangers, or to those who are in need of shelter. Let our defence not be wanting to wards, or our protection to the defenceless.[1] To ransom captives is a great work of pity, and also to visit and comfort the sick who are in poverty. If the helpless or strangers die, we should not permit them to lie unburied. These are the works, these the duties, of pity; and if any one undertakes these, he will offer unto God a true and acceptable sacrifice. This victim is more adapted for an offering to God, who is not appeased with the blood of a sheep, but with the piety of man, whom God, because He is just, follows up with His own law, and with His own condition. He shows mercy to him whom He sees to be merciful; He is inexorable to him whom He sees to be harsh to those who entreat him. Therefore, that we may be able to do all these things, which are pleasing to God, money is to be despised, and to be transferred to heavenly treasures, where neither thief can break through, nor rust corrupt, nor tyrant take away, but it may be preserved for us under the guardianship of God to our eternal wealth.

CHAP. LXVI. — OF FAITH IN RELIGION, AND OF FORTITUDE.

Faith also is a great part of justice; and this ought especially to be preserved by us, who bear the name of faith, especially in religion, because God is before and to be preferred to man. And if it is a glorious thing to undergo death in behalf of friends, of parents, and of children, that is, in behalf of man, and if he who has done this obtains lasting memory and praise, how much more so in behalf of God, who is able to bestow eternal life in return for temporal death? Therefore, when a necessity of this kind happens, that we are compelled to turn aside from God, and to pass over to the rites of the heathens, no fear, no terror should turn us aside from guarding the faith delivered to us. Let God be before our eyes, in our heart, by whose inward help we may overcome the pain of our flesh, and the torments applied to our body. Then let us think of nothing else but the rewards of an immortal life. And thus, even though our limbs should be torn in pieces, or burnt, we shall easily endure all things which the madness of tyrannical cruelty shall contrive against us. Lastly, let us strive to undergo death itself, not unwillingly or timidly, but willingly and undauntedly, as those who know what glory we are about to have in the presence of God, having triumphed over the world and coming to the things promised us; with what good things and how great blessedness we shall be compensated for these brief evils of punishments, and the injuries of this life. But if the opportunity of this glory shall be wanting, faith will have its reward even in peace.

Therefore let it be observed in all the duties of life, let it be observed in marriage. For it is not sufficient if you abstain from another's bed, or from the brothel. Let him who has a wife seek nothing further, but, content with her alone, let him guard the mysteries of the marriage-bed chaste and undefiled. For he is equally an adulterer in the sight of God and impure, who, having thrown off the yoke, wantons in strange pleasure either with a free woman or a slave. But as a woman is bound by the bonds of chastity not to desire any other man, so let the husband be bound by the same law, since God has joined together the husband and the wife in the union of one body. On this account He has commanded that the wife shall not be put away unless convicted of adultery, and that the bond of the conjugal compact shall never be dissolved, unless unfaithfulness have broken it.[2] This also is added for the completion of chastity, that

[1] Viduis.

[2] [The law of divorce in Christian States. Sanderson, v. iv. p. 135.]

there should be an absence not only of the offence, but even of the thought. For it is evident that the mind is polluted by the desire, though unaccomplished; and so that a just man ought neither to do, nor to wish to do, that which is unjust. Therefore the conscience must be cleansed; for God, who cannot be deceived, inspects it. The breast must be cleared from every stain, that it may be a temple of God, which is enlightened not by the gleam of gold or ivory, but by the brightness of faith and purity.

CHAP. LXVII. — OF REPENTANCE, THE IMMORTALITY OF THE SOUL, AND OF PROVIDENCE.

But it is true all these things are difficult to man, nor does the condition of his frailty permit that any one should be without blemish. Therefore the last remedy is this, that we have recourse to repentance, which has not the least place among the virtues, because it is a correction of oneself; that when we have happened to fail either in deed or in word, we may immediately come to a better mind, and confess that we have offended, and entreat pardon from God, which according to His mercy He will not deny, except to those who persist in their error. Great is the aid, great the solace of repentance. That is the healing of wounds and offences, that hope, that the harbour of safety; and he who takes away this cuts off from himself the way of salvation, because no one can be so just that repentance is never necessary for him. But we, even though there is no offence of ours, yet ought to confess to God, and to entreat pardon for our faults, and to give thanks even in evils. Let us always offer this obedience to our Lord. For humility is dear and lovely in the sight of God; for since He rather receives the sinner who confesses his fault, than the just man who is haughty, how much more will He receive the just man who confesses, and exalt him in His heavenly kingdom in proportion to his humility! These are the things which the worshipper of God ought to hold forth; these are the victims, this the sacrifice, which is acceptable; this is true worship, when a man offers upon the altar of God the pledges of his own mind. That supreme Majesty rejoices in such a worshipper as this, as it takes him as a son and bestows upon him the befitting reward of immortality, concerning which I must now speak, and refute the persuasion of those who think that the soul is destroyed together with the body. For inasmuch as they neither knew God nor were able to perceive the mystery of the world, they did not even comprehend the nature of man and of the soul. For how could they see the consequences, who did not hold the main point?[1] Therefore, in denying the existence of a providence, they plainly denied the existence of God, who is the fountain and source of all things. It followed that they should either affirm that those things which exist have always existed, or were produced of their own accord, or arose from a meeting together of minute seeds.

It cannot be said that that which exists, and is visible, always existed; for it cannot exist of itself without some beginning. But nothing can be produced of its own accord, because there is no nature without one who generates it. But how could there be original[2] seeds, since both the seeds arise from objects,[3] and, in their turn, objects from seeds? Therefore there is no seed which has not origin. Thus it came to pass, that when they supposed that the world was produced by no providence, they did not suppose that even man was produced by any plan.[4] But if no plan was made use of in the creation of man, therefore the soul cannot be immortal. But others, on the other hand, thought there was but one God, and that the world was made by Him, and made for the sake of men, and that souls are immortal. But though they entertained true sentiments, nevertheless they did not perceive the causes, or reasons, or issues of this divine work and design, so as to complete the whole mystery of the truth, and to comprise it within some limit. But that which they were not able to do, because they did not hold the truth in its integrity,[5] must be done by us, who know it on the announcement of God.

CHAP. LXVIII. — OF THE WORLD, MAN, AND THE PROVIDENCE OF GOD.

Let us therefore consider what was the plan of making this so great and so immense a work. God made the world, as Plato thought, but he does not show why He made it. Because He is good, he says, and envying no one, He made the things which are good. But we see that there are both good and evil things in the system of nature. Some perverse person may stand forth, such as that atheist Theodorus was, and answer Plato: Nay, because He is evil, He made the things which are evil. How will he refute him? If God made the things which are good, whence have such great evils burst forth, which, for the most part, even prevail over those which are good? They were contained, he says, in the matter. If there were evil, therefore there were also good things; so that either God made nothing, or if He made only good things, the evil things which were not made are more eternal than

[1] Summam. Lactantius uses this word to express a compendious summary of divine mysteries.

[2] Semina principalia.

[3] Ex rebus.

[4] Aliquâ ratione.

[5] Perpetuo, i.e., without intermission.

the good things which had a beginning. Therefore the things which at one time began will have an end, and those which always existed will be permanent. Therefore evils are preferable. But if they cannot be preferable, they cannot indeed be more eternal. Therefore they either always existed, and God has been inactive,[1] or they both flowed from one source. For it is more in accordance with reason that God made all things, than that He made nothing.

Therefore, according to the sentiments of Plato, the same God is both good, because He made good things, and evil, because He made evil things. And if this cannot be so, it is evident that the world was not made by God on this account, because He is good. For He comprised all things, both good and evil; nor did He make anything for its own sake, but on account of something else. A house is built not for this purpose only, that there may be a house, but that it may receive and shelter an inhabitant. Likewise a ship is built not for this purpose, that it may appear only to be a ship, but that men may be able to sail in it. Vessels also are made, not only that the vessels may exist, but that they may receive things which are necessary for use. Thus also God must have made the world for some use. The Stoics say that it was made for the sake of men; and rightly so. For men enjoy all these good things which the world contains in itself. But they do not explain why men themselves were made, or what advantage Providence, the Maker of all things, has in them.

Plato also affirms that souls are immortal, but why, or in what manner, or at what time, or by whose instrumentality they attain to immortality, or what is the nature of that great mystery, why those who are about to become immortal are previously born mortal, and then, having completed the course[2] of their temporal life, and having laid aside the covering[3] of their frail bodies, are transferred to that eternal blessedness, — of all this he has no comprehension. Finally, he did not explain the judgment of God, nor the distinction between the just and the unjust, but supposed that the souls which have plunged themselves into crimes are condemned thus far, that they may be reproduced in the lower animals, and thus atone for their offences, until they again return to the forms of men, and that this is always taking place, and that there is no end of this transmigration. In my opinion, he introduces some sport resembling a dream, in which there appears to be neither plan, nor government of God, nor any design.

[1] Otiosus.
[2] Decurso . . . spatio. The expression is borrowed from a chariot race.
[3] Corporum exuviis.

CHAP. LXIX. — THAT THE WORLD WAS MADE ON ACCOUNT OF MAN, AND MAN ON ACCOUNT OF GOD.

I will now say what is that chief[4] point which not even those who spoke the truth were able to connect together, bringing into one view causes and reasons. The world was made by God, that men might be born; again, men are born, that they may acknowledge God as a Father, in whom is wisdom; they acknowledge Him, that they may worship Him, in whom is justice; they worship Him, that they may receive the reward of immortality; they receive immortality, that they may serve God for ever. Do you see how closely connected the first are with the middle, and the middle with the last? Let us look into them separately, and see whether they are consistent[5] with each other. God made the world on account of man. He who does not see this, does not differ much from a beast. Who but man looks up to the heaven? who views with admiration the sun, who the stars, who all the works of God? Who inhabits the earth? who receives the fruit from it? Who has in his power the fishes, who the winged creatures, who the quadrupeds, except man? Therefore God made all things on account of man, because all things have turned out for the use of man.

The philosophers saw this, but they did not see the consequence, that He made man himself on His own account. For it was befitting, and pious, and necessary, that since He contrived such great works for the sake of man, when He gave him so much honour, and so much power, that he should bear rule in the world, man should both acknowledge God, the Author of such great benefits, who made the world itself on his account, and should pay Him the worship and honour due to Him. Here Plato erred; here he lost the truth which he had at first laid hold of, when he was silent concerning the worship of that God whom he confessed to be the framer and parent of all things, and did not understand that man is bound to God by the ties of piety, whence religion itself receives its name, and that this is the only thing on account of which souls become immortal. He perceived, however, that they are eternal, but he did not descend by the regular gradations to that opinion. For the middle arguments being taken away, he rather fell into the truth, as though by some abrupt precipice; nor did he advance further, since he had found the truth by accident, and not by reason. Therefore God is to be worshipped, that by means of religion, which is also justice, man may receive from God immortality, nor is there any other reward of a pious mind; and if this is

[4] Summa.
[5] Utrumne illis ratio subsistat.

invisible, it cannot be presented by the invisible God with any reward but that which is invisible.

CHAP. LXX. — THE IMMORTALITY OF THE SOUL IS CONFIRMED.

It may in truth be collected from many arguments that souls are eternal. Plato says that that which always moves by itself, and has no beginning of motion, also has no end; but that the soul of man always moves by itself, and because it is flexible for reflection, subtle for discovery, easy of perception, adapted to learning, and because it retains the past, comprehends the present, foresees the future, and embraces the knowledge of many subjects and arts, that it is immortal, since it contains nothing which is mixed with the contagion of earthly weight. Moreover, the eternity of the soul is understood from virtue and pleasure. Pleasure is common to all animals, virtue belongs only to man; the former is vicious, the latter is honourable; the former is in accordance with nature, the latter is opposed to nature, unless the soul is immortal. For in defence of faith and justice, virtue neither fears want, nor is alarmed at exile, nor dreads imprisonment, nor shrinks from pain, nor refuses death; and because these things are contrary to nature, either virtue is foolishness, if it stands in the way of advantages, and is injurious to life; or if it is not foolishness, then the soul is immortal, and despises present goods, because other things are preferable which it attains after the dissolution of the body. But that is the greatest proof of immortality, that man alone has the knowledge of God. In the dumb animals there is no notion[1] of religion, because they are earthly and bent down to the earth. Man is upright, and beholds the heaven for this purpose, that he may seek God. Therefore he cannot be other than immortal, who longs for the immortal. He cannot be liable to dissolution, who is connected[2] with God both in countenance and mind. Finally, man alone makes use of the heavenly element, which is fire. For if light is through fire, and life through light, it is evident that he who has the use of fire is not mortal, since this is closely connected, this is intimately related to Him without whom neither light nor life can exist.

But why do we infer from arguments that souls are eternal, when we have divine testimonies? For the sacred writings and the voices of the prophets teach this. And if this appears to any one insufficient, let him read the poems of the Sibyls, let him also weigh the answers of the Milesian Apollo, that he may understand that Democritus, and Epicurus, and Dicæarchus raved, who alone of all mortals denied that which is evident. Having proved the immortality of the soul, it remains to teach by whom, and to whom, and in what manner, and at what time, it is given. Since fixed and divinely appointed times have begun to be filled up, a destruction and consummation of all things must of necessity take place, that the world may be renewed by God. But that time is at hand, as far as may be collected from the number of years, and from the signs which are foretold by the prophets. But since the things which have been spoken concerning the end of the world and the conclusion of the times are innumerable, those very things which are spoken are to be laid down without adornment, since it would be a boundless task to bring forward the testimonies. If any one wishes for them, or does not place full confidence in us, let him approach to the very shrine of the heavenly letters, and being more fully instructed through their trustworthiness, let him perceive that the philosophers have erred, who thought either that this world was eternal, or that there would be numberless thousands of years from the time when it was prepared. For six thousand years have not yet been completed, and when this number shall be made up, then at length all evil will be taken away, that justice alone may reign. And how this will come to pass, I will explain in few words.

CHAP. LXXI. — OF THE LAST TIMES.

These things are said by the prophets, but as seers, to be about to happen. When the last end shall begin to approach to the world, wickedness will increase; all kinds of vices and frauds will become frequent; justice will perish; faith, peace, mercy, modesty, truth, will have no existence; violence and daring will abound; no one will have anything, unless it is acquired by the hand, and defended by the hand. If there shall be any good men, they will be esteemed as a prey and a laughing-stock. No one will exhibit filial affection to parents, no one will pity an infant or an old man; avarice and lust will corrupt all things. There will be slaughter and bloodshed. There will be wars, and those not only between foreign and neighbouring states, but also intestine wars. States will carry on wars among themselves, every sex and age will handle arms. The dignity of government will not be preserved, nor military discipline; but after the manner of robbery, there will be depredation and devastation. Kingly power will be multiplied, and ten men will occupy, portion out, and devour the world. There will arise another by far more powerful and wicked, who, having destroyed three, will obtain Asia, and having reduced and subdued the others under his own

[1] Suspicio.
[2] Cum Deo communis est.

power, will harass all the earth. He will appoint new laws, abrogate old ones; he will make the state his own, and will change the name and seat of the government.

Then there will be a dreadful and detestable time, in which no one would choose to live. In fine, such will be the condition of things, that lamentation will follow the living, and congratulation the dead. Cities and towns will be destroyed, at one time by fire and the sword, at another by repeated earthquakes; now by inundation of waters, now by pestilence and famine. The earth will produce nothing, being barren either through excessive cold or heat. All water will be partly changed into blood, partly vitiated by bitterness, so that none of it can be useful for food, or wholesome for drinking. To these evils will also be added prodigies from heaven, that nothing may be wanting to men for causing fear. Comets will frequently appear. The sun will be overshadowed with perpetual paleness. The moon will be stained with blood, nor will it repair the losses of its light taken away. All the stars will fall, nor will the seasons preserve their regularity, winter and summer being confused. Then both the year, and the month, and the day will be shortened. And Trismegistus has declared that this is the old age and decline of the world. And when this shall have come, it must be known that the time is at hand in which God will return to change the world. But in the midst of these evils there will arise an impious king, hostile not only to mankind, but also to God. He will trample upon, torment, harass and put to death those who have been spared by that former tyrant. Then there will be ever-flowing tears, perpetual wailings and lamentations, and useless prayers to God; there will be no rest from fear, no sleep for a respite. The day will always increase disaster, the night alarm. Thus the world will be reduced almost to solitude, certainly to fewness of men. Then also the impious man will persecute the just and those who are dedicated to God, and will give orders that he himself shall be worshipped as God. For he will say that he is Christ, though he will be His adversary.[1] That he may be believed, he will receive the power of doing wonders, so that fire may descend from heaven, the sun retire from his course, and the image which he shall have set up may speak. And by these prodigies he shall entice many to worship him, and to receive his sign in their hand or forehead. And he who shall not worship him and receive his sign will die with refined tortures. Thus he will destroy nearly two parts, the third will flee into desolate solitudes. But he, frantic and raging with implacable anger, will lead an army and besiege the mountain to which the righteous shall have fled. And when they shall see themselves besieged, they will implore the aid of God with a loud voice, and God shall hear them, and shall send to them a deliverer.

CHAP. LXXII. — OF CHRIST DESCENDING FROM HEAVEN TO THE GENERAL JUDGMENT, AND OF THE MILLENARIAN REIGN.[2]

Then the heaven shall be opened in a tempest,[3] and Christ shall descend with great power, and there shall go before Him a fiery brightness and a countless host of angels, and all that multitude of the wicked shall be destroyed, and torrents of blood shall flow, and the leader himself shall escape, and having often renewed his army, shall for the fourth time engage in battle, in which, being taken, with all the other tyrants, he shall be delivered up to be burnt. But the prince also of the demons himself, the author and contriver of evils, being bound with fiery chains, shall be imprisoned, that the world may receive peace, and the earth, harassed through so many years, may rest. Therefore peace being made, and every evil suppressed, that righteous King and Conqueror will institute a great judgment on the earth respecting the living and the dead, and will deliver all the nations into subjection to the righteous who are alive, and will raise the *righteous* dead to eternal life, and will Himself reign with them on the earth, and will build the holy city, and this kingdom of the righteous shall be for a thousand years. Throughout that time the stars shall be more brilliant, and the brightness of the sun shall be increased, and the moon shall not be subject to decrease. Then the rain of blessing shall descend from God at morning and evening, and the earth shall bring forth all her fruit without the labour of men. Honey shall drop from rocks, fountains of milk and wine shall abound. The beasts shall lay aside their ferocity and become mild, the wolf shall roam among the flocks without doing harm, the calf shall feed with the lion, the dove shall be united with the hawk, the serpent shall have no poison; no animal shall live by bloodshed. For God shall supply to all abundant and harmless[4] food. But when the thousand years shall be fulfilled, and the prince of the demons loosed, the nations will rebel against the righteous, and an innumerable multitude will come to storm the city of the saints. Then the last judgment of God will come to pass against the nations. For He will shake the earth from its foundations, and the cities shall be overthrown, and He shall rain upon the wicked fire with brimstone and hail, and they shall be on fire, and

[1] [See Hippolytus, vol. v. pp. 190–250.]

[2] [See vol. i. p. 209.]

[3] In tempestate; others read "intempestâ nocte."

[4] Innocentem, "without injury to any."

slay each other. But the righteous shall for a little space be concealed under the earth, until the destruction of the nations is accomplished, and after the third day they shall come forth, and see the plains covered with carcases. Then there shall be an earthquake, and the mountains shall be rent, and valleys shall sink down to a profound depth, and into this the bodies of the dead shall be heaped together, and its name shall be called Polyandrion.[1] After these things God will renew the world, and transform the righteous into the forms of angels, that, being presented with the garment of immortality, they may serve God for ever; and this will be the kingdom of God, which shall have no end. Then also the wicked shall rise again, not to life but to punishment; for God shall raise these also, when the second resurrection takes place, that, being condemned to eternal torments and delivered to eternal fires, they may suffer the punishments which they deserve for their crimes.

CHAP. LXXIII. — THE HOPE OF SAFETY IS IN THE RELIGION AND WORSHIP OF GOD.

Wherefore, since all these things are true and certain, in harmony with the predicted announcement of the prophets, since Trismegistus and Hystaspes and the Sibyls have foretold the same things, it cannot be doubted that all hope of life and salvation is placed in the religion of God alone. Therefore, unless a man shall have received Christ, whom God has sent, and is about to send for our redemption, unless he shall have known the Supreme God through Christ, unless he shall have kept His commandments and law, he will fall into those punishments of which we have spoken. Therefore frail things must be despised, that we may gain those which are substantial; earthly things must be scorned, that we may be honoured with heavenly things; temporal things must be shunned, that we may reach those which are eternal. Let every one train himself to justice, mould himself to self-restraint, prepare himself for the contest, equip himself for virtue, that if by any chance an adversary shall wage war, he may be driven from that which is upright and good by no force, no terror, and no tortures, may give[2] himself up to no senseless fictions, but in his uprightness acknowledge the true and only God, may cast away pleasures, by the attractions of which the lofty soul is depressed to the earth, may hold fast innocency, may be of service to as many as possible, may gain for himself incorruptible treasures by good works, that he may be able, with God for his judge, to gain for the merits of his virtue either the crown of faith, or the reward of immortality.

[1] A name sometimes given to cemeteries, because many men (πολλοὶ ἄνδρες) are borne thither.

[2] Se substernet.

ELUCIDATIONS

I.

(Princes and kings, p. 13.)

How memorable the histories, moreover, of Nebuchadnezzar[1] and his decrees; of Darius[2] and his also; but especially of Cyrus and his great monumental edict![3] The beautiful narratives of the Queen of Sheba and of the Persian consort of Queen Esther (probably Xerxes) are also manifestations of the ways of Providence in giving light to the heathen world through that "nation of priests" in Israel.

But Lactantius, who uses the Sibyls so freely, should not have omitted to show what Sibylline oracles God drew forth from "the princes of this world" also, by the illumination of the *pharos* which he established in Sion, "to be a light to lighten the Gentiles" until the great Epiphany should rise upon them in "the dayspring from on high."

I extract from a paradoxical but most entertaining author, whom I have often quoted, certain extracts from Philo, which I translate from his note in the *Soirées*. Thus: —

"Agrippa," says Philo,[4] "having visited Jerusalem in Herod's time, was enchanted by the religion of the Jews, and could never cease to speak of it. . . . Augustus ordered that every day,

[1] Dan. ii. 47, iii. 29, and iv. [2] Dan. vi. 25. [3] Ezra i. 2. [4] In his *Discourse to Caligula*.

at his own expense, and under the legal forms, a bull and *two lambs* should be offered in holocaust to the Most High God on the altar at Jerusalem, though he knew that it contained no image, whether exposed or within the veil; for this great prince, surpassed by none in the philosophic spirit, felt the actual necessity in this world of an altar dedicated to a God invisible."

Philo also says: —

"Your great-grandmother Julia[1] also made superb presents to the temple; and although women very reluctantly detach themselves from images, and rarely conceive of anything apart from sensation, this lady, nevertheless, greatly superior to her sex in culture and in natural endowments, arrived at that point in which she preferred to contemplate such things in the mind rather than in sensible objects, regarding these as mere shadows of the realities."

In the same discourse, wasting words on Caligula, Philo reminds him that Augustus "not only *admired*, nay, rather, he adored (ἐθαύμαζε καὶ προσέκυνει, κ.τ.λ.), this custom of employing *no sort of image to represent, materially, a nature invisible in itself.*" Poor De Maistre, who quotes this testimony against images from Philo with intense appreciation, will yet sophisticate himself and others into the very contrary in behalf of his one predominant idea of (προσκύνησις) canine self-abasement to the decrees of the Vatican. On this account I am forced to consider him a sophist as well as a fanatic; but I delight to render justice to his genius, for, wherever he talks and reasons *as a Christian* merely, he fascinates and instructs me. He never conceived of "Catholicity," and lived under the delusion of the Decretals, a disciple of the Jesuits.

II.

(Therefore they were neglected for many ages, p. 116.)

The explicit statements of Lactantius, and his profuse quotations from the *Sibyllina*, persuade me that these curious fragments deserve a degree of scientific attention which they have not yet received. The Fathers all cite them, when it must have exposed them to scorn and overwhelming refutation had their quotations not been found in the *Sibylline* books of their adversaries. The influence of the Jewish religion upon the Gentiles under the Babylonian and Medo-Persian monarchies must have been considerable, but after Alexander's time it was vastly increased. Many versions of select prophets were doubtless produced in Greek before the authorized Septuagint. These were soon embedded in the Sibyls' books; and I cannot think the interpolations of early Christians were all frauds, by any means. Their numerous marginal annotations crept into other copies; and very likely, in the time of our author, they were inextricably confused with the text in the greater part of the "editions," so to speak, then current with booksellers.

But in vol. viii. we shall have occasion to recur again to this interesting inquiry.

III.

(We made proclamation before him as children, p. 117.)

"Sicut pueri." This is *not* according to the Septuagint, ὡς παιδίον. It is not the Vulgate, of course; but its radical difference with that raises interesting inquiries: Is it a specimen of one of many African or old Italic versions? Does our author endeavour to translate from the Septuagint? May he not have had in hand a copy of Isaiah from among those which preceded the Septuagint?

The Septuagint reading finds its key in cap. lii. 7, and in the tenth verse, where the "Arm of the Lord" ("His Holy Arm") is introduced as the personal Logos Incarnate. The thirteenth and fourteenth verses predict the amazing sequel, and its practical and blessed results; and then

[1] i.e., Livia, wife and empress of Augustus.

begins cap. liii., "Who hath believed" our message. To whom is "the Arm of the Lord" revealed? "*Going* before Him (i.e., as heralds), we have proclaimed *Him* as a child, and, as *it were*, a root in a thirsty land; He has no form nor glory," etc. In other words, "We have prophesied of Him who is elsewhere predicted ("unto us a child is born") as one who from His childhood is as a rush without water, — prematurely withered, — a man of sorrows, and the Carpenter's Son."

It does not hint, therefore, the "obscurity" of the Messiah's birth, but rather what Irenæus insists upon, i.e., His (premature) old age; the worn and stricken appearance of senility in comparative youth.[1] This is just what the messengers (Isa. lii. 7) had said in their proclamation (Isa. lii. 14) just before: "His visage was so marred more than any man, and His form more than the sons of men."

IV.

(There was darkness, etc., pp. 122, 240.)

In former instances, where thought has turned to Phlegon the Trallian,[2] I have failed to refer to an author whose excess of candour sometimes gives away more than is called for, in questions on which adversaries have contrived to fasten undue importance, in order to elicit indiscreet defences. But it is due to my readers that I should refer them to a most learned work, to be found in public libraries only, by my revered friend and instructor Dr. Jarvis. The sixth chapter (part ii.) of his *Chronological Introduction to Church History*[3] is devoted to this matter, and I can do no better than give the summary of its contents as follows: —

> "Who Phlegon was; his work lost; extracts from it by Julius Africanus and Eusebius; their works, containing these extracts, lost; all we know is from versions and later writers; collation of extracts as given by the Armenian version of the *Chronicon* of Eusebius, St. Jerome's Latin version, the *Chronographia* of Syncellus, and the *Chronicon Paschale*; extract by Syncellus from Julius Africanus; remarks upon it; testimony of Origen concerning Phlegon's account; of John Philoponus (St. Maximus) Malala; summary of the whole; account of Phlegon's testimony; not noticed by the learned and voluminous writers of the fourth and fifth centuries when they speak of the darkness, etc.; Dr. Lardner's judgment[4] adopted."

Lardner's view, it will be observed, is thus sustained by an independent and most competent critic. This decision puts honour on the early writers: he thinks they were unwilling to claim a corroboration from evidence about which they were not well assured.

V.

(Divine and ethnic oracles, p. 210, note 2; p. 112, note 9.)

The whole subject of ethnic oracles needs fresh study and illustration. Nothing would be more fascinating in theological inquiry, and Divine Inspiration might be richly illustrated by it, as anatomical science is clarified by "comparative anatomy." I commend this subject to men of faith, learning, and intellectual vigour. Notably, let it be observed: (1) That Balaam's ass is instanced by St. Peter as miraculously enabled to rebuke the madness of his master; and the same Apostle shortly before gives us the law as to divine inspiration in contrast.[5] (2) Balaam himself, as mechanically as the beast he rode,[6] had his own mouth opened (see Num. xxiv. 16–19). (3) The wicked Caiaphas in like manner (St. John xi. 51, 52) spake prophetically, "not of himself." (4) St. Paul (Acts xvii. 28) quotes a heathen oracle very much as does our author.[7]

[1] Vol. i. p. 391, note 12, this series.

[2] See vol. iii. Elucidation V. p. 58.

[3] P. 419.

[4] *Works*, ed. London, 1788, vol. vii. p. 385.

[5] Comp. 2 Pet. i. 18-21 with ii. 16.

[6] P. 174, note 2, *supra*.

[7] See p. 140, note 10, *supra*.

Now, in view of the boldness with which the early Christians follow the example of the Apostle in quoting the *Orphica* and *Sibyllina*, I cannot imagine that these citations were not honestly believed by them to be oracles of a certain sort, by which God permitted the heathen to be enlightened.[1] Observe our author's moderate but most pregnant remark about such inspiration (on p. 170, *supra*, note 8), "*almost* with a divine voice;" then (on p. 192) compare other *almost* inspired words of poor Tully (at note 2), and of Seneca also.[2]

Finally, and to close the subject, the reader will readily forgive me for introducing the following citations from the "Warburton Lecture" of Dr. Edersheim, on *Prophecy and History*[3] *in Relation to the Messiah*. Discussing the *pseudepigraphic writings* (in Lecture Eleventh), he says as follows:[4]—

"The Sibylline oracles, in Greek hexameters, consist, in their present form, of twelve books. *They are full of interpolations*, the really ancient portions forming part of the first two books and the largest part of book third (verses 97–807). These sections *are deeply imbued with the Messianic spirit*.[5] They date from about the year 140 before our era, while another small portion of the same book is supposed to date from the year 32 B.C.

"As regards the promise of the Messiah, we turn in the first place, and with special interest, to the *Sibylline Oracles*. In the third book of these (such portions as I shall quote date from about 140 B.C.) the Messiah is described as 'the King sent from heaven, who would judge every man in blood and splendour of fire.' And the Vision of Messianic times opens with a reference to 'the King whom God will send from the Sun,' where we cannot fail to perceive a reference to the *Seventy-second* Psalm,[6] especially as we remember that the Greek of the Seventy, *which must have been present to the Hellenist Sibyl*, fully adapted the Messianic application of the passage to a *premundane* Messiah. We also think of the picture drawn in the prophecies of Isaiah. According to the Sibylline books, King Messiah was not only to come, but He was to be specifically sent of God. He is *supermundane*, a King and a Judge[7] of superhuman glory and splendour. And, indeed, that a superhuman kingdom, such as the Sibylline oracles paint, should have a superhuman king, seems only a natural and necessary inference. . . . If, as certain modern critics contend, the book of Daniel is not authentic,[8] but dates from Maccabean times, . . . it may well be asked *to what king* the Sibylline oracles point, for they certainly date from that period; and what is the relationship between the (supposed Maccabean) prophecies of the book of Daniel and the *certainly Messianic* anticipations of the undoubted literature of that period?"

Dr. Edersheim gives us the reference in the margin, to which I would call attention, as directing to the whole *pseudepigraphic* literature.[9] But who can wonder, after what we thus learn, that Constantine[10] was so profoundly impressed with Virgil's *Pollio?* In spite of all that has been said,[11] I cannot but see Isaiah in its entire spirit.

---

1 See p. 219, note 3.

2 Compare Cyprian (vol. v. p. 502, this series), and note his judicious reference to the inspiration of Balaam by the extreme instance of the miraculous voice of a dumb beast. Also, see vol. ii. Elucidation XIII. p. 346, this series.

3 Republished, New York, Randolph, 1885.

4 Pp. 339, 343.

5 Note, these are the "really ancient" portions.

6 Verses 5, 6, etc., to the end.

7 Ps. lxxii. 1, 2.

8 An absurdity *pulverized* by the faith and learning of Dr. Pusey.

9 *Pseudepigrapha*. O. F. Fritzsche, Lips., 1871, *Codex Pseudepigr. Vet. Test.*, ed. 1722.; J. A. Fabricius, *Messias Judæorum*, Hilgenfeld, Lips., 1869; also Drummond, *The Jewish Messiah;* and compare Jellinek, *Bet-ha-Midrash*, six parts, 1857–73.

10 See the Greek of Constantine's quotations in Heyne's *Virgil*, excursus i. tom. i. p. 164.

11 Heyne (Lips., 1788), vol. i. pp. 66–70.

A TREATISE ON THE ANGER OF GOD

ADDRESSED TO DONATUS.[1]

CHAP. I. — OF DIVINE AND HUMAN WISDOM.

I HAVE often observed, Donatus, that many persons hold this opinion, which some philosophers also have maintained, that God is not subject to anger; since the divine nature is either altogether beneficent, and that it is inconsistent with His surpassing and excellent power to do injury to any one; or, at any rate, He takes no notice of us at all, so that no advantage comes to us from His goodness, and no evil from His ill-will. But the error of these men, because it is very great, and tends to overthrow the condition of human life, must be refuted by us, lest you yourself also should be deceived, being incited by the authority of men who deem themselves wise. Nor, however, are we so arrogant as to boast that the truth is comprehended by our intellect; but we follow the teaching of God, who alone is able to know and to reveal secret things. But the philosophers, being destitute of this teaching, have imagined that the nature of things can be ascertained by conjecture. But this is impossible; because the mind of man, enclosed in the dark abode of the body, is far removed from the perception of truth: and in this the divine nature differs from the human, that ignorance is the property of the human, knowledge of the divine nature.

On which account we have need of some light to dispel the darkness by which the reflection of man is overspread, since, while we live in mortal flesh, we are unable to divine by our senses. But the light of the human mind is God, and he who has known and admitted Him into his breast will acknowledge the mystery of the truth with an enlightened heart; but when God and heavenly instruction are removed, all things are full of errors. And Socrates, though he was the most learned of all the philosophers, yet, that he might prove the ignorance of the others, who thought that they possessed something, rightly said that he knew nothing, except one thing — that he knew nothing. For he understood that that learning had nothing certain, nothing true in itself; nor, as some imagine, did he pretend[2] to learning that he might refute others, but he saw the truth in some measure. And he testified even on his trial (as is related by Plato) that there was no human wisdom. He so despised, derided, and cast aside the learning in which the philosophers then boasted, that he professed that very thing as the greatest learning, that he had learnt that he knew nothing. If, therefore, there is no human wisdom, as Socrates taught, as Plato handed down, it is evident that the knowledge of the truth is divine, and belongs to no other than to God. Therefore God must be known, in whom alone is the truth. He is the Parent of the world, and the Framer of all things; who is not seen with the eyes, and is scarcely distinguished by the mind; whose religion is accustomed to be attacked in many ways by those who have neither been able to attain true wisdom, nor to comprehend the system of the great and heavenly secret.

CHAP. II. — OF THE TRUTH AND ITS STEPS, AND OF GOD.

For since there are many steps by which the ascent is made to the abode of truth, it is not easy for any one to reach the summit. For when the eyes are darkened by the brightness of the truth, they who are unable to maintain a firm step fall back to the level ground.[3] Now the first step is to understand false religions, and to throw aside the impious worship of gods which are made by the hand of man. But the second step is to perceive with the mind that there is but one Supreme God, whose power and providence made the world from the beginning, and afterwards continues to govern it. The third step is to know His Servant and Messenger,[4]

---

[1] [Of this Donatus, see (*On the Persecutors*) cap. 16, *infra;* also cap. 35. He was a confessor and sore sufferer under Diocletian.]

[2] Simulavit: others read "dissimulavit," concealed his knowledge.

[3] Revolvuntur in planum.

[4] Thus our Lord Himself speaks, John xvii. 3: "This is life eternal, that they may know Thee, the only true God, and Jesus Christ, whom Thou hast sent." [The Jehovah-Angel, vol. i. pp. 223-226, this series, and *sparsim.*]

whom He sent as His ambassador to the earth, by whose teaching being freed from the error in which we were held entangled, and formed to the worship of the true God, we might learn righteousness. From all of these steps, as I have said, there is a rapid and easy gliding to a downfall,[1] unless the feet are firmly planted with unshaken stedfastness.

We see those shaken off from the first step, who, though they understand things which are false, do not, however, discover that which is true; and though they despised earthly and frail images, do not betake themselves to the worship of God, of whom they are ignorant. But viewing with admiration the elements of the universe, they worship the heaven, the earth, the sea, the sun, the moon, and the other heavenly bodies.

But we have already reproved their ignorance in the second book of the *Divine Institutes*.[2] But we say that those fall from the second step, who, though they understand that there is but one Supreme God, nevertheless, ensnared by the philosophers, and captivated by false arguments, entertain opinions concerning that excellent majesty far removed from the truth; who either deny that God has any figure, or think that He is moved by no affection, because every affection is a sign of weakness, which has no existence in God. But they are precipitated from the third step, who, though they know the Ambassador of God, who is also the Builder of the divine and immortal temple,[3] either do not receive Him, or receive Him otherwise than faith demands; whom we have partly refuted in the fourth book of the above-named work.[4] And we will hereafter refute more carefully, when we shall begin to reply to all the sects, which, while they dispute,[5] have destroyed the truth.

But now we will argue against those who, falling from the second step, entertain wrong sentiments respecting the Supreme God. For some say that He neither does a kindness to any one, nor becomes angry, but in security and quietness enjoys the advantages of His own immortality. Others, indeed, take away anger, but leave to God kindness; for they think that a nature excelling in the greatest virtue, while it ought not to be malevolent, ought also to be benevolent. Thus all the philosophers are agreed on the subject of anger, but are at variance respecting kindness. But, that my speech may descend in order to the proposed subject, a division of this kind must be made and followed by me, since anger and kindness are different, and opposed to one another. Either anger must be attributed to God, and kindness taken from Him; or both alike must be taken from Him; or anger must be taken away, and kindness attributed to Him; or neither must be taken away. The nature of the case admits of nothing else besides these; so that the truth, which is sought for, must necessarily be found in some one of these. Let us consider them separately, that reason and arrangement may conduct us to the hiding-place of truth.

1 Ad ruinam.
2 Ch. v. and vi. pp. 47, 48.
3 The temple built of living stones, 1 Pet. ii. 5.
4 Ch. x., etc., p. 108.
5 Dum disputant; other editions read, "dum dissipant."

CHAP. III. — OF THE GOOD AND EVIL THINGS IN HUMAN AFFAIRS, AND OF THEIR AUTHOR.

First, no one ever said this respecting God, that He is only subject to anger, and is not influenced by kindness. For it is unsuitable to God, that He should be endowed with a power of this kind, by which He may injure and do harm, but be unable to profit and to do good. What means, therefore, what hope of safety, is proposed to men, if God is the author of evils only? For if this is so, that venerable majesty will now be drawn out, not to the power of the judge, to whom it is permitted to preserve and set at liberty, but to the office of the torturer and executioner. But whereas we see that there are not only evils in human affairs, but also goods, it is plain that if God is the author of evils, there must be another who does things contrary to God, and gives to us good things. If there is such a one, by what name must he be called? Why is he who injures us more known to us than He who benefits us? But if this can be nothing besides God, it is absurd and vain to suppose that the divine power, than which nothing is greater or better, is able to injure, but unable to benefit; and accordingly no one has ever existed who ventured to assert this, because it is neither reasonable nor in any way credible. And because this is agreed upon, let us pass on and seek after the truth elsewhere.

CHAP. IV. — OF GOD AND HIS AFFECTIONS, AND THE CENSURE OF EPICURUS.

That which follows is concerning the school of Epicurus; that as there is no anger in God, so indeed there is no kindness. For when Epicurus thought that it was inconsistent with God to injure and to inflict harm, which for the most part arises from the affection of anger, he took away from Him beneficence also, since he saw that it followed that if God has anger, He must also have kindness. Therefore, lest he should concede to Him a vice, he deprived Him also of virtue.[6] From this, he says, He is happy and uncorrupted, because He cares about nothing, and neither takes trouble Himself nor occasions it to another. Therefore He is not God, if He

6 [Ne illi vitium concederet etiam virtutis fecit expertem.]

is neither moved, which is peculiar to a living being, nor does anything impossible for man, which is peculiar to God, if He has no will at all, no action, in short, no administration, which is worthy of God. And what greater, what more worthy administration can be attributed to God, than the government of the world, and especially of the human race, to which all earthly things are subject?

What happiness, then, can there be in God, if He is always inactive, being at rest and unmoveable? if He is deaf to those who pray to Him, and blind to His worshippers? What is so worthy of God, and so befitting to Him, as providence? But if He cares for nothing, and foresees nothing, He has lost all His divinity. What else does he say, who takes from God all power and all substance, except that there is no God at all? In short, Marcus Tullius relates that it was said by Posidonius,[1] that Epicurus understood that there were no gods, but that he said those things which he spoke respecting the gods for the sake of driving away odium; and so that he leaves the gods in words, but takes them away in reality, since he gives them no motion, no office. But if this is so, what can be more deceitful than him? And this ought to be foreign to the character of a wise and weighty man. But if he understood one thing and spoke another, what else is he to be called than a deceiver, double-tongued, wicked, and moreover foolish? But Epicurus was not so crafty as to say those things with the desire of deceiving, when he consigned these things also by his writings to everlasting remembrance; but he erred through ignorance of the truth. For, being led from the beginning by the probability[2] of a single opinion, he necessarily fell into those things which followed. For the first opinion was, that anger was not consistent with the character of God. And when this appeared to him to be true and unassailable,[3] he was unable to refuse the consequences; because one affection being removed, necessity itself compelled him to remove from God the other affections also. Thus, he who is not subject to anger is plainly uninfluenced by kindness, which is the opposite feeling to anger. Now, if there is neither anger nor kindness in Him, it is manifest that there is neither fear, nor joy, nor grief, nor pity. For all the affections have one system, one motion,[4] which cannot be the case with God. But if there is no affection in God, because whatever is subject to affections is weak, it follows that there is in Him neither the care of anything, nor providence.

The disputation of the wise man[5] extends thus far: he was silent as to the other things which follow; namely, that because there is in Him neither care nor providence, therefore there is no reflection nor any perception in Him, by which it is effected that He has no existence at all. Thus, when he had gradually descended, he remained on the last step, because he now saw the precipice. But what does it avail to have remained silent, and concealed the danger? Necessity compelled him even against his will to fall. For he said that which he did not mean, because he so arranged his argument that he necessarily came to that point which he wished to avoid. You see, therefore, to what point he comes, when anger is removed and taken away from God. In short, either no one believes that, or a very few, and they the guilty and the wicked, who hope for impunity for their sins. But if this also is found to be false, that there is neither anger nor kindness in God, let us come to that which is put in the third place.

CHAP. V.—THE OPINION OF THE STOICS CONCERNING GOD; OF HIS ANGER AND KINDNESS.

The Stoics and some others are supposed to have entertained much better sentiments respecting the divine nature, who say that there is kindness in God, but not anger. A very pleasing and popular speech, that God is not subject to such littleness of mind as to imagine that He is injured by any one, since it is impossible for Him to be injured; so that that serene and holy majesty is excited, disturbed, and maddened, which is the part of human frailty. For they say that anger is a commotion and perturbation of the mind, which is inconsistent with God. Since, when it falls upon the mind of any one, as a violent tempest it excites such waves that it changes the condition of the mind, the eyes gleam, the countenance trembles, the tongue stammers, the teeth chatter, the countenance is alternately stained now with redness spread over it, now with white paleness. But if anger is unbecoming to a man, provided he be of wisdom and authority, how much more is so foul a change unbecoming to God! And if man, when he has authority and power, inflicts widespread injury through anger, sheds blood, overthrows cities, destroys communities, reduces provinces to desolation, how much more is it to be believed that God, since He has power over the whole human race, and over the universe itself, would have been about to destroy all things if He were angry.

Therefore they think that so great and so pernicious an evil ought to be absent from Him. And if anger and excitement are absent from

1 [Disciple of Panætius the Rhodian, a Stoic, third century B.C.]
2 Verisimilitudine, i.e., likeness of truth.
3 Inexpugnabile, impregnable.
4 Commotio.

5 Epicurus: it seems to be spoken with some irony.

Him, because it is disfiguring and injurious, and He inflicts injury on no one, they think that nothing else remains, except that He is mild, calm, propitious, beneficent, the preserver. For thus at length He may be called the common Father of all, and the best and greatest, which His divine and heavenly nature demands. For if among men it appears praiseworthy to do good rather than to injure, to restore to life[1] rather than to kill, to save rather than to destroy, and innocence is not undeservedly numbered among the virtues, — and he who does these things is loved, esteemed, honoured, and celebrated with all blessings and vows, — in short, on account of his deserts and benefits is judged to be most like to God; how much more right is it that God Himself, who excels in divine and perfect virtues, and who is removed from all earthly taint, should conciliate[2] the whole race of man by divine and heavenly benefits! Those things are spoken speciously and in a popular manner, and they allure many to believe them; but they who entertain these sentiments approach nearer indeed to the truth, but they partly fail, not sufficiently considering the nature of the case. For if God is not angry with the impious and the unrighteous, it is clear that He does not love the pious and the righteous. Therefore the error of those is more consistent who take away at once both anger and kindness. For in opposite matters it is necessary to be moved to both sides or to neither. Thus, he who loves the good also hates the wicked, and he who does not hate the wicked does not love the good; because the loving of the good arises from the hatred of the wicked, and the hating of the wicked has its rise from the love of the good. There is no one who loves life without a hatred of death, nor who is desirous of light, but he who avoids darkness. These things are so connected by nature, that the one cannot exist without the other.

If any master has in his household a good and a bad servant, it is evident that he does not hate them both, or confer upon both benefits and honours; for if he does this, he is both unjust and foolish. But he addresses the one who is good with friendly words, and honours him, and sets him over his house and household, and all his affairs; but punishes the bad one with reproaches, with stripes, with nakedness, with hunger, with thirst, with fetters: so that the latter may be an example to others to keep them from sinning, and the former to conciliate them; so that fear may restrain some, and honour may excite others. He, therefore, who loves also hates, and he who hates also loves; for there are those who ought to be loved, and there are those who ought to be hated. And as he who loves confers good things on those whom he loves, so he who hates inflicts evils upon those whom he hates; which argument, because it is true, can in no way be refuted. Therefore the opinion of those is vain and false, who, when they attribute the one to God, take away the other, not less than the opinion of those who take away both. But the latter,[3] as we have shown, in part do not err, but retain that which is the better of the two; whereas the former,[4] led on by the accurate method of their reasoning, fall into the greatest error, because they have assumed premises which are altogether false. For they ought not to have reasoned thus: Because God is not liable to anger, therefore He is not moved by kindness; but in this manner: Because God is moved by kindness, therefore He is also liable to anger. For if it had been certain and undoubted that God is not liable to anger, then the other point would necessarily be arrived at. But since the question as to whether God is angry is more open to doubt, while it is almost perfectly plain that He is kind, it is absurd to wish to subvert that which is certain by means of an uncertainty, since it is easier to confirm uncertain things by means of those which are certain.

CHAP. VI. — THAT GOD IS ANGRY.

These are the opinions entertained by the philosophers respecting God. But if we have discovered that these things which have been spoken are false, there remains that one last resource, in which alone the truth can be found, which has never been embraced by philosophers, nor at any time defended: that it follows that God is angry, since He is moved by kindness. This opinion is to be maintained and asserted by us; for[5] this is the sum and turning-point on which the whole of piety and religion depend: and no honour can be due to God, if He affords nothing to His worshippers; and no fear, if He is not angry with him who does not worship Him.[6]

CHAP. VII. — OF MAN, AND THE BRUTE ANIMALS, AND RELIGION.

Though philosophers have often turned aside from reason through their ignorance of the truth, and have fallen into inextricable errors (for that is wont to happen to these which happens to a traveller ignorant of the way, and not confessing that he is ignorant, — namely, that he wanders about, while he is ashamed to inquire from those

[1] Vivificare.

[2] Promereri.

[3] The Stoics. [Encountered first by St. Paul, Acts xvii. 18.]

[4] The Epicureans. [*Ibid.*]

[5] In eo enim summa omnis et cardo religionis pietatisque versatur.

[6] [This fear of the Lord is *filial*, not *servile;* and this anger is likewise twofold, including fatherly and corrective indignation, and the wrath of the magistrate, which inflicts penalty and retribution. Compare Ps. vii. 11; also p. 104, note 1, *supra*.]

whom he meets), no philosopher, however, has ever made the assertion that there is no difference between man and the brutes. Nor has any one at all, provided that he wished to appear wise, reduced a rational animal to the level of the mute and irrational; which some ignorant persons do, resembling the brutes themselves, who, wishing to give themselves up to the indulgence of their appetite and pleasure, say that they are born on the same principle as all living animals, which it is impious for man to say. For who is so unlearned as not to know, who is so void of understanding as not to perceive, that there is something divine in man? I do not as yet come to the excellences of the soul and of the intellect, by which there is a manifest affinity between man and God. Does not the position of the body itself, and the fashion of the countenance, declare that we are not on a level with the dumb creation? Their nature is prostrated to the ground and to their pasture, and has nothing in common with the heaven, which they do not look upon. But man, with his erect position, with his elevated countenance raised to the contemplation of the universe, compares his features with God, and reason recognises reason.[1]

And on this account there is no animal, as Cicero says,[2] except man, which has any knowledge of God. For he alone is furnished with wisdom, so that he alone understands religion; and this is the chief or only difference between man and the dumb animals. For the other things which appear to be peculiar to man, even if there are not such in the dumb animals, nevertheless may appear to be similar. Speech is peculiar to man; yet even in these there is a certain resemblance to speech. For they both distinguish one another by their voices; and when they are angry, they send forth a sound resembling altercation; and when they see one another after an interval of time, they show the office of congratulation by their voice. To us, indeed, their voices appear uncouth,[3] as ours perhaps do to them; but to themselves, who understand one another, they are words. In short, in every affection they utter distinct expressions of voice[4] by which they may show their state of mind. Laughter also is peculiar to man; and yet we see certain indications of joy in other animals, when they use passionate gestures[5] with a view to sports, hang down[6] their ears, contract their mouth, smooth their forehead, relax their eyes to sportiveness. What is so peculiar to man as reason and the foreseeing of the future? But there are animals which open several outlets in different directions from their lairs, that if any danger comes upon them, an escape may be open for them shut in; but they would not do this unless they possessed intelligence and reflection. Others are provident for the future, as

> "Ants, when they plunder a great heap of corn, mindful of the winter, and lay it up in their dwelling;"[7]

again, —

> "As bees, which alone know a country and fixed abodes; and mindful of the winter which is to come, they practise labour in the summer, and lay up their gains as a common stock."[8]

It would be a long task if I should wish to trace out the things most resembling the skill of man, which are accustomed to be done by the separate tribes of animals. But if, in the case of all these things which are wont to be ascribed to man, there is found to be some resemblance even in the dumb animals, it is evident that religion is the only thing of which no trace can be found in the dumb animals, nor any indication. For justice is peculiar to religion, and to this no other animal attains. For man alone bears rule; the other animals are subjected[9] to him. But the worship of God is ascribed to justice; and he who does not embrace this, being far removed from the nature of man, will live the life of the brutes under the form of man. But since we differ from the other animals almost in this respect alone, that we alone of all perceive the divine might and power, while in the others there is no understanding of God, it is surely impossible that in this respect either the dumb animals should have more wisdom, or human nature should be unwise, since all living creatures, and the whole system of nature, are subject to man on account of his wisdom. Wherefore if reason, if the force of man in this respect, excels and surpasses the rest of living creatures, inasmuch as he alone is capable of the knowledge of God, it is evident that religion can in no way be overthrown.

CHAP. VIII. — OF RELIGION.

But religion is overthrown if we believe Epicurus speaking thus: —

> "For the nature of gods must ever in itself of necessity enjoy immortality together with supreme repose, far removed and withdrawn from our concerns; since, exempt from every pain, exempt from all dangers, strong in its own resources, not wanting aught of us, it is neither gained by favours nor moved by anger."[10]

Now, when he says these things, does he think that any worship is to be paid to God, or does

1 The reason of man, man's rational nature, recognises the divine reason, i.e., God. [Confert cum Deo vultum et rationem ratio cognoscit. Hence Milton's "human face divine."]
2 *De Legibus*, i. 8.
3 Incondita, "unformed, or rude." [See p. 77, *supra*.]
4 [Vol. vi. note 3, p. 452, this series.]
5 Ad lusum gestiunt.
6 Demulcent.
7 Virg., *Æn.*, iv. 402.
8 Virg., *Georg.*, iv. 155.
9 Conciliata sunt.
10 Lucret., ii. 646.

he entirely overthrow religion? For if God confers nothing good on any one, if He repays the obedience of His worshipper with no favour, what is so senseless, what so foolish, as to build temples, to offer sacrifices, to present gifts, to diminish our property, that we may obtain nothing?[1] But (it will be said) it is right that an excellent nature should be honoured. What honour can be due to a being who pays no regard to us, and is ungrateful? Can we be bound in any manner to him who has nothing in common with us? "Farewell to God," says Cicero,[2] "if He is such as to be influenced by no favour, and by no affection of men. For why should I say 'may He be propitious?' for He can be propitious to no one." What can be spoken more contemptible with respect to God? Farewell to Him, he says, that is, let Him depart and retire, since He is able to profit no one. But if God takes no trouble, nor occasions trouble to another, why then should we not commit crimes as often as it shall be in our power to escape the notice of men,[3] and to cheat the public laws? Wherever we shall obtain a favourable opportunity of escaping notice, let us take advantage of the occasion: let us take away the property of others, either without bloodshed or even with blood, if there is nothing else besides the laws to be reverenced.

While Epicurus entertains these sentiments, he altogether destroys religion; and when this is taken away, confusion and perturbation of life will follow. But if religion cannot be taken away without destroying our hold of wisdom, by which we are separated from the brutes, and of justice, by which the public life may be more secure, how can religion itself be maintained or guarded without fear? For that which is not feared is despised, and that which is despised is plainly not reverenced. Thus it comes to pass that religion, and majesty, and honour exist together with fear; but there is no fear where no one is angry. Whether, therefore, you take away from God kindness, or anger, or both, religion must be taken away, without which the life of men is full of folly, of wickedness, and enormity. For conscience greatly curbs men, if we believe that we are living in the sight of God; if we imagine not only that the actions which we perform are seen from above, but also that our thoughts and our words are heard by God. But it is profitable to believe this, as some imagine, not for the sake of the truth, but of utility, since laws cannot punish conscience unless some terror from above hangs over to restrain offences. Therefore religion is altogether false, and there is no divinity; but all things are made up by skilful men, in order that they may live more uprightly and innocently. This is a great question, and foreign to the subject which we have proposed; but because it necessarily occurs, it ought to be handled, however briefly.

CHAP. IX. — OF THE PROVIDENCE OF GOD, AND OF OPINIONS OPPOSED TO IT.

When the philosophers of former times had agreed in their opinions respecting providence, and there was no doubt but that the world was set in order by God and reason, and was governed by reason, Protagoras, in the times of Socrates, was the first of all who said that it was not clear to him whether there was any divinity or not. And this disputation of his was judged so impious, and so contrary to the truth and to religion, that the Athenians both banished him from their territories, and burnt in a public assembly those books of his in which these statements were contained. But there is no need to speak respecting his opinions, because he pronounced nothing certain. After these things Socrates and his disciple Plato, and those who flowed forth from the school of Plato like rivulets into different directions, namely, the Stoics and Peripatetics, were of the same opinion as those who went before them.[4]

Afterwards Epicurus said that there was indeed a God, because it was necessary that there should be in the world some being of surpassing excellence, distinction, and blessedness; yet that there was no providence, and thus that the world itself was ordered by no plan, nor art, nor workmanship, but that the universe was made up of certain minute and indivisible seeds. But I do not see what can be said more repugnant to the truth. For if there is a God, as God He is manifestly provident; nor can divinity be attributed to Him in any other way than if He retains the past, and knows the present, and foresees the future. Therefore, in taking away providence, he also denied the existence of God. But when he openly acknowledged the existence of God, at the same time he also admitted His providence; for the one cannot exist at all, or be understood, without the other. But in those later times in which philosophy had now lost its vigour,[5] there lived a certain Diagoras of Melos,[6] who altogether denied the existence of God, and on account of this sentiment was called atheist;[7] also Theodorus[6] of Cyrene: both of whom, because they were unable to discover anything new, all things having already been said and found out, preferred even, in opposition to the truth, to deny that in which all pre-

1 i.e., without any result.
2 *De Nat. Deor.*, i. 44.
3 Hominum conscientiam fallere.

4 [A beautiful formula of the history of Greek philosophy.]
5 Defloruerat.
6 [Vol. vi. p. 421.]
7 ἄθεος.

ceding philosophers had agreed without any ambiguity. These are they who attacked providence, which had been asserted and defended through so many ages by so many intellects. What then? Shall we refute those trifling and inactive philosophers by reason, or by the authority of distinguished men, or rather by both? But we must hasten onwards, lest our speech should wander too far from our subject.

CHAP. X. — OF THE ORIGIN OF THE WORLD, AND THE NATURE OF AFFAIRS, AND THE PROVIDENCE OF GOD.

They who do not admit that the world was made by divine providence, either say that it is composed of first principles coming together at random, or that it suddenly came into existence by nature, but hold, as Straton [1] does, that nature has in itself the power of production and of diminution, but that it has neither sensibility nor figure, so that we may understand that all things were produced spontaneously, without any artificer or author. Each opinion is vain and impossible. But this happens to those who are ignorant of the truth, that they devise anything, rather than perceive that which the nature of the subject [2] requires. First of all, with respect to those minute seeds, by the meeting together of which they say that the whole world came into existence,[3] I ask where or whence they are. Who has seen them at any time? Who has perceived them? Who has heard them? Had none but Leucippus [4] eyes? Had he alone a mind, who assuredly alone of all men was blind and senseless, since he spoke those things which no sick man could have uttered in his ravings,[5] or one asleep in his dreams?

The ancient philosophers argued that all things were made up of four elements.[6] He would not admit this, lest he should appear to tread in the footsteps of others; but he held that there were other first principles of the elements themselves, which can neither be seen, nor touched, nor be perceived by any part of the body. They are so minute, he says, that there is no edge of a sword so fine that they can be cut and divided by it. From which circumstance he gave them the name of atoms. But it occurred to him, that if they all had one and the same nature, they could not make up different objects of so great a variety as we see to be present in the world. He said, therefore, that there were smooth and rough ones, and round, and angular, and hooked. How much better had it been to be silent, than to have a tongue for such miserable and empty uses! And, indeed, I fear lest he who thinks these things worthy of refutation, should appear no less to rave. Let us, however, reply as to one who says something.[7] If they are soft [8] and round, it is plain that they cannot lay hold of one another, so as to make some body; as, though any one should wish to bind together millet into one combination,[9] the very softness of the grains would not permit them to come together into a mass. If they are rough, and angular, and hooked, so that they may be able to cohere, then they are divisible, and capable of being cut; for hooks and angles must project,[10] so that they may possibly be cut off.

Therefore that which is able to be cut off and torn away, will be able both to be seen and held. "These," he says, "flutter about with restless motions through empty space, and are carried hither and thither, just as we see little particles of dust in the sun when it has introduced its rays and light through a window. From these there arise trees and herbs, and all fruits of the earth; from these, animals, and water, and fire, and all things are produced, and are again resolved into the same elements." This can be borne as long as the inquiry is respecting small matters. Even the world itself was made up of these. He has reached to the full extent of perfect madness: it seems impossible that anything further should be said, and yet he found something to add. "Since everything," he says, "is infinite, and nothing can be empty, it follows of necessity that there are innumerable worlds." What force of atoms had been so great, that masses so incalculable should be collected from such minute elements? And first of all I ask, What is the nature or origin of those seeds? For if all things are from them, whence shall we say that they themselves are? What nature supplied such an abundance of matter for the making of innumerable worlds? But let us grant that he raved with impunity concerning worlds; let us speak respecting this in which we are, and which we see. He says that all things are made from minute bodies which are incapable of division.

If this were so, no object would ever need the seed of its own kind. Birds would be born without eggs, or eggs without bringing forth; likewise the rest of the living creatures without coition: trees and the productions of the earth would not have their own seeds, which we daily handle and sow. Why does a corn-field arise from grain, and again grain from a corn-field? In short, if the meeting together and collecting

1 [Peripatetic; succeeded Theophrastus B.C. 238.]
2 Ratio.
3 Coiisse.
4 [Leucippus, anterior to B.C. 470, author of the atomic theory.]
5 Delirare posset.
6 [See Tayler Lewis, *Plato contra Atheos*, p. 119.]

7 i.e., something to the purpose.
8 Lenia; others read "lævia," smooth.
9 Coagmentationem.
10 Eminere, "to stand out prominently."

of atoms would effect all things, all things would grow together in the air, since atoms flutter about through empty space. Why cannot the herb, why cannot the tree or grain, arise or be increased without earth, without roots, without moisture, without seed? From which it is evident that nothing is made up from atoms, since everything has its own peculiar and fixed nature, its own seed, its own law given from the beginning. Finally, Lucretius, as though forgetful of atoms,[1] which he was maintaining, in order that he might refute those who say that all things are produced from nothing, employed these arguments, which might have weighed against himself. For he thus spoke: —

> "If things came from nothing, any kind might be born of anything; nothing would require seed."[2]

Likewise afterwards: —

> "We must admit, therefore, that nothing can come from nothing, since things require seed before they can severally be born, and be brought out into the buxom fields of air."[3]

Who would imagine that he had brain when he said these things, and did not see that they were contrary to one another? For that nothing is made by means of atoms, is apparent from this, that everything has a definite[4] seed, unless by chance we shall believe that the nature both of fire and water is derived from atoms. Why should I say, that if materials of the greatest hardness are struck together with a violent blow, fire is struck out? Are atoms concealed in the steel, or in the flint? Who shut them in? Or why do they not leap forth spontaneously? Or how could the seeds of fire remain in a material of the greatest coldness?

I leave the subject of the flint and steel. If you hold in the sun an orb of crystal filled with water, fire is kindled from the light which is reflected from the water, even in the most severe cold. Must we then believe that fire is contained in the water? And yet fire cannot be kindled from the sun even in summer. If you shall breathe upon wax, or if a light vapour shall touch anything — either the hard surface[5] of marble or a plate of metal — water is gradually condensed by means of the most minute drops. Also from the exhalation of the earth or sea mist is formed, which either, being dispersed, moistens whatever it has covered, or being collected, is carried aloft by the wind to high mountains, and compressed into cloud, and sends down great rains. Where, then, do we say that fluids are produced? Is it in the vapour? Or in the exhalation? Or in the wind? But nothing can be formed in that which is neither touched nor seen. Why should I speak of animals, in whose bodies we see nothing formed without plan, without arrangement, without utility, without beauty, so that the most skilful and careful marking out[6] of all the parts and members repels the idea of accident and chance? But let us suppose it possible that the limbs, and bones, and nerves, and blood should be made up of atoms. What of the senses, the reflection, the memory, the mind, the natural capacity: from what seeds can they be compacted?[7] He says, From the most minute. There are therefore others of greater size. How, then, are they indivisible?

In the next place, if the things which are not seen are formed from invisible seeds, it follows that those which are seen are from visible seeds. Why, then, does no one see them? But whether any one regards the invisible parts which are in man, or the parts which can be touched, and which are visible, who does not see that both parts exist in accordance with design?[8] How, then, can bodies which meet together without design effect anything reasonable?[9] For we see that there is nothing in the whole world which has not in itself very great and wonderful design. And since this is above the sense and capacity of man, to what can it be more rightly attributed than to the divine providence? If a statue, the resemblance of man, is made by the exercise of design and art, shall we suppose that man himself is made up of fragments which come together at random? And what resemblance to the truth is there in the thing produced,[10] when the greatest and most surpassing skill[11] can imitate nothing more than the mere outline and extreme lineaments[12] of the body? Was the skill of man able to give to his production any motion or sensibility? I say nothing of the exercise of the sight, of hearing, and of smelling, and the wonderful uses of the other members, either those which are in sight or those which are hidden from view. What artificer could have fabricated either the heart of man, or the voice, or his very wisdom? Does any man of sound mind, therefore, think that that which man cannot do by reason and judgment, may be accomplished by a meeting together of atoms everywhere adhering to each other? You see into what foolish ravings they have fallen, while they are unwilling to assign to God the making and the care of all things.

Let us, however, concede to them that the things which are earthly are made from atoms: are the things also which are heavenly? They

1 [Vol. vi. p. 445, note 18.]
2 Lucret., i. 160.
3 *Ibid.*, i. 206.
4 Certum.
5 Crustam marmoris.
6 Descriptio.
7 Coagmentari.
8 Ratio.
9 Rationale.
10 Ficto.
11 Artificium.
12 Umbram et extrema lineamenta.

say that the gods are without contamination, eternal, and blessed; and they grant to them alone an exemption, so that they do not appear to be made up of a meeting together of atoms. For if the gods also had been made up of these, they would be liable to be dispersed, the seeds at length being resolved, and returning to their own nature. Therefore, if there is something which the atoms could not produce, why may we not judge in the same way of the others? But I ask why the gods did not build for themselves a dwelling-place before those first elements produced the world? It is manifest that, unless the atoms had come together and made the heaven, the gods would still be suspended through the midst of empty space. By what counsel, then, by what plan, did the atoms from a confused mass collect themselves, so that from some the earth below was formed into a globe, and the heaven stretched out above, adorned with so great a variety of constellations that nothing can be conceived more embellished? Can he, therefore, who sees such and so great objects, imagine that they were made without any design, without any providence, without any divine intelligence, but that such great and wonderful things arose out of fine and minute atoms? Does it not resemble a prodigy, that there should be any human being who might say these things, or that there should be those who might believe them — as Democritus, who was his hearer, or Epicurus, to whom all folly flowed forth from the fountain of Leucippus? But, as others say, the world was made by Nature, which is without perception and figure.[1] But this is much more absurd. If Nature made the world, it must have made it by judgment and intelligence; for it is he that makes something who has either the inclination to make it, or knowledge. If nature is without perception and figure, how can that be made by it which has both perception and figure, unless by chance any one thinks that the fabric of animals, which is so delicate, could have been formed and animated by that which is without perception, or that that figure of heaven, which is prepared with such foresight for the uses of living beings, suddenly came into existence by some accident or other, without a builder, without an artificer?[2]

"If there is anything," says Chrysippus, "which effects those things which man, though he is endowed with reason, cannot do, that assuredly is greater, and stronger, and wiser than man." But man cannot make heavenly things; therefore that which shall produce or has produced these things surpasses man in art, in design, in skill, and in power. Who, therefore, can it be but God? But Nature, which they suppose to be, as it were, the mother of all things, if it has not a mind, will effect nothing, will contrive nothing; for where there is no reflection there is neither motion nor efficacy. But if it uses counsel for the commencement of anything, reason for its arrangement, art for its accomplishment, energy for its consummation, and power to govern and control, why should it be called Nature rather than God? Or if a concourse of atoms, or Nature without mind, made those things which we see, I ask why it was able to make the heaven, but unable to make a city or a house?[3] Why it made mountains of marble, but did not make columns and statues? But ought not atoms to have come together to effect these things, since they leave no position untried? For concerning Nature, which has no mind, it is no wonder that it forgot to do these things. What, then, is the case? It is plain that God, when He commenced this work of the world, — than which nothing can be better arranged with respect to order, nor more befitting as to utility, nor more adorned as to beauty, nor greater as to bulk, — Himself made the things which could not be made by man; and among these also man himself, to whom He gave a portion of His own wisdom, and furnished him with reason, as much as earthly frailty was capable of receiving, that he might make for himself the things which were necessary for his own uses.

But if in the commonwealth of this world, so to speak, there is no providence which rules, no God who administers, no sense at all prevails in this nature of things. From what source therefore will it be believed that the human mind, with its skill and its intelligence, had its origin? For if the body of man was made from the ground, from which circumstance man received his name;[4] it follows that the soul, which has intelligence, and is the ruler of the body, which the limbs obey as a king and commander, which can neither be looked upon nor comprehended, could not have come to man except from a wise nature. But as mind and soul govern everybody, so also does God govern the world. For it is not probable that lesser and humble things bear rule, but that greater and highest things do not bear rule. In short, Marcus Cicero, in his *Tusculan Disputations*,[5] and in his *Consolation*, says: "No origin of souls can be found on earth. For there is nothing, he says, mixed and compound[6] in souls, or which may appear to be produced and made up from the earth; nothing moist or airy,[7] or of the nature of fire.

1 [See p. 97, note 4, *supra*.]
2 [See Cicero's judgment, p. 99, note 6, *supra*.]
3 [See Dionysius, cap. ii. p. 85, vol. vi., this series.]
4 Homo ab humo.
5 [Book i. cap. 27.]
6 Concretum.
7 Flabile.

For in these natures there is nothing which has the force of memory, of mind and reflection, which both retains the past and foresees the future, and is able to comprise the present; which things alone are divine. For no source will ever be found from which they are able to come to man, unless it be from God." Since, therefore, with the exception of two or three vain calumniators, it is agreed upon that the world is governed by providence, as also it was made, and there is no one who ventures to prefer the opinion of Diagoras and Theodorus, or the empty fiction of Leucippus, or the levity of Democritus and Epicurus, either to the authority of those seven ancient men who were called wise,[1] or to that of Pythagoras or of Socrates or Plato, and the other philosophers who judged that there is a providence; therefore that opinion also is false, by which they think that religion was instituted by wise men for the sake of terror and fear, in order that ignorant men might abstain from sins.

But if this is true, it follows that we are derided by the wise men of old. But if they invented religion for the sake of deceiving us, and moreover of deceiving the whole human race, therefore they were not wise, because falsehood is not consistent with the character of the wise man. But grant that they were wise; what great success in falsehood was it, that they were able to deceive not only the unlearned, but Plato also, and Socrates, and so easily to delude Pythagoras, Zeno, and Aristotle, the chiefs of the greatest sects? There is therefore a divine providence, as those men whom I have named perceived, by the energy and power of which all things which we see were both made and are governed. For so vast a system of things,[2] such arrangement and such regularity in preserving the settled orders and times, could neither at first have arisen without a provident artificer, or have existed so many ages without a powerful inhabitant, or have been perpetually governed without a skilful and intelligent[3] ruler; and reason itself declares this. For whatever exists which has reason, must have arisen from reason. Now reason is the part of an intelligent and wise nature; but a wise and intelligent nature can be nothing else than God. Now the world, since it has reason, by which it is both governed and kept together, was therefore made by God. But if God is the maker and ruler of the world, then religion is rightly and truly established; for honour and worship are due to the author and common parent of all things.

CHAP. XI.—OF GOD, AND THAT THE ONE GOD, AND BY WHOSE PROVIDENCE THE WORLD IS GOVERNED AND EXISTS.

Since it is agreed upon concerning providence, it follows that we show whether it is to be believed that it belongs to many, or rather to one only. We have sufficiently taught, as I think, in our *Institutions*, that there cannot be many gods; because, if the divine energy and power be distributed among several, it must necessarily be diminished. But that which is lessened is plainly mortal; but if He is not mortal, He can neither be lessened nor divided. Therefore there is but one God, in whom complete energy and power can neither be lessened nor increased. But if there are many, while they separately have something of power and authority, the sum itself decreases; nor will they separately be able to have the whole, which they have in common with others: so much will be wanting to each as the others shall possess. There cannot therefore be many rulers in this world, nor many masters in one house, nor many pilots in one ship, nor many leaders in one herd or flock, nor many queens in one swarm. But there could not have been many suns in heaven, as there are not several souls in one body; so entirely does the whole of nature agree in unity. But if the world

"Is nourished by a soul,
A spirit whose celestial flame
Glows in each member of the frame,
And stirs the mighty whole,"[4]

it is evident from the testimony of the poet, that there is one God who inhabits the world, since the whole body cannot be inhabited and governed except by one mind. Therefore all divine power must be in one person, by whose will and command all things are ruled; and therefore He is so great, that He cannot be described in words by man, or estimated by the senses. From what source, therefore, did the opinion or persuasion[5] respecting many gods come to men? Without doubt, all those who are worshipped as gods were men, and were also the earliest and greatest kings; but who is ignorant that they were invested with divine honours after death, either on account of the virtue by which they had profited the race of men, or that they obtained immortal memory on account of the benefits and inventions by which they had adorned human life? And not only men, but women also. And this, both the most ancient writers of Greece, whom they call *theologi*,[6] and also Roman writers following and imitating the

[1] [P. 101, *supra;* also vol. v. p. 11, note 2.]
[2] Tanta rerum magnitudo.
[3] Sentiente; others read "sciente."

[4] Virg., *Æn.*, vi. 726.
[5] Persuasiove; most editions read "persuasione," but the meaning is not so good.
[6] θεολόγοι.

Greeks, teach; of whom especially Euhemerus and our Ennius, who point out the birthdays, marriages, offspring, governments, exploits, deaths, and tombs [1] of all of them. And Tullius, following them, in his third book, *On the Nature of the Gods*, destroyed the public religions; but neither he himself nor any other person was able to introduce the true one, of which he was ignorant. And thus he himself testified that that which was false was evident; that the truth, however, lay concealed. "Would to heaven," he says, "that I could as easily discover true things as refute those that are false!" [2] And this he proclaimed not with dissimulation as an Academic, but truly and in accordance with the feeling of his mind, because the truth cannot be uprooted from human perceptions: that which the foresight of man was able to attain to, he attained to, that he might expose false things. For whatever is fictitious and false, because it is supported by no reason, is easily destroyed. There is therefore one God, the source and origin of all things, as Plato both felt and taught in the *Timæus*, whose majesty he declares to be so great, that it can neither be comprehended by the mind nor be expressed by the tongue.

Hermes bears the same testimony, whom Cicero asserts [3] to be reckoned by the Egyptians among the number of the gods. I speak of him who, on account of his excellence and knowledge of many arts, was called Trismegistus; and he was far more ancient not only than Plato, but than Pythagoras, and those seven wise men.[4] In Xenophon,[5] Socrates, as he discourses, says that "the form of God ought not to be inquired about;" and Plato, in his *Book of Laws*,[6] says: "What God is, ought not to be the subject of inquiry, because it can neither be found out nor related." Pythagoras also admits that there is but one God, saying that there is an incorporeal mind, which, being diffused and stretched through all nature, gives vital perception to all living creatures; but Antisthenes, in his *Physics*, said that there was but one natural God, although the nations and cities have gods of their own people. Aristotle, with his followers the Peripatetics, and Zeno with his followers the Stoics, say nearly the same things. Truly it would be a long task to follow up the opinions of all separately, who, although they used different names, nevertheless agreed in one power which governed the world. But, however, though philosophers and poets, and those, in short, who worship the gods, often acknowledge the Supreme God, yet no one ever inquired into, no one discussed, the subject of His worship and honours; with that persuasion, in truth, with which, always believing Him to be bounteous and incorruptible, they think [7] that He is neither angry with any one, nor stands in need of any worship. Thus there can be no religion where there is no fear.[8]

CHAP. XII. — OF RELIGION AND THE FEAR OF GOD.

Now, since we have replied to the impious and detestable wisdom,[9] or rather senselessness of some, let us return to our proposed subject. We have said that, if religion is taken away, neither wisdom nor justice can be retained: wisdom, because the understanding of the divine nature, in which we differ from the brutes, is found in man alone; justice, because unless God, who cannot be deceived, shall restrain our desires, we shall live wickedly and impiously. Therefore, that our actions should be viewed by God, pertains not only to the usefulness of common life, but even to the truth; because, if religion and justice are taken away, having lost our reason, we either descend to the senselessness [10] of the herds; or to the savageness of the beasts, yea, even more so, since the beasts spare animals of their own kind. What will be more savage, what more unmerciful, than man, if, the fear of a superior being taken away, he shall be able either to escape the notice of or to despise the might of the laws? It is therefore the fear of God alone which guards the mutual society of men, by which life itself is sustained, protected, and governed. But that fear is taken away if man is persuaded that God is without anger; for that He is moved and indignant when unjust actions are done, not only the common advantage, but even reason itself, and truth, persuade us. We must again return to the former subjects, that, as we have taught that the world was made by God, we may teach why it was made.

CHAP. XIII. — OF THE ADVANTAGE AND USE OF THE WORLD AND OF THE SEASONS.

If any one considers the whole government of the world, he will certainly understand how true is the opinion of the Stoics, who say that the world was made on our account. For all the things of which the world is composed, and which it produces from itself, are adapted to the use of man. Man, accordingly, uses fire for the purpose of warmth and light, and of softening his food, and for the working of iron; he uses

1 Sepulcra; others read "simulacra."
2 *De Nat. Deor.*, i. 32. [See p. 29, note 2, *supra.*]
3 *Ibid.*, iii. 22.
4 [P. 268, note 1, *supra.*]
5 *Memor.*, iv. 3.
6 Lib. vii.
7 Arbitrantur; some editions have "arbitrabantur," which appears preferable.
8 ["The fear of the Lord is the beginning of wisdom" (Prov. ix. 10). See p. 262, cap. 6, note 6, *supra.*]
9 Prudentiæ; another reading is "imprudentiæ."
10 Stultitiam.

springs for drinking, and for baths; he uses rivers for irrigating the fields, and assigning boundaries to countries; he uses the earth for receiving a variety of fruits, the hills for planting vineyards, the mountains for the use of trees and firewood,[1] the plains for crops of grain; he uses the sea not only for commerce, and for receiving supplies from distant countries, but also for abundance of every kind of fish. But if he makes use of these elements to which he is nearest, there is no doubt that he uses the heaven also, since the offices even of heavenly things are regulated for the fertility of the earth from which we live. The sun, with its ceaseless courses and unequal intervals,[2] completes its annual circles, and either at his rising draws forth the day for labour, or at his setting brings on the night for repose; and at one time by his departure farther towards the south, at another time by his approach nearer towards the north, he causes the vicissitudes of winter and summer, so that both by the moistures and frosts of winter the earth becomes enriched for fruitfulness, and by the heats of summer either the produce of grass[3] is hardened by maturity, or that which is in moist places, being seethed and heated, becomes ripened. The moon also, which governs the time of night, regulates her monthly courses by the alternate loss and recovery of light,[4] and by the brightness of her shining illumines the nights obscure with gloomy darkness, so that journeys in the summer heat, and expeditions, and works, may be performed without labour and inconvenience; since

> "By night the light stubble, by night
> The dry meadows are better mown."[5]

The other heavenly bodies also, either at their rising or setting, supply favourable times[6] by their fixed positions.[7] Moreover, they also afford guidance to ships, that they may not wander through the boundless deep with uncertain course, since the pilot duly observing them arrives at the harbour of the shore at which he aims.[8] Clouds are attracted by the breath of the winds, that the fields of sown grain may be watered with showers, that the vines may abound with produce, and the trees with fruits. And these things are exhibited by a succession of changes throughout the year, that nothing may at any time be wanting by which the life of men is sustained. But[9] (it is said) the same earth nourishes the other living creatures, and by the produce of the same even the dumb animals are fed. Has not God laboured also for the sake of the dumb animals? By no means; because they are void of reason. On the contrary, we understand that even these themselves in the same manner were made by God for the use of man, partly for food, partly for clothing, partly to assist him in his work; so that it is manifest that the divine providence wished to furnish and adorn the life of men with an abundance of objects and resources, and on this account He both filled the air with birds, and the sea with fishes, and the earth with quadrupeds. But the Academics, arguing against the Stoics, are accustomed to ask why, if God made all things for the sake of men, many things are found even opposed, and hostile, and injurious to us, as well in the sea as on the land. And the Stoics, without any regard to the truth, most foolishly repelled this. For they say that there are many things among natural productions,[10] and reckoned among animals, the utility of which hitherto[11] escapes notice, but that this is discovered in process of the times, as necessity and use have already discovered many things which were unknown in former ages. What utility, then, can be discovered in mice, in beetles, in serpents, which are troublesome and pernicious to man? Is it that some medicine lies concealed in them? If there is any, it will at some time be found out, namely, as a remedy against evils, whereas they complain that it is altogether evil. They say that the viper, when burnt and reduced to ashes, is a remedy for the bite of the same beast. How much better had it been that it should not exist at all, than that a remedy should be required against it drawn from itself?

They might then have answered with more conciseness and truth after this manner. When God had formed man as it were His own image, that which was the completion of His workmanship, He breathed wisdom into him alone, so that he might bring all things into subjection to his own authority and government, and make use of all the advantages of the world. And yet He set before him both good and evil things, inasmuch as He gave to him wisdom, the whole nature of which is employed in discerning things evil and good: for no one can choose better things, and know what is good, unless he at the same time knows to reject and avoid the things which are evil.[12] They are both mutually connected with each other, so that, the one being taken away, the other must also be taken away. Therefore, good and evil things being set before it, then at length wisdom discharges its office, and desires

1 Lignorum.
2 Spatiis. The word properly refers to a racecourse.
3 Herbidæ fruges.
4 Amissi ac recepti luminis vicibus.
5 Virg., *Georg.*, i. 289.
6 Opportunitates temporum.
7 Certis stationibus. Others read "sationibus," for certain kinds of sowing; but "statio" is applied to the stars by Seneca and Pliny.
8 Designati.
9 An objection is here met and answered.

10 Gignentium.
11 Adhuc, omitted in many manuscripts.
12 [I have heretofore noted the elements of a *theodicy* to be found in Lactantius.]

the good for usefulness, but rejects the evil for safety. Therefore, as innumerable good things have been given which it might enjoy, so also have evils, against which it might guard. For if there is no evil, no danger — nothing, in short, which can injure man — all the material of wisdom is taken away, and will be unnecessary for man. For if only good things are placed in sight, what need is there of reflection, of understanding, of knowledge, of reason? since, wherever he shall extend his hand, that is befitting and adapted to nature; so that if any one should wish to place a most exquisite dinner before infants, who as yet have no taste, it is plain that each will desire that to which either impulse, or hunger, or even accident, shall attract them; and whatever they shall take, it will be useful and salutary to them. What injury will it therefore be for them always to remain as they are, and always to be infants and unacquainted with affairs? But if you add a mixture either of bitter things, or things useless, or even poisonous, they are plainly deceived through their ignorance of good and evil, unless wisdom is added to them, by which they may have the rejection of evil things and the choice of good things.

You see, therefore, that we have greater need of wisdom on account of evils; and unless these things had been proposed to us, we should not be a rational animal. But if this account is true, which the Stoics were in no manner able to see, that argument also of Epicurus is done away. God, he says, either wishes to take away evils, and is unable; or He is able, and is unwilling; or He is neither willing nor able, or He is both willing and able. If He is willing and is unable, He is feeble, which is not in accordance with the character of God; if He is able and unwilling, He is envious, which is equally at variance with God; if He is neither willing nor able, He is both envious and feeble, and therefore not God; if He is both willing and able, which alone is suitable to God, from what source then are evils? or why does He not remove them? I know that many of the philosophers, who defend providence, are accustomed to be disturbed by this argument, and are almost driven against their will to admit that God takes no interest in anything, which Epicurus especially aims at; but having examined the matter, we easily do away with this formidable argument. For God is able to do whatever He wishes, and there is no weakness or envy in God. He is able, therefore, to take away evils; but He does not wish to do so, and yet He is not on that account envious. For on this account He does not take them away, because He at the same time gives wisdom, as I have shown; and there is more of goodness and pleasure in wisdom than of annoyance in evils. For wisdom causes us even to know God, and by that knowledge to attain to immortality, which is the chief good. Therefore, unless we first know evil, we shall be unable to know good. But Epicurus did not see this, nor did any other, that if evils are taken away, wisdom is in like manner taken away; and that no traces of virtue remain in man, the nature of which consists in enduring and overcoming the bitterness of evils. And thus, for the sake of a slight gain[1] in the taking away of evils, we should be deprived of a good, which is very great, and true, and peculiar to us. It is plain, therefore, that all things are proposed for the sake of man, as well evils as also goods.

CHAP. XIV. — WHY GOD MADE MAN.

It follows that I show for what purpose God made man himself. As He contrived the world for the sake of man, so He formed man himself on His own account, as it were a priest of a divine temple, a spectator of His works and of heavenly objects. For he is the only being who, since he is intelligent and capable of reason, is able to understand God, to admire His works, and perceive His energy and power; for on this account he is furnished with judgment, intelligence, and prudence. On this account he alone, beyond the other living creatures, has been made with an upright body and attitude, so that he seems to have been raised up for the contemplation of his Parent.[2] On this account he alone has received language, and a tongue the interpreter of his thought, that he may be able to declare the majesty of his Lord. Lastly, for this cause all things were placed under his control, that he himself might be under the control of God, their Maker and Creator. If God, therefore, designed man to be a worshipper of Himself, and on this account gave him so much honour, that he might rule over all things; it is plainly most just that he should worship Him[3] who bestowed upon him such great gifts, and love man, who is united with us in the participation of the divine justice. For it is not right that a worshipper of God should be injured by a worshipper of God. From which it is understood that man was made for the sake of religion and justice. And of this matter Marcus Tullius is a witness in his books respecting the Laws, since he thus speaks:[4] "But of all things concerning which learned men dispute, nothing is of greater consequence than that it should be altogether understood that we are born to justice." And if this is most true, it follows that God will have all men to be just,

[1] Propter exiguum compendium sublatorum malorum.
[2] [I cease to note this perpetually recurrent thought. It had profoundly impressed our author as an element of natural religion.]
[3] Et Deum colere, etc. Some editions read, "et eum, qui tanta præstiterit," omitting the word "colere."
[4] i. 10.

that is, to have God and man as objects of their affection; to honour God in truth as a Father, and to love man as a brother: for in these two things the whole of justice is comprised. But he who either fails to acknowledge God or acts injuriously to man, lives unjustly and contrary to his nature, and in this manner disturbs the divine institution and law.

CHAP. XV. — WHENCE SINS EXTENDED TO MAN.

Here perhaps some one may ask, Whence sins extended to man, or what perversion distorted the rule of the divine institution to worse things, so that, though he was born to justice, he nevertheless performs unjust works. I have already in a former place explained, that God at the same time set before him good and evil, and that He loves the good, and hates the evil which is contrary to this; but that He permitted the evil on this account, that the good also might shine forth, since, as I have often taught, we understand that the one cannot exist without the other; in short, that the world itself is made up of two elements opposing and connected with one another, of fire and moisture, and that light could not have been made unless there has also been darkness, since there cannot be a higher place without a lower, nor a rising without a setting, nor warmth without cold, nor softness without hardness. Thus also we are composed of two substances equally opposed to one another — soul and body: the one of which is assigned to the heaven, because it is slight and not to be handled; the other to the earth, because it is capable of being laid hold of: the one is firm[1] and eternal, the other frail and mortal. Therefore good clings to the one, and evil to the other: light, life, and justice to the one; darkness, death, and injustice to the other. Hence there arose among men the corruption of their nature, so that it was necessary that a law should be established, by which vices might be prohibited, and the duties of virtue be enjoined. Since, therefore, there are good and evil things in the affairs of men, the nature of which I have set forth, it must be that God is moved to both sides, both to favour when He sees that just things are done, and to anger when He perceives unjust things.

But Epicurus opposes us, and says: "If there is in God the affection of joy leading Him to favour, and of hatred influencing Him to anger, He must of necessity have both fear, and inclination, and desire, and the other affections which belong to human weakness." It does not follow that he who is angry must fear, or that he who feels joy must grieve; in short, they who are liable to anger are less timid, and they who are of a joyful temperament are less affected with grief. What need is there to speak of the affections of humanity, to which our nature yields? Let us weigh the divine necessity; for I am unwilling to speak of nature, since it is believed that our God was never born. The affection of fear has a subject-matter in man, but it has none in God. Man, inasmuch as he is liable to many accidents and dangers, fears lest any greater violence should arise which may strike, despoil, lacerate, dash down, and destroy him. But God, who is liable neither to want, nor injury, nor pain, nor death, can by no means fear, because there is nothing which can offer violence to Him. Also the reason and cause of desire is manifest in man. For, inasmuch as he was made frail and mortal, it was necessary that another and different sex should be made, by union with which offspring might be produced to continue the perpetuity of his race. But this desire has no place in God, because frailty and death are far removed from Him; nor is there with Him any female in whose union He is able to rejoice; nor does He stand in need of succession, since He will live for ever. The same things may be said respecting envy and passion, to which, from sure and manifest causes, man is liable, but to which God is by no means liable. But, in truth, favour and anger and pity have their substance[2] in God, and that greatest and matchless power employs them for the preservation of the world.

CHAP. XVI. — OF GOD, AND HIS ANGER AND AFFECTIONS.

Some one will ask what this substance is. First of all, when evils befall them, men in their dejected state for the most part have recourse to God: they appease and entreat Him, believing that He is able to repel injuries from them. He has therefore an occasion of exercising pity; for He is not so unmerciful and a despiser of men as to refuse aid to those who are in distress. Very many, also, who are persuaded that justice is pleasing to God, both worship Him who is Lord and Parent of all, and with continual prayers and repeated vows offer gifts and sacrifices, follow up His name with praises, striving to gain His favour by just and good works. There is therefore a reason, on account of which God may and ought to favour them. For if there is nothing so befitting God as beneficence, and nothing so unsuited to His character as to be ungrateful, it is necessary that He should make some return for the services of those who are excellent, and who lead a holy life, that He may not be liable to the charge of ingratitude, which is worthy of blame[3] even in the case of

[1] Solidum.

[2] Materia. Subjective existence.

[3] Criminosa.

a man. But, on the contrary, others are daring[1] and wicked, who pollute all things with their lusts, harass with slaughters, practise fraud, plunder, commit perjury, neither spare relatives nor parents, neglect the laws, and even God Himself. Anger, therefore, has a befitting occasion[2] in God.

For it is not right that, when He sees such things, He should not be moved, and arise to take vengeance upon the wicked, and destroy the pestilent and guilty, so as to promote the interests of all good men. Thus even in anger itself there is also contained a showing of kindness.[3] Therefore the arguments are found to be empty and false, either of those who, when they will not admit that God is angry, will have it that He shows kindness, because this, indeed, cannot take place without anger; or of those who think that there is no emotion of the mind in God. And because there are some affections to which God is not liable, as desire, fear, avarice, grief, and envy, they have said that He is entirely free from all affection. For He is not liable to these, because they are vicious affections; but as to those which belong to virtue, — that is, anger towards the wicked, regard towards the good, pity towards the afflicted, — inasmuch as they are worthy of the divine power, He has affections of His own,[4] both just and true. And if He is not possessed of them, the life of man will be thrown into confusion, and the condition of things will come to such disturbance that the laws will be despised and overpowered, and audacity alone reign, so that no one can at length be in safety unless he who excels[5] in strength. Thus all the earth will be laid waste, as it were, by a common robbery. But now, since the wicked expect punishment, and the good hope for favour, and the afflicted look for aid, there is place for virtues, and crimes are more rare. But[6] it is said, ofttimes the wicked are more prosperous, and the good more wretched, and the just are harassed with impunity by the unjust. We will hereafter consider why these things happen. In the meantime let us explain respecting anger, whether there be any in God; whether He takes no notice at all, and is unmoved at those things which are done with impiety.

CHAP. XVII. — OF GOD, HIS CARE AND ANGER.

God, says Epicurus, regards nothing; therefore He has no power. For he who has power must of necessity regard affairs. For if He has power, and does not use it, what so great cause is there that, I will not say our race, but even the universe itself, should be contemptible in His sight? On this account he says He is pure[7] and happy, because He is always at rest.[8] To whom, then, has the administration of so great affairs been entrusted,[9] if these things which we see to be governed by the highest judgment are neglected by God? or how can he who lives and perceives be at rest? For rest belongs either to sleep or to death. But sleep has not rest. For when we are asleep, the body indeed is at rest, but the soul is restless and agitated: it forms for itself images which it may behold, so that it exercises its natural power of motion by a variety of visions, and calls itself away from false things, until the limbs are satiated, and receive vigour from rest. Therefore eternal rest belongs to death alone. Now if death does not affect God, it follows that God is never at rest. But in what can the action of God consist, but in the administration of the world? But if God carries on the care of the world, it follows that He cares for the life of men, and takes notice of the acts of individuals, and He earnestly desires that they should be wise and good. This is the will of God, this the divine law; and he who follows and observes this is beloved by God. It is necessary that He should be moved with anger against the man who has broken or despised this eternal and divine law. If, he says, God does harm to any one, therefore He is not good. They are deceived by no slight error who defame all censure, whether human or divine, with the name of bitterness and malice, thinking that He ought to be called injurious[10] who visits the injurious with punishment. But if this is so, it follows that we have injurious laws, which enact punishment for offenders, and injurious judges who inflict capital punishments on those convicted of crime. But if the law is just which awards to the transgressor his due, and if the judge is called upright and good when he punishes crimes, — for he guards the safety of good men who punishes the evil, — it follows that God, when He opposes the evil, is not injurious; but he himself is injurious who either injures an innocent man, or spares an injurious person that he may injure many.

I would gladly ask from those who represent God as immoveable,[11] if any one had property, a house, a household[12] of slaves, and his slaves, despising the forbearance of their master, should attack all things, and themselves take the enjoyment of his goods, if his household should honour them, while the master was despised by

1 Facinorosi.
2 Materia.
3 Gratificatio.
4 Proprios.
5 Prævaleat.
6 An objection is here met and answered.
7 Incorruptus.
8 Quietus.
9 Cessit.
10 Nocentes.
11 Immobilem: not subject to emotions.
12 Familiam.

all, insulted, and deserted: could he be a wise man who should not avenge the insults, but permit those over whom he had power to have the enjoyment of his property? Can such forbearance be found in any one? If, indeed, it is to be called forbearance, and not rather a kind of insensible stupor. But it is easy to endure contempt. What if those things were done which are spoken of by Cicero?[1] "For I ask, if any head of a family,[2] when his children had been put to death by a slave, his wife slain and his house set on fire, should not exact most severe punishment from that slave, whether he would appear to be kind and merciful, or inhuman and most cruel?" But if to pardon deeds of this kind is the part of cruelty rather than of kindness,[3] it is not therefore the part of goodness in God not to be moved at those things which are done unjustly. For the world is, as it were, the house of God, and men, as it were, His slaves; and if His name is a mockery to them, what kind or amount of forbearance is it to give[4] up His own honours, to see wicked and unjust things done, and not to be indignant, which is peculiar and natural to Him who is displeased with sins! To be angry, therefore, is the part of reason: for thus faults are removed, and licentiousness is curbed; and this is plainly in accordance with justice and wisdom.

But the Stoics did not see that there is a distinction between right and wrong, that there is a just and also an unjust anger; and because they did not find a remedy for the matter, they wished altogether to remove it. But the Peripatetics said that it was not to be cut out, but moderated; to whom we have made a sufficient reply in the sixth book of the *Institutions*.[5] Now, that the philosophers were ignorant of the nature of anger, is plain from their definitions, which Seneca enumerated in the books which he composed on the subject of anger. "Anger is," he says, "the desire of avenging an injury." Others, as Posidonius says, describe it as the desire of punishing him by whom you think that you have been unfairly injured. Some have thus defined it: "Anger is an incitement of the mind to injure him who either has committed an injury, or who has wished to do so." The definition of Aristotle does not differ greatly from ours;[6] for he says that "anger is the desire of requiting pain." This is the unjust anger, concerning which we spoke before, which is contained even in the dumb animals; but it is to be restrained in man, lest he should rush to some very great evil through rage. This cannot exist in God, because He cannot be injured;[7] but it is found in man, inasmuch as he is frail. For the inflicting[8] of injury inflames[9] anguish, and anguish produces a desire of revenge. Where, then, is that just anger against offenders? For this is evidently not the desire of revenge, inasmuch as no injury precedes. I do not speak of those who sin against the laws; for although a judge may be angry with these without incurring blame, let us, however, suppose that he ought to be of a sedate mind when he sentences the guilty to punishment, because he is the executor[10] of the laws, not of his own spirit or power; for so they wish it who endeavour to extirpate anger. But I speak of those in particular who are in our own power, as slaves, children, wives, and pupils; for when we see these offend, we are incited to restrain them.

For it cannot fail to be, that he who is just and good is displeased with things which are bad, and that he who is displeased with evil is moved when he sees it practised. Therefore we arise to take vengeance, not because we have been injured, but that discipline may be preserved, morals may be corrected, and licentiousness be suppressed. This is just anger; and as it is necessary in man for the correction of wickedness, so manifestly is it necessary in God, from whom an example comes to man. For as we ought to restrain those who are subject to our power, so also ought God to restrain the offences of all. And in order that He may do this, He must be angry; because it is natural for one who is good to be moved and incited at the fault of another. Therefore they ought to have given this definition: Anger is an emotion of the mind arousing itself for the restraining of faults.[11] For the definition given by Cicero, "Anger is the desire of taking vengeance," does not differ much from those already mentioned.[12] But that anger which we may call either fury or rage ought not to exist even in man, because it is altogether vicious; but the anger which relates to the correction of vices ought not to be taken away from man; nor can it be taken away from God, because it is both serviceable for the affairs of men, and necessary.

CHAP. XVIII. — OF THE PUNISHMENT OF FAULTS, THAT IT CANNOT TAKE PLACE WITHOUT ANGER.

What need is there, they say, of anger, since faults can be corrected without this affection? But there is no one who can calmly see any one committing an offence. This may perhaps be

1 In *Catal.*, iv. 6.
2 Paterfamilias, the master of a house.
3 Pietatis.
4 Ut cedat.
5 [Cap. 15, p. 179, *supra*.]
6 [See p. 277, note 6, *infra*. But he should say *indignation*, not *anger*.]
7 Illæsibilis est. Others read "stabilis est," he is firm. The reading of the text is confirmed by "læsio" in the next clause.
8 Læsio.
9 Inurit, "burns in."
10 Minister.
11 [See note 6, *supra*.]
12 [P. 260, etc., *supra*.]

possible in him who presides over the laws, because the deed is not committed before his eyes, but it is brought before him as a doubtful matter from another quarter. Nor can any wickedness be so manifest, that there is no place for a defence; and therefore it is possible that a judge may not be moved against him who may possibly be found to be innocent; and when the detected crime shall have come to light, he now no longer uses his own opinion, but that of the laws. It may be granted that he does that which he does without anger; for he has that which he may follow. We, undoubtedly, when an offence is committed by our household at home, whether we see or perceive it, must be indignant; for the very sight of a sin is unbecoming. For he who is altogether unmoved either approves of faults, which is more disgraceful and unjust, or avoids the trouble of reproving them, which a tranquil spirit and a quiet mind despises and refuses, unless anger shall have aroused and incited it. But when any one is moved, and yet through unseasonable leniency grants pardon more frequently than is necessary, or at all times, he evidently both destroys the life of those whose audacity he is fostering for greater crimes, and furnishes himself with a perpetual source of annoyances. Therefore the restraining of one's anger in the case of sins is faulty.

Archytas of Tarentum is praised, who, when he had found everything ruined[1] on his estate, rebuking the fault of his bailiff, said, "Wretch, I would have beaten you to death if I had not been angry." They consider this to be a singular example of forbearance; but influenced by authority, they do not see how foolishly he spoke and acted. For if (as Plato says) no prudent man punishes because there is an offence, but to prevent the occurrence of an offence, it is evident how evil an example this wise man put forth. For if slaves shall perceive that their master uses violence when he is not angry, and abstains from violence[2] when he is angry, it is evident that they will not commit slight offences, lest they should be beaten; but will commit the greatest offences, that they may arouse the anger of the perverse man, and escape with impunity. But I should praise him if, when he was enraged, he had given space to his anger, that the excitement of his mind might calm down through the interval of time, and his chastisement might be confined within moderate limits. Therefore, on account of the magnitude of the anger, punishment ought not to have been inflicted, but to have been delayed, lest it should inflict[3] upon the offender pain greater than is just, or occasion an outburst of fury in the punisher. But now, how is it equitable or wise, that any one should be punished on account of a slight offence, and should be unpunished on account of a very great one? But if he had learned the nature and causes of things, he never would have professed so unsuitable a forbearance, that a wicked slave should rejoice that his master has been angry with him. For as God has furnished the human body with many and various senses which are necessary for the use of life, so also He has assigned to the soul various affections by which the course of life might be regulated; and as He has given desire for the sake of producing offspring, so has He given anger for the sake of restraining faults.

But they who are ignorant of the ends of good and evil things, as they employ sensual desire for the purposes of corruption and pleasure, in the same manner make use of anger and passion for the inflicting of injury, while they are angry with those whom they regard with hatred. Therefore they are angry even with those who commit no offence, even with their equals, or even with their superiors. Hence they daily rush to monstrous[4] deeds; hence tragedies often arise. Therefore Archytas would be deserving of praise, if, when he had been enraged against any citizen or equal who injured him, he had curbed himself, and by forbearance mitigated the impetuosity of his fury. This self-restraint is glorious, by which any great evil which impends is restrained; but it is a fault not to check the faults of slaves and children; for through their escaping without punishment they will proceed to greater evil. In this case anger is not to be restrained; but even if it is in a state of inactivity,[5] it must be aroused. But that which we say respecting man, we also say respecting God, who made man like to Himself. I omit making mention of the figure of God, because the Stoics say that God has no form, and another great subject will arise if we should wish to refute them. I only speak respecting the soul. If it belongs[6] to God to reflect, to be wise, to understand, to foresee, to excel, and of all animals man alone has these qualities, it follows that he was made after the likeness of God; but on this account he goes on to vice, because, being mingled with frailty derived from earth, he is unable to preserve pure and uncontaminated that which he has received from God, unless he is imbued with the precepts of justice by the same God.

CHAP. XIX. — OF THE SOUL AND BODY, AND OF PROVIDENCE.

But since he is made up, as we have said, of two parts, soul and body, the virtues are con-

1 Corrupta esse omnia.
2 Parcere.
3 Inureret, i.e., should burn in, or brand.
4 Immania, i.e., of an inhuman character.
5 Jacet.
6 Deo subjacet.

tained in the one, and vices in the other, and they mutually oppose each other. For the good properties of the soul, which consist in restraining lusts, are contrary to the body; and the good properties of the body, which consist in every kind of pleasure, are hostile to the soul. But if the virtue of the soul shall have resisted the desires, and suppressed them, he will be truly like to God. From which it is evident that the soul of man, which is capable of divine virtue, is not mortal. But there is this distinction, that since virtue is attended with bitterness, and the attraction of pleasure is sweet, great numbers are overcome and are drawn aside to the pleasantness; but they who have given themselves up to the body and earthly things are pressed to the earth, and are unable to attain to the favour of the divine bounty, because they have polluted themselves with the defilements of vices. But they who, following God, and in obedience to Him, have despised the desires of the body, and, preferring virtue to pleasures, have preserved innocence and righteousness, these God recognises as like to Himself.

Since, therefore, He has laid down a most holy law, and wishes all men to be innocent and beneficent, is it possible that He should not be angry when He sees that His law is despised, that virtue is rejected, and pleasure made the object of pursuit? But if He is the governor of the world, as He ought to be, He surely does not despise that which is even of the greatest importance in the whole world. If He has foresight, as it is befitting that God should have, it is plain that He consults the interests of the human race, in order that our life may be more abundantly supplied, and better, and safer. If He is the Father and God of all, He is undoubtedly delighted with the virtues of men, and provoked by their vices. Therefore He loves the just, and hates the wicked. There is no need (one says) of hatred; for He once for all has fixed a reward for the good, and punishment for the wicked. But if any one lives justly and innocently, and at the same time neither worships God nor has any regard for Him, as Aristides, and Timon,[1] and others of the philosophers, will he escape[2] with impunity, because, though he has obeyed the law of God, he has nevertheless despised God Himself? There is therefore something on account of which God may be angry with one rebelling against Him, as it were, in reliance upon His integrity. If He can be angry with this man on account of his pride, why not more so with the sinner, who has despised the law together with the Lawgiver? The judge cannot pardon offences, because he is subject to the will of another. But God can pardon, because He is Himself the arbitrator[3] and judge of His own law; and when He laid down this, He did not surely deprive Himself of all power, but He has the liberty of bestowing pardon.

CHAP. XX. — OF OFFENCES, AND THE MERCY OF GOD.

If He is able to pardon, He is therefore able also to be angry. Why, then, some one will say, does it often occur, that they who sin are prosperous, and they who live piously are wretched? Because fugitives and disinherited[4] persons live without restraint, and they who are under the discipline of a father or master live in a more strict and frugal manner. For virtue is proved and fixed[5] by means of ills; vices by means of pleasure. Nor, however, ought he who sins to hope for lasting impunity, because there is no lasting happiness.

> "But, in truth, the last day is always to be looked for by man; and no one ought to be called happy before his death and last funeral rites,"[6]

as the not inelegant poet says. It is the end which proves happiness, and no one is able to escape the judgment of God, either when alive or after death. For He has the power both to cast down the living from on high, and to punish the dead with eternal torments. Nay, he says, if God is angry, He ought to have inflicted vengeance at once, and to have punished every one according to his desert. But (it is replied) if He had done this, no one would survive. For there is no one who offends in no respect, and there are many things which excite to the commission of sin — age, intemperance, want, opportunity, reward. To such an extent is the frailty of the flesh with which we are clothed liable to sin, that unless God were indulgent to this necessity, perhaps too few would live. On this account He is most patient, and restrains His anger. For because there is in Him perfect virtue, it follows of necessity that His patience also is perfect, which is itself also a virtue. How many men, from having been sinners, have afterwards become righteous; from being injurious, have become good; from being wicked, have become temperate! How many who were in early life base, and condemned by the judgment of all, afterwards have turned out praiseworthy? But it is plain that this could not happen if punishment followed every offence.

---

1 Others read "Cimon." If the reading Timon be retained, the reference is not to Timon who is called "the Misanthrope," but to Timon the philosopher of Phlius, who lived in the time of Ptolemy Philadelphus, and belonged to the sect of the Sceptics.

2 Cedetne huic impune.

3 Disceptator.

4 Abdicati.

5 Constat.

6 Ovid., *Metam.*, iii. 153.

["Ultima semper
Expectanda dies homini est; dicique beatus
Ante obitum nemo," etc.]

The public laws condemn those who are manifestly guilty; but there are great numbers whose offences are concealed, great numbers who restrain the accuser either by entreaties or by reward, great numbers who elude justice by favour or influence. But if the divine censure should condemn all those who escape the punishment of men, there would be few or even no men on the earth. In short, even that one reason for destroying the human race might have been a just one, that men, despising the living God, pay divine honour to earthly and frail images, as though they were of heaven, adoring works made by human hands. And though God their Creator made them of elevated countenance and upright figure, and raised them to the contemplation of the heaven and the knowledge of God, they have preferred, like cattle, to bend themselves to the earth.[1] For he is low, and curved, and bent downward, who, turning away from the sight of heaven and God his Father, worships things of the earth, which he ought to have trodden upon, that is, things made and fashioned from earth. Therefore, amidst such great impiety and such great sins of men, the forbearance of God attains this object, that men, condemning the errors of their past life, correct themselves. In short, there are many who are just and good; and these, having laid aside the worship of earthly things, acknowledge the majesty of the one and only God. But though the forbearance of God is very great and most useful; yet, although late, He punishes the guilty, and does not suffer them to proceed further, when He sees that they are incorrigible.

CHAP. XXI. — OF THE ANGER OF GOD AND MAN.

There remains one question, and that the last. For some one will perhaps say, that God is so far from being angry, that in His precepts He even forbids man to be angry. I might say that the anger of man ought to be curbed, because he is often angry unjustly; and he has immediate emotion, because he is only for a time.[2] Therefore, lest those things should be done which the low, and those of moderate station, and great kings do in their anger, his rage ought to have been moderated and suppressed, lest, being out of his mind,[3] he should commit some inexpiable crime. But God is not angry for a short time,[4] because He is eternal and of perfect virtue, and He is never angry unless deservedly. But, however, the matter is not so; for if He should altogether prohibit anger, He Himself would have been in some measure the censurer of His own workmanship, since He from the beginning had inserted anger in the liver[5] of man, since it is believed that the cause of this emotion is contained in the moisture of the gall. Therefore He does not altogether prohibit anger, because that affection is necessarily given, but He forbids us to persevere in anger. For the anger of mortals ought to be mortal; for if it is lasting, enmity is strengthened to lasting destruction. Then, again, when He enjoined us to be angry, and yet not to sin,[6] it is plain that He did not tear up anger by the roots, but restrained it, that in every correction we might preserve moderation and justice. Therefore He who commands us to be angry is manifestly Himself angry; He who enjoins us to be quickly appeased is manifestly Himself easy to be appeased: for He has enjoined those things which are just and useful for the interests of society.[7]

But because I had said that the anger of God is not for a time[8] only, as is the case with man, who becomes inflamed with an immediate[9] excitement, and on account of his frailty is unable easily to govern himself, we ought to understand that because God is eternal, His anger also remains to eternity; but, on the other hand, that because He is endued with the greatest excellence, He controls His anger, and is not ruled by it, but that He regulates it according to His will. And it is plain that this is not opposed to that which has just been said. For if His anger had been altogether immortal, there would be no place after a fault for satisfaction or kind feeling, though He Himself commands men to be reconciled before the setting of the sun.[10] But the divine anger remains for ever against those who ever sin. Therefore God is appeased not by incense or a victim, not by costly offerings, which things are all corruptible, but by a reformation of the morals: and he who ceases to sin renders the anger of God mortal. For this reason He does not immediately[11] punish every one who is guilty, that man may have the opportunity of coming to a right mind,[12] and correcting himself.

CHAP. XXII. — OF SINS, AND THE VERSES OF THE SIBYLS RESPECTING THEM RECITED.

This is what I had to say, most beloved Donatus, respecting the anger of God, that you might know how to refute those who represent God as being without emotions.[13] It only remains that, after the practice of Cicero, I should use an

1 [The degradation of the mind of man to the worship of stocks and stones impresses our author as against nature.]
2 Temporalis.
3 Mentis impos, i.e., not having possession of his mind, opposed to "mentis compos." Some editions add, "in bile."
4 Ad præsens.
5 As supposed to be the seat of the passions.
6 [Ps. iv. 4, *Vulgate*, and Ephes., as below.]
7 Rebus communibus.
8 Temporalem.
9 Præsentaneâ. The word is applied to a remedy which operates instantaneously.
10 See Eph. iv. 26.
11 Ad præsens.
12 Resipiscendi.
13 Immobilem.

epilogue by way of peroration. As he did in the *Tusculan Disputations*,[1] when discoursing on the subject of death, so we in this work ought to bring forward divine testimonies, which may be believed, to refute the persuasion of those who, believing that God is without anger, destroy all religion, without which, as we have shown, we are either equal to the brutes in savageness, or to the cattle in foolishness; for it is in religion only — that is, in the knowledge of the Supreme God — that wisdom consists. All the prophets, being filled with the Divine Spirit, speak nothing else than of the favour of God towards the righteous, and His anger against the ungodly. And their testimony is indeed sufficient for us; but because it is not believed by those who make a display of wisdom by their hair and dress,[2] it was necessary to refute them by reason and arguments. For they act so preposterously,[3] that human things give authority to divine things, whereas divine things ought rather to give authority to human. But let us now leave these things, lest we should produce no effect upon them, and the subject should be indefinitely drawn out. Let us therefore seek those testimonies which they can either believe, or at any rate not oppose.

Authors of great number and weight have made mention of the Sibyls; of the Greeks, Aristo the Chian, and Apollodorus the Erythræan; of our writers, Varro and Fenestella. All these relate that the Erythræan Sibyl was distinguished and noble beyond the rest. Apollodorus, indeed, boasts of her as his own citizen and countrywoman. But Fenestella also relates that ambassadors were sent by the senate to Erythræ, that the verses of this Sibyl might be conveyed to Rome, and that the consuls Curio and Octavius might take care that they should be placed in the Capitol, which had then been restored under the care of Quintus Catulus. In her writings, verses of this kind are found respecting the Supreme God and Maker of the world: —

> "The incorruptible and eternal Maker who dwells in the heaven, holding forth good to the good, a much greater reward, but stirring up anger and rage against the evil and unjust."

Again, in another place, enumerating the deeds by which God is especially moved to anger, she introduced these things: —

> "Avoid unlawful services, and serve the living God. Abstain from adultery and impurity; bring up a pure generation of children; do not kill: for the Immortal will be angry with every one who may sin."

Therefore He is angry with sinners.

CHAP. XXIII. — OF THE ANGER OF GOD AND THE PUNISHMENT OF SINS, AND A RECITAL OF THE VERSES OF THE SIBYLS RESPECTING IT; AND, MOREOVER, A REPROOF AND EXHORTATION.

But because it is related by most learned men that there have been many Sibyls, the testimony of one may not be sufficient to confirm the truth, as we purpose to do. The volumes, indeed, of the Cumæan Sibyl, in which are written the fates of the Romans are kept secret; but the writings of all the others are, for the most part, not prohibited from being in common use. And of these another, denouncing the anger of God against all nations on account of the impiety of men, thus began: —

> "Since great anger is coming upon a disobedient world, I disclose the commands of God to the last age, prophesying to all men from city to city."

Another *Sibyl* also said, that the deluge was caused by the indignation of God against the unrighteous in a former age, that the wickedness of the human race might be extinguished: —

> "From the time when, the God of heaven being enraged against the cities themselves and all men, a deluge having burst forth, the sea covered the earth."

In like manner she foretold a conflagration about to take place hereafter, in which the impiety of men should again be destroyed: —

> "And at some time, God no longer soothing His anger, but increasing it, and destroying the race of men, and laying waste the whole of it by fire."

From which mention is thus made concerning Jupiter by Ovid:[4] —

> "He remembers also that it is fated that the time shall come in which the sea, the earth, and the palace of heaven, being caught by fire, shall be burnt, and the curiously wrought framework of the world[5] be in danger."

And this must come to pass at the time when the honour and worship of the Supreme shall have perished among men. The same *Sibyl*, however, testifying that He was appeased by reformation[6] of conduct and self-improvement, added these things: —

> "But, ye mortals, in pity[7] turn yourselves now, and do not lead the great God to every kind of anger."

And also a little later: —

> "He will not destroy, but will again restrain His anger, if you all practise valuable piety in your minds."

Then another Sibyl declares that the Father of heavenly and earthly things ought to be loved, lest His indignation should arise, to the destruction of men: —

> "Lest by chance the immortal God should be angry, and destroy the whole race of men, their life and shameless race, it is befitting that we love the wise, ever-living God the Father."

---

1 [Book i., concluding chapters.]

2 The philosophers wore long hair and cloaks. See *Instit.*, iii. 25. [Needlessly repeated. See p. 95, *supra*; also 137.]

3 Præpostere, i.e., in a reversed order, putting the last first.

4 *Metam.*, i. 256.

5 Moles operosa laboret.

6 Pœnitentiâ factorum.

7 ἐλεεῖ. Others read, ὦ μέλεοι, "O wretched."

From these things it is evident that the arguments of the philosophers are vain, who imagine that God is without anger, and among His other praises reckon that which is most useless, detracting from Him that which is most salutary for human affairs, by which majesty itself exists. For this earthly kingdom and government, unless guarded by fear, is broken down. Take away anger from a king, and he will not only cease to be obeyed, but he will even be cast down headlong from his height. Yea, rather take away this affection from any person of low degree, and who will not plunder him? Who will not deride him? Who will not treat him with injury? Thus he will be able to have neither clothing, nor an abode, nor food, since others will deprive him of whatever he has; much less can we suppose that the majesty of the heavenly government can exist without anger and fear. The Milesian Apollo being consulted concerning the religion of the Jews, inserted these things in his answer: —

> "God, the King and Father of all, before whom the earth trembles, and the heaven and sea, and whom the recesses of Tartarus and the demons dread."

If He is so mild, as the philosophers will have it, how is it that not only the demons and ministers of such great power, but even the heaven and earth, and the whole system of the universe, tremble at His presence? For if no one submits to the service of another except by compulsion, it follows that all government exists by fear, and fear by anger. For if any one is not aroused against one who is unwilling to obey, it will not be possible for him to be compelled to obedience. Let any one consult his own feelings; he will at once understand that no one can be subdued to the command of another without anger and chastisement. Therefore, where there shall be no anger, there will be no authority. But God has authority; therefore also He must have anger, in which authority consists. Therefore let no one, induced by the empty prating [1] of the philosophers, train himself to the contempt of God, which is the greatest impiety. We all are bound both to love Him, because He is our Father; and to reverence Him, because He is our Lord: both to pay Him honour, because He is bounteous; and to fear Him, because He is severe: each character in Him is worthy of reverence.[2] Who can preserve his piety, and yet fail to love the parent of his life? or who can with impunity despise Him who, as ruler of all things, has true and everlasting power over all? If you consider Him in the character of Father, He supplies to us our entrance to the light which we enjoy: through Him we live, through Him we have entered into the abode [3] of this world. If you contemplate Him as God, it is He who nourishes us with innumerable resources: it is He who sustains us, we dwell in His house, we are His household; [4] and if we are less obedient than was befitting, and less attentive to our duty [5] than the endless merits of our Master and Parent demanded: nevertheless it is of great avail to our obtaining pardon, if we retain the worship and knowledge of Him; if, laying aside low and earthly affairs and goods, we meditate upon heavenly and divine things which are everlasting. And that we may be able to do this, God must be followed by us, God must be adored and loved; since there is in Him the substance [6] of things, the principle [7] of the virtues, and the source of all that is good.

For what is greater in power than God, or more perfect in reason, or brighter in clearness? And since He begat us to wisdom, and produced us to righteousness, it is not allowable for man to forsake God, who is the giver of intelligence and life, and to serve earthly and frail things, or, intent upon seeking temporal goods, to turn aside from innocence and piety. Vicious and deadly pleasures do not render a man happy; nor does opulence, which is the inciter of lusts; nor empty ambition; nor frail honours, by which the human soul, being ensnared and enslaved to the body, is condemned [8] to eternal death: but innocence and righteousness alone, the lawful and due reward of which is immortality, which God from the beginning appointed for holy and uncorrupted minds, which keep themselves pure and uncontaminated from vices, and from every earthly impurity. Of this heavenly and eternal reward they cannot be partakers, who have polluted their conscience by deeds of violence, frauds, rapine, and deceits; and who, by injuries inflicted upon men, by impious actions, have branded themselves [9] with indelible stains. Accordingly it is befitting that all who wish deservedly to be called wise, who wish to be called men, should despise frail things, should trample upon earthly things, and should look down upon base [10] things, that they may be able to be united in a most blissful relationship with God.

Let impiety and discords be removed; let turbulent and deadly dissensions be allayed,[11] by which human societies and the divine union of the public league are broken in upon, divided, and dispersed; as far as we can, let us aim at

1 Vaniloquentia.
2 Venerabilis.

3 Hospitium, i.e., a place of hospitality.
4 Familia, "a household of slaves."
5 Officiosa, i.e., familia.
6 Materia rerum.
7 Ratio virtutum.
8 Æterna morte damnatur.
9 Ineluibiles sibi maculas inusserunt.
10 Humilia.
11 Sopiantur, i.e., be lulled to sleep.

being good and bounteous: if we have a supply of wealth and resources, let it not be devoted to the pleasure of a single person, but bestowed on the welfare of many. For pleasure is as shortlived as the body to which it does service. But justice and kindness are as immortal as the mind and soul, which by good works attain to the likeness of God. Let God be consecrated by us, not in temples, but in our heart. All things which are made by the hand are destructible.[1] Let us cleanse this temple, which is defiled not by smoke or dust, but by evil thoughts; which is lighted not by blazing tapers,[2] but by the brightness and light of wisdom. And if we believe that God is always present in this temple, to whose divinity the secrets of the heart are open, we shall so live as always to have Him propitious, and never to fear His anger.

[1] Destructilia. The word is used by Prudentius.
[2] [See p. 163, *supra*. See note below.]

NOTE BY THE AMERICAN EDITOR

It is worth while to direct attention to (book vi. cap. 2) what our author has said of "*true* worship," just now, when the most violent and persistent efforts are made to sensualize Christian worship, and to explain away the testimony of the Ante-Nicene Fathers on this important subject. The argument of our author, in its entire drift, is as applicable to our own times as to his; and, deeply as I value beauty in the public worship of God, I cannot, as a Nicene Catholic, do less than adopt the universal sentiment of the early Fathers as to the limits of decoration.

ON THE WORKMANSHIP OF GOD,

OR THE FORMATION OF MAN

A TREATISE ADDRESSED TO HIS PUPIL DEMETRIANUS.

CHAP. I.—THE INTRODUCTION, AND EXHORTATION TO DEMETRIANUS.[1]

How disturbed I am, and in the greatest necessities, you will be able to judge from this little book which I have written to you, Demetrianus, almost in unadorned words, as the mediocrity of my talent permitted, that you might know my daily pursuit, and that I might not be wanting to you, even now an instructor, but of a more honourable subject and of a better system. For if you afforded yourself a ready hearer in literature, which did nothing else than form the style, how much more teachable ought you to be in these true studies, which have reference even to the life! And I now profess to you, that I am hindered by no necessity of circumstance or time from composing something by which the philosophers of our sect[2] which we uphold may become better instructed and more learned for the future, although they now have a bad reputation, and are commonly reproved, as living otherwise than is befitting for wise men, and as concealing their vices under the covering of a name; whereas they ought either to have remedied them, or to have altogether avoided them, that they might render the name of wisdom happy and uncorrupted, their life itself agreeing with their precepts. I, however, shrink from no labour that I may at once instruct ourselves and others. For I am not able to forget myself, and especially at that time when it is most necessary for me to remember; as also you do not forget yourself, as I hope and wish. For although the necessity of the state may turn you aside from true and just works, yet it is impossible that a mind conscious of rectitude should not from time to time look to the heaven.

I indeed rejoice that all things which are esteemed blessings turn out prosperously to you, but only on condition of their changing nothing of your state of mind. For I fear lest custom and the pleasantness of these subjects should, as usually happens, creep by degrees into your mind. Therefore I advise you,

"And repeating it, will again and again advise you,"[3]

not to believe that you have these enjoyments of the earth as great or true blessings, since they are not only deceitful because they are doubtful, but also treacherous because they are pleasant. For you know how crafty that wrestler and adversary of ours is, and also often violent, as we now see that he is. He employs all these things which are able to entice as snares, and with such subtilty that they escape the notice of the eyes of the mind, so that they cannot be avoided by the foresight of man. Therefore it is the highest prudence to advance step by step, since he occupies the passes on both sides, and secretly places stumbling-blocks for our feet. Accordingly I advise you, either to disregard, if you are able according to your virtue, your prosperity in which you live, or not to admire it greatly. Remember your true parent, and in what[4] city you have given your name, and of what rank you have been. You understand assuredly what I say. For I do not charge you with pride, of which there is not even a suspicion in your case; but the things which I say are to be referred to the mind, not to the body, the whole system of which has been arranged on this account, that it may be in subjection to the soul as to a master, and may be ruled by its will. For it is in a certain manner an earthen vessel in which the soul, that is, the true man himself, is contained, and that vessel indeed not made by Prometheus, as the poets say, but by that supreme Creator and Artificer of the world, God, whose divine providence and most perfect excellence it is neither

---

[1] [Of whom, *infra.*]

[2] [Nostræ sectæ. Perhaps adopted pleasantly from Acts xxviii. 22.] i.e., Christians.

[3] Virg., *Æn.*, iii. 436.

[4] i.e., have been initiated by baptism. [Philipp. iii. 20. *Greek.*]

possible to comprehend by the perception, nor to express in word.

I will attempt, however, since mention has been made of the body and soul, to explain the nature of each, as far as the weakness of my understanding sees through; and I think that this duty is especially to be undertaken on this account, because Marcus Tullius, a man of remarkable talent, in his fourth book on the Republic, when he had attempted to do this, concluded a subject of wide extent within narrow limits, lightly selecting the chief points. And that there might be no excuse, because he had not followed up this subject, he testified that neither inclination nor attention had been wanting to him. For in his first book concerning the Laws, when he was concisely summing up the same subject, he thus spoke: "Scipio, as it appears to me, has sufficiently expressed this subject in those books which you have read." Afterwards, however, in his second book concerning the Nature of the Gods, he endeavoured to follow up the same subject more extensively. But since he did not express it sufficiently even there, I will approach this office, and will take upon myself boldly to explain that which a man of the greatest eloquence has almost left untouched. Perhaps you may blame me for attempting to discuss something in matters of obscurity, when you see that there have been men of such rashness who are commonly called philosophers, that they scrutinized those things which God willed to be abstruse and hidden, and investigated the nature of things in heaven and on earth, which are far removed from us, and cannot be examined[1] by the eyes, nor touched by the hand, nor perceived by the senses; and yet they so dispute concerning the nature of these things, as to wish that the things which they bring forward may appear to be proved and known. What reason is there, I pray, why any one should think it an invidious thing in us, if we wish to look into and contemplate the system of our body,[2] which is not altogether obscure, because from the very offices of the limbs, and the uses of the several parts, it is permitted us to understand with what great power of providence each part has been made?

CHAP. II. — OF THE PRODUCTION OF THE BEASTS AND OF MAN.

For our Creator and Parent, God, has given to man perception and reason, that it might be evident from this that we are descended from Him, because He Himself is intelligence, He Himself is perception and reason. Since He did not give that power of reason to the other animals, He provided beforehand in what manner their life might be more safe. For He clothed them all with their own natural hair,[3] in order that they might more easily be able to endure the severity of frosts and colds. Moreover, He has appointed to every kind its own peculiar defence for the repelling of attacks from without; so that they may either oppose the stronger animals with natural weapons, or the feebler ones may withdraw themselves from danger by the swiftness of their flight, or those which require at once both strength and swiftness may protect themselves by craft, or guard themselves in hiding-places.[4] And so others of them either poise themselves aloft with light plumage, or are supported by hoofs,[5] or are furnished with horns; some have arms in their mouth — namely, their teeth[6] — or hooked talons on their feet; and none of them is destitute of a defence for its own protection.

But if any fall as a prey to the greater animals, that their race might not utterly perish, they have either been banished to that region where the greater ones cannot exist, or they have received a more abundant fruitfulness in production, that food might be supplied from them to the beasts which are nourished by blood, and yet their very multitude might survive the slaughter inflicted upon them, so as to preserve the race.[7] But He made man — reason being granted to him, and the power of perceiving and speaking being given to him — destitute of those things which are given to the other animals, because wisdom was able to supply those things which the condition of nature had denied to him. He made him naked and defenceless, because he could be armed by his talent, and clothed by his reason.[8] But it cannot be expressed how wonderfully the absence of those things which are given to the brutes contributes to the beauty of man. For if He had given to man the teeth of wild beasts, or horns, or claws, or hoofs, or a tail, or hairs of various colour, who cannot perceive how misshapen an animal he would be, as the dumb animals, if they were made naked and defenceless? For if you take from these the natural clothing of their body, or those things by which they are armed of themselves, they can be neither beautiful nor safe, so that they appear wonderfully furnished if you think of utility, and wonderfully adorned if you think of appearance: in such a wonderful manner is utility combined with beauty.

But with reference to man, whom He formed

---

1 Contrectari.

2 [The argument from design is unanswerable, and can never be obsolete. The objections are frivolous, and belong to Cicero's "minute philosophers."] Of whom, see *Tuscul. Quæst.*, book i. cap. 23.]

3 Omnes enim suis ex se pilis. Others read, "pellibus texit."

4 [ποδωκίην λὰγωοῖς. — ANAC., *Ode* i. 3.]

5 [Φύσις κέρατα ταύροις ὁπλὰς δ' ἔδωκεν ἵπποις. — ANAC., *Ode* i. 1, 2.]

6 [λέουσι χάσμ' ὀδόντων. — *Ib.*, 4.]

7 [" The survival of the fittest." The cant of our day anticipated.]

8 [τοῖς ἀνδράσιν φρόνημα. — *Ib.*, 5. See p. 172, note 5, *supra*.]

an eternal and immortal being, He did not arm him, as the others, without, but within; nor did He place his protection in the body, but in the soul: since it would have been superfluous, when He had given him that which was of the greatest value, to cover him with bodily defences, especially when they hindered the beauty of the human body. On which account I am accustomed to wonder at the senselessness of the philosophers who follow Epicurus, who blame the works of nature, that they may show that the world is prepared and governed by no providence;[1] but they ascribe the origin of all things to indivisible and solid bodies, from the fortuitous meetings of which they say that all things are and were produced. I pass by the things relating to the work itself with which they find fault, in which matter they are ridiculously mad; I assume that which belongs to the subject of which we are now treating.

CHAP. III. — OF THE CONDITION OF THE BEASTS AND MAN.

They complain that man is born in a more feeble and frail condition than that in which the other animals are born: for that these, as soon as they are produced from the womb, immediately raise themselves on their feet, and express their joy by running to and fro, and are at once fit for enduring the air, inasmuch as they have come forth to the light protected by natural coverings; but man, on the contrary, being naked and defenceless, is cast forth, and driven, as it were, from a shipwreck, to the miseries of this life; who is neither able to move himself from the place where he has been born,[2] nor to seek the nourishment of milk, nor to endure the injury of time. Therefore they say that Nature is not the mother of the human race, but a stepmother, who has dealt so liberally with the dumb creation, but has so produced man, that, without resources, and without strength, and destitute of all aid, he can do nothing else than give tokens[3] of the state of his frailty by wailing and lamentations; "as well he may, whose destiny it is to go through in life so many ills."[4]

And when they say these things they are believed to be very wise, because every one without consideration is displeased with his own condition; but I contend that they are never more foolish than when they say these things.[1] For when I consider the condition of things, I understand that nothing ought to have been otherwise than it is — not to say could have been otherwise, for God is able to do all things: but it must be, that that most provident majesty made that which was better and more right.

I should like, therefore, to ask those censurers of the divine works, what they think to be wanting in man, on account of his being born in a more feeble condition. Do they think that men are, on this account, brought up worse? Or that they advance the less to the greatest strength of age? Or that weakness is a hindrance to their growth or safety, since reason bestows[5] the things which are wanting? But, they say, the bringing up of man costs the greatest labours: in truth, the condition of the brute creation is better, because all these, when they have brought forth their young, have no care except for their own food; from which it is effected that, their teats being spontaneously distended, the nourishment of milk is supplied to their offspring, and that they seek this nourishment by the compulsion of nature, without any trouble on the part of the mothers. How is it with birds, which have a different nature? do they not undergo the greatest labours in bringing up their young, so that they sometimes appear to have something of human intelligence? For they either build their nests of mud, or construct them with twigs and leaves, and they sit upon the eggs without taking food; and since it has not been given to them to nourish their young from their own bodies, they convey to them food, and spend whole days in going to and fro in this manner; but by night they defend, cherish, and protect them. What more can men do? unless it be this only, that they do not drive away their young when grown up, but retain them bound by perpetual relationship and the bond of affection. Why should I say that the offspring of birds is much more fragile than that of man? Inasmuch as they do not bring forth the animal itself from the body of the mother, but that which, being warmed by the nourishment and heat of the body of the mother, produces the animal; and this, even when animated by breath, being unfledged and tender, is not only without the power of flying, but even of walking. Would he not, therefore, be most senseless, if any one should think that nature has dealt badly with birds, first, because they are twice born, and then because they are so weak, that they have to be nourished by food sought with labour by their parents? But they select the stronger, and pass by the more feeble animals.

I ask, therefore, from those who prefer the condition of the beasts to their own, what they would choose if God should give them the choice: would they prefer the wisdom of man

[1] [The admirable investigations of the modern atheists are so many testimonies against their own theories when they come to talk of *force*, etc., instead of God. P. 97, note 4, *supra*.]
[2] Effusus est.
[3] Ominari.
[4] Lucret., v. 228.
[5] Dependit.

together with his weakness, or the strength of the beasts together with their nature? In truth, they are not so much like the beasts as not to prefer even a much more fragile condition, provided that it be human, to that strength of theirs unattended with reason. But, in truth, prudent men neither desire the reason of man together with frailty, nor the strength of the dumb animals without reason. Therefore it is nothing so repugnant or contradictory,[1] that either reason or the condition of nature should of necessity prepare each animal. If it is furnished with natural protection, reason is superfluous. For what will it contrive?[2] What will it do? Or what will it plan? Or in what will it display that light of the intellect, when Nature of its own accord grants those things which are able to be the result of reason? But if it be endued with reason, what need will there be of defences for the body, when reason once granted is able to supply the office of nature? And this has such power for the adorning and protection of man, that nothing greater or better can be given by God. Finally, since man is possessed of a body which is not great, and of slight strength, and of infirm health, nevertheless, since he has received that which is of greater value, he is better equipped than the other animals, and more adorned. For though he is born frail and feeble, yet he is safe from all the dumb animals, and all those which are born with greater strength, though they are able to bear patiently the inclemency of the sky, yet are unable to be safe from man. Thus it comes to pass that reason bestows more on man than nature does on the dumb animals; since, in their case, neither greatness of strength nor firmness of body can prevent them from being oppressed by us, or from being made subject to our power.

Can any one, then, when he sees that even elephants,[3] with their vast bodies and strength, are subservient to man, complain respecting God, the Maker of all things, because he has received moderate strength, and a small body; and not estimate according to their deserts the divine benefits towards himself, which is the part of an ungrateful man, or (to speak more truly) of a madman? Plato, I believe, that he might refute these ungrateful men, gave thanks to nature that he was born a man.[4] How much better and more soundly did he act, who perceived that the condition of man was better, than they did who would have preferred that they had been born beasts! For if God should happen to change them into those animals whose condition they prefer to their own, they would now immediately desire to return to their previous state, and would with great outcries eagerly demand their former condition, because strength and firmness of body are not of such consequence that you should be without the office of the tongue; or the free course of birds through the air, that you should be without the hands. For the hands are of greater service than the lightness and use of the wings; the tongue is of greater service than the strength of the whole body. What madness is it, therefore, to prefer those things which, if they were given, you would refuse to receive!

CHAP. IV. — OF THE WEAKNESS OF MAN.

They also complain that man is liable to diseases, and to untimely death. They are indignant, it appears, that they are not born gods. By no means, they say; but we show from this, that man was made with no foresight, which ought to have been otherwise. What if I shall show, that this very thing was foreseen with great reason, that he might be able to be harassed by diseases, and that his life might often be cut short in the midst of its course? For, since God had known that the animal which He had made, of its own accord passed to death, that it might be capable of receiving death itself, which is the dissolution of nature, He gave to it frailty, which might find an approach for death in order to the dissolution of the animal. For if it had been of such strength that disease and sickness could not approach it, not even could death, since death is the consequence of diseases. But how could a premature death be absent from him, for whom a mature death had been appointed? Assuredly they wish that no man should die, unless when he has completed his hundredth year. How can they maintain their consistency in so great an opposition of circumstances? For, in order that no one may be capable of dying before a hundred years, something of the strength which is immortal must be given to him; and when this is granted, the condition of death must necessarily be excluded. But of what kind can that be, which can render a man firm and impregnable against diseases and attacks from without? For, inasmuch as he is composed of bones, and nerves, and flesh, and blood, which of these can be so firm as to repel frailty and death? That man, therefore, may not be liable to dissolution before that time which they think ought to have been appointed for him, of what material will they assign to him a body? All things which can be seen and touched are frail. It remains that they seek something from heaven, since there is nothing on earth which is not weak.

Since, therefore, man had to be so formed by

---

1 Contrarium.
2 Excogitabit.
3 Boves Lucas. Elephants are said to have been so called, because they were first seen by the Romans in Lucania.
4 Some editions here add: "But what is the nature of this, it does not belong to the present subject to consider."

God, that he should at some time be mortal, the matter itself required that he should be made with a frail and earthly body. It is necessary, therefore, that he should at some time receive death, since he is possessed of a body; for every body is liable to dissolution and to death. Therefore they are most foolish who complain of premature death, since the condition of nature makes a place for it. Thus it will follow that he is subject also to diseases; for nature does not admit that infirmity can be absent from that body which is at some time to undergo dissolution. But let us suppose it to be possible, as they wish, that man is not born under those conditions by which he is subject to disease or death, unless, having completed the course of his life, he shall have arrived at the extremity of old age. They do not, therefore, see what would be the consequence if it were so arranged, that it would be plainly impossible to die at another time; but if any one can be deprived of nourishment by another, it will be possible for him to die. Therefore the case requires that man, who cannot die before an appointed day, should have no need of the nourishment of food, because it may be taken from him; but if he shall have no need of food, he will now not be a man, but will become a god. Therefore, as I have already said, they who complain of the frailty of man, make this complaint especially, that they were not born immortal and everlasting. No one ought to die unless he is old. On this account, in truth, he ought to die, because he is not God. But mortality cannot be united with immortality: for if a man is mortal in old age, he cannot be immortal in youth; neither is the condition of death foreign to him who is at some time about to die; nor is there any immortality to which a limit is appointed. Thus it comes to pass, that the exclusion of immortality for ever, and the reception of mortality for a time, place man in such a condition that he is at some time mortal.

Therefore the necessity is in all points suitable,[1] that he ought not to have been otherwise than he is, and that it was impossible. But they do not see the order of consequences, because they have once committed an error in the main point itself. For the divine providence having been excluded from the affairs of men, it necessarily followed that all things were produced of their own accord. Hence they invented the notion of those blows and fortuitous meetings together of minute seeds, because they did not see the origin of things. And when they had thrown themselves into this difficulty, necessity now compelled them to think that souls were born together with bodies, and in like manner were extinguished together with bodies; for they had made the assumption, that nothing was made by the divine mind. And they were unable to prove this in any other way, than by showing that there were some things in which the system of providence appeared to be at fault.[2] Therefore they blamed those things in which providence wonderfully expressed its divinity, as those things which I have related concerning diseases and premature death; whereas they ought to have considered, these things being assumed, what would be the necessary consequences (but those things which I have spoken are the consequences) if he were not liable to diseases, and did not require a dwelling, nor clothing. For why should he fear the winds, or rains, or colds, the power of which consists in this, that they bring diseases? For on this account he has received wisdom, that he may guard his frailty against things that would injure him. The necessary consequence is, that since he is liable to diseases for the sake of retaining his wisdom, he must also be liable to death; because he to whom death does not come, must of necessity be firm. But infirmity has in itself the condition of death; but where there shall be firmness, neither can old age have any place, nor death, which follows old age.

Moreover, if death were appointed for a fixed age, man would become most arrogant, and would be destitute of all humanity. For almost all the rights of humanity, by which we are united with one another, arise from fear and the consciousness of frailty. In short, all the more feeble and timid animals herd together, that, since they are unable to protect themselves by strength, they may protect themselves by their multitude; but the stronger animals seek solitudes, since they trust in their force and strength.[3] If man also, in the same manner, had sufficient strength for the repelling of dangers, and did not stand in need of the assistance of any other, what society would there be? Or what system? What humanity? Or what would be more harsh than man? What more brutal? What more savage? But since he is feeble, and not able to live by himself apart from man, he desires society, that his life, passed in intercourse with others, may become both more adorned and more safe. You see, therefore, that the whole reason of man centres most of all in this, that he is born naked and fragile, that he is attacked by diseases, that he is punished by premature death. And if these things should be taken away from man, reason also, and wisdom, must necessarily be taken away. But I am discussing too long respecting things which are manifest, since it is clear that nothing ever was made, or could have been made, without providence. And if

[1] Quadrat.

[2] Claudicare.

[3] [The disposition, even among men, to herd together in artificial societies, is instinctively repugnant to the stronger natures.]

I should now wish to discuss respecting all its works in order, the subject would be infinite. But I have purposed to speak so much concerning the body of man only, that I may show in it the power of divine providence, how great it has been in those things only which are easy of comprehension and open; for those things which relate to the soul can neither be subjected to the eyes, nor comprehended. Now we speak concerning the vessel itself of man, which we see.

CHAP. V. — OF THE FIGURES AND LIMBS OF ANIMALS.

In the beginning, when God was forming the animals, He did not wish to conglobate [1] and collect them into a round shape, that they might be able easily to put themselves in motion for walking, and to turn themselves in any direction; but from the highest part of the body He lengthened out the head. He also carried out to a greater length some of the limbs, which are called feet, that, being fixed on the ground with alternate motions, they might lead forward the animal wherever his inclination had borne him, or the necessity of seeking food had called him. Moreover, He made four limbs standing out from the very vessel of the body: two behind, which are in all animals — the feet; also two close to the head and neck, which supply various uses to animals. For in cattle and wild beasts they are feet like the hinder ones; but in man they are hands, which are produced not for walking, but for acting and controlling.[2] There is also a third class, in which those former limbs are neither feet nor hands; but wings, which, having feathers arranged in order, supply the use of flying.[3] Thus one formation has different forms and uses; and that He might firmly hold together the density itself of the body, by binding together greater and small bones, He compacted a kind of keel, which we call the spine; and He did not think fit to form it of one continued bone, lest the animal should not have the power of walking and bending itself. From its middle part, as it were, He has extended in a different direction transverse and flat bones, by which, being slightly curved, and almost drawn together to themselves as into a circle, the inward organs [4] may be covered, that those parts which needed to be soft and less strong might be protected by the encircling of a solid framework.[5] But at the end of that joining together which we have said to resemble the keel of a ship, He placed the head, in which might be the government of the whole living creature; and this name was given to it, as indeed Varro writes to Cicero, because from this the senses and the nerves take their beginning.

But those parts, which we have said to be lengthened out from the body, either for the sake of walking, or of acting, or of flying, He would have to consist of bones, neither too long, for the sake of rapidity of motion, nor too short, for the sake of firmness, but of a few, and those large. For either they are two as in man, or four as in a quadruped. And these He did not make solid, lest in walking sluggishness and weight should retard; but He made them hollow, and full of marrow within, to preserve the vigour of the body. And again, He did not make them equally extended to the end; but He conglobated their extremities with coarse knots, that they might be able more easily to be bound with sinews, and to be turned more easily, from which they are called joints.[6] These knots He made firmly solid, and covered with a soft kind of covering, which is called cartilage; for this purpose, that they might be bent without galling or any sense of pain. He did not, however, form these after one fashion. For He made some simple and round into an orb, in those joints at least in which it was befitting that the limbs should move in all directions, as in the shoulders, since it is necessary that the hands should move and be twisted about in any direction; but others He made broad, and equal, and round towards one part, and that plainly in those places where only it was necessary for the limbs to be bent, as in the knees, and in the elbows, and in the hands themselves. For as it was at the same time pleasant to the sight, and useful, that the hands should move in every direction from that position from which they spring; so assuredly, if this same thing should happen to the elbows, a motion of that kind would be at once superfluous and unbecoming. For then the hand, having lost the dignity which it now has, through its excessive flexibility,[7] would appear like the trunk of an elephant; and man would be altogether snake-handed,[8] — an instance of which has been wonderfully effected in that monstrous beast. For God, who wished to display His providence and power by a wonderful variety of many things, inasmuch as He had not extended the head of that animal to such a length that he might be able to touch the earth with his mouth, which would have been horrible and hideous, and because He had so armed the mouth itself with extended tusks, that even if he touched the earth the tusks would still deprive him of the power of feeding, He lengthened out

[1] Conglobare, "to gather into a ball."
[2] Temperandum. Others read "tenendum."
[3] [But, query, Is there not an unsolved mystery about birds and flying? They seem to me to be sustained in the air by some faculty not yet understood.]
[4] Viscera. This word includes the heart, lungs, liver, stomach, and intestines.
[5] Cratis, properly "wicker-work."
[6] Vertibula.
[7] Mobilitas.
[8] Anguimanus, — a word applied by Lucretius to the elephant.

between these from the top of the forehead a soft and flexible limb, by which he might be able to grasp and lay hold of anything, lest the prominent magnitude of the tusks, or the shortness of the neck, should interfere with the arrangement for taking food.

CHAP. VI. — OF THE ERROR OF EPICURUS, AND OF THE LIMBS AND THEIR USE.

I cannot here be prevented from again showing the folly of Epicurus. For all the ravings of Lucretius [1] belong to him, who, in order that he might show that animals are not produced by any contrivance of the divine mind, but, as he is wont to say, by chance, said that in the beginning of the world innumerable other animals of wonderful form and magnitude were produced; but that they were unable to be permanent, because either the power of taking food, or the method of uniting and generating, had failed them. It is evident that, in order to make a place for his atoms flying about through the boundless and empty space, he wished to exclude the divine providence. But when he saw that a wonderful system of providence is contained in all things which breathe, what vanity was it (O mischievous one!) to say that there had been animals of immense size, in which the system of production ceased!

Since, therefore, all things which we see are produced with reference to a plan — for nothing but a plan [2] can effect this very condition of being born — it is manifest that nothing could have been born without a plan. For it was previously foreseen in the formation of everything, how it should use the service of the limbs for the necessaries of life; and how the offspring, being produced from the union of bodies, might preserve all living creatures by their several species. For if a skilful architect, when he designs to construct some great building, first of all considers what will be the effect [3] of the complete building, and previously ascertains by measurement what situation is suitable for a light weight, in what place a massive part of the structure will stand, what will be the intervals between the columns, what or where will be the descents and outlets of the falling waters and the reservoirs, — he first, I say, foresees these things, that he may begin together with the very foundations whatever things are necessary for the work when now completed, — why should any one suppose that, in the contrivance of animals, God did not foresee what things were necessary for living, before giving life itself? For it is manifest that life could not exist, unless those things by which it exists were previously arranged.[4]

Therefore Epicurus saw in the bodies of animals the skill of a divine plan; but that he might carry into effect that which he had before imprudently assumed, he added another absurdity agreeing with the former. For he said that the eyes were not produced for seeing, nor the ears for hearing, nor the feet for walking, since these members were produced before there was the exercise of seeing, hearing, and walking; but that all the offices of these members arose from them after their production.[5] I fear lest the refutation of such extravagant and ridiculous stories should appear to be no less foolish; but it pleases me to be foolish, since we are dealing with a foolish man, lest he should think himself too clever.[6] What do you say, Epicurus? Were not the eyes produced for seeing? Why, then, do they see? Their use, he says, afterwards showed itself. Therefore they were produced for the sake of seeing, since they can do nothing else but see. Likewise, in the case of the other limbs, use itself shows for what purpose they were produced. For it is plain that this use could have no existence, unless all the limbs had been made with such arrangement and foresight, that they might be able to have their use.

For what if you should say, that birds were not made to fly, nor wild beasts to rage, nor fishes to swim, nor men to be wise, when it is evident that living creatures are subject to that natural disposition and office to which each was created? But it is evident that he who has lost the main point itself of the truth must always be in error. For if all things are produced not by providence, but by a fortuitous meeting together of atoms, why does it never happen by chance, that those first principles meet together in such a way as to make an animal of such a kind, that it might rather hear with its nostrils, smell with its eyes, and see [7] with its ears? For if the first principles leave no kind of position untried, monstrous productions of this kind ought daily to have been brought forth, in which the arrangement of the limbs might be distorted,[8] and the use far different from that which prevails. But since all the races of animals, and all the limbs, observe their own laws and arrangements, and the uses assigned to them, it is plain that nothing is made by chance, since a perpetual arrangement of the divine plan is preserved. But we will refute Epicurus at another time. Now let

---

1 [Yet Lucretius has originality and genius of an order far nobler than that of moderns who copy his follies.]

2 Ratio. Nearly equivalent in this place to "providentia."

3 Summa. [Wisd. xi. 20.]

4 [The amazing *proportions* imparted to all things created, in correspondence with their relations to man and to the earth, is beautifully hinted by our author.]

5 [The snout of the elephant and the neck of the giraffe were developed from their necessities, etc. *Modern Science, passim.*]

6 [In our days reproduced as *progress.*]

7 Cerneret, "to see so as to distinguish;" a stronger word than "video."

8 Præposterus; having the last first, and the first last.

us discuss the subject of providence, as we have begun.

CHAP. VII. — OF ALL THE PARTS OF THE BODY.

God therefore connected and bound together the parts which strengthen[1] the body, which we call bones, being knotted and joined to one another by sinews, which the mind might make use of, as bands,[2] if it should wish to hasten forward or to lag behind; and, indeed, without any labour or effort, but with a very slight inclination, it might moderate and guide the mass of the whole body. But He covered these with the inward organs,[3] as was befitting to each place, that the parts which were solid might be enclosed and concealed. Also He mixed with the inward organs, veins as streams divided through the whole body, through which the moisture and the blood, running in different directions, might bedew all the limbs with the vital juices; and He fashioned these inward organs after that manner which was befitting to each kind and situation, and covered them with skin drawn over them, which He either adorned with beauty only, or covered with thick hair, or fenced with scales, or adorned with brilliant feathers. But that is a wonderful contrivance of God, that one arrangement and one state exhibits innumerable varieties of animals. For in almost all things which breathe there is the same connection and arrangement of the limbs. For first of all is the head, and annexed to this the neck; also the breast adjoined to the neck, and the shoulders projecting from it, the belly adhering to the breast; also the organs of generation subjoined to the belly; in the last place, the thighs and feet. Nor do the limbs only keep their own course and position in all, but also the parts of the limbs. For in the head itself alone the ears occupy a fixed position, the eyes a fixed position, likewise the nostrils, the mouth also, and in it the teeth and tongue. And though all these things are the same in all animals, yet there is an infinite and manifold diversity of the things formed; because those things of which I have spoken, being either more drawn out or more contracted, are comprehended by lineaments differing in various ways. What! is not that divine, that in so great a multitude of living creatures each animal is most excellent in its own class and species? — so that if any part should be taken from one to another, the necessary result would be, that nothing would be more embarrassed for use, nothing more unshapely to look upon; as if you should give a prolonged neck to an elephant, or a short neck to a camel; or if you should attach feet or hair to serpents, in which the length of the body equally stretched out required nothing else, except that being marked as to their backs with spots, and supporting themselves by their smooth scales, with winding courses they should glide into slippery tracts. But in quadrupeds the same designer lengthened out the arrangement of the spine, which is drawn out from the top of the head to a greater length on the outside of the body, and pointed it into a tail, that the parts of the body which are offensive might either be covered on account of their unsightliness, or be protected on account of their tenderness, so that by its motion certain minute and injurious animals might be driven away from the body; and if you should take away this member, the animal would be imperfect and weak. But where there is reason and the hand, that is not so necessary as a covering of hair. To such an extent are all things most befittingly arranged, each in its own class, that nothing can be conceived more unbecoming than a quadruped which is naked, or a man that is covered.

But, however, though nakedness itself on the part of man tends in a wonderful manner to beauty, yet it was not adapted to his head; for what great deformity there would be in this, is evident from baldness. Therefore He clothed the head with hair; and because it was about to be on the top, He added it as an ornament, as it were, to the highest summit of the building. And this ornament is not collected into a circle, or rounded into the figure of a cap, lest it should be unsightly by leaving some parts bare; but it is freely poured forth in some places, and withdrawn in others, according to the comeliness of each place. Therefore, the forehead entrenched by a circumference, and the hair put forth from the temples before the ears, and the uppermost parts of these being surrounded after the manner of a crown, and all the back part of the head covered, display an appearance of wonderful comeliness. Then the nature of the beard contributes in an incredible degree to distinguish the maturity of bodies, or to the distinction of sex, or to the beauty of manliness and strength; so that it appears that the system of the whole work would not have been in agreement, if anything had been made otherwise than it is.

CHAP. VIII. — OF THE PARTS OF MAN: THE EYES AND EARS.

Now I will show the plan of the whole man, and will explain the uses and habits of the several members which are exposed to view in the body, or concealed. When, therefore, God had determined of all the animals to make man alone heavenly, and all the rest earthly, He

1 Solidamenta corporis.
2 Retinaculis.
3 Visceribus.

raised him erect[1] to the contemplation of the heaven, and made him a biped, doubtless that he might look to the same quarter from which he derives his origin; but He depressed the others to the earth, that, inasmuch as they have no expectation of immortality, being cast down with their whole body to the ground, they might be subservient to their appetite and food. And thus the right reason and elevated position of man alone, and his countenance, shared with and closely resembling God his Father, bespeak his origin and Maker.[2] His mind, nearly divine, because it has obtained the rule not only over the animals which are on the earth, but even over his own body, being situated in the highest part, the head, as in a lofty citadel, looks out upon and observes all things. He formed this its palace, not drawn out and extended, as in the case of the dumb animals, but like an orb and a globe, because all[3] roundness belongs to a perfect plan and figure. Therefore the mind and that divine fire is covered with it,[4] as with a vault;[5] and when He had covered its highest top with a natural garment, He alike furnished and adorned the front part, which is called the face, with the necessary services of the members.

And first, He closed the orbs of the eyes with concave apertures, from which boring[6] Varro thought that the forehead[7] derived its name; and He would have these to be neither less nor more than two, because no number is more perfect as to appearance than that of two: as also He made the ears two, the doubleness[8] of which bears with it an incredible degree of beauty, both because each part is adorned with a resemblance, and that voices coming from both sides[9] may more easily be collected. For the form itself is fashioned after a wonderful manner: because He would not have their apertures to be naked and uncovered, which would have been less becoming and less useful; since the voice might fly beyond the narrow space of simple caverns, and be scattered, did not the apertures themselves confine it, received through hollow windings and kept back from reverberation, like those small vessels, by the application of which narrow-mouthed vessels are accustomed to be filled.

These ears, then, which have their name from the drinking[10] in of voices, from which Virgil says,[11]

"And with these ears I drank in his voice;"

or because the Greeks call the voice itself αὐδήν, from hearing, — the ears (*aures*) were named as though *audes* by the change of a letter, — God would not form of soft skins, which, hanging down and flaccid, might take away beauty; nor of hard and solid bones, lest, being stiff and immoveable, they should be inconvenient for use. But He designed that which might be between these, that a softer cartilage might bind them, and that they might have at once a befitting and flexible firmness. In these the office of hearing only is placed, as that of seeing is in the eyes, the acuteness of which is especially inexplicable and wonderful; for He covered their orbs, presenting the similitude of gems in that part with which they had to see, with transparent membranes, that the images of objects placed opposite them, being refracted[12] as in a mirror, might penetrate to the innermost perception. Through these membranes, therefore, that faculty which is called the mind sees those things which are without; lest you should happen to think that we see either by the striking[13] of the images, as the philosophers discuss, since the office of seeing ought to be in that which sees, not in that which is seen; or in the tension of the air together with the eyesight; or in the outpouring of the rays: since, if it were so, we should see the ray towards which we turn with our eyes, until the air, being extended together with the eyesight, or the rays being poured out, should arrive at the object which was to be seen.

But since we see at the same moment of time, and for the most part, while engaged on other business, we nevertheless behold all things which are placed opposite to us, it is more true and evident that it is the mind which, through the eyes, sees those things which are placed opposite to it, as though through windows covered with pellucid crystal or transparent stone;[14] and therefore the mind and inclination are often known from the eyes. For the refutation of which Lucretius[15] employed a very senseless argument. For if the mind, he says, sees through the eyes, it would see better if the eyes were torn out and dug up, inasmuch as doors being torn up together with the door-posts let in more light than if they were covered. Truly his eyes, or rather those of Epicurus who taught him, ought to have been dug out, that they might not see, that the torn-out orbs, and the burst fibres of the eyes, and the blood flowing through the veins, and the flesh increasing from wounds, and the scars drawn over at last can admit no light; unless by chance he would have it that eyes are produced resembling ears, so that we should see

1 Rigidum.
2 [An amusing persistency in the enforcement of this idea.]
3 Omnis. Others read "orbis."
4 i.e., the head.
5 Cœlo. Some believed that the soul was of fire.
6 Foratu, "the process of boring;" foramen, "the aperture thus made."
7 Frontem.
8 Duplicitas.
9 Altrinsecus.
10 Hauriendis, from which "aures" is said to be formed.
11 *Æneid*, iv. 359. [The English verb *bother* (= both ear) is an amusing comment on the adaptation of ears to unwelcome voices.]

12 Refulgentes.
13 Imaginum incursione.
14 According to some, "talc."
15 iii. 368.

not so much with eyes as with apertures, than which there can be nothing more unsightly or more useless. For how little should we be able to see, if from the innermost recesses of the head the mind should pay attention through slight fissures of caverns; as, if any one should wish to look through a stalk of hemlock, he would see no more than the capability of the stalk itself admitted! For sight, therefore, it was rather needful that the members should be collected together into an orb, that the sight might be spread in breadth and the parts which adjoined them in the front of the face, that they might freely behold all things. Therefore the unspeakable power of the divine providence made two orbs most resembling each other, and so bound them together that they might be able not only to be altogether turned, but to be moved and directed with moderation.[1] And He willed that the orbs themselves should be full of a pure and clear moisture, in the middle part of which sparks of lights might be kept shut up, which we call the pupils, in which, being pure and delicate, are contained the faculty and method of seeing. The mind therefore directs itself through these orbs that it may see, and the sight of both the eyes is mingled and joined together in a wonderful manner.

CHAP. IX. — OF THE SENSES AND THEIR POWER.

It pleases me in this place to censure the folly of those who, while they wish to show that the senses are false, collect many instances in which the eyes are deceived; and among them this also, that all things appear double to the mad and intoxicated, as though the cause of that error were obscure. For it happens on this account, because there are two eyes. But hear how it happens. The sight of the eyes consists in the exertion of the soul. Therefore, since the mind, as has been above said, uses the eyes as windows, this happens not only to those who are intoxicated or mad, but even to those who are of sound mind, and sober. For if you place any object too near, it will appear double, for there is a certain interval and space in which the sight of the eyes meets together. Likewise, if you call the soul back as if to reflection, and relax the exertion of the mind, then the sight of each eye is drawn asunder, and they each begin to see separately.

If you, again, exert the mind and direct the eyesight, whatever appeared double unites into one. What wonder, therefore, if the mind, impaired by poison and the powerful influence of wine, cannot direct itself to seeing, as the feet cannot to walking when they are weak through the numbness of the sinews, or if the force of madness raging against the brain disunites the agreement of the eyes? Which is so true, that in the case of one-eyed[2] men, if they become either mad or intoxicated, it can by no means happen that they see any object double. Wherefore, if the reason is evident why the eyes are deceived, it is clear that the senses are not false: for they either are not deceived if they are pure and sound; or if they are deceived, yet the mind is not deceived which recognises their error.

CHAP. X. — OF THE OUTER LIMBS OF MAN, AND THEIR USE.

But let us return to the works of God. That the eyes, therefore, might be better protected from injury, He concealed them with the coverings of the eyelashes,[3] from which Varro thinks that the eyes[4] derived their name. For even the eyelids themselves, in which there is the power of rapid motion, and to which throbbing[5] gives their name, being protected by hairs standing in order, afford a most becoming fence to the eyes; the continual motion of which, meeting with incomprehensible rapidity, does not impede the course of the sight, and relieves the eyes.[6] For the pupil — that is, the transparent membrane — which ought not to be drained and to become dry, unless it is cleansed by continual moisture so that it shines clearly, loses its power.[7] Why should I speak of the summits of the eyebrows themselves, furnished with short hair? Do they not, as it were by mounds, both afford protection to the eyes, so that nothing may fall into them from above,[8] and at the same time ornament? And the nose, arising from the confines of these, and stretched out, as it were, with an equal ridge, at once serves to separate and to protect the two eyes. Below also, a not unbecoming swelling of the cheeks, gently rising after the similitude of hills, makes the eyes safer on every side; and it has been provided by the great Artificer, that if there shall happen to be a more violent blow, it may be repelled by the projecting parts. But the upper part of the nose as far as the middle has been made solid; but the lower part has been made with a softened cartilage annexed to it, that it may be pliant[9] to the use of the fingers. Moreover, in this, though a single member, three offices are placed: one, that of drawing the breath; the second, that of smelling; the third, that the secretions of the brain may escape through its caverns. And in how wonderful, how divine a manner did God

[1] Cum modo: "in a measured degree."

[2] Luscis.

[3] Ciliorum. The word properly denotes the edge of the eyelid, in which the eyelash is fixed; said to be derived from "cilleo," to move.

[4] Oculi, as though derived from "occulere," to conceal.

[5] Palpitatio. Hence "palpebræ," the eyelids.

[6] Reficit obtutum.

[7] Obsolescit.

[8] [Xenophon, *Memorabilia*, i. 4.]

[9] Tractabilis.

contrive these also, so that the very cavity of the nose should not deform the beauty of the face: which would certainly have been the case if one single aperture only were open. But He enclosed and divided that, as though by a wall drawn through the middle, and made it most beautiful by the very circumstance of its being double.[1] From which we understand of how much weight the twofold number, made firm by one simple connection, is to the perfection of things.

For though the body is one, yet the whole could not be made up of single members, unless it were that there should be parts on the right hand or on the left. Therefore, as the two feet and also hands not only avail to some utility and practice either of walking or of doing something, but also bestow an admirable character and comeliness; so in the head, which is, as it were, the crown of the divine work, the hearing has been divided by the great Artificer into two ears, and the sight into two eyes, and the smelling into two nostrils, because the brain, in which is contained the system of the sensation, although it is one, yet is divided into two parts by the intervening membrane. But the heart also, which appears to be the abode of wisdom, although it is one, yet has two recesses within, in which are contained the living fountains of blood, divided by an intervening barrier: that as in the world itself the chief control, being twofold from simple matter, or simple from a twofold matter, governs and keeps together the whole; so in the body, all the parts, being constructed of two, might present an inseparable unity. Also how useful and how becoming is the appearance and the opening of the mouth transversely cannot be expressed; the use of which consists in two offices, that of taking food and speaking.

The tongue enclosed within, which by its motions divides the voice into words, and is the interpreter of the mind, cannot, however, by itself alone fulfil the office of speaking, unless it strikes its edge against the palate, unless aided by striking against the teeth or by the compression of the lips. The teeth, however, contribute more to speaking: for infants do not begin to speak before they have teeth; and old men, when they have lost their teeth, so lisp that they appear to have returned afresh to infancy. But these things relate to man alone, or to birds, in which the tongue, being pointed and vibrating with fixed motions, expresses innumerable inflexions of songs and various kinds of sounds. It has, moreover, another office also, which it exercises in all, and this alone in the dumb animals, that it collects the food when bruised and ground by the teeth, and by its force presses it down when collected into balls, and transmits it to the belly. Accordingly, Varro thinks that the name of tongue was given to it from binding[2] the food. It also assists the beasts in drinking: for with the tongue stretched out and hollowed they draw water; and when they have taken it in the hollow[3] of the tongue, lest by slowness and delay it should flow away, they dash[4] it against the palate with swift rapidity. This, therefore, is covered by the concave part of the palate as by a shell,[5] and God has surrounded it with the enclosure of the teeth as with a wall.

But He has adorned the teeth themselves, which are arranged in order in a wonderful manner, lest, being bare and exposed,[6] they should be a terror rather than an ornament, with soft gums, which are so named from producing teeth, and then with the coverings of the lips; and the hardness of the teeth, as in a millstone, is greater and rougher than in the other bones, that they might be sufficient for bruising the food and pasture. But how befittingly has He divided[7] the lips themselves, which as it were before were united! the upper of which, under the very middle of the nostrils, He has marked with a kind of slight cavity, as with a valley: He has gracefully spread out[8] the lower for the sake of beauty. For, as far as relates to the receiving of flavour, he is deceived, whoever he is, who thinks that this sense resides in the palate; for it is the tongue by which flavours are perceived, and not the whole of it: for the parts of it which are more tender on either side, draw in the flavour with the most delicate perceptions. And though nothing is diminished from that which is eaten or drunk, yet the flavour in an indescribable manner penetrates to the sense, in the same way in which the taking of the smell detracts nothing from any material.

And how beautiful the other parts are can scarcely be expressed. The chin, gently drawn down from the cheeks, and the lower part of it so closed that the lightly imprinted division appears to mark its extreme point: the neck stiff and well rounded: the shoulders let down as though by gentle ridges from the neck: the fore-arms[9] powerful, and braced[10] by sinews for firmness: the great strength of the upper-arms[11] standing out with remarkable muscles: the useful and becoming bending of the elbows. What shall I say of the hands, the ministers of reason and wisdom? Which the most skilful Creator made with a flat and moderately concave bend, that if

1 Ipsa duplicitate.

2 Lingua, as though from "ligando."
3 Linguæ sinu.
4 Complodunt.
5 Testudine.
6 Restricti.
7 Intercidit.
8 Foras molliter explicavit.
9 Brachia. The fore-arms, from the hand to the elbow.
10 Substricta.
11 Lacerti. The arm from the elbow to the shoulder.

anything was to be held, it might conveniently rest upon them, and terminated them in the fingers; in which it is difficult to explain whether the appearance or the usefulness is greater. For the perfection and completeness of their number, and the comeliness of their order and gradation, and the flexible bending of the equal joints, and the round form of the nails, comprising and strengthening the tips of the fingers with concave coverings, lest the softness of the flesh should yield in holding any object, afford great adornment. But this is convenient for use in wonderful ways, that one separated from the rest rises together with the hand itself, and is enlarged[1] in a different direction, which, offering itself as though to meet the others, possesses all the power of holding and doing either alone, or in a special manner, as the guide and director of them all; from which also it received the name of thumb,[2] because it prevails among the others by force and power. It has two joints standing out, not as the others, three; but one is annexed by flesh to the hand for the sake of beauty: for if it had been with three joints, and itself separate, the foul and unbecoming appearance would have deprived the hand of all grace.

Again, the breadth of the breast, being elevated, and exposed to the eyes, displays a wonderful dignity of its condition; of which this is the cause, that God appears to have made man only, as it were, reclining with his face upward: for scarcely any other animal is able to lie upon its back. But He appears to have formed the dumb animals as though lying on one side, and to have pressed them to the earth. For this reason He gave them a narrow breast, and removed from sight, and prostrate[3] towards the earth. But He made that of man open and erect, because, being full of reason given from heaven, it was not befitting that it should be humble or unbecoming. The nipples also gently rising, and crowned with darker and small orbs, add something of beauty; being given to females for the nourishment of their young, to males for grace only, that the breast might not appear misshapen, and, as it were, mutilated. Below this is placed the flat surface of the belly, about the middle of which the navel distinguishes by a not unbecoming mark, being made for this purpose, that through it the young, while it is in the womb, may be nourished.

CHAP. XI. — OF THE INTESTINES IN MAN, AND THEIR USE.

It necessarily follows that I should begin to speak of the inward parts also, to which has been assigned not beauty, because they are concealed from view, but incredible utility, since it was necessary that this earthly body should be nourished with some moisture from food and drink, as the earth itself is by showers and frosts. The most provident Artificer placed in the middle of it a receptacle for articles of food, by means of which, when digested and liquefied, it might distribute the vital juices to all the members. But since man is composed of body and soul, that receptacle of which I have spoken above affords nourishment only to the body; to the soul, in truth, He has given another abode. For He has made a kind of intestines soft and thin,[4] which we call the lungs, into which the breath might pass by an alternate interchange;[5] and He did not form this after the fashion of the uterus, lest the breath should all at once be poured forth, or at once inflate it. And on this account He did not make it a full intestine,[6] but capable of being inflated, and admitting the air, so that it might gradually receive the breath; while the vital air is spread through that thinness, and might again gradually give it back, while it spreads itself forth from it: for the very alternation of blowing and breathing,[7] and the process of respiration, support life in the body.

Since, therefore, there are in man two receptacles, — one of the air which nourishes the soul,[8] the other of the food which nourishes the body, — there must be two tubes[9] through the neck for food, and for breath, the upper of which leads from the mouth to the belly, the lower from the nostrils to the lungs. And the plan and nature of these are different: for the passage which is from the mouth has been made soft, and which when closed always adheres[10] to itself, as the mouth itself; since drink and food, being corporeal, make for themselves a space for passage, by moving aside and opening the gullet. The breath, on the other hand, which is incorporeal and thin, because it was unable to make for itself a space, has received an open way, which is called the windpipe. This is composed of flexible and soft bones, as though of rings fitted together after the manner of a hemlock stalk,[11] and adhering together; and this passage is always open. For the breath can have no cessation in passing; because it, which is always passing to and fro, is checked as by a kind of obstacle through means of a portion of a member usefully sent down from the brain, and which is called the uvula, lest, drawn by pestilential air,

---

1 Maturius funditur.
2 i.e., pollex, as though from "polleo," to prevail.
3 Abjectum.
4 Rarum, i.e., loose in texture.
5 Reciprocâ vicissitudine.
6 Ne plenum quidem. Some editions omit "ne," but it seems to be required by the sense; the lungs not being compact and solid, as the liver, but of a slighter substance.
7 Flandi et spirandi. The former word denotes the process of sending forth, the latter of inhaling, the air.
8 Animam, the vital principle, as differing from the rational.
9 Fistulas.
10 Cohæreat sibi.
11 In cicutæ modum.

it should come with impetuosity and spoil the slightness[1] of its abode, or bring the whole violence of the injury upon the inner receptacles. And on this account also the nostrils are slightly open, which are therefore so named, because either smell or breath does not cease to flow[2] through these, which are, as it were, the doors of this tube. Yet this breathing-tube lies open[3] not only to the nostrils, but also to the mouth in the extreme regions of the palate, where the risings of[4] the jaws, looking towards the uvula, begin to raise themselves into a swelling. And the reason of this arrangement is not obscure: for we should not have the power of speaking if the windpipe were open to the nostrils only, as the path of the gullet is to the mouth only; nor could the breath proceeding from it cause the voice, without the service of the tongue.

Therefore the divine skill opened a way for the voice from that breathing-tube, so that the tongue might be able to discharge its office, and by its strokes divide into words the even[5] course of the voice itself. And this passage, if by any means it is intercepted, must necessarily cause dumbness. For he is assuredly mistaken, whoever thinks that there is any other cause why men are dumb. For they are not tongue-tied, as is commonly believed; but they pour forth that vocal breath through the nostrils, as though bellowing,[6] because there is either no passage at all for the voice to the mouth, or it is not so open as to be able to send forth the full voice. And this generally comes to pass by nature; sometimes also it happens by accident that this entrance is blocked up and does not transmit the voice to the tongue, and thus makes those who can speak dumb. And when this happens, the hearing also must necessarily be blocked up; so that because it cannot emit the voice, it is also incapable of admitting it. Therefore this passage has been opened for the purpose of speaking. It also affords this advantage, that in frequenting the bath,[7] because the nostrils are not able to endure the heat, the hot air is taken in by the mouth; also, if phlegm contracted by cold shall have happened to stop up the breathing pores of the nostrils, we may be able to draw the air through the mouth, lest, if the passage[8] should be obstructed, the breath should be stifled. But the food being received into the stomach, and mixed with the moisture of the drink, when it has now been digested by the heat, its juice, being in an indescribable manner diffused through the limbs, bedews and invigorates the whole body.

The manifold coils also of the intestines, and their length rolled together on themselves, and yet fastened with one band, are a wonderful work of God. For when the stomach has sent forth from itself the food softened, it is gradually thrust forth through those windings of the intestines, so that whatever of the moisture by which the body is nourished is in them, is divided to all the members. And yet, lest in any place it should happen to adhere and remain fixed, which might have taken place on account of the turnings of the coils,[9] which often turn back to themselves, and which could not have happened without injury, He has spread over[10] these from within a thicker juice, that the secretions of the belly might more easily work their way through the slippery substance to their outlets. It is also a most skilful arrangement, that the bladder, which birds do not use, though it is separated from the intestines, and has no tube by which it may draw the urine from them, is nevertheless filled and distended with moisture. And it is not difficult to see how this comes to pass. For the parts of the intestines which receive the food and drink from the belly are more open than the other coils, and much more delicate. These entwine themselves around and encompass the bladder; and when the meat and the drink have arrived at these parts in a mixed state, the excrement becomes more solid, and passes through, but all the moisture is strained through those tender parts,[11] and the bladder, the membrane of which is equally fine and delicate, absorbs and collects it, so as to send it forth where nature has opened an outlet.

CHAP. XII. — DE UTERO, ET CONCEPTIONE ATQUE SEXIBUS.[12]

De utero quoque et conceptione, quoniam de internis loquimur, dici necesse est, ne quid præterisse videamur; quæ quamquam in operto latent, sensum tamen atque intelligentiam latere non possunt. Vena in maribus, quæ seminium continet, duplex est, paulo interior, quam illud humoris obscœni receptaculum. Sicut enim renes duo sunt, itemque testes, ita et venæ seminales duæ, in una tamen compage cohærentes; quod videmus in corporibus animalium, cùm interfecta[13] patefiunt. Sed illa dexterior masculinum continet semen, sinisterior fœmininum; et omnino in toto corpore pars dextra masculina est, sinistra vero fœminina. Ipsum semen quidam putant ex medullis tantum, qui-

[1] Teneritudinem domicilii.
[2] Nare; hence "nares," the nostrils.
[3] Interpatet.
[4] Colles faucium. Others read "toles," i.e., the tonsils.
[5] Inoffensum tenorem, i.e., without obstruction, not striking against any object — smooth.
[6] Quasi mugiens.
[7] In lavacris celebrandis.
[8] Obstructâ meandi facultate.
[9] Voluminum flexiones.
[10] Oblevit ea intrinsecus crassiore succo.
[11] Per illam teneritudinem.
[12] It has been judged advisable not to translate this and the first part of the next chapter.
[13] Alii legunt "intersecta."

dam ex omni corpore ad venam genitalem confluere, ibique concrescere. Sed hoc, humana mens, quomodo fiat, non potest comprehendere. Item in fœminis uterus in duas se dividit partes, quæ in diversum diffusæ ac reflexæ, circumplicantur, sicut arietis cornua. Quæ pars in dextram retorquetur, masculina est; quæ in sinistram, fœminina.

Conceptum igitur Varro et Aristoteles sic fieri arbitrantur. Aiunt non tantum maribus inesse semen, verum etiam fœminis, et inde plerumque matribus similes procreari; sed earum semen sanguinem esse purgatum, quod si recte cum virili mixtum sit, utraque concreta et simul coagulata informari: et primum quidem cor hominis effingi, quod in eo sit et vita omnis et sapientia; denique totum opus quadragesimo die consummari. Ex abortionibus hæc fortasse collecta sunt. In avium tamen fœtibus primum oculos fingi dubium non est, quod in ovis sæpe deprehendimus. Unde fieri non posse arbitror, quin fictio a capite sumat exordium.

Similitudines autem in corporibus filiorum sic fieri putant. Cum semina inter se permixta coalescunt, si virile superaverit, patri similem provenire, seu marem, seu fœminam; si muliebre prævaluerit, progeniem cujusque sexus ad imaginem respondere maternam. Id autem prævalet e duobus, quod fuerit uberius; alterum enim quodammodo amplectitur et includit: hinc plerumque fieri, ut unius tantum lineamenta prætendat. Si vero æqua fuerit ex pari semente permixtio, figuras quoque misceri, ut soboles illa communis aut neutrum referre videatur, quia totum ex altero non habet; aut utrumque, quia partem de singulis mutuata est. Nam in corporibus animalium videmus aut confundi parentum colores, ac fieri tertium neutri generantium simile; aut utriusque sic exprimi, ut discoloribus membris per omne corpus concors mixtura varietur. Dispares quoque naturæ hoc modo fieri putantur. Cum forte in lævam uteri partem masculinæ stirpis semen inciderit, marem quidem gigni opinatio est; sed quia sit in fœminina parte conceptus, aliquid in se habere fœmineum, supra quam decus virile patiatur; vel formam insignem, vel nimium candorem, vel corporis levitatem, vel artus delicatos, vel staturam brevem, vel vocem gracilem, vel animum imbecillum, vel ex his plura. Item, si partem in dextram semen fœminini sexus influxerit, fœminam quidem procreari; sed quoniam in masculina parte concepta sit, habere in se aliquid virilitatis, ultra quam sexus ratio permittat; aut valida membra, aut immoderatam longitudinem, aut fuscum colorem, aut hispidam faciem, aut vultum indecorum, aut vocem robustam, aut animum audacem, aut ex his plura.

Si verò masculinum in dexteram, fœmininum in sinistram pervenerit, utrosque fœtus recte provenire; ut et fœminis per omnia naturæ suæ decus constet, et maribus tam mente, quam corpore robur virile servetur. Istud vero ipsum quam mirabile institutum Dei, quod ad conservationem generum singulorum, duos sexus maris ac fœminæ machinatus est; quibus inter se per voluptatis illecebras copulatis, successiva soboles pareretur, ne omne genus viventium conditio mortalitatis extingueret. Sed plus roboris maribus attributum est, quo facilius ad patientiam jugi maritalis fœminæ cogerentur. Vir itaque nominatus est, quod major in eo vis est, quàm in fœmina; et hinc virtus nomen accepit. Item mulier (ut Varro interpretatur) a mollitie, immutata et detracta littera, velut *mollier;* cui suscepto fœtu, cùm partus appropinquare jam cœpit, turgescentes mammæ dulcibus succis distenduntur, et ad nutrimenta nascentis fontibus lacteis fœcundum pectus exuberat. Nec enim decebat aliud quàm ut sapiens animal a corde alimoniam duceret. Idque ipsum solertissimè comparatum est, ut candens ac pinguis humor teneritudinem novi corporis irrigaret, donec ad capiendos fortiores cibos, et dentibus instruatur, et viribus roboretur. Sed redeamus ad propositum, ut cætera, quæ supersunt, breviter explicemus.

CHAP. XIII. — OF THE LOWER MEMBERS.

Poteram nunc ego ipsorum quoque genitalium membrorum mirificam rationem tibi exponere, nisi me pudor ab hujusmodi sermone revocaret: itaque a nobis indumento verecundiæ, quæ sunt pudenda velentur. Quod ad hanc rem attinet, queri satis est, homines impios ac profanos summum nefas admittere, qui divinum et admirabile Dei opus, ad propagandam successionem inexcogitabili ratione provisum et effectum, vel ad turpissimos quæstus, vel ad obscœnæ libidinis pudenda opera convertunt, ut jam nihil aliud ex re sanctissima petant, quam inanem et sterilem voluptatem.

How is it with respect to the other parts of the body? Are they without order and beauty? The flesh rounded off into the *nates*, how adapted to the office of sitting! and this also more firm than in the other limbs, lest by the pressure of the bulk of the body it should give way to the bones. Also the length of the thighs drawn out, and strengthened by broader muscles, in order that it might more easily sustain the weight of the body; and as this is gradually contracted, it is bounded[1] by the knees, the comely joints[2] of which supply a bend which is most adapted for walking and sitting. Also the legs not drawn out in an equal manner, lest an unbecoming figure should deform the feet; but they are at once strengthened and adorned by

[1] Genua determinant.
[2] Nodi.

well-turned[1] calves gently standing out and gradually diminishing.

But in the soles of the feet there is the same plan as in the hands, but yet very different: for since these are, as it were, the foundations of the whole body,[2] the admirable Artificer has not made them of a round appearance, lest man should be unable to stand, or should need other feet for standing, as is the case with quadrupeds; but He has formed them of a longer and more extended shape, that they might make the body firm by their flatness,[3] from which circumstance their name was given to them. The toes are of the same number with the fingers, for the sake of appearance rather than utility; and on this account they are both joined together, and short, and put together by gradations; and that which is the greatest of these, since it was not befitting that it should be separated from the others, as in the hand, has been so arranged in order, that it appears to differ from the others in magnitude and the small space which intervenes. This beautiful union[4] of them strengthens the pressure of the feet with no slight aid; for we cannot be excited to running, unless, our toes being pressed against the ground, and resting upon the soil, we take an impetus and a spring. I appear to have explained all things of which the plan is capable of being understood. I now come to those things which are either doubtful or obscure.

CHAP. XIV. — OF THE UNKNOWN PURPOSE OF SOME OF THE INTESTINES.

It is evident that there are many things in the body, the force and purpose of which no one can perceive but He who made them. Can any one suppose that he is able to relate what is the advantage, and what the effect, of that slight transparent membrane by which the stomach is netted over and covered? What the twofold resemblance of the kidneys? which Varro says are so named because streams of foul moisture arise from these; which is far from being the case, because, rising on either side of the spine, they are united, and are separated from the intestines. What is the use of the spleen? What of the liver? Organs which appear as it were to be made up[5] of disordered blood. What of the very bitter moisture of the gall? What of the heart? unless we shall happen to think that they ought to be believed, who think that the affection of anger is placed in the gall, that of fear in the heart, of joy in the spleen. But they will have it that the office of the liver is, by its embrace and heat, to digest the food in the stomach; some think that the desires of the amorous passions are contained in the liver.

First of all, the acuteness of the human sense is unable to perceive these things, because their offices lie concealed; nor, when laid open, do they show their uses. For, if it were so, perhaps the more gentle animals would either have no gall at all, or less than the wild beasts; the more timid ones would have more heart, the more lustful would have more liver, the more playful more spleen. As, therefore, we perceive that we hear with our ears, that we see with our eyes, that we smell with our nostrils; so assuredly we should perceive that we are angry with the gall, that we desire with the liver, that we rejoice with the spleen. Since, therefore, we do not at all perceive from what part those affections come, it is possible that they may come from another source, and that those organs may have a different effect to that which we suppose. We cannot prove, however, that they who discuss these things speak falsely. But I think that all things which relate to the motions of the mind and soul, are of so obscure and profound a nature, that it is beyond the power of man to see through them clearly. This, however, ought to be sure and undoubted, that so many objects and so many organs have one and the same office — to retain the soul in the body. But what office is particularly assigned to each, who can know, except the Designer, to whom alone His own work is known?

CHAP. XV. — OF THE VOICE.

But what account can we give of the voice? Grammarians, indeed, and philosophers, define the voice to be air struck by the breath; from which words[6] derive their name: which is plainly false. For the voice is not produced outside of the mouth, but within, and therefore that opinion is more probable, that the breath, being compressed, when it has struck against the obstacle presented by the throat, forces out the sound of the voice: as when we send down the breath into an open hemlock stalk, having applied it to the lips, and the breath, reverberating from the hollow of the stalk, and rolled back from the bottom, while it returns[7] to that descending through meeting with itself, striving for an outlet, produces a sound; and the wind, rebounding by itself, is animated into vocal breath. Now, whether this is true, God, who is the designer, may see. For the voice appears to arise not from the mouth, but from the innermost breast. In fine, even when the mouth is closed, a sound such as is possible is emitted from the nostrils.

1 Teretes.
2 Corporis. Other editions have "operis," i.e., of the whole work.
3 Planitie, hence "planta."
4 Germanitas, "a brotherhood, or close connection."
5 Concreta esse. [See p. 180, note 1, *supra*.]
6 Verba: as though derived from "verbero," to strike.
7 Dum ad descendentem occursu suo redit. Others read, "Dum descendentem reddit."

Moreover, also, the voice is not affected by that greatest breath with which we gasp, but with a light and not compressed breath, as often as we wish. It has not therefore been comprehended in what manner it takes place, or what it is altogether. And do not imagine that I am now falling into the opinion of the Academy, for all things are not incomprehensible. For as it must be confessed that many things are unknown, since God has willed that they should exceed the understanding of man; so, however, it must be acknowledged that there are many which may both be perceived by the senses and comprehended by the reason. But we shall devote an entire treatise to the refutation of the philosophers. Let us therefore finish the course over which we are now running.

CHAP. XVI. — OF THE MIND AND ITS SEAT.

That the nature of the mind is also incomprehensible, who can be ignorant, but he who is altogether destitute of mind, since it is not known in what place the mind is situated, or of what nature it is? Therefore various things have been discussed by philosophers concerning its nature and place. But I will not conceal what my own sentiments are: not that I should affirm that it is so — for in a doubtful matter it is the part of a foolish person to do this; but that when I have set forth the difficulty of the matter, you may understand how great is the magnitude of the divine works. Some would have it, that the seat of the mind is in the breast. But if this is so, how wonderful is it, that a faculty which is situated in an obscure and dark habitation should be employed in so great a light of reason and intelligence; then that the senses from every part of the body come together to it, so that it appears to be present in any quarter of the limbs! Others have said that its seat is in the brain: and, indeed, they have used probable arguments, saying that it was doubtless befitting that that which had the government of the whole body should especially have its abode in the highest place, as though in the citadel of the body; and that nothing should be in a more elevated position than that which governs the whole by reason, just as the Lord Himself, and Ruler of the universe, is in the highest place. Then they say that the organs which are the ministers of each sense, that is, of hearing, and seeing, and smelling, are situated in the head, and that the channels of all these lead not to the breast, but to the brain: otherwise we must be more slow in the exercise of our senses, until the power of sensation by a long course should descend through the neck even to the breast. These, in truth, do not greatly err, or perchance not at all.

For the mind, which exercises control over the body, appears to be placed in the highest part, the head, as God is in heaven; but when it is engaged in any reflection, it appears to pass to the breast, and, as it were, to withdraw to some secret recess, that it may elicit and draw forth counsel, as it were, from a hidden treasury. And therefore, when we are intent upon reflection, and when the mind, being occupied, has withdrawn itself to the inner depth,[1] we are accustomed neither to hear the things which sound about us, nor to see the things which stand in our way. But whether this is the case, it is assuredly a matter of admiration how this takes place, since there is no passage from the brain to the breast. But if it is not so, nevertheless it is no less a matter of admiration that, by some divine plan or other, it is caused that it appears to be so. Can any fail to admire that that living and heavenly faculty which is called the mind or the soul, is of such volubility[2] that it does not rest even then when it is asleep; of such rapidity, that it surveys the whole heaven at one moment of time; and, if it wills, flies over seas, traverses lands and cities, — in short, places in its own sight all things which it pleases, however far and widely they are removed?

And does any one wonder if the divine mind of God, being extended[3] through all parts of the universe, runs to and fro, and rules all things, governs all things, being everywhere present, everywhere diffused; when the strength and power of the human mind, though enclosed within a mortal body, is so great, that it can in no way be restrained even by the barriers of this heavy and slothful body, to which it is bound, from bestowing upon itself, in its impatience of rest, the power of wandering without restraint? Whether, therefore, the mind has its dwelling in the head or in the breast, can any one comprehend what power of reason effects, that that incomprehensible faculty either remains fixed in the marrow of the brain, or in that blood divided into two parts[4] which is enclosed in the heart; and not infer from this very circumstance how great is the power of God, because the soul does not see itself, or of what nature or where it is; and if it did see, yet it would not be able to perceive in what manner an incorporeal substance is united with one which is corporeal? Or if the mind has no fixed locality, but runs here and there scattered through the whole body, — which is possible, and was asserted by Xenocrates, the disciple of Plato, — then, inasmuch as intelligence is present in every part of

---

1 In altum se abdiderit. [An interesting "evolution from self-consciousness," not altogether to be despised. In connection with the tripartite nature of man (of which see vol. iii. p. 474), we may well inquire as to the seat of the ψυχὴ and the πνεῦμα, severally, on this hint.]

2 Mobilitatis.

3 Intenta discurrit. [2 Chron. xvi. 9; Zech. iv. 10.]

4 Bipartito.

the body, it cannot be understood what that mind is, or what its qualities are, since its nature is so subtle and refined, that, though infused into solid organs by a living and, as it were, ardent perception, it is mingled with all the members.

But take care that you never think it probable, as Aristoxenus said, that the mind has no existence, but that the power of perception exists from the constitution of the body and the construction of the organs, as harmony does in the case of the lyre. For musicians call the stretching and sounding of the strings to entire strains, without any striking of notes in agreement with them, harmony. They will have it, therefore, that the soul in man exists in a manner like that by which harmonious modulation exists on the lyre; namely, that the firm uniting of the separate parts of the body and the vigour of all the limbs agreeing together, makes that perceptible motion, and adjusts[1] the mind, as well-stretched things produce harmonious sound. And as, in the lyre, when anything has been interrupted or relaxed, the whole method of the strain is disturbed and destroyed; so in the body, when any part of the limbs receives an injury, the whole are weakened, and all being corrupted and thrown into confusion, the power of perception is destroyed: and this is called death. But he, if he had possessed any mind, would never have transferred harmony from the lyre to man. For the lyre cannot of its own accord send forth a sound, so that there can be in this any comparison and resemblance to a living person; but the soul both reflects and is moved of its own accord. But if there were in us anything resembling harmony, it would be moved by a blow from without, as the strings of the lyre are by the hands; whereas without the handling of the artificer, and the stroke of the fingers, they lie mute and motionless. But doubtless he[2] ought to have beaten by the hand, that he might at length observe; for his mind, badly compacted from his members, was in a state of torpor.

CHAP. XVII. — OF THE SOUL, AND THE OPINION OF PHILOSOPHERS CONCERNING IT.

It remains to speak of the soul, although its system and nature cannot be perceived. Nor, therefore, do we fail to understand that the soul is immortal, since whatever is vigorous and is in motion by itself at all times, and cannot be seen or touched, must be eternal. But what the soul is, is not yet agreed upon by philosophers, and perhaps will never be agreed upon. For some have said that it is blood, others that it is fire, others wind, from which it has received its name of *anima*, or *animus*, because in Greek the wind is called *anemos*,[3] and yet none of these appears to have spoken anything. For if the soul appears to be extinguished when the blood is poured forth through a wound, or is exhausted by the heat of fevers, it does not therefore follow that the system of the soul is to be placed in the material of the blood; as though a question should arise as to the nature of the light which we make use of, and the answer should be given that it is oil, for when that is consumed the light is extinguished: since they are plainly different, but the one is the nourishment of the other. Therefore the soul appears to be like light, since it is not itself blood, but is nourished by the moisture of the blood, as light is by oil.

But they who have supposed it to be fire made use of this argument, that when the soul is present the body is warm, but on its departure the body grows cold. But fire is both without perception and is seen, and burns when touched. But the soul is both endowed with perception and cannot be seen, and does not burn. From which it is evident that the soul is something like God. But they who suppose that it is wind are deceived by this, because we appear to live by drawing breath from the air. Varro gives this definition: "The soul is air conceived in the mouth, warmed in the lungs, heated in the heart, diffused into the body." These things are most plainly false. For I say that the nature of things of this kind is not so obscure, that we do not even understand what cannot be true. If any one should say to me that the heaven is of brass, or crystal, or, as Empedocles says, that it is frozen air, must I at once assent because I do not know of what material the heaven is? For as I know not this, I know that. Therefore the soul is not air conceived in the mouth, because the soul is produced much before air can be conceived in the mouth. For it is not introduced into the body after birth, as it appears to some philosophers, but immediately after conception, when the divine necessity has formed the offspring in the womb; for it so lives within the bowels of its mother, that it is increased in growth, and delights to bound with repeated beatings. In short, there must be a miscarriage if the living young within shall die. The other parts of the definition have reference to this, that during those nine months in which we were in the womb we appear to have been dead. None, therefore, of these three opinions is true. We cannot, however, say that they who held these sentiments were false to such an extent that they said nothing at all; for we live at once by the blood, and heat, and breath. But since the soul

1 Concinnet.
2 Aristoxenus, whose opinion has been mentioned above.
3 ἄνεμος.

exists in the body by the union of all these, they did not express what it was in its own proper sense;[1] for as it cannot be seen, so it cannot be expressed.

CHAP. XVIII. — OF THE SOUL AND THE MIND, AND THEIR AFFECTIONS.

There follows another, and in itself an inexplicable inquiry: Whether the soul and the mind are the same, or there be one faculty by which we live, and another by which we perceive and have discernment.[2] There are not wanting arguments on either side. For they who say that they are one faculty make use of this argument, that we cannot live without perception, nor perceive without life, and therefore that that which is incapable of separation cannot be different; but that whatever it is, it has the office of living and the method of perception. On which account two[3] Epicurean poets speak of the mind and the soul indifferently. But they who say that they are different argue in this way: That the mind is one thing, and the soul another, may be understood from this, that the mind may be extinguished while the soul is uninjured, which is accustomed to happen in the case of the insane; also, that the soul is put to rest[4] by death, the mind by sleep, and indeed in such a manner that it is not only ignorant of what is taking place,[5] or where it is, but it is even deceived by the contemplation of false objects. And how this takes place cannot accurately be perceived; why it takes place can be perceived. For we can by no means rest unless the mind is kept occupied by the similitudes[6] of visions. But the mind lies hid, oppressed with sleep, as fire buried[7] by ashes drawn over it; but if you stir it a little it again blazes, and, as it were, wakes up.[8] Therefore it is called away by images,[9] until the limbs, bedewed with sleep, are invigorated; for the body while the perception is awake, although it lies motionless, yet is not at rest, because the perception burns in it, and vibrates as a flame, and keeps all the limbs bound to itself.

But when the mind is transferred from its application to the contemplation of images, then at length the whole body is resolved into rest. But the mind is transferred from dark thought, when, under the influence of darkness, it has begun to be alone with itself. While it is intent upon those things concerning which it is reflecting, sleep suddenly creeps on, and the thought itself imperceptibly turns aside to the nearest appearances:[10] thus it begins also to see those things which it had placed before its eyes. Then it proceeds further, and finds diversions[11] for itself, that it may not interrupt the most healthy repose of the body. For as the mind is diverted in the day by true sights, so that it does not sleep; so is it diverted in the night by false sights, so that it is not aroused. For if it perceives no images, it will follow of necessity either that it is awake, or that it is asleep in perpetual death. Therefore the system of dreaming has been given by God for the sake of sleeping; and, indeed, it has been given to all animals in common; but this especially to man, that when God gave this system on account of rest, He left to Himself the power of teaching man future events by means of the dream.[12] For narratives often testify that there have been dreams which have had an immediate and a remarkable accomplishment,[13] and the answers of our prophets have been after the character of a dream.[14] On which account they are not always true, nor always false, as Virgil testified,[15] who supposed that there were two gates for the passage of dreams. But those which are false are seen for the sake of sleeping; those which are true are sent by God, that by this revelation we may learn impending goods or evils.

CHAP. XIX. — OF THE SOUL, AND IT GIVEN BY GOD.

A question also may arise respecting this, whether the soul is produced from the father, or rather from the mother, or indeed from both. But I think that this judgment is to be formed as though in a doubtful matter.[16] For nothing is true of these three opinions, because souls are produced neither from both nor from either. For a body may be produced from a body, since something is contributed from both; but a soul cannot be produced from souls, because nothing can depart from a slight and incomprehensible subject. Therefore the manner of the production of souls belongs entirely to God alone.

> "In fine, we are all sprung from a heavenly seed, all
> all have that same Father."

as Lucretius[17] says. For nothing but what is mortal can be generated from mortals. Nor ought he to be deemed a father who in no way

---

1 Proprie.

2 [See cap. 16, p. 296, note 1, *supra;* also vol. ii. p. 102, note 2, this series.]

3 Lucretius is undoubtedly one of the poets here referred to; some think that Virgil, others that Horace, is the second.

4 Sopiatur.

5 Quid fiat. Others read "quid faciat."

6 Imaginibus.

7 Sopitus.

8 Evigilat.

9 Simulacris.

10 Species.

11 Avocamenta.

12 Thus Joseph and Daniel were interpreters of dreams; and the prophet Joel (ii. 28) foretells this as a mark of the last days, "Your old men shall dream dreams, your young men shall see visions."

13 Quorum præsens et admirabilis fuerit eventus. [A sober view of the facts revealed in Scripture, and which, in the days of miracles, influenced so many of the noblest minds in the Church.]

14 Ex parte somnii constiterunt. Some editions read, "ex parte somniis constituerunt."

15 *Æneid*, vi. 894.

16 Sed ego id in eo jure ab ancipiti vindico.

17 ii. 991.

perceives that he has transmitted or breathed a soul from his own; nor, if he perceives it, comprehends in his mind when or in what manner that effect is produced.

From this it is evident that souls are not given by parents, but by one and the same God and Father of all, who alone has the law and method of their birth, since He alone produces them. For the part of the earthly parent is nothing more than with a sense of pleasure to emit the moisture of the body, in which is the material of birth, or to receive it; and to this work man's power is limited,[1] nor has he any further power. Therefore men wish for the birth of sons, because they do not themselves bring it about. Everything beyond this is the work of God, — namely, the conception itself, and the moulding of the body, and the breathing in of life, and the bringing forth in safety, and whatever afterwards contributes to the preservation of man: it is His gift that we breathe, that we live, and are vigorous. For, besides that we owe it to His bounty that we are safe in body, and that He supplies us with nourishment from various sources, He also gives to man wisdom, which no earthly father can by any means give; and therefore it often happens that foolish sons are born from wise parents, and wise sons from foolish parents, which some persons attribute to fate and the stars. But this is not now the time to discuss the subject of fate. It is sufficient to say this, that even if the stars hold together the efficacy of all things, it is nevertheless certain that all things are done by God, who both made and set in order the stars themselves. They are therefore senseless who detract this power from God, and assign it to His work.

He would have it, therefore, to be in our own power, whether we use or do not use this divine and excellent gift of God. For, having granted this, He bound man himself by the mystery[2] of virtue, by which he might be able to gain life. For great is the power, great the reason, great the mysterious purpose of man; and if any one shall not abandon this, nor betray his fidelity and devotedness, he must be happy: he, in short, to sum up the matter in few words, must of necessity resemble God. For he is in error whosoever judges of[3] man by his flesh. For this worthless body[4] with which we are clothed is the receptacle of man.[5] For man himself can neither be touched, nor looked upon, nor grasped, because he lies hidden within this body, which is seen. And if he shall be more luxurious and delicate in this life than its nature demands, if he shall despise virtue, and give himself to the pursuit of fleshly lusts, he will fall and be pressed down to the earth; but if (as his duty is) he shall readily and constantly maintain his position, which is right for him, and he has rightly obtained,[6] — if he shall not be enslaved to the earth, which he ought to trample upon and overcome, he will gain eternal life.

CHAP. XX. — OF HIMSELF AND THE TRUTH.

These things I have written to you, Demetrianus, for the present in few words, and perhaps with more obscurity than was befitting, in accordance with the necessity of circumstances and the time, with which you ought to be content, since you are about to receive more and better things if God shall favour us. Then, accordingly, I will exhort you with greater clearness and truth to the learning of true philosophy. For I have determined to commit to writing as many things as I shall be able, which have reference to the condition of a happy life; and that indeed against the philosophers, since they are pernicious and weighty for the disturbing of the truth. For the force of their eloquence is incredible, and their subtlety in argument and disputation may easily deceive any one; and these we will refute partly by our own weapons, but partly by weapons borrowed from their mutual wrangling, so that it may be evident that they rather introduced error than removed it.

Perhaps you may wonder that I venture to undertake so great a deed. Shall we then suffer the truth to be extinguished or crushed? I, in truth, would more willingly fail even under this burthen. For if Marcus Tullius, the unparalleled example of eloquence itself, was often vanquished by men void of learning and eloquence, — who, however, were striving for that which was true, — why should we despair that the truth itself will by its own peculiar force and clearness avail against deceitful and captious eloquence? They indeed are wont to profess themselves advocates of the truth; but who can defend that which he has not learned, or make clear to others that which he himself does not know? I seem to promise a great thing; but there is need of the favour of Heaven, that ability and time may be given us for following our purpose. But if life is to be wished for by a wise man, assuredly I should wish to live for no other reason than that I may effect something which may be worthy of life, and which may be useful to my readers, if

[1] Et citra hoc opus homo resistit. The compound word "resistit" is used for the simple *sistit* — "stands."

[2] Sacramento.

[3] Metitur, "measures."

[4] Corpusculum. The diminutive appears to imply contempt.

[5] The expression is too general, since the body as well as the soul is a true part of man's nature. [Perhaps so; but Lactantius is thinking of St. Paul's expression (Philipp. iii. 21), "the body of our *humiliation*."]

[6] Quem rectum rectè sortitus est. In some editions the word "recte" is omitted.

not for eloquence, because there is in me but a slight stream of eloquence, at any rate for living, which is especially needful. And when I have accomplished this, I shall think that I have lived enough, and that I have discharged the duty of a man, if my labour shall have freed some men from errors, and have directed them to the path which leads to heaven.

GENERAL NOTE BY THE AMERICAN EDITOR.

JUST here I economize a little spare room to note the cynical Gibbon's ideas about Lactantius and his works. He quotes him freely, and recognises his Ciceronian Latinity, and even the elegance of his rhetoric, and the spirit and eloquence with which he can garnish the "dismal tale" of coming judgments, based on the Apocalypse. But then, again[1] he speaks of him as an "obscure rhetorician," and affects a doubt as to his sources of information, notably in doubting the conversation between Galerius and Diocletian which forced the latter to abdicate. This is before he decides to attribute the work on the *Deaths of Persecutors* to somebody else, or, rather, to quote its author ambiguously as Cæcilius. And here we may insert what he says on this subject, as follows: —

"It is certain that this . . . was composed and published while Licinius, sovereign of the East, still preserved the friendship of Constantine and of the Christians. Every reader of taste must perceive that the style is of a very different and inferior character to that of Lactantius; and such, indeed, is the judgment of Le Clerc[2] and Lardner.[3] Three arguments (from the title of the book and from the names of Donatus and Cæcilius) are produced by the advocates of Lactantius.[4] Each of these proofs is, singly, weak and defective; *but their concurrence has great weight.* I have often fluctuated, and shall *tamely*[5] follow the Colbert MS. in calling the author, whoever he was, *Cæcilius.*"

After this the critic adheres to this ambiguity. I have no wish to argue otherwise. Quite as important are his notes on the *Institutes.* He states the probable conjecture of *two* original editions, — the one under Diocletian, and the other under Licinius. Then he says:[6] —

"I am *almost* convinced that Lactantius dedicated his *Institutions* to the sovereign of Gaul at a time when Galerius, Maximin, and even Licinius, persecuted the Christians; that is, between the years A.D. 306 and A.D. 311."

On the dubious passages[7] he remarks:[8] —

"The first and most important of these is, indeed, wanting in twenty-eight MSS., but is found in nineteen. If we weigh the comparative value of those MSS., one, . . . in the King of France's library,[9] may be alleged in its favour. But the passage is omitted in the correct MS. of Bologna, which the Père de Montfaucon[10] ascribes to the sixth or seventh century. The taste of most of the editors[11] has *felt* the genuine style of Lactantius."

Do not many indications point to the natural suggestion of a *third* original edition, issued after the conversion of Constantine? Or the questionable passages may be the interpolations of Lactantius himself.

---

1 Cap. xiv. (vol. i.) p. 452.
2 *Bibliothèque Ancienne et Mod.*, tom. iii. p. 438.
3 *Credib.*, part ii. vol. vii. p. 94.
4 The Père Lestocq, tom. ii. pp. 46–60.
5 This word is italicized by Gibbon.
6 Vol. ii. cap. 20.
7 *Inst.*, i. 1 and vii. 27.
8 Vol. ii. cap. 20.
9 Now (1880) a thousand years old.
10 *Diarium Italicum*, p. 409.
11 "Except Isæus," says Gibbon, who refers to the edition of our author by Dufresnoy, tom. i. p. 596.

OF THE MANNER IN WHICH THE PERSECUTORS DIED.[1]

ADDRESSED TO DONATUS.

CHAP. I.

THE Lord has heard those supplications which you, my best beloved Donatus,[2] pour forth in His presence all the day long, and the supplications of the rest of our brethren, who by a glorious confession have obtained an everlasting crown, the reward of their faith. Behold, all the adversaries are destroyed, and tranquillity having been re-established throughout the Roman empire, the late oppressed Church arises again, and the temple of God, overthrown by the hands of the wicked, is built with more glory than before. For God has raised up princes to rescind the impious and sanguinary edicts of the tyrants and provide for the welfare of mankind; so that now the cloud of past times is dispelled, and peace and serenity gladden all hearts. And after the furious whirlwind and black tempest, the heavens are now become calm, and the wished-for light has shone forth; and now God, the hearer of prayer, by His divine aid has lifted His prostrate and afflicted servants from the ground, has brought to an end the united devices of the wicked, and wiped off the tears from the faces of those who mourned. They who insulted over the Divinity, lie low; they who cast down the holy temple, are fallen with more tremendous ruin; and the tormentors of just men have poured out their guilty souls amidst plagues inflicted by Heaven, and amidst deserved tortures. For God delayed to punish them, that, by great and marvellous examples, He might teach posterity that He alone is God, and that with fit vengeance He executes judgment on the proud, the impious, and the persecutors.[3]

Of the end of those men I have thought good to publish a narrative, that all who are afar off, and all who shall arise hereafter, may learn how the Almighty manifested His power and sovereign greatness in rooting out and utterly destroying the enemies of His name. And this will become evident, when I relate *who* were the persecutors of the Church from the time of its first constitution, and *what* were the punishments by which the divine Judge, in His severity, took vengeance on them.

CHAP. II.

In the latter days of the Emperor Tiberius, in the consulship of Ruberius Geminus and Fufius Geminus, and on the tenth of the kalends of April,[4] as I find it written, Jesus Christ was crucified by the Jews.[5] After He had risen again on the third day, He gathered together His apostles, whom fear, at the time of His being laid hold on, had put to flight; and while He sojourned with them forty days, He opened their hearts, interpreted to them the Scripture, which hitherto had been wrapped up in obscurity, ordained and fitted them for the preaching of His word and doctrine, and regulated all things concerning the institutions of the New Testament; and this having been accomplished, a cloud and whirlwind enveloped Him, and caught Him up from the sight of men unto heaven.

His apostles were at that time eleven in number, to whom were added Matthias, in the room of the traitor Judas, and afterwards Paul. Then were they dispersed throughout all the earth to preach the Gospel, as the Lord their Master had commanded them; and during twenty-five years, and until the beginning of the reign of the Emperor Nero, they occupied themselves in laying the foundations of the Church in every province and city. And while Nero reigned, the Apostle Peter came to Rome, and, through the power of God committed unto him, wrought certain miracles, and, by turning many to the true religion, built up a faithful and stedfast temple

---

1 [Not "*the* persecutors," but only some of them. This treatise is, in fact, a most precious relic of antiquity, and a striking narrative of the events which led to the "conversion of the Empire," so called. Its historical character is noted by Gibbon, *D. and F.*, vol. ii. 20, n. 40.]

2 [See cap. 16, *infra*.]

3 [Let any one who visits Rome stand before the Arch of Constantine, and, while he looks upon it (as the mark of an epoch), let him at the same time behold the Colosseum close at hand, and there let him recall this noble chapter.]

4 23d of March.

5 [Elucidation, p. 322.]

unto the Lord. When Nero heard of those things, and observed that not only in Rome, but in every other place, a great multitude revolted daily from the worship of idols, and, condemning their old ways, went over to the new religion, he, an execrable and pernicious tyrant, sprung forward to raze the heavenly temple and destroy the true faith. He it was who first persecuted the servants of God; he crucified Peter, and slew Paul:[1] nor did he escape with impunity; for God looked on the affliction of His people; and therefore the tyrant, bereaved of authority, and precipitated from the height of empire, suddenly disappeared, and even the burial-place of that noxious wild beast was nowhere to be seen. This has led some persons of extravagant imagination to suppose that, having been conveyed to a distant region, he is still reserved alive; and to him they apply the Sibylline verses concerning

> "The fugitive, who slew his own mother, being to come from the uttermost boundaries of the earth;"

as if he who was the first should also be the last persecutor, and thus prove the forerunner of Antichrist! But we ought not to believe those who, affirming that the two prophets Enoch and Elias have been translated into some remote place that they might attend our Lord when He shall come to judgment,[2] also fancy that Nero is to appear hereafter as the forerunner of the devil, when he shall come to lay waste the earth and overthrow mankind.

CHAP. III.

After an interval of some years from the death of Nero, there arose another tyrant no less wicked (Domitian), who, although his government was exceedingly odious, for a very long time oppressed his subjects, and reigned in security, until at length he stretched forth his impious hands against the Lord. Having been instigated by evil demons to persecute the righteous people, he was then delivered into the power of his enemies, and suffered due punishment. To be murdered in his own palace was not vengeance ample enough: the very memory of his name was erased. For although he had erected many admirable edifices, and rebuilt the Capitol, and left other distinguished marks of his magnificence, yet the senate did so persecute his name, as to leave no remains of his statues, or traces of the inscriptions put up in honour of him; and by most solemn and severe decrees it branded him, even after death, with perpetual infamy. Thus, the commands of the tyrant having been rescinded, the Church was not only restored to her former state, but she shone forth with additional splendour, and became more and more flourishing. And in the times that followed, while many well-deserving princes guided the helm of the Roman empire, the Church suffered no violent assaults from her enemies, and she extended her hands unto the east and unto the west, insomuch that now there was not any the most remote corner of the earth to which the divine religion had not penetrated, or any nation of manners so barbarous that did not, by being converted to the worship of God, become mild and gentle.[3]

CHAP. IV.

This long peace,[4] however, was afterwards interrupted. Decius appeared in the world, an accursed wild beast, to afflict the Church, — and *who* but a bad man would persecute religion? It seems as if he had been raised to sovereign eminence, at once to rage against God, and at once to fall; for, having undertaken an expedition against the Carpi, who had then possessed themselves of Dacia and Moefia, he was suddenly surrounded by the barbarians, and slain, together with great part of his army; nor could he be honoured with the rites of sepulture, but, stripped and naked, he lay to be devoured by wild beasts and birds,[5] — a fit end for the enemy of God.

CHAP. V.

And presently Valerian also, in a mood alike frantic, lifted up his impious hands to assault God, and, although his time was short, shed much righteous blood. But God punished him in a new and extraordinary manner, that it might be a lesson to future ages that the adversaries of Heaven always receive the just recompense of their iniquities. He, having been made prisoner by the Persians, lost not only that power which he had exercised without moderation, but also the liberty of which he had deprived others; and he wasted the remainder of his days in the vilest condition of slavery: for Sapores, the king of the Persians, who had made him prisoner, whenever he chose to get into his carriage or to mount on horseback, commanded the Roman to stoop and present his back; then, setting his foot on the shoulders of Valerian, he said, with a smile of reproach, "*This* is true, and not what the Romans delineate on board or plaster." Valerian lived for a considerable time under the well-merited insults of his conqueror; so that the Roman name remained long the scoff and derision of the barbarians: and this also was added to the severity of his punishment, that although he had an emperor for his son, he found no one to revenge his captivity and most abject and ser-

[1] [St. Peter, as a Jew, could be thus dealt with; St. Paul, as a Roman, was beheaded. See p. 120, note 7, *supra*.]

[2] [Note the incredulity of Lactantius. But see vol. iv. p. 219.]

[3] [See especially vol. iv. p. 141 for the intermediary pauses of persecutions, while yet in many places Christians "died daily."]

[4] [Most noteworthy in corroboration of the earlier Fathers.]

[5] [Jer. xxii. 19 and xxxvi. 30.]

vile state; neither indeed was he ever demanded back. Afterward, when he had finished this shameful life under so great dishonour, he was flayed, and his skin, stripped from the flesh, was dyed with vermilion, and placed in the temple of the gods of the barbarians, that the remembrance of a triumph so signal might be perpetuated, and that this spectacle might always be exhibited to our ambassadors, as an admonition to the Romans, that, beholding the spoils of their captived emperor in a Persian temple, they should not place too great confidence in their own strength.

Now since God so punished the sacrilegious, is it not strange that any one should afterward have dared to do, or even to devise, aught against the majesty of the one God, who governs and supports all things?

CHAP. VI.

Aurelian might have recollected the fate of the captived emperor, yet, being of a nature outrageous and headstrong, he forgot both *his* sin and its punishment, and by deeds of cruelty irritated the divine wrath. He was not, however, permitted to accomplish what he had devised; for just as he began to give a loose to his rage, he was slain. His bloody edicts had not yet reached the more distant provinces, when he himself lay all bloody on the earth at Cænophrurium in Thrace, assassinated by his familiar friends, who had taken up groundless suspicions against him.

Examples of such a nature, and so numerous, ought to have deterred succeeding tyrants; nevertheless they were not only not dismayed, but, in their misdeeds against God, became more bold and presumptuous.

CHAP. VII.

While Diocletian, that author of ill, and deviser of misery, was ruining all things, he could not withhold his insults, not even against God. This man, by avarice partly, and partly by timid counsels, overturned the Roman empire. For he made choice of three persons to share the government with him; and thus, the empire having been quartered, armies were multiplied, and each of the four princes strove to maintain a much more considerable military force than any sole emperor had done in times past.[1] There began to be fewer men who paid taxes than there were who received wages; so that the means of the husbandmen being exhausted by enormous impositions, the farms were abandoned, cultivated grounds became woodland, and universal dismay prevailed. Besides, the provinces were divided into minute portions, and many presidents and a multitude of inferior officers lay heavy on each territory, and almost on each city. There were also many stewards of different degrees, and deputies of presidents. Very few civil causes came before them: but there were condemnations daily, and forfeitures frequently inflicted; taxes on numberless commodities, and those not only often repeated, but perpetual, and, in exacting them, intolerable wrongs.

Whatever was laid on for the maintenance of the soldiery might have been endured; but Diocletian, through his insatiable avarice, would never allow the sums of money in his treasury to be diminished: he was constantly heaping together extraordinary aids and free gifts, that his original hoards might remain untouched and inviolable. He also, when by various extortions he had made all things exceedingly dear, attempted by an ordinance to limit their prices. Then much blood was shed for the veriest trifles; men were afraid to expose aught to sale, and the scarcity became more excessive and grievous than ever, until, in the end, the ordinance, after having proved destructive to multitudes, was from mere necessity abrogated. To this there were added a certain endless passion for building, and on that account, endless exactions from the provinces for furnishing wages to labourers and artificers, and supplying carriages and whatever else was requisite to the works which he projected. *Here* public halls, *there* a circus, *here* a mint, and *there* a workhouse for making implements of war; in one place a habitation for his empress, and in another for his daughter. Presently great part of the city was quitted, and all men removed with their wives and children, as from a town taken by enemies; and when those buildings were completed, to the destruction of whole provinces, he said, "They are not right, let them be done on another plan." Then they were to be pulled down, or altered, to undergo perhaps a future demolition. By such folly was he continually endeavouring to equal Nicomedia with the city Rome in magnificence.

I omit mentioning how many perished on account of their possessions or wealth; for such evils were exceedingly frequent, and through their frequency appeared almost lawful. But this was peculiar to him, that whenever he saw a field remarkably well cultivated, or a house of uncommon elegance, a false accusation and a capital punishment were straightway prepared against the proprietor; so that it seemed as if Diocletian could not be guilty of rapine without also shedding blood.

CHAP. VIII.

What was the character of his brother in empire, Maximian, called *Herculius?* Not unlike to that of Diocletian; and, indeed, to render

1 [See p. 12, note 1, *supra*.]

their friendship so close and faithful as it was, there must have been in them a sameness of inclinations and purposes, a corresponding will and unanimity in judgment. Herein alone they were different, that Diocletian was more avaricious and less resolute, and that Maximian, with less avarice, had a bolder spirit, prone not to good, but to evil. For while he possessed Italy, itself the chief seat of empire, and while other very opulent provinces, such as Africa and Spain, were near at hand, he took little care to preserve those treasures which he had such fair opportunities of amassing. Whenever he stood in need of more, the richest senators were presently charged, by suborned evidences, as guilty of aspiring to the empire; so that the chief luminaries of the senate were daily extinguished. And thus the treasury, delighting in blood, overflowed with ill-gotten wealth.

Add to all this the incontinency of that pestilent wretch, not only in debauching males, which is hateful and abominable, but also in the violation of the daughters of the principal men of the state; for wherever he journeyed, virgins were suddenly torn from the presence of their parents. In such enormities he placed his supreme delight, and to indulge to the utmost his lust and flagitious desires was in his judgment the felicity of his reign.

I pass over Constantius, a prince unlike the others, and worthy to have had the sole government of the empire.

CHAP. IX.

But the other Maximian (Galerius), chosen by Diocletian for his son-in-law, was worse, not only than those two princes whom our own times have experienced, but worse than all the bad princes of former days. In this wild beast there dwelt a native barbarity and a savageness foreign to Roman blood; and no wonder, for his mother was born beyond the Danube, and it was an inroad of the Carpi that obliged her to cross over and take refuge in New Dacia. The form of Galerius corresponded with his manners. Of stature tall, full of flesh, and swollen to a horrible bulk of corpulency; by his speech, gestures, and looks, he made himself a terror to all that came near him. His father-in-law, too, dreaded him excessively. The cause was this. Narseus, king of the Persians, emulating the example set him by his grandfather Sapores, assembled a great army, and aimed at becoming master of the eastern provinces of the Roman empire. Diocletian, apt to be low-spirited and timorous in every commotion, and fearing a fate like that of Valerian, would not in person encounter Narseus; but he sent Galerius by the way of Armenia, while he himself halted in the eastern provinces, and anxiously watched the event. It is a custom amongst the barbarians to take everything that belongs to them into the field. Galerius laid an ambush for them, and easily overthrew men embarrassed with the multitude of their followers and with their baggage. Having put Narseus to flight, and returned with much spoil, his own pride and Diocletian's fears were greatly increased. For after this victory he rose to such a pitch of haughtiness as to reject the appellation of Cæsar;[1] and when he heard that appellation in letters addressed to him, he cried out, with a stern look and terrible voice, "How long am I to be *Cæsar?*" Then he began to act extravagantly, insomuch that, as if he had been a second Romulus, he wished to pass for and to be called the offspring of Mars; and that he might appear the issue of a divinity, he was willing that his mother Romula should be dishonoured with the name of adulteress. But, not to confound the chronological order of events, I delay the recital of his actions; for indeed afterwards, when Galerius got the title of emperor, his father-in-law having been divested of the imperial purple, he became altogether outrageous, and of unbounded arrogance.

While by such a conduct, and with such associates, Diocles—for *that* was the name of Diocletian before he attained sovereignty—occupied himself in subverting the commonweal, there was no evil which his crimes did not deserve: nevertheless he reigned most prosperously, as long as he forbore to defile his hands with the blood of the just; and what cause he had for persecuting them, I come now to explain.

CHAP. X.

Diocletian, as being of a timorous disposition, was a searcher into futurity, and during his abode in the East he began to slay victims, that from their livers he might obtain a prognostic of events; and while he sacrificed, some attendants of his, who were Christians, stood by, and they put the *immortal sign* on their foreheads. At this the demons were chased away, and the holy rites interrupted. The soothsayers trembled, unable to investigate the wonted marks on the entrails of the victims. They frequently repeated the sacrifices, as if the former had been unpropitious; but the victims, slain from time to time, afforded no tokens for divination. At length Tages, the chief of the soothsayers,[2] either from guess or from his own observation, said, "There are profane persons here, who obstruct the rites." Then Diocletian, in furious passion, ordered not only all who were assisting at the holy ceremonies, but also

[1] [On which see cap. 20, *infra*, and preceding chapters.]
[2] [Nothing easier than for these to pretend such a difficulty, in order to incite the emperor to severities. They may have found it convenient to represent the sign of the cross as the source of their inability to give oracles.]

all who resided within the palace, to sacrifice, and, in case of their refusal, to be scourged. And further, by letters to the commanding officers, he enjoined that all soldiers should be forced to the like impiety, under pain of being dismissed the service. Thus far his rage proceeded; but at that season he did nothing more against the law and religion of God. After an interval of some time he went to winter in Bithynia; and presently Galerius Cæsar came thither, inflamed with furious resentment, and purposing to excite the inconsiderate old man to carry on that persecution which he had begun against the Christians. I have learned that the cause of his fury was as follows.

CHAP. XI.

The mother of Galerius, a woman exceedingly superstitious, was a votary of the gods of the mountains. Being of such a character, she made sacrifices almost every day, and she feasted her servants on the meat offered to idols: but the Christians of her family would not partake of those entertainments; and while she feasted with the Gentiles, they continued in fasting and prayer. On this account she conceived ill-will against the Christians, and by woman-like complaints instigated her son, no less superstitious than herself, to destroy them. So, during the whole winter, Diocletian and Galerius held councils together, at which no one else assisted; and it was the universal opinion that their conferences respected the most momentous affairs of the empire. The old man long opposed the fury of Galerius, and showed how pernicious it would be to raise disturbances throughout the world and to shed so much blood; that the Christians were wont with eagerness to meet death; and that it would be enough for him to exclude persons of that religion from the court[1] and the army. Yet he could not restrain the madness of that obstinate man. He resolved, therefore, to take the opinion of his friends. Now this was a circumstance in the bad disposition of Diocletian, that whenever he determined to do good, he did it without advice, that the praise might be all his own; but whenever he determined to do ill, which he was sensible would be blamed, he called in many advisers, that his own fault might be imputed to other men: and therefore a few civil magistrates, and a few military commanders, were admitted to give their counsel; and the question was put to them according to priority of rank. Some, through personal ill-will towards the Christians, were of opinion that they ought to be cut off, as enemies of the gods and adversaries of the established religious ceremonies. Others thought differently, but, having understood the will of Galerius, they, either from dread of displeasing or from a desire of gratifying him, concurred in the opinion given against the Christians. Yet not even then could the emperor be prevailed upon to yield his assent. He determined above all to consult his gods; and to that end he despatched a soothsayer to inquire of Apollo at Miletus, whose answer was such as might be expected from an enemy of the divine religion. So Diocletian was drawn over from his purpose. But although he could struggle no longer against his friends, and against Cæsar and Apollo, yet still he attempted to observe such moderation as to command the business to be carried through without bloodshed; whereas Galerius would have had all persons burnt alive who refused to sacrifice.

CHAP. XII.

A fit and auspicious day was sought out for the accomplishment of this undertaking; and the festival of the god Terminus, celebrated on the seventh of the kalends of March,[2] was chosen, in preference to all others, to terminate, as it were, the Christian religion.

> "That day, the harbinger of death, arose,
> First cause of ill, and long enduring woes;"

of woes which befell not only the Christians, but the whole earth. When that day dawned, in the eighth consulship of Diocletian and seventh of Maximian, suddenly, while it was yet hardly light, the prefect, together with chief commanders, tribunes, and officers of the treasury, came to the church in Nicomedia, and the gates having been forced open, they searched everywhere for an image of the Divinity. The books of the Holy Scriptures were found, and they were committed to the flames; the utensils and furniture of the church were abandoned to pillage: all was rapine, confusion, tumult. That church, situated on rising ground, was within view of the palace; and Diocletian and Galerius stood, as if on a watch-tower, disputing long whether it ought to be set on fire. The sentiment of Diocletian prevailed, who dreaded lest, so great a fire being once kindled, some part of the city might be burnt; for there were many and large buildings that surrounded the church. Then the Pretorian Guards came in battle array, with axes and other iron instruments, and having been let loose everywhere, they in a few hours levelled that very lofty edifice with the ground.[3]

CHAP. XIII.

Next day an edict was published, depriving the Christians of all honours and dignities;

[1] [A just statement of Diocletian's earlier disposition. See. vol. vi. p. 158, the beautiful letter of Theonas.]

[2] 23d of February.

[3] [See cap. 15, *infra*.]

ordaining also that, without any distinction of rank or degree, they should be subjected to tortures, and that every suit at law should be received against them; while, on the other hand, they were debarred from being plaintiffs in questions of wrong, adultery, or theft; and, finally, that they should neither be capable of freedom, nor have right of suffrage. A certain person tore down this edict, and cut it in pieces, improperly indeed, but with high spirit, saying in scorn, "These are the triumphs of Goths and Sarmatians." Having been instantly seized and brought to judgment, he was not only tortured, but burnt alive, in the forms of law; and having displayed admirable patience under sufferings, he was consumed to ashes.

CHAP. XIV.

But Galerius, not satisfied with the tenor of the edict, sought in another way to gain on the emperor. That he might urge him to excess of cruelty in persecution, he employed private emissaries to set the palace on fire; and some part of it having been burnt, the blame was laid on the Christians as public enemies; and the very appellation of *Christian* grew odious [1] on account of that fire. It was said that the Christians, in concert with the eunuchs, had plotted to destroy the princes; and that both of the princes had well-nigh been burnt alive in their own palace. Diocletian, shrewd and intelligent as he always chose to appear, suspected nothing of the contrivance, but, inflamed with anger, immediately commanded that all his own domestics should be tortured to force a confession of the plot. He sat on his tribunal, and saw innocent men tormented by fire to make discovery. All magistrates, and all who had superintendency in the imperial palace, obtained special commissions to administer the torture; and they strove with each other *who* should be first in bringing to light the conspiracy. No circumstances, however, of the fact were detected anywhere; for no one applied the torture to any domestics of Galerius. He himself was ever with Diocletian, constantly urging him, and never allowing the passions of the inconsiderate old man to cool. Then, after an interval of fifteen days, he attempted a second fire; but that was perceived quickly, and extinguished. Still, however, its author remained unknown. On that very day, Galerius, who in the middle of winter had prepared for his departure, suddenly hurried out of the city, protesting that he fled to escape being burnt alive.

CHAP. XV.

And now Diocletian raged, not only against his own domestics, but indiscriminately against all; and he began by forcing his daughter Valeria and his wife Prisca to be polluted by sacrificing. Eunuchs, once the most powerful, and who had chief authority at court and with the emperor, were slain. Presbyters and other officers of the Church were seized, without evidence by witnesses or confession, condemned, and together with their families led to execution. In burning alive, no distinction of sex or age was regarded; and because of their great multitude, they were not burnt one after another, but a herd of them were encircled with the same fire; and servants, having millstones tied about their necks, were cast into the sea. Nor was the persecution less grievous on the rest of the people of God; for the judges, dispersed through all the temples, sought to compel every one to sacrifice. The prisons were crowded; tortures, hitherto unheard of, were invented; and lest justice should be inadvertently administered to a Christian, altars were placed in the courts of justice, hard by the tribunal, that every litigant might offer incense before his cause could be heard. Thus judges were no otherwise approached than divinities. Mandates also had gone to Maximian Herculius and Constantius, requiring their concurrence in the execution of the edicts; for in matters even of such mighty importance their opinion was never once asked. Herculius, a person of no merciful temper, yielded ready obedience, and enforced the edicts throughout his dominions of Italy. Constantius, on the other hand, lest he should have seemed to dissent from the injunctions of his superiors, permitted the demolition of churches, — mere walls, and capable of being built up again, — but he preserved entire that true temple of God, which is the human body.[2]

CHAP. XVI.

Thus was all the earth afflicted; and from east to west, except in the territories of Gaul, three ravenous wild beasts continued to rage.

> "Had I a hundred mouths, a hundred tongues,
> A voice of brass, and adamantine lungs,
> Not half the dreadful scene could I disclose,"

or recount the punishments inflicted by the rulers in every province on religious and innocent men.

But what need of a particular recital of those things, especially to you, my best beloved Donatus,[3] who above all others was exposed to the storm of that violent persecution? For when you had fallen into the hands of the prefect Flaccinian, no puny murderer, and afterwards of Hierocles, who from a deputy became president of Bithynia, the author and adviser of the persecution, and last of all into the hands of his suc-

[1] [That it had become in some degree popular, see evidence, vol. vi. pp. 158-160.]

[2] [Truly an eloquent passage, and a tribute to Constantius, which Constantine, in filial humour, must have relished.]

[3] [See p. 301, *supra*.]

cessor Priscillian, you displayed to mankind a pattern of invincible magnanimity. Having been nine times exposed to racks and diversified torments, nine times by a glorious profession of your faith you foiled the adversary; in nine combats you subdued the devil and his chosen soldiers; and by nine victories you triumphed over this world and its terrors. How pleasing the spectacle to God, when He beheld you a conqueror, yoking in your chariot not white horses, nor enormous elephants, but those very men who had led captive the nations! After this sort to lord it over the lords of the earth is triumph indeed! Now, by your valour were they conquered, when you set at defiance their flagitious edicts, and, through stedfast faith and the fortitude of your soul, you routed all the vain terrors of tyrannical authority. Against you neither scourges, nor iron claws, nor fire, nor sword, nor various kinds of torture, availed aught; and no violence could bereave you of your fidelity and persevering resolution. This it is to be a disciple of God, and this it is to be a soldier of Christ; a soldier whom no enemy can dislodge, or wolf snatch, from the heavenly camp; no artifice ensnare, or pain of body subdue, or torments overthrow. At length, after those nine glorious combats, in which the devil was vanquished by you, he dared not to enter the lists again with one whom, by repeated trials, he had found unconquerable; and he abstained from challenging you any more, lest you should have laid hold on the garland of victory already stretched out to you; an unfading garland, which, although you have not at present received it, is laid up in the kingdom of the Lord for your virtue and deserts. But let us now return to the course of our narrative.

CHAP. XVII.

The wicked plan having been carried into execution, Diocletian, whom prosperity had now abandoned, set out instantly for Rome, *there* to celebrate the commencement of the twentieth year of his reign. That solemnity was performed on the twelfth of the kalends of December;[1] and suddenly the emperor, unable to bear the Roman freedom of speech, peevishly and impatiently burst away from the city. The kalends of January[2] approached, at which day the consulship, for the ninth time, was to be offered to him; yet, rather than continue thirteen days longer in Rome, he chose that his first appearance as consul should be at Ravenna. Having, however, begun his journey in winter, amidst intense cold and incessant rains, he contracted a slight but lingering disease: it harassed him without intermission, so that he was obliged for the most part to be carried in a litter. Then, at the close of summer, he made a circuit along the banks of the Danube, and so came to Nicomedia. His disease had now become more grievous and oppressing; yet he caused himself to be brought out, in order to dedicate that circus which, at the conclusion of the twentieth year of his reign, he had erected. Immediately he grew so languid and feeble, that prayers for his life were put up to all the gods. Then suddenly, on the ides of December,[3] there was heard in the palace sorrow, and weeping, and lamentation, and the courtiers ran to and fro; there was silence throughout the city, and a report went of the death, and even of the burial, of Diocletian: but early on the morrow it was suddenly rumoured that he still lived. At this the countenance of his domestics and courtiers changed from melancholy to gay. Nevertheless there were who suspected his death to be kept secret until the arrival of Galerius Cæsar, lest in the meanwhile the soldiery should attempt some change in the government; and this suspicion grew so universal, that no one would believe the emperor alive, until, on the kalends of March,[4] he appeared in public, but so wan, his illness having lasted almost a year, as hardly to be known again. The fit of stupor, resembling death, happened on the ides of December; and although he in some measure recovered, yet he never attained to perfect health again, for he became disordered in his judgment, being at certain times insane and at others of sound mind.

CHAP. XVIII.

Within a few days Galerius Cæsar arrived, not to congratulate his father-in-law on the re-establishment of his health, but to force him to resign the empire. Already he had urged Maximian Herculius to the like purpose, and by the alarm of civil wars terrified the old man into compliance; and he now assailed Diocletian. At first, in gentle and friendly terms, he said that age and growing infirmities disabled Diocletian for the charge of the commonweal, and that he had need to give himself some repose after his labours. Galerius, in confirmation of his argument, produced the example of Nerva, who laid the weight of empire on Trajan.

But Diocletian made answer, that it was unfit for one who had held a rank, eminent above all others and conspicuous, to sink into the obscurity of a low station; neither indeed was it safe, because in the course of so long a reign he must unavoidably have made many enemies. That the case of Nerva was very different: he, after

1 20th of November.
2 1st of January.
3 13th of December.
4 1st of March.

having reigned a single year, felt himself, either from age or from inexperience in business, unequal to affairs so momentous, and therefore threw aside the helm of government, and returned to that private life in which he had already grown old. But Diocletian added, that if Galerius wished for the title of emperor, there was nothing to hinder its being conferred on him and Constantius, as well as on Maximian Herculius.

Galerius, whose imagination already grasped at the whole empire, saw that little but an unsubstantial name would accrue to him from this proposal, and therefore replied that the settlement made by Diocletian himself ought to be inviolable; a settlement which provided that there should be two of higher rank vested with supreme power, and two others of inferior, to assist them. Easily might concord be preserved between *two* equals, never amongst *four;*[1] that he, if Diocletian would not resign, must consult his own interests, so as to remain no longer in an inferior rank, and the last of that rank; that for fifteen years past he had been confined, as an exile, to Illyricum and the banks of the Danube, perpetually struggling against barbarous nations, while others, at their ease, governed dominions more extensive than his, and better civilized.

Diocletian already knew, by letters from Maximian Herculius, all that Galerius had spoken at their conference, and also that he was augmenting his army; and now, on hearing his discourse, the spiritless old man burst into tears, and said, "Be it as you will."

It remained to choose *Cæsars* by common consent. "But," said Galerius, "why ask the advice of Maximian and Constantius, since they must needs acquiesce in whatever we do?"—"Certainly they will," replied Diocletian, "for we must elect their sons."

Now Maximian Herculius had a son, Maxentius, married to the daughter of Galerius, a man of bad and mischievous dispositions, and so proud and stubborn withal, that he would never pay the wonted obeisance either to his father or father-in-law, and on that account he was hated by them both. Constantius also had a son, Constantine, a young man of very great worth, and well meriting the high station of *Cæsar*. The distinguished comeliness of his figure, his strict attention to all military duties, his virtuous demeanour and singular affability, had endeared him to the troops, and made him the choice of every individual. He was then at court, having long before been created by Diocletian a tribune of the first order.

"What is to be done?" said Galerius, "for *that* Maxentius deserves not the office. He who, while yet a private man, has treated me with contumely, how will he act when once he obtains power?"—"But Constantine is amiable, and will so rule as hereafter, in the opinion of mankind, to surpass the mild virtues of his father."—"Be it so, if my inclinations and judgment are to be disregarded. Men ought to be appointed who are at my disposal, who will dread me, and never do anything unless by my orders."—"Whom then shall we appoint?"—"Severus."—"How! that dancer, that habitual drunkard, who turns night into day, and day into night?"—"He deserves the office, for he has approved himself a faithful paymaster and purveyor of the army; and, indeed, I have already despatched him to receive the purple from the hands of Maximian."—"Well, I consent; but whom else do you suggest?"—"Him," said Galerius, pointing out Daia, a young man, half-barbarian. Now Galerius had lately bestowed part of his own name on that youth, and called him *Maximin*, in like manner as Diocletian formerly bestowed on Galerius the name of *Maximian*, for the omen's sake, because Maximian Herculius had served him with unshaken fidelity.—"Who is that you present?"—"A kinsman of mine."—"Alas!" said Diocletian, heaving a deep sigh, "you do not propose men fit for the charge of public affairs!"—"I have tried them."—"Then do *you* look to it, who are about to assume the administration of the empire: as for *me*, while I continued emperor, long and diligent have been my labours in providing for the security of the commonweal; and now, should anything disastrous ensue, the blame will not be mine."

CHAP. XIX.

Matters having been thus concerted, Diocletian and Galerius went in procession to publish the nomination of *Cæsars*. Every one looked at Constantine; for there was no doubt that the choice would fall on him. The troops present, as well as the chief soldiers of the other legions, who had been summoned to the solemnity, fixed their eyes on Constantine, exulted in the hope of his approaching election, and occupied themselves in prayers for his prosperity. Near three miles from Nicomedia there is an eminence, on the summit of which Galerius formerly received the purple; and *there* a pillar, with the statue of Jupiter, was placed. Thither the procession went. An assembly of the soldiers was called. Diocletian, with tears, harangued them, and said that he was become infirm, that he needed repose after his fatigues, and that he would resign the empire into hands more vigorous and able, and at the same time appoint new *Cæsars*. The spectators, with the utmost earnestness, waited for the nomination. Suddenly he declared that

[1] [See p. 303, *supra.*]

the *Cæsars* were Severus and Maximin. The amazement was universal. Constantine stood near in public view, and men began to question amongst themselves whether his name too had not been changed into *Maximin;* when, in the sight of all, Galerius, stretching back his hand, put Constantine aside, and drew Daia forward, and, having divested him of the garb of a private person, set him in the most conspicuous place. All men wondered who he could be, and from whence he came; but none ventured to interpose or move objections, so confounded were their minds at the strange and unlooked-for event. Diocletian took off his purple robe, put it on Daia, and resumed his own original name of Diocles. He descended from the tribunal, and passed through Nicomedia in a chariot; and then this old emperor, like a veteran soldier freed from military service, was dismissed into his own country; while Daia, lately taken from the tending of cattle in forests to serve as a common soldier, immediately made one of the life-guard, presently a tribune, and next day *Cæsar*, obtained authority to trample under foot and oppress the empire of the East; a person ignorant alike of war and of civil affairs, and from a herdsman become a leader of armies.

CHAP. XX.

Galerius having effected the expulsion of the two old men, began to consider himself alone as the sovereign of the Roman empire. Necessity had required the appointment of Constantius to the first rank; but Galerius made small account of one who was of an easy temper, and of health declining and precarious. He looked for the speedy death of Constantius. And although that prince should recover, it seemed not difficult to force him to put off the imperial purple; for what else could he do, if pressed by his three colleagues to abdicate? Galerius had Licinius ever about his person, his old and intimate acquaintance, and his earliest companion in arms, whose counsels he used in the management of all affairs; yet he would not nominate Licinius to the dignity of *Cæsar*, with the title of *son*, for he purposed to nominate him, in the room of Constantius, to the dignity of *emperor*, with the title of *brother*, while he himself might hold sovereign authority, and rule over the whole globe with unbounded licence. After that, he meant to have solemnized the *vicennial* festival; to have conferred on his son Candidianus, then a boy of nine years of age, the office of *Cæsar;* and, in conclusion, to have resigned, as Diocletian had done. And thus, Licinius and Severus being emperors, and Maximin and Candidianus in the next station of *Cæsars*, he fancied that, environed as it were by an impregnable wall, he should lead an old age of security and peace. Such were his projects; but God, whom he had made his adversary, frustrated all those imaginations.

CHAP. XXI.

Having thus attained to the highest power, he bent his mind to afflict that empire into which he had opened his way. It is the manner and practice of the Persians for the people to yield themselves slaves to their kings, and for the kings to treat their people as slaves. This flagitious man, from the time of his victories over the Persians, was not ashamed incessantly to extol such an institution, and he resolved to establish it in the Roman dominions; and because he could not do this by an express law, he so acted, in imitation of the Persian kings, as to bereave men of their liberties. He first of all degraded those whom he meant to punish; and then not only were inferior magistrates put to the torture by him, but also the chief men in cities, and persons of the most eminent rank, and this too in matters of little moment, and in civil questions. Crucifixion was the punishment ready prepared in capital cases; and for lesser crimes, fetters. Matrons of honourable station were dragged into workhouses; and when any man was to be scourged, there were four posts fixed in the ground, and to them he was tied, after a manner unknown in the chastisement of slaves. What shall I say of his apartment for sport, and of his favourite diversions? He kept bears, most resembling himself in fierceness and bulk, whom he had collected together during the course of his reign. As often as he chose to indulge his humour, he ordered some particular bear to be brought in, and men were thrown to that savage animal, rather to be swallowed up than devoured; and when their limbs were torn asunder, he laughed with excessive complacency: nor did he ever sup without being spectator of the effusion of human blood. Men of private station were condemned to be burnt alive; and he began this mode of execution by edicts against the Christians, commanding that, after torture and condemnation, they should be burnt at a slow fire. They were fixed to a stake, and first a moderate flame was applied to the soles of their feet, until the muscles, contracted by burning, were torn from the bones; then torches, lighted and put out again, were directed to all the members of their bodies, so that no part had any exemption. Meanwhile cold water was continually poured on their faces, and their mouths moistened, lest, by reason of their jaws being parched, they should expire. At length they did expire, when, after many hours, the violent heat had consumed their skin and penetrated into their intestines. The dead carcases were laid on a funeral pile, and wholly burnt; their bones were gathered, ground to powder, and thrown into the river, or into the sea.

CHAP. XXII.

And now *that* cruelty, which he had learned in torturing the Christians, became habitual, and he exercised it against all men indiscriminately.[1] He was not wont to inflict the slighter sorts of punishment, as to banish, to imprison, or to send criminals to work in the mines; but to burn, to crucify, to expose to wild beasts, were things done daily, and without hesitation. For smaller offences, those of his own household and his stewards were chastised with lances, instead of rods; and, in great offences, to be beheaded was an indulgence shown to very few; and it seemed as a favour, on account of old services, when one was permitted to die in the easiest manner. But these were slight evils in the government of Galerius, when compared with what follows. For eloquence was extinguished, pleaders cut off, and the learned in the laws either exiled or slain. Useful letters came to be viewed in the same light as magical and forbidden arts; and all who possessed them were trampled upon and execrated, as if they had been hostile to government, and public enemies. Law was dissolved, and unbounded licence permitted to judges, — to judges chosen from amongst the soldiery, rude and illiterate men, and let loose upon the provinces, without assessors to guide or control them.

CHAP. XXIII.

But that which gave rise to public and universal calamity, was the tax imposed at once on each province and city. Surveyors having been spread abroad, and occupied in a general and severe scrutiny, horrible scenes were exhibited, like the outrages of victorious enemies, and the wretched state of captives. Each spot of ground was measured, vines and fruit-trees numbered, lists taken of animals of every kind, and a capitation-roll made up. In cities, the common people, whether residing within or without the walls, were assembled, the market-places filled with crowds of families, all attended with their children and slaves, the noise of torture and scourges resounded, sons were hung on the rack to force discovery of the effects of their fathers, the most trusty slaves compelled by pain to bear witness against their masters, and wives to bear witness against their husbands. In default of all other evidence, men were tortured to speak against themselves; and no sooner did agony oblige them to acknowledge what they had not, but those imaginary effects were noted down in the lists. Neither youth, nor old age, nor sickness, afforded any exemption. The diseased and the infirm were carried in; the age of each was estimated; and, that the capitation-tax might be enlarged, years were added to the young and struck off from the old. General lamentation and sorrow prevailed. Whatever, by the laws of war, conquerors had done to the conquered, the like did this man presume to perpetrate against Romans and the subjects of Rome, because his forefathers had been made liable to a like tax imposed by the victorious Trajan, as a penalty on the Dacians for their frequent rebellions. After this, money was levied for each head, as if a price had been paid for liberty to exist; yet full trust was not reposed on the same set of surveyors, but others and others still were sent round to make further discoveries; and thus the tributes were redoubled, not because the new surveyors made any fresh discoveries, but because they added at pleasure to the former rates, lest they should seem to have been employed to no purpose. Meanwhile the number of animals decreased, and men died; nevertheless taxes were paid even for the dead, so that no one could either live or cease to live without being subject to impositions. There remained mendicants alone, from whom nothing could be exacted, and whom their misery and wretchedness secured from ill-treatment. But this pious man had compassion on them, and determining that they should remain no longer in indigence, he caused them all to be assembled, put on board vessels, and sunk in the sea. So merciful was he in making provision that under his administration no man should want! And thus, while he took effectual measures that none, under the feigned pretext of poverty, should elude the tax, he put to death a multitude of real wretches, in violation of every law of humanity.

CHAP. XXIV.

Already the judgment of God approached him, and that season ensued in which his fortunes began to droop and to waste away. While occupied in the manner that I have described above, he did not set himself to subvert or expel Constantius, but waited for his death, not imagining, however, that it was so nigh. Constantius, having become exceedingly ill, wrote to Galerius, and requested that his son Constantine might be sent to see him. He had made a like request long before, but in vain; for Galerius meant nothing less than to grant it. On the contrary, he laid repeated snares for the life of that young man, because he durst not use open violence, lest he should stir up civil wars against himself, and incur that which he most dreaded, the hate

[1] [A course of conduct which, providentially, tended to stop the chronic severity against believers.]

and resentment of the army. Under pretence of manly exercise and recreation, he made him combat with wild beasts: but this device was frustrated; for the power of God protected Constantine, and in the very moment of jeopardy rescued him from the hands of Galerius. At length, Galerius, when he could no longer avoid complying with the request of Constantius, one evening gave Constantine a warrant to depart, and commanded him to set out next morning with the imperial despatches. Galerius meant either to find some pretext for detaining Constantine, or to forward orders to Severus for arresting him on the road. Constantine discerned his purpose; and therefore, after supper, when the emperor was gone to rest, he hasted away, carried off from the principal stages all the horses maintained at the public expense, and escaped. Next day the emperor, having purposely remained in his bed-chamber until noon, ordered Constantine to be called into his presence; but he learnt that Constantine had set out immediately after supper. Outrageous with passion, he ordered horses to be made ready, that Constantine might be pursued and dragged back; and hearing that all the horses had been carried off from the great road, he could hardly refrain from tears. Meanwhile Constantine, journeying with incredible rapidity, reached his father, who was already about to expire. Constantius recommended his son to the soldiers, delivered the sovereign authority into his hands, and then died, as his wish had long been, in peace and quiet.

Constantine Augustus, having assumed the government, made it his first care to restore the Christians to the exercise of their worship and to their God; and so began his administration by reinstating [1] the holy religion.

CHAP. XXV.

Some few days after, the portrait of Constantine, adorned with laurels, was brought to the pernicious wild beast, that, by receiving that symbol, he might acknowledge Constantine in the quality of *emperor*. He hesitated long whether to receive it or not, and he was about to commit both the portrait and its bearer to the flames, but his confidants dissuaded him from a resolution so frantic. They admonished him of the danger, and they represented that, if Constantine came with an armed force, all the soldiers, against whose inclination obscure or unknown *Cæsars* had been created, would acknowledge him, and crowd eagerly to his standard. So Galerius, although with the utmost unwillingness, accepted the portrait, and sent the imperial purple to Constantine, that he might seem of his own accord to have received that prince into partnership of power with him. And now his plans were deranged, and he could not, as he intended formerly, admit Licinius, without exceeding the limited number of emperors. But *this* he devised, that Severus, who was more advanced in life, should be named *emperor*, and that Constantine, instead of the title of *emperor*, to which he had been named, should receive that of *Cæsar* in common with Maximin Daia, and so be degraded from the second place to the fourth.

CHAP. XXVI.

Things seemed to be arranged in some measure to the satisfaction of Galerius, when another alarm was brought, that his son-in-law Maxentius had been declared *emperor* at Rome. The cause was this: Galerius having resolved by permanent taxes to devour the empire, soared to such extravagance in folly, as not to allow an exemption from that thraldom even to the Roman people. Tax-gatherers therefore were appointed to go to Rome, and make out lists of the citizens. Much about the same time Galerius had reduced the Pretorian Guards. There remained at Rome a few soldiers of that body, who, profiting of the opportunity, put some magistrates to death, and, with the acquiescence of the tumultuary populace, clothed Maxentius in the imperial purple. Galerius, on receiving this news, was disturbed at the strangeness of the event, but not much dismayed. He hated Maxentius, and he could not bestow on him the dignity of *Cæsar*, already enjoyed by two (Daia and Constantine); besides, he thought it enough for him to have once bestowed that dignity against his inclination. So he sent for Severus, exhorted him to regain his dominion and sovereignty, and he put under his command that army which Maximian Herculius had formerly commanded, that he might attack Maxentius at Rome. *There* the soldiers of Maximian had been oftentimes received with every sort of luxurious accommodation, so that they were not only interested to preserve the city, but they also longed to fix their residence in it.

Maxentius well knew the enormity of his own offences; and although he had as it were an hereditary claim to the services of his father's army, and might have hoped to draw it over to himself, yet he reflected that this consideration might occur to Galerius also, and induce him to leave Severus in Illyricum, and march in person with his own army against Rome. Under such apprehensions, Maxentius sought to protect himself from the danger that hung over him. To his father, who since his abdication resided in Campania, he sent the purple, and saluted him again *Augustus*. Maximian, given to change,

[1] [Re-establishing (Edin.) is too strong a term. He refers to the restoration, from ruins, of churches, etc. (cap. 12, p. 305, *supra*). See caps. 34, 48, *infra*.]

eagerly resumed that purple of which he had unwillingly divested himself. Meanwhile Severus marched on, and with his troops approached the walls of the city. Presently the soldiers raised up their ensigns, abandoned Severus, and yielded themselves to Maxentius, against whom they had come. What remained but flight for Severus, thus deserted? He was encountered by Maximian, who had resumed the imperial dignity. On this he took refuge in Ravenna, and shut himself up *there* with a few soldiers. But perceiving that he was about to be delivered up, he voluntarily surrendered himself, and restored the purple to him from whom he had received it; and after this he obtained no other grace but that of an easy death, for he was compelled to open his veins, and in that gentle manner expired.

CHAP. XXVII.

But Maximian, who knew the outrageous temper of Galerius, began to consider that, fired with rage on hearing of the death of Severus, he would march into Italy, and that possibly he might be joined by Daia, and so bring into the field forces too powerful to be resisted. Having therefore fortified Rome, and made diligent provision for a defensive war, Maximian went into Gaul, that he might give his younger daughter Fausta in marriage to Constantine, and thus win over that prince to his interest. Meantime Galerius assembled his troops, invaded Italy, and advanced towards Rome, resolving to extinguish the senate and put the whole people to the sword. But he found everything shut and fortified against him. There was no hope of carrying the place by storm, and to besiege it was an arduous undertaking; for Galerius had not brought with him an army sufficient to invest the walls. Probably, having never seen Rome, he imagined it to be little superior in size to those cities with which he was acquainted. But some of his legions, detesting the wicked enterprise of a father against his son-in-law, and of Romans against Rome, renounced his authority, and carried over their ensigns to the enemy. Already had his remaining soldiers begun to waver, when Galerius, dreading a fate like that of Severus, and having his haughty spirit broken and humiliated, threw himself at the feet of his soldiers, and continued to beseech them that he might not be delivered to the foe, until, by the promise of mighty largesses, he prevailed on them. Then he retreated from Rome, and fled in great disorder. Easily might he have been cut off in his flight, had any one pursued him even with a small body of troops. He was aware of his danger, and allowed his soldiers to disperse themselves, and to plunder and destroy far and wide, that, if there were any pursuers, they might be deprived of all means of subsistence in a ruined country. So the parts of Italy through which that pestilent band took its course were wasted, all things pillaged, matrons forced, virgins violated, parents and husbands compelled by torture to disclose where they had concealed their goods, and their wives and daughters; flocks and herds of cattle were driven off like spoils taken from barbarians. And thus did he, once a Roman emperor, but now the ravager of Italy, retire into his own territories, after having afflicted all men indiscriminately with the calamities of war. Long ago, indeed, and at the very time of his obtaining sovereign power, he had avowed himself the enemy of the Roman name; and he proposed that the empire should be called, not the *Roman*, but the *Dacian* empire.

CHAP. XXVIII.

After the flight of Galerius, Maximian, having returned from Gaul, held authority in common with his son; but more obedience was yielded to the young man than to the old: for Maxentius had most power, and had been longest in possession of it; and it was to him that Maximian owed on this occasion the imperial dignity. The old man was impatient at being denied the exercise of uncontrolled sovereignty, and envied his son with a childish spirit of rivalry; and therefore he began to consider how he might expel Maxentius and resume his ancient dominion. This appeared easy, because the soldiers who deserted Severus had originally served in his own army. He called an assembly of the people of Rome, and of the soldiers, as if he had been to make an harangue on the calamitous situation of public affairs. After having spoken much on that subject, he stretched his hands towards his son, charged him as author of all ills and prime cause of the calamities of the state, and then tore the purple from his shoulders. Maxentius, thus stripped, leaped headlong from the tribunal, and was received into the arms of the soldiers. Their rage and clamour confounded the unnatural old man, and, like another Tarquin the Proud, he was driven from Rome.

CHAP. XXIX.

Then Maximian returned into Gaul; and after having made some stay in those quarters, he went to Galerius, the enemy of his son, that they might confer together, as he pretended, about the settlement of the commonweal; but his true purpose was, under colour of reconciliation, to find an opportunity of murdering Galerius, and of seizing his share of the empire, instead of his own, from which he had been everywhere excluded.

Diocles was at the court of Galerius when Maximian arrived; for Galerius, meaning now to invest Licinius with the ensigns of supreme power in the room of Severus, had lately sent for Diocles to be present at the solemnity. So it was performed in presence both of him and of Maximian; and thus there were six who ruled the empire at one and the same time.[1]

Now the designs of Maximian having been frustrated, he took flight, as he had done twice before, and returned into Gaul, with a heart full of wickedness, and intending by treacherous devices to overreach Constantine, who was not only his own son-in-law, but also the child of his son-in-law; and that he might the more successfully deceive, he laid aside the imperial purple. The Franks had taken up arms. Maximian advised the unsuspecting Constantine not to lead all his troops against them, and he said that a few soldiers would suffice to subdue those barbarians. He gave this advice that an army might be left for him to win over to himself, and that Constantine, by reason of his scanty forces, might be overpowered. The young prince believed the advice to be judicious, because given by an aged and experienced commander; and he followed it, because given by a father-in-law. He marched, leaving the most considerable part of his forces behind. Maximian waited a few days; and as soon as, by his calculation, Constantine had entered the territory of the barbarians, he suddenly resumed the imperial purple, seized the public treasures, after his wont made ample donatives to the soldiery, and feigned that such disasters had befallen Constantine as soon after befell himself. Constantine was presently informed of those events, and, by marches astonishingly rapid, he flew back with his army. Maximian, not yet prepared to oppose him, was overpowered at unawares, and the soldiers returned to their duty. Maximian had possessed himself of Marseilles (he fled thither), and shut the gates. Constantine drew nigh, and seeing Maximian on the walls, addressed him in no harsh or hostile language, and demanded what he meant, and what it was that he wanted, and why he had acted in a way so peculiarly unbecoming him. But Maximian from the walls incessantly uttered abuse and curses against Constantine. Then, of a sudden, the gates on the opposite side having been unbarred, the besiegers were admitted into the city. The rebel emperor, and unnatural parent and a perfidious father-in-law, was dragged into the presence of Constantine, heard a recital made of his crimes, was divested of his imperial robe, and, after this reprimand, obtained his life.

[1] [See pp. 303 (cap. vii.) and 308, at note 1, *supra*.]

CHAP. XXX.

Maximian, having thus forfeited the respect due to an emperor and a father-in-law, grew impatient at his abased condition, and, emboldened by impunity, formed new plots against Constantine. He addressed himself to his daughter Fausta, and, as well by entreaties as by the soothing of flattery, solicited her to betray her husband. He promised to obtain for her a more honourable alliance than that with Constantine; and he requested her to allow the bed-chamber of the emperor to be left open, and to be slightly guarded. Fausta undertook to do whatever he asked, and instantly revealed the whole to her husband. A plan was laid for detecting Maximian in the very execution of his crime. They placed a base eunuch to be murdered instead of the emperor. At the dead of night Maximian arose, and perceived all things to be favourable for his insidious purpose. There were few soldiers on guard, and these too at some distance from the bed-chamber. However, to prevent suspicion, he accosted them, and said that he had had a dream which he wished to communicate to his son-in-law. He went in armed, slew the eunuch, sprung forth exultingly, and avowed the murder. At that moment Constantine showed himself on the opposite side with a band of soldiers; the dead body was brought out of the bed-chamber; the murderer, taken in the fact, all aghast,

> "Stood like a stone, silent and motionless;"

while Constantine upbraided him for his impiety and enormous guilt. At last Maximian obtained leave that the manner of his death should be at his own choice, and he strangled himself.

Thus that mightiest sovereign of Rome—who ruled so long with exceeding glory, and who celebrated his twentieth anniversary—thus that most haughty man had his neck broken, and ended his detestable life by a death base and ignominious.

CHAP. XXXI.

From Maximian, God, the avenger of religion and of His people, turned his eyes to Galerius, the author of the accursed persecution, that in his punishment also He might manifest the power of His majesty. Galerius, too, was purposing to celebrate his twentieth anniversary; and as, under that pretext, he had, by new taxes payable in gold and silver, oppressed the provinces, so now, that he might recompense them by celebrating the promised festival, he used the like pretext for repeating his oppressions. Who can relate in fit terms the methods used to harass mankind in levying the tax, and especially with regard to corn and the other fruits of the earth? The officers, or rather the executioners, of all the different magistrates, seized on each individual, and would never let go their hold. No man knew to whom he ought to make payment first. There was no dispensation given to those who had nothing; and they were required, under pain of being variously tortured, instantly to pay, notwithstanding their inability. Many guards were set round, no breathing time was granted, or, at any season of the year, the least respite from exactions. Different magistrates, or the officers of different magistrates, frequently contended for the right of levying the tax from the same persons. No threshing-floor without a tax-gatherer, no vintage without a watch, and nought left for the sustenance of the husbandman! That food should be snatched from the mouths of those who had earned it by toil, was grievous: the hope, however, of being afterwards relieved, might have made that grievance supportable; but it was necessary for every one who appeared at the anniversary festival to provide robes of various kinds, and gold and silver besides. And one might have said, "How shall I furnish myself with those things, O tyrant void of understanding, if you carry off the whole fruits of my ground, and violently seize its expected produce?" Thus, throughout the dominions of Galerius, men were spoiled of their goods, and all was raked together into the imperial treasury, that the emperor might be enabled to perform his vow of celebrating a festival which he was doomed never to celebrate.

CHAP. XXXII.

Maximin Daia was incensed at the nomination of Licinius to the dignity of *emperor*, and he would no longer be called *Cæsar*, or allow himself to be ranked as third in authority. Galerius, by repeated messages, besought Daia to yield, and to acquiesce in *his* arrangement, to give place to age, and to reverence the grey hairs of Licinius. But Daia became more and more insolent. He urged that, as it was he who first assumed the purple, so, by possession, he had right to priority in rank; and he set at nought the entreaties and the injunctions of Galerius. That brute animal was stung to the quick, and bellowed when the mean creature whom he had made *Cæsar*, in expectation of his thorough obsequiousness, forgot the great favour conferred on him, and impiously withstood the requests and will of his benefactor. Galerius at length, overcome by the obstinacy of Daia, abolished the subordinate title of *Cæsar*, gave to himself and Licinius that of *the Augusti*, and to Daia and Constantine that of *sons of the Augusti*. Daia, some time after, in a letter to Galerius, took occasion to observe, that at the last general muster he had been saluted by his army under the title of *Augustus*. Galerius, vexed and grieved at this, commanded that all the four should have the appellation of *emperor*.[1]

CHAP. XXXIII.

And now, when Galerius was in the eighteenth year of his reign, God struck him with an incurable plague. A malignant ulcer formed itself low down in his secret parts, and spread by degrees. The physicians attempted to eradicate it, and healed up the place affected. But the sore, after having been skinned over, broke out again; a vein burst, and the blood flowed in such quantity as to endanger his life. The blood, however, was stopped, although with difficulty. The physicians had to undertake their operations anew, and at length they cicatrized the wound. In consequence of some slight motion of his body, Galerius received a hurt, and the blood streamed more abundantly than before. He grew emaciated, pallid, and feeble, and the bleeding then stanched. The ulcer began to be insensible to the remedies applied, and a gangrene seized all the neighbouring parts. It diffused itself the wider the more the corrupted flesh was cut away, and everything employed as the means of cure served but to aggravate the disease.

"The masters of the healing art withdrew."

Then famous physicians were brought in from all quarters; but no human means had any success. Apollo and Æsculapius were besought importunately for remedies: Apollo did prescribe, and the distemper augmented. Already approaching to its deadly crisis, it had occupied the lower regions of his body: his bowels came out, and his whole seat putrefied. The luckless physicians, although without hope of overcoming the malady, ceased not to apply fomentations and administer medicines. The humours having been repelled, the distemper attacked his intestines, and worms were generated in his body. The stench was so foul as to pervade not only the palace, but even the whole city; and no wonder, for by that time the passages from his bladder and bowels, having been devoured by the worms, became indiscriminate, and his body, with intolerable anguish, was dissolved into one mass of corruption.[2]

"Stung to the soul, he bellowed with the pain,
So roars the wounded bull."— PITT.

They applied warm flesh of animals to the chief seat of the disease, that the warmth might draw out those minute worms; and accordingly, when the dressings were removed, there issued forth an innumerable swarm: nevertheless the

---

[1] [One wonders that this history was not more efficacious in enforcing the hint on p. 12, at note 1, *supra*.]
[2] [Acts xii. 23.]

prolific disease had hatched swarms much more abundant to prey upon and consume his intestines. Already, through a complication of distempers, the different parts of his body had lost their natural form: the superior part was dry, meagre, and haggard, and his ghastly-looking skin had settled itself deep amongst his bones; while the inferior, distended like bladders, retained no appearance of joints. These things happened in the course of a complete year; and at length, overcome by calamities, he was obliged to acknowledge God, and he cried aloud, in the intervals of raging pain, that he would re-edify the Church which he had demolished, and make atonement for his misdeeds; and when he was near his end, he published an edict of the tenor following: —

CHAP. XXXIV.

"Amongst our other regulations for the permanent advantage of the commonweal, we have hitherto studied to reduce all things to a conformity with the ancient laws and public discipline of the Romans.

"It has been our aim in an especial manner, that the Christians also, who had abandoned the religion of their forefathers, should return to right opinions. For such wilfulness and folly had, we know not how, taken possession of them, that instead of observing those ancient institutions, which possibly their own forefathers had established, they, through caprice, made laws to themselves, and drew together into different societies many men of widely different persuasions.

"After the publication of our edict, ordaining the Christians to betake themselves to the observance of the ancient institutions, many of them were subdued through the fear of danger, and moreover many of them were exposed to jeopardy; nevertheless, because great numbers still persist in their opinions, and because we have perceived that at present they neither pay reverence and due adoration to the gods, nor yet worship their own God, therefore we, from our wonted clemency in bestowing pardon on all, have judged it fit to extend our indulgence to those men, and to permit them again to be Christians, and to establish the places of their religious assemblies; yet so as that they offend not against good order.

"By another mandate we purpose to signify unto magistrates how they ought herein to demean themselves.

"Wherefore it will be the duty of the Christians, in consequence of this our toleration, to pray to their God for our welfare, and for that of the public, and for their own; that the commonweal may continue safe in every quarter, and that they themselves may live securely in their habitations."

CHAP. XXXV.

This edict was promulgated at Nicomedia on the day preceding the kalends of May,[1] in the eighth consulship of Galerius, and the second of Maximin Daia. Then the prison-gates having been thrown open, you, my best beloved Donatus,[2] together with the other confessors for the faith, were set at liberty from a jail, which had been your residence for six years. Galerius, however, did not, by publication of this edict, obtain the divine forgiveness. In a few days after he was consumed by the horrible disease that had brought on an universal putrefaction. Dying, he recommended his wife and son to Licinius, and delivered them over into his hands. This event was known at Nicomedia before the end of the month.[3] His vicennial anniversary was to have been celebrated on the ensuing kalends of March.[4]

CHAP. XXXVI.

Daia, on receiving this news, hasted with relays of horses from the East, to seize the dominions of Galerius, and, while Licinius lingered in Europe, to arrogate to himself all the country as far as the narrow seas of Chalcedon. On his entry into Bithynia, he, with the view of acquiring immediate popularity, abolished Galerius' tax, to the great joy of all. Dissension arose between the two emperors, and almost an open war. They stood on the opposite shores with their armies. Peace, however, and amity were established under certain conditions. Licinius and Daia met on the narrow sees, concluded a treaty, and in token of friendship joined hands. Then Daia, believing all things to be in security, returned (to Nicomedia), and was in his new dominions what he had been in Syria and Egypt. First of all, he took away the toleration and general protection granted by Galerius to the Christians, and, for this end, he secretly procured addresses from different cities, requesting that no Christian church might be built within their walls; and thus he meant to make that which was his own choice appear as if extorted from him by importunity. In compliance with those addresses, he introduced a new mode of government in things respecting religion, and for each city he created a high priest, chosen from among the persons of most distinction. The office of those men was to make daily sacrifices to all their gods, and, with the aid of the former priests, to prevent the Christians from erecting churches, or from worshipping God either publicly or in private; and he authorized them to compel the Christians to sacrifice to idols, and,

1 30th of April.
2 [See p. 301, *supra*, and p. 316, *infra*.]
3 May.
4 1st of March following.

on their refusal, to bring them before the civil magistrate; and, as if this had not been enough, in every province he established a superintendent priest, one of chief eminence in the state; and he commanded that all those priests newly instituted should appear in white habits, that being the most honourable distinction of dress.[1] And as to the Christians, he purposed to follow the course that he had followed in the East, and, affecting the show of clemency, he forbade the slaying of God's servants, but he gave command that they should be mutilated. So the confessors for the faith had their ears and nostrils slit, their hands and feet lopped off, and their eyes dug out of the sockets.

CHAP. XXXVII.

While occupied in this plan, he received letters from Constantine which deterred him from proceeding in its execution, so for a time he dissembled his purpose; nevertheless any Christian that fell within his power was privily thrown into the sea. Neither did he cease from his custom of sacrificing every day in the palace. It was also an invention of his to cause all animals used for food to be slaughtered, not by cooks, but by priests at the altars; so that nothing was ever served up, unless foretasted, consecrated, and sprinkled with wine, according to the rites of paganism; and whoever was invited to an entertainment must needs have returned from it impure and defiled. In all things else he resembled his preceptor Galerius. For if aught chanced to have been left untouched by Diocles and Maximian, *that* did Daia greedily and shamelessly carry off. And now the granaries of each individual were shut, and all warehouses sealed up, and taxes, not yet due, were levied by anticipation. Hence famine, from neglect of cultivation, and the prices of all things enhanced beyond measure. Herds and flocks were driven from their pasture for the daily sacrifice. By gorging his soldiers with the flesh of sacrifices, he so corrupted them, that they disdained their wonted pittance in corn, and wantonly threw it away. Meanwhile Daia recompensed his body-guards, who were very numerous, with costly raiment and gold medals, made donatives in silver to the common soldiers and recruits, and bestowed every sort of largess on the barbarians who served in his army. As to grants of the property of living persons, which he made to his favourites whenever they chose to ask what belonged to another, I know not whether the same thanks might not be due to him that are given to merciful robbers, who spoil without murdering.

[1] [Singular that he does not assert that in this he imitated the Christian discipline.]

CHAP. XXXVIII.

But *that* which distinguished his character, and in which he transcended all former emperors, was his desire of debauching women. What else can I call it but a blind and headstrong passion? Yet such epithets feebly express my indignation in reciting his enormities. The magnitude of the guilt overpowers my tongue, and makes it unequal to its office. Eunuchs and panders made search everywhere, and no sooner was any comely face discovered, than husbands and parents were obliged to withdraw. Matrons of quality and virgins were stripped of their robes, and all their limbs were inspected, lest any part should be unworthy of the bed of the emperor. Whenever a woman resisted, death by drowning was inflicted on her; as if, under the reign of this adulterer, chastity had been treason. Some men there were, who, beholding the violation of wives whom for virtue and fidelity they affectionately loved, could not endure their anguish of mind, and so killed themselves. While this monster ruled, it was singular deformity alone which could shield the honour of any female from his savage desires. At length he introduced a custom prohibiting marriage unless with the imperial permission; and he made this an instrument to serve the purposes of his lewdness. After having debauched freeborn maidens, he gave them for wives to his slaves. His courtiers also imitated the example of the emperor, and violated with impunity the beds of their dependants. For who was there to punish such offences? As for the daughters of men of middle rank, any who were inclined took them by force. Ladies of quality, who could not be taken by force, were petitioned for, and obtained from the emperor by way of free gift. Nor could a father oppose this; for the imperial warrant having been once signed, he had no alternative but to die, or to receive some barbarian as his son-in-law. For hardly was there any person in the life-guard except of those people, who, having been driven from their habitations by the Goths in the twentieth year of Diocletian, yielded themselves to Galerius, and entered into his service. It was ill for humankind, that men who had fled from the bondage of barbarians should thus come to lord it over the Romans. Environed by such guards, Daia oppressed and insulted the Eastern empire.

CHAP. XXXIX.

Now Daia, in gratifying his libidinous desires, made his own will the standard of right; and therefore he would not refrain from soliciting the widow of Galerius, the Empress Valeria, to whom he had lately given the appellation of mother. After the death of her husband, she had repaired to Daia, because she imagined that she might live with more security in his dominions than elsewhere, especially as he was a married man; but the flagitious creature became instantly inflamed with a passion for her. Valeria was still in weeds, the time of her mourning not being yet expired. He sent a message to her proposing marriage, and offering, on her compliance, to put away his wife. She frankly returned an answer such as she alone could dare to do: first, that she would not treat of marriage while she was in weeds, and while the ashes of Galerius, *her* husband, and, by adoption, the father of Daia, were yet warm; next, that he acted impiously, in proposing to divorce a faithful wife to make room for another, whom in her turn he would also cast off; and, lastly, that it was indecent, unexampled, and unlawful for a woman of her title and dignity to engage a second time in wedlock.[1] This bold answer having been reported to Daia, presently his desires changed into rage and furious resentment. He pronounced sentence of forfeiture against the princess, seized her goods, removed her attendants, tortured her eunuchs to death, and banished her and her mother Prisca: but he appointed no particular place for her residence while in banishment; and hence he insultingly expelled her from every abode that she took in the course of her wanderings; and, to complete all, he condemned the ladies who enjoyed most of her friendship and confidence to die on a false accusation of adultery.

CHAP. XL.

There was a certain matron of high rank who already had grandchildren by more than one son. Her Valeria loved like a second mother, and Daia suspected that her advice had produced that refusal which Valeria gave to his matrimonial offers; and therefore he charged the president Eratineus to have her put to death in a way that might injure her fame. To her two others, equally noble, were added. One of them, who had a daughter a Vestal virgin at Rome, maintained an intercourse by stealth with the banished Valeria. The other, married to a senator, was intimately connected with the empress. Excellent beauty and virtue proved the cause of their death. They were dragged to the tribunal, not of an upright judge, but of a robber. Neither indeed was there any accuser, until a certain Jew, one charged with other offences, was induced, through hope of pardon, to give false evidence against the innocent. The equitable and vigilant magistrate conducted him out of the city under a guard, lest the populace should have stoned him. This tragedy was acted at Nicæa. The Jew was ordered to the torture till he should speak as he had been instructed, while the torturers by blows prevented the women from speaking in their own defence. The innocent were condemned to die. Then there arose wailing and lamentation, not only of the senator, who attended on his well-deserving consort, but amongst the spectators also, whom this proceeding, scandalous and unheard of, had brought together; and, to prevent the multitude from violently rescuing the condemned persons out of the hands of the executioners, military commanders followed with light infantry and archers. And thus, under a guard of armed soldiers, they were led to punishment. Their domestics having been forced to flee, they would have remained without burial, had not the compassion of friends interred them by stealth. Nor was the promise of pardon made good to the feigned adulterer, for he was fixed to a gibbet, and then he disclosed the whole secret contrivance; and with his last breath he protested to all the beholders that the women died innocent.

CHAP. XLI.

But the empress, an exile in some desert region of Syria, secretly informed her father Diocletian of the calamity that had befallen her. He despatched messengers to Daia, requesting that his daughter might be sent to him. He could not prevail. Again and again he entreated; yet she was not sent. At length he employed a relation of his, a military man high in power and authority, to implore Daia by the remembrance of past favours. This messenger, equally unsuccessful in his negotiation as the others, reported to Diocletian that his prayers were vain.

CHAP. XLII.

At this time, by command of Constantine, the statues of Maximian Herculius were thrown down, and his portraits removed; and, as the two old emperors were generally delineated in one piece, the portraits of both were removed at the same time. Thus Diocletian lived to see a disgrace which no former emperor had ever seen, and, under the double load of vexation of spirit and bodily maladies, he resolved to die. Tossing to and fro, with his soul agitated by grief, he could neither eat nor take rest. He sighed, groaned, and wept often, and incessantly threw himself into various postures, now on his couch, and now on the ground. So he, who for twenty years was the most prosperous of emperors, having been cast down into the obscurity of a private station, treated in the most contumelious manner, and compelled to abhor life, became incapable of receiving nourishment, and, worn out with anguish of mind, expired.

1 [Language greatly the product of Christian influences.]

CHAP. XLIII.

Of the adversaries of God there still remained one, whose overthrow and end I am now to relate.

Daia had entertained jealousy and ill-will against Licinius from the time that the preference was given to him by Galerius; and those sentiments still subsisted, notwithstanding the treaty of peace lately concluded between them. When Daia heard that the sister of Constantine was betrothed to Licinius, he apprehended that the two emperors, by contracting this affinity, meant to league against him; so he privily sent ambassadors to Rome, desiring a friendly alliance with Maxentius: he also wrote to him in terms of cordiality. The ambassadors were received courteously, friendship established, and in token of it the effigies of Maxentius and Daia were placed together in public view. Maxentius willingly embraced this, as if it had been an aid from heaven; for he had already declared war against Constantine, as if to revenge the death of his father Maximian. From this appearance of filial piety a suspicion arose, that the detestable old man had but feigned a quarrel with his son that he might have an opportunity to destroy his rivals in power, and so make way for himself and his son to possess the whole empire. This conjecture, however, had no foundation; for his true purpose was to have destroyed his son and the others, and then to have reinstated himself and Diocletian in sovereign authority.

CHAP. XLIV.

And now a civil war broke out between Constantine and Maxentius. Although Maxentius kept himself within Rome, because the soothsayers had foretold that if he went out of it he should perish, yet he conducted the military operations by able generals. In forces he exceeded his adversary; for he had not only his father's army, which deserted from Severus, but also his own, which he had lately drawn together out of Mauritania and Italy. They fought, and the troops of Maxentius prevailed. At length Constantine, with steady courage and a mind prepared for every event, led his whole forces to the neighbourhood of Rome, and encamped them opposite to the Milvian bridge. The anniversary of the reign of Maxentius approached, that is, the sixth of the kalends of November,[1] and the fifth year of his reign was drawing to an end.

Constantine was directed in a dream to cause *the heavenly sign* to be delineated on the shields of his soldiers, and so to proceed to battle. He did as he had been commanded, and he marked on their shields the letter X, with a perpendicular line drawn through it and turned round thus at ☧ the top, being the cipher of CHRIST. Having this sign, his troops stood to arms. The enemies advanced, but without their emperor, and they crossed the bridge. The armies met, and fought with the utmost exertions of valour, and firmly maintained their ground. In the meantime a sedition arose at Rome, and Maxentius was reviled as one who had abandoned all concern for the safety of the commonweal; and suddenly, while he exhibited the Circensian games on the anniversary of his reign, the people cried with one voice, "Constantine cannot be overcome!" Dismayed at this, Maxentius burst from the assembly, and having called some senators together, ordered the Sibylline books to be searched. In them it was found that:—

> "On the same day the enemy of the Romans should perish."

Led by this response to the hopes of victory, he went to the field. The bridge in his rear was broken down. At sight of that the battle grew hotter. The hand of the Lord prevailed, and the forces of Maxentius were routed. He fled towards the broken bridge; but the multitude pressing on him, he was driven headlong into the Tiber.

This destructive war being ended, Constantine was acknowledged as emperor, with great rejoicings, by the senate and people of Rome. And now he came to know the perfidy of Daia; for he found the letters written to Maxentius, and saw the statues and portraits of the two associates which had been set up together. The senate, in reward of the valour of Constantine, decreed to him the title of *Maximus* (the Greatest), a title which Daia had always arrogated to himself. Daia, when he heard that Constantine was victorious and Rome freed, expressed as much sorrow as if he himself had been vanquished; but afterwards, when he heard of the decree of the senate, he grew outrageous, avowed enmity towards Constantine, and made his title of *the Greatest* a theme of abuse and raillery.

CHAP. XLV.

Constantine having settled all things at Rome, went to Milan about the beginning of winter. Thither also Licinius came to receive his wife Constantia. When Daia understood that they were busied in solemnizing the nuptials, he moved out of Syria in the depth of a severe winter, and by forced marches he came into Bithynia with an army much impaired; for he lost all his beasts of burden, of whatever kind, in consequence of excessive rains and snow, miry ways, cold and fatigue. Their carcases, scattered about the

[1] 27th of October.

roads, seemed an emblem of the calamities of the impending war, and the presage of a like destruction that awaited the soldiers. Daia did not halt in his own territories; but immediately crossed the Thracian Bosphorus, and in a hostile manner approached the gates of Byzantium. There was a garrison in the city, established by Licinius to check any invasion that Daia might make. At first Daia attempted to entice the soldiers by the promise of donatives, and then to intimidate them by assault and storm. Yet neither promises nor force availed aught. After eleven days had elapsed, within which time Licinius might have learned the state of the garrison, the soldiers surrendered, not through treachery, but because they were too weak to make a longer resistance. Then Daia moved on to Heraclea (otherwise called Perinthus), and by delays of the like nature before that place lost some days. And now Licinius by expeditious marches had reached Adrianople, but with forces not numerous. Then Daia, having taken Perinthus by capitulation, and remained there for a short space, moved forwards eighteen miles to the first station. Here his progress was stopped; for Licinius had already occupied the second station, at the distance also of eighteen miles. Licinius, having assembled what forces he could from the neighbouring quarters, advanced towards Daia rather indeed to retard his operations than with any purpose of fighting, or hope of victory: for Daia had an army of seventy thousand men, while he himself had scarce thirty thousand; for his soldiers being dispersed in various regions, there was not time, on that sudden emergency, to collect all of them together.

CHAP. XLVI.

The armies thus approaching each other, seemed on the eve of a battle. Then Daia made this vow to Jupiter, that if he obtained victory he would extinguish and utterly efface the name of the Christians. And on the following night an angel of the Lord seemed to stand before Licinius while he was asleep, admonishing him to arise immediately, and with his whole army to put up a prayer to the Supreme God, and assuring him that by so doing he should obtain victory. Licinius fancied that, hearing this, he arose, and that his monitor, who was nigh him, directed how he should pray, and in what words. Awaking from sleep, he sent for one of his secretaries, and dictated these words exactly as he had heard them: —

"Supreme God, we beseech Thee; Holy God, we beseech Thee; unto Thee we commend all right; unto Thee we commend our safety; unto Thee we commend our empire. By Thee we live, by Thee we are victorious and happy. Supreme Holy God, hear our prayers; to Thee we stretch forth our arms. Hear, Holy Supreme God."

Many copies were made of these words, and distributed amongst the principal commanders, who were to teach them to the soldiers under their charge. At this all men took fresh courage, in the confidence that victory had been announced to them from heaven. Licinius resolved to give battle on the kalends of May;[1] for precisely eight years before Daia had received the dignity of *Cæsar*, and Licinius chose that day in hopes that Daia might be vanquished on the anniversary of *his* reign, as Maxentius had been on *his*. Daia, however, purposed to give battle earlier, to fight on the day before those kalends,[2] and to triumph on the anniversary of his reign. Accounts came that Daia was in motion; the soldiers of Licinius armed themselves, and advanced. A barren and open plain, called *Campus Serenus*, lay between the two armies. They were now in sight of one another. The soldiers of Licinius placed their shields on the ground, took off their helmets, and, following the example of their leaders, stretched forth their hands towards heaven. Then the emperor uttered the prayer, and they all repeated it after him. The host, doomed to speedy destruction, heard the murmur of the prayers of their adversaries. And now, the ceremony having been thrice performed, the soldiers of Licinius became full of courage, buckled on their helmets again, and resumed their shields. The two emperors advanced to a conference: but Daia could not be brought to peace; for he held Licinius in contempt, and imagined that the soldiers would presently abandon an emperor parsimonious in his donatives, and enter into the service of one liberal even to profusion. And indeed it was on this notion that he began the war. He looked for the voluntary surrender of the armies of Licinius; and, thus reinforced, he meant forthwith to have attacked Constantine.

CHAP. XLVII.

So the two armies drew nigh; the trumpets gave the signal; the military ensigns advanced; the troops of Licinius charged. But the enemies, panic-struck, could neither draw their swords nor yet throw their javelins. Daia went about, and, alternately by entreaties and promises, attempted to seduce the soldiers of Licinius. But he was not hearkened to in any quarter, and they drove him back. Then were the troops of Daia slaughtered, none making resistance; and such numerous legions, and forces so mighty, were mowed down by an inferior enemy. No one called to mind his reputation, or former valour, or the honourable rewards which had been conferred on him. The Supreme God did so place their necks under the sword of their

[1] 1st of May. [As to the angel, see Gibbon, cap. xx. note 41.]
[2] 30th of April. [Note these dates, p. 315.]

foes, that they seemed to have entered the field, not as combatants, but as men devoted to death. After great numbers had fallen, Daia perceived that everything went contrary to his hopes; and therefore he threw aside the purple, and having put on the habit of a slave, hasted across the Thracian Bosphorus. One half of his army perished in battle, and the rest either surrendered to the victor or fled; for now that the emperor himself had deserted, there seemed to be no shame in desertion. Before the expiration of the kalends of May, Daia arrived at Nicomedia, although distant one hundred and sixty miles from the field of battle. So in the space of one day and two nights he performed that journey. Having hurried away with his children and wife, and a few officers of his court, he went towards Syria; but having been joined by some troops from those quarters, and having collected together a part of his fugitive forces, he halted in Cappadocia, and then he resumed the imperial garb.

CHAP. XLVIII.

Not many days after the victory, Licinius, having received part of the soldiers of Daia into his service, and properly distributed them, transported his army into Bithynia, and having made his entry into Nicomedia, he returned thanks to God, through whose aid he had overcome; and on the ides of June,[1] while he and Constantine were consuls for the third time, he commanded the following edict for the restoration of the Church, directed to the president of the province, to be promulgated: —

"When we, Constantine and Licinius, emperors, had an interview at Milan, and conferred together with respect to the good and security of the commonweal, it seemed to us that, amongst those things that are profitable to mankind in general, the reverence paid to the Divinity merited our first and chief attention, and that it was proper that the Christians and all others should have liberty to follow that mode of religion which to each of them appeared best; so that that God, who is seated in heaven, might be benign and propitious to us, and to every one under our government. And therefore we judged it a salutary measure, and one highly consonant to right reason, that no man should be denied leave of attaching himself to the rites of the Christians, or to whatever other religion his mind directed him, that thus the supreme Divinity, to whose worship we freely devote ourselves, might continue to vouchsafe His favour and beneficence to us. And accordingly we give you to know that, without regard to any provisos in our former orders to you concerning the Christians, all who choose that religion are to be permitted, freely and absolutely, to remain in it, and not to be disturbed any ways, or molested. And we thought fit to be thus special in the things committed to your charge, that you might understand that the indulgence which we have granted in matters of religion to the Christians is ample and unconditional; and perceive at the same time that the open and free exercise of their respective religions is granted to all others, as well as to the Christians. For it befits the well-ordered state and the tranquillity of our times that each individual be allowed, according to his own choice, to worship the Divinity; and we mean not to derogate aught from the honour due to any religion or its votaries. Moreover, with respect to the Christians, we formerly gave certain orders concerning the places appropriated for their religious assemblies; but now we will that all persons who have purchased such places, either from our exchequer or from any one else, do restore them to the Christians, without money demanded or price claimed, and that this be performed peremptorily and unambiguously; and we will also, that they who have obtained any right to such places by form of gift do forthwith restore them to the Christians: reserving always to such persons, who have either purchased for a price, or gratuitously acquired them, to make application to the judge of the district, if they look on themselves as entitled to any equivalent from our beneficence.

"All those places are, by your intervention, to be immediately restored to the Christians. And because it appears that, besides the places appropriated to religious worship, the Christians did possess other places, which belonged not to individuals, but to their society in general, that is, to their churches, we comprehend all such within the regulation aforesaid, and we will that you cause them all to be restored to the society or churches, and *that* without hesitation or controversy: Provided always, that the persons making restitution without a price paid shall be at liberty to seek indemnification from our bounty. In furthering all which things for the behoof of the Christians, you are to use your utmost diligence, to the end that our orders be speedily obeyed, and our gracious purpose in securing the public tranquillity promoted. So shall that divine favour which, in affairs of the mightiest importance, we have already experienced, continue to give success to us, and in our successes make the commonweal happy. And that the tenor of this our gracious ordinance may be made known unto all, we will that you cause it by your authority to be published everywhere."

Licinius having issued this ordinance, made an harangue, in which he exhorted the Christians to rebuild their religious edifices.

And thus, from the overthrow of the Church

[1] 13th of June. [Note the rise of *general* toleration.]

until its restoration, there was a space of ten years and about four months.

CHAP. XLIX.

While Licinius pursued with his army, the fugitive tyrant retreated, and again occupied the passes of mount Taurus; and there, by erecting parapets and towers, attempted to stop the march of Licinius. But the victorious troops, by an attack made on the right, broke through all obstacles, and Daia at length fled to Tarsus. *There*, being hard pressed both by sea and land, he despaired of finding any place for refuge; and in the anguish and dismay of his mind, he sought death as the only remedy of those calamities that God had heaped on him. But first he gorged himself with food, and large draughts of wine, as those are wont who believe that they eat and drink for the last time; and so he swallowed poison. However, the force of the poison, repelled by his full stomach, could not immediately operate, but it produced a grievous disease, resembling the pestilence; and his life was prolonged only that his sufferings might be more severe. And now the poison began to rage, and to burn up everything within him, so that he was driven to distraction with the intolerable pain; and during a fit of frenzy, which lasted four days, he gathered handfuls of earth, and greedily devoured it. Having undergone various and excruciating torments, he dashed his forehead against the wall, and his eyes started out of their sockets. And now, become blind, he imagined that he saw God, with His servants arrayed in white robes, sitting in judgment on him. He roared out as men on the rack are wont, and exclaimed that not he, but others, were guilty. In the end, as if he had been racked into confession, he acknowledged his own guilt, and lamentably implored Christ to have mercy upon him. Then, amidst groans, like those of one burnt alive, did he breathe out his guilty soul in the most horrible kind of death.

CHAP. L.

Thus did God subdue all those who persecuted His name, so that neither root nor branch of them remained; for Licinius, as soon as he was established in sovereign authority, commanded that Valeria should be put to death. Daia, although exasperated against her, never ventured to do this, not even after his discomfiture and flight, and when he knew that his end approached. Licinius commanded that Candidianus also should be put to death. He was the son of Galerius by a concubine, and Valeria, having no children, had adopted him. On the news of the death of Daia, she came in disguise to the court of Licinius, anxious to observe what might befall Candidianus. The youth, presenting himself at Nicomedia, had an outward show of honour paid to him, and, while he suspected no harm, was killed. Hearing of this catastrophe, Valeria immediately fled. The Emperor Severus left a son, Severianus, arrived at man's estate, who accompanied Daia in his flight from the field of battle. Licinius caused him to be condemned and executed, under the pretence that, on the death of Daia, he had intentions of assuming the imperial purple. Long before this time, Candidianus and Severianus, apprehending evil from Licinius, had chosen to remain with Daia; while Valeria favoured Licinius, and was willing to bestow on him that which she had denied to Daia, all rights accruing to her as the widow of Galerius. Licinius also put to death Maximus, the son of Daia, a boy eight years old, and a daughter of Daia, who was seven years old, and had been betrothed to Candidianus. But before their death, their mother had been thrown into the Orontes, in which river she herself had frequently commanded chaste women to be drowned. So, by the unerring and just judgment of God, all the impious received according to the deeds that they had done.

CHAP. LI.

Valeria, too, who for fifteen months had wandered under a mean garb from province to province, was at length discovered in Thessalonica, was apprehended, together with her mother Prisca, and suffered capital punishment. Both the ladies were conducted to execution; a fall from grandeur which moved the pity of the multitude of beholders that the strange sight had gathered together. They were beheaded, and their bodies cast into the sea. Thus the chaste demeanour of Valeria, and the high rank of her and her mother, proved fatal to both of them.[1]

CHAP. LII.

I relate all those things on the authority of well-informed persons; and I thought it proper to commit them to writing exactly as they happened, lest the memory of events so important should perish, and lest any future historian of the persecutors should corrupt the truth, either by suppressing their offences against God, or the judgment of God against them. To His everlasting mercy ought we to render thanks, that, having at length looked on the earth, He deigned to collect again and to restore His flock, partly laid waste by ravenous wolves, and partly scattered abroad, and to extirpate those noxious wild beasts who had trod down its pastures, and destroyed its resting-places.[2] Where now are

[1] [See cap. 39, p. 317, *supra*.]
[2] [Let us recall our Lord's forewarning: Matt. x. 16 and Luke x. 3.]

the surnames of the *Jovii* and the *Herculii*, once so glorious and renowned amongst the nations; surnames insolently assumed at first by Diocles and Maximian, and afterwards transferred to their successors? The Lord has blotted them out and erased them from the earth. Let us therefore with exultation celebrate the triumphs of God, and oftentimes with praises make mention of His victory; let us in our prayers, by night and by day, beseech Him to confirm for ever that peace which, after a warfare of ten years, He has bestowed on His own: and do you, above all others, my best beloved Donatus, who so well deserve to be heard, implore the Lord that it would please Him propitiously and mercifully to continue His pity towards His servants, to protect His people from the machinations and assaults of the devil, and to guard the now flourishing churches in perpetual felicity.

ELUCIDATION

(On the tenth of the kalends of April, p. 301.)

SERIOUS difficulties are encountered by the learned in reconciling Lactantius with himself, if, indeed, the fault be not one of his copyists rather than his own. In the fourth book of the *Institutes* [1] his language is thus given by Baluzius: [2] —

"Extremis temporibus Tiberii Cæsaris, *ut scriptum legimus*, Dominus noster Jesus Christus, a Judæis cruciatus est *post diem decimum kalendarum Aprilis*, duobus Geminis consulibus."

Lactantius was writing in Nicomedia, and may have quoted from memory what he had read, perhaps in the report of Pilate himself. The expression *post diem decimum kalendarum Aprilis* is ambiguous: and Jarvis says, "My impression is, that it means 'after the tenth day before the kalends of April;' that is, after the 23d of March." [3]

But here our author says, according to the accurate edition of Walchius [4] (A.D. 1715), —

"Exinde tetrarchas habuerunt usque ad Herodem, qui fuit sub imperio Tiberii Cæsaris: cujus anno quinto decimo, id est duobus Geminis consulibus, *ante diem septimam Calendarum Aprilium*, Judæi Christum cruci affixerunt."

But here, on the authority of forty manuscripts, Du Fresnoy reads, "*ante* diem decimam," which he labours to reconcile with "*post* diem decimum," as above. Jarvis adheres to the reading *septimam*, supported by more than fifty manuscripts, and decides for the 23d of March.

He cites Augustine to the same effect in the noted passage: [5] —

"Ille autem mense conceptum et passum esse Christum, et Paschæ observatio et dies ecclesiis notissimus Nativitatis ejus ostendit. Qui enim mense nono natus est octavo kalendas Janvarias profecto mense primo conceptus est circa octavum kalendas Aprilis, quod tempus passionis ejus fuit."

This, Augustine considers to be "seething a kid in mother's milk," after a mystical sense; cruelly making the cross to coincide with the maternity of the Virgin, who beheld her Son an innocent victim on the anniversary of her salutation by the angel.

---

[1] See note 1, p. 109. [2] As cited by Jarvis, *Introd.*, p. 379. [3] Baluz., *Miscellanea*, tom. i. p. 2. [4] *Opp.*, ed. Walchii, p. 435. [5] *Quæstt. in Exod.*, lib. ii., *Opp.*, tom. iii. p. 337.

FRAGMENTS OF LACTANTIUS

I. Fear, love, joy, sadness, lust, eager desire, anger, pity, emulation, admiration, — these motions or affections of the mind exist from the beginning of man's creation by the Lord; and they were usefully and advantageously introduced into human nature, that by governing himself by these with method, and in accordance with reason, man may be able, by acting manfully, to exercise those good qualities, by means of which he would justly have deserved to receive from the Lord eternal life. For these affections of the mind being restrained within their proper limits, that is, being rightly employed, produce at present good qualities, and in the future eternal rewards. But when they advance [1] beyond their boundaries, that is, when they turn aside to an evil course, then vices and iniquities come forth, and produce everlasting punishments.[2]

II. Within our memory, also, Lactantius speaks of metres, — the pentameter (he says) and the tetrameter.[3]

III. Firmianus, writing to Probus on the metres of comedies, thus speaks: "For as to the question which you proposed concerning the metres of comedies, I also know that many are of opinion that the plays of Terence in particular have not the metre of Greek comedy, — that is, of Menander, Philemon, and Diphilus, which consist of trimeter verses; for our ancient writers of comedies, in the modulation of their plays, preferred to follow Eupolis, Cratinus, and Aristophanes, as has been before said." That there is a measure — that is, metre [4] — in the plays of Terence and Plautus, and of the other comic and tragic writers, let these declare: Cicero, Scaurus, and Firmianus.[5]

IV. We will bring forward the sentiments of our Lactantius, which he expressed in words in his third volume to Probus on this subject. The Gauls, he says, were from ancient times called Galatians, from the whiteness of their body; and thus the Sibyl terms them. And this is what the poet intended to signify when he said, —

> "Gold collars deck their milk-white necks,"[6]

when he might have used the word *white*. It is plain that from this the province was called Galatia, in which, on their arrival in it, the Gauls united themselves with Greeks, from which circumstance that region was called Gallogræcia, and afterwards Galatia. And it is no wonder if he said this concerning the Galatians, and related that a people of the West, having passed over so great a distance in the middle of the earth, settled in a region of the East.[7]

---

1 Affluentes.

2 From *Muratorii Antiquit. Ital. med. æv.*

3 From *Maxim. Victorin. de carmine heroico.* Cf. Hieron., *Catal.*, c. 80. We have also another treatise, which is entitled "On Grammar."

4 μέτρον.

5 From Rufinus, the grammarian, on *Comic Metres*, p. 2712.

6 Virg., *Æn.*, viii. 660.

7 From Hieron., *Commentar. in ep. ad Gal.*, l. ii., opp. ed. Vallars. viii. 1, p. 426. Hieron., *De Viris Illus.*, c. 80: we have "four books of epistles to Probus."

THE PHŒNIX

BY AN UNCERTAIN AUTHOR. ATTRIBUTED TO LACTANTIUS.[1]

THERE is a happy spot, retired[2] in the first East, where the great gate of the eternal pole lies open. It is not, however, situated near to his rising in summer or in winter, but where the sun pours the day from his vernal chariot. There a plain spreads its open tracts; nor does any mound rise, nor hollow valley open[3] itself. But through twice six ells that place rises above the mountains, whose tops are thought to be lofty among us. Here is the grove of the sun; a wood stands planted with many a tree, blooming with the honour of perpetual foliage. When the pole had blazed with the fires of Phaethon, that place was uninjured by the flames; and when the deluge had immersed the world in waves, it rose above the waters of Deucalion. No enfeebling diseases, no sickly old age, nor cruel death, nor harsh fear, approaches hither, nor dreadful crime, nor mad desire of riches, nor Mars, nor fury, burning with the love of slaughter.[4] Bitter grief is absent, and want clothed in rags, and sleepless cares, and violent hunger. No tempest rages there, nor dreadful violence of the wind; nor does the hoar-frost cover the earth with cold dew. No cloud extends its fleecy[5] covering above the plains, nor does the turbid moisture of water fall from on high; but there is a fountain in the middle, which they call by the name of "living;"[6] it is clear, gentle, and abounding with sweet waters, which, bursting forth once during the space of each[7] month, twelve times irrigates all the grove with waters. Here a species of tree, rising with lofty stem, bears mellow fruits not about to fall on the ground. This grove, these woods, a single[8] bird, the phœnix, inhabits,—single, but it lives reproduced by its own death. It obeys and submits[9] to Phœbus, a remarkable attendant. Its parent nature has given it to possess this office. When at its first rising the saffron morn grows red, when it puts to flight the stars with its rosy light, thrice and four times she plunges her body into the sacred waves, thrice and four times she sips water from the living stream.[10] She is raised aloft, and takes her seat on the highest top of the lofty tree, which alone looks down upon the whole grove; and turning herself to the fresh risings of the nascent Phœbus, she awaits his rays and rising beam. And when the sun has thrown back the threshold of the shining gate, and the light gleam[11] of the first light has shone forth, she begins to pour strains of sacred song, and to hail[12] the new light with wondrous voice, which neither the notes of the nightingale[13] nor the flute of the Muses can equal with Cyrrhæan[14] strains. But neither is it thought that the dying swan can imitate it, nor the tuneful strings of the lyre of Mercury. After that Phœbus has brought back his horses to the open heaven,[15] and continually advancing, has displayed[16] his whole orb; she applauds with thrice-repeated flapping of her wings, and having thrice adored the fire-bearing head, is silent. And she also distinguishes the swift hours by sounds not liable to error by day and night: an overseer[17] of the groves, a venerable priestess of the wood, and alone admitted to thy secrets, O Phœbus. And when she has

1 [A curious expansion of the fable so long supposed to be authentic history of a natural wonder, and probably derived from Oriental tales corroborated by travellers. See vol. i. p. 12; also iii. 554. Yezeedee bird-worship may have sprung out of it.]

2 Remotus. The reference is supposed to be to Arabia, though some think that India is pointed out as the abode of the phœnix.

3 Hiat.

4 Cædis amore furor. There is another reading, "cedit."

5 Vellera, "thin fleecy clouds." So Virg., *Georg.*, i. 397; Tenuia nec lanæ per cœlum vellera ferri.

6 Vivum.

7 Per singula tempora mensum.

8 Unica, "the only one." It was supposed that only one phœnix lived at one time. So the proverb, "Phœnice rarior."

9 Birds were considered sacred to peculiar gods; thus the phœnix was held sacred to Phœbus. [Layard, *Nineveh*, vol. ii. p. 462.]

10 Gurgite.

11 Aura. So Virg., *Æneid*, vi. 204: "Discolor unde auri per ramos aura refulsit."

12 Ciere.

13 Aëdoniæ voces. The common reading is "Ædoniæ," contrary to the metre.

14 i.e., strains of Apollo and the Muses, for Cyrrha is at the foot of Parnassus, their favourite haunt.

15 Aperta Olympi, when he has mounted above the horizon.

16 Protulit.

17 Antistes.

now accomplished the thousand years of her life, and length of days has rendered her burdensome,[1] in order that she may renew the age which has glided by, the fates pressing[2] her, she flees from the beloved couch of the accustomed grove. And when she has left the sacred places, through a desire of being born[3] again, then she seeks this world, where death reigns. Full of years, she directs her swift flight into Syria, to which Venus herself has given the name of Phœnice;[4] and through trackless deserts she seeks the retired groves in the place, where a remote wood lies concealed through the glens. Then she chooses a lofty palm, with top reaching to the heavens, which has the pleasing[5] name of phœnix from the bird, and where[6] no hurtful living creature can break through, or slimy serpent, or any bird of prey. Then Æolus shuts in the winds in hanging caverns, lest they should injure the bright[7] air with their blasts, or lest a cloud collected by the south wind through the empty sky should remove the rays of the sun, and be a hindrance[8] to the bird. Afterwards she builds for herself either a nest or a tomb, for she perishes that she may live; yet she produces herself. Hence she collects juices and odours, which the Assyrian gathers from the rich wood, which the wealthy Arabian gathers; which either the Pygmæan[9] nations, or India crops, or the Sabæan land produces from its soft bosom. Hence she heaps together cinnamon and the odour of the far-scented amomum, and balsams with mixed leaves. Neither the twig of the mild cassia nor of the fragrant acanthus is absent, nor the tears and rich drop of frankincense. To these she adds tender ears[10] of flourishing spikenard, and joins the too pleasing pastures[11] of myrrh. Immediately she places her body about to be changed on the strewed nest, and her quiet limbs on such[12] a couch. Then with her mouth she scatters juices around and upon her limbs, about to die with her own funeral rites. Then amidst various odours she yields up[13] her life, nor fears the faith of so great a deposit. In the meantime, her body, destroyed by death, which proves the source of life,[14] is hot, and the heat itself produces a flame; and it conceives fire afar off from the light of heaven: it blazes, and is dissolved into burnt ashes. And these ashes collected in death it fuses,[15] as it were, into a mass, and has an effect[16] resembling seed. From this an animal is said to arise without limbs, but the worm is said to be of a milky colour. And it suddenly increases vastly with an imperfectly formed[17] body, and collects itself into the appearance of a well-rounded egg. After this it is formed again, such as its figure was before, and the phœnix, having burst her shell,[18] shoots forth, even as caterpillars[19] in the fields, when they are fastened by a thread to a stone, are wont to be changed into a butterfly. No food is appointed for her in our world, nor does any one make it his business to feed her while unfledged. She sips the delicate[20] ambrosial dews of heavenly nectar which have fallen from the star-bearing pole. She gathers these; with these the bird is nourished in the midst of odours, until she bears a natural form. But when she begins to flourish with early youth, she flies forth now about to return to her native abode. Previously, however, she encloses in an ointment of balsam, and in myrrh and dissolved[21] frankincense, all the remains of her own body, and the bones or ashes, and relics[22] of herself, and with pious mouth brings it into a round form,[23] and carrying this with her feet, she goes to the rising of the sun, and tarrying at the altar, she draws it forth in the sacred temple. She shows and presents herself an object of admiration to the beholder; such great beauty is there, such great honour abounds. In the first place, her colour is like the brilliancy[24] of that which the seeds of the pomegranate when ripe take under the smooth rind;[25] such colour as is contained in the leaves which the poppy produces in the fields, when Flora spreads her garments beneath the blushing sky. Her shoulders and beautiful breasts shine with this covering; with this her head, with this her neck, and the upper parts of her back shine. And her tail is extended, varied with yellow metal, in the spots of which mingled purple blushes. Between her wings there is a bright[26] mark above, as[27] Iris on high is wont to paint a cloud from above. She gleams resplendent with a mingling of the green emerald, and a shining beak[28] of pure horn opens itself. Her eyes are large;[29] you might

1 Gravem, i.e., a burden to herself.
2 Fatis urgentibus; others read "spatiis vergentibus."
3 Studio renascendi.
4 Venus was worshipped in Syro-Phœnice.
5 Gratum; others read "Graium," Grecian.
6 Quà; another reading is "quam," that which.
7 Purpureum. There may be a reference to the early dawn.
8 Obsit.
9 Some ancient writers place these fabulous people in India, others beyond Arabia.
10 Aristas. The word is sometimes applied, as here, to spikenard.
11 Et sociat myrrhæ pascua grata nimis; another reading is, "et sociam myrrhæ vim, Panachaia tuæ."
12 In talique toro; others, "vitalique toro," i.e., on a death-bed.
13 Commendat.
14 Genitali, "productive;" observe the antithesis.
15 Conflat.
16 Effectum; others read, "ad fœtum seminis instar habent.
17 Cum corpore curto; others read, "cum tempore certo."
18 Ruptis exuviis. The same word is used by Virgil to describe the serpent slipping its skin—"positis exuviis."
19 Tineæ.
20 Tenues; others read "teneri."
21 Thure soluto.
22 Exuvias suas.
23 In formam conglobat.
24 Quem croceum. The word is properly used to denote the colour of saffron: it is also applied to other bright colours.
25 Sub cortice lævi; the common reading is "sub sidere cæli."
26 Clarum insigne; others read, "aurum . . . insigneque."
27 Ceu; others read, "seu."
28 Gemmea cuspis. Her beak is of horn, but bright and transparent as a gem.
29 Ingentes oculi; others read, "oculos."

believe that they were two jacinths;[1] from the middle of which a bright flame shines. An irradiated crown is fitted[2] to the whole of her head, resembling on high the glory of the head of Phœbus.[3] Scales cover her thighs spangled with yellow metal, but a rosy[4] colour paints her claws with honour. Her form is seen to blend the figure of the peacock with that of the painted bird of Phasis.[5] The winged creature which is produced in the lands of the Arabians, whether it be beast or bird, can scarcely equal her magnitude.[6] She is not, however, slow, as birds which through the greatness of their body have sluggish motions, and a very heavy[7] weight. But she is light and swift, full of royal beauty. Such she always shows herself[8] in the sight of men. Egypt comes hither to such a wondrous[9] sight, and the exulting crowd salutes the rare bird. Immediately they carve her image on the consecrated marble, and mark both the occurrence and the day with a new title. Birds of every kind assemble together; none is mindful of prey, none of fear. Attended by a chorus of birds, she flies through the heaven, and a crowd accompanies her, exulting in the pious duty. But when she has arrived at the regions of pure ether, she presently returns;[10] afterwards she is concealed in her own regions. But oh, bird of happy lot and fate,[11] to whom the god himself granted to be born from herself! Whether it be female, or male, or neither, or both, happy she, who enters into[12] no compacts of Venus. Death is Venus to her; her only pleasure is in death: that she may be born, she desires previously to die. She is an offspring to herself, her own father and heir, her own nurse, and always a foster-child to herself. She is herself indeed, but not the same, since she is herself, and not herself, having gained eternal life by the blessing of death.

---

1 Hyacinthos; gems of this colour.

2 Æquatur.

3 i.e., the rays of the sun.

4 Roseus; others read, "roseo honore."

5 The pheasant.

6 Magniciem. Some take this as denoting the name of a bird, but no such bird is known.

7 Pergrave pondus; others read, "per grave pondus," by reason of the heavy weight.

8 Se exhibet; others read, "se probat."

9 Tanti ad miracula visus. [Deut. iv. 17.]

10 Inde; others read, "ille," but the allusion is very obscure.

11 Fili, "the thread," i.e., of fate.

12 Colit. [Badger's *Nestorians*, vol. i. p. 122.]

A POEM ON THE PASSION OF THE LORD

FORMERLY ASCRIBED TO LACTANTIUS.

WHOEVER you are who approach, and are entering the precincts [1] of the middle of the temple, stop a little and look upon me, who, though innocent, suffered for your crime; lay me up in your mind, keep me in your breast. I am He who, pitying the bitter misfortunes of men, came hither as a messenger [2] of offered peace, and as a full atonement [3] for the fault of men.[4] Here the brightest light from above is restored to the earth; here is the merciful image of safety; here I am a rest to you, the right way, the true redemption, the banner [5] of God, and a memorable sign of fate. It was on account of you and your life that I entered the Virgin's womb, was made man, and suffered a dreadful death; nor did I find rest anywhere in the regions of the earth, but everywhere threats, everywhere labours. First of all a wretched dwelling [6] in the land of Judæa was a shelter for me at my birth, and for my mother with me: here first, amidst the outstretched sluggish cattle, dry grass gave me a bed in a narrow stall. I passed my earliest years in the Pharian [7] regions, being an exile in the reign of Herod; and after my return to Judæa I spent the rest of my years, always engaged [8] in fastings, and the extremity of poverty itself, and the lowest circumstances; always by healthful admonitions applying the minds of men to the pursuit of genial uprightness, uniting with wholesome teaching many evident miracles: on which account impious Jerusalem, harassed by the raging cares of envy and cruel hatred, and blinded by madness, dared to seek for me, though innocent, by deadly punishment, a cruel death on the dreadful cross. And if you yourself wish to discriminate these things more fully,[9] and if it delights you to go through all my groans, and to experience griefs with me, put together [10] the designs and plots, and the impious price of my innocent blood, and the pretended kisses of a disciple,[11] and the insults and strivings of the cruel multitude; and, moreover, the blows, and tongues prepared [12] for accusations. Picture to your mind both the witnesses, and the accursed [13] judgment of the blinded Pilate, and the immense cross pressing my shoulders and wearied back, and my painful steps to a dreadful death. Now survey me from head to foot, deserted as I am, and lifted up afar from my beloved mother. Behold and see my locks clotted with blood, and my blood-stained neck under my very hair, and my head drained [14] with cruel thorns, and pouring down like rain [15] from all sides a stream [16] of blood over my divine face. Survey my compressed and sightless eyes, and my afflicted cheeks; see my parched tongue poisoned with gall, and my countenance pale with death. Behold my hands pierced with nails, and my arms drawn out, and the great wound in my side; see the blood streaming from it, and my perforated [17] feet, and blood-stained limbs. Bend your knee, and with lamentation adore the venerable wood of the cross, and with lowly countenance stooping [18] to the earth, which is wet with innocent blood, sprinkle it with rising tears, and at times [19] bear me and my admonitions in your devoted heart. Follow the footsteps of my life, and while you look upon my torments and cruel death, remembering my innumerable pangs of body and soul, learn to endure hardships,[20] and to watch over your own safety. These memorials,[21] if at any time you find pleasure in thinking over them, if in your mind there is any confidence to bear *anything* like my *suffer-*

---

1 Limina, "the threshold."
2 Interpres.
3 Venia, "remission."
4 Communis culpæ.
5 Vexillum.
6 Magalia.
7 i.e., Egypt.
8 Secutus.
9 Latius, "more widely," "in greater detail."
10 Collige.
11 Clientis. The "cliens" is one who puts himself under the protection of a "patronus." Here it is used of a follower.
12 Promptas.
13 Infanda, "unspeakable," "wicked."
14 Haustum.
15 Pluens.
16 Vivum cruorem.
17 Fossos.
18 Terram petens.
19 Nonnunquam; others read, "nunquam non," always.
20 Adversa.
21 Monumenta.

ings),[1] if the piety due, and gratitude worthy of my labours shall arise, will be incitements[2] to true virtue, and they will be shields against the snares of an enemy, aroused[3] by which you will be safe, and as a conqueror bear off the palm in every contest. If these memorials shall turn away your senses, which are devoted to a perishable[4] world, from the fleeting shadow of earthly beauty, the result will be, that you will not venture,[5] enticed by empty hope, to trust the frail[6] enjoyments of fickle fortune, and to place your hope in the fleeting years of life. But, truly, if you thus regard this perishable world,[7] and through your love of a better country deprive yourself[8] of earthly riches and the enjoyment of present things,[9] the prayers of the pious will bring you up[10] in sacred habits, and in the hope of a happy life, amidst severe punishments, will cherish you with heavenly dew, and feed you with the sweetness of the promised good. Until the great favour of God shall recall your happy[11] soul to the heavenly regions,[12] your body being left after the fates of death. Then freed from all labour, then joyfully beholding the angelic choirs, and the blessed companies of saints in perpetual bliss, it shall reign with me in the happy abode of perpetual peace.

1 Meorum.
2 Stimuli.
3 Acer.
4 Labilis orbis amicos sensus.
5 Auseris, an unusual form.
6 Occiduis rebus.
7 Ista caduca sæcula.
8 Exutum.
9 Rerum usus.
10 Extollent. The reading is uncertain; some editions have "expolient."
11 Purpuream, "bright, or shining."
12 Sublimes ad auras.

GENERAL NOTE.

THERE is no MS. authority for ascribing the above to Lactantius. "It does not, in the least, come up to the purity and eloquence of his style," says Dupin; and the same candid author notes the "adoration of the cross" as fatal to any such claim.[1]

Of the following poem, on Easter, Dupin says: "It is attributed to Venantius upon the testimony of some MSS. in the Vatican Library." This writer became known to Gregory of Tours, who died about A.D. 595, and seems to have succeeded him as bishop, dying soon after. Bede quotes his verse on St. Alban,[2] —

"Albanum egregium fecunda Britannia profert,"

but styles him "presbyter Fortunatus." He was the author of a poem on *St. Martin*, and another, *In Laude Virginum*. His works were edited by Brouverius, a Jesuit.

1 Note 18, p. 327.
2 The reader will be pleased with a reference, on p. 330, *infra*, to the (then recent) conversion of our Saxon forefathers in Kent.

POEM OF VENANTIUS HONORIUS[1] CLEMENTIANUS FORTUNATUS, ON EASTER

THE seasons blush varied with the flowery, fair weather,[2] and the gate of the pole lies open with greater light. His path in the heaven raises the fire-breathing[3] sun higher, who goes forth on his course,[4] and enters the waters of the ocean. Armed with rays traversing the liquid elements, in this[5] brief night he stretches out the day in a circle. The brilliant firmament[6] puts forth its clear countenance, and the bright stars show their joy. The fruitful earth pours forth its gifts with varied increase,[7] when the year has well returned its vernal riches.[8] Soft beds of violets paint the purple plain; the meadows are green with plants,[9] and the plant shines with its leaves. By degrees gleaming brightness of the flowers[10] comes forth; all the herbs smile with their blossoms.[11] The seed being deposited, the corn springs up far and wide[12] in the fields, promising to be able to overcome the hunger of the husbandman. Having deserted its stem, the vine-shoot bewails its joys; the vine gives water only from the source from which it is wont to give wine. The swelling bud, rising with tender down from the back of its mother, prepares its bosom for bringing forth. Its foliage[13] having been torn off in the wintry season, the verdant grove now renews its leafy shelter. Mingled together, the willow, the fir, the hazel, the osier,[14] the elm, the maple, the walnut, each tree applauds, delightful with its leaves. Hence the bee, about to construct its comb, leaving the hive, humming over the flowers, carries off honey with its leg. The bird which, having closed its song, was dumb, sluggish with the wintry cold, returns to its strains. Hence Philomela attunes her notes with her own instruments,[15] and the air becomes sweeter with the re-echoed melody. Behold, the favour of the reviving world bears witness that all gifts have returned together with its Lord. For in honour of Christ rising triumphant after *His descent to* the gloomy Tartarus, the grove on every side with its leaves *expresses approval,* the plants with their flowers express approval.[16] The light, the heaven, the fields, and the sea duly praise the God ascending above the stars, having crushed the laws of hell. Behold, He who was crucified reigns as God over all things, and all created objects offer prayer to their Creator. Hail, festive day, to be reverenced throughout the world,[17] on which God has conquered hell, and gains the stars! The changes of the year and of the months, the bounteous light of the days, the splendour of the hours, all things with voice applaud.[18] Hence, in honour of you, the wood with its foliage applauds; hence the vine, with its silent shoot, gives thanks. Hence the thickets now resound with the whisper of birds; amidst these the sparrow sings with exuberant[19] love. O Christ, Thou Saviour of the world, merciful Creator and Redeemer, the only offspring from the Godhead of the Father, flowing in an indescribable[20] manner from the heart of Thy Parent, Thou self-existing Word, and powerful from the mouth of Thy Father, equal to Him, of one mind with Him, His fellow, coeval with the Father, from whom at first[21] the world derived its origin! Thou

1 Venantius Honorius, to whom this poem is ascribed, was an Italian presbyter and poet In some editions the title is *De Resurrectione*. It was addressed to the bishop Felix.

2 Florigero sereno.

3 Ignivomus.

4 Vagus.

5 Hac in nocte brevi. Other editions read, "adhuc nocte brevi."

6 Æthera, an unusual form.

7 Fœtu; others read "cultu."

8 Cum bene vernales reddidit annus opes. Another reading is, "cum bene vernarit; reddit et annus opes."

9 Herbis.

10 Stellantia lumina florum.

11 Floribus; another reading is, "arridentque oculis."

12 Late; others read, "lactens," juicy.

13 Foliorum crine revulso; others read, "refuso."

14 Siler, supposed to be the osier, but the notices of the tree are too scanty to enable us to identify it. See Conington, *Virg. Georg.*, ii. 12.

15 Suis attemperat organa cannis. "Canna" seems to be used for "gutturis canna," the windpipe; "organum," often used for a musical instrument.

16 Favent.

17 Toto venerabilis ævo. [Rev. i. 10. Easter in Patmos, I suppose.]

18 Mobilitas anni, mensum, lux alma dierum
Horarum splendor, stridula cuncta favent.

There are great variations in the readings of this passage. Some read
"Nobilitas anni, mensum decus, alma dierum,
Horarum splendor, scriptula, puncta fovent."

19 Nimio; another reading is, "minimus."

20 Irrecitabiliter.

21 Principe.

dost suspend the firmament,[1] Thou heapest together the soil, Thou dost pour forth the seas, by whose[2] government all things which are fixed in their places flourish. Who seeing that the human race was plunged in the depth[3] *of misery*, that Thou mightest rescue man, didst Thyself also become man: nor wert Thou willing only to be born with a body,[4] but Thou becamest flesh, which endured to be born and to die. Thou dost undergo[5] funeral obsequies, Thyself the author of life and *framer* of the world, Thou dost enter[6] the path of death, in giving the aid of salvation. The gloomy chains of the infernal law yielded, and chaos feared to be pressed by the presence[7] of the light. Darkness perishes, put to flight by the brightness of Christ; the thick pall of eternal[8] night falls. But restore the promised[9] pledge, I pray Thee, O power benign! The third day has returned; arise, my buried One; it is not becoming that Thy limbs should lie in the lowly sepulchre, nor that worthless stones should press *that which is* the ransom[10] of the world. It is unworthy that a stone should shut in with a confining[11] rock, and cover Him in whose fist[12] all things are enclosed. Take away the linen clothes, I pray; leave the napkins in the tomb: Thou art sufficient for us, and without Thee there is nothing. Release the chained shades of the infernal prison, and recall to the upper regions[13] whatever sinks to the lowest depths. Give back Thy face, that the world may see the light; give back the day which flees from us at Thy death. But returning, O holy conqueror! Thou didst altogether fill the heaven![14] Tartarus lies depressed, nor retains its rights. The ruler of the lower regions, insatiably opening his hollow jaws, who has always been a spoiler, becomes[15] a prey to Thee. Thou rescuest an innumerable people from the prison of death, and they follow in freedom to the place whither their leader[16] approaches. The fierce monster in alarm vomits forth the multitude whom he had swallowed up, and the Lamb[17] withdraws the sheep from the jaw of the wolf. Hence re-seeking the tomb from the lower regions,[18] having resumed Thy flesh, as a warrior Thou carriest back ample trophies to the heavens. Those whom chaos held in punishment[19] he[20] has now restored; and those whom death might seek, a new life holds. Oh, sacred King, behold a great part of Thy triumph shines forth, when the sacred laver blesses pure souls! A host, clad in white,[21] come forth from the bright waves, and cleanse their old[22] fault in a new stream. The white garment also designates bright souls, and the shepherd has enjoyments from the snow-white flock. The priest Felix is added sharing[23] in this reward, who wishes to give double talents to his Lord. Drawing those who wander in Gentile error to better things, that a beast of prey may not carry them away, He guards the fold of God. Those whom guilty Eve had before infected, He now restores, fed[24] with abundant milk at the bosom of the Church. By cultivating rustic hearts with mild conversations, a crop is produced from a briar by the bounty of Felix. The Saxon, a fierce nation, living as it were after the manner of wild beasts, when you, O sacred One! apply a remedy, the beast of prey resembles[25] the sheep. About to remain with you through an age with the return[26] of a hundred-fold, you fill the barns with the produce of an abundant harvest. May this people, free from stain, be strengthened[27] in your arms, and may you bear to the stars a pure pledge to God. May one crown be bestowed on you from on high *gained* from yourself,[28] may another flourish gained from your people.

1 Æthera.
2 Quo moderante; others read, "quæ moderata."
3 Profundo.
4 Cum corpore; others read, "nostro e corpore nasci."
5 Pateris vitæ auctor; others have "patris novus auctor."
6 Intras; others, "intra."
7 Luminis ore.
8 Æternæ; another reading is, "et tetræ."
9 Pollicitam; others have "sollicitam."
10 Pretium mundi.
11 Rupe vetante.
12 Pugillo. Thus Prov. xxx. 4: "Who hath gathered the wind in His fists?"
13 Revoca sursum.
14 Olympum; others read, "in orbem," returning to the world.
15 Fit; others read, "sit."
16 Auctor.
17 i.e., "the Lamb of God."
18 [Post Tartara. Vol. iv. p. 140; v. pp. 153, 161, 174, this series.]
19 Pœnale.
20 Iste; another reading is, "in te."
21 An allusion to the white garments in which the newly baptized were arrayed.
22 Vetus vitium, "original sin;" as it was termed, "peccatum originis."
23 Consors; others read "concors," harmonious.
24 Pastos; others, "pastor."
25 Reddit.
26 Centeno reditu.
27 Vegetetur; another reading is, "agitetur."
28 De te; others read, "detur et," with injury to the metre.

GENERAL NOTE.

A FINE passage illustrating the gush of early Christian devotion at Easter, "breaking into all the heavenly joy of the new creation," will be found in Professor Milligan's remarkable work on *The Resurrection of our Lord* (London, Macmillan, 1884). The author is "professor of divinity and biblical criticism in the University of Aberdeen."

ASTERIUS URBANUS

INTRODUCTORY NOTICE

TO

ASTERIUS URBANUS

[*Circa* A.D. 232.] Finding these fragments relegated, by the Edinburgh editors, to a place (unaccountably chosen) among the spurious Decretals,[1] and dismissed as of dubious character, it looked as if modern light had been shed upon this author, and as if he had better, perhaps, be classed with the apocryphal works of our concluding volume. But, after considerable inquiry, I see no reason to dismiss Asterius from the respectable position assigned him by Lardner;[2] and I now wish I had appended these fragments to those of the Roman presbyter Caius, to which the reader is referred.[3] It is true, Lardner is quite undecided as to this author, though he accepts Tillemont's conjecture as probable; viz., that the Asterius Urbanus mentioned by Eusebius is the author of the fragments, and that his work against the Montanists was written in the eleventh year of the Emperor Alexander, *circa* 232. It is doubtful whether the author was a presbyter or a bishop. On some occasions he seems to have been at Ancyra in Galatia, where he reluctantly consented to write his treatise at the solicitation of the presbytery there, and particularly of Abercius[4] Marcellus, to whom it is inscribed.

The translator is not named, but here follows the very unsatisfactory preface of the Edinburgh edition: —

Nothing is known of Asterius Urbanus. The name occurs in Fragment IV.;[5] and from the allusion made to him there, some have inferred that he was the author of the work against the Montanists, from which Eusebius has made these extracts. The inference is unfounded. There is no clue to the authorship. It has been attributed by different critics to Apollinaris, Apollonius, and Rhodon.

---

1 Edin. ed., vol. ix. p 224.

2 *Credib.*, vol. ii. p. 410.

3 Vol v. p 599, this series. See note 3, p 335, *infra*.

4 Or *Avircius*. See p. 335, note 2, *infra*.

5 Translated p. 336, *infra*.

THE EXTANT WRITINGS OF ASTERIUS URBANUS[1]

I. THE EXORDIUM.

Having now for a very long and surely a very sufficient period had the charge pressed upon me by thee, my dear Avircius[2] Marcellus, to write some sort of treatise against the heresy that bears the name of Miltiades,[3] I have somehow been very doubtfully disposed toward the task up till now; not that I felt any difficulty in refuting the falsehood, and in bearing my testimony to the truth, but that I was apprehensive and fearful lest I should appear to any to be adding some new word or precept[4] to the doctrine of the Gospel of the New Testament, with respect to which indeed it is not possible for one who has chosen to have his manner of life in accordance with the Gospel itself, either to add anything to it or to take away anything from

Being recently, however, at Ancyra, a town of Galatia, and finding the church in Pontus[5] greatly agitated[6] by this new prophecy, as they call it, but which should rather be called this false prophecy, as shall be shown presently, I discoursed to the best of my ability, with the help of God, for many days in the church, both on these subjects and on various others[7] which were brought under my notice by them. And this I did in such manner that the church rejoiced and was strengthened in the truth, while the adversaries[8] were forthwith routed, and the opponents put to grief. And the presbyters of the place accordingly requested us to leave behind us some memorandum of the things which we alleged in opposition to the adversaries of the truth, there being present also our fellow-presbyter Zoticus Otrenus.[9] This, however, we did not; but we promised, if the Lord gave us opportunity, to write down the matters here, and send them to them with all speed.

II. FROM BOOK I.

Now the attitude of opposition[10] which they have assumed, and this new heresy of theirs which puts them in a position of separation from the Church, had their origin in the following manner. There is said to be a certain village called Ardaba[11] in the Mysia, which touches Phrygia.[12] There, they say, one of those who had been but recently converted to the faith, a person of the name of Montanus, when Gratus was proconsul of Asia, gave the adversary entrance against himself by the excessive lust of his soul after taking the lead. And this person was carried away in spirit;[13] and suddenly being seized with a kind of frenzy and ecstasy, he raved, and began to speak and to utter strange things, and to prophesy in a manner contrary to the custom of the Church, as handed down from early times and preserved thenceforward in a continuous succession. And among those who were present on that occasion, and heard those spurious utterances, there were some who were indignant, and rebuked him as one frenzied, and under the power of demons, and possessed by the spirit of delusion, and agitating the multitude, and debarred him from speaking any more; for they were mindful of the Lord's

---

1 Being fragments of three books to Abercius Marcellus against the Montanists. Gallandi, vol. iii. p. 273, from Eusebius, *Hist. Eccl.*, v. ch. 16, 17.

2 The manuscripts write the name Ἀουίρκιος, Avircius: but Nicephorus (book iv.) gives it as Ἀβέρκιος, Abercius.

3 Nicephorus adds ἴσον δ' εἰπεῖν Μοντανόν, which seems, however, to be but a scholium. It may appear difficult to account for the fact that the name of Miltiades rather than that of Montanus is associated with the heresy of the Cataphrygians, and some consequently have conjectured that we should read here *Alcibiades*, as that is a name mentioned in concert with Montanus and Theodotus in Euseb. v. 3. In the Muratorian fragment, however, as given above among the writings of Caius, we find again a Miltiades named among the heretics. [Vol. v. p. 604, this series.]

4 ἐπισυγγράφειν ἢ ἐπιδιατάσσεσθαι.

5 κατὰ πόντον. But the Codex Regius reads κατὰ τόπον, the church *of the place*, i.e., the church of Ancyra itself. This reading is confirmed by Nicephorus, book iv. 23, and is adopted by the Latin interpreter.

6 διατεθρυλλημένην, "ringing with it," "deafened by it."

7 ἕκαστά τε. Others propose ἑκάστοτε, "constantly," "daily."

8 ἀντιθέτους. Others read ἀντιθέους, "the enemies of God."

9 Ζωτικοῦ τοῦ Ὀτρηνοῦ. Nicephorus reads Ὀστρηνοῦ. [Compare p. 336, *infra*. This looks like a bishop or a presbyter attending Asterius (compare Cyprian, vol. v. p. 319, note 7, this series), and is a token that our author was a bishop.]

10 ἔνστασις.

11 Ἀρδαβαῦ. One codex makes it Ἀρδαβᾶβ.

12 ἐν τῇ κατὰ τὴν Φρυγιαν Μυσίᾳ. Rufinus renders it, *apud Phrygiam Mysiæ civitatem*; others render it, *apud Mysiam Phrygiæ*; Migne takes it as defining this Mysia to be the Asiatic one, in distinction from the European territory, which the Latins called Mœsia, but the Greeks also Μυσία.

13 πνευματοφορηθῆναι.

distinction [1] and threatening, whereby He warned them to be on their guard vigilantly against the coming of the false prophets. But there were others too, who, as if elated by the Holy Spirit and the prophetic gift, and not a little puffed up, and forgetting entirely the Lord's distinction, challenged the maddening and insidious and seductive spirit, being themselves cajoled and misled by him, so that there was no longer any checking him to silence.[2] And thus by a kind of artifice, or rather by such a process of craft, the devil having devised destruction against those who were disobedient *to the Lord's warning*, and being unworthily honoured by them, secretly excited and inflamed their minds that had already left the faith which is according to truth, in order to play the harlot with error.[3] For he stirred up two others also, women, and filled them with the spurious spirit, so that they too spoke in a frenzy and unseasonably, and in a strange manner, like the person already mentioned, while the spirit called them happy as they rejoiced and exulted proudly at his working, and puffed them up by the magnitude of his promises; while, on the other hand, at times also he condemned them skilfully and plausibly, in order that he might seem to them also to have the power of reproof.[4] And those few who were thus deluded were Phrygians. But the same arrogant spirit taught them to revile the Church universal under heaven, because that false spirit of prophecy found neither honour from it nor entrance into it. For when the faithful throughout Asia met together often and in many places of Asia for deliberation on this subject, and subjected those novel doctrines to examination, and declared them to be spurious, and rejected them as heretical, they were in consequence of that expelled from the Church and debarred from communion.[5]

III. FROM BOOK II.

Wherefore, since they stigmatized us as slayers of the prophets[6] because we did not receive their loquacious[7] prophets, — for they say that these are they whom the Lord promised to send to the people, — let them answer us in the name of God, and tell us, O friends, whether there is any one among those who began to speak from Montanus and the women onward that was persecuted by the Jews or put to death by the wicked? There is not one. Not even one of them is there who was seized and crucified for the name[8] *of Christ*. No; certainly not. Neither assuredly was there one of these women who was ever scourged in the synagogues of the Jews, or stoned. No; never anywhere. It is indeed by another kind of death that Montanus and Maximilla are said to have met their end. For the report is, that by the instigation of that maddening spirit both of them hung themselves; not together indeed, but at the particular time of the death of each,[9] as the common story goes. And thus they died, and finished their life like the traitor Judas. Thus, also, the general report gives it that Theodotus — that astonishing person who was, so to speak, the first procurator[10] of their so-called prophecy, and who, as if he were sometime taken up and received into the heavens, fell into spurious ecstasies,[11] and gave himself wholly over to the spirit of delusion — was at last tossed by him[12] into the air, and met his end miserably. People say then that this took place in the way we have stated. But as we did not see[13] them ourselves, we do not presume to think that we know any of these things with certainty. And it may therefore have been in this way perhaps, and perhaps in some other way, that Montanus and Theodotus and the woman mentioned above perished.

IV.

And let not the spirit of Maximilla say (as it is found in the same book of Asterius Urbanus[14]), "I am chased like a wolf from the sheep; I am no wolf. I am word, and spirit, and power." But let him clearly exhibit and prove the power in the spirit. And by the spirit let him constrain to a confession those who were present at that time for the very purpose of trying and holding converse with the talkative spirit — those men so highly reputed as men and bishops — namely, Zoticus of the village of Comana,[15] and Julian

1 *διαστολῆς*.
2 *εἰς τὸ μηκέτι κωλύεσθαι σιωπᾶν*.
3 *τὴν ἀποκεκοιμημένην*, etc.; the verb being used literally of the wife who proves false to her marriage vow.
4 *ἐλεγκτικόν*. Montanus, that is to say, or the demon that spake by Montanus, knew that it had been said of old by the Lord, that when the Spirit came He would convince or reprove the world of sin; and hence this false spirit, with the view of confirming his hearers in the belief that he was the true Spirit of God, sometimes rebuked and condemned them. See a passage in Ambrose's *Epistle to the Thessal.*, ch. v. (Migne).
5 [Vol. ii. pp. 4, 5.]
6 [Compare Num. xvi. 41.]
7 *αμετροφώνους*. So Homer in the *Iliad* calls Thersites *ἀμετροεπής*, "unbridled of tongue," and thus also *mendacious*.

8 *τοῦ ὀνόματος*. Nicephorus reads *τοῦ νόμου*, "for the law." [Compare Tertullian, vol. iii. cap. 28, p. 624.]
9 *κατὰ δὲ τὸν ἑκαστοῦ τελευτῆς καιρόν*.
10 *οἷον ἐπίτροπον*. Rufinus renders it, "veluti primogenitum prophetiæ ipsorum." Migne takes it as meaning *steward*, manager of a common fund established among the Montanists for the support of their prophets. Eusebius (v. 18) quotes Apollonius as saying of Montanus, that he *established exactors of money, and provided salaries for those who preached his doctrine.*
11 *παρεκστῆναι*.
12 *δισκευθέντα*, "pitched like a quoit."
13 The text is, *ἀλλὰ μὴν ἄνευ*. But in various codices we have the more correct reading, *ἀλλὰ μὴ ἄνευ*.
14 These words are apparently a scholium, which Eusebius himself or some old commentator had written on the margin of his copy We gather also from them that Asterius Urbanus was credited with the authorship of these three books, and not Apollinaris, as some have supposed.
15 Comana seems to have been a town of Pamphylia. At least a bishop of Comana is mentioned in the epistle of the bishops of Pamphylia to Leo Augustus, cited in the third part of the *Council of Chalcedon*, p. 391. [See p. 335, note 9, *supra*.]

of Apamea, whose mouths Themison[1] and his followers bridled, and prevented the false and seductive spirit from being confuted by them.

V.

And has not the falsity of this also been made manifest already? For it is now upwards of thirteen years since the woman died, and there has arisen neither a partial nor a universal war in the world. Nay, rather there has been steady and continued peace to the Christians by the mercy of God.

VI. FROM BOOK III.

But as they have been refuted in all their allegations, and are thus at a loss what to say, they try to take refuge in their martyrs. For they say that they have many martyrs, and that this is a sure proof of the power of their so-called prophetic spirit. But this allegation, as it seems, carries not a whit more truth with it than the others. For indeed some of the other heresies have also a great multitude of martyrs; but yet certainly we shall not on that account agree with them, neither shall we acknowledge that they have truth in them. And those first heretics, who from the heresy of Marcion are called Marcionites, allege that they have a great multitude of martyrs for Christ. But yet they do not confess Christ Himself according to truth.

VII.

Hence, also, whenever those who have been called to martyrdom for the true faith by the Church happen to fall in with any of those so-called martyrs of the Phrygian heresy, they always separate from them, and die without having fellowship with them, because they do not choose to give their assent to the spirit of Montanus and the women. And that this is truly the case, and that it has actually taken place in our own times at Apamea, a town on the Mæander, in the case of those who suffered martyrdom with Caius[2] and Alexander, natives of Eumenia, is clear to all.

VIII.

As I found these things in a certain writing of theirs directed against the writing of our brother Alcibiades,[3] in which he proves the impropriety of a prophet's speaking in ecstasy, I made an abridgment of that work.

IX.

But the false prophet falls into a spurious ecstasy, which is accompanied by a want of all shame and fear. For beginning with a voluntary (designed) rudeness, he ends with an involuntary madness of soul, as has been already stated. But they will never be able to show that any one of the Old Testament prophets, or any one of the New, was carried away in spirit after this fashion. Nor will they be able to boast that Agabus, or Judas, or Silas, or the daughters of Philip, or *the woman* Ammia in Philadelphia, or Quadratus, or indeed any of the others who do not in any respect belong to them, were moved in this way.

X.

For if, after Quadratus and the woman Ammia in Philadelphia, as they say, the women who attached themselves to Montanus succeeded to the gift of prophecy, let them show us which of them thus succeeded Montanus and his women. For the apostle deems that the gift of prophecy should abide in all the Church up to the time of the final advent. But they will not be able to show the gift to be in their possession even at the present time, which is the fourteenth year only from the death of Maximilla.[4]

[1] Themison was a person of note among the Montanists, who boasted of himself as a confessor and martyr, and had the audacity to write a catholic epistle to the churches like an apostle, with the view of commending the new prophecy to them. See Euseb., v. 18.

[2] ἐν τοῖς περὶ Γάϊον . . . μαρτυρήσασι. It may be intended for, "In the case of the martyrs Caius and Alexander.

[3] Migne is of opinion that there has been an interchange of names between this passage and the Exordium, and that we should read Miltiades here, and Alcibiades there. But see Exordium, note 3, p. 335. [And compare Eusebius, book v. cap. 3, where two of this name are mentioned; also *Ibid.*, cap. 17.]

[4] This seems to be the sense of the text, which appears to be imperfect here: ἀλλ' οὐκ ἂν ἔχοιεν δεῖξαι τεσσαρεσκαιδέκατον ἤδη που τοῦτο ἔτος ἀπὸ τῆς Μαξιμίλλης τελευτῆς.

GENERAL NOTE.

THE reader will do well to turn back to my Introductory Notice to the *Epistle of Hermas*,[1] and also to the elucidations[2] which are appended to that Epistle. If any value attaches to this fragment, it must be found in its illustrations of Hermas and Tertullian. These, in turn, shed light on it.

[1] Vol. ii. p. 3, this series.

[2] *Ibid.*, p. 56.

ELUCIDATION

(Aviricius Marcellus, p. 335, *supra.*)

LIKE his great predecessor in Patristic research (Bishop Pearson), the learned and indefatigable Bishop Lightfoot will leave us gold-dust in the mere sweepings of his literary work. His recent voluminous edition of the *Apostolic Fathers*[1] is encyclopedic in its treatment of the subject; and I had hardly corrected the last proofs of the fragments ascribed to Asterius Urbanus when I discovered, in one of his notes on Polycarp, a most brilliant elucidation of a matter which I had supposed involved in twofold obscurity. Asterius is a mere name embedded in Eusebius, and in his fragments there preserved is embedded the yet obscurer name of Aviricius Marcellus, which the reader will find, with its various spellings, in one of the translator's notes.[2] Who could have supposed that even the learning and ingenuity of Lightfoot could fish out of very dark waters such shining booty as fills the network about "Abercius of Hierapolis?" While he does not even name Asterius, the mere *nominis umbra* of Aviricius Marcellus is material for a truly remarkable dissertation covering nine pages of fine print, and enabling us to conclude that this Aviricius is none other than the same "bishop of Hierapolis" about whom there is such a long story in the Bollandist *Acta Sanctorum*.[3] The story is a silly legend, but Lightfoot understands the art *ex fumo dare lucem;* and any one who enjoys following up such elaborations will find most curious and delightful reading in the pages to which I have referred. Our Aviricius, then, was bishop of "Hieropolis of Lesser Phrygia," not of Hierapolis on the Mæander, and flourished about A.D. 163, during the reign of M. Aurelius. This date, therefore, must correct the conjecture of Tillemont and the date which I had accepted from him on the authority of Dr. Lardner.[4]

---

1 London, Macmillans, 1885. Refer to part ii. vol. i. pp. 476–485.

2 See p. 335, *supra*, note 2.

3 Lightfoot also gives a reference to Migne's *Patrologia*, vol. cxv. p. 1211.

4 See p. 333, *supra*. "There is no clue to the authorship" of the fragments, says the translator; but, under the lead of a Lightfoot, who may not hope to find one? I commend the quarry to studious readers.

VICTORINUS

[TRANSLATED BY THE REV. ROBERT ERNEST WALLIS, PH.D.]

ON THE CREATION OF THE WORLD[1]

To me, as I meditate and consider in my mind concerning the creation of this world in which we are kept enclosed, even such is the rapidity of that creation; as is contained in the book of Moses, which he wrote about its creation, and which is called Genesis. God produced that entire mass for the adornment of His majesty in six days; on the seventh to which He consecrated it . . . with a blessing. For this reason, therefore, because in the septenary number of days both heavenly and earthly things are ordered, in place of the beginning I will consider of this seventh day after the principle of all matters pertaining to the number of seven; and as far as I shall be able, I will endeavour to portray the day of *the divine* power to that consummation.

In the beginning God made the light, and divided it in the exact measure of twelve hours by day and by night, for this reason, doubtless, that day might bring over the night as an occasion of rest for men's labours; that, again, day might overcome, and thus that labour might be refreshed with this alternate change of rest, and that repose again might be tempered by the exercise of day. "On the fourth day He made two lights in the heaven, the greater and the lesser, that the one might rule over the day, the other over the night,"[2] — *the lights of* the sun and moon; and He placed the rest of the stars in heaven, that they might shine upon the earth, and by their positions distinguish the seasons, and years, and months, and days, and hours.

Now is manifested the reason of the truth why the fourth day is called the Tetras, why we fast even to the ninth hour, or even to the evening, or why there should be a passing over even to the next day. Therefore this world of ours is composed of four elements — fire, water, heaven, earth. These four elements, therefore, form the quaternion of times or seasons. The sun, also, and the moon constitute throughout the space of the year four seasons — of spring, summer, autumn, winter; and these seasons make a quaternion. And to proceed further still from that principle, lo, there are four living creatures before God's throne,[3] four Gospels, four rivers flowing in paradise;[4] four generations of people from Adam to Noah, from Noah to Abraham, from Abraham to Moses, from Moses to Christ the Lord, the Son of God; and four living creatures, *viz.*, a man, a calf, a lion, an eagle; and four rivers, the Pison, the Gihon, the Tigris, and the Euphrates. The man Christ Jesus, the originator of these things whereof we have above spoken, was taken prisoner by wicked hands, by a quaternion *of soldiers*. Therefore on account of His captivity by a quaternion, on account of the majesty of His works, — that the seasons also, wholesome to humanity, joyful for the harvests, tranquil for the tempests, may roll on, — therefore we make *the fourth day* a station or a supernumerary fast.

On the fifth day the land and water brought forth their progenies. On the sixth day the things that were wanting were created; and thus God raised up man from the soil, as lord of all the things which He created upon the earth and the water. Yet He created angels and archangels before He created man, placing spiritual beings before earthly ones. For light was made before sky and the earth. This sixth day is called *parasceve*,[5] that is to say, the preparation of the kingdom. For He perfected Adam, whom *He made* after His image and likeness. But for this reason He completed His works before He created angels and fashioned man, lest perchance they should falsely assert that they had been His helpers. On this day also, on account of the passion of the Lord Jesus Christ, we make either a station to God, or a fast. On the seventh day He rested from all His works, and blessed it, and sanctified it. On the former day we are accustomed to fast rigorously, that on the Lord's day we may go forth

[1] A fragment by the martyr Victorinus, bishop of Petau, who flourished towards the end of the third century. [He died in the persecution A.D. 304. For the text and full annotations, see Routh, iii. 451–483. His See must not be confounded with the Gallic Poictiers. He was of Petau in Austria (*Pannonia Superior*), as Launoy demonstrated A.D. 1653.]

[2] Gen i 16, 17.

[3] Rev. iv. 6. [See vol. v. note 3, p. 618, this series.]

[4] Gen. ii. 10.

[5] παρασκευή.

to our bread with giving of thanks. And let the *parasceve* become a rigorous fast, lest we should appear to observe any Sabbath with the Jews, which Christ Himself, the Lord of the Sabbath, says by His prophets that "His soul hateth;"[1] which Sabbath He in His body abolished, although, nevertheless, He had formerly Himself commanded Moses that circumcision should not pass over the eighth day, which day very frequently happens on the Sabbath, as we read written in the Gospel.[2] Moses, foreseeing the hardness of that people, on the Sabbath raised up his hands, therefore, and thus *figuratively* fastened himself to a cross.[3] And in the battle they were sought for by the foreigners on the Sabbath-day, that they might be taken captive, and, as if by the very strictness of the law, might be fashioned to the avoidance of its teaching.[4]

And thus in the sixth Psalm for the eighth day,[5] David asks the Lord that He would not rebuke him in His anger, nor judge him in His fury; for this is indeed the eighth day of that future judgment, which will pass beyond the order of the sevenfold arrangement. Jesus also, the son of Nave, the successor of Moses, himself broke the Sabbath-day; for on the Sabbath-day he commanded the children of Israel[6] to go round the walls of the city of Jericho with trumpets, and declare war against the aliens. Matthias[7] also, prince of Judah, broke the Sabbath; for he slew the prefect of Antiochus the king of Syria on the Sabbath, and subdued the foreigners by pursuing them. And in Matthew we read, that it is written Isaiah also and the rest of his colleagues broke the Sabbath[8] — that that true and just Sabbath should be observed in the seventh millenary of years. Wherefore to those seven days the Lord attributed to each a thousand years; for thus went the warning: "In Thine eyes, O Lord, a thousand years are as one day."[9] Therefore in the eyes of the Lord each thousand of years is ordained, for I find that the Lord's eyes are seven.[10] Wherefore, as I have narrated, that true Sabbath will be in the seventh millenary of years, when Christ with His elect shall reign. Moreover, the seven heavens agree with those days; for thus we are warned: "By the word of the Lord were the heavens made, and all the powers of them by the spirit of His mouth."[11] There are seven spirits. Their names are the spirits which abode on the Christ of God, as was intimated in Isaiah the prophet: "And there rests upon Him the spirit of wisdom and of understanding, the spirit of counsel and might, the spirit of wisdom[12] and of piety, and the spirit of God's fear hath filled Him."[13] Therefore the highest heaven is the heaven of wisdom; the second, of understanding; the third, of counsel; the fourth, of might; the fifth, of knowledge; the sixth, of piety; the seventh, of God's fear. From this, therefore, the thunders bellow, the lightnings are kindled,[14] the fires are heaped together; fiery darts[15] appear, stars gleam, the anxiety caused by the dreadful comet is aroused.[16] Sometimes it happens that the sun and moon approach one another, and cause those more than frightful appearances, radiating with light in the field of their aspect. But the author of the whole creation is Jesus. His name is the Word; for thus His Father says: "My heart hath emitted a good word."[17] John the evangelist thus says: "In the beginning was the Word, and the Word was with God, and the Word was God. The same was in the beginning with God. All things were made by Him, and without Him was nothing made that was made."[18] Therefore, first, was made the creation; secondly, man, the lord of the human race, as says the apostle.[19] Therefore this Word, when it made light, is called Wisdom; when it made the sky, Understanding; when it made land and sea, Counsel; when it made sun and moon and other bright things, Power; when it calls forth land and sea, Knowledge; when it formed man, Piety; when it blesses and sanctifies man, it has the name of God's fear.

Behold the seven horns of the Lamb,[20] the seven eyes of God[21] — the seven eyes are the seven spirits of the Lamb;[22] seven torches burning before the throne of God[22] seven golden candlesticks,[23] seven young sheep,[24] the seven women in Isaiah,[25] the seven churches in Paul,[26] seven deacons,[27] seven angels,[28] seven trumpets,[29] seven seals to the book, seven periods of seven days with which Pentecost is completed, the seven weeks in Daniel,[30] also the forty-three weeks in Daniel;[31] with Noah, seven of all clean

1 Isa. i. 13, 14.
2 John vii. 22.
3 Exod. xxii. 9, 12.
4 1 Macc. ii. 31–41.
5 Ps. vi. 1; [also Ps. xii. On *Sheminith*, 1 Chron. xv. 21].
6 Josh. vi. 4.
7 Mattathias, interp. Vulg.
8 Matt. xii. 5.
9 Ps. xc. 4.
10 Zech. iv. 10.
11 Ps. xxxiii. 6. [*Seven*, say the Rabbis. Vol. ii. note 7, p. 438, this series.]
12 Probably "knowledge."
13 Isa. xi. 2, 3.
14 Or, "the rivers are spread abroad."
15 Trabes. [There is no proof of seven heavens in Scripture.]
16 Coma horribilis curabitur.
17 Ps. xlv. 1. [Vol. i. p. 213, this series.]
18 John i. 1, 2, 3.
19 1 Cor. xv. 45–47.
20 Rev. v. 6.
21 Zech. iv. 10.
22 Rev. iv. 5.
23 Rev. i. 13.
24 Lev. xxiii. 18.
25 Isa. iv. 1.
26 Acts vi. 3?
27 Acts vi. 3.
28 Rev. *passim*.
29 Josh. vi.; Rev. viii.
30 Dan. ix. 25.
31 Dan. ix.

things in the ark;[1] seven revenges of Cain,[2] seven years for a debt to be acquitted,[3] the lamp with seven orifices,[4] seven pillars of wisdom in the house of Solomon.[5]

Now, therefore, you may see that it is being told you of the unerring glory of God in providence; yet, as far as my small capacity shall be able, I will endeavour to set it forth. That He might re-create that Adam by means of the week, and bring aid to His entire creation, was accomplished by the nativity of His Son Jesus Christ our Lord. Who, then, that is taught in the law of God, who that is filled with the Holy Spirit, does not see in his heart, that on the same day on which the dragon seduced Eve, the angel Gabriel brought the glad tidings to the Virgin Mary; that on the same day the Holy Spirit overflowed the Virgin Mary, on which He made light; that on that day He was incarnate in flesh, in which He made the land and water; that on the same day He was put to the breast, on which He made the stars; that on the same day He was circumcised,[6] on which the land and water brought forth their offspring; that on the same day He was incarnated, on which He formed man out of the ground; that on the same day Christ was born, on which He formed man; that on that day He suffered, on which Adam fell; that on the same day He rose again from the dead, on which He created light? He, moreover, consummates His humanity in the number seven: of His nativity, His infancy, His boyhood, His youth, His young-manhood, His mature age, His death. I have also set forth His humanity to the Jews in these manners: since He is hungry, is thirsty; since He gave food and drink; since He walks, and retired; since He slept upon a pillow;[7] since, moreover, He walks upon the stormy seas with His feet, He commands the winds, He cures the sick and restores the lame, He raises the blind by His speech,[8] — see ye that He declares Himself to them to be the Lord.

The day, as I have above related, is divided into two parts by the number twelve — by the twelve hours of day and night; and by these hours too, months, and years, and seasons, and ages are computed. Therefore, doubtless, there are appointed also twelve angels of the day and twelve angels of the night, in accordance, to wit, with the number of hours. For these are the twenty-four witnesses of the days and nights[9] which sit before the throne of God, having golden crowns on their heads, whom the Apocalypse of John the apostle and evangelist calls elders, for the reason that they are older both than the other angels and than men.

1 Gen. vii. 2.
2 Gen. iv. 15.
3 Deut. xv. 1.
4 Zech. iv. 2.
5 Prov. xi. 1.
6 Ea die in sanguine.
7 Mark iv. 38.
8 "He makes the deaf to hear, and recalls the dead:" this is inserted conjecturally by Routh.
9 Rev. iv. 4.

COMMENTARY ON THE APOCALYPSE OF THE BLESSED JOHN

FROM THE FIRST CHAPTER.

1. "THE Revelation of Jesus Christ, which God gave to Him, and showed unto His servants things which must shortly come to pass, and signified it. Blessed are they who read and hear the words of this prophecy, and keep the things which are written."] The beginning of the book promises blessing to him that reads and hears and keeps, that he who takes pains about the reading may thence learn *to do* works, and may keep the precepts.

4. "Grace unto you, and peace, from Him which is, and which was, and which is to come."] *He is*, because He endures continually; *He was*, because with the Father He made all things, and has at this time taken a beginning from the Virgin; *He is to come*, because assuredly *He will come* to judgment.

"And from the seven spirits which are before His throne."] We read of a sevenfold spirit in Isaiah,[1]—namely, the spirit of wisdom and of understanding, the spirit of counsel and might, of knowledge and of piety, and the spirit of the fear of the Lord.

5. "And from Jesus Christ, who is the faithful Witness, the first-begotten of the dead."] In taking upon Him manhood, He gave a testimony in the world, wherein also having suffered, He freed us by His blood from sin; and having vanquished hell, He was the first who rose from the dead, and "death shall have no more dominion over Him,"[2] but by His own reign the kingdom of the world is destroyed.

6. "And He made us a kingdom and priests unto God and His Father."] That is to say, a Church of all believers; as also the Apostle Peter says: "A holy nation, a royal priesthood."[3]

7. "Behold, He shall come with clouds, and every eye shall see Him."] For He who at first came hidden in the manhood that He had undertaken, shall after a little while come to judgment manifest in majesty and glory. And what saith He?

12. "And I turned, and saw seven golden candlesticks; and in the midst of the seven golden candlesticks one like unto the Son of man."] He says that He was like Him after His victory over death, when He had ascended into the heavens, after the union in His body of the power which He received from the Father with the spirit of His glory.

13. "As it were the Son of man walking in the midst of the golden candlesticks."] He says, in the midst of the churches, as it is said in Solomon, "I will walk in the midst of the paths of the just,"[4] whose antiquity is immortality, and the fountain of majesty.

"Clothed with a garment down to the ankles."] In the long, that is, the priestly garment, these words very plainly deliver the flesh which was not corrupted in death, and has the priesthood through suffering.

"And He was girt about the paps with a golden girdle."] His paps are the two testaments, and the golden girdle is the choir of saints, as gold tried in the fire. Otherwise the golden girdle bound around His breast indicates the enlightened conscience, and the pure and spiritual apprehension that is given to the churches.

14. "And His head and His hairs were white as it were white wool, and as it were snow."] On the head the whiteness is shown; "but the head of Christ is God."[5] In the white hairs is the multitude of abbots[6] like to wool, in respect of simple sheep; to snow, in respect of the innumerable crowd of candidates taught from heaven.

"His eyes were as a flame of fire."] God's precepts are those which minister light to believers, but to unbelievers burning.

16. "And in His face was brightness as the sun."] That which He called *brightness* was

[1] Isa. xi. 2. [P. 342, *supra*.]
[2] Rom. vi. 9.
[3] 1 Pet. ii. 9.
[4] Prov. viii. 20.
[5] 1 Cor. xi. 3.
[6] [*Abba* = father. Fathers, rather.]

the appearance of that in which He spoke to men face to face. But the glory of the *sun* is less than the glory of the Lord. Doubtless on account of its rising and setting, and rising again, that He was born and suffered and rose again, therefore the Scripture gave this similitude, likening His face to the glory of the sun.

15. "His feet were like unto yellow brass, as if burned in a furnace."] He calls the apostles His feet, who, being wrought by suffering, preached His word in the whole world; for He rightly named those by whose means the preaching went forth, feet. Whence also the prophet anticipated this, and said: "We will worship in the place where His feet have stood."[1] Because where they first of all stood and confirmed the Church, that is, in Judea, all the saints shall assemble together, and will worship their Lord.

16. "And out of His mouth was issuing a sharp two-edged sword."] By the twice-sharpened sword going forth out of His mouth is shown, that it is He Himself who has both now declared the word of the Gospel, and previously by Moses declared the knowledge of the law to the whole world. But because from the same word, as well of the New as of the Old Testament, He will assert Himself upon the whole human race, therefore He is spoken of as two-edged. For the sword arms the soldier, the sword slays the enemy, the sword punishes the deserter. And that He might show to the apostles that He was announcing judgment, He says: "I came not to send peace, but a sword."[2] And after He had completed His parables, He says to them: "Have ye understood all these things? And they said, We have. And He added, Therefore is every scribe instructed in the kingdom of God like unto a man that is a father of a family, bringing forth from his treasure things new and old,"[3] — the new, the evangelical words of the apostles; the old, the precepts of the law and the prophets: and He testified that these proceeded out of His mouth. Moreover, He also says to Peter: "Go thou to the sea, and cast a hook, and take up the fish that shall first come up; and having opened its mouth, thou shalt find a *stater* (that is, two *denarii*), and thou shalt give it for me and for thee."[4] And similarly David says by the Spirit: "God spake once, twice I have heard the same."[5] Because God once decreed from the beginning what shall be even to the end. Finally, as He Himself is the Judge appointed by the Father, on account of His assumption of humanity, wishing to show that men shall be judged by the word that He had declared, He says: "Think ye that I will judge you at the last day? Nay, but the word," says He, "which I have spoken unto you, that shall judge you in the last day."[6] And Paul, speaking of Antichrist to the Thessalonians, says: "Whom the Lord Jesus will slay by the breath of His mouth."[7] And Isaiah says: "By the breath of His lips He shall slay the wicked."[8] This, therefore, is the two-edged sword issuing out of His mouth.

15. "And His voice as it were the voice of many waters."] The many waters are understood to be many peoples, or the gift of baptism that He sent forth by the apostles, saying: "Go ye, teach all nations, baptizing them in the name of the Father, and of the Son, and of the Holy Ghost."[9]

16. "And He had in His right hand seven stars."] He said that in His right hand He had seven stars, because the Holy Spirit of sevenfold agency was given into His power by the Father. As Peter exclaimed to the Jews: "Being at the right hand of God exalted, He hath shed forth this Spirit received from the Father, which ye both see and hear."[10] Moreover, John the Baptist had also anticipated this, by saying to his disciples: "For God giveth not the Spirit by measure *unto Him*. The Father," says he, "loveth the Son, and hath given all things into His hands."[11] Those seven stars are the seven churches, which he names in his addresses by name, and calls them to whom he wrote epistles. Not that they are themselves the only, or even the principal churches; but what he says to one, he says to all. For they are in no respect different, that on that ground any one should prefer them to the larger number of similar small ones. In the whole world Paul taught that all the churches are arranged by sevens, that they are called seven, and that the Catholic Church is one. And first of all, indeed, that he himself also might maintain the type of seven churches, he did not exceed that number. But he wrote to the Romans, to the Corinthians, to the Galatians, to the Ephesians, to the Thessalonians, to the Philippians, to the Colossians; afterwards he wrote to individual persons, so as not to exceed the number of seven churches. And abridging in a short space his announcement, he thus says to Timothy: "That thou mayest know how thou oughtest to behave thyself in the Church of the living God."[12] We read also that this typical number is announced by the Holy Spirit by the mouth of Isaiah: "Of seven women which took hold of one man."[13] The one man is

1 Ps. cxxxii. 7.
2 Matt. x. 34.
3 Matt. xiii. 51, 52.
4 Matt. xvii. 27.
5 Ps. lxii. 11.

6 John xii. 48.
7 2 Thess. ii. 8.
8 Isa. xi. 4.
9 Matt xxviii. 19.
10 Acts ii. 33.
11 John iii. 34, 35. [Compare Wordsworth on the Apocalypse.]
12 1 Tim. iii. 15.
13 Isa. iv. 1.

Christ, not born of seed; but the seven women are seven churches, receiving His bread, and clothed with his apparel, who ask that their reproach should be taken away, only that His name should be called upon them. The bread is the Holy Spirit, which nourishes to eternal life, promised to them, that is, by faith. And His garments wherewith they desire to be clothed are the glory of immortality, of which Paul the apostle says: "For this corruptible must put on incorruption, and this mortal must put on immortality."[1] Moreover, they ask that their reproach may be taken away—that is, that they may be cleansed from their sins: for the reproach is the original sin which is taken away in baptism, and they begin to be called Christian men, which is, "Let thy name be called upon us." Therefore in these seven churches, of one Catholic Church are believers, because it is one in seven by the quality of faith and election. Whether writing to them who labour in the world, and live[2] of the frugality of their labours, and are patient, and when they see certain men in the Church wasters, and pernicious, they hear them, lest there should become dissension, he yet admonishes them by love, that in what respects their faith is deficient they should repent; or to those who dwell in cruel places among persecutors, that they should continue faithful; or to those who, under the pretext of mercy, do unlawful sins in the Church, and make them manifest to be done by others; or to those that are at ease in the Church; or to those who are negligent, and Christians only in name; or to those who are meekly instructed, that they may bravely persevere in faith; or to those who study the Scriptures, and labour to know the mysteries of their announcement, and are unwilling to do God's work that is mercy and love: to all he urges penitence, to all he declares judgment.

FROM THE SECOND CHAPTER.

2. "I know thy works, and thy labour, and thy patience."] In the first epistle He speaks thus: I know that thou sufferest and workest, I see that thou art patient; think not that I am staying long from thee.

"And that thou canst not bear them that are evil, and who say that they are Jews and are not, and thou has found them liars, and thou hast patience for My name's sake."] All these things tend to praise, and that no small praise; and it behoves such men, and such a class, and such elected persons, by all means to be admonished, that they may not be defrauded of such privileges granted to them of God. These few things He said that He had against them.

4, 5. "And thou hast left thy first love: remember whence thou hast fallen."] He who falls, falls from a height: therefore He said *whence:* because, even to the very last, works of love must be practised; and this is the principal commandment. Finally, unless this is done, He threatened to remove their candlestick out of its place, that is, to disperse the congregation.

6. "This thou hast also, that thou hatest the deeds of the Nicolaitanes."] But because thou thyself hatedst those who hold the doctrines of the Nicolaitanes, thou expectest praise. Moreover, to hate the works of the Nicolaitanes, which He Himself also hated, this tends to praise. But the works of the Nicolaitanes were in that time false and troublesome men, who, as ministers under the name of Nicolaus, had made for themselves a heresy, to the effect that what had been offered to idols might be exorcised and eaten, and that whoever should have committed fornication might receive peace on the eighth day. Therefore He extols those to whom He is writing; and to these men, being such and so great, He promised the tree *of life*, which is in the paradise of His God.

The following epistle unfolds the mode of life and habit of another order which follows. He proceeds to say:—

9. "I know thy tribulation and thy poverty, but thou art rich."] For He knows that with such men there are riches hidden with Him, and that they deny the blasphemy of the Jews, who say that they are Jews and are not; but they are the synagogue of Satan, since they are gathered together by Antichrist; and to them He says:—

10. "Be thou faithful unto death."] That they should continue to be faithful even unto death.

11. "He that shall overcome, shall not be hurt by the second death."] That is, he shall not be chastised in hell.

The third order of the saints shows that they are men who are strong in faith, and who are not afraid of persecution; but because even among them there are some who are inclined to unlawful associations, He says:—

14–16. "Thou hast there some who hold the doctrine of Balaam, who taught in the case of Balak that he should put a stumbling-block before the children of Israel, to eat and to commit fornication. So also hast thou them who hold the doctrine of the Nicolaitanes; but I will fight with them with the sword of my mouth."] That is, I will say what I shall command, and I will tell you what you shall do. For Balaam,[3] with his doctrine, taught Balak to cast a stumbling-block before the eyes of the children of Israel, to eat what was sacrificed to idols, and to

[1] 1 Cor. xv. 53.
[2] Operantur, conjectured to be "vivunt."

[3] Num. xxiii. [Wordsworth, ed. 1852, pp. 78–92.]

commit fornication, — a thing which is known to have happened of old. For he gave this advice to the king of the Moabites, and they caused stumbling to the people. Thus, says He, ye have among you those who hold such doctrine; and under the pretext of mercy, you would corrupt others.

17. "To him that overcometh I will give the hidden manna, and I will give him a white stone."] The hidden manna is immortality; the white gem is adoption to *be* the son of God; the new name written on the stone is "Christian."

The fourth class intimates the nobility of the faithful, who labour daily, and do greater works. But even among them also He shows that there are men of an easy disposition to grant unlawful peace, and to listen to new forms of prophesying; and He reproves and warns the others to whom this is not pleasing, who know the wickedness opposed to them: for which evils He purposes to bring upon the head of the faithful both sorrows and dangers; and therefore He says: —

24. "I will not put upon you any other burden."] That is, I have not given you laws, observances, and duties, which is another burden.

25, 26. "But that which ye have, hold fast until I come; and he that overcometh, to him will I give power over all peoples."] That is, him I will appoint as judge among the rest of the saints.

28. "And I will give him the morning star."] To wit, the first resurrection. He promised the morning star, which drives away the night, and announces the light, that is, the beginning of day.

FROM THE THIRD CHAPTER.

The fifth class, company, or association of saints, sets forth men who are careless, and who are carrying on in the world other transactions than those which they ought — Christians only in name. And therefore He exhorts them that by any means they should be turned away from negligence, and be saved; and to this effect He says: —

2. "Be watchful, and strengthen the other things which were ready to die; for I have not found thy works perfect before God."] For it is not enough for a tree to live and to have no fruit, even as it is not enough to be called a Christian and to confess Christ, but not to have Himself in our work, that is, not to do His precepts.

The sixth class is the mode of life of the best election. The habit of saints is set forth; of those, to wit, who are lowly in the world, and unskilled in the Scriptures, and who hold the faith immoveably, and are not at all broken down by any chance, or withdrawn from the faith by any fear. Therefore He says to them: —

8. "I have set before thee an open door, because thou hast kept the word of my patience."] In such little strength.

10. "And I will keep thee from the hour of temptation."] That they may know His glory to be of this kind, that they are not indeed permitted to be given over to temptation.

12. "He that overcometh shall be made a pillar in the temple of God."] For even as a pillar is an ornament of the building, so he who perseveres shall obtain a nobility in the Church.

Moreover, the seventh association of the Church declares that they are rich men placed in positions of dignity, but believing that they are rich, among whom indeed the Scriptures are discussed in their bedchamber, while the faithful are outside; and they are understood by none, although they boast themselves, and say that they know all things, — endowed with the confidence of learning, but ceasing from its labour. And thus He says: —

15. "That they are neither cold nor hot."] That is, neither unbelieving nor believing, for they are all things to all men. And because he who is neither cold nor hot, but lukewarm, gives nausea, He says: —

16. "I will vomit thee out of My mouth."] Although nausea is hateful, still it hurts no one; so also is it with men of this kind when they have been cast forth. But because there is time of repentance, He says: —

18. "I persuade thee to buy of Me gold tried in the fire."] That is, that in whatever manner you can, you should suffer for the Lord's name tribulations and passions.

"And anoint thine eyes with eye-salve."] That what you gladly know by the Scripture, you should strive also to do the work of the same. And because, if in these ways men return out of great destruction to great repentance, they are not only useful to themselves, but they are able also to be of advantage to many, He promised them no small reward, — to sit, namely, on the throne of judgment.

FROM THE FOURTH CHAPTER.

"After this, I beheld, and, lo, a door was opened in heaven."] The new testament is announced as an open door in heaven.

"And the first voice which I heard *was*, as it were, of a trumpet talking with me, saying, Come up hither."] Since the door is shown to be opened, it is manifest that previously it had been closed to men. And it was sufficiently and fully laid open when Christ ascended with His body to the Father into heaven. Moreover, the first voice which he had heard when he says that it spoke with him, without contradiction condemns those who say that one spoke in the prophets, another in the Gospel; since it is rather He Himself who comes, that is the same who spoke in the prophets. For John was of the circumcision, and all that people which had heard the announcement of the Old Testament was edified with his word.

"That very same voice," said he, "that I had heard, that said unto me, Come up hither."] That is the Spirit, whom a little before he confesses that he had seen walking as the Son of man in the midst of the golden candlesticks. And he now gathers from Him what had been foretold in similitudes by the law, and associates with this scripture all the former prophets, and opens up the Scriptures. And because our Lord invited in His own name all believers into heaven, He forthwith poured out the Holy Spirit, who should bring them to heaven. He says:—

2. "Immediately I was in the Spirit."] And since the mind of the faithful is opened by the Holy Spirit, and that is manifested to them which was also foretold to the fathers, he distinctly says:—

"And, behold, a throne was set in heaven."] The throne set: what is it but the throne of judgment and of the King?

3. "And He that sate upon the throne was, to look upon, like a jasper and a sardine stone."] Upon the throne he says that he saw the likeness of a jasper and a sardine stone. The jasper is of the colour of water, the sardine of fire. These two are thence manifested to be placed as judgments upon God's tribunal until the consummation of the world, of which judgments one is already completed in the deluge of water, and the other shall be completed by fire.

"And there was a rainbow about the throne."] Moreover, the rainbow round about the throne has the same colours. The rainbow is called a bow from what the Lord spake to Noah and to his sons,[1] that they should not fear any further deluge in the generation of God, but fire. For thus He says: I will place my bow in the clouds, that ye may now no longer fear water, but fire.

6. "And before the throne there was, as it were, a sea of glass like to crystal."] That is the gift of baptism which He sheds forth through His Son in time of repentance, before He executes judgment. It is therefore before the throne, that is, the judgment. And when he says a sea of glass like to crystal, he shows that it is pure water, smooth, not agitated by the wind, not flowing down as on a slope, but given to be immoveable as the house of God.

"And round about the throne were four living creatures."] The four living creatures are the four Gospels.

7–10. "The first living creature was like to a lion, and the second was like to a calf, and the third had a face like to a man, and the fourth was like to a flying eagle; and they had six wings, and round about and within they were full of eyes; and they had no rest, saying, Holy, holy, holy, Lord Omnipotent. And the four and twenty elders, falling down before the throne, adored God."] The four and twenty elders are the twenty-four books of the prophets and of the law, which give testimonies of the judgment. Moreover, also, they are the twenty-four fathers—twelve apostles and twelve patriarchs. And in that the living creatures are different in appearance, this is the reason: the living creature like to a lion designates Mark, in whom is heard the voice of the lion roaring in the desert. And in the figure of a man, Matthew strives to declare to us the genealogy of Mary, from whom Christ took flesh. Therefore, in enumerating from Abraham to David, and thence to Joseph, he spoke of Him as if of a man: therefore his announcement sets forth the image of a man. Luke, in narrating the priesthood of Zacharias as he offers a sacrifice for the people, and the angel that appears to him with respect of the priesthood, and the victim in the same description bore the likeness of a calf. John the evangelist, like to an eagle hastening on uplifted wings to greater heights, argues about the Word of God. Mark, therefore, as an evangelist thus beginning, "The beginning of the Gospel of Jesus Christ, as it is written in Isaiah the prophet;"[2] "The voice of one crying in the wilderness,"[3]—has the effigy of a lion. And Matthew, "The book of the generation of Jesus Christ, the son of David, the son of Abraham:"[4] this is the form of a man. But Luke said, "There was a priest, by name Zachariah, of the course of Abia, and his wife was of the daughters of Aaron:"[5] this is the likeness of a calf. But John, when he begins, "In the beginning was the Word, and the Word was with God, and the Word was God,"[6] sets forth the likeness of a flying eagle. Moreover, not only do the evangelists express their four similitudes in their *respective* openings of the Gospels, but also the Word itself of God the Father Omnipotent, which is His Son our Lord Jesus Christ, bears the same likeness in the time of His advent. When He preaches to us, He is, as it were, a lion and a lion's whelp. And when for man's salvation He was made man to overcome death, and to set all men free, and that He offered

[1] Gen. ix. [Wordsworth, Lect. iv.]

[2] Mark i. 3. [On the *Zoa*, see p. 341, *supra*.]
[3] Isa. xl. 3.
[4] Matt. i. 1.
[5] Luke i. 5.
[6] John i. 1.

Himself a victim to the Father on our behalf, He was called a calf. And that He overcame death and ascended into the heavens, extending His wings and protecting His people, He was named a flying eagle. Therefore these announcements, although they are four, yet are one, because it proceeded from one mouth. Even as the river in paradise, although it is one, was divided into four heads. Moreover, that for the announcement of the New Testament those living creatures had eyes within and without, shows the spiritual providence which both looks into the secrets of the heart, and beholds the things which are coming after that are within and without.

8. "Six wings."] These are the testimonies of the books of the Old Testament. Thus, twenty and four make as many as there are elders sitting upon the thrones. But as an animal cannot fly unless it have wings, so, too, the announcement of the New Testament gains no faith unless it have the fore-announced testimonies of the Old Testament, by which it is lifted from the earth, and flies. For in every case, what has been told before, and is afterwards found to have happened, that begets an undoubting faith. Again, also, if wings be not attached to the living creatures, they have nothing whence they may draw their life. For unless what the prophets foretold had been consummated in Christ, their preaching was vain. For the Catholic Church holds those things which were both before predicted and afterwards accomplished. And it flies, because the living animal is reasonably lifted up from the earth. But to heretics who do not avail themselves of the prophetic testimony, to them also there are present living creatures; but they do not fly, because they are of the earth. And to the Jews who do *not* receive the announcement of the New Testament there are present wings; but they do not fly, that is, they bring a vain prophesying to men, not adjusting facts to their words. And the books of the Old Testament that are received are twenty-four, which you will find in the epitomes of Theodore. But, moreover (as we have said), four and twenty elders, patriarchs and apostles, are to judge His people. For to the apostles, when they asked, saying, "We have forsaken all that we had, and followed Thee: what shall we have?" our Lord replied, "When the Son of man shall sit upon the throne of His glory, ye also shall sit upon twelve thrones, judging the twelve tribes of Israel."[1] But of the fathers also who should judge, says the patriarch Jacob, "Dan also himself shall judge his people among his brethren, even as one of the tribes in Israel."[2]

5. "And from the throne proceeded lightnings, and voices, and thunders, and seven torches of fire burning."] And the lightnings, and voices, and thunders proceeding from the throne of God, and the seven torches of fire burning, signify announcements, and promises of adoption, and threatenings. For lightnings signify the Lord's advent, and the voices the announcements of the New Testament, and the thunders, that the words are from heaven. The burning torches of fire *signify* the gift of the Holy Spirit, that it is given by the wood of the passion. And when these things were doing, he says that all the elders fell down and adored the Lord; while the living creatures—that is, of course, the actions recorded in the Gospels and the teaching of the Lord—gave Him glory and honour.[3] In that they had fulfilled the word that had been previously foretold by them, they worthily and with reason exult, feeling that they have ministered the mysteries and the word of the Lord. Finally, also, because He had come who should remove death, and who alone was worthy to take the crown of immortality, all for the glory of His most excellent doing had crowns.

10. "And they cast their crowns under His feet."] That is, on account of the eminent glory of Christ's victory, they cast all their victories under His feet. This is what in the Gospel the Holy Spirit consummated by showing. For when about finally to suffer, our Lord had come to Jerusalem, and the people had gone forth to meet Him, some strewed the road with palm branches cut down, others threw down their garments, doubtless these were setting forth two peoples—the one of the patriarchs, the other of the prophets; that is to say, of the great men who had any kind of palms of their victories against sin, and cast them under the feet of Christ, the victor of all. And the palm and the crown signify the same things, and these are not given save to the victor.

FROM THE FIFTH CHAPTER.

1. "And I saw in the right hand of Him that sate upon the throne, a book written within and without, sealed with seven seals."] This book signifies the Old Testament, which has been given into the hands of our Lord Jesus Christ, who received from the Father judgment.

2, 3. "And I saw an angel full of strength proclaiming with a loud voice, Who is worthy to open the book, and to loose the seals thereof? And no one was found worthy, neither in the earth nor under the earth, to open the book."] Now to open the book is to overcome death for man.

[1] Matt. xix. 27, 28.
[2] Gen. xlix. 16.

[3] The living creatures are held to be the Gospels, or the acts and teaching of our Lord narrated in them. [Wordsworth, Lect. iv.]

4. "There was none found worthy to do this."] Neither among the angels of heaven, nor among men in earth, nor among the souls of the saints in rest, save Christ the Son of God alone, whom he says that he saw as a Lamb standing as it were slain, having seven horns. What had not been then announced, and what the law had contemplated for Him by its various oblations and sacrifices, it behoved Himself to fulfil. And because He Himself was the testator, who had overcome death, it was just that Himself should be appointed the Lord's heir, that He should possess the substance of the dying man, that is, the human members.

5. "Lo, the Lion of the tribe of Judah, the root of David, hath prevailed."] We read in Genesis that this lion of the tribe of Judah hath conquered, when the patriarch Jacob says, "Judah, thy brethren shall praise thee; thou hast lain down and slept, and hast risen up again as a lion, and as a lion's whelp."[1] For He is called a lion for the overcoming of death; but for the suffering for men He was led as a lamb to the slaughter. But because He overcame death, and anticipated the duty of the executioner, He was called as it were slain. He therefore opens and seals again the testament, which He Himself had sealed. The legislator Moses intimating this, that it behoved Him to be sealed and concealed, even to the advent of His passion, veiled his face, and so spoke to the people; showing that the words of his announcement were veiled even to the advent of His time. For he himself, when he had read to the people, having taken the wool purpled with the blood of the calf, with water sprinkled the whole people, saying, "This is the blood of His testament who hath purified you."[2] It should therefore be observed that the Man is accurately announced, and that all things combine into one. For it is not sufficient that that law is spoken of, but it is named as a testament. For no law is called a testament, nor is any thing else called a testament, save what persons make who are about to die. And whatever is within the testament is sealed, even to the day of the testator's death. Therefore it is with reason that it is only sealed by the Lamb slain, who, as it were a lion, has broken death in pieces, and has fulfilled what had been foretold; and has delivered man, that is, the flesh, from death, and has received as a possession the substance of the dying person, that is, of the human members; that as by one body all men had fallen under the obligation of its death, also by one body all believers should be born again unto life, and rise again. Reasonably, therefore, His face is opened and unveiled to Moses; and therefore He is called Apocalypse, Revelation. For now His book is unsealed—now the offered victims are perceived—now the fabrication of the priestly chrism; moreover the testimonies are openly understood.

8, 9. "Twenty-four elders and four living creatures, having harps and phials, and singing a new song."] The proclamation of the Old Testament associated with the New, points out the Christian people singing a new song, that is, bearing their confession publicly. It is a new thing that the Son of God should become man. It is a new thing to ascend into the heavens with a body. It is a new thing to give remission of sins to men. It is a new thing for men to be sealed with the Holy Spirit. It is a new thing to receive the priesthood of sacred observance, and to look for a kingdom of unbounded promise. The harp, and the chord stretched on its wooden frame, signifies the flesh of Christ linked with the wood of the passion. The phial signifies *the* Confession,[3] and the race of the new Priesthood. But it is the praise of many angels, yea, of all, the salvation of all, and the testimony of the universal creation, bringing to our Lord thanksgiving for the deliverance of men from the destruction of death. The unsealing of the seals, as we have said, is the opening of the Old Testament, and the foretelling of the preachers of things to come in the last times, which, although the prophetic Scripture speaks by single seals, yet by all the seals opened at once, prophecy takes its rank.

FROM THE SIXTH CHAPTER.

1, 2. "And when the Lamb had opened one of the seven seals, I saw, and heard one of the four living creatures saying, Come and see. And, lo, a white horse, and He who sate upon him had a bow."] The first seal being opened, he says that he saw a white horse, and a crowned horseman having a bow. For this was at first done by Himself. For after the Lord ascended into heaven and opened all things, He sent the Holy Spirit, whose words the preachers sent forth as arrows reaching to the human heart, that they might overcome unbelief. And the crown on the head is promised to the preachers by the Holy Spirit. The other three horses very plainly signify the wars, famines, and pestilences announced by our Lord in the Gospel. And thus he says that one of the four living creatures said (because all four are one), "Come and see." "Come" is said to him that is invited to faith; "see" is said to him who saw not. Therefore the white horse is the word of preaching with the Holy Spirit sent into the world. For the Lord says, "This Gospel shall be preached

[1] Gen. xlix. 8, 9.
[2] Ex. xxiv. 7, 8.
[3] [The Creed and the evangelical priests. Vol. ii. note 4, p. 173.]

throughout the whole world for a testimony to all nations, and then shall come the end."[1]

3, 4. "And when He had opened the second seal, I heard the second living creature saying, Come and see. And there went out another horse that was red, and to him that sate upon him was given a great sword."] The red horse, and he that sate upon him, having a sword, signify the coming wars, as we read in the Gospel: "For nation shall rise against nation, and kingdom against kingdom; and there shall be great earthquakes in *divers* places."[2] This is the ruddy horse.

5. "And when He had opened the third seal, I heard the third living creature saying, Come and see. And, lo, a black horse; and he who sate upon it had a balance in his hand."] The black horse signifies famine, for the Lord says, "There shall be famines in *divers* places;" but the word is specially extended to the times of Antichrist, when there shall be a great famine, and when all shall be injured. Moreover, the balance in the hand is the examining scales, wherein He might show forth the merits of every individual. He then says:—

6. "Hurt not the wine and the oil."] That is, strike not the spiritual man with thy inflictions. This is the black horse.

7, 8. "And when He had opened the fourth seal, I heard the fourth living creature saying, Come and see. And, lo, a pale horse; and he who sate upon him was named Death."] For the pale horse and he who sate upon him bore the name of Death. These same things also the Lord had promised among the rest of the coming destructions — great pestilences and deaths; since, moreover, he says:—

"And hell followed him."] That is, it was waiting for the devouring of many unrighteous souls. This is the pale horse.

9. "And when He had opened the fifth seal, I saw under the altar the souls of them that were slain."] He relates that he saw under the altar of God, that is, under the earth, the souls of them that were slain. For both heaven and earth are called God's altar, as saith the law, commanding in the symbolical form of the truth two altars to be made, — a golden one within, and a brazen one without. But we perceive that the golden altar is thus called heaven, by the testimony that our Lord bears to it; for He says, "When thou bringest thy gift to the altar" (assuredly our gifts are the prayers which we offer), "and there rememberest that thy brother hath ought against thee, leave there thy gift before the altar."[3] Assuredly prayers ascend to heaven. Therefore heaven is understood to be the golden altar which was within; for the priests also were accustomed to enter once in the year — as they who had the anointing — to the golden altar, the Holy Spirit signifying that Christ should do this once for all. As the golden altar is acknowledged to be heaven, so also by the brazen altar is understood the earth, under which is the Hades, — a region withdrawn from punishments and fires, and a place of repose for the saints, wherein indeed the righteous are seen and heard by the wicked, but they cannot be carried across to them. He who sees all things would have us to know that these saints, therefore — that is, the souls of the slain — are asking for vengeance for their blood, that is, of their body, from those that dwell upon the earth; but because in the last time, moreover, the reward of the saints will be perpetual, and the condemnation of the wicked shall come, it was told them to wait. And for a solace to their body, there were given unto each of them white robes. They received, says he, white robes, that is, the gift of the Holy Spirit.

12. "And I saw, when he had opened the sixth seal, there was a great earthquake."] In the sixth seal, then, was a great earthquake: this is that very last persecution.

"And the sun became black as sackcloth of hair."] The sun becomes as sackcloth; that is, the brightness of doctrine will be obscured by unbelievers.

"And the entire moon became as blood."] By the moon of blood is set forth the Church of the saints as pouring out her blood for Christ.

13. "And the stars fell to the earth."] The falling of the stars are the faithful who are troubled for Christ's sake.

"Even as a fig-tree casteth her untimely figs."] The fig-tree, when shaken, loses its untimely figs — when men are separated from the Church by persecution.

14. "And the heaven withdrew as a scroll that is rolled up."] For the heaven to be rolled away, that is, that the Church shall be taken away.

"And every mountain and the islands were moved from their places."] Mountains and islands removed from their places intimate that in the last persecution all men departed from their places; that is, that the good will be removed, seeking to avoid the persecution.

FROM THE SEVENTH CHAPTER.

2. "And I saw another angel ascending from the east, having the seal of the living God."] He speaks of Elias the prophet, who is the precursor of the times of Antichrist, for the restoration and establishment of the churches from the great and intolerable persecution. We read

[1] Matt. xxiv. 14.
[2] Luke xxi. 10, 11.
[3] Matt. v. 23, 24.

that these things are predicted in the opening of the Old and New Testament; for He says by Malachi: "Lo, I will send to you Elias the Tishbite, to turn the hearts of the fathers to the children, according to the time of calling, to recall the Jews to the faith of the people that succeed them."[1] And to that end He shows, as we have said, that the number of those that shall believe, of the Jews and of the nations, is a great multitude which no man was able to number. Moreover, we read in the Gospel that the prayers of the Church are sent from heaven by an angel, and that they are received against wrath, and that the kingdom of Antichrist is cast out and extinguished by holy angels; for He says: "Pray that ye enter not into temptation: for there shall be a great affliction, such as has not been from the beginning of the world; and except the Lord had shortened those days, no flesh should be saved."[2] Therefore He shall send these seven great archangels to smite the kingdom of Antichrist; for He Himself also thus said: "Then the Son of man shall send His messengers; and they shall gather together His elect from the four corners of the wind, from the one end of heaven even to the other end thereof."[3] For, moreover, He previously says by the prophet: "Then shall there be peace for our land, when there shall arise in it seven shepherds and eight attacks of men; and they shall encircle Assur," that is, Antichrist, "in the trench of Nimrod,"[4] that is, in the nation of the devil, by the spirit of the Church. Similarly when the keepers of the house shall be moved. Moreover, the Lord Himself, in the parable to the apostles, when the labourers had come to Him and said, "Lord, did not we sow good seed in Thy field? whence, then, hath it tares? answered them, An enemy hath done this. And they said to Him, Lord, wilt Thou, then, that we go and root them up? And He said, Nay, but let both grow together until the harvest; and in the time of the harvest I will say to the reapers, that they gather the tares and make bundles of them, and burn them with fire everlasting, but that they gather the wheat into my barns."[5] The Apocalypse here shows, therefore, that these reapers, and shepherds, and labourers, are the angels. And the trumpet is the word of power. And although the same thing recurs in the phials, still it is not said as if it occurred twice, but because what is decreed by the Lord to happen shall be once for all; for this cause it is said twice. What, therefore, He said too little in the trumpets, is here found in the phials. We must not regard the order of what is said, because frequently the Holy Spirit, when He has traversed even to the end of the last times, returns again to the same times, and fills up what He had *before* failed to say.[6] Nor must we look for order in the Apocalypse; but we must follow the meaning of those things which are prophesied. Therefore in the trumpets and phials is signified either the desolation of the plagues that are sent upon the earth, or the madness of Antichrist himself, or the cutting off of the peoples, or the diversity of the plagues, or the hope in the kingdom of the saints, or the ruin of states, or the great overthrow of Babylon, that is, the Roman state.

9. "After this I beheld, and, lo, a great multitude, which no man was able to number, of every nation, tribe, and people, and tongue, clothed with white robes."] What the great multitude out of every tribe implies, is to show the number of the elect out of all believers, who, being cleansed by baptism in the blood of the Lamb, have made their robes white, keeping the grace which they have received.

FROM THE EIGHTH CHAPTER.

1. "And when He had opened the seventh seal, there was silence in heaven for about half an hour."] Whereby is signified the beginning of everlasting rest; but it is described as partial, because the silence being interrupted, he repeats it in order. For if the silence had continued, here would be an end of his narrative.

13. "And I saw an angel flying through the midst of heaven."] By the angel flying through the midst of heaven is signified the Holy Spirit bearing witness in two of the prophets that a great wrath of plagues was imminent. If by any means, even in the last times, any one should be willing to be converted, any one might even still be saved.

FROM THE NINTH CHAPTER.

13, 14. "And I heard a voice from the four horns of the golden altar which is in the presence of God, saying to the sixth angel which had the trumpet, Loose the four angels."] That is, the four corners of the earth which hold the four winds.

"Which are bound in the great river Euphrates."] By the corners of the earth, or the four winds across the river Euphrates, are *meant* four nations, because to every nation is sent an angel; as said the law, "He determined them by the number of the angels of God,"[7] until the number of the saints should be filled up. They do not overpass their bounds, because at the last they shall come with Antichrist.

---

1 Mal. iv. 5, 6.
2 Mark xiii. 18–20.
3 Mark xiii. 27.
4 Mic. v. 5, 6.
5 Matt. xiii. 27–30.
6 [The rule of Mede's "Synchronisms."]
7 Deut. xxxii. 8.

FROM THE TENTH CHAPTER.

1, 2. "I saw another mighty angel coming down from heaven, clothed with a cloud; and a rainbow was upon his head, and his face was as it were the sun, and his feet as pillars of fire: and he had in his hand an open book: and he set his right foot upon the sea, and his left foot upon the earth."] He signifies that that mighty angel who, he says, descended from heaven, clothed with a cloud, is our Lord, as we have above narrated.

"His face was as it were the sun."] That is, with respect to the resurrection.

"Upon his head was a rainbow."] He points to the judgment which is executed by Him, or shall be.

"An open book."] A revelation of works in the future judgment, or the Apocalypse which John received.

"His feet,"] as we have said above, are the apostles. For that both things in sea and land are trodden under foot by Him, signifies that all things are placed under His feet. Moreover, he calls Him an angel, that is, a messenger, to wit, of the Father; for He is called the Messenger of great counsel. He says also that He cried with a loud voice. The great voice is to tell the words of the Omnipotent God of heaven to men, and to bear witness that after penitence is closed there will be no hope subsequently.

3. "Seven thunders uttered their voices."] The seven thunders uttering their voices signify the Holy Spirit of sevenfold power, who through the prophets announced all things to come, and by His voice John gave his testimony in the world; but because he says that he was about to write the things which the thunders had uttered, that is, whatever things had been obscure in the announcements of the Old Testament; he is forbidden to write them, but he was charged to leave them sealed, because he is an apostle, nor was it fitting that the grace of the subsequent stage should be given in the first. "The time," says he, "is at hand."[1] For the apostles, by powers, by signs, by portents, and by mighty works, have overcome unbelief. After them there is now given to the same completed Churches the comfort of having the prophetic Scriptures subsequently interpreted, for I said that after *the apostles* there would be interpreting prophets.

For the apostle says: "And he placed in the Church indeed, first, apostles; secondly, prophets; thirdly, teachers,"[2] and the rest. And in another place he says: "Let the prophets speak two or three, and let the others judge."[3] And he says: "Every woman that prayeth or prophesieth with her head uncovered, dishonoureth her head."[4] And when he says, "Let the prophets speak two or three, and let the others judge," he is not speaking in respect of the Catholic prophecy of things unheard and unknown, but of things both announced and known. But let them judge whether or not the interpretation is consistent with the testimonies of the prophetic utterance.[5] It is plain, therefore, that to John, armed as he was with superior virtue, this was not necessary, although the body of Christ, which is the Church, adorned with His members, ought to respond to its position.

10. "I took the book from the hand of the angel, and ate it up."] To take the book and eat it up, is, when exhibition of a thing is made to one, to commit it to memory.

"And it was in my mouth as sweet as honey."] To be sweet in the mouth is the reward of the preaching of the speaker, and is most pleasant to the hearers; but it is most bitter both to those that announce it, and to those that persevere in its commandments through suffering.

11. "And He says unto me, Thou must again prophesy to the peoples, and to the tongues, and to the nations, and to many kings."] He says this, because when John said these things he was in the island of Patmos, condemned to the labour of the mines by Cæsar Domitian. There, therefore, he saw the Apocalypse; and when grown old, he thought that he should at length receive his quittance by suffering, Domitian being killed, all his judgments were discharged. And John being dismissed from the mines, thus subsequently delivered the same Apocalypse which he had received from God. This, therefore, is what He says: Thou must again prophesy to all nations, because thou seest the crowds of Antichrist rise up; and against them other crowds shall stand, and they shall fall by the sword on the one side and on the other.

FROM THE ELEVENTH CHAPTER.

1. "And there was shown unto me a reed like unto a rod: and the angel stood, saying, Rise, and measure the temple of God, and the altar, and them that worship therein."] A reed was shown like to a rod. This itself is the Apocalypse which he subsequently exhibited to the churches; for the Gospel of the complete faith he subsequently wrote for the sake of our salvation. For when Valentinus, and Cerinthus, and Ebion, and others of the school of Satan, were scattered abroad throughout the world, there assembled together to him from the neighbouring provinces all the bishops, and compelled

[1] Rev. i. 3, xxii. 10.
[2] 1 Cor. xii. 28.
[3] 1 Cor. xiv. 29.
[4] 1 Cor. xi. 5.
[5] [Some excuse for Tertullian's lapse is found in the prevailing uncertainty about the withdrawal of prophetic gifts.]

him himself also to draw up his testimony. Moreover, we say that the measure of God's temple is the command of God to confess the Father Almighty, and that His Son Christ was begotten by the Father before the beginning of the world, and was made man in very soul and flesh, both of them having overcome misery and death; and that, when received with His body into heaven by the Father, He shed forth the Holy Spirit, the gift and pledge of immortality, that He was announced by the prophets, He was described by the law, He was God's hand, and the Word of the Father from God, Lord over all, and founder of the world: this is the reed and the measure of faith; and no one worships the holy altar save he who confesses this faith.

2. "The court which is within the temple leave out."] The space which is called the court is the empty altar within the walls: these being such as were not necessary, he commanded to be ejected from the Church.

"It is given to be trodden down by the Gentiles."] That is, to the men of this world, that it may be trodden under foot by the nations, or with the nations. Then he repeats about the destruction and slaughter of the last time, and says: —

3. "They shall tread the holy city down for forty and two months; and I will give to my two witnesses, and they shall predict a thousand two hundred and threescore days clothed in sackcloth."] That is, three years and six months: these make forty-two months. Therefore their preaching is three years and six months, and the kingdom of Antichrist as much again.

5. "If any man will hurt them, fire proceedeth out of their mouth, and devoureth their enemies."] That fire proceedeth out of the mouth of those prophets against the adversaries, bespeaks the power of the world. For all afflictions, however many there are, shall be sent by their messengers in their word. Many think that there is Elisha, or Moses, with Elijah; but both of these died; while the death of Elijah is not heard of, with whom all our ancients have believed that it was Jeremiah. For even the very word spoken to him testifies to him, saying, "Before I formed thee in the belly I knew thee; and before thou camest forth out of the womb I sanctified thee, and I ordained thee a prophet unto the nations."[1] But he was not a prophet unto the nations; and thus the truthful word of God makes it necessary, which it has promised to set forth, that he should be a prophet to the nations.

4. "These are the two candlesticks standing before the Lord of the earth."] These two candlesticks and two olive trees He has to this end spoken of, and admonished you that if, when you have read of them elsewhere, you have not understood, you may understand here. For in Zechariah, one of the twelve prophets, it is thus written: "These are the two olive trees and two candlesticks which stand in the presence of the Lord of the earth;"[2] that is, they are in paradise. Also, in another sense, standing in the presence of the lord of the earth, that is, in the presence of Antichrist. Therefore they must be slain by Antichrist.

7. "And the beast which ascendeth from the abyss."] After many plagues completed in the world, in the end he says that a beast ascended from the abyss. But that he shall ascend from the abyss is proved by many testimonies; for he says in the thirty-first chapter of Ezekiel: "Behold, Assur was a cypress in Mount Lebanon." Assur, deeply rooted, was a lofty and branching cypress — that is, a numerous people — in Mount Lebanon, in the kingdom of kingdoms, that is, of the Romans. Moreover, that he says he was beautiful in offshoots, he says he was strong in armies. The water, he says, shall nourish him, that is, the many thousands of men which were subjected to him; and the abyss increased him, that is, belched him forth. For even Isaiah speaks almost in the same words; moreover, that he was in the kingdom of the Romans, and that he was among the Cæsars. The Apostle Paul also bears witness, for he says to the Thessalonians: "Let him who now restraineth restrain, until he be taken out of the way; and then shall appear that Wicked One, even he whose coming is after the working of Satan, with signs and lying wonders."[3] And that they might know that he should come who then was the prince, he added: "He already endeavours after the secret of mischief"[4] — that is, the mischief which he is about to do he strives to do secretly; but he is not raised up by his own power, nor by that of his father, but by command of God, of which thing Paul says in the same passage: "For this cause, because they have not received the love of God, He will send upon them a spirit of error, that they all may be persuaded of a lie, who have not been persuaded of the truth."[5] And Isaiah saith: "While they waited for the light, darkness arose upon them."[6] Therefore the Apocalypse sets forth that these prophets are killed by the same, and on the fourth day rise again, that none might be found equal to God.

8. "And their dead bodies shall lie in the streets of the great city, which spiritually is called

[1] Jer i. 5.

[2] Zech. iv. 14.
[3] 2 Thess. ii. 7, 8, 9.
[4] 2 Thess. ii. 10.
[5] 2 Thess. ii. 11.
[6] Isa. lix. 9.

Sodom and Egypt."] But He calls Jerusalem Sodom and Egypt, since it had become the heaping up of the persecuting people. Therefore it behoves us diligently, and with the utmost care, to follow the prophetic announcement, and to understand what the Spirit from the Father both announces and anticipates, and how, when He has gone forward to the last times, He again repeats the former ones. And now, what He will do once for all, He sometimes sets forth as if it were done; and unless you understand this as sometimes done, and sometimes as about to be done, you will fall into a great confusion. Therefore the interpretation of the following sayings has shown therein, that not the order of the reading, but the order of the discourse, must be understood.

19. "And the temple of God was opened which is in heaven."] The temple opened is a manifestation of our Lord. For the temple of God is the Son, as He Himself says: "Destroy this temple, and in three days I will raise it up." And when the Jews said, "Forty and six years was this temple in building," the evangelist says, "He spake of the temple of His body."[1]

"And there was seen in His temple the ark of the Lord's testament."] The preaching of the Gospel and the forgiveness of sins, and all the gifts whatever that came with Him, he says, appeared therein.

FROM THE TWELFTH CHAPTER.

1. "And there was seen a great sign in heaven. A woman clothed with the sun, and the moon under her feet, and on her head a crown of twelve stars. And being with child, she cried out travailing, and bearing torments that she might bring forth."] The woman clothed with the sun, and having the moon under her feet, and wearing a crown of twelve stars upon her head, and travailing in her pains, is the ancient Church of fathers, and prophets, and saints, and apostles,[2] which had the groans and torments of its longing until it saw that Christ, the fruit of its people according to the flesh long promised to it, had taken flesh out of the selfsame people. Moreover, being clothed with the sun intimates the hope of resurrection and the glory of the promise. And the moon intimates the fall of the bodies of the saints under the obligation of death, which never can fail. For even as life is diminished, so also it is increased. Nor is the hope of those that sleep extinguished absolutely, as some think, but they have in their darkness a light such as the moon. And the crown of twelve stars signifies the choir of fathers, according to the fleshly birth, of whom Christ was to take flesh.

3. "And there appeared another sign in heaven; and behold a red dragon, having seven heads."] Now, that he says that this dragon was of a red colour — that is, of a purple colour — the result of his work gave him such a colour. For from the beginning (as the Lord says) he was a murderer; and he has oppressed the whole of the human race, not so much by the obligation of death, as, moreover, by the various forms of destruction and fatal mischiefs. His seven heads were the seven kings of the Romans, of whom also is Antichrist, as we have said above.

"And ten horns."] He says that the ten kings in the latest times are the same as these, as we shall more fully set forth there.

4. "And his tail drew the third part of the stars of heaven, and cast them upon the earth."] Now, that he says that the dragon's tail drew the third part of the stars of heaven, this may be taken in two ways. For many think that he may be able to seduce the third part of the men who believe.[3] But it should more truly be understood, that of the angels that were subject to him, since he was still a prince when he descended from his estate, he seduced the third part; therefore what we said above, the Apocalypse says.

"And the dragon stood before the woman who was beginning to bring forth, that, when she had brought forth, he might devour her child."] The red dragon standing and desiring to devour her child when she had brought him forth, is the devil, — to wit, the traitor angel, who thought that the perishing of all men would be alike by death; but He, who was not born of seed, owed nothing to death: wherefore he could not devour Him — that is, detain Him in death — for on the third day He rose again. Finally, also, and before He suffered, he approached to tempt Him as man; but when he found that He was not what he thought Him to be, he departed from Him, even till the time. Whence it is here said: —

5. "And she brought forth a son, who begins to rule all nations with a rod of iron."] The rod of iron is the sword of persecution.

"I saw that all men withdrew from his abodes."] That is, the good will be removed, flying from persecution.[4]

"And her son was caught up to God, and to His throne."] We read also in the Acts of the Apostles that He was caught up to God's throne, just as speaking with the disciples He was caught up to heaven.

6. "But the woman fled into the wilderness, and there were given to her two great eagle's

[1] John ii. 19, 20, 21.

[2] [No hint here that this was a manifestation of the Blessed Virgin, the modern fiction of Rome. See vol. vi p. 355, this series.]

[3] [A noteworthy testimony to primitive interpretation.]

[4] [Compare Tertullian, *De Fuga*, vol iv. p. 117, this series.]

wings."] The aid of the great eagle's wings — to wit, the gift of prophets — was given to that Catholic Church, whence in the last times a hundred and forty-four thousands of men should believe on the preaching of Elias; but, moreover, he here says that the rest of the people should be found alive on the coming of the Lord. And the Lord says in the Gospel: "Then let them which are in Judea flee to the mountains;"[1] that is, as many as should be gathered together in Judea, let them go to that place which they have ready, and let them be supported there for three years and six months from the presence of the devil.

14. "Two great wings"] are the two prophets — Elias, and the prophet who shall be with him.

15. "And the serpent cast out of his mouth after the woman water as a flood, that he might carry her away with the flood."] He signifies by the water which the serpent cast out of his mouth, the people who at his command would persecute her.

16. "And the earth helped the woman, and opened her mouth, and swallowed up the flood which the dragon cast out of his mouth."] That the earth opened her mouth and swallowed up the waters, sets forth the vengeance for the present troubles. Although, therefore, it may signify this woman bringing forth, it shows her afterwards flying when her offspring is brought forth, because both things did not happen at one time; for we know that Christ was born, but that the time should arrive that she should flee from the face of the serpent: (we do not know) that this has happened as yet. Then he says: —

7–9. "There was a battle in heaven: Michael and his angels fought with the dragon; and the dragon warred, and his angels, and they prevailed not; nor was their place found any more in heaven. And that great dragon was cast forth, that old serpent: he was cast forth into the earth."] This is the beginning of Antichrist; yet previously Elias must prophesy, and there must be times of peace. And afterwards, when the three years and six months are completed in the preaching of Elias, he also must be cast down from heaven, where up till that time he had had the power of ascending; and all the apostate angels, as well as Antichrist, must be roused up from hell. Paul the apostle says: "Except there come a falling away first, and the man of sin shall appear, the son of perdition; and the adversary who exalted himself above all which is called God, or which is worshipped."[2]

FROM THE THIRTEENTH CHAPTER.[3]

1. "And I saw a beast rising up from the sea, like unto a leopard."] This signifies the kingdom of that time of Antichrist, and the people mingled with the variety of nations.

2. "His feet were as the feet of a bear."] A strong and most unclean beast, the feet are to be understood as his leaders.

"And his mouth as the mouth of a lion."] That is, his mouth armed for blood is his bidding, and a tongue which will proceed to nothing else than to the shedding of blood.

* * * * * * * *

18. "His number is the name of a man, and his number is Six hundred threescore and six."] As they have it reckoned from the Greek characters, they thus find it among many to be *τειταν*, for *τειταν* has this number, which the Gentiles call Sol and Phœbus; and it is reckoned in Greek thus: *τ* three hundred, *ε* five, *ι* ten, *τ* three hundred, *α* one, *ν* fifty, — which taken together become six hundred and sixty-six. For as far as belongs to the Greek letters, they fill up this number and name; which name if you wish to turn into Latin, it is understood by the antiphrase DICLUX, which letters are reckoned in this manner: since D figures five hundred, I one, C a hundred, L fifty, V five, X ten, — which by the reckoning up of the letters makes similarly six hundred and sixty-six, that is, what in Greek gives *τειταν*, to wit, what in Latin is called DICLUX; by which name, expressed by antiphrases, we understand Antichrist, who, although he be cut off from the supernal light, and deprived thereof, yet transforms himself into an angel of light, daring to call himself light.[4] Moreover, we find in a certain Greek codex *αντεμος*, which letters being reckoned up, you will find to give the number as above: *α* one, *ν* fifty, *τ* three hundred, *ε* five, *μ* forty, *ο* seventy, *ς* two hundred, — which together makes six hundred and sixty-six, according to the Greeks. Moreover, there is another name in Gothic of him, which will be evident of itself, that is, *γενσήρικος*, which in the same way you will reckon in Greek letters: *γ* three, *ε* five, *ν* fifty, *σ* two hundred, *η* eight, *ρ* a hundred, *ι* ten, *κ* twenty, *ο* seventy, *ς* also two hundred, which, as has been said above, make six hundred and sixty-six.

11. "And I saw another beast coming up out of the earth."] He is speaking of the great and false prophet who is to do signs, and portents, and falsehoods before him in the presence of men.

"And he had two horns like a lamb — that is, the appearance within of a man — and he spoke like a dragon."] But the devil speaks full of malice; for he shall do these things in the presence of men, so that even the dead appear to rise again.

[1] Luke xxi. 21.

[2] 2 Thess. ii. 3, 4.

[3] [The Edinburgh edition seems to follow the confusion of MSS., introducing here the seventeenth chapter, out of place.]

[4] [But see Irenæus, vol. i. p. 559.]

13. "And he shall make fire come down from heaven in the sight of men."] Yes (as I also have said), in the sight of men. Magicians do these things, by the aid of the apostate angels, even to this day. He shall cause also that a golden image of Antichrist shall be placed in the temple at Jerusalem, and that the apostate angel should enter, and thence utter voices and oracles. Moreover, he himself shall contrive that his servants and children should receive as a mark on their foreheads, or on their right hands, the number of his name, lest any one should buy or sell them. Daniel had previously predicted his contempt and provocation of God. "And he shall place," says he, "his temple within Samaria, upon the illustrious and holy mountain that is at Jerusalem, an image such as Nebuchadnezzar had made."[1] Thence here he places, and by and by here he renews, that of which the Lord, admonishing His churches concerning the last times and their dangers, says: "But when ye shall see the contempt which is spoken of by Daniel the prophet standing in the holy place, let him who readeth understand."[2] It is called a contempt when God is provoked, because idols are worshipped instead of God, or when the dogma of heretics is introduced in the churches. But it is a turning away because stedfast men, seduced by false signs and portents, are turned away from their salvation.

FROM THE FOURTEENTH CHAPTER.

6. "And I saw an angel flying through the midst of heaven."] The angel flying through the midst of heaven, whom he says that he saw, we have already treated of above, as being the same Elias who anticipates the kingdom of Antichrist in his prophecy.

8. "And another angel following him."] The other angel following, he speaks of as the same prophet who is the associate of his prophesying. But that he says,—

15. "Thrust in thy sharp sickle, and gather in the grapes of the vine,"] he signifies it of the nations that should perish on the advent of the Lord. And indeed in many forms he shows this same thing, as if to the dry harvest, and the seed for the coming of the Lord, and the consummation of the world, and the kingdom of Christ, and the future appearance of the kingdom of the blessed.

19, 20. "And the angel thrust in the sickle, and reaped the vine of the earth, and cast it into the wine-press of the wrath of God. And the wine-press of His fury was trodden down without the city."] In that he says that it was cast into the wine-press of the wrath of God, and trodden down without the city, the treading of the wine-press is the retribution on the sinner.

"And blood went out from the wine-press, even unto the horse-bridles."] The vengeance of shed blood, as was before predicted, "In blood thou hast sinned, and blood shall follow thee."[3]

"For a thousand and six hundred furlongs."] That is, through all the four parts of the world: for there is a quadrate put together by fours, as in four faces and four appearances, and wheels by fours; for forty times four is one thousand six hundred. Repeating the same persecution, the Apocalypse says:—

FROM THE FIFTEENTH CHAPTER.

1. "And I saw another great and wonderful sign, seven angels having the seven last plagues; for in them is completed the indignation of God."] For the wrath of God always strikes the obstinate people with seven plagues, that is, perfectly, as it is said in Leviticus; and these shall be in the last time, when the Church shall have gone out of the midst.

2. "Standing upon the sea of glass, having harps."] That is, that they stood stedfastly in the faith upon their baptism, and having their confession in their mouth, that they shall exult in the kingdom before God. But let us return to what is set before us.

FROM THE SEVENTEENTH CHAPTER.

1–6. "There came one of the seven angels, which have the seven bowls, and spake with me, saying, Come, I will show thee the judgment of that great whore who sitteth upon many waters. And I saw the woman drunk with the blood of the saints, and with the blood of the martyrs."] The decrees of that senate are always accomplished against all, contrary to the preaching of the true faith; and now already mercy being cast aside, itself here gave the decree among all nations.

3. "And I saw the woman herself sitting upon the scarlet-coloured beast, full of names of blasphemy."] But to sit upon the scarlet beast, the author of murders, is the image of the devil. Where also *is treated* of his captivity, concerning which we have fully considered. I remember, indeed, that this is called Babylon also in the Apocalypse, on account of confusion; and in Isaiah also; and Ezekiel called it Sodom. In fine, if you compare what is said against Sodom, and what Isaiah says against Babylon, and what the Apocalypse says, you will find that they are all one.[4]

9. "The seven heads are the seven hills, on

[1] Dan. xi. 45.
[2] Matt. xxiv. 15; Dan. ix. 27.
[3] Ezek. xxxv. 6.
[4] [Apparently in conflict with what our author says *supra*, pp. 352 and 355.]

which the woman sitteth."] That is, the city of Rome.

10. "And there are seven kings: five have fallen, and one is, and the other is not yet come; and when he is come, he will be for a short time."] The time must be understood in which the written Apocalypse was published, since then reigned Cæsar Domitian; but before him had been Titus his brother, and Vespasian, Otho, Vitellius, and Galba. These are the five who have fallen. One remains, under whom the Apocalypse was written — Domitian, to wit. "The other has not yet come," speaks of Nerva; "and when he is come, he will be for a short time," for he did not complete the period of two years.

11. "And the beast which thou sawest is of the seven."] Since before those kings Nero reigned.

"And he is the eighth."] He says only when this beast shall come, reckon it the eighth place, since in that is the completion. He added: —

"And shall go into perdition."] For that ten kings received royal power when he shall move from the east, he says. He shall be sent from the city of Rome with his armies. And Daniel sets forth the ten horns and the ten diadems. And that these are eradicated from the former ones, — that is, that three of the principal leaders are killed by Antichrist: that the other seven give him honour and wisdom and power, of whom he says: —

16. "These shall hate the whore, to wit, the city, and shall burn her flesh with fire."] Now that one of the heads was, as it were, slain to death, and that the stroke of his death was directed, he speaks of Nero. For it is plain that when the cavalry sent by the senate was pursuing him, he himself cut his throat. Him therefore, when raised up, God will send as a worthy king, but worthy in such a way as the Jews merited. And since he is to have another name, He shall also appoint another name, that so the Jews may receive him as if he were the Christ. Says Daniel: "He shall not know the lust of women, although before he was most impure, and he shall know no God of his fathers: for he will not be able to seduce the people of the circumcision, unless he is a judge of the law."[1] Finally, also, he will recall the saints, not to the worship of idols, but to undertake circumcision, and, if he is able, to seduce any; for he shall so conduct himself as to be called Christ by them. But that he rises again from hell, we have said above in the word of Isaiah: "Water shall nourish him, and hell hath increased him;" who, however, must come with name unchanged, and doings unchanged, as says the Spirit.

FROM THE NINETEENTH CHAPTER.

11. "And I saw heaven opened, and behold a white horse; and he that sate upon him was called Faithful and True."] The horse, and He that sits upon him, sets forth our Lord coming to His kingdom with the heavenly army. Because from the sea of the north, which is the Arabian Sea, even to the sea of Phœnice, and even to the ends of the earth, they will command these greater parts in the coming of the Lord Jesus, and all the souls of the nations will be assembled to judgment.

FROM THE TWENTIETH CHAPTER.

1–3. "And I saw an angel come down from heaven, having the key of the abyss, and a chain in his hand. And he held the dragon, that old serpent, which is called the Devil and Satan, and bound him for a thousand years, and cast him into the abyss, and shut him up, and set a seal upon him, that he should deceive the nations no more, till the thousand years should be finished: after this he must be loosed a little season."] Those years wherein Satan is bound are in the first advent of Christ, even to the end of the age; and they are called a thousand, according to that mode of speaking, wherein a part is signified by the whole, just as is that passage, "the word which He commanded for a thousand generations,"[2] although they are not a thousand. Moreover that he says, "and he cast him into the abyss," he says this, because the devil, excluded from the hearts of believers, began to take possession of the wicked, in whose hearts, blinded day by day, he is shut up as if in a profound abyss. And he shut him up, says he, and put a seal upon him, that he should not deceive the nations until the thousand years should be finished. "He shut the door upon him," it is said, that is, he forbade and restrained his seducing those who belong to Christ. Moreover, he put a seal upon him, because it is hidden who belong to the side of the devil, and who to that of Christ. For we know not of those who seem to stand whether they shall not fall, and of those who are down it is uncertain whether they may rise. Moreover, that he says that he is bound and shut up, that he may not seduce the nations, the nations signify the Church, seeing that of them it itself is formed, and which being seduced, he previously held until, he says, the thousand years should be completed, that is, what is left of the sixth day, to wit, of the sixth age, which subsists for a thousand years; after this he must be loosed for a little season. The little season signifies three years and six months, in which with all his power the devil will avenge himself under Anti-

[1] Dan. xi. 37.

[2] Ps. cv. 8.

christ against the Church. Finally, he says, after that the devil shall be loosed, and will seduce the nations in the whole world, and will entice war against the Church, the number of whose foes shall be as the sand of the sea.[1]

4, 5. "And I saw thrones, and them that sate upon them, and judgment was given unto them; and *I saw* the souls of them that were slain on account of the testimony of Jesus, and for the word of God, and which had not worshipped the beast nor his image, nor have received his writing on their forehead or in their hand; and they reigned with Christ for a thousand years: the rest of them lived not again until the thousand years were finished. This is the first resurrection."] There are two resurrections. But the first resurrection is now of the souls that are by the faith, which does not permit men to pass over to the second death. Of this resurrection the apostle says: "If ye have risen with Christ, seek those things which are above." [2]

6. "Blessed and holy is he who has part in this resurrection: on them the second death shall have no power, but they shall be priests of God and Christ, and they shall reign with Him a thousand years."] I do not think the reign of a thousand years is eternal; or if it is thus to be thought of, they cease to reign when the thousand years are finished. But I will put forward what my capacity enables me to judge. The tenfold number signifies the decalogue, and the hundredfold sets forth the crown of virginity: for he who shall have kept the undertaking of virginity completely, and shall have faithfully fulfilled the precepts of the decalogue, and shall have destroyed the untrained nature or impure thoughts within the retirement of the heart, that they may not rule over him, this is the true priest of Christ, and accomplishing the millenary number thoroughly, is thought to reign with Christ; and truly in his case the devil is bound. But he who is entangled in the vices and the dogmas of heretics, in his case the devil is loosed. But that it says that when the thousand years are finished he is loosed, so the number of the perfect saints being completed, in whom there is the glory of virginity in body and mind, by the approaching advent of the kingdom of the hateful one, many, seduced by that love of earthly things, shall be overthrown, and together with him shall enter the lake of fire.

8–10. "And they went up upon the breadth of the earth, and compassed the camp of the saints about, and the beloved city; and fire came down from God out of heaven, and devoured them. And the devil who seduced them was cast into the lake of fire and brimstone, where both the beast and the false prophet shall be tormented day and night for ever and ever."] This belongs to the last judgment. And after a little time the earth was made holy, as being at least that wherein lately had reposed the bodies of the virgins, when they shall enter upon an eternal kingdom with an immortal King, as they who are not only virgins in body, but, moreover, with equal inviolability have protected themselves, both in tongue and thought, from wickedness; and these, it shows, shall dwell in rejoicing for ever with the Lamb.

FROM THE TWENTY-FIRST AND TWENTY-SECOND CHAPTERS.

16. "And the city is placed in a square."] The city which he says is squared, he says also is resplendent with gold and precious stones, and has a sacred street, and a river through the midst of it, and the tree of life on either side, bearing twelve manner of fruits throughout the twelve months; and that the light of the sun is not there, because the Lamb is the light of it; and that its gates were of single pearls; and that there were three gates on each of the four sides, and that they could not be shut. I say, in respect of the square city, he shows forth the united multitude of the saints, in whom the faith could by no means waver. As Noah is commanded to make the ark of squared beams,[3] that it might resist the force of the deluge, by the precious stones he sets forth the holy men who cannot waver in persecution, who could not be moved either by the tempest of persecutors, or be dissolved from the true faith by the force of the rain, because they are associated of pure gold, of whom the city of the great King is adorned. Moreover, the streets set forth their hearts purified from all uncleanness, transparent with glowing light, that the Lord may justly walk up and down in them. The river of life sets forth that the grace of spiritual doctrine flowed through the minds of the faithful, and that manifold flourishing forms of odours germinated therein. The tree of life on either bank sets forth the Advent of Christ, according to the flesh, who satisfied the peoples wasted with famine, *that* received life from One by the wood of the Cross, with the announcement of God's word. And *in* that he says that the sun is not necessary in the city, *he* shows, evidently, that the Creator as the immaculate light shines in the midst of it, whose brightness no mind has been able to conceive, nor tongue to tell.

In that he says there are three gates placed on each of the four sides, of single pearls, I think that these are the four virtues,[4] to wit, prudence, fortitude, justice, temperance, which are associated with one another. And, being involved

1 [Compare vol. v. pp. 207, 215, caps. 15 and 54.]
2 Col. iii. 1.
3 Gen. vi. 14, LXX.
4 [Called the *philosophical* virtues. Vol. ii. note 7, p. 502.]

together, they make the number twelve. But the twelve gates we believe to be the number of the apostles, who, shining in the four virtues as precious stones, manifesting the light of their doctrine among the saints, cause it to enter the celestial city, that by intercourse with them the choir of angels may be gladdened. And that the gates cannot be shut, it is evidently shown that the doctrine of the apostles can be separated from rectitude by no tempest of contradiction. Even though the floods of the nations and the vain superstitions of heretics should revolt against their true faith, they are overcome, and shall be dissolved as the foam, because Christ is the Rock [1] by which, and on which, the Church is founded.[2] And thus it is overcome by no traces of maddened men. Therefore they are not to be heard who assure themselves that there is to be an earthly reign of a thousand years; who think, *that is to say*, with the heretic Cerinthus.[3] For the kingdom of Christ is now eternal in the saints, although the glory of the saints shall be manifested after the resurrection.

1 [From a Western theologian of the date of our author. This is emphatic.]

2 [Compare vol. v. p. 561, Elucidation VII.]

3 [Here is evidence that Cerinthus (see vol. i. 351, 352) and other heretics had disgusted the Church even with the less carnal views of the Millenium entertained by the better "Chiliasts," such as Commodian. See vol. iv. pp. 212 and 218.]

GENERAL NOTES BY THE AMERICAN EDITOR.

1. THE whole subject of the Apocalypse is so treated,[1] in the *Speaker's Commentary*, as to elucidate many questions suggested by the primitive commentators of this series, and to furnish the latest judgments of critics on the subject. It is so immense a matter, however, as to render annotations on patristic *specialties* impossible in a work like this. Every reader must feel how apposite is the sententious saying of Augustine: "Apocalypsis Joannis tot habet sacramenta quot verba."

2. *The seven spirits*, p. 344, ver. 4. That is, the one Spirit in His seven-fold gifts. He now fulfils the promise of Christ, "He shall show you things to come." Without this complement the Church would lack assurance that her great Head upon the throne has ordered and limited the whole course of this world for her conflicts and her final triumph by the Spirit's power. St. John's rapture was the Spirit's work: "I was in the Spirit on the Lord's day."[2] The whole Apocalypse is an Easter sermon (on the text, i. 18) and an Easter song (vers. 9–14, and *passim*). It supplements the appearances of the risen Redeemer for *identification*, by a manifestation, which is the Church's assurance of His *glorification*, and of His perpetual work in her and for her, as well as of His presence with her, by the Spirit.

3. *Seven golden candlesticks*, p. 344, ver. 12. The symbol of the seven-fold Spirit in the Church. On the Arch of Titus this symbol had just been set up as proof of its removal from the Mosaic Church. It is now found to be transferred to the "seven churches," a symbol of the Catholic Church [3] or "the communion of saints." The threatening of removal from particular churches derives force from the (then) recent removal out of Jerusalem.

4. *All the saints shall assemble*, p. 345, ver. 15. Our author clings to the purer Chiliasm of Commodian, to which Augustine had now given the death-blow by his famous retractation.[4]

5. *New forms of prophesying*, p. 347, ver. 17. A retrospective glance at Montanism, and a *caveat* against the mistakes of Tertullian.

6. *I will vomit thee*, p. 347, ver. 17. Bishop Wordsworth suggests, that, if the canon of Scripture compiled by the church of Laodicea lacks the Apocalypse, its terrible reproof of that church may have influenced its unwillingness to accept it. Accordingly she was *vomited*, and perished in the Saracen invasion.

7. *That is the Spirit*, p. 348, ver. 1. Christ's divine nature as distinguished from his flesh.[5] "In a word," says Professor Milligan,[6] "πνευμα is a short expression for our Lord's resurrection state." A truth, but based on the distinction between the flesh of Christ and His spiritual nature as the Word. See Tertullian,[7] vol. iii. p. 609, note 5, and p. 610, note 5; also 2 Cor. iii. 17–18.

8. *The genealogy of Mary*, p. 348, vers. 7–10. It is remarkable that St. Matthew should be credited with this, and not St. Luke, who in the sixteenth century [8] began to be regarded as giving the ancestry of Mary. See Africanus [9] on the subject, and my elucidation,[10] in which I followed Wordsworth. Though I had already prepared the pages of Victorinus for the press, I failed to note at that time this modification of the general truth, that antiquity regards both genealogies as those of Joseph.

9. *Dan himself*, p. 349, ver. 8. Here is a touch of Chiliasm again, i.e., of the better sort. Even Dan is promised a restoration; and the use of Gen. xlix. 16 for that intent is noteworthy, as compared with Rev. vii. 5–8, where Dan is omitted. But Hippolytus takes a very different view of the same text.[11]

10. *Hades*, p. 351. "A region withdrawn from punishment and fires," says our author. He identifies it with paradise, and shows that in his day the Latin churches knew of no purgatorial fires. He knows of nothing but a place for those "who die in the Lord," and a place for the wicked. It is perpetually overlooked, that, in the fiction of "purgatory," it is only the righteous who are entitled to it; none but those dying in full communion with the Church having any portion in it, or any title to Masses for their repose. Of all this our author had no conception.[12]

11. *To take the book and eat it up*, p. 353, ver. 10. We must not fail to note with this the passage Jer. xv. 16, where the Revised Version pedantically sacrifices the Septuagint reading, ὁ λόγος σου, (which is followed by the Vulgate), distinguishing "sermones tui" from "Verbum tuum." The Seventy have testified to this distinction in their day, and their copies of the Hebrew must have supported it. So understood, what riches in the text of Jeremiah!

12. *Thessalonians*, p. 354, ver. 7. On which much that is suggestive is said by St. Augustine, though he confesses, concerning what St. Paul had said to the Thessalonians, "Ego prorsus quid dixerit me fateor ignorare." See *De Civ. Dei*, lib. xx. cap. 19, p. 685, ed. Migne.

13. *The woman*, p. 355, ver. 1. Compare vol. vi. p. 337, note 4, and Elucidation II. p. 355. It is quite important to observe the voice of antiquity on a matter which, in our own times, has been made a stumbling-block to souls by a wanton, personal act of the Bishop of Rome and his dogma of "Immaculate Conception."

14. *The hope of those that sleep*, p. 355, ver. 1. To make our author consistent with himself (see note 10, *supra*), we should read thus: "But they have in their darkness a light (some think) such as the moon." Here, however, it seems to me, he is giving his mind to "the Church of fathers and prophets" exclusively, in which *its* "saints and apostles" were for a time waiting and looking for the Man-child. Even that Church of the Hebrews had, in Hades, light "like that of the moon," where they reposed in Abraham's bosom; but Christ removed them into a fairer region, i.e., Paradise, when He illuminated Hades, and then became "the first-fruits of them that slept." Such seems to be the sense.

15. *In a certain Greek codex*, p. 357, ver. 18. Can αντεμος here be a reference to Anthemius, of the kindred of Julian (*d.* A.D. 472)? His history, mixed up with that of Ricimer, connects with Genseric, who died A.D. 477.

16. *Sea of the north*, p. 358, ver. 11. The Mediterranean, near Mount Carmel, is "the sea of Phœnice," I suppose; but how the Arabian Gulf can be called the sea of the north, I do not comprehend. As Routh says, the manuscripts must have been much corrupted.

17. *Two resurrections*, p. 359, ver. 5. Here our author, who is supposed to be the contemporary of St. Augustine, accepts his final judgment.[13] But Victorinus was a Chiliast of the better sort, according to St. Jerome. This confirms the corruption of the MSS. Indeed, if the Victorinus mentioned by Jerome be the same as our author, the mention of Genseric proves the subsequent interpolation of his works.

18. It is evident that the fragment which is here preserved, if, indeed, it be the work of Caius Marius Victorinus, surnamed Afer, is full of the corrections of some pious disciple of St. Augustine who lived much later. The reader must consult Lardner,[14] and compare Routh, whose notes on this treatise are indeed few. He does not think the reference to *abbots* [15] of any consequence in determining its age, because he finds *albatorum* elsewhere sustained as the true reading, i.e., those "*made white* in the blood of the Lamb." But the great probability that there were two authors of the name living in different ages seems more than suspected by the learned. Dupin, who calls him *Marius* without the *Caius* (changed to *Fabius* by the English translator), leaves one yet more in a mist as to the identity of our author with the one he writes about.

1 By William Lee, D.D., archdeacon of Dublin.

2 The Lord's day is here the Paschal feast, "the Great Sunday," probably. See Eichhorn in Rosenmüller, *Scholia*, tom. v. p. 626.

3 P. 345, sec. 16.

4 *Civ. Dei*, xx. cap. 7, p. 667, ed. Migne.

5 See vol. iii. note 5, pp. 624, 630.

6 *Ut supra*, p. 249, note 15.

7 See Kaye's *Tertullian*, p. 530, for a brief comment on this and its supposed scriptural base.

8 Virtually in the fifteenth, as Annius published his theory in 1502, and wrote, no doubt, before that century began. Vol. vi. p. 139.

9 Vol. vi. p. 126, this series.

10 Vol. vi. p. 139.

11 Vol v p 207, this series.

12 Compare vol. iii. p. 428, Elucidation VIII.

13 See p. 360, note 2.

14 *Credib.*, vol. iv. p. 254.

15 P 344 note 6 *supra*

DIONYSIUS

INTRODUCTORY NOTICE

TO

DIONYSIUS, BISHOP OF ROME

[A.D. 259–269.] Dionysius is no exception to the rule that Latin Christianity had no place in Rome till after the Nicene Council. He was a Greek by birth, and reflects the spirit and orthodoxy of the Greek Fathers; and what we have from him is written in the Greek language. We find it in Athanasius, where, remarks Waterland,[1] its genuineness cannot be suspected, because "Athanasius did not entirely approve of it, and would certainly never have forged an interpretation different from his own." He concurred with the Easterns in the discipline of Paul of Samosata. Waterland says of the following fragment: "*It is of admirable use* for showing the doctrine of the Trinity as professed by the Church of Christ at that time."

The purely receptive character of the Roman See during the Ante-Nicene period must be sufficiently apparent to the possessors of the volumes of this series. Until after the Council of Nice, as a Roman pontiff has testified, she was unfelt in the churches as a teaching church.[2] Irenæus has justly stated her case: as the *focus* of the empire, she was the natural centre of exchange and social commerce among all nations. Thither all Christians converged, and there at all times might be found representatives of all the churches,—those of Gaul and Britain; those of Asia Minor and Syria; those of Alexandria and Egypt; those of North Africa, where Latin Christianity had begun to exist, and where it had reached a vigorous maturity at the Nicene period. Hence, from all these churches came into Rome *a Catholic testimony*, which was thus preserved at the metropolis by the pressure from without.

This is the fact which gives importance to the earliest dogmatic testimony proceeding from the See of Rome.[3] Dionysius has the great distinction of sustaining the orthodoxy which Hippolytus and other comprovincial bishops had established against the heresy of two of his predecessors; and this little essay, embedded in the works of Athanasius, comes forth as a genuine "bee" out of his precious amber, sweet with the honey of truth, and pungent with the sting of an acute and piercing testimony against error.

For the necessary preface to this essay or synodical letter, the reader must turn to the history of Dionysius of Alexandria, surnamed the Great, and to the letters he wrote to his namesake of Rome.[4] For a complete view of the whole matter, and for the originals of both these great prelates, the student will not fail to consult Routh.[5] Athanasius, the touchstone of orthodoxy, does not altogether commend the idioms of either; but he sustains the essential orthodoxy of both with that vast sweep of genius which could insist upon Nicene idioms after the council, but sustain those who, in defective language, fought previously for essential truth.

---

1 *Works*, vol. iii. p. 318.

2 Vol. iv. p. 170, this series. Compare Irenæus, vol. i. pp. 415–460, this series.

3 Novatian (vol. v. p. 607, this series) must not be overlooked, but he is valued merely as a personal witness.

4 See pp. 78 and 92, vol. vi., this series.

5 *Reliqu. Sac.*, vol. iii. pp. 221–250.

For a just view of Novatian and of the orthodoxy of Rome in the times of Dionysius, as that unhappy but competent witness sets it forth, the reader would do well to consult Dr. Waterland.[1] For a vindication of the Alexandrian Dionysius, to whom his contemporaries gave the surname *Magnus*, see the same lucid expounder of antiquity.[2] For a sententious statement of the *subordination* of the Son, on which so much hinges in these inquiries, consult the same theologian.[3]

I might have suffixed this essay to the works of the great Dionysius but for several important considerations: (1) I was glad to give due prominence to this exceptional voice from old Rome, and to place Dionysius with due dignity before the reader; (2) as the Bishop of Rome was without a hearing at Nicæa, I was anxious to show what good Sylvester would have said had he been able to attend the council; (3) I was not willing, therefore, to hide this writer's light under the bushel of the pages devoted to the Alexandrian school; (4) I was anxious to close this important volume by a just exhibition of the Ante-Nicene doctrine, previous to the compilation of the Great Symbol; (5) I considered it judicious to elucidate Dionysius by the doctrines of Athanasius, to whom we owe the preservation of the fragment itself; and (6) I felt that here was the place to record the "Athanasian Confession" (so called), which, apocryphal though it be, as a "creed" under his name is allowed to embody the principles for which the whole life of Athanasius was a contest unparalleled in the history of Christianity.

---

[1] *Works*, vol. iii. pp. 57, 119, 139, 214, 274, 454–459.

[2] *Ib.*, pp. 43, 111, 274.

[3] *Works*, iii. p. 23.

AGAINST THE SABELLIANS[1]

1. Now truly it would be just to dispute against those who, by dividing and rending the monarchy, which is the most august announcement of the Church of God, into, as it were, three powers, and distinct substances (*hypostases*), and three deities, destroy it.[2] For I have heard that some who preach and teach the word of God among you are teachers of this opinion, who indeed diametrically, so to speak, are opposed to the opinion of Sabellius. For he blasphemes in saying that the Son Himself is the Father, and *vice versâ ;* but these in a certain manner announce three gods, in that they divide the holy unity into three different substances, absolutely separated from one another. For it is essential that the Divine Word should be united to the God of all, and that the Holy Spirit should abide and dwell in God; and thus that the Divine Trinity should be reduced and gathered into one, as if into a certain head — that is, into the omnipotent God of all. For the doctrine of the foolish Marcion, which cuts and divides the monarchy into three elements, is assuredly of the devil, and is not of Christ's true disciples, or of those to whom the Saviour's teaching is agreeable. For these indeed rightly know that the Trinity is declared in the divine Scripture, but that the doctrine that there are three gods is neither taught in the Old nor in the New Testament.

2. But neither are they less to be blamed who think that the Son was a creation, and decided that the Lord was made just as one of those things which really were made; whereas the divine declarations testify that He was begotten, as is fitting and proper, but not that He was created or made. It is therefore not a trifling, but a very great impiety, to say that the Lord was in any wise made with hands. For if the Son was made, there was a time when He was not; but He always was, if, as He Himself declares,[3] He is undoubtedly in the Father. And if Christ is the Word, the Wisdom, and the Power, — for the divine writings tell us that Christ is these, as ye yourselves know, — assuredly these are powers of God. Wherefore, if the Son was made, there was a time when these were not in existence;[4] and thus there was a time when God was without these things, which is utterly absurd. But why should I discourse at greater length to you about these matters, since ye are men filled with the Spirit, and especially understanding what absurd results follow from the opinion which asserts that the Son was made? The leaders of this view seem to me to have given very little heed to these things, and for that reason to have strayed absolutely, by explaining the passage otherwise than as the divine and prophetic Scripture demands. "The Lord created me the beginning of His ways."[5] For, as ye know, there is more than one signification of the word "created;" and in this place "created" is the same as "set over" the works made by Himself — made, I say, by the Son Himself. But this "created" is not to be understood in the same manner as "made." For to make and to create are different from one another. "Is not He Himself thy Father, that hath possessed thee and created thee?"[6] says Moses in the great song of Deuteronomy. And thus might any one reasonably convict these men. Oh reckless and rash men! was then "the first-born of every creature"[7] something made? — "He who was begotten from the womb before the morning star?"[8] — He who in the person of Wisdom says, "Before all the hills He begot me?"[9] Finally, any one may read in many parts of the divine utterances that the Son is said to have been begotten, but never that He was made. From which considerations, they who dare to say that His divine and inexplicable generation was a creation, are openly convicted of thinking that which is false concerning the generation of the Lord.

3. That admirable and divine unity, therefore,

[1] A fragment of an epistle or treatise of Dionysius, bishop of Rome. [From the epistle of St. Athanasius, *De Decretis Nicænæ Synodi*, cap. xxvi. p 231, ed. Benedict.]
[2] Athan., *Ep. de decret. Nic. Syn.*, 4. 26.
[3] John xiv. 11. [See vol. v. Elucidation V. p. 156.]
[4] [He quotes the formula, afterwards notorious, ἦν ὅτε οὐκ ἦν.]
[5] Prov. viii. 22.
[6] Deut. xxxii. 6.
[7] Col. i. 15. [See vol. v. Elucidation XI. p. 159.]
[8] Ps. cx. 3, LXX.
[9] Prov. viii. 25.

must neither be separated into three divinities, nor must the dignity and eminent greatness of the Lord be diminished by *having applied to it* the name of creation, but we must believe on God the Father Omnipotent, and on Christ Jesus His Son, and on the Holy Spirit. Moreover, that the Word is united to the God of all, because He says, "I and the Father are one;"[1] and, "I am in the Father, and the Father is in Me."[2] Thus doubtless will be maintained in its integrity *the doctrine of* the divine Trinity, and the sacred announcement of the monarchy.

[1] John x. 30.
[2] John xiv. 10.

ELUCIDATIONS.

I.

THE Confession, improperly called "the Creed of Athanasius," is acknowledged to embody the (Athanasian) doctrine of the Nicene Council; and I append it here as an index to the state of theology at the period which is the limit of our series. Nothing is properly a "creed" which has never been accepted as such by the whole Church, and the Greeks knew no other creed than that called *Nicene*. The Anglo-American Church has ceased to recite this Confession in public worship, but does not depart from it as doctrine. The "Reformed" communion in America[1] retains it among her liturgical forms, and I suppose the same is true of the Lutherans. It is a Western Confession, and, like the *Te Deum*, is a hymn rather than a symbol, though breathing the spirit of the Creed.

Usher adopts A.D. 447 as its date, and Beveridge assigns it to the fourth century. Dupin gives it a later origin than Usher, and a considerable number of eminent authorities agree with him in the date A.D. 484.

What are called the anathemas are the *enacting clauses* (so to speak), and, like the same in the Nicene Creed, may be regarded as no part of the Confession itself. If they have disappeared from the Great Symbol itself, as unsuitable to liturgical recitation, why not apply the same rule here?

CONFESSION OF OUR CHRISTIAN FAITH, COMMONLY CALLED THE CREED OF ST. ATHANASIUS.

Quicunque vult.

¶ *Whosoever will be saved: before all things it is necessary that he hold the Catholick Faith.*

Which Faith except everyone do keep whole and undefiled: without doubt he shall perish everlastingly.

I.

And the Catholick Faith is this: That we worship one God in Trinity, and Trinity in Unity;

Neither confounding the Persons: nor dividing the Substance.

For there is one Person of the Father, another of the Son: and another of the Holy Ghost.

But the God-head of the Father, of the Son, and of the Holy Ghost, is all one: the Glory equal, the Majesty co-eternal.

Such as the Father is, such is the Son: and such is the Holy Ghost.

The Father un-create, the Son un-create: and the Holy Ghost un-create.

The Father incomprehensible, the Son incomprehensible: and the Holy Ghost incomprehensible.

The Father eternal, the Son eternal: and the Holy Ghost eternal.

And yet they are not three eternals: but one eternal.

As also there are not three incomprehensibles, nor three un-created: but one un-created, and one incomprehensible.

So likewise the Father is Almighty, the Son Almighty: and the Holy Ghost Almighty.

[1] Commonly called "the Dutch Church;" i.e., the Church of Holland.

And yet they are not three Almighties: but one Almighty.

So the Father is God, the Son is God: and the Holy Ghost is God.

And yet they are not three Gods: but one God.

So likewise the Father is Lord, the Son is Lord: and the Holy Ghost is Lord.

And yet not three Lords: but one Lord.

For like as we are compelled by the Christian verity: to acknowledge every Person by Himself to be God and Lord;

So we are forbidden by the Catholick Religion: to say, there be three Gods, or three Lords.

The Father is made of none: neither created, nor begotten.

The Son is of the Father alone: not made, nor created, but begotten.

The Holy Ghost is of the Father *and of the Son:*[1] neither made, nor created, nor begotten, but proceeding.

So there is one Father, not three Fathers; one Son, not three Sons: one Holy Ghost, not three Holy Ghosts.

And in this Trinity none is afore, or after other: none is greater, or less than another;

But the whole three Persons are co-eternal together: and co-equal.

So that in all things, as is aforesaid: the Unity in Trinity, and the Trinity in Unity, is to be worshipped.

¶ *He therefore that will be saved: must thus think of the Trinity.*

II.

Furthermore, it is necessary to everlasting salvation: that he also believe rightly the Incarnation of our Lord Jesus Christ.

For the right Faith is, that we believe and confess: that our Lord Jesus Christ, the Son of God, is God and Man;

God, of the Substance of the Father, begotten before the worlds: and Man, of the Substance of His Mother, born in the world;

Perfect God, and perfect Man: of a reasonable soul and human flesh subsisting;

Equal to the Father, as touching His God-head· and inferior to the Father, as touching His Manhood.

Who although He be God and Man: yet He is not two, but one Christ;

One; not by conversion of the God-head into flesh: but by taking of the Manhood into God;

One altogether; not by confusion of Substance: but by unity of Person.

For as the reasonable soul and flesh is one man: so God and Man is one Christ;

Who suffered for our Salvation: descended into hell, rose again the third day from the dead.

He ascended into heaven, He sitteth on the right hand of the Father, God Almighty: from whence He shall come to judge the quick and the dead.

At whose coming all men shall rise again with their bodies: and shall give account for their own works.

And they that have done good shall go into life everlasting: and they that have done evil into everlasting fire.

¶ *This is the Catholick Faith: which except a man believe faithfully, he cannot be saved.*

II.

It is with regret that I am forced to take exception to the most useful *Ecclesiastical History* of the learned Professor Schaff, in this connection. I quote from that work[2] as follows: —

"He, Dionysius, maintained distinctly, in (*a*) controversy with Dionysius of Alexandria, at once the unity of essence and the real personal distinction, etc., . . . and avoided tritheism, Sabellianism, and (*b*) *subordinationism,* with the instinct of orthodoxy, and also with the art of anathematizing, (*c*) already familiar to (*d*) the popes."

Such a paragraph must convey to the youthful student a great confusion of ideas; all the greater, because the same valuable work elsewhere invites him to conclusions quite the reverse. Thus, (*a*) there was no *controversy* whatever between the two Dionysii; with a holy jealousy they entered into fraternal explanations of the same truth, held by each, but by neither very *technically* elucidated. The *mere* reader would probably infer that the greater of the two was guilty of tritheism or Sabellianism, although that is not the meaning of these unguarded expressions. But (*b*) the "subordinationism" which he repudiated was the doctrine of the *subjection* of the Son, not of the *subordination,* which orthodoxy has always maintained. Again, (*c*) I see no such "anathe-

[1] The words italicized have never been accepted by the whole Church.

[2] Vol. ii. p. 570.

matizing" in the letter of Dionysius as is here charged; indeed, it contains no *anathema* [1] whatever, much less the artificial cursing of the Papacy which is thus assumed. And last, (*d*) what can be meant by the expression, "already familiar *to the popes?*" The learned pages of the same author sufficiently prove that there were no such things [2] as "popes" till a much later period of history; and, as to the "art of anathematizing," if it existed at all in those days, we find it much more freely exemplified by the Greek Fathers than by bishops of Rome. I say, *if it existed at all*, because the *primitive* anathema was a purely scriptural enforcement of St. Paul's great canon (Gal. i. 8, 9); while the "*art* of anathematizing," so justly credited to "the popes," was a vindictive and monstrous assertion, at a later date, of prerogatives which they impiously arrogated to themselves, against other churches.

[1] "*Culpandi* sunt" is quite strong enough for the original, καταμέμφοιτο. Routh, *R. S.*, iii. p. 374.

[2] The word existed, but then, and long afterwards, was universally applied to all bishops.

THE TEACHING OF THE TWELVE APOSTLES

INTRODUCTORY NOTICE

TO

THE TEACHING OF THE TWELVE APOSTLES

THE interest so generally excited in the learned world by the ("Bryennios") discovery of a very primitive document, rendered it indispensable that this republication should be enriched by it, in connection with the *Apostolic Constitutions* (so called), which had been reserved for the concluding volume of the series. The critics were greatly divided as to the genuineness of the *Bryennios* MS.; and, in order to gain time, I had relegated the *Constitutions*, with this document as its sequel or its preface, to a place with the *Apocrypha*. Dissatisfied with my own impressions and conjectures, I soon decided that the task of editing the *Teaching*, as the Bryennios document is entitled, must be entrusted to an "expert," and that, if possible, it should be taken in hand with the *Constitutions*. In order to give sufficient time, I entrusted the task, a year ago, to the well-qualified head and hands of Professor Riddle of Hartford, who most kindly accepted my proposals, and who now enables me to present his completed work to the public with the volume to which it properly belongs. It will be hailed by literary men generally as a timely reviewal of the whole subject, nor should I be surprised to find Dr. Riddle's estimate of the *Teaching* accepted as the most important contribution yet made to the literature of inquiry touching its worth and character. Appearing, as it does in this place, in close relations with the *Constitutions*, and with the editorial comparisons so felicitously introduced by the learned annotator, the student will find himself in a position to weigh and to decide for himself all the questions that have been raised in previous examinations of the case. Without risking any judgment of my own upon the decisions which have been reached by Dr. Riddle in the exercise of his great critical skill, I cannot withhold an expression of gratitude for the impartiality and scientific conscientiousness with which he has handled the matter. Uninfluenced by prepossessions, he presents the case with judicial calmness and with due consideration of what others have suggested. I am gratified to find that impressions of my own are strengthened by his conclusions. In an early notice of the Bryennios discovery, contributed to a leading publication, I stated my surmise that the *Teaching*, and its parallels in the *Constitutions* and other primitive writings, would prove to be based upon some original document, common to all. Even Lactantius, in his *Institutes*, shapes his instructions to Constantine by the *Duæ Viæ*, which seem to have been formulated in the earliest ages for the training of catechumens. The elementary nature and the "childishness" of the work are thus accounted for, and I am sure that the "mystagogic" teaching of Cyril receives light from this view of the matter. This work was "food for lambs:" it was not meant to meet the wants of those "of full age." It may prove, as Dr. Riddle hints, that the *Teaching* as we have it, in the Bryennios document, is tainted by the views of some nascent sect or heresy, or by the incompetency of some obscure local church as yet unvisited by learned teachers and evangelists. It seems to me not improbably influenced by views of the *charismata*, which ripened into Montanism, and which are illustrated by the warnings and admonitions of Hermas.[1]

---

1 The reader has observed that all my notes, except the "General Notes," are bracketed when they illustrate any other text except that of my own original prefaces, elucidations, etc. This rule will apply to Professor Riddle's work, as well as to that of the Edinburgh translator's.

INTRODUCTORY NOTICE BY PROFESSOR M. B. RIDDLE, D.D.

SECTION 1.—THE DISCOVERY OF THE CODEX, AND ITS CONTENTS.

In 1873 Philotheos Bryennios, then Head Master of the higher Greek school at Constantinople, but now Metropolitan of Nicomedia, discovered a remarkable collection of manuscripts in the library of the Jerusalem Monastery of the Most Holy Sepulchre at Constantinople. This collection is bound in one volume, and written by the same hand. It is signed "Leon, notary and sinner," and bears the Greek date of 6564 = A.D. 1056. There is no reason to doubt the age of the manuscripts. The documents have been examined by Professor Albert L. Long of Robert College, Constantinople;[1] and some of the pages, reproduced by photography, were published by the Johns Hopkins University, Baltimore, April, 1885. The jealousy of its guardians does not imply any lack of confidence in the age and value of the Codex. The contents of the 120 folios (240 pp.) are as follows:—

I. Synopsis of the Old and New Testaments, by St. Chrysostom (fol. 1–32).
II. The Epistle of Barnabas (fol. 33–51*b*).
III. The two Epistles of Clement to the Corinthians (fol. 51*b*–76*a*).
IV. The Teaching of the Twelve Apostles (fol. 76*a*–80).
V. The Epistle of Mary of Cassoboli to Ignatius (fol. 81–82*a*).
VI. Twelve Epistles of Ignatius (fol. 82*a*–120*a*).

The last part of fol. 120*a* contains the signature and date; then follows an account of the genealogy of Joseph, continued on the other page of the leaf.

Schaff (p. 6) gives a facsimile of fol. 120*a*.

Of these, I. supplies some unpublished portions, and furnishes matter for textual criticism. II. gives the second Greek copy of Barnabas, also furnishing new readings. III. is very valuable; the text of both Epistles is now complete. Two-fifths of that of the second was previously unknown.[2] The value for purposes of textual criticism is also great. IV. is the *Teaching*, the value of which is discussed below. V. and VI. both belong to the Ignatian literature, and furnish new readings, which have already appeared in the editions of Funk (*Opera Patr. Apost.*, ii., Tübingen, 1881) and Lightfoot (*Epistles of St. Ignatius*, London and Cambridge, 1885).

SECTION 2.—PUBLICATION OF THE DISCOVERED WORKS: THE EFFECT.

In 1875 Bryennios, who had been chosen Metropolitan of Serræ during his absence at the Old Catholic conference in Bonn, published at Constantinople the two Epistles of Clement, with prolegomena and notes; giving the text found in the Jerusalem Codex, as he termed it. All patristic scholars welcomed his work, which bore every mark of care and learning; showing the results of his contact, as a student, with German methods. Bishop Lightfoot and many others at once made use of this new material. The remaining contents of the Codex were named in the volume of Bryennios, and some interest awakened by the mention of the *Teaching*. The learned Metropolitan furnished new readings from other parts of the Codex to German scholars. At the close of 1883 he published in Constantinople the text of the *Teaching*, with prolegomena and notes. A copy of the volume was received in Germany in January, 1884; was translated into German, and published Feb. 3, 1884; translated from German into English, and published in

[1] See New-York *Independent*, July 31, 1884.

[2] See this volume, *infra*, the Second Epistle of Clement, so called.

America, Feb. 28, 1884; Archdeacon Farrar published (*Contemporary Review*) a version from the Greek in May, 1884. Before the close of the year the literature on the subject, exclusive of newspaper articles, covered fifty titles (given by Schaff) in Western Europe and America.[1]

SECTION 3.—CONTENTS OF TEACHING, AND RELATION TO OTHER WORKS.

In the Babel of conflicting opinions, it is best to notice first the obvious internal phenomena. The first part of the *Teaching* (now distinguished as chaps. i.–vi.) sets forth the duty of the Christian; in chaps. vii.–x., xiv., we find a directory for worship; chaps. xi.–xiii., xv., give advice respecting church officers, extraordinary and local, and the reception of Christians; the closing chapter (xvi.) enjoins watchfulness in view of the coming of Christ, which is then described.

The amount of matter is not so great as that of the Sermon on the Mount.

The peculiarities of language are marked, but can only be indicated here in footnotes. They point to a period of transition from New-Testament usage to that of ecclesiastical Greek. The citations from the Scriptures resemble those of the Apostolic Fathers. The Gospel of Matthew is most frequently used, especially chaps. v.–vii. and xxiv.; but some of the passages fairly imply a knowledge of the Gospel of Luke. There are some remarkable correspondences with expressions and thoughts found in the Gospel of John, while there is good reason for inferring the writer's acquaintance with all the groups of Pauline Epistles. His allusions to the other New-Testament books are less marked. There is nothing to prove that he did not know all of our canonical books. If an early date is accepted, the tone of the whole opposes the tendency-theory of the Tübingen school.

The most striking internal phenomena are, however, the correspondences of this document with early Christian writings, from A.D. 125 to the fourth century. With the so-called *Epistle to Barnabas*, chaps. xviii.–xx., the resemblances are so marked as to demand a critical theory which can account for them. A few passages in the *Shepherd of Hermas* show some resemblance; but only two sentences, in Commandment Second, are verbally the same. There is a still greater agreement with the so-called *Apostolical Church Order*, of Egyptian origin, probably as old as the third century. It is now known in the Coptic (Memphitic), and also in Arabic and Greek.[2] The first thirteen canons correspond quite closely, both in order and words, with chaps. i.–iv. of the *Teaching*.

Most noteworthy, however, is the parallel with the *Apostolic Constitutions*, vii. 1–32, which contain more than half the *Teaching*, in precisely the same order, with very close verbal resemblances. The parts omitted are in most cases such as had lost their pertinence in the fourth century, while they seem appropriate to a much earlier period. The details will be found in the footnotes to the *Teaching* in this volume. These phenomena have called forth voluminous discussions, and are the most important facts in determining the authenticity and age of the *Teaching*.

SECTION 4.—AUTHENTICITY.

By this is meant, in this case, the substantial identity of the recently discovered document with the work known and referred to by early Christian writers under the same (or a similar) title. Of apostolic origin no one should presume to speak, since the text of the document makes no such claim, and internal evidence is obviously against such a suggestion. On the other hand, there is no reason for doubting the age of the Codex, or the accuracy of the edition published by Bryennios.

Eusebius (*d.* 340) of Cæsarea, in the famous passage of his history (iii. 25) which treats of the canonical books of the New Testament, names among the "spurious" works (νόθοι) "the so-called *Teachings of the Apostles*" (τῶν ἀποστόλων αἱ λεγόμεναι διδαχαί). The plural form does

[1] See Bibliography at the close of vol. viii., this series.

[2] The *Church Order* is to be distinguished from the Ethiopic collection of Apostolic canons; see Introductory Notice to *Apostolic Constitutions*.

not forbid a reference to the work under discussion, since Athanasius (*d.* 373) has a notice clearly pointing to the same writing, in which he uses the singular (*Festal Epistle*, 39). Rufinus (*d.* 410) speaks of a brief work called *The Two Ways*, or *The Judgment of Peter;* and this fact, in view of the contents of the *Teaching*, furnishes one of the most important data for the critical discussion. The last notice of the *Teaching* was made by Nicephorus (*d.* 828) more than two hundred years before Leon made this copy. Clement of Alexandria (*d. circa* 216) and Irenæus (*mart.* 202) use expressions that may indicate an acquaintance with this writing. The more extended correspondences with Barnabas and later disciplinary works are noticed above (sec. 3). The existence of an old Latin translation of the *Teaching*, of the tenth century, a fragment of which has been preserved, furnishes general evidence to the authenticity of the Greek copy, but by its variations suggests the presence of many textual corruptions. Its closer correspondence with Barnabas has led to the theory that the translator used both documents. Others suppose that its form points to a document which was the common source of the Greek form of the *Teaching* and of Barnabas.

The various theories based on the above facts cannot even be stated. The following positions seem, on the whole, most tenable: —

1. The Greek Codex presents substantially the writing referred to by Eusebius and Athanasius.

2. Owing to an absence of other copies, we cannot determine the purity of the text; but there is every probability of many minor corruptions.

3. This probability calls for care that we do not infer too much from verbal resemblances.

4. The resemblances to book vii., *Apostolic Constitutions*, are, however, of such a character as establish, not only a literary connection between the two works, but also the priority of the *Teaching*.

5. In the case of Barnabas, the resemblances can be accounted for (*a*) by accepting the priority of the *Teaching*, or (*b*) by assuming a common (earlier and unknown) source, or (*c*) by accepting the priority of Barnabas, and assuming such corruptions in the Greek copy of the *Teaching* as will account for the supposed marks of its priority. Despite the general adoption of (*a*), there remains a strong probability that (*b*) is the correct solution of the problem.

6. The *Duæ Viæ*, spoken of by Rufinus, may be the common source. We have no positive evidence, but the "two ways" form so prominent a topic in most of these documents which indicate literary relationship, as to encourage this theory. If there was a common source, it probably contained only matter similar to chaps. i.–v., which was variously used by the subsequent compilers. Here a number of theories have been suggested.[1] None of them, however, necessarily call for a very late date of the *Teaching*, or compel us to deny that Eusebius and Athanasius referred to substantially the same work as that now existing in the Codex at Constantinople. Many resemblances have been noticed in other works. Probably in the course of a few years all the data will have been collected, and a well-defined result based upon them. But, even in this period of discussion, there is remarkable agreement among critics in regard to the main question of authenticity.

SECTION 5.—TIME AND PLACE OF COMPOSITION.

Granting the general authenticity of the Greek work, the time of composition must be at least as early as the first half of the second century. If the *Teaching* is older than Barnabas, then it cannot be later than A.D. 120. If both are from a common source, the interval of time was probably not very great.[2] The document itself bears many marks of an early date: —

(1) Its simplicity, almost amounting to childishness, not only discountenances all idea of

[1] Compare the detailed discussions of Harnack, Holtzmann, Warfield, and most recently McGiffert, *Andover Review*, vol. v. pp. 430–442.

[2] For the various dates, see p. 375.

forgery, but points to the sub-apostolic age, during which Christianity manifested this characteristic. The fact is an important one in the discussion of the canon of the New Testament.

(2) The undeveloped Christian thought, as well as the indications of undeveloped heresy,[1] confirms this position. Christianity was at first a life, for which the Apostles furnished a basis of revealed thought. But the Christians of the sub-apostolic age had not consciously assimilated the thought to any large extent, while their ethical striving was stimulated by the gross sins surrounding them.[2]

(3) The Church polity indicated in the *Teaching* is less developed than that of the genuine Ignatian Epistles, and shows the existence of extraordinary travelling teachers ("Apostles" and "Prophets," chap. xi.). This points to a date not later than the first half of the second century, probably as early as the first quarter.[3]

Most of these phenomena would, however, consist with a date as late as that of the Ignatian Epistles on the theory that the *Teaching* was written for a community of Christians in some obscure locality. But this theory must admit that there existed for a long time great variety of Church polity and worship.[4] Of this there is, indeed, considerable evidence. The undeveloped form of the doctrinal elements of the work constitutes the most serious objection to the theory of a late origin. On the other hand, it seems on many accounts improbable that the work, in its present form, was written earlier than the beginning of the second century: (1) Such a document would not be penned during the lifetime of any of the Apostles. (2) There is no allusion in chap. xvi. to the destruction of Jerusalem. If the author was a Jewish Christian, as seems most probable, such silence implies an interval of at least one generation. (3) The position of the document in the Codex is *after* the Clementine Epistles, and *before* the Ignatian. This probably marks the chronological position. (4) The extreme simplicity scarcely consists with the view that the author was nearly contemporary with the Apostles.

Bryennios and Harnack assign, as the date, between 120 and 160; Hilgenfeld, 160 and 190; English and American scholars vary between A.D. 80 and 120. Until the priority to Barnabas is more positively established, the two may be regarded as of the same age, about 120, although a date slightly later is not impossible. All attempts to discover the author are, with our present lack of data, necessarily futile. Even the region in and for which it was composed cannot be determined. Jewish-Christian tendencies are not sufficiently indicated to warrant the assumption of a polemical aim.[5] The document has been assigned to Alexandria, to Antioch, to Jerusalem; indeed, many other places have been named. In favour of the Syrian origin is the literary connection with the *Apostolic Constitutions*, while the correspondences with the Epistle to Barnabas suggest Egypt as the locality. If the *Teaching* and Barnabas have a common basis, e.g., the *Duæ Viæ*, the last may be assigned to Egypt, and the *Teaching*, in its present form, to Syria. The Palestinian origin is urged by those who lay stress upon the absence of Pauline doctrine in the *Teaching*. [If meant for catechumens only, this fact is sufficiently accounted for.]

The question is still an open one.

As regards the doctrine, polity, usages, and ethics expressed and implied in the *Teaching*, the reader can judge for himself. The writer is of the opinion that the work represents, on many of these points, only a very small fraction of the Christians during the second century, and that, while it casts some light upon usages of that period, it cannot be regarded as an authoritative witness concerning the universal faith and practice of believers at the date usually assigned to it. The few notices of it, and its early disappearance, confirm this position. The theory of a composite origin also accords with this estimate of the document as a whole.

[1] [Note this mark of a possibly corrupted source.]

[2] [See Apostolic Fathers, *passim*.]

[3] [Compare Rev. ii. 2 and 9.]

[4] [In obscure regions such an admission is clearly consistent with apostolic experience. Compare 1 Cor. iv. 16, 17, xi. 34; Gal. iv. 9.]

[5] [Compare 1 John iv. 1; Titus i. 10.]

The version of the *Teaching* here given is that of Professor Isaac H. Hall and Mr. John T. Napier, which first appeared in the *Sunday-School Times* (Philadelphia), April 12, 1884. It is now republished by permission of the editor of that periodical and of the joint authors. A few slight changes have been made, some of them in accordance with suggestions from Professor Hall, others to indicate correspondences with book vii. of *Apostolic Constitutions*.

The division of verses agrees with that of Harnack as given by Schaff. The headings to the chapters have been inserted by the editor. The Scripture references have been selected and verified. The notes have been kept within narrow limits. They serve to indicate the relation of the matter to that in other early writings, mainly the *Apostolic Constitutions*, and to give various readings and renderings. Occasionally explanations and comments have been inserted. In dealing with this, as with most other books, the best method of study is historico-exegetical. To read the book intelligently is better than to read about it. The editor has sought to furnish some help in this method.

THE TEACHING OF THE TWELVE APOSTLES

THE LORD'S TEACHING THROUGH THE TWELVE APOSTLES TO THE NATIONS.[1]

CHAP. I. — THE TWO WAYS; THE FIRST COMMANDMENT.

1 THERE are two ways,[2] one of life and one
of death;[3] but a great difference between the
2 two ways. The way of life, then, is this: First,
thou shalt love God[4] who made thee; second,
thy neighbour as thyself;[5] and all things whatsoever thou wouldst should not occur to thee, thou
3 also to another do not do.[6] And of these sayings[7] the teaching is this: Bless them that curse
you, and pray for your enemies, and fast for them
that persecute you.[8] For what thank *is there*,
if ye love them that love you? Do not also the
Gentiles do the same?[9] But do ye love them
that hate you; and ye shall not have an enemy.[10]
4 Abstain thou from fleshly and worldly lusts.[11] If
one give thee a blow upon thy right cheek, turn
to him the other also;[12] and thou shalt be perfect. If one impress thee for one mile, go with
him two.[13] If one take away thy cloak, give him
also thy coat.[14] If one take from thee thine own,
ask it not back,[15] for indeed thou art not able.
5 Give to every one that asketh thee, and ask
it not back;[16] for the Father willeth that to all
should be given of our own blessings (free gifts).[17]
Happy *is* he that giveth according to the commandment; for he is guiltless. Woe to him that
receiveth; for if one having need receiveth, he is
guiltless; but he *that receiveth* not having need,
shall pay the penalty, why he received and for
what, and, coming into straits (confinement),[18]
he shall be examined concerning the things
which he hath done, and he shall not escape
thence until he pay back the last farthing.[19] But 6
also now concerning this, it hath been said, Let
thine alms sweat[20] in thy hands, until thou know
to whom thou shouldst give.

CHAP. II.[21] — THE SECOND COMMANDMENT: GROSS SIN FORBIDDEN.

And the second commandment of the Teach- 1
ing; Thou shalt not commit murder, thou shalt 2
not commit adultery,[22] thou shalt not commit
pæderasty,[23] thou shalt not commit fornication,
thou shalt not steal,[24] thou shalt not practise
magic, thou shalt not practise witchcraft, thou
shalt not murder a child by abortion nor kill
that which is begotten.[25] Thou shalt not covet
the things of thy neighbour,[26] thou shalt not for- 3
swear thyself,[27] thou shalt not bear false witness,[28]
thou shalt not speak evil, thou shalt bear no
grudge.[29] Thou shalt not be double-minded nor 4
double-tongued; for to be double-tongued is a

---

[1] The longer title is supposed to be the original one: the shorter, a popular abridgment. The latter has no real connection with Acts ii. 42. Many hold that the term "nations" (or "Gentiles") points to a Jewish Christian as the author (so Bryennios), though this is denied by others (so Brown). A similar diversity of opinion exists as to the class of readers; but, if the early date is accepted, the more probable theory is, that the first part at least of the manual was for the instruction of catechumens of Gentile birth (so Bryennios, Schaff). Others extend it to Gentile Christians.

[2] This phrase connects the book with the *Duæ Viæ*; see Introductory Notice. *Barnabas* has "light" and "darkness" for "life" and "death."

[3] Deut. xxx. 15, 19; Jer. xxi. 8; Matt. vii. 13, 14.

[4] Comp. Deut. vi. 5, which is fully cited in *Apostolic Constitutions*, vii. 2, though the verb here is more exactly cited from LXX.

[5] Lev. xix. 18; Matt. xxii. 37, 39. Comp. Mark xii. 30, 31.

[6] Comp. Tobit iv. 15; and Matt. vii. 12; Luke vi. 31.

[7] These Old-Testament commands are thus taught by the Lord.

[8] Matt. v. 44. But the last clause is added, and is of unknown origin; not found in *Apostolic Constitutions*.

[9] Matt. v. 46, 47; Luke vi. 32. The two passages are combined.

[10] So *Apostolic Constitutions*. Comp. 1 Pet. iii. 13.

[11] 1 Pet. ii. 11. The Codex has σωματικῶν, "bodily;" but editors correct to κοσμικῶν.

[12] Matt. v. 39; Luke vi. 29.

[13] Matt. v. 41.

[14] Matt. v. 40; Luke vi. 29.

[15] Luke vi. 30. The last clause is a peculiar addition; "art not able," since thou art a Christian; otherwise it is a commonplace observation.

[16] Luke vi. 30. The rest of the sentence is explained by the parallel passage in *Apostolic Constitutions*, which cites Matt. v. 45.

[17] Bryennios finds a parallel (or citation) in *Hermas*, Commandment Second, p. 20, vol. ii. *Ante-Nicene Fathers*. The remainder of this chapter has no parallel in *Apostolic Constitutions*.

[18] Gr. ἐν συνοχῇ. Probably = imprisonment; see next clause.

[19] Matt. v. 26.

[20] Codex: ἱδρωτάτω, which in this connection is unintelligible. Bryennios corrects into ἱδρωσάτω, rendered as above. There are various other conjectural emendations. The verse probably forbids indiscriminate charity, pointing to an early abuse of Christian liberality.

[21] The chapter, except this opening sentence and part of verse 7, is found in *Apostolic Constitutions*, vii. 2–5; but the precepts are separated and enlarged upon.

[22] Ex. xx. 13, 14.

[23] Or, "corrupt boys," as in the version of *Apostolic Constitutions*.

[24] Ex. xx. 15.

[25] Comp. Ex. xxi. 22, 23. The Codex reads γεννηθέντα, which Schaff renders "the new-born child." Bryennios substitutes γεννηθέν, which is accepted by most editors, and rendered as above.

[26] Ex. xx. 17.

[27] Matt. v. 34.

[28] Ex. xx. 16

[29] Rendered "nor shalt thou be mindful of injuries" in version of *Apostolic Constitutions*.

5 snare of death.[1] Thy speech shall not be false,
6 nor empty, but fulfilled by deed.[2] Thou shalt
not be covetous, nor rapacious, nor a hypocrite,
nor evil disposed, nor haughty. Thou shalt not
7 take evil counsel against thy neighbour.[3] Thou
shalt not hate any man; but some thou shalt
reprove,[4] and concerning some thou shalt pray,
and some thou shalt love more than thy own
life.[5]

CHAP. III.[6] — OTHER SINS FORBIDDEN.

1 My child,[7] flee from every evil thing, and from
2 every likeness of it. Be not prone to anger, for
anger leadeth the way to murder; neither jealous, nor quarrelsome, nor of hot temper; for
3 out of all these murders are engendered. My
child, be not a lustful one; for lust leadeth the
way to fornication; neither a filthy talker, nor
of lofty eye; for out of all these adulteries are
4 engendered. My child, be not an observer of
omens, since it leadeth the way to idolatry;
neither an enchanter, nor an astrologer, nor a
purifier, nor be willing to look at these things;
5 for out of all these idolatry is engendered. My
child, be not a liar, since a lie leadeth the way
to theft; neither money-loving, nor vainglorious,
6 for out of all these thefts are engendered. My
child, be not a murmurer, since it leadeth the
way to blasphemy; neither self-willed nor evil-
minded, for out of all these blasphemies are en-
7 gendered. But be thou meek, since the meek
8 shall inherit the earth.[8] Be long-suffering and
pitiful and guileless and gentle and good and
always trembling at the words which thou hast
9 heard.[9] Thou shalt not exalt thyself,[10] nor give
over-confidence to thy soul. Thy soul shall not
be joined with lofty ones, but with just and lowly
10 ones shall it have its intercourse. The workings
that befall thee receive as good, knowing that
apart from God nothing cometh to pass.[11]

CHAP. IV.[12] — VARIOUS PRECEPTS.

1 My child, him that speaketh to thee the word
of God remember night and day; and thou
shalt honour him as the Lord;[13] for *in the place*
whence lordly rule is uttered,[14] there is the Lord.
And thou shalt seek out day by day the faces of 2
the saints, in order that thou mayest rest upon[15]
their words. Thou shalt not long for[16] division, 3
but shalt bring those who contend to peace.
Thou shalt judge righteously, thou shalt not
respect persons in reproving for transgressions.
Thou shalt not be undecided whether it shall be 4
or no.[17] Be not a stretcher forth of the hands 5
to receive and a drawer of them back to give.[18]
If thou hast *aught*, through thy hands thou shalt 6
give ransom for thy sins.[19] Thou shalt not hesi- 7
tate to give, nor murmur when thou givest; for
thou shalt know who is the good repayer of the
hire. Thou shalt not turn away from him that 8
is in want, but thou shalt share all things with
thy brother, and shalt not say that they are thine
own; for if ye are partakers in that which is
immortal, how much more in things which are
mortal?[20] Thou shalt not remove thy hand from 9
thy son or from thy daughter, but from *their*
youth shalt teach *them* the fear of God.[21] Thou 10
shalt not enjoin aught in thy bitterness upon thy
bondman or maidservant, who hope in the same
God, lest ever they shall fear not God who is
over both;[22] for he cometh not to call according
to the outward appearance, but unto them whom
the Spirit hath prepared. And ye bondmen shall 11
be subject to your[23] masters as to a type of God,
in modesty and fear.[24] Thou shalt hate all hy- 12
pocrisy and everything which is not pleasing to
the Lord. Do thou in no wise forsake the com- 13
mandments of the Lord; but thou shalt keep
what thou hast received, neither adding *thereto*
nor taking away *therefrom*.[25] In the church[26] 14
thou shalt acknowledge thy transgressions, and
thou shalt not come near for thy prayer[27]
with an evil conscience.[28] This is the way of
life.[29]

---

1 So *Barnabas*, xix.

2 Verse 5, except the first clause, occurs only here.

3 Latter half of verse 6 in *Barnabas*, xix.

4 Lev. xix. 17; *Apostolic Constitutions*.

5 Or, "soul." The last part of the clause is found in *Barnabas;* but "and concerning some . . . pray, and some" has no parallel. An interesting verse in its literary history.

6 About one-half of the matter of this chapter is to be found, in well-nigh the same order, scattered through *Apostolic Constitutions*, vii. 6–8. The precepts are aimed at minor sins, and require no particular comment. This chapter has the largest number of Greek words not found in the New Testament.

7 The address "my child" does not occur in the parallel passages.

8 Matt. v. 5.

9 Isa. lxvi. 2, 5; *Apostolic Constitutions*, vii. 8.

10 Comp. Luke xviii. 14.

11 Ecclus. ii. 4. So Bryennios. Comp. last part of *Apostolic Constitutions*, vii. 8.

12 This chapter, with the exception of a few clauses and words, is found in *Apostolic Constitutions*, vii. 9–17. There are verbal variations, but the order is exact. In *Barnabas* not so much of the matter is found. There is, however, even greater verbal agreement in many cases, though the order is quite different. Two important clauses (verses 8, 14) find an exact parallel only in *Barnabas*. One phrase is peculiar to the *Teaching;* see ver. 14.

13 Comp. Heb. xiii. 7. In *Apostolic Constitutions* there is a transposition of words.

14 Schaff: "The Lordship is spoken of." *Apostolic Constitutions*, "where the doctrine concerning God is," etc.

15 Or, "acquiesce in" (*Apostolic Constitutions*).

16 Some read ποιήσεις, "make," as in *Apostolic Constitutions* and *Barnabas*, instead of ποθήσεις, Codex.

17 Comp. Ecclus. i. 28. The verse occurs in *Barnabas;* and in *Apostolic Constitutions* "in thy prayer" is inserted, which is probably the sense here.

18 Ecclus. iv. 31. The Greek word συσπῶν occurs here and in *Barnabas*, but not in *Apostolic Constitutions*.

19 *Apostolic Constitutions* adds, in explanation, Prov. xvi. 6.

20 Comp. Acts iv. 32; Rom. xv. 27. The latter half of the verse is in *Barnabas* (not in *Apostolic Constitutions*), but with the substitution of "incorruptible" and "corruptible."

21 Comp. Eph. vi. 4.

22 Comp. Eph. vi. 9; Col. iv. 1.

23 Codex reads "our;" editors correct to "your."

24 Comp. Eph. vi. 5; Col. iii. 22.

25 Deut. xii. 32.

26 "In the congregation;" i.e., assembly of believers. This phrase is omitted in both *Barnabas* and *Apostolic Constitutions*. Comp. Jas. v. 16.

27 Or, "to thy *place of* prayer" (Schaff).

28 So *Barnabas;* but *Apostolic Constitutions*, "in the day of thy bittterness."

29 So *Apostolic Constitutions;* but *Barnabas*, "the way of light." See note on chap. i. 1.

CHAP. V.[1] — THE WAY OF DEATH.

1 And the way of death[2] is this: First of all it is
evil and full of curse:[3] murders,[4] adulteries,
lusts, fornications, thefts, idolatries, magic arts,
witchcrafts, rapines, false witnessings, hypocrisies,
double-heartedness, deceit, haughtiness, depravity, self-will, greediness, filthy talking, jealousy,
2 over-confidence, loftiness, boastfulness; persecutors of the good,[5] hating truth, loving a lie,
not knowing a reward for righteousness, not
cleaving[6] to good nor to righteous judgment,
watching not for that which is good, but for that
which is evil; from whom meekness and endurance are far, loving vanities, pursuing requital,
not pitying a poor man, not labouring for the afflicted, not knowing Him that made them, murderers of children, destroyers of the handiwork
of God, turning away from him that is in want,
afflicting him that is distressed, advocates of the
rich, lawless judges of the poor, utter sinners.[7]
Be delivered, children, from all these.[8]

CHAP. VI.[9] — AGAINST FALSE TEACHERS, AND FOOD OFFERED TO IDOLS.

1 See that no one cause thee to err[10] from this
way of the Teaching, since apart from God it
2 teacheth thee. For if thou art able to bear all
the yoke[11] of the Lord, thou wilt be perfect; but
if thou art not able, what thou art able that do.
3 And concerning food,[12] bear what thou art able;
but against that which is sacrificed to idols[13] be
exceedingly on thy guard; for it is the service
of dead gods.[14]

CHAP. VII. — CONCERNING BAPTISM.

And concerning baptism,[15] thus baptize ye:[16] 1
Having first said all these things, baptize into
the name of the Father, and of the Son, and of
the Holy Spirit,[17] in living water.[18] But if thou 2
have not living water, baptize into other water;
and if thou canst not in cold, in warm. But if 3
thou have not either, pour out water thrice[19] upon
the head into the name of Father and Son and
Holy Spirit. But before the baptism let the 4
baptizer fast, and the baptized, and whatever
others can; but thou shalt order the baptized to
fast one or two days before.[20]

CHAP. VIII.[21] — CONCERNING FASTING AND PRAYER (THE LORD'S PRAYER).

But let not your fasts be with the hypocrites;[22] 1
for they fast on the second and fifth day of the
week; but do ye fast on the fourth *day* and
the Preparation (Friday).[23] Neither pray as the 2
hypocrites; but as the Lord commanded in His
Gospel,[24] thus pray: Our Father who art in
heaven, hallowed be Thy name. Thy kingdom
come. Thy will be done, as in heaven, *so* on
earth. Give us to-day our daily (needful)
bread,[25] and forgive us our debt as we also forgive
our debtors. And bring us not into temptation,
but deliver us from the evil *one* (or, evil); for
Thine is the power and the glory for ever.[26]
Thrice in the day thus pray.[27] 3

CHAP. IX.[28] — THE THANKSGIVING (EUCHARIST).

Now concerning the Thanksgiving (Eucha- 1
rist), thus give thanks. First, concerning the 2

---

1 This chapter finds nearly exact parallels in *Barnabas*, xx., and *Apostolic Constitutions*, vii. 18, but with curious variations.

2 *Barnabas* has "darkness," but afterwards "way of eternal death."

3 Not in *Apostolic Constitutions*, and no exact parallel in *Barnabas*

4 Of the twenty-two sins named in this verse, *Barnabas* gives fourteen, in differing order, and in the singular; *Apostolic Constitutions* gives all but one (ὕψος, "loftiness," "haughtiness"), in the same order, and with the same change from plural to singular.

5 This verse appears almost word for word in *Barnabas*, with two additional clauses

6 The *Apostolic Constitutions* give a parallel from this point; verbally exact from the phrase, "not for that which is good."

7 The word πανθαμαρτητοι occurs only here, and in the parallel passage in *Barnabas* (rendered in this edition "who are in every respect transgressors," vol. i. p. 149), and in *Apostolic Constitutions* (rendered "full of sin"). A similar term occurs in the recently recovered portion of 2 Clement, xviii., where Bishop Lightfoot renders, as above, "an utter sinner."

8 Found *verbatim* in *Apostolic Constitutions*, not in *Barnabas*; with the latter there is no further parallel, except a few phrases in chap. xvi. 2, 3 (which see).

9 Of this chapter, two phrases and one entire clause are found in *Apostolic Constitutions*, vii. 19-21.

10 Comp. Matt. xxiv. 4 (Greek); Revised Version, "lead you astray;" *Apostolic Constitutions*, vii. 19.

11 Or, "the whole yoke." Those who accept the Jewish-Christian authorship refer this to the ceremonial law. It seems quite as likely to mean ascetic regulations. Of these there are many traces, even in the New-Testament churches.

12 *Apostolic Constitutions*. vii. 20, begins with a similar phrase, but is explicitly against asceticism in this respect. The precepts here do not indicate any such spirit as that opposed by Paul.

13 Comp. Acts xv. 20, 29; 1 Cor. viii. 4, etc., x. 18, etc. (Rom. xiv. 20 refers to ascetic abstinence.) This prohibition had a necessary permanence; comp. *Apostolic Constitutions*, vii. 21.

14 Comp. the same phrase in 2 Clement, iii. This chapter closes the first part of the *Teaching*, that supposed to be intended for catechumens. The absence of doctrinal statement does not necessarily prove the existence of a circle of Gentile Christians where the Pauline theology was unknown. If such a circle existed, emphasizing the ethical side of Christianity to the exclusion of its doctrinal basis, it disappeared very soon. From the nature of the case, that kind of Christianity is intellectually weak and necessarily short-lived.

15 Verse 1 is found, well-nigh entire, in *Apostolic Constitutions*, vii. 22, but besides this only a few words of verses 2 and 4. The chapter has naturally called out much discussion as to the mode of baptism.

16 [Elucidation I.]

17 Matt. xxviii. 19.

18 Probably *running water*.

19 The previous verses point to immersion; this permits pouring in certain cases, which indicates that this mode was not unknown. The trine application of the water, and its being poured on the head, are both significant.

20 The fasting of the baptized is enjoined in *Apostolic Constitutions*, but that of the baptizer (and others) is peculiar to this document.

21 The entire chapter is found almost *verbatim* in *Apostolic Constitutions*, vii 23, 24.

22 Comp. Matt. vi. 16.

23 The reasons for fasting on Wednesday and Friday are given in *Apostolic Constitutions* (the days of betrayal and of burial). Monday and Thursday were the Jewish fast-days. The word "Preparation" (day before the Jewish sabbath) occurs in Matt. xxvii. 62, etc., and for some time retained a place in Christian literature.

24 Matt. vi. 5, 9-13. This form of the Lord's Prayer is evidently cited from Matthew, not from Luke. The textual variations are slight. The citation is of importance, as proving that the writer used this Gospel, and that the liturgical use of the Lord's Prayer was common.

25 On this phrase, comp. Revised Version, Matt. vi. 11; Luke xi. 3 (text, margin, and American appendix).

26 The variation in the form of the doxology confirms the judgment of textual criticism, which omits it in Matt. vi. 13. All early liturgical literature tends in the same direction; comp. *Apostolic Constitutions*, vii. 24.

27 This is in accordance with Jewish usage. Dan. vi. 10; Ps. lv. 17. Comp. Acts iii. 1, x. 9.

28 The eucharistic prayers of this and the following chapter are only partially reproduced in *Apostolic Constitutions*, vii. 25, 26; that of verse 2 has no parallel.

cup:[1] We thank thee, our Father, for the holy
vine of David Thy servant,[2] which Thou madest
known to us through Jesus Thy Servant; to Thee
3 be the glory for ever. And concerning the broken
bread:[3] We thank Thee, our Father, for the life
and knowledge which Thou madest known to us
through Jesus Thy Servant; to Thee be the glory
4 for ever. Even as this broken *bread* was scattered over the hills,[4] and was gathered together
and became one, so let Thy Church be gathered
together from the ends of the earth into Thy
kingdom;[5] for Thine is the glory and the power
5 through Jesus Christ for ever. But let no one
eat or drink of your Thanksgiving (Eucharist),
but they who have been baptized into the name
of the Lord; for concerning this also the Lord
hath said, Give not that which is holy to the
dogs.[6]

CHAP. X.[7] — PRAYER AFTER COMMUNION.

1 But after ye are filled,[8] thus give thanks:
2 We thank Thee, holy Father, for Thy holy name
which Thou didst cause to tabernacle in our
hearts, and for the knowledge and faith and immortality, which Thou madest known to us
through Jesus Thy Servant; to Thee be the glory
3 for ever. Thou, Master almighty, didst create
all things for Thy name's sake; Thou gavest
food and drink to men for enjoyment, that
they might give thanks to Thee; but to us
Thou didst freely give spiritual food and drink
4 and life eternal through Thy Servant.[9] Before all
things we thank Thee that Thou art mighty; to
5 Thee be the glory for ever. Remember, Lord,
Thy Church, to deliver it from all evil and to
make it perfect in Thy love, and gather it from
the four winds, sanctified for Thy kingdom which
Thou hast prepared for it;[10] for Thine is the
6 power and the glory for ever. Let grace come,
and let this world pass away.[11] Hosanna to the
God (Son)[12] of David! If any one is holy, let
him come; if any one is not so, let him repent.[13]
Maran atha.[14] Amen. But permit the prophets 7
to make Thanksgiving as much as they desire.[15]

CHAP. XI.[16] — CONCERNING TEACHERS, APOSTLES, AND PROPHETS.

Whosoever, therefore, cometh and teacheth 1
you all these things that have been said before,
receive him.[17] But if the teacher himself turn[18] 2
and teach another doctrine to the destruction
of this, hear him not; but *if he teach* so as to
increase righteousness and the knowledge of the
Lord, receive him as the Lord. But concern- 3
ing the apostles and prophets, according to the
decree of the Gospel, thus do. Let every apostle 4
that cometh to you be received as the Lord.[19]
But he shall not remain *except* one day; but if 5
there be need, also the next; but if he remain
three days, he is a false prophet. And when the 6
apostle goeth away, let him take nothing but
bread until he lodgeth;[20] but if he ask money,
he is a false prophet. And every prophet that 7
speaketh in the Spirit[21] ye shall neither try nor
judge; for every sin shall be forgiven, but this
sin shall not be forgiven.[22] But not every one 8
that speaketh in the Spirit is a prophet; but only
if he hold the ways of the Lord. Therefore from
their ways shall the false prophet and the prophet
be known. And every prophet who ordereth a 9
meal[23] in the Spirit eateth not from it, except
indeed he be a false prophet; and every prophet 10
who teacheth the truth, if he do not what he
teacheth, is a false prophet. And every prophet, 11
proved true,[24] working unto the mystery of the
Church in the world,[25] yet not teaching *others* to

[1] This is a variation from the order of the New Testament and of all liturgies: probably this led to its omission in *Apostolic Constitutions*. The word "for" may be substituted for "concerning" here and in verse 3. [Possibly a *response* for recipients.]

[2] Peculiar to this passage, but derived from a common scriptural figure and from the paschal formula. Comp. especially John xv. 1; Matt. xxvi. 29; Mark xiv. 25.

[3] The word κλάσμα is found in the accounts of the feeding of the multitude (Matt. xiv. 20, xv. 37, and parallels); it was naturally applied to the broken bread of the Eucharist.

[4] This reference to "hills," or "mountains," is used as an argument against the Egyptian origin of the *Teaching*.

[5] This part of the verse is found in *Apostolic Constitutions*. Schaff properly calls attention to the distinction here made between "Thy Church" and "Thy kingdom."

[6] Matt. vii. 6.

[7] This post-communion thanksgiving is found in *Apostolic Constitutions*, vii. 26, but with many omissions, alterations, and additions. Still, the correspondence in thought and language is very remarkable. Schaff cites a similar prayer at the Passover (after the Hallel cup).

[8] "After the participation" (*Apostolic Constitutions*) points to a distinct eucharistic service. Here the Lord's Supper is evidently connected with the *Agape* [a noteworthy suggestion]; comp. 1 Cor. xi. 20–22, 33. This is an evidence of early date; comp. Justin Martyr, *Apol.*, i. chaps. 64–66, where the Lord's Supper is shown to be distinct (*Ante-Nicene Fathers*, i. pp. 185, 186).

[9] This last clause has no parallel in *Apostolic Constitutions*, and points to an earlier and more spiritual conception of the Eucharist. Verse 4 also is peculiar to this passage.

[10] The above rendering follows Bryennios; that of Harnack (formerly accepted by Hall and Napier) is: "Gather it, sanctified, from the four winds, into Thy kingdom," etc. The phrase "from the four winds" recalls Matt. xxiv. 31.

[11] This is peculiar; but comp. 1 Cor. vii. 31 for the last clause.

[12] The Codex reads τῷ θεῷ, which Bryennios alters to τῷ υἱῷ. The former is the more difficult reading, and is defended by Harnack.

[13] This exhortation indicates a mixed assembly; comp. *Apostolic Constitutions*. [If so, it belongs to the *Agape*.]

[14] 1 Cor. xvi. 22, Revised Version, margin: "That is, *our Lord cometh*." Comp. Rev. xxii. 20.

[15] A limitation as compared with 1 Cor. xiv. 29, 31, and yet indicating a combination of extemporaneous devotion with the liturgical form. The verse prepares the way for the next chapter.

[16] The *Apostolic Constitutions* (vii. 27) present scarcely any parallel to this chapter, which points to an earlier period, when ecclesiastical polity was less developed, and the travelling "Apostles" and "Prophets" here spoken of were numerous. [Elucidation II.]

[17] This refers to all teachers, more fully described afterwards.

[18] Lit. "being turned;" i.e., turned from the truth, perverted.

[19] Matt. x. 40. The mention of apostles here has caused much discussion, but there are many indications that travelling evangelists were thus termed for some time after the apostolic age. Bishop Lightfoot has shown, that, even in the New Testament, a looser use of the term applied it to others than the Twelve. Comp. Rom. xvi. 7; 1 Cor. xv. 5, 7 (?); Gal. i. 19; 1 Thess. ii. 6: also, as applied to Barnabas, Acts xiv. 4, 14.

[20] Reach a place where he can lodge.

[21] Under the influence of the charismatic gift spoken of in 1 Cor. xii. 3, xiv. 2. Another indication of an early date.

[22] Probably a reference to the sin against the Holy Spirit. Matt. xii. 31, 32; Mark iii. 29, 30.

[23] Probably a love-feast, commanded by the prophet in his peculiar utterance.

[24] ἀληθινός, "genuine."

[25] ποιῶν εἰς μυστήριον κοσμικὸν ἐκκλησίας, "working unto a worldly mystery of (the) Church," or "making assemblies for a worldly mystery." Either rendering is grammatical: neither is very intelligible. The paraphrase in the above version presents one lead-

do what he himself doeth, shall not be judged
among you, for with God he hath his judgment;
12 for so did also the ancient prophets. But whoever saith in the Spirit, Give me money, or
something else, ye shall not listen to him; but
if he saith to you to give for others' sake who
are in need, let no one judge him.

CHAP. XII.[1] — RECEPTION OF CHRISTIANS.

1 But let every one that cometh in the name of
the Lord be received,[2] and afterward ye shall
prove and know him; for ye shall have under-
2 standing right and left. If he who cometh is a
wayfarer, assist him as far as ye are able; but
he shall not remain with you, except for two or
3 three days, if need be. But if he willeth to abide
with you, being an artisan, let him work and eat;[3]
4 but if he hath no trade, according to your understanding see to it that, as a Christian,[4] he shall
5 not live with you idle. But if he willeth not so
to do, he is a Christ-monger.[5] Watch that ye
keep aloof from such.

CHAP. XIII.[6] — SUPPORT OF PROPHETS.

1 But every true prophet that willeth to abide
2 among you[7] is worthy of his support.[8] So also
a true teacher is himself worthy, as the workman,
3 of his support.[9] Every first-fruit, therefore, of
the products of wine-press and threshing-floor,
of oxen and of sheep, thou shalt take and give
to the prophets, for they are your high priests.[10]
4 But if ye have not a prophet, give it to the poor.
5 If thou makest a batch of dough, take the first-
fruit and give according to the commandment.
So also when thou openest a jar of wine or of 6
oil, take the first-fruit and give it to the prophets;
and of money (silver) and clothing and every 7
possession, take the first-fruit, as it may seem
good to thee, and give according to the commandment.

CHAP. XIV.[11] — CHRISTIAN ASSEMBLY ON THE LORD'S DAY.

But every Lord's day[12] do ye gather yourselves 1
together, and break bread, and give thanksgiving
after having confessed your transgressions,[13] that
your sacrifice may be pure.[14] But let no one that 2
is at variance[15] with his fellow come together
with you, until they be reconciled, that your sacrifice may not be profaned. For this is that 3
which was spoken by the Lord: In every place
and time offer to me a pure sacrifice;[16] for I am
a great King, saith the Lord, and my name is
wonderful among the nations.[17]

CHAP. XV.[18] — BISHOPS AND DEACONS; CHRISTIAN REPROOF.

Appoint, therefore, for yourselves, bishops and 1
deacons worthy of the Lord, men meek, and not
lovers of money,[19] and truthful and proved; for
they also render to you the service[20] of prophets
and teachers. Despise them not therefore, for 2
they are your honoured ones, together with the
prophets and teachers. And reprove one another, 3
not in anger, but in peace, as ye have *it* in the Gospel;[21] but to every one that acts amiss[22] against
another, let no one speak, nor let him hear aught
from you until he repent. But your prayers and 4
alms and all your deeds so do, as ye have *it* in
the Gospel of our Lord.[23]

---

ing view of this difficult passage: the mystery is the Church, and a worldly one, because the Church is in the world. The other leading view joins ἐκκλησίας (as accusative) with ποιῶν, "making assemblies for a worldly mystery." So Bryennios, who regards the worldly mystery as a symbolical act of the prophet. Others suggest, as the mystery for which the assemblies are called, revelation of future events, celibacy, the Eucharist, the ceremonial law. It seems, at all events, to point to incipient fanaticism on the part of the prophets of those days. [Elucidation III.] This was likely to take the form either of asceticism or of extravagant predictions and mystical fancies about the Church in the world. Did we know the place and the time more accurately, we might decide which was meant. This caution was evidently needed: Let God judge such extravagances.

1 Verse 1 is almost identical with the beginning of *Apostolic Constitutions*, vii. 28; the remaining verses have no parallel.

2 All professed Christians are meant.

3 Comp. 2 Thess. iii. 10.

4 The term occurs only here in the *Teaching*.

5 "Christ-trafficker." The abuse of Christian fellowship and hospitality naturally followed the remarkable extension of Christianity. This expressive term was coined to designate the class of idlers who would make gain out of their professed Christianity. It occurs in the longer form of the Ignatian Epistles (*Trallians*, vi.) and in literature of the fourth century.

6 A large part of this chapter is found in *Apostolic Constitutions*, vii. 28, 29, but with modifications and additions indicating a later date.

7 "Who will settle among you" (Hitchcock and Brown). The itinerant prophets might become stationary, we infer. Chaps. xi.–xv. point to a movement from an itinerant and extraordinary ministry to a more settled one.

8 Lit., "nourishment," "food."

9 Matt. x. 10; comp. Luke x. 7.

10 This phrase, indicating a sacerdotal view of the ministry, seems to point to a later date than that claimed for the *Teaching*. Some regard it as an interpolation: others take it in a figurative sense. In *Apostolic Constitutions* the sacerdotal view is more marked. [1 Pet. ii. 9. If the *plebs* = "priests," prophets = "high priests."] Here the term is restricted to the prophets; compare Schaff *in loco*.

11 Verses 1 and 3 are given substantially in *Apostolic Constitutions*, vii. 30. This chapter would seem to belong more properly before chap. viii.; but the same order of topics is followed in *Apostolic Constitutions*, — a remarkable proof of literary connection.

12 Comp. Rev. i. 10. Here the full form is κατὰ κυριακὴν δὲ Κυρίου. If the early date is allowed, this verse confirms the view that from the first the Lord's Day was observed, and that, too, by a eucharistic celebration.

13 Comp. chap. iv. 14. No parallel in *Apostolic Constitutions*.

14 On this spiritual sense of "sacrifice," comp. Rom. xii. 1; Phil. ii. 17; Heb. xiii. 15; 1 Pet. ii. 5.

15 "That hath the (or, any) dispute" (ἀμφιβολίαν); comp. Matt. v. 23, 24.

16 [See Mal. i. 11. See Irenæus, cap. xvii. 5, vol. i. p. 484.]

17 Mal. i. 11, 14. Quoted in *Apostolic Constitutions* and by several Ante-Nicene Fathers, with the same reference to the Eucharist.

18 The larger part of verse 1, and a clause from verses 2, 3, respectively, are found in *Apostolic Constitutions*, vii. 31. Verses 1, 2, both in the use of terms and in the Church polity indicated, point to an early date: (1) There are evident marks of a transition from extraordinary to ordinary ministers. (2) The distinction between bishops and elders does not appear [1 Pet. v. 1. Vol. i. p. 16, this series], and yet it is found in Ignatius. (3) The word χειροτονέω is here used in the sense of "elect" or "appoint" (by show of hands), and not in that of "ordain" (by laying on of hands). The former is the New-Testament sense (Acts xiv. 23; 2 Cor. viii. 19), also in Ignatius; the latter sense is found in *Apostolic Canons*, i. (4) The choice by the people also indicates an early period.

19 Comp. 1 Tim. iii. 4

20 Or, "ministry." This clause and the following verse indicate that the extraordinary ministers were as yet more highly regarded.

21 Comp. Matt. xviii. 15–17.

22 The word ἀστοχέω, occurring here, means "to miss the mark;" in New Testament, "to err" or, "swerve." See 1 Tim. i. 6, vi. 21; 2 Tim. ii. 18.

23 The reference here is probably to the Sermon on the Mount: Matt. v.–vii., especially to chap. vi.

CHAP. XVI.[1] — WATCHFULNESS; THE COMING OF THE LORD.

1 Watch for your life's sake.[2] Let not your
lamps be quenched, nor your loins unloosed;[3]
but be ye ready, for ye know not the hour in
2 which our Lord cometh.[4] But often shall ye
come together, seeking the things which are befitting to your souls: for the whole time of your
faith will not profit you,[5] if ye be not made per-
3 fect in the last time. For in the last days[6] false
prophets and corrupters shall be multiplied, and
the sheep shall be turned into wolves, and love
4 shall be turned into hate;[7] for when lawlessness
increaseth, they shall hate and persecute and
betray one another,[8] and then shall appear the
world-deceiver[9] as Son of God,[10] and shall do
signs and wonders,[11] and the earth shall be delivered into his hands, and he shall do iniquitous
things which have never yet come to pass since
5 the beginning. Then shall the creation of men
come into the fire of trial,[12] and many shall be
made to stumble and shall perish; but they that
endure in their faith shall be saved[13] from under
the curse itself.[14] And then shall appear the 6
signs of the truth;[15] first, the sign of an outspreading[16] in heaven; then the sign of the
sound of the trumpet; and the third, the resurrection of the dead; yet not of all, but as it is 7
said: The Lord shall come and all His saints
with Him.[17] Then shall the world see the Lord 8
coming upon the clouds of heaven.[18]

---

[1] The resemblance between this chapter and *Apostolic Constitutions*, vii. 31, 32, is mainly in order of topics and in the identity of some phrases and terms. Verses 3 and 4 (to the word "world-deceiver") are reproduced almost *verbatim*. That the writer of the *Teaching* used Matt. xxiv. is extremely probable, but the connection of *Apostolic Constitutions* with this passage is evident. In *Barnabas*, iv., there are a few corresponding phrases.

[2] Or, "over your life;" the clause occurs *verbatim* in *Apostolic Constitutions*.

[3] Comp. Luke xii. 35, which is exactly cited in *Apostolic Constitutions*.

[4] Matt. xxiv. 42.

[5] Here *Barnabas*, iv., furnishes a parallel.

[6] This reference to the last days as present or impending is an evidence of early date; comp. *Barnabas*, iv., and many passages in the New Testament. The mistake has been in measuring God's prophetic chronology by our mathematical standard of years.

[7] Comp. Matt. xxiv. 11, 12.

[8] Comp. Matt. xxiv. 10.

[9] ὁ κοσμοπλάνος, found only here and in *Apostolic Constitutions*, vii. 32. Comp. 2 Thess. ii. 3, 4, 8; Rev. xii. 9.

[10] Not found in *Apostolic Constitutions*. The expression plainly implies the belief that Jesus Christ was Son of God.

[11] Comp. Matt. xxiv. 24. The rest of the verse has no parallel.

[12] Comp. 1 Pet. iv. 12, where πύρωσις also occurs.

[13] Comp. Matt x. 22 and similar passages; none of them directly cited here.

[14] ὑπ' αὐτοῦ τοῦ καταθέματος, "from under the curse itself;" namely, that which has just been described. Bryennios and others render "by the curse Himself;" that is, Christ, whom they were tempted to revile. All other interpretations either rest on textual emendations or are open to grammatical objections. Of the two given above, that of Hall and Napier seems preferable.

[15] "Truth" might refer to Christ Himself, but the personal advent is spoken of in verse 8; it is better, then, to refer it to the truth respecting the *parousia* held by the early Christians. For this belief they were mocked, and hence dwelt upon it and the prophecies respecting it. The verse is probably based upon Matt. xxiv. 30, 31; but some find here, as in verse 4, an allusion to Paul's eschatological statements in the Epistles to the Thessalonians.

[16] Professor Hall now prefers to render ἐκπετάσεως, "outspreading," instead of "unrolling," as in his version originally. Hitchcock and Brown, Schaff, and others, prefer "opening;" that is, the apparent opening in heaven through which the Lord will descend. "Outspreading" is usually explained (so Professor Hall) as meaning the expanded sign of the cross in the heavens, the patristic interpretation of Matt. xxiv 30. Bryennios and Farrar refer it to the flying forth of the saints to meet the Lord. There are other interpretations based on textual emendations. As the word is very rare, it is difficult to determine the exact sense. "Opening" seems lexically allowable and otherwise free from objection.

[17] Zech. xiv. 5. This citation is given substantially in *Apostolic Constitutions*. As here used, it seems to point to the first resurrection. Comp. 1 Thess. iv. 17; 1 Cor. xv. 23; Rev. xx. 5. Probably it is based upon the Pauline eschatology rather than upon that of the Apocalypse. At all events, there is no allusion to the millennial statement of the latter. Since there was in the early Church, in connection with the expectation of the speedy coming of Christ, a marked tendency to Chiliasm, the silence respecting the millennium may indicate that the writer was not acquainted with the Apocalypse. This inference is allowable, however, only on the assumption of the early date of the *Teaching*.

[18] Comp. Matt. xxiv. 30. The conclusion is abrupt, and in *Apostolic Constitutions* the New-Testament doctrine of future punishment and reward is added. The absence of all reference to the destruction of Jerusalem would indicate that some time had elapsed since that event. An interval of from thirty to sixty years may well be claimed.

ELUCIDATIONS

I.

(Thus baptize ye, p. 379.)

If we compare this chapter with the corresponding one in the *Apostolic Constitutions*, the *Teaching* seems to me to be a somewhat abridged form of a common original. This being designed for the *catechumens*, there is an omission of what they are afterwards to know. A form originally drawn up for clergy and people has been very inartificially expurgated for the instruction of young disciples. This appears from the ninth chapter (p. 380), where only certain receptive or responsive forms are given. The liturgy of the *Apostolic Constitutions*, book viii., embodies what was studiously kept from all but the τέλειοι, i.e., those "of full age."

II.

(Concerning apostles, p. 380, note 16.)

The reference to "apostles," probably itinerant, in Rev. ii. 2, corresponds with this. There were officers known in the Apostolic day (compare 2 Cor. viii. 23, *Greek*) as ἀπόστολοι ἐκκλησιῶν, for the *pseud-apostles* of the Apocalypse could not have pretended what they did had it been otherwise. Neither would it have been needful to "*try* those who said they were apostles," in that case: the mere assertion of such a pretence would have sufficiently convicted them.

The very childish directions (suited to mere *catechumens*) given in the text illustrates Rev ii. 2, and is, so far, evidence of the very early origin of the *Teaching*.

The name *apostles* was made *technical* by Christ Himself: "He *named* them Apostles" (Luke vi. 13). And the word is never used in the loose way which Bishop Lightfoot hazardously suggests, as I must venture to believe.

III.

(Incipient fanaticism, p. 381, note 25.)

Unquestionably, for even in St. Paul's day his admonitions imply nothing less. See 1 Cor. cap. xiv., *passim*. But, as in the Introductory Notice [1] I hinted my suspicions of incipient Montanism in the *Teaching*, so I am strengthened in this idea by the learned critic to whose note I venture to append this remark for the purpose of asking a reference to my annotations of Hermas in vol. ii. of this series. May I also ask a reference to the same volume, pp. 4, 5, and 6? The "meal" (note 23, p. 380) of the *Teaching* is doubtless the *Agape*, which had been abused at so early a day, that St. Peter [2] himself was forced to denounce the "false prophets" who polluted this feast of charity.

---

[1] P. 371, *supra*.

[2] 2 Pet. ii. 13. Compare 1 John iv. 1.

CONSTITUTIONS OF THE HOLY APOSTLES

[EDITED, WITH NOTES, BY JAMES DONALDSON, D.D.]

INTRODUCTORY NOTICE

TO

CONSTITUTIONS OF THE HOLY APOSTLES

HAVING learned from the erudite Beveridge what I long supposed to be a just view of the *Constitutions*, I have found in the recent literature of the subject not a little to increase my confidence in the general conclusions to which he was led by all that could be known in his times. The treatise of Krabbe guided me to some results of more modern investigations; and Dr. Bunsen, though not apart from his critics, has enabled me still further to correct some of my impressions. But, in connection with the late discovery of Bryennios, the field of discussion and inquiry has been so much enlarged, that I have felt it due to the readers and students of this republication to invoke the aid of Professor Riddle, who is able to enrich the work with the results of genuine learning and much patient research. Whatever may be my own convictions on some subordinate points, I have been glad to secure the judgment of a critical scholar who, I am persuaded, aims to shed upon the subject the colourless light of scientific investigation. This is all I can desire, anxious only to see facts clearly established and historic truth illustrated, no matter to what results they may seem to point. Where the professor's decisions coincide with my own impressions, I am naturally gratified by his valued and independent corroboration: where the case is otherwise, I am hardly less gratified to present my indulgent readers with opinions deserving of their highest respect, and by which they will be stimulated, as well as influenced, in forming convictions for themselves.

The *Constitutions* are so full of material on which it is well for one in my position not to speak very freely in such a work as this, that I rejoice all the more to confide the task of annotation almost exclusively to another and to one from whom American Christians must ever be glad to hear on subjects requiring in an almost equal degree the skill of an expert critic and the candour of a conscientious Christian.

I prefix Professor Riddle's PREFACE to the Introductory Notice of the Edinburgh editor, as follows: —

NEW interest has been awakened in the *Apostolic Constitutions* by the discovery of an ancient manuscript in Constantinople.[1] While it does not contain the *Constitutions*, it affords much material for discussion respecting the sources and authorship of this compilation. The so-called *Teaching of the Twelve Apostles*, found in the Codex at Constantinople, and published by Bryennios in 1883, is recognised as the basis of the seventh book of the *Constitutions*. The verbal coincidences, the order of topics, and other obvious phenomena, leave little room for reasonable doubt on this point. That the reader may be in possession of the main facts, the corresponding portions have been indicated both in book vii. of the *Constitutions* and in the version of the *Teaching* inserted in this volume. This literary connection has some bearing on

---

[1] See the brief account prefixed to the version of the *Teaching*, p. 372, *supra*.

the discussion as to the age of the *Constitutions*. If the *Teaching* is substantially the early work bearing that name, then some of the references by early writers which have been applied to the larger work must now be regarded as pointing to the *Teaching;* still, this only bears against the theory of a date as early as the third century. The new critical material furnished by the Bryennios manuscript for the Ignatian controversy has a bearing on the question respecting the work before us. The opinion has been strengthened (see below), that the same hand enlarged the Ignatian Epistles and adapted earlier matter (such as the *Teaching*) for the *Apostolic Constitutions.*

We may accept as established the following positions: —

1. The *Apostolic Constitutions* are a compilation, the material being derived from sources differing in age.

2. The first six books are the oldest; the seventh, in its present form, somewhat later, but, from its connection with the *Teaching*, proven to contain matter of a very ancient date. The eighth book is of latest date.

3. It now seems to be generally admitted that the entire work is not later than the fourth century, although the usual allowance must be made for later textual changes, whether by accident or design.

Dr. Von Drey [1] regards the first six books as of Eastern origin (mainly Syrian), and to be assigned to the second half of the third century. The seventh and eighth were more recent, he thinks, but united with the others before A.D. 325. With this, Schaff (in his *Church History*, vol. ii., rev. ed., p. 185) substantially agreed; but, in his later work on the *Teaching*, seems to assign the completion of the compilation to a date somewhat later. This is the view of Harnack, who, "by a critical analysis and comparison, comes to the conclusion [2] that pseudo-Clement, *alias* pseudo-Ignatius, was a Eusebian, a semi-Arian, and rather worldly-minded anti-ascetic Bishop of Syria, a friend of the Emperor Constantius between 340 and 360; that he enlarged and adapted the *Didascalia* of the third and the *Didache* of the second century, as well as the Ignatian Epistles, to his own view of morals, worship, and discipline, and clothed them with Apostolic authority." [3]

This is, at all events, a more reasonable view than that of Krabbe, who assigns the first six books to the end of the third century, and the eighth to the beginning of the fifth. The latter, it is true, he regards a compilation from older sources. The purpose of the whole, in his view, was to confirm the episcopal hierarchy, and to establish the unity of the Catholic Church on the basis of the unity of the priesthood, etc. But it is now generally held that the purpose of the compilation was merely to present a manual of instruction, worship, polity, and usage for both clergy and laity. Had it been designed to further some ecclesiastical tendency, it would be far less valuable, since it would less fairly reproduce the ecclesiastical life of the age or ages in which it originated. Bishop Beveridge at first attributed the *Constitutions* to Clemens Alexandrinus (end of second century), but afterwards accepted the third century as the more probable date. The views now prevalent do full justice to his opinions, but seem to be better sustained in detail.

The collection of *Canons* at the close of the *Constitutions* is undoubtedly a compilation. Some are evidently much more ancient than others, and there is every evidence that various collections or recensions existed. That of Dionysius (about A.D. 500), in Latin, contained fifty canons; that of John (Scholasticus) of Antioch (about A.D. 565) contained eighty-five canons: and "it is undeniable that the Greek copy which Dionysius had before him belonged to a differ-

[1] *Neue Untersuchungen über die Constitut. u. Kanones der Ap.*, Tübingen, 1832. Hefele (*Conciliengeschichte*, i., Freiburg, 1855, 2d ed., 1873, Edinb. trans., 1871, p. 449) speaks of this as the best work on the subject.

[2] [Needless to say that this seems to me utterly inconsistent with admitted facts.]

[3] Schaff, *The Teaching of the Twelve Apostles*, New York, 1885, pp. 134, 135. Comp. Harnack on the *Teaching* in *Texte und Untersuchungen, u. s. w.*, ii. pp. 246–268, Leipzig, 1884. Bishop Lightfoot (*Epistles of St. Ignatius*, London and Cambridge, 1885), differs from Harnack, who further discusses the topic in the *Expositor*, January, 1886.

ent family of collections from that used by John Scholasticus, for they differ frequently, if not essentially, both in text and in the way of numbering the canons." [1]

Bishop Beveridge sought to trace these *Canons* to the synods of the first two centuries, while Daillé held that the collection was made as late as the fifth century. The latter view is not generally accepted, though the existence of a variety of collections tells against some of the views of Bishop Beveridge.[2] It is impossible to enter into a full discussion here. It seemed better to annotate the *Canons* from the results of Drey and Hefele, two most candid and scholarly Roman-Catholic investigators.[3] The brief notes indicate the sources according to these authors. The reader will at once perceive from the views thus suggested, as well as from the contents of the *Canons*, that, while some canons are presumably quite ancient, a number belong to the fourth century, and that, as a complete collection, they cannot antedate the compilation of the *Apostolic Constitutions*. Indeed, Drey, who accepts the latter as Ante-Nicene (see above), thinks five of the canons (30, 67, 74, 81, 83) were derived from the canons of the Fourth Œcumenical Council at Chalcedon, A.D. 451, and quite a number of others he traces to synods and councils of the fourth century. Hefele doubts the positions taken by Drey in regard to most of these. He does not, however, insist that the collection is Ante-Nicene, while he traces the origin of many of the canons to the *Apostolic Constitutions*.

[The following is Dr. Donaldson's INTRODUCTORY NOTICE: —]

THERE has always existed a great diversity of opinion as to the author and date of the *Apostolical Constitutions*. Earlier writers were inclined to assign them to the apostolic age, and to Clement; but much discussion ensued, and the questions to which they give rise are still unsettled.

The most peculiar opinion in regard to them is that of Whiston, who devoted a volume (vol. iii.) of his *Primitive Christianity Revived* to prove that "they are the most sacred of the canonical books of the New Testament;" for "these sacred Christian laws or constitutions were delivered at Jerusalem, and in Mount Sion, by our Saviour to the eleven apostles there assembled after His resurrection."

Krabbe, who wrote an elaborate treatise on the origin and contents of the *Apostolical Constitutions*, tried to show that the first seven books were written "towards the end of the third century." The eighth book, he thinks, must have been written at the end of the fourth or beginning of the fifth.

Bunsen thinks that, if we expunge a few interpolations of the fourth and fifth centuries, "we find ourselves unmistakeably in the midst of the life of the Church of the second and third centuries." [4] "I think," he says, "I have proved in my analysis, more clearly than has been hitherto done, the Ante-Nicene origin of a book, or rather books, called by an early fiction *Apostolical Constitutions*, and consequently the still higher antiquity of the materials, both ecclesiastical and literary, which they contain. I have shown that the compilers made use of the Epistle of Barnabas,[5] which belongs to the first half of the second century; that the eighth is an extract or transcript of Hippolytus; and that the first six books are so full of phrases found in the second interpolation of the Ignatian Epistles, that their last compiler, the author of the present text, must either have lived soon after that interpolation was made, or *vice versâ*, or the interpolator and compiler must have been one and the same person.[6] This last circumstance renders it probable

[1] Hefele, *History of Councils*, i. p. 460.

[2] The Ethiopic form of these *Canons* has recently appeared in an English translation (*Journal of Society of Biblical Literature and Exegesis*, 1885, pp. 63–72). Professor George H. Schodde, Ph D., the translator, has made use of the edition of Winand Fell (Cologne, 1871) with a Latin version. The *Canons* in this form contain most of the matter given in the Edinburgh version from the Greek, and in the same order. But the number is only fifty-seven, in many cases several Greek canons being combined as one in the Ethiopic. Some modifications are found, but very little that differs materially from the Greek. This collection is not part of the Apostolical Church Order published by Tattam, Lagarde, Harnack, and others. Comp. Schaff, *Teaching*, pp. 237–247.

[3] [However candid, even Hefele, unquestionably learned, has been enslaved to "Infallibility," and was never a freeman.]

[4] *Christianity and Mankind*, vol. ii. p. 405.

[5] [Evidently the *Teaching* must now be substituted for the Epistle of Barnabas. — R.]

[6] [So Harnack, most decidedly; but Bishop Lightfoot opposes this view. — R.]

that at least the first six books of the Greek compilation, like the Ignatian forgeries,[1] were the produce of Asia Minor. Two points are self-evident — their Oriental origin, and that they belong neither to Antioch nor to Alexandria. I suppose nobody now will trace them to Palestine."[2]

Modern critics are equally at sea in determining the date of the collections of canons given at the end of the eighth book. Most believe that some of them belong to the apostolic age, while others are of a comparatively late date. The subject is very fully discussed in Krabbe.

Bovius first gave a complete edition of the *Constitutions* (Venice, 1563), but only in a Latin form. The Greek was first edited by the Jesuit Turrianus (Venice, 1563). It was reprinted several times. Cotelerius gave it in his *Apostolical Fathers*. In the second edition of this work, as prepared by Clericus (1724), the readings of two Vienna manuscripts were given. These V. MSS. and Oxford MS. of book viii. are supposed by Bunsen to be nearer the original than the others, alike in what they give and in what they omit. The *Constitutions* have been edited by Ültzen (1853), and by Lagarde in Bunsen's *Analecta Ante-Nicæna*, vol. ii. (1854). Lagarde has partially introduced readings from the Syriac, Arabic, Æthiopic, and Coptic forms of the *Constitutions*. Whiston devoted the second volume of his *Primitive Christianity* to the *Constitutions* and *Canons*, giving both the Greek and English. It is his translation which we have republished, with considerable alterations. We have not deemed it necessary to give a tithe of the various readings, but have confined ourselves to those that seem important. We have also given no indication of the Syriac form of the first six books. We shall give this form by itself. The translation of Whiston was reprinted by Irah Chase, D.D., very carefully revised, with a translation of Krabbe's *Essay on the Origin and Contents of the Constitutions*, and his *Dissertation on the Canons* (New York, 1848).[3]

---

1 [Bunsen's magisterial views on many subjects are swept away by the recent work of Bishop Lightfoot on the Ignatian literature.]

2 *Christianity and Mankind*, vol. ii. p. 418.

3 [A valuable work, apart from many of Dr. Chase's personal ideas not generally received by critics.]

CONSTITUTIONS OF THE HOLY APOSTLES[1]

BOOK I.

CONCERNING THE LAITY.

SEC. I. — GENERAL COMMANDMENTS.

THE apostles and elders to all those who from among the Gentiles have believed in the Lord Jesus Christ; grace and peace from Almighty God, through our Lord Jesus Christ, be multiplied unto you in the acknowledgment of Him.

The Catholic Church is the plantation of God, and His beloved vineyard;[2] containing those who have believed in His unerring divine religion; who are the heirs by faith of His everlasting kingdom; who are partakers of His divine influence, and of the communication of the Holy Spirit; who are armed through Jesus, and have received His fear into their hearts; who enjoy the benefit of the sprinkling of the precious and innocent blood of Christ; who have free liberty to call Almighty God, Father; being fellow-heirs and joint-partakers of His beloved Son: hearken to this holy doctrine, you who enjoy His promises, as being delivered by the command of your Saviour, and agreeable to His glorious words. Take care, ye children of God, to do all things in obedience to God; and in all things please Christ our Lord.[3] For if any man follows unrighteousness, and does those things that are contrary to the will of God, such a one will be esteemed by God as the disobedient heathen.

CONCERNING COVETOUSNESS.

I. Abstain, therefore, from all unlawful desires and injustice. For it is written in the law, "Thou shalt not covet thy neighbour's wife, nor his field, nor his man-servant, nor his maid-servant, nor his ox, nor his ass, nor anything that is thy neighbour's;"[4] for all coveting of these things is from the evil one. For he that covets his neighbour's wife, or his man-servant, or his maid-servant, is already in his mind an adulterer and a thief; and if he does not repent, is condemned by our Lord Jesus Christ: through whom[5] glory be to God for ever, Amen. For He says in the Gospel, recapitulating, and confirming, and fulfilling the ten commandments of the law: "It is written in the law, Thou shalt not commit adultery: but I say unto you, that is, I said in the law, by Moses. But now I say unto you myself, Whosoever shall look on his neighbour's wife to lust after her, hath committed adultery with her already in his heart."[6] Such a one is condemned of adultery, who covets his neighbour's wife in his mind. But does not he that covets an ox or an ass design to steal them? to apply them to his own use, and to lead them away? Or, again, does not he that covets a field, and continues in such a disposition, wickedly contrive how to remove the landmarks, and to compel the possessor to part with somewhat for nothing? For as the prophet somewhere speaks: "Woe to those who join house to house, and lay field to field, that they may deprive their neighbour of somewhat which was his."[7] Wherefore he says: "Must you alone inhabit the earth? For these things have been heard in the ears of the Lord of hosts." And elsewhere: "Cursed be he who removeth his neighbour's landmarks: and all the people shall say, Amen."[8] Wherefore Moses says: "Thou shalt not remove thy neighbour's landmarks[9] *which thy fathers have set.*"[10] Upon this account, therefore, terrors, death, tribunals, and condemnations follow such as these from God. But as to those who are obedient to God, there is one law of God, *simple,*[10] true, living, which is this: "Do not that to another which thou hatest another should do to thee."[11] Thou

[1] [On the titlepage of the Edinburgh edition is subjoined: "by Clement, bishop and citizen of Rome."]

[2] Isa. v. 7, 2.

[3] The reading of the V. MSS. The others read, "Christ our God."

[4] Ex. xx. 17.

[5] "To whom" in V. MSS., and "to God" is omitted.

[6] Matt. v. 28.

[7] Isa. v. 8.

[8] Deut. xxvii. 17.

[9] Deut. xix. 14.

[10] Omitted in V. MSS.

[11] Tob. iv. 16.

wouldst not that any one should look upon thy wife with an evil design to corrupt her; do not thou, therefore, look upon thy neighbour's wife with a wicked intention. Thou wouldst not that thy garment should be taken away; do not thou, therefore, take away another's. Thou wouldst not be beaten, reproached, affronted; do not thou, therefore, serve any other in the like manner.

THAT WE OUGHT NOT TO RETURN INJURIES, NOR REVENGE OURSELVES ON HIM THAT DOES US WRONG.

II. But if any one curse thee, do thou bless him. For it is written in the book of Numbers: "He that blesseth thee is blessed, and he that curseth thee is cursed."[1] In the same manner it is written in the Gospel: "Bless them that curse you."[2] Being injured, do not avenge yourselves, but bear it with patience; for the Scripture speaks thus: "Say not thou, I will avenge myself on my enemy for what injuries he has offered me; but acquiesce under them, that the Lord may right thee, and bring vengeance upon him who injures thee."[3] For so says He again in the Gospel: "Love your enemies, do good to them that hate you, and pray for them which despitefully use you and persecute you; and ye shall be the children of your Father which is in heaven: for He maketh His sun to shine on the evil and on the good, and raineth on the just and unjust."[4] Let us therefore, beloved, attend to these commandments, that we may be found to be the children of light by doing them. Bear, therefore, with one another, ye servants and sons of God.

SEC. II. — COMMANDMENTS TO MEN.

CONCERNING THE ADORNMENT OF OURSELVES, AND THE SIN WHICH ARISES FROM THENCE.

Let the husband not be insolent nor arrogant towards his wife; but compassionate, bountiful, willing to please his own wife *alone*,[5] and treat her honourably and obligingly, endeavouring to be agreeable to her; (III.) not adorning thyself in such a manner as may entice another woman to thee. For if thou art overcome by her, and sinnest with her, eternal death will overtake thee from God; and thou wilt be punished with sensible and bitter torments. Or if thou dost not perpetrate such a wicked act, but shakest her off, and refusest her, in this case thou art not wholly innocent, even though thou art not guilty of the crime itself, but only in so far as through thy adorning thou didst entice the woman to desire thee. For thou art the cause that the woman was so affected, and by her lusting after thee was guilty of adultery with thee: yet art thou not so guilty, because thou didst not send to her, who was ensnared by thee; nor didst thou desire her. Since, therefore, thou didst not deliver up thyself to her, thou shalt find mercy with the Lord thy God, who hath said, "Thou shalt not commit adultery," and, "Thou shalt not covet."[6] For if such a woman, upon sight of thee, or unseasonable meeting with thee, was smitten in her mind, and sent to thee, but thou as a religious person didst refuse her,[7] if she was wounded in her heart by thy beauty, and youth, and adorning, and fell in love with thee, thou wilt be found guilty of her transgressions, as having been the occasion of scandal to her,[8] *and shalt inherit a woe*.[9] Wherefore pray thou to the Lord God that no mischief may befall thee upon this account: for thou art not to please men, so as to commit sin; but God, so as to attain holiness of life, and be partaker of everlasting rest. That beauty which God and nature has bestowed on thee, do not further beautify; but modestly diminish it before men. Thus, do not thou permit the hair of thy head to grow too long, but rather cut it short; lest by a nice combing thy hair, and wearing it long, and anointing thyself, thou draw upon thyself such ensnared or ensnaring women. Neither do thou wear over-fine garments to seduce any; neither do thou, with an evil subtilty, affect over-fine stockings or shoes for thy feet, but only such as suit the measures of decency and usefulness. Neither do thou put a gold ring upon thy fingers; for all these ornaments are the signs of lasciviousness, which if thou be solicitous about in an indecent manner, thou wilt not act as becomes a good man: for it is not lawful for thee, a believer and a man of God, to permit the hair of thy head to grow long, and to brush it up together, nor to suffer it to spread abroad, nor to puff it up, nor by nice combing and platting to make it curl and shine; since that is contrary to the law, which says thus, in its additional precepts: "You shall not make to yourselves curls and round rasures."[10] Nor may men destroy the hair of their beards, and unnaturally change the form of a man. For the law says: "Ye shall not mar your beards."[10] For God the Creator has made this decent for women, but has determined that it is unsuitable for men. But if thou do these things to please men, in contradiction to the law, thou wilt be abominable with God, who created thee after His own image.

[1] Num. xxiv. 9.
[2] Luke vi. 28.
[3] Prov. xx. 22.
[4] Matt. v. 44, 45.
[5] Omitted in V. MSS.
[6] Ex. xx. 14, 17.
[7] The V. MSS. add: "didst abstain from her, and didst not sin against her."
[8] Matt. xviii 7.
[9] Not in V. MSS.
[10] Lev. xix. 27, xxi. 5.

If, therefore, thou wilt be acceptable to God, abstain from all those things which He hates, and do none of those things that are unpleasing to Him.

THAT WE OUGHT NOT TO BE OVER-CURIOUS ABOUT THOSE WHO LIVE WICKEDLY, BUT TO BE INTENT UPON OUR OWN PROPER EMPLOYMENT.

IV. Thou shalt not be as a wanderer and gadder abroad, rambling about the streets, without just cause, to spy out such as live wickedly. But by minding thy own trade and employment, endeavour to do what is acceptable to God. And keeping in mind the oracles of Christ, meditate in the same continually. For so the Scripture says to thee: "Thou shalt meditate in His law day and night; when thou walkest in the field, and when thou sittest in thine house, and when thou liest down, and when thou risest up, that thou mayest have understanding in all things."[1] Nay, although thou beest rich, and so dost not want a trade for thy maintenance, be not one that gads about, and walks abroad at random; but either go to some that are believers, and of the same religion, and confer and discourse with them about the lively oracles of God:—

WHAT BOOKS OF SCRIPTURE WE OUGHT TO READ.

V. Or if thou stayest at home, read the books of the Law, of the Kings, with the Prophets; sing the hymns of David; and peruse diligently the Gospel, which is the completion of the other.

THAT WE OUGHT TO ABSTAIN FROM ALL THE BOOKS OF THOSE THAT ARE OUT OF THE CHURCH.

VI. Abstain from all the heathen books. For what hast thou to do with such foreign discourses, or laws, or false prophets, which subvert the faith of the unstable? For what defect dost thou find in the law of God, that thou shouldest have recourse to those heathenish fables? For if thou hast a mind to read history, thou hast the books of the Kings; if books of wisdom or poetry, thou hast those of the Prophets, of Job, and the Proverbs, in which thou wilt find greater depth of sagacity than in all the heathen poets and sophisters, because these are the words of the Lord, the only wise God. If thou desirest something to sing, thou hast the Psalms; if the origin of things, thou hast Genesis; if laws and statutes, thou hast the glorious law of the Lord God. Do thou therefore utterly abstain from all strange and diabolical books. Nay, when thou readest the law, think not thyself bound to observe the additional precepts; though not all of them, yet some of them. Read those barely for the sake of history, in order to the knowledge of them, and to glorify God that He has delivered thee from such great and so many bonds. Propose to thyself to distinguish what rules were from the law of nature, and what were added afterwards, or were such additional rules as were introduced and given in the wilderness to the Israelites after the making of the calf; for the law contains those precepts which were spoken by the Lord God before the people fell into idolatry, and made a calf like the Egyptian Apis — that is, the ten commandments. But as to those bonds which were further laid upon them after they had sinned, do not thou draw them upon thyself: for our Saviour came for no other reason but that *He might deliver those that were obnoxious thereto from the wrath which was reserved for them, that*[2] He might fulfil the Law and the Prophets, and that He might abrogate or change those secondary bonds which were superadded to the rest of the law. For therefore did He call to us, and say, "Come un*to me*,[2] all ye that labour and are heavy laden, and I will give you rest."[3] When, therefore, thou hast read the Law, which is agreeable to the Gospel and to the Prophets, read also the books of the Kings, that thou mayest thereby learn which of the kings were righteous, and how they were prospered by God, and how the promise of eternal life continued with them from Him; but those kings which went a-whoring from God did soon perish in their apostasy by the righteous judgment of God, and were deprived of His life, inheriting, instead of rest, eternal punishment. Wherefore by reading these books thou wilt be mightily strengthened in the faith, and edified in Christ, whose body and member thou art. Moreover, when thou walkest abroad in public, and hast a mind to bathe, make use of that bath which is appropriated to men, lest, by discovering thy body in an unseemly manner to women, or by seeing a sight not seemly for men, either thou beest ensnared, or thou ensnarest and enticest to thyself *those women who easily yield to such temptations*.[2] Take care, therefore, and avoid such things, lest thou admit a snare upon thy own soul.

CONCERNING A BAD WOMAN.

VII. For let us learn what the sacred word says in the book of Wisdom: "My son, keep my words, and hide my commandments with thee. Say unto Wisdom, Thou art my sister; and make understanding familiar with thee: that she may keep thee from the strange and wicked woman, in case such a one accost thee with sweet words.

[1] Josh. i. 8; Deut. vi. 7.

[2] Omitted in V. MSS.
[3] Matt. xi. 28.

For from the window of her house she looks into the street, to see if she can espy some young man among the foolish children, without understanding, walking in the market-place, in the meeting of the street near her house, and talking in the dusk of the evening, or in the silence and darkness of the night. A woman meets him in the appearance of an harlot, who steals away the hearts of young persons. She rambles about, and is dissolute; her feet abide not in her house: sometimes she is without, sometimes in the streets, and lieth in wait at every corner. Then she catches him, and kisses him, and with an impudent face says unto him, I have peace-offerings with me; this day do I pay my vows: therefore came I forth to meet thee; earnestly I have desired thy face, and I have found thee. I have decked my bed with coverings; with tapestry from Egypt have I adorned it. I have perfumed my bed with saffron, and my house with cinnamon. Come, let us take our fill of love until the morning; come, let us solace ourselves with love," etc. To which he adds: "With much discourse she seduced him, with snares from her lips she forced him. He goes after her like a silly bird."[1] And again: "Do not hearken to a wicked woman; for though the lips of an harlot are like drops from an honey-comb, which for a while is smooth in thy throat, yet afterwards thou wilt find her more bitter than gall, and sharper than any two-edged sword."[2] And again: "But get away quickly, and tarry not; fix not thine eyes upon her: for she hath thrown down many wounded; yea, innumerable multitudes have been slain by her."[3] "If not," says he, "yet thou wilt repent at the last, when thy flesh and thy body are consumed, and wilt say, How have I hated instruction, and my heart has avoided the reproofs of the righteous! I have not hearkened to the voice of my instructor, nor inclined mine ear to my teacher. I have almost been in all evil."[4] But we will make no more quotations; and if we have omitted any, be so prudent as to select the most valuable out of the Holy Scriptures, and confirm yourselves with them, rejecting all things that are evil, that so you may be found holy with God in eternal life.

SEC. III. — COMMANDMENTS TO WOMEN.

CONCERNING THE SUBJECTION OF A WIFE TO HER HUSBAND, AND THAT SHE MUST BE LOVING AND MODEST.

VIII. Let the wife be obedient to her own proper husband, because "the husband is the head of the wife."[5] But Christ is the head of that husband who walks in the way of righteousness; and "the head of Christ is God," even His Father. Therefore, O wife, next after the Almighty, our God and Father, the Lord of the present world and of the world to come, the Maker of everything that breathes, and of every power; and after His beloved Son, our Lord Jesus Christ, through whom[6] glory be to God, do thou fear thy husband, and reverence him, pleasing him alone, rendering thyself acceptable to him in the several affairs of life, that so on thy account thy husband may be called blessed, according to the Wisdom of Solomon, which thus speaks: "Who can find a virtuous woman? for such a one is more precious than costly stones. The heart of her husband doth safely trust in her, so that she shall have no need of spoil: for she does good to her husband all the days of her life. She buyeth wool and flax, and worketh profitable things with her hands. She is like the merchants' ships, she bringeth her food from far. She riseth also while it is yet night, and giveth meat to her household, and food to her maidens. She considereth a field, and buyeth it; with the fruit of her hands she planteth a vineyard. She girdeth her loins with strength, and strengtheneth her arms. She tasteth that it is good to labour; her lamp goeth not out all the whole night. She stretcheth out her arms for useful work, and layeth her hands to the spindle. She openeth her hands to the needy; yea, she reacheth forth her hands to the poor. Her husband takes no care of the affairs of his house; for all that are with her are clothed with double garments. She maketh coats for her husband, clothings of silk and purple. Her husband is eminent in the gates, when he sitteth with the elders of the land. She maketh fine linen, and selleth it to the Phœnicians, and girdles to the Canaanites. She is clothed with glory and beauty, and she rejoices in the last days. She openeth her mouth with wisdom and discretion, and puts her words in order. The ways of her household are strict; she eateth not the bread of idleness. She will open her mouth with wisdom and caution, and upon her tongue are the laws of mercy. Her children arise up and praise her for her riches, and her husband joins in her praises. Many daughters have obtained wealth and done worthily, but thou surpassest and excellest them all. May lying flatteries and the vain beauty of a wife be far from thee. For a religious wife is blessed. Let her praise the fear of the Lord:[7] give her of the fruits of her lips, and let her husband be praised in the gates."[8] And again: "A virtuous wife is a crown to her husband."[9] And

[1] Prov. vii. 1, etc.
[2] Prov. v. 3, 4.
[3] Prov. vii. 25, 26.
[4] Prov. v. 11, etc.
[5] 1 Cor. xi. 3.
[6] "To whom be glory," V. MSS.
[7] [The incorrect rendering of the LXX. is here cited, as given in the text. — R.]
[8] Prov. xxxi. 10, etc.
[9] Prov. xii. 4.

again: "Many wives have built an house."[1] You have learned what great commendations a prudent and loving wife receives from the Lord God. If thou desirest to be one of the faithful, and to please the Lord, O wife, do not superadd ornaments to thy beauty, in order to please other men; neither affect to wear fine broidering, garments, or shoes, to entice those who are allured by such things. For although thou dost not these wicked things with design of sinning thyself, but only for the sake of ornament and beauty, yet wilt thou not so escape future punishment, as having compelled another to look so hard at thee as to lust after thee, and as not having taken care both to avoid sin thyself, and the affording scandal to others. But if thou yield thyself up, and commit the crime, thou art both guilty of thy own sin, and the cause of the ruin of the other's soul also. Besides, when thou hast committed lewdness with one man, and beginnest to despair, thou wilt again turn away from thy duty, and follow others, and grow past feeling; as says the divine word: "When a wicked man comes into the depth of evil, he becomes a scorner, and then disgrace and reproach come upon him."[2] For such a woman afterward being wounded, ensnares without restraint the souls of the foolish. Let us learn, therefore, how the divine word triumphs over such women, saying: "I hated a woman who is a snare and net to the heart of men worse than death; her hands are fetters."[3] And in another passage: "As a jewel of gold in a swine's snout, so is beauty in a wicked woman."[4] And again: "As a worm in wood, so does a wicked woman destroy her husband."[5] And again: "It is better to dwell in the corner of the house-top, than with a contentious and an angry woman."[6] You, therefore, who are Christian women, do not imitate such as these. But thou who designest to be faithful to thine own husband, take care to please him alone. And when thou art in the streets, cover thy head; for by such a covering thou wilt avoid being viewed of idle persons. Do not paint thy face, which is God's workmanship; for there is no part of thee which wants ornament, inasmuch as all things which God has made are very good. But the lascivious additional adorning of what is already good is an affront to the bounty of the Creator. Look downward when thou walkest abroad, veiling thyself as becomes women.

[1] [A.V., "Every wise woman buildeth her house."—R.] Prov. xiv. 1.
[2] Prov. xviii. 3.
[3] Eccles. vii. 26.
[4] Prov. xi. 22.
[5] Prov. xii. 4 in LXX.
[6] Prov. xxi. 9, 19.

THAT A WOMAN MUST NOT BATHE WITH MEN.

IX. Avoid also that disorderly practice of bathing in the same place with men; for many are the nets of the evil one. And let not a Christian woman bathe with an hermaphrodite; for if she is to veil her face, and conceal it with modesty from strange men, how can she bear to enter naked into the bath together with men? But if the bath be appropriated to women, let her bathe orderly, modestly, and moderately. But let her not bathe without occasion, nor much, nor often, nor in the middle of the day, nor, if possible, every day; and let the tenth hour of the day be the set time for such seasonable bathing. For it is convenient that thou, who art a Christian woman, shouldst ever constantly avoid a curiosity which has many eyes.

CONCERNING A CONTENTIOUS AND BRAWLING WOMAN.

X. But as to a spirit of contention, be sure to curb it as to all men, but principally as to thine husband; lest, if he be an unbeliever or an heathen, he may have an occasion of scandal or of blaspheming God, and thou be partaker of a woe from God. For, says He, "Woe to him by whom My name is blasphemed among the Gentiles;"[7] and lest, if thy husband be a Christian, he be forced, from his knowledge of the Scriptures, to say that which is written in the book of Wisdom: "It is better to dwell in the wilderness, than with a contentious and an angry woman."[8] You wives, therefore, demonstrate your piety by your modesty and meekness to all without the Church, whether they be women or men, in order to their conversion and improvement in the faith. And since we have warned you, and instructed you briefly, whom we do esteem our sisters, daughters, and members, as being wise yourselves, persevere all your lives in an unblameable course of life. Seek to know such kinds of learning whereby you may arrive at the kingdom of our Lord, and please Him, and so rest for ever and ever. Amen.

[7] Isa. lii. 5.
[8] Prov. xxi. 19.

CONSTITUTIONS OF THE HOLY APOSTLES

BOOK II.

OF BISHOPS, PRESBYTERS, AND DEACONS.

SEC. I. — ON EXAMINING CANDIDATES FOR THE EPISCOPAL OFFICE.

THAT A BISHOP MUST BE WELL INSTRUCTED AND EXPERIENCED IN THE WORD.

I. BUT concerning bishops, we have heard from our Lord, that a pastor who is to be ordained a bishop for the churches in every parish, must be unblameable, unreprovable, free from all kinds of wickedness common among men, not under fifty years of age; for such a one is in good part past youthful disorders, and the slanders of the heathen, as well as the reproaches which are sometimes cast upon many persons by some false brethren, who do not consider the word of God in the Gospel: "Whosoever speaketh an idle word shall give an account thereof to the Lord in the day of judgment." [1] And again: "By thy words thou shalt be justified, and by thy words thou shalt be condemned." [2] Let him therefore, *if it is possible*, be well educated; *but if he be unlettered, let him at any rate be* [3] skilful in the word, and of competent age. But if in a small parish one advanced in years is not to be found,[4] let some younger person, who has a good report among his neighbours, and is esteemed by them worthy of the office of a bishop, — who has carried himself from his youth with meekness and regularity, like a much elder person, — after examination, and a general good report, be ordained in peace. For Solomon at twelve years of age was king of Israel,[5] and Josiah at eight years of age reigned righteously,[6] and in like manner Joash governed the people at seven years of age.[7] Wherefore, although the person be young, let him be meek, gentle, and quiet. For the Lord God says by Esaias: "Upon whom will I look, but upon him who is humble and quiet, and always trembles at my words?" [8] In like manner it is in the Gospel also: "Blessed are the meek: for they shall inherit the earth." [9] Let him also be merciful; for again it is said: "Blessed are the merciful: for they shall obtain mercy." [10] *Let him also be a peacemaker; for again it is said: "Blessed are the peacemakers: for they shall be called the sons of God."* [11] Let him also be one of a good conscience, purified from all evil, and wickedness, and unrighteousness; for it is said again: "Blessed are the pure in heart: for they shall see God." [12]

WHAT OUGHT TO BE THE CHARACTERS OF A BISHOP AND OF THE REST OF THE CLERGY.

II. Let him therefore be sober, prudent, decent, firm, stable, not given to wine; no striker, but gentle; not a brawler, not covetous; "not a novice, lest, being puffed up with pride, he fall into condemnation, and the snare of the devil: for every one that exalteth himself shall be abased." [13] Such a one a bishop ought to be, who has been the "husband of one wife," [14] who also has herself had no other husband, "ruling well his own house." [15] In this manner let examination be made when he is to receive ordination, and to be placed in his bishopric, whether he be grave, faithful, decent; whether he hath a grave and faithful wife, or has formerly had such a one; whether he hath educated his children piously, and has "brought them up in the nurture and admonition of the Lord;" [16] whether his domestics do fear and reverence

---

[1] Matt. xii. 36.
[2] Matt. xii. 37.
[3] The words in italics occur only in the V. MSS.
[4] The V. MSS. read: "But if in a small parish one advanced in years is not to be found whom his neighbours testify to be worthy of the office of bishop, and wise enough to be appointed to it, and if there be a young man who has carried," etc.
[5] 1 Kings xii. (LXX.).
[6] 2 Kings xxii. 1.
[7] 2 Chron. xxiv. 1; 2 Kings xi. 3, 4.
[8] Isa. lxvi. 2.
[9] Matt. v. 5.
[10] Matt. v. 7.
[11] From the V. MSS.; Matt. v. 9.
[12] Matt. v. 8.
[13] 1 Tim. iii. 6; Luke xiv. 11.
[14] 1 Tim. iii. 2.
[15] 1 Tim. iii. 4.
[16] Eph. vi. 4.

him, and are all obedient to him: for if those who are immediately about him for worldly concerns are seditious and disobedient, how will others not of his family, when they are under his management, become obedient to him?

IN WHAT THINGS A BISHOP IS TO BE EXAMINED BEFORE HE IS ORDAINED.

III. Let examination also be made whether he be unblameable as to the concerns of this life; for it is written: "Search diligently for all the faults of him who is to be ordained for the priesthood." [1]

SEC. II. — ON THE CHARACTER AND TEACHING OF THE BISHOP.

On which account let him also be void of anger; for Wisdom says: "Anger destroys even the prudent." [2] Let him also be merciful, of a generous and loving temper; for our Lord says: "By this shall all men know that ye are my disciples, if ye love one another." [3] Let him be also ready to give, a lover of the widow and the stranger; ready to serve, and minister, and attend; resolute in his duty; and let him know who is the most worthy of his assistance.

THAT CHARITABLE DISTRIBUTIONS ARE NOT TO BE MADE TO EVERY WIDOW, BUT THAT SOMETIMES A WOMAN WHO HAS A HUSBAND IS TO BE PREFERRED; AND THAT NO DISTRIBUTIONS ARE TO BE MADE TO ANY ONE WHO IS GIVEN TO GLUTTONY, DRUNKENNESS, AND IDLENESS.

IV. For if there be a widow who is able to support herself, and another woman who is not a widow, but is needy by reason of sickness, or the bringing up many children, or infirmity of her hands, let him stretch out his hand in charity rather to this latter. But if any one be in want by gluttony, drunkenness, or idleness, he does not deserve any assistance, or *to be esteemed a member of* the Church of God. For the Scripture, speaking of such persons, says: "The slothful hideth his hand in his bosom, and is not able to bring it to his mouth again." [4] And again: "The sluggard folds up his hands, and eats his own flesh." [5] "For every drunkard and whoremonger shall come to poverty, and every drowsy person shall be clothed with tatters *and rags*." [6] And in another passage: "If thou give thine eyes to drinking and cups, thou shalt afterwards walk more naked than a pestle." [7] For certainly idleness is the mother of famine.

THAT A BISHOP MUST BE NO ACCEPTER OF PERSONS IN JUDGMENT; THAT HE MUST POSSESS A GENTLE DISPOSITION, AND BE TEMPERATE IN HIS MODE OF LIFE.

V. A bishop must be no accepter of persons; neither revering nor flattering a rich man contrary to what is right, nor overlooking nor domineering over a poor man. For, says God to Moses, "Thou shalt not accept the person of the rich, nor shalt thou pity a poor man in his cause: for the judgment is the Lord's." [8] And again: "Thou shalt with exact justice follow that which is right." [9] Let a bishop be frugal, and contented with a little in his meat and drink, that he may be ever in a sober frame, and disposed to instruct and admonish the ignorant; and let him not be costly in his diet, a pamperer of himself, given to pleasure, or fond of delicacies. Let him he patient and gentle in his admonitions, well instructed himself, meditating in and diligently studying the Lord's books, and reading them frequently, that so he may be able carefully to interpret the Scriptures, expounding the Gospel in correspondence with the prophets and with the law; and let the expositions from the law and the prophets correspond to the Gospel. For the Lord Jesus says: "Search the Scriptures; for they are those which testify of me." [10] And again: "For Moses wrote of me." [11] But, above all, let him carefully distinguish between the original law and the additional precepts, and show which are the laws for believers, and which the bonds for the unbelievers, lest any should fall under those bonds. Be careful, therefore, O bishop, to study the word, that thou mayest be able to explain everything exactly, and that thou mayest copiously nourish thy people with much doctrine, and enlighten them with the light of the law; for God says: "Enlighten yourselves with the light of knowledge, while we have yet opportunity." [12]

THAT A BISHOP MUST NOT BE GIVEN TO FILTHY LUCRE, NOR BE A SURETY NOR AN ADVOCATE.

VI. Let not a bishop be given to filthy lucre, especially before the Gentiles, rather suffering than offering injuries; not covetous, nor rapacious; no purloiner; no admirer of the rich, nor hater of the poor; no evil-speaker, nor false witness; not given to anger; no brawler; not entangled with the affairs of this life; not a surety for any one, nor an accuser in suits about money; not ambitious; not double-minded, nor double-tongued; not ready to hearken to calumny or evil-speaking; not a dissembler; not addicted to the heathen festivals; not given to vain

1 Lev. xxi. 17, etc.
2 Prov. xv. 1 (LXX.).
3 John xiii. 35.
4 Prov. xix. 24.
5 Eccles. iv. 5.
6 Not in V. MSS. Prov. xxiii. 21.
7 Prov. xxiii. 31 (LXX.). The word translated "pestle" has also been rendered "upper room," and some suppose it corrupt.

8 Lev. xix. 15; Ex. xxiii. 3.
9 Deut. i. 17, xvi. 20.
10 John v. 39.
11 John v. 46.
12 Hos. x. 12.

deceits; not eager after worldly things, nor a lover of money. For all these things are opposite to God, and pleasing to demons. Let the bishop earnestly give all these precepts in charge to the laity also, persuading them to imitate his conduct. For, says He, "Do ye make the children of Israel pious."[1] Let him be prudent, humble, apt to admonish with the instructions of the Lord, well-disposed, one who has renounced all the wicked projects of this world, and all heathenish lusts; let him be orderly, sharp in observing the wicked, and taking heed of them, but yet a friend to all; just, discerning; and whatsoever qualities are commendable among men, let the bishop possess them in himself. For if the pastor be unblameable as to any wickedness, he will compel his own disciples, and by his very mode of life press them to become worthy imitators of his own actions. As the prophet somewhere says, "And it will be, as is the priest, so is the people;"[2] for our Lord and Teacher Jesus Christ, *the Son*[3] of God, began first to do, and then to teach, *as Luke somewhere says:*[4] "*which Jesus began to do and to teach.*"[3] Wherefore he says: "Whosoever shall do and teach, he shall be called great in the kingdom of God."[5] For you bishops are to be guides and watchmen to the people, as you yourselves have Christ for your guide and watchman. Do you therefore become good guides and watchmen to the people of God. For the Lord says by Ezekiel, speaking to every one of you: "Son of man, I have given thee for a watchman to the house of Israel; and thou shalt hear the word from my mouth, and shalt observe, and shalt declare it from me. When I say unto the wicked, Thou shalt surely die; if thou dost not speak to warn the wicked from his wickedness, that wicked man shall die in his iniquity, and his blood will I require at thine hand. But if thou warn the wicked from his way, that he may turn from it, and he does not turn from it, he shall die in his iniquity, and thou hast delivered thy soul."[6] "In the same manner, if the sword of war be approaching, and the people set a watchman to watch, and he see the same approach, and does not forewarn them, and the sword come and take one of them, he is taken away in his iniquity; but his blood shall be required at the watchman's hand, because he did not blow the trumpet. But if he blew the trumpet, and he who heard it would not take warning, and the sword come and take him away, his blood shall be upon him, because he heard the trumpet and took not warning. But he who took warning has delivered his soul; and the watchman, because he gave warning, shall surely live."[7] The sword here is the judgment; the trumpet is the holy Gospel; the watchman is the bishop, who is set in the Church, who is obliged by his preaching to testify *and vehemently to forewarn*[3] concerning that judgment. If ye do not declare and testify this to the people, the sins of those who are ignorant of it will be found upon you. Wherefore do you warn and reprove the uninstructed with boldness, teach the ignorant, confirm those that understand, bring back those that go astray. If we repeat the very same things on the same occasions, brethren, we shall not do amiss. For by frequent hearing it is to be hoped that some will be made ashamed, and at least do some good action, and avoid some wicked one. For says God by the prophet: "Testify those things to them; perhaps they will hear thy voice."[8] And again: "If perhaps they will hear, if perhaps they will submit."[9] Moses also says to the people: "*If hearing thou wilt hear the Lord God, and do that which is good and right in His eyes.*"[10] *And again:*[3] "Hear, O Israel; the Lord our God is one Lord."[11] And our Lord is often recorded in the Gospel to have said: "He that hath ears to hear, let him hear."[12] And wise Solomon says: "My son, hear the instruction of thy father, and reject not the laws of thy mother."[13] And, indeed, to this day men have not heard; for while they seem to have heard, they have not heard aright, as appears by their having left the one and only true God, and their being drawn into destructive and dangerous heresies, concerning which we shall speak again afterwards.

SEC. III. — HOW THE BISHOP IS TO TREAT THE INNOCENT, THE GUILTY, AND THE PENITENT.

WHAT OUGHT TO BE THE CHARACTER OF THE INITIATED.

VII. Beloved, be it known to you that those who are baptized into the death of our Lord Jesus are obliged to go on no longer in sin; for as those who are dead cannot work wickedness any longer, so those who are dead with Christ cannot practise wickedness. We do not therefore believe, brethren, that any one who has received the washing of life continues in the practice of the licentious acts of transgressors. Now he who sins after his baptism, unless he repent and forsake his sins, shall be condemned to hell-fire.

1 Lev. xv. 31.
2 Hos iv. 9.
3 Not in V. MSS.
4 Acts i. 1.
5 Matt. v. 19.
6 Ezek. xxxiii. 7, etc.
7 Ezek. xxxiii. 2, etc.
8 Jer. xxvi.
9 Ezek. ii. 7, iii. 11.
10 Ex. xv. 26.
11 Deut. vi. 4; Mark xii. 29.
12 Matt. xi., xiii.
13 Prov. i. 8.

CONCERNING A PERSON FALSELY ACCUSED, OR A PERSON CONVICTED.

VIII. But if any one be maliciously prosecuted by the heathen, because he will not still go along with them to the same excess of riot, let him know that such a one is blessed of God, according as our Lord says in the Gospel: "Blessed are ye when men shall reproach you, or persecute you, or say all manner of evil against you falsely, for my sake. Rejoice and be exceeding glad, for your reward is great in heaven."[1] If, therefore, any one be slandered and falsely accused, such a one is blessed; for the Scripture says, "A man that is a reprobate is not tried by God."[2] But if any one be convicted as having done a wicked action, such a one not only hurts himself, but occasions the whole body of the Church and its doctrine to be blasphemed; as if we Christians did not practise those things that we declare to be good and honest, and we ourselves shall be reproached by the Lord, that "they say and do not."[3] Wherefore the bishop must boldly reject such as these upon full conviction, unless they change their course of life.

THAT A BISHOP OUGHT NOT TO RECEIVE BRIBES.

IX. For the bishop must not only himself give no offence, but must be no respecter of persons; in meekness instructing those that offend. But if he himself has not a good conscience, and is a respecter of persons for the sake of filthy lucre and receiving of bribes, and spares the open offender, and permits him to continue in the Church, he disregards the voice of God and of our Lord, which says, "Thou shalt exactly execute right judgment."[4] "Thou shalt not accept persons in judgment: thou shalt not justify the ungodly."[5] "Thou shalt not receive gifts against any one's life; for gifts do blind the eyes of the wise, and pervert the words of the righteous."[6] And elsewhere He says: "Take away from among yourselves that wicked person."[7] And Solomon says in his Proverbs: "Cast out a pestilent fellow from the congregation, and strife will go out along with him."[8]

THAT A BISHOP WHO BY WRONG JUDGMENT SPARES AN OFFENDER IS HIMSELF GUILTY.

X. But he who does not consider these things, will, contrary to justice, spare him who deserves punishment; as Saul spared Agag,[9] and Eli[10] his sons, "who knew not the Lord." Such a one profanes his own dignity, and that Church of God which is in his parish. Such a one is esteemed unjust before God and holy men, as affording occasion of scandal to many of the newly baptized, and to the catechumens; as also to the youth of both sexes, to whom a woe belongs, and "a mill-stone about his neck,"[11] and drowning, on account of his guilt. For, observing what a person their governor is, through his wickedness and neglect of justice they will grow sceptical, and, indulging the same disease, will be compelled to perish with him; as was the case of the people joining with Jeroboam,[12] and those which were in the conspiracy with Corah.[13] But if the offender sees that the bishop and deacons are innocent and unblameable, and the flock pure, he will either not venture to despise their authority, and to enter into the Church of God at all, as one smitten by his own conscience: or if he values nothing, and ventures to enter in, either he will be convicted immediately, as Uzza[14] at the ark, when he touched it to support it; and as Achan,[15] when he stole the accursed thing; and as Gehazi,[16] when he coveted the money of Naaman, and so will be immediately punished: or else he will be admonished by the pastor, and drawn to repentance. For when he looks round the whole Church one by one, and can spy no blemish, neither in the bishop nor in the people who are under his care, he will be put to confusion, and pricked at the heart, and in a peaceable manner will go his way with shame and many tears, and the flock will remain pure. He will apply himself to God with tears, and will repent of his sins, and have hope. Nay, the whole flock, at the sight of his tears, will be instructed, because a sinner avoids destruction by repentance.

HOW A BISHOP OUGHT TO JUDGE OFFENDERS.

XI. Upon this account, therefore, O bishop, endeavour to be pure in thy actions, and to adorn thy place and dignity, which is that of one sustaining the character of God among men, as being set over all men, over priests, kings, rulers, fathers, children, teachers, and in general over all those who are subject to thee: and so sit in the Church when thou speakest, as having authority to judge offenders. For to you, O bishops, it is said: "Whatsoever ye shall bind on earth shall be bound in heaven; and whatsoever ye shall loose on earth shall be loosed in heaven."[17]

1 Matt. v. 11, 12.
2 This passage is not found in Scripture. Some compare Jas. i. 12 and Heb. xii. 8.
3 Matt. xxiii. 3.
4 Deut. xvi. 20, i. 17.
5 Ex. xxiii. 7, LXX.
6 Ex. xxiii. 8.
7 Deut. xxvii. 25, xvi. 19, xvii. 7.
8 Prov. xxii. 10.
9 1 Sam. xv.
10 1 Sam. ii.
11 Matt. xviii. 6, 7.
12 1 Kings xii.
13 Num. xvi.
14 2 Sam. vi.
15 Josh. vii.
16 2 Kings v.
17 Matt. xviii. 18.

INSTRUCTION AS TO HOW A BISHOP OUGHT TO BEHAVE HIMSELF TO THE PENITENT.

XII. Do thou therefore, O bishop, judge with authority like God, yet receive the penitent; for God is a God of mercy. Rebuke those that sin, admonish those that are not converted, exhort those that stand to persevere in their goodness, receive the penitent; for the Lord God has promised with an oath to afford remission to the penitent for what things they have done amiss. For He says by Ezekiel: "Speak unto them, As I live, saith the Lord, I would not the death of a sinner, but that the wicked turn from his evil way, and live. Turn ye therefore from your evil ways; for why will ye die, O house of Israel?"[1] Here *the word*[2] affords hope to sinners, that if they will repent they shall have hope of salvation, lest otherwise out of despair they yield themselves up to their transgressions; but that, having hope of salvation, they may be converted, and may address to God with tears, on account of their sins, and may repent from their hearts, and so appease His displeasure towards them; so shall they receive a pardon from Him, as from a merciful Father.

THAT WE OUGHT TO BEWARE HOW WE MAKE TRIAL OF ANY SINFUL COURSE.

XIII. Yet it is very necessary that those who are yet innocent should continue so, and not make an experiment what sin is, that they may not have occasion for trouble, sorrow, and those lamentations which are in order to forgiveness. For how dost thou know, O man, when thou sinnest, whether thou shalt live any number of days in this present state, that thou mayest have time to repent? For the time of thy departure out of this world is uncertain; and if thou diest in sin, there will remain no repentance for thee; as God says by David, "In the grave who will confess to Thee?"[3] It behoves us, therefore, to be ready in the doing of our duty, that so we may await our passage into another world without sorrow. Wherefore also the Divine Word exhorts, *speaking to thee by the wise Solomon*,[2] "Prepare thy works against thy exit, and provide all beforehand in the field,"[4] lest some of the things necessary to thy journey be wanting; as the oil of piety was deficient in the five foolish virgins[5] mentioned in the Gospel, when they, on account of their having extinguished their lamps of divine knowledge, were shut out of the bride-chamber. Wherefore he who values the security of his soul will take care to be out of danger, by keeping free from sin, that so he may preserve the advantage of his former good works to himself. Do thou, therefore, so judge as executing judgment for God. For, as the Scripture says, "the judgment is the Lord's."[6] In the first place, therefore, condemn the guilty person with authority; afterwards try to bring him home with mercy and compassion, and readiness to receive him, promising him salvation if he will change his course of life, and become a penitent; and when he does repent, and has submitted to his chastisement, receive him: remembering that our Lord has said, "There is joy in heaven over one sinner that repenteth."[7]

CONCERNING THOSE WHO AFFIRM THAT PENITENTS ARE NOT TO BE RECEIVED INTO THE CHURCH. THAT A RIGHTEOUS PERSON, ALTHOUGH HE CONVERSE WITH A SINNER, WILL NOT PERISH WITH HIM. THAT NO PERSON IS PUNISHED FOR ANOTHER, BUT EVERY ONE MUST GIVE AN ACCOUNT OF HIMSELF. THAT WE MUST ASSIST THOSE WHO ARE WEAK IN THE FAITH; AND THAT A BISHOP MUST NOT BE GOVERNED BY ANY TURBULENT PERSON AMONG THE LAITY.

XIV. But if thou refusest to receive him that repents, thou exposest him to those who lie in wait to destroy, forgetting what David says: "Deliver not my soul, which confesses to Thee, unto destroying beasts."[8] Wherefore Jeremiah, when he is exhorting men to repentance, says thus: "Shall not he that falleth arise? or he that turneth away, cannot he return? Wherefore have my people gone back by a shameless backsliding? and they are hardened in their purpose.[9] Turn, ye backsliding children, and I will heal your backslidings."[10] Receive, therefore, without any doubting, him that repents. Be not hindered by such unmerciful men, who say that we must not be defiled with such as those, nor so much as speak to them: for such advice is from men that are unacquainted with God and His providence, and are unreasonable judges, and unmerciful brutes. These men are ignorant that we ought to avoid society with offenders, not in discourse, but in actions: for "the righteousness of the righteous shall be upon him, and the wickedness of the wicked shall be upon him."[11] And again: "If a land sinneth against me by trespassing grievously, and I stretch out my hand upon it, and break the staff of bread upon it, and send famine upon it, and destroy man and beast therein: though these three men, Noah, Job, and Daniel, were in the midst of it, they shall only save their own souls

1 Ezek. xxxiii. 11.
2 Not in V. MSS.
3 Ps. vi. 5.
4 Prov. xxiv. 27.
5 Matt. xxv.
6 Deut. i. 17.
7 Luke xv. 7.
8 Ps. lxxiv. 19.
9 Jer. viii. 4, 5.
10 Jer. iii. 22.
11 Ezek. xviii. 20.

by their righteousness, saith the Lord God."[1] The Scripture most clearly shows that a righteous man that converses with a wicked man does not perish with him. For in the present world the righteous and the wicked are mingled together in the common affairs of life, but not in holy communion; and in this the friends and favourites of God are guilty of no sin. For they do but imitate "their Father which is in heaven, who maketh His sun to rise on the righteous and unrighteous, and sendeth His rain on the evil and on the good;"[2] and the righteous man undergoes no peril on this account. For those who conquer and those who are conquered are in the same place of running, but only those who have bravely undergone the race are where the garland is bestowed; and "no one is crowned, unless he strive lawfully."[3] For every one shall give account of himself, and God will not destroy the righteous with the wicked; for with Him it is a constant rule, that innocence is never punished. For neither did He drown Noah, nor burn up Lot, nor destroy Rahab for company. And if you desire to know how this matter was among us, Judas was one of us, and took the like part of the ministry which we had; and Simon the magician received the seal of the Lord. Yet both the one and the other proving wicked, the former hanged himself, and the latter, as he flew in the air in a manner unnatural, was dashed against the earth. Moreover, Noah and his sons with him were in the ark; but Ham, who alone was found wicked, received punishment in his son.[4] But if fathers are not punished for their children, nor children for their fathers, it is thence clear that neither will wives be punished for their husbands, nor servants for their masters, nor one relation for another, nor one friend for another, nor the righteous for the wicked. But every one will be required an account of his own doing. For neither was punishment inflicted on Noah for the world, nor was Lot destroyed by fire for the Sodomites, nor was Rahab slain for the inhabitants of Jericho, nor Israel for the Egyptians. For not the dwelling together, but the agreement in their sentiments, alone could condemn the righteous with the wicked. We ought not therefore to hearken to such persons who call for death, and hate mankind, and love accusations, and under fair pretences bring men to death. For one man shall not die for another, but "every one is held with the chains of his own sins."[5] And, "behold, the man and his work is before his face."[6] Now we ought to assist those who are with us,[7] and are in danger, and fall, and, as far as lies in our power, to reduce them to sobriety by our exhortations, and so save them from death. For "the whole have no need of the physician, but the sick;"[8] since "it is not pleasing in the sight of your Father that one of these little ones should perish."[9] For we ought not to establish the will of hard-hearted men, but the will of the God and Father of the universe, which is revealed to us by Jesus Christ our Lord, to whom be glory for ever. Amen.

For it is not equitable that thou, O bishop, who art the head, shouldst submit to the tail, that is, to some seditious person among the laity, to the destruction of another, but to God alone. For it is thy privilege to govern those under thee, but not to be governed by them. For neither does a son, who is subject by the course of generation, govern his father; nor a slave, who is subject by law, govern his master; nor does a scholar govern his teacher, nor a soldier his king, nor any of the laity his bishop. For that there is no reason to suppose that such as converse with the wicked, in order to their instruction in the word, are defiled by or partake of their sins, Ezekiel, as it were on purpose preventing the suspicions of ill-disposed persons, says thus: "Why do you speak this proverb concerning the land of Israel? The fathers have eaten sour grapes, and the children's teeth are set on edge. As I live, saith the Lord God, ye shall not henceforth have occasion to use this proverb in Israel. For all souls are mine, in like manner as the soul of the father, so also the soul of the son is mine: the soul that sinneth, it shall die. But the man who is righteous, and does judgment and justice" (and so the prophet reckons up the rest of the virtues, and then adds for a conclusion, "Such a one is just"), "he shall surely live, saith the Lord God. And if he beget a son who is a robber, a shedder of blood, and walks not in the way of his righteous father" (and when the prophet had added what follows, he adds in the conclusion), "he shall certainly not live: he has done all this wickedness; he shall surely die; his blood shall be upon him. Yet they will ask thee, Why? Does not the son bear the iniquity of the father; or his righteousness, having exercised righteousness and mercy himself? And thou shalt say unto them, The soul that sinneth, it shall die. The son shall not bear the iniquity of the father, and the father shall not bear the iniquity of the son. The righteousness of the righteous shall be upon him, and the wickedness of the wicked shall be upon

1 Ezek. xiv. 13, 14.
2 Matt. v. 45.
3 2 Tim. ii. 5.
4 A various reading gives: "Ham, one of his sons, who alone was found wicked, received punishment."
5 Prov v. 22.
6 Isa. lxii. 11.
7 One V. MS. reads: "those who are sick."
8 Matt. ix. 12.
9 Matt. xviii. 14.

him."[1] And a little after he says: "When the righteous turneth away from his righteousness, and committeth iniquity, all his righteousness, by reason of all his wickedness which he has committed, shall not be mentioned to him: in his iniquity which he hath committed, and in his sin which he hath sinned, in them shall he die." And a little after he adds: "When the wicked turneth away from his wickedness which he hath committed, and doth judgment and justice, he hath preserved his soul, he hath turned away from all his ungodliness which he hath done; he shall surely live, he shall not die." And afterwards: "I will judge every one of you according to his ways, O house of Israel, saith the Lord God."

THAT A PRIEST MUST NEITHER OVERLOOK OFFENCES, NOR BE RASH IN PUNISHING THEM.

XV. Observe, you who are our beloved sons, how merciful yet righteous the Lord our God is; how gracious and kind to men; and yet most certainly "He will not acquit the guilty:"[2] though He welcomes the returning sinner, and revives him, leaving no room for suspicion to such as wish to judge sternly and to reject offenders entirely, and to refuse to vouchsafe to them exhortations which might bring them to repentance. In contradiction to such, God by Isaiah says to the bishops: "Comfort ye, comfort ye my people, ye priests: speak comfortably to Jerusalem." It therefore behoves you, upon hearing those words of His, to encourage those who have offended, and lead them to repentance, and afford them hope, and not vainly to suppose that you shall be partakers of their offences on account of such your love to them. Receive the penitent with alacrity, and rejoice over them, and with mercy and bowels of compassion judge the sinners. For if a person was walking by the side of a river, and ready to stumble, and thou shouldest push him and thrust him into the river, instead of offering him thy hand for his assistance, thou wouldst be guilty of the murder of thy brother; whereas thou oughtest rather to lend thy helping hand as he was ready to fall, lest he perish without remedy, that both the people may take warning, and the offender may not utterly perish. It is thy duty, O bishop, neither to overlook the sins of the people, nor to reject those who are penitent, that thou mayst not unskilfully destroy the Lord's flock, or dishonour His new name, which is imposed on His people, and thou thyself beest reproached as those ancient pastors were, of whom God speaks thus to Jeremiah: "Many shepherds have destroyed my vineyard; they have polluted my heritage."[3] And in another passage: "My anger is waxed hot against the shepherds, and against the lambs shall I have indignation."[4] And elsewhere: "Ye are the priests that dishonour my name."[5]

[1] Ezek. xviii. 2, etc.
[2] Nah. i. 3.

OF REPENTANCE, THE MANNER OF IT, AND RULES ABOUT IT.

XVI. When thou seest the offender, with severity command him to be cast out; and as he is going out, let the deacons also treat him with severity, and then let them go and seek for him, and detain him out of the Church; and when they come in, let them entreat thee for him. For our Saviour Himself entreated His Father for those who had sinned, as it is written in the Gospel: "Father, forgive them; for they know not what they do."[6] Then order the offender to come in; and if upon examination thou findest that he is penitent, and fit to be received at all into the Church when thou hast afflicted him his days of fasting, according to the degree of his offence — as two, three, five, or seven weeks — so set him at liberty, and speak such things to him as are fit to be said in way of reproof, instruction, and exhortation to a sinner for his reformation, that so he may continue privately in his humility, and pray to God to be merciful to him, saying: "If Thou, O Lord, shouldest mark iniquities, O Lord, who should stand? For with Thee there is propitiation."[7] Of this sort of declaration is that which is said in the book of Genesis to Cain: "Thou hast sinned; be quiet;"[8] that is, do not go on in sin. For that a sinner ought to be ashamed for his own sin, that oracle of God delivered to Moses concerning Miriam is a sufficient proof, when he prayed that she might be forgiven. For says God to him: "If her father had spit in her face, should she not be ashamed? Let her be shut out of the camp seven days, and afterwards let her come in again."[9] We therefore ought to do so with offenders, when they profess their repentance, — namely, to separate them some determinate time, according to the proportion of their offence, and afterwards, like fathers to children, receive them again upon their repentance.

THAT A BISHOP MUST BE UNBLAMEABLE, AND A PATTERN FOR THOSE WHO ARE UNDER HIS CHARGE.

XVII. But if the bishop himself be an offender, how will he be able any longer to prosecute the

[3] Jer. xii. 10.
[4] Zech. x. 3.
[5] Mal. i. 6.
[6] Luke xxiii. 34.
[7] Ps. cxxx. 3.
[8] Gen. iv. 7, LXX.
[9] [Num. xii. 14.—R.]

offence of another? Or how will he be able to reprove another, either he or his deacons, if by accepting of persons, or receiving of bribes, they have not all a clear conscience? For when the ruler asks, and the judge receives, judgment is not brought to perfection; but when both are "companions of thieves, and regardless of doing justice to the widows,"[1] those who are under the bishop will not be able to support and vindicate him: for they will say to him what is written in the Gospel, "Why beholdest thou the mote that is in thy brother's eye, but considerest not the beam that is in thine own eye?"[2] Let the bishop, therefore, with his deacons, dread to hear any such thing; that is, let him give no occasion for it. For an offender, when he sees any other doing as bad as himself, will be encouraged to do the very same things; and then the wicked one, taking occasion from a single instance, works in others, which God forbid: and by that means the flock will be destroyed. For the greater number of offenders there are, the greater is the mischief that is done by them: for sin which passes without correction grows worse and worse, and spreads to others; since "a little leaven infects the whole lump,"[3] and one thief spreads the abomination over a whole nation, and "dead flies spoil the whole pot of sweet ointment;"[4] and "when a king hearkens to unrighteous counsel, all the servants under him are wicked."[5] So one scabbed sheep, if not separated from those that are whole, infects the rest with the same distemper; and a man infected with the plague is to be avoided by all men; and a mad dog is dangerous to every one that he touches. If, therefore, we neglect to separate the transgressor from the Church of God, we shall make the "Lord's house a den of thieves."[6] For it is the bishop's duty not to be silent in the case of offenders, but to rebuke them, to exhort them, to beat them down, to afflict them with fastings, that so he may strike a pious dread into the rest: for, as He says, "make ye the children of Israel pious."[7] For the bishop must be one who discourages sin by his exhortations, and sets a pattern of righteousness, and proclaims those good things which are prepared by God, and declares that wrath which will come at the day of judgment, lest he contemn and neglect the plantation of God; and, on account of his carelessness, hear that which is said in Hosea: "Why have ye held your peace at impiety, and have reaped the fruit thereof?"[8]

[1] Isa. i. 23.
[2] Luke vi. 41.
[3] Gal. v. 9.
[4] Eccles. x. 1.
[5] Prov. xxix. 12.
[6] Matt. xxi. 13.
[7] Lev. xv. 31.
[8] Hos. x. 13, LXX.

THAT A BISHOP MUST TAKE CARE THAT HIS PEOPLE DO NOT SIN, CONSIDERING THAT HE IS SET FOR A WATCHMAN AMONG THEM.

XVIII. Let the bishop, therefore, extend his concern to all sorts of people: to those who have not offended, that they may continue innocent; to those who offend, that they may repent. For to you does the Lord speak thus: "Take heed that ye offend not one of these little ones."[9] It is your duty also to give remission to the penitent. For as soon as ever one who has offended says, in the sincerity of his soul, "I have sinned against the Lord," the Holy Spirit answers, "The Lord also hath forgiven thy sin; be of good cheer, thou shalt not die."[10] Be sensible, therefore, O bishop, of the dignity of thy place, that as thou hast received the power of binding, so hast thou also that of loosing. Having therefore the power of loosing, know thyself, and behave thyself in this world as becomes thy place, being aware that thou hast a great account to give. "For to whom," as the Scripture says, "men have entrusted much, of him they will require the more."[11] For no one man is free from sin, excepting Him that was made man for us; since it is written: "No man is pure from filthiness; no, not though he be but one day old."[12] Upon which account the lives and conduct of the ancient holy men and patriarchs are described; not that we may reproach them from our reading, but that we ourselves may repent, and have hope that we also shall obtain forgiveness. For their blemishes are to us both security and admonition, because we hence learn, when we have offended, that if we repent we shall have pardon. For it is written: "Who can boast that he has a clean heart? and who dare affirm that he is pure from sin?"[13] No man, therefore, is without sin. Do thou therefore labour to the utmost of thy power to be unblameable; and be solicitous of all the parts of thy flock, lest any one be scandalized on thy account, and thereby perish. For the layman is solicitous only for himself, but thou for all, as having a greater burden, and carrying a heavier load. For it is written: "And the Lord said unto Moses, Thou and Aaron shall bear the sins of the priesthood."[14] Since, therefore, thou art to give an account of all, take care of all. Preserve those that are sound, admonish those that sin; and when thou hast afflicted them with fasting, give them ease by remission; and when with tears the offender begs readmission, receive him, and let the whole Church pray for him; and when by imposition

[9] Matt. xviii. 10.
[10] 2 Sam. xii. 13.
[11] Luke xii. 48.
[12] Job xiv. 4, LXX.
[13] Prov. xx. 9.
[14] Num. xviii. 1.

of thy hand thou hast admitted him, give him leave to abide afterwards in the flock. But for the drowsy and the careless, do thou endeavour to convert and confirm, and warn and cure them, as sensible how great a reward thou shalt have for doing so, and how great danger thou wilt incur if thou beest negligent therein. For Ezekiel speaks thus to those overseers who take no care of the people: "Woe unto the shepherds of Israel, for they have fed themselves; the shepherds feed not the sheep, but themselves. Ye eat the milk, and are clothed with the wool; ye slay the strong, ye do not feed the sheep. The weak have ye not strengthened, neither have ye healed that which was sick, neither have ye bound up that which was broken, neither have ye brought again that which was driven away, neither have ye sought that which was lost; but violently ye chastised them with insult: and they were scattered, because there was no shepherd; and they became meat to all the beasts of the forest." And again: "The shepherds did not search for my sheep; and the shepherds fed themselves, but they fed not my sheep." And a little after: "Behold, I am against the shepherds, and I will require my sheep at their hands, and cause them to cease from feeding my sheep, neither shall the shepherds feed themselves any more; and I will deliver my sheep out of their hands, and they shall not be meat for them." And he also adds, speaking to the people: "Behold, I will judge between sheep and sheep, and between rams and rams. Seemed it a small thing unto you to have eaten up the good pasture, and to have trodden down with your feet the residue of your pasture, and that the sheep have eaten what was trodden down with your feet?" And a little after He adds: "And ye shall know that I am the Lord, and you the sheep of my pasture; ye are my men, and I am your God, saith the Lord God."[1]

THAT A SHEPHERD WHO IS CARELESS OF HIS SHEEP WILL BE CONDEMNED, AND THAT A SHEEP WHICH WILL NOT BE LED BY THE SHEPHERD IS TO BE PUNISHED.

XIX. Hear, O ye bishops; and hear, O ye of the laity, how God speaks: "I will judge between ram and ram, and between sheep and sheep." And He says to the shepherds: "Ye shall be judged for your unskilfulness, and for destroying the sheep." That is, I will judge between one bishop and another, and between one lay person and another, and between one ruler and another (for these sheep and these rams are not irrational, but rational creatures): lest at any time a lay person should say, I am a sheep and not a shepherd, and I am not concerned for myself; let the shepherd look to that, for he alone will be required to give an account for me. For as that sheep that will not follow its good shepherd is exposed to the wolves, to its destruction; so that which follows a bad shepherd is also exposed to unavoidable death, since his shepherd will devour him. Wherefore care must be had to avoid destructive shepherds.

HOW THE GOVERNED ARE TO OBEY THE BISHOPS WHO ARE SET OVER THEM.

XX. As to a good shepherd, let the lay person honour him, love him, reverence him as his lord, as his master, as the high priest of God, as a teacher of piety. For he that heareth him, heareth Christ; and he that rejecteth him, rejecteth Christ; and he who does not receive Christ, does not receive His God and Father: for, says He, "He that heareth you, heareth me; and he that rejecteth you, rejecteth me; and he that rejecteth me, rejecteth Him that sent me."[2] In like manner, let the bishop love the laity as his children, fostering and cherishing them with affectionate diligence; as eggs, in order to the hatching of young ones; or as young ones, taking them in his arms, to the rearing them into birds: admonishing all men; reproving all who stand in need of reproof; reproving, that is, but not striking; beating them down to make them ashamed, but not overthrowing them; warning them in order to their conversion; chiding them in order to their reformation and better course of life; watching the strong, that is, keeping him firm in the faith who is already strong; feeding the people peaceably; strengthening the weak, that is, confirming with exhortation that which is tempted; healing that which is sick, that is, curing by instruction that which is weak in the faith through doubtfulness of mind; binding up that which is broken, that is, binding up by comfortable admonitions that which is gone astray, or wounded, bruised, or broken by their sins, and put out of the way; easing it of its offences, and giving hope: by this means restore it in strength to the Church, bringing it back into the flock. Bring again that which is driven away, that is, do not permit that which is in its sins, and is cast out by way of punishment, to continue excluded; but receiving it, and bringing it back, restore it to the flock, that is, to the people of the undefiled Church. Seek for that which is lost, that is, do not suffer that which desponds of its salvation, by reason of the multitude of its offences, utterly to perish. Do thou search for that which is grown sleepy, drowsy, and sluggish, and that which is unmindful of its own life, through the depth of its sleep, and which is at a great dis-

[1] Ezek. xxxiv. 2, etc.

[2] Luke x. 16.

tance from its own flock, so as to be in danger of falling among the wolves, and being devoured by them. Bring it back by admonition, exhort it to be watchful; and insinuate hope, not permitting it to say that which was said by some: "Our impieties are upon us, and we pine away in them; how shall we then live?"[1] As far as possible, therefore, let the bishop make the offence his own, and say to the sinner, Do thou but return, and I will undertake to suffer death for thee, as our Lord suffered death for me, and for all men. For "the good shepherd lays down his life for the sheep; but he that is an hireling, and not the shepherd, whose own the sheep are not, seeth the wolf coming, that is, the devil, and he leaveth the sheep, and fleeth, and the wolf seizes upon them."[2] We must know, therefore, that God is very merciful to those who have offended, and hath promised repentance with an oath. But he who has offended, and is unacquainted with this promise of God concerning repentance, and does not understand His long-suffering and forbearance, and besides is ignorant of the Holy Scriptures, which proclaim repentance, inasmuch as he has never learned them from you, perishes through his folly. But do thou, like a compassionate shepherd, and a diligent feeder of the flock, search out, and keep an account of thy flock. Seek that which is wanting;[3] as the Lord God our gracious Father has sent His own Son, the good Shepherd and Saviour, our Master Jesus, and has commanded Him to "leave the ninety-nine upon the mountains, and to go in search after that which was lost, and when He had found it, to take it upon His shoulders, and to carry it into the flock, rejoicing that He had found that which was lost."[4] In like manner, be obedient, O bishop, and do thou seek that which was lost, guide that which has wandered out of the right way, bring back that which is gone astray: for thou hast authority to bring them back, and to deliver those that are broken-hearted by remission. For by thee does our Saviour say to him who is discouraged under the sense of his sins, "Thy sins are forgiven thee: thy faith hath saved thee; go in peace."[5] But this peace and haven of tranquillity is the Church of Christ, into which do thou, when thou hast loosed them from their sins, restore them, as being now sound and unblameable, of good hope, diligent, laborious in good works. As a skilful and compassionate physician, heal all such as have wandered in the ways of sin; for "they that are whole have no need of a physician, but they that are sick. For the Son of man came to save and to seek that which was lost."[6] Since thou art therefore a physician of the Lord's Church, provide remedies suitable to every patient's case. Cure them, heal them by all means possible; restore them sound to the Church. Feed the flock, "not with insolence and contempt, as lording it over them,"[7] but as a gentle shepherd, "gathering the lambs into thy bosom, and gently leading those which are with young."[8]

THAT IT IS A DANGEROUS THING TO JUDGE WITHOUT HEARING BOTH SIDES, OR TO DETERMINE OF PUNISHMENT AGAINST A PERSON BEFORE HE IS CONVICTED.

XXI. Be gentle, gracious, mild, without guile, without falsehood; not rigid, not insolent, not severe, not arrogant, not unmerciful, not puffed up, not a man-pleaser, not timorous, not double-minded, not one that insults over the people that are under thee, not one that conceals the divine laws and the promises to repentance, not hasty in thrusting out and expelling, but steady, not one that delights in severity, not heady. Do not admit less evidence to convict any one than that of three witnesses, and those of known and established reputation; inquire whether they do not accuse out of ill-will or envy: for there are many that delight in mischief, forward in discourse, slanderous, haters of the brethren, making it their business to scatter the sheep of Christ; whose affirmation if thou admittest without nice scanning the same, thou wilt disperse thy flock, and betray it to be devoured by wolves, that is, by demons and wicked men, or rather not men, but wild beasts in the shape of men — by the heathen, by the Jews, and by the atheistic heretics. For those destroying wolves soon address themselves to any one that is cast out of the Church, and esteem him as a lamb delivered for them to devour, reckoning his destruction their own gain. For he that is "their father, the devil, is a murderer."[9] He also who is separated unjustly by thy want of care in judging will be overwhelmed with sorrow, and be disconsolate, and so will either wander over to the heathen, or be entangled in heresies, and so will be altogether estranged from the Church and from hope in God, and will be entangled in impiety, whereby thou wilt be guilty of his perdition: for it is not fair to be too hasty in casting out an offender, but slow in receiving him when he returns; to be forward in cutting off, but unmerciful when he is sorrowful, and ought to be healed. For of such as these speaks the divine Scripture: "Their feet run to mischief; they are hasty to shed blood. Destruction and misery are in their

1 Ezek. xxxiii. 10.
2 John x. 11, 12.
3 Matt. xviii. 12.
4 Luke xv. 4, etc.
5 Luke v. 20; Matt. ix. 2; Mark v. 34.
6 Matt. ix. 12; Luke xix. 10.
7 Ezek. xxxiv. 4.
8 Matt. xx. 25; Isa. xl. 11.
9 John viii. 44.

ways, and the way of peace have they not known. The fear of God is not before their eyes."[1] Now the way of peace is our Saviour Jesus Christ, who has taught us, saying: "Forgive, and ye shall be forgiven. Give, and it shall be given to you;"[2] that is, give remission of sins, and your offences shall be forgiven you. As also He instructed us by His prayer to say unto God: "Forgive us our debts, as we forgive our debtors."[3] If, therefore, you do not forgive offenders, how can you expect the remission of your own sins? Do not you rather bind yourselves faster, by pretending in your prayers to forgive, when you really do not forgive? Will you not be confronted with your own words, when you say you forgive and do not forgive? For know ye, that he who casts out one who has not behaved himself wickedly, or who will not receive him that returns, is a murderer of his brother, and sheds his blood, as Cain did that of his brother Abel, and his "blood cries to God,"[4] and will be required. For a righteous man unjustly slain by any one will be in rest with God for ever. The same is the case of him who without cause is separated by his bishop. He who has cast him out as a pestilent fellow when he was innocent, is more furious than a murderer. Such a one has no regard to the mercy of God, nor is mindful of His goodness to those that are penitent, nor keeping in his eye the examples of those who, having been once great offenders, received forgiveness upon their repentance. Upon which account, he who casts off an innocent person is more cruel than he that murders the body. In like manner, he who does not receive the penitent, scatters the flock of Christ, being really against Him. For as God is just in judging of sinners, so is He merciful in receiving them when they return. For David, the man after God's own heart, in his hymns ascribes both mercy and judgment to Him.

THAT DAVID, THE NINEVITES, HEZEKIAH, AND HIS SON MANASSEH, ARE EMINENT EXAMPLES OF REPENTANCE. THE PRAYER OF MANASSEH, KING OF JUDAH.

XXII. It is also thy duty, O bishop, to have before thine eyes the examples of those that have gone before, and to apply them skilfully to the cases of those who want words of severity or of consolation. Besides, it is reasonable that in thy administration of justice thou shouldest follow the will of God; and as God deals with sinners, and with those who return, that thou shouldest act accordingly in thy judging. Now, did not God by Nathan reproach David for his offence? And yet as soon as he said he repented, He delivered him from death, saying, "Be of good cheer; thou shalt not die."[5] So also, when God had caused Jonah[6] to be swallowed up by the sea and the whale, upon his refusal to preach to the Ninevites, when yet he prayed to Him out of the belly of the whale, He retrieved his life from corruption. And when Hezekiah had been puffed up for a while, yet, as soon as he prayed with lamentation, He remitted his offence. But, O ye bishops, hearken to an instance useful upon this occasion. For it is written thus in the fourth book of Kings and the second book of Chronicles: "And Hezekiah died; and Manasseh his son reigned. He was twelve years old when he began to reign, and he reigned fifty and five years in Jerusalem; and his mother's name was Hephzibah. And he did evil in the sight of the Lord: he did not abstain from the abominations of the heathen, whom the Lord destroyed from the face of the children of Israel. And Manasseh returned and built the high places which Hezekiah his father had overthrown; and he reared pillars for Baal, and set up an altar for Baal, and made groves, as did Ahab king of Israel. And he made altars in the house of the Lord, of which the Lord spake to David and to Solomon his son, saying, Therein will I put my name. And Manasseh set up altars, and by them served Baal, and said, My name shall continue for ever.[7] And he built altars to the host of heaven in the two courts of the house of the Lord; and he made his children pass through the fire in a place named Ge Benennom;[8] and he consulted enchanters, and dealt with wizards and familiar spirits, and with conjurers and observers of times, and with teraphim. And he sinned exceedingly in the eyes of the Lord, to provoke Him to anger. And he set a molten and a graven image, the image of his grove, which he made in the house of the Lord, wherein the Lord had chosen to put His name in Jerusalem, the holy city, for ever, and had said, I will no more remove my foot from the land of Israel, which I gave to their fathers; only if they will observe to do according to all that I have commanded them, and according to all the precepts that my servant Moses commanded them. And they hearkened not. And Manasseh seduced them to do more evil before the Lord than did the nations whom the Lord cast out from the face of the children of Israel. And the Lord spake concerning Manasseh and concerning His people by the hand of His servants the prophets, saying, Because Manasseh king of Judah

[1] Prov. i. 16; Isa. lix. 7, 8; Ps. xxxvi. 1; Rom. iii. 15.
[2] Luke vi. 37, 38.
[3] Matt. vi. 12.
[4] Gen. iv. 10.
[5] 2 Sam. xii. 13.
[6] Jonah i. 17, and ii.
[7] From "said" to "ever" is not in Scripture.
[8] Taken from 2 Chron. xxiii. 3, LXX., instead of the reading of the MSS., "Gebanai."

has done all these wicked abominations in a higher degree than the Amorite did which was before him, and hath made Judah to sin with his idols, thus saith the Lord God of Israel, Behold, I bring evils upon Jerusalem and Judah, that whosoever heareth of them, both his ears shall tingle. And I will stretch over Jerusalem the line of Samaria, and the plummet of the house of Ahab; and I will blot out Jerusalem as a table-book is blotted out by wiping it. And I will turn it upside down; and I will give up the remnant of my inheritance, and will deliver them into the hands of their enemies, and they shall become a prey and a spoil to all their enemies, because of all the evils which they have done in mine eyes, and have provoked me to anger from the day that I brought their fathers out of the land of Egypt even until this day. Moreover, Manasseh shed innocent blood very much, till he had filled Jerusalem from one end to another, beside his sins wherewith he made Judah to sin in doing evil in the sight of the Lord. And the Lord brought upon him the captains of the host of the king of Assyria, and they caught Manasseh in bonds, and they bound him in fetters of brass, and brought him to Babylon; and he was bound and shackled with iron all over in the house of the prison. And bread made of bran was given unto him scantily, and by weight, and water mixed with vinegar but a little and by measure, so much as would keep him alive; and he was in straits and sore affliction. And when he was violently afflicted, he besought the face of the Lord his God, and humbled himself greatly before the face of the Lord God of his fathers. And he prayed unto the Lord, saying, O Lord, almighty God of our fathers Abraham, Isaac, and Jacob, and of their righteous seed, who hast made heaven and earth, with all the ornament thereof, who hast bound the sea by the word of Thy commandment, who hast shut up the deep, and sealed it by Thy terrible and glorious name, whom all men fear and tremble before Thy power; for the majesty of Thy glory cannot be borne, and Thine angry threatening towards sinners is insupportable. But Thy merciful promise is unmeasurable and unsearchable; for Thou art *the most high Lord*,[1] of great compassion, long-suffering, very merciful, and repentest of the evils of men. Thou, O Lord, according to Thy great goodness, hast promised repentance and forgiveness to them that have sinned against Thee, and of Thine infinite mercy hast appointed repentance unto sinners, that they may be saved. Thou therefore, O Lord, that art the God of the just, has not appointed repentance to the just as to Abraham and Isaac and Jacob, which have not sinned against Thee; but Thou hast appointed repentance unto me that am a sinner: for I have sinned above the number of the sands of the sea. My transgressions, O Lord, are multiplied; my transgressions are multiplied, and I am not worthy to behold and see the height of heaven for the multitude of mine iniquity. I am bowed down with many iron bands; for I have provoked Thy wrath, and done evil before Thee, setting up abominations, and multiplying offences. Now, therefore, I bow the knee of mine heart, beseeching Thee of grace. I have sinned, O Lord, I have sinned, and I acknowledge mine iniquities; wherefore I humbly beseech Thee, forgive me, O Lord, forgive me, and destroy me not with mine iniquities. Be not angry with me for ever, by reserving evil for me; neither condemn me into the lower part of the earth. For Thou art the God, even the God of them that repent, and in me Thou wilt show Thy goodness; for Thou wilt save me that am unworthy, according to Thy great mercy. Therefore I will praise Thee for ever all the days of my life; for all the powers of the heavens do praise Thee, and Thine is the glory for ever and ever. Amen. And the Lord heard his voice, and had compassion upon him. And there appeared a flame of fire about him, and all the iron shackles and chains which were about him fell off; and the Lord healed Manasseh from his affliction, and brought him back to Jerusalem unto his kingdom: and Manasseh knew that the Lord He is God alone. And he worshipped the Lord God alone with all his heart, and with all his soul, all the days of his life; and he was esteemed righteous. And he took away the strange gods and the graven image out of the house of the Lord, and all the altars which he had built in the house of the Lord, and all the altars in Jerusalem, and he cast them out of the city. And he repaired the altar of the Lord, and sacrificed thereon peace-offerings and thank-offerings. And Manasseh spake to Judah to serve the Lord God of Israel. And he slept in peace with his fathers; and Amon his son reigned in his stead. And he did evil in the sight of the Lord according to all things that Manasseh his father had done in the former part of his reign. And he provoked the Lord his God to anger."[2]

Ye have heard, our beloved children, how the Lord God for a while punished him that was addicted to idols, and had slain many innocent persons; and yet that He received him when he repented, and forgave him his offences, and restored him to his kingdom. For He not only forgives the penitent, but reinstates them in their former dignity.

[1] Not in MSS.

[2] 2 Kings xx., xxi.; 2 Chron. xxxii., xxxiii.

AMON MAY BE AN EXAMPLE TO SUCH AS SIN WITH AN HIGH HAND.

XXIII. There is no sin more grievous than idolatry, for it is an impiety against God: and yet even this sin has been forgiven, upon sincere repentance. But if any one sin in direct opposition, and on purpose to try whether God will punish the wicked or not, such a one shall have no remission, although he say with himself, "All is well, and I will walk according to the conversation of my evil heart." Such a one was Amon the son of Manasseh. For the Scripture says: "And Amon reasoned an evil reasoning of transgression, and said, My father from his childhood was a great transgressor, and repented in his old age; and now I will walk as my soul lusteth, and afterwards I will return unto the Lord. And he did evil in the sight of the Lord above all that were before him. And the Lord God soon destroyed him utterly from His good land. And his servants conspired against him, and slew him in his own house, and he reigned two years only."

THAT CHRIST JESUS OUR LORD CAME TO SAVE SINNERS BY REPENTANCE.

XXIV. Take heed, therefore, ye of the laity, lest any one of you fix the reasoning of Amon in his heart, and be suddenly cut off, and perish. In the same manner, let the bishop take all the care he can that those which are yet innocent may not fall into sin; and let him heal and receive those which turn from their sins. But if he is pitiless, and will not receive the repenting sinner, he will sin against the Lord his God, pretending to be more just than God's justice, and not receiving him whom He has received, through Christ; for whose sake He sent His Son upon earth to men, as a man; for whose sake God was pleased that He, who was the Maker of man and woman, should be born of a woman; for whose sake He did not spare Him from the cross, from death, and burial, but permitted Him to die, who by nature could not suffer, His beloved Son, God the Word, the Angel of His great council, that he might deliver those from death who were obnoxious to death. Him do those provoke to anger who do not receive the penitent. For He was not ashamed of me, Matthew, who had been formerly a publican; and admitted of Peter, when he had through fear denied Him three times, but had appeased Him by repentance, and had wept bitterly; nay, He made him a shepherd to His own lambs. Moreover, He ordained Paul, our fellow-apostle, to be of a persecutor an apostle, and declared him a chosen vessel, even when he had heaped many mischiefs upon us before, and had blasphemed His sacred name. He says also to another, a woman that was a sinner: "Thy sins, which are many, are forgiven, for thou lovest much."[1] And when the elders had set another woman which had sinned before Him, and had left the sentence to Him, and were gone out, our Lord, the Searcher of the hearts, inquiring of her whether the elders had condemned her, and being answered No, He said unto her: "Go thy way therefore, for neither do I condemn thee."[2] This Jesus, O ye bishops, our Saviour, our King, and our God, ought to be set before you as your pattern; and Him you ought to imitate, in being meek, quiet, compassionate, merciful, peaceable, without passion, apt to teach, and diligent to convert, willing to receive and to comfort; no strikers, not soon angry, not injurious, not arrogant, not supercilious, not wine-bibbers, not drunkards, not vainly expensive, not lovers of delicacies, not extravagant, using the gifts of God not as another's, but as their own, as good stewards appointed over them, as those who will be required by God to give an account of the same.

SEC. IV.—ON THE MANAGEMENT OF THE RESOURCES COLLECTED FOR THE SUPPORT OF THE CLERGY, AND THE RELIEF OF THE POOR.

Let the bishop esteem such food and raiment sufficient as suits necessity and decency. Let him not make use of the Lord's goods as another's, but moderately; "for the labourer is worthy of his reward."[3] Let him not be luxurious in diet, or fond of idle furniture, but contented with so much alone as is necessary for his sustenance.

OF FIRST-FRUITS AND TITHES, AND AFTER WHAT MANNER THE BISHOP IS HIMSELF TO PARTAKE OF THEM, OR TO DISTRIBUTE THEM TO OTHERS.

XXV. Let him use those tenths and first-fruits, which are given according to the command of God, as a man of God; as also let him dispense in a right manner the free-will offerings which are brought in on account of the poor, to the orphans, the widows, the afflicted, and strangers in distress, as having that God for the examiner of his accounts who has committed the disposition to him. Distribute to all those in want with righteousness, and yourselves use the things which belong to the Lord, but do not abuse them; eating of them, but not eating them all up by yourselves: communicate with those that are in want, and thereby show yourselves unblameable before God. For if you shall consume them by yourselves, you will be reproached by God, who says to such unsatiable people, who

[1] Luke vii. 47.
[2] John viii. 11.
[3] Luke x. 7.

alone devour all, "Ye eat up the milk, and clothe yourselves with the wool;" [1] and in another passage, "Must you alone live upon the earth?" [2] Upon which account you are commanded in the law, "Thou shalt love thy neighbour as thyself." [3] Now we say these things, not as if you might not partake of the fruits of your labours; for it is written, "Thou shalt not muzzle the mouth of the ox which treadeth out the corn;" [4] but that you should do it with moderation and righteousness. As, therefore, the ox that labours in the threshing-floor without a muzzle eats indeed, but does not eat all up; so do you who labour in the threshing-floor, that is, in the Church of God, eat of the Church: which was also the case of the Levites, who served in the tabernacle of the testimony, which was in all things a type of the Church. Nay, further, its very name implied that that tabernacle was fore-appointed for a testimony of the Church. Here, therefore, the Levites also, who attended upon the tabernacle, partook of those things that were offered to God by all the people,—namely, gifts, offerings, and first-fruits, and tithes, and sacrifices, and oblations, without disturbance, they and their wives, and their sons and their daughters. Since their employment was the ministration to the tabernacle, therefore they had not any lot or inheritance in the land among the children of Israel, because the oblations of the people were the lot of Levi, and the inheritance of their tribe. You, therefore, O bishops, are to your people priests and Levites, ministering to the holy tabernacle, the holy Catholic Church; who stand at the altar of the Lord your God, and offer to Him reasonable and unbloody sacrifices through Jesus the great High Priest. You are to the laity prophets, rulers, governors, and kings; the mediators between God and His faithful people, who receive and declare His word, well acquainted with the Scriptures. Ye are the voice of God, and witnesses of His will, who bear the sins of all, and intercede for all; whom, as you have heard, the word severely threatens if you hide the key of knowledge from men, who are liable to perdition if you do not declare His will to the people that are under you; who shall have a certain reward from God, and unspeakable honour and glory, if you duly minister to the holy tabernacle. For as yours is the burden, so you receive as your fruit the supply of food and other necessaries. For you imitate Christ the Lord; and as He "bare the sins of us all upon the tree" at His crucifixion, the innocent for those who deserved punishment, so also you ought to make the sins of the people your own. For concerning our Saviour it is said in Isaiah, "He bears our sins, and is afflicted for us." [5] And again: "He bare the sins of many, and was delivered for our offences." [6] As, therefore, you are patterns for others, so have you Christ for your pattern. As, therefore, He is concerned for all, so be you for the laity under you. For do not thou imagine that the office of a bishop is an easy or light burden. As, therefore, you bear the weight, so have you a right to partake of the fruits before others, and to impart to those that are in want, as being to give an account to Him, who without bias will examine your accounts. For those who attend upon the Church ought to be maintained by the Church, as being priests, Levites, presidents, and ministers of God; as it is written in the book of Numbers concerning the priests: "And the Lord said unto Aaron, Thou, and thy sons, and the house of thy family, shall bear the iniquities of the holy things of your priesthood." [7] "Behold, I have given unto you the charge of the first-fruits, from all that are sanctified to me by the children of Israel; I have given them for a reward to thee, and to thy sons after thee, by an ordinance for ever. This shall be yours out of the holy things, out of the oblations, and out of the gifts, and out of all the sacrifices, and out of every trespass-offering, and sin-offerings; and all that they render unto me out of all their holy things, they shall belong to thee, and to thy sons: in the sanctuary shall they eat them." [8] And a little after: "All the first-fruits of the oil, and of the wine, and of the wheat, all which they shall give unto the Lord, to thee have I given them; and all that is first ripe, to thee have I given it, and every devoted thing. Every first-born of man and of beast, clean and unclean, and of sacrifice, with the breast, and the right shoulder, all these appertain to the priests, and to the rest of those belonging to them, even to the Levites." [9]

Hear this, you of the laity also, the elect Church of God. For the people were formerly called "the people of God," [10] and "an holy nation." [11] You, therefore, are the holy and sacred "Church of God, enrolled in heaven, a royal priesthood, an holy nation, a peculiar people," [12] a bride adorned for the Lord God, a great Church, a faithful Church. Hear attentively now what was said formerly: oblations and tithes belong to Christ our High Priest, and to those who minister to Him. Tenths of salvation are the first letter of the name of Jesus. Hear, O thou Holy Catholic Church, who hast escaped the ten plagues, and hast received the ten com-

[1] Ezek. xxxiv. 3.
[2] Isa. v. 8.
[3] Lev. xix. 18.
[4] Deut. xxv. 4; 1 Cor. ix. 9.
[5] Isa. liii. 4.
[6] Isa. liii. 12.
[7] Num. xviii. 1.
[8] Num. xviii. 8, etc.
[9] Num. xviii. 12, etc.
[10] Ex. xix. 5, 6.
[11] Heb. xii. 23.
[12] 1 Pet. ii. 9.

mandments, and hast learned the law, and hast kept the faith, and hast believed in Jesus, *and hast known the decad, and hast believed in the iota which is the first letter of the name of Jesus*,[1] and art named after His name, and art established, and shinest in the consummation of His glory. Those which were then the sacrifices now are prayers, and intercessions, and thanksgivings. Those which were then first-fruits, and tithes, and offerings, and gifts, now are oblations, which are presented by holy bishops to the Lord God, through Jesus Christ, who has died for them. For these are your high priests, as the presbyters are your priests, and your present deacons instead of your Levites; as are also your readers, your singers, your porters, your deaconesses, your widows, your virgins, and your orphans: but He who is above all these is the High Priest.

ACCORDING TO WHAT PATTERNS AND DIGNITY EVERY ORDER OF THE CLERGY IS APPOINTED BY GOD.

XXVI. The bishop, he is the minister of the word, the keeper of knowledge, the mediator between God and you in the several parts of your divine worship. He is the teacher of piety; and, next after God, he is your father, who has begotten you again to the adoption of sons by water and the Spirit. He is your ruler and governor; he is your king and potentate; he is, next after God, your earthly god, who has a right to be honoured by you. For concerning him, and such as he, it is that God pronounces, "I have said, Ye are gods; and ye are all children of the Most High."[2] And, "Ye shall not speak evil of the gods."[3] For let the bishop preside over you as one honoured with the authority of God, which he is to exercise over the clergy, and by which he is to govern all the people. But let the deacon minister to him, as Christ does to His Father;[4] and let him serve him unblameably in all things, as Christ does nothing of Himself, but does always those things that please His Father. Let also the deaconess be honoured by you in the place of the Holy Ghost, and not do or say anything without the deacon; as neither does the Comforter say or do anything of Himself, but gives glory to Christ by waiting for His pleasure. And as we cannot believe on Christ without the teaching of the Spirit, so let not any woman address herself to the deacon or bishop without the deaconess. Let the presbyters be esteemed by you to represent us the apostles, and let them be the teachers of divine knowledge; since our Lord, when He sent us, said, "Go ye, and make disciples of all nations, baptizing them in the name of the Father, and of the Son, and of the Holy Ghost: teaching them to observe all things whatsoever I have commanded you."[5] Let the widows and orphans be esteemed as representing the altar of burnt-offering; and let the virgins be honoured as representing the altar of incense, and the incense itself.

THAT IT IS A HORRIBLE THING FOR A MAN TO THRUST HIMSELF INTO ANY SACERDOTAL OFFICE, AS DID CORAH AND HIS COMPANY, SAUL AND UZZIAH.

XXVII. As, therefore, it was not lawful for one of another tribe, that was not a Levite, to offer anything, or to approach the altar without the priest, so also do you do nothing without the bishop;[6] for if any one does anything without the bishop, he does it to no purpose. For it will not be esteemed as of any avail to him. For as Saul, when he had offered without Samuel, was told, "It will not avail for thee;"[7] so every person among the laity, doing anything without the priest, labours in vain. And as Uzziah the king,[8] who was not a priest, and yet would exercise the functions of the priests, was smitten with leprosy for his transgression; so every lay person shall not be unpunished who despises God, and is so mad as to affront His priests, and unjustly to snatch that honour to himself: not imitating Christ, "who glorified not Himself to be made an high priest;"[9] but waited till He heard from His Father, "The Lord sware, and will not repent, Thou art a priest for ever, after the order of Melchizedek."[10] If, therefore, Christ did not glorify Himself without the Father, how dare any man thrust himself into the priesthood who has not received that dignity from his superior, and do such things which it is lawful only for the priests to do? Were not the followers of Corah, even though they were of the tribe of Levi, consumed with fire, because they rose up against Moses and Aaron, and meddled with such things as did not belong to them? And Dathan and Abiram went down quick into hell; and the rod that budded put a stop to the madness of the multitude, and demonstrated who was the high priest ordained by God.[11] You ought therefore, brethren, to bring your sacrifices and your oblations to the bishop, as to your high priest, either by yourselves or by the deacons; and do you bring not those only, but also your first-fruits, and your tithes, and your free-will offerings to him. For he knows who they are that are in affliction, and gives to every one as is convenient,

---

1 Inserted from V. MSS.
2 Ps. lxxxii. 6.
3 Ex. xxii. 28.
4 The V. MSS. read, "as the powers do to God," which, Ültzen remarks, is an orthodox correction of an Arian opinion.
5 Matt. xxviii. 19.
6 One V. MS. reads "priest."
7 1 Sam. xiii. 13.
8 2 Chron. xxvi.
9 Heb. v. 5.
10 Ps. cx. 4.
11 Num. xvi.

that so one may not receive alms twice or oftener the same day, or the same week, while another has nothing at all. For it is reasonable rather to supply the wants of those who really are in distress, than of those who only appear to be so.

OF AN ENTERTAINMENT, AND AFTER WHAT MANNER EACH DISTINCT ORDER OF THE CLERGY IS TO BE TREATED BY THOSE WHO INVITE THEM TO IT.

XXVIII. If any determine to invite elder women to an entertainment of love, or a feast, as our Saviour calls it,[1] let them most frequently send to such a one whom the deacons know to be in distress. But let what is the pastor's due, I mean the first-fruits,[2] be set apart in the feast for him, even though he be not at the entertainment, as being your priest, and in honour of that God who has entrusted him with the priesthood. But as much as is given to every one of the elder women, let double so much be given to the deacons, in honour of Christ. Let also a double portion be set apart for the presbyters, as for such who labour continually about the word and doctrine, upon the account of the apostles of our Lord, whose place they sustain, as the counsellors of the bishop and the crown of the Church. For they are the Sanhedrim and senate of the Church. If there be a reader there, let him receive a single portion, in honour of the prophets, and let the singer and the porter have as much. Let the laity, therefore, pay proper honours in their presents, and utmost marks of respect to each distinct order. But let them not on all occasions trouble their governor, but let them signify their desires by those who minister to him, that is, by the deacons, with whom they may be more free. For neither may we address ourselves to Almighty God, but only by Christ. In the same manner, therefore, let the laity make known all their desires to the bishop by the deacon, and accordingly let them act as he shall direct them. For there was no holy thing offered or done in the temple formerly without the priest. "For the priest's lips shall keep knowledge, and they shall seek the law at his mouth," as the prophet somewhere says, "for he is the messenger of the Lord Almighty."[3] For if the worshippers of demons, in their hateful, abominable, and impure performances, imitate the sacred rules till this very day (it is a wide comparison indeed, and there is a vast distance between their abominations and God's sacred worship), in their mockeries of worship they neither offer nor do anything without their pretended priest, but esteem him as the very mouth of their idols of stone, waiting to see what commands he will lay upon them. And whatsoever he commands them, that they do, and without him they do nothing; and they honour him, their pretended priest, and esteem his name as venerable in honour of lifeless statues, and in order to the worship of wicked spirits. If these heathens, therefore, who give glory to lying vanities, and place their hope upon nothing that is firm, endeavour to imitate the sacred rules, how much more reasonable is it that you, who have a most certain faith and undoubted hope, and who expect glorious, and eternal, and never-failing promises, should honour the Lord God in those set over you, and esteem your bishop to be the mouth of God!

WHAT IS THE DIGNITY OF A BISHOP AND OF A DEACON.

XXIX. For if Aaron, because he declared to Pharaoh the words of God from Moses, is called a prophet; and Moses himself is called a god to Pharaoh, on account of his being at once a king and a high priest, as God says to him, "I have made thee a god to Pharaoh, and Aaron thy brother shall be thy prophet;"[4] why do not ye also esteem the mediators of the word to be prophets, and reverence them as gods?

AFTER WHAT MANNER THE LAITY ARE TO BE OBEDIENT TO THE DEACON.

XXX. For now the deacon is to you Aaron, and the bishop Moses. If, therefore, Moses was called a god by the Lord, let the bishop be honoured among you as a god, and the deacon as his prophet. For as Christ does nothing without His Father, so neither does the deacon do anything without his bishop; and as the Son without His Father is nothing, so is the deacon nothing without his bishop; and as the Son is subject to His Father, so is every deacon subject to his bishop; and as the Son is the messenger and prophet of the Father, so is the deacon the messenger and prophet of his bishop. Wherefore let all things that he is to do with any one be made known to the bishop, and be finally ordered by him.

THAT THE DEACON MUST NOT DO ANYTHING WITHOUT THE BISHOP.

XXXI. Let him not do anything at all without his bishop, nor give anything without his consent. For if he gives to any one as to a person in distress without the bishop's knowledge, he gives it so that it must tend to the reproach of the bishop, and he accuses him as careless of the distressed. But he that casts reproach on his bishop, either by word or deed, opposes God, not hearkening to what He says: "Thou shalt not speak evil of the gods."[5] For He did not make that law concerning deities of wood and

[1] Luke xiv. 13.
[2] [Compare *Teaching*, chap. xiii. p. 381. — R.]
[3] Mal. ii. 7.
[4] Ex. vii. 1.
[5] Ex. xxii. 28.

of stone, which are abominable, because they are falsely called gods, but concerning the priests and the judges, to whom He also said, "Ye are gods, and children of the Most High." [1]

THAT THE DEACON MUST NOT MAKE ANY DISTRIBUTIONS WITHOUT THE CONSENT OF THE BISHOP, BECAUSE THAT WILL TURN TO THE REPROACH OF THE BISHOP.

XXXII. If therefore, O deacon, thou knowest any one to be in distress, put the bishop in mind of him, and so give to him; but do nothing in a clandestine way, so as may tend to his reproach, lest thou raise a murmur against him; for the murmur will not be against him, but against the Lord God: and the deacon, with the rest, will hear what Aaron and Miriam heard, when they spake against Moses: "How is it that ye were not afraid to speak against my servant Moses?" [2] And again, Moses says to those who rose up against him: "Your murmuring is not against us, but against the Lord our God." [3] For if he that calls one of the laity Raka,[4] or fool, shall not be unpunished, as doing injury to the name [5] of Christ, how dare any man speak against his bishop, by whom the Lord gave the Holy Spirit among you upon the laying on of his hands, by whom ye have learned the sacred doctrines, and have known God, and have believed in Christ, by whom ye were known of God, by whom ye were sealed with the oil of gladness and the ointment of understanding, by whom ye were declared to be the children of light, by whom the Lord in your illumination testified by the imposition of the bishop's hands, and sent out His sacred voice upon every one of you, saying, "Thou art my son, this day have I begotten thee?" [6] By thy bishop, O man, God adopts thee for His child. Acknowledge, O son, that right hand which was a mother to thee. Love him who, after God, is become a father to thee, and honour him.

AFTER WHAT MANNER THE BISHOPS ARE TO BE HONOURED, AND TO BE REVERENCED AS OUR SPIRITUAL PARENTS.

XXXIII. For if the divine oracle says, concerning our parents according to the flesh, "Honour thy father and thy mother, that it may be well with thee;" [7] and, "He that curseth his father or his mother, let him die the death;" [8] how much more should the word exhort you to honour your spiritual parents, and to love them as your benefactors and ambassadors with God, who have regenerated you by water, and endued you with the fulness of the Holy Spirit, who have fed you with the word as with milk, who have nourished you with doctrine, who have confirmed you by their admonitions, who have imparted to you the saving body and precious blood of Christ, who have loosed you from your sins, who have made you partakers of the holy and sacred eucharist, who have admitted you to be partakers and fellow-heirs of the promise of God! Reverence these, and honour them with all kinds of honour; for they have obtained from God the power of life and death, in their judging of sinners, and condemning them to the death of eternal fire, as also of loosing returning sinners from their sins, and of restoring them to a new life.

THAT PRIESTS ARE TO BE PREFERRED BEFORE RULERS AND KINGS.

XXXIV. Account these worthy to be esteemed your rulers and your kings, and bring them tribute as to kings; for by you they and their families ought to be maintained. As Samuel made constitutions for the people concerning a king,[9] in the first book of Kings, and Moses did so concerning priests in Leviticus, so do we also make constitutions for you concerning bishops. For if there the multitude distributed the inferior services in proportion to so great a king, ought not therefore the bishop much more now to receive of you those things which are determined by God for the sustenance of himself and of the rest of the clergy belonging to him? But if we may add somewhat further, let the bishop receive more than the other received of old: for he only managed the affairs of the soldiery, being entrusted with war and peace for the preservation of men's bodies; but the other is entrusted with the exercise of the priestly office in relation to God, in order to preserve both body and soul from dangers. By how much, therefore, the soul is more valuable than the body, so much the priestly office is beyond the kingly. For it binds and looses those that are worthy of punishment or of remission. Wherefore you ought to love the bishop as your father, and fear him as your king, and honour him as your lord, bringing to him your fruits and the works of your hands, for a blessing upon you, giving to him your first-fruits, and your tithes, and your oblations, and your gifts, as to the priest of God; the first-fruits of your wheat, and wine, and oil, and autumnal fruits, and wool,[10] and all things which the Lord God gives thee. And thy offering shall be accepted as a savour of a sweet smell to the Lord thy God; and the Lord will bless the works of thy hands, and will multiply

1 Ps. lxxxii. 6.
2 Num. xii. 8.
3 Ex. xvi. 8.
4 Matt. v. 22.
5 Capellius reads, "the law of Christ."
6 Ps. ii. 7.
7 Ex. xx. 12.
8 Ex. xxi. 17.
9 1 Sam. viii.
10 One V. MS. reads "olives" instead of "wool."

the good things of the land. "For a blessing is upon the head of him that giveth." [1]

THAT BOTH THE LAW AND THE GOSPEL PRESCRIBE OFFERINGS.

XXXV. Now you ought to know, that although the Lord has delivered you from the additional bonds, and has brought you out of them to your refreshment, and does not permit you to sacrifice irrational creatures for sin-offerings, and purifications, and scapegoats, and continual washings and sprinklings, yet has He nowhere freed you from those oblations which you owe to the priests, nor from doing good to the poor. For the Lord says to you in the Gospel: "Unless your righteousness abound more than that of the scribes and Pharisees, ye shall by no means enter into the kingdom of heaven." [2] Now herein will your righteousness exceed theirs, if you take greater care of the priests, the orphans, and the widows; as it is written: "He hath scattered abroad; he hath given to the poor; his righteousness remaineth for ever." [3] And again: "By acts of righteousness and faith iniquities are purged." [4] And again: "Every bountiful soul is blessed." [5] So therefore shalt thou do as the Lord has appointed, and shalt give to the priest what things are due to him, the first-fruits of thy floor, and of thy wine-press, and sin-offerings, as to the mediator between God and such as stand in need of purgation and forgiveness. For it is thy duty to give, and his to administer, as being the administrator and disposer of ecclesiastical affairs. Yet shalt thou not call thy bishop to account, nor watch his administration, how he does it, when, or to whom, or where, or whether he do it well or ill, or indifferently; for he has One who will call him to an account, the Lord God, who put this administration into his hands, and thought him worthy of the priesthood of so great dignity.

THE RECITAL OF THE TEN COMMANDMENTS, AND AFTER WHAT MANNER THEY DO HERE PRESCRIBE TO US.

XXXVI. Have before thine eyes the fear of God, and always remember the ten commandments of God, — to love the one and only Lord God with all thy strength; to give no heed to idols, or any other beings, as being lifeless gods, or irrational beings or dæmons. Consider the manifold workmanship of God, which received its beginning through Christ. Thou shalt observe the Sabbath, on account of Him who ceased from His work of creation, but ceased not from His work of providence: it is a rest for meditation of the law, not for idleness of the hands. Reject every unlawful lust, everything destructive to men, and all anger. Honour thy parents, as the authors of thy being. Love thy neighbour as thyself. Communicate the necessaries of life to the needy. Avoid swearing falsely, and swearing often, and in vain; for thou shalt not be held guiltless. Do not appear before the priests empty, and offer thy free-will offerings continually. Moreover, do not leave the church of Christ; but go thither in the morning before all thy work, and again meet there in the evening, to return thanks to God that He has preserved thy life. Be diligent, and constant, and laborious in thy calling. Offer to the Lord thy free-will offerings; for says He, "Honour the Lord with the fruit of thy honest labours." [6] If thou art not able to cast anything considerable into the Corban,[7] yet at least bestow upon the strangers one, or two, or five mites. "Lay up to thyself heavenly treasure, which neither the moth nor thieves can destroy." [8] And in doing this, do not judge thy bishop, or any of thy neighbours among the laity; for if thou judge thy brother, thou becomest a judge, without being constituted such by anybody, for the priests are only entrusted with the power of judging. For to them it is said, "Judge righteous judgment;" [9] and again, "Approve yourselves to be exact money-changers." [10] For to you this is not entrusted; for, on the contrary, it is said to those who are not of the dignity of magistrates or ministers: "Judge not, and ye shall not be judged." [11]

SEC. V. — ON ACCUSATIONS, AND THE TREATMENT OF ACCUSERS.

CONCERNING ACCUSERS AND FALSE ACCUSERS, AND HOW A JUDGE IS NOT RASHLY EITHER TO BELIEVE THEM OR DISBELIEVE THEM, BUT AFTER AN ACCURATE EXAMINATION.

XXXVII. But it is the duty of the bishop to judge rightly, as it is written, "Judge righteous judgment;" [12] and elsewhere, "Why do ye not even of yourselves judge what is right?" [13] Be ye therefore as skilful dealers in money: for as these reject bad money, but take to themselves what is current, in the same manner it is the bishop's duty to retain the unblameable, but either to heal, or, if they be past cure, to cast off those that are blameworthy, so as not to be hasty in cutting off, nor to believe all accusations; for it sometimes happens that some, either

1 Prov. xi. 26.
2 Matt. v. 20.
3 Ps cxii. 9.
4 Prov. xvi. 6.
5 Prov. xi. 25.
6 Prov. iii. 9.
7 The V. MSS. read: "Casting into the treasury whatever you can bestow."
8 Matt. vi. 20.
9 Deut. i. 16, xvi. 18.
10 Zech. vii. 9.
11 Luke vi. 37.
12 John vii. 24.
13 Luke xii. 57.

through passion or envy, do insist on a false accusation against a brother, as did the two elders in the case of Susanna in Babylon,[1] and the Egyptian woman in the case of Joseph.[2] Do thou therefore, as a man of God, not rashly receive such accusations, lest thou take away the innocent and slay the righteous; for he that will receive such accusations is the author of anger rather than of peace. But where there is anger, there the Lord is not; for that anger, which is the friend of Satan — I mean that which is excited unjustly by the means of false brethren — never suffers unanimity to be in the Church. Wherefore, when you know such persons to be foolish, quarrelsome, passionate, and such as delight in mischief, do not give credit to them; but observe such as they are, when you hear anything from them against their brother: for murder is nothing in their eyes, and they cast a man down in such a way as one would not suspect. Do thou therefore consider diligently the accuser,[3] wisely observing his mode of life, what, and of what sort it is; and in case thou findest him a man of veracity, do according to the doctrine of our Lord,[4] and taking him who is accused, rebuke him, that he may repent, when nobody is by. But if he be not persuaded, take with thee one or two more, and so show him his fault, and admonish him with mildness and instruction; for "wisdom will rest upon an heart that is good, but is not understood in the heart of the foolish."[5]

THAT SINNERS ARE PRIVATELY TO BE REPROVED, AND THE PENITENT TO BE RECEIVED, ACCORDING TO THE CONSTITUTION OF OUR LORD.

XXXVIII. If, therefore, he be persuaded by the mouth of you three, it is well. But if any one hardens himself, "tell it to the Church: but if he neglects to hear the Church, let him be to thee as an heathen man and a publican;"[6] and receive him no longer into the Church as a Christian, but reject him as an heathen. But if he be willing to repent, receive him. For the Church does not receive an heathen or a publican to communion, before they every one repent of their former impieties; for our Lord Jesus, the Christ of God, has appointed place for the acceptance of men upon their repentance.

EXAMPLES OF REPENTANCE.

XXXIX. For I Matthew, one of those twelve which speak to you in this doctrine, am an apostle, having myself been formerly a publican, but now have obtained mercy through believing, and have repented of my former practices, and have been vouchsafed the honour to be an apostle and preacher of the word. And Zacchæus, whom the Lord received upon his repentance and prayers to Him, was also himself in the same manner a publican at first. And, besides, even the soldiers and multitude of publicans, who came to hear the word of the Lord about repentance, heard this from the prophet John, after he had baptized them: "Do nothing more than that which is appointed you."[7] In like manner, life is not refused to the heathen, if they repent and cast away their unbelief. Esteem, therefore, every one that is convicted of any wicked action, and has not repented, as a publican or an heathen. But if he afterward repents, and turns from his error, then, as we receive the heathen, when they wish to repent, into the Church indeed to hear the word, but do not receive them to communion until they have received the seal of baptism, and are made complete Christians; so do we also permit such as these to enter only to hear, until they show the fruit of repentance, that by hearing the word they may not utterly and irrecoverably perish. But let them not be admitted to communion in prayer; and let them depart after the reading of the law, and the prophets, and the Gospel, that by such departure they may be made better in their course of life, by endeavouring to meet every day about the public assemblies, and to be frequent in prayer, that they also may be at length admitted, and that those who behold them may be affected, and be more secured by fearing to fall into the same condition.

THAT WE ARE NOT TO BE IMPLACABLE TO HIM WHO HAS ONCE OR TWICE OFFENDED.

XL. But yet do not thou, O bishop, presently abhor any person who has fallen into one or two offences, nor shalt thou exclude him from the word of the Lord, nor reject him from common intercourse, since neither did the Lord refuse to eat with publicans and sinners; and when He was accused by the Pharisees on this account, He said: "They that are well have no need of the physician, but they that are sick."[8] Do you, therefore, live and dwell with those who are separated from you for their sins; and take care of them, comforting them, and confirming them, and saying to them: "Be strengthened, ye weak hands and feeble knees."[9] For we ought to comfort those that mourn, and afford encouragement to the fainthearted, lest by immoderate sorrow they degenerate into distraction, since "he that is fainthearted is exceedingly distracted."[10]

---

1 Hist. Susanna.
2 Gen. xxxix.
3 The MSS. read, "the accused."
4 Matt. xviii. 15.
5 Prov. xiv. 32.
6 Matt. xviii. 17.
7 Luke iii. 13.
8 Matt. ix. 12.
9 Isa. xxxv. 3.
10 Prov. xiv. 29, LXX.

AFTER WHAT MANNER WE OUGHT TO RECEIVE A PENITENT; HOW WE OUGHT TO DEAL WITH OFFENDERS, AND WHEN THEY ARE TO BE CUT OFF FROM THE CHURCH.

XLI. But if any one returns, and shows forth the fruit of repentance, then do ye receive him to prayer, as the lost son, the prodigal, who had consumed his father's substance with harlots, who fed swine, and desired to be fed with husks, and could not obtain it. This son, when he repented, and returned to his father, and said, "I have sinned against Heaven, and before thee, and am no more worthy to be called thy son;"[1] the father, full of affection to his child, received him with music, and restored him his old robe, and ring, and shoes, and slew the fatted calf, and made merry with his friends. Do thou therefore, O bishop, act in the same manner. And as thou receivest an heathen after thou hast instructed and baptized him, so do thou let all join in prayers for this man, and restore him by imposition of hands to his ancient place among the flock, as one purified by repentance; and that imposition of hands shall be to him instead of baptism: for by the laying on of our hands the Holy Ghost was given to believers. And in case some one of those brethren who had stood immoveable accuse thee, because thou art reconciled to him, say to him: "Thou art always with me, and all that I have is thine. It was meet to make merry and be glad: for this thy brother was dead, and is alive again; he was lost, and is found." For that God does not only receive the penitent, but restores them to their former dignity, holy David is a sufficient witness, who, after his sin in the matter of Uriah, prayed to God, and said: "Restore unto me the joy of Thy salvation, and uphold me with Thy free Spirit."[2] And again: "Turn Thy face from my sins, and blot out all mine offences. Create in me a clean heart, O God, and renew a right spirit in my inward parts. Cast me not away from Thy presence, and take not Thy Holy Spirit from me." Do thou therefore, as a compassionate physician, heal all that have sinned, making use of saving methods of cure; not only cutting and searing, or using corrosives, but binding up, and putting in tents, and using gentle healing medicines, and sprinkling comfortable words. If it be an hollow wound, or great gash, nourish it with a suitable plaister, that it may be filled up, and become even with the rest of the whole flesh. If it be foul, cleanse it with corrosive powder, that is, with the words of reproof. If it have proud flesh, eat it down with a sharp plaister—the threats of judgment. If it spreads further, sear it, and cut off the putrid flesh, mortifying him with fastings. But if, after all that thou hast done, thou perceivest that from the feet to the head there is no room for a fomentation, or oil, or bandage, but that the malady spreads and prevents all cure, as a gangrene which corrupts the entire member; then, with a great deal of consideration, and the advice of other skilful physicians, cut off the putrefied member, that the whole body of the Church be not corrupted. Be not therefore ready and hasty to cut off, nor do thou easily have recourse to the saw, with its many teeth; but first use a lancet to lay open the wound, that the inward cause whence the pain is derived being drawn out, may keep the body free from pain. But if thou seest any one past repentance, and he is become insensible, then cut off the incurable from the Church with sorrow and lamentation. For: "Take out from among yourselves that wicked person."[3] And: "Ye shall make the children of Israel to fear."[4] And again: "Thou shalt not accept the persons of the rich in judgment."[5] And: "Thou shalt not pity a poor man in his cause: for the judgment is the Lord's."[6]

THAT A JUDGE MUST NOT BE A RESPECTER OF PERSONS.

XLII. But if the slanderous accusation be false, and you that are the pastors, with the deacons, admit of that falsehood for truth, either by acceptance of persons or receiving of bribes, as willing to do that which will be pleasing to the devil, and so you thrust out from the Church him that is accused, but is clear of the crime, you shall give an account in the day of the Lord. For it is written: "The innocent and the righteous thou shalt not slay."[7] "Thou shalt not take gifts to smite the soul: for gifts blind the eyes of the wise, and destroy the words of the righteous."[8] And again: "They that justify the wicked for gifts, and take away the righteousness of the righteous from him."[9] Be careful, therefore, not to condemn any persons unjustly, and so to assist the wicked. For "woe to him that calls evil good, and good evil; bitter sweet, and sweet bitter; that puts light for darkness, and darkness for light."[10] *Take care, therefore, lest by any means ye become acceptors of persons, and thereby fall under this voice of the Lord.*[11] For if you condemn others unjustly, you pass sentence against yourselves. For the Lord says: "With what judgment ye judge, ye shall be judged; and as you condemn, you shall be

1 Luke xv. 21.
2 Ps. li.
3 Deut. xvii. 7.
4 Lev. xv. 31.
5 Deut. i. 17; Lev. xix. 15.
6 Ex. xxiii. 3.
7 Ex. xxiii. 7, 8.
8 Deut. xxvii. 25, xvi. 19.
9 Isa. v. 23.
10 Isa. v. 20.
11 This sentence follows the passage from Isa. v. 23 in most MSS. One V. MS. has the order adopted in the text.

condemned."[1] If, therefore, ye judge without respect of persons, ye will discover that accuser who bears false witness against his neighbour, and will prove him to be a sycophant, a spiteful person, and a murderer, causing perplexity by accusing the man as if he were wicked, inconstant in his words, contradicting himself in what he affirms, and entangled with the words of his own mouth; for his own lips are a dangerous snare to him: whom, when thou hast convicted him of speaking falsely, thou shalt judge severely, and shalt deliver him to the fiery sword, and thou shalt do to him as he wickedly proposed to do to his brother; for as much as in him lay he slew his brother, by forestalling the ears of the judge.[2] Now it is written, that "he that sheddeth man's blood, for that his own blood shall be shed."[3] And: "Thou shalt take away that innocent blood, which was shed without cause, from thee."[4]

AFTER WHAT MANNER FALSE ACCUSERS ARE TO BE PUNISHED.

XLIII. Thou shalt therefore cast him out of the congregation as a murderer of his brother. Some time afterwards, if he says that he repents, mortify him with fastings, and afterwards ye shall lay your hands upon him and receive him, but still securing him, that he does not disturb anybody a second time. But if, when he is admitted again, he be alike troublesome, and will not cease to disturb and to quarrel with his brother, spying faults out of a contentious spirit, cast him out as a pernicious person, that he may not lay waste the Church of God. For such a one is the raiser of disturbances in cities; for he, though he be within, does not become the Church, but is a superfluous and vain member, casting a blot, as far as in him lies, on the body of Christ. For if such men as are born with superfluous members of their body, which hang to them as fingers, or excrescences of flesh, cut them away from themselves on account of their indecency, whereby the unseemliness vanishes, and the man recovers his natural good shape by the means of the surgeon; how much more ought you, the pastors of the Church (for the Church is a perfect body, and sound members; of such as believe in God, in the fear of the Lord, and in love), to do the like when there is found in it a superfluous member with wicked designs, and rendering the rest of the body unseemly, and disturbing it with sedition, and war, and evil-speaking; causing fears, disturbances, blots, evil-speaking, accusations, disorders, and doing the like works of the devil, as if he were ordained by the devil to cast a reproach on the Church by calumnies, and mighty disorders, and strife, and division! Such a one, therefore, when he is a second time cast out of the Church, is justly cut off entirely from the congregation of the Lord. And now the Church of the Lord will be more beautiful than it was before, when it had a superfluous, and to itself a disagreeable member. Wherefore henceforward it will be free from blame and reproach, and become clear of such wicked, deceitful, abusive, unmerciful, traitorous persons; of such as are "haters of those that are good, lovers of pleasure,"[5] affecters of vain-glory, deceivers, and pretenders to wisdom; of such as make it their business to scatter, or rather utterly to disperse, the lambs of the Lord.

SEC. VI. — THE DISPUTES OF THE FAITHFUL TO BE SETTLED BY THE DECISIONS OF THE BISHOP, AND THE FAITHFUL TO BE RECONCILED.

Do thou therefore, O bishop, together with thy subordinate clergy, endeavour rightly to divide the word of truth. For the Lord says: "If you walk cross-grained to me, I will walk cross-grained to you."[6] And elsewhere: "With the holy Thou wilt be holy, and with the perfect man Thou wilt be perfect, and with the froward Thou wilt be froward."[7] Walk therefore holily, that you may rather appear worthy of praise from the Lord than of complaint from the adversary.

THAT THE DEACON IS TO EASE THE BURTHEN OF THE BISHOPS, AND TO ORDER THE SMALLER MATTERS HIMSELF.

XLIV. Be ye of one mind, O ye bishops, one with another, and be at peace with one another; sympathize with one another, love the brethren, and feed the people with care; with one consent teach those that are under you to be of the same sentiments and to be of the same opinions about the same matters, "that there may be no schisms among you; that ye may be one body and one spirit, perfectly joined together in the same mind and in the same judgment,"[8] according to the appointment of the Lord. And let the deacon refer all things to the bishop, as Christ does to His Father. But let him order such things as he is able by himself, receiving power from the bishop, as the Lord did from His Father the power of creation and of providence. But the weighty matters let the bishop judge; but let the deacon be the bishop's ear, and eye, and mouth, and heart, and soul, that the bishop may not be distracted with many cares, but with such only as are more considerable, as Jethro did appoint for Moses, and his counsel was received.[9]

---

1 Matt. vii. 2; Luke vi. 37.
2 Deut. xix. 19.
3 Gen. ix. 6.
4 Deut. xix. 13.
5 2 Tim. iii. 3, 4.
6 Lev. xxvi. 27, 28.
7 Ps. xviii. 26.
8 1 Cor. i. 10; Eph. iv. 4.
9 Ex. xviii.

THAT CONTENTIONS AND QUARRELS ARE UNBECOMING CHRISTIANS.

XLV. It is therefore a noble encomium for a Christian to have no contest with any one;[1] but if by any management or temptation a contest arises with any one, let him endeavour that it may be composed, though thereby he be obliged to lose somewhat; and let it not come before an heathen tribunal. Nay, indeed, you are not to permit that the rulers of this world should pass sentence against your people; for by them the devil contrives mischief to the servants of God, and occasions a reproach to be cast upon us, as though we had not "one wise man that is able to judge between his brethren," or to decide their controversies.

THAT BELIEVERS OUGHT NOT TO GO TO LAW BEFORE UNBELIEVERS: NOR OUGHT ANY UNBELIEVER TO BE CALLED FOR A WITNESS AGAINST BELIEVERS.

XLVI. Let not the heathen therefore know of your differences among one another, nor do you receive unbelievers as witnesses against yourselves, nor be judged by them, nor owe them anything on account of tribute or fear; but "render to Cæsar the things that are Cæsar's, and unto God the things that are God's,"[2] as tribute, taxes, or poll-money, as our Lord by giving a piece of money was freed from disturbance.[3] Choose therefore rather to suffer harm, and to endeavour after those things that make for peace, not only among the brethren, but also among the unbelievers. For by suffering loss in the affairs of this life, thou wilt be sure not to suffer in the concerns of piety, and wilt live religiously, and according to the command of Christ.[4] But if brethren have lawsuits one with another, which God forbid, you who are the rulers ought thence to learn that such as these do not do the work of brethren *in the Lord*, but rather of public enemies; and one of the parties will be found to be mild, gentle, and the child of light; but the other unmerciful, insolent, and covetous. Let him, therefore, who is condemned be rebuked, let him be separated, let him undergo the punishment of his hatred to his brother. Afterwards, when he repents, let him be received; and so, when they have learned prudence, they will ease your judicatures. It is also a duty to forgive each other's trespasses — not the duty of those that judge, but of those that have quarrels; as the Lord determined when I Peter asked Him, "How oft shall my brother sin against me, and I forgive him? Till seven times?" He replied, "I say not unto thee, Until seven times, but until seventy times seven."[5] For so would our Lord have us to be truly His disciples, and never to have anything against anybody; as, for instance, anger without measure, passion without mercy, covetousness without justice, hatred without reconciliation. Draw by your instruction those who are angry to friendship, and those who are at variance to agreement. For the Lord says: "Blessed are the peacemakers, for they shall be called the children of God."[6]

THAT THE JUDICATURES OF CHRISTIANS OUGHT TO BE HELD ON THE SECOND DAY OF THE WEEK.

XLVII. Let your judicatures be held on the second day of the week, that if any controversy arise about your sentence, having an interval till the Sabbath,[7] you may be able to set the controversy right, and to reduce those to peace who have the contests one with another against the Lord's day. Let also the deacons and presbyters be present at your judicatures, to judge without acceptance of persons, as men of God, with righteousness. When, therefore, both the parties are come, according as the law says,[8] those that have the controversy shall stand severally in the middle of the court; and when you have heard them, give your votes holily, endeavouring to make them both friends before the sentence of the bishop, that judgment against the offender may not go abroad into the world; knowing that he has in the court the Christ of God as conscious of and confirming his judgment. But if any persons are accused by any one, and their fame suffers as if they did not walk uprightly in the Lord, in like manner you shall hear both parties — the accuser and accused; but not with prejudice, nor with hearkening to one part only, but with righteousness, as passing a sentence concerning eternal life or death. For says God: "He shall prosecute that which is right justly."[9] For he that is justly punished and separated by you is rejected from eternal life and glory; he becomes dishonourable among holy men, and one condemned of God.

THAT THE SAME PUNISHMENT IS NOT TO BE INFLICTED FOR EVERY OFFENCE, BUT DIFFERENT PUNISHMENTS FOR DIFFERENT OFFENDERS.

XLVIII. Do not pass the same sentence for every sin, but one suitable to each crime, distinguishing all the several sorts of offences with much prudence, the great from the little. Treat a wicked action after one manner, and a wicked word after another; a bare intention still other-

1 1 Cor. vi. 1, etc.
2 Matt. xxii. 21.
3 Matt. xvii. 24, etc.
4 One V. MS. reads "God" instead of "Christ."
5 Matt. xviii. 21, 22.
6 Matt. v. 9.
7 [i.e., Saturday.]
8 Deut. xix. 17.
9 Deut. xvi. 20.

wise. So also in the case of a contumely or suspicion. And some thou shalt curb by threatenings alone; some thou shalt punish with fines to the poor; some thou shalt mortify with fastings; and others thou shalt separate according to the greatness of their several crimes. For the law did not allot the same punishment to every offence, but had a different regard to a sin against God, against the priest, against the temple, or against the sacrifice; from a sin against the king, or ruler, or a soldier, or a fellow-subject; and so were the offences different which were against a servant, a possession, or a brute creature. And again, sins were differently rated according as they were against parents and kinsmen, and those differently which were done on purpose from those that happened involuntarily. Accordingly the punishments were different: as death either by crucifixion or by stoning, fines, scourgings, or the suffering the same mischiefs they had done to others. Wherefore do you also allot different penalties to different offences, lest any injustice should happen, and provoke God to indignation. For of what unjust judgment soever you are the instruments, of the same you shall receive the reward from God. "For with what judgment ye judge ye shall be judged." [1]

WHAT ARE TO BE THE CHARACTERS OF ACCUSERS AND WITNESSES.

XLIX. When, therefore, you are set down at your tribunal, and the parties are both of them present (for we will not call them brethren until they receive each other in peace), examine diligently concerning those who appear before you; and first concerning the accuser, whether this be the first person he has accused, or whether he has advanced accusations against some others before, and whether this contest and accusation of theirs does not arise from some quarrel, and what sort of life the accuser leads. Yet, though he be of a good conscience, do not give credit to him alone, for that is contrary to the law; but let him have others to join in his testimony, and those of the same course of life. As the law says: "At the mouth of two or three witnesses everything shall be established." [2] But why did we say that the character of the witnesses was to be inquired after, of what sort it is? Because it frequently happens that two and more testify for mischief, and with joint consent prefer a lie; as did the two elders against Susanna in Babylon,[3] and the sons of transgressors against Naboth in Samaria,[4] and the multitude of the Jews against our Lord at Jerusalem,[5] and against Stephen His first martyr.[6] Let the witnesses therefore be meek, free from anger, full of equity, kind, prudent, continent, free from wickedness, faithful, religious; for the testimony of such persons is firm on account of their character, and true on account of their mode of life. But as to those of a different character, do not ye receive their testimony, although they seem to agree together in their evidence against the accused; for it is ordained in the law: "Thou shalt not be with a multitude for wickedness; thou shalt not receive a vain report; thou shalt not consent with a multitude to pervert judgment." [7] You ought also particularly to know him that is accused; what he is in his course and mode of life; whether he have a good report as to his life; whether he has been unblameable; whether he has been zealous in holiness; whether he be a lover of the widows, a lover of the strangers, a lover of the poor, and a lover of the brethren; whether he be not given to filthy lucre; whether he be not an extravagant person, or a spendthrift; whether he be sober, and free from luxury, or a drunkard, or a glutton; whether he be compassionate and charitable.

THAT FORMER OFFENCES DO SOMETIMES RENDER AFTER ACCUSATIONS CREDIBLE.

L. For if he has been before addicted to wicked works, the accusations which are now brought against him will thence in some measure appear to be true, unless justice do plainly plead for him. For it may be, that though he had formerly been an offender, yet that he may not be guilty of this crime of which he is accused. Wherefore be exactly cautious about such circumstances, and so render your sentences, when pronounced against the offender convicted, safe and firm. And if, after his separation, he begs pardon, and falls down before the bishop, and acknowledges his fault, receive him. But neither do you suffer a false accuser to go unpunished, that he may not calumniate another who lives well, or encourage some other person to do like him. Nor, to be sure, do ye suffer a person convicted to go off clear, lest another be ensnared in the same crimes. For neither shall a witness of mischiefs be unpunished, nor shall he that offends be without censure.

AGAINST JUDGING WITHOUT HEARING BOTH SIDES.

LI. We said before that judgment ought not to be given upon hearing only one of the parties; for if you hear one of them when the other is not there, and so cannot make his defence to the accusation brought against him, and rashly

1 Matt. vii. 2.
2 Deut. xix. 15.
3 Susanna 28.
4 1 Kings xxi.
5 Matt. xxvi.
6 Acts vi. and vii.
7 Ex. xxiii. 2.

give your votes for condemnation, you will be found guilty of that man's destruction, and partaker with the false accuser before God, the just Judge. For "as he that holdeth the tail of a dog, so is he that presides at unjust judgment."[1] But if ye become imitators of the elders in Babylon, who, when they had borne witness against Susanna, unjustly condemned her to death, you will become obnoxious to their judgment and condemnation. For the Lord by Daniel delivered Susanna from the hand of the ungodly, but condemned to the fire those elders who were guilty of her blood, and reproaches you by him, saying: "Are ye so foolish, ye children of Israel? Without examination, and without knowing the truth, have ye condemned a daughter of Israel? Return again to the place of judgment, for these men have borne false witness against her."[2]

THE CAUTION OBSERVED AT HEATHEN TRIBUNALS BEFORE THE CONDEMNATION OF CRIMINALS AFFORDS CHRISTIANS A GOOD EXAMPLE.

LII. Consider even the judicatures of this world, by whose power we see murderers, adulterers, wizards, robbers of sepulchres, and thieves brought to trial; and those that preside, when they have received their accusations from those that brought them, ask the malefactor whether those things be so. And though he does not deny the crimes, they do not presently send him out to punishment; but for several days they make inquiry about him with a full council, and with the veil interposed. And he that is to pass the final decree and suffrage of death against him, lifts up his hands to the sun, and solemnly affirms that he is innocent of the blood of the man. Though they be heathens, and know not the Deity, nor the vengeance which will fall upon men from God on account of those that are unjustly condemned, they avoid such unjust judgments.

THAT CHRISTIANS OUGHT NOT TO BE CONTENTIOUS ONE WITH ANOTHER.

LIII. But you who know who our God is, and what are His judgments, how can you bear to pass an unjust judgment, since your sentence will be immediately known to God? And if you have judged righteously, you will be deemed worthy of the recompenses of righteousness, both now and hereafter; but if unrighteously, you will partake of the like. We therefore advise you, brethren, rather to deserve commendation from God than rebukes; for the commendation of God is eternal life to men, as is His rebuke everlasting death. Be ye therefore righteous judges, peacemakers, and without anger. For "he that is angry with his brother without a cause is obnoxious to the judgment."[3] But if it happens that by any one's contrivance you are angry at anybody, "let not the sun go down upon your wrath;"[4] for says David, "Be angry and sin not;"[5] that is, be soon reconciled, lest your wrath continue so long that it turn to a settled hatred, and work sin. "For the souls of those that bear a settled hatred are to death,"[6] says Solomon. But our Lord and Saviour Jesus Christ says in the Gospels: "If thou bring thy gift to the altar, and there rememberest that thy brother hath ought against thee, leave there thy gift before the altar, and go thy way; first be reconciled to thy brother, and then come and offer thy gift to God."[7] Now the gift to God is every one's prayer and thanksgiving. If, therefore, thou hast anything against thy brother, or he has anything against thee, neither will thy prayers be heard, nor will thy thanksgivings be accepted, by reason of that hidden anger. But it is your duty, brethren, to pray continually. Yet, because God hears not those which are at enmity with their brethren by unjust quarrels, even though they should pray three times an hour, it is our duty to compose all our enmity and littleness of soul, that we may be able to pray with a pure and unpolluted heart. For the Lord commanded us to love even our enemies, and by no means to hate our friends. And the lawgiver says: "Thou shalt not hate any man; thou shalt not hate thy brother in thy mind. Thou shalt certainly reprove thy brother, and not incur sin on his account."[8] "Thou shalt not hate an Egyptian, for thou wast a sojourner with him. Thou shalt not hate an Idumæan, for he is thy brother."[9] And David says: "If I have repaid those that requited me evil."[10] Wherefore, if thou wilt be a Christian, follow the law of the Lord: "Loose every band of wickedness;"[11] for the Lord has given thee authority to remit those sins to thy brother which he has committed against thee as far as "seventy times seven,"[12] that is, four hundred and ninety times. How oft, therefore, hast thou remitted to thy brother, that thou art unwilling to do it now, when thou also hast heard Jeremiah saying, "Do not any of you impute the wickedness of his neighbour in your hearts?"[13] But thou rememberest injuries, and keepest enmity, and comest into judgment, and art suspicious of His anger, and thy prayer is hindered. Nay, if thou hast re-

[1] Prov. xxvi. 17.
[2] Susanna 48.

[3] Matt. v. 22.
[4] Eph. iv. 26.
[5] Ps. iv. 4.
[6] Prov. xii. 28, LXX.
[7] Matt. v. 23, 24.
[8] Lev. xix. 17.
[9] Deut. xxiii. 7.
[10] Ps. vii. 4.
[11] Isa. lviii. 6.
[12] Matt. xviii. 22.
[13] Zech. viii. 17.

mitted to thy brother four hundred and ninety times, do thou still multiply thy acts of gentleness more, to do good for thy own sake. Although he does not do so, yet, however, do thou endeavour to forgive thy brother for God's sake, "that thou mayest be the son of thy Father which is in heaven,"[1] and when thou prayest, mayest be heard as a friend of God.

THAT THE BISHOPS MUST BY THEIR DEACON PUT THE PEOPLE IN MIND OF THE OBLIGATION THEY ARE UNDER TO LIVE PEACEABLY TOGETHER.

LIV. Wherefore, O bishop, when you are to go to prayer after the lessons, and the psalmody, and the instruction out of the Scriptures, let the deacon stand nigh you, and with a loud voice say: Let none have any quarrel with another; let none come in hypocrisy; that if there be any controversy found among any of you, they may be affected in conscience, and may pray to God, and be reconciled to their brethren. For if, upon coming into any one's house, we are to say, "Peace be to this house,"[2] like sons of peace bestowing peace on those who are worthy, as it is written, "He came and preached peace to you that are nigh, and them that are far off, whom the Lord knows to be His,"[3] much more is it incumbent on those that enter into the Church of God before all things to pray for the peace of God. But if he prays for it upon others, much more let himself be within the same, as a child of light; for he that has it not within himself is not fit to bestow it upon others. Wherefore, before all things, it is our duty to be at peace in our own minds; for he that does not find any disorder in himself will not quarrel with another, but will be peaceable, friendly, gathering the Lord's people, and a fellow-worker with him, in order to the increasing the number of those that shall be saved in unanimity. For those who contrive enmities, and strifes, and contests, and lawsuits, are wicked, and aliens from God.

AN ENUMERATION OF THE SEVERAL INSTANCES OF DIVINE PROVIDENCE, AND HOW IN EVERY AGE FROM THE BEGINNING OF THE WORLD GOD HAS INVITED ALL MEN TO REPENTANCE.

LV. For God, being a God of mercy from the beginning, called every generation to repentance by righteous men and prophets. He instructed those before the flood by Abel, and Sem, and Seth, also by Enos, and by Enoch that was translated; those at the flood by Noah; the inhabitants of Sodom by hospitable Lot; those after the flood by Melchizedek, and the patriarchs, and Job the beloved of God; the Egyptians by Moses; the Israelites by him, and Joshua, and Caleb, and Phineas, and the rest; those after the law by angels and prophets, and the same by His own incarnation[4] of the Virgin; those a little before His bodily appearance by John His forerunner, and the same by the same person after Christ's birth, saying, "Repent ye, for the kingdom of heaven is at hand;"[5] those after His passion by us, the twelve apostles, and Paul the chosen vessel. We therefore, who have been vouchsafed the favour of being the witnesses of His appearance, together with James the brother of our Lord, and the other seventy-two disciples, and his seven deacons, have heard from the mouth of our Lord Jesus Christ, and by exact knowledge declare "what is the will of God, that good, and acceptable, and perfect will"[6] which is made known to us by Jesus; that none should perish, but that all men with one accord should believe in Him, and send unanimously praise to Him, and thereby live for ever.

THAT IT IS THE WILL OF GOD THAT MEN SHOULD BE OF ONE MIND IN MATTERS OF RELIGION, IN ACCORD WITH THE HEAVENLY POWERS.

LVI. For this is that which our Lord taught us when we pray to say to His Father, "Thy will be done, as in heaven, so upon earth;"[7] that as the heavenly natures of the incorporeal powers do all glorify God with one consent, so also upon earth all men with one mouth and one purpose may glorify the only, the one, and the true God, by Christ His only-begotten. It is therefore His will that men should praise Him with unanimity, and adore Him with one consent.[8] For this is His will in Christ, that those who are saved by Him may be many; but that you do not occasion any loss or diminution to Him, nor to the Church, or lessen the number by one soul of man, as destroyed by you, which might have been saved by repentance; and which therefore perishes not only by its own sin, but also by your treachery besides, whereby you fulfil that which is written, "He that gathereth not with me, scattereth."[9] Such a one is a disperser of the sheep, an adversary, an enemy of God, a destroyer of those lambs whose Shepherd was the Lord, and we were the collectors out of various nations and tongues, by much pains and danger, and perpetual labour, by watchings, by fastings, by lyings on the ground, by persecutions, by stripes, by imprisonments, that we might do the will of God, and fill the feast-chamber with guests to sit down at His

[1] Matt. v. 45.
[2] Matt. x. 12.
[3] Isa. lvii. 19; Eph. ii. 17; 2 Tim. ii. 19.

[4] One V. MS. inserts, "of the Holy Spirit and."
[5] Matt. iii. 2.
[6] Rom. xii. 2.
[7] Matt. vi. 10.
[8] "And adore him with one consent" is omitted in one V. MS.
[9] Matt. xii. 30.

table, that is, the holy and Catholic Church, with joyful and chosen people, singing hymns and praises to God that has called them by us to life. And you, as much as in you lies, have dispersed them. Do you also of the laity be at peace with one another, endeavouring like wise men to increase the Church, and to turn back, and tame, and restore those which seem wild. For this is the greatest reward by His promise from God, "If thou fetch out the worthy and precious from the unworthy, thou shalt be as my mouth."[1]

SEC. VII. — ON ASSEMBLING IN THE CHURCH.

AN EXACT DESCRIPTION OF A CHURCH AND THE CLERGY, AND WHAT THINGS IN PARTICULAR EVERY ONE IS TO DO IN THE SOLEMN ASSEMBLIES OF THE CLERGY AND LAITY FOR RELIGIOUS WORSHIP.

LVII. But be thou, O bishop, holy, unblameable, no striker, not soon angry, not cruel; but a builder up, a converter, apt to teach, forbearing of evil, of a gentle mind, meek, long-suffering, ready to exhort, ready to comfort, as a man of God.

When thou callest an assembly of the Church as one that is the commander of a great ship, appoint the assemblies to be made with all possible skill, charging the deacons as mariners to prepare places for the brethren as for passengers, with all due care and decency. And first, let the building be long, with its head to the east, with its vestries on both sides at the east end, and so it will be like a ship. In the middle let the bishop's throne be placed, and on each side of him let the presbytery sit down; and let the deacons stand near at hand, in close and small girt garments, for they are like the mariners and managers of the ship: with regard to these, let the laity sit on the other side, with all quietness and good order. And let the women sit by themselves, they also keeping silence. In the middle, let the reader stand upon some high place: let him read the books of Moses, of Joshua the son of Nun, of the Judges, and of the Kings and of the Chronicles, and those written after the return from the captivity; and besides these, the books of Job and of Solomon, and of the sixteen prophets. But when there have been two lessons severally read, let some other person sing the hymns of David, and let the people join at the conclusions of the verses. Afterwards let our Acts be read, and the Epistles of Paul our fellow-worker, which he sent to the churches under the conduct of the Holy Spirit; and afterwards let a deacon or a presbyter read the Gospels, both those which I Matthew and John have delivered to you, and those which the fellow-workers of Paul received and left to you, Luke and Mark. And while the Gospel is read, let all the presbyters and deacons, and all the people, stand up in great silence; for it is written: "Be silent, and hear, O Israel."[2] And again: "But do thou stand there, and hear."[3] In the next place, let the presbyters one by one, not all together, exhort the people, and the bishop in the last place, as being the commander. Let the porters stand at the entries of the men, and observe them. Let the deaconesses also stand at those of the women, like shipmen. For the same description and pattern was both in the tabernacle of the testimony and in the temple of God.[4] But if any one be found sitting out of his place, let him be rebuked by the deacon, as a manager of the foreship, and be removed into the place proper for him; for the Church is not only like a ship, but also like a sheepfold. For as the shepherds place all the brute creatures distinctly, I mean goats and sheep, according to their kind and age, and still every one runs together, like to his like; so is it to be in the Church. Let the young persons sit by themselves, if there be a place for them; if not, let them stand upright. But let those that are already stricken in years sit in order. For the children which stand, let their fathers and mothers take them to them. Let the younger women also sit by themselves, if there be a place for them; but if there be not, let them stand behind the women. Let those women which are married, and have children, be placed by themselves; but let the virgins, and the widows, and the elder women, stand or sit before all the rest; and let the deacon be the disposer of the places, that every one of those that comes in may go to his proper place, and may not sit at the entrance. In like manner, let the deacon oversee the people, that nobody may whisper, nor slumber, nor laugh, nor nod; for all ought in the church to stand wisely, and soberly, and attentively, having their attention fixed upon the word of the Lord. After this, let all rise up with one consent, and looking towards the east, after the catechumens and penitents are gone out, pray to God eastward, who ascended up to the heaven of heavens to the east; remembering also the ancient situation of paradise in the east, from whence the first man, when he had yielded to the persuasion of the serpent, and disobeyed the command of God, was expelled. As to the deacons, after the prayer is over, let some of them attend upon the oblation of the Eucharist, ministering to the Lord's body with fear. Let others of them watch the multitude, and keep them silent. But let

[1] Jer. xv. 19.

[2] Deut. xxvii. 9.

[3] Deut. v. 31.

[4] Deut. xxiii. 1. "And in the temple of God" is omitted in one V. MS.

that deacon who is at the high priest's hand say to the people, Let no one have any quarrel against another; let no one come in hypocrisy. Then let the men give the men, and the women give the women, the Lord's kiss. But let no one do it with deceit, as Judas betrayed the Lord with a kiss. After this let the deacon pray for the whole Church, for the whole world, and the several parts of it, and the fruits of it; for the priests and the rulers, for the high priest and the king, and the peace of the universe. After this let the high priest pray for peace upon the people, and bless them, as Moses commanded the priests to bless the people, in these words: "The Lord bless thee, and keep thee: the Lord make His face to shine upon thee,[1] and give thee peace."[2] Let the bishop pray for the people, and say: "Save Thy people, O Lord, and bless Thine inheritance, which Thou hast obtained with the precious blood of Thy Christ, and hast called a royal priesthood, and an holy nation."[3] After this let the sacrifice follow, the people standing, and praying silently; and when the oblation has been made, let every rank by itself partake of the Lord's body and precious blood in order, and approach with reverence and holy fear, as to the body of their king. Let the women approach with their heads covered, as is becoming the order of women; but let the door be watched, lest any unbeliever, or one not yet initiated, come in.[4]

OF COMMENDATORY LETTERS IN FAVOUR OF STRANGERS, LAY PERSONS, CLERGYMEN, AND BISHOPS; AND THAT THOSE WHO COME INTO THE CHURCH ASSEMBLIES ARE TO BE RECEIVED WITHOUT REGARD TO THEIR QUALITY.

LVIII. If any brother, man or woman, come in from another parish, bringing recommendatory letters, let the deacon be the judge of that affair, inquiring whether they be of the faithful, and of the Church? whether they be not defiled by heresy? and besides, whether the party be a married woman or a widow? And when he is satisfied in these questions, that they are really of the faithful, and of the same sentiments in the things of the Lord, let him conduct every one to the place proper for him. And if a presbyter comes from another parish, let him be received to communion by the presbyters; if a deacon, by the deacons; if a bishop, let him sit with the bishop, and be allowed the same honour with himself; and thou, O bishop, shalt desire him to speak to the people words of instruction: for the exhortation and admonition of strangers is very acceptable, and exceeding profitable. For, as the Scripture says, "no prophet is accepted in his own country."[5] Thou shalt also permit him to offer the Eucharist; but if, out of reverence to thee, and as a wise man, to preserve the honour belonging to thee, he will not offer, at least thou shalt compel him to give the blessing to the people. But if, after the congregation is sat down, any other person comes upon you of good fashion and character in the world, whether he be a stranger, or one of your own country, neither do thou, O bishop, if thou art speaking the word of God, or hearing him that sings or reads, accept persons so far as to leave the ministry of the word, that thou mayest appoint an upper place for him; but continue quiet, not interrupting thy discourse, nor thy attention. But let the brethren receive him by the deacons; and if there be not a place, let the deacon by speaking, but not in anger, raise the junior, and place the stranger there. And it is but reasonable that one that loves the brethren should do so of his own accord; but if he refuse, let him raise him up by force, and set him behind all, that the rest may be taught to give place to those that are more honourable. Nay, if a poor man, or one of a mean family, or a stranger, comes upon you, whether he be old or young, and there be no place, the deacon shall find a place for even these, and that with all his heart; that, instead of accepting persons before men, his ministration towards God may be well-pleasing. The very same thing let the deaconess do to those women, whether poor or rich, that come unto them.

THAT EVERY CHRISTIAN OUGHT TO FREQUENT THE CHURCH DILIGENTLY BOTH MORNING AND EVENING.

LIX. When thou instructest the people, O bishop, command and exhort them to come constantly to church morning and evening every day, and by no means to forsake it on any account, but to assemble together continually; neither to diminish the Church by withdrawing themselves, and causing the body of Christ to be without its member. For it is not only spoken concerning the priests, but let every one of the laity hearken to it as concerning himself, considering that it is said by the Lord: "He that is not with me is against me, and he that gathereth not with me scattereth abroad."[6] Do not you therefore scatter yourselves abroad, who are the members of Christ, by not assembling together, since you have Christ your head, according to His promise, present, and communicating to you.[7] Be not careless of yourselves,

[1] One V. MS. inserts, "and pity thee: the Lord lift His countenance upon thee."
[2] Num. vi. 24, etc.
[3] Ps. xxviii. 9; Acts xx. 28; 1 Pet. i. 19, ii. 9.
[4] [Note all this as bearing upon the ceremonial of the Latin Mass, which reverses these primitive precepts in divers points.]

[5] Luke iv. 24; John iv. 44.
[6] Matt. xii. 30.
[7] Matt. xxviii. 20. [Compare vol. i. pp. 185, 186, this series.]

neither deprive your Saviour of His own members, neither divide His body nor disperse His members, neither prefer the occasions of this life to the word of God; but assemble yourselves together every day, morning and evening, singing psalms and praying in the Lord's house: in the morning saying the sixty-second Psalm, and in the evening the hundred and fortieth, but principally on the Sabbath-day. And on the day of our Lord's resurrection, which is the Lord's day, meet more diligently, sending praise to God that made the universe by Jesus, and sent Him to us, and condescended to let Him suffer, and raised Him from the dead. Otherwise what apology will he make to God who does not assemble on that day to hear the saving word concerning the resurrection, on which we pray thrice standing in memory of Him who arose in three days, in which is performed the reading of the prophets, the preaching of the Gospel, the oblation of the sacrifice, the gift of the holy food?

THE VAIN ZEAL WHICH THE HEATHENS AND JEWS SHOW IN FREQUENTING THEIR TEMPLES AND SYNAGOGUES IS A PROPER EXAMPLE AND MOTIVE TO EXCITE CHRISTIANS TO FREQUENT THE CHURCH.

LX. And how can he be other than an adversary to God, who takes pains about temporary things night and day, but takes no care of things eternal? who takes care of washings and temporary food every day, but does not take care of those that endure for ever? How can such a one even now avoid hearing that word of the Lord, "The Gentiles are justified more than you?"[1] as He says, by way of reproach, to Jerusalem, "Sodom is justified rather than thou." For if the Gentiles every day, when they arise from sleep, run to their idols to worship them, and before all their work and all their labours do first of all pray to them, and in their feasts and in their solemnities do not keep away, but attend upon them; and not only those upon the place, but those living far distant do the same; and in their public shows all come together, as into a synagogue: in the same manner those which are vainly called Jews, when they have worked six days, on the seventh day rest, and come together into their synagogue, never leaving nor neglecting either rest from labour or assembling together, while yet they are deprived of the efficacy of the word in their unbelief, nay, and of the force of that name Judah, by which they call themselves, — for Judah is interpreted *Confession*, — but these do not confess to God (having unjustly occasioned the suffering on the cross), so as to be saved on their repentance; — if, therefore, those who are not saved frequently assemble together for such purposes as do not profit them, what apology wilt thou make to the Lord God who forsakest His Church, not imitating so much as the heathen, but by such thy absence growest slothful, or turnest apostate, or actest wickedness? To whom the Lord says by Jeremiah: "Ye have not kept my ordinances; nay, ye have not walked according to the ordinances of the heathen, and you have in a manner exceeded them."[2] And again: "Israel has justified his soul more than treacherous Judah."[3] And afterwards: "Will the Gentiles change their gods which are not gods?[4] Wherefore pass over to the isles of Chittim, and behold, and send to Kedar, and observe diligently whether such things have been done. For those nations have not changed their ordinances; but," says He, "my people has changed its glory for that which will not profit."[5] How, therefore, will any one make his apology who has despised or absented himself from the church of God?

THAT WE MUST NOT PREFER THE AFFAIRS OF THIS LIFE TO THOSE WHICH CONCERN THE WORSHIP OF GOD.

LXI. But if any one allege the pretence of his own work, and so is a despiser, "offering pretences for his sins," let such a one know that the trades of the faithful are works by the by, but the worship of God is their great work. Follow therefore your trades as by the by, for your maintenance, but make the worship of God your main business; as also our Lord said: "Labour not for the meat which perishes, but for that which endureth unto everlasting life."[6] And again: "This is the work of God, that ye believe on Him whom He hath sent."[7] Endeavour therefore never to leave the Church of God; but if any one overlooks it, and goes either into a polluted temple of the heathens, or into a synagogue of the Jews or heretics, what apology will such a one make to God in the day of judgment, who has forsaken the oracles of the living God, and the living and quickening oracles, such as are able to deliver from eternal punishment, and has gone into an house of demons, or into a synagogue of the murderers of Christ, or the congregation of the wicked? — not hearkening unto him that says: "I have hated the congregation of the wicked, and I will not enter with the ungodly. I have not sat with the assembly of vanity, neither will I sit with the ungodly."[8] And again: "Blessed is the

[1] Ezek. xvi. 52.

[2] Ezek. v. 7, xvi. 47.
[3] Jer. iii. 11.
[4] One V. MS. inserts here, "and elsewhere through another."
[5] Jer. ii. 11, 10.
[6] John vi. 27.
[7] John vi. 29.
[8] Ps. xxvi. 5, 4.

man that hath not walked in the counsel of the ungodly, nor stood in the way of sinners, and hath not sat in the seat of the scornful; but his delight is in the law of the Lord, and in His law will he meditate day and night."[1] But thou, forsaking the gathering together of the faithful, the Church of God, and His laws, hast respect to those "dens of thieves," calling those things holy which He has called profane, and making such things unclean which He has sanctified. And not only so, but thou already runnest after the pomps of the Gentiles, and hastenest to their theatres, being desirous to be reckoned one of those that enter into them, and to partake of unseemly, not to say abominable words; not hearkening to Jeremiah, who says, "O Lord, I have not sat in their assemblies, for they are scorners; but I was afraid because of Thy hand;"[2] nor to Job, who speaks in like manner, "If I have gone at any time with the scornful; for I shall be weighed in a just balance."[3] But why wilt thou be a partaker of the heathen oracles, which are nothing but dead men declaring by the inspiration of the devil deadly things, and such as tend to subvert the faith, and to draw those that attend to them to polytheism? Do you therefore, who attend to the laws of God, esteem those laws more honourable than the necessities of this life, and pay a greater respect to them, and run together to the Church of the Lord, "which He has purchased with the blood of Christ, the beloved, the first-born of every creature."[4] For this Church is the daughter of the Highest, which has been in travail of you by the word of grace, and has "formed Christ in you," of whom you are made partakers, and thereby become His holy and chosen members, "not having spot or wrinkle, or any such thing; but as being holy and unspotted in the faith, ye are complete in Him, after the image of God that created you."[5]

THAT CHRISTIANS MUST ABSTAIN FROM ALL THE IMPIOUS PRACTICES OF THE HEATHENS.

LXII. Take heed, therefore, not to join yourselves in your worship with those that perish, which is the assembly of the Gentiles, to your deceit and destruction. For there is no fellowship between God and the devil; for he that assembles himself with those that favour the things of the devil, will be esteemed one of them, and will inherit a woe. Avoid also indecent spectacles: I mean the theatres and the pomps of the heathens; their enchantments, observations of omens, soothsayings, purgations, divinations, observations of birds; their necromancies and invocations. For it is written: "There is no divination in Jacob, nor soothsaying in Israel."[6] And again: "Divination is iniquity."[7] And elsewhere: "Ye shall not be soothsayers, and follow observers of omens, nor diviners, nor dealers with familiar spirits. Ye shall not preserve alive wizards."[8] Wherefore Jeremiah exhorts, saying: "Walk ye not according to the ways of the heathen, and be not afraid of the signs of heaven."[9] So that it is the duty of a believer to avoid the assemblies of the ungodly, of the heathen, and of the Jews, and of the rest of the heretics, lest by uniting ourselves to them we bring snares upon our own souls; that we may not by joining in their feasts, which are celebrated in honour of demons, be partakers with them in their impiety. You are also to avoid their public meetings, and those sports which are celebrated in them. For a believer ought not to go to any of those public meetings, unless to purchase a slave, and save a soul,[9] and at the same time to buy such other things as suit their necessities. Abstain, therefore, from all idolatrous pomp and state, all their public meetings, banquets, duels, and all shows belonging to demons.

SEC. VIII. — ON THE DUTY OF WORKING FOR A LIVELIHOOD.

THAT A CHRISTIAN WHO WILL NOT WORK MUST NOT EAT, AS PETER AND THE REST OF THE APOSTLES WERE FISHERMEN, BUT PAUL AND AQUILA TENTMAKERS, JUDE THE SON OF JAMES AN HUSBANDMAN.

LXIII. Let the young persons of the Church endeavour to minister diligently in all necessaries: mind your business with all becoming seriousness, that so you may always have sufficient to support yourselves and those that are needy, and not burden the Church of God. For we ourselves, besides our attention to the word of the Gospel, do not neglect our inferior employments. For some of us are fishermen, some tentmakers, some husbandmen, that so we may never be idle. So says Solomon somewhere: "Go to the ant, thou sluggard; consider her ways diligently, and become wiser than she. For she, having neither field, overseer, nor ruler, prepareth her food in the summer, and layeth up a great store in the harvest. Or else go to the bee, and learn how laborious she is, and her work how valuable it is, whose labours both kings and mean men make use of for their health. She is desirable and glorious, though she be weak in strength, yet by honouring wisdom she is improved, etc. How long wilt thou lie on thy bed, O sluggard? When wilt thou

[1] Ps. i. 1, 2.
[2] Jer. xv. 17.
[3] Job xxxi. 5, 6.
[4] *Vid.* Acts xx. 28; Col. i. 15.
[5] Eph. v. 27.
[6] Num. xxiii. 23.
[7] 1 Sam. xv. 23, LXX.
[8] Lev. xix. 26; Deut. xviii. 10.
[9] Jer. x. 2. [Slaves were bought to be baptized. Elucid., p. 425.]

awake out of thy sleep? Thou sleepest awhile, thou liest down awhile, thou slumberest awhile, thou foldest thy hands on thy breast to sleep awhile. Then poverty comes on thee like an evil traveller, and want as a swift racer. But if thou beest diligent, thy harvest shall come as a fountain, and want shall fly from thee as an evil runagate."[1] And again: "He that manageth his own land shall be filled with bread."[2] And elsewhere he says: "The slothful has folded his own hands together, and has eaten his own flesh."[3] And afterwards: "The sluggard hides his hand; he will not be able to bring it to his mouth."[4] And again: "By slothfulness of the hands a floor will be brought low."[5] Labour therefore continually; for the blot of the slothful is not to be healed. But "if any one does not work, let not such a one eat"[6] among you. For the Lord our God hates the slothful. For no one of those who are dedicated to God ought to be idle.

[1] Prov. vi. 6, etc., LXX.
[2] Prov. xii. 11.
[3] Eccles. iv. 5.
[4] Prov. xix. 24.
[5] Eccles. x. 18.
[6] 2 Thess. iii. 10.

ELUCIDATION

(To purchase a slave, and save a soul, p. 424.)

THE calm and patient course of the Church in gradually obliterating slavery has been well defended by the pious Spanish Ultramontane writer Jacques Balmès.[1] Of course, he imagines that "the Catholic Church," which wrought the change, was his own Tridentine Communion.[2] Lecky's remarks on the gladiators and slavery as the product of famines and distress are worthy of note, and even he is forced to recognise the ameliorating influences of Christianity from the beginning.[3] He says: —

"Christianity for the first time made charity a rudimentary virtue, giving it a foremost place in the moral type and in the exhortations of its teachers. Besides its general influence in stimulating the affections, it effected a complete revolution in this sphere, by representing the poor as the special representatives of the Christian founder, and thus making the love of Christ rather than the love of man the principle of charity. Even in the days of persecution, collections for the relief of the poor were made at the Sunday meetings. The *agapæ*, or feasts of love, were intended mainly for the poor; and food that was saved by the fasts was devoted to their benefit. A vast organization of charity, presided over by the bishops, and actively directed by the deacons, soon ramified over Christendom, till the bond of charity became the bond of unity, and the most distant sections of the Christian Church corresponded by the interchange of mercy.[4] Long before the era of Constantine it was observed that the charities of the Christians were so extensive — it may perhaps be said so excessive — that they drew very many impostors to the Church; and, when the victory of Christianity was achieved, the enthusiasm for charity displayed itself in the erection of numerous institutions that were altogether unknown to the pagan world."

[1] See his chapter (xvii.) *Moyens employés par l'église pour affranchir les esclaves, Civilisation Européene*, vol. i. p. 222, Paris, 1851.
[2] The countrymen of Balmès, on the contrary, were the authors of the negro slavery of modern times.
[3] *History of European Morals*, vol. ii. p. 84.
[4] See also Elucidation XII. vol. v. p. 563.

CONSTITUTIONS OF THE HOLY APOSTLES

BOOK III.

SEC. I.—CONCERNING WIDOWS.

THE AGE AT WHICH WIDOWS SHOULD BE CHOSEN.

I. CHOOSE your "widows not under sixty years of age,"[1] that in some measure the suspicion of a second marriage may be prevented by their age. But if you admit one younger into the order of widows, and she cannot bear her widowhood in her youth, and marries, she will procure indecent reflections on the glory of the order of the widows, and shall give an account to God; not because she married a second time, but because she has "waxed wanton against Christ,"[2] and not kept her promise, *because she did not come and keep her promise with faith and the fear of God.*[3] Wherefore such a promise ought not to be rashly made, but with great caution: "for it is better for her not to vow, than to vow and not to pay."[4] But if any younger woman, who has lived but a while with her husband, and has lost him by death or some other occasion, and remains by herself, having the gift of widowhood, she will be found to be blessed, and to be like the widow of Sarepta, belonging to Sidon, with whom the holy prophet of God, Elijah,[5] lodged. Such a one may also be compared to "Anna, the daughter of Phanuel, of the tribe of Aser, which departed not from the temple, but continued in supplications and prayers night and day, who was fourscore years old, and had lived with an husband seven years from her virginity, who glorified the coming of Christ, and gave thanks to the Lord, and spake concerning Him to all those who looked for redemption in Israel."[6] Such a widow will have a good report, and will be honoured, having both glory with men upon earth, and eternal praise with God in heaven.

[1] *Vid.* 1 Tim. v. 9.
[2] 1 Tim. v. 11.
[3] Not in one V. MS.
[4] Eccles. v. 5.
[5] 1 Kings xvii. 9.
[6] Luke ii. 36, etc.

THAT WE MUST AVOID THE CHOICE OF YOUNGER WIDOWS, BECAUSE OF SUSPICION.

II. But let not the younger widows be placed in the order of widows, lest, under pretence of inability to contain in the flower of their age, they come to a second marriage, and become subject to imputation. But let them be assisted and supported, that so they may not, under pretence of being deserted, come to a second marriage, and so be ensnared in an unseemly imputation. For you ought to know this, that once marrying according to the law is righteous, as being according to the will of God; but second marriages, after the promise, are wicked, not on account of the marriage itself, but because of the falsehood. Third marriages are indications of incontinency. But such marriages as are beyond the third are manifest fornication, and unquestionable uncleanness. For God in the creation gave one woman to one man; for "they two shall be one flesh."[7] But to the younger women let a second marriage be allowed after the death of their first husband, lest they fall into the condemnation of the devil, and many snares, and foolish lusts, which are hurtful to souls, and which bring upon them punishment rather than rest.

WHAT CHARACTER THE WIDOWS OUGHT TO BE OF, AND HOW THEY OUGHT TO BE SUPPORTED BY THE BISHOP.

III. But the true widows are those which have had only one husband, having a good report among the generality for good works; widows indeed, sober, chaste, faithful, pious, who have brought up their children well, and have entertained strangers unblameably, which are to be supported as devoted to God. Besides, do thou, O bishop, be mindful of the needy, both reaching out thy helping hand and making provision

[7] Gen. ii. 24.

for them as the steward of God, distributing seasonably the oblations to every one of them, to the widows, the orphans, the friendless, and those tried with affliction.

THAT WE OUGHT TO BE CHARITABLE TO ALL SORTS OF PERSONS IN WANT.

IV. For what if some are neither widows nor widowers, but stand in need of assistance, either through poverty or some disease, or the maintenance of a great number of children? It is thy duty to oversee all people, and to take care of them all. For they that give gifts do not of their own head give them to the widows, but barely bring them in, calling them free-will offerings, that so thou that knowest those that are in affliction mayest as a good steward give them their portion of the gift. For God knows the giver, though thou distributest it to those in want when he is absent. And he has the reward of well-doing, but thou the blessedness of having dispensed it with a good conscience. But do thou tell them who was the giver, that they may pray for him by name. For it is our duty to do good to all men, not fondly preferring one or another, whoever they be. For the Lord says: "Give to every one that asketh of thee."[1] It is evident that it is meant of every one that is really in want, whether he be friend or foe, whether he be a kinsman or a stranger, whether he be single or married. For in all the Scripture the Lord gives us exhortations about the needy, saying first by Isaiah: "Deal thy bread to the hungry, and bring the poor which have no covering into thine house. If thou seest the naked, do thou cover him; and thou shalt not overlook those which are of thine own family and seed."[2] And then by Daniel He says to the potentate: "Wherefore, O king, let my counsel please thee, and purge thy sins by acts of mercy, and thine iniquities by bowels of compassion to the needy."[3] And He says by Solomon: "By acts of mercy and of faith iniquities are purged."[4] And He says again by David: "Blessed is he that has regard to the poor and needy; the Lord shall deliver him in the evil day."[5] And again: "He hath dispersed abroad, he hath given to the needy, his righteousness remaineth for ever."[6] And Solomon says: "He that hath mercy on the poor lendeth to the Lord;[7] according to his gift it shall be repaid him again."[8] And afterwards: "He that stoppeth his ear, that he may not hear him that is in want, he also shall call himself, and there shall be none to hear him."[9]

THAT THE WIDOWS ARE TO BE VERY CAREFUL OF THEIR BEHAVIOR.

V. Let every widow be meek, quiet, gentle, sincere, free from anger, not talkative, not clamorous, not hasty of speech, not given to evil-speaking, not captious, not double-tongued, not a busybody. If she see or hear anything that is not right, let her be as one that does not see, and as one that does not hear. And let the widow mind nothing but to pray for those that give, and for the whole Church; and when she is asked anything by any one, let her not easily answer, excepting questions concerning the faith, and righteousness, and hope in God, remitting those that desire to be instructed in the doctrines of godliness to the governors. Let her only answer so as may tend to the subversion of the error of polytheism, and let her demonstrate the assertion concerning the monarchy of God. But of the remaining doctrines let her not answer anything rashly, lest by saying anything unlearnedly she should make the word to be blasphemed. For the Lord has taught us that the word is like "a grain of mustard seed,"[10] which is of a fiery nature, which if any one uses unskilfully, he will find it bitter. For in the mystical points we ought not to be rash, but cautious; for the Lord exhorts us, saying: "Cast not your pearls before swine, lest they trample them with their feet, and turn again and rend you."[11] For unbelievers, when they hear the doctrine concerning Christ not explained as it ought to be, but defectively, and especially that concerning His incarnation or His passion, will rather reject it with scorn, and laugh at it as false, than praise God for it. And so the aged women will be guilty of rashness, and of causing blasphemy, and will inherit a woe. For says He, "Woe to him by whom my name is blasphemed among the Gentiles."[12]

THAT WOMEN OUGHT NOT TO TEACH, BECAUSE IT IS UNSEEMLY; AND WHAT WOMEN FOLLOWED OUR LORD.

VI. We do not permit our "women to teach in the Church,"[13] but only to pray and hear those that teach; for our Master and Lord, Jesus Himself, when He sent us the twelve to make disciples of the people and of the nations, did nowhere send out women to preach, although He did not want such. For there were with us the mother of our Lord and His sisters; also Mary Magdalene, and Mary the mother of James, and Martha and Mary the sisters of Lazarus; Salome, and certain others. For, had it been necessary for women to teach, He Himself had first com-

[1] Luke vi. 30.
[2] Isa. lviii 7.
[3] Dan. iv. 27.
[4] Prov. xvi. 6.
[5] Ps. xli. 1.
[6] Ps. cxii. 9.
[7] Instead of "Lord," one V. MS. reads "God."
[8] Prov. xix. 17.
[9] Prov. xxi. 13.

[10] Matt. xiii. 31.
[11] Matt. vii. 6.
[12] Isa. lii. 5.
[13] 1 Cor. xiv. 34.

manded these also to instruct the people with us. For "if the head of the wife be the man,"[1] it is not reasonable that the rest of the body should govern the head. Let the widow therefore own herself to be the "altar of God," and let her sit in her house, and not enter into the houses of the faithful, under any pretence, to receive anything; for the altar of God never runs about, but is fixed in one place. Let, therefore, the virgin and the widow be such as do not run about, or gad to the houses of those who are alien from the faith. For such as these are gadders and impudent: they do not make their feet to rest in one place, because they are not widows, but purses ready to receive, triflers, evil-speakers, counsellors of strife, without shame, impudent, who being such, are not worthy of Him that called them. For they do not come to the common station of the congregation on the Lord's day,[2] as those that are watchful; but either they slumber, or trifle, or allure men, or beg, or ensnare others, bringing them to the evil one; not suffering them to be watchful in the Lord, but taking care that they go out as vain as they came in, because they do not hear the word of the Lord either taught or read. For of such as these the prophet Isaiah says: "Hearing ye shall hear, and shall not understand; and seeing ye shall see, and not perceive: for the heart of this people is waxen gross,[3] *and they hear heavily with their ears.*"[4]

WHAT ARE THE CHARACTERS OF WIDOWS FALSELY SO CALLED.

VII. In the same manner, therefore, the ears of the hearts of such widows as these are stopped, that they will not sit within in their cottages to speak to the Lord, but will run about with the design of getting, and by their foolish prattling fulfil the desires of the adversary. Such widows, therefore, are not affixed to the altar of Christ: for there are some widows which esteem gain their business; and since they ask without shame, and receive without being satisfied, render the generality more backward in giving. For when they ought to be content with their subsistence from the Church, as having moderate desires, on the contrary, they run from one of their neighbours' houses[5] to another, and disturb them, heaping up to themselves plenty of money, and lend at bitter usury, and are only solicitous about mammon, whose bag is their god; who prefer eating and drinking before all virtue, saying, "Let us eat and drink, for to-morrow we die;"[6] who esteem these things as if they were durable and not perishing things. For she that uses herself to nothing but talking of money, worships mammon instead of God, — that is, is a servant to gain, but cannot be pleasing to God, nor resigned to His worship; not being able to intercede with Him continuously on account that her mind and disposition run after money: for "where the treasure is, there will the heart be also."[7] For she is thinking in her mind whither she may go to receive, or that a certain woman her friend has forgot her, and she has somewhat to say to her. She that thinks of such things as these will no longer attend to her prayers, but to that thought which offers itself; so that though sometimes she would pray for anybody, she will not be heard, because she does not offer her petition to the Lord with her whole heart, but with a divided mind. But she that will attend to God will sit within, and mind the things of the Lord day and night, offering her sincere petition with a mouth ready to utter the same without ceasing. As therefore Judith, most famous for her wisdom, and of a good report for her modesty, "prayed to God night and day for Israel;"[8] so also the widow who is like to her will offer her intercession without ceasing for the Church to God. And He will hear her, because her mind is fixed on this thing alone, and is not disposed to be either insatiable, or covetous, or expensive; when her eye is pure, and her hearing clean, and her hands undefiled, and her feet quiet, and her mouth prepared for neither gluttony nor trifling, but speaking the things that are fit, and partaking of only such things as are necessary for her maintenance. So, being grave, and giving no disturbance, she will be pleasing to God; and as soon as she asks anything, the gift will come to her: as He says, "While thou art speaking, I will say, Behold, I am here."[9] Let such a one also be free from the love of money, free from arrogance, not given to filthy lucre, not insatiable, not gluttonous, but continent, meek, giving nobody disturbance, pious, modest, sitting at home, singing, and praying, and reading, and watching, and fasting; speaking to God continually in songs and hymns. And let her take wool, and rather assist others than herself want from them; being mindful of that widow who is honoured in the Gospel with the Lord's testimony, who, coming into the temple, "cast into the treasury two mites, which make a farthing. And Christ our Lord and Master, and Searcher of hearts, saw her, and said, Verily I say unto you, that this widow hath cast into the treasury more than they all: for all they have cast in of their

[1] 1 Cor. xi. 3.
[2] "On the Lord's day" not in one V. MS.
[3] Isa. vi. 9, 10.
[4] Inserted from one V. MS.
[5] Probably the reading should be, "they go round the houses of the rich."
[6] Isa. xxii. 13; 1 Cor. xv. 32.
[7] Matt. vi. 21.
[8] Judith ix. 1, etc.
[9] Isa. lviii. 9.

abundance, but this woman of her penury hath cast in all the living that she had."[1]

The widows therefore ought to be grave, obedient to their bishops, and their presbyters, and their deacons, and besides these to the deaconesses, with piety, reverence, and fear; not usurping authority, nor desiring to do anything beyond the constitution without the consent of the deacon: as, suppose, the going to any one to eat or drink with him, or to receive anything from anybody. But if without direction she does any one of these things, let her be punished with fasting, or else let her be separated on account of her rashness.

THAT THE WIDOWS OUGHT NOT TO ACCEPT OF ALMS FROM THE UNWORTHY NO MORE THAN THE BISHOP, OR ANY OTHER OF THE FAITHFUL.

VIII. For how does such a one know of what character the person is from whom she receives? or from what sort of ministration he supplies her with food, whether it does not arise from rapine or some other ill course of life? while the widow does not remember that if she receives in a way unworthy of God, she must give an account for every one of these things. For neither will the priests at any time receive a free-will offering from such a one, as, suppose, from a rapacious person or from a harlot. For it is written, "Thou shalt not covet the goods that are thy neighbour's;"[2] and, "Thou shalt not offer the hire of an harlot to the Lord God."[3] From such as these no offerings ought to be accepted, nor indeed from those that are separated from the Church. Let the widows also be ready to obey the commands given them by their superiors, and let them do according to the appointment of the bishop, being obedient to him as to God; for he that receives from such a one who is worthy of blame, or from one excommunicated, and prays for him, while he purposes to go on in a wicked course, and while he is not willing at any time to repent, holds communion with him in prayer, and grieves Christ, who rejects the unrighteous, and confirms them by means of the unworthy gift, and is defiled with them, not suffering them to come to repentance, so as to fall down before God with lamentation, and pray to Him.

THAT WOMEN OUGHT NOT TO BAPTIZE, BECAUSE IT IS IMPIOUS, AND CONTRARY TO THE DOCTRINE OF CHRIST.

IX. Now, as to women's baptizing, we let you know that there is no small peril to those that undertake it. Therefore we do not advise you to it; for it is dangerous, or rather wicked and impious. For if the "man be the head of the woman,"[4] and he be originally ordained for the priesthood, it is not just to abrogate the order of the creation, and leave the principal to come to the extreme part of the body. For the woman is the body of the man, taken from his side, and subject to him, from whom she was separated for the procreation of children. For says He, "He shall rule over thee."[5] For the principal part of the woman is the man, as being her head. But if in the foregoing constitutions we have not permitted them to teach, how will any one allow them, contrary to nature, to perform the office of a priest? For this is one of the ignorant practices of the Gentile atheism, to ordain women priests to the female deities, not one of the constitutions of Christ. For if baptism were to be administered by women, certainly our Lord would have been baptized by His own mother, and not by John; or when He sent us to baptize, He would have sent along with us women also for this purpose. But now He has nowhere, either by constitution or by writing, delivered to us any such thing; as knowing the order of nature, and the decency of the action;[6] as being the Creator of nature, and the Legislator of the constitution.

THAT A LAYMAN OUGHT NOT TO DO ANY OFFICE OF THE PRIESTHOOD: HE OUGHT NEITHER TO BAPTIZE, NOR OFFER, NOR LAY ON HANDS, NOR GIVE THE BLESSING.

X. Neither do we permit the laity to perform any of the offices belonging to the priesthood; as, for instance, neither the sacrifice, nor baptism, nor the laying on of hands, nor the blessing, whether the smaller or the greater: for "no one taketh this honour to himself, but he that is called of God."[7] For such sacred offices are conferred by the laying on of the hands of the bishop. But a person to whom such an office is not committed, but he seizes upon it for himself, he shall undergo the punishment of Uzziah.[8]

THAT NONE BUT A BISHOP AND PRESBYTER, NONE EVEN OF THE INFERIOR RANKS OF THE CLERGY, ARE PERMITTED TO DO THE OFFICES OF THE PRIESTS; THAT ORDINATION BELONGS WHOLLY TO THE BISHOP, AND TO NOBODY ELSE.

XI. Nay, further, we do not permit to the rest of the clergy to baptize, — as, for instance, neither to readers, nor singers, nor porters, nor ministers, — but to the bishops and presbyters alone, yet so that the deacons are to minister to them

[1] Mark xii. 42; Luke xxi. 3, 4.
[2] Ex. xx. 17.
[3] Deut. xxiii. 18.
[4] 1 Cor. xi. 3.
[5] Gen. iii. 16.
[6] [" The eternal fitness of things."]
[7] Heb. v. 4.
[8] 2 Chron. xxvi.

therein. But those who venture upon it shall undergo the punishment of the companions of Corah.[1] We do not permit presbyters to ordain deacons, or deaconesses, or readers, or ministers, or singers, or porters, but only bishops; for this is the ecclesiastical order and harmony.

THE REJECTION OF ALL UNCHARITABLE ACTIONS.

XII. Now, as concerning envy, or jealousy, or evil-speaking, or strife, or the love of contention, we have said already to you, that these are alien from a Christian, and chiefly in the case of widows. But because the devil, who works in men, is in his conduct cunning, and full of various devices, he goes to those that are not truly widows, as formerly to Cain (for some say they are widows, but do not perform the injunctions agreeable to the widowhood; as neither did Cain discharge the duties due to a brother: for they do not consider how it is not the name of widowhood that will bring them to the kingdom of God, but true faith and holy[2] works). But if any one possesses the name of widowhood, but does the works of the adversary, her widowhood will not be imputed, but she will be thrust out of the kingdom, and delivered to eternal punishment. For we hear that some widows are jealous, envious calumniators, and envious at the quiet of others. Such widows as these are not the disciples of Christ, nor of His doctrine; for it becomes them, when one of their fellow-widows is clothed by any one, or receives money, or meat, or drink, or shoes, at the sight of the refreshment of their sister to say: —

HOW THE WIDOWS ARE TO PRAY FOR THOSE THAT SUPPLY THEIR NECESSITIES.

XIII. Thou art blessed, O God, who hast refreshed my fellow-widow. Bless, O Lord, and glorify him that has bestowed these things upon her, and let his good work ascend in truth to Thee, and remember him for good in the day of his visitation. And as for my bishop, who *has so well performed his duty to Thee, and*[3] has ordered such a seasonable alms to be bestowed on my fellow-widow, who was naked, do Thou increase his *glory, and give him a*[3] crown of rejoicing in the day of the revelation of Thy visitation. In the same manner, let the widow who has received the alms join with the other in praying for him who ministered to her.

THAT SHE WHO HAS BEEN KIND TO THE POOR OUGHT NOT TO MAKE A STIR AND TELL ABROAD HER NAME, ACCORDING TO THE CONSTITUTION OF THE LORD.

XIV. But if any woman has been good, let her, as a prudent person, conceal her own name, not sounding a trumpet before her, that her alms may be with God in secret, as the Lord says: "Thou, when thou doest thine alms, let not thy left hand know what thy right hand doth, that thine alms may be in secret."[4] And let the widow pray for him that gave her the alms, whosoever he be, as being the holy altar of Christ;[5] and "the Father, who seeth in secret, will render to him that did good openly." But those widows which will not live according to the command of God, are solicitous and inquisitive what deaconess it is that gives the charity, and what widows receive it. And when she has learned those things, she murmurs at the deaconess who distributed the charity, saying, Dost not thou see that I am in more distress, and want of thy charity? Why, therefore, hast thou preferred her before me? She says these things foolishly, not understanding that this does not depend on the will of man, but the appointment of God. For if she is herself a witness that she was nearer, and, upon inquiry, was in greater want, and more naked than the other, she ought to understand who it is that made this constitution, and to hold her peace, and not to murmur at the deaconess who distributed the charity, but to enter into her own house, and to cast herself prostrate on her face to make supplication to God that her sin may be forgiven her. For God commanded the deaconess who brought the charity not to proclaim the same, and this widow murmured because she did not publish her name, that so she might know it, and run to receive; nay, did not only murmur, but also cursed her, forgetting Him that said: "He that blesseth thee is blessed, and he that curseth thee is cursed."[6] But the Lord says: "When ye enter into an house, say, Peace be to this house. And if the son of peace be there, your peace shall rest upon it; but if it be not worthy, your peace shall return to you."[7]

THAT IT DOES NOT BECOME US TO REVILE OUR NEIGHBOURS, BECAUSE CURSING IS CONTRARY TO CHRISTIANITY.

XV. If, therefore, peace returns upon those that sent it, nay, upon those that before had actually given it, because it did not find persons fit to receive it, much rather will a curse return upon the head of him that unjustly sent it, because he to whom it was sent was not worthy to receive it: for all those who abuse others without a cause curse themselves, as Solomon says: "As birds and sparrows fly away, so the curse causeless shall not come upon any one."[8] And again he says: "Those that bring re-

[1] Num. xvi.
[2] Instead of "holy," one V. MS. reads "divine."
[3] Not in one V. MS.

[4] Matt. vi. 3, 4.
[5] Instead of "Christ," one V. MS. reads "of God."
[6] Gen. xxvii. 29.
[7] Luke x. 5, 6; Matt. x. 12, 13.
[8] Prov. xxvi. 2.

proaches are exceeding foolish."[1] But as the bee, a creature as to its strength feeble, if she stings any one, loses her sting, and becomes a drone; in the same manner you also, whatsoever injustice you do to others, will bring it upon yourselves. "He hath graven and digged a pit, and he shall fall into the same ditch that he has made."[2] And again: "He that diggeth a pit for his neighbour, shall fall into it."[3] Wherefore he that avoids a curse, let him not curse another; for "what thou hatest should be done to thee, do not thou to another."[4] Wherefore admonish the widows that are feeble-minded, strengthen those of them that are weak, and praise such of them as walk in holiness. Let them rather bless, and not calumniate. Let them make peace, and not stir up contention.

SEC. II. — ON DEACONS AND DEACONESSES, THE REST OF THE CLERGY, AND ON BAPTISM.

Let not therefore either a bishop, or a presbyter, or a deacon, or any one else of the sacerdotal catalogue, defile his tongue with calumny, lest he inherit a curse instead of a blessing; and let it also be the bishop's business and care that no lay person utter any curse: for he ought to take care of all, — of the clergy, of the virgins, of the widows, of the laity. For which reason, O bishop, do thou ordain thy fellow-workers, the labourers for life and for righteousness, such deacons as are pleasing to God, such whom thou provest to be worthy among all the people, and such as shall be ready for the necessities of their ministration. Ordain also a deaconess who is faithful and holy, for the ministrations towards women. For sometimes he cannot send a deacon, who is a man, to the women, on account of unbelievers. Thou shalt therefore send a woman, a deaconess, on account of the imaginations of the bad. For we stand in need of a woman, a deaconess, for many necessities; and first in the baptism of women, the deacon shall anoint only their forehead with the holy oil, and after him the deaconess shall anoint them:[5] for there is no necessity that the women should be seen by the men; but only in the laying on of hands the bishop shall anoint her head, as the priests and kings were formerly anointed, not because those which are now baptized are ordained priests, but as being Christians, or anointed, from Christ the Anointed, "a royal priesthood, and an holy nation, the Church of God, the pillar and ground of the marriage-chamber,"[6] who formerly were not a people, but now are beloved and chosen, upon whom is called His new name,[7] as Isaiah the prophet witnesses, saying: "And they shall call the people by His new name, which the Lord shall name for them."[8]

CONCERNING THE SACRED INITIATION OF HOLY BAPTISM.

XVI. Thou therefore, O bishop, according to that type, shalt anoint the head of those that are to be baptized, whether they be men or women, with the holy oil, for a type of the spiritual baptism. After that, either thou, O bishop, or a presbyter that is under thee, shall in the solemn form name over them the Father, and Son, and Holy Spirit, and shall dip them in the water; and let a deacon receive the man, and a deaconess the woman, that so the conferring of this inviolable seal may take place with a becoming decency. And after that, let the bishop anoint those that are baptized with ointment.

WHAT IS THE MEANING OF BAPTISM INTO CHRIST, AND ON WHAT ACCOUNT EVERYTHING IS THERE SAID OR DONE.

XVII. This baptism, therefore, is given into the death of Jesus:[9] the water is instead of the burial, and the oil instead of the Holy Ghost; the seal instead of the cross; the ointment is the confirmation of the confession; the mention of the Father as of the Author and Sender; the joint mention of the Holy Ghost as of the witness; the descent into the water the dying together with Christ; the ascent out of the water the rising again with Him. The Father is the God over all; Christ is the only-begotten God, the beloved Son, the Lord of glory; the Holy Ghost is the Comforter, who is sent by Christ, and taught by Him, and proclaims Him.

OF WHAT CHARACTER HE OUGHT TO BE WHO IS INITIATED.

XVIII. But let him that is to be baptized be free from all iniquity; one that has left off to work sin, the friend of God, the enemy of the devil, the heir of God the Father, the fellow-heir of His Son; one that has renounced Satan, and the demons, and Satan's deceits; chaste, pure, holy, beloved of God, the son of God, praying as a son to his father, and saying, as from the common congregation of the faithful, thus: "Our Father, which art in heaven, hallowed be Thy name; Thy kingdom come; Thy will be done on earth, as it is in heaven; give us this day our daily bread; and forgive us our debts, as we forgive our debtors; and lead us not into temptation, but deliver us from the evil

[1] Prov. x. 18.
[2] Ps. vii. 15.
[3] Prov. xxvi. 27.
[4] Tob. iv. 16.
[5] [Compare Jas. v. 14.]
[6] 1 Pet. ii. 9; 1 Tim. iii. 15.
[7] The words from "upon whom" to the end of the chapter are omitted in one V. MS.
[8] Isa. lxii. 2.
[9] *Vid.* Rom. vi. 3.

one: for Thine is the kingdom, and the power, and the glory, for ever. Amen."[1]

WHAT ARE THE CHARACTERS OF A DEACON.

XIX. Let the deacons be in all things unspotted, as the bishop himself is to be, only more active; in number according to the largeness of the Church, that they may minister to the infirm as workmen that are not ashamed. And let the deaconess be diligent in taking care of the women; but both of them ready to carry messages, to travel about, to minister, and to serve, as spake Isaiah concerning the Lord, saying: "To justify the righteous, who serves many faithfully."[2] Let every one therefore know his proper place, and discharge it diligently with one consent, with one mind, as knowing the reward of their ministration; but let them not be ashamed to minister to those that are in want, as even our "Lord Jesus Christ came not to be ministered unto, but to minister, and to give His life a ransom for many."[3] So therefore ought they also to do, and not to scruple it, if they should be obliged to lay down their life for a brother. For the Lord and our Saviour Jesus Christ did not scruple to "lay down His life," as Himself says, "for His friends."[4] If, therefore, the Lord of heaven and earth underwent all His sufferings for us, how then do you make a difficulty to minister to such as are in want, who ought to imitate Him who underwent servitude, and want, and stripes, and the cross for us? We ought therefore also to serve the brethren, in imitation of Christ. For says He: "He that will be great among you, let him be your minister; and he that will be first among you, let him be your servant."[5] For so did He really, and not in word only, fulfil the prediction of, "serving many faithfully."[6] For "when He had taken a towel, He girded Himself. Afterward He puts water into a bason; and as we were sitting at meat, He came and washed the feet of us all, and wiped them with the towel."[7] By doing this He demonstrated to us His kindness and brotherly affection, that so we also might do the same to one another. If, therefore, our Lord and Master so humbled Himself, how can you, the labourers of the truth, and administrators of piety, be ashamed to do the same to such of the brethren as are weak and infirm? Minister therefore with a kind mind, not murmuring nor mutinying; for ye do not do it on the account of man, but on the account of God, and shall receive from Him the reward of your ministry in the day of your visitation. It is your duty who are deacons to visit all those who stand in need of visitation. And tell your bishop of all those that are in affliction; for you ought to be like his soul and senses—active *and attentive in all things to him*[8] as to your bishop, *and father*[8] and master.

THAT A BISHOP OUGHT TO BE ORDAINED BY THREE OR BY TWO BISHOPS, BUT NOT BY ONE; FOR THAT WOULD BE INVALID.

XX. We command that a bishop be ordained by three bishops, or at least by two; but it is not lawful that he be set over you by one; for the testimony of two or three witnesses is more firm and secure. But a presbyter and a deacon are to be ordained by one bishop and the rest of the clergy. Nor must either a presbyter or a deacon ordain from the laity into the clergy; but the presbyter is only to teach, to offer, to baptize, to bless the people, and the deacon is to minister to the bishop, and to the presbyters, that is, to do the office of a ministering deacon, but not to meddle with the other offices.

[1] Matt. vi. 9, etc.
[2] Isa. liii. 11, LXX.
[3] Matt. xx. 28.
[4] John xv. 13.
[5] Matt. xx. 26, 27.
[6] Isa. liii. 11.
[7] John xiii. 4, 5.
[8] The portions in italics are not in one V. MS.

CONSTITUTIONS OF THE HOLY APOSTLES

BOOK IV.

SEC. I. — ON HELPING THE POOR.

THOSE WHO HAVE NO CHILDREN SHOULD ADOPT ORPHANS, AND TREAT THEM AS THEIR OWN CHILDREN.

I. WHEN any Christian becomes an orphan, whether it be a young man or a maid, it is good that some one of the brethren who is without a child should take the young man, and esteem him in the place of a son; and he that has a son about the same age, and that is marriageable, should marry the maid to him: for they which do so perform a great work, and become fathers to the orphans, and shall receive the reward of this charity from the Lord God. But if any one that walks in the way of man-pleasing is rich, and therefore is ashamed of orphans, the Father of orphans and Judge of widows will make provision for the orphans, but himself shall have such an heir as will spend what he has spared; and it shall happen to him according as it is said: "What things the holy people have not eaten, those shall the Assyrians eat." As also Isaiah says: "Your land, strangers devour it in your presence."[1]

HOW THE BISHOP OUGHT TO PROVIDE FOR THE ORPHANS.

II. Do you therefore, O bishops, be solicitous about their maintenance, being in nothing wanting to them; exhibiting to the orphans the care of parents; to the widows the care of husbands; to those of suitable age, marriage; to the artificer, work; to the unable, commiseration; to the strangers, an house; to the hungry, food; to the thirsty, drink; to the naked, clothing; to the sick, visitation; to the prisoners, assistance. Besides these, have a greater care of the orphans, that nothing may be wanting to them; and that as to the maiden, till she arrives at the age of marriage, and ye give her in marriage to a brother: to the young man assistance, that he may learn a trade, and may be maintained by the advantage arising from it; that so, when he is dextrous in the management of it, he may thereby be enabled to buy himself the tools of his trade, that so he may no longer burden any of the brethren, or their sincere love to him, but may support himself: for certainly he is a happy man who is able to support himself, and does not take up the place of the orphan, the stranger, and the widow.

WHO OUGHT TO BE SUPPORTED ACCORDING TO THE LORD'S CONSTITUTION.

III. Since even the Lord said: "The giver was happier than the receiver."[2] For it is again said by Him: "Woe to those that have, and receive in hypocrisy; or who are able to support themselves, yet will receive of others: for both of them shall give an account to the Lord God in the day of judgment." But an orphan who, by reason of his youth, or he that by the feebleness of old age, or the incidence of a disease, or the bringing up of many children, receives alms, such a one shall not only not be blamed, but shall be commended: for he shall be esteemed an altar to God, and be honoured by God, because of his zealous and constant prayers for those that give to him; not receiving idly, but to the uttermost of his power recompensing what is given him by his prayer. Such a one therefore shall be blessed by God in eternal life. But he that hath, and receives in hypocrisy or through idleness, instead of working and assisting others, shall be obnoxious to punishment before God, because he has snatched away the morsel of the needy.[3]

OF THE LOVE OF MONEY.

IV. For he that has money and does not bestow it upon others, nor use it himself, is like the serpent, which they say sleeps over the treasures; and of him is that scripture true which says, "He has gathered riches of which he shall not

---

1 Isa. i. 7.

2 Acts xx. 35.

3 [The early Church had a constant struggle with professional paupers. This entire book is a valuable contribution to social ethics. The problems of to-day confronted the Church then. Few wiser counsels have been recorded. — R.]

taste;"[1] and they will be of no use to him when he perishes justly. For it says, "Riches will not profit in the day of wrath." For such a one has not believed in God, but in his own gold; esteeming that his God, and trusting therein. Such a one is a dissembler of the truth, an accepter of persons, unfaithful, cheating, fearful, unmanly, light, of no value, a complainer, ever in pain, his own enemy, and nobody's friend. Such a one's money shall perish, and a man that is a stranger shall consume it, either by theft while he is alive, or by inheritance when he is dead. "For riches unjustly gotten shall be vomited up."[2]

WITH WHAT FEAR MEN OUGHT TO PARTAKE OF THE LORD'S OBLATIONS.

V. We exhort, therefore, the widows and orphans to partake of those things that are bestowed upon them with all fear, and all pious reverence, and to return thanks to God who gives food to the needy, and to lift up their eyes to Him. For, says He, "Which of you shall eat, or who shall drink without Him? For He openeth His hand, and filleth every living thing with His kindness: giving wheat to the young men, and wine to the maidens, and oil for the joy of the living, grass for the cattle, and green herb for the service of men, flesh for the wild beasts, seeds for the birds, and suitable food for all creatures."[3] Wherefore the Lord says:[4] "Consider the fowls *of heaven*,[5] that they sow not, *neither do they reap* nor gather into barns, and your Father feedeth them. Are not ye much better than they? Be not therefore solicitous, saying, What shall we eat? or what shall we drink? For your Father knoweth that ye have need of all these things."[6] Since ye therefore enjoy such a providential care from Him, and are partakers of the good things that are derived from Him, you ought to return praise to Him that receives the orphan and the widow, to Almighty God, through His beloved Son Jesus Christ our Lord; through whom[7] glory be to God in spirit and truth for ever. Amen.

WHOSE OBLATIONS ARE TO BE RECEIVED, AND WHOSE NOT TO BE RECEIVED.

VI. Now the bishop ought to know whose oblations he ought to receive, and whose he ought not. For he is to avoid corrupt dealers, and not receive their gifts. "For a corrupt dealer shall not be justified from sin."[8] For of them it was that Isaiah reproached Israel, and said, "Thy corrupt dealers mingle wine with water."[9] He is also to avoid fornicators, for "thou shalt not offer the hire of an harlot to the Lord."[10] He is also to avoid extortioners, and such as covet other men's goods, and adulterers; for the sacrifices of such as these are abominable with God. Also those that oppress the widow and overbear the orphan, and fill prisons with the innocent, and abuse their own servants wickedly, I mean with stripes, and hunger, and hard service, nay, destroy whole cities; do thou, O bishop, avoid such as these, and their odious oblations. Thou shalt also refuse rogues, and such pleaders that plead on the side of injustice, and idol-makers, and thieves, and unjust publicans, and those that deceive by false balances and deceitful measures, and a soldier who is a false accuser and not content with his wages, but does violence to the needy, a murderer, a cut-throat, and an unjust judge, a subverter of causes, him that lies in wait for men, a worker of abominable wickedness, a drunkard, a blasphemer, a sodomite, an usurer, and every one that is wicked and opposes the will of God. For the Scripture says that all such as these are abominable with God. For those that receive from such persons, and thereby support the widows and orphans, shall be obnoxious to the judgment-seat of God; as Adonias the prophet, in the book of Kings, when he disobeyed God, and both "eat bread and drank water in the place which the Lord had forbid him,"[11] because of the impiety of Jeroboam, was slain by a lion. For the bread which is distributed to the widows from labour is better, though it be short and little, than that from injustice and false accusation, though it be much and fine. For the Scripture says: "Better is a little to the righteous, than much riches of the sinners."[12] Now, although a widow, who eats and is filled from the impious, pray for them, she shall not be heard. For God, who knows the heart, with judgment has declared concerning the impious, saying, "If Moses and Samuel stand before my face in their behalf, I will not hear them;"[13] and, "Pray thou not for this people, and do not ask mercy for them, and do not intercede with me for them, for I will not hear thee."[14]

THAT THE OBLATIONS OF THE UNWORTHY, WHILE THEY ARE SUCH, DO NOT ONLY NOT PROPITIATE GOD, BUT, ON THE CONTRARY, PROVOKE HIM TO INDIGNATION.

VII. And not these only, but those that are in sin and have not repented, will not only not be

[1] Job xx. 18, LXX.; Prov. xi. 4.
[2] Job xx. 15, LXX.
[3] Eccles. ii. 25, LXX.; Ps. cxlv. 16; Zech. ix. 17, LXX.; Ps. civ. 14, 15.
[4] One V. MS. reads, "Thus also did the Lord exhort His disciples, saying."
[5] The words in italics are not in one V. MS.
[6] Matt. vi. 26, 31, 32.
[7] One V. MS. reads, "with whom be glory to Him, with the Spirit."
[8] Ecclus. xxvi. 29.
[9] Isa. i. 22.
[10] Deut. xxiii. 18.
[11] 1 Kings xiii.
[12] Ps. xxxvii. 16.
[13] Jer. xv. 1.
[14] Jer. vii. 16.

heard when they pray, but will provoke God to anger, as putting Him in mind of their own wickedness. Avoid therefore such ministrations, as you would the price of a dog and the hire of an harlot; for both of them are forbidden by the laws. For neither did Elisha receive the presents which were brought by Hazael,[1] nor Ahijah those from Jeroboam;[2] but if the prophets of God did not admit of presents from the impious, it is reasonable, O bishops, that neither should you. Nay, when Simon the magician offered money to me Peter and John,[3] and tried to obtain the invaluable grace by purchase, we did not admit it, but bound him with everlasting maledictions, because he thought to possess the gift of God, not by a pious mind towards God, but by the price of money. Avoid therefore such oblations to God's altar as are not from a good conscience. For says He: "Abstain from all injustice, and thou shalt not fear, and trembling shall not come nigh thee."[4]

THAT IT IS BETTER TO AFFORD, THOUGH IT BE INCONSIDERABLE AND FEW, CONTRIBUTIONS TO THE WIDOWS FROM OUR OWN LABOURS, THAN THOSE WHICH ARE MANY AND LARGE RECEIVED FROM THE UNGODLY; FOR IT IS BETTER TO PERISH BY FAMINE THAN TO RECEIVE AN OBLATION FROM THE UNGODLY.

VIII. But if ye say that those who give alms are such as these, and if we do not receive from them, whence shall we administer to the widows? And whence shall the poor among the people be maintained? Ye shall hear from us, that therefore have ye received the gift of the Levites, the oblations of your people, that ye might have enough for yourselves, and for those that are in want; and that ye might not be so straitened as to receive from the wicked. But if the churches be so straitened, it is better to perish than to receive anything from the enemies of God, to the reproach and abuse of His friends. For of such as these the prophet speaks: "Let not the oil of a sinner moisten my head."[5] Do ye therefore examine such persons, and receive from such as walk holily, and supply the afflicted. But receive not from those that are excommunicated, until they are thought worthy to become the members of the Church. But if a gift be wanting, inform the brethren, and make a collection from them, and thence minister to the orphans and widows in righteousness.

THAT THE PEOPLE OUGHT TO BE EXHORTED BY THE PRIEST TO DO GOOD TO THE NEEDY, AS SAYS SOLOMON THE WISE.

IX. Say unto the people under thee what Solomon the wise says: "Honour the Lord out of thy just labours, and pay thy first-fruits to Him out of thy fruits of righteousness, that thy garners may be filled with fulness of wheat, and thy presses may burst out with wine."[6] Therefore maintain and clothe those that are in want from the righteous labour of the faithful. And such sums of money as are collected from them in the manner aforesaid, appoint to be laid out in the redemption of the saints, the deliverance of slaves, and of captives, and of prisoners, and of those that have been abused, and of those that have been condemned by tyrants to single combat and death on account of the name of Christ. For the Scripture says: "Deliver those that are led to death, and redeem those that are ready to be slain, do not spare."[7]

A CONSTITUTION, THAT IF ANY ONE OF THE UNGODLY BY FORCE WILL CAST MONEY TO THE PRIESTS, THEY SPEND IT IN WOOD AND COALS, BUT NOT IN FOOD.

X. But if at any time you be forced unwillingly to receive money from any ungodly person, lay it out in wood and coals, that so neither the widow nor the orphan may receive any of it, or be forced to buy with it either meat or drink, which it is unfit to do. For it is reasonable that such gifts of the ungodly should be fuel for the fire, and not food for the pious. And this method is plainly appointed by the law,[8] when it calls a sacrifice kept too long a thing not fit to be eaten, and commands it to be consumed with fire. For such oblations are not evil in their nature, but on account of the mind of those that bring them. And this we ordain, that we may not reject those that come to us, as knowing that the common conversation of the pious has often been very profitable to the ungodly, but religious communion with them is alone hurtful. And so much, beloved, shall suffice to have spoken to you in order to your security.

SEC. II. — ON DOMESTIC AND SOCIAL LIFE.

OF PARENTS AND CHILDREN.

XI. Ye fathers, educate your children in the Lord, bringing them up in the nurture and admonition of the Lord; and teach them such trades as are agreeable and suitable to the word, lest

---

1 2 Kings viii. [Offerings to God are privileges of saints.]
2 1 Kings xiv.
3 Acts viii.
4 Isa. liv. 14.
5 Ps. cxli. 5.
6 Prov. iii. 9, etc.
7 Prov. xxiv. 11.
8 Lev. xix. 6.

they by such opportunity become extravagant, and continue without punishment from their parents, and so get relaxation before their time, and go astray from that which is good. Wherefore be not afraid to reprove them, and to teach them wisdom with severity. For your corrections will not kill them, but rather preserve them. As Solomon says somewhere in the book of Wisdom: "Chasten thy son, and he will refresh thee; so wilt thou have good hope of him. Thou verily shalt smite him with the rod, and shalt deliver his soul from death."[1] And again, says the same Solomon thus, "He that spareth his rod, hateth his son;"[2] and afterwards, "Beat his sides whilst he is an infant, lest he be hardened and disobey thee."[3] He, therefore, that neglects to admonish and instruct his own son, hates his own child. Do you therefore teach your children the word of the Lord. Bring them under with cutting stripes, and make them subject from their infancy, teaching them the Holy Scriptures, which are Christian and divine, and delivering to them every sacred writing, "not giving them such liberty that they get the mastery,"[4] and act against your opinion, not permitting them to club together for a treat with their equals. For so they will be turned to disorderly courses, and will fall into fornication; and if this happen by the carelessness of their parents, those that begat them will be guilty of their souls. For if the offending children get into the company of debauched persons by the negligence of those that begat them, they will not be punished alone by themselves; but their parents also will be condemned on their account. For this cause endeavour, at the time when they are of an age fit for marriage, to join them in wedlock, and settle them together, lest in the heat and fervour of their age their course of life become dissolute, and you be required to give an account by the Lord God in the day of judgment.

OF SERVANTS AND MASTERS.

XII. But as to servants, what can we say more than that the slave bring a good will to his master, with the fear of God, although he be impious and wicked,[5] but yet not to yield any compliance as to his worship? And let the master love his servant, although he be his superior. Let him consider wherein they are equal, even as he is a man. And let him that has a believing master[6] love him both as his master, and as of the same faith, and as a father, but still with the preservation of his authority as his master: "not as an eye-servant, but as a lover of his master; as knowing that God will recompense to him for his subjection."[7] In like manner, let a master who has a believing servant love him as a son or as a brother, on account of their communion in the faith, but still preserving the difference of a servant.

IN WHAT THINGS WE OUGHT TO BE SUBJECT TO THE RULERS OF THIS WORLD.

XIII. Be ye subject to all royal power and dominion in things which are pleasing to God, as to the ministers of God, and the punishers of the ungodly.[8] Render all the fear that is due to them, all offerings, all customs, all honour, gifts, and taxes.[9] For this is God's command, that you owe nothing to any one but the pledge of love, which God has commanded by Christ.[10]

OF VIRGINS.

XIV. Concerning virginity we have received no commandment;[11] but we leave it to the power of those that are willing, as a vow: exhorting them so far in this matter that they do not promise anything rashly; since Solomon says, "It is better not to vow, than to vow and not pay."[12] Let such a virgin, therefore, be holy in body and soul, as the temple of God,[13] as the house of Christ, as the habitation of the Holy Spirit. For she that vows ought to do such works as are suitable to her vow; and to show that her vow is real, and made on account of leisure for piety, not to cast a reproach on marriage. Let her not be a gadder abroad, nor one that rambles about unseasonably; not double-minded, but grave, continent, sober, pure, avoiding the conversation of many, and especially of those that are of ill reputation.[14]

---

1 Prov. xxix. 17, xix. 18, xxiii. 14.
2 Prov. xiii. 24.
3 Ecclus. xxx. 12.
4 Ecclus. xxx. 11.
5 See Eph. vi. 5; 1 Pet. ii. 18.
6 Col. iv. 1. See 1 Tim. vi. 2.
7 Eph. vi. 6; Col. iii. 22, 24.
8 See 1 Pet. ii. 13; Tit. iii. 1.
9 Rom. xiii. 1, 4, 7.
10 Rom. xiii. 8.
11 See 1 Cor. vii. 25.
12 Eccles. v. 5.
13 1 Cor. vii. 34.
14 [The absence of any marked ascetic tone in this passage is in sharp contrast with the pseudo-Clementine Epistles concerning virginity. See vol. viii. — R.]

CONSTITUTIONS OF THE HOLY APOSTLES

BOOK V.

SEC. I. — CONCERNING THE MARTYRS.

THAT IT IS REASONABLE FOR THE FAITHFUL TO SUPPLY THE WANTS OF THOSE WHO ARE AFFLICTED FOR THE SAKE OF CHRIST BY THE UNBELIEVERS, ACCORDING TO THE CONSTITUTION OF THE LORD.

I. IF any Christian, on account of the name of Christ, and love and faith towards God, be condemned by the ungodly to the games, to the beasts, or to the mines, do not ye overlook him; but send to him from your labour and your very sweat for his sustenance, and for a reward to the soldiers, that he may be eased and be taken care of; that, as far as lies in your power, your blessed brother may not be afflicted: for he that is condemned for the name of the Lord God is an holy martyr, a brother of the Lord, the son of the Highest, a receptacle of the Holy Spirit, by whom every one of the faithful has received the illumination of the glory of the holy Gospel, by being vouchsafed the incorruptible crown, and the testimony of Christ's sufferings, and the fellowship of His blood, to be made conformable to the death of Christ for the adoption of children. For this cause do you, all ye of the faithful, by your bishop, minister to the saints of your substance and of your labour. But if any one has not, let him fast a day, and set apart that, and order it for the saints. But if any one has superfluities, let him minister more to them according to the proportion of his ability. But if he can possibly sell all his livelihood, and redeem them out of prison, he will be blessed, and a friend of Christ. For if he that gives his goods to the poor be perfect, supposing his knowledge of divine things, much more is he so that does it on account of the martyrs. For such a one is worthy of God, and will fulfil His will by supplying those who have confessed Him before nations and kings, and the children of Israel; concerning whom our Lord declared, saying: "Whosoever shall confess me before men, him will I also confess before my Father."[1] And if these be such as to be attested to by Christ before His Father, you ought not to be ashamed to go to them in the prisons. For if you do this, it will be esteemed to you for a testimony, because the real trial was to them a testimony; and your readiness will be so to you, as being partakers of their combat: for the Lord speaks somewhere to such as these, saying: "Come, ye blessed of my Father, inherit the kingdom prepared for you from the foundation of the world. For I was an hungry, and ye gave me meat; I was thirsty, and ye gave me drink; I was a stranger, and ye took me in; naked, and ye clothed me; I was sick, and ye visited me; I was in prison, and ye came unto me. Then shall the righteous answer, and say, Lord, when saw we Thee an hungered, and fed Thee? or thirsty, and gave Thee drink? When saw we Thee naked, and clothed Thee? or sick, and visited Thee? When saw we Thee a stranger, and took Thee in? or in prison, and came unto Thee? And He will answer and say unto them, Inasmuch as ye have done it unto one of the least of these my brethren, ye have done it unto me. And these shall go away into life everlasting. Then shall He say unto them on His left hand, Depart from me, ye cursed, into everlasting fire, prepared for the devil and his angels. For I was hungry, and ye gave me no meat; I was thirsty, and ye gave me no drink; I was a stranger, and ye took me not in; naked, and ye clothed me not; sick, and in prison, and ye visited me not. Then shall they also answer and say, Lord when saw we Thee hungry, or thirsty, or a stranger, or naked, or sick, or in prison, and did not minister unto Thee? Then shall He answer and say unto them, Verily I say unto you, Inasmuch as ye have not done it unto one of the least of these, neither have ye done it unto me. And these shall go away unto everlasting punishment."[2]

[1] Matt. x. 32.

[2] Matt. xxv. 34, etc. Portions of the passage from Matthew are omitted in one V. MS.; and the conclusion, beginning with "Then shall they also," is entirely omitted. [The citation is quite accurate; ver. 46 is divided, doubtless for the sake of emphasis, and slightly modified. — R.]

THAT WE ARE TO AVOID INTERCOURSE WITH FALSE BRETHREN WHEN THEY CONTINUE IN THEIR WICKEDNESS.

II. But if any one who calls himself a brother is seduced by the evil one, and acts wickedness, and is convicted and condemned to death as an adulterer, or a murderer, depart from him, that ye may be secure, and none of you may be suspected as a partner in such an abominable practice; and that no evil report may be spread abroad, as if all Christians took a pleasure in unlawful actions. Wherefore keep far from them. But do you assist with all diligence those that for the sake of Christ are abused by the ungodly and shut up in prison, or who are given over to death, or bonds, or banishment, in order to deliver your fellow-members from wicked hands. And if any one who accompanies with them is caught, and falls into misfortune, he is blessed, because he is partaker with the martyr, and is one that imitates the sufferings of Christ; for we ourselves also, when we oftentimes received stripes from Caiaphas, and Alexander, and Annas, for Christ's sake, "went out rejoicing that we were counted worthy to suffer such things for our Saviour."[1] Do you also rejoice when ye suffer such things, for ye shall be blessed in that day.[2]

THAT WE OUGHT TO AFFORD AN HELPING HAND TO SUCH AS ARE SPOILED FOR THE SAKE OF CHRIST, ALTHOUGH WE SHOULD INCUR DANGER OURSELVES.

III. Receive also those that are persecuted on account of the faith, and who "fly from city to city"[3] on account of the Lord's commandment; and assist them as martyrs, rejoicing that ye are made partakers of their persecution, as knowing that they are esteemed blessed by the Lord; for Himself says: "Blessed are ye when men shall reproach you, and persecute you, and say all manner of evil against you falsely, for my sake. Rejoice, and be exceeding glad, because your reward is great in heaven: for so persecuted they the prophets which were before us."[4] And again: "If they have persecuted me, they will also persecute you."[5] And afterwards: "If they persecute you in this city, flee ye to another. For in the world ye have tribulation: for they shall deliver you into the synagogues; and ye shall be brought before rulers and kings for my sake, and for a testimony to them."[6] And, "He that endureth unto the end, the same shall be saved."[7] For he that is persecuted for the sake of the faith, and bears witness in regard to Him, *Christ*, and endures, is truly a man of God.

THAT IT IS AN HORRIBLE AND DESTRUCTIVE THING TO DENY CHRIST.

IV. But he that denies himself to be a Christian, that he may not be hated of men, and so loves his own life more than he does the Lord, in whose hand his breath is, is wretched and miserable, as being detestable and abominable, who desires to be the friend of men, but is the enemy of God, having no longer his portion with the saints, but with those that are accursed; choosing instead of the kingdom of the blessed, that eternal fire which is prepared for the devil and his angels: not being any longer hated by men, but rejected by God, and cast out from His presence. For of such a one our Lord declared, saying: "Whosoever shall deny me before men, and shall be ashamed of my name, I also will deny and be ashamed of him before my Father which is in heaven."[8] And again He speaks thus to us ourselves, His disciples: "He that loveth father or mother more than me, is not worthy of me; and he that loveth son or daughter more than me, is not worthy of me; and he that taketh not his cross, and followeth after me, is not worthy of me. He that findeth his life, shall lose it; and he that loseth his life for my sake, shall find it. For what is a man profited, if he shall gain the whole world, and lose his own soul? or what shall a man give in exchange for his soul?"[9] And afterwards: "Fear not them that kill the body, but are not able to kill the soul; but rather fear Him who is able to destroy both soul and body in hell."[10]

THAT WE OUGHT TO IMITATE CHRIST IN SUFFERING, AND WITH ZEAL TO FOLLOW HIS PATIENCE.

V. Every one therefore who learns any art, when he sees his master by his diligence and skill perfecting his art, does himself earnestly endeavour to make what he takes in hand like to it. If he is not able, he is not perfected in his work. We therefore who have a Master, our Lord Jesus Christ, why do we not follow His doctrine?—since He renounced repose, pleasure, glory, riches, pride, the power of revenge, His mother and brethren, nay, and moreover His own life, on account of His piety towards His Father, and His love to us the race of mankind; and suffered not only persecution and stripes, reproach and mockery, but also crucifixion, that He might save the penitent, both Jews and Gentiles. If therefore He for our sakes renounced His repose, was not ashamed

1 Acts iv. 6, v. 40, 41.
2 *Vid.* Luke vi. 22, 23.
3 Matt. x. 23.
4 Matt. v. 11, 12.
5 John xv. 20.
6 Matt. x. 23, 17; John xvi. 33.
7 Matt. x. 22.
8 Matt. x. 33; Luke ix. 26.
9 Matt. x. 37, xvi. 26.
10 Matt. x. 28.

of the cross, and did not esteem death inglorious, why do not we imitate His sufferings, and renounce on His account even our own life, with that patience which He gives us? For He did all for our sakes, but we do it for our own sakes: for He does not stand in need of us, but we stand in need of His mercy. He only requires the sincerity and readiness of our faith, as the Scripture says: "If thou beest righteous, what doest thou give to Him? or what will He receive at thy hand? Thy wickedness is to a man like thyself, and thy righteousness to a son of man." [1]

THAT A BELIEVER OUGHT NEITHER RASHLY TO RUN INTO DANGER THROUGH SECURITY, NOR TO BE OVER-TIMOROUS THROUGH PUSILLANIMITY, BUT TO FLY AWAY FOR FEAR; YET THAT IF HE DOES FALL INTO THE ENEMY'S HAND, TO STRIVE EARNESTLY, UPON ACCOUNT OF THE CROWN THAT IS LAID UP FOR HIM.

VI. Let us therefore renounce our parents, and kinsmen, and friends, and wife, and children, and possessions, and all the enjoyments of life, when any of these things become an impediment to piety. For we ought to pray that we may not enter into temptation; but if we be called to martyrdom, with constancy to confess His precious name, and if on this account we be punished, let us rejoice, as hastening to immortality. When we are persecuted, let us not think it strange; let us not love the present world, nor the praises which come from men, nor the glory and honour of rulers, according as some of the Jews wondered at the mighty works of our Lord, yet did not believe on Him, for fear of the high priests and the rest of the rulers: "For they loved the praise of men more than the praise of God." [2] But now, by confessing a good confession, we not only save ourselves, but we confirm those who are newly illuminated, and strengthen the faith of the catechumens. But if we remit any part of our confession, and deny godliness by the faintness of our persuasion, and the fear of a very short punishment, we not only deprive ourselves of everlasting glory, but we shall also become the causes of the perdition of others; and shall suffer double punishment, as affording suspicion, by our denial that that truth which we gloried in so much before is an erroneous doctrine. Wherefore neither let us be rash and hasty to thrust ourselves into dangers, for the Lord says: "Pray that ye fall not into temptation: the spirit indeed is willing, but the flesh is weak." [3] Nor let us, when we do fall into dangers, be fearful or ashamed of our profession. For if a person, by the denial of his own hope, which is Jesus the Son of God, should be delivered from a temporary death, and the next day should fall dangerously sick upon his bed, with a distemper in his bowels, his stomach, or his head, or any of the incurable diseases, as a consumption, or gangrene, or looseness, or iliac passion, or dropsy, or colic, and has a sudden catastrophe, and departs this life; is not he deprived of the things present, and loses those eternal? Or rather, he is within the verge of eternal punishment, "and goes into outer darkness, where is weeping and gnashing of teeth." [4] But let him who is vouchsafed the honour of martyrdom rejoice with joy in the Lord, as obtaining thereby so great a crown, and departing out of this life by his confession. Nay, though he be but a catechumen, let him depart without trouble; for his suffering for Christ will be to him a more genuine baptism, because he does really die with Christ, but the rest only in a figure. Let him therefore rejoice in the imitation of his Master, since is it thus ordained: "Let every one be perfect, as his Master is." [5] Now his and our Master, Jesus the Lord, was smitten for our sake: He underwent reproaches and revilings with long-suffering. He was spit upon, He was smitten on the face, He was buffeted; and when He had been scourged, He was nailed to the cross. He had vinegar and gall to drink; and when He had fulfilled all things that were written, He said to His God and Father, "Into Thy hands I commend my spirit." [6] Wherefore let him that desires to be His disciple earnestly follow His conflicts: let him imitate His patience, knowing that, although he be burned in the fire by men, he will suffer nothing, like the three children; [7] or if he does suffer anything, he shall receive a reward from the Lord, believing in the one and the only true God and Father, through Jesus Christ, the great High Priest, and Redeemer of our souls, and rewarder of our sufferings. To whom be glory for ever. Amen.

SEVERAL DEMONSTRATIONS CONCERNING THE RESURRECTION, CONCERNING THE SIBYL, AND WHAT THE STOICS SAY CONCERNING THE BIRD CALLED THE PHŒNIX.

VII. For the Almighty God Himself will raise us up through our Lord Jesus Christ, according to His infallible promise, and grant us a resurrection with all those that have slept from the beginning of the world; and we shall then be such as we now are in our present form, without any defect or corruption. For we shall rise incorruptible: whether we die at sea, or are scat-

[1] Job xxxv. 7, 8. One V. MS. reads "piety," instead of "wickedness," in the last sentence.
[2] John xii. 43.
[3] Matt. xxvi. 41. [See *De Fuga*, vol. iv. p. 119.]
[4] Matt. viii. 12.
[5] Luke vi. 40.
[6] Luke xxiii. 46.
[7] Dan. iii.

tered on the earth, or are torn to pieces by wild beasts and birds, He will raise us by His own power; for the whole world is held together by the hand of God. Now He says: "An hair of your head shall not perish."[1] Wherefore He exhorts us, saying: "In your patience possess ye your souls."[2] But as concerning the resurrection of the dead, and the recompense of reward for the martyrs, Gabriel speaks to Daniel: "And many of them that sleep shall arise out of the dust of the earth, some to everlasting life, and some to shame and everlasting contempt. And they that understand shall shine as the sun, and as the firmament, and as the stars."[3] Therefore the most holy Gabriel foretold that the saints should shine like the stars: for His sacred name did witness to them, that they might understand the truth. Nor is a resurrection only declared for the martyrs, but for all men, righteous and unrighteous, godly and ungodly, that every one may receive according to his desert. For God, says the Scripture, "will bring every work into judgment, with every secret thing, whether it be good or whether it be evil."[4] This resurrection was not believed by the Jews, when of old they said, "Our bones are withered, and we are gone."[5] To whom God answered, and said: "Behold, I open your graves, and will bring you out of them; and I will put my Spirit into you, and ye shall live: and ye shall know that I the Lord have spoken it, and will do it." And He says by Isaiah: "The dead shall rise, and those that are in the graves shall be raised up. And those that rest in the earth shall rejoice, for the dew which is from Thee shall be healing to them."[6] There are indeed many and various things said concerning the resurrection, and concerning the continuance of the righteous in glory, and concerning the punishment of the ungodly, their fall, rejection, condemnation, shame, "eternal fire, and endless worm."[7] Now that, if it had pleased Him that all men should be immortal, it was in His power, He showed in the examples of Enoch and Elijah, while He did not suffer them to have any experience of death. Or if it had pleased Him in every generation to raise those that died, that this also He was able to do He hath made manifest both by Himself and by others; as when He raised the widow's son[8] by Elijah, and the Shunammite's son[9] by Elisha. But we are persuaded that death is not a retribution of punishment, because even the saints have undergone it; nay, even the Lord of the saints, Jesus Christ, the life of them that believe, and the resurrection of the dead. Upon this account, therefore, according to the ancient practice, for those who live in the great city, after the combats He brings a dissolution for a while, that, when He raises up every one, He may either reject him or crown him. For He that made the body of Adam out of the earth will raise up the bodies of the rest, and that of the first man, after their dissolution, (to pay what is owing to the rational nature of man; we mean the continuance in being through all ages. He, therefore, who brings on the dissolution, will Himself procure the resurrection. And He that said, "The Lord took dust from the ground, and formed man, and breathed into his face the breath of life, and man became a living soul,"[10] added after the disobedience, "Earth thou art, and unto earth shalt thou return;"[11] the same promised us a resurrection afterwards.[12]) For says He: "All that are in the graves shall hear the voice of the Son of God, and they that hear shall live."[13] Besides these arguments, we believe there is to be a resurrection also from the resurrection of our Lord. For it is He that raised Lazarus, when he had been in the grave four days,[14] and Jairus' daughter,[15] and the widow's son.[16] It is He that raised Himself by the command of the Father in the space of three days, who is the pledge of our resurrection. For says He: "I am the resurrection and the life."[17] Now He that brought Jonas[18] in the space of three days, alive and unhurt, out of the belly of the whale, and the three children out of the furnace of Babylon, and Daniel out of the mouth of the lions,[19] does not want power to raise us up also. But if the Gentiles laugh at us, and disbelieve our Scriptures, let at least their own prophetess Sibylla[20] oblige them to believe, who says thus to them in express words:—

"But when all things shall be reduced to dust and ashes,
And the immortal God who kindled the fire shall have quenched it,
God shall form those bones and that ashes into a man again,
And shall place mortal men again as they were before.
And then shall be the judgment, wherein God will do justice,
And judge the world again. But as many mortals as have sinned through impiety
Shall again be covered under the earth;
But so many as have been pious shall live again in the world.

1 Luke xxi. 18.
2 Luke xxi. 19.
3 Dan. xii. 2, 3.
4 Eccles. xii. 14.
5 Ezek. xxxvii. 11, etc.
6 Isa. xxvi. 19.
7 Isa. lxvi. 24.
8 1 Kings xvii.
9 2 Kings iv.
10 Gen. ii. 7.
11 Gen. iii. 19.
12 The part within parentheses is not in one of the V. MSS.
13 John v. 25.
14 John xi.
15 Mark v.
16 Luke vii.
17 John xi. 25.
18 Jonah ii.
19 Dan. iii., vi.
20 [Compare pp. 256, 257, *supra*.]

When God puts His Spirit into them, and gives those
at once that are godly both life and favour,
Then shall all see themselves."[1]

If, therefore, this prophetess confesses the resurrection, and does not deny the restoration of all things, and distinguishes the godly from the ungodly, it is in vain for them to deny our doctrine. Nay, indeed, they say they can show a resemblance of the resurrection, while they do not themselves believe the things they declare: for they say that there is a bird single in its kind which affords a copious demonstration of the resurrection, which they say is without a mate, and the only one in the creation. They call it a phœnix, and relate that every five hundred years it comes into Egypt, to that which is called the altar of the sun, and brings with it a great quantity of cinnamon, and cassia, and balsam-wood, and standing towards the east, as they say, and praying to the sun, of its own accord is burnt, and becomes dust; but that a worm arises again out of those ashes, and that when the same is warmed it is formed into a new-born phœnix; and when it is able to fly, it goes to Arabia, which is beyond the Egyptian countries. If, therefore, as even themselves say, a resurrection is exhibited by the means of an irrational bird, wherefore do they vainly disparage our accounts, when we profess that He who by His power brings that into being which was not in being before, is able to restore this body, and raise it up again after its dissolution? For on account of this full assurance of hope we undergo stripes, and persecutions, and deaths. Otherwise we should to no purpose undergo such things if we had not a full assurance of these promises, whereof we profess ourselves to be the preachers. As, therefore, we believe Moses when he says, "In the beginning God made the heaven and the earth;"[2] and we know that He did not want matter, but by His will alone brought those things into being which Christ was commanded to make; we mean the heaven, the earth, the sea, the light, the night, the day, the luminaries, the stars, the fowls, the fishes, and four-footed beasts, the creeping things, the plants, and the herbs; so also will He raise all men up by His will, as not wanting any assistance. For it is the work of the same power to create the world and to raise the dead. And then He made man, who was not a man before, of different parts, giving to him a soul made out of nothing. But now He will restore the bodies, which have been dissolved, to the souls that are still in being: for the rising again belongs to things laid down, not to things which have no being. He therefore that made the original bodies out of nothing, and fashioned various *forms* of them, will also again revive and raise up those that are dead. For He that formed man in the womb out of a little seed, and created in him a soul which was not in being before, — as He Himself somewhere speaks to Jeremiah, "Before I formed thee in the womb I knew thee;"[3] and elsewhere, "I am the Lord who established the heaven, and laid the foundations of the earth, and formed the spirit of man in him,"[4] — will also raise up all men, as being His workmanship; as also the divine Scripture testifies that God said to Christ, His only-begotten, "Let us make man after our image, and after our likeness. And God made man: after the image of God made He him; male and female made He them."[5] And the most divine and patient Job, of whom the Scripture says that it is written, that "he was to rise again with those whom the Lord raises up,"[6] speaks to God thus: "Hast not Thou milked me like milk, and curdled me like cheese? Thou hast clothed me with skin and flesh, and hast fenced me with bones and sinews. Thou hast granted me life and favour, and Thy visitation hath preserved my spirit. Having these things within me, I know that Thou canst do all things, and that nothing is impossible with Thee."[7] Wherefore also[8] our Saviour and Master Jesus Christ says, that "what is impossible with men is possible with God."[9] And David, the beloved of God, says: "Thine hands have made me, and fashioned me."[10] And again: "Thou knowest my frame."[11] And afterward: "Thou hast fashioned me, and laid Thine hand upon me. The knowledge of Thee is declared to be too wonderful for me; it is very great, I cannot attain unto it."[12] "Thine eyes did see my substance, being yet imperfect; and all men shall be written in Thy book."[13] Nay, and Isaiah says in his prayer to Him: "We are the clay, and Thou art the framer of us."[14] If, therefore, man be His workmanship, made by Christ, by Him most certainly will he after he is dead be raised again, with intention either of being crowned for his good actions or punished for his transgressions. But if He, being the legislator, judges with righteousness; as He punishes the ungodly, so does He do good to and saves the faithful. And those saints who for His sake have been slain by men, "some of them He will make light as the stars, and make others bright as the luminaries,"[15] as Gabriel said to Daniel.

---

1 *Orac. Sibyl.*, l. iv. *in fin.* [See p. 324, *supra*.]
2 Gen. i. 1.
3 Jer. i. 5.
4 Zech. xii. 1.
5 Gen. i. 26, 27.
6 *In fin.* Job in LXX.
7 Job x. 10.
8 The words from "Wherefore also" to "possible with God" are omitted in one V. MS., and noticed as spurious in the other.
9 Luke xviii. 27.
10 Ps. cxix. 73.
11 Ps. ciii. 14.
12 Ps. cxxxix. 5, 6.
13 Ps. cxxxix. 16.
14 Isa. lxiv. 8.
15 Dan. xii. 3.

All we of the faithful, therefore, who are the disciples of Christ, believe His promises. For He that has promised it cannot lie; as says the blessed prophet David: "The Lord is faithful in all His words, and holy in all His works."[1] For He that framed for Himself a body out of a virgin, is also the Former of other men. And He that raised Himself from the dead, will also raise again all that are laid down. He who raises wheat out of the ground with many stalks from one grain, He who makes the tree that is cut down send forth fresh branches, He that made Aaron's dry rod put forth buds,[2] will raise us up in glory; He that raised Him up that had the palsy whole,[3] and healed him that had the withered hand,[4] He that supplied a defective part to him that was born blind from clay and spittle,[5] will raise us up; He that satisfied five thousand men with five loaves and two fishes, and caused a remainder of twelve baskets,[6] and out of water made wine,[7] and sent a piece of money out of a fish's mouth[8] by me Peter to those that demanded tribute, will raise the dead. For we testify all these things concerning Him, and the prophets testify the other. We who have eaten and drunk with Him, and have been spectators of His wonderful works, and of His life, and of His conduct, and of His words, and of His sufferings, and of His death, and of His resurrection from the dead, and who associated with Him forty days after His resurrection,[9] and who received a command from Him to preach the Gospel to all the world, and to make disciples of all nations,[10] and to baptize them into His death by the authority of the God of the universe, who is His Father, and by the testimony of the Spirit, who is His Comforter, — we teach you all these things which He appointed us by His constitutions, before "He was received up in our sight into heaven,"[11] to Him that sent Him. And if you will believe, you shall be happy; but if you will not believe, we shall be found innocent, and clear from your incredulity.

CONCERNING JAMES THE BROTHER OF THE LORD, AND STEPHEN THE FIRST MARTYR.

VIII. Now concerning the martyrs, we say to you that they are to be had in all honour with you, as we honour the blessed James the bishop, and the holy Stephen our fellow-servant. For these are reckoned blessed by God, and are honoured by holy men, who were pure from all transgressions, immoveable when tempted to sin, or persuaded from good works, without dispute deserving encomiums: of whom also David speaks, "Precious in the sight of the Lord is the death of His holy ones;"[12] and Solomon says, "The memory of the just is with encomiums:"[13] of whom also the prophet speaks, "Righteous men are taken away."[14]

CONCERNING FALSE MARTYRS.

IX. These things we have said concerning those that in truth have been martyrs for Christ, but not concerning false martyrs, concerning whom the oracle speaks, "The name of the ungodly is extinguished."[13] For "a faithful witness will not lie, but an unjust witness inflames lies."[15] For he that departs this life in his testimony without lying, for the sake of the truth, is a faithful martyr, worthy to be believed in such things wherein he strove for the word of piety by his own blood.

SEC. II. — ALL ASSOCIATION WITH IDOLS IS TO BE AVOIDED.

A MORAL ADMONITION, THAT WE ARE TO ABSTAIN FROM VAIN TALKING, OBSCENE TALKING, JESTING, DRUNKENNESS, LASCIVIOUSNESS, AND LUXURY.

X. Now we exhort you, brethren and fellow-servants, to avoid vain talk and obscene discourses, and jestings, drunkenness, lasciviousness, luxury, unbounded passions, with foolish discourses, since we do not permit you so much as on the Lord's days, which are days of joy, to speak or act anything unseemly; for the Scripture somewhere says: "Serve the Lord with fear, and rejoice unto Him with trembling."[16] Even your very rejoicings therefore ought to be done with fear and trembling: for a Christian who is faithful ought neither to repeat an heathen hymn nor an obscene song, because he will be obliged by that hymn to make mention of the idolatrous names of demons; and instead of the Holy Spirit, the wicked one will enter into him.

AN ADMONITION INSTRUCTING MEN TO AVOID THE ABOMINABLE SIN OF IDOLATRY.

XI. You are also forbidden to swear by them, or to utter their abominable names through your mouth, and to worship them, or fear them as gods; for they are not gods, but either wicked demons or the ridiculous contrivances of men. For somewhere God says concerning the Israelites: "They have forsaken me, and sworn by them that are no gods."[17] And afterwards: "I

[1] Ps. cxlv. 17.
[2] Num. xvii. 8.
[3] Matt. ix. 2, etc.
[4] Mark iii. 1, etc.
[5] John ix. 1, etc.
[6] Matt. xiv. 17, etc.
[7] John ii. 3, etc.
[8] Matt. xvii. 24, etc.
[9] Acts i. 3.
[10] Matt. xxviii. 19.
[11] Acts i. 9.
[12] Ps. cxvi. 15.
[13] Prov. x. 7.
[14] Isa. lvii. 1, LXX.
[15] Prov. xiv. 5.
[16] Ps. ii. 11.
[17] Jer. v. 7.

will take away the names of your idols out of their mouth."[1] And elsewhere: "They have provoked me to jealousy with them that are no gods; they have provoked me to anger with their idols."[2] And in all the Scriptures these things are forbidden by the Lord God.

THAT WE OUGHT NOT TO SING AN HEATHEN OR AN OBSCENE SONG, NOR TO SWEAR BY AN IDOL; BECAUSE IT IS AN IMPIOUS THING, AND CONTRARY TO THE KNOWLEDGE OF GOD.

XII. Nor do the legislators give us only prohibitions concerning idols, but also warn us concerning the luminaries, not to swear by them, nor to serve them. For they say: "Lest, when thou seest the sun, and the moon, and the stars, thou shouldest be seduced to worship them."[3] And elsewhere: "Do not ye learn to walk after the ways of the heathen, and be not afraid of the signs of heaven."[4] For the stars and the luminaries were given to men to shine upon them, but not for worship; although the Israelites, by the perverseness of their temper, "worshipped the creature instead of the Creator,"[5] and acted insultingly to their Maker, and admired the creature more than is fit. And sometimes they made a calf, as in the wilderness;[6] sometimes they worshipped Baalpeor;[7] another time Baal,[8] and Thamuz,[9] and Astarte of Sidon;[10] and again Moloch and Chamos;[11] another time the sun,[12] as it is written in Ezekiel; nay, and besides, brute creatures, as among the Egyptians Apis, and the Mendesian goat, and gods of silver and gold, as in Judea. On account of all which things He threatened them, and said by the prophet: "Is it a small thing to the house of Judah to do these abominations which they have done? For they have filled the land with their wickedness, to provoke me to anger: and, behold, they are as those that mock. And I will act with anger. Mine eye shall not spare, neither will I have mercy; and they shall cry in mine ears with a great voice, and I will not hearken unto them."[13] Consider, beloved, how many things the Lord declares against idolaters, and the worshippers of the sun and moon. Wherefore it is the duty of a man of God, as he is a Christian, not to swear by the sun, or by the moon, or by the stars; nor by the heaven, nor by the earth, nor by any of the elements, whether small or great. For if our Master charged us not to swear by the true God, that our word might be firmer than an oath, nor by heaven itself, for that is a piece of heathen wickedness, nor by Jerusalem, nor by the sanctuary of God, nor the altar, nor the gift, nor the gilding of the altar, nor one's own head,[14] for this custom is a piece of Judaic corruption, and on that account was forbidden; and if He exhorts the faithful that their yea be yea, and their nay, nay, and says that "what is more than these is of the evil one," how much more blameable are those who appeal to deities falsely so called as the objects of an oath, and who glorify imaginary beings instead of those that are real, whom God for their perverseness "delivered over to foolishness, to do those things that are not convenient!"[15]

SEC. III. — ON FEAST DAYS AND FAST DAYS.

A CATALOGUE OF THE FEASTS OF THE LORD WHICH ARE TO BE KEPT, AND WHEN EACH OF THEM OUGHT TO BE OBSERVED.

XIII. Brethren, observe the festival days; and first of all the birthday which you are to celebrate on the twenty-fifth of the ninth month; after which let the Epiphany be to you the most honoured, in which the Lord made to you a display of His own Godhead, and let it take place on the sixth of the tenth month; after which the fast of Lent is to be observed by you as containing a memorial of our Lord's mode of life and legislation. But let this solemnity be observed before the fast of the passover, beginning from the second day of the week, and ending at the day of the preparation. After which solemnities, breaking off your fast, begin the holy week of the passover, fasting in the same all of you with fear and trembling, praying in them for those that are about to perish.

CONCERNING THE PASSION OF OUR LORD, AND WHAT WAS DONE ON EACH DAY OF HIS SUFFERINGS; AND CONCERNING JUDAS, AND THAT JUDAS WAS NOT PRESENT WHEN THE LORD DELIVERED THE MYSTERIES TO HIS DISCIPLES.

XIV. For they began to hold a council against the Lord on the second day of the week, in the first month, which is Xanthicus; and the deliberation continued on the third day of the week; but on the fourth day they determined to take away His life by crucifixion. And Judas knowing this, who for a long time had been perverted, but was then smitten by the devil himself with the love of money, although he had been long entrusted with the purse,[16] and used to steal what was set apart for the needy, yet was he not cast off by the Lord, through much long-suffering;

1 Zech. xiii. 2.
2 Deut. xxxii. 21.
3 Deut. iv. 19.
4 Jer. x. 2.
5 Rom. i. 25.
6 Ex. xxxii. 4.
7 Num. xxv. 3.
8 Judg. ii. 13.
9 Ezek. viii. 14.
10 1 Kings xi. 5.
11 1 Kings xi. 7.
12 Ezek. viii. 16.
13 Ezek. viii. 17, 18.
14 Matt. v. 34, xxiii. 16.
15 Rom. i. 28.
16 John xii. 6.

nay, and when we were once feasting with Him, being willing both to reduce him to his duty and instruct us in His own foreknowledge, He said: "Verily, verily, I say unto you, that one of you will betray me;" and every one of us saying, "Is it I?"[1] And the Lord being silent, I, who was one of the twelve, and more beloved by Him than the rest, arose up from lying in His bosom, and besought Him to tell who it should be that should betray Him. Yet neither then did our good Lord declare His name, but gave two signs of the betrayer: one by saying, "he that dippeth with me in the dish;" a second, "to whom I shall give the sop when I have dipped it." Nay, although he himself said, "Master, is it I?" the Lord did not say Yes, but, "Thou hast said." And being willing to affright him in the matter, He said: "Woe to that man by whom the Son of man is betrayed! good were it for him if he had never been born. Who, when he had heard that, went his way, and said to the priests, What will ye give me, and I will deliver Him unto you? And they bargained with him for thirty pieces of silver."[2] And the scripture was fulfilled, which said, "And they took[3] the thirty pieces of silver, the price of Him that was valued, whom they of the children of Israel did value, and gave them for the house of the potter."[4] And on the fifth day of the week, when we had eaten the passover with Him, and when Judas had dipped his hand into the dish, and received the sop, and was gone out by night, the Lord said to us: "The hour is come that ye shall be dispersed, and shall leave me alone;"[5] and every one vehemently affirming that they would not forsake Him, I Peter adding this promise, that I would even die with Him, He said, "Verily I say unto thee, Before the cock crows, thou shalt thrice deny that thou knowest me."[6] And when He had delivered to us the representative mysteries of His precious body and blood, Judas not being present with us, He went out to the Mount of Olives, near the brook Cedron, where there was a garden;[7] and we were with Him, and sang an hymn according to the custom.[8] And being separated not far[9] from us, He prayed to His Father, saying: "Father, remove this cup away from me; yet not my will, but Thine be done."[10] And when He had done this thrice, while we out of despondency of mind were fallen asleep, He came and said: "The hour is come, and the Son of man is betrayed into the hands of sinners. And behold Judas, and with him a multitude of ungodly men,"[11] to whom he shows the signal by which he was to betray Him — a deceitful kiss. But they, when they had received the signal agreed on, took hold of the Lord; and having bound Him, they led Him to the house of Caiaphas the high priest, wherein were assembled many, not the people, but a great rout, not an holy council, but an assembly of the wicked and council of the ungodly, who did many things against Him, and left no kind of injury untried, spitting upon Him, cavilling at Him, beating Him, smiting Him on the face, reviling Him, tempting Him, seeking vain divination instead of true prophecies from Him, calling Him a deceiver, a blasphemer, a transgressor of Moses, a destroyer of the temple, a taker away of sacrifices, an enemy to the Romans, an adversary to Cæsar. And these reproaches did these bulls and dogs[12] in their madness cast upon Him, till it was very early in the morning, and then they lead Him away to Annas, who was father-in-law to Caiaphas; and when they had done the like things to Him there, it being the day of the preparation, they delivered Him to Pilate the Roman governor, accusing Him of many and great things, none of which they could prove. Whereupon the governor, as out of patience with them, said: "I find no cause against Him."[13] But they bringing two lying witnesses, wished to accuse the Lord falsely; but they being found to disagree, and so their testimony not conspiring together, they altered the accusation to that of treason, saying, "This fellow says that He is a king, and forbids to give tribute to Cæsar."[14] And themselves became accusers, and witnesses, and judges, and authors of the sentence, saying, "Crucify Him, crucify Him;"[15] that it might be fulfilled which is written by the prophets concerning Him, "Unjust witnesses were gathered together against me, and injustice lied to itself;"[16] and again, "Many dogs compassed me about, the assembly of the wicked laid siege against me;"[17] and elsewhere, "My inheritance became to me as a lion in a wood, and has sent forth her voice against me."[18] Pilate therefore, disgracing his authority by his pusillanimity, convicts himself of wickedness by regarding the multitude more than this just person, and bearing witness to Him that He was innocent, yet as guilty delivering Him up to the punishment of the cross, although the Romans had made laws that no man unconvicted should be put to death. But

1 Matt. xxvi. 21, 22; John xiii. 21, etc.
2 Matt. xxvi. 15.
3 The words from "And they took" to "house of the potter" are wanting in one V. MS. The other reads "field" of the potter, instead of "house."
4 Matt. xxvii. 9, 10.
5 John xvi. 32; Matt. xxvi. 31.
6 Luke xxii. 34.
7 John xviii. 1.
8 Matt. xxvi. 30.
9 "Not far," the reading of the V. MSS. The others read: "And being separated from us, He prayed earnestly."
10 Luke xxii. 42; Matt. xxvi. 39, 42.
11 Luke xxii. 47; Matt. xxvi. 47.
12 Ps. xxii. 12, 16.
13 Luke xxiii. 14; John xviii. 38.
14 Luke xxiii. 2.
15 Luke xxiii. 21.
16 Ps. xxvii. 12.
17 Ps. xxii. 16.
18 Jer. xii. 8.

the executioners took the Lord of glory and nailed Him to the cross, crucifying Him indeed at the sixth hour, but having received the sentence of His condemnation at the third hour. After this they gave to Him vinegar to drink, mingled with gall. Then they divided His garments by lot. Then they crucified two malefactors with Him, on each side one, that it might be fulfilled which was written: "They gave me gall to eat, and when I was thirsty they gave me vinegar to drink."[1] And again: "They divided my garment among themselves, and upon my vesture have they cast lots."[2] And in another place: "And I was reckoned with the transgressors."[3] Then there was darkness for three hours, from the sixth to the ninth, and again light in the evening; as it is written: "It shall not be day nor night, and at the evening there shall be light."[4] All which things,[5] when those malefactors saw that were crucified with Him, the one of them reproached Him as though He was weak and unable to deliver Himself; but the other rebuked the ignorance of his fellow, and turning to the Lord, as being enlightened by Him, and acknowledging who He was that suffered, he prayed that He would remember him in His kingdom hereafter.[6] He then presently granted him the forgiveness of his former sins, and brought him into paradise to enjoy the mystical good things; who also cried out about the ninth hour, and said to His Father: "My God! my God! why hast Thou forsaken me?"[7] And a little afterward, when He had cried with a loud voice, "Father, forgive them, for they know not what they do,"[8] and had added, "Into Thy hands I commit my spirit," He gave up the ghost,[9] and was buried before sunset in a new sepulchre. But when the first day of the week dawned He arose from the dead, and fulfilled those things which before His passion He foretold to us, saying: "The Son of man must continue in the heart of the earth three days and three nights."[10] And when He was risen from the dead, He appeared first to Mary Magdalene, and Mary the mother of James, then to Cleopas in the way, and after that to us His disciples, who had fled away for fear of the Jews, but privately were very inquisitive about Him.[11] But these things are also written in the Gospel.

[1] Ps. lxix. 21.
[2] Ps. xxii. 18.
[3] Isa. liii. 12.
[4] Zech. xiv. 7. The V. MSS. read: "On that day there will not be light, but there will be cold and frost for one day."
[5] The words from "All which things" to "mystical good things" are omitted in one V. MS.
[6] Luke xxiii. 39, etc.
[7] Matt. xxvii. 46.
[8] Luke xxiii. 34.
[9] Luke xxiii. 46.
[10] Matt. xii. 40.
[11] Mark xvi. 9; John xx. 11, etc.; Luke xxiv. 18; Mark xvi. 14.

OF THE GREAT WEEK, AND ON WHAT ACCOUNT THEY ENJOIN US TO FAST ON WEDNESDAY AND FRIDAY.

XV. He therefore charged us Himself to fast these six days on account of the impiety and transgression of the Jews, commanding us withal to bewail over them, and lament for their perdition. For even He Himself "wept over them, because they knew not the time of their visitation."[12] But He commanded us to fast on the fourth and sixth days of the week; the former on account of His being betrayed, and the latter on account of His passion. But He appointed us to break our fast on the seventh day at the cock-crowing, but to fast on the Sabbath-day. Not that the Sabbath-day is a day of fasting, being the rest from the creation, but because we ought to fast on this one Sabbath only, while on this day the Creator was under the earth. For on their very feast-day they apprehended the Lord, that that oracle might be fulfilled which says: "They placed their signs in the middle of their feast, and knew them not."[13] Ye ought therefore to bewail over them, because when the Lord came they did not believe on Him, but rejected His doctrine, judging themselves unworthy of salvation. You therefore are happy who once were not a people, but are now an holy nation, delivered from the deceit of idols, from ignorance, from impiety, who once had not obtained mercy, but now have obtained mercy through your hearty obedience: for to you, the converted Gentiles, is opened the gate of life, who formerly were not beloved, but are now beloved; a people ordained for the possession of God, to show forth His virtues, concerning whom our Saviour said, "I was found of them that sought me not; I was made manifest to them that asked not after me. I said, Behold me, to a nation which did not call upon my name."[14] For when ye did not seek after Him, then were ye sought for by Him; and you who have believed in Him have hearkened to His call, and have left the madness of polytheism, and have fled to the true monarchy, to Almighty God, through Christ Jesus, and are become the completion of the number of the saved — "ten thousand times ten thousand, and thousands of thousands;"[15] as it is written in David, "A thousand[16] shall fall beside thee, and ten thousand at thy right hand;"[17] and again, "The chariots of God are by tens of thousands, and thousands of the prosperous."[18] But unto unbelieving Israel

[12] Luke xix. 44.
[13] Ps. lxxiv. 4.
[14] Isa. lxv. 1.
[15] Dan. vii. 10.
[16] The words from "A thousand" to "of the prosperous" are not in the V. MSS.
[17] Ps. xci. 7.
[18] Ps. lxviii. 17.

He says: "All the day long have I stretched out mine hands to a disobedient and gainsaying people, which go in a way that is not good, but after their own sins, a people provoking me before my face."[1]

AN ENUMERATION OF THE PROPHETICAL PREDICTIONS WHICH DECLARE CHRIST, WHOSE COMPLETION THOUGH THE JEWS SAW, YET OUT OF THE EVIL TEMPER OF THEIR MIND THEY DID NOT BELIEVE HE WAS THE CHRIST OF GOD, AND CONDEMNED THE LORD OF GLORY TO THE CROSS.

XVI. See how the people provoked the Lord by not believing in Him! Therefore He says: "They provoked the Holy Spirit, and He was turned to be their enemy."[2] For blindness is cast upon them, by reason of the wickedness of their mind, because when they saw Jesus they did not believe Him to be the Christ of God, who was before all ages[3] begotten of Him, His only-begotten Son, God the Word, whom they did not own through their unbelief, neither on account of His mighty works, nor yet on account of the prophecies which were written concerning Him. For that He was to be born of a virgin, they read this prophecy: "Behold, a virgin shall be with child, and shall bring forth a Son, and they shall call His name Emanuel."[4] "For to us a Child is born, to us a Son is given, whose government is upon His shoulders; and His name is called the Angel of His Great Council, the Wonderful Counsellor, the Mighty God, the Potentate, the Prince of Peace, the Father of the Future Age."[5] Now, that because of their exceeding great wickedness they would not believe in Him, the Lord shows in these words: "Who hath believed our report? and to whom hath the arm of the Lord been revealed?"[6] And afterward: "Hearing ye shall hear, and shall not understand; and seeing ye shall see, and shall not perceive: for the heart of this people is waxed gross."[7] Wherefore knowledge was taken from them, because seeing they overlooked, and hearing they heard not. But to you, the converted of the Gentiles, is the kingdom given, because you, who knew not God, have believed by preaching, and "have known Him, or rather are known of Him,"[8] through Jesus, the Saviour and Redeemer of those that hope in Him. For ye are translated from your former vain and tedious mode of life, and have contemned the lifeless idols, and despised the demons, which are in darkness, and have run to the "true light,"[9] and by it have "known the one and only true God and Father,"[10] and so are owned to be heirs of His kingdom. For since ye have "been baptized into the Lord's death,"[11] and into His resurrection, as "new-born babes,"[12] ye ought to be wholly free from all sinful actions; "for you are not your own, but His that bought you"[13] with His own blood. For concerning the former Israel the Lord speaks thus, on account of their unbelief: "The kingdom of God shall be taken from them, and given to a nation bringing forth the fruits thereof;"[14] that is to say, that having given the kingdom to you, who were once far estranged from Him, He expects the fruits of your gratitude and probity. For ye are those that were once sent into the vineyard, and did not obey, but these they that did obey;[15] but you have repented of your denial, and you work therein now. But they, being uneasy on account of their own covenants, have not only left the vineyard uncultivated, but have also killed the stewards of the Lord of the vineyard,[16] — one with stones, another with the sword; one they sawed asunder,[17] another they slew in the holy place, "between the temple and the altar;"[18] nay, at last they "cast the Heir Himself out of the vineyard, and slew Him."[19] And by them He was rejected as an unprofitable stone,[20] but by you was received as the corner-stone. Wherefore He says concerning you: "A people whom I knew not have served me, and at the hearing of the ear have they obeyed me."[21]

HOW THE PASSOVER OUGHT TO BE CELEBRATED.

XVII. It is therefore your duty, brethren, who are redeemed by the precious blood of Christ, to observe the days of the passover exactly, with all care, after the vernal equinox, lest ye be obliged to keep the memorial of the one passion twice in a year. Keep it once only in a year for Him that died but once.

Do not you yourselves compute, but keep it when your brethren of the circumcision do so: keep it together with them; and if they err in their computation, be not you concerned. Keep your nights of watching in the middle of the days of unleavened bread. And when the Jews are feasting, do you fast and wail over them, because on the day of their feast they crucified Christ;

1 Isa. lxv. 2.
2 Isa. lxiii. 10.
3 One V. MS. omits "ages," and the other "begotten of Him."
4 Isa. vii. 14; Matt. i. 23.
5 Isa. ix. 6. [Justin Martyr, p. 236, n. 8, vol. i., this series.]
6 Isa. liii. 1.
7 Isa. vi. 9, 10.
8 Gal. iv. 9.
9 John i. 9.
10 John xvii. 3.
11 Rom. vi. 3.
12 1 Pet. ii. 2.
13 1 Cor. vi. 19, 20.
14 Matt. xxi. 43.
15 Matt. xxi. 28, etc.
16 Matt. xxi. 35.
17 Heb. xi. 37.
18 Matt. xxiii. 35.
19 Matt. xxi. 39.
20 Matt. xxi. 42.
21 Ps. xviii. 43, 44.

and while they are lamenting and eating unleavened bread in bitterness, do you feast.[1] But no longer be careful to keep the feast with the Jews, for we have now no communion with them; for they have been led astray in regard to the calculation itself, which they think they accomplish perfectly, that they may be led astray on every hand, and be fenced off from the truth. But do you observe carefully the vernal equinox, which occurs on the twenty-second of the twelfth month, which is Dystros (March), observing carefully until the twenty-first of the moon, lest the fourteenth of the moon shall fall on another week, and an error being committed, you should through ignorance celebrate the passover twice in the year, or celebrate the day of the resurrection of our Lord on any other day than a Sunday.

A CONSTITUTION CONCERNING THE GREAT PASSOVER WEEK.

XVIII. Do you therefore fast on the days of the passover, beginning from the second day of the week until the preparation, and the Sabbath, six days, making use of only bread, and salt, and herbs, and water for your drink; but do you abstain on these days from wine and flesh, for they are days of lamentation and not of feasting. Do ye who are able fast the day of the preparation and the Sabbath-day entirely, tasting nothing till the cock-crowing of the night; but if any one is not able to join them both together, at least let him observe the Sabbath-day; for the Lord says somewhere, speaking of Himself: "When the bridegroom shall be taken away from them, in those days shall they fast."[2] In these days, therefore, He was taken from us by the Jews, falsely so named, and fastened to the cross, and "was numbered among the transgressors."[3]

CONCERNING THE WATCHING ALL THE NIGHT OF THE GREAT SABBATH, AND CONCERNING THE DAY OF THE RESURRECTION.

XIX. Wherefore we exhort you to fast on those days, as we also fasted till the evening, when He was taken away from us; but on the rest of the days, before the day of the preparation, let every one eat at the ninth hour, or at the evening, or as every one is able. But from the even of the fifth day till cock-crowing break your fast when it is daybreak of the first day of the week, which is the Lord's day. From the even till cock-crowing keep awake, and assemble together in the church, watch and pray, and entreat God; reading, when you sit up all night, the Law, the Prophets, and the Psalms, until cock-crowing, and baptizing your catechumens, and reading the Gospel with fear and trembling, and speaking to the people such things as tend to their salvation: put an end to your sorrow, and beseech God that Israel may be converted, and that He will allow them place of repentance, and the remission of their impiety; for the judge, who was a stranger, "washed his hands, and said, I am innocent of the blood of this just person: see ye to it. But Israel cried out, His blood be on us, and on our children."[4] And when Pilate said, "Shall I crucify your king? they cried out, We have no king but Cæsar: crucify Him, crucify Him; for every one that maketh himself a king speaketh against Cæsar." And, "If thou let this man go, thou art not Cæsar's friend."[5] And Pilate the governor and Herod the king commanded Him to be crucified; and that oracle was fulfilled which says, "Why did the Gentiles rage, and the people imagine vain things? The kings of the earth set themselves, and the rulers were gathered together against the Lord, and against His Christ;"[6] and, "They cast away the Beloved, as a dead man, who is abominable."[7] And since He was crucified on the day of the Preparation, and rose again at break of day on the Lord's day, the scripture was fulfilled which saith, "Arise, O God; judge the earth: for Thou shalt have an inheritance in all the nations;"[8] and again, "I will arise, saith the Lord; I will put Him in safety, I will wax bold through Him;"[9] and, "But Thou, Lord, have mercy upon me, and raise me up again, and I shall requite them."[10] For this reason do you also, now the Lord is risen, offer your sacrifice, concerning which He made a constitution by us, saying, "Do this for a remembrance of me;"[11] and thenceforward leave off your fasting, and rejoice, and keep a festival, because Jesus Christ, the pledge of our resurrection, is risen from the dead. And let this be an everlasting ordinance till the consummation of the world, until the Lord come. For to Jews the Lord is still dead, but to Christians He is risen: to the former, by their unbelief; to the latter, by their full assurance of faith. For the hope in Him is immortal and eternal life. After eight days let there be another feast observed with honour, the eighth day itself, on which He gave me Thomas, who was hard of belief, full assurance, by showing me the print of the nails, and the wound made in His side by the spear.[12] And again, from the first Lord's

1 This italicized passage does not occur in the MSS., but is taken from Epiphanius. It is believed to be genuine, in which case what follows must be regarded as the work of the interpolator. [See Epiphanius, tom. iv. p. 29, ed. Oehler, 1861.]
2 Matt. ix. 15; Mark ii. 20; Luke v. 35.
3 Isa. liii. 12.
4 Matt. xxvii. 24, 25.
5 John xix. 15, 6, 12.
6 Ps. ii. 1, 2.
7 Isa. xiv. 19.
8 Ps. lxxxii. 8.
9 Ps. xii. 5.
10 Ps. xli. 10.
11 Luke xxii. 19.
12 John xx. 25.

day count forty days, from the Lord's day till the fifth day of the week, and celebrate the feast of the ascension of the Lord, whereon He finished all His dispensation and constitution, and returned to that God and Father that sent Him, and sat down at the right hand of power, and remains there until His enemies are put under His feet; who also will come at the consummation of the world with power and great glory, to judge the quick and the dead, and to recompense to every one according to his works. And then shall they see the beloved Son of God whom they pierced;[1] and when they know Him, they shall mourn for themselves, tribe by tribe, and their wives apart.[2]

A PROPHETIC PREDICTION CONCERNING CHRIST JESUS.

XX. For even now, on the tenth day of the month Gorpiæus, when they assemble together, they read the Lamentations of Jeremiah, in which it is said, "The Spirit before our face, Christ the Lord was taken in their destructions;"[3] and Baruch, in whom it is written, "This is our God; no other shall be esteemed with Him. He found out every way of knowledge, and showed it to Jacob His son, and Israel His beloved. Afterwards He was seen upon earth, and conversed with men."[4] And when they read them, they lament and bewail, as themselves suppose, that desolation which happened by Nebuchadnezzar; but, as the truth shows, they unwillingly make a prelude to that lamentation which will overtake them. But after ten days from the ascension, which from the first Lord's day is the fiftieth day, do ye keep a great festival: for on that day, at the third hour, the Lord Jesus sent on us the gift of the Holy Ghost, and we were filled with His energy, and we "spake with new tongues, as that Spirit did suggest to us;"[5] and we preached both to Jews and Gentiles, that He is the Christ of God, who is "determined by Him to be the Judge of quick and dead."[6] To Him did Moses bear witness, and said: "The Lord received fire from the Lord, and rained it down."[7] Him did Jacob see as a man, and said: "I have seen God face to face, and my soul is preserved."[8] Him did Abraham entertain, and acknowledge to be the Judge, and his Lord.[9] Him did Moses see in the bush;[10] concerning Him did he speak in Deuteronomy: "A Prophet will the Lord your God raise up unto you out of your brethren, like unto me; Him shall ye hear in all things, whatsoever He shall say unto you. And it shall be, that every soul that will not hear that Prophet, shall be destroyed from among his people."[11] Him did Joshua the son of Nun see, as the captain of the Lord's host, in armour, for their assistance against Jericho; to whom he fell down, and worshipped, as a servant does to his master.[12] Him Samuel knew as the "Anointed of God,"[13] and thence named the priests and the kings the anointed. Him David knew, and sung an hymn concerning Him, "A song concerning the Beloved;"[14] and adds in his person, and says, "Gird Thy sword upon Thy thigh, O Thou who art mighty in Thy beauty and renown: go on, and prosper, and reign, for the sake of truth, and meekness, and righteousness; and Thy right hand shall guide Thee after a wonderful manner. Thy darts are sharpened, O Thou that art mighty; the people shall fall under Thee in the heart of the king's enemies. Wherefore God, Thy God, hath anointed Thee with the oil of gladness above Thy fellows." Concerning Him also spake Solomon, as in His person: "The Lord created me the beginning of His ways, for His works: before the world He founded me, in the beginning before He made the earth, before the fountains of waters came, before the mountains were fastened; He begat me before all the hills."[15] And again: "Wisdom built herself an house."[16] Concerning Him also Isaiah said: "A Branch shall come out of the root of Jesse, and a Flower shall spring out of his root." And, "There shall be a root of Jesse; and He that is to rise to reign over the Gentiles, in Him shall the Gentiles trust."[17] And Zechariah says: "[18] Behold, thy King cometh unto thee, just, and having salvation; meek, and riding upon an ass, and upon a colt, the foal of an ass."[19] Him Daniel describes as "the Son of man coming to the Father,"[20] and receiving all judgment and honour from Him; and as "the stone cut out of the mountain without hands, and becoming a great mountain, and filling the whole earth,"[21] dashing to pieces the many governments of the smaller countries, and the polytheism of gods, but preaching the one God, and ordaining the monarchy of the Romans. Concerning Him also did Jeremiah prophesy, saying: "The Spirit before His face, Christ the Lord, was taken in their snares: of whom we said, Under His shadow

1 Zech. xii. 10; John xix. 37.
2 The words "and their wives apart" are not in one V. MS.
3 Lam. iv. 20.
4 Bar. iii. 35-37.
5 Acts ii. 4.
6 Acts x. 42.
7 Gen. xix. 24.
8 Gen. xxxii. 30.
9 Gen. xviii. 25, 27.
10 Ex. iii. 2.
11 Deut. xviii. 15.
12 Josh. v. 14.
13 1 Sam. xii. 3.
14 Ps. xlv.
15 Prov. viii. 22-25.
16 Prov. ix. 1.
17 Isa. xi. 1, 10.
18 One V. MS. inserts: "Rejoice greatly, O daughter of Zion."
19 Zech. ix. 9.
20 Dan. vii. 13.
21 Dan. ii. 34.

we shall live among the Gentiles."[1] Ezekiel also, and the following prophets, affirm everywhere that He is the Christ, the Lord, the King, the Judge, the Lawgiver, the Angel of the Father, the only-begotten God. Him therefore do we also preach to you, and declare Him to be God the Word, who ministered to His God and Father for the creation of the universe. By believing in Him you shall live, but by disbelieving you shall be punished. For "he that is disobedient to the Son shall not see life, but the wrath of God abideth on him."[2] Therefore, after you have kept the festival of Pentecost, keep one week more festival, and after that fast; for it is reasonable to rejoice for the gift of God, and to fast after that relaxation: for both Moses and Elijah fasted forty days, and Daniel for "three weeks of days did not eat desirable bread, and flesh and wine did not enter into his mouth."[3] And blessed Hannah, when she asked for Samuel, said: "I have not drunk wine nor strong drink, and I pour out my soul before the Lord."[4] And the Ninevites, when they fasted three days and three nights,[5] escaped the execution of wrath. And Esther, and Mordecai, and Judith,[6] by fasting, escaped the insurrection of the ungodly Holofernes and Haman. And David says: "My knees are weak through fasting, and my flesh faileth for *want of* oil."[7] Do you therefore fast, and ask your petitions of God. We enjoin you to fast every fourth day of the week, and every day of the preparation, and the surplusage of your fast bestow upon the needy; every Sabbath-day excepting one, and every Lord's day, hold your solemn assemblies, and rejoice: for he will be guilty of sin who fasts on the Lord's day, being the day of the resurrection, or during the time of Pentecost, or, in general, who is sad on a festival day to the Lord. For on them we ought to rejoice, and not to mourn.

1 Lam. iv. 20.
2 John iii. 36.
3 Ex. xxxiv. 28; 1 Kings xix. 8; Dan. x. 2, 3.
4 1 Sam. i. 15.
5 Jonah iii. 5.
6 Esth. iv. 16; Judith viii. 6.
7 Ps. cix. 24.

CONSTITUTIONS OF THE HOLY APOSTLES

BOOK VI.

SEC. I.—ON HERESIES.

WHO THEY WERE THAT VENTURED TO MAKE SCHISMS, AND DID NOT ESCAPE PUNISHMENT.

I. ABOVE all things, O bishop, avoid the sad and dangerous and most atheistical heresies, eschewing them as fire that burns those that come near to it. Avoid also schisms: for it is neither lawful to turn one's mind towards wicked heresies, nor to separate from those of the same sentiment out of ambition. For some who ventured to set up such practices of old did not escape punishment. For Dathan and Abiram,[1] who set up in opposition to Moses, were swallowed up into the earth. But Corah, and those two hundred and fifty who with him raised a sedition against Aaron, were consumed by fire. Miriam also, who reproached Moses, was cast out of the camp for seven days; for she said that Moses had taken an Ethiopian to wife.[2] Nay, in the case of Azariah and Uzziah,[3] the latter of which was king of Judah, but venturing to usurp the priesthood, and desiring to offer incense, which it was not lawful for him to do, was hindered by Azariah the high priest, and the fourscore priests; and when he would not obey he found the leprosy to arise in his forehead, and he hastened to go out, because the Lord had reproved him.

THAT IT IS NOT LAWFUL TO RISE UP EITHER AGAINST THE KINGLY OR THE PRIESTLY OFFICE.

II. Let us therefore, beloved, consider what sort of glory that of the seditious is, and what their condemnation. For if he that rises up against kings is worthy of punishment, even though he be a son or a friend, how much more he that rises up against the priests! For by how much the priesthood is more noble than the royal power, as having its concern about the soul, so much has he a greater punishment who ventures to oppose the priesthood, than he who ventures to oppose the royal power, although neither of them goes unpunished. For neither did Absalom nor Abdadan[4] escape without punishment; nor Corah and Dathan.[1] The former rose against David, and strove concerning the kingdom; the latter against Moses, concerning pre-eminence. And they both spake evil; Absalom of his father David, as of an unjust judge, saying to every one: "Thy words are good, but there is no one that will hear thee, and do thee justice. Who will make me a ruler?"[5] But Abdadan: "I have no part in David, nor any inheritance in the son of Jesse."[6] It is plain that he could not endure to be under David's government, of whom God spake: "I have found David the son of Jesse, a man after my heart, who will do all my commands."[7] But Dathan and Abiram, and the followers of Corah, said to Moses: "Is it a small thing that thou hast brought us out of the land of Egypt, out of a land flowing with milk and honey? And why hast thou put out our eyes? And wilt thou rule over us?" And they gathered together against him a great congregation; and the followers of Corah said: "Has God spoken alone to Moses? Why is it that He has given the high-priesthood to Aaron alone? Is not all the congregation of the Lord holy? And why is Aaron alone possessed of the priesthood?"[8] And before this, one said: "Who made thee a ruler and a judge over us?"[9]

CONCERNING THE VIRTUE OF MOSES AND THE INCREDULITY OF THE JEWISH NATION, AND WHAT WONDERFUL WORKS GOD DID AMONG THEM.

III. And they raised a sedition against Moses the servant of God, the meekest of all men,[10] and faithful, and affronted[11] so great a man with the highest ingratitude; him who was their lawgiver, and guardian, and high priest, and king, the ad-

---

1 Num. xvi.
2 Num. xii. 1.
3 2 Chron. xxvi.

4 2 Sam. xviii.-xx.
5 2 Sam. xv. 3.
6 2 Sam. xx. 1.
7 Acts xiii. 22.
8 Num. xvi. 13, xii. 2, xvi. 3.
9 Ex. ii. 14.
10 Num. xii. 3.
11 The words from "and affronted" to "by his holiness" are not in one V. MS.

ministrator of divine things; one that showed as a creator the mighty works of the Creator; the meekest man, freest from arrogance, and full of fortitude, and most benign in his temper; one who had delivered them from many dangers, and freed them from several deaths by his holiness; who had done so many signs and wonders from God before the people, and had performed glorious and wonderful works for their benefit; who had[1] brought the ten plagues upon the Egyptians; who had divided the Red Sea, and had separated the waters as a wall on this side and on that side, and had led the people through them as through a dry wilderness,[2] and had drowned Pharaoh and the Egyptians, and all that were in company with them;[3] and had made the fountain sweet for them with wood, and had brought water out of the stony rock for them when they were thirsty;[4] and had given them manna out of heaven, and had distributed flesh to them out of the air;[5] and had afforded them a pillar of fire in the night to enlighten and conduct them, and a pillar of a cloud to shadow them in the day, by reason of the violent heat of the sun;[6] and had exhibited to them the law of God, engraven from the mouth, and hand, and writing of God, in tables of stone, the perfect number of ten commandments;[7] "to whom God spake face to face, as if a man spake to his friend;"[8] of whom He said, "And there arose not a prophet like unto Moses."[9] Against him arose the followers of Corah, and the Reubenites,[10] and threw stones at Moses, who prayed, and said: "Accept not Thou their offering."[11] And the glory of God appeared, and sent some down into the earth, and burnt up others with fire; and so, as to those ringleaders of this schismatical deceit which said, "Let us make ourselves a leader,"[12] the earth opened its mouth, and swallowed them up, and their tents, and what appertained to them, and they went down alive into hell; but He destroyed the followers of Corah with fire.

SEC. II. — HISTORY AND DOCTRINES OF HERESIES.

THAT SCHISM IS MADE NOT BY HIM WHO SEPARATES HIMSELF FROM THE UNGODLY, BUT WHO DEPARTS FROM THE GODLY.

IV. If therefore God inflicted punishment immediately on those that made a schism on account of their ambition, how much rather will He do it upon those who are the leaders of impious heresies! Will not He inflict severer punishment on those that blaspheme His providence or His creation? But do you, brethren, who are instructed out of the Scripture, take care not to make divisions in opinion, nor divisions in unity. For those who set up unlawful opinions are marks of perdition to the people. In like manner, do not you of the laity come near to such as advance doctrines contrary to the mind of God; nor be you partakers of their impiety. For says God: "Separate yourselves from the midst of these men, lest you perish together with them."[13] And again: "Depart from the midst of them, and separate yourselves, says the Lord, and touch not the unclean thing, and I will receive you."[14]

UPON WHAT ACCOUNT ISRAEL, FALSELY SO NAMED, IS REJECTED BY GOD, DEMONSTRATED FROM THE PROPHETIC PREDICTIONS.

V. For those are most certainly to be avoided who blaspheme God. The greatest part of the ungodly, indeed, are ignorant of God; but these men, as fighters against God, are possessed with a wilful evil disposition, as with a disease. For from the wickedness of these heretics "pollution is gone out upon all the earth,"[15] as says the prophet Jeremiah. For the wicked synagogue is now cast off by the Lord God, and His house is rejected by Him, as He somewhere speaks: "I have forsaken mine house, I have left mine inheritance."[16] And again, says Isaiah: "I will neglect my vineyard, and it shall not be pruned nor digged, and thorns shall spring up upon it, as upon a desert; and I will command the clouds that they rain no rain upon it."[17] He has therefore "left His people as a tent in a vineyard, and as a garner in a fig or olive yard, and as a besieged city."[18] He has taken away from them the Holy Spirit, and the prophetic rain, and has replenished His Church with spiritual grace, as the "river of Egypt in the time of first-fruits;"[19] and has advanced the same "as an house upon an hill, or as an high mountain; as a mountain fruitful for milk and fatness, wherein it has pleased God to dwell. For the Lord will inhabit therein to the end."[20] And He says in Jeremiah: "Our sanctuary is an exalted throne of glory."[21] And He says in Isaiah: "And it shall come to pass in the last days, that the mountain of the Lord shall be glorious, and the house of the Lord shall

1 The words from "who had" to "Egyptians" are not in one V. MS.
2 Ex. vii., etc.
3 Ex. xiv. 28.
4 Ex. xvii. 6.
5 Ex. xvi.
6 Ex. xiii. 21.
7 Ex. xxxi., etc.
8 Ex. xxxiii. 11.
9 Deut. xxxiv 10.
10 Num. xiv. 10.
11 Num. xvi. 15.
12 Num. xiv. 5.

13 Num. xvi. 21.
14 2 Cor. vi. 17.
15 Jer. xxiii. 15.
16 Jer. xii. 7.
17 Isa v. 6.
18 Isa. i. 8.
19 See Ecclus. xxiv. 25.
20 Ps. lxviii. 16.
21 Jer. xvii. 12.

be upon the top of the mountains, and shall be advanced above the hills."[1] Since, therefore, He has forsaken His people, He has also left His temple desolate, and rent the veil of the temple, and took from them the Holy Spirit; for says He, "Behold, your house is left unto you desolate."[2] And He has bestowed upon you, the converted of the Gentiles, spiritual grace, as He says by Joel: "And it shall come to pass after these things, saith God, that I will pour out of my Spirit upon all flesh; and your sons shall prophesy, and your daughters shall see visions, and your old men shall dream dreams."[3] For God has taken away all the power and efficacy of His word, and such like visitations, from that people, and has transferred it to you, the converted of the Gentiles. For on this account the devil himself is very angry at the holy Church of God: he is removed to you, and has raised against you adversities, seditions, and reproaches, schisms, and heresies. For he had before subdued that people to himself, by their slaying of Christ. But you who have left his vanities he tempts in different ways, as he did the blessed Job.[4] For indeed he opposed that great high priest Joshua the son of Josedek;[5] and he oftentimes sought to sift us, that our faith might fail.[6] But our Lord and Master, having brought him to trial, said unto him: "The Lord rebuke thee, O devil; and the Lord, who hath chosen Jerusalem, rebuke thee. Is not this plucked out of the fire as a brand?"[7] And who said then to those that stood by the high priest, "Take away his ragged garments from him;" and added, "Behold, I have taken thine iniquities away from thee;" He will say now, as He said formerly of us when we were assembled together, "I have prayed that your faith may not fail."[8]

THAT EVEN AMONG THE JEWS THERE AROSE THE DOCTRINE OF SEVERAL HERESIES HATEFUL TO GOD.

VI. For even the Jewish nation had wicked heresies: for of them were the Sadducees, who do not confess the resurrection of the dead; and the Pharisees, who ascribe the practice of sinners to fortune and fate; and the Basmotheans, who deny providence, and say that the world is made by spontaneous motion, and take away the immortality of the soul; and the Hemerobaptists, who every day, unless they wash, do not eat, — nay, and unless they cleanse their beds and tables, or platters and cups and seats, do not make use of any of them; and those who are newly risen amongst us, the Ebionites, who will have the Son of God to be a mere man, begotten by human pleasure, and the conjunction of Joseph and Mary. There are also those that separate themselves from all these, and observe the laws of their fathers, and these are the Essenes. These, therefore, arose among the former people. And now the evil one, who is wise to do mischief, and as for goodness, knows no such good thing, has cast out some from among us, and has wrought by them heresies and schisms.

WHENCE THE HERESIES SPRANG, AND WHO WAS THE RINGLEADER OF THEIR IMPIETY.

VII. Now the original of the new heresies began thus: the devil entered into one Simon, of a village called Gitthæ, a Samaritan, by profession a magician, and made him the minister of his wicked design.[9] For when Philip our fellow-apostle,[10] by the gift of the Lord and the energy of His Spirit, performed the miracles of healing in Samaria, insomuch that the Samaritans were affected, and embraced the faith of the God of the universe, and of the Lord Jesus, and were baptized into His name; nay, and that Simon himself, when he saw the signs and wonders which were done without any magic ceremonies, fell into admiration, and believed, and was baptized, and continued in fasting and prayer, — we heard of the grace of God which was among the Samaritans by Philip, and came down[11] to them; and enlarging much upon the word of doctrine, we laid our hands upon all that were baptized, and we conferred upon them the participation of the Spirit. But when Simon saw that the Spirit was given to believers by the imposition of our hands, he took money, and offered it to us, saying, "Give me also the power, that on whomsoever I also shall lay my hand, he may receive the Holy Ghost;"[12] being desirous that as the devil[13] deprived Adam by his tasting of the tree of that immortality which was promised him, so also that Simon might entice us by the receiving of money, and might thereby cut us off from the gift of God,[14] that so by exchange we might sell to him for money the inestimable gift of the Spirit. But as we were all troubled at this offer, I Peter, with a fixed attention on that malicious serpent which was in him, said to Simon: "Let thy money go with thee to perdition, because thou hast thought to purchase the gift of God with money. Thou hast no part in this matter, nor lot in this faith;

1 Isa ii. 2.
2 Matt. xxiii. 38.
3 Joel ii. 28.
4 Job i., etc.
5 Zech. iii. 1.
6 Luke xxii. 31.
7 Zech. iii. 2, etc.
8 Luke xxii. 32.
9 Acts viii.
10 [Either an ignorant error or a peculiar use of a technical word (p. 383, *supra*) to signify a missionary. See the note, book viii. sec. 3, cap. 17, *infra*.]
11 [Were sent, rather. See Acts viii. 14.]
12 Acts viii. 19.
13 "The devil:" this reading is adopted from the V. MSS.
14 The V. MSS. insert here: "Simon, therefore, being moved by the devil, brought the money."

for thy heart is not right in the sight of God. Repent therefore of this thy wickedness, and pray to the Lord, if perhaps the thought of thine heart may be forgiven thee. For I perceive thou art in the gall of bitterness and the bond of iniquity."[1] But then Simon was terrified, and said: "I entreat you, pray ye to the Lord for me, that none of those things which ye have spoken come upon me."[2]

WHO WERE THE SUCCESSORS OF SIMON'S IMPIETY, AND WHAT HERESIES THEY SET UP.

VIII. But when we went forth among the Gentiles to preach the word of life, then the devil wrought in the people to send after us false apostles to the corrupting of the word; and they sent forth one Cleobius, and joined him with Simon, and these became disciples to one Dositheus, whom they despising, put him down from the principality. Afterwards also others were the authors of absurd doctrines: Cerinthus, and Marcus, and Menander, and Basilides, and Saturnilus. Of these some own the doctrine of many gods, some only of three, but contrary to each other, without beginning, and ever with one another, and some of an infinite number of them, and those unknown ones also. And some reject marriage; and their doctrine is, that it is not the appointment of God; and others abhor some kinds of food: some are impudent in uncleanness, such as those who are falsely called Nicolaitans. And Simon meeting me Peter, first at Cæsarea Stratonis (where the faithful Cornelius, a Gentile, believed on the Lord Jesus by me), endeavoured to pervert the word of God; there being with me the holy children, Zacchæus, who was once a publican, and Barnabas; and Nicetas and Aquila, brethren of Clement the bishop and citizen of Rome, who was the disciple of Paul, our fellow-apostle and fellow-helper in the Gospel. I thrice discoursed before them with him concerning the true Prophet, and concerning the monarchy of God; and when I had overcome him by the power of the Lord, and had put him to silence, I drove him away into Italy.

HOW SIMON, DESIRING TO FLY BY SOME MAGICAL ARTS, FELL DOWN HEADLONG FROM ON HIGH AT THE PRAYERS OF PETER, AND BRAKE HIS FEET, AND HANDS, AND ANKLE-BONES.

IX. Now when he was in Rome, he mightily disturbed the Church, and subverted many, and brought them over to himself, and astonished the Gentiles with his skill in magic, insomuch that once, in the middle of the day, he went into their theatre, and commanded the people that they should bring me also by force into the theatre, and promised he would fly in the air; and when all the people were in suspense at this, I prayed by myself. And indeed he was carried up into the air by demons, and did fly on high in the air, saying that he was returning into heaven, and that he would supply them with good things from thence. And the people making acclamations to him, as to a god, I stretched out my hands to heaven, with my mind, and besought God through the Lord Jesus to throw down this pestilent fellow, and to destroy the power of those demons that made use of the same for the seduction and perdition of men, to dash him against the ground, and bruise him, but not to kill him. And then, fixing my eyes on Simon, I said to him: "If I be a man of God, and a real apostle of Jesus Christ, and a teacher of piety, and not of deceit, as thou art, Simon, I command the wicked powers of the apostate from piety, by whom Simon the magician is carried, to let go their hold, that he may fall down headlong from his height, that he may be exposed to the laughter of those that have been seduced by him." When I had said these words, Simon was deprived of his powers, and fell down headlong with a great noise, and was violently dashed against the ground, and had his hip and ankle-bones broken; and the people cried out, saying, "There is one only God, whom Peter rightly preaches in truth." And many left him; but some who were worthy of perdition continued in his wicked doctrine. And after this manner the most atheistical heresy of the Simonians was first established in Rome; and the devil wrought by the rest of the false apostles[3] also.

HOW THE HERESIES DIFFER FROM EACH OTHER, AND FROM THE TRUTH.

X. Now all these had one and the same design of atheism, to blaspheme Almighty God, to spread their doctrine that He is an unknown being, and not the Father of Christ, nor the Creator of the world; but one who cannot be spoken of, ineffable, not to be named, and begotten by Himself; that we are not to make use of the law and the prophets; that there is no providence and no resurrection to be believed; that there is no judgment nor retribution; that the soul is not immortal; that we must only indulge our pleasures, and turn to any sort of worship without distinction. Some of them say that there are many gods, some that there are three gods without beginning, some that there are two unbegotten gods, some that there are innumerable Æons. Further, some of them teach that men are not to marry, and must ab-

[1] Acts viii. 20, etc.
[2] Acts viii. 24.

[3] [2 Cor. xi. 13. See p. 457, *infra*.]

stain from flesh and wine, affirming that marriage, and the begetting of children, and the eating of certain foods, are abominable; that so, as sober persons, they may make their wicked opinions to be received as worthy of belief. And some of them absolutely prohibit the eating of flesh, as being the flesh not of brute animals, but of creatures that have a rational soul, as though those that ventured to slay them would be charged with the crime of murder. But others of them affirm that we must only abstain from swine's flesh, but may eat such as are clean by the law; and that we ought to be circumcised, according to the law, and to believe in Jesus as in an holy man and a prophet. But others teach that men ought to be impudent in uncleanness, and to abuse the flesh, and to go through all unholy practices, as if this were the only way for the soul to avoid the rulers of this world. Now all these are the instruments of the devil, and the children of wrath.

SEC. III. — THE HERESIES ATTACKED BY THE APOSTLES.

AN EXPOSITION OF THE PREACHING OF THE APOSTLES.

XI. But we, who are the children of God and the sons of peace, do preach the holy and right word of piety, and declare one only God, the Lord of the law and of the prophets, the Maker of the world, the Father of Christ; not a being that caused Himself, or begat Himself, as they suppose, but eternal, and without original, and inhabiting light inaccessible; not two or three, or manifold, but eternally one only; not a being that cannot be known or spoken of, but who was preached by the law and the prophets; the Almighty, the Supreme Governor of all things, the All-powerful Being; the God and Father of the Only-begotten, and of the First-born of the whole creation; one God, the Father of one Son, not of many; the Maker of one Comforter by Christ, the Maker of the other orders, the one Creator of the several creatures by Christ, the same their Preserver and Legislator by Him; the cause of the resurrection, and of the judgment, and of the retribution which shall be made by Him: that this same Christ was pleased to become man, and went through life without sin, and suffered, and rose from the dead, and returned to Him that sent Him. We also say that every creature of God is good, and nothing abominable; that everything for the support of life, when it is partaken of righteously, is very good: for, according to the Scripture, "all things were very good."[1] We believe that lawful marriage, and the begetting of children, is honourable and undefiled; for difference of sexes was formed in Adam and Eve for the increase of mankind. We acknowledge with us a soul that is incorporeal and immortal, — not corruptible as bodies are, but immortal, as being rational and free. We abhor all unlawful mixtures, and that which is practised by some against nature as wicked and impious. We profess there will be a resurrection both of the just and unjust, and a retribution. We profess that Christ is not a mere man, but God the Word, and man the Mediator between God and men, the High Priest of the Father; nor are we circumcised with the Jews, as knowing that He is come "to whom the inheritance was reserved,"[2] and on whose account the families were kept distinct — "the expectation of the Gentiles," Jesus Christ, who sprang out of Judah,[3] the Son from the branch, the flower from Jesse, whose government is upon His shoulder.[4]

FOR THOSE THAT CONFESS CHRIST, BUT ARE DESIROUS TO JUDAIZE.

XII. But because this heresy did then seem the more powerful to seduce men, and the whole Church was in danger,[5] we the twelve assembled together at Jerusalem (for Matthias was chosen to be an apostle in the room of the betrayer, and took the lot of Judas; as it is said, "His bishopric[6] let another take"). We deliberated, together with James the Lord's brother, what was to be done; and it seemed good to him and to the elders to speak to the people words of doctrine. For certain men likewise went down from Judea to Antioch, and taught the brethren who were there, saying: "Unless ye be circumcised after the manner of Moses, and walk according to the other customs which he ordained, ye cannot be saved."[7] When, therefore, there had been no small dissension and disputation, the brethren which were at Antioch, when they knew that we were all met together about this question, sent out unto us men who were faithful and understanding in the Scriptures to learn concerning this question. And they, when they were come to Jerusalem, declared to us what questions were arisen in the church of Antioch, — namely, that some said men ought to be circumcised, and to observe the other purifications. And when some said one thing, and some another, I Peter stood up, and said unto them: "Men and brethren, ye know how that from ancient days God made choice among you that the Gentiles should hear the word of the Gospel by my mouth, and believe; and God, which knoweth the hearts, bare

[1] Gen. i. 31.

[2] Gen. xlix. 10.
[3] Gen. xlix. 9.
[4] Isa. xi. 1, ix. 6.
[5] Acts xv.
[6] Ps. cix. 8; Acts i. 20. [The name common to apostles and elders.]
[7] Acts xv. 1.

them witness.[1] For an angel of the Lord appeared on a certain time to Cornelius,[2] who was a centurion of the Roman government, and spake to him concerning me, that he should send for me, and hear the word of life from my mouth. He therefore sent for me from Joppa to Cæsarea Stratonis; and when I was ready to go to him, I would have eaten. And while they made ready I was in the upper room praying; and I saw heaven opened, and a vessel, knit at the four corners like a splendid sheet, let down to the earth, wherein were all manner of four-footed beasts, and creeping things of the earth, and fowls of the heaven. And there came a voice out of heaven to me, saying, Arise, Peter; kill, and eat. And I said, By no means, Lord: for I have never eaten anything common or unclean. And there came a voice a second time, saying, What God hath cleansed, that call not thou common. And this was done thrice, and the vessel was received up again into heaven. But as I doubted what this vision should mean, the Spirit said to me, Behold, men seek thee; but rise up, and go thy way with them, nothing doubting, for I have sent them.[3] These men were those which came from the centurion, and so by reasoning I understood the word of the Lord which is written: 'Whosoever shall call on the name of the Lord shall be saved.'[4] And again: 'All the ends of the earth shall remember, and turn unto the Lord, and all the families of the heathen shall worship before Him: for the kingdom is in the Lord's, and He is the governor of the nations.'[5] And observing that there were expressions everywhere concerning the calling of the Gentiles, I rose up, and went with them, and entered into the man's house. And while I was preaching the word, the Holy Spirit fell upon him, and upon those that were with him, as it did upon us at the beginning; and He put no difference between us and them, purifying their hearts by faith. And I perceived that God is no respecter of persons; but that in every nation he that feareth Him, and worketh righteousness, will be accepted with Him. But even the believers which were of the circumcision were astonished at this. Now therefore why tempt ye God, to lay an heavy yoke upon the neck of the disciples, which neither we nor our fathers were able to bear? But by the grace of the Lord, we believe we shall be saved, even as they.[6] For the Lord has loosed us from our bonds, and has made our burden light, and has loosed the heavy yoke from us by His clemency." While I spake these things, the whole multitude kept silence. But James the Lord's brother answered and said: "Men and brethren, hearken unto me; Simeon hath declared how God at first visited to take out a people from the Gentiles for His name. And to this agree the words of the prophets; as it is written: 'Afterwards I will return, and will raise again and rebuild the tabernacle of David, which is fallen down; and I will rebuild its ruins, and will again set it up, that the residue of men may seek after the Lord, and all the nations upon whom my name is called, saith the Lord, who doth these things.'[7] Known unto God are all His works from the beginning of the world. Wherefore my sentence is, that we do not trouble those who from among the Gentiles turn unto God: but to charge them that they abstain from the pollutions of the Gentiles, and from what is sacrificed to idols, and from blood, and from things strangled, and from fornication; which laws were given to the ancients who lived before the law, under the law of nature, Enos, Enoch, Noah, Melchizedek, Job, and if there be any other of the same sort."[8] Then it seemed good to us the apostles, and to James the bishop, and to the elders, with the whole Church, to send men chosen from among our own selves, with Barnabas, and Paul of Tarsus, the apostle of the Gentiles, and Judas who was called Barsabbas, and Silas, chief men among the brethren, and wrote by their hand, as follows: "The apostles, and elders, and brethren,[9] to the brethren of Antioch, Syria, and Cilicia of the Gentiles, send greeting: Since we have heard that some from us have troubled you with words, subverting your souls, to whom we gave no such commandment, it has seemed good to us, when we were met together with one accord, to send chosen men to you, with our beloved Barnabas and Paul, men that have hazarded their lives for our Lord Jesus Christ, by whom ye sent unto us. We have sent also with them Judas and Silas, who shall themselves declare the same things by mouth. For it seemed good to the Holy Ghost, and to us, to lay no other burden upon you than these necessary things; that ye abstain from things offered to idols, and from blood, and from things strangled, and from fornication: from which things if ye keep yourselves, ye shall do well. Fare ye well."[10] We accordingly sent this epistle; but we ourselves remained in Jerusalem many days, consulting together for the public benefit, for the well ordering of all things.

THAT WE MUST SEPARATE FROM HERETICS.

XIII. But after a long time we visited the brethren, and confirmed them with the word of

1 Acts. xv. 7, 8.
2 Acts x.
3 Acts x. 13, etc.
4 Joel ii. 32.
5 Ps. xxii. 27, 28.
6 Acts xi. 15, x. 34, 35, 45, xv. 9, 10.
7 Amos ix. 11.
8 Acts xv. 13, etc.
9 [Compare Elucidation III. vol. v. p. 411, this series.]
10 Acts xv. 23, etc.

piety, and charged them to avoid those who, under the name of Christ and Moses, war against Christ and Moses, and in the clothing of sheep hide the wolf. For these are false Christs, and false prophets, and false apostles, deceivers and corrupters, portions of foxes, the destroyers of the herbs of the vineyards: "for whose sake the love of many will wax cold. But he that endureth stedfast to the end, the same shall be saved.[1] Concerning whom, that He might secure us, the Lord declared, saying: "There will come to you men in sheep's clothing, but inwardly they are ravening wolves. Ye shall know them by their fruits; take care of them. For false Christs and false prophets shall arise and shall deceive many."[2]

WHO WERE THE PREACHERS OF THE CATHOLIC DOCTRINE, AND WHICH ARE THE COMMANDMENTS GIVEN BY THEM.

XIV. On whose account also we, who are now assembled in one place, — Peter and Andrew; James and John, sons of Zebedee; Philip and Bartholomew; Thomas and Matthew; James the son of Alphæus, and Lebbæus who is surnamed Thaddæus; and Simon the Canaanite,[3] and Matthias, who instead of Judas was numbered with us; and James the brother of the Lord and bishop of Jerusalem, and Paul the teacher of the Gentiles, the chosen vessel, having all met together, have written to you this Catholic doctrine for the confirmation of you, to whom the oversight of the universal Church is committed: wherein we declare unto you, that there is only one God Almighty, besides whom there is no other, and that you must worship and adore Him alone, through Jesus Christ our Lord, in the most holy Spirit;[4] that you are to make use of the sacred Scriptures, the law, and the prophets; to honour your parents; to avoid all unlawful actions; to believe the resurrection and the judgment, and to expect the retribution; and to use all His creatures with thankfulness, as the works of God, and having no evil in them; to marry after a lawful manner, for such marriage is unblameable. For "the woman is suited to the man by the Lord;"[5] and the Lord says: "He that made them from the beginning, made them male and female; and said, For this cause shall a man leave his father and his mother, and shall cleave unto his wife: and they two shall be one flesh."[6] Nor let it be esteemed lawful after marriage to put her away who is without blame. For says He: "Thou shalt take care to thy spirit, and shalt not forsake the wife of thy youth; for she is the partner[7] of thy life, and the remains of thy spirit. I and no other have made her."[8] For the Lord says: "What God has joined together, let no man put asunder."[9] For the wife is the partner of life, united by God unto one body from two. But he that divides that again into two which is become one, is the enemy of the creation of God, and the adversary of His providence. In like manner, he that retains her that is corrupted is a transgressor of the law of nature; since "he that retains an adulteress is foolish and impious."[10] For says He, "Cut her off from thy flesh;"[11] for she is not an help, but a snare, bending her mind from thee to another. Nor be ye circumcised in your flesh, but let the circumcision which is of the heart by the Spirit suffice for the faithful; for He says, "Be ye circumcised to your God, and be circumcised in the foreskin of your heart."[12]

THAT WE OUGHT NOT TO REBAPTIZE, NOR TO RECEIVE THAT BAPTISM WHICH IS GIVEN BY THE UNGODLY, WHICH IS NOT BAPTISM, BUT A POLLUTION.

XV. Be ye likewise contented with one baptism alone, that which is into the death of the Lord; not that which is conferred by wicked heretics, but that which is conferred by unblameable priests, "in the name of the Father, and of the Son, and of the Holy Ghost:"[13] and let not that which comes from the ungodly be received by you, nor let that which is done by the godly be disannulled by a second. For as there is one God, one Christ, and one Comforter, and one death of the Lord in the body, so let that baptism which is unto Him be but one. But those that receive polluted baptism from the ungodly will become partners in their opinions. For they are not priests. For God says to them: "Because thou hast rejected knowledge, I will also reject thee from the office of a priest to me."[14] Nor indeed are those that are baptized by them initiated, but are polluted, not receiving the remission of sins, but the bond of impiety. And, besides, they that attempt to baptize those already initiated crucify the Lord afresh, slay Him a second time, laugh at divine and ridicule holy things, affront the Spirit, dishonour the sacred blood of Christ as common blood, are impious against Him that sent, Him that suffered, and Him that witnessed. Nay, he that, out of contempt, will not be baptized, shall be

1 Matt. xxiv. 12, 13.
2 Matt. vii. 15, xxiv. 24.
3 Matt. x. 2.
4 One V. MS. reads as follows: "And our Lord Jesus Christ, and the most holy Spirit."
5 Prov. xix. 14.
6 Matt. xix. 4, 5.
7 The words from "for she is the partner" to "made her" are omitted in one V. MS.
8 Mal. ii. 15, 14.
9 Matt. xix. 6.
10 Prov. xviii. 22.
11 Ecclus. xxv. 26.
12 Jer. iv. 4.
13 Matt. xxviii. 19.
14 Hos. iv. 6. [Compare vol. v. p. 565, this series.]

condemned as an unbeliever, and shall be reproached as ungrateful and foolish. For the Lord says: "Except a man be baptized of water and of the Spirit, he shall by no means enter into the kingdom of heaven."[1] And again: "He that believeth and is baptized shall be saved; but he that believeth not shall be damned."[2] But he that says, When I am dying I will be baptized, lest I should sin and defile my baptism, is ignorant of God, and forgetful of his own nature. For "do not thou delay to turn unto the Lord, for thou knowest not what the next day will bring forth."[3] Do you also baptize your infants, and bring them up in the nurture and admonition of God. For says He: "Suffer the little children to come unto me, and forbid them not."[4]

CONCERNING BOOKS WITH FALSE INSCRIPTIONS.

XVI. We have sent all these things to you, that ye may know our opinion, what it is; and that ye may not receive those books which obtain in our name, but are written by the ungodly. For you are not to attend to the names of the apostles, but to the nature of the things, and their settled opinions. For we know that Simon and Cleobius, and their followers, have compiled poisonous books under the name of Christ and of His disciples, and do carry them about in order to deceive you who love Christ, and us His servants. And among the ancients also some have written apocryphal books of Moses, and Enoch, and Adam, and Isaiah, and David, and Elijah, and of the three patriarchs, pernicious and repugnant to the truth. The same things even now have the wicked heretics done, reproaching the creation, marriage, providence, the begetting of children, the law, and the prophets; inscribing certain barbarous names, and, as they think, of angels, but, to speak the truth, of demons, which suggest things to them: whose doctrine eschew, that ye may not be partakers of the punishment due to those that write such things for the seduction and perdition of the faithful and unblameable disciples of the Lord Jesus.

MATRIMONIAL PRECEPTS CONCERNING CLERGYMEN.

XVII. We have already said, that a bishop, a presbyter, and a deacon, when they are constituted, must be but once married, whether their wives be alive or whether they be dead; and that it is not lawful for them, if they are unmarried when they are ordained, to be married afterwards; or if they be then married, to marry a second time, but to be content with that wife which they had when they came to ordination.[5] We also appoint that the ministers, and singers, and readers, and porters, shall be only once married. But if they entered into the clergy before they were married, we permit them to marry, if they have an inclination thereto, lest they sin and incur punishment.[6] But we do not permit any one of the clergy to take to wife either a courtesan, or a servant, or a widow, or one that is divorced, as also the law says. Let the deaconess be a pure virgin; or, at the least, a widow who has been but once married, faithful, and well esteemed.[7]

AN EXHORTATION COMMANDING TO AVOID THE COMMUNION OF THE IMPIOUS HERETICS.

XVIII. Receive ye the penitent, for this is the will of God in Christ. Instruct the catechumens in the elements of religion, and then baptize them. Eschew the atheistical heretics, who are past repentance, and separate them from the faithful, and excommunicate them from the Church of God, and charge the faithful to abstain entirely from them, and not to partake with them either in sermons or prayers: for these are those that are enemies to the Church, and lay snares for it; who corrupt the flock, and defile the heritage of Christ, pretenders only to wisdom, and the vilest of men; concerning whom Solomon the wise said: "The wicked doers pretend to act piously." For, says he, "there is a way which seemeth right to some, but the ends thereof look to the bottom of hell."[8] These are they concerning whom the Lord declared His mind with bitterness and severity, saying that "they are false Christs and false teachers;"[9] who have blasphemed the Spirit of grace, and done despite to the gift they had from Him after the grace *of baptism*, "to whom forgiveness shall not be granted, neither in this world nor in that which is to come;"[10] who are both more wicked than the Jews and more atheistical than the Gentiles; who blaspheme the God over all, and tread under foot His Son, and do despite to the doctrine of the Spirit; who deny the words of God, or pretend hypocritically to receive them, to the affronting of God, and the deceiving of those that come among them; who abuse the Holy Scriptures, and as for righteousness, they do not so much as know what it is; who spoil the Church of God, as the "little foxes do the vineyard;"[11] whom we exhort you to avoid, lest you lay traps for your own souls. "For he that walketh with wise men shall be wise, but he that walketh

1 John iii. 5.
2 Mark xvi. 16.
3 Ecclus. v. 7; Prov. xxvii. 1, iii. 28.
4 Matt. xix. 14.
5 1 Tim. iii. 2, 12; Tit. i. 6.
6 [See Elucidation XIII. vol. v. p. 160, this series.]
7 Lev. xxi. 7, 14; 1 Tim. v. 9.
8 Prov. xiv. 12.
9 Matt. xxiv. 24.
10 Matt. xii. 32.
11 *Vid.* Cant. ii. 15.

with the foolish shall be known."[1] For we ought neither to run along with a thief, nor put in our lot with an adulterer; since holy David says: "O Lord, I have hated them that hate Thee, and I am withered away on account of Thy enemies. I hated them with a perfect hatred: they were to me as enemies."[2] And God reproaches Jehoshaphat with his friendship towards Ahab, and his league with him and with Ahaziah, by Jonah the prophet: "Art thou in friendship with a sinner? Or dost thou aid him that is hated by the Lord?"[3] "For this cause the wrath of the Lord would be upon thee suddenly, but that thy heart is found perfect with the Lord. For this cause the Lord hath spared thee; yet are thy works shattered, and thy ships broken to pieces."[4] Eschew therefore their fellowship, and estrange yourselves from their friendship. For concerning them did the prophet declare, and say: "It is not lawful to rejoice with the ungodly,"[5] says the Lord. For these are hidden wolves, dumb dogs, that cannot bark, who at present are but few, but in process of time, when the end of the world draws nigh, will be more in number and more troublesome, of whom said the Lord, "Will the Son of man, when He comes, find faith on the earth?"[6] and, "Because iniquity shall abound, the love of many shall wax cold;" and, "There shall come false Christs and false prophets, and shall show signs in the heaven, so as, if it were possible, to deceive the elect:"[7] from whose deceit God, through Jesus Christ, who is our hope, will deliver us. For we ourselves, as we passed through the nations, and confirmed the churches, curing some with much exhortation and healing words, restored them again when they were in the certain way to death. But those that were incurable we cast out from the flock, that they might not infect the lambs, which were found with their scabby disease, but might continue before the Lord God pure and undefiled, sound and unspotted. And this we did in every city, everywhere through the whole world, and have left to you the bishops and to the rest of the priests this very Catholic doctrine worthily and righteously, as a memorial or confirmation to those who have believed in God; and we have sent it by our fellow-minister Clement, our most faithful and intimate son in the Lord, together with Barnabas, and Timothy our most dearly beloved son, and the genuine Mark, together with whom we recommend to you also Titus and Luke, and Jason and Lucius, and Sosipater.[8]

SEC. IV. — OF THE LAW.

By whom also we exhort you in the Lord to abstain from your old conversation, vain bonds, separations, observances, distinction of meats, and daily washings: for "old things are passed away; behold, all things are become new."[9]

TO THOSE THAT SPEAK EVIL OF THE LAW.

XIX. For since ye have known God through Jesus Christ, and all His dispensation, as it has been from the beginning, that He gave a plain law to assist the law of nature,[10] such a one as is pure, saving, and holy, in which His own name was inscribed,[11] perfect, which is never to fail, being complete in ten commands, unspotted, converting souls;[12] which, when the Hebrews forgot, He put them in mind of it by the prophet Malachi, saying, "Remember ye the law of Moses, the man of God, who gave you in charge commandments and ordinances."[13] Which law is so very holy and righteous, that even our Saviour, when on a certain time He healed one leper, and afterwards nine, said to the first, "Go, show thyself to the high priest, and offer the gift which Moses commanded for a testimony unto them;"[14] and afterwards to the nine, "Go, show yourselves to the priests."[15] For He nowhere has dissolved the law, as Simon pretends, but fulfilled it; for He says: "One iota, or one tittle, shall not pass from the law until all be fulfilled." For says He, "I come not to dissolve the law, but to fulfil it."[16] For Moses himself, who was at once the lawgiver, and the high priest, and the prophet, and the king, and Elijah, the zealous follower of the prophets, were present at our Lord's transfiguration in the mountain,[17] and witnesses of His incarnation and of His sufferings, as the intimate friends of Christ, but not as enemies and strangers. Whence it is demonstrated that the law is good and holy, as also the prophets.

WHICH IS THE LAW OF NATURE, AND WHICH IS THAT AFTERWARDS INTRODUCED, AND WHY IT WAS INTRODUCED.

XX. Now the law is the decalogue, which the Lord promulgated to them with an audible voice,[18] before the people made that calf which represented the Egyptian Apis.[19] And the law is righteous, and therefore is it called the law, because judgments are thence made according

1 Prov. xiii. 20.
2 Ps cxxxix. 21, 22.
3 2 Chron. xix. 2.
4 2 Chron xx. 37.
5 *Vid.* Isa. lvii. 21.
6 Luke xviii. 8.
7 Matt. xxiv. 12, 24.
8 Rom. xvi. 21.

9 2 Cor. v. 17.
10 Isa. viii. 20, LXX.
11 Deut. xii. 5.
12 Ps. xix. 7.
13 Mal. iv. 4.
14 Matt. viii. 4; Mark i. 44.
15 Luke xvii. 14.
16 Matt. v. 18, 17.
17 Luke ix. 30.
18 Ex. xx.
19 Ex. xxxii.

to the law of nature, which the followers of Simon abuse, supposing they shall not be judged thereby, and so shall escape punishment. This law is good, holy, and such as lays no compulsion in things positive. For He says: "If thou wilt make me an altar, thou shalt make it of earth."[1] It does not say, "Make one," but, "If thou wilt make." It does not impose a necessity, but gives leave to their own free liberty. For God does not stand in need of sacrifices, being by nature above all want. But knowing that, as of old, Abel, beloved of God, and Noah and Abraham, and those that succeeded, without being required, but only moved of themselves by the law of nature, did offer sacrifice to God out of a grateful mind; so He did now permit the Hebrews, not commanding, but, if they had a mind, permitting them; and if they offered from a right intention, showing Himself pleased with their sacrifices. Therefore He says: "If thou desirest to offer, do not offer to me as to one that stands in need of it, for I stand in need of nothing; for the world is mine, and the fulness thereof."[2] But when this people became forgetful of that, and called upon a calf as God, instead of the true God, and to him did ascribe the cause of their coming out of Egypt, saying, "These are thy gods, O Israel, which have brought thee out of the land of Egypt;"[3] and when these men had committed wickedness with the "similitude of a calf that eateth hay," and denied God who had visited them by Moses[4] in their afflictions, and had done signs with his hand and rod, and had smitten the Egyptians with ten plagues; who had divided the waters of the Red Sea into two parts; who had led them in the midst of the water, as a horse upon the ground; who had drowned their enemies, and those that laid wait for them; who at Marah had made sweet the bitter fountain; who had brought water out of the sharp rock till they were satisfied; who had overshadowed them with a pillar of a cloud on account of the immoderate heat, and with a pillar of fire which enlightened and guided them when they knew not which way they were to go; who gave them manna from heaven, and gave them quails for flesh from the sea;[5] who gave them the law in the mountain; whose voice He had vouchsafed to let them hear; Him did they deny, and said to Aaron, "Make us gods who shall go before us;"[6] and they made a molten calf, and sacrificed to an idol; — then was God angry, as being ungratefully treated by them, and bound them with bonds which could not be loosed, with a mortifying burden and a hard collar, and no longer said, "If thou makest," but, "Make an altar," and sacrifice perpetually; for thou art forgetful and ungrateful. Offer burnt-offerings therefore continually, that thou mayest be mindful of me. For since thou hast wickedly abused thy power, I lay a necessity upon thee for the time to come, and I command thee to abstain from certain meats; and I ordain thee the distinction of clean and unclean creatures, although every creature is good, as being made by me; and I appoint thee several separations, purgations, frequent washings and sprinklings, several purifications, and several times of rest; and if thou neglectest any of them, I determine that punishment which is proper to the disobedient, that being pressed and galled by thy collar, thou mayest depart from the error of polytheism, and laying aside that, "These are thy gods, O Israel,"[3] mayest be mindful of that, "Hear, O Israel, the Lord thy God is one Lord;"[7] and mayest run back again to that law which is inserted by me in the nature of all men, "that there is only one God in heaven and on earth, and to love Him with all thy heart, and all thy might, and all thy mind," and to fear none but Him, nor to admit the names of other gods into thy mind, nor to let thy tongue utter them out of thy mouth. He bound them for the hardness of their hearts, that by sacrificing, and resting, and purifying themselves, and by similar observances, they might come to the knowledge of God, who ordained these things for them.

THAT WE WHO BELIEVE IN CHRIST ARE UNDER GRACE, AND NOT UNDER THE SERVITUDE OF THAT ADDITIONAL LAW.

XXI. "But blessed are your eyes, for they see; and your ears, for they hear."[8] Yours, I say, who have believed in the one God, not by necessity, but by a sound understanding, in obedience to Him that called you. For you are released from the bonds, and freed from the servitude. For says He:[9] "I call you no longer servants, but friends; for all things that I have heard of my Father have I made known unto you."[10] For to them that would not see nor hear, not for the want of those senses, but for the excess of their wickedness, "I gave statutes that were not good, and judgments whereby they would not live;"[11] they are looked upon as not good, as burnings and a sword, and medicines are esteemed enemies by the sick, and impossible to be observed on account of their

1 Ex. xx. 24.
2 Ps. l. 12.
3 Ex. xxxii. 4.
4 Ex. iv., etc.
5 Num. xi. 31.
6 Ex. xxxii. 1.
7 Deut. vi. 4.
8 Matt. xiii. 16.
9 One V. MS. reads: "Thus also said the Lord to us His disciples."
10 John xv. 15.
11 Ezek. xx. 25.

obstinacy: whence also they brought death upon them being not obeyed.

THAT THE LAW FOR SACRIFICES IS ADDITIONAL, WHICH CHRIST WHEN HE CAME TOOK AWAY.

XXII. You therefore are blessed who are delivered from the curse. For Christ, the Son of God, by His coming has confirmed and completed the law, but has taken away the additional precepts, although not all of them, yet at least the more grievous ones; having confirmed the former, and abolished the latter, and has again set the free-will of man at liberty, not subjecting him to the penalty of a temporal death, but giving laws to him according to another constitution. Wherefore He says: "If any man will come after me, let him come."[1] And again: "Will ye also go away?"[2] And besides, before His coming He refused the sacrifices of the people, while they frequently offered them, when they sinned against Him, and thought He was to be appeased by sacrifices, but not by repentance. For thus He speaks: "Why dost thou bring to me frankincense from Saba, and cinnamon from a remote land? Your burnt-offerings are not acceptable, and your sacrifices are not sweet to me."[3] And afterwards: "Gather your burnt-offerings, together with your sacrifices, and eat flesh. For I did not command you, when I brought you out of the land of Egypt, concerning burnt-offerings and sacrifices."[4] And He says by Isaiah: "To what purpose do ye bring me a multitude of sacrifices? saith the Lord. I am full of the burnt-offerings of rams, and I will not accept the fat of lambs, and the blood of bulls and of goats. Nor do you come and appear before me; for who hath required these things at your hands? Do not go on to tread my courts any more. If you bring me fine flour, it is vain: incense is an abomination unto me: your new moons, and your Sabbaths, and your great day, I cannot bear them: your fasts, and your rests, and your feasts, my soul hateth them; I am over-full of them."[5] And He says by another: "Depart from me; the sound of thine hymns, and the psalms of thy musical instruments, I will not hear."[6] And Samuel says to Saul, when he thought to sacrifice: "Obedience is better than sacrifice, and hearkening than the fat of rams. For, behold, the Lord does not so much delight in sacrifice, as in obeying Him."[7] And He says by David: "I will take no calves out of thine house, nor he-goats out of thy flock. If I should be hungry, I would not tell thee; for the whole world is mine, and the fulness thereof. Shall I eat the flesh of bulls, or drink the blood of goats? Sacrifice to God the sacrifice of praise, and pay thy vows to the Most High."[8] And in all the Scriptures in like manner He refuses their sacrifices on account of their sinning against Him. For "the sacrifices of the impious are an abomination with the Lord, since they offer them in an unlawful manner."[9] And again: "Their sacrifices are to them as bread of lamentation; all that eat of them shall be defiled."[10] If, therefore, before His coming He sought for "a clean heart and a contrite spirit"[11] more than sacrifices, much rather would He abrogate those sacrifices, I mean those by blood, when He came. Yet He so abrogated them as that He first fulfilled them. For He was both circumcised, and sprinkled, and offered sacrifices and whole burnt-offerings, and made use of the rest of their customs. And He that was the Lawgiver became Himself the fulfilling of the law; not taking away the law of nature, but abrogating those additional laws that were afterwards introduced, although not all of them neither.

HOW CHRIST BECAME A FULFILLER OF THE LAW, AND WHAT PARTS OF IT HE PUT A PERIOD TO, OR CHANGED, OR TRANSFERRED.

XXIII. For He did not take away the law of nature, but confirmed it. For He that said in the law, "The Lord thy God is one Lord;"[12] the same says in the Gospel, "That they might know Thee, the only true God."[13] And He that said, "Thou shalt love thy neighbour as thyself,"[14] says in the Gospel, renewing the same precept, "A new commandment I give unto you, that ye love one another."[15] He who then forbade murder, does now forbid causeless anger.[16] He that forbade adultery, does now forbid all unlawful lust. He that forbade stealing, now pronounces him most happy who supplies those that are in want out of his own labours.[17] He that forbade hatred, now pronounces him blessed that loves his enemies.[18] He that forbade revenge, now commands long-suffering;[19] not as if just revenge were an unrighteous thing, but because long-suffering is more excellent. Nor did He make laws to root out our natural passions, but only to forbid the excess of them.[20]

1 Matt. xvi. 24.
2 John vi. 67.
3 Jer. vi. 20.
4 Jer. vii. 21, 22.
5 Isa. i. 11, etc.
6 Amos v. 23.
7 1 Sam. xv. 22.
8 Ps. l. 9, 12, etc.
9 Prov. xxi. 27.
10 Hos. ix. 4.
11 Ps. li. 10, 17.
12 Deut. vi. 4.
13 John xvii. 3.
14 Lev. xix. 18.
15 John xiii. 34.
16 Matt. v. 22.
17 Acts xx. 35.
18 Matt. v. 7.
19 Matt. v. 43.
20 Matt. v. 38.

He who had commanded to honour our parents, was Himself subject to them.[1] He who had commanded to keep the Sabbath, by resting thereon for the sake of meditating on the laws, has now commanded us to consider of the law of creation, and of providence every day, and to return thanks to God. He abrogated circumcision when He had Himself fulfilled it. For He it was "to whom the inheritance was reserved, who was the expectation of the nations."[2] He who made a law for swearing rightly, and forbade perjury, has now charged us not to swear at all.[3] He has in several ways changed baptism, sacrifice, the priesthood, and the divine service, which was confined to one place: for instead of daily baptisms, He has given only one, which is that into His death. Instead of one tribe, He has appointed that out of every nation the best should be ordained for the priesthood; and that not their bodies should be examined for blemishes, but their religion and their lives. Instead of a bloody sacrifice, He has appointed that reasonable and unbloody mystical one of His body and blood, which is performed to represent the death of the Lord by symbols. Instead of the divine service confined to one place, He has commanded and appointed that He should be glorified from sunrising to sunsetting in every place of His dominion.[4] He did not therefore take away the law from us, but the bonds. For concerning the law Moses says: "Thou shalt meditate on the word which I command thee, sitting in thine house, and rising up, and walking in the way."[5] And David says: "His delight is in the law of the Lord, and in His law will he meditate day and night."[6] For everywhere would he have us subject to His laws, but not transgressors of them. For says He: "Blessed are the undefiled in the way, who walk in the law of the Lord. Blessed are they that search out His testimonies; with their whole heart shall they seek Him."[7] And again: "Blessed are we, O Israel, because those things that are pleasing to God are known to us."[8] And the Lord says: "If ye know these things, happy are ye if ye do them."[9]

THAT IT PLEASED THE LORD THAT THE LAW OF RIGHTEOUSNESS SHOULD BE DEMONSTRATED BY THE ROMANS.

XXIV. Nor does He desire that the law of righteousness should only be demonstrated by us; but He is pleased that it should appear and shine by means of the Romans. For these Romans, believing in the Lord, left off their polytheism and injustice, and entertain the good, and punish the bad. But they hold the Jews under tribute, and do not suffer them to make use of their own ordinances.

HOW GOD, ON ACCOUNT OF THEIR IMPIETY TOWARDS CHRIST, MADE THE JEWS CAPTIVES, AND PLACED THEM UNDER TRIBUTE.

XXV. Because, indeed, they drew servitude upon themselves voluntarily, when they said, "We have no king but Cæsar;"[10] and, "If we do not slay Christ, all men will believe in Him, and the Romans will come and will take away both our place and nation."[11] And so they prophesied unwittingly. For accordingly the nations believed on Him, and they themselves were deprived by the Romans of their power, and of their legal worship; and they have been forbidden to slay whom they please, and to sacrifice when they will. Wherefore they are accursed, as not able to perform the things they are commanded to do. For says He: "Cursed be he that does not continue in all things that are written in the book of the law to do them."[12] Now it is impossible in their dispersion, while they are among the heathen, for them to perform all things in their law. For the divine Moses forbids both to rear an altar out of Jerusalem, and to read the law out of the bounds of Judea.[13] Let us therefore follow Christ, that we may inherit His blessings. Let us walk after the law and the prophets by the Gospel. Let us eschew the worshippers of many gods, and the murderers of Christ, and the murderers of the prophets, and the wicked and atheistical heretics. Let us be obedient to Christ as to our King, as having authority to change several constitutions, and having, as a legislator, wisdom to make new constitutions in different circumstances; yet so that everywhere the laws of nature be immutably preserved.

SEC. V. — THE TEACHING OF THE APOSTLES IN OPPOSITION TO JEWISH AND GENTILE SUPERSTITIONS, ESPECIALLY IN REGARD TO MARRIAGE AND FUNERALS.

THAT WE OUGHT TO AVOID THE HERETICS AS THE CORRUPTERS OF SOULS.

XXVI. Do you therefore, O bishops, and ye of the laity, avoid all heretics who abuse the law and the prophets. For they are enemies to God Almighty, and disobey Him, and do not confess

1 Luke ii. 51.
2 Gen. xlix. 10.
3 Matt. v. 33.
4 Ps. cxiii. 3; Mal. i. 11.
5 Deut. vi. 6.
6 Ps. i. 2.
7 Ps. cxix. 1, 2.
8 Bar. iv. 4.
9 John xiii. 17.
10 John xix. 15.
11 John xi. 48.
12 Deut. xxvii. 26; Gal. iii. 10.
13 Deut. xii. [See on Liturgies, *infra*.]

Christ to be the Son of God. For they also deny His generation according to the flesh; they are ashamed of the cross; they abuse His passion and His death; they know not His resurrection; they take away His generation before all ages. Nay, some of them are impious after another manner, imagining the Lord to be a mere man, supposing Him to consist of a soul and body. But others of them suppose that Jesus Himself is the God over all, and glorify Him as His own Father, and suppose Him to be both the Son and the Comforter; than which doctrines what can be more detestable? Others, again, of them do refuse certain meats, and say that marriage with the procreation of children is evil, and the contrivance of the devil; and being ungodly themselves, they are not willing to rise again from the dead on account of their wickedness. Wherefore also they ridicule the resurrection, and say, We are holy people, unwilling to eat and to drink; and they fancy that they shall rise again from the dead demons without flesh, who shall be condemned for ever in eternal fire. Fly therefore from them, lest ye perish with them in their impieties.

OF SOME JEWISH AND GENTILE OBSERVANCES.

XXVII. Now if any persons keep to the Jewish customs and observances concerning the natural emission and nocturnal pollutions, and the lawful conjugal acts,[1] let them tell us whether in those hours or days, when they undergo any such thing, they observe not to pray, or to touch a Bible, or to partake of the Eucharist? And if they own it to be so, it is plain they are void of the Holy Spirit, which always continues with the faithful. For concerning holy persons Solomon says: "That every one may prepare himself, that so when he sleeps it may keep him, and when he arises it may talk with him."[2] For if thou thinkest, O woman, when thou art seven days in thy separation, that thou art void of the Holy Spirit, then if thou shouldest die suddenly thou wilt depart void of the Spirit, and without assured hope in God; or else thou must imagine that the Spirit always is inseparable from thee, as not being in a place. But thou standest in need of prayer and the Eucharist, and the coming of the Holy Ghost, as having been guilty of no fault in this matter. For neither lawful mixture, nor child-bearing, nor the menstrual purgation, nor nocturnal pollution, can defile the nature of a man, or separate the Holy Spirit from him. Nothing but impiety and unlawful practice can do that. For the Holy Spirit always abides with those that are possessed of it, so long as they are worthy; and those from whom it is departed, it leaves them desolate, and exposed to the wicked spirit. Now every man is filled either with the holy or with the unclean spirit; and it is not possible to avoid the one or the other, unless they can receive opposite spirits. For the Comforter hates every lie, and the devil hates all truth. But every one that is baptized agreeably to the truth is separated from the diabolical spirit, and is under the Holy Spirit; and the Holy Spirit remains with him so long as he is doing good, and fills him with wisdom and understanding, and suffers not the wicked spirit to approach him, but watches over his goings. Thou therefore, O woman, if, as thou sayest, in the days of thy separation thou art void of the Holy Spirit, thou art then filled with the unclean one; for by neglecting to pray and to read thou wilt invite him to thee, though he were unwilling. For this spirit, of all others, loves the ungrateful, the slothful, the careless, and the drowsy, since he himself by ingratitude was distempered with an evil mind, and was thereby deprived by God of his dignity; having rather chosen to be a devil than an archangel. Wherefore, O woman, eschew such vain words, and be ever mindful of God that created thee, and pray to Him. For He is thy Lord, and the Lord of the universe; and meditate in His laws without observing any such things, such as the natural purgation, lawful mixture, child-birth, a miscarriage, or a blemish of the body; since such observations are the vain inventions of foolish men, and such inventions as have no sense in them. Neither the burial of a man, nor a dead man's bone, nor a sepulchre, nor any particular sort of food, nor the nocturnal pollution, can defile the soul of man; but only impiety towards God, and transgression, and injustice towards one's neighbour; I mean rapine, violence, or if there be anything contrary to His righteousness, adultery or fornication. Wherefore, beloved, avoid and eschew such observations, for they are heathenish. For we do not abominate a dead man, as do they, seeing we hope that he will live again. Nor do we hate lawful mixture; for it is their practice to act impiously in such instances. For the conjunction of man and wife, if it be with righteousness, is agreeable to the mind of God. "For He that made them at the beginning made them male and female; and He blessed them, and said, Increase and multiply, and fill the earth."[3] If, therefore, the difference of sexes was made by the will of God for the generation of multitudes, then must the conjunction of male and female be also acceptable to His mind.

OF THE LOVE OF BOYS, ADULTERY, AND FORNICATION.

XXVIII. But we do not say so of that mixture that is contrary to nature, or of any unlawful

[1] Lev. xv.
[2] Prov. vi. 22.
[3] Matt. xix. 4; Gen. i. 28.

practice; for such are enmity to God. For the sin of Sodom is contrary to nature, as is also that with brute beasts. But adultery and fornication are against the law; the one whereof is impiety, the other injustice, and, in a word, no other than a great sin. But neither sort of them is without its punishment in its own proper nature. For the practisers of one sort attempt the dissolution of the world, and endeavour to make the natural course of things to change for one that is unnatural; but those of the second sort — the adulterers — are unjust by corrupting others' marriages, and dividing into two what God hath made one, rendering the children suspected, and exposing the true husband to the snares of others. And fornication is the destruction of one's own flesh, not being made use of for the procreation of children, but entirely for the sake of pleasure, which is a mark of incontinency, and not a sign of virtue. All these things are forbidden by the laws; for thus say the oracles: "Thou shalt not lie with mankind as with womankind."[1] "For such a one is accursed, and ye shall stone them with stones: they have wrought abomination."[2] "Every one that lieth with a beast, slay ye him: he has wrought wickedness in his people."[3] "And if any one defile a married woman, slay ye them both: they have wrought wickedness; they are guilty; let them die."[4] And afterwards: "There shall not be a fornicator among the children of Israel, and there shall not be an whore among the daughters of Israel. Thou shalt not offer the hire of an harlot to the Lord thy God upon the altar, nor the price of a dog."[5] "For the vows arising from the hire of an harlot are not clean."[6] These things the laws have forbidden, but they have honoured marriage, and have called it blessed, since God has blessed it, who joined male and female together.[7] And wise Solomon somewhere says: "A wife is suited to her husband by the Lord."[8] And David says: "Thy wife is like a flourishing vine in the sides of thine house; thy children like olive-branches round about thy table. Behold, thus shall the man be blessed that feareth the Lord."[9] Wherefore "marriage is honourable"[10] and comely, and the begetting of children pure, for there is no evil in that which is good. Therefore neither is the natural purgation abominable before God, who has ordered it to happen to women within the space of thirty days for their advantage and healthful state, who do less move about, and keep usually at home in the house. Nay, moreover, even in the Gospel, when the woman with the perpetual purgation of blood[11] touched the saving border of the Lord's garment in hope of being healed, He was not angry at her, nor did complain of her at all; but, on the contrary, He healed her, saying, "Thy faith hath saved thee." When the natural purgations do appear in the wives, let not their husbands approach them, out of regard to the children to be begotten; for the law has forbidden it, for it says: "Thou shalt not come near thy wife when she is in her separation."[12] Nor, indeed, let them frequent their wives' company when they are with child.[13] For they do this not for the begetting of children, but for the sake of pleasure. Now a lover of God ought not to be a lover of pleasure.

HOW WIVES OUGHT TO BE SUBJECT TO THEIR OWN HUSBANDS, AND HUSBANDS OUGHT TO LOVE THEIR OWN WIVES.

XXIX. Ye wives, be subject to your own husbands, and have them in esteem, and serve them with fear and love, as holy Sarah honoured Abraham. For she could not endure to call him by his name, but called him lord, when she said, "My lord is old."[14] In like manner, ye husbands, love your own wives as your own members, as partners in life, and fellow-helpers for the procreation of children. For says He, "Rejoice with the wife of thy youth. Let her conversation be to thee as a loving hind, and a pleasant foal; let her alone guide thee, and be with thee at all times: for if thou beest every way encompassed with her friendship, thou wilt be happy in her society."[15] Love them therefore as your own members, as your very bodies; for so it is written, "The Lord has testified between thee and between the wife of thy youth; and she is thy partner, and another has not made her: and she is the remains of thy spirit;" and, "Take heed to your spirit, and do not forsake the wife of thy youth."[16] An husband, therefore, and a wife, when they company together in lawful marriage, and rise from one another, may pray without any observations, and without washing are clean. But whosoever corrupts and defiles another man's wife, or is defiled with an harlot, when he arises up from her, though he should wash himself in the entire ocean and all the rivers, cannot be clean.

---

1 Lev. xviii. 22.
2 Lev. xx. 13.
3 Ex. xxii. 19.
4 Lev. xx. 10; Deut. xxii. 22.
5 Deut. xxiii. 17, 18.
6 Prov. xix. 13, LXX.
7 Gen. i. 28.
8 Prov. xix. 14.
9 Ps. cxxviii. 3, 4.
10 Heb. xiii. 4.
11 Matt. ix. 22.
12 Lev. xviii. 19; Ezek. xviii. 6.
13 [But if this be otherwise done, it may be well to compare Lactantius as to a question of actual crime. See p. 190, n. 1, *supra*.]
14 1 Pet. iii. 6.
15 Prov. v. 18, etc.
16 Mal. ii. 14, 15, 16.

SEC. VI. — CONCLUSION OF THE WORK.

THAT IT IS THE CUSTOM OF JEWS AND GENTILES TO OBSERVE NATURAL PURGATIONS, AND TO ABOMINATE THE REMAINS OF THE DEAD; BUT THAT ALL THIS IS CONTRARY TO CHRISTIANITY.

XXX. Do not therefore keep any such observances about legal and natural purgations, as thinking you are defiled by them. Neither do you seek after Jewish separations, or perpetual washings, or purifications upon the touch of a dead body. But without such observations assemble in the dormitories, reading the holy books, and singing for the martyrs which are fallen asleep, and for all the saints from the beginning of the world, and for your brethren that are asleep in the Lord, and offer the acceptable Eucharist, the representation of the royal body of Christ, both in your churches and in the dormitories; and in the funerals of the departed, accompany them with singing, if they were faithful in Christ. For "precious in the sight of the Lord is the death of His saints."[1] And again: "O my soul, return unto thy rest, for the Lord hath done thee good."[2] And elsewhere: "The memory of the just is with encomiums."[3] And, "The souls of the righteous are in the hands of God."[4] For those that have believed in God, although they are asleep, are not dead. For our Saviour says to the Sadducees: "But concerning the resurrection of the dead, have ye not read that which is written, I am the God of Abraham, and the God of Isaac, and the God of Jacob? God, therefore, is not the God of the dead, but of the living; for all live to Him."[5] Wherefore, of those that live with God, even their very relics are not without honour. For even Elisha the prophet, after he was fallen asleep, raised up a dead man who was slain by the pirates of Syria.[6] For his body touched the bones of Elisha, and he arose and revived. Now this would not have happened unless the body of Elisha were holy. And chaste Joseph embraced Jacob after he was dead upon his bed;[7] and Moses and Joshua the son of Nun carried away the relics of Joseph,[8] and did not esteem it a defilement. Whence you also, O bishops, and the rest, who without such observances touch the departed, ought not to think yourselves defiled. Nor abhor the relics of such persons, but avoid such observances, for they are foolish. And adorn yourselves with holiness and chastity, that ye may become partakers of immortality, and partners of the kingdom of God, and may receive the promise of God, and may rest for ever, through Jesus Christ our Saviour.

To Him, therefore, who is able to open the ears of your hearts to the receiving the oracles of God administered to you both by the Gospel and by the teaching of Jesus Christ of Nazareth; who was crucified under Pontius Pilate and Herod, and died, and rose again from the dead, and will come again at the end of the world with power and great glory, and will raise the dead, and put an end to this world, and distribute to every one according to his deserts: to Him that has given us Himself for an earnest of the resurrection; who was taken up into the heavens by the power of His God and Father in our sight, who ate and drank with Him for forty days after He arose from the dead; who is sat down on the right hand of the throne of the majesty of Almighty God upon the cherubim; to whom it was said, "Sit Thou on my right hand, until I make Thine enemies Thy footstool;"[9] whom the most blessed Stephen saw standing at the right hand of power, and cried out, and said, "Behold, I see the heavens opened, and the Son of man standing at the right hand of God,"[10] as the High Priest of all the rational orders, — through Him, worship, and majesty, and glory be given to Almighty God, both now and for evermore.[11] Amen.

1 Ps. cxvi. 15.
2 Ps. cxvi. 7.
3 Prov. x. 7.
4 Wisd. iii. 1.
5 Ex. iii. 6; Luke xx. 38.
6 2 Kings xiii. 21.
7 Gen. l. 1.
8 Ex. xiii. 19; Josh. xxiv. 32.
9 Ps. cx. 1.
10 Acts vii. 56.
11 One V. MS. reads: "to Him be worship, and majesty, and glory, along with the Father and the co-eternal Spirit, for ever and ever. Amen."

CONSTITUTIONS OF THE HOLY APOSTLES

BOOK VII.

CONCERNING THE CHRISTIAN LIFE, AND THE EUCHARIST, AND THE INITIATION INTO CHRIST.

SEC. I. — ON THE TWO WAYS,[1] — THE WAY OF LIFE AND THE WAY OF DEATH.

THAT THERE ARE TWO WAYS, — THE ONE NATURAL, OF LIFE, AND THE OTHER INTRODUCED AFTERWARDS, OF DEATH; AND THAT THE FORMER IS FROM GOD, AND THE LATTER OF ERROR, FROM THE SNARES OF THE ADVERSARY.

I. THE lawgiver Moses said to the Israelites, "Behold, I have set before your face the way of life and the way of death;"[2] and added, "Choose life, that thou mayest live."[3] Elijah the prophet also said to the people: "How long will you halt with both your legs? If the Lord be God, follow Him."[4] The Lord Jesus also said justly: "No one can serve two masters: for either he will hate the one, and love the other; or else he will hold to the one, and despise the other."[5] We also, following our teacher Christ, "who is the Saviour of all men, especially of those that believe,"[6] are obliged to say that there are two ways — the one of life, the other of death;[7] which have no comparison one with another, for they are very different,[8] or rather entirely separate; and the way of life is that of nature, but that of death was afterwards introduced, — it not being according to the mind of God, but from the snares of the adversary.[9]

MORAL EXHORTATIONS OF THE LORD'S CONSTITUTIONS AGREEING WITH THE ANCIENT PROHIBITIONS OF THE DIVINE LAWS. THE PROHIBITION OF ANGER, SPITE, CORRUPTION, ADULTERY, AND EVERY FORBIDDEN ACTION.

II. The first way, therefore, is that of life; and is this,[10] which the law also does appoint: "To love the Lord God with all thy mind, and with all thy soul, who is the one and only God, besides whom there is no other;"[11] "and thy neighbour as thyself."[12] "And whatsoever thou wouldest not should be done to thee, that do not thou to another."[13] "Bless them that curse you; pray for them that despitefully use you."[14] "Love your enemies; for what thanks is it if ye love those that love you? for even the Gentiles do the same."[15] "But do ye love those that hate you, and ye shall have no enemy." For says He, "Thou shalt not hate any man; no, not an Egyptian, nor an Edomite;"[16] for they are all the workmanship of God. Avoid not the persons, but the sentiments, of the wicked. "Abstain from fleshly and worldly lusts."[17] "If any one gives thee a stroke on thy right cheek, turn to him the other also."[18] Not that revenge is evil, but that patience is more honourable. For David says, "If I have made returns to them that repaid me evil."[19] "If any one compel thee to go a mile, go with him twain."[20] And, "He that will sue thee at the law, and take away thy coat, let him have thy cloak also."[21] "And from him that taketh thy goods, require them not again."[22] "Give to him that asketh thee, and from him that would borrow of thee do not shut thy hand."[23] For "the righteous man is pitiful, and lendeth."[24] For your Father would have you give to all, who Himself "maketh His sun to rise on the evil and on the good, and sendeth His rain on the just and on the unjust."[25] It is therefore reasonable to give to all out of thine own labours; for says He, "Honour the Lord out of thy right-

1 [See pp. 377, *etc.*, *supra*.]
2 Deut. xxx. 15.
3 Deut. xxx. 19.
4 1 Kings xviii. 21.
5 Matt. vi. 24.
6 1 Tim. iv. 10.
7 [See *Teaching*, i. 1. — R.]
8 [*Teaching*, i. 1. — R.]
9 The Greek words properly mean: "Introduced was the way of death; not of that death which exists according to the mind of God, but that which has arisen from the plots of the adversary."
10 [The larger half of chap. i., *Teaching*, is found in the first half of this chapter; but the matter peculiar to each is of about the same extent. — R.]
11 Deut. vi. 5; Mark xii. 32.
12 Lev. xix. 18.
13 Tob. iv. 15.
14 Matt. v. 44.
15 Luke vi. 32; Matt. v. 46, 47.
16 Deut. xxiii. 7.
17 1 Pet. ii. 11.
18 Matt. v. 39; Luke vi. 29.
19 Ps. vii. 4.
20 Matt. v. 41.
21 Matt. v. 40; Luke vi. 29.
22 Luke vi. 30.
23 Matt. v. 42.
24 Ps. cxii. 5.
25 Matt. v. 45.

eous labours,"[1] but so that the saints be preferred.[2] "Thou shalt not kill;"[3] that is, thou shalt not destroy a man like thyself: for thou dissolvest what was well made. Not as if all killing were wicked, but only that of the innocent: but the killing which is just is reserved to the magistrates alone. "Thou shalt not commit adultery:" for thou dividest one flesh into two. "They two shall be one flesh:"[4] for the husband and wife are one in nature, in consent, in union, in disposition, and the conduct of life; but they are separated in sex and number. "Thou shalt not corrupt boys:"[5] for this wickedness is contrary to nature, and arose from Sodom, which was therefore entirely consumed with fire sent from God.[6] "Let such a one be accursed: and all the people shall say, So be it."[7] "Thou shalt not commit fornication:" for says He, "There shall not be a fornicator among the children of Israel."[8] "Thou shalt not steal:" for Achan, when he had stolen in Israel at Jericho, was stoned to death;[9] and Gehazi, who stole, and told a lie, inherited the leprosy of Naaman;[10] and Judas, who stole the poor's money, betrayed the Lord of glory to the Jews,[11] and repented, and hanged himself, and burst asunder in the midst, and all his bowels gushed out;[12] and Ananias, and Sapphira his wife, who stole their own goods, and "tempted the Spirit of the Lord," were immediately, at the sentence of Peter our fellow-apostle, struck dead.[13]

THE PROHIBITION OF CONJURING, MURDER OF INFANTS, PERJURY, AND FALSE WITNESS.

III. Thou shalt not use magic.[14] Thou shalt not use witchcraft; for He says, "Ye shall not suffer a witch to live."[15] Thou shall not slay thy child by causing abortion, nor kill that which is begotten; for "everything that is shaped, and has received a soul from God, if it be slain, shall be avenged, as being unjustly destroyed."[16] "Thou shalt not covet the things that belong to thy neighbour, as his wife, or his servant, or his ox, or his field." "Thou shalt not forswear thyself;" for it is said, "Thou shalt not swear at all."[17] But if that cannot be avoided, thou shalt swear truly; for "every one that swears by Him shall be commended."[18] "Thou shalt not bear false witness;" for "he that falsely accuses the needy provokes to anger Him that made him."[19]

THE PROHIBITION OF EVIL-SPEAKING AND PASSION, OF DECEITFUL CONDUCT, OR IDLE WORDS, LIES, COVETOUSNESS, AND HYPOCRISY.

IV. Thou shalt not speak evil;[20] for says He, "Love not to speak evil, lest thou beest taken away." Nor shalt thou be mindful of injuries; for "the ways of those that remember injuries are unto death."[21] Thou shalt not be double-minded nor double-tongued; for "a man's own lips are a strong snare to him,"[22] and "a talkative person shall not be prospered upon earth."[23] Thy words shall not be vain; for "ye shall give an account of every idle word."[24] Thou shalt not tell lies: for says He, "Thou shalt destroy all those that speak lies."[25] Thou shalt not be covetous nor rapacious: for says He, "Woe to him that is covetous towards his neighbour with an evil covetousness."[26]

THE PROHIBITION OF MALIGNITY, ACCEPTATION OF PERSONS, WRATH, MALICE, AND ENVY.

V. Thou shalt not be an hypocrite, lest thy "portion be with them."[27] Thou shalt not be ill-natured nor proud: for "God resisteth the proud."[28] "Thou shalt not accept persons in judgment; for the judgment is the Lord's." "Thou shalt not hate any man; thou shalt surely reprove thy brother, and not become guilty on his account;"[29] and, "Reprove a wise man, and he will love thee."[30] Eschew all evil, and all that is like it: for says He, "Abstain from injustice, and trembling shall not come nigh thee."[31] Be not soon angry, nor spiteful, nor passionate, nor furious, nor daring, lest thou undergo the fate of Cain, and of Saul, and of Joab: for the first of these slew his brother Abel, because Abel was found to be preferred before him with God, and because Abel's sacrifice was preferred;[32] the second persecuted holy David, who had slain Goliah the Philistine, being envious of the praises of the women who danced;[33] the third slew two gen-

1 Prov. iii. 9.
2 Gal. vi. 10.
3 [Ex. xx. 13. Five brief precepts, of which this is the first, are common to *Teaching*, ii. 2, and the rest of this chapter. — R.]
4 Gen. ii. 24.
5 Lev. xviii. 22.
6 Gen. xix.
7 Deut. xxvii.
8 Deut. xxiii. 17.
9 Josh. vii.
10 2 Kings v.
11 John xii. 6.
12 Matt. xxvii. 5; Acts i. 18.
13 Acts v.
14 [Seven brief clauses of *Teaching*, ii. 2, 3, are found in this chapter. — R.]
15 Ex. xxii. 18.
16 Ex. xxi. 23, LXX.
17 Matt. v. 34.
18 Ps. lxiii. 11.
19 Prov. xiv. 31.
20 [Chap. iv. also contains seven clauses found in *Teaching* (ii. 3-6), while chap. v. has but five and a verbal resemblance; chap. ii. of the *Teaching* is, however, almost entirely given in these passages. — R.]
21 Prov. xii. 28, LXX.
22 Prov. vi. 2.
23 Ps. cxl. 11.
24 Matt. xii. 36; Lev. xix. 11.
25 Ps. v. 6.
26 Hab. ii. 9.
27 Matt. xxiv. 51.
28 1 Pet. v. 5.
29 Deut. i. 17; Lev. xix. 17.
30 Prov. ix. 8.
31 Isa. liv. 14.
32 Gen. iv.
33 1 Sam. xvii., xviii.

erals of armies — Abner of Israel, and Amasa of Judah.[1]

CONCERNING AUGURY AND ENCHANTMENTS.

VI. Be not a diviner, for that leads to idolatry;[2] for says Samuel, "Divination is sin;"[3] and, "There shall be no divination in Jacob, nor soothsaying in Israel."[4] Thou shalt not use enchantments or purgations for thy child. Thou shall not be a soothsayer nor a diviner by great or little birds. Nor shalt thou learn wicked arts; for all these things has the law forbidden.[5] Be not one that wishes for evil, for thou wilt be led into intolerable sins. Thou shalt not speak obscenely, nor use wanton glances, nor be a drunkard; for from such causes arise whoredoms and adulteries. Be not a lover of money, lest thou "serve mammon instead of God."[6] Be not vainglorious, nor haughty, nor highminded. For from all these things arrogance does spring. Remember him who said: "Lord, my heart is not haughty, nor mine eyes lofty: I have not exercised myself in great matters, nor in things too high for me; but I was humble."[7]

THE PROHIBITION OF MURMURING, INSOLENCE, PRIDE, AND ARROGANCE.

VII. Be not a murmurer, remembering the punishment which those underwent who murmured against Moses. Be not self-willed, be not malicious, be not hard-hearted, be not passionate, be not mean-spirited; for all these things lead to blasphemy. But be meek, as were Moses and David,[8] since "the meek shall inherit the earth."[9]

CONCERNING LONG-SUFFERING, SIMPLICITY, MEEKNESS, AND PATIENCE.

VIII. Be slow to wrath; for such a one is very prudent, since "he that is hasty of spirit is a very fool."[10] Be merciful; for "blessed are the merciful: for they shall obtain mercy."[11] Be sincere, quiet, good, "trembling at the word of God."[12] Thou shalt not exalt thyself, as did the Pharisee; for "every one that exalteth himself shall be abased,"[13] and "that which is of high esteem with man is abomination with God."[14] Thou shalt not entertain confidence in thy soul; for "a confident man shall fall into mischief."[15] Thou shalt not go along with the foolish, but with the wise and righteous; for "he that walketh[16] with wise men shall be wise, but he that walketh with the foolish shall be known."[17] Receive the afflictions that fall upon thee with an even mind, and the chances of life without over-much sorrow, knowing that a reward shall be given to thee by God, as was given to Job and to Lazarus.[18]

THAT IT IS OUR DUTY TO ESTEEM OUR CHRISTIAN TEACHERS ABOVE OUR PARENTS — THE FORMER BEING THE MEANS OF OUR WELL-BEING, THE OTHER ONLY OF OUR BEING.

IX. Thou shalt honour him that speaks to thee the word of God, and be mindful of him day and night; and thou shalt reverence him,[19] not as the author of thy birth, but as one that is made the occasion of thy well-being. For where the doctrine concerning God is, there God is present. Thou shalt every day seek the face of the saints, that thou mayest acquiesce in their words.

THAT WE OUGHT NOT TO DIVIDE OURSELVES FROM THE SAINTS, BUT TO MAKE PEACE BETWEEN THOSE THAT QUARREL, TO JUDGE RIGHTEOUSLY, AND NOT TO ACCEPT PERSONS.

X. Thou shalt not make schisms among the saints, but be mindful of the followers of Corah.[20] Thou shalt make peace between those that are at variance, as Moses did when he persuaded them to be friends.[21] Thou shalt judge righteously; for "the judgment is the Lord's."[22] Thou shalt not accept persons when thou reprovest for sins; but do as Elijah and Micaiah did to Ahab, and Ebedmelech the Ethiopian to Zedekiah, and Nathan to David, and John to Herod.[23]

CONCERNING HIM THAT IS DOUBLE-MINDED AND DESPONDING.

XI. Be not of a doubtful mind in thy prayer, whether it shall be granted or no. For the Lord said to me Peter upon the sea: "O thou of little faith, wherefore didst thou doubt?"[24] "Be not thou ready to stretch out thy hand to receive, and to shut it when thou shouldst give."[25]

[1] 2 Sam. iii., xx.
[2] [Chaps. vi.-viii. contain passages parallel to nearly one-half of chap. iii., *Teaching*, and in the same order. — R.]
[3] 1 Sam. xv. 23.
[4] Num. xxiii. 23.
[5] Lev. xix. 26, 31; Deut. xviii. 10, 11.
[6] Matt. vi. 24.
[7] Ps. cxxxi. 1.
[8] Num. xii. 3; Ps. cxxxi. 1.
[9] Matt. v. 5.
[10] Prov. xiv. 29, LXX.
[11] Matt. v. 7.
[12] Isa. lxvi. 2.
[13] Luke xviii. 14.
[14] Luke xvi. 15.
[15] Prov. xiii. 17, LXX.
[16] The words from "for he that walketh" to "be known" are omitted in one V. MS.
[17] Prov. xiii. 20.
[18] Job xlii.; Luke xvi.
[19] [Chaps. ix.-xvii. contain nearly every clause of *Teaching*, chap. iv., in the same order, and with every appearance of a designed enlargement of that passage. — R.]
[20] Num. xvi.
[21] Ex. ii. 13.
[22] Deut. i. 17.
[23] 1 Kings xviii., xxi., xxii.; 2 Sam. xii.; Matt. xiv.
[24] Matt. xiv. 31.
[25] Ecclus. iv. 31.

CONCERNING DOING GOOD.

XII. If thou hast by the work of thy hands, give, that thou mayest labour for the redemption of thy sins; for "by alms and acts of faith sins are purged away."[1] Thou shalt not grudge to give to the poor, nor when thou hast given shalt thou murmur; for thou shalt know who will repay thee thy reward. For says he: "He that hath mercy on the poor man lendeth to the Lord; according to his gift, so shall it be repaid him again."[2] Thou shalt not turn away from him that is needy; for says he: "He that stoppeth his ears, that he may not hear the cry of the needy, himself also shall call, and there shall be none to hear him."[3] Thou shalt communicate in all things to thy brother, and shalt not say *thy goods* are thine own; for the common participation of the necessaries of life is appointed to all men by God. Thou shalt not take off thine hand from thy son or from thy daughter, but shalt teach them the fear of God from their youth; for says he: "Correct thy son, so shall he afford thee good hope."[4]

HOW MASTERS OUGHT TO BEHAVE THEMSELVES TO THEIR SERVANTS, AND HOW SERVANTS OUGHT TO BE SUBJECT.

XIII. Thou shalt not command thy man-servant, or thy maid-servant, who trust in the same God, with bitterness of soul, lest they groan against thee, and wrath be upon thee from God. And, ye servants, "be subject to your masters,"[5] as to the representatives of God, with attention and fear, "as to the Lord, and not to men."[6]

CONCERNING HYPOCRISY, AND OBEDIENCE TO THE LAWS, AND CONFESSION OF SINS.

XIV. Thou shalt hate all hypocrisy; and whatsoever is pleasing to the Lord, that shalt thou do. By no means forsake the commands of the Lord. But thou shalt observe what things thou hast received from Him, neither adding to them nor taking away from them. "For thou shalt not add unto His words, lest He convict thee, and thou becomest a liar."[7] Thou shalt confess thy sins unto the Lord thy God; and thou shalt not add unto them, that it may be well with thee from the Lord thy God, who willeth not the death of a sinner, but his repentance.

CONCERNING THE OBSERVANCE DUE TO PARENTS.

XV. Thou shalt be observant to thy father and mother as the causes of thy being born, that thou mayest live long on the earth which the Lord thy God giveth thee. Do not overlook thy brethren or thy kinsfolk; for "thou shalt not overlook those nearly related to thee."[8]

CONCERNING THE SUBJECTION DUE TO THE KING AND TO RULERS.

XVI. Thou shalt fear the king, knowing that his appointment is of the Lord. His rulers thou shalt honour as the ministers of God, for they are the revengers of all unrighteousness; to whom pay taxes, tribute, and every oblation with a willing mind.

CONCERNING THE PURE CONSCIENCE OF THOSE THAT PRAY.

XVII. Thou shalt not proceed to thy prayer in the day of thy wickedness, before thou hast laid aside thy bitterness. This is the way of life, in which may ye be found, through Jesus Christ our Lord.

THAT THE WAY WHICH WAS AFTERWARD INTRODUCED BY THE SNARES OF THE ADVERSARY IS FULL OF IMPIETY AND WICKEDNESS.

XVIII. But the way of death[9] is known by its wicked practices: for therein is the ignorance of God, and the introduction of many evils, and disorders, and disturbances; whereby come murders, adulteries, fornications, perjuries, unlawful lusts, thefts, idolatries, magic arts, witchcrafts, rapines, false-witnesses, hypocrisies, double-heartedness, deceit, pride, malice, insolence, covetousness, obscene talk, jealousy, confidence, haughtiness, arrogance, impudence, persecution of the good, enmity to truth, love of lies, ignorance of righteousness. For they who do such things do not adhere to goodness, or to righteous judgment: they watch not for good, but for evil; from whom meekness and patience are far off, who love vain things, pursuing after reward, having no pity on the poor, not labouring for him that is in misery, nor knowing Him that made them; murderers of infants, destroyers of the workmanship of God, that turn away from the needy, adding affliction to the afflicted, the flatterers of the rich, the despisers of the poor, full of sin. May you, children, be delivered from all these.

THAT WE MUST NOT TURN FROM THE WAY OF PIETY EITHER TO THE RIGHT HAND OR TO THE LEFT. AN EXHORTATION OF THE LAWGIVER.

XIX. See that no one seduce thee[10] from piety; for says He: "Thou mayst not turn aside from

[1] Prov. xvi. 6; Dan. iv. 27.
[2] Prov. xix. 17.
[3] Prov. xxi. 13.
[4] Prov. xix. 18.
[5] Eph. vi. 5.
[6] Eph. vi. 7.
[7] Prov. xxx. 6.
[8] Isa. lviii. 7.
[9] [For the remarkable agreement of this chapter with *Teaching*, chap. v., see the latter: comp. also *Barnabas*, xx. — R.]
[10] [Chaps. xix.-xxi. have few parallels with the *Teaching*. — R.]

it to the right hand, or to the left, that thou mayst have understanding in all that thou doest."[1] For if thou dost not turn out of the right way, thou wilt not be ungodly.

SEC. II. — ON THE FORMATION OF THE CHARACTER OF BELIEVERS, AND ON GIVING OF THANKS TO GOD.

THAT WE OUGHT NOT TO DESPISE ANY OF THE SORTS OF FOOD THAT ARE SET BEFORE US, BUT GRATEFULLY AND ORDERLY TO PARTAKE OF THEM.

XX. Now concerning the several sorts of food, the Lord says to thee, "Ye shall eat the good things of the earth;"[2] and, "All sorts of flesh shall ye eat, as the green herb;"[3] but, "Thou shalt pour out the blood."[4] For "not those things that go into the mouth, but those that come out of it, defile a man;"[5] I mean blasphemies, evil-speaking, and if there be any other thing of the like nature.[6] But "do thou eat the fat of the land with righteousness."[7] For "if there be anything pleasant, it is His; and if there be anything good, it is His. Wheat for the young men, and wine to cheer the maids." For "who shall eat or who shall drink without Him?"[8] Wise Ezra[9] does also admonish thee, and say: "Go your way, and eat the fat, and drink the sweet, and be not sorrowful."[10]

THAT WE OUGHT TO AVOID THE EATING OF THINGS OFFERED TO IDOLS.

XXI. But do ye abstain from things offered to idols;[11] for they offer them in honour of demons, that is, to the dishonour of the one God, that ye may not become partners with demons.

A CONSTITUTION OF OUR LORD, HOW WE OUGHT TO BAPTIZE, AND INTO WHOSE DEATH.

XXII. Now concerning baptism,[12] O bishop, or presbyter, we have already given direction, and we now say, that thou shalt so baptize as the Lord commanded us, saying: "Go ye, and teach all nations, baptizing them in the name of the Father, and of the Son, and of the Holy Ghost (teaching them to observe all things whatsoever I have commanded you):"[13] of the Father who sent, of Christ who came, of the Comforter who testified. But thou shalt beforehand anoint the person with the holy oil, and afterward baptize him with the water, and in the conclusion shalt seal him with the ointment; that the anointing with oil may be the participation of the Holy Spirit, and the water the symbol of the death *of Christ*, and the ointment the seal of the covenants. But if there be neither oil nor ointment, water is sufficient both for the anointing, and for the seal, and for the confession of Him that is dead, or indeed is dying together *with Christ*. But before baptism, let him that is to be baptized fast; for even the Lord, when He was first baptized by John, and abode in the wilderness, did afterward fast forty days and forty nights.[14] But He was baptized, and then fasted, not having Himself any need of cleansing, or of fasting, or of purgation, who was by nature pure and holy; but that He might testify the truth to John, and afford an example to us. Wherefore our Lord was not baptized into His own passion, or death, or resurrection — for none of those things had then happened — but for another purpose. Wherefore He by His own authority fasted after His baptism, as being the Lord of John. But he who is to be initiated into His death ought first to fast, and then to be baptized. For it is not reasonable that he who has been buried *with Christ*, and is risen again with Him, should appear dejected at His very resurrection. For man is not lord of our Saviour's constitution, since one is the Master and the other the servant.

WHICH DAYS OF THE WEEK WE ARE TO FAST, AND WHICH NOT, AND FOR WHAT REASONS.

XXIII. But let not your fasts be with the hypocrites;[15] for they fast on the second and fifth days of the week. But do you either fast the entire five days, or on the fourth day of the week, and on the day of the Preparation, because on the fourth day the condemnation went out against the Lord, Judas then promising to betray Him for money; and you must fast on the day of the Preparation, because on that day the Lord suffered the death of the cross under Pontius Pilate. But keep the Sabbath, and the Lord's day festival; because the former is the memorial of the creation, and the latter of the resurrection. But there is one only Sabbath to be observed by you in the whole year, which is that of our Lord's burial, on which men ought to keep a fast, but not a festival. For inasmuch as the Creator was then under the earth, the sorrow for Him is more forcible than the joy for the creation; for the Creator is more honourable by nature and dignity than His own creatures.

1 Deut. v. 32.
2 Isa. i. 19.
3 Gen. ix. 3.
4 Deut. xv. 23.
5 Matt. xv. 11.
6 Mark vii. 22.
7 Zech. ix. 17.
8 Eccles. ii. 25, LXX.
9 The words from "Wise Ezra" to "sorrowful" are not in one V. MS.
10 Neh. viii. 10.
11 1 Cor. x. 20.
12 [Comp., with this chapter, *Teaching*, chap. vii. — R.]
13 Matt. xxviii. 19.
14 Matt. iii., iv.
15 [Comp. the few but remarkable resemblances of *Teaching*, chap. viii., with chaps. xxiii., xxiv., here. — R.]

WHAT SORT OF PEOPLE OUGHT TO PRAY THAT PRAYER THAT WAS GIVEN BY THE LORD.

XXIV. Now, "when ye pray, be not ye as the hypocrites;" [1] but as the Lord has appointed us in the Gospel, so pray ye: "Our Father which art in heaven, hallowed be Thy name; Thy kingdom come; Thy will be done, as in heaven, so on earth; give us this day our daily bread; and forgive us our debts, as we forgive our debtors; and lead us not into temptation, but deliver us from evil; for Thine is the kingdom for ever. Amen." [2] Pray thus thrice in a day, preparing yourselves beforehand, that ye may be worthy of the adoption of the Father; lest, when you call Him Father unworthily, you be reproached by Him, as Israel once His first-born son was told: "If I be a Father, where is my glory? And if I be a Lord, where is my fear?" [3] For the glory of fathers is the holiness of their children, and the honour of masters is the fear of their servants, as the contrary is dishonour and confusion. For says He: "Through you my name is blasphemed among the Gentiles." [4]

A MYSTICAL THANKSGIVING.

XXV. Be ye always thankful, as faithful and honest servants; and concerning the eucharistical thanksgiving say thus: [5] We thank Thee, our Father, for that life which Thou hast made known to us by Jesus Thy Son, by whom Thou madest all things, and takest care of the whole world; whom Thou hast sent to become man for our salvation; whom Thou hast permitted to suffer and to die; whom Thou hast raised up, and been pleased to glorify, and hast set Him down on Thy right hand; by whom Thou hast promised us the resurrection of the dead. Do thou, O Lord Almighty, everlasting God, so gather together Thy Church from the ends of the earth into Thy kingdom, as this *corn* was once scattered, and is now become one loaf. We also, our Father, thank Thee for the precious blood of Jesus Christ, which was shed for us, and for His precious body, whereof we celebrate this representation, as Himself appointed us, "to show forth His death." [6] For through Him glory is to be given to Thee for ever. Amen. Let no one eat of these things that is not initiated; but those only who have been baptized into the death of the Lord. But if any one that is not initiated conceal himself, and partake of the same, "he eats eternal damnation;" [7] because, being not of the faith of Christ, he has partaken of such things as it is not lawful for him to partake of, to his own punishment. But if any one is a partaker through ignorance, instruct him quickly, and initiate him, that he may not go out and despise you.

A THANKSGIVING AT THE DIVINE PARTICIPATION.

XXVI. After the participation,[8] give thanks in this manner: We thank thee, O God and Father of Jesus our Saviour, for Thy holy name, which Thou hast made to inhabit among us; and that knowledge, faith, love, and immortality which Thou hast given us through Thy Son Jesus. Thou, O Almighty Lord, the God of the universe, hast created the world, and the things that are therein, by Him; and hast planted a law in our souls, and beforehand didst prepare things for the convenience of men. O God of our holy and blameless fathers, Abraham, and Isaac, and Jacob, Thy faithful servants; Thou, O God, who art powerful, faithful, and true, and without deceit in Thy promises; who didst send upon earth Jesus Thy Christ to live with men, as a man, when He was God the Word, and man, to take away error by the roots: do Thou even now, through Him, be mindful of this Thy holy Church, which Thou hast purchased with the precious blood of Thy Christ, and deliver it from all evil, and perfect it in Thy love and Thy truth, and gather us all together into Thy kingdom which Thou hast prepared. Let this Thy kingdom come.[9] "Hosanna to the Son of David. Blessed be He that cometh in the name of the Lord" [10] — God the Lord, who was manifested to us in the flesh. If any one be holy, let him draw near; but if any one be not such, let him become such by repentance. Permit also to your presbyters to give thanks.

A THANKSGIVING ABOUT THE MYSTICAL OINTMENT.

XXVII. Concerning the ointment give thanks in this manner: We give Thee thanks, O God, the Creator of the whole world, both for the fragrancy of the ointment, and for the immortality which Thou hast made known to us by Thy Son Jesus. For Thine is the glory and the power for ever. Amen. Whosoever comes to you,[11] and gives thanks in this manner, receive him as a disciple of Christ. But if he preach another doctrine, different from that which Christ by us has delivered to you, such a one you must not permit to give thanks; for such a one rather affronts God than glorifies Him.

---

[1] Matt. vi. 5.
[2] Matt. vi. 9, etc.
[3] Mal. i. 6.
[4] Isa. lii. 5.
[5] [See the eucharistic prayer in *Teaching*, chap. ix. The correspondences and divergences are alike interesting. — R.]
[6] 1 Cor. xi. 26.
[7] 1 Cor. xi. 59 [See Elucidation I. p. 382, *supra*.]
[8] [Comp. *Teaching*, chap. x. — R.]
[9] ["Maran atha," as in *Teaching*. — R.]
[10] 1 Cor. xvi. 22; Matt. xxi. 9; Mark xi. 10. [Comp. John xii. 13. — R.]
[11] [Comp. *Teaching*, chap. xi., where, however, only a few phrases correspond. — R.]

THAT WE OUGHT NOT TO BE INDIFFERENT ABOUT COMMUNICATING.

XXVIII. But whosoever comes to you, let him be first examined, and then received; for ye have understanding, and are able to know the right hand from the left,[1] and to distinguish false teachers from true teachers. But when a teacher comes to you, supply him with what he wants with all readiness. And even when a false teacher comes, you shall give him for his necessity, but shall not receive his error. Nor indeed may ye pray together with him, lest ye be polluted as well as he. Every true prophet or teacher[2] that comes to you is worthy of his maintenance, as being a labourer in the word of righteousness.[3]

A CONSTITUTION CONCERNING OBLATIONS.

XXIX. All the first-fruits of the winepress, the threshing-floor, the oxen, and the sheep, shalt thou give to the priests,[4] that thy storehouses and garners and the products of thy land may be blessed, and thou mayst be strengthened with corn and wine and oil, and the herds of thy cattle and flocks of thy sheep may be increased. Thou shalt give the tenth of thy increase to the orphan, and to the widow, and to the poor, and to the stranger. All the first-fruits of thy hot bread, of thy barrels of wine, or oil, or honey, or nuts, or grapes, or the first-fruits of other things, shalt thou give to the priests; but those of silver, and of garments, and of all sort of possessions, to the orphan and to the widow.

HOW WE OUGHT TO ASSEMBLE TOGETHER, AND TO CELEBRATE THE FESTIVAL DAY OF OUR SAVIOUR'S RESURRECTION.

XXX. On the day of the resurrection of the Lord,[5] that is, the Lord's day, assemble yourselves together, without fail, giving thanks to God, and praising Him for those mercies God has bestowed upon you through Christ, and has delivered you from ignorance, error, and bondage, that your sacrifice may be unspotted, and acceptable to God, who has said concerning His universal Church: "In every place shall incense and a pure sacrifice be offered unto me; for I am a great King, saith the Lord Almighty, and my name is wonderful among the heathen."[6]

WHAT QUALIFICATIONS THEY OUGHT TO HAVE WHO ARE TO BE ORDAINED.

XXXI. Do you first ordain bishops worthy of the Lord,[7] and presbyters and deacons, pious men, righteous, meek, free from the love of money, lovers of truth, approved, holy, not accepters of persons, who are able to teach the word of piety, and rightly dividing the doctrines of the Lord.[8] And do ye honour such as your fathers, as your lords, as your benefactors, as the causes of your well-being. Reprove ye one another, not in anger, but in mildness, with kindness and peace. Observe all things that are commanded you by the Lord. Be watchful for your life.[9] "Let your loins be girded about, and your lights burning, and ye like unto men who wait for their Lord, when He will come, at even, or in the morning, or at cock-crowing, or at midnight. For at what hour they think not, the Lord will come; and if they open to Him, blessed are those servants, because they were found watching. For He will gird Himself, and will make them to sit down to meat, and will come forth and serve them."[10] Watch therefore, and pray, that ye do not sleep unto death. For your former good deeds will not profit you, if at the last part of your life you go astray from the true faith.

A PREDICTION CONCERNING FUTURITIES.

XXXII. For in the last days false prophets shall be multiplied, and such as corrupt the word; and the sheep shall be changed into wolves, and love into hatred: for through the abounding of iniquity the love of many shall wax cold. For men shall hate, and persecute, and betray one another. And then shall appear the deceiver of the world, the enemy of the truth, the prince of lies,[11] whom the Lord Jesus "shall destroy with the spirit of His mouth, who takes away the wicked with His lips; and many shall be offended at Him. But they that endure to the end, the same shall be saved. And then shall appear the sign of the Son of man in heaven;"[12] and afterwards shall be the voice of a trumpet by the archangel;[13] and in that interval shall be the revival of those that were asleep. And then shall the Lord come, and all His saints with Him,[14] with a great concussion above the clouds, with the angels of His power,[15] in the throne of His kingdom, to condemn *the devil*, the deceiver of the world, and to render to every one according to his deeds. "Then shall the wicked go away into everlasting punishment, but the righteous shall go into life eternal,"[16] to inherit those things "which eye hath not seen, nor ear heard, nor

1 [This sentence is found in *Teaching*, chap. xii. — R.]
2 [Part of this sentence has a parallel in *Teaching*, chap. xiii., but there is an obvious difference of circumstances. Chap. xxix. presents more parallel passages. — R.]
3 Matt. x. 41.
4 Num. xviii.
5 [The resemblance to *Teaching*, chap. xiv., is marked. — R.]
6 Mal. i. 11, 14.
7 [Comp. text and notes, *Teaching*, chap. xv. — R.]

8 2 Tim. ii. 15.
9 [This clause is found *verbatim* in *Teaching*, chap. xvi. There is a resemblance also, in order of topics, from this point down to the phrase "above the clouds;" see chap. xxxii. No further correspondences appear. — R.]
10 Luke xii. 35, 37; Mark xiii. 35.
11 2 Thess. ii.
12 Isa. xi. 4; Matt. xxiv.
13 1 Thess. iv. 16.
14 [Zech. xiv. 5. — R.]
15 Matt. xvi. 27.
16 Matt. xxv. 46.

have entered into the heart of man, such things as God hath prepared for them that love Him;"[1] and they shall rejoice in the kingdom of God, which is in Christ Jesus. Since we are vouchsafed such great blessings from Him, let us become His suppliants, and call upon Him by continual prayer, and say:—

A PRAYER DECLARATIVE OF GOD'S VARIOUS PROVIDENCE.

XXXIII. Our eternal Saviour, the King of gods, who alone art almighty, and the Lord, the God of all beings, and the God of our holy and blameless fathers, and of those before us; the God of Abraham, and of Isaac, and of Jacob; who art merciful and compassionate, long-suffering, and abundant in mercy; to whom every heart is naked, and by whom every heart is seen, and to whom every secret thought is revealed: to Thee do the souls of the righteous cry aloud, upon Thee do the hopes of the godly trust, Thou Father of the blameless, Thou hearer of the supplication of those that call upon Thee with uprightness, and who knowest the supplications that are not uttered: for Thy providence reaches as far as the inmost parts of mankind; and by Thy knowledge Thou searchest the thoughts of every one, and in every region of the whole earth the incense of prayer and supplication is sent up to Thee. O Thou who hast appointed this present world as a place of combat to righteousness, and hast opened to all the gate of mercy, and hast demonstrated to every man by implanted knowledge, and natural judgment, and the admonitions of the law, how the possession of riches is not everlasting, the ornament of beauty is not perpetual, our strength and force are easily dissolved; and that all is vapour and vanity; and that only the good conscience of faith unfeigned passes through the midst of the heavens, and returning with truth, takes hold of the right hand of the joy[2] which is to come. And withal, before the promise of the restoration of all things is accomplished, the soul itself exults in hope, and is joyful. For from that truth which was in our forefather Abraham, when he changed his way Thou didst guide him by a vision, and didst teach him what kind of state this world is; and knowledge went before his faith, and faith was the consequence of his knowledge; and the covenant did follow after his faith. For Thou saidst: "I will make thy seed as the stars of heaven, and as the sand which is by the sea-shore."[3] Moreover, when Thou hadst given him Isaac, and knewest him to be like him in his mode of life, Thou wast then called his God, saying: "I will be a God to thee, and to thy seed after thee."[4] And when our father Jacob was sent into Mesopotamia, Thou showedst him Christ, and by him speakest, saying: "Behold, I am with thee, and I will increase thee, and multiply thee exceedingly."[5] And so spakest Thou to Moses, Thy faithful and holy servant, at the vision of the bush: "I am He that is; this is my name for ever, and my memorial for generations of generations."[6] O Thou great protector of the posterity of Abraham, Thou art blessed for ever.

A PRAYER DECLARATIVE OF GOD'S VARIOUS CREATION.

XXXIV. Thou art blessed, O Lord, the King of ages, who by Christ hast made the whole world, and by Him in the beginning didst reduce into order the disordered parts; who dividedst the waters from the waters by a firmament, and didst put into them a spirit of life; who didst fix the earth, and stretch out the heaven, and didst dispose every creature by an accurate constitution. For by Thy power, O Lord, the world is beautified, the heaven is fixed as an arch over us, and is rendered illustrious with stars for our comfort in the darkness. The light also and the sun were begotten for days and the production of fruit, and the moon for the change of seasons, by its increase and diminutions; and one was called Night, and the other Day. And the firmament was exhibited in the midst of the abyss, and Thou commandedst the waters to be gathered together, and the dry land to appear. But as for the sea itself, who can possibly describe it, which comes with fury from the ocean, yet runs back again, being stopped by the sand at Thy command? For Thou hast said: "Thereby shall her waves be broken."[7] Thou hast also made it capable of supporting little and great creatures, and made it navigable for ships. Then did the earth become green, and was planted with all sorts of flowers, and the variety of several trees; and the shining luminaries, the nourishers of those plants, preserve their unchangeable course, and in nothing depart from Thy command. But where Thou biddest them, there do they rise and set for signs of the seasons and of the years, making a constant return of the work of men. Afterwards the kinds of the several animals were created—those belonging to the land, to the water, to the air, and both to air and water; and the artificial wisdom of Thy providence does still impart to every one a suitable providence. For as He was not unable to produce different kinds, so neither has He disdained to exercise a

1 1 Cor. ii. 9.
2 A conjecture of Cotelerius is adopted. The MSS. read "nourishment" instead of "joy."
3 Gen. xiii. 16, xxii. 17.
4 Gen. xxvi. 3.
5 Gen. xvii. 7, xxviii. 15, xlviii. 4.
6 Ex. iii. 14, 15.
7 Job xxxviii. 11.

different providence towards every one. And at the conclusion of the creation Thou gavest direction to Thy Wisdom, and formedst a reasonable creature as the citizen of the world, saying, "Let us make man after our image, and after our likeness;"[1] and hast exhibited him as the ornament of the world, and formed him a body out of the four elements, those primary bodies, but hadst prepared a soul out of nothing, and bestowedst upon him his five senses, and didst set over his sensations a mind as the conductor of the soul. And besides all these things, O Lord God, who can worthily declare the motion of the rainy clouds, the shining of the lightning, the noise of the thunder, in order to the supply of proper food, and the most agreeable temperature of the air? But when man was disobedient, Thou didst deprive him of the life which should have been his reward. Yet didst Thou not destroy him for ever, but laidst him to sleep for a time; and Thou didst by oath call him to a resurrection, and loosedst the bond of death, O Thou reviver of the dead, through Jesus Christ, who is our hope.

A PRAYER, WITH THANKSGIVING, DECLARATIVE OF GOD'S PROVIDENCE OVER THE BEINGS HE HAS MADE.

XXXV. Great art thou, O Lord Almighty, and great is Thy power, and of Thy understanding there is no number. Our Creator and Saviour, rich in benefits, long-suffering, and the bestower of mercy, who dost not take away Thy salvation from Thy creatures: for Thou art good by nature, and sparest sinners, and invitest them to repentance; for admonition is the effect of Thy bowels of compassion. For how should we abide if we were required to come to judgment immediately, when, after so much long-suffering, we hardly get clear of our miserable condition? The heavens declare Thy dominion, and the earth shakes with earthquakes, and, hanging upon nothing, declares Thy unshaken stedfastness. The sea raging with waves, and feeding a flock of ten thousand creatures, is bounded with sand, as standing in awe at Thy command, and compels all men to cry out: "How great are Thy works, O Lord! in wisdom hast Thou made them all: the earth is full of Thy creation."[2] And the bright host of angels and the intellectual spirits say to Palmoni,[3] "There is but one holy Being;"[4] and the holy seraphim, together with the six-winged cherubim, who sing to Thee their triumphal song, cry out with never-ceasing voices, "Holy, holy, holy, Lord God of hosts! heaven and earth are full of Thy glory;"[5] and the other multitudes of the orders, angels archangels, thrones, dominions, principalities, authorities, and powers cry aloud, and say, "Blessed be the glory of the Lord out of His place."[6] But Israel, Thy Church on earth, taken out of the Gentiles, emulating the heavenly powers night and day, with a full heart and a willing soul sings, "The chariot of God is ten thousandfold thousands of them that rejoice: the Lord is among them in Sinai, in the holy place."[7] The heaven knows Him who fixed it as a cube of stone, in the form of an arch, upon nothing, who united the land and water to one another, and scattered the vital air all abroad, and conjoined fire therewith for warmth, and the comfort against darkness. The choir of stars strikes us with admiration, declaring Him that numbers them, and showing Him that names them; the animals declare Him that puts life into them; the trees show Him that makes them grow: all which creatures, being made by Thy word, show forth the greatness of Thy power. Wherefore every man ought to send up an hymn from his very soul to Thee, through Christ, in the name of all the rest, since He has power over them all by Thy appointment. For Thou art kind in Thy benefits, and beneficent in Thy bowels of compassion, who alone art almighty: for when Thou willest, to be able is present with Thee; for Thy eternal power both quenches flame, and stops the mouths of lions, and tames whales, and raises up the sick, and overrules the power of all things, and overturns the host of enemies, and casts down a people numbered in their arrogance. Thou art He who art in heaven, He who art on earth, He who art in the sea, He who art in finite things, Thyself unconfined by anything. For of Thy majesty there is no boundary; for it is not ours, O Lord, but the oracle of Thy servant, who said, "And thou shalt know in thine heart that the Lord thy God He is God in heaven above, and on earth beneath, and there is none other besides Thee:"[8] for there is no God besides Thee alone, there is none holy besides Thee, the Lord, the God of knowledge, the God of the saints, holy above all holy beings; for they are sanctified by Thy hands. Thou art glorious, and highly exalted, invisible by nature, and unsearchable in Thy judgments; whose life is without want, whose duration can never alter or fail, whose operation is without toil, whose greatness is unlimited, whose excellency is perpetual, whose habitation is inaccessible, whose dwelling is unchangeable, whose knowledge is without beginning, whose truth is immutable, whose work is without assistants, whose dominion cannot be

1 Gen. i. 26.
2 Ps. civ. 24.
3 [i.e., "the wonderful Numberer;" *Eng.*, *marg.*]
4 Dan. viii. 13. [Not according to Heb. nor LXX. as now.]
5 Isa. vi. 3.
6 Ezek. iii. 12.
7 Ps. lxvii. 17.
8 Deut. iv. 39.

taken away, whose monarchy is without succession, whose kingdom is without end, whose strength is irresistible, whose army is very numerous: for Thou art the Father of wisdom, the Creator of the creation, by a Mediator, as the cause; the Bestower of providence, the Giver of laws, the Supplier of want, the Punisher of the ungodly, and the Rewarder of the righteous; the God and Father of Christ, and the Lord of those that are pious towards Him, whose promise is infallible, whose judgment without bribes, whose sentiments are immutable, whose piety is incessant, whose thanksgiving is everlasting, through whom [1] adoration is worthily due to Thee from every rational and holy nature.

A PRAYER COMMEMORATIVE OF THE INCARNATION OF CHRIST, AND HIS VARIOUS PROVIDENCE TO THE SAINTS.

XXXVI. O Lord Almighty, Thou hast created the world by Christ, and hast appointed the Sabbath in memory thereof, because that on that day Thou hast made us rest from our works, for the meditation upon Thy laws. Thou hast also appointed festivals for the rejoicing of our souls, that we might come into the remembrance of that wisdom which was created by Thee; how He submitted to be made of a woman on our account; [2] He appeared in life, and demonstrated Himself in His baptism; how He that appeared is both God and man; He suffered for us by Thy permission, and died, and rose again by Thy power: on which account we solemnly assemble to celebrate the feast of the resurrection on the Lord's day, and rejoice on account of Him who has conquered death, and has brought life and immortality to light. For by Him Thou hast brought home the Gentiles to Thyself for a peculiar people, the true Israel, beloved of God, and seeing God. For Thou, O Lord, broughtest our fathers out of the land of Egypt, and didst deliver them out of the iron furnace, from clay and brick-making, and didst redeem them out of the hands of Pharaoh, and of those under him, and didst lead them through the sea as through dry land, and didst bear their manners in the wilderness, and bestow on them all sorts of good things. Thou didst give them the law or decalogue, which was pronounced by Thy voice and written with Thy hand. Thou didst enjoin the observation of the Sabbath, not affording them an occasion of idleness, but an opportunity of piety, for their knowledge of Thy power, and the prohibition of evils; having limited them as within an holy circuit for the sake of doctrine, for the rejoicing upon the seventh period. On this account was there appointed one week, and seven weeks, and the seventh month, and the seventh year, and the revolution of these, the jubilee, which is the fiftieth year for remission, that men might have no occasion to pretend ignorance.[3] On this account He permitted men every Sabbath to rest, that so no one might be willing to send one word out of his mouth in anger on the day of the Sabbath. For the Sabbath is the ceasing of the creation, the completion of the world, the inquiry after laws, and the grateful praise to God for the blessings He has bestowed upon men. All which the Lord's day excels,[4] and shows the Mediator Himself, the Provider, the Lawgiver, the Cause of the resurrection, the First-born of the whole creation, God the Word, and man, who was born of Mary alone, without a man, who lived holily, who was crucified under Pontius Pilate, and died, and rose again from the dead. So that the Lord's day commands us to offer unto Thee, O Lord, thanksgiving for all.[5] For this is the grace afforded by Thee, which on account of its greatness has obscured all other blessings.

A PRAYER CONTAINING THE MEMORIAL OF HIS PROVIDENCE, AND AN ENUMERATION OF THE VARIOUS BENEFITS AFFORDED THE SAINTS BY THE PROVIDENCE OF GOD THROUGH CHRIST.

XXXVII. Thou who hast fulfilled Thy promises made by the prophets, and hast had mercy on Zion, and compassion on Jerusalem, by exalting the throne of David, Thy servant, in the midst of her, by the birth of Christ, who was born of his seed according to the flesh, of a virgin alone; do Thou now, O Lord God, accept the prayers which proceed from the lips of Thy people which are of the Gentiles, which call upon Thee in truth, as Thou didst accept of the gifts of the righteous in their generations. In the first place Thou did respect the sacrifice of Abel,[6] and accept it as Thou didst accept of the sacrifice of Noah when he went out of the ark;[7] of Abraham, when he went out of the land of the Chaldeans;[8] of Isaac at the Well of the Oath;[9] of Jacob in Bethel;[10] of Moses in the desert;[11] of Aaron between the dead and the living;[12] of Joshua the son of Nun in Gilgal;[13] of Gideon at the rock, and the fleeces, before his sin;[14] of Manoah and his wife in the field; of Samson in his thirst before the transgression;[15] of Jephtha

1 One V. MS. reads, "with whom."
2 Prov. viii. 22, LXX.

3 Lev. xxiii., xxv.
4 [Vol. vi. p. 149, note 8, this series.]
5 [Justin Martyr, vol. i. p. 186, this series.]
6 Gen. iv.
7 Gen. viii.
8 Gen. xii.
9 Gen. xxvi.
10 Gen. xxxv.
11 Ex. iii.
12 Num. xvi.
13 Josh. v.
14 Judg. vi., viii.
15 Judg. xiii., xv., xvi.

in the war before his rash vow; of Barak and Deborah in the days of Sisera;[1] of Samuel in Mizpeh;[2] of David in the threshing-floor of Ornan the Jebusite;[3] of Solomon in Gibeon and in Jerusalem:[4] of Elijah in Mount Carmel;[5] of Elisha at the barren fountain;[6] of Jehoshaphat in war;[7] of Hezekiah in his sickness, and concerning Sennacherib;[8] of Manasseh in the land of the Chaldeans, after his transgression;[9] of Josiah in Phassa;[10] of Ezra at the return;[11] of Daniel in the den of lions;[12] of Jonah in the whale's belly;[13] of the three children in the fiery furnace;[14] of Hannah in the tabernacle before the ark;[15] of Nehemiah at the rebuilding of the walls;[16] of Zerubbabel; of Mattathias and his sons in their zeal;[17] of Jael in blessings. Now also do Thou receive the prayers of Thy people which are offered to Thee with knowledge, through Christ in the Spirit.

A PRAYER FOR THE ASSISTANCE OF THE RIGHTEOUS.

XXXVIII. We give Thee thanks for all things, O Lord Almighty, that Thou hast not taken away Thy mercies and Thy compassions from us; but in every succeeding generation Thou dost save, and deliver, and assist, and protect: for Thou didst assist in the days of Enos and Enoch, in the days of Moses and Joshua, in the days of the judges, in the days of Samuel and of Elijah and of the prophets, in the days of David and of the kings, in the days of Esther and Mordecai, in the days of Judith, in the days of Judas Maccabeus and his brethren, and in our days hast Thou assisted us by Thy great High Priest, Jesus Christ Thy Son. For He has delivered us from the sword, and hath freed us from famine, and sustained us; has delivered us from sickness, has preserved us from an evil tongue. For all which things do we give Thee thanks through Christ, who has given us an articulate voice to confess withal, and added to it a suitable tongue as an instrument to modulate withal, and a proper taste, and a suitable touch, and a sight for contemplation, and the hearing of sounds, and the smelling of vapours, and hands for work, and feet for walking. And all these members dost Thou form from a little drop in the womb; and after the formation dost Thou bestow on it an immortal soul, and producest it into the light as a rational creature, even man. Thou hast instructed him by Thy laws, improved him by Thy statutes; and when Thou bringest on a dissolution for a while, Thou hast promised a resurrection. Wherefore what life is sufficient, what length of ages will be long enough, for men to be thankful? To do it worthily it is impossible, but to do it according to our ability is just and right. For Thou hast delivered us from the impiety of polytheism, and from the heresy of the murderers of Christ; Thou hast delivered us from error and ignorance; Thou hast sent Christ among men as a man, being the only begotten God; Thou hast made the Comforter to inhabit among us; Thou hast set angels over us; Thou hast put the devil to shame; Thou hast brought us into being when we were not; Thou takest care of us when made; Thou measurest out life to us; Thou affordest us food; Thou hast promised repentance. Glory and worship be to Thee for all these things, through Jesus Christ,[18] now and ever, and through all ages. Amen. Meditate on these things, brethren; and the Lord be with you upon earth, and in the kingdom of His Father, who both sent Him, and has "delivered us by Him from the bondage of corruption into His glorious liberty;"[19] and has promised life to those who through Him have believed in the God of the whole world.

SEC. III. — ON THE INSTRUCTION OF CATECHUMENS, AND THEIR INITIATION INTO BAPTISM.

Now, after what manner those ought to live that are initiated into Christ, and what thanksgivings they ought to send up to God through Christ, has been said in the foregoing directions. But it is reasonable not to leave even those who are not yet initiated without assistance.

HOW THE CATECHUMENS ARE TO BE INSTRUCTED IN THE ELEMENTS.

XXXIX. Let him, therefore, who is to be taught the truth in regard to piety be instructed before his baptism in the knowledge of the unbegotten God, in the understanding of His only begotten Son, in the assured acknowledgment of the Holy Ghost. Let him learn the order of the several parts of the creation, the series of providence, the different dispensations of Thy laws. Let him be instructed why the world was made, and why man was appointed to be a citizen therein;

1 Judg. xi., iv.
2 1 Sam. vii.
3 1 Chron. xxi.
4 1 Kings iii., viii.
5 1 Kings xviii.
6 2 Kings ii.
7 2 Chron. xviii.
8 2 Kings xx., xix. [Curiously enough, the chronological order, according to the best recent authorities, is that indicated above: the sickness (2 Kings xx.) preceded the invasion of Sennacherib (chap. xix.). Monumental evidence confirms this view. — R.]
9 2 Chron. xxxiii.
10 2 Chron. xxxv. Cotelerius conjectures "in his passover," instead of "in Phassa." [A very probable textual emendation. — R.]
11 Ezra viii.
12 Dan. vi. 16.
13 Jonah ii.
14 Dan. iii.
15 1 Sam. i.
16 Neh. iii.
17 1 Macc. i., etc.
18 One V. MS. reads, "with Christ and the Holy Spirit."
19 Rom. viii. 21.

let him also know his own nature, of what sort it is; let him be taught how God punished the wicked with water and fire, and did glorify the saints in every generation — I mean Seth, and Enos, and Enoch, and Noah, and Abraham and his posterity, and Melchizedek, and Job, and Moses, and Joshua, and Caleb, and Phineas the priest, and those that were holy in every generation; and how God still took care of and did not reject mankind, but called them from their error and vanity to the acknowledgment of the truth at various seasons, reducing them from bondage and impiety unto liberty and piety, from injustice to righteousness, from death eternal to everlasting life. Let him that offers himself to baptism learn these and the like things during the time that he is a catechumen; and let him who lays his hands upon him adore God, the Lord of the whole world, and thank Him for His creation, for His sending Christ His only begotten Son, that He might save man by blotting out his transgressions, and that He might remit ungodliness and sins, and might "purify him from all filthiness of flesh and spirit,"[1] and sanctify man according to the good pleasure of His kindness, that He might inspire him with the knowledge of His will, and enlighten the eyes of his heart to consider of His wonderful works, and make known to him the judgments of righteousness, that so he might hate every way of iniquity, and walk in the way of truth, that he might be thought worthy of the laver of regeneration, to the adoption of sons, which is in Christ, that "being planted together in the likeness of the death of Christ,"[2] in hopes of a glorious communication, he may be mortified to sin, and may live to God, as to his mind, and word, and deed, and may be numbered together in the book of the living. And after this thanksgiving, let him instruct him in the doctrines concerning our Lord's incarnation, and in those concerning His passion, and resurrection from the dead, and assumption.

A CONSTITUTION HOW THE CATECHUMENS ARE TO BE BLESSED BY THE PRIESTS IN THEIR INITIATION, AND WHAT THINGS ARE TO BE TAUGHT THEM.

XL. And when it remains that the catechumen is to be baptized, let him learn what concerns the renunciation of the devil, and the joining himself with Christ; for it is fit that he should first abstain from things contrary, and then be admitted to the mysteries. He must beforehand purify his heart from all wickedness of disposition, from all spot and wrinkle, and then partake of the holy things; for as the skilfullest husbandman does first purge his ground of the thorns which are grown up therein, and does then sow his wheat, so ought you also to take away all impiety from them, and then to sow the seeds of piety in them, and vouchsafe them baptism. For even our Lord did in this manner exhort us, saying first, "Make disciples of all nations;"[3] and then He adds this, "and baptize them into the name of the Father, and of the Son, and of the Holy Ghost." Let, therefore, the candidate for baptism declare thus in his renunciation:[4] —

THE RENUNCIATION OF THE ADVERSARY, AND THE DEDICATION TO THE CHRIST OF GOD.

XLI. I renounce Satan, and his works, and his pomps, and his worships, and his angels, and his inventions, and all things that are under him. And after his renunciation let him in his consociation say: And I associate myself to Christ, and believe, and am baptized into one unbegotten Being, the only true God Almighty, the Father of Christ, the Creator and Maker of all things, from whom are all things; and into the Lord Jesus Christ, His only begotten Son, the First-born of the whole creation, who before the ages was begotten by the good pleasure of the Father, by whom all things were made, both those in heaven and those on earth, visible and invisible; who in the last days descended from heaven, and took flesh, and was born of the holy Virgin Mary, and did converse holily according to the laws of His God and Father, and was crucified under Pontius Pilate, and died for us, and rose again from the dead after His passion the third day, and ascended into the heavens, and sitteth at the right hand of the Father, and again is to come at the end of the world with glory to judge the quick and the dead, of whose kingdom there shall be no end. And I am baptized into the Holy Ghost, that is, the Comforter, who wrought in all the saints from the beginning of the world, but was afterwards sent to the apostles by the Father, according to the promise of our Saviour and Lord, Jesus Christ; and after the apostles, to all those that believe in the Holy Catholic Church; into the resurrection of the flesh, and into the remission of sins, and into the kingdom of heaven, and into the life of the world to come. And after this vow, he comes in order to the anointing with oil.

A THANKSGIVING CONCERNING THE ANOINTING WITH THE MYSTICAL OIL.

XLII. Now this is blessed by the high priest for the remission of sins, and the first preparation for baptism. For he calls thus upon the unbegotten God, the Father of Christ, the King of all sensible and intelligible natures, that He would sanctify the oil in the name of the Lord

[1] 2 Cor. vii. 1.
[2] Rom. vi. 5.
[3] Matt. xxviii. 19.
[4] [Compare Justin Martyr, vol. i. p. 183, this series.]

Jesus, and impart to it spiritual grace and efficacious strength, the remission of sins, and the first preparation for the confession of baptism, that so the candidate for baptism, when he is anointed, may be freed from all ungodliness, and may become worthy of initiation, according to the command of the Only-begotten.

A THANKSGIVING CONCERNING THE MYSTICAL WATER.

XLIII. After this he comes to the water, and blesses and glorifies the Lord God Almighty, the Father of the only begotten God;[1] and the priest returns thanks that He has sent His Son to become man on our account, that He might save us; that He has permitted that He should in all things become obedient to the laws of that incarnation, to preach the kingdom of heaven, the remission of sins, and the resurrection of the dead. Moreover, he adores the only begotten God Himself, after His Father, and for Him, giving Him thanks that He undertook to die for all men by the cross, the type of which He has appointed to be the baptism of regeneration. He glorifies Him also, for that God who is the Lord of the whole world, in the name of Christ, and by His Holy Spirit, has not cast off mankind, but has suited His providence to the difference of seasons: at first giving to Adam himself paradise for an habitation of pleasure, and afterwards giving a command on account of providence, and casting out the offender justly, but through His goodness not utterly casting him off, but instructing his posterity in succeeding ages after various manners; on whose account, in the conclusion of the world, He has sent His Son to become man for man's sake, and to undergo all human passions without sin. Him, therefore, let the priest even now call upon in baptism, and let him say: Look down from heaven, and sanctify this water, and give it grace and power, that so he that is to be baptized, according to the command of Thy Christ, may be crucified with Him, and may die with Him, and may be buried with Him, and may rise with Him to the adoption which is in Him, that he may be dead to sin and live to righteousness. And after this, when he has baptized him in the name of the Father, and of the Son, and of the Holy Ghost, he shall anoint him with ointment, and shall add as follows:—

A THANKSGIVING CONCERNING THE MYSTICAL OINTMENT.

XLIV. O Lord God, who art without generation, and without a superior, the Lord of the whole world, who hast scattered the sweet odour of the knowledge of the Gospel among all nations, do Thou grant at this time that this ointment may be efficacious upon him that is baptized, that so the sweet odour of Thy Christ may continue upon him firm and fixed; and that now he has died with Him, he may arise and live with Him. Let him say these and the like things, for this is the efficacy of the laying on of hands on every one; for unless there be such a recital made by a pious priest over every one of these, the candidate for baptism does only descend into the water as do the Jews, and he only puts off the filth of the body, not the filth of the soul. After this let him stand up, and pray that prayer which the Lord taught us. But, of necessity, he who is risen again ought to stand up and pray, because he that is raised up stands upright. Let him, therefore, who has been dead with Christ, and is raised up with Him, stand up. But let him pray towards the east.[2] For this also is written in the second book of the Chronicles, that after the temple of the Lord was finished by King Solomon, in the very feast of dedication the priests and the Levites and the singers stood up towards the east, praising and thanking God with cymbals and psalteries, and saying, "Praise the Lord, for He is good; for His mercy endureth for ever."[3]

A PRAYER FOR THE NEW FRUITS.

XLV. But let him pray thus after the foregoing prayer, and say: O God Almighty, the Father of Thy Christ, Thy only begotten Son, give me a body undefiled, a heart pure, a mind watchful, an unerring knowledge, the influence of the Holy Ghost for the obtaining and assured enjoying of the truth, through Thy Christ, by whom[4] glory be to Thee, in the Holy Spirit, for ever. Amen. We have thought it reasonable to make these constitutions concerning the catechumens.

SEC. IV. — ENUMERATION ORDAINED BY APOSTLES.

WHO WERE THEY THAT THE HOLY APOSTLES SENT AND ORDAINED?

XLVI. Now concerning those bishops which have been ordained in our lifetime, we let you know that they are these:—James the bishop of Jerusalem, the brother of our Lord;[5] upon whose death the second was Simeon the son of Cleopas; after whom the third was Judas the son of James. Of Cæsarea of Palestine, the

---

[1] One V. MS. has "Son" instead of "God." Cotelerius remarks that this change was made in the interests of orthodoxy; for the expression "only begotten God" had become common with the Arians. [Comp. John i. 18, where the most weighty ancient authorities read μονογενης θεός instead of ὁ μονογενὴς υἱός; see Revised Version, margin, *in loco*.—R.]

[2] [Compare vol. ii. p. 535 and vol. iii. p. 31.]

[3] 2 Chron. v. 13.

[4] One V. MS. reads, "with whom glory be to Thee, along with the Holy Spirit."

[5] [An incidental proof of the early origin of this compilation is furnished by the clear distinction it makes between James the son of Alphæus and James the brother of our Lord. The theory of Jerome, which identifies them, was later.—R.]

first was Zacchæus, who was once a publican; after whom was Cornelius, and the third Theophilus. Of Antioch, Euodius, ordained by me Peter; and Ignatius by Paul. Of Alexandria, Annianus was the first, ordained by Mark the evangelist; the second Avilius by Luke, who was also an evangelist. Of the church of Rome, Linus the son of Claudia was the first, ordained by Paul;[1] and Clemens, after Linus' death, the second, ordained by me Peter.[2] Of Ephesus, Timotheus, ordained by Paul; and John, by me John. Of Smyrna, Aristo the first; after whom Stratæas the son of Lois;[3] and the third Aristo. Of Pergamus, Gaius. Of Philadelphia, Demetrius, by me. Of Cenchrea, Lucius, by Paul. Of Crete, Titus. Of Athens, Dionysius. Of Tripoli in Phœnicia, Marathones. Of Laodicea in Phrygia, Archippus.[4] Of Colossæ, Philemon.[5] Of Borea in Macedonia, Onesimus, once the servant of Philemon.[6] Of the churches of Galatia, Crescens.[7] Of the parishes of Asia, Aquila and Nicetas. Of the church of Æginæ, Crispus. These are the bishops who are entrusted by us with the parishes in the Lord; whose doctrine keep ye always in mind, and observe our words. And may the Lord be with you now, and to endless ages, as Himself said to us when He was about to be taken up to His own God and Father. For says He, "Lo, I am with you all the days, until the end of the world. Amen."[8]

SEC. V. — DAILY PRAYERS.

A MORNING PRAYER.

XLVII. "Glory be to God in the highest, and upon earth peace, good-will among men."[9] We praise Thee, we sing hymns to Thee, we bless Thee, we glorify Thee, we worship Thee by Thy great High Priest; Thee who art the true God, who art the One Unbegotten, the only inaccessible Being. For Thy great glory, O Lord and heavenly King, O God the Father Almighty, O Lord God,[10] the Father of Christ the immaculate Lamb, who taketh away the sin of the world, receive our prayer, Thou that sittest upon the cherubim. For Thou only art holy, Thou only art the Lord Jesus, the Christ of the God of all created nature, and our King, by whom glory, honour, and worship be to Thee.

AN EVENING PRAYER.

XLVIII. "Ye children, praise the Lord: praise the name of the Lord."[11] We praise Thee, we sing hymns to Thee, we bless Thee for Thy great glory, O Lord our King, the Father of Christ the immaculate Lamb, who taketh away the sin of the world. Praise becomes Thee, hymns become Thee, glory becomes Thee, the God and Father,[12] through the Son, in the most holy Spirit, for ever and ever. Amen. "Now, O Lord, lettest Thou Thy servant depart in peace, according to Thy word; for mine eyes have seen Thy salvation, which Thou hast prepared before the face of all people, a light for the revelation to the Gentiles, and the glory of Thy people Israel."[13]

A PRAYER AT DINNER.

XLIX. Thou art blessed, O Lord, who nourishest me from my youth, who givest food to all flesh. Fill our hearts with joy and gladness, that having always what is sufficient for us, we may abound to every good work, in Christ Jesus our Lord, through whom[14] glory, honour, and power be to Thee for ever. Amen.

1 2 Tim. iv. 21.
2 [Noteworthy, and to be recalled hereafter. See vol. iii. p. 258.]
3 2 Tim. i. 5.
4 [Comp. Col. iv. 16, 17, whence this is probably derived. — R.]
5 Philem. 1.
6 [Philem. 10. — R.]
7 [Comp. 2 Tim. iv. 10. — R.]
8 Matt. xxviii. 20.
9 Luke ii. 14.
10 One V. MS. gives a more orthodox form to this prayer: "O Lord, only begotten Son, and Holy Spirit, Lord God, the Lamb of God, the Son of the Father, who takest away the sins of the world, receive our prayer. Thou who sittest at the right hand of the Father, have mercy upon us, for Thou only art holy; Thou only art Christ, Jesus Christ, to the glory of God the Father. Amen."
11 Ps. cxiii. 1.
12 One V. MS. omits "the God and;" then reads, "to Father, Son, and Holy Ghost."
13 Luke ii. 29, etc.
14 One V. MS. reads, "with whom."

GENERAL NOTE.

Comparing the *Teaching* with chapters xxv. and xxvi. of these *Constitutions*, it seems to me that the nature of the eucharistic (thanksgiving) prayers becomes apparent. They presuppose the formulas to be found in the eighth book of the *Constitutions*,[1] and are such instructions as were imparted only to *catechumens;* the part peculiar to presbyters being withheld, of course, as *esoteric* mysteries, until further knowledge was canonically appropriate. See Elucidation IV. vol. vi. p. 236; and in this volume, Elucidation I. p. 382. The Bryennios MS. is cleared from nearly all difficulties by Dr. Riddle's lucid notes, when compared with corresponding passages in the *Constitutions*, or illustrated by such as are supplementary.

1 Beginning p. 479, *infra*.

CONSTITUTIONS OF THE HOLY APOSTLES

BOOK VIII.

CONCERNING GIFTS, AND ORDINATIONS, AND THE ECCLESIASTICAL CANONS.

SEC. I.—ON THE DIVERSITY OF SPIRITUAL GIFTS.

ON WHOSE ACCOUNT THE POWERS OF MIRACLES ARE PERFORMED.

I. JESUS CHRIST, our God and Saviour, delivered to us the great mystery of godliness, and called both Jews and Gentiles to the acknowledgment of the one and only[1] true God His Father,[2] as Himself somewhere says, when He was giving thanks for the salvation of those that had believed, "I have manifested Thy name to men, I have finished the work Thou gavest me;"[3] and said concerning us to His Father, "Holy Father, although the world has not known Thee, yet have I known Thee; and these have known Thee."[4] With good reason did He say to all of us together, when we were perfected concerning those gifts which were given from Him by the Spirit: "Now these signs shall follow them that have believed in my name: they shall cast out devils; they shall speak with new tongues; they shall take up serpents; and if they drink any deadly thing, it shall by no means hurt them: they shall lay their hands on the sick, and they shall recover."[5] These gifts were first bestowed on us the apostles when we were about to preach the Gospel to every creature, and afterwards were of necessity afforded to those who had by our means believed; not for the advantage of those who perform them, but for the conviction of the unbelievers, that those whom the word did not persuade, the power of signs might put to shame: for signs are not for us who believe, but for the unbelievers, both for the Jews and Gentiles. For neither is it any profit to us to cast out demons, but to those who are so cleansed by the power of the Lord; as the Lord[6] Himself somewhere instructs us, and shows, saying: "Rejoice ye, not because the spirits are subject unto you; but rejoice, because your names are written in heaven."[7] Since the former is done by His power, but this by our good disposition and diligence, yet (it is manifest) by His assistance. It is not therefore necessary that every one of the faithful should cast out demons, or raise the dead, or speak with tongues; but such a one only who is vouchsafed this gift, for some cause which may be advantage to the salvation of the unbelievers, who are often put to shame, not with the demonstration of the world, but by the power of the signs; that is, such as are worthy of salvation: for all the ungodly are not affected by wonders; and hereof God Himself is a witness, as when He says in the law: "With other tongues will I speak to this people, and with other lips, and yet will they by no means believe."[8] For neither did the Egyptians believe in God, when Moses had done so many signs and wonders;[9] nor did the multitude of the Jews believe in Christ, as they believed Moses, who yet had healed every sickness and every disease among them.[10] Nor were the former shamed by the rod which was turned into a living serpent, nor by the hand which was made white with leprosy, nor by the river Nile turned into blood; nor the latter by the blind who recovered their sight, nor by the lame who walked, nor by the dead who were raised.[11] The one was resisted by Jannes and Jambres, the other by Annas and Caiaphas.[12] Thus signs do not shame all into belief, but only those of a good disposition; for whose sake also it is that God is pleased, as a wise steward of a family, to appoint miracles to be wrought, not

[1] The words "one and only" are omitted in the Syriac and Coptic.
[2] One V. MS. omits "His Father." The Syriac and Coptic have "the only Father."
[3] John xvii. 6, 4.
[4] John xvii. 11, 25.
[5] Mark xvi. 17, 18.
[6] The Coptic reads "our God."
[7] Luke x. 20.
[8] Isa. xxviii. 11; 1 Cor. xiv. 21.
[9] Ex. vii. and iv.
[10] Deut. xviii. 15, etc.
[11] Matt. xi. 5.
[12] 2 Tim. iii. 8.

by the power of men, but by His own will. Now we say these things, that those who have received such gifts may not exalt themselves against those who have not received them; such gifts, we mean, as are for the working of miracles. For otherwise there is no man who has believed in God through Christ,[1] that has not received some spiritual gift: for this very thing, having been delivered from the impiety of polytheism, and having believed in God the Father through Christ,[2] this is a gift of God. And the having cast off the veil of Judaism, and having believed that, by the good pleasure of God, His only begotten Son, who was before all ages,[3] was in the last time born of a virgin,[4] without the company of a man, and that He lived as a man, yet without sin, and fulfilled all that righteousness which is of the law; and that, by the permission of God, He who was God the Word endured the cross, and despised the shame; and that He died, and was buried, and rose within three days; and that after His resurrection, having continued forty days with His apostles, and completed His whole constitutions, He was taken up in their sight to His God and Father, who sent Him: he who has believed these things, not at random and irrationally, but with judgment and full assurance, has received the gift of God. So also has He who is delivered from every heresy. Let not, therefore, any one that works signs and wonders judge any one of the faithful who is not vouchsafed the same: for the gifts of God which are bestowed by Him through Christ are various; and one man receives one gift, and another another. For perhaps one has the word of wisdom, and another the word of knowledge;[5] another, discerning of spirits; another, foreknowledge of things to come; another, the word of teaching; another, long-suffering; another, continence according to the law: for even Moses, the man of God, when he wrought signs in Egypt, did not exalt himself against his equals: and when he was called a god, he did not arrogantly despise his own prophet Aaron.[6] Nor did Joshua the son of Nun, who was the leader of the people after him, though in the war with the Jebusites he had made the sun stand still over against Gibeon, and the moon over against the valley of Ajalon,[7] because the day was not long enough for their victory, insult over Phineas or Caleb. Nor did Samuel, who had done so many surprising things, disregard David the beloved of God: yet they were both prophets, and the one was high priest, and the other was king. And when there were only seven thousand holy men in Israel who had not bowed the knee to Baal,[8] Elijah alone among them, and his disciple Elisha, were workers of miracles. Yet neither did Elijah despise Obadiah the steward, who feared God, but wrought no signs; nor did Elisha despise his own disciple when he trembled at the enemies.[9] Moreover, neither did the wise Daniel who was twice delivered from the mouths of the lions, nor the three children who were delivered from the furnace of fire,[10] despise the rest of their fellow-Israelites: for they knew that they had not escaped these terrible miseries by their own might; but by the power of God did they both work miracles, and were delivered from miseries. Wherefore let none of you exalt himself against his brother, though he be a prophet, or though he be a worker of miracles: for if it happens that there be no longer an unbeliever, all the power of signs will thenceforwards be superfluous. For to be pious is from any one's good disposition; but to work wonders is from the power of Him that works them by us: the first of which respects ourselves; but the second respects God that works them, for the reasons which we have already mentioned. Wherefore neither let a king despise his officers that are under him, nor the rulers those who are subject. For where there are none to be ruled over, rulers are superfluous; and where there are no officers, the kingdom will not stand. Moreover, let not a bishop be exalted against his deacons and presbyters, nor the presbyters against the people: for the subsistence of the congregation depends on each other. For the bishops and the presbyters are the priests with relation to the people; and the laity are the laity with relation to the clergy. And to be a Christian is in our own power; but to be an apostle, or a bishop, or in any other such office, is not in our own power, but at the disposal of God, who bestows the gifts. And thus much concerning those who are vouchsafed gifts and dignities.

CONCERNING UNWORTHY BISHOPS AND PRESBYTERS.

II. We add, in the next place, that neither is every one that prophesies holy, nor every one that casts out devils religious: for even Balaam the son of Beor the prophet did prophesy,[11] though he was himself ungodly; as also did Caiaphas, the falsely-named high priest.[12] Nay, the devil foretells many things, and the demons, about Him; and yet for all that, there is not a spark of piety in them: for they are oppressed

1 Instead of "Christ," the Coptic reads, "through His Holy Son."
2 The Coptic reads, "and in Christ and the Holy Spirit."
3 The Coptic reads, "and His only begotten Son, who was with the Father and the life-giving Holy Spirit before all the ages."
4 The Coptic reads, "spotless virgin."
5 1 Cor. xii. 8.
6 Ex. vii. 1.
7 Josh. x.
8 1 Kings xix. 18; Rom. xi. 4.
9 2 Kings vi.
10 Dan. vi. 16, iii.
11 Num. xxiii. and xxiv.
12 John xi. 51. [See on the *Sibyllina, passim.*]

with ignorance, by reason of their voluntary wickedness. It is manifest, therefore, that the ungodly, although they prophesy, do not by their prophesying cover their own impiety; nor will those who cast out demons be sanctified by the demons being made subject to them: for they only mock one another, as they do who play childish tricks for mirth, and destroy those who give heed to them. For neither is a wicked king any longer a king, but a tyrant; nor is a bishop oppressed with ignorance or an evil disposition a bishop, but falsely so called, being not one sent out by God, but by men, as Ananiah and Samœah in Jerusalem, and Zedekiah and Achiah the false prophets in Babylon.[1] And indeed Balaam the prophet, when he had corrupted Israel by Baal-peor, suffered punishment;[2] and Caiaphas at last was his own murderer; and the sons of Sceva, endeavouring to cast out demons, were wounded by them, and fled away in an unseemly manner;[3] and the kings of Israel and of Judah, when they became impious, suffered all sorts of punishments. It is therefore evident how bishops and presbyters, also falsely so called, will not escape the judgment of God. For it will be said to them even now: "O ye priests that despise my name,[4] I will deliver you up to the slaughter, as I did Zedekiah and Achiah, whom the king of Babylon fried in a frying-pan," as says Jeremiah the prophet.[5] We say these things, not in contempt of true prophecies, for we know that they are wrought in holy men by the inspiration of God, but to put a stop to the boldness of vainglorious men; and add this withal, that from such as these God takes away His grace: for "God resisteth the proud, but giveth grace to the humble."[6] Now Silas and Agabus prophesied in our times;[7] yet did they not equal themselves to the apostles, nor did they exceed their own measures though they were beloved of God. Now women prophesied also. Of old, Miriam the sister of Moses and Aaron,[8] and after her Deborah,[9] and after these Huldah[10] and Judith[11] — the former under Josiah, the latter under Darius. The mother of the Lord did also prophesy, and her kinswoman Elisabeth, and Anna;[12] and in our time the daughters of Philip:[13] yet were not these elated against their husbands, but preserved their own measures.[14] Wherefore if among you also there be a man or a woman, and such a one obtains any gift, let him be humble, that God may be pleased with him. For says He: "Upon whom will I look, but upon him that is humble and quiet, and trembles at my words?"[15]

SEC. II. — ELECTION AND ORDINATION OF BISHOPS: FORM OF SERVICE ON SUNDAYS.

THAT TO MAKE CONSTITUTIONS ABOUT THE OFFICES TO BE PERFORMED IN THE CHURCHES IS OF GREAT CONSEQUENCE.

III. We have now finished the first part of this discourse concerning gifts, whatever they be, which God has bestowed upon men according to His own will; and how He rebuked the ways of those who either attempted to speak lies, or were moved by the spirit of the adversary; and that God often employed the wicked[16] for prophecy and the performance of wonders. But now our discourse hastens as to the principal part, that is, the constitution of ecclesiastical affairs, that so, when ye have learned this constitution from us, ye who are ordained bishops by us at the command of Christ, may perform all things according to the commands delivered you, knowing that he that heareth us heareth Christ, and he that heareth Christ heareth His God and Father,[17] to whom be glory for ever. Amen.

CONCERNING ORDINATIONS.

IV. Wherefore we, the twelve apostles of the Lord, who are now together, give you in charge those divine constitutions concerning every ecclesiastical form, there being present with us Paul the chosen vessel, our fellow-apostle, and James the bishop, and the rest of the presbyters, and the seven deacons.[18] In the first place, therefore, I Peter say,[19] *that a bishop to be ordained is to be*, as we have already, all of us, appointed, unblameable in all things, a select person,[20] *chosen by the whole people, who, when he is named and approved, let the people assemble, with the presbytery and bishops* that are present, *on the Lord's day*, and let them give their consent. *And let the principal of the bishops ask the presbytery and*

---

1 Jer. xxviii. and xxix.
2 Num. xxv. and xxxi.
3 Acts xix. 14.
4 Mal. i. 6.
5 Jer. xxix. 22.
6 1 Pet. v. 5.
7 Acts [xi. 28] xv. 32, xxi. 10.
8 Ex. xv. 20.
9 Judg. iv. 4.
10 2 Kings xxii. 14.
11 Judith viii.
12 Luke i. and ii.
13 Acts xxi. 9.
14 [The compiler has forgotten that few of these had husbands, at least at the time when they are reported to have prophesied. — R.]

15 Isa. lxvi. 2.
16 We have adopted the reading of one V. MS., ἀπεχρήσατο. It means more than is in the text — that God used the wicked in a way in which they would not be naturally used; lit., "abused," or "misused." The other MSS. and the Coptic read ἀπεχαρίσατο, "gave His gifts to the wicked for prophecy." Whiston has tried to make sense by giving a new meaning to ἀπεχαρίσατο, "taking away His grace from the wicked."
17 Luke x. 16.
18 The Coptic and one V. MS. omit from the commencement of the chapter to "deacons." The V. MS. has: "Peter, the chief of the apostles, proclaimed the Gospel to Pontus, Galatia, Cappadocia, Asia, Bithynia, and finally in Rome, where he was crucified by the prefect in the reign of Nero, and where also he is buried."
19 From this to the end of ch. xxvi., only small portions of what is now in the received text occur in the Coptic version. The Oxford MS. is also deficient. It has only a portion of the fifth, nothing of ch. vi. to xvi., and only a single sentence in ch. xxii. The portions in Coptic are printed in italics.
20 Omitted in one V. MS.

people whether this be the person whom they desire for their ruler. And if they give their consent, let him ask further whether he has a good testimony from all men as to his worthiness for so great and glorious an authority; whether all things relating to his piety towards God be right; whether justice towards men has been observed by him; whether the affairs of his family have been well ordered by him; whether he has been unblameable in the course of his life. And if all the assembly together do according to truth, and not according to prejudice, witness that he is such a one, let them the third time, as before God the Judge, and Christ, the Holy Ghost being also present, as well as all the holy and ministering spirits, *ask again whether he be truly worthy of this ministry, that so "in the mouth of two or three witnesses every word may be established."*[1] *And if they agree the third time that he is worthy, let them all be demanded their vote; and when they all give it willingly,* let them be heard. And *silence being made, let one of the principal bishops, together with two others, stand near to the altar, the rest of the bishops and presbyters praying silently, and the deacons holding the divine Gospels open upon the head of him that is to be ordained,* and say to God thus:[2] —

THE FORM OF PRAYER FOR THE ORDINATION OF A BISHOP.

v. O Thou the great Being, O Lord God Almighty, who alone art unbegotten, and ruled over by none; who always art, and wast before the world; who standest in need of nothing, and art above all cause and beginning; who only art true, who only art wise; who alone art the most high; who art by nature invisible; whose knowledge is without beginning; who only art good, and beyond compare; who knowest all things before they are; who art acquainted with the most secret things; who art inaccessible, and without a superior; the God and Father of Thy only begotten Son, of our God and Saviour; the Creator of the whole world by Him; whose providence provides for and takes the care of all; the Father of mercies, and God of all consolation;[4] who dwellest in the highest heavens,[5] and yet lookest down on things below: Thou who didst appoint the rules of the Church, by the coming of Thy Christ in the flesh; of which the Holy Ghost is the witness, by Thy apostles, and by us the bishops, who by Thy grace are here present; who hast fore-ordained priests from the beginning for the government of Thy people — Abel in the first place, Seth and Enos, and Enoch and Noah, and Melchisedec and Job; who didst appoint Abraham, and the rest of the patriarchs, with Thy faithful servants Moses and Aaron, and Eleazar and Phineas; who didst choose from among them rulers and priests in the tabernacle of Thy testimony; who didst choose Samuel for a priest and a prophet; who didst not leave Thy sanctuary without ministers; who didst delight in those whom Thou chosest to be glorified in. Do Thou, by us, pour down the influence of Thy free Spirit, through the mediation of Thy Christ, which is committed to Thy beloved Son Jesus Christ; which He bestowed according to Thy will on the holy apostles of Thee the eternal God. Grant by Thy name, O God, who searchest the hearts, that this Thy servant, whom Thou hast chosen to be a bishop, may feed Thy holy flock, and discharge the office of an high priest to Thee, and minister to Thee, unblameably night and day; that he may appease Thee, and gather together the number of those that shall be saved, and may

OXFORD MS.[3]

v. God and Father of our Lord Jesus Christ, the Father of mercies and the God of all consolation, who knowest all things before they take place; Thou who didst appoint the rules of the Church through the word of Thy grace; who didst appoint beforehand the race righteous from the beginning that came from Abraham to be rulers, and didst constitute them priests, not leaving Thy sanctuary without ministers; who from the foundation of the world didst delight in those whom Thou chosest to be glorified in; and now pour down the influence of Thy free Spirit, which through Thy beloved Son Jesus Christ Thou hast bestowed on Thy holy apostles, who set up the Church in the place of the sanctuary, to unending glory and praise of Thy name: O Thou, who knowest the hearts of all, grant that this Thy servant whom Thou hast chosen to the holy office of Thy bishop, may discharge the duty of a high priest to Thee, and minister to Thee unblameably night and day; that he may appease Thee unceasingly, and present to Thee the gifts of Thy holy Church, and in the spirit of the high-priesthood have power to remit sins according to Thy commandment, to give lots according to Thy injunction, to loose every bond according to the power which Thou hast given to the apostles, and be well-pleasing to Thee, in meekness and a pure heart offering a smell of sweet savour through Thy Son Jesus Christ our Lord, with whom to Thee be glory, power, and honour, along with the Holy Spirit, now and for ever. Amen.

[1] Matt. xviii. 16.
[2] The Coptic has, "let the bishop pray for him."
[3] The Oxford MS. has this chapter in an abbreviated form as in the parallel columns.
[4] 2 Cor. i. 3.
[5] Ps. cxiii. 5.

offer to Thee the gifts of Thy holy Church. Grant to him, O Lord Almighty, through Thy Christ, the fellowship of the Holy Spirit, that so he may have power to remit sins according to Thy command; to give forth lots according to Thy command; to loose every bond, according to the power which Thou gavest the apostles; that he may please Thee in meekness and a pure heart, with a stedfast, unblameable, and unreprovable mind; to offer to Thee a pure and unbloody sacrifice, which by Thy Christ Thou hast appointed as the mystery of the new covenant, for a sweet savour, through Thy holy child Jesus Christ, our God and Saviour, through whom[1] glory, honour, and worship be to Thee in the Holy Spirit, now and always, and for all ages. And when he has prayed for these things, let the rest of the priests add, Amen; and together with them all the people. *And after the prayer let one of the bishops elevate the sacrifice upon the hands of him that is ordained, and* early in the morning *let him be placed in his throne, in a place set apart for him among the rest of the bishops, they* all *giving him the kiss in the Lord.*[2] *And after the reading of the* Law[3] and the Prophets, and our Epistles, and Acts, and the Gospels, *let him that is ordained salute the Church, saying, The grace of our Lord Jesus Christ, the love of God and the Father, and the fellowship of the Holy Ghost, be with you all; and let them all answer, And with Thy Spirit. And after these words let him speak to the people the words of exhortation; and when he has ended his word of doctrine* (I Andrew[4] the brother of Peter speak), all standing up, *let the deacon ascend upon some high seat, and proclaim,* Let none of the hearers, *let none of the unbelievers stay;* and silence being made, let him say:—

THE DIVINE LITURGY, WHEREIN IS THE BIDDING PRAYER FOR THE CATECHUMENS.

VI. Ye catechumens, pray, and let all the faithful pray for them in their mind, saying: Lord, have mercy upon them. And let the deacon bid prayers for them, saying: Let us all pray unto God for the catechumens, that He that is good, He that is the lover of mankind, will mercifully hear their prayers and their supplications, and so accept their petitions as to assist them and give them those desires of their hearts which are for their advantage, and reveal to them the Gospel of His Christ; give them illumination and understanding, instruct them in the knowledge of God, teach them His commands and His ordinances, implant in them His pure and saving fear, open the ears of their hearts, that they may exercise themselves in His law day and night; strengthen them in piety, unite them to and number them with His holy flock; vouchsafe them the laver of regeneration, and the garment of incorruption, which is the true life; and deliver them from all ungodliness, and give no place to the adversary against them; "and cleanse them from all filthiness of flesh and spirit, and dwell in them, and walk in them, by His Christ; bless their goings out and their comings in, and order their affairs for their good."[5] Let us still earnestly put up our supplications for them, that they may obtain the forgiveness of their transgressions by their admission, and so may be thought worthy of the holy mysteries, and of constant communion with the saints. Rise up, ye catechumens, beg for yourselves the peace of God through His Christ, a peaceable day, and free from sin, and the like for the whole time of your life, and your Christian ends of it; a compassionate and merciful God; and the forgiveness of your transgressions. Dedicate yourselves to the only unbegotten God, through His Christ. Bow down your heads, and receive the blessing. But at the naming of every one by the deacon, as we said before, let the people say, Lord, have mercy upon him; and let the children say it first. And as they have bowed down their heads, let the bishop who is newly ordained bless them with this blessing: O God Almighty, unbegotten and inaccessible, who only art the true God, the God and Father of Thy Christ, Thy only begotten Son; the God[6] of the Comforter, and Lord of the whole world; who by Christ didst appoint Thy disciples to be teachers for the teaching of piety; do Thou now also look down upon Thy servants, who are receiving instruction in the Gospel of Thy Christ, and "give them a new heart, and renew a right spirit in their inward parts,"[7] that they may both know and do Thy will with full purpose of heart, and with a willing soul. Vouchsafe them an holy admission, and unite them to Thy holy Church, and make them partakers of Thy divine mysteries, through Christ, who is our hope, and who died for them; by whom glory and worship be given to Thee in the Holy Spirit for ever. Amen. And after this, let the deacon say: Go out, ye catechumens, in peace. And after they are gone out, let him say: Ye energumens, afflicted with unclean spirits, pray, and let us all earnestly pray for them, that God, the lover of mankind, will

1 One V. MS. reads, "with whom."
2 The Coptic inserts, "let the holy Gospels be read."
3 The Coptic reads "Gospel" instead of "Law."
4 One V. MS. has the following note: "Andrew the brother of Peter preaches the Gospel to the Scythians, Sogdiani, and Thracians, who on account of preaching Christ is crowned with the martyrdom of the cross by Ægæa the proconsul, and was buried in Patræ. Afterwards he was removed to Constantinople by the Emperor Constantine."

5 2 Cor. vii. 1, vi. 16; Ps. cxxi. 8.
6 One V. MS. has προβολεύς, "the sender forth," or "producer," instead of "God."
7 Ps. li. 10.

by Christ rebuke the unclean and wicked spirits, and deliver His supplicants from the dominion of the adversary. May He that rebuked the legion of demons, and the devil, the prince of wickedness,[1] even now rebuke these apostates from piety, and deliver His own workmanship from his power, and cleanse those creatures which He has made with great wisdom. Let us still pray earnestly for them. Save them, O God, and raise them up by Thy power. Bow down your heads, ye energumens, and receive the blessings. And let the bishop add this prayer, and say: —

FOR THE ENERGUMENS.

VII. Thou, who hast bound the strong man, and spoiled all that was in his house, who hast given us power over serpents and scorpions to tread upon them, and upon all the power of the enemy;[2] who hast delivered the serpent, that murderer of men, bound to us, as a sparrow to children, whom all things dread, and tremble before the face of Thy power;[3] who hast cast him down as lightning from heaven to earth,[4] not with a fall from a place, but from honour to dishonour, on account of his voluntary evil disposition; whose look dries the abysses, and threatening melts the mountains, and whose truth remains for ever; whom the infants praise, and sucking babes bless; whom angels sing hymns to, and adore; who lookest upon the earth, and makest it tremble; who touchest the mountains, and they smoke; who threatenest the sea, and driest it up, and makest all its rivers as desert, and the clouds are the dust of His feet; who walkest upon the sea as upon the firm ground;[5] Thou only begotten God,[6] the Son of the great Father, rebuke these wicked spirits, and deliver the works of Thy hands from the power of the adverse spirit. For to Thee is due glory, honour, and worship, and by Thee to Thy Father, in the Holy Spirit, for ever. Amen. And let the deacon say: Go out, ye energumens. And after them, let him cry aloud: Ye that are to be illuminated, pray. Let all us, the faithful, earnestly pray for them, that the Lord will vouchsafe that, being initiated into the death of Christ, they may rise with Him, and become partakers of His kingdom, and may be admitted to the communion of His mysteries; unite them to, number them among, those that are saved in His holy Church. Save them, and raise them up by Thy grace. And being sealed to God through His Christ, let them bow down their heads, and receive this blessing from the bishop: —

FOR THE BAPTIZED.

VIII. Thou who hast formerly said by Thy holy prophets to those that be initiated, "Wash ye, become clean,"[7] and hast appointed spiritual regeneration by Christ, do Thou now also look down upon these that are baptized, and bless them, and sanctify them, and prepare them that they may become worthy of Thy spiritual gift, and of the true adoption of Thy spiritual mysteries, of being gathered together with those that are saved through Christ our Saviour; by whom glory, honour, and worship be to Thee, in the Holy Ghost, for ever. Amen. And let the deacon say: Go out, ye that are preparing for illumination. And after that let him proclaim: Ye penitents, pray; let us all earnestly pray for our brethren in the state of penitence, that God, the lover of compassion, will show them the way of repentance, and accept their return and their confession, and bruise Satan under their feet suddenly,[8] and redeem them from the snare of the devil, and the ill-usage of the demons, and free them from every unlawful word, and every absurd practice and wicked thought; forgive them all their offences, both voluntary and involuntary, and blot out that handwriting which is against them,[9] and write them in the book of life;[10] cleanse them from all filthiness of flesh and spirit,[11] and restore and unite them to His holy flock. For He knoweth our frame. For who can glory that he has a clean heart? And who can boldly say, that he is pure from sin?[12] For we are all among the blameworthy. Let us still pray for them more earnestly, for there is joy in heaven over one sinner that repenteth,[13] that, being converted from every evil work, they may be joined to all good practice; that God, the lover of mankind, will suddenly accept their petitions, will restore[14] to them the joy of His salvation, and strengthen them with His free Spirit;[15] that they may not be any more shaken,[16] but be admitted to the communion of His most holy things, and become partakers of His divine mysteries, that appearing worthy of His adoption, they may obtain eternal life. Let us all still earnestly say on their account: Lord, have mercy upon them. Save them, O God, and raise them up by Thy mercy. Rise up, and bow your heads to God through His Christ, and receive the blessings. Let the bishop then add this prayer: —

---

1 Mark v. 9; Zech. iii. 2.
2 Matt. xii. 29; Luke x. 19.
3 Job xl. 24, LXX.
4 Luke x. 18.
5 Ps. cvi. 9; Isa. li. 10; Ps. xcvii. 5; Isa. lxiv. 1; Ps. cxvii. 2, viii. 2, xcvii. 4, civ. 32; Nah. i. 4, 3; Job ix. 8, LXX.
6 [Comp. note 1, p. 477, book vii. chap. xliii. — R.]
7 Isa. i. 16.
8 Rom. xvi. 20.
9 Col. ii. 13, 14.
10 Phil. iv. 3.
11 2 Cor. vii. 1.
12 Prov. xx. 9.
13 Luke xv. 7.
14 The V. MSS. read, "restore them to their former position, and give them the joy," etc.
15 Ps. li. 12.
16 The V. MSS. add, "in their footsteps, but may be deemed worthy to be admitted," etc.

IMPOSITION OF HANDS; PRAYER FOR PENITENTS.

IX. Almighty, eternal God, Lord of the whole world, the Creator and Governor of all things, who hast exhibited man as the ornament of the world through Christ, and didst give him a law both naturally implanted and written, that he might live according to law, as a rational creature; and when he had sinned, Thou gavest him Thy goodness as a pledge in order to his repentance: Look down upon these persons who have bended the neck of their soul and body to Thee; for Thou desirest not the death of a sinner, but his repentance, that he turn from his wicked way, and live.[1] Thou who didst accept the repentance of the Ninevites, who willest that all men be saved, and come to the acknowledgment of the truth;[2] who didst accept of that son who had consumed his substance in riotous living,[3] with the bowels of a father, on account of his repentance; do Thou now accept of the repentance of Thy supplicants: for there is no man that will not sin; for "if Thou, O Lord, markest iniquities, O Lord, who shall stand? For with Thee there is propitiation."[4] And do Thou restore them to Thy holy Church, into their former dignity and honour, through Christ our God and Saviour, by whom glory and adoration be to Thee, in the Holy Ghost, for ever. Amen. Then let the deacon say, Depart, ye penitents; and let him add, Let none of those who ought not to come draw near. All we of the faithful, let us bend our knee: let us all entreat God through His Christ; let us earnestly beseech God through His Christ.

THE BIDDING PRAYER FOR THE FAITHFUL.

X. Let us pray for the peace and happy settlement of the world, and of the holy churches; that the God of the whole world may afford us His everlasting peace, and such as may not be taken away from us; that He may preserve us in a full prosecution of such virtue as is according to godliness. Let us pray for the Holy Catholic and Apostolic Church which is spread from one end of the earth to the other; that God would preserve and keep it unshaken, and free from the waves of this life, until the end of the world, as founded upon a rock; and for the holy parish in this place, that the Lord of the whole world may vouchsafe us without failure to follow after His heavenly hope, and without ceasing to pay Him the debt of our prayer. Let us pray for every episcopacy which is under the whole heaven, of those that rightly divide the word of Thy truth. And let us pray for our bishop James,[5] and his parishes; let us pray for our bishop Clement, and his parishes; let us pray for our bishop Euodius, and his parishes; let us pray for our bishop Annianus, and his parishes: that the compassionate God may grant them to continue in His holy churches in health, honour, and long life, and afford them an honourable old age in godliness and righteousness. And let us pray for our presbyters, that the Lord may deliver them from every unreasonable and wicked action, and afford them a presbyterate in health and honour. Let us pray for all the deacons and ministers in Christ, that the Lord may grant them an unblameable ministration. Let us pray for the readers, singers, virgins, widows, and orphans. Let us pray for those that are in marriage and in child-bearing, that the Lord may have mercy upon them all. Let us pray for the eunuchs who walk holily. Let us pray for those in a state of continence and piety. Let us pray for those that bear fruit in the holy Church, and give alms to the needy. And let us pray for those who offer sacrifices and oblations to the Lord our God, that God, the fountain of all goodness, may recompense them with His heavenly gifts, and "give them in this world an hundredfold, and in the world to come life everlasting;"[6] and bestow upon them for their temporal things, those that are eternal; for earthly things, those that are heavenly. Let us pray for our brethren newly enlightened, that the Lord may strengthen and confirm them. Let us pray for our brethren exercised with sickness, that the Lord may deliver them from every sickness and every disease, and restore them sound into His holy Church. Let us pray for those that travel by water or by land. Let us pray for those that are in the mines, in banishments, in prisons, and in bonds, for the name of the Lord. Let us pray for those that are afflicted with bitter servitude. Let us pray for our enemies, and those that hate us. Let us pray for those that persecute us for the name of the Lord, that the Lord may pacify their anger, and scatter their wrath against us. Let us pray for those that are without, and are wandered out of the way, that the Lord may convert them. Let us be mindful of the infants of the Church, that the Lord may perfect them in His fear, and bring them to a complete age. Let us pray one for another, that the Lord may keep us and preserve us by His grace to the end, and deliver us from the evil one, and from all the scandals of those that work iniquity, and preserve us unto His heavenly kingdom. Let us pray for every Christian soul. Save us, and raise us up, O God, by Thy mercy. Let us rise up, and let us pray earnestly, and dedicate ourselves and one another to the living God, through His Christ. And let the high priest add this prayer, and say: —

[1] Ezek. xviii. and xxxiii.
[2] Jonah iii.; 1 Tim. ii. 4.
[3] Luke xv.
[4] [Ps. cxxx. 3, 4. — R.]
[5] [This is "James, the Lord's brother;" Gal. i. 19. An incidental proof of the Eastern and Ante-Nicene origin of book viii. also. — R.]
[6] Matt. xix. 29.

THE FORM OF PRAYER FOR THE FAITHFUL.

XI. O Lord Almighty, the Most High, who dwellest on high, the Holy One, that restest among the saints, without beginning, the Only Potentate, who hast given to us by Christ the preaching of knowledge, to the acknowledgment of Thy glory and of Thy name, which He has made known to us, for our comprehension, do Thou now also look down through Him upon this Thy flock, and deliver it from all ignorance and wicked practice, and grant that we may fear Thee in earnest, and love Thee with affection, and have a due reverence of Thy glory. Be gracious and merciful to them, and hearken to them when they pray unto Thee; and keep them, that they may be unmoveable, unblameable, and unreprovable, that they may be holy in body and spirit, not having spot or wrinkle, or any such thing; but that they may be complete, and none of them may be defective or imperfect. O our support, our powerful God, who dost not accept persons, be Thou the assister of this Thy people,[1] which Thou hast redeemed with the precious blood of Thy Christ; be Thou their protector, aider, provider, and guardian, their strong wall of defence, their bulwark and security. For "none can snatch out of Thy hand:"[2] for there is no other God like Thee; for on Thee is our reliance. "Sanctify them by Thy truth: for Thy word is truth."[3] Thou who dost nothing for favour, Thou whom none can deceive, deliver them from every sickness, and every disease, and every offence, every injury and deceit, "from fear of the enemy, from the dart that flieth in the day, from the mischief that walketh about in darkness;"[4] and vouchsafe them that everlasting life which is in Christ Thy only begotten Son, our God and Saviour, through whom glory and worship be to Thee, in the Holy Spirit, now and always, and for ever and ever. Amen. And after this let the deacon say, Let us attend. And let the bishop salute the church, and say, The peace of God be with you all. And let the people answer, And with thy spirit; and *let the deacon say to all, Salute ye one another with the holy kiss. And let the clergy salute the bishop, the men of the laity salute the men, the women the women. And let the children stand at the reading-desk; and let another deacon stand by them, that they may not be* disorderly.[5] *And let other deacons walk about and watch the men and women, that no tumult may be made, and that no one nod, or whisper, or slumber; and let* the deacons[6] *stand at the doors of the men, and the* sub-*deacons at those of the women, that no one go out, nor a door be opened, although it be for one of the faithful, at the time of the oblation. But let one of the sub-deacons bring water to wash the hands of the priests, which is a symbol of the purity of those souls that are devoted to God.*

THE CONSTITUTION OF JAMES THE BROTHER OF JOHN, THE SON OF ZEBEDEE.

XII. And I James,[7] the brother of John, the son of Zebedee, say, that *the deacon shall* immediately *say, Let none of the catechumens, let none of the hearers, let none of the unbelievers, let none of the heterodox, stay here.* You who have prayed the foregoing prayer, depart.[8] *Let the mothers receive their children; let no one have anything against any one; let no one come in hypocrisy; let us stand upright before the Lord with fear and trembling, to offer. When this is done, let the deacons bring the gifts to the bishop at the altar; and let the presbyters stand on his right hand, and on his left, as disciples stand before their Master. But let two of the deacons, on each side of the altar, hold a fan, made up of thin membranes, or of the feathers of the peacock, or of fine cloth, and let them silently drive away the small animals that fly about, that they may not come near to the cups. Let the high priest, therefore,* together with the priests, *pray*[9] by himself; and let him put on his shining garment, and stand at the altar, and make the sign of the cross upon his forehead with his hand,[10] and say: The grace of Almighty God, and the love of our Lord Jesus Christ, and the fellowship of the Holy Ghost, be with you all. And let all with one voice say: And with thy spirit. The high priest: Lift up your mind. All the people: We lift it up unto the Lord. The high priest: Let us give thanks to the Lord. All the people: It is meet and right so to do. Then let the high priest say: It is very meet and right before all things to sing an hymn to Thee, who art the true God, who art before all beings, "from whom the whole family in heaven and earth is named;"[11] who only art unbegotten, and without beginning, and without a ruler, and without a master; who standest in need of nothing; who art the bestower of everything that is good; who art beyond all cause and generation; who art alway and immutably the same; from whom all things came into being, as from their proper original. For Thou art eternal knowledge, ever-

1 The V. MSS. insert, "whom Thou hast selected out of myriads."
2 John x. 29.
3 John xvii. 17.
4 Ps. lxiv. 1, xci. 5, 6.
5 The meaning in Coptic seems to be uncertain.
6 The Coptic reads, "sub-deacons."

7 One V. MS. gives the following note: "James the son of Zebedee, brother of John, preached the Gospel in Judea, was slain with the sword by Herod the tetrarch, and lies in Cæsarea.
8 [N.B.—No non-communicating attendance permitted.]
9 The Coptic adds, "over the oblation, that the Holy Spirit may descend upon it, making the bread the body of Christ, and the cup the blood of Christ; and prayers being ended." It then goes on with the words in italics in ch. xiii.
10 The common text has, "before all the people," omitted by one V. MS.
11 Eph. iii. 15.

lasting sight, unbegotten hearing, untaught wisdom, the first by nature, and the measure of being, and beyond all number; who didst bring all things out of nothing into being by Thy only begotten Son, but didst beget Him before all ages by Thy will, Thy power, and Thy goodness, without any instrument, the only begotten Son, God the Word, the living Wisdom, "the First-born of every creature, the angel of Thy Great Counsel,"[1] and Thy High Priest, but the King and Lord of every intellectual and sensible nature, who was before all things, by whom were all things. For Thou, O eternal God, didst make all things by Him, and through Him it is that Thou vouchsafest Thy suitable providence over the whole world; for by the very same that Thou bestowedst being, didst Thou also bestow well-being: the God and Father of Thy only begotten Son, who by Him didst make before all things the cherubim and the seraphim, the æons and hosts, the powers and authorities, the principalities and thrones, the archangels and angels; and after all these, didst by Him make this visible world, and all things that are therein. For Thou art He who didst frame the heaven as an arch, and "stretch it out like the covering of a tent,"[2] and didst found the earth upon nothing by Thy mere will; who didst fix the firmament, and prepare the night and the day; who didst bring the light out of Thy treasures, and on its departure didst bring on darkness, for the rest of the living creatures that move up and down in the world; who didst appoint the sun in heaven to rule over the day, and the moon to rule over the night, and didst inscribe in heaven the choir of stars to praise Thy glorious majesty; who didst make the water for drink and for cleansing, the air in which we live for respiration and the affording of sounds, by the means of the tongue, which strikes the air, and the hearing, which co-operates therewith, so as to perceive speech when it is received by it, and falls upon it; who madest fire for our consolation in darkness, for the supply of our want, and that we might be warmed and enlightened by it; who didst separate the great sea from the land, and didst render the former navigable and the latter fit for walking, and didst replenish the former with small and great living creatures, and filledst the latter with the same, both tame and wild; didst furnish it with various plants, and crown it with herbs, and beautify it with flowers, and enrich it with seeds; who didst ordain the great deep, and on every side madest a mighty cavity for it, which contains seas of salt waters heaped together,[3] yet didst Thou every way bound them with barriers of the smallest sand;[4] who sometimes dost raise it to the height of mountains by the winds, and sometimes dost smooth it into a plain; sometimes dost enrage it with a tempest, and sometimes dost still it with a calm, that it may be easy to seafaring men in their voyages; who didst encompass this world, which was made by Thee through Christ, with rivers, and water it with currents, and moisten it with springs that never fail, and didst bind it round with mountains for the immoveable and secure consistence of the earth: for Thou hast replenished Thy world, and adorned it with sweet-smelling and with healing herbs, with many and various living creatures, strong and weak, for food and for labour, tame and wild; with the noises of creeping things, the sounds of various sorts of flying creatures; with the circuits of the years, the numbers of months and days, the order of the seasons, the courses of the rainy clouds, for the production of the fruits and the support of living creatures. Thou hast also appointed the station of the winds, which blow when commanded by Thee, and the multitude of the plants and herbs. And Thou hast not only created the world itself, but hast also made man for a citizen of the world, exhibiting him as the ornament of the world; for Thou didst say to Thy Wisdom: "Let us make man according to our image, and according to our likeness; and let them have dominion over the fish of the sea, and over the fowls of the heaven."[5] Wherefore also Thou hast made him of an immortal soul, and of a body liable to dissolution — the former out of nothing, the latter out of the four elements — and hast given him as to his soul rational knowledge, the discerning of piety and impiety, and the observation of right and wrong; and as to his body, Thou hast granted him five senses and progressive motion: for Thou, O God Almighty, didst by Thy Christ plant a paradise in Eden,[6] in the east, adorned with all plants fit for food, and didst introduce him into it, as into a rich banquet. And when Thou madest him, Thou gavest him a law implanted within him, that so he might have at home and within himself the seeds of divine knowledge; and when Thou hadst brought him into the paradise of pleasure, Thou allowedst him the privilege of enjoying all things, only forbidding the tasting of one tree, in hopes of greater blessings; that in case he would keep that command, he might receive the reward of it, which was immortality. But when he neglected that command, and tasted of the forbidden fruit, by the seduction of the serpent and the counsel of his wife, Thou didst justly cast him out of paradise. Yet of Thy goodness

[1] Col. i. 15; Isa. ix. 6, LXX.
[2] Gen. i.; 4 Esd. xvi. 60; Ps. civ. 2.
[3] Job xxxviii.
[4] Jer. v. 22.
[5] Gen. i. 26.
[6] Gen. ii. 8.

Thou didst not overlook him, nor suffer him to perish utterly, for he was Thy creature; but Thou didst subject the whole creation to him, and didst grant him liberty to procure himself food by his own sweat and labours, whilst Thou didst cause all the fruits of the earth to spring up, to grow, and to ripen. But when Thou hadst laid him asleep for a while, Thou didst with an oath call him to a restoration again, didst loose the bond of death, and promise him life after the resurrection. And not this only; but when Thou hadst increased his posterity to an innumerable multitude, those that continued with Thee Thou didst glorify, and those who did apostatize from Thee Thou didst punish. And while Thou didst accept of the sacrifice of Abel[1] as of an holy person, Thou didst reject the gift of Cain, the murderer of his brother, as of an abhorred wretch. And besides these, Thou didst accept of Seth and Enos,[2] and didst translate Enoch:[3] for Thou art the Creator of men, and the giver of life, and the supplier of want, and the giver of laws, and the rewarder of those that observe them, and the avenger of those that transgress them; who didst bring the great flood upon the world by reason of the multitude of the ungodly,[4] and didst deliver righteous Noah from that flood by an ark,[5] with eight souls, the end of the foregoing generations, and the beginning of those that were to come; who didst kindle a fearful fire against the five cities of Sodom, and "didst turn a fruitful land into a salt lake for the wickedness of them that dwelt therein,"[6] but didst snatch holy Lot out of the conflagration. Thou art He who didst deliver Abraham from the impiety of his forefathers, and didst appoint him to be the heir of the world, and didst discover to him Thy Christ; who didst aforehand ordain Melchisedec an high priest for Thy worship;[7] who didst render Thy patient servant Job the conqueror of that serpent who is the patron of wickedness; who madest Isaac the son of the promise, and Jacob the father of twelve sons, and didst increase his posterity to a multitude, and bring him into Egypt with seventy-five souls.[8] Thou, O Lord, didst not overlook Joseph, but grantedst him, as a reward of his chastity for Thy sake, the government over the Egyptians. Thou, O Lord, didst not overlook the Hebrews when they were afflicted by the Egyptians, on account of the promises made unto their fathers; but Thou didst deliver them, and punish the Egyptians.[9] And when men had corrupted the law of nature, and had sometimes esteemed the creation the effect of chance, and sometimes honoured it more than they ought, and equalled it to the God of the universe, Thou didst not, however, suffer them to go astray, but didst raise up Thy holy servant Moses, and by him didst give the written law for the assistance of the law of nature,[10] and didst show that the creation was Thy work, and didst banish away the error of polytheism. Thou didst adorn Aaron and his posterity with the priesthood, and didst punish the Hebrews when they sinned, and receive them again when they returned to Thee. Thou didst punish the Egyptians with a judgment of ten plagues, and didst divide the sea, and bring the Israelites through it, and drown and destroy the Egyptians who pursued after them. Thou didst sweeten the bitter water with wood; Thou didst bring water out of the rock of stone; Thou didst rain manna from heaven, and quails, as meat out of the air; Thou didst afford them a pillar of fire by night to give them light, and a pillar of a cloud by day to overshadow them from the heat; Thou didst declare Joshua to be the general of the army, and didst overthrow the seven nations of Canaan by him;[11] Thou didst divide Jordan, and dry up the rivers of Etham;[12] Thou didst overthrow walls without instruments or the hand of man.[13] For all these things, glory be to Thee, O Lord Almighty. Thee do the innumerable hosts of angels, archangels, thrones, dominions, principalities, authorities, and powers, Thine everlasting armies, adore. The cherubim and the six-winged seraphim, with twain covering their feet, with twain their heads, and with twain flying,[14] say, together with thousand thousands of archangels, and ten thousand times ten thousand of angels,[15] incessantly, and with constant and loud voices, and let all the people say it with them: "Holy, holy, holy, Lord of hosts, heaven and earth are full of His glory: be Thou blessed for ever. Amen."[16] And afterwards let the high priest say: For Thou art truly holy, and most holy, the highest and most highly exalted for ever. Holy also is Thy only begotten Son our Lord and God, Jesus Christ, who in all things ministered to His God and Father, both in Thy various creation and Thy suitable providence, and has not overlooked lost mankind. But after the law of nature, after the exhortations in the positive law, after the prophetical reproofs and the government of the angels, when men had perverted both the positive law and that of nature, and had cast out of their mind the memory of the flood, the burn-

---

1 Gen. iv.
2 Ecclus. xlix. 16.
3 Gen. iv. and v.
4 Gen. vi. and vii.
5 1 Pet. iii. 20.
6 Gen. xix.; Wisd. x. 6; Ps. cvii. 34.
7 Gen. xii., etc.
8 Gen. xlvi. 27, LXX.
9 Ex. i, etc.
10 See Isa. viii. 20, LXX.
11 Josh. iii. 10, etc.
12 Ps. lxxiv. 15.
13 Josh. vi.
14 Isa. vi. 2.
15 Dan. vii. 10.
16 Isa. vi. 3; Rom. i. 25.

ing of Sodom, the plagues of the Egyptians, and the slaughters of the inhabitants of Palestine, and being just ready to perish universally after an unparalleled manner, He was pleased by Thy good will to become man, who was man's Creator; to be under the laws, who was the Legislator; to be a sacrifice, who was an High Priest; to be a sheep, who was the Shepherd. And He appeased Thee, His God and Father, and reconciled Thee to the world, and freed all men from the wrath to come, and was made of a virgin, and was in flesh, being God the Word, the beloved Son, the first-born of the whole creation, and was, according to the prophecies which were foretold concerning Him by Himself, of the seed of David and Abraham, of the tribe of Judah. And He was made in the womb of a virgin, who formed all mankind that are born into the world; He took flesh, who was without flesh; He who was begotten before time, was born in time; He lived holily, and taught according to the law; He drove away every sickness and every disease from men, and wrought signs and wonders among the people; and He was partaker of meat, and drink, and sleep, who nourishes all that stand in need of food, and "fills every living creature with His goodness;"[1] "He manifested His name to those that knew it not;"[2] He drave away ignorance; He revived piety, and fulfilled Thy will; He finished the work which Thou gavest Him to do; and when He had set all these things right, He was seized by the hands of the ungodly, of the high priests and priests, falsely so called, and of the disobedient people, by the betraying of him who was possessed of wickedness as with a confirmed disease; He suffered many things from them, and endured all sorts of ignominy by Thy permission; He was delivered to Pilate the governor, and He that was the Judge was judged, and He that was the Saviour was condemned; He that was impassible was nailed to the cross, and He who was by nature immortal died, and He that is the giver of life was buried, that He might loose those for whose sake He came from suffering and death, and might break the bonds of the devil, and deliver mankind from his deceit. He arose from the dead the third day; and when He had continued with His disciples forty days, He was taken up into the heavens, and is sat down on the right hand of Thee, who art His God and Father. Being mindful, therefore, of those things that He endured for our sakes, we give Thee thanks, O God Almighty, not in such a manner as we ought, but as we are able, and fulfil His constitution: "For in the same night that He was betrayed, He took bread"[3] in His holy and undefiled hands, and, looking up to Thee His God and Father, "He brake it, and gave it to His disciples, saying, This is the mystery of the new covenant: take of it, and eat. This is my body, which is broken for many, for the remission of sins."[4] In like manner also "He took the cup," and mixed it of wine and water, and sanctified it, and delivered it to them, saying: "Drink ye all of this; for this is my blood which is shed for many, for the remission of sins: do this in remembrance of me. For as often as ye eat this bread and drink this cup, ye do show forth my death until I come." Being mindful, therefore, of His passion, and death, and resurrection from the dead, and return into the heavens, and His future second appearing, wherein He is to come with glory and power to judge the quick and the dead, and to recompense to every one according to his works, we offer to Thee, our King and our God, according to His constitution, this bread and this cup, giving Thee thanks, through Him, that Thou hast thought us worthy to stand before Thee, and to sacrifice to Thee; and we beseech Thee that Thou wilt mercifully look down upon these gifts which are here set before Thee, O Thou God, who standest in need of none of our offerings. And do Thou accept them, to the honour of Thy Christ, and send down upon this sacrifice Thine Holy Spirit, the Witness of the Lord Jesus' sufferings, that He may show this bread to be the body of Thy Christ, and the cup to be the blood of Thy Christ, that those who are partakers thereof may be strengthened for piety, may obtain the remission of their sins, may be delivered from the devil and his deceit, may be filled with the Holy Ghost, may be made worthy of Thy Christ, and may obtain eternal life upon Thy reconciliation to them, O Lord Almighty. We further pray unto Thee, O Lord, for thy holy Church spread from one end of the world to another, which Thou hast purchased with the precious blood of Thy Christ, that Thou wilt preserve it unshaken and free from disturbance until the end of the world; for every episcopate who rightly divides the word of truth. We further pray to Thee for me, who am nothing, who offer to Thee, for the whole presbytery, for the deacons and all the clergy, that Thou wilt make them wise, and replenish them with the Holy Spirit. We further pray to Thee, O Lord, "for the king and all in authority,"[5] for the whole army, that they may be peaceable towards us, that so, leading the whole time of our life in quietness and unanimity, we may glorify Thee through Jesus Christ, who is our hope. We further offer to Thee also for all those holy persons who have pleased Thee from the beginning of the world—patri-

1 Ps. cv. 16.
2 John xvii. 6, 4.
3 1 Cor. xi. 23.
4 Matt. xxvi.; Mark xiv.; Luke xxii.
5 1 Tim. ii. 2.

archs, prophets, righteous men, apostles, martyrs, confessors, bishops, presbyters, deacons, sub-deacons, readers, singers, virgins, widows, and lay persons, with all whose names Thou knowest. We further offer to Thee for this people, that Thou wilt render them, to the praise of Thy Christ, "a royal priesthood and an holy nation;" [1] for those that are in virginity and purity; for the widows of the Church; for those in honourable marriage and child-bearing; for the infants of Thy people; that Thou wilt not permit any of us to "become castaways." We further beseech Thee also for this city and its inhabitants; for those that are sick; for those in bitter servitude; for those in banishments; for those in prison; for those that travel by water or by land; that Thou, the helper and assister of all men, wilt be their supporter. We further also beseech Thee for those that hate us and persecute us for Thy name's sake; for those that are without, and wander out of the way; that Thou wilt convert them to goodness, and pacify their anger. We further also beseech Thee for the catechumens of the Church, and for those that are vexed by the adversary, and for our brethren the penitents, that Thou wilt perfect the first in the faith, that Thou wilt deliver the second from the energy of the evil one, and that Thou wilt accept the repentance of the last, and forgive both them and us our offences. We further offer to Thee also for the good temperature of the air, and the fertility of the fruits, that so, partaking perpetually of the good things derived from Thee, we may praise Thee without ceasing, "who gavest food to all flesh." [2] We further beseech Thee also for those who are absent on a just cause, that Thou wilt keep us all in piety, and gather us together in the kingdom of Thy Christ, the God of all sensible and intelligent nature, our King; that Thou wouldst keep us immoveable, unblameable, and unreprovable: for to Thee belongs all glory, and worship, and thanksgiving, honour and adoration, the Father, with the Son, and to the Holy Ghost, both now and always, and for everlasting, and endless ages for ever. And let all the people say, Amen. And let the bishop say, "The peace of God be with you all." And let all the people say, "And with thy spirit." And let the deacon proclaim again: —

THE BIDDING PRAYER FOR THE FAITHFUL AFTER THE DIVINE OBLATION.

XIII. Let us still further beseech God through His Christ, and let us beseech Him on account of the gift which is offered to the Lord God, that the good God will accept it, through the mediation of His Christ, upon His heavenly altar, for a sweet-smelling savour. Let us pray for this church and people. Let us pray for every episcopate, every presbytery, all the deacons and ministers in Christ, for the whole congregation, that the Lord will keep and preserve them all. Let us pray "for kings and those in authority," that they may be peaceable toward us, "that so we may have and lead a quiet and peaceable life in all godliness and honesty." [3] Let us be mindful of the holy martyrs, that we may be thought worthy to be partakers of their trial. Let us pray for those that are departed in the faith. Let us pray for the good temperature of the air, and the perfect maturity of the fruits. Let us pray for those that are newly enlightened, that they may be strengthened in the faith, and all may be mutually comforted by one another.[4] Raise us up, O God, by Thy grace. Let us stand up, and dedicate ourselves to God, through His Christ. And let the bishop say: O God, who art great, and whose name is great, who art great in counsel and mighty in works, the God and Father of Thy holy child Jesus, our Saviour; look down upon us, and upon this Thy flock, which Thou hast chosen by Him to the glory of Thy name; and sanctify our body and soul, and grant us the favour to be "made pure from all filthiness of flesh and spirit," [5] and may obtain the good things laid up for us, and do not account any of us unworthy; but be Thou our comforter, helper, and protector, through Thy Christ, with whom glory, honour, praise, doxology, and thanksgiving be to Thee and to the Holy Ghost for ever. Amen. And after that all have said Amen, let the deacon say: Let us attend. And let the bishop speak thus to the people: Holy things for holy persons. And let the people answer: There is One that is holy; there is one Lord, one Jesus Christ, blessed for ever, to the glory of God the Father. Amen. "Glory to God in the highest, and on earth peace, good-will among men. Hosanna to the son of David! Blessed be He that cometh in the name of the Lord," being the Lord God who appeared to us, "Hosanna in the highest." [6] *And after that, let the bishop partake, then the presbyters, and deacons, and* [7] sub-deacons, and the readers, and the singers, and the ascetics; and then of the women, the deaconesses, and the virgins, and the widows; then the children; *and then all the people in order, with reverence and godly fear, without tumult. And let the bishop give the oblation, saying, The body of Christ; and let him that receiveth say, Amen.*

---

[1] 1 Pet. ii. 9.

[2] Ps. cxxxvi. 25.

[3] 1 Tim. ii. 2.

[4] This is not a fair translation of the Greek, which, as the text stands, does not make sense. One V. MS. reads, "Let us beseech in behalf of one another."

[5] 2 Cor. vii. 1.

[6] Luke ii. 14; Matt. xxi. 9.

[7] The Coptic adds, "the rest of the clergy in their order."

And let the deacon take *the cup; and when he gives* it, *say, The blood of Christ, the cup of life; and let him that drinketh say, Amen.*[1] And let the thirty-third psalm be said, while the rest are partaking; *and when all,*[2] both men and women, *have partaken,* let the deacons carry what remains into the vestry. *And when the singer has done, let the deacon say:* —

THE BIDDING PRAYER AFTER THE PARTICIPATION.

XIV. *Now we have received the precious body and* the precious *blood of Christ, let us give thanks to Him who has thought us worthy to partake of these His holy*[3] *mysteries;* and let us beseech Him that it may not be to us for condemnation, but for salvation, to the advantage of soul and body, to the preservation of piety, to the remission of sins, and to the life of the world to come. Let us arise, and by the grace of Christ let us dedicate ourselves to God, to the only unbegotten God, and to His Christ. And let the bishop give thanks: —

THE FORM OF PRAYER AFTER THE PARTICIPATION.

XV. O Lord God Almighty, the Father of Thy Christ, Thy blessed Son, who hearest those who call upon Thee with uprightness, who also knowest the supplications of those who are silent; we thank Thee that Thou hast thought us worthy to partake of Thy holy mysteries, which Thou hast bestowed upon us, for the entire confirmation of those things we have rightly known, for the preservation of piety, for the remission of our offences; for the name of thy Christ is called upon us, and we are joined To Thee. O Thou that hast separated us from the communion of the ungodly, unite us with those that are consecrated to Thee in holiness; confirm us in the truth, by the assistance of Thy Holy Spirit; reveal to us what things we are ignorant of, supply what things we are defective in, confirm us in what things we already know, preserve the priests blameless in Thy worship; keep the kings in peace, and the rulers in righteousness, the air in a good temperature, the fruits in fertility, the world in an all-powerful providence; pacify the warring nations, convert those that are gone astray, sanctify Thy people, keep those that are in virginity, preserve those in the faith that are in marriage, strengthen those that are in purity, bring the infants to complete age, confirm the newly admitted; instruct the catechumens, and render them worthy of admission; and gather us all together into Thy kingdom of heaven, by Jesus Christ our Lord, with whom glory, honour, and worship be to Thee, in the Holy Ghost, for ever. Amen. And *let the deacon say: Bow down to*[4] God through His Christ, *and receive the blessing.* And let the bishop add this prayer, and say: O God Almighty, the true God, to whom nothing can be compared, who art everywhere, and present in all things, and art in nothing as one of the things themselves; who art not bounded by place, nor grown old by time; who art not terminated by ages, nor deceived by words; who art not subject to generation, and wantest no guardian; who art above all corruption, free from all change, and invariable by nature; "who inhabitest light inaccessible;"[5] who art by nature invisible, and yet art known to all reasonable natures who seek Thee with a good mind, and art comprehended by those that seek after Thee with a good mind; the God of Israel, Thy people which truly see, and which have believed in Christ: Be gracious to me, and hear me, for Thy name's sake, and bless those that bow down their necks unto Thee, and grant them the petitions of their hearts, which are for their good, and do not reject any one of them from Thy kingdom; but sanctify, guard, cover, and assist them; deliver them from the adversary and every enemy; keep their houses, and guard "their comings in and their goings out."[6] For to Thee belongs the glory, praise, majesty, worship, and adoration, and to Thy Son Jesus, Thy Christ, our Lord and God and King, and to the Holy Ghost, now and always, for ever and ever. Amen. *And*[7] *the deacon shall say, Depart in peace.*[8] *These constitutions concerning this mystical worship, we,* the apostles, *do ordain for you, the bishops, presbyters, and deacons.*

SEC. III. — ORDINATION AND DUTIES OF THE CLERGY.

CONCERNING THE ORDINATION OF PRESBYTERS — THE CONSTITUTION OF JOHN, WHO WAS BELOVED BY THE LORD.

XVI. Concerning the ordination of presbyters, I[9] who am loved by the Lord make this constitution for you the bishops: *When thou ordainest a presbyter, O bishop, lay thy hand upon his head,*

1 The Coptic has, "and let them sing psalms during the distribution, until the whole congregation has received it."
2 The Coptic has, "let all the women receive it also."
3 The Coptic, "these His holy and immortal mysteries, which are numbered in heaven."

4 The Coptic has, "the Lord."
5 1 Tim. vi. 16.
6 Ps. cxxi. 8.
7 The Coptic adds: "And let the presbyters and deacons watch the few fragments that are left, that they may perceive that there is nothing superfluous; lest they fall into the great judgment, like the sons of Aaron and Eli, whom the Holy Spirit destroyed, because they did not refrain from despising the sacrifice of the Lord: how much more those who despise the body and blood of the Lord, thinking that to be merely material food which they receive, and not spiritual!"
8 The Coptic inserts, "when they have been blessed."
9 One V. MS. has this note: "John the evangelist, the brother of James, was banished by Domitian to the island of Patmos, and there composed the Gospel according to him. He died a natural death, in the third year of Trajan's reign, in Ephesus. His remains were sought, but have not been found."

in the presence of the presbyters and deacons,[1] and pray, saying: O Lord Almighty, our God, who hast created all things by Christ, and dost in like manner take care of the whole world by Him; for He who had power to make different creatures, has also power to take care of them, according to their different natures; on which account, O God, Thou takest care of immortal beings by bare preservation, but of those that are mortal by succession — of the soul by the provision of laws, of the body by the supply of its wants. Do Thou therefore now also look down upon Thy holy Church, and increase the same, and multiply those that preside in it, and grant them power, that they may labour both in word and work for the edification of Thy people. Do Thou now also look down upon this Thy servant, who is put into the presbytery by the vote and determination of the whole clergy; and do Thou replenish him with the Spirit of grace and counsel, to assist and govern Thy people with a pure heart, in the same manner as Thou didst look down upon Thy chosen people, and didst command Moses to choose elders, whom Thou didst fill with Thy Spirit.[2] Do Thou also now, O Lord, grant this, and preserve in us the Spirit of Thy grace, that this person, being filled with the gifts of healing and the word of teaching, may in meekness instruct Thy people, and sincerely serve Thee with a pure mind and a willing soul, and may fully discharge the holy ministrations for Thy people, through Thy Christ, with whom glory, honour, and worship be to Thee, and to the Holy Ghost, for ever. Amen.

CONCERNING THE ORDINATION OF DEACONS — THE CONSTITUTION OF PHILIP.

XVII. Concerning the ordination of deacons, I Philip[3] make this constitution: Thou shalt ordain a deacon, O bishop, by laying thy hands upon him in the presence of the whole presbytery, and of the deacons, and shalt pray, and say: —

THE FORM OF PRAYER FOR THE ORDINATION OF A DEACON.

XVIII. O God Almighty, the true and faithful God, who art rich unto all that call upon Thee in truth, who art fearful in counsels, and wise in understanding, who art powerful and great, hear our prayer, O Lord, and let Thine ears receive our supplication, and "cause the light of Thy countenance to shine upon this Thy servant," who is to be ordained for Thee to the office of a deacon; and replenish him with Thy Holy Spirit, and with power, as Thou didst replenish Stephen, who was Thy martyr, and follower of the sufferings of Thy Christ.[4] Do Thou render him worthy to discharge acceptably the ministration of a deacon, steadily, unblameably, and without reproof, that thereby he may attain an higher degree, through the mediation of Thy only begotten Son, with whom glory, honour, and worship be to Thee and the Holy Spirit for ever. Amen.

CONCERNING THE DEACONESS — THE CONSTITUTION OF BARTHOLOMEW.

XIX. Concerning a deaconess, I Bartholomew[5] make this constitution: O bishop, thou shalt lay thy hands upon her in the presence of the presbytery, and of the deacons and deaconesses, and shalt say: —

THE FORM OF PRAYER FOR THE ORDINATION OF A DEACONESS.

XX. O Eternal God, the Father of our Lord Jesus Christ, the Creator of man and of woman, who didst replenish with the Spirit Miriam, and Deborah, and Anna, and Huldah;[6] who didst not disdain that Thy only begotten Son should be born of a woman; who also in the tabernacle of the testimony, and in the temple, didst ordain women to be keepers of Thy holy gates, — do Thou now also look down upon this Thy servant, who is to be ordained to the office of a deaconess, and grant her Thy Holy Spirit, and "cleanse her from all filthiness of flesh and spirit,"[7] that she may worthily discharge the work which is committed to her to Thy glory, and the praise of Thy Christ, with whom glory and adoration be to Thee and the Holy Spirit for ever. Amen.

CONCERNING THE SUB-DEACONS — THE CONSTITUTION OF THOMAS.

XXI. Concerning the sub-deacons, I Thomas[8] make this constitution for you the bishops:[9] When thou dost ordain a sub-deacon,[10] O bishop, thou shalt lay thy hands upon him, and say: O Lord God, the Creator of heaven and earth, and of all things that are therein; who also in the tabernacle of the testimony didst appoint overseers and keepers of Thy holy vessels;[11] do Thou now look down upon this Thy servant, appointed

[1] The Coptic adds: "While you pray, he is ordained; and thou shalt ordain the deacon also according to this constitution alone."

[2] Ex. xviii., xxiv., xxviii.

[3] One V. MS. has the following note: "Philip having proclaimed the life-giving word to the Asiatic diocese, has been buried in Hierapolis of Phrygia along with his daughters, having been crowned with martyrdom in the reign of the Emperor Domitian. Philip, who has the daughters, is one of the seven; it was he also who baptized the eunuch."

[4] Acts vi. and vii.

[5] One V. MS. has the following note: "Bartholomew preached the Gospel according to Matthew to the Indians, who also has been buried in India."

[6] Ex. xv. 20; Judg. iv. 4; Luke ii. 36; 2 Kings xxii. 14.

[7] 2 Cor. vii. 1.

[8] One V. MS. has the following note: "Thomas preached to the Parthians, Medes, Persians, Germans, Hyrcanians, Bactrians, Bardians, who also, having been a martyr, lies in Edessa of Osdroene."

[9] The words "for you the bishops" are omitted in the Oxford MS.

[10] [See vol. v. Elucidation XIV. p. 417.]

[11] Num. iii.; 1 Chron. vi.

a sub-deacon; and grant him the Holy Spirit, that he may worthily handle the vessels of Thy ministry, and do Thy will always, through Thy Christ, with whom glory, honour, and worship be to Thee and to the Holy Spirit for ever. Amen.

CONCERNING THE READERS — THE CONSTITUTION OF MATTHEW.

XXII. Concerning readers,[1] I Matthew, also called Levi, who was once a tax-gatherer, make a constitution: Ordain a reader by laying thy hands upon him, and pray unto God, and say: O Eternal God, who art plenteous in mercy and compassions, who hast made manifest the constitution of the world by Thy operations therein, and keepest the number of Thine elect, do Thou also now look down upon Thy servant, who is to be entrusted to read Thy Holy Scriptures to Thy people, and give him Thy Holy Spirit, the prophetic Spirit. Thou who didst instruct Esdras Thy servant to read Thy laws to the people,[2] do Thou now also at our prayers instruct Thy servant, and grant that he may without blame perfect the work committed to him, and thereby be declared worthy of an higher degree, through Christ, with whom glory and worship be to Thee and to the Holy Ghost for ever. Amen.

CONCERNING THE CONFESSORS — THE CONSTITUTION OF JAMES THE SON OF ALPHEUS.

XXIII. And I James, the son of Alphæus, make a constitution in regard to confessors: *A confessor is not ordained; for he is so by choice and patience, and is worthy of great honour, as having confessed the name of God, and of His Christ, before nations and kings. But if there be occasion,* he is to be ordained[3] *either a bishop, priest, or deacon. But if any one of the confessors who is not ordained snatches to himself any such dignity upon account of his confession, let the same person be deprived and rejected; for he is not in such an office, since he has denied the constitution of Christ, and is "worse than an infidel."*[4]

THE SAME APOSTLE'S CONSTITUTION CONCERNING VIRGINS.

XXIV. I, the same, make a constitution in regard to virgins: *A virgin is not ordained, for we have no such command from the Lord;*[5] *for this is a state of voluntary trial, not for the reproach of marriage, but on account of leisure for piety.*

[1] The Oxford MS. has no part of this chapter. It reads: "A reader is appointed when the bishop gives him a book; for there is no imposition of hands."
[2] Neh. viii.
[3] The Coptic reads, "let him be ordained."
[4] 1 Tim. v. 8.
[5] 1 Cor. vii. 25.

THE CONSTITUTION OF LEBBÆUS, WHO WAS SURNAMED THADDÆUS, CONCERNING WIDOWS.

XXV. And I Lebbæus,[6] surnamed Thaddæus, make this constitution in regard to widows: *A widow is not ordained; yet if she has lost her husband a great while, and has lived soberly and unblameably, and has taken extraordinary care of her family, as Judith*[7] *and Anna*[8] *— those women of great reputation — let her be chosen into the order of widows. But if she has lately lost her yokefellow, let her not be believed, but let her* youth *be judged of by the time; for the affections do sometimes grow aged with men, if they be not restrained by a better bridle.*

THE SAME APOSTLE CONCERNING THE EXORCIST.

XXVI. I the same make a constitution in regard to an exorcist. *An exorcist is not ordained. For it is a trial of voluntary goodness, and of the grace of God through Christ by the inspiration of the Holy Spirit. For he who has received the gift of healing is declared by revelation from God, the grace which is in him being manifest to all. But if there be occasion for him,* he must be ordained[9] *a bishop, or a presbyter, or a deacon.*

SIMON THE CANAANITE CONCERNING THE NUMBER NECESSARY FOR THE ORDINATION OF A BISHOP.

XXVII.[10] And I Simon the Canaanite[11] make a constitution to determine by how many a bishop ought to be elected. Let a bishop be ordained by three or two bishops; but if any one be ordained by one bishop, let him be deprived, both himself and he that ordained him. But if there be a necessity that he have only one to ordain him, because more bishops cannot come together, as in time of persecution, or for such like causes, let him bring the suffrage of permission from more bishops.

THE SAME APOSTLE'S CANONS CONCERNING BISHOPS, PRESBYTERS, DEACONS, AND THE REST OF THE CLERGY.

XXVIII. Concerning[12] the canons I the same make a constitution. A bishop blesses, but does not receive the blessing. He lays on hands, or-

[6] The two V. MSS. have the following note: "Thaddæus, also called Lebbæus, and who was surnamed Judas the Zealot, preached the truth to the Edessenes and the people of Mesopotamia when Abgarus ruled over Edessa, and has been buried in Berytus of Phœnicia."
[7] Judith xvi. 21, 23.
[8] Luke ii. 36, etc.
[9] The Coptic has, "let him be ordained."
[10] Ch. xxvii., xxviii., xxx.-xxxiv., and ch. xlii.-xlvii., occur in Syriac and Coptic, as well as in the Greek MSS.
[11] One V. MS. has the following note: "Simon the Canaanite, preacher of the truth, is crowned with martyrdom in Judea in the reign of Domitian."
[12] The words from "concerning" to "constitution" are omitted in the Oxford MS., in Syriac, and Coptic.

dains, offers, receives the blessing from bishops, but by no means from presbyters. A bishop deprives any clergyman who deserves deprivation, excepting a bishop; for of himself he has not power to do that. A presbyter blesses, but does not receive the blessing; yet does he receive the blessing from the bishop or a fellow-presbyter. In like manner does he give it to a fellow-presbyter. He lays on hands, but does not ordain; he does not deprive, yet does he separate those that are under him, if they be liable to such a punishment. A deacon does not bless, does not give the blessing, but receives it from the bishop and presbyter: he does not baptize, he does not offer; but when a bishop or presbyter has offered, he distributes to the people, not as a priest, but as one that ministers to the priests. But it is not lawful for any one of the other clergy to do the work of a deacon. A deaconess does not bless, nor perform anything belonging to the office of presbyters or deacons, but only is to keep the doors, and to minister to the presbyters in the baptizing of women, on account of decency. A deacon separates a sub-deacon, a reader, a singer, and a deaconess, if there be any occasion, in the absence of a presbyter. It is not lawful for a sub-deacon to separate either one of the clergy or laity; nor for a reader, nor for a singer, nor for a deaconess, for they are the ministers to the deacons.

SEC. IV. — CERTAIN PRAYERS AND LAWS.

CONCERNING THE BLESSING OF WATER AND OIL — THE CONSTITUTION OF MATTHIAS.

XXIX.[1] Concerning the water and the oil, I Matthias make a constitution. Let the bishop bless the water, or the oil. But if he be not there, let the presbyter bless it, the deacon standing by. But if the bishop be present, let the presbyter and deacon stand by, and let him say thus: O Lord of hosts, the God of powers, the creator of the waters, and the supplier of oil, who art compassionate, and a lover of mankind, who hast given water for drink and for cleansing, and oil to give man a cheerful and joyful countenance;[2] do Thou now also sanctify this water and this oil through Thy Christ, in the name of him or her that has offered them, and grant them a power to restore health, to drive away diseases, to banish demons, and to disperse all snares through Christ our hope, with whom glory, honour, and worship be to Thee, and to the Holy Ghost, for ever. Amen.

THE SAME APOSTLE'S CONSTITUTION CONCERNING FIRST-FRUITS AND TITHES.

XXX. I[3] the same make a constitution in regard to first-fruits and tithes. Let all first-fruits be brought to the bishop, and to the presbyters, and to the deacons,[4] for their maintenance; but let all the tithe be for the maintenance of the rest of the clergy, and of the virgins and widows, and of those under the trial of poverty. For the first-fruits belong to the priests, and to those deacons that minister to them.

THE SAME APOSTLE'S CONSTITUTIONS CONCERNING THE REMAINING OBLATIONS.

XXXI. I the same make a constitution in regard to remainders. Those eulogies which remain at the mysteries, let the deacons distribute them among the clergy, according to the mind of the bishop or the presbyters: to a bishop, four parts; to a presbyter, three[5] parts; to a deacon, two[6] parts; and to the rest of the sub-deacons, or readers, or singers, or deaconesses, one part. For this is good and acceptable in the sight of God, that every one be honoured according to his dignity; for the Church is the school, not of confusion, but of good order.

VARIOUS CANONS OF PAUL THE APOSTLE CONCERNING THOSE THAT OFFER THEMSELVES TO BE BAPTIZED — WHOM WE ARE TO RECEIVE, AND WHOM TO REJECT.

XXXII. *I also, Paul,*[7] *the least of the apostles, do make the following constitutions for you, the bishops, and presbyters, and deacons, concerning canons.* Those that first come to the mystery of godliness, let them be brought to the bishop or to the presbyters by the deacons, and let them be examined as to the causes wherefore they come to the word of the Lord; and let those that bring them exactly inquire about their character, and give them their testimony. Let their manners and their life be inquired into, and whether they be slaves or freemen. And if any one be a slave, let him be asked who is his master. If he be slave to one of the faithful, let his master be asked if he can give him a good character. If he cannot, let him be rejected, until he show himself to be worthy to his master. But if he does give him a good character, let him be admitted. But if he be household slave

[1] This chapter is not found in the Coptic and Syriac. One V. MS. has the following note: "Matthew (probably a mistake for Matthias) taught the doctrines of Christ in Judea, and was one of the seventy disciples. After the ascension of Christ he was numbered with the twelve apostles, instead of Judas, who was the betrayer. He lies in Jerusalem."

[2] Ps. civ. 15.

[3] The Oxford MS. reads: "I the same, Simon the Canaanite, make a constitution."

[4] "Deacons" omitted in Oxford MS. and in Coptic.

[5] "Two," Oxford MS.

[6] "One," Oxford MS.

[7] One V. MS. has the following instead of the title: "Paul, the teacher of the Gentiles, having proclaimed the Gospel of Christ to the Gentiles from Jerusalem even to Illyricum, was cut off in Rome while teaching the truth, by Nero and King Agrippa, being beheaded, and has been buried in Rome itself."

to an heathen, let him be taught to please his master, that the word be not blasphemed. If, then, he have a wife, or a woman hath an husband, let them be taught to be content with each other; but if they be unmarried, let them learn not to commit fornication, but to enter into lawful marriage. But if his master be one of the faithful, and knows that he is guilty of fornication, and yet does not give him a wife, or to the woman an husband, let him be separated; but if any one hath a demon, let him indeed be taught piety, but not received into communion before he be cleansed; yet if death be near, let him be received. If any one be a maintainer of harlots, let him either leave off to prostitute women, or else let him be rejected. If a harlot come, let her leave off whoredom, or else let her be rejected. If a maker of idols come, let him either leave off his employment, or let him be rejected. If one belonging to the theatre[1] come, whether it be man or woman, or charioteer, or dueller, or racer, or player of prizes, or Olympic gamester, or one that plays on the pipe, on the lute, or on the harp at those games, or a dancing-master, or an huckster,[2] either let them leave off their employments, or let them be rejected. If a soldier come, let him be taught to "do no injustice, to accuse no man falsely, and to be content with his allotted wages:"[3] if he submit to those rules, let him be received; but if he refuse them, let him be rejected. He that is guilty of sins not to be named, a sodomite, an effeminate person, a magician, an enchanter, an astrologer, a diviner, an user of magic verses, a juggler, a mountebank, one that makes amulets, a charmer, a soothsayer, a fortune-teller, an observer of palmistry; he that, when he meets you, observes defects in the eyes or feet of the birds or cats, or noises, or symbolical sounds: let these be proved for some time, for this sort of wickedness is hard to be washed away; and if they leave off those practices, let them be received; but if they will not agree to that, let them be rejected. Let a concubine, who is slave to an unbeliever, and confines herself to her master alone, be received;[4] but if she be incontinent with others, let her be rejected. If one of the faithful hath a concubine, if she be a bond-servant, let him leave off that way, and marry in a legal manner: if she be a free woman, let him marry her in a lawful manner; if he does not, let him be rejected. Let him that follows the Gentile customs, or Jewish fables, either reform, or let him be rejected. If any one follows the sports of the theatre, their huntings, or horse-races, or combats, either let him leave them off, or let him be rejected. Let him who is to be a catechumen be a catechumen for three years; but if any one be diligent, and has a good-will to his business, let him be admitted: for it is not the length of time, but the course of life, that is judged. Let him that teaches, although he be one of the laity, yet, if he be skilful in the word and grave in his manners, teach; for "they shall be all taught of God."[5] Let all the faithful, whether men or women, when they rise from sleep, before they go to work, when they have washed themselves, pray; but if any catechetic instruction be held, let the faithful person prefer the word of piety before his work. Let the faithful person, whether man or woman, treat servants kindly, as we have ordained in the foregoing books, and have taught in our epistles.[6]

UPON WHICH DAYS SERVANTS ARE NOT TO WORK.

XXXIII. I Peter and Paul do make the following constitutions. Let the slaves work five days; but on the Sabbath-day and the Lord's day let them have leisure to go to church for instruction in piety. We have said that the Sabbath is on account of the creation, and the Lord's day of the resurrection. Let slaves rest from their work all the great week, and that which follows it—for the one in memory of the passion, and the other of the resurrection; and there is need they should be instructed who it is that suffered and rose again, and who it is permitted Him to suffer, and raised Him again. Let them have rest from their work on the Ascension, because it was the conclusion of the dispensation by Christ. Let them rest at Pentecost, because of the coming of the Holy Spirit, which was given to those that believed in Christ. Let them rest on the festival of His birth, because on it the unexpected favour was granted to men, that Jesus Christ, the Logos of God, should be born of the Virgin Mary,[7] for the salvation of the world.[8] Let them rest on the festival of Epiphany, because on it a manifestation took place of the divinity of Christ, for the Father bore testimony to Him at the baptism; and the Paraclete, in the form of a dove, pointed out to the bystanders Him to whom testimony was borne. Let them rest on the days of the apostles: for they were appointed your teachers *to bring you* to Christ, and made you worthy of the Spirit. Let them rest on the day of the first[9] martyr Stephen, and of the other holy martyrs who preferred Christ to their own life.

1 [Note this uniform testimony of antiquity against theatricals in all forms.]
2 [Purveyors to the play-house.]
3 Luke iii. 14.
4 [Compare vol. v. p. 130, note 1.]
5 John vi. 45.
6 Eph. vi.; Col. iv.; Philem.
7 The Coptic adds, "the holy mother of God."
8 [Compare vol. iii. pp. 164, 352.
9 One V. MS., Coptic, and Syriac omit "first."

AT WHAT HOURS, AND WHY, WE ARE TO PRAY.

XXXIV. Offer up your prayers in the morning, at the third hour, the sixth, the ninth, the evening, and at cock-crowing: in the morning, returning thanks that the Lord has sent you light, that He has brought you past the night, and brought on the day; at the third hour, because at that hour the Lord received the sentence of condemnation from Pilate; at the sixth, because at that hour He was crucified;[1] at the ninth, because all things were in commotion at the crucifixion of the Lord, as trembling at the bold attempt of the impious Jews, and not bearing the injury offered to their Lord; in the evening, giving thanks that He has given you the night to rest from the daily labours; at cock-crowing, because that hour brings the good news of the coming on of the day for the operations proper for the light. But if it be not possible to go to the church on account of the unbelievers, thou, O bishop, shalt assemble them in a house, that a godly man may not enter into an assembly of the ungodly. For it is not the place that sanctifies the man, but the man the place. And if the ungodly possess the place, do thou avoid it, because it is profaned by them. For as holy priests sanctify a place, so do the profane ones defile it. If it be not possible to assemble either in the church or in a house, let every one by himself sing, and read, and pray, or two or three together. For "where two or three are gathered together in my name, there am I in the midst of them."[2] Let not one of the faithful pray with a catechumen, no, not in the house: for it is not reasonable that he who is admitted should be polluted with one not admitted. Let not one of the godly pray with an heretic, no, not in the house. For "what fellowship hath light with darkness?"[3] Let Christians, whether men or women, who have connections with slaves, either leave them off, or let them be rejected.

THE CONSTITUTION OF JAMES THE BROTHER OF CHRIST CONCERNING EVENING PRAYER.

XXXV. I James,[4] the brother of Christ according to the flesh, but His servant as the only begotten God, and one appointed bishop of Jerusalem by the Lord Himself, and the Apostles, do ordain thus: When it is evening, thou, O bishop, shalt assemble the church; and after the repetition of the psalm at the lighting up the lights, the deacon shall bid prayers for the catechumens, the energumens, the illuminated, and the penitents, as we have formerly said. But after the dismission of these, the deacon shall say: So many as are of the faithful, let us pray to the Lord. And after the bidding prayer, which is formerly set down, he shall say: —

THE BIDDING PRAYER FOR THE EVENING.

XXXVI. Save us, O God, and raise us up by Thy Christ. Let us stand up, and beg for the mercies of the Lord, and His compassions, for the angel of peace, for what things are good and profitable, for a Christian departure out of this life, an evening and a night of peace, and free from sin; and let us beg that the whole course of our life may be unblameable. Let us dedicate ourselves and one another to the living God through His Christ. And let the bishop add this prayer, and say: —

THE THANKSGIVING FOR THE EVENING.

XXXVII. O God, who art without beginning and without end, the Maker of the whole world by Christ, and the Provider for it, but before all[5] His God and Father, the Lord[6] of the Spirit, and the King of intelligible and sensible beings; who hast made the day for the works of light, and the night for the refreshment of our infirmity, — for "the day is Thine, the night also is Thine: Thou hast prepared the light and the sun,"[7] — do Thou now, O Lord, Thou lover of mankind, and Fountain of all good, mercifully accept of this our evening thanksgiving. Thou who hast brought us through the length of the day, and hast brought us to the beginnings of the night, preserve us by Thy Christ, afford us a peaceable evening, and a night free from sin, and vouchsafe us everlasting life by Thy Christ, through whom glory, honour, and worship be to Thee in[8] the Holy Spirit for ever. Amen. And let the deacon say: Bow down for the laying on of hands. And let the bishop say: O God of our fathers, and Lord of mercy, who didst form man of Thy wisdom a rational creature, and beloved of God more than the other beings upon this earth, and didst give him authority to rule over the creatures upon the earth, and didst ordain by Thy will rulers and priests — the former for the security of life, the latter for a regular worship, — do Thou now also look down, O Lord Almighty, and cause Thy face to shine upon Thy people, who bow down the neck of their heart, and bless them by Christ; through whom Thou hast enlightened us with the light of

[1] The Syriac and Coptic add: "and His side being wounded, blood and water came forth."

[2] Matt. xviii. 20. [A token that much of these constitutions is truly primitive.]

[3] 2 Cor. vi. 14. [Compare p. 483, *supra*: Energumens?]

[4] The words from "I James" to "ordain thus" are omitted in the V. MSS., and the following words are given instead in the two V. MSS.: "James, the brother of the Lord, has been killed with stones (the other MS. reads, 'with sticks') by the Jews in Jerusalem on account of the doctrines of Christ." Ch. XXXV.-XLI. are omitted in the Oxford MS., and in Syriac and Coptic.

[5] "Before all" is omitted in one V. MS.

[6] One V. MS. reads "sender forth" instead of "Lord."

[7] Ps. lxxiv. 16.

[8] One V. MS. reads "with" instead of "in."

knowledge, and hast revealed Thyself to us; with whom worthy adoration is due from every rational and holy nature to Thee, and to the Spirit, who is the Comforter, for ever. Amen. And let the deacon say: "Depart in peace." In like manner, in the morning, after the repetition of the morning psalm, and his dismission of the catechumens, the energumens, the candidates for baptism, and the penitents, and after the usual bidding of prayers, that we may not again repeat the same things, let the deacon add after the words, Save us, O God, and raise us up by Thy grace: Let us beg of the Lord His mercies and His compassions, that this morning and this day may be with peace and without sin, as also all the time of our sojourning; that He will grant us His angel of peace, a Christian departure out of this life, and that God will be merciful and gracious. Let us dedicate ourselves and one another to the living God through His Only-begotten. And let the bishop add this prayer, and say: —

THE THANKSGIVING FOR THE MORNING.

XXXVIII. O God, the God of spirits and of all flesh, who art beyond compare, and standest in need of nothing, who hast given the sun to have rule over the day, and the moon and the stars to have rule over the night, do Thou now also look down upon us with gracious eyes, and receive our morning thanksgivings, and have mercy upon us; for we have not "spread out our hands unto a strange God;" [1] for there is not among us any new God, but Thou, the eternal God, who art without end, who hast given us our being through Christ, and given us our well-being through Him. Do Thou vouchsafe us also, through Him, eternal life; with whom glory, and honour, and worship be to Thee and to the Holy Spirit for ever. Amen. And let the deacon say: Bow down for the laying on of hands. And let the bishop add this prayer, saying: —

THE IMPOSITION OF HANDS FOR THE MORNING.

XXXIX. O God, who art faithful and true, who "hast mercy on thousands and ten thousands of them that love Thee," [2] the lover of the humble, and the protector of the needy, of whom all things stand in need, for all things are subject to Thee; look down upon this Thy people, who bow down their heads to Thee, and bless them with spiritual blessing. "Keep them as the apple of an eye," [3] preserve them in piety and righteousness, and vouchsafe them eternal life in Christ Jesus Thy beloved Son, with whom glory, honour, and worship be to Thee and to the Holy Spirit, now and always, and for ever and ever. Amen. And let the deacon say: "Depart in peace." And when the first-fruits are offered, the bishop gives thanks in this manner: —

THE FORM OF PRAYER FOR THE FIRST-FRUITS.

XL. We give thanks to Thee, O Lord Almighty, the Creator of the whole world, and its Preserver, through Thy only begotten Son Jesus Christ our Lord, for the first-fruits which are offered to Thee, not in such a manner as we ought, but as we are able. For what man is there that can worthily give Thee thanks for those things Thou hast given them to partake of? The God of Abraham, and of Isaac, and of Jacob, and of all the saints, who madest all things fruitful by Thy word, and didst command the earth to bring forth various fruits for our rejoicing and our food; who hast given to the duller and more sheepish sort of creatures juices — herbs to them that feed on herbs, and to some flesh, to others seeds, but to us corn, as advantageous and proper food, and many other things — some for our necessities, some for our health, and some for our pleasure. On all these accounts, therefore, art Thou worthy of exalted hymns of praise for Thy beneficence by Christ, through whom [4] glory, honour, and worship be to Thee, in the Holy Spirit, for ever. Amen. Concerning those that are at rest in Christ: After the bidding prayer, that we may not repeat it again, the deacon shall add as follows: —

THE BIDDING PRAYER FOR THOSE DEPARTED.

XLI. Let us pray for our brethren that are at rest [5] in Christ, that God, the lover of mankind, who has received his soul, may forgive him every sin, voluntary and involuntary, and may be merciful and gracious to him, and give him his lot in the land of the pious that are sent into the bosom of Abraham, and Isaac, and Jacob, with all those that have pleased Him and done His will from the beginning of the world, whence all sorrow, grief, and lamentation are banished. Let us arise, let us dedicate ourselves and one another to the eternal God, through that Word which was in the beginning. And let the bishop say: O Thou who art by nature immortal, and hast no end of Thy being, from whom every creature, whether immortal or mortal, is derived; who didst make man a rational creature, the citizen of this world, in his constitution mortal, and didst add the promise of a resurrection; who didst not suffer Enoch and Elijah to taste of death; "the God of Abraham, the God of Isaac, and the God of Jacob, who art the God of them,

[1] Ps. xliv. 20.
[2] Ex. xxxiv. and xx.
[3] Ps. xvii. 8.
[4] One V. MS. reads, "with whom," and "with the Holy Spirit."
[5] [They are "at rest." Yet this prayer, and wherefore? See St. Augustine, *Confessions* (ed. Migne), p. 765, Nebridius.]

not as of dead, but as of living persons: for the souls of all men live with Thee, and the spirits of the righteous are in Thy hand, which no torment can touch;"[1] for they are all sanctified under Thy hand: do Thou now also look upon this Thy servant, whom Thou hast selected and received into another state, and forgive him if voluntarily or involuntarily he has sinned, and afford him merciful angels, and place him in the bosom of the patriarchs, and prophets, and apostles, and of all those that have pleased Thee from the beginning of the world, where there is no grief, sorrow, nor lamentation; but the peaceable region of the godly, and the undisturbed land of the upright, and of those that therein see the glory of Thy Christ; by whom[2] glory, honour, and worship, thanksgiving, and adoration be to Thee, in the Holy Spirit, for ever. Amen. And let the deacon say: Bow down, and receive the blessing. And let the bishop give thanks for them, saying as follows: "O Lord, save Thy people, and bless Thine inheritance,"[3] which Thou hast purchased with the precious blood of Thy Christ. Feed them under Thy right hand, and cover them under Thy wings, and grant that they may "fight the good fight, and finish their course, and keep the faith"[4] immutably, unblameably, and unreprovably, through our Lord Jesus Christ, Thy beloved Son, with whom glory, honour, and worship be to Thee and to the Holy Spirit for ever. Amen.

HOW AND WHEN WE OUGHT TO CELEBRATE THE MEMORIALS OF THE FAITHFUL DEPARTED, AND THAT WE OUGHT THEN TO GIVE SOMEWHAT OUT OF THEIR GOODS TO THE POOR.

XLII. Let the third day of the departed be celebrated with psalms, and lessons, and prayers, on account of Him who arose within the space of three days; and let the ninth day be celebrated in remembrance of the living, and of the departed; and the fortieth[5] day according to the ancient pattern: for so did the people lament Moses, and the anniversary day in memory of him.[6] And let alms be given to the poor out of his goods for a memorial of him.[7]

THAT MEMORIALS OR MANDATES DO NOT AT ALL PROFIT THE UNGODLY WHO ARE DEAD.

XLIII. These things we say concerning the pious; for as to the ungodly, if thou givest all the world to the poor, thou wilt not benefit him at all. For to whom the Deity was an enemy while he was alive, it is certain it will be so also when he is departed; for there is no unrighteousness with Him. For "the Lord[8] is righteous, and has loved righteousness."[9] And, "Behold the man and his work."[10]

CONCERNING DRUNKARDS.

XLIV. Now, when you are invited to their memorials, do you feast with good order, and the fear of God, as disposed to intercede for those that are departed. For since you are the presbyters and deacons of Christ, you ought always to be sober, both among yourselves and among others, that so you may be able to warn the unruly. Now the Scripture says, "The men in power are passionate. But let them not drink wine, lest by drinking they forget wisdom, and are not able to judge aright."[11] Wherefore[12] both the presbyters and the deacons are those of authority in the Church next to God Almighty and His beloved Son.[13] We say this, not they are not to drink at all, otherwise it would be to the reproach of what God has made for cheerfulness, but that they be not disordered with wine. For the Scripture does not say, Do not drink wine; but what says it? "Drink not wine to drunkenness;" and again, "Thorns spring up in the hand of the drunkard."[14] Nor do we say this only to those of the clergy, but also to every lay Christian, upon whom the name of our Lord Jesus Christ is called. For to them also it is said, "Who hath woe? who hath sorrow? who hath uneasiness? who hath babbling? who hath red eyes? who hath wounds without cause? Do not these things belong to those that tarry long at the wine, and that go to seek where drinking meetings are?"[15]

CONCERNING THE RECEIVING SUCH AS ARE PERSECUTED FOR CHRIST'S SAKE.

XLV. Receive ye those that are persecuted[16] on account of the faith, and who fly from city to city,[17] as mindful of the words of the Lord. For, knowing that though "the spirit be willing, the flesh is weak,"[18] they fly away, and prefer the spoiling of their goods, that they may preserve the name of Christ in themselves without denying it. Supply them therefore with what they want, and thereby fulfil the commandment of the Lord.

---

1 Matt. xxii. 32; Wisd. iii. 1.
2 "With whom," one V. MS.
3 Ps. xxviii. 9.
4 2 Tim. iv. 7.
5 The Syriac and a Greek marginal reading give "the thirtieth."
6 Deut. xxxiv. 8. [Comp. Aug., *Confess.* (ed. Migne), p. 778.]
7 [The "month's mind" was anciently of this sort, with no reference to purgatorial penalties. "Credo jam feceris quod rogo."—Aug.]
8 The Syriac and the Oxford MS. read "God" instead of "Lord."
9 Ps. xi. 7.
10 Isa. lxii. 11.
11 Prov. xxxi. 4, LXX.
12 The Syriac, the Coptic, and the Oxford MS. add, "the bishops." The Coptic omits "the deacons."
13 The Coptic adds, "Jesus Christ and the Holy Spirit."
14 Prov. xxiii.; Ecclus. xxxi. 25-31; Eph. v. 18; Prov. xxvi. 9.
15 Prov. xxiii. 29, 30.
16 [A token of the early origin of what is genuine in these interpolated *Constitutions.*]
17 Matt. x. 23.
18 Matt. xxvi. 41.

SEC. V. — ALL THE APOSTLES URGE THE OBSERVANCE OF THE ORDER OF THE CHURCH.

THAT EVERY ONE OUGHT TO REMAIN IN THAT RANK WHEREIN HE IS PLACED, BUT NOT SNATCH SUCH OFFICES TO HIMSELF WHICH ARE NOT ENTRUSTED TO HIM.

XLVI. Now this we all in common do charge you, that every one remain in that rank which is appointed him, and do not transgress his proper bounds; for they are not ours, but God's. For says the Lord: "He that heareth you, heareth me; and he that heareth me, heareth Him that sent me." And, "He that despiseth you, despiseth me; and he that despiseth me, despiseth Him that sent me."[1] For if those things that are without life do observe good order, as the night, the day, the sun, the moon, the stars, the elements, the seasons, the months, the weeks, the days, and the hours, and are subservient to the uses appointed them, according to that which is said, "Thou hast set them a bound which they shall not pass;"[2] and again, concerning the sea, "I have set bounds thereto, and have encompassed it with bars and gates; and I said to it, Hitherto shalt thou come, and thou shalt go no farther;"[3] how much more ought ye not to venture to remove those things which we, according to God's will, have determined for you! But because many think this a small matter, and venture to confound the orders, and to remove the ordination which belongs to them severally, snatching to themselves dignities which were never given them, and allowing themselves to bestow that authority in a tyrannical manner which they have not themselves, and thereby provoke God to anger (as did the followers of Corah and King Uzziah,[4] who, having no authority, usurped the high-priesthood without commission from God; and the former were burnt with fire, and the latter was struck with a leprosy in his forehead); and provoke Christ Jesus to anger, who has made this constitution; and also grieve the Holy Spirit, and make void His testimony: therefore, foreknowing the danger that hangs over those who do such things, and the neglect about the sacrifices and eucharistical offices which will arise from their being impiously offered by those who ought not to offer them; who think the honour of the high-priesthood, which is an imitation of the great High Priest Jesus Christ our King, to be a matter of sport; we have found it necessary to give you warning in this matter also. For some are already turned aside after their own vanity. We say that Moses the servant of God ("to whom God spake face to face, as if a man spake to his friend;"[5] to whom He said, "I know thee above all men;" to whom He spake directly, and not by obscure methods, or dreams, or angels, or riddles), — this person, when he made constitutions and divine laws, distinguished what things were to be performed by the high priests, what by the priests, and what by the Levites; distributing to every one his proper and suitable office in the divine service. And those things which are allotted for the high priests to do, those might not be meddled with by the priests; and what things were allotted to the priests, the Levites might not meddle with; but every one observed those ministrations which were written down and appointed for them. And if any would meddle beyond the tradition, death was his punishment. And Saul's example does show this most plainly, who, thinking he might offer sacrifice without the prophet and high priest Samuel,[6] drew upon himself a sin and a curse without remedy. Nor did even his having anointed him king discourage the prophet. But God showed the same by a more visible effect in the case of Uzziah,[7] when He without delay exacted the punishment due to this transgression, and he that madly coveted after the high-priesthood was rejected from his kingdom also. As to those things that have happened amongst us, you yourselves are not ignorant of them. For ye know undoubtedly that those that are by us named bishops, and presbyters, and deacons, were made by prayer, and by the laying on of hands; and that by the difference of their names is showed the difference of their employments. For not every one that will is ordained, as the case was in that spurious and counterfeit priesthood of the calves under Jeroboam;[8] but he only who is called of God. For if there were no rule or distinction of orders, it would suffice to perform all the offices under one name. But being taught by the Lord the series of things, we distributed the functions of the high-priesthood to the bishops, those of the priesthood to the presbyters, and the ministration under them both to the deacons; that the divine worship might be performed in purity. For it is not lawful for a deacon to offer the sacrifice, or to baptize, or to give either the greater or the lesser blessing. Nor may a presbyter perform ordination; for it is not agreeable to holiness to have this order perverted. For "God is not the God of confusion,"[9] that the subordinate persons should tyrannically assume to themselves the functions belonging to their superiors, forming a new scheme of laws to their own mischief, not knowing that "it is hard for them to

1 Luke x. 16; Matt. x. 40; John xiii. 20.
2 Ps. civ. 9.
3 Job xxxviii. 10, 11.
4 Num. xvi.; 2 Chron. xxvi.
5 Num. xii. 7, 8; Ex. xxxiii. 11, 17.
6 1 Sam. xiii.
7 2 Chron. xxvi.
8 1 Kings xiii. 33.
9 1 Cor. xiv. 33. [See p. 500, note 6, *infra.*]

kick against the pricks;"[1] for such as these do not fight against us, or against the bishops, but against the universal Bishop and the High Priest of the Father, Jesus Christ our Lord.[2] High priests, priests, and Levites were ordained by Moses,[3] the most beloved of God. By our Saviour[4] were we apostles, thirteen in number, ordained; and by the apostles I James, and I Clement, and others with us, were ordained, that we may not make the catalogue of all those bishops over again. And in common, presbyters, and deacons, and sub-deacons, and readers, were ordained by all of us. The great High Priest therefore, who is so by nature, is Christ the only begotten; not having snatched that honour to Himself, but having been appointed such by the Father; who being made man for our sake, and offering the spiritual sacrifice to His God and Father, before His suffering gave it us alone in charge to do this, although there were others with us who had believed in Him. But he that believes is not presently appointed a priest, or obtains the dignity of the high-priesthood. But after His ascension we offered, according to His constitution, the pure and unbloody sacrifice; and ordained bishops, and presbyters, and deacons, seven in number: one of which was Stephen,[5] that blessed martyr, who was not inferior to us as to his pious disposition of mind towards God; who showed so great piety towards God, by his faith and love towards our Lord Jesus Christ, as to give his life for Him, and was stoned to death by the Jews, the murderers of the Lord. Yet still this so great and good a man, who was fervent in spirit, who saw Christ on the right hand of God, and the gates of heaven opened, does nowhere appear to have exercised functions which did not appertain to his office of a deacon, nor to have offered the sacrifices, nor to have laid hands upon any, but kept his order of a deacon unto the end. For so it became him, who was a martyr for Christ, to preserve good order. But if some do blame Philip[6] our deacon, and Ananias[7] our faithful brother, that the one did baptize the eunuch, and the other me Paul, these men do not understand what we say. For we have affirmed only that no one snatches the sacerdotal dignity to himself, but either receives it from God, as Melchisedec and Job, or from the high priest, as Aaron from Moses. Wherefore Philip and Ananias did not constitute themselves, but were appointed by Christ, the High Priest of that God to whom no being is to be compared.

[1] Acts ix. 5. [See Acts xxvi. 14, where the clause is genuine. In ix. 5 it is a later interpolation of the Vulgate and Erasmus. — R.]
[2] The Coptic adds, "the Son of God, and true God."
[3] Ex. xxviii. and xxix.
[4] The Coptic adds "God."
[5] Acts vi. and vii.
[6] One V. MS. has the following note: "That he who baptized the Ethiopian eunuch was not the Apostle Philip, but one of those who were chosen along with St. Stephen to be deacons, and who also had four daughters, as says Luke in the Acts." [See pp. 452, 492, *supra.*]
[7] Acts viii. and ix.

THE ECCLESIASTICAL CANONS OF THE SAME HOLY APOSTLES.[1]

XLVII. 1. Let a bishop be ordained by two or three bishops.

2. A presbyter by one bishop, as also a deacon, and the rest of the clergy.[2]

3. If any bishop or presbyter, otherwise than our Lord has ordained concerning the sacrifice, offer other things at the altar *of God*, as honey, milk, or strong beer instead of wine, any necessaries, or birds, or animals, or pulse, otherwise than is ordained, let him be deprived; excepting grains of new corn, or ears of wheat, or bunches of grapes in their season.[3]

4. For it is not lawful to offer anything besides these at the altar, and oil for the holy lamp, and incense in the time of the divine oblation.

5. But let all other fruits be sent to the house of the bishop, as first-fruits to him and to the presbyters, but not to the altar. Now it is plain that the bishop and presbyters are to divide them to the deacons and to the rest of the clergy.

6. Let not a bishop, a priest, or a deacon[4] cast off his own wife under pretence of piety; but if he does cast her off, let him be suspended. If he go on in it, let him be deprived.

7. Let not a bishop, a priest, or deacon undertake the cares of this world; but if he do, let him be deprived.[5]

8. If any bishop, or presbyter, or deacon shall celebrate the holiday of the passover before the vernal equinox with the Jews, let him be deprived.[6]

9. If any bishop, or presbyter, or deacon, or any one of the catalogue of the priesthood, when the oblation is over, does not communicate, let

[1] [The brief notes on these canons have been mainly derived from the text and notes appended to Hefele's *History of Christian Councils*, vol. i. pp. 450–492, Edinburgh translation. — R.]
[2] [Comp. *Apostolic Constitutions*, iii. 20, viii. 4, 27, on these two canons. — R.]
[3] [This canon, and the two following ones, which explain it, point to some early heretical customs. The *Apostolic Constitutions* furnish no exact parallel. Canon 4 was joined with 3 in the Greek text. Dionysius divided them: hence a variation in number exists from this point. — R.]
[4] [Dionysius omits *aut diaconus*. — R.]
[5] [Comp. *Apostolic Constitutions*, ii. 6. — R.]
[6] [This points to a discussion in the third century. — R.]

him give his reason; and if it be just, let him be forgiven; but if he does not do it, let him be suspended, as becoming the cause of damage to the people, and occasioning a suspicion against him that offered, as of one that did not rightly offer.[1]

10. All those of the faithful that enter *into the holy church of God*, and hear the sacred Scriptures, but do not stay during prayer and the holy communion, must be suspended, as causing disorder in the church.

11. If any one, even in the house, prays with a person excommunicate, let him also be suspended.

12. If any clergyman prays with one deprived as with a clergyman, let himself also be deprived.

13. If any clergyman or layman who is suspended, or ought not to be received,[2] goes away, and is received in another city without commendatory letters, let both those who received him and he that was received be suspended. But if he be already suspended, let his suspension be lengthened, as lying to and deceiving the Church of God.

14. A bishop ought not to leave his own parish and leap to another, although the multitude should compel him, unless there be some good reason forcing him to do this, as that he can contribute much greater profit to the people of the new parish by the word of piety; but this is not to be settled by himself, but by the judgment of many bishops, and very great supplication.

15. If any presbyter or deacon, or any one of the catalogue of the clergy, leaves his own parish and goes to another, and, entirely removing himself, continues in that other parish without the consent of his own bishop, him we command no longer to go on in his ministry, especially in case his bishop calls upon him to return, and he does not obey, but continues in his disorder. However, let him communicate there as a layman.

16. But if the bishop with whom they are undervalues the deprivation decreed against them, and receives them as clergymen, let him be suspended as a teacher of disorder.

17. He who has been twice married after his baptism, or has had a concubine, cannot be made a bishop, or presbyter, or deacon, or indeed any one of the sacerdotal catalogue.[3]

18. He who has taken a widow, or a divorced woman, or an harlot, or a servant, or one belonging to the theatre, cannot be either a bishop, priest, or deacon, or indeed any one of the sacerdotal catalogue.

19. He who has married two sisters, or his brother's or sister's daughter, cannot be a clergyman.

20. Let a clergyman who becomes a surety be deprived.

21. Let an eunuch, if he be such by the injury of men, or his *virilia* were taken away in the persecution, or he was born such, and yet is worthy of episcopacy, be made a bishop.

22. Let not him who has disabled himself be made a clergyman; for he is a self-murderer, and an enemy to the creation of God.[4]

23. If any one who is of the clergy disables himself, let him be deprived, for he is a murderer of himself.

24. Let a layman who disables himself be separated for three years, for he lays a snare for his own life.[5]

25. Let a bishop, or presbyter, or deacon who is taken in fornication, or perjury, or stealing, be deprived, *but not suspended; for the Scripture says: "Thou shalt not avenge twice for the same crime by affliction."*[6]

26. In like manner also as to the rest of the clergy.

27. Of those who come into the clergy unmarried, we permit only the readers and singers, if they have a mind, to marry afterward.[7]

28. We command that a bishop, or presbyter, or deacon who strikes the faithful that offend, or the unbelievers who do wickedly, and thinks to terrify them by such means, be deprived, for our Lord has nowhere taught us such things. On the contrary, "when Himself was stricken, He did not strike again; when He was reviled, He reviled not again; when He suffered, He threatened not."[8]

29. If any bishop, or presbyter, or deacon who is deprived justly for manifest crimes, does venture to meddle with that ministration which was once entrusted to him, let the same person be entirely cut off from the Church.

30. If any bishop obtains that dignity by money, or even a presbyter or deacon, let him and the person that ordained him be deprived; and let him be entirely cut off from communion, as Simon Magus was by *me* Peter.[9]

31. If any bishop makes use of the rulers of this world, and by their means obtains to be a bishop of a church, let him be deprived and suspended, and all that communicate with him.

---

1 [Canons 9–16 agree with those of the Council of Antioch, A.D. 341; but there is a difference of opinion on the question of priority. — R.]

2 Dionysius Exiguus translates "*communicans*," in which case the Greek reading must be δεκτός, or, "who can be received."

3 [Canons 17, 18, 20, agree with *Apostolic Constitutions*, vi. 17, ii. 6. — R.]

4 [After Origen. Comp. Melito, vol. viii., this series.]

5 [Canons 21–24 agree with the first of the Nicene Council (Hefele, *Christian Councils*, i. pp. 375, 376). Some hold that canon to refer to these; others find in the enlarged application of Canon 24 a proof of the later date of this collection. — R.]

6 Nah. i. 9. [Canons 25, 26, are referred to by Basil the Great (*Ad Amphilochium*, iii.). In the Greek collection 26 is joined with 25. — R.]

7 [*Apostolic Constitutions*, vi. 17. — R.]

8 1 Pet. ii. 23. [This canon seems of late origin, probably from Synod of Constantinople, A.D. 394. — R.]

9 [The closing clause points to a comparatively late date, as do the contents of Canon 31. — R.]

32. If any presbyter despises his own bishop, and assembles separately, and fixes another altar, when he has nothing to condemn in his bishop either as to piety or righteousness, let him be deprived as an ambitious person; for he is a tyrant, and the rest of the clergy, whoever join themselves to him. And let the laity be suspended. But let these things be done after one, and a second, or even a third admonition from the bishop.[1]

33. If any presbyter or deacon be put under suspension by his bishop, it is not lawful for any other to receive him, but for him only who put him under suspension, unless it happens that he who put him under suspension die.

34. Do not ye receive any stranger, whether bishop, or presbyter, or deacon, without commendatory letters; and when such are offered, let them be examined. And if they be preachers of piety, let them be received; but if not, supply their wants, but do not receive them to communion: for many things are done by surprise.

35. The bishops of every country ought to know who is the chief among them, and to esteem him as their head, and not to do any great thing without his consent; but every one to manage only the affairs that belong to his own parish, and the places subject to it. But let him not do anything without the consent of all; for it is by this means there will be unanimity, and God will be glorified by Christ, in the Holy Spirit.

36. A bishop must not venture to ordain out of his own bounds for cities or countries that are not subject to him. But if he be convicted of having done so without the consent of such as governed those cities or countries, let him be deprived, both the bishop himself and those whom he has ordained.

37. If any bishop that is ordained does not undertake his office, nor take care of the people committed to him, let him be suspended until he do undertake it; and in the like manner a presbyter and a deacon. But if he goes, and is not received, not because of the want of his own consent, but because of the ill temper of the people, let him continue bishop; but let the clergy of that city be suspended, because they have not taught that disobedient people better.

38. Let a synod of bishops be held twice in the year, and let them ask one another the doctrines of piety; and let them determine the ecclesiastical disputes that happen — once in the fourth week of Pentecost, and again on the twelfth of the month Hyperberetæus.

39. Let the bishop have the care of ecclesiastical revenues, and administer them as in the presence of God. But it is not lawful for him to appropriate any part of them to himself, or to give the things of God to his own kindred. But if they be poor, let him support them as poor; but let him not, under such pretences, alienate the revenues of the Church.

40. Let not the presbyters and deacons do anything without the consent of the bishop, for it is he who is entrusted with the people of the Lord, and will be required to give an account of their souls. Let the proper goods of the bishop, if he has any, and those belonging to the Lord, be openly distinguished, that he may have power when he dies to leave his own goods as he pleases, and to whom he pleases; that, under pretence of the ecclesiastical revenues, the bishop's own may not come short, who sometimes has a wife and children, or kinsfolk, or servants. For this is just before God and men, that neither the Church suffer any loss by the not knowing which revenues are the bishop's own, nor his kindred, under pretence of the Church, be undone, or his relations fall into lawsuits, and so his death be liable to reproach.[2]

41. We command that the bishop have power over the goods of the Church; for if he be entrusted with the precious souls of men, much more ought he to give directions about goods, that they all be distributed to those in want, according to his authority, by the presbyters and deacons, and be used for their support with the fear of God, and with all reverence. He is also to partake of those things he wants, if he does want them, for his necessary occasions, and those of the brethren who live with him, that they may not by any means be in straits: for the law of God appointed that those who waited at the altar should be maintained by the altar; since not so much as a soldier does at any time bear arms against the enemies at his own charges.

42. Let a bishop, or presbyter, or deacon who indulges himself in dice or drinking, either leave off those practices, or let him be deprived.[3]

43. If a sub-deacon, a reader, or a singer does the like, either let him leave off, or let him be suspended; and so for one of the laity.

44. Let a bishop, or presbyter, or deacon who requires usury of those he lends to, either leave off to do so, or let him be deprived.

45. Let a bishop, or presbyter, or deacon who only prays with heretics, be suspended; but if he also permit them to perform any part of the office of a clergyman, let him be deprived.[4]

1 [Canons 32–41 also agree with those of Antioch; see note on Canon 9. Some of the regulations have, however, an earlier date: whether they existed in this form before that time, is open to discussion. — R.]

2 [This canon is divided by most editors of the Greek text; forming, in their enumeration, Canons 38 and 39. — R.]

3 [Hefele and others regard Canons 42–44 as among the most ancient of this collection, and of unknown origin. — R.]

4 [The substance of this canon is very ancient, Hefele thinks; but Drey derives it from Canons 9, 33, 34, of the Synod of Laodicea, about A.D. 363. — R.]

46. We command that a bishop, or presbyter, or deacon who receives the baptism, or the sacrifice of heretics, be deprived: "For what agreement is there between Christ and Belial? or what part hath a believer with an infidel?"[1]

47. If a bishop or presbyter rebaptizes him who has had true baptism, or does not baptize him who is polluted by the ungodly, let him be deprived, as ridiculing the cross and the death of the Lord, and not distinguishing between real priests and counterfeit ones.

48. If a layman divorces his own wife, and takes another, or one divorced by another, let him be suspended.[2]

49. If any bishop or presbyter does not baptize according to the Lord's constitution, into the Father, the Son, and the Holy Ghost, but into three beings without beginning, or into three Sons, or three Comforters, let him be deprived.[3]

50. If any bishop or presbyter does not perform the three immersions of the one admission, but one immersion, which is given into the death of Christ, let him be deprived; for the Lord did not say, "Baptize into my death," but, "Go ye and make disciples of all nations, baptizing them into the name of the Father, and of the Son, and of the Holy Ghost." Do ye, therefore, O bishops, baptize thrice into one Father, and Son, and Holy Ghost, according to the will of Christ, and our constitution by the Spirit.[4]

51. If any bishop, or presbyter, or deacon, or indeed any one of the sacerdotal catalogue, abstains from marriage, flesh, and wine, not for his own exercise, but because he abominates these things, forgetting that "all things were very good,"[5] and that "God made man male and female,"[6] and blasphemously abuses the creation, either let him reform, or let him be deprived, and be cast out of the Church; and the same for one of the laity.[7]

52. If any bishop or presbyter does not receive him that returns from his sin, but rejects him, let him be deprived; because he grieves Christ, who says, "There is joy in heaven over one sinner that repenteth."[8]

53. If any bishop, or presbyter, or deacon does not on festival days partake of flesh or wine, let him be deprived, as "having a seared conscience,"[9] and becoming a cause of scandal to many.

54. If any one of the clergy be taken eating in a tavern, let him be suspended, excepting when he is forced to bait at an inn upon the road.[10]

55. If any one of the clergy abuses his bishop unjustly, let him be deprived; for says the Scripture, "Thou shalt not speak evil of the ruler of thy people."[11]

56. If any one of the clergy abuses a presbyter or a deacon, let him be separated.

57. If any one of the clergy mocks at a lame, a deaf, or a blind man, or at one maimed in his feet, let him be suspended; and the like for the laity.

58. Let a bishop or presbyter who takes no care of the clergy or people, and does not instruct them in piety, be separated; and if he continues in his negligence, let him be deprived.[12]

59. If any bishop or presbyter, when any one of the clergy is in want, does not supply his necessity, let him be suspended; and if he continues in it, let him be deprived, as having killed his brother.[13]

60. If any one publicly reads in the Church the spurious books of the ungodly, as if they were holy, to the destruction of the people and of the clergy, let him be deprived.[14]

61. If there be an accusation against a Christian for fornication, or adultery, or any other forbidden action, and he be convicted, let him not be promoted into the clergy.

62. If any one of the clergy for fear of men,

---

1 2 Cor. vi. 5. [Drey regards this as very ancient; but Hefele derives it and the following one from the *Apostolic Constitutions*, vi. 15. — R.]

2 [Very ancient, of unknown origin; repeated in canons of Elvira and Arles. — R.]

3 [From *Apostolic Constitutions*, vi. 11, 26. — R.]

4 [This canon, the last of those in the collection of Dionysius, is regarded as among the most recent. Of unknown origin. — R.] At the end of this canon, in the collection of John of Antioch, the following words are added: "Let him that is baptized be taught that the Father was not crucified, nor endured to be born of man, nor indeed that the Holy Spirit became man, or even endured suffering, for He was not made flesh; but the only begotten Son ransomed the world from the wrath which lay upon it: for He became man through His love of man, having fashioned a body for Himself from a virgin. For Wisdom built a house for herself as a Creator; but He willingly endured the cross, and rescued the world from the wrath that lies on it, namely, those who are baptized into the name of the Father, and the Son, and the Holy Spirit. But let those who do not thus baptize be suspended, as being ignorant of the mystery of piety." The same collection gives the following as Canon 51: "He who says that the Father suffered is more impious than the Jews, nailing along with Christ the Father also. He who denies that the only begotten Son was made flesh for us, and endured the cross, fights with God, and is an enemy of the saints. He that names the Holy Spirit Father or Son, is ignorant and foolish; for the Son is Creator along with the Father, and has the same throne, and is Lawgiver along with Him, and Judge, and the cause of the resurrection; and the Holy Spirit is the same in substance: for the Godhead has three Persons, the same in substance. For in our day Simon the magician gave forth *his doctrines*, drawing the speechless, delusive, unstable, and wicked spirit to himself, and babbling that there is one God with three names, and sometimes erasing the passion and birth of Christ. Do you, then, most beloved ones, baptize into one Father, and Son, and the Holy Spirit as third, according to the will of the Lord, and our constitution made in the spirit."

5 Gen. i. 31.

6 Gen. i. 26.

7 [Canons 51–53 are from the *Apostolic Constitutions*: the first from vi. 8, 10, 26; the second from ii. 12, 13; the third from v. 20. — R.]

8 Luke xv. 7.

9 1 Tim. iv. 2.

10 [Canons 54–57 are of unknown origin; the first is deemed ancient, while the conduct forbidden in the others points to a more recent date. Drey thinks the distinctions of the clergy also point to a later date. — R.]

11 Ex. xxii. 28.

12 [Canon 58 is supposed to refer to the absence of bishops at the imperial city, which prevailed in the middle of the fourth century. — R.]

13 [Canon 59 resembles the twenty-fifth canon of Synod of Antioch; see on Canon 9. — R.]

14 [Of doubtful origin, but resembling *Apostolic Constitutions*, vi. 16, though probably of later date. — R.]

as of a Jew, or a Gentile, or an heretic, shall deny the name of Christ, let him be suspended; but if he deny the name of a clergyman, let him be deprived; but when he repents, let him be received as one of the laity.[1]

63. If any bishop, or presbyter, or deacon, or indeed any one of the sacerdotal catalogue, eats flesh with the blood of its life, or that which is torn by beasts, or which died of itself, let him be deprived; for this the law itself has forbidden.[2] But if he be one of the laity, let him be suspended.[3]

64. If any one of the clergy be found to fast on the Lord's day, or on the Sabbath-day, excepting one only, let him be deprived; but if he be one of the laity, let him be suspended.[4]

65. If any one, either of the clergy or laity, enters into a synagogue of the Jews or heretics to pray, let him be deprived and suspended.[5]

66. If any one of the clergy strikes one in a quarrel, and kills him by that one stroke, let him be deprived, on account of his rashness; but if he be one of the laity, let him be suspended.[6]

67. If any one has offered violence to a virgin not betrothed, and keeps her, let him be suspended. But it is not lawful for him to take another to wife; but he must retain her whom he has chosen, although she be poor.[7]

68. If any bishop, or presbyter, or deacon, receives a second ordination from any one, let him be deprived, and the person who ordained him, unless he can show that his former ordination was from the heretics; for those that are either baptized or ordained by such as these, can be neither Christians nor clergymen.[8]

69. If any bishop, or presbyter, or deacon, or reader, or singer, does not fast the fast of forty days, or the fourth day of the week, and the day of the Preparation, let him be deprived, except he be hindered by weakness of body. But if he be one of the laity, let him be suspended.[9]

70. If any bishop, or any other of the clergy, fasts with the Jews, or keeps the festivals with them, or accepts of the presents from their festivals, as unleavened bread or some such thing, let him be deprived; but if he be one of the laity, let him be suspended.[10]

71. If any Christian carries oil into an heathen temple, or into a synagogue of the Jews, or lights up lamps in their festivals, let him be suspended.

72. If any one, either of the clergy or laity, takes away from the holy Church an honeycomb, or oil, let him be suspended, and let him add the fifth part to that which he took away.[11]

73. A vessel of silver, or gold, or linen, which is sanctified, let no one appropriate to his own use, for it is unjust; but if any one be caught, let him be punished with suspension.[12]

74. If a bishop be accused of any crime by credible and faithful persons, it is necessary that he be cited by the bishops; and if he comes and makes his apology, and yet is convicted, let his punishment be determined. But if, when he is cited, he does not obey, let him be cited a second time, by two bishops sent to him. But if even then he despises them, and will not come, let the synod pass what sentence they please against him, that he may not appear to gain advantage by avoiding their judgment.[13]

75. Do not ye receive an heretic in a testimony against a bishop; nor a Christian if he be single. For the law says, "In the mouth of two or three witnesses every word shall be established."[14]

76. A bishop must not gratify his brother, or his son, or any other kinsman, with the episcopal dignity, or ordain whom he pleases; for it is not just to make heirs to episcopacy, and to gratify human affections in divine matters. For we must not put the Church of God under the laws of inheritance; but if any one shall do so, let his ordination be invalid, and let him be punished with suspension.[15]

77. If any one be maimed in an eye, or lame of his leg, but is worthy of the episcopal dignity, let him be made a bishop; for it is not a blemish of the body that can defile him, but the pollution of the soul.[16]

78. But if he be deaf and blind, let him not be made a bishop; not as being a defiled person, but that the ecclesiastical affairs may not be hindered.

79. If any one hath a demon, let him not be made one of the clergy. Nay, let him not pray with the faithful; but when he is cleansed, let him be received; and if he be worthy, let him be ordained.[17]

---

1 [Canons 61, 62, are of unknown origin. — R.]

2 Gen. ix.; Lev. xvii.

3 [Canon 63 is regarded as very ancient. — R.]

4 [Canon 64 is numbered as 66 in Hefele's edition, being preceded by Canons 65 and 66 as given above. It is from *Apostolic Constitutions*, v. 20. — R.]

5 [Canon 65 is from *Apostolic Constitutions*, ii. 61. — R.]

6 [Of unknown but probably late origin. — R.]

7 [Drey makes this one of the most recent canons of the collection. — R.]

8 [Of unknown origin, probably recent. — R.]

9 [Drey considers Canon 69 to be very ancient, but also intimates that it and Canon 70 were taken from the pseudo-Ignatian Epistle to the Philippians; see the same, chap. xiii., latter half, vol. i. p. 119, of this series. — R.]

10 [With Canons 70, 71, compare Synod of Elvira (A.D. 305 or 306), Canons 49, 50, in Hefele, vol. i. pp. 158, 159. Drey, however, derives them from Canons 37–39 of Laodicea (A.D. 363). — R.]

11 Lev. v. 16. [It is argued from the theft forbidden that this canon is more recent; its origin is unknown. — R.]

12 [The wealth here implied points to a comparatively late origin; Hefele assigns it to the second half of the third century, but Drey gives a later date. — R.]

13 [Hefele thinks both this and the following canon to be later than the Nicæan Council. Drey, however, derives Canon 74 from the council at Chalcedon (A.D. 451), a view opposed by both Bickell and Hefele. — R.]

14 Deut. xix. 15. [According to Drey this canon is from the Council of Constantinople (sixth canon), in A.D. 381. — R.]

15 [Drey derives this from Canon 23, Synod of Antioch, A.D. 341. — R.]

16 [Hefele: "The Canons 77–79, inclusive, belong to the first three centuries of the Church; their origin is unknown." — R.]

17 [Comp. *Apostolic Constitutions*, viii. 32, p. 495, from which this may have been taken. — R.]

80. It is not right to ordain him bishop presently who is just come in from the Gentiles, and baptized; or from a wicked mode of life: for it is unjust that he who has not yet afforded any trial of himself should be a teacher of others, unless it anywhere happens by divine grace.[1]

81. We have said that a bishop ought not to let himself into public administrations, but to attend on all opportunities upon the necessary affairs of the Church.[2] Either therefore let him agree not to do so, or let him be deprived. For "no one can serve two masters,"[3] according to the Lord's admonition.[4]

82. We do not permit servants to be ordained into the clergy without their masters' consent; for this would grieve those that owned them. For such a practice would occasion the subversion of families. But if at any time a servant appears worthy to be ordained into an high office, such as our Onesimus appeared to be, and if his master allows of it, and gives him his freedom, and dismisses him from his house, let him be ordained.[5]

83. Let a bishop, or presbyter, or deacon, who goes to the army, and desires to retain both the Roman government and the sacerdotal administration, be deprived. For "the things of Cæsar belong to Cæsar, and the things of God to God."[6]

84. Whosoever shall abuse the king[7] or the governor unjustly, let him suffer punishment; and if he be a clergyman, let him be deprived; but if he be a layman, let him be suspended.

85. Let the following books be esteemed venerable and holy by you, both of the clergy and laity. Of the Old Covenant: the five books of Moses — Genesis, Exodus, Leviticus, Numbers, and Deuteronomy; one of Joshua the son of Nun, one of the Judges, one of Ruth, four of the Kings, two of the Chronicles, two of Ezra, one of Esther, *one of Judith*, three of the Maccabees, one of Job, one hundred and fifty psalms; three books of Solomon — Proverbs, Ecclesiastes, and the Song of Songs; sixteen prophets. And besides these, take care that your young persons learn the Wisdom of the very learned Sirach. But our sacred books, that is, those of the New Covenant, are these: the four Gospels of Matthew, Mark, Luke, and John; the fourteen Epistles of Paul; two Epistles of Peter, three of John, one of James, one of Jude; two Epistles of Clement; and the Constitutions dedicated to you the bishops by me Clement, in eight books; which it is not fit to publish before all, because of the mysteries contained in them; and the Acts of us the Apostles.[8]

Let these canonical rules be established by us for you, O ye bishops; and if you continue to observe them, ye shall be saved, and shall have peace; but if you be disobedient, you shall be punished, and have everlasting war one with another, and undergo a penalty suitable to your disobedience.

Now, God who alone is unbegotten, and the Maker of the whole world, unite you all through His peace, in the Holy Spirit; perfect you unto every good work, immoveable, unblameable, and unreprovable; and vouchsafe to you eternal life with us, through the mediation of His beloved Son Jesus Christ our God and Saviour; with whom glory be to Thee, the God over all, and the Father, in the Holy Spirit the Comforter, now and always, and for ever and ever. Amen.

The end of the Constitutions of the Holy Apostles by Clement, which are the Catholic doctrine.

---

1 [Drey regards Canon 80 as an imitation of the second canon of Nicæa, which is, however, much fuller; comp. Hefele, i. p. 377. On the principle, comp. 1 Tim. iii. 6 and similar passages. — R.]

2 Can. iv. *prius*.

3 Matt. vi. 24.

4 [The contents of this canon point to a late date. Drey regards it as an abridgment of the third canon of Chalcedon (A.D. 451). — R.]

5 [Of unknown origin and date. — R.]

6 Matt. xxii. 21. [This also Drey traces to the Council of Chalcedon, A.D. 451 (Canon 7); but Hefele opposes this view here, as in the case of the other canons (30, 67, 74, 81) which Drey derives from that source. — R.]

7 [Or rather, "the emperor" (βασιλέα having that sense). Hefele refers this to the time of the Arian struggle, when the emperors were involved in ecclesiastical controversies. — R.]

8 [Hefele: "This is probably the least ancient canon in the whole collection." With this opinion there is general concurrence, since the mention of the *Constitutions* among the canonical books indicates the hand of the last compiler of that collection of writings. Whoever he was, he was not Clement of Rome. — R.]

ELUCIDATIONS

I.

(The Bidding Prayer, etc., p. 485.)

THE PAULINE NORM.[1]

1. *Supplications.*
2. *Prayers, Psalms, Hymns, and Spiritual Songs.*
3. *Intercessions.*
4. *General Thanksgiving.* The Kiss of Peace.
5. *Anaphora.*[2]

The Lord Jesus the same night in which He was betrayed took bread:
And when He had given thanks, He brake it,
And said, Take, eat: this is my Body, which is broken for you:
This do in remembrance of Me.
After the same manner also He took the cup, when He had supped,
Saying, This cup is the New Testament in my Blood:
This do ye, as oft as ye drink it, in remembrance of Me.
For as often as ye eat this Bread, and drink this Cup, ye do show the Lord's death till He come.

6. *Our Father*, etc.[3]
7. *Communion.*

Let us note also that the Apostle had "delivered" unto the Corinthians (1 Cor. xi. 23), as doubtless to others (vii. 17), certain institutions which he *ordained* in all the churches, and for departing from which he censures the Corinthians in this place (ver. 17 compared with ver. 2) in certain particulars. In chap. xiv., at ver. 40, he refers to these ordinances as a *τάξις*, in the performance of which they were to proceed (*κοσμίως*) with due order, *becomingly;* not with mere decency, but with a beautiful decorum of service.

Finally, let me suggest that there are fragments of the Apostle's (*παράδοσεις*) instructions everywhere scattered through his Epistles, such as the minute canon[4] concerning the veiling of women in acts of worship, insisting upon it with a length of argument which in one of the Apostolic Fathers would be considered childish. He also insisted that his *τάξις* is from the Lord.

---

[1] 1 Tim. ii. 1–3. Compare (*ποιεῖσθαι*) the Greek here with that of the LXX. in Ex. xxix. 36, 38, 39, 41; also Ex. x. 25, and so throughout the Old Testament. Note also Eph. v. 19 and Col. iii. 16; and the kiss, 1 Cor. xvi. 20.

[2] 1 Cor. xi. 23. To me there is great significance in the fact that the Apostle *received this* as an original Gospel from the Lord Himself. Truly (2 Cor. xi. 5) he was not "a whit behind" even that chief Apostle who reclined in the bosom of the Great High Priest and adorable Lamb of God as He instituted the feast.

[3] Matt. vi. 9. For this we have the important testimony of Gregory the Great, as preserved to his day: that the Apostles (SS. Peter and Paul must have been primarily in his mind, of course) delivered no other "custom" to the churches (i.e., as essential) than the words of Institution and the Lord's Prayer. He says: —

"Orationem Dominicam, *mox post precem*, dicimus, quia *mos Apostolorum erat*, ad ipsam solummodo orationem oblationis hostiam consecrare." — *Epist. ad Joann. Episc. Syrac.*, lib. ix. Ep. xii., *Opp.*, tom. iii. p. 958, ed. Migne.

Now, for the sense of *post precem* in the above, we have Justin Martyr for a primitive witness of Roman usage. He speaks of the words of Institution expressly (vol. i. cap. lxvi. p. 185) as "the Prayer of the Logos" (δι' εὐχῆς Λόγου), in the use of which he makes the essential act of the Oblation to consist. Liturgic fulness may or may not require more, but the essentials are thus simple. So far, the Roman Missal to this day sustains the words of Gregory. It is overloaded with ceremonial, but does not include the noble features on which the Greeks lay so great stress; i.e., the conjoint Oblation and Invocation. See 1 Pet. ii. 5.

[4] 1 Cor. xi. 5, 6. Here men are equally enjoined not to follow the Jewish rite of covering their heads in prayer.

Fragments of the primitive hymns are also scattered through the Apostles' writings, as, e.g., —

> *Ἔγειραι ὁ καθεύδων,*
> *καὶ ἀνάστα ἐκ τῶν νεκρῶν,*
> *καὶ ἐπιφαύσει σοι ὁ Χριστός.*[1]

Of such passages the formula (*διὸ λέγει*) "It saith" seems to be a frequent index.

May we not conclude also that the sublime prayer and doxology of Eph. iii. 14–21 is a quotation from the Apostle's own eucharistic *τάξις* for the whole state of Christ's Church militant?

Might not the same be more constantly used in our days as an intercession for the whole flock of the one Shepherd?

II.

(Fulfil His constitution, p. 489.)

The Pauline Norm being borne in mind, we shall best comprehend this Clementine liturgy, as to its primitive claims, by taking the testimony of Justin, writing in Rome to the Antonines A.D. 160. Referring to the *Apology* in our first volume, we observe that the order kept up in his day was this: —

1. Prayers for all estates of men.
2. The kiss of peace.
3. Oblation of bread and wine.
4. Thanksgiving.
5. Words of institution.
6. The prayer ending with *Amen*.
7. Communion.

Now, a century later, we may suppose the *original* of this *Clementine* to have taken a fuller shape; of which still later this *Clementine* is the product.[2]

Bear in mind that the early Roman use was (Greek) borrowed wholly from the East;[3] and, comparing the testimony of Justin with the *Pauline Norm*, may we not suppose that this norm in Rome was augmented by the *Eastern uses*, and so preserves a true name in that of the first Bishop of Rome, who accepted it from Jerusalem or Antioch?

III.

(That He may show this bread, etc., p. 489.)

From a recent essay by Dr. Williams, the erudite bishop of Connecticut, I am permitted to cite, as follows: —

Compare the original texts thus: —

CLEMENTINE.[4]	IRENÆUS.[5]
ὅπως αποφηνη τὸν αρτον τοῦτον σῶμα τοῦ Χριστοῦ σου καὶ τὸ ποτήριον τοῦτον αἶμα τοῦ Χριστοῦ σου ινα οἱ μεταλαβόντες, κ.τ.λ.	*ὅπως ἀποφηνῃ τὴν θυσίαν ταύτην, καὶ τὸν ἄρτον σῶμα τοῦ Χριστοῦ, καὶ τὸ ποτήριον τὸ αἷμα του Χριστοῦ ἵνα οἱ μεταλαβόντες, κ.τ.λ.*

---

1 Eph. v. 14.

2 See the Greek in Hammond, p. 3, and the learned *Introduction*, p. lxx.

3 Hammond, *Introduction*, p. lxix.

4 See translation, p. 489, *supra*.

5 See translation, vol. i. (Fragment xxxvii.) p. 574, this series.

Bishop Williams then proceeds to inquire : —

"How is this striking agreement to be explained? Does Irenæus quote from the Clementine, or the Clementine from him? Or is it not much more likely that they are independent witnesses to primitive uses, going back to the period of the persecutions, and extending 'far beyond the limits of Syria or Palestine'?"[1]

I shall recur to these passages in the elucidations to *Early Liturgies* (*infra*) : but here I beg the reader to consult Pfaff, to whom we owe the discovery of the fragment cited from Irenæus; also Grabe, in the same volume of Pfaff, whom I have already introduced to the reader.[2]

POSTSCRIPT.

THE American editor had been promised the aid of his beloved friend the Rev. Dr. Hobart in the elucidation of the liturgies; but a sudden and almost fatal prostration of his health has deprived the reader of the admirable comments with which he would have enriched these pages, had Providence permitted.

[1] For purposes of comparison on many points connected with this inquiry, see the *Fragment of an Ancient East-Syrian Liturgy* in Hammond's *Appendix*, published separately, Oxford, 1879.

[2] Concerning Pfaff, see p. 536, *infra*, and vol. i. p. 574, note 5, this series.

AN ANCIENT HOMILY

COMMONLY STYLED

THE SECOND EPISTLE OF CLEMENT

INTRODUCTORY NOTICE

TO THE HOMILY KNOWN AS

THE SECOND EPISTLE OF CLEMENT

It is gratifying that our series is marked by tokens of critical progress, and not less cheering tokens of scientific research. The clearing-up of much that has perplexed us about Hermas; the Bryennios discovery; and, not least, the completion of this fragment, which has long been a scandal to patristic inquiry, — are surely such tokens. They enrich the reader with definite ideas on many collateral subjects. May they not stimulate American scholarship and American affluence to fresh enterprises of the same character for the advancement of learning, and the glory of the world's Redeemer and Illuminator?

The very early date to which this homily is now assigned makes its slightest allusions to the New-Testament canon of very great importance. I have ventured to indicate a few such, even where they may be mere *allusions*, not textual quotations: as, e.g., on p. 517, at notes 20 and 22, slight indications of a reference to the Second Epistle of St. Peter and to the Apocalypse.[1]

I shall have occasion to refer to this work in the elucidation of the *Liturgies* which are to follow. If it be, as Bishop Lightfoot supposes, a homily of the second century, it may lend important retrospective aid to the student of these volumes in other particulars; but, having entrusted this interesting relic to the editorial care of a most competent scholar, I shall not presume to anticipate his judgment in any matter.

---

[1] If this reference to 2 Pet. iii. 9 be probable, it is one of the earliest testimonies to the genuine character of that Epistle. The true Clement has two references to the same (pp. 8 and 11, vol. i., this series), and Justin also (vol. i. p. 240) is credited with a similar reference to 2 Peter and the Apocalypse. See Lardner, *Credib.*, vol. ii. p. 123 et seq.

INTRODUCTORY NOTICE BY PROFESSOR M. B. RIDDLE, D.D.

SECTION I.—TEXT.

In this volume, pp. 372–376, will be found a brief account of the Codex discovered by Bryennios, now Metropolitan of Nicomedia. It remains in the library of the Jerusalem Monastery of the Holy Sepulchre at Constantinople. While the publication of the Greek text of the *Teaching* awakened unusual interest, the recovery of that document has not been the only valuable result of this important discovery. The Codex, as was speedily known, contains the only complete copy of the Greek text of the two Epistles of Clement. The *lacunæ* previously existing in the genuine Epistle were not extensive; but, as now appears, the Alexandrian manuscript contains only three-fifths of the second Epistle. The entire Greek text of both Epistles was given to the public by Bryennios[1] in 1875.

This at once led to a revision of some recent editions, notably those of Hilgenfeld,[2] and of Gebhardt and Harnack.[3] Many monographs soon appeared. But the discovery of a new (Syriac) source for the text in 1876, while not affecting the general problem, gave to patristic scholars more abundant critical material. Bishop Lightfoot's Appendix[4] contains the most convenient and accessible collation of this material, as well as the most clear statements on all points affected by the two discoveries. The Syriac manuscript, containing a version of the two Epistles of Clement, was purchased by the Cambridge University Library in 1876, from the collection of "the late Oriental scholar M. Jules Mohl of Paris" (Lightfoot). It embraces the entire New Testament, except the Apocalypse, in the Harkleian recension of the Philoxenian (or later) Syriac version; but the scribe has inserted the two Epistles of Clement (entire) between the Catholic and Pauline Epistles. The value of the manuscript for New-Testament criticism is great, and the phenomena it presents interesting, as bearing on the discussion of the New-Testament canon; but the paucity of sources for the text of the Clementine Epistles gives special importance to the discovery of a version of these writings so soon after the recovery of the entire Greek text. A discussion of the textual questions is forbidden by the limits of this Introductory Notice, but a few points may be stated:—

1. A comparison of the three authorities (the Alexandrian, the Constantinopolitan, and the Syriac), in the parts they in common contain, shows that the first is most trustworthy, and that the Syriac is usually more correct than the Constantinopolitan.

2. Hence, in the recovered portions, the authority of the Syriac is very valuable in correcting the obvious blunders of the Greek copy. This should teach caution in accepting the text of the *Teaching*, where the same Greek manuscript is our only authority.

3. The genuine Epistle of Clement, which stands next in age to the canonical books of the New Testament, now stands next in accuracy of text also. Doubt in regard to textual questions decreases as the critical material increases.

---

1 The full title of his edition, in English form, is as follows: "The two Epistles of our holy father Clement Bishop of Rome to the Corinthians; from a manuscript in the Library of the Most Holy Sepulchre in Fanar of Constantinople; now for the first time published complete, with prolegomena and notes, by Philotheos Bryennios, Metropolitan of Serræ. Constantinople, 1875."

2 *Novum Test. extra canonem receptum* (2d ed., Leipzig, 1876). Pp. xliv.-xlix., 69-106, contain prolegomena, text, and notes, 2 Clement.

3 *Patrum Apost. Opera*, 2d ed., Leipzig, 1876.

4 *St. Clement of Rome.* An Appendix containing the newly recovered portions, with introductions, notes, and translations. London, 1877. The original volume, London, 1869.

SECTION 2.—PLACE AND DATE OF COMPOSITION; AUTHOR.

The recovery of the entire text of the *Second Epistle* settles the question as to the *purpose* of the work. As was previously surmised, it is a homily (comp. chaps. xvii., xix., xx.); moreover, it was "read" by the author at public worship after the Scripture lesson (see chap. xix). But as to *place, date,* and *author,* there is still diversity of opinion. The three questions are closely related. The view of Bishop Lightfoot seems, on the whole, most tenable. He regards the homily as of Corinthian origin, delivered, in all probability, between A.D. 120 and 140, but the work of an unknown author, who seems to have been one of the presbyters of the church,—possibly the bishop. The allusions to the athletic games are in favour of Corinth. On this theory the title is thus accounted for: The genuine Epistle of Clement was addressed to the Corinthians, and read in the church of that city from time to time. This homily was probably read in the same manner, and at length united in a manuscript copy with the other. Each was "to the Corinthians:" hence it was gradually inferred that both were Epistles of Clement. Of this succession or movement Lightfoot finds some indications in the manuscript authorities.

The internal evidence of an early date has been increased by the discovery of the concluding portion, but there is nothing to determine the exact time of composition. The distinction made in chap. xiv. between the Old and New Testaments, as well as the use of the Gospel of the Egyptians (at the close of chap. xii.), taken in connection with the unmistakeable citations of New-Testament passages as of Divine authority, point to the first half of the second century as the probable period. The absence of all direct opposition to Gnosticism points to an origin within the same limits. All these considerations make against the view of Hilgenfeld, who attributes the homily to Clement of Alexandria, thus assigning it to the latter half of the second century.

In regard to the author, nothing further is learned from the newly recovered portion, except the fact that he was a preacher. Even this does not determine his ecclesiastical position, since at that early date much freedom of utterance was permitted in Christian assemblies. It is, however, very probable that the author was a presbyter; and it is not improbable that he was the chief presbyter, or local bishop.

The homily is still attributed to a person named Clement, but there are three theories as to what Clement. (1) Bryennios stands almost alone in claiming that the document is the work of Clemens Romanus. The internal evidence against this view was quite sufficient before the full text of the two Epistles was known; now it is to be regarded as abundantly conclusive. Even the English version of the two writings will suggest to the intelligent reader the points of difference. (2) As intimated above, Hilgenfeld regards Clement of Alexandria as the author; but this places the homily too late. Moreover, the writings of the Alexandrian Father stand immensely above this feeble, commonplace, and chaotic production. Even the citation from the Gospel of the Egyptians, common to both,[1] is differently used by the two authors; Clement of Alexandria opposing the interpretation favoured in this homily, as well as objecting to the authority of that apocryphal Gospel. Hilgenfeld's argument from the word φιλοσοφεῖν, in chap. xix., is invalidated by the improbability of that reading; see note *in loco.* (3) The most plausible view, as Bishop Lightfoot admits, is that of Harnack. He assigns the homily to a third Clement, referred to, as he supposes, in the *Shepherd of Hermas,*[2] and living somewhat later than Clement of Rome. In favour of this may be urged: some similarity to the *Shepherd of Hermas,* the probability that at the date of the later writing Clement of Rome was not living, and the easy explanation it affords of the traditional title. But, while a third Clement may have lived at Rome, we have no evidence other than the doubtful hint in the *Shepherd.* The allusion in that work seems far more appropriate to the well-known Clement of Rome. The argument from the later date of the *Shepherd* proves very little; not only is the date uncertain, but the visions are placed

[1] See chap. xii., and Clem. Alex., *Stromata,* iii. 13, vol. ii. p. 398.

[2] See Vision II. 4, vol. ii. p. 12.

quite early. The editor of this series, while accepting A.D. 160 as the probable date of the *Shepherd*, regards it as a compilation, introducing "Hermas and Clement to identify the times which are idealized in his allegory." [1] The view of Bishop Lightfoot, therefore, seems to be the safest.

SECTION 3.—CHARACTER AND CONTENTS.

The style of the homily is poor. It abounds in connectives, which link unconnected ideas; its thought is feeble, its theology peculiar though not false, its arrangement confused. While it furnishes some historical data for practical theology, it is, in homiletical method and matter, in sharp contrast with the Apostolic writings and with the homilies of Origen. Though referring to Scripture, it has none of the virtues of the expository discourse; though hortatory in tone, it has little of the unity and directness of better sermons of that class. Its chief excellence is its brevity.

It is difficult to make an analysis of the contents. The theme is the duty of fulfilling the commands of Christ.

(1) This obedience is the true confession of Christ, answering to the greatness of His salvation; mainly in chaps. i.–iv.

(2) Thus the Christian shows his opposition to the world; chaps. v.–viii.

(3) This obedience will be rewarded in the future world; chaps. ix.–xvii.

(4) The conclusion: the preacher's confession (xviii.), justification of his exhortation (xix.); concluding word of consolation, with doxology (xx.). But the treatment is not strictly logical, nor are the parts clearly distinguished.

The theology shows no traces of heresy, nor does it sharply oppose any false doctrinal views. It lacks the dogmatic precision of a later age, but emphasizes rigid views of the relation of the sexes. "Repentance and good works seem to be the main articles of its creed. Of regeneration there seems to be no definite idea: to be called is the same as to be saved. The Church is pre-existent; the kingdom of God is in the future; no worth is left to this world or to the life in it. The principal argument urged in favour of standing firm in faith is the good issue of it in the next life" (C. J. H. Ropes).

The hints given in regard to public worship agree with the famous description of Justin Martyr,[2] and there are indications that the early freedom of exhortation had not yet disappeared. Bishop Lightfoot aptly concludes his dissertation with these words: "The homily itself, as a literary work, is almost worthless. As the earliest example of its kind, however, and as the product of an important age of which we possess only the scantiest remains, it has the highest value. Nor will its intellectual poverty blind us to its true grandeur, as an example of the lofty moral earnestness and the triumphant faith which subdued a reluctant world, and laid it prostrate at the foot of the cross." [3]

SECTION 4.—THE VERSION IN THIS VOLUME.

Greater unity would have been secured by a new translation of the entire work. Since, however, this was not possible, the aim of the editor has been to give the reader, as far as practicable, the benefit of the light shed upon the whole by the recently discovered authorities. The portion already translated in the Edinburgh volume has been supplied with critical annotations, and a few exegetical points have been treated. The recent editions of the Greek text have, of course, been consulted.

The newly recovered portion has been re-translated. Bishop Lightfoot's version is so excel-

---

1 See vol. ii. p. 4; and comp. Lightfoot, *Appendix*, pp. 316, 317.

2 *First Apology*, ch. lxvii. (vol. i. p. 186).

3 St. Clement, *Appendix*, p. 317.

lent that the temptation to use it was very great. It has, of course, influenced the editor in many places. But the following version differs from it mainly in two respects: (1) An effort has been made to preserve the verbal correspondences between the language of the homily and that of the New Testament: hence the English word used in the Revised Version as an equivalent of a Greek term is given here as a similar equivalent. (2) The view of the Greek tenses indicated in Lightfoot's renderings does not always accord with that of the editor.

It may be added, that Professor C. J. H. Ropes of Bangor, Me., kindly sent, for use in the preparation of the Epistle for this volume, his manuscript translation and notes. These have been very helpful, and are entitled to this acknowledgment. It will be found that the American translation is less paraphrastic than the Edinburgh. The new portions, both text and notes, have been printed without brackets when they are the work of the editor. The rare additions of the general editor are always bracketed, that the reader may readily recognise to whom the literary responsibility in each case properly belongs.

The following is the Edinburgh INTRODUCTORY NOTICE: —

THE first certain reference which is made by any early writer to this so-called Epistle of Clement is found in these words of Eusebius (*Hist. Eccl.*, iii. 38): "We must know that there is also a second Epistle of Clement. But we do not regard it as being equally notable with the former, since we know of none of the ancients that have made use of it." Several critics in modern times have endeavoured to vindicate the authenticity of this Epistle. But it is now generally regarded as one of the many writings which have been falsely ascribed to Clement. Besides the want of external evidence, indicated even by Eusebius in the above extract, the diversity of style clearly points to a different writer from that of the first Epistle. A commonly accepted opinion among critics at the present day is, that this is not an Epistle at all, but a fragment of one of the many homilies falsely ascribed to Clement. There can be no doubt, however, that in the catalogue of writings contained in the Alexandrian MS. it is both styled an Epistle, and, as well as the other which accompanies it, is attributed to Clement. As the MS. is certainly not later than the fifth century, the opinion referred to must by that time have taken firm root in the Church; but in the face of internal evidence, and in want of all earlier testimony, such a fact goes but a small way to establish its authenticity.

THE HOMILY[1]

CHAP. I. — WE OUGHT TO THINK HIGHLY OF CHRIST.

BRETHREN, it is fitting that you should think of Jesus Christ as of God, — as the Judge of the living and the dead. And it does not become us[2] to think lightly[3] of our salvation; for if we think little[3] of Him, we shall also hope but to obtain little *from Him*. And those of us[4] who hear carelessly of these things, as if they were of small importance, commit sin, not knowing whence we have been called, and by whom, and to what place, and how much Jesus Christ submitted to suffer for our sakes. What return, then, shall we make to Him? or what fruit that shall be worthy of that which He has given to us? For,[5] indeed, how great are the benefits[6] which we owe to Him! He has graciously given us light; as a Father, He has called us sons; He has saved us when we were ready to perish. What praise, then, shall we give to Him, or what return shall we make for the things which we have received?[7] We were deficient[8] in understanding, worshipping stones and wood, and gold, and silver, and brass, the works of men's hands;[9] and our whole life was nothing else than death. Involved in blindness, and with such darkness[10] before our eyes, we have received sight, and through His will have laid aside that cloud by which we were enveloped. For He had compassion on us, and mercifully saved us, observing the many errors in which we were entangled, as well as the destruction to which we were exposed,[11] and that we had[12] no hope of salvation except it came to us from Him. For He called us when we were not,[13] and willed that out of nothing we should attain a real existence.[14]

CHAP. II. — THE CHURCH, FORMERLY BARREN, IS NOW FRUITFUL.

"Rejoice, thou barren that bearest not; break forth and cry, thou that travailest not; for she that is desolate hath many more children than she that hath an husband."[15] In that He said, "Rejoice, thou barren that bearest not," He referred to us, for our Church was barren before that children were given to her. But when He said, "Cry out, thou that travailest not," He means this, that we should sincerely offer up our prayers to God, and should not, like women in travail, show signs of weakness.[16] And in that He said, "For she that is desolate hath many more children than she that hath an husband," *He means* that[17] our people seemed to be outcast from God, but now, through believing, have become more numerous than those who are reckoned to possess God.[18] And another Scripture saith, "I came not to call the righteous, but sinners."[19] This means that those who are perishing must be saved. For it is indeed a great and admirable thing to establish, not the things which are standing, but those that are falling. Thus also did Christ desire[20] to save the things which were perishing,[21] and has saved many by coming and calling us when hastening to destruction.[22]

---

1 No title, not even a letter, is preserved in the MS. [In C (= MS. at Constantinople found by Bryennios) the title is Κλήμεντος πρὸς Κορινθίους Β', corresponding to that of the First Epistle. In S (= Syriac MS. at Cambridge) there is a subscription to the First Epistle ascribing it to Clement, then these words: "Of the same the Second Epistle to the Corinthians." At the close this subscription occurs: "Here endeth the Second Epistle of Clement to the Corinthians." — R.]

2 [C has here, and in many other places, ὑμᾶς instead of ἡμᾶς. This substitution of the second person plural is one of its marked peculiarities. — R.]

3 [Literally, "little things;" Lightfoot, "mean things." — R.]

4 [Lightfoot follows the Syriac, and renders: "And they that listen, as concerning mean things, do wrong; and we ourselves do wrong, not knowing," etc. But the briefer reading of the Greek MSS. is *lectio difficilior*. — R.]

5 [Only S has γάρ. A has δέ, which the Edinburgh translators have rendered "for." So twice in chap. iii. — R.]

6 Literally, "holy things."

7 Comp. Ps. cxvi. 12.

8 Literally, "lame."

9 Literally, "of men." [Compare Arnobius, vol. vi. p. 423.]

10 Literally, "being full of such darkness in our sight."

11 Literally, "having beheld in us much error and destruction."

12 [C, S (apparently), and recent editors have ἔχοντας, "*even* when we had," instead of ἔχοντες (A), as above paraphrased. — R.]

13 Comp. Hos. ii. 23; Rom. iv. 17, ix. 25.

14 Literally, "willed us from not being to be." [Comp. n. 4, p. 365.]

15 Isa. liv. 1; Gal. iv. 27. [R. V., "the husband." — R.]

16 Some render, "should not cry out, like women in travail." The text is doubtful. [Lightfoot: "Let us not, like women in travail, grow weary of offering up our prayers with simplicity to God." — R.]

17 [ἐπεί, "since;" hence Lightfoot renders, "He so spake, because." — R.]

18 It has been remarked that the writer here implies he was a Gentile.

19 Matt. ix. 13; Luke v. 32. [The briefer form given above is that of the correct text in Matthew and Mark (ii. 17), not Luke. — R.]

20 [ἠθέλησε, "willed." — R.] [Noteworthy. 2 Pet. iii. 9.]

21 Comp. Matt. xviii. 11. [Luke xix. 10. — R.]

22 Literally, "already perishing." [Rev. iii. 2.]

CHAP. III. — THE DUTY OF CONFESSING CHRIST.

Since, then, He has displayed so great mercy towards us, and especially in this respect, that we who are living should not offer sacrifices to gods that are dead, or pay them worship, but should attain through Him to the knowledge of the true Father,[1] whereby shall we show that we do indeed know Him,[2] but by not denying Him through whom this knowledge has been attained? For He Himself declares,[3] "Whosoever shall confess Me before men, him will I confess before My Father."[4] This, then, is our reward if we shall confess Him by whom we have been saved. But in what way shall we confess Him? By doing what He says, and not transgressing His commandments, and by honouring Him not with our lips only, but with all our heart and all our mind.[5] For He says[6] in Isaiah, "This people honoureth Me with their lips, but their heart is far from Me."[7]

CHAP. IV. — TRUE CONFESSION OF CHRIST.

Let us, then, not only call Him Lord, for that will not save us. For He saith, "Not every one that saith to Me, Lord, Lord, shall be saved, but he that worketh righteousness."[8] Wherefore, brethren, let us confess Him by[9] our works, by loving one another, by not committing adultery, or speaking evil of one another, or cherishing envy; but being continent, compassionate, and good. We ought also to sympathize with one another, and not be avaricious. By such[10] works let us confess Him,[11] and not by those that are of an opposite kind. And it is not fitting that we should fear men, but rather God. For this reason, if we should do such *wicked* things, the Lord hath said, "Even though ye were gathered together to Me[12] in My very bosom, yet if ye were not to keep My commandments, I would cast you off, and say unto you, Depart from Me; I know you not whence ye are, ye workers of iniquity."[13]

CHAP. V. — THIS WORLD SHOULD BE DESPISED.

Wherefore, brethren, leaving *willingly* our sojourn in this present world, let us do the will of Him that called us, and not fear to depart out of this world. For the Lord saith, "Ye shall be as lambs in the midst of wolves."[14] And Peter answered and said unto Him,[15] "What, then, if the wolves shall tear in pieces the lambs?" Jesus said unto Peter, "The lambs have no cause after they are dead to fear[16] the wolves; and in like manner, fear not ye them that kill you, and can do nothing more unto you; but fear Him who, after you are dead, has power over both soul and body to cast them into hell-fire."[17] And consider,[18] brethren, that the sojourning in the flesh in this world is but brief and transient, but the promise of Christ is great and wonderful, even the rest of the kingdom to come, and of life everlasting.[19] By what course of conduct, then, shall we attain these things, but by leading a holy and righteous life, and by deeming these worldly things as not belonging to us, and not fixing our desires upon them? For if we desire to possess them, we fall away from the path of righteousness.[20]

CHAP. VI. — THE PRESENT AND FUTURE WORLDS ARE ENEMIES TO EACH OTHER.

Now the Lord declares, "No servant can serve two masters."[21] If we desire, then, to serve both God and mammon, it will be unprofitable for us. "For what will it profit if a man gain the whole world, and lose his own soul?"[22] This world and the next are two enemies. The one urges to[23] adultery and corruption, avarice and deceit; the other bids farewell to these things. We cannot therefore be the friends of both; and it behoves us, by renouncing the one, to make sure[24] of the other. Let us reckon[25] that it is better to hate the things present, since they are trifling, and transient, and corruptible; and to love those *which are to come*, as being good and incorruptible. For if we do the will of Christ, we shall find rest; otherwise, nothing shall deliver us from eternal punishment, if we disobey His commandments. For thus also saith the Scripture in Ezekiel, "If Noah, Job, and Daniel should rise up, they should not deliver their children in captivity."[26] Now, if men

1 [Literally, "the Father of the truth." The best editions have a period here. — R.]

2 Literally, "what is the knowledge which is towards Him." [C, with Bryennios. Hilgenfeld reads τῆς ἀληθείας, "what is the knowledge of the truth," instead of ἡ πρὸς αὐτόν, A, S, Lightfoot, and earlier editors. — R.]

3 [λέγει δὲ καὶ αὐτός, "Yea, He Himself saith," Lightfoot. — R.]

4 Matt. x. 32.

5 Comp. Matt. xxii. 37.

6 ["Now He saith also." — R.]

7 Isa. xxix. 13.

8 Matt. vii. 21, loosely quoted.

9 [Literally, "in." — R.]

10 [A defect in A was thus supplied, but "these" is now accepted; so C, S. — R.]

11 Some read "God." ["Him" is correct. — R.]

12 Or, "with Me." [This is the more exact rendering of μετ' ἐμοῦ. — R.]

13 The first part of this sentence is not found in Scripture; for the second, comp. Matt. vii. 23, Luke xiii. 27. [The first part is not even identified as a citation from an apocryphal book. — R.]

14 Matt. x. 16.

15 No such conversation is recorded in Scripture. [Comp. note 13. — R.]

16 Or, "Let not the lambs fear."

17 Matt. x. 28; Luke xii. 4, 5.

18 Or, "know."

19 The text and translation are here doubtful. [All doubt has been removed; the above rendering is substantially correct. — R.]

20 [More exactly, "the righteous path," τῆς ὁδοῦ τῆς δικαίας. — R.]

21 Matt. vi. 24; Luke xvi. 13.

22 Matt. xvi. 26. [The citation is not exactly according to any evangelist. Literally, "For what advantage is it, if any one gain the whole (C omits 'whole') world, but forfeit his life," or "soul." — R.]

23 Literally, "speaks of." [So Lightfoot. — R].

24 Or, "enjoy." [Lightfoot: "but must bid farewell to the one, and hold companionship with the other;" thus preserving the correspondence with the preceding sentence. — R.]

25 The MS. has, "we reckon." [So C and S, but Lightfoot retains the subjunctive. — R.]

26 Ezek. xiv. 14, 20.

so eminently righteous [1] are not able by their righteousness to deliver their children, how can we hope to [2] enter into the royal residence [3] of God unless we keep our baptism holy and undefiled? Or who shall be our advocate, unless we be found possessed of works of holiness and righteousness? [4]

CHAP. VII. — WE MUST STRIVE IN ORDER TO BE CROWNED.

Wherefore, then, my brethren, let us struggle [5] with all earnestness, knowing that the contest is *in our case* close at hand, and that many undertake long voyages to strive for a corruptible reward; [6] yet all are not crowned, but those only that have laboured hard and striven gloriously. Let us therefore so strive, that we may all be crowned. Let us run the straight [7] course, even the race that is incorruptible; and let us in great numbers set out [8] for it, and strive that we may be crowned. And should we not all be able to obtain the crown, let us at least come near to it. We must remember [9] that he who strives in the corruptible contest, if he be found acting unfairly,[10] is taken away and scourged, and cast forth from the lists. What then think ye? If one does anything unseemly in the incorruptible contest, what shall *he* have to bear? For of those who do not preserve the seal [11] *unbroken, the Scripture* saith,[12] "Their worm shall not die, and their fire shall not be quenched, and they shall be a spectacle to all flesh." [13]

CHAP. VIII. — THE NECESSITY OF REPENTANCE WHILE WE ARE ON EARTH.

As long, therefore, as we are upon earth, let us practise repentance, for we are as clay in the hand of the artificer. For as the potter, if he make a vessel, and it be distorted or broken in his hands, fashions it over again; but if he have before this cast it into the furnace of fire, can no longer find any help for it: so let us also, while we are in this world, repent with our whole heart of the evil deeds we have done in the flesh, that we may be saved by the Lord, while we have yet an opportunity of repentance. For after we have gone out of the world, no further power of confessing or repenting will there belong to us. Wherefore, brethren, by doing the will of the Father, and keeping the flesh holy, and observing the commandments of the Lord, we shall obtain eternal life. For the Lord saith in the Gospel, "If ye have not kept that which was small, who will commit to you the great? For I say unto you, that he that is faithful in that which is least, is faithful also in much." [14] This, then, is what He means: "Keep the flesh holy and the seal undefiled, that ye [15] may receive eternal life." [16]

CHAP. IX. — WE SHALL BE JUDGED IN THE FLESH.

And let no one of you say that this very flesh shall not be judged, nor rise again. Consider ye [17] in what *state* ye were saved, in what ye received sight,[18] if not while ye were in this flesh. We must therefore preserve the flesh as the temple of God. For as ye were called in the flesh, ye shall also come *to be judged* in the flesh. As Christ [19] the Lord who saved us, though He was first a Spirit,[20] became flesh, and thus called us, so shall we also receive the reward in this flesh. Let us therefore love one another, that we may all attain to the kingdom of God. While we have an opportunity of being healed, let us yield ourselves to God that healeth us, and give to Him a recompense. Of what sort? Repentance out of a sincere heart; for He knows all things beforehand, and is acquainted with what is in our hearts. Let us therefore give Him praise,[21] not with the mouth only, but also with the heart, that He may accept us as sons. For the Lord has said, "Those are My brethren who do the will of My Father." [22]

CHAP. X. — VICE IS TO BE FORSAKEN, AND VIRTUE FOLLOWED.

Wherefore, my brethren, let us do the will of the Father who called us, that we may live; and let us earnestly [23] follow after virtue, but forsake

---

1 [Literally, "But if even such righteous men." — R.]
2 Literally, "with what confidence shall we."
3 Wake translates "kingdom," as if the reading had been βασιλείαν; but the MS. has βασίλειον, "palace." [Lightfoot gives the former rendering, though accepting βασίλειον. — R.]
4 [Literally, "holy and righteous works." — R.]
5 [ἀγωνισωμεθα, "let us strive," as in the games. — R.]
6 Literally, "that many set sail for corruptible contests," referring probably to the concourse at the Isthmian games.
7 Or, "Let us place before us." [The latter rendering is that of the reading found in A and C, and now accepted by many editors (θῶμεν); but Lightfoot adheres to θέωμεν (so S), and holds the former reading to be a corruption. — R.]
8 Or, "set sail."
9 Literally, "know."
10 Literally, "if he be found corrupting."
11 Baptism is probably meant. [See Eph. i. 13 and Acts xix. 6.]
12 [Or, "He saith;" "unbroken" is not necessary. — R.]
13 Isa. lxvi. 24.
14 Comp. Luke xvi. 10-12.
15 MS. has "we," which is corrected by all editors as above. [The newly discovered authorities have the second person; most recent editors, however, adopt the first person, as *lectio difficilior*. So Lightfoot; but Hilgenfeld restores ἀπολάβητε in his second edition. — R.]
16 Some have thought this a quotation from an unknown apocryphal book, but it seems rather an explanation of the preceding words.
17 [Editors differ as to the punctuation. Lightfoot: "Understand ye. In what were ye saved? In what did ye recover your sight? if ye were not in the flesh." Hilgenfeld puts a comma after γνῶτε (understand ye), and a period after ἐσώθητε (saved). — R.]
18 Literally, "looked up." [Both senses of ἀναβλέπειν occur in New Testament. — R.]
19 The MS. has εἱς, "one," which Wake follows, but it seems clearly a mistake for ὡς. [Lightfoot reads ει, with a Syriac fragment; both C and S have εἶς. — R.]
20 [C has here the curious reading λόγος instead of πνεῦμα, but all editors retain the latter. — R.]
21 [A reads "eternal," and C, S, "praise;" Lightfoot and others combine the two, "eternal praise." — R.]
22 Matt. xii. 50.
23 Literally, "rather."

every wicked tendency[1] which would lead us into transgression; and flee from ungodliness, lest evils overtake us. For if we are diligent in doing good, peace will follow us. On this account, such men cannot find it, i.e., *peace*, as are[2] influenced by human terrors, and prefer rather present enjoyment to the promise which shall afterwards be fulfilled. For they know not what torment present enjoyment incurs, or what felicity is involved in the future promise. And if, indeed, they themselves only did such things, it would be *the more* tolerable; but now they persist in imbuing innocent souls with their pernicious doctrines,[3] not knowing that they shall receive a double condemnation, both they and those that hear them.

CHAP. XI. — WE OUGHT TO SERVE GOD, TRUSTING IN HIS PROMISES.

Let us therefore serve God with a pure heart, and we shall be righteous; but if we do not serve Him, because we believe not the promise of God, we shall be miserable. For the prophetic word also declares, "Wretched are those of a double mind, and who doubt in their heart, who say, All these things have we heard even in the times of our fathers; but though we have waited day by day, we have seen none of them *accomplished*. Ye fools! compare yourselves to a tree; take, for instance, the vine. First of all it sheds its leaves, then the bud appears; after that the sour grape, and then the fully-ripened fruit. So, likewise, my people have borne disturbances and afflictions, but afterwards shall they receive their good things."[4] Wherefore, my brethren, let us not be of a double mind, but let us hope and endure, that we also may obtain the reward. For He is faithful who has promised that He will bestow on every one a reward according to his works. If, therefore, we shall do righteousness in the sight of God, we shall enter into His kingdom, and shall receive the promises, "which ear hath not heard, nor eye seen, neither have entered into the heart of man."[5]

CHAP. XII. — WE ARE CONSTANTLY TO LOOK FOR THE KINGDOM OF GOD.

Let us expect, therefore, hour by hour, the kingdom of God in love and righteousness, since we know not the day of the appearing of God. For the Lord Himself, being asked by one when His kingdom would come, replied, "When two shall be one, and that which is without as that which is within, and the male with the female, neither male nor female."[6] Now, two are one when we speak the truth one to another, and there is unfeignedly one soul in two bodies. And "that which is without as that which is within" meaneth this: He calls the soul "that which is within," and the body "that which is without." As, then, thy body is visible to sight, so also let thy soul be manifest by good works. And "the male with the female, neither male nor female," this[7] . . .

[The newly recovered portion follows:][8] —

. . . meaneth,[9] that a brother seeing a sister should think nothing[10] about her as of a female, nor *she*[11] think anything about him as of a male. If ye do these things, saith He,[12] the kingdom of my Father shall come.

CHAP. XIII. — DISOBEDIENCE CAUSETH GOD'S NAME TO BE BLASPHEMED.[13]

Therefore, brethren,[14] let us now at length repent; let us be sober unto what is good; for we are full of much folly and wickedness. Let us blot out from us our former sins, and repenting from the soul let us be saved; and let us not become[15] men-pleasers, nor let us desire to please only one another,[16] but also the men that are without, by our righteousness, that the Name[17]

---

1 Literally, "malice, as it were, the precursor of our sins." Some deem the text corrupt.

2 Literally, according to the MS., "it is not possible that a man should find it who *are*" — the passage being evidently corrupt. [The evidence of C and S does not clear up the difficulty here, the reading of these authorities being substantially that of A. Lightfoot renders: "For for this cause is a man unable to attain happiness, seeing that they call in the fears of men," etc. Hilgenfeld (2d ed.) assumes here a considerable gap in all the authorities, and inserts two paragraphs, cited in other authors as from Clement. The first and longer passage is from John of Damascus, and it may be accounted for as a loose citation from chap. xx. in the recovered portion of this Epistle. The other is from pseudo-Justin (*Questions to the Orthodox*, 74). This was formerly assigned by both Hilgenfeld and Lightfoot (against Harnack) to the *First Epistle of Clement*, lviii., in that portion wanting in A. But the recovered chapters (lviii.-lxiii.) contain, according to C and S, no such passage. Lightfoot thinks the reference in pseudo-Justin is to chap. xvi. of this homily, and that the mention of the Sibyl in the same author is not necessarily part of the citation from Clement. Comp. Lightfoot, pp. 308, 447, 448, 458, 459, and Hilgenfeld, 2d ed., pp. xlviii., 77. — R.]

3 [Lightfoot, more literally, "but now they continue teaching evil to innocent souls." — R.]

4 The same words occur in Clement's first epistle, chap. xxiii.

5 1 Cor. ii. 9.

6 These words are quoted (Clem. Alex., *Strom.*, iii. 9, 13) from the Gospel according to the Egyptians, no longer extant.

7 Thus ends the MS., but what followed will be found in Clem. Alex. as just cited.

8 For details respecting the version here given, see Introductory Notice, pp. 514, 515.

9 Or, more correctly, both here and above, "by this He meaneth."

10 All editors read οὐδὲν φρονῇ, but C has φρονεῖ, which is ungrammatical. In this clause, after ἵνα we would expect μηδέν; but, as Lightfoot suggests, οὐδὲν may be combined as a substantive idea with θηλυκόν; comp. the use of οὐ with participles.

11 For μηδὲ (so C) Gebhardt would substitute μηδ' ἥδε, while S supplies in full, *quum soror videbit fratrem*, an obvious interpretament.

12 This seems to be an explanation of the saying above referred to, and not a citation; similar cases occur in the homily.

13 The headings to the chapters have been supplied by the editor, but in so rambling a discourse they are in some cases necessarily unsatisfactory.

14 Hilgenfeld reads μου instead of οὖν; so S apparently. The chapters are usually introduced with οὖν (nine times) or ωστε (five times).

15 γινώμεθα; Lightfoot, "be found."

16 Literally, "ourselves," ἑαυτοῖς; but the reciprocal sense is common in Hellenistic Greek, and is here required by the context.

17 Comp. Acts v. 41, where the correct text omits αὐτοῦ. The Revised Version properly capitalizes "Name" in that passage.

be not blasphemed on account of us.[1] For the Lord also saith, "Continually[2] My name is blasphemed among all the Gentiles,"[3] and again, "Woe[4] to him on account of whom My name is blasphemed." Wherein is it blasphemed? In your not doing what I desire.[5] For the Gentiles, when they hear from our mouth the oracles of God,[6] marvel at them as beautiful and great; afterwards, when they have learned that our works are not worthy of the words we speak, they then turn themselves to blasphemy, saying that it is some fable and delusion. For when they hear from us that God saith,[7] "There is no thank unto you, if ye love them that love you; but there is thank unto you, if ye love your enemies and them that hate you;"[8] when they hear these things, they marvel at the excellency of the goodness; but when they see that we not only do not love them that hate us, but not even them that love us, they laugh us to scorn, and the Name is blasphemed.

CHAP. XIV. — THE LIVING CHURCH IS THE BODY OF CHRIST.

Wherefore,[9] brethren, if we do the will of God our Father, we shall be of the first Church, that is, spiritual, that hath been created before the sun and moon;[10] but if we do not the will of the Lord, we shall be of the scripture that saith, "My house was made a den of robbers."[11] So then let us choose to be of the Church of life,[12] that we may be saved. I do not, however, suppose ye are ignorant that the living Church is the body of Christ;[13] for the Scripture saith, "God made man, male and female."[14] The male is Christ, the female is the Church. And the Books[15] and the Apostles *plainly declare*[16] that the Church is not of the present, but from the beginning.[17] For she was spiritual, as our Jesus also was, but was manifested in the last days that He[18] might save us. Now the Church, being spiritual, was manifested in the flesh of Christ, *thus* signifying to us that, if any of us keep[19] her in the flesh and do not corrupt her, he shall receive her again[20] in the Holy Spirit: for this flesh is the copy of the spirit. No one then who corrupts the copy, shall partake of the original.[21] This then is what He meaneth, "Keep the flesh,[22] that ye may partake of the spirit." But if we say that the flesh is the Church and the spirit Christ,[23] then he that hath shamefully used the flesh hath shamefully used the Church. Such a one then shall not partake of the spirit, which is Christ. Such life and incorruption this flesh[24] can partake of, when the Holy Spirit is joined to it. No one can utter or speak "what the Lord hath prepared" for His elect.[25]

CHAP. XV. — FAITH AND LOVE THE PROPER RETURN TO GOD.

Now I do not think I have given you any light counsel concerning self-control,[26] which if any one do he will not repent of it, but will save both himself and me who counselled him. For it is no light reward to turn again a wandering and perishing soul that it may be saved.[27] For this is the recompense[28] we have to return to God who created us, if he that speaketh and heareth both speaketh and heareth with faith and love. Let us therefore abide in the things which we believed, righteous and holy, that with boldness we may ask of God who saith, "While thou art yet speaking, I will say, Lo, I am here."[29] For this saying is the sign of a great promise; for the Lord saith of Himself that He is more ready to give than he that asketh *to ask*.[30] Being

---

1 C here, and in many other cases, reads ὑμᾶς; a comparison of MSS. shows that it is a correction of the scribe.

2 Lightfoot renders διὰ παντός, "every way;" but the temporal sense is common in Hellenistic Greek, and here required by the Hebrew.

3 Isa. lii 5, with πασῖν inserted.

4 Lightfoot reads, καὶ πάλιν Οὐαί, following the Syriac. C has καὶ Διό. There is difficulty in identifying this second quotation; comp. Ezek. xxxvi. 20-23. Lightfoot thinks it probable that the preacher used two different forms of Isa. lii. 5

5 This sentence is not part of the citation, but an explanation, the words being used as if spoken by God. The Syriac text seeks to avoid this difficulty by reading, "by our not doing what we say."

6 Here τὰ λόγια τοῦ Θεοῦ is used of the Scriptures, and with distinct reference to the New Testament; see next note.

7 In view of the connection, this must mean "God in His oracles;" a significant testimony to the early belief in the inspiration of the Gospels.

8 Luke vi. 27, 32, freely combined; comp. Matt. v. 44, 46. The use of χάρις ὑμῖν shows that the quotation is from the former Gospel.

9 ὥστε, as at the beginning of chaps. vii., x.

10 Comp. Ps. lxxii. (LXX. lxxi.) 5, 17.

11 Jer. vii. 11. Comp. Matt. xxi. 13: Mark xi. 17: Luke xix. 46.

12 Harnack says, "The Jewish synagogue is the church of death." Lightfoot, more correctly, accepts a contrast "between mere external membership in the visible body and spiritual communion in the celestial counterpart."

13 Comp. Eph. i. 23 and many similar passages.

14 Gen. i. 27; comp. Eph. v. 31-33.

15 The reference here is probably to the Old-Testament "books," while the term "Apostles" may mean the New Testament in whole or part. The more direct reference probably is to Genesis and Ephesians.

16 Lightfoot inserts in brackets λέγουσιν, δῆλον, rendering as above. Hilgenfeld suggests φασὶν οἴδατε, "Ye know that the books, etc., say that." Bryennios joins this sentence to the preceding, taking the whole as dependent on ἀγνοεῖν. Ropes renders accordingly, making a parenthesis from "for the Scripture" to "the Church." In any case a verb of saying must be supplied, as in the Syriac.

17 ἄνωθεν has a local and a temporal sense; the latter is obviously preferable here.

18 "Jesus" is the subject of the latter part of the sentence.

19 "Keep her pure;" comp. chap. viii. Lightfoot renders τηρεῖν, "guard," here and elsewhere.

20 The verb corresponds with that rendered "partake" in what follows.

21 "Copy," ἀντίτυπος, ἀντίτυπον. Comp. Heb. ix. 24; 1 Pet iii. 21. Our use of "antitype" is different. The antithesis here is αὐθεντικόν, the original, or archetype. This mystical interpretation has a Platonic basis.

22 Comp. the close of chap. viii.

23 Lightfoot calls attention to the confusion of metaphors; but there is also evidence of that false exegesis which made "flesh" and "spirit" equivalent to "body" and "soul," — an error which always leads to further mistakes.

24 Here the word "flesh" is used in an ambiguous sense.

25 1 Cor. ii. 9.

26 περὶ ἐγκρατείας, "temperance" in the wide New-Testament sense. Lightfoot, "continence;" in these days the prominent danger was from libidinous sins.

27 Comp. Jas. v. 19, 20, with which our passage has many verbal correspondences.

28 "A favorite word with our author, especially in this connection." — LIGHTFOOT.

29 Isa. lviii. 9, LXX.

30 εἰς τὸ διδόναι τοῦ αἰτοῦντος; the sense of the elliptical construction is obviously as above.

therefore partakers of so great kindness, let us not be envious of one another [1] in the obtaining of so many good things. For as great as is the pleasure which these sayings have for them that have done them, so great is the condemnation they have for them that have been disobedient.

CHAP. XVI. — THE EXCELLENCE OF ALMSGIVING.

Wherefore, brethren, having received no small occasion [2] for repentance, while we have the opportunity,[3] let us turn unto God that called us, while we still have Him as One that receiveth us. For if we renounce [4] these enjoyments and conquer our soul in not doing these its evil desires, we shall partake of the mercy of Jesus. But ye know that the day of judgment even now "cometh as a burning oven," [5] and some "of the heavens shall melt," and all the earth *shall be* as lead melting on the fire,[6] and then the hidden and open works of men shall appear. Almsgiving therefore is a good thing, as repentance from sin; fasting is better than prayer, but almsgiving than both; [7] "but love covereth a multitude of sins." [8] But prayer out of a good conscience delivereth from death. Blessed is every one that is found full of these; for almsgiving lighteneth the burden of sin.[9]

CHAP. XVII. — THE DANGER OF IMPENITENCE.

Let us therefore repent from the whole heart, that no one of us perish by the way. For if we have commandments that we should also practise this,[10] to draw away men from idols and instruct them, how much more ought a soul already knowing God not to perish! Let us therefore assist one another that we may also lead up those weak as to what is good,[11] in order that all may be saved; and let us convert and admonish one another.[12] And let us not think to give heed and believe now only, while we are admonished by the presbyters, but also when we have returned home,[13] remembering the commandments [14] of the Lord; and let us not be dragged away by worldly lusts, but coming [15] more frequently let us attempt to make advances in the commandments of the Lord, that all being of of the same mind [16] we may be gathered together unto life. For the Lord said, "I come to gather together all the nations, tribes, and tongues." [17] This He speaketh of the day of His appearing, when He shall come and redeem us, each one according to his works.[18] And the unbelievers "shall see His glory," and strength; and they shall think it strange when they see the sovereignty [19] of the world in Jesus, saying, Woe unto us, Thou wast *He*,[20] and we did not know and did not believe, and we did not obey the presbyters when they declared unto us concerning our salvation. And "their worm dieth not, and their fire is not quenched, and they shall be for a spectacle unto all flesh." [21] He speaketh of that day of judgment, when they shall see those among us [22] that have been ungodly and acted deceitfully with the commandments of Jesus Christ. But the righteous who have done well and endured torments and hated the enjoyments of the soul, when they shall behold those that have gone astray and denied Jesus through their words or through their works, how that they are punished with grievous torments in unquenchable fire, shall be giving glory to God, saying, There will be hope for him that hath served God with his whole heart.

CHAP. XVIII. — THE PREACHER CONFESSETH HIS OWN SINFULNESS.

Let us also become of the number of them that give thanks, that have served God, and not of the ungodly that are judged. For I myself also, being an utter sinner,[23] and not yet escaped from temptation, but still being in the midst of the engines [24] of the devil, give diligence to fol-

---

1 ἑαυτοῖς. Here again in the reciprocal sense; comp. chap. xiii.

2 ἀφορμὴν λαβόντες, as in Rom. vii. 8, 11.

3 καιρὸν ἔχοντες, "seeing that we have time" (Lightfoot). But "opportunity" is more exact.

4 ἀποταξώμεθα, "bid farewell to;" comp. chap. vi.

5 Comp. Mal. iv. 1.

6 Comp. Isa. xxxiv. 4, which resembles the former clause, and 2 Pet. iii. 7, 10, where the same figures occur. The text seems to be corrupt: τινες ("some") is sustained by both the Greek and the Syriac, but this limitation is so peculiar as to awaken suspicion; still, the notion of several heavens might have been in the author's mind.

7 Comp. Tobit xii. 8, 9; but the position given to almsgiving seems to be contradicted by the next sentence. Lightfoot seems to suspect a corruption of text here also, but in the early Church there was often an undue emphasis placed upon almsgiving.

8 1 Pet. iv. 8. Comp. Prov. x. 12; Jas. v. 20.

9 Literally, "becometh a lightener (κούφισμα) of sin;" comp. Ecclus. iii. 30.

10 Lightfoot, with Syriac, reads ἵνα καὶ τοῦτο πράσσωμεν. C omits ἵνα, and reads πράσσομεν, "If we have commandments and practise this."

11 Here Lightfoot thinks a verb has probably fallen out of the text.

12 Bryennios thus connects: "in order that all may be saved, and may convert," etc.

13 "This clearly shows that the work before us is a sermon delivered in church" (Lightfoot). The preacher is himself one of "the presbyters;" comp. chap. xix. It is possible, but cannot be proven, that he was the head of the presbyters, the parochial bishop.

14 ἐνταλμάτων, not the technical word for the commandments of the Decalogue (ἐντολαί).

15 Syriac, "praying," which Lightfoot thinks may be correct; but προσερχόμενοι might very easily be mistaken for προσευχόμενοι. The former means coming in worship; comp. Heb. x. 1, 22.

16 2 Cor. xiii. 11; Phil. ii. 2.

17 Isa. lxvi. 18. But "tribes" is inserted; comp. Dan. iii. 7. The phrase "shall see His glory" is from the passage in Isaiah. The language seems to be put into the mouth of Christ by the preacher.

18 This implies various degrees of reward among these redeemed.

19 τὸ βασίλειον; not exactly "the kingdom," rather "the kingly rule." ἐν τῷ Ἰησοῦ is rightly explained by Lightfoot, "in the hands, in the power, of Jesus;" ξενισθήσονται is rendered above "shall think it strange," as in 1 Pet. iv. 4, 12.

20 "He" is properly supplied, as frequently in the Gospels. There seems to be a reminiscence of John viii. 24 and similar passages.

21 Isa. lxvi. 24; comp. chap. vii. above.

22 C reads ὑμιν, as often, for ἡμῖν, Syriac, accepted by all editors.

23 πανθαμαρτωλός, occurring only here; but a similar word, πανθαμάρτητος, occurs in the *Teaching*, v. 2, *Apostolical Constitutions*, vii. 18, and *Barnabas*, xx.

24 τοῖς ὀργάνοις; comp. Ignat., *Rom.*, iv., *Ante-Nicene Fathers*, i. p. 75, where the word is rendered "instruments," and applied to the teeth of the wild beasts in the amphitheatre. Here Lightfoot renders "engines," regarding the metaphor as military.

low after righteousness, that I may have strength to come even near it,[1] fearing the judgment to come.

CHAP. XIX. — HE JUSTIFIETH HIS EXHORTATION.

Wherefore, brethren and sisters,[2] after the God of truth *hath been heard*,[3] I read to you an entreaty[4] that ye may give heed to the things that are written, in order that ye may save both yourselves and him that readeth among you. For as a reward I ask of you that ye repent with the whole heart, thus giving to yourselves salvation and life. For by doing this we shall set a goal[5] for all the young who are minded to labour[6] on behalf of piety and the goodness of God. And let us not, unwise ones that we are, be affronted and sore displeased, whenever some one admonisheth and turneth us from iniquity unto righteousness. For sometimes while we are practising evil things we do not perceive it on account of the double-mindedness and unbelief that is in our breasts, and we are "darkened in our understanding"[7] by our vain lusts. Let us then practise righteousness that we may be saved unto the end. Blessed are they that obey these ordinances. Even if for a little time they suffer evil in the world,[8] they shall enjoy the immortal fruit of the resurrection. Let not then the godly man be grieved, if he be wretched in the times that now are; a blessed time waits for him. He, living again above with the fathers, shall be joyful for an eternity without grief.

CHAP. XX. — CONCLUDING WORD OF CONSOLATION. DOXOLOGY.

But neither let it trouble your understanding, that we see the unrighteous having riches and the servants of God straitened. Let us therefore, brethren and sisters, be believing: we are striving in the contest[9] of the living God, we are exercised by the present life, in order that we may be crowned by that to come. No one of the righteous received fruit speedily, but awaiteth it. For if God gave shortly the recompense of the righteous, straightway we would be exercising ourselves in business, not in godliness; for we would seem to be righteous, while pursuing not what is godly but what is gainful. And on this account Divine judgment surprised a spirit that was not righteous, and loaded it with chains.[10]

To the only God invisible,[11] the Father of truth, who sent forth to us the Saviour and Prince of incorruption,[12] through whom also He manifested to us the truth and the heavenly life, to Him be the glory for ever and ever. Amen.[13]

---

1 The phrase κἂν ἐγγὺς αὐτῆς implies a doubt of attaining the aim, in accord with the tone of humility which obtains in this chapter.

2 Comp. the opening sentence of *Barnabas*, "Sons and daughters," *Ante-Nicene Fathers*, i. p. 137; see also chap. xx.

3 If any doubt remained as to the character of this writing, it would be removed by this sentence. The passage is elliptical, μετὰ τὸν θεὸν τῆς ἀληθείας, but there is no doubt as to the meaning. The Scripture was read, and listening to it was regarded as hearing the voice of God, whose words of truth were read. Then followed the sermon or exhortation; comp. Justin, *First Apology*, chap. lxvii. (vol. i. p. 186). That lessons from some at least of the New Testament were included at the date of this homily, seems quite certain; comp. the references to the New Testament in chaps. ii., iii., iv., and elsewhere. It is here implied that this homily was written and "read."

4 The word ἔντευξις, here used, means intercession, or supplication, to God (comp. 1 Tim. ii. 1, iv. 5) in early Christian literature: but the classical sense is "entreaty:" so in the opening sentence of Justin, *First Apology* (vol. i. p.163, where it is rendered "petition").

5 Lightfoot, with Syriac and most editors, reads σκοπόν; but C has κόπον, so Bryennios.

6 C had originally φιλοσοφεῖν (accepted by Hilgenfeld), but was corrected to φιλοπονεῖν. The latter is confirmed by the Syriac, and now generally accepted, though Hilgenfeld uses the other reading to support his view that Clement of Alexandria was the author.

7 Eph. iv. 18.

8 C inserts τούτῳ; so Bryennios, Hilgenfeld, and others. Lightfoot omits, with Syriac. The punctuation above given is that of Bryennios and Lightfoot. Hilgenfeld joins this clause with what precedes.

9 πεῖραν ἀθλοῦμεν; the construction is classical, and the figure common in all Greek literature.

10 The verbs here are aorists, and have been rendered by the English past tense; the present participle (μὴ ὂν δίκαιον) describing the character of the "spirit" must, according to English usage, conform to the main verbs. Lightfoot says, "The aorist here has its common *gnomic* sense;" and he therefore interprets the passage as a general statement: "Sordid motives bring their own punishment in a judicial blindness." But this gnomic sense of the aorist is not common. C reads δεσμός, which yields this sense: "and a chain weighed *upon him*." Hilgenfeld refers the passage to those Christians who suffered persecution for other causes than those of righteousness. Harnack thinks the author has in mind Satan, as the prince of avarice, and regards him as already loaded with chains. If the aorist is taken in its usual sense, this is the preferable explanation; but the meaning is obscure.

11 1 Tim. i. 17.

12 Acts iii. 15, v. 31; comp. Heb. ii. 10.

13 The doxology is interesting, as indicating the early custom of thus closing a homily. The practice, fitting in itself, naturally followed the examples in the Epistles.

THE NICENE CREED

THE CREED

As set forth at Nicæa,[1] *A.D. 325.*

We believe in one God, the Father Almighty, Maker of all things, visible and invisible:

And in one Lord Jesus Christ, the Son of God, begotten of the Father, only begotten, that is, of the substance of the Father;

God of God; Light of light; very God of very God; begotten, not made; being of one substance with the Father,

By whom all things were made, both things in heaven and things in earth:

Who for us men and for our salvation came down, and was incarnate, and was made man:

He suffered, and rose again the third day:

And ascended into heaven:

And shall come again to judge the quick and the dead.

And in the Holy Ghost, etc.[2]

THE RATIFICATION.

And those who say *There was a time when He was not*, or that *Before He was begotten He was not*, or that *He was made out of nothing*; or who say that *The Son of God is of any other substance*, or that *He is changeable* or *unstable*, — these the Catholic and Apostolic Church anathematizes.

ADDENDA,

As authorized at Constantinople, A.D. 381.

(*a*) Of heaven and earth.

(*b*) Begotten of the Father before all worlds.

(*c*) By the Holy Ghost of the Virgin Mary.

(*d*) Was crucified also for us, under Pontius Pilate,

(*e*) And was buried.

(*f*) Sitteth on the right hand of the Father,

(*g*) Whose kingdom shall have no end.

(*h*) The Lord, the Giver of life,

Who proceedeth from the Father;[3]

Who with the Father and the Son together is worshipped and glorified;

---

[1] It was the old Creed of Jerusalem slightly amended, and made the liturgic symbol of Christendom, and the exponent of Catholic orthodoxy. Compare the Creed of Cæsarea, Burbidge, p. 334. But see this whole subject admirably illustrated for popular study by Burbidge, *Liturgies and Offices of the Church*, p. 330, etc., London, Bells, 1885.

[2] Here the κ.τ.λ. is to be understood, as in the liturgies where a known form is begun and left imperfect. The clauses (see Cyril of Jerusalem, *Catechet.*, lect. xviii.) are found in the Creed of Jerusalem, thus: "In one baptism of repentance for the remission of sins, and in one Holy Catholic Church; and in the resurrection of the flesh; and in eternal life."

[3] The addition of the *Filioque*, in the West, is theologically true, but of no authority here. See Pearson, *On the Creed*.

Who spake by the prophets:
In one Holy Catholic and Apostolic Church.
We acknowledge one baptism for the remission of sins.
We look for the resurrection of the dead,
And the life of the world to come. Amen.

This Nicæno-Constantinopolitan Creed was solemnly ratified by the Council of Ephesus (A.D. 431) with the decree[1] that "No one[2] shall be permitted to introduce, write, or compose *any other faith*,[3] besides that which was defined by the holy Fathers assembled in the city of Nice, with *the presence of* the Holy Ghost."

[1] Canon vii.

[2] *No one.* This re-affirms the action of Nicæa itself, and forbids the imposition of anything novel as a creed by any authority whatever. Nothing, therefore, which has not been set forth by Nicene authority (or by the supplementing and co-equal councils of the whole Church, from the same primitive sources) can be a creed, strictly speaking. It may be an orthodox confession, like the *Quicunque Vult*, but cannot be imposed in terms of communion, any more than the *Te Deum*.

[3] *Any other faith.* The composition and setting forth of *another faith*, as terms of communion, by Pius IV., bishop of Rome, A.D. 1564, and its acceptance, with additional dogmas, at the opening of the Vatican Council (so-called), A.D. 1869, brought the whole Papal communion under this anathema of Ephesus.

EARLY LITURGIES

INTRODUCTORY NOTICE

TO

EARLY LITURGIES

It is in curious contrast with the work of Brett and others like-minded that we have in these Edinburgh translations a reflection from the minds of divines who are unused to liturgies, and who have no interest in their elucidation. For the mere reader this is not an advantage; but the student who goes to the originals will find that it affords at times no inconsiderable help. These translations are "inartificially drawn," as the lawyers say. They are so much Greek and Latin rendered grammatically by competent scholars, who have no theories to sustain, and who are equally devoid of *technique* and of a disposition to exhibit it for the support of preconceptions. Not infrequently one gets a new view of certain stereotyped expressions from the way in which they are here handled. The liturgiologist finds his researches freshened by etymologies he had hardly thought of, here literally rendered. Of course, these are mere specimens, and no one can use them for argument, except by comparison with the Greek, or the Latin of Renaudot, or the originals in Syriac or Coptic; but they will prove very useful in many ways. The whole science is in its infancy; and we have no specimen of a primitive liturgy unless it be the Clementine, so called. The specimens here given are like cloth of gold (Ps. xlv. 13), moth-eaten and patched, and spangled over with tinsel; and the true artist has only the one object in view, — to restore it, that is, to the king's daughter, as it was aforetime.

The following is the announcement of the Messrs. Clark in the Edinburgh edition: "The Liturgy of St. James has been translated by William Macdonald, M.A.; that of the Evangelist Mark by George Ross Merry, B.A.; and that of the Holy Apostles by Dr. Donaldson."

It will be observed that the translations are given in the Edinburgh series with hardly a line of comment, and with no editorial helps to the reader whatever. These have been scantily supplied, here and there, where the case seemed to require some elucidation; and in a few instances I have ventured to reduce a word or two in the rendering to liturgical phraseology.

The interest which has recently been awakened in *liturgiology*, and which exists among the learned so generally, will justify me in stating somewhat at large the considerations which are prerequisites to an intelligent study of these compilations. I shall not depart from my rule, nor formulate my personal convictions; but I must indicate sources of information not mentioned by the Edinburgh editors, only remarking, that, while they have cited the learned and excellent Dr. Neale, with others who advance untenable claims in some instances, I shall refer to writers of a more moderate school, such as have taken a less narrow and more historic view of the whole matter. By claiming too much, and by reading their own ideas back into the ancient exemplars, many good and learned men have overdone their argument, and confused scriptural simplicity with the artificial systems of post-Nicene ages. Earnest and worthy of respect as they are, I must therefore prefer a class of writers who breathe the spirit of the ante-Nicene Fathers as better elucidating the primitive epoch and its principles, alike in doctrine and worship.

Hippolytus, in a few terse sentences, has pointed out the epoch of David, in its vast import, as the dawning of Christianity itself.[1] More elaborately, a recent writer of great erudition has expounded the same historic fact, and given us the pivot of Hebrew history on which turns the whole system of that "goodly fellowship of prophets" who heralded the Sun of righteousness as successive constellations rise before the day. The learned Dean Payne-Smith, more minutely than Hippolytus, identifies Samuel, the master of David, as the great instrument of God in shaping the institutions of Moses to be a prelude to the Advent; in other words, transforming a local and tribal religion into that of Catholicity. The value of the Dean's condensed and luminous elaboration of this cardinal truth can hardly be overstated.

But, to go behind even the Dean's stand-point, we shall better comprehend the era of which, under God, Samuel was the author, by noting the immense importance of that specific Mosaic ordinance which not only made it possible, but which proves that an all-wise *prolepsis* governed the whole law of Moses. We generally conceive of the Mosaic system as one of unlimited hecatombs and burnt-offerings. On the contrary, it was a system restricting and limiting the unsystematized primeval institution of sacrifice, which had done its work by passing into the universal religions and rituals of Gentilism.[2] When the seminal idea of expiation, atonement, and the blood of innocence as a propitiation for guilt, was communicated to all the families of the earth, the Mosaic institutions limited sacrifices for the faithful, and localized them with marvellous significance. Previously the faithful everywhere had imitated the sacrifices of their fathers, Noah and Abraham, who reared their altars everywhere, as Job also did, — wherever they dwelt or sojourned. Now mark the first step towards a more spiritual worship, based, nevertheless, on the fundamental principle of sacrifice. Moses ordains as follows: —

1. "When ye go over Jordan, and dwell in the land which the Lord your God giveth you, . . . then *there shall be a place* which the Lord your God shall choose to cause His name to dwell there; *thither shall ye bring all that I command you*, your burnt-offerings," etc.[3]

2. "Take heed to thyself that thou offer not thy burnt-offerings in every place that thou seest; but *in the place which the Lord shall choose* in one of the tribes, *there* thou shalt offer thy burnt-offerings, and there thou shalt do all that I command thee."[4]

3. "If the place which the Lord thy God hath chosen to put His name there, be too far from thee" [i.e., *for frequent sacrifices; observe, nevertheless, the law as to the sanctity of blood in thy common use of meats, and forbear to sacrifice, till the opportunity comes*], "only thy *holy things* which thou hast, and thy vows, thou shalt take, and *go unto the place which the Lord shall choose;* and thou shalt offer thy burnt-offerings, the flesh and the blood, upon the altar of the Lord thy God."[5]

4. "Three times in a year shall all thy males appear before the Lord thy God, *in the place which He shall choose*."[6]

5. "Thou mayest not sacrifice THE PASSOVER within any of thy gates; . . . but *at the place which the Lord thy God shall choose* to place His name in, *there thou shalt sacrifice the Passover*."

Note, further, that all this provision and *pre*vision was part of the great Messianic system, which reached its crisis in the time of David, as prophetic of "the Son of David."

It was the office of Samuel to take the Mosaic ordinances just there, and to shape them for the advent of the Lamb of God, for His sacrifice upon Calvary, and for the setting-up of His universal kingdom.

The Institutions of Samuel, therefore, were *in essence* institutions for the Gospel-day, and they were completed by the anointing of David as king, and by his prophetic mission to provide the Psalter (of which more, by and by); then the Ark came out of curtains, and the Lord chose and appointed *the place* of which Moses had spoken, — none other than the spot where Abraham had rehearsed in type the Sacrifice and Resurrection of Christ, according as it was written:[7]

---

1 Vol. v. note 2, p. 170.
2 Vol. vi. p. 542, Elucidation VI.
3 Deut. xii. 6.
4 Deut. xii. 24.
5 Deut. xii. 21, xiv. 24.
6 Exod. xxiii. 17; Deut. xvi. 16.
7 Gen. xxii. 14.

"Jehovah-Jireh . . . *in the mount of the Lord* it shall be seen." Thus, all sacrifice acceptable to God was shown to have reference to the Paschal Lamb, who on that mount of the Lord should be sacrificed, and rise again, as was accomplished in a figure aforetime.[1]

And next, the Psalmist commemorates the putting away of the migratory Tabernacle, and the *rest* of the Ark of the Covenant in the place designed for the grand accomplishment of redemption ("the sure mercies of David"), as follows:[2] —

"He refused the tabernacle of Joseph, and chose not the tribe of Ephraim: but chose the tribe of Judah, *the Mount Zion* which He loved. And He built His sanctuary like high palaces, like the earth which He hath established for ever."

Thus, localized sacrifice was made to designate *the spot* where the one propitiatory sacrifice should be offered, "for the sins of the whole world;" and that spot in turn interpreted the great canon of redemption,[3] —

"Without shedding of blood is no remission:"

and all this, being accomplished in the Messiah, passed away for ever. The veil of the Temple was rent when Jesus cried, "It is finished."

And now let us note the "Institutions of Samuel." The localizing of the Temple-worship made way for the clearer revelation of spiritual sacrifices: the Temple itself was to be supplied with an expository liturgy. Moreover, a liturgical system, revolving about the central worship of the Temple, was to be brought to every man's door by the establishment of the synagogue for the villages of Israel.[4] The synagogue-worship became, therefore, the education and preparation of the faithful for the simple and spiritual worship of the new law. This our Lord Himself expounded in the grand Catholicity of His words to the outcast Samaritans: —

"The hour cometh, when ye shall neither in this mountain, nor yet at Jerusalem, worship the Father. . . . But the hour cometh, and now is, when the true worshippers shall worship the Father in spirit and in truth,"[5] etc.

We have seen that the hour promised by Malachi was supposed by the Ante-Nicene Fathers to be here intended: "My name shall be great among the Gentiles; and *in every place* incense shall be offered unto My name, and a pure offering."[6]

The student of this series must have observed that the primitive writers were universally impressed with these principles,[7] and they are essential to the study of the liturgies here introduced into the series by the Edinburgh editors. For other purposes, expounding the prophetic system, on a text of St. Peter, Dean Payne-Smith has incidentally elucidated these ideas so fully, and with such originality, that I leave the student to consult his pages,[8] with only the following important hints to those who may fail to see them: —

1. We find the prophet Samuel instituting "Schools of the Prophets," out of which grew the synagogue system supplying the Rabbinical education to Israel, and furnishing chiefs to the synagogues. See Acts iii. 24; and compare 1 Sam. x. 5, xix. 20, and Chron. ix. 22.[9]

2. We find the institution of choral worship and the chanting of hymns — e.g., of Moses and Miriam, and Hannah (Samuel's mother) — in full operation under Samuel.

3. We find David at this juncture inspired, as "the sweet singer of Israel," to supply the Psalter, which in divers arrangements has continued among Christians to be the marrow of public worship "in every place," and throughout the world.

4. The reading of the law and the prophets was now set in order; and not only was the Temple supplied with teachers, but also the villages in every tribe.[10]

5. Thus the Christian Church was provided with a system of worship from the hour of its

---

1 Heb. xi. 19.
2 Ps. lxxviii. 67-69.
3 Heb. ix. 22.
4 Ps. lxxxiii. 12, lxxiv. 6.
5 John iv. 21-23.
6 Mal. i. 11.
7 This series *passim;* but, e.g., vol. i. pp. 138, 482, and v. p. 290, note 8.
8 As above mentioned in his work on *Prophecy*. See p. 530.
9 See also Cruden on the word "school" in his *Concordance*.
10 Dean Smith, *Prophecy*, etc., p. 124.

institution,[1] the synaxis succeeding the synagogue; the "ministration of the word" being enriched by Gospels and Epistles, by psalms and hymns and spiritual songs, and by "the prayers" (based upon the *Shemone esre*)[2] which now began to be composed and multiplied in the churches. Touching "free prayer" as exemplified in the first ages, see St. Cyprian's *Epistles* more especially:[3] "Let us pray for the lapsed," etc.

6. It is most significant, that, as St. Paul was not present at the institution of the Lord's Supper, he was, nevertheless, "not behind the chiefest of the Apostles," even in this. He also "received" the whole knowledge of the institution, and became, in so far, the author of an original Gospel in his details of Christ's great oblation of Himself. Hereupon, he adds the sacrificial expositions[4] of the Epistle to the Hebrews, and "delivered the ordinances" to *every church*[5] (κατὰ τάξιν), providing for order and decorum in divine offices.

This he seems to have done as "Liturge" and "Hierurge," or evangelical priest,[6] "*ministering in sacrifice*[7] the Gospel of God," etc.

Compare, then, with the Scriptures, Justin Martyr's account of the early worship of Christians; and after consulting the (so-called) "Clementine Liturgy,"[8] the student will be qualified to form an enlightened judgment upon the primitive and the interpolated elements of the following liturgies. For we must bear in mind that they are reflected from MSS., not one of which has any claim to represent the *Ante-Nicene* period. To purify them, therefore, by Scripture, and the truly primitive testimonies of this series, is a task yet remaining to be accomplished, and one which may well invoke the most conscientious and patient labours of the most learned in the land.

Here follows the Edinburgh INTRODUCTORY NOTICE: —

THE word *Liturgy* has a special meaning as applied to the following documents. It denotes the service used in the celebration of the Eucharist.

Various liturgies have come down to us from antiquity; and their age, authorship, and genuineness have been matter of keen discussion. In our own country two writers on this subject stand specially prominent: the Rev. William Palmer, M.A., who in his *Origines Liturgicæ*[9] gave a dissertation on Primitive Liturgies; and the Rev. J. Mason Neale, who devoted a large portion of his life to liturgies, edited four of them in his *Tetralogia Liturgica*,[10] five of them in his *Liturgies of St. Mark, St. James, St. Clement, St. Chrysostom, and St. Basil*,[11] and discussed them in a masterly manner in several works, but especially in his *General Introduction to a History of the Holy Eastern Church*.[12]

Ancient liturgies are generally divided into four families, — the Liturgy of the Jerusalem Church,[13] adopted throughout the East; the Alexandrian,[14] used in Egypt and the neighbouring countries; and the Roman and Gallican Liturgies. To these Neale has added a fifth, the Liturgy of Persia or Edessa.

There is also a liturgy not included in any of these families — the Clementine. It seems never to have been used in any public service. It forms part of the eighth book of the *Apostolical Constitutions*.[15]

1 Acts i. 4 (Greek), 14, ii. 1, 42, iv. 24.
2 Vol. v. Elucidation III. p. 559.
3 *Ibid.*, Elucidation VI. p. 412.
4 See Field, *Epistle to the Hebrews*, London, Rivingtons, 1882.
5 1 Cor. vii. 17, xi. 2, 25, 33, etc., xiv. 34-40.
6 See vol. v. p. 409.
7 Revised Version of 1881.
8 See *Apostolic Constitutions*, p. 489, *supra*.
9 Oxford, 1832.
10 London, 1849.
11 Second ed. London, 1868.
12 London, 1850.
13 [Or of St. James, so called.]
14 [Called the Liturgy of St. Mark.]
15 [It is most valuable, and indicates the usages of a period near the age of Justin Martyr. It is typical of an original from which the Liturgy of St. James itself is derived. It was probably used in Gaul, if not also in Rome.]

The age ascribed to these documents depends very much on the temperament and inclination of the inquirer. Those who have great reverence for them think that they must have had an apostolic origin, that they contain the apostolic form, first handed down by tradition, and then committed to writing, but they allow that there is a certain amount of interpolation and addition of a date later than the Nicene Council. Such words as "consubstantial" and "mother of God" bear indisputable witness to this. Others think that there is no real historical proof of their early existence at all, — that they all belong to a late date, and bear evident marks of having been written long after the age of the apostles.[1]

There can scarcely be a doubt that they were not committed to writing till a comparatively late day. Those who think that their origin was apostolic allow this. "The period," says Palmer,[2] "when liturgies were first committed to writing is uncertain, and has been the subject of some controversy. Le Brun contends that no liturgy was written till the fifth century; but his arguments seem quite insufficient to prove this, and he is accordingly opposed by Muratori and other eminent ritualists. It seems certain, on the other hand, that the liturgy of the *Apostolical Constitutions* was written at the end of the third or beginning of the fourth century; and there is no reason to deny that others may have been written about the same time, or not long after."

Neale[3] sums up the results of his study in the following words: "I shall content myself therefore with assuming, (1) that these liturgies, though not composed by the Apostles whose names they bear, were the legitimate development of their unwritten tradition respecting the Christian Sacrifice; the words, probably, in the most important parts, the general tenor in all portions, descending unchanged from the apostolic authors. (2) That the Liturgy of St. James is of earlier date, as to its main fabric, than A.D. 200; that the Clementine Office is at least not later than 260; that the Liturgy of St. Mark is nearly coeval with that of St. James; while those of St. Basil and St. Chrysostom are to be referred respectively to the saints by whom they purport to be composed. In all these cases, several manifest insertions and additions do not alter the truth of the general statement."

1. The Roman Liturgy. The first writer who is supposed to allude to a Roman Liturgy is Innocentius, in the beginning of the fifth century; but it may well be doubted whether his words refer to any liturgy now extant.[4] Some have attributed the authorship of the Roman Liturgy to Leo the Great, who was made bishop of Rome in A.D. 451; some to Gelasius, who was made bishop of Rome in A.D. 492; and some to Gregory the First, who was made bishop of Rome in A.D. 590. Such being the opinions of those who have given most study to the subject, we have not deemed it necessary to translate it, though Probst, in his *Liturgie der drei ersten christlichen Jahrhunderte*,[5] probably out of affection for his own Church, has given it a place beside the Clementine and those of St. James and St. Mark.

2. The Gallican has still less claim to antiquity. In fact, Daniel marks it among the spurious.[6] Mabillon tries to prove that three ecclesiastics had a share in the authorship of this liturgy: Musæus, presbyter of Marseilles, who died after the middle of the fifth century; Sidonius, bishop of Auvergne, who died A.D. 494; and Hilary, bishop of Poictiers, who died A.D. 366.[7] Palmer strives to show with great ingenuity that it is not improbable that the Gallican Liturgy may have been originally derived from St. John; but his arguments are merely conjectures.

3. The Liturgy of St. James, the Liturgy of the Church of Jerusalem. Asseman, Zaccaria, Dr. Brett, Palmer, Trollope, and Neale, think that the main structure of this liturgy is the work of St. James, while they admit that it contains some evident interpolations. Leo Allatius, Bona, Bellar-

---

1 [A fair view of their origin is to be found in Sir William Palmer's *Origines Liturgicæ*, Oxford, 1832.]

2 *Origines Liturgicæ*, p. 11.

3 *General Introduction to the History of the Holy Eastern Church*, p. 319.

4 [If Justin Martyr describes the liturgy used in Rome, when he lived there under the Antonines, then it was nearly identical with the "Clementine," and had reached them from the East. See vol. i. p. 185, this series.]

5 Tübingen, 1870.

6 νόθοι. *Codex Liturgicus*, vol. iv. p. 35, note.

7 Palmer, vol. i. p. 144.

mine, Baronius, and some others, think that the whole is the genuine production of the apostle. Cave, Fabricius, Dupin, Le Nourry, Basnage, Tillemont, and many others, think that it is entirely destitute of any claim to an apostolic origin, and that it belongs to a much later age.[1]

"From the Liturgy of St. James," says Neale, "are derived, on the one hand, the forty Syro-Jacobite offices: on the other, the Cæsarean office, or Liturgy of St. Basil, with its offshoots; that of St. Chrysostom, and the Armeno-Gregorian."[2]

There are only two manuscripts of the Greek Liturgy of St. James, — one of the tenth, the other of the twelfth century, — with fragments of a third.[3] The first edition appeared at Rome in 1526. In more recent times it has been edited by Rev. W. Trollope, M.A.,[4] Neale in the two works mentioned above, and Daniel in his *Codex Liturgicus*. Bishop Rattray edited the *Anaphora*,[5] and attempted to separate the original from the interpolations, "though," says Neale, "the supposed restoration is unsatisfactory enough." Bunsen, in his *Analecta Ante-Nicæna*,[6] has tried to restore the *Anaphora* to the state in which it may have been in the fourth century, "as far as was possible — *quantum fieri potuit*."

4. The Liturgy of St. Mark, the liturgy of the church of Alexandria. The same difference of opinion exists in regard to the age and genuineness of this liturgy as we found existing in regard to that of St. James, and the same scholars occupy the same relative position.

The offshoots from St. Mark's Liturgy are St. Basil, St. Cyril, and St. Gregory, and the Ethiopic Canon or Liturgy of All Apostles. In regard to the Liturgy of St. Cyril, Neale says that it is "to all intents and purposes the same as that of St. Mark; and it seems highly probable that the Liturgy of St. Mark came, as we have it now, from the hands of St. Cyril, or, to use the expression of Abu'lberkat, that Cyril 'perfected' it."[7]

There is only one manuscript of the Liturgy of St. Mark, probably belonging to the twelfth century. The first edition appeared at Paris in 1583. The liturgy is given in Renaudot's *Liturgiarum Orientalium Collectio*, tom. i. pp. 120–148,[8] in Neale's two works, and in Daniel's *Codex Liturgicus*.

5. The Liturgy of the Apostles Adæus and Maris. This liturgy has been brought prominently forward by Neale, who says: "It is generally passed over as of very inferior importance, and Renaudot alone seems to have been prepared to acknowledge in some degree its great antiquity."[9] He thinks that it is "one of the earliest, and perhaps the very earliest, of the many formularies of the Christian Sacrifice."[10] It is one of the three Nestorian liturgies, the other two being that of Nestorius and that of Theodore the interpreter.

A Latin translation of it is given in Renaudot's *Collectio*,[11] which is reprinted in Daniel's *Codex Liturgicus*. It is from this version that our translation is made. Several prayers and hymns are indicated only by the initial words, and the rubrical directions are probably of a much later date than the text.

The Liturgies are divided into two parts, — the part before "Lift we up our hearts," and the part after this. The first is termed the Proanaphoral Part, the second the Anaphora.

Trollope describes what he conceives to be the form of worship in the early Church, thus:[12] "The service of this day divided itself into two parts; at the latter of which, called in the Eastern

---

1 [Here the *weight* of authorities is clearly on this side.]

2 *General Introd.*, p. 317.

3 [Palmer gives proof of its currency at an early period in some details. *O. S.*, vol. i. p. 42.]

4 Edinburgh, T. & T. Clark, 1848.

5 London, 1744.

6 Vol. iii. [Grabe also attempted this.]

7 *General Introd.*, p. 324. [From the poverty of MS. authority, we can only form a judgment by comparison with the Clementine and with other more fully represented originals.]

8 Editio secunda correctior. Francofurti ad Moenum, 1847.

9 *General Introd.*, p. 319.

10 *Ibid.*, p. 323.

11 Tom. ii. pp. 578–592, ed. sec.

12 *Introduction*, p. 11.

churches *Liturgia mystica*, and in the Western *Missa fidelium*, none but perfect and approved Christians were allowed to be present. To the *Missa Catechumenorum*, or that part of the service which preceded the prayers peculiar to communicants only, not only believers, but Gentiles, were admitted, in the hope that some might possibly become converts to the faith. After the Psalms and Lessons with which the service commenced, as on ordinary occasions, a section from the Acts of the Apostles or the Epistles was read; after which the deacon or presbyter read the Gospel. Then followed an exhortation from one or more of the presbyters; and the bishop or president delivered a *Homily* or *Sermon*, explanatory, it should seem, of the Scripture which had been read, and exciting the people to an imitation of the virtues therein exemplified. When the preacher had concluded his discourse with a doxology in praise of the Holy Trinity, a deacon made proclamation for all infidels and non-communicants to withdraw; then came the dismissal of the several classes of catechumens, energumens, competents, and penitents, after the prayers for each respectively, as on ordinary days; and the *Missa fidelium* commenced. This office consisted of two parts, essentially distinct: viz., of *prayers for the faithful*, and for mankind in general, introductory to the Oblation; and the *Anaphora* or *Oblation* itself. The introductory part varied considerably in the formularies of different churches; but in the *Anaphora* all the existing liturgies so closely agree, in substance at least, if not in words, that they can only be reasonably referred to the same common origin.[1] Their arrangement, indeed, is not always the same; but the following essential points belong, without exception, to them all:— 1. The Kiss of Peace; 2. The form beginning, *Lift up your hearts;* 3. The Hymn, *Therefore with angels*, etc.; 4. Commemoration of the words of Institution; 5. The Oblation; 6. Prayer of Consecration; 7. Prayers for the Church on Earth; 8. Prayers for the Dead; 9. The Lord's Prayer; 10. Breaking of the Bread; 11. Communion."

Neale gives a more minute account of the different parts of the service. He divides the *Proanaphoral* portion into parts in the following manner:[2] —

"1. Liturgy (or *Missa*) of the Catechumens.	I. The Preparatory Prayers. II. The Initial Hymn or Introit. III. The Little Entrance. IV. The Trisagion. V. The Lections. VI. The Prayers after the Gospel, and expulsion of the Catechumen.
"Liturgy (or *Missa*) of the Faithful.	I. The Prayers for the Faithful. II. The Great Entrance. III. The Offertory. IV. The Kiss of Peace. V. The Creed."

The *Anaphora* he divides into four parts in the following manner:[3] —

"The great Eucharistic Prayer.	I. The Preface. II. The Prayer of the Triumphal Hymn. III. The Triumphal Hymn. IV. Commemoration of Our Lord's Life. V. Commemoration of Institution.
"The Consecration.	VI. Words of Institution of the Bread. VII. Words of Institution of the Wine. VIII. Oblation of the Body and Blood. IX. Introductory Prayer for the Descent of the Holy Ghost. X. Prayer for the Sanctification of Elements.

1 [Hence the value of these liturgies is to be sought in the points of their agreement and their comparative concord with the Clementine.]

2 *General Introduction*, p. 359.

3 *Ibid.*, p. 463.

"The great Intercessory Prayer.	XI. General Intercession for Quick and Dead. XII. Prayer before the Lord's Prayer. XIII. The Lord's Prayer. XIV. The Embolismus.
"The Communion.	XV. The Prayer of Inclination. XVI. The *Holy Things for Holy Persons.* XVII. The Fraction. XVIII. The Confession. XIX. The Communion. XX. The Antidoron: and Prayers of Thanksgiving."

The whole subject is discussed by Mr. Neale with extraordinary minuteness, fulness of detail, and perfect mastery of his subject; and to his work we refer those who wish to prosecute the study of the subject.[1]

GENERAL NOTE BY THE AMERICAN EDITOR.

I HAVE found a few less noted works most useful in my own studies, which began with Palmer's *Origines* on their first publication, followed up by *Brett*, and then by *Renaudot*. The publications of Drs. Neale and Littledale are sufficiently referred to elsewhere; and I purposely omit the mention of many purely Anglican authorities, as well as costly works from other European sources.

1. Freeman's *Principles of Divine Service*, etc.[2] A work of incomparable utility to those who would comprehend the Jewish ritual and its preparations for Christian worship.

2. Badger's *Nestorians and their Rituals*.[3]

3. Warren's *Liturgy and Ritual of the Celtic Church*;[4] replete with information hitherto inaccessible.

4. Scudamore's *Notitia Eucharistica*;[5] Anglican, but full of general information.

5. Trevor's *Catholic Doctrine of Sacrifice*, etc.;[6] a candid and learned study of this subject, and free from fanatical or visionary conceptions.

6. Hammond's *Liturgies*, etc.,[7] elsewhere spoken of.

7. Burbidge, *Liturgies and Offices*,[8] of which I have only lately discovered the value.

8. Field's *Apostolic Liturgy and the Ep. to the Hebrews*;[9] open to some objections, but full of valuable and suggestive information.

9. Pfaffius, Christ. Math. His invaluable *Dissertatio de Oblatione*, etc.[10] A high Lutheran authority of great learning.

10. Marriott's *Testimony of the Catacombs*;[11] learned and instructive.

---

1 [A very fair reviewal of Neale's theoretical statements may be found in Hammond's *Liturgies, Eastern and Western*, Oxford, 1878.]

2 Oxford, Parker, 1855.

3 London, Masters, 1852.

4 Oxford, University Press, 1881.

5 London, Rivingtons, 1872.

6 Oxford, Parker, 1876.

7 Oxford, University Press, 1878. Also *Ancient Liturgy of Antioch*, Oxford, 1879.

8 London, Bells, 1885.

9 London, Rivingtons, 1882.

10 The Hague, Scheurler, 1715. Let me give the title of this rare book more fully, thus: *S. Irenæi Fragmenta Anecdota*, etc., *quæ illustravit, denique Liturgia Græca Jo. Ern. Grabii, et dissertatione de præjudiciis theologicis auxit Christoph. Matth. Pfaffius.* Of whom see Lardner, *Credib.*, i. 17. See vol. i. p. 574, note 5.

11 London, Hatchards, 1870. Valuable for its study of the "Autun Inscription."

EARLY LITURGIES[1]

THE DIVINE LITURGY OF JAMES, THE HOLY APOSTLE AND BROTHER OF THE LORD.

I.

The Priest.[2]

I. O SOVEREIGN Lord our God, contemn me not, defiled with a multitude of sins: for, behold, I have come to this Thy divine and heavenly mystery, not as being worthy; but looking only to Thy goodness, I direct my voice to Thee: God be merciful to me, a sinner; I have sinned against Heaven, and before Thee, and am unworthy to come into the presence of this Thy holy and spiritual table, upon which Thy only-begotten Son, and our Lord Jesus Christ, is mystically set forth as a sacrifice for me, a sinner, and stained with every spot. Wherefore I present to Thee this supplication and thanksgiving, that Thy Spirit the Comforter may be sent down upon me, strengthening and fitting me for this service; and count me worthy to make known without condemnation the word, delivered from Thee by me to the people, in Christ Jesus our Lord, with whom Thou art blessed, together with Thy all-holy, and good, and quickening, and consubstantial[3] Spirit, now and ever, and to all eternity. Amen.

Prayer of the standing beside the altar.

II. Glory to the Father, and to the Son, and to the Holy Spirit, the triune light of the Godhead, which is unity subsisting in trinity, divided, yet indivisible: for the Trinity is the one God Almighty, whose glory the heavens declare, and the earth His dominion, and the sea His might, and every sentient and intellectual creature at all times proclaims His majesty: for all glory becomes Him, and honour and might, greatness and magnificence, now and ever, and to all eternity. Amen.

Prayer of the incense at the beginning.[4]

III. Sovereign Lord Jesus Christ, O Word of God, who didst freely offer Thyself a blameless sacrifice upon the cross to God even the Father, the coal of double nature, that didst touch the lips of the prophet with the tongs, and didst take away his sins, touch also the hearts of us sinners, and purify us from every stain, and present us holy beside Thy holy altar, that we may offer Thee a sacrifice of praise: and accept from us, Thy unprofitable servants, this incense as an odour of a sweet smell, and make fragrant the evil odour of our soul and body, and purify us with the sanctifying power of Thy all-holy Spirit: for Thou alone art holy, who sanctifiest, and art communicated to the faithful; and glory becomes Thee, with Thy eternal Father, and Thy all-holy, and good, and quickening Spirit, now and ever, and to all eternity. Amen.

Prayer of the commencement.

IV. O beneficent King eternal, and Creator of the universe, receive Thy Church, coming unto Thee through Thy Christ: fulfil to each what is profitable; lead all to perfection, and make us perfectly worthy of the grace of Thy sanctification, gathering us together within Thy holy Church, which Thou hast purchased by the precious blood of Thy only-begotten Son, and our Lord and Saviour Jesus Christ, with whom Thou art blessed and glorified, together with Thy all-holy, and good, and quickening Spirit, now and ever, and to all eternity. Amen.

The Deacon.

V. Let us again pray to the Lord.

The Priest, prayer of the incense at the entrance of the congregation.

God, who didst accept the gifts of Abel, the sacrifice of Noah and of Abram, the incense of

[1] [This title is misleading, as we have no copies of the originals of these liturgies, and they are encrusted with the ideas of later ages. I shall distinguish between the interpolations legitimately made by councils and the manifest corruptions which contradict Scripture and ancient authors. N.B.: I print the deacon's parts as such.]

[2] [*A Lavabo:* he prepares himself by the prayer for purification.]

[3] [Here is a token of theological but legitimate interpolation.]

[4] [On the lawful and unlawful additions to these liturgies, see Hickes' *Christian Priesthood* (Oxford, 1847), p. 151.]

Aaron and of Zacharias, accept also from the hand of us sinners this incense for an odour of a sweet smell, and for remission of our sins, and those of all Thy people; for blessed art Thou, and glory becomes Thee, the Father, and the Son, and the Holy Spirit, now and ever.

The Deacon.

Sir, pronounce the blessing.[1]

The Priest prays.

Our Lord and God, Jesus Christ, who through exceeding goodness and love not to be restrained wast crucified, and didst not refuse to be pierced by the spear and nails; who didst provide this mysterious and awful service as an everlasting memorial for us perpetually: bless Thy ministry in Christ the God, and bless our entrance, and fully complete the presentation of this our service by Thy unutterable compassion, now and ever, and to all eternity. Amen.

The responsive prayer from the Deacon.

VI. The Lord bless us, and make us worthy seraphically to offer gifts, and to sing the oft-sung hymn of the divine Trisagion, by the fulness and exceeding abundance of all the perfection of holiness, now and ever.

Then the Deacon begins to sing in the entrance.[2]

Thou who art the only-begotten Son and Word of God, immortal; who didst submit for our salvation to become flesh of the holy God-mother,[3] and ever-virgin Mary; who didst immutably become man and wast crucified, O Christ our God, and didst by Thy death tread death under foot; who art one of the Holy Trinity, glorified together with the Father and the Holy Spirit, save us.

The Priest says this prayer from the gates to the altar.

VII. God Almighty, Lord great in glory, who hast given to us an entrance into the Holy of Holies, through the sojourning among men of Thy only-begotten Son, our Lord, and God, and Saviour Jesus Christ, we supplicate and invoke Thy goodness, since we are fearful and trembling when about to stand at Thy holy altar; send forth upon us, O God, Thy good grace, and sanctify our souls, and bodies, and spirits, and turn our thoughts to piety, in order that with a pure conscience we may bring unto Thee gifts, offerings, and fruits for the remission of our transgressions, and for the propitiation of all Thy people, by the grace and mercies and loving-kindness of Thy only-begotten Son, with whom Thou art blessed to all eternity. Amen.

After the approach to the altar, the Priest says:—

VIII. Peace be to all.

The People.

And to thy spirit.

The Priest.

The Lord bless us all, and sanctify us for the entrance and celebration of the divine and pure mysteries, giving rest to the blessed souls among the good and just, by His grace and loving-kindness, now and ever, and to all eternity. Amen.

Then the Deacon says the bidding prayer.[4]

IX. In peace let us beseech the Lord.

For the peace that is from above, and for God's love to man, and for the salvation of our souls, let us beseech the Lord.

For the peace of the whole world, for the unity of all the holy churches of God, let us beseech the Lord.

For the remission of our sins, and forgiveness of our transgressions, and for our deliverance from all tribulation, wrath, danger, and distress, and from the uprising of our enemies, let us beseech the Lord.

Then the Singers sing the Trisagion Hymn.

Holy God, holy mighty, holy immortal, have mercy upon us.

Then the Priest prays, bowing.

X. O compassionate and merciful, long-suffering, and very gracious and true God, look from Thy prepared dwelling-place, and hear us Thy suppliants, and deliver us from every temptation of the devil and of man; withhold not Thy aid from us, nor bring on us chastisements too heavy for our strength: for we are unable to overcome what is opposed to us; but Thou art able, Lord, to save us from everything that is against us. Save us, O God, from the difficulties of this world, according to Thy goodness, in order that, having drawn nigh with a pure conscience to Thy holy altar, we may send up to Thee without condemnation the blessed hymn Trisagion, together with the heavenly powers, and that, having performed the service, well pleasing to Thee and divine, we may be counted worthy of eternal life.

(*Aloud.*)

Because Thou art holy, Lord our God, and dwellest and abidest in holy places, we send up the praise and the hymn Trisagion to Thee, the Father, and the Son, and the Holy Spirit, now and ever, and to all eternity.

---

1 This is addressed to the priest. Some translate, "O Lord, bless us." [This latter is the more primitive idea.]

2 [The *Lesser Entrance* with the Holy Gospels.]

3 [The *Theotoce* or *Deipara*. Of course, added after the Council of Chalcedon.]

4 [See a specimen of the unlimited capacity for extension of these prayers, in vol. v. p. 412, Elucidation VI., this series.]

The People.

Amen.

The Priest.

XI. Peace be to all.

The People.

And to thy spirit.

The Singers.

Alleluia.

Then there are read in order[1] *the holy oracles of the Old Testament, and of the prophets; and the incarnation of the Son of God is set forth, and His sufferings and resurrection from the dead, His ascension into heaven, and His second appearing with glory; and this takes place daily in the holy and divine service.*[2]

After the reading and instruction the Deacon says: —

XII. Let us all say, Lord, be merciful.[3]

Lord Almighty, the God of our fathers;

We beseech Thee, hear us.

For the peace which is from above, and for the salvation of our souls;

Let us beseech the Lord.

For the peace of the whole world, and the unity of all the holy churches of God;

Let us beseech the Lord.

For the salvation and help of all the Christ-loving people;

We beseech Thee, hear us.

For our deliverance from all tribulation, wrath, danger, distress, from captivity, bitter death, and from our iniquities;

We beseech Thee, hear us.

For the people standing round, and waiting for the rich and plenteous mercy that is from Thee;

We beseech Thee, be merciful and gracious.

Save Thy people, O Lord, and bless Thine inheritance.

Visit Thy world in mercy and compassion.

Exalt the horn of Christians by the power of the precious and quickening cross.

We beseech Thee, most merciful Lord, hear us praying to Thee, and have mercy upon us.

The People (thrice).

Lord, have mercy upon us.

[1] [At great length. Cf. Justin Martyr, vol. i. p. 186, this series.]

[2] [The reading of the Scriptures in the common tongue is a very precious part of the daily offices in the East.]

[3] [Frequent *Amens* are to be supposed.]

The Deacon.

XIII. For the remission of our sins, and forgiveness of our transgressions, and for our deliverance from all tribulation, wrath, danger, and distress, let us beseech the Lord.

Let us all entreat from the Lord, that we may pass the whole day, perfect, holy, peaceful, and without sin.

Let us entreat from the Lord a messenger of peace, a faithful guide, a guardian of our souls and bodies.

Let us entreat from the Lord forgiveness and remission of our sins and transgressions.

Let us entreat from the Lord the things which are good and proper for our souls, and peace for the world.

Let us entreat from the Lord, that we may spend the remaining period of our life in peace and health.

Let us entreat that the close of our lives may be Christian, without pain and without shame, and a good plea at the dread and awful judgment-seat of Christ.

The Priest.

XIV. For Thou art the gospel and the light, Saviour and keeper of our souls and bodies, God, and Thy only-begotten Son, and Thy all-holy Spirit, now and ever.

The People.

Amen.[4]

The Priest.

God, who hast taught us Thy divine and saving oracles, enlighten the souls of us sinners for the comprehension of the things which have been before spoken, so that we may not only be seen to be hearers of spiritual things, but also doers of good deeds, striving after guileless faith, blameless life, and pure conversation.

(Aloud.)

In Christ Jesus our Lord, with whom Thou art blessed, together with Thy all-holy, good, and quickening Spirit, now and always, and for ever.

The People.

Amen.

The Priest.

XV. Peace be to all.

[4] [Here there is an evident interpolation, not Mariolatrous, yet not primitive, as follows:] —

The Priest.

Commemorating with all the holy and just, our all-holy, pure, most glorious Lady, the God-mother, and ever-virgin Mary, let us devote ourselves, and one another, and our whole life, to Christ our God.

The People.

To Thee, Lord.

The People.

And to Thy spirit.

The Deacon.

Let us bow our heads to the Lord.

The People.

To Thee, Lord.

The Priest prays, saying: —

O Sovereign giver of life, and provider of good things, who didst give to mankind the blessed hope of eternal life, our Lord Jesus Christ, count us worthy in holiness, and perfect this Thy divine service to the enjoyment of future blessedness.

(*Aloud.*)

So that, guarded by Thy power at all times, and led into the light of truth, we may send up the praise and the thanksgiving to Thee, the Father, the Son, and the Holy Spirit, now and ever.

The People.

Amen.

The Deacon.

XVI. Let none remain of the catechumens, none of the unbaptized, none of those who are unable to join with us in prayer. Look at one another.[1] The door.
All erect:[2] let us again pray to the Lord.

II.[3]

The Priest says the prayer of incense.

Sovereign Almighty, King of Glory, who knowest all things before their creation, manifest Thyself to us calling upon Thee at this holy hour, and redeem us from the shame of our transgressions; cleanse our mind and our thoughts from impure desires, from worldly deceit, from all influence of the devil; and accept from the hands of us sinners this incense, as Thou didst accept the offering of Abel, and Noah, and Aaron, and Samuel, and of all Thy saints, guarding us from everything evil, and preserving us for continually pleasing, and worshipping, and glorifying Thee, the Father, and Thy only-begotten Son, and Thy all-holy Spirit, now and always, and for ever.

And the Readers begin the Cherubic Hymn.

Let all mortal flesh be silent, and stand with fear and trembling, and meditate nothing earthly within itself: —

For the King of kings and Lord of lords, Christ our God, comes forward to be sacrificed, and to be given for food to the faithful; and the bands of angels go before Him with every power and dominion, the many-eyed cherubim, and the six-winged seraphim, covering their faces, and crying aloud the hymn, Alleluia, Alleluia, Alleluia.

The Priest, bringing in the holy gifts,[4] says this prayer: —

XVII. O God, our God, who didst send forth the heavenly bread, the food of the whole world, our Lord Jesus Christ, to be a Saviour, and Redeemer, and Benefactor, blessing and sanctifying us, do Thou Thyself bless this offering, and graciously receive it to Thy altar above the skies:

Remember in Thy goodness and love those who have brought it, and those for whom they have brought it, and preserve us without condemnation in the service of Thy divine mysteries: for hallowed and glorified is Thy all-honoured and great name, Father, and Son, and Holy Spirit, now and ever, and to all eternity.

The Priest.

Peace be to all.

The Deacon.

Sir, pronounce the blessing.

The Priest.

Blessed be God, who blesseth and sanctifieth us all at the presentation of the divine and pure mysteries, and giveth rest to the blessed souls among the holy and just, now and always, and to all eternity.

The Deacon.

XVIII. Let us attend in wisdom.

The Priest begins.

I believe in one God, Father Almighty, Maker of heaven and earth, and in one Lord Jesus Christ, the Son of God: *and the rest of the Creed.*

Then he prays, bowing his neck.

XIX. God and Sovereign of all, make us, who are unworthy, worthy of this hour, lover of mankind; that being pure from all deceit and all hypocrisy, we may be united with one another by the bond of peace and love, being confirmed by the sanctification of Thy divine knowledge through Thine only-begotten Son, our Lord and Saviour Jesus Christ, with whom Thou art blessed, together with Thy all-holy, and good, and quickening Spirit, now and ever, and to all eternity. Amen.

1 [So as to be sure no enemy was among the faithful.]
2 These clauses are elliptical. After "prayer" supply "remain;" the door is for "shut the door;" and "all erect," for "stand all erect."
3 [Here begins the Liturgy of the Faithful.]
4 [Here is the *Great Entrance*, or bringing-in of the unconsecrated elements. It has a symbolical meaning (Heb. i. 6) now forgotten; and here, instead of the glorified Christ, no doubt the superstitious do adore bread and wine in ignorance.]

The Deacon.

XX. Let us stand well, let us stand reverently, let us stand in the fear of God, and with compunction of heart. In peace let us pray to the Lord.

The Priest.

For God of peace, mercy, love, compassion, and loving-kindness art Thou, and Thine only-begotten Son, and Thine all-holy Spirit, now and ever.

The People.

Amen.

The Priest.

Peace be to all.

The People.

And to thy spirit.

The Deacon.

Let us salute one another with an holy kiss.[1] Let us bow our heads to the Lord.

The Priest bows, saying this prayer:—

XXI. Only Lord and merciful God, on those who are bowing their necks before Thy holy altar, and seeking the spiritual gifts that come from Thee, send forth Thy good grace; and bless us all with every spiritual blessing, that cannot be taken from us, Thou, who dwellest on high, and hast regard unto things that are lowly.

(*Aloud.*)

For worthy of praise and worship and most glorious is Thy all-holy name, Father and Son and Holy Spirit, now and always, and to all eternity.

The Deacon.

Sir, pronounce the blessing.

The Priest.

The Lord will bless us, and minister with us all by His grace and loving-kindness.

And again.

The Lord will bless us, and make us worthy to stand at His holy altar, at all times, now and always, and for ever.

And again.

Blessed be God, who blesseth and sanctifieth us all in our attendance upon, and service of, His pure mysteries, now and always, and for ever.

The Deacon makes the Universal Litany.

XXII. In peace let us pray to the Lord.

The People.

O Lord, have mercy.

The Deacon.

Save us, have mercy upon us, pity and keep us, O God, by Thy grace.

For the peace that is from above, and the loving-kindness of God, and the salvation of our souls;

Let us beseech the Lord.

For the peace of the whole world, and the unity of all the holy churches of God;

Let us beseech the Lord.

For those who bear fruit, and labour honourably in the holy churches of God; for those who remember the poor, the widows and the orphans, the strangers and needy ones; and for those who have requested us to mention them in our prayers;

Let us beseech the Lord.

For those who are in old age and infirmity, for the sick and suffering, and those who are troubled by unclean spirits, for their speedy cure from God and their salvation;

Let us beseech the Lord.

For those who are passing their days in virginity, and celibacy, and discipline, and for those in holy matrimony; and for the holy fathers and brethren agonizing in mountains,[2] and dens, and caves of the earth;

Let us beseech the Lord.

For Christians sailing, travelling, living among strangers, and for our brethren in captivity, in exile, in prison, and in bitter slavery, their peaceful return;

Let us beseech the Lord.

For the remission of our sins, and forgiveness of our transgressions, and for our deliverance from all tribulation, wrath, danger, and constraint, and uprising against us of enemies;

Let us beseech the Lord.

For favourable weather, peaceful showers, beneficent dews, abundance of fruits, the perfect close of a good season, and for the crown of the year;

Let us beseech the Lord.

For our fathers and brethren present, and praying with us in this holy hour, and at every season, their zeal, labour, and earnestness;

Let us beseech the Lord.

1 [The sexes sat apart, the salutations of each confined to its own: an apostolic feature. 1 Pet. v. 14 *et alibi;* and see Clementine, p. 486, *supra*. Note that beautiful tribute of Augustine to the purity of primitive rites, "Honesta utrinsque sexus discretione," *Civ. Dei*, lib. ii. cap. xxviii. p. 77, ed. Migne.] See vol. ii. 291 and iii. 686, this series.]

2 [A token of the Ante-Nicene age, though some think of the later asceticism.]

For every Christian soul in tribulation and distress, and needing the mercy and succour of God; for the return of the erring, the health of the sick, the deliverance of the captives, the rest of the fathers and brethren that have fallen asleep aforetime;

Let us beseech the Lord.

For the hearing and acceptance of our prayer before God, and the sending down on us His rich mercies and compassion.

Let us beseech the Lord.[1]

And for the offered, precious, heavenly, unutterable, pure, glorious, dread, awful, divine gifts, and the salvation of the priest who stands by and offers them;

Let us offer supplication to God the Lord.

The People.

O Lord, have mercy.

(*Thrice.*)

Then the Priest makes the sign of the cross on the gifts,[2] *and, standing, speaks separately thus:* —

XXIII. Glory to God in the highest, and on earth peace, good-will among men, etc.

(*Thrice.*)

Lord, Thou wilt open my lips, and my mouth shall show forth Thy praise.

(*Thrice.*)

Let my mouth be filled with Thy praise, O Lord, that I may tell of Thy glory, of Thy majesty, all the day.

(*Thrice.*)

Of the Father. Amen. And of the Son. Amen. And of the Holy Spirit. Amen. Now and always, and to all eternity. Amen.

And bowing to this side and to that,[3] *he says:* —

XXIV. Magnify the Lord with me, and let us exalt His name together.

And they answer, bowing: —

The Holy Ghost shall come upon thee, and the power of the Highest shall overshadow thee.[4]

Then the Priest, at great length: —

O Sovereign Lord, who hast visited us in compassion and mercies, and hast freely given to us, Thy humble and sinful and unworthy servants, boldness to stand at Thy holy altar, and to offer to Thee this dread and bloodless sacrifice for our sins, and for the errors of the people, look upon me Thy unprofitable servant, and blot out my transgressions for Thy compassion's sake; and purify my lips and heart from all pollution of flesh and spirit; and remove from me every shameful and foolish thought, and fit me by the power of Thy all-holy Spirit for this service; and receive me graciously by Thy goodness as I draw nigh to Thy altar.

And be pleased, O Lord, that these gifts brought by our hands may be acceptable, stooping to my weakness; and cast me not away from Thy presence, and abhor not my unworthiness; but pity me according to Thy great mercy, and according to the multitude of Thy mercies pass by my transgressions, that, having come before Thy glory without condemnation, I may be counted worthy of the protection of Thy only-begotten Son, and of the illumination of Thy all-holy Spirit, that I may not be as a slave of sin cast out, but as Thy servant may find grace and mercy and forgiveness of sins before Thee, both in the world that now is and in that which is to come.

I beseech Thee, Almighty Sovereign, all-powerful Lord, hear my prayer; for Thou art He who workest all in all, and we all seek in all things the help and succour that come from Thee and Thy only-begotten Son, and the good and quickening and consubstantial Spirit, now and ever.

XXV. O God, who through Thy great and unspeakable love didst send forth Thy only-begotten Son into the world, in order that He might turn back the lost sheep, turn not away us sinners, laying hold of Thee by this dread and bloodless sacrifice; for we trust not in our own righteousness, but in Thy good mercy, by which Thou purchasest our race.

We entreat and beseech Thy goodness that it may not be for condemnation to Thy people that this mystery for salvation has been administered by us, but for remission of sins, for renewal of souls and bodies, for the well-pleasing of Thee, God and Father, in the mercy and love of Thy only-begotten Son, with whom Thou art blessed, together with Thy all-holy and good and quickening Spirit, now and always, and for ever.[5]

XXVI. O Lord God, who didst create us, and bring us into life, who hast shown to us ways to salvation, who hast granted to us a revelation of heavenly mysteries, and hast appointed us to this ministry in the power of Thy all-holy Spirit, grant, O Sovereign, that we may become servants of Thy new testament, ministers of Thy pure

[1] [Here an interpolation as follows: "Let us commemorate our all-holy, pure, most glorious, blessed lady, God-mother, and ever-virgin Mary, and all the holy and just, that we may all find mercy through their prayers and intercessions." On which, and like interpolations (the Clementine free from all this), see Scudamore, p. 381.]

[2] [Strongly censured by Hickes as a superstitious innovation (p. 153), with other evils introduced after the pseudo-Council of Nice, A.D. 787, of which this is the least.]

[3] [The Gospel and the Epistle sides.]

[4] ["And Mary said, My soul doth magnify," etc.]

[5] [In such places *Amens* are to be supposed.]

mysteries, and receive us as we draw near to Thy holy altar, according to the greatness of Thy mercy, that we may become worthy of offering to Thee gifts and sacrifices for our transgressions and for those of the people; and grant to us, O Lord, with all fear and a pure conscience to offer to Thee this spiritual and bloodless sacrifice, and graciously receiving it unto Thy holy and spiritual altar above the skies for an odour of a sweet spiritual smell, send down in answer on us the grace of Thy all-holy Spirit.

And, O God, look upon us, and have regard to this our reasonable service, and accept it, as Thou didst accept the gifts of Abel, the sacrifices of Noah, the priestly offices of Moses and Aaron, the peace-offerings of Samuel, the repentance of David, the incense of Zacharias. As Thou didst accept from the hand of Thy apostles this true service, so accept also in Thy goodness from the hands of us sinners these offered gifts; and grant that our offering may be acceptable, sanctified by the Holy Spirit, as a propitiation [1] for our transgressions and the errors of the people; and for the rest of the souls [2] that have fallen asleep aforetime; that we also, Thy humble, sinful, and unworthy servants, being counted worthy without guile to serve Thy holy altar, may receive the reward of faithful and wise stewards, and may find grace and mercy in the terrible day of Thy just and good retribution.

Prayer of the veil.[3]

XXVII. We thank Thee, O Lord our God, that Thou hast given us boldness for the entrance of Thy holy places, which Thou hast renewed to us as a new and living way through the veil of the flesh [4] of Thy Christ. We therefore, being counted worthy to enter into the place of the tabernacle of Thy glory, and to be within the veil, and to behold the Holy of Holies, cast ourselves down before Thy goodness:

Lord, have mercy on us: since we are full of fear and trembling, when about to stand at Thy holy altar, and to offer this dread and bloodless sacrifice for our own sins and for the errors of the people: [5] send forth, O God, Thy good grace, and sanctify our souls, and bodies, and spirits; and turn our thoughts to holiness, that with a pure conscience we may bring to Thee a peace-offering, the sacrifice of praise:

(*Aloud.*)

By the mercy and loving-kindness of Thy only-begotten Son, with whom Thou art blessed, together with Thy all-holy, and good, and quickening Spirit, now and always:

The People.

Amen.

The Priest.

Peace be to all.

The Deacon.

Let us stand reverently, let us stand in the fear of God, and with contrition: let us attend to the holy communion service, to offer peace to God.

The People.

The offering of peace, the sacrifice of praise.

The Priest. [*A veil is now withdrawn from the oblation of bread and wine.*]

And, uncovering the veils that darkly invest in symbol [6] this sacred ceremonial, do Thou reveal it clearly to us: fill our intellectual vision with absolute light, and having purified our poverty from every pollution of flesh and spirit, make it worthy of this dread and awful approach: for Thou art an all-merciful and gracious God, and we send up the praise and the thanksgiving to Thee, Father, Son, and Holy Spirit, now, and always, and for ever.

III.

THE ANAPHORA.

Then he says aloud:—

XXVIII. The love of the Lord and Father, the grace of the Lord and Son, and the fellowship and the gift of the Holy Spirit, be with us all.

The People.

And with thy spirit.

The Priest.

Let us lift up our minds and our hearts.[7]

The People.

It is becoming and right.

Then the Priest prays.

Verily it is becoming and right, proper and due to praise Thee, to sing of Thee, to bless Thee, to worship Thee, to glorify Thee, to give Thee thanks, Maker of every creature visible and invisible, the treasure of eternal good things, the fountain of life and immortality, God and Lord of all:

Whom the heavens of heavens praise, and all the host of them; the sun, and the moon, and all the choir of the stars; earth, sea, and all that is in them; Jerusalem, the heavenly assembly,

1 [Propitiation, not expiation.]

2 [See vol. v. pp. 222–223.]

3 [See Field on "the meaning of the veil," p. 294, where he differs from authors who make it a late innovation; also pp. 448, 449.]

4 [This great primitive thought has been frittered away by references to the veil covering the oblation.]

5 [Based on Heb. v. 1–3.]

6 [See more on the veil in Field, p. 492.]

7 [The *Sursum corda*, found in all liturgies.]

and church of the first-born that are written in heaven; spirits of just men and of prophets; souls of martyrs and of apostles; angels, archangels, thrones, dominions, principalities, and authorities, and dread powers; and the many-eyed cherubim, and the six-winged seraphim, which cover their faces with two wings, their feet with two, and with two they fly, crying one to another with unresting lips, with unceasing praises:

(Aloud.)

With loud voice singing the victorious hymn of Thy majestic glory, crying aloud, praising, shouting, and saying: —

The People.

Holy, holy, holy, O Lord of Sabaoth, the heaven and the earth are full of Thy glory. Hosanna in the highest; blessed is He that cometh in the name of the Lord. Hosanna in the highest.[1]

The Priest, making the sign of the cross[2] on the gifts, says: —

XXIX. Holy art Thou, King of eternity, and Lord and giver of all holiness; holy also Thy only-begotten Son, our Lord Jesus Christ, by whom Thou hast made all things; holy also Thy Holy Spirit, which searches all things, even Thy deep things, O God: holy art Thou, almighty, all-powerful, good, dread, merciful, most compassionate to Thy creatures; who didst make man from earth after Thine own image and likeness; who didst give him the joy of paradise; and when he transgressed Thy commandment, and fell away, didst not disregard nor desert him, O Good One, but didst chasten him as a merciful father, call him by the law, instruct him by the prophets; and afterwards didst send forth Thine only-begotten Son Himself, our Lord Jesus Christ, into the world, that He by His coming might renew and restore Thy image;

Who, having descended from heaven, and become flesh of the Holy Spirit and Virgin God-mother[3] Mary, and having sojourned among men, fulfilled the dispensation for the salvation of our race; and being about to endure His voluntary and life-giving death by the cross, He the sinless for us the sinners, in the night in which He was betrayed, nay, rather delivered Himself up for the life and salvation of the world,

Then the Priest holds the bread in his hand, and says: —

XXX. Having taken the bread in His holy and pure and blameless and immortal hands, lifting up His eyes to heaven, and showing it to Thee, His God and Father, He gave thanks, and hallowed, and brake, and gave it to us,[4] His disciples and apostles, saying: —

The Deacons say:[5] —

For the remission of sins and life everlasting.

Then he says aloud: —

Take, eat: this is my body, broken for you, and given for remission of sins.

The People.

Amen.

Then he takes the cup, and says: —

In like manner, after supper, He took the cup, and having mixed wine and water, lifting up His eyes to heaven, and presenting it to Thee, His God and Father, He gave thanks, and hallowed and blessed it, and filled it with the Holy Spirit, and gave it to us His disciples, saying, Drink ye all of it; this is my blood of the new testament shed for you and many, and distributed for the remission of sins.

The People.

Amen.

The Priest.

This do in remembrance of me; for as often as ye eat this bread, and drink this cup, ye do show forth the Lord's death, and confess His resurrection, till He come.

The Deacons say: —

We believe and confess:

The People.

We show forth Thy death, O Lord, and confess Thy resurrection.

The Priest (Oblation).

XXXI. Remembering, therefore, His life-giving sufferings, His saving cross, His death and His burial, and resurrection from the dead on the third day, and His ascension into heaven, and sitting at the right hand of Thee, our God and Father, and His second glorious and awful appearing, when He shall come with glory to judge the quick and the dead, and render to every one according to His works; even we, sinful men, offer unto Thee, O Lord, this dread and bloodless sacrifice, praying that Thou wilt not deal with us after our sins, nor reward us according to our iniquities;

But that Thou, according to Thy mercy and

---

1 [See Hammond's *Lit. of Antioch*, etc., p. 15, note 29.]
2 [Compare the Clementine, p. 488; and note differences.]
3 [A token of Post-Nicene origin. Vol. v. p. 259, Elucid. I.]

4 [Supposed by some to be a relic of the original formula as the Apostles delivered it. On the *synaxis*, see vol. v. p. 259, Elucid. II.].
5 [These abrupt interjections of the deacon are made while the priest proceeds. This logically *follows* what the priest subjoins.]

Thy unspeakable loving-kindness, passing by and blotting out the handwriting against us Thy suppliants, wilt grant to us Thy heavenly and eternal gifts (which eye hath not seen, and ear hath not heard, and which have not entered into the heart of man[1]) that thou hast prepared, O God, for those who love Thee; and reject not, O loving Lord, the people for my sake, or for my sin's sake:

Then he says, thrice:—

For Thy people and Thy Church supplicate Thee.

The People.

Have mercy on us, O Lord our God, Father Almighty.

Again the Priest says (Invocation):—

XXXII. Have mercy upon us, O God Almighty.

Have mercy upon us, O God our Saviour.

Have mercy upon us, O God, according to Thy great mercy, and send forth on us, and on these offered gifts, Thy all-holy Spirit.

Then, bowing his neck, he says:—

The sovereign and quickening Spirit, that sits upon the throne with Thee, our God and Father, and with Thy only-begotten Son, reigning with Thee; the consubstantial[2] and co-eternal; that spoke in the law and in the prophets, and in Thy New Testament; that descended in the form of a dove on our Lord Jesus Christ at the river Jordan, and abode on Him; that descended on Thy apostles in the form of tongues of fire in the upper room of the holy and glorious Zion on the day of Pentecost: this Thine all-holy Spirit, send down, O Lord, upon us, and upon these offered holy gifts;

And rising up, he says aloud:—

That coming, by His holy and good and glorious appearing, He may sanctify this bread, and make it the holy body of Thy Christ.[3]

The People.

Amen.

The Priest.

And this cup the precious blood of Thy Christ.

The People.

Amen.

The Priest by himself standing.

XXXIII. That they may be to all that partake of them for remission of sins, and for life everlasting, for the sanctification of souls and of bodies, for bearing the fruit of good works, for the stablishing of Thy Holy Catholic Church, which Thou hast founded on the Rock of Faith,[4] that the gates of hell may not prevail against it; delivering it from all heresy and scandals, and from those who work iniquity, keeping it till the fulness of the time.

And having bowed, he says:—

XXXIV. We present them to Thee also, O Lord, for the holy places, which Thou hast glorified by the divine appearing of Thy Christ, and by the visitation of Thy all-holy Spirit; especially for the glorious Zion, the mother of all the churches;[5] and for Thy Holy, Catholic, and Apostolic Church throughout the world: even now, O Lord, bestow upon her the rich gifts of Thy all-holy Spirit.

Remember also, O Lord, our holy fathers and brethren in it, and the bishops in all the world, who rightly divide the word of Thy truth.

Remember also, O Lord, every city and country, and those of the true faith dwelling in them, their peace and security.

Remember, O Lord, Christians sailing, travelling, sojourning in strange lands; our fathers and brethren, who are in bonds, prison, captivity, and exile; who are in mines, and under torture, and in bitter slavery.

Remember, O Lord, the sick and afflicted, and those troubled by unclean spirits, their speedy healing from Thee, O God, and their salvation.

Remember, O Lord, every Christian soul in affliction and distress, needing Thy mercy and succour, O God; and the return of the erring.

Remember, O Lord, our fathers and brethren, toiling hard, and ministering unto us, for Thy holy name's sake.

Remember all, O Lord, for good: have mercy on all, O Lord, be reconciled to us all: give peace to the multitudes of Thy people: put away scandals: bring wars to an end: make the uprising of heresies to cease: grant Thy peace and Thy love to us, O God our Saviour, the hope of all the ends of the earth.

Remember, O Lord, favourable weather, peaceful showers, beneficent dews, abundance of fruits, and to crown the year with Thy goodness; for the eyes of all wait on Thee, and Thou givest their food in due season: thou openest Thy hand, and fillest every living thing with gladness.

Remember, O Lord, those who bear fruit, and labour honourably in the holy[6] of Thy Church;

---

1 To conceive. [A feeble interpolation in the Edinburgh edition.]

2 [Post-Nicene, but legitimate.]

3 [Understood mystically and spiritually down to a late period, even in the West. See Ratramni *De Corpore et Sanguine*, Oxon., 1838. Note the inference as to time of sanctification.]

4 [See vol. v. Elucidation VII. p. 561.]

5 [An honorary title conceded to Jerusalem by the Second General Council: *τῆς δέ γε μητρὸς ἀπασῶν τῶν ἐκκλησιῶν*.]

6 Services. [Otherwise, "who do good works in Thy holy churches."]

and those who forget not the poor, the widows, the orphans, the strangers, and the needy; and all who have desired us to remember them in our prayers.

Moreover, O Lord, be pleased to remember those who have brought these offerings this day to Thy holy altar, and for what each one has brought them or with what mind, and those persons who have just now been mentioned to Thee.

Remember, O Lord, according to the multitude of Thy mercy and compassion, me also, Thy humble and unprofitable servant; and the deacons who surround Thy holy altar, and graciously give them a blameless life, keep their ministry undefiled, and purchase for them a good degree, that we may find mercy and grace, with all the saints that have been well pleasing to Thee since the world began, to generation and generation — grandsires, sires, patriarchs, prophets, apostles, martyrs, confessors, teachers, saints, and every just spirit made perfect in the faith of Thy Christ.

XXXV. [1] Hail, Mary, highly favoured: the Lord is with Thee; blessed art thou among women, and blessed the fruit of thy womb, for thou didst bear the Saviour of our souls.[2]

The Deacons.

XXXVI. Remember us, O Lord God.

The Priest, bowing, says: —

Remember, O Lord God, the spirits and all flesh, of whom we have made mention, and of whom we have not made mention, who are of the true faith, from righteous Abel unto this day: unto them do Thou give rest there in the land of the living, in Thy kingdom, in the joy of paradise, in the bosom of Abraham, and of Isaac, and of Jacob, our holy fathers; whence pain, and grief, and lamentation have fled: there the light of Thy countenance looks upon them, and enlightens them for ever.[3]

Make the end of our lives Christian, acceptable, blameless, and peaceful, O Lord, gathering us together, O Lord, under the feet of Thine elect, when Thou wilt, and as Thou wilt; only without shame and transgressions, through Thy only-begotten Son, our Lord and God and Saviour Jesus Christ: for He is the only sinless one who hath appeared on the earth.

The Deacon..

And *let us pray:* —

For the peace and establishing of the whole world, and of the holy churches of God, and for the purposes for which each one made his offering, or according to the desire he has: and for the people standing round, and for all men, and all women:

The People.

And for all men and all women. (*Amen.*)

The Priest says aloud: —

Wherefore, both to them and to us, do Thou in Thy goodness and love:

The People.

Forgive, remit, pardon, O God, our transgressions, voluntary and involuntary: in deed and in word: in knowledge and in ignorance: by night and by day: in thought and intent: in Thy goodness and love, forgive us them all.

The Priest.

Through the grace and compassion and love of Thy only-begotten Son, with whom Thou art blessed and glorified, together with the all-holy, and good, and quickening Spirit, now and ever, and to all eternity.

The People.

Amen.

The Priest.

XXXVII. Peace be to all:

The People.

And to thy spirit.

The Deacon.

Again, and continually, in peace let us pray to the Lord.

For the gifts to the Lord God presented and sanctified, precious, heavenly, unspeakable, pure, glorious, dread, awful, divine;

Let us pray.

That the Lord our God, having graciously received them to His altar that is holy and above the heavens, rational and spiritual, for the odour of a sweet spiritual savour, may send down in answer upon us the divine grace and the gift of the all-holy Spirit;

Let us pray.

---

[1] [The Angelical Salutation is here an evident interpolation, marring the grand unities of the liturgy.]

[2] [I place in a note what follows:] —

Then the Priest says aloud: —

Hail in the highest, our all-holy, pure, most blessed, glorious Lady, the God-mother and ever-virgin Mary.

The Singers.

Verily it is becoming to bless Thee, the God-bearing, the ever-blessed, and all-blameless, and mother of our God, more honourable than the cherubim, and incomparably more glorious than the seraphim: thee, who didst bear with purity God the Word, thee the true God-mother, we magnify.

And again they sing: —

In thee, highly favoured, all creation rejoices, the host of angels, and the race of men; hallowed temple, and spiritual paradise, pride of virgins, of whom God was made flesh and our God, who was before eternity, became a little child: for He made Thy womb His throne, and Thy bowels *more capacious* than the heavens. In thee, O highly favoured one, all creation rejoices: glory unto thee.

[3] [A prayer entirely corresponding with the primitive ideas. See vol. vi. p. 488, and elucidation, p. 541.]

Having prayed for the unity of the faith, and the communion of His all-holy and adorable Spirit;

Let us commend ourselves and one another, and our whole life, to Christ our God:

The People.

Amen.

The Priest prays.

XXXVIII. God and Father of our Lord and God and Saviour Jesus Christ, the glorious Lord, the blessed essence, the bounteous goodness, the God and Sovereign of all, who art blessed to all eternity, who sittest upon the cherubim, and art glorified by the seraphim, before whom stand thousand thousands and ten thousand times ten thousand hosts of angels and archangels: Thou hast accepted the gifts, offerings, and fruits brought unto Thee as an odour of a sweet spiritual smell, and hast been pleased to sanctify them, and make them perfect, O good One, by the grace of Thy Christ, and by the presence of Thy all-holy Spirit.

Sanctify also, O Lord, our souls, and bodies, and spirits, and touch our understandings, and search our consciences, and cast out from us every evil imagination, every impure feeling, every base desire, every unbecoming thought, all envy, and vanity, and hypocrisy, all lying, all deceit, every worldly affection, all covetousness, all vainglory, all indifference, all vice, all passion, all anger, all malice, all blasphemy, every motion of the flesh and spirit that is not in accordance with Thy holy will:

(*Aloud.*)

And count us worthy, O loving Lord, with boldness, without condemnation, in a pure heart, with a contrite spirit, with unshamed face, with sanctified lips, to dare to call upon Thee, the holy God, Father in heaven, and to say,

The People.

Our Father, which art in heaven: hallowed be Thy name; *and so on to the doxology.*

The Priest, bowing, says (*the Embolism* [1]): —

And lead us not into temptation, Lord, Lord of Hosts, who knowest our frailty, but deliver us from the evil one and his works, and from all his malice and craftiness, for the sake of Thy holy name, which has been placed upon our humility:

(*Aloud.*)

For Thine is the kingdom, the power, and the glory, Father, Son, and Holy Spirit, now and for ever.

The People.

Amen.

The Priest.

XXXIX. Peace be to all.

The People.

And to thy spirit.

The Deacon.

Let us bow our heads to the Lord.

The People.

To Thee, O Lord.

The Priest prays, speaking thus: —

To Thee, O Lord, we Thy servants have bowed our heads before Thy holy altar, waiting for the rich mercies that are from Thee.

Send forth upon us, O Lord, Thy plenteous grace and Thy blessing; and sanctify our souls, bodies, and spirits, that we may become worthy communicants and partakers of Thy holy mysteries, to the forgiveness of sins and life everlasting:

(*Aloud.*)

For adorable and glorified art Thou, our God, and Thy only-begotten Son, and Thy all-holy Spirit, now and ever.

The People.

Amen.

The Priest says aloud: —

And the grace and the mercies of the holy and consubstantial, and uncreated, and adorable Trinity, shall be with us all.[2]

The People.

And with thy spirit.

The Deacon.

In the fear of God, let us attend.

The Priest says secretly: [3] —

O holy Lord, that abidest in holy places, sanctify us by the word of Thy grace, and by the visitation of Thy all-holy Spirit: for Thou, O Lord, hast said, Ye will be holy, for I am holy. O Lord our God, incomprehensible Word of God, one in substance with the Father and the Holy Spirit, co-eternal and indivisible, accept the pure hymn, in Thy holy and bloodless sacrifices; with the cherubim, and seraphim, and from me, a sinful man, crying and saying: —

He takes up the gifts and saith aloud: —

XL. The holy things unto holy.

1 [In all early liturgies always following the Lord's Prayer, to accentuate the petition against the evil one. It hurls back his "fiery darts," as it were; whence this name.]

2 [Duplicated, with other parts, in the Greek copies.]

3 [The taking-up of the gifts is here erroneously introduced in the Edinburgh edition.]

The People.

One *only is* holy, one Lord Jesus Christ, to the glory of God the Father, to whom be glory to all eternity.

The Deacon.

XLI. For the remission of our sins, and the propitiation of our souls, and for every soul in tribulation and distress, needing the mercy and succour of God, and for the return of the erring, the healing of the sick, the deliverance of the captives, the rest of our fathers and brethren, who have fallen asleep aforetime;

Let us all say fervently, Lord, have mercy:

The People (twelve times).

Lord, have mercy.[1]

Then the Priest breaks the bread, and holds the half in his right hand, and the half in his left, and dips that in his right hand in the chalice, saying:—

The union of the all-holy body and precious blood of our Lord and God and Saviour, Jesus Christ.

Then he makes the sign of the cross on that in his left hand: then with that which has been signed the other half: then forthwith he begins to divide, and before all to give to each chalice a single piece, saying:—

It has been made one, and sanctified, and perfected, in the name of the Father, and of the Son, and of the Holy Spirit, now and ever.

And when he makes the sign of the cross on the bread, he says:—

Behold the Lamb of God, the Son of the Father, that taketh away the sin of the world, sacrificed for the life and salvation of the world.

And when he gives a single piece to each chalice, he says:—

A holy portion of Christ, full of grace and truth, of the Father, and of the Holy Spirit, to whom be the glory and the power to all eternity.

Then he begins to divide, and to say:—

XLII. The Lord is my Shepherd, I shall not want. In green pastures, *and so on.*[2]

Then,

I will bless the Lord at all times, *and so on.*[3]

Then,

I will extol Thee, my God, O King, *and so on.*[4]

Then,

O praise the Lord, all ye nations, *and so on.*[5]

The Deacon.

Sir, pronounce the blessing.

The Priest.

The Lord will bless us, and keep us without condemnation for the communion of His pure gifts, now and always, and for ever.

And when they have filled,[6] the Deacon says:—

Sir, pronounce the blessing.

The Priest says:—

The Lord will bless us, and make us worthy with the pure touchings of our fingers to take the live coal, and place it upon the mouths of the faithful for the purification and renewal of their souls and bodies, now and always.

Then,

O taste and see that the Lord is good; who is parted and not divided; distributed to the faithful and not expended; for the remission of sins, and the life everlasting; now and always, and for ever.

The Deacon.

In the peace of Christ, let us sing:

The Singers.

O taste and see that the Lord is good.

The Priest says the prayer before the communion.

O Lord our God, the heavenly bread, the life of the universe, I have sinned against Heaven, and before Thee, and am not worthy to partake of Thy pure mysteries; but as a merciful God, make me worthy by Thy grace, without condemnation to partake of Thy holy body and precious blood, for the remission of sins, and life everlasting.[7]

XLIII. *Then he distributes to the clergy; and when the deacons take the disks[8] and the chalices for distribution to the people, the Deacon, who takes the first disk, says:—*

Sir, pronounce the blessing.

The Priest replies:—

Glory to God who has sanctified and is sanctifying us all.

The Deacon says:—

Be Thou exalted, O God, over the heavens, and Thy glory over all the earth, and Thy kingdom endureth to all eternity.[9]

---

1 [The publican's prayer, adapted to the Christian worship: ἱλάσθητί μοι, is the plea for mercy through propitiation. Luke xviii. 13.]
2 Ps. xxiii.
3 Ps. xxxiv.
4 Ps. cxlv.

5 Ps. cxvii.
6 [Here the chalice is filled for participation.]
7 [Here the presbyter receives.]
8 Or patens.
9 [Here are difficulties explained by Drs. Neale and Littledale in their *Translation*, etc., p. 60.]

And when the Deacon is about to put it on the side-table,[1] *the Priest says:* —

Blessed be the name of the Lord our God for ever.

The Deacon.

In the fear of God, and in faith and love, draw nigh.

The People.

Blessed is He that cometh in the name of the Lord.[2]

And again, when he sets down the disk upon the side-table, he says: —

Sir, pronounce the blessing.

The Priest.

Save Thy people, O God, and bless Thine inheritance.

The Priest again.[3]

Glory to our God, who has sanctified us all.

And when he has put the chalice back on the holy table, the Priest says: —

Blessed be the name of the Lord to all eternity.

The Deacons and the People say: —

Fill our mouths with Thy praise, O Lord, and fill our lips with joy, that we may sing of Thy glory, of Thy greatness all the day.

And again: —

We render thanks to Thee, Christ our God, that Thou hast made us worthy to partake of Thy body and blood, for the remission of sins, and for life everlasting. Do Thou, in Thy goodness and love, keep us, we pray Thee, without condemnation.

The prayer of incense at the last entrance.

XLIV. We render thanks to Thee, the Saviour and God of all, for all the good things Thou hast given us, and for the participation of Thy holy and pure mysteries, and we offer to Thee this incense, praying: Keep us under the shadow of Thy wings, and count us worthy till our last breath to partake of Thy holy rites for the sanctification of our souls and bodies, for the inheritance of the kingdom of heaven: for Thou, O God, art our sanctification, and we send up praise and thanksgiving to Thee, Father, Son, and Holy Spirit.

The Deacon begins in the entrance.

Glory to Thee, glory to Thee, glory to Thee, O Christ the King, only-begotten Word of the Father, that Thou hast counted us, Thy sinful and unworthy servants, worthy to enjoy thy pure mysteries for the remission of sins, and for life everlasting: glory to Thee.[4]

And when he has made the entrance, the Deacon begins to speak thus: —

XLV. Again and again, and at all times, in peace, let us beseech the Lord.

That the participation of His Holy rites may be to us for the turning away from every wicked thing, for our support on the journey to life everlasting, for the communion and gift of the Holy Spirit;

Let us pray.

The Priest prays.

Commemorating our all-holy, pure, most glorious, blessed Lady, the God-Mother and Ever-Virgin Mary,[5] and all the saints that have been well-pleasing to Thee since the world began, let us devote ourselves, and one another, and our whole life, to Christ our God:

The People.

To Thee, O Lord.

The Priest.

XLVI. O God, who through Thy great and unspeakable love didst condescend to the weakness of Thy servants, and hast counted us worthy to partake of this heavenly table, condemn not us sinners for the participation of Thy pure mysteries; but keep us, O good One, in the sanctification of Thy Holy Spirit, that being made holy, we may find part and inheritance with all Thy saints that have been well-pleasing to Thee since the world began, in the light of Thy countenance, through the mercy of Thy only-begotten Son, our Lord and God and Saviour Jesus Christ, with whom Thou art blessed, together with Thy all-holy, and good, and quickening Spirit: for blessed and glorified is Thy all-precious and glorious name, Father, Son, and Holy Spirit, now and ever, and to all eternity.

The People.

Amen.

The Priest.

Peace be to all.

The People.

And to thy spirit.

The Deacon.

XLVII. Let us bow our heads to the Lord.

The Priest.

O God, great and marvellous, look upon Thy servants, for we have bowed our heads to Thee. Stretch forth Thy hand, strong and full of bless-

1 [The side-table or credence.]
2 [Here the laity are communicated.]
3 [Compare Neale's *Tetralogia Liturgica*, p. 192.]

4 [Here are confusions; but see Neale and Littledale, p. 62, note 20.]
5 [Interpolated, but not Mariolatrous: the *Theotoce* is commemorated, not adored.]

ings, and bless Thy people. Keep Thine inheritance, that always and at all times we may glorify Thee, our only living and true God, the holy and consubstantial[1] Trinity, Father, Son, and Holy Ghost, now and ever, and to all eternity.

(*Aloud.*)

For unto Thee is becoming and is due praise from us all, and honour, and adoration, and thanksgiving, Father, Son, and Holy Spirit, now and ever.

The Deacon.

XLVIII. In the peace of Christ let us sing:

And again he says:—

In the peace of Christ let us go on:

The People.

In the name of the Lord. Sir, pronounce the blessing.[2]

Dismission prayer, spoken by the Deacon.

Going on from glory to glory, we praise Thee, the Saviour of our souls. Glory to Father, and Son, and Holy Spirit now and ever, and to all eternity. We praise Thee, the Saviour of our souls.

The Priest says a prayer from the altar to the sacristy.

XLIX. Going on from strength to strength, and having fulfilled all the divine service in Thy temple, even now we beseech Thee, O Lord our God, make us worthy of perfect loving-kindness; make straight our path: root us in Thy fear, and make us worthy of the heavenly kingdom, in Christ Jesus our Lord, with whom Thou art blessed, together with Thy all-holy, and good, and quickening Spirit, now and always, and for ever.

The Deacon.

L. Again and again, and at all times, in peace let us beseech the Lord.

Prayer said in the sacristy after the dismissal.

Thou hast given unto us, O Lord, sanctification in the communion of the all-holy body and precious blood of Thy only-begotten Son, our Lord Jesus Christ; give unto us also the grace of Thy good Spirit, and keep us blameless in the faith, lead us unto perfect adoption and redemption, and to the coming joys of eternity; for Thou art our sanctification and light, O God, and Thy only-begotten Son, and Thy all-holy Spirit, now and ever, and to all eternity. Amen.

The Deacon.

In the peace of Christ let us keep watch.

The Priest.

Blessed is God, who blesseth and sanctifieth through the communion of the holy, and quickening, and pure mysteries, now and ever, and to all eternity. Amen.

Then the prayer of propitiation.

O Lord Jesus Christ, Son of the living God, Lamb and Shepherd, who takest away the sin of the world, who didst freely forgive their debt to the two debtors, and gavest remission of her sins to the woman that was a sinner, who gavest healing to the paralytic, with the remission of his sins; forgive, remit, pardon, O God, our offences, voluntary and involuntary, in knowledge and in ignorance, by transgression and by disobedience, which Thy all-holy Spirit knows better than Thy servants do:

And if men, carnal and dwelling in this world, have in aught erred from Thy commandments, either moved by the devil, whether in word or in deed, or if they have come under a curse, or by reason of some special vow, I entreat and beseech Thy unspeakable loving-kindness, that they may be set free from their word, and released from the oath and the special vow, according to Thy goodness.

Verily, O Sovereign Lord, hear my supplication on behalf of Thy servants, and do Thou pass by all their errors, remembering them no more; forgive them every transgression, voluntary and involuntary; deliver them from everlasting punishment: for Thou art He that hast commanded us, saying, Whatsoever things ye bind upon earth, shall be bound in heaven; and whatsoever things ye loose upon earth, shall be loosed in heaven: for thou art our God, a God able to pity, and to save and to forgive sins; and glory is due unto Thee, with the eternal Father, and the quickening Spirit, now and ever, and to all eternity. Amen.

1 [A legitimate addition, according to the primitive laws.]
2 [Which must here be given.]

THE DIVINE LITURGY OF THE HOLY APOSTLE AND EVANGELIST MARK,[1] THE DISCIPLE OF THE HOLY PETER.[2]

The Priest.

I. Peace be to all.

The People.

And to thy spirit.

The Deacon.

Pray.

The People.

Lord, have mercy; Lord, have mercy; Lord, have mercy.

The Priest prays secretly.[3]

We give Thee thanks, yea, more than thanks, O Lord our God, the Father of our Lord and God and Saviour Jesus Christ, for all Thy goodness at all times and in all places, because Thou hast shielded, rescued, helped, and guided us all the days of our lives, and brought us unto this hour, permitting us again to stand before Thee in Thy holy place, that we may implore forgiveness of our sins and propitiation to all Thy people. We pray and beseech Thee, merciful God, to grant in Thy goodness that we may spend this holy day[4] and all the time of our lives without sin, in fulness of joy, health, safety, holiness, and reverence of Thee. But all envy, all fear, all temptation, all the influence of Satan, all the snares of wicked men, do Thou, O Lord, drive away from us, and from Thy Holy Catholic and Apostolic Church. Bestow upon us, O Lord, what is good and meet. Whatever sin we commit in thought, word, or deed, do Thou in Thy goodness and mercy be pleased to pardon. Leave us not, O Lord, while we hope in Thee; nor lead us into temptation, but deliver us from the evil one and from his works, through the grace, mercy, and love of Thine only-begotten Son.

(*In a loud voice.*)

Through whom and with whom be glory and power to Thee, in Thy most holy, good, and life-giving Spirit, now, henceforth, and for evermore.

The People.

Amen.

The Priest.

II. Peace be to all.

The People.

And to thy spirit.

The Deacon.

Pray for the king.[5]

The People.

Lord, have mercy;[6] Lord, have mercy; Lord, have mercy.

The Priest prays.

O God, Sovereign Lord, the Father of our Lord and God and Saviour Jesus Christ, we pray and beseech Thee to grant that our king may enjoy peace, and be just and brave. Subdue under him, O God, all his adversaries and enemies. Gird on thy shield and armour, and rise to his aid. Give him the victory, O God, that his heart may be set on peace and the praise of Thy holy name, that we too[7] in his peaceful reign[8] may spend a calm and tranquil life in all reverence and godly fear, through the grace, mercy, and love of Thine only-begotten Son:

(*In a loud voice.*)

Through whom and with whom be glory and power to Thee, with Thy most holy, good, and life-giving Spirit, now, henceforth, and for evermore.

The People.

Amen.

The Priest.

III. Peace be to all.

The People.

And to thy spirit.

The Deacon.

Pray for the *papas*[9] and the bishop.

The People.

Lord, have mercy; Lord, have mercy; Lord, have mercy.

1 [The only authority for this valuable relic is a single codex of the twelfth century, i.e., the *Codex Rossanensis*, found at Rossano, in Calabria. It was deposited in the Basilian monastery at Rome, and first published A.D. 1583, at Paris. See Hammond, pp. xlv., li.]

2 [Elucidation I.]

3 [i.e., μυστικῶς = arcane. — HEDERIC.]

4 [This implies that the Eucharist was not (originally) celebrated every day, as a rule. See Justin Martyr, vol. i. note 1, p. 186.]

5 Rather "for the emperor," says Renaudot; and the word βασιλεύς will stand this meaning.

6 [The (κύριε ἐλέησον) Kyrie Eleëson.]

7 [According to 1 Tim. ii. 2.]

8 [Suits the first years of Diocletian.]

9 The Patriarch of Alexandria is meant. The word πάπας was used at first to designate all bishops; but its application gradually became more restricted, and so here the Patriarch of Alexandria is called πάπας, as being superior to the bishops of his patriarchate. [See vol. v. p. 154, and vol. vi., Introd.]

The Priest.

O Sovereign and Almighty God, the Father of our Lord, God, and Saviour Jesus Christ, we pray and beseech Thee to defend in Thy good mercy our most holy and blessed high priest our Father *in God* Δ, and our most reverend Bishop Δ. Preserve them for us through many years in peace, while they according to Thy holy and blessed will fulfil the sacred priesthood committed to their care, and dispense aright the word of truth; with all the orthodox bishops, elders, deacons, sub-deacons, readers, singers, and laity, with the entire body of the Holy and only Catholic Church. Graciously bestow upon them peace, health, and salvation. The prayers they offer up for us, and we for them, do Thou, O Lord, receive at Thy holy, heavenly, and reasonable altar. But all the enemies of Thy Holy Church put Thou speedily under their feet, through the grace, mercy, and love of Thine only-begotten Son:

(*Aloud.*)

Through whom and with whom be glory and power to Thee, with Thy all-holy, good, and life-giving Spirit, now, henceforth, and for evermore.

The People.

Amen.

The Priest.

IV. Peace be to all.

The People.

And to thy spirit.

The Deacon.

Stand[1] and pray.

The People.

Lord have mercy (*thrice*).

The Priest offers up the prayer of entrance,[2] and for incense.

The Priest.

O Sovereign Lord our God, who hast chosen the lamp of the twelve apostles with its twelve lights, and hast sent them forth to proclaim throughout the whole world and teach the Gospel of Thy kingdom, and to heal sickness and every weakness among the people, and hast breathed upon their faces and said unto them, Receive the Holy Spirit the Comforter: whosesoever sins ye remit, they are remitted unto them; and whosesoever sins ye retain, they are retained: Breathe also Thy Holy Spirit upon us Thy servants, who, standing around, are about to enter on Thy holy service,[3] upon the bishops, elders, deacons, readers, singers, and laity, with the entire body of the Holy Catholic and Apostolic Church.

From the curse and execration, from condemnation, imprisonment, and banishment, and from the portion of the adversary;

O Lord, deliver us.

Purify our lives and cleanse our hearts from all pollution and from all wickedness, that with pure heart and conscience we may offer to Thee this incense for a sweet-smelling savour, and for the remission of our sins and the sins of all Thy people, through the grace, mercy, and love of Thine only-begotten Son:

(*Aloud.*)

Through whom and with whom be the glory and the power to Thee, with Thy all-holy, good, and life-giving Spirit, now, henceforth, and for evermore.

The People.

Amen.

The Deacon.

V. Stand.

They sing:—

Only-begotten Son and Word,[4] etc.

The Gospel is carried in, and the Deacon says:—

Let us pray.

The Priest.

Peace be to all.

The People.

And to thy spirit.

The Deacon.

Let us pray.

The People.

Lord, have mercy.

The Priest says the prayer of the Trisagion.

O Sovereign Lord Christ Jesus, the co-eternal Word of the eternal Father, who wast made in all things like as we are, but without sin, for the salvation of our race; who hast sent forth Thy holy disciples and apostles to proclaim and teach the Gospel of Thy kingdom, and to heal all disease, all sickness among Thy people, be pleased now, O Lord, to send forth Thy light and Thy truth. Enlighten the eyes of our minds, that we may understand Thy divine oracles. Fit us to become hearers, and not only hearers, but doers of Thy word, that we, becoming fruitful, and yielding good fruit from thirty to an hundred fold, may be deemed worthy of the kingdom of heaven.

---

[1] [See vol. iii. p. 689, this series.]

[2] This is the Little Entrance. [The priest and deacon come from the prothesis bearing the Gospels. See p. 538, *supra*.]

[3] [Bestowing what is meet.] The text here is defective. Some suppose that a sentence has been lost.

[4] Given in full in chap. vi. of the Liturgy of James, p. 538, *supra*. [It is so worded that it must be dated later than the Council of Ephesus, A.D. 431.]

(*Aloud.*)

Let Thy mercy speedily overtake us, O Lord. For Thou art the bringer of good tidings, the Saviour and Guardian of our souls and bodies; and we offer glory, thanks, and the *Trisagion* to Thee, the Father, Son, and Holy Ghost, now, henceforth, and for evermore.

The People.

Amen. Holy God, holy mighty, holy immortal. Holy, holy, holy,[1] etc.

VI. *After the Trisagion the Priest makes the sign of the cross over the people, and says:* —

Peace be to all.

The People.

And to thy spirit.

Then follow the Let us attend;[2] *The Apostle and Prologue of the Hallelujah.*[3] *The Deacons, after a prescribed form, say:* —

Lord, bless us.[4]

The Priest says: —

May the Lord[5] in His mercy bless and help us, now, henceforth, and for evermore.

The Priest, before the Gospel is read, offers incense,[6] *and says:* —

Accept at Thy holy, heavenly, and reasonable altar, O Lord, the incense we offer in presence of Thy sacred glory. Send down upon us in return the grace of Thy Holy Spirit, for Thou art blessed, and let Thy glory encircle us.

VII. *The Deacon, when he is about to read the Gospel, says:* —

Lord, bless us.

The Priest.

May the Lord, who is the blessed God, bless and strengthen us, and make us hearers of His holy Gospel, now, henceforth, and for evermore. Amen.

The Deacon.

Stand and let us hear the holy Gospel.

The Priest.

Peace be to all.

The People.

And to thy spirit.

VIII. *The Deacon reads the Gospel, and the Priest says the prayer of the Collect.*[7]

Look down in mercy and compassion, O Lord, and heal the sick among Thy people.

May all our brethren who have gone or who are about to go abroad, safely reach their destination in due season.

Send down the gracious rain upon the thirsty lands, and make the rivers[8] flow in full stream, according to Thy grace.

The fruits of the land do Thou, O Lord, fill with seed and make ripe for the harvest.

In peace, courage, justice, and tranquillity preserve the kingdom of Thy servant, whom Thou hast deemed worthy to reign over this land.

From evil days, from famine and pestilence, from the assault of barbarians, defend, O Lord, this Christ-loving city, lowly and worthy of Thy compassion, as Thou didst spare Nineveh of old.

For Thou art full of mercy and compassion, and rememberest not the iniquities of men against them.

Thou hast said through Thy prophet Isaiah, — I will defend this city, to save it for mine own sake, and for my servant David's sake.

Wherefore we pray and beseech Thee to defend in Thy good mercy this city, for the sake of the martyr and evangelist Mark, who has shown us the way of salvation through the grace, mercy, and love of Thine only-begotten Son.

(*Aloud.*)

Through whom and with whom be glory and power to Thee, with Thy all-holy, good, and life-giving Spirit.

The Deacon.

IX. Begin.

Then they say the verse.[9] *The Deacon says — The three.*[10]

The Priest.

O Sovereign and Almighty God, the Father of our Lord Jesus Christ, we pray and beseech Thee to fill our hearts with the peace of heaven, and to bestow moreover the peace of this life. Preserve for us through many years our most holy and blessed *Papas* Δ,[11] and our most pious Bishop Δ, while they, according to Thy holy and blessed will, peacefully fulfil the holy priesthood committed to their care, and dispense aright the word of truth, with all the orthodox bishops, elders, deacons, sub-deacons,[12] readers, singers, with the entire body of the holy Catholic and Apostolic Church. Bless our meetings, O Lord.

---

1 [The *Trisagion* is found in all the liturgies, which proves a common source and original.]

2 πρόσχωμεν.

3 [*The Apostle* means that the Epistle is read, and there is a prayer said (μυστικῶς), followed by the outburst of Hallelujah.]

4 See note 1, p. 538. ["Sir, bless us" (in ordinary renderings) is a Western form.]

5 [Here, the deacon's words having been correctly given, the blessing of the priests shows the force of his expression.]

6 [I have frequently noted the Ante-Nicene ignorance of this rite among Christians, in order to illustrate these later usages as without apostolic warrant. See Irenæus, note 9, p. 484.]

7 τὴν συνάπτην.

8 [The waters of *the* river, rather, with reference to the Nile.]

9 [The anthem, probably.]

10 Probably by *the three* are meant three prayers. [See Hammond, note 1, p. 177.]

11 Patriarch.

12 [Vol. v. p. 417, Elucidation XIV.]

Grant that we may hold them without let or hindrance, according to Thy holy will. Be pleased to give to us, and Thy servants after us for ever, houses of praise and prayer. Rise, O Lord, and let Thine enemies be scattered. Let all who hate Thy holy name be put to flight. Bless Thy faithful and orthodox people. Multiply them by thousands and tens of thousands.

Let no deadly sin prevail against them, or against Thy holy people, through the grace, mercy, and love of Thine only-begotten Son.

(*Aloud.*)

Through whom and with whom be glory and power to Thee, with Thy all-holy, good, and life-giving Spirit.

The People.

Amen.

The Priest.

Peace be to all.

The People.

And to thy spirit.

The Deacon.

Take care that none of the catechumens [1] —

II.

Then they sing the Cherubic hymn.[2]

X. *The Priest offers incense at the entrance,*[3] *and prays:* —

O Lord our God, who lackest nothing, accept this incense offered by an unworthy hand, and deem us all worthy of Thy blessing, for Thou art our sanctification, and we ascribe glory to Thee.

The holy things are carried to the altar, and the Priest prays thus: —

O holy, highest, awe-inspiring God, who dwellest among the saints, sanctify us, and deem us worthy of Thy reverend priesthood. Bring us to Thy precious altar with a good conscience, and cleanse our hearts from all pollution. Drive away from us all unholy thoughts, and sanctify our souls and minds. Grant that, with reverence of Thee, we may perform the service of our holy fathers, and propitiate Thy presence through all time; for Thou art He who blesseth and sanctifieth all things, and to Thee we ascribe glory and thanks.

The Deacon.

XI. Salute one another.

The Priest says the prayer of salutation.

O Sovereign and Almighty Lord, look down from heaven on Thy Church, on all Thy people, and on all Thy flock. Save us all, Thy unworthy servants, the sheep of Thy fold. Give us Thy peace, Thy help, and Thy love, and send to us the gift of Thy Holy Spirit, that with a pure heart and a good conscience we may salute one another with an holy kiss, without hypocrisy, and with no hostile purpose, but guileless and pure in one spirit, in the bond of peace and love, one body and one spirit, in one faith, even as we have been called in one hope of our calling, that we may all meet in the divine and boundless love, in Christ Jesus our Lord, with whom Thou art blessed.

Then the Priest offers the incense, and says: —

The incense is offered to Thy name. Let it ascend, we implore Thee, from the hands of Thy poor and sinful servants to Thy heavenly altar for a sweet-smelling savour, and the propitiation of all Thy people. For all glory, honour, adoration, and thanks are due unto Thee, the Father, Son, and Holy Ghost, now, henceforth, and for evermore. Amen.

After the Salutation,[4] *the Deacon in a loud voice says:* —

XII. Stand and make the offering duly.[5]

The Priest, making the sign of the cross over the disks and chalices, says in a loud voice (the Nicene Creed): —

I believe in one God, etc.

The Deacon.

Stand for prayer.

The Priest.

Peace be to all.

The Deacon.

Pray for those who present the offering.

The Priest says the prayer of the Oblation.[6]

O Sovereign Lord, Christ Jesus the Word, who art equal in power with the Father and the Holy Spirit, the great high priest; the bread that came down from heaven, and saved our souls from ruin; who gavest Thyself, a spotless Lamb, for the life of the world . . .

We pray and beseech Thee, O Lord, in Thy mercy, to let Thy presence rest upon this bread and these chalices [7] on the all-holy table, while angels, archangels, and Thy holy priests stand round and minister for Thy glory and the renewing of our souls, through the grace, mercy, and love of Thine only-begotten Son, through

[1] Some such word as *remain* is intentionally omitted. [See p. 540, *supra.*]

[2] [See p. 540, *supra.*]

[3] [The *Great Entrance;* p. 540, *supra.*]

[4] [See p. 541, *supra.*]

[5] [i.e., in due order; in your turn.]

[6] τῆς προθέσεως.

[7] [ἐπι τὸν ἄρτον τοῦτον και ἐπὶ τὰ ποτήρια ταῦτα. Most noteworthy language in this place.]

whom and with whom be glory and power to Thee.

And when the People say,

And from the Holy Spirit was He made flesh;

The Priest makes the sign of the cross,[1] *and says:—*

And was crucified for us.

The Priest makes the sign of the cross again,[1] *and says:—*

And to the Holy Spirit.

III.

XIII.[2] *In like manner also, as after the Creed,*[3] *he makes the sign of the cross upon the People, and says aloud:—*

The Lord be with all.

The People.

And with thy spirit.

The Priest.

Let us lift up our hearts.

The People.

We lift them up to the Lord.

The Priest.

Let us give thanks to the Lord.

The People.

It is meet and right.[4]

The Priest begins the Anaphòral prayer.

O Lord God, Sovereign and Almighty Father, truly it is meet and right, holy and becoming, and good for our souls, to praise, bless, and thank Thee; to make open confession to Thee by day and night with voice, lips, and heart without ceasing;

To Thee who hast made the heaven, and all that is therein; the earth, and all that is therein;

The sea, fountains, rivers, lakes, and all that is therein;

To Thee who, after Thine own image and likeness, hast made man, upon whom Thou didst also bestow the joys of Paradise;

And when he trespassed against Thee, Thou didst neither neglect nor forsake him, good Lord,

But didst recall him by Thy law, instruct him by Thy prophets, restore and renew him by this awful, life-giving, and heavenly mystery.

And all this Thou hast done by Thy Wisdom and the Light of truth, Thine only-begotten Son, our Lord, God, and Saviour Jesus Christ,

Through whom, thanking Thee with Him and the Holy Spirit,

We offer this reasonable and bloodless sacrifice, which all nations, from the rising to the setting of the sun, from the north and the south, present to Thee, O Lord; for great is Thy name among all peoples, and in all places are incense, sacrifice, and oblation offered to Thy holy name.[5]

XIV. We pray and beseech Thee, O *lover of men, O good* Lord,[6] remember in Thy good mercy the Holy and only Catholic and Apostolic Church throughout the whole world, and all Thy people, and all the sheep of this fold.[7] Vouchsafe to the hearts of all of us the peace of heaven, but grant us also the peace of this life.

Guide and direct in all peace the king,[8] army, magistrates, councils,[9] peoples, and neighbourhoods, and all our outgoings and incomings.

O King of Peace, grant us Thy peace in unity and love. May we be Thine, O Lord; for we know no other God but Thee, and name no other name but Thine. Give life unto the souls of all of us, and let no deadly sin prevail against us, or against all Thy people.

Look down in mercy and compassion, O Lord, and heal the sick among Thy people. Deliver them and us, O Lord, from sickness and disease, and drive away the spirit of weakness.

Raise up those who have been long afflicted, and heal those who are vexed with unclean spirits.

Have mercy on all who are in prison, or in mines, or on trial, or condemned, or in exile, or crushed by cruel bondage or tribute. Deliver them, O Lord, for Thou art our God, who settest the captives free; who raisest up the downtrodden; who givest hope to the hopeless, and help to the helpless; who liftest up the fallen; who givest refuge to the shipwrecked, and vengeance to the oppressed.

Pity, relieve, and restore every Christian soul that is afflicted or wandering.

But do Thou, O Lord, the physician of our souls and bodies, the guardian of all flesh, look down, and by Thy saving power heal all the diseases of soul and body.

Guide and prosper our brethren who have gone or who are about to go abroad. Whether they travel by land, or river, or lake, by public road, or in whatever way journeying, bring them everywhere to a safe and tranquil haven. Be pleased to be with them by land and sea, and restore them in health and joy to joyful and healthful homes.

---

1 [Two after the Creed and one before.]

2 [The Anaphora.]

3 [I have supposed the adverb ὥσπερ (*as*) in this place, for obvious reasons. It is implied in the text.]

4 [See p. 543, *supra*. Here the Edinburgh inserts: "*The Deacon*. . . ."]

5 [The reference to Mal. i. 11, always noteworthy. Vol. i. p. 484.]

6 [Here I supply an omission, in italics.]

7 [και πάντων τῶν ποιμνίων σου. John x. 16.]

8 Or emperor. [See p. 551, notes 5, 7.]

9 βουλάς, senates.

Ever defend, O Lord, our journey through this life from trouble and storm.

Send down rich and copious showers on the dry and thirsty lands.

Gladden and revive the face of the earth, that it may spring forth and rejoice in the raindrops.

Make the waters of the river flow in full stream.

Gladden and revive the face of the earth with the swelling waters.

Fill all the channels of the streams, and multiply the fruits of the earth.

Bless, O Lord, the fruits of the earth, and keep them safe and unharmed. Fill them with seed, and make them ripe for the harvest.

Bless even now, O Lord, Thy yearly crown of blessing for the sake of the poor of Thy people, the widow, the orphan, and the stranger, and for the sake of all of us who have our hope in Thee and call upon Thy holy name; for the eyes of all are upon Thee, and Thou givest them bread in due season.

O Thou who givest food to all flesh, fill our hearts with joy and gladness, that at all times, having all sufficiency, we may abound to every good work in Christ Jesus our Lord.

O King of kings and Lord of lords, defend the kingdom of Thy servant, our orthodox and Christ-loving sovereign,[1] whom Thou hast deemed worthy to reign over this land in peace, courage, and justice.

Subdue under him, O Lord, every enemy and adversary, whether at home or abroad. Gird on Thy shield and armour, and rise to his aid. Draw Thy sword, and help him to fight against them that persecute him. Shield him in the day of battle, and grant that the fruit of his loins may sit upon his throne.

Be kind to him, O Lord, for the sake of Thy Holy and Apostolic Church, and all Thy Christ-loving people, that we too in his peaceful reign may live a calm and tranquil life, in all reverence and godliness.

O Lord our God, give peace to the souls of our fathers and brethren who have fallen asleep in Jesus, remembering our forefathers of old, our fathers, patriarchs, prophets, apostles, martyrs, confessors, bishops, and the souls of all the holy and just men who have died in the Lord.

Especially remember those whose memory we this day *celebrate*, and our holy father Mark,[2] the apostle and evangelist, who has shown us the way of salvation.[3]

The Deacon.

Lord, bless us.

The Priest.

The Lord will bless thee in His grace, now, henceforth, and for evermore.

The Deacon reads the record of the dead.[4]

The Priest bows and prays.

XV. Give peace, O Sovereign Lord our God, to the souls of all who dwell in the tabernacles of Thy saints. Graciously bestow upon them in Thy kingdom Thy promised blessing, which eye hath not seen, and ear hath not heard, nor has it entered into the heart of man what Thou, O God, hast prepared for those who love Thy holy name. Give peace to their souls, and deem them worthy of the kingdom of heaven.[5]

Grant that we may end our lives as Christians, acceptable unto Thee and without sin, and be pleased to give us part and lot with all Thy saints.

Accept, O God, by Thy ministering archangels at Thy holy, heavenly, and reasonable altar in the spacious heavens, the thank-offerings of those who offer sacrifice and oblation, and of those who desire to offer much or little, in secret or openly, but have it not to give.

Accept the thank-offerings of those who have presented them this day, as Thou didst accept the gifts of Thy righteous Abel:

The Priest offers incense, and says:[6] —

As Thou didst accept the sacrifice of our father Abraham, the incense of Zacharias, the alms of Cornelius, and the widow's two mites, accept also the thank-offerings of these, and give them for the things of time the things of eternity, and for the things of earth the things of heaven. Defend, O Lord, our most holy and blessed *Papas*[7] Δ, whom Thou hast fore-ordained to rule over Thy Holy Catholic and Apostolic Church, and our most pious Bishop Δ, that they through many years of peace may, according to Thy holy and blessed will, fulfil the sacred priesthood committed to their care, and dispense aright the word of truth.

Remember the orthodox bishops everywhere, the elders, deacons, sub-deacons, readers, singers, monks,[8] virgins, widows, and laity.

Remember, O Lord, the holy city[9] of our God, Jesus Christ; and the imperial city;[10] and this city of ours, and all cities and all lands, and the peace and safety of those who dwell therein in the orthodox faith of Christ.

---

1 [Evidently after Constantine.]

2 [Elucid. II. Such passages indicate, of course, how St. Mark's name came to be given to this liturgy. Here is interpolated:] —

Hail! thou art highly favoured; the Lord is with thee; blessed art thou among women, and blessed is the fruit of thy womb, because thou hast brought forth the Saviour of our souls.

Aloud.

Especially *remember* our all-holy, pure, and blessed Lady, Mary the Virgin Mother of God.

3 [Hammond's note is important, p. 182; and see Elucid. II.]

4 τὰ δίπτυχα. [See the note of Hammond, *Glossary*, p. 378.]

5 [See Burbidge, p. 34 and *passim* to p. 253.]

6 [Burbidge, p. 185.]

7 The Patriarch.

8 [Subsequent to *Antony*. Vol. vi. p. 279.]

9 [Jerusalem: a token of antiquity.]

10 [Rome, no doubt.]

Be mindful, O Lord, of the return of the backsliding, and of every Christian soul that is afflicted and oppressed, and in need of Thy divine mercy and help.

Be mindful, O Lord, of our brethren in captivity. Grant that they may find mercy and compassion with those who have led them captive.

Be mindful also of us, O Lord, Thy sinful and unworthy servants, and blot out our sins in Thy goodness and mercy.

Be mindful also of me, Thy lowly, sinful, and unworthy servant, and in Thy mercy blot out my sins.

Be with us, O Lord, who minister unto Thy holy name.

Bless our meetings, O Lord.

Utterly uproot idolatry from the world.[1]

Crush under our feet Satan, and all his wicked influence.

Humble now, as at all times, the enemies of Thy Church.

Lay bare their pride.

Speedily show them their weakness.

Bring to nought the wicked plots they contrive against us.

Arise, O Lord, and let Thine enemies be scattered, and let all who hate Thy holy name be put to flight.

Do Thou bless a thousand times ten thousand Thy faithful and orthodox people while they do Thy holy will.

The Deacon.

Let those who are seated stand.

The Priest says the following prayer: —

Deliver the captive; rescue the distressed; feed the hungry; comfort the faint-hearted; convert the erring; enlighten the darkened; raise the fallen; confirm the wavering; heal the sick; and guide them all, good Lord, into the way of salvation, and into Thy sacred fold. Deliver us from our iniquities; protect and defend us at all times.

The Deacon.

Turn to the east.

The Priest bows and prays.

For Thou art far above all principality, and power, and might, and dominion, and every name that is named, not only in this world, but in that which is to come. Round Thee stand ten thousand times ten thousand, and thousands of thousands of holy angels and hosts of archangels; and Thy two most honoured creatures, the many-eyed cherubim and the six-winged seraphim. With twain they cover their faces, and with twain they cover their feet, and with twain they do fly; and they cry one to another for ever with the voice of praise, and glorify Thee, O Lord, singing aloud the triumphal and thrice-holy[2] hymn to Thy great glory: —

Holy, holy, holy, Lord God of Sabaoth. Heaven and earth are full of Thy glory.

(*Aloud.*)

Thou dost ever sanctify all men; but with all who glorify Thee, receive also, O Sovereign Lord, our sanctification, who with them celebrate Thy praise, and say: —

The People.

Holy, holy, holy Lord.

The Priest makes the sign of the cross over the sacred mysteries.

XVI. For truly heaven and earth are full of Thy glory, through the manifestation of our Lord and God and Saviour Jesus Christ. Fill, O God, this sacrifice with Thy blessing, through the inspiration of Thy all-holy Spirit. For the Lord Himself, our God and universal King, Christ Jesus, reclining at meat the same night on which He delivered Himself up for our sins and died in the flesh for all, took bread in His holy, pure, and immaculate hands, and lifting His eyes to His Father, our God, and the God of all, gave thanks; and when He had blessed, hallowed, and broken the bread, gave it to His holy and blessed disciples and apostles, saying: —

(*Aloud.*)

Take, eat.

The Deacon.

Pray earnestly.

The Priest (aloud).

For this is my body, which is broken for you, and divided for the remission of sins.

The People.

Amen.

The Priest prays.

After the same manner also, when He had supped, He took the cup of wine mingled with water, and lifting His eyes to Thee, His Father, our God, and the God of all, gave thanks; and when He had blessed and filled it with the Holy Spirit, gave it to His holy and blessed disciples and apostles, saying: —

(*Aloud.*)

Drink ye all of it.

The Deacon.

Pray earnestly again.

---

[1] [Agrees with the *partial* triumphs of A.D 325.]

[2] The Trisagion.

The Priest (aloud).

For this is my blood of the new testament, which is shed for you and for many, and distributed among you for the remission of sins.

The People.

Amen.

The Priest prays thus: —

This do ye in remembrance of me; for as often as ye eat this bread and drink this cup, ye do show forth my death and acknowledge my resurrection and ascension until I come. O Sovereign and Almighty Lord, King of heaven, while we show forth[1] the death of Thine only-begotten Son, our Lord, God, and Saviour Jesus Christ, and acknowledge His blessed resurrection from the dead on the third day, we do also openly declare His ascension into heaven, and His sitting on the right hand of Thee, God and Father, and await His second terrible and dreadful coming, in which He will come to judge righteously the quick and the dead, and to render to each man according to his works.

XVII. O Lord our God, we have placed before Thee what is Thine from Thine own mercies. We pray and beseech Thee, O good and merciful God, to send down from Thy holy heaven, from the mansion Thou hast prepared, and from Thine infinite bosom, the Paraclete Himself,[2] holy, powerful, and life-giving, the Spirit of truth, who spake in the law, the apostles, and prophets; who is everywhere present, and filleth all things, freely working sanctification in whom He will with Thy good pleasure; one in His nature; manifold in His working; the fountain of divine blessing; of like substance[3] with Thee, and proceeding from Thee; sitting with Thee on the throne of Thy kingdom, and with Thine only-begotten Son, our Lord and God and Saviour Jesus Christ. Send down upon us also, and upon this bread and upon these chalices, Thy Holy Spirit, that by His all-powerful and divine influence He may sanctify and consecrate them, and make this bread the body.[2]

The People.

Amen.

The Priest (aloud).

And this cup the blood of the new testament, of the very Lord, and God, and Saviour, and universal King Christ Jesus.

The Deacon.

Deacons, come down.

The Priest (aloud).

That to all of us who partake thereof they may tend unto faith, sobriety, healing, temperance, sanctification, the renewal of soul, body, and spirit, participation in the blessedness of eternal life and immortality, the glory of Thy most holy name, and the remission of sins, that Thy most holy, precious, and glorious name may be praised and glorified in this as in all things.

The People.

As it was and is.

The Priest.

XVIII. Peace be to all.

The Deacon.

Pray.

The Priest prays in secret.

O God of light, Father of life, Author of grace, Creator of worlds, Founder of knowledge, Giver of wisdom, Treasure of holiness, Teacher of pure prayers, Benefactor of our souls, who givest to the faint-hearted who put their trust in Thee those things into which the angels desire to look: O Sovereign Lord, who hast brought us up from the depths of darkness to light, who hast given us life from death, who hast graciously bestowed upon us freedom from slavery, who hast scattered the darkness of sin within us, through the presence of Thine only-begotten Son, do Thou now also, through the visitation of Thy all-holy Spirit, enlighten the eyes of our understanding, that we may partake without fear of condemnation of this heavenly and immortal food, and sanctify us wholly in soul, body, and spirit, that with Thy holy disciples and apostles we may say this prayer to Thee: Our Father who art in heaven, etc.

(Aloud.)

And grant, O Sovereign Lord, in Thy mercy, that we with freedom of speech, without fear of condemnation, with pure heart and enlightened soul, with face that is not ashamed, and with hallowed lips, may venture to call upon Thee, the holy God who art in heaven, as our Father, and say: —

The People.

Our Father who art in heaven, etc.

The Priest prays:[4] —

Verily, Lord, Lord, lead us not into temptation, but deliver us from evil; for Thy abundant mercy showeth that we through our great infirmity are unable to resist it.

Grant that we may find a way whereby we may be able to withstand temptation; for Thou hast given us power to tread upon serpents, and scorpions, and all the power of the enemy.

---

1 [The Oblation, κατ' ἐξοχήν.]

2 [The Invocation.]

3 [On all this, see Hammond, notes 1 and 2, p. 187.]

4 [The Embolisms = ejaculations.]

(Aloud.)

For Thine is the kingdom and power.

The People.

Amen.

The Priest.

XIX. Peace be to all.

The Deacon.

Bow your heads to Jesus.[1]

The People.

Thou, Lord.

The Priest prays.

O Sovereign and Almighty Lord,[2] who sittest upon the cherubim, and art glorified by the seraphim; who hast made the heaven out of waters, and adorned it with choirs of stars; who hast placed an unbodied host of angels in the highest heavens to sing Thy praise for ever; before Thee have we bowed our souls and bodies in token of our bondage. We beseech Thee to repel the dark assaults of sin from our understanding, and to gladden our minds with the divine radiance of Thy Holy Spirit, that, filled with the knowledge of Thee, we may worthily partake of the mercies set before us, the pure body and precious blood of Thine only-begotten Son, our Lord and God and Saviour Jesus Christ. Pardon all our sins in Thy abundant and unsearchable goodness, through the grace, mercy, and love of Thine only-begotten Son:[3]

(Aloud.)

Through whom and with whom be glory and power to Thee, with the all-holy, good, and life-giving Spirit.

The Priest.

XX. Peace be to all.

The Deacon.

With the fear of God.

The Priest prays.

O holy, highest, awe-inspiring God, who dwellest among the saints, sanctify us by the word of Thy grace and by the inspiration of Thy all-holy Spirit; for Thou hast said, O Lord our God, Be ye holy; for I am holy. O Word of God, past finding out, consubstantial[4] and co-eternal with the Father and the Holy Spirit, and sharer of their sovereignty, accept the pure song which cherubim and seraphim, and the unworthy lips of Thy sinful and unworthy servant, sing aloud.

The People.

Lord, have mercy; Lord, have mercy; Lord, have mercy.

1 [Phil. ii. 10. See Hammond, note 1, p. 48.]
2 [Prayer of Humble Access.]
3 [Compare Hammond, p. 79.]
4 [Post-Nicene.]

The Priest (aloud).

Holy things for the holy.[5]

The People.

One Father holy, one Son holy, one Spirit holy, in the unity of the Holy Spirit. Amen.[6]

The Deacon.

For salvation and help.

The Priest makes the sign of the cross upon the people, and saith in a loud voice:—

The Lord be with all.

The Priest breaks the bread, and saith:—

Praise ye God.

The Priest divides it among those present, and saith:—

The Lord will bless and help you through His great *mercy*.

The Priest says:—

Command.

The Clergy say:—

The Holy Spirit commands and sanctifies.

The Priest.

Lo, they are sanctified and consecrated.

The Clergy.

One holy[7] Father, etc. (*thrice*).

The Priest says:—

The Lord be with all.

The Clergy.

And with thy spirit.

The Priest says:—

The Lord Himself hath blessed it.

The Priest partakes, and prays.

According to Thy loving-kindness,[8] etc.

Or,

As the hart panteth after the water-brooks,[9] etc.

When he gives the bread to the clergy, he says:—

The holy body.

And when he gives the chalice, he says:—

The precious blood of our Lord, and God, and Saviour.

5 [Elucidation III.]
6 [Perhaps the Triad is meant at note 10, p. 553.]
7 [See p. 567, *infra*.]
8 [Ps. xlii.]
9 [Ps. xlii. 1.]

IV.

After the service is completed, the Deacon says:—

XXI. Stand for prayer.[1]

The Priest.

Peace be to all.

The Deacon.

Pray.

The Priest says the prayer of thanksgiving.

O Sovereign Lord our God, we thank Thee that we have partaken of Thy holy, pure, immortal, and heavenly mysteries, which Thou hast given for our good, and for the sanctification and salvation of our souls and bodies. We pray and beseech Thee, O Lord, to grant in Thy good mercy, that by partaking of the holy body and precious blood of Thine only-begotten Son, we may have faith that is not ashamed, love that is unfeigned, fulness of holiness, power to eschew evil and keep Thy commandments, provision for eternal life, and an acceptable defence before the awful tribunal of Thy Christ:

In a loud voice.

Through whom and with whom be glory and power to Thee, with Thy all-holy, good, and life-giving Spirit.

The Priest then turns to the people, and says:—

XXII. O mightiest King, co-eternal with the Father, who by Thy might hast vanquished hell and trodden death under foot, who hast bound the strong man, and by Thy miraculous power and the enlightening radiance of Thy unspeakable Godhead hast raised Adam from the tomb, send forth Thy invisible right hand, which is full of blessing, and bless us all.

Pity us, O Lord, and strengthen us by Thy divine power.

Take away from us the sinful and wicked influence of carnal desire.

Let the light shine into our souls, and dispel the surrounding darkness of sin.

[1] [Post-Communion.]

Unite us to the all-blessed assembly that is well-pleasing unto Thee; for through Thee and with Thee, all praise, honour, power, adoration, and thanksgiving are due unto the Father and the Holy Spirit, now, henceforth, and for evermore.

The Deacon.

Depart in peace:

The People.

In the name of the Lord.

The Priest (aloud).

XXIII. The love of God the Father; the grace of the Son, our Lord Jesus Christ; the communion and gift of the All-holy Spirit, be with us all, now, henceforth, and for evermore.

The People.

Amen. Blessed be the name of the Lord.

The Priest prays in the sacristy, and says:—

O Lord, Thou hast given us sanctification by partaking of the all-holy body and precious blood of Thine only-begotten Son; give us the grace and gift of the All-holy Spirit. Enable us to lead blameless lives; and guide us unto the perfect redemption, and adoption, and the everlasting joys of the world to come. For Thou art our sanctification, and we ascribe glory unto Thee, the Father, and the Son, and the All-holy Spirit, now, henceforth, and for evermore.

The People.

Amen.

The Priest.

Peace be to all.

The People.

And to thy spirit.

The Priest dismisses them, and says:—

May God bless, who blesseth and sanctifieth, who defendeth and preserveth us all through the partaking of His holy mysteries; and who is blessed for ever. Amen.

THE LITURGY OF THE BLESSED APOSTLES.

COMPOSED BY ST. ADÆUS AND ST. MARIS, TEACHERS OF THE EASTERNS.[1]

I.[2] *First:* Glory to God in the highest, etc. Our Father which art in heaven.

Prayer.

Strengthen, O our Lord and God, our weakness through Thy mercy, that we may administer the holy mystery which has been given for the renovation and salvation of our degraded nature, through the mercies of Thy beloved Son the Lord of all.

On common days.

Adored, glorified, lauded, celebrated, exalted, and blessed in heaven and on earth, be the adorable and glorious name of Thine ever-glorious Trinity, O Lord of all.

On common days they sing the Psalm (xv.), Lord, who shall dwell in Thy tabernacle? *entire with its canon,*[3] *of the mystery of the sacraments.*

(*Aloud.*)

Who shall shout with joy? etc.

Prayer.

II. Before the resplendent throne of Thy majesty, O Lord, and the exalted and sublime throne of Thy glory, and on the awful seat of the strength of Thy love and the propiatory altar which Thy will hath established, in the region of Thy pasture,[4] with thousands of cherubim praising Thee, and ten thousands of seraphim sanctifying Thee, we draw near, adore, thank, and glorify Thee always, O Lord of all.

On commemorations and Fridays.

Thy name, great and holy, illustrious and blessed, the blessed and incomprehensible name of Thy glorious Trinity, and Thy kindness to our race, we ought at all times to bless, adore, and glorify, O Lord of all.

Responsory[5] *at the chancel, as above.*

Who commanded, etc.
To the priest, etc.

Prayer.

How breathes in us, O our Lord and God, the sweet fragrance of the sweetness of Thy love; illumined are our souls, through the knowledge of Thy truth: may we be rendered worthy of receiving the manifestation of Thy beloved from Thy holy heavens: there shall we render thanks unto Thee, and, in the meantime, glorify Thee without ceasing in Thy Church, crowned and filled with every aid and blessing, because Thou art Lord and Father, Creator of all.

III. *Prayer of Incense.*

We shall repeat the hymn to Thy glorious Trinity, O Father, Son, and Holy Ghost.

On fast-days.

And on account, etc.

At the commemoration of saints.

Thou, O Lord, art truly the raiser up of our bodies: Thou art the good Saviour of our souls, and the secure preserver of our life; and we ought to thank Thee continually, to adore and glorify Thee, O Lord of all.

At the lessons.[6]

Holy art Thou, worthy of praise, mighty, immortal, who dwellest in the holies, and Thy will resteth in them: have regard unto us, O Lord; be merciful unto us, and pity us, as Thou art our helper in all circumstances, O Lord of all.

IV. *At the apostle.*[7]

Enlighten, O our Lord and God, the movements of our meditations to hear and understand the sweet listenings to Thy life-giving and divine

---

1 [Here the Edinburgh editors give the following title from their copy, without stating whence it is: "The Liturgy of the Holy Apostles, or Order of the Sacraments."]

2 [I have made slight corrections, after Renaudot, as given in Hammond, from *Litt. Orient. Coll.*, tom. ii pp. 578–592.]

3 Suicer says that a canon is a psalm or hymn (*canticum*) wont to be sung on certain days, ordinarily and as if by rule. He quotes Zonaras, who says that a canon is metrical, and is composed of nine odes. See Sophocles, *Glossary of Byzantine Greek*, Introduction, § 43. The canon of the Nestorian Church is somewhat different. See Neale, *General Introduction to the History of the Eastern Church*, p 979.

4 [Rev. v. 6. The Apocalypse saturates these liturgies.]

5 "The psalm, or verses of a psalm, sung after the Epistle, was always entitled *gradual*, from being chanted on the steps (*gradus*) of the pulpit. When sung by one person without interruption, it was called *tractus;* when chanted alternately by several singers, it was termed *responsory*." — PALMER, *Origines Liturgicæ*, vol. ii. p .46, note.

6 i.e., while the lesson from the Old Testament is read. [But the Malabar Liturgy and Dr. Badger's translation insert before this, according to Hammond, the *Sanctus Deus, Sanctus fortis*, etc.]

7 i.e., while the lesson from the Apostolical Epistles is read.

commands; and grant unto us through Thy grace and mercy to gather from them the assurance of love, and hope, and salvation suitable to soul and body, and we shall sing to Thee everlasting glory without ceasing and always, O Lord of all.

On fast-days.

To Thee, the wise governor, etc.

v. *Descending, he shall salute the Gospel, saying this prayer before the altar.*

Thee, the renowned seed of Thy Father, and the image of the person of Thy Father, who wast revealed in the body of our humanity, and didst arise to us in the light of Thy annunciation, Thee we thank, adore, etc.

And after the proclamation:[1] —

Thee, O Lord God Almighty, we beseech and entreat, perfect with us Thy grace, and pour out through our hands Thy gift, the pity and compassion of Thy divinity. May they be to us for the propitiation of the offences of Thy people, and for the forgiveness of the sins of the entire flock of Thy pasture, through Thy grace and tender mercies, O good friend of men, O Lord of all.

vi. *The Deacons say:* —

Bow your heads.

The Priest says this secret prayer in the sanctuary:[2] —

O Lord God Omnipotent, Thine is the Holy Catholic Church, inasmuch as Thou, through the great passion of Thy Christ, didst buy the sheep of Thy pasture; and from the grace of the Holy Spirit, who is indeed of one nature with Thy glorious divinity, are granted the degrees of the true priestly ordination; and through Thy clemency Thou didst vouchsafe, O Lord, to make our weakness spiritual members in the great body of Thy Holy Church, that we might administer spiritual aid to faithful souls. Now, O Lord, perfect Thy grace with us, and pour out Thy gift through our hands: and may Thy tender mercies and the clemency of Thy divinity be upon us, and upon the people whom Thou hast chosen for Thyself.

(*Aloud.*)

And grant unto us, O Lord, through Thy clemency, that we may all together, and equally every day of our life, please Thy divinity, and be rendered worthy of the aid of Thy grace to offer Thee praise, honour, thanksgiving, and adoration at all times, O Lord.

[1] Renaudot understands by the proclamation the reading aloud of the Gospel. [According to Hammond, the deacon's bidding prayer, during which, in Dr. Badger's translation the Offertory is said also.]

[2] Bema.

vii. *And the Deacons ascend to the altar, and say:* —

He who has not received baptism, etc.[3]

And the Priest begins the responsory of the mysteries,[4] *and the Sacristan and Deacon place the disk and the chalice upon the altar. The Priest crosses his hands, and says:*[5] —

We offer praise to Thy glorious Trinity at all times and for ever.

And proceeds: —

May Christ, who was offered for our salvation, and commanded us to commemorate His death and His resurrection, Himself receive this sacrifice from the hands of our weakness, through His grace and mercies for ever. Amen.

And proceeds: —

Laid are the renowned holy and life-giving mysteries upon the altar of the mighty Lord, even until His advent, for ever. Amen.

Praise, etc.
Thy memory, etc.
Our Father, etc.
The apostles of the Father, etc.
Upon the holy altar, etc.
They who have slept, etc.
Matthew, Mark, Luke, etc.[6]

THE CREED.[7]

viii. *The Priest draws near to celebrate, and thrice bows before the altar, the middle of which he kisses, then the right and the left horn of the altar; and bows to the Gospel side, and says:* —

Bless, O Lord, etc.

Pray for me, my fathers, brethren, and masters, that God may grant unto me the capability and power to perform this service to which I have drawn near, and that this oblation may be accepted from the hands of my weakness, for myself, for you, and for the whole body of the Holy Catholic Church, through His grace and mercies for ever. Amen.

And they respond: —

May Christ listen to thy prayers, and be pleased with thy sacrifice, receive thy oblation, and honour thy priesthood, and grant unto us, through thy mediation,[8] the pardon of our offences, and the forgiveness of our sins, through His grace and mercies for ever.

[3] The Malabar Liturgy fills up, "let him depart."

[4] [Here begins the Liturgy of the Faithful.]

[5] [The Offertory.]

[6] [Here the Edinburgh editors insert the title of this liturgy given on p. 561, *supra*, and add: "In the Syriac copy, 70, *Biblioth. Reg.*, this title does not occur, the service going forward without interruption. — ETHERIDGE." See Elucidation IV.]

[7] [According to Badger.]

[8] [2 Cor. v. 19, 20.]

Presently he bows at the other side, uttering the same words; and they respond in the same manner: then he bows to the altar, and says:—

God, Lord of all, be with us through His grace and mercies for ever. Amen.

And bowing towards the Deacon, who is on the left (Epistle side), he says:—

God, the Lord of all, confirm thy words, and secure to thee peace, and accept this oblation from my hands for me, for thee, for the whole body of the Holy Catholic Church, and for the entire world, through His grace and mercies for ever.

He kneels at the altar, and says in secret:—

IX. O our Lord and God, look not on the multitude of our sins, and let not Thy dignity be turned away on account of the heinousness of our iniquities; but through Thine unspeakable grace sanctify this sacrifice of Thine, and grant through it power and capability, so that Thou mayest forget our many sins, and be merciful when Thou shalt appear at the end of time, in the man whom Thou hast assumed from among us, and we may find before Thee grace and mercy, and be rendered worthy to praise Thee with spiritual[1] assemblies.

He rises, and says this prayer in secret:—

We thank Thee, O our Lord and God, for the abundant riches of Thy grace to us:

And he proceeds:—

Us who were sinful and degraded, on account of the multitude of Thy clemency, Thou hast made worthy to celebrate the holy mysteries of the body and blood of Thy Christ. We beg aid from Thee for the strengthening of our souls, that in perfect love and true faith we may administer Thy gift to us.

Canon.

And we shall ascribe to Thee praise, glory, thanksgiving, and adoration, now, always, and for ever and ever.

He signs himself with the sign of the cross, and they respond:—

Amen.

X. *And he proceeds:—*

Peace be with you:

They respond:—

With thee and with thy spirit.

[1] Intellectualibus. [This prayer not well rendered.]

And they give the (kiss of) peace to each other, and say:—

For all:[2]

The Deacon says:—

Let us thank, entreat, and beseech.

The Priest says this prayer in secret:—

O Lord, mighty God, help my weakness through Thy clemency and the aid of Thy grace; and make me worthy of offering before Thee this oblation, as for the common aid of all, and to the praise of Thy Trinity, O Father, Son, and Holy Ghost.

Another prayer.[3]

O our Lord and God, restrain our thoughts, that they wander not amid the vanities of this world. O Lord our God, grant that I may be united to the affection of Thy love, unworthy though I be. Glory be to Thee, O Christ.

Ascend into the chamber of Thy renowned light, O Lord; sow in me the good seed of humility; and under the wings of Thy grace hide me through Thy mercy. If Thou wert to mark iniquities, O Lord, who shall stand? Because there is mercy with Thee.

[*The Priest says the following prayer in secret:*[4]—

O mother of our Lord Jesus Christ, beseech for me the only-begotten Son, who was born of thee, to forgive me my offences and my sins, and to accept from my feeble and sinful hands this sacrifice which my weakness offers upon this altar, through thy intercession for me, O holy mother.]

XI. *When the Deacon shall say*, With watchfulness and care, etc., *immediately the Priest rises up and uncovers the sacraments, taking away the veil with which they were covered: he blesses the incense, and says a canon with a loud voice:—*

The grace of our Lord Jesus Christ, and the love of God the Father, and the communion of the Holy Ghost, be with us all, now, etc.[5]

He signs the sacraments, and they respond:—

Amen.

The Priest proceeds:—

Lift up your minds:

They respond:—

They are towards Thee, O God of Abraham, Isaac, and Israel, O glorious King.

[2] i.e., Catholics. But the word *Catholics* is omitted in most MSS.
[3] Which is said also in the Liturgy of Nestorius.
[4] In another MS. [Evidently corrupt and mediæval.]
[5] [Here begins the Anaphora.]

The Priest.

The oblation is offered to God, the Lord of all.

They respond:—

It is meet and right.

The Deacon.

Peace be with you.

The Priest puts on the incense, and says this prayer:—

O Lord, Lord, grant me an open countenance before Thee, that with the confidence which is from Thee we may fulfil this awful and divine sacrifice with consciences free from all iniquity and bitterness. Sow in us, O Lord, affection, peace, and concord towards each other, and toward every one.

And standing, he says in secret:[1] —

Worthy of glory from every mouth, and of thanksgiving from all tongues, and of adoration and exaltation from all creatures, is the adorable and glorious name of Father, Son, and Holy Ghost, who created the world through His grace, and its inhabitants through His clemency, who saved men through His mercy, and showed great favour towards mortals. Thy majesty, O Lord, thousands of thousands of heavenly *spirits*, and ten thousand myriads of holy angels, hosts of spirits, ministers of fire and spirit, bless and adore; with the holy cherubim and the spiritual seraphim they sanctify and celebrate Thy name, crying and praising, without ceasing crying unto each other.

They say with a loud voice:—

Holy, holy, holy, Lord God Almighty; full are the heavens and the earth of His glory.

The Priest in secret:—

Holy, holy, holy art Thou, O Lord God Almighty; the heavens and the earth are full of His glory and the nature of His essence, as they are glorious with the honour of His splendour; *as it is written*, The heaven and the earth are full of me, saith the mighty Lord.

Holy art Thou, O God *our* Father, truly the only one, of whom the whole family in heaven and earth is named. Holy art Thou, Eternal Son, through whom all things were made. Holy art Thou, Holy, Eternal Spirit, through whom all things are sanctified.

Woe to me, woe to me, who have been astonied, because I am a man of polluted lips, and dwell among a people of polluted lips, and my eyes have seen the King, the mighty Lord. How terrible to-day is this place! For this is none other than the house of God and the gate of heaven; because Thou hast been seen eye to eye, O Lord.

Now, I pray, may Thy grace be with us, O Lord; purge away our impurities, and sanctify our lips; unite the voices of our insignificance with the sanctification of seraphim and archangels. Glory be to Thy tender mercies, because Thou hast associated the earthly with the heavenly.[2]

And he proceeds, saying in secret this prayer, in a bowing posture:—

XII. And with those heavenly powers we give Thee thanks, even we, Thine insignificant, pithless, and feeble servants; because Thou hast granted unto us Thy great grace which cannot be repaid. For indeed Thou didst take upon Thee our human nature, that Thou mightest bestow life on us through Thy divinity; Thou didst exalt our low condition; Thou didst raise our ruined state; Thou didst rouse up our mortality; Thou didst wash away our sins; Thou didst blot out the guilt of our sins; Thou didst enlighten our intelligence, and Thou didst condemn our enemy, O Lord our God; and Thou didst cause the insignificance of our pithless nature to triumph.

Here follow the words of institution,[3] *after which:—*

Through the tender mercies of Thy grace poured out, O clement One, pardon our offences and sins; blot out my offences in the judgment. And on account of all Thy aids and Thy favours to us, we shall ascribe unto Thee praise,[4] honour, thanksgiving, and adoration, now, always, and for ever and ever.

The Priest signs the sacraments. The response is made.

Amen.

The Deacon.

In your minds. Pray for peace with us.

The Priest says this prayer[5] *bowing, and in a low voice:—*

O Lord God Almighty, accept this oblation for the whole Holy Catholic Church, and for all

[1] [The Preface.]

[2] Spiritualibus. [Note 3, p. 545, *supra*.]

[3] [See Hammond, p. 274.]

[4] Hymnum.

[5] In another MS. that prayer begins thus:—

O Lord God Almighty, hear the voice of my cry before Thee at this time. Give ear, O Lord, and hear my groanings before Thy majesty, and accept the entreaty of me, a sinner, with which I call upon Thy grace, at this hour at which the sacrifice is offered to Thy Father. Have mercy on all creatures; spare the guilty; convert the erring; restore the oppressed; on the disquieted bestow rest; heal the weak; console the afflicted; and perfect the alms of those who work righteousness on account of Thy holy name. Have mercy on me also, a sinner, through Thy grace. O Lord God Almighty, may this oblation be accepted for the entire Holy Catholic Church; and for priests, kings, princes, *and the rest as above.*

the pious and righteous fathers who have been pleasing to Thee, and for all the prophets and apostles, and for all the martyrs and confessors, and for all that mourn, that are in straits, and are sick, and for all that are under difficulties and trials, and for all the weak and the oppressed, and for all the dead that have gone from amongst us; then for all that ask a prayer from our weakness, and for me, a degraded and feeble sinner. O Lord our God, according to Thy mercies and the multitude of Thy favours, look upon Thy people, and on me, a feeble man, not according to my sins and my follies, but that they may become worthy of the forgiveness of their sins through this holy body, which they receive with faith, through the grace of Thy mercy for ever and ever. Amen.

The Priest says this prayer of inclination in secret:—

XIII. Do Thou, O Lord, through Thy many and ineffable mercies, make the memorial good and acceptable *with that of*[1] all the pious and righteous fathers who have been pleading before Thee in the commemoration of the body and blood of Thy Christ, which we offer to Thee upon Thy pure and holy altar, as Thou hast taught us; and grant unto us Thy rest all the days of this life.

He proceeds with the Great Oblation:—

O Lord our God, bestow on us Thy rest and peace all the days of this life, that all the inhabitants of the earth may know Thee, that Thou art the only true God the Father, and Thou didst send our Lord Jesus Christ, Thy Son and Thy beloved; and He Himself our Lord and God came and taught us all purity and holiness. Make remembrance of prophets, apostles, martyrs, confessors, bishops, doctors, priests, deacons, and all the sons of the Holy Catholic Church who have been signed with the sign of life, of holy baptism. We also, O Lord:

He proceeds:—

We, Thy degraded, weak, and feeble servants who are congregated in Thy name, and now stand before Thee, and have received with joy the form which is from Thee, praising, glorifying, and exalting, commemorate and celebrate this great, awful, holy, and divine mystery of the passion, death, burial, and resurrection of our Lord and Saviour Jesus Christ.

And may Thy Holy Spirit come, O Lord,[2] and rest upon this oblation of Thy servants which they offer, and bless and sanctify it; and may it be unto us, O Lord, for the propitiation of our offences and the forgiveness of our sins, and for a grand hope of resurrection from the dead, and for a new life in the kingdom of the heavens, with all who have been pleasing before Him. And on account of the whole of Thy wonderful dispensation towards us, we shall render thanks unto Thee, and glorify Thee without ceasing in Thy Church, redeemed by the precious blood of Thy Christ, with open mouths and joyful countenances:

Canon.

Ascribing praise,[3] honour, thanksgiving, and adoration to Thy holy, loving, and life-giving name, now, always, and for ever.

The Priest signs the mysteries with the cross, and they respond:—

Amen.

The Priest bows himself and kisses the altar, first in the middle, then at the two sides right and left, and says this prayer:[4]*—*

Have mercy upon me, O God, *down to the words*, and sinners shall be converted unto Thee: *and* unto Thee lift I up mine eyes,[5] *down to* have mercy upon us, O Lord, have mercy upon us. *Also* stretch forth Thy hand, and let Thy right hand save me, O Lord; may Thy mercies remain upon me, O Lord, for ever, and despise not the works of Thy hands.[6]

Then he says this prayer:—

XIV. O Christ, peace of those in heaven and great rest of those below,[7] grant that Thy rest and peace may dwell in the four parts of the world,[8] but especially in Thy Holy Catholic Church; grant that the priesthood with the government may have peace; cause wars to cease from the ends of the earth, and scatter the nations that delight in wars,[9] that we may enjoy the blessing of living in tranquillity and peace, in all temperance and fear of God. Spare the offences and sins of the dead, through Thy grace and mercies for ever.

And to those who are around the altar he says:—

Bless, O Lord. Bless, O Lord.

And he puts on the incense with which he fumes himself, and says:—

Sweeten, O Lord our God, the unpleasing savour[10] of our souls through the sweetness of Thy

1 [Italics mine, conjecturally.]
2 [The Invocation.]

3 Hymnum.
4 In another MS., says the Psalm li.
5 Ps. cxxiii.
6 [From Ps. cxxxviii. 7, 8.]
7 i.e., the dead.
8 [The first words of Dr. Butler's *Ancient Geography* teaches that the ancients knew but three; but see p. 555, lines 7, 8.]
9 Lit. "wish for wars."
10 [So the true reading (Badger), though Edinburgh editors follow the illogical emendation (*jucundum*) of Renaudot.]

love, and through it cleanse me from the stains of my sin, and forgive me my offences and sins, whether known or unknown to me.

A second time he takes the incense with both hands, and censes the mysteries; presently he says: —

The clemency of Thy grace, O our Lord and God, gives us access to these renowned, holy, life-giving, and divine mysteries, unworthy though we be.

The Priest repeats these words once and again, and at each interval unites his hands over his breast in the form of a cross. He kisses the altar in the middle, and receives with both hands the upper oblation; and looking up, says: —

Praise be to Thy holy name, O Lord Jesus Christ, and adoration to Thy majesty, always and for ever. Amen.

For He is the living and life-giving bread which cometh down from heaven, and giveth life to the whole world, of which they who eat die not; and they who receive it are saved by it, and do not see corruption, and live through it for ever; and Thou art the antidote of our mortality,[1] and the resurrection of our entire frame.[2]

XV.[3] * * *

XVI. Praise to Thy holy name, O Lord. (*As above.*)

The Priest kisses the host[4] *in the form of a cross; in such a way, however, that his lips do not touch it, but appear to kiss it; and he says:* —

Glory to Thee, O Lord; glory to Thee, O Lord, on account of Thine unspeakable gift to us, for ever.

Then he draws nigh to the fraction of the host,[4] *which he accomplishes with both his hands, saying:* —

We draw nigh, O Lord, with true faith, and break with thanksgiving and sign through Thy mercy the body and blood of our Life-giver, Jesus Christ, in the name of the Father, Son, and Holy Ghost.

And, naming the Trinity, he breaks the host,[4] *which he holds in his hands, into two parts: and the one which is in his left hand he lays down on the disk; with the other, which he holds in his right hand, he signs the chalice, saying:* —

The precious blood is signed with the holy body of our Lord Jesus Christ. In the name of the Father, and the Son, and the Holy Ghost for ever.

And they respond: —

Amen.

Then he dips it even to the middle in the chalice, and signs with it the body which is in the paten, saying: —

The holy body is signed with the propitiatory blood of our Lord Jesus Christ. In the name of the Father, and of the Son, and of the Holy Ghost for ever.

And they respond: —

Amen.

And he unites the two parts, the one with the other, saying: —

Divided, sanctified, completed, perfected, united, and commingled have been these renowned, holy, life-giving, and divine mysteries, the one with the other, in the adorable and glorious name of Thy glorious Trinity, O Father, Son, and Holy Ghost, that they may be to us, O Lord, for the propitiation of our offences and the forgiveness of our sins; also for the grand hope of a resurrection from the dead, and of a new life in the kingdom of the heavens, for us and for the Holy Church of Christ our Lord, here and in every place whatsoever, now and always, and for ever.

XVII. *In the meantime he signs the host*[5] *with his right thumb in the form of a cross from the lower part to the upper, and from the right to the left, and thus forms a slight fissure in it where it has been dipped in the blood. He puts a part of it into the chalice in the form of a cross: the lower part is placed towards the priest, the upper towards the chalice, so that the place of the fissure looks to the chalice. He bows, and rising, says:* —

Glory be to Thee, O Lord Jesus Christ, who hast made me, unworthy though I be, through Thy grace, a minister and mediator of Thy renowed, holy, life-giving, and divine mysteries: through the grace of Thy mercy, make me worthy of the pardon of my offences and the forgiveness of my sins.

---

1 [The reference to John vi. 32–40 is clear.]

2 In another MS. there is a different reading: — "Glory to Thee, O God the Father, who didst send Thine only-begotten Son for our salvation, and He Himself before He suffered," etc.

3 In the MS. of Elias, which we have followed, there is a defect, seeing that the whole recitation of the words of Christ is omitted through the fault of the transcriber, or because these ought to have been taken from another source, namely, from the Liturgy of Theodorus or Nestorius. In that which the Patriarch Joseph wrote at Rome, 1697, that entire passage is remodelled according to the Chaldean missal published at Rome, as in the mass, a translation of which was edited by Alexius Menesius. Since there were no other codices at hand, in this place it seemed good to place asterisks to indicate the defects.

4 [Renaudot supplies the Latin word *hostiam*. It is not the early patristic word, much less is it scriptural for θυσία.]

5 [*Ut supra*, note 4, this page; also Burbidge, p. 95, note 2.]

He signs himself with the sign of the cross on his forehead, and does the same to those standing round him.[1]

The Deacons approach, and he signs each one of them on the forehead, saying:—

Christ accept thy ministry: Christ cause thy face to shine: Christ save thy life: Christ make thy youth to grow.

And they respond:—

Christ accept thy oblation.

XVIII. *All return to their own place; and the Priest, after bowing, rises and says, in the tone of the Gospel:—*

The grace of our Lord Jesus Christ, and the love of God the Father, and the communion of the Holy Ghost, be with us all.

The Priest signs himself, and lifts up his hand over his head, so that it should be in the air, and the people be partakers in the singing:—

The Deacon says:—

We all with fear, etc.

And at these words:—

He hath given to us His mysteries:

The Priest begins to break[2] *the body, and says:—*

Be merciful, O Lord, through Thy clemency to the sins and follies of Thy servants, and sanctify our lips through Thy grace, that they may give the fruits of glory and praise to Thy divinity, with all Thy saints in Thy kingdom.

And, raising his voice, he says:—

And make us worthy, O Lord our God, to stand before Thee continually without stain, with pure heart, with open countenance, and with the confidence which is from Thee, mercifully granted to us: and let us all with one accord invoke Thee, and say thus: Our Father, etc.

The People say:—

Our Father, etc.

The Priest.[3]

O Lord God Almighty, O Lord and our good God, who art full of mercy, we beg Thee, O Lord our God, and beseech the clemency of Thy goodness; lead us not into temptation, but deliver and save us from the evil one and his hosts; because Thine is the kingdom, the power, the strength, the might, and the dominion in heaven and on earth, now and always.

He signs himself, and they respond:—

Amen.

XIX. *And he proceeds:—*

Peace be with you.

They respond:—

With thee and with thy spirit.

He proceeds:—

It is becoming that the holy things should be to the holy in perfection.

And they say:—

One holy Father: one holy Son: one Holy Ghost. Glory be to the Father, and to the Son, and to the Holy Ghost, for ever and ever. Amen.

The Deacon.

Praise ye.

And they say the responsory. And when the Deacon comes to carry the chalice, he says:—

Let us pray for peace with us.

The Priest says:—

The grace of the Holy Ghost be with thee, with us, and with those who receive Him.

And he gives the chalice to the Deacon. The Deacon says:—

Bless, O Lord.

The Priest.

The gift of the grace of our Life-giver and Lord Jesus Christ be completed, in mercies, with all.

And he signs the people with the cross. In the meantime the responsories are said.

Brethren, receive the body of the Son, cries the Church, and drink ye His chalice with faith in the house of His kingdom.

On feast-days.

Strengthen, O Lord, etc.

On the Lord's day.

O Lord Jesus Christ, etc.

Daily.

The mysteries which we have received, etc.

The responsories being ended, the Deacon says:—

All therefore, etc.

---

1 In another MS.:—

He signs his forehead with the sign of the cross, and says:—

Glory to Thee, O Lord, who didst create me by Thy grace. Glory to Thee, O Lord, who didst call me by Thy mercy. Glory to Thee, O Lord, who didst appoint me the mediator of Thy gift; and on account of all the benefits to my weakness, ascribed unto Thee be praise, honour, thanksgiving, and adoration, now, etc.

2 [Not κλᾶν, but μέλιζειν. The second *fraction* for communicating the faithful with the *Humble Access.*]

3 [Adds the Embolisms.]

And they respond: —

Glory be to Himself on account of His ineffable gift.

The Deacon.

Let us pray for peace with us.

The Priest at the middle of the altar says this prayer:[1] —

XX. It is meet, O Lord, just and right in all days, times, and hours, to thank, adore, and praise the awful name of Thy majesty, because Thou hast through Thy grace, O Lord, made us, mortal men possessing a frail nature, worthy to sanctify Thy name with the heavenly[2] beings, and to become partakers of the mysteries of Thy gift, and to be delighted with the sweetness of Thy oracles. And voices of glory and thanksgiving we ever offer up to Thy sublime divinity, O Lord.

Another.

Christ, our God, Lord, King, Saviour, and Life-giver, through His grace has made us worthy to receive His body and His precious and all-sanctifying blood. May He grant unto us that we may be pleasing unto Him in our words, works, thoughts, and deeds, so that that pledge which we have received may be to us for the pardon of our offences, the forgiveness of our sins, and the grand hope of a resurrection from the dead, and a new and true life in the kingdom of the heavens, with all who have been pleasing before Him, through His grace and His mercies for ever.

On ordinary days.

Praise, O Lord, honour, blessing, and thanksgiving we ought to ascribe to Thy glorious Trinity for the gift of Thy holy mysteries, which Thou hast given to us for the propitiation of our offences, O Lord of all.

[1] [Beginning the Post-Communion.]
[2] Spiritualibus.

Another.

Blessed be Thy adorable honour, from Thy glorious place, O Christ, the propitiator of our offences and our sins, and who takest away our follies through Thy renowned, holy, life-giving, and divine mysteries. Christ the hope of our nature always and for ever. Amen.

Obsignation or final benediction.

May our Lord Jesus Christ, to whom we have ministered, and whom we have seen and honoured in His renowned, holy, life-giving, and divine mysteries, Himself render us worthy of the splendid glory of His kingdom, and of gladness with His holy angels, and for confidence before Him, that we may stand at His right hand.

And on our entire congregation may His mercies and compassion be continually poured out, now and always, and ever.

On the Lord's day and on feast-days.

May He Himself who blessed us with all spiritual blessings in the heavens, through Jesus Christ our Lord, and prepared us for His kingdom, and called us to the desirable good things which neither cease nor perish, as He promised to us in His life-giving Gospel, and said to the blessed congregation of His disciples — Verily, verily I say unto you, that every one who eateth my body and drinketh my blood, abideth in me, and I in him, and I will raise him up at the last day; and he cometh not to judgment, but I will make him pass from death to eternal life:

May He Himself now bless this congregation, and maintain our position, and render glorious our people who have come and rejoiced in receiving His renowned, holy, life-giving, and divine mysteries; and may ye be sealed and guarded by the holy sign of the Lord's cross from all evils, secret and open, now and always.

ELUCIDATIONS

I.

(Disciple of the holy Peter, p. 551.)

THE early use of the originals of this liturgy in the Alexandrian patriarchate accounts for its bearing the name of St. Mark, — "sister's son to Barnabas," as St. Paul calls him.[1] That he was St. Peter's pupil may be inferred from that Apostle's language,[2] — "Marcus, my son." See Clement's testimony concerning him (with Eusebius) in vol. ii. pp. 579, 580, this series. That he founded the "Evangelical See," though resting on great historic authority,[3] seems to be doubted in our times by some.

[1] Col. iv. 10.
[2] Compare Acts xii. 12. St. Peter may have baptized him then.
[3] Lardner's quotations from Jerome, *Credib.*, vol. iv. p. 442 *et alibi.*

II.

(Our holy father Mark, p. 556.)

While St. Mark could not have written this, it may, of course, have been added at a very early date.[1] This most touching prayer bears marks of great antiquity, the reference to our "Christ-loving sovereign" comporting better with the early enthusiasm inspired by Constantine's conversion than with the disappointments incurred under his Arianizing or apostate successors. Now, this commemoration of St. Mark would of itself attach his name to the liturgy.

But here is the place to note the principles of these primitive prayers for saints departed. (1) They could only be offered in behalf of the holy dead who had fallen asleep in full communion with Christ and His Church; (2) They were not prayers for their deliverance out of one place into another; (3) They recognised the *repose* (not yet the *triumph*) of the faithful departed as incomplete, and hence (4) invoked for them a blessed consummation of peace and joy in the resurrection.

Now, all this is fatal to the Roman dogmas and usages, because (1) they thus include St. Mark and the Blessed Virgin in these commemorations; while Rome teaches, not only that these great saints went immediately to the excellent glory, and there have reigned with Christ ever since they died, but (2) that on this very ground, and that of their *supererogatory* merits, the Pontiff holds a purse[2] of their excessive righteousness to dispense to meaner Christians.

St. Augustine speaks of his dear Nebridius as in Abraham's bosom,[3] but finds comfort in commemorating him and Monica his mother, "because it is so comfortable." This is his idea, in a word: "Et credo jam feceris quod te rogo, sed (Ps. cxix. 108) *voluntaria* oris mei, approba, Domine."

III.

(Holy things for the holy, p. 559.)

Bingham[4] has so fully elucidated this by quotations from Chrysostom (Hom. vii.) and others, that one might think it useless to attach to it any other meaning than that which Chrysostom understands in it; viz., "Holy things for holy persons." It occurs just before the communicating of the faithful, and has nothing whatever to do with the "elevation of the host,"—a Western ceremony of the fourteenth century.[5] Yet, in an otherwise (generally) useful manual of liturgies, an attempt is made to give it this meaning; and the preceding prayer of "Intense Adoration," addressed to the Great High Priest in the heavens, is debased to eke out the weak idea. Nothing could be more averse to the primitive principle of worship;[6] but it is sufficient to note the fact that the "elevation of the host" revolutionized the eucharistic worship of the West as soon as it was established. (1) It abolished the Eucharist practically as the *synaxis*, or communion of the faithful, and made it only a sacrifice *for* them in their behalf; (2) not to be eaten and received, but to be gazed at; (3) not for all the faithful at all times, excluding even catechumens from beholding it, but to be displayed to all eyes in pompous ceremonials, carried through the streets, and dispensed only in half-communion, once a year, to the individual communicant. All these ancient liturgies, corrupted as they are in all the MSS. we possess, are yet liturgies for communicating the faithful, in their turns,[7] one and all; and, so far, they are true to the Scriptures and the precepts of Christ and His Apostles. But well does the pious Hirscher exclaim, with reference to

---

1 As with Moses, Exod. xxxiv. 5.
2 Bellarmine, *De Indulg.*, i. 2.
3 *Confessions*, ix. 3, 12, *et alibi.*
4 *Antiqu.*, book i. cap. iv. sec. 5; book xiii. cap. vi. sec. 7; book xv. cap. iii. sec. 31.
5 See Roman Mass, Hammond, p. 334.
6 As illustrated in Freeman's important work. See p. 536, note 2.
7 See *Apostolic Constitutions*, pp. 490, 548, *supra.*

the Mass, as he was obliged to celebrate it in his own gorgeous cathedral at Freiburg in the Breisgau: "What would an Apostle think we were doing, should he enter during our ceremonies?" Also, "I know all that can be said in their favour. I know just as well that by them *the spirit is turned apart from internal godliness*, and borne away; and that, with such appeals to sense, withdrawal from things of sense becomes impossible. . . . God is a Spirit: He looks to be adored *in spirit and in truth*, and all ceremonial which dulls the adoration [1] of the spirit is odious to God. To glorify self, as His minister, before the King of kings, before the majesty of the Creator, before His Christ, naked and crucified,—is it not an absurdity, a ceremony of contradictions? The people no longer comprehend the ceremonial . . . to see them satisfied by mere corporal attendance, is it not deplorable? They do not understand Latin. Is it not melancholy that they take no real part in the touching offices of the Holy Week? Is not a deplorable indifference the result; in France, for example? Nay, at Rome also?" [2]

His remonstrances were vain; he was cruelly censured, yet he died in the Papal communion. Dear Hirscher! The venerable man kissed me when I parted from him in 1851,[3] and gave me his blessing with a primitive spirit of Christian charity. I gratefully quote him here.

In Germany a passing stranger often sees the pious peasantry at Mass, singing with all their hearts their beautiful German hymns. It misleads, however. They are not attending to the Mass, but consoling themselves by spiritual songs, while it goes on without their assistance. The bell rings: they adore the host, but that is all their relation to the worship of the Christian liturgies. Hirscher loved their hymns, but bewailed the utter loss of their liturgic communion, once common to the faithful.[4]

IV.

(Teachers of the Easterns, etc., p. 561.)

The apostle Thaddeus is called *Addai* in Syriac. Maris is said to have been one of the seventy disciples, but his name is not on the list ascribed to Hippolytus. He was the first bishop of the people now called "Nestorians," but whom Dr. Badger [5] prefers to call "the Christians of Assyria."

We have this liturgy in another form in Dr. Badger's important work, *Nestorians and their Rituals*. He selects that called "the Liturgy of Nestorius" from three which are in use among the Assyrians, but criticises the translation of Renaudot as not entirely faultless. It is selected by Dr. Badger because of its reputed Nestorianism; while Hammond gives us what is here translated, in Renaudot's Latin.[6] We must bear in mind, that, since the Ephesine Council (A.D. 431), these Christians have been separated from the communion of Eastern orthodoxy.

The Malabar Liturgy should be carefully compared with this by the student. A convenient translation of it is to be found in Neale and Littledale. A most important fact, by the way, is noted in their translation;[7] viz., that in this Malabar "the invocation of the Holy Ghost, *contrary to the use of every other Oriental liturgy*, preceded the words of institution;" that is to say, in the work of *the Portuguese revisers*, a work from which Dr. Neale and his colleague feel justified in making "a considerable alteration" as to the order of the prayers.

The words of institution are found in the Malabar, and suggest that they belong not less to this Liturgy of the Assyrians, though, *ex summa verecundia*,[8] they are omitted from the transcript, as the Lord's Prayer is omitted in the Clementine.

---

[1] The "Intense Adoration" of the liturgies.

[2] *Die Christlichen Zustände der Gegenwart*, Freiburg, 1850. My translation appeared in Oxford in 1852, and is often advertised in old book catalogues as *Sympathies of the Continent; or, Proposals for a New Reformation*.

[3] On St. Bartholomew's Day.

[4] See his *Study of the Eucharist*. He tried to revive primitive views of the Eucharist in this excellent work on the subject.

[5] See his contribution to the Liverpool Church Congress of 1869. Bartlett & Co., London.

[6] P. 267.

[7] P. 165, ed. of 1869.

[8] Hammond, p. lx., *Introduction*.

The normal form of this corrupted liturgy is credited with extreme antiquity by Dr. Neale. To his learned and cogent reasoning on the subject the student should by all means refer.[1]

V.

(For all the prophets and confessors, p. 565.)

These commemorations of the dead, it will be noted, are in behalf of the most glorious apostles and saints, and for martyrs who go straight to glory. Obviously, as Usher has said,[2] for whatever purpose, then, the departed were commemorated, it was not to change their estate before the resurrection, much less to relieve them from purgatorial penalties. This comes out in the "Liturgy of St. Chrysostom" (so called), where it is said: "We offer to Thee this reasonable service for those who have fallen asleep in faith, . . . patriarchs, apostles, evangelists, martyrs, . . . and every *just one made perfect in* the faith: *especially* our all-holy, undefiled, most blessed Lady, *Theotokos* and ever-virgin Mary," etc. But she, they tell us, was *assumed* into glory, like Christ Himself, and reigns with Him as "Queen of Angels," etc. See Elucidation II. p. 569.

VI.

(The propitiatory blood, etc., p. 566.)

The peril of confounding the early use of this idea of propitiation with the mediæval theory, which is quite another, is well pointed out and enforced by Burbidge.[3] The primitive writers and the ancient liturgies "do not regard the Eucharist as being *itself* a propitiatory offering," but it is the perpetual pleading of the blood of propitiation once offered. Thus St. Chrysostom: "We do not offer another sacrifice, but *always the same.*" So far, his words might be quoted to favour the Middle-Age doctrine; but he guards himself, and adds:[4] "or, *rather, we make a memorial* of the sacrifice."

The rhetoric of the liturgies and of the Fathers was unhappily made into the logic of the Schoolmen, and hence the stupendous system of propitiatory Masses, with Masses for the dead, and that traffic in Masses which so fearfully defiles the priesthood of Western Europe and the Spanish and Portuguese colonies in America. In vain does the pious Hirscher complain:[5] "The rich, then, are the happy sinners in this respect: they can buy innumerable Masses, and establish them in perpetuity; their privileges have no limit, and their advantages over the poor extend through all eternity." His book was put into the Index (Acts xvi. 19, xix. 27), but it was never answered.

VII.

Let me now recur to Elucidation III. on p. 507, to which I would here add the following from Bishop Williams, as there quoted:—

"In both the Mozarabic and the Gallican Liturgies there was an invocation as well as an oblation. Irenæus[6] says (and he, writing at Lyons, must have in mind the Gallican Liturgy), 'The bread which is of the earth, having received the *invocation of God*, is no longer common bread, but the Eucharist.' The word translated 'invocation' is ἐπίκλησιν; and it is worthy of notice that Basil and Cyril of Jerusalem use the same word in evidently the same technical sense (Harvey's *Irenæus*, vol. ii. pp. 205–207 and notes). In another passage Irenæus[7] speaks even more distinctly: 'We offer to God the bread and the cup of blessing, giving thanks to Him for that He hath commanded the earth to bring forth these fruits for our nourishment; and, having finished the offering,

[1] *General Introduction*, etc., vol. i. p. 319, etc., ed. 1850.
[2] See vol. vi. Elucidation IV. p. 541, this series.
[3] *Liturgies*, etc., p. 11. See also pp. 96, 110.
[4] *Opp.*, tom. xii. p. 131, ed. Migne.
[5] *Christliche Zustände*, etc., p. 74.
[6] See vol. i. p. 486, note 6, this series.
[7] Fragment xxxvii. vol. i. p. 574, this series.

we invoke the Holy Spirit that He may exhibit (or declare, ἀποφήνῃ) this sacrifice and bread the body of Christ, and the cup the blood of Christ, that they who shall receive these antitypes may obtain remission of sins and everlasting life' (Harvey's *Irenæus*, vol. ii. p. 502). This passage is a remarkable one. It proves beyond question, that, in the time of Irenæus (*d.* A.D. 202 or 208), the Liturgy of Gaul contained an invocation of the Holy Ghost following the oblation of the bread and cup. Moreover, when we compare the words of Irenæus with those of the Clementine Liturgy, their agreement is too clear and precise to be explained as a mere chance-matter. The liturgy reads, 'Send down Thy Holy Spirit on this sacrifice, the witness of the sufferings of the Lord Jesus, that He may exhibit (ἀποφήνῃ) this bread, the body of Thy Christ, and this cup, the blood of Thy Christ, that they who shall receive,'[1] etc. Irenæus says as above, using the same word (ἀποφήνῃ), a word which is found, it is believed, in no liturgy but the Clementine."

Now I humbly suggest that Justin Martyr and Irenæus *concur* in giving us evidence that the *Clementine Liturgy* is substantially that which was used in Rome and Gaul in their times. The latter may have received it from Polycarp. The use of the Roman and the Greek churches was uniform in his day, as may be inferred from the intercourse of Polycarp and Victor.[2]

[1] See p. 489, *supra*.

[2] Fragment iii. vol. i. p. 568, this series.

INDEXES

LACTANTIUS

INDEX OF SUBJECTS

LACTANTIUS, VENANTIUS

INDEX OF TEXTS

VENANTIUS, ASTERIUS URBANUS, VICTORINUS, DIONYSIUS OF ROME

INDEX OF SUBJECTS

ASTERIUS URBANUS, VICTORINUS, DIONYSIUS OF ROME

INDEX OF TEXTS

APOSTOLICAL TEACHING, CONSTITUTIONS, AND CANONS, AND THE CLEMENTINE HOMILY

INDEX OF SUBJECTS

APOSTOLICAL TEACHING, CONSTITUTIONS, AND CANONS, AND THE CLEMENTINE HOMILY

INDEX OF TEXTS

EARLY LITURGIES

INDEX OF SUBJECTS

EARLY LITURGIES

INDEX OF TEXTS

[These Liturgies furnish endless allusions to texts of Scripture not fully quoted.]